CAMBRID(
B

Literary Studies

This series provides a high-quality selection of early printings of literary works, textual editions, anthologies and literary criticism which are of lasting scholarly interest. Ranging from Old English to Shakespeare to early twentieth-century work from around the world, these books offer a valuable resource for scholars in reception history, textual editing, and literary studies.

Illustrations of the Literary History of the Eighteenth Century

The subtitle of this eight-volume set is *Consisting of Authentic Memoirs and Original Letters of Eminent Persons, and Intended as a Sequel to the 'Literary Anecdotes'*, which had been published in nine volumes by the author, editor and publisher John Nichols (1745–1826) between 1812 and 1815, and are also reissued in this series. Like its predecessor set, these 'illustrations' are a useful source of biographical material on authors and publishers at a time when many of the literary genres we take for granted, such as the novel, the autobiography and the analytical history, were first being developed. The volumes were published between 1817 and 1858, the project being continued after Nichols' death by his son and grandson. Among the 'eminent persons' included in Volume 6 are the poet Anna Seward, Dr Johnson, the bibliographer Thomas Dibdin, and King George III.

Cambridge University Press has long been a pioneer in the reissuing of out-of-print titles from its own backlist, producing digital reprints of books that are still sought after by scholars and students but could not be reprinted economically using traditional technology. The Cambridge Library Collection extends this activity to a wider range of books which are still of importance to researchers and professionals, either for the source material they contain, or as landmarks in the history of their academic discipline.

Drawing from the world-renowned collections in the Cambridge University Library and other partner libraries, and guided by the advice of experts in each subject area, Cambridge University Press is using state-of-the-art scanning machines in its own Printing House to capture the content of each book selected for inclusion. The files are processed to give a consistently clear, crisp image, and the books finished to the high quality standard for which the Press is recognised around the world. The latest print-on-demand technology ensures that the books will remain available indefinitely, and that orders for single or multiple copies can quickly be supplied.

The Cambridge Library Collection brings back to life books of enduring scholarly value (including out-of-copyright works originally issued by other publishers) across a wide range of disciplines in the humanities and social sciences and in science and technology.

Illustrations of
the Literary History
of the
Eighteenth Century

*Consisting of Authentic Memoirs
and Original Letters of Eminent Persons,
and Intended as a Sequel to the 'Literary Anecdotes'*

VOLUME 6

JOHN NICHOLS

CAMBRIDGE
UNIVERSITY PRESS

CAMBRIDGE
UNIVERSITY PRESS

University Printing House, Cambridge, CB2 8BS, United Kingdom

Cambridge University Press is part of the University of Cambridge.
It furthers the University's mission by disseminating knowledge in the pursuit of
education, learning and research at the highest international levels of excellence.

www.cambridge.org
Information on this title: www.cambridge.org/9781108077392

© in this compilation Cambridge University Press 2015

This edition first published 1831
This digitally printed version 2015

ISBN 978-1-108-07739-2 Paperback

Wm Gifford

Born 1756, ____ Died 1826.

Published Jan.ᵗ.1832, by J.B. Nichols. Parliament Street.

ILLUSTRATIONS

OF THE

LITERARY HISTORY

OF THE

EIGHTEENTH CENTURY.

CONSISTING OF

𝔄uthentic 𝔐emoirs and 𝔒riginal 𝔏etters

OF

EMINENT PERSONS;

AND INTENDED AS A SEQUEL TO

𝔗he 𝔏iterary 𝔄necdotes.

By JOHN NICHOLS, F.S.A.

VOLUME VI.

LONDON:

PRINTED BY AND FOR J. B. NICHOLS AND SON,

25, PARLIAMENT-STREET, WESTMINSTER.

1831.

DEDICATION.

A 2

PREFACE.

———◆———

THE contents of the present volume consist principally of selections from the yet far from exhausted stores of literary correspondence possessed by the late Mr. Nichols. Three series of letters are included, which would probably have been published before, had they not in the original appeared too extensive to become only portions of a volume. These are the correspondence with Mr. Gough of three eminent antiquaries: Mr. Essex, the Cambridge architect; Mr. Brooke, Somerset Herald; and the Rev. Samuel Denne. In a careful revision of the originals, for the purpose of abridgement and condensation, it has been endeavoured to omit matter already published; and indeed to retain only such portions as might be conducive to some useful purpose, if not (as in most cases) from their biographical or literary information, at least from containing intelligent and sensible remarks.

The letters of Lord Camelford are from the papers consigned to Mr. Nichols by the family of his kind friend, and assistant in this Work, Mr. Justice Hardinge. They are the composition of a highly cultivated mind, of a literary turn, and polished by an intercourse with the best society of Europe; and, although their theme is in a great degree politics,

they will not be perused with less interest on that
account, when it is recollected that the writer was
a cousin of the Prime Minister of the period, and
an eye-witness of those first stages of the French
Revolution which furnish a principal topic for his
remarks.

The biographical memoirs have in many cases
been compiled from a variety of sources, and are
therefore generally entitled to the term " original ; "
when not original, additional facts have in almost
every case been introduced.   The autobiography of
Mr. Chafin, a clerical country squire, who in his old
age turned author, after a life spent in pursuits of a
very opposite character, will be found to possess
many of the charms usually characteristic of that
description of writing.

The following distinct articles, (most of them embracing auxiliary notices of other literary characters,) have been contributed by the Rev. James
Ford, late of Ipswich, and now Vicar of Navestock
in Essex.

George Richard Savage Nassau, Esq.
The Rev. William Clubbe, LL. B. and John Clubbe, M. D.
The Rev. Samuel Darby, A. M.
The Rev. John Price, Keeper of the Bodleian.
Richard Beatniffe, author of the Norfolk Tour.
The Rev. John Brand, the Mathematician.
The Rev. Richard Canning, A. M. editor of the second edition
    of the Suffolk Traveller.
Edmund Gillingwater, historian of Lowestoft and Bury.
The Rev. Thomas Bishop, D.D.
Biographical notices of the Dawson family.
The Rev. George Burton, A.M.
Mr. John Mole.

In the article which commences this volume, that of the great critical autocrat Mr. Gifford, the Editors were indebted to the late William Bulmer, Esq. both for the communication of additional information on Mr. Gifford's dramatic labours, and for the poetical trifles which at once show the good-nature of the writer's disposition, and his talents in extempore versification.

John Turner, Esq. a Commissioner of Bankrupts, has kindly contributed a portrait of his late father the Rev. Baptist Noel Turner, as well as the use of the MSS. left by that gentleman.

The Rev. Charles Turnor, F. S. A. obligingly revised the memoir of his late brother, Edmund Turnor, Esq. F. R. S. & S. A.; as did Richard Edward Kerrich, Esq. that of his late father, the Principal Librarian of Cambridge University.

The Rev. Thomas Harwood, B. D. F. S. A. of Lichfield, considerably amended the articles on the Rev. Theophilus Buckeridge, the topographer, and on Mr. Greene, the virtuoso, of that city.

The memoir of the Rev. Thomas Leman, F. S. A. was compiled with some difficulty; but at length greatly enriched by the assistance and inquiries of the Rev. Joseph Hunter, F. S. A. of Bath, and by the contribution of some letters and anecdotes by James Norris Brewer, Esq. F. S. A.

The interesting letters of Mr. Murphy, the architect and traveller, have been supplied by Thomas Crofton Croker, Esq. F. S. A.; and for a copy of

the agreements between Bishop Percy and Tonson
the bookseller Mr. Nichols was indebted to Mr.
Upcott, of the London Institution, in whose possession the originals, among many other documents
of a similar description, are deservedly preserved.

Jan. 1, 1831.

(ix)

CONTENTS

OF THE

SIXTH VOLUME.

———◆———

Page.

Page.

xiv   CONTENTS.

LIST OF PORTRAITS.

[The Binder is desired to notice five starred leaves are to be
inserted after p. 434; there is a cancel of pp. 637-8.]

ADDITIONS.

P. 40. " The history of Mr. Hellins was in every respect similar to that of his friend [the Rev. Malachy] Hitchins. He was the son of a poor labourer at Ash Raigney, or Ring's Ash, in Devonshire, and was actually bound a parish apprentice to a cooper at Chumleigh. His master was fond of the boy, and finding him diligent, indulged his inclination for study, which lay wholly in arithmetic. When out of his time he ventured to open a school at Bishop's Tawton in the same county. He had not, however, been long settled there, when Dr. Maskelyne wanting an assistant in the Royal Observatory, Mr. Hellins was recommended to him, and the situation being most acceptable, he went to Greenwich, and continued there for some years. Dr. Maskelyne was so well pleased with his conduct and love of science that he gave him much valuable instruction, introduced him to several of his friends, and lastly advised him to enter into the church. With this view he retired into Devonshire, where he studied the learned languages and theology with such diligence as to pass a very close examination before Bishop Ross with marked approbation. His first appointment was to the curacy of Constantine in Cornwall; from whence he removed into Northamptonshire, to engage in the education of the young Earl of Pomfret, who, on coming of age, gave him the Vicarage of Potterspury." *Memoir of Davies Gilbert, Esq. Pr. R. S. in the Imperial Magazine for July* 1823.

P. 45. The Rev. Malachy Hitchins " was for a long series of years the principal calculator of the Nautical Almanac and the Tables for the Board of Longitude; but, though a mathematician of the first order, he never published any distinct work. Many of his solutions are to be found in the Lady's Diary, and other Miscellanies. He was entirely self-taught, even in classical learning; for, though he proceeded to the degree of B. A. at Exeter college, Oxford, his preparatory acquirements were all the result of laborious and unassisted application. His outset in life was of course very humble; but, by becoming assistant to Benjamin Donne in making the actual survey of Devon, he had opportunities of gaining the rudiments of science, which he duly improved, till qualified for the University." *Ibid.*

It is highly to the credit of the late President of the Royal Society to have been the friend and patron of Hitchins, Hellins, and, above all, of Davy.

ILLUSTRATIONS

OF THE

LITERATURE

OF THE

EIGHTEENTH CENTURY.

WILLIAM GIFFORD, Esq.

WILLIAM GIFFORD, the Juvenal of the 18th Century, the founder, and for twenty years the conductor, of the Quarterly Review, published in 1802 a most interesting piece of autobiography. This beautifully artless and honourable narrative, although it has perhaps been more frequently perused than almost any other similar production, none of his friends will be sorry to see inserted in the present Work. Of his early life, therefore, it will, in this introductory memoir, be necessary to notice only the principal events.

Mr. Gifford was born at Ashburton in Devonshire in 1756. His parents were of an inferior station in society; and, losing them both before he had attained his thirteenth year, he was left dependant on the charity of a far from indulgent godfather. After but little education at the free-school of his native town, he was first apprenticed to the master of a coasting vessel, in which he endured great hardships for nearly a twelvemonth; and afterwards to a shoe-maker, whom he served for five years.

In his twentieth year his attempts at verse attracted the notice of Mr. Cookesley, a surgeon in the town ; and the remarkable instance he displayed of thirst for knowledge, struggling with almost overwhelming circumstances, prompted that benevolent gentleman to raise a subscription for relieving him from his apprenticeship, and supplying him with proper means of instruction. In little more than two years he was pronounced fit for the University ; and, by the interest of one of his patrons, obtained the situation of Bible-reader at Exeter-college, Oxford. His finances were then proposed to be increased by a translation of Juvenal's Satires, to be published by subscription; but the design was thwarted by the death of his friend Mr. Cookesley ; and not resumed until after a lapse of twenty years. He was, however, soon enabled to provide himself for his wants, by being allowed to take some pupils; and it was not long after that he was introduced, by an accidental circumstance, to the patronage of Lord Grosvenor. That generous nobleman, after the first exposition of the youthful student's circumstances, charged himself with his support and establishment; and received him under his own roof. Mr. Gifford continued to reside with his Lordship; and as tutor to the present Earl Grosvenor, both at home and in two successive tours on the continent, he spent many years.

Mr. Gifford did not appear as an author until 1794, when his first publication was his Satire, intituled, "The Baviad," levelled at the taste for maudlin poetry then fashionable *. That taste it was so

---

* " In 1785," says Mr. Gifford in his Preface, " a few English of both sexes, whom chance had jumbled together at Florence, took a fancy to while away their time in scribbling high panegyrics on themselves, and complimentary canzonettas on two or three Italians, who understood too little of the language to be

successful in banishing from the British Parnassus, that in the following year he was encouraged again to wield the same weapon for the amendment of dramatic poetry *. This was in "The Mæviad," an

disgusted with them. In this there was not much harm; but as folly is progressive, they soon wrought themselves into an opinion that they really deserved the fine things which were mutually said and sung of each other. About the same period a daily paper, called 'The World,' was in fashion, and much read. This paper was equally lavish of its praise and abuse, and its conductors took upon themselves to direct the taste of the town, by prefixing a short panegyric to every trifle that appeared in their own columns. The first cargo of Della Cruscan poetry was given to the public through the medium of this paper. There was a specious brilliancy in these exotics which dazzled the native grubs, who had scarce ever ventured beyond a sheep, and a crook, and a rose-tree grove; with an ostentatious display of ' blue hills,' and ' crashing torrents,' and ' petrifying suns.' From admiration to imitation is but a step. Honest Yenda tried his hand at a descriptive ode, and succeeded beyond his hopes : Anna Matilda followed ; in a word,

————————————— " Contagio labem
Hanc dedit in plures, sicut grex totus in agris
Unius scabie cadit, et porrigine porci.

" While the epidemic malady was spreading from fool to fool, Della Crusca came over, and immediately announced himself by a sonnet to love. Anna Matilda answered it; and the ' two great luminaries of the age,' as Mr. Bell calls them, fell desperately in love with each other. From that period not a day passed without an amatory epistle fraught with thunder, lightning, *et quicquid habent telorum armamentaria cœli.* The fever turned to frenzy: Laura-Maria, Carlos, Orlando, Adelaide, and a thousand other nameless names, caught the infection, and from one end of the kingdom to another, all was nonsense and Della Crusca. Even then I waited with a patience which I can better account for than excuse, for some one (abler than myself) to step forth to correct this depravity of the public taste, and check the inundation of absurdity that was bursting upon us from a thousand springs. As no one appeared, and as the evil grew every day more alarming (for now bed-ridden old women, and girls at their sampler, began to rave), I determined, without much confidence of success, to try what could be effected by my feeble powers ; and accordingly wrote the following poem."

* " I know not," Mr. Gifford declares in the preface to this Satire, " if the stage has been so low since the days of Gammar Gurton as at this hour. It seems as if all the block-

4 ILLUSTRATIONS OF LITERATURE.

imitation of the tenth Satire of the first book of
Horace. Never was satire better employed, or
more powerfully directed, than it was in both these
instances, but the effect was not equal; for while
the triumph of the Baviad was signally decisive,
that of the Mæviad was only partial. Not that
the execution of the latter failed; on the contrary,
of the two the Mæviad excels in pointed wit and
dignified severity of language; but, as unfortunately the malady opposed had its seat more in the
public manners than in the affectation of individuals,
it was not so easily expelled.

The next object of Mr. Gifford's satyric muse
was a writer who had made himself notorious by
the most scurrilous attacks on all that was good and
great in the Kingdom. Mr. Gifford, who well
knew the man, his history *, and his habits, discharged against him one of his sharpest arrows, in
the form of an " Epistle to Peter Pindar." Wol-
cott, though a lampooner of others, could not bear
to be satirized himself; and, stung to the soul by

heads in the kingdom had started up and exclaimed, *una voce*,
' Come! let us write for the theatres.' In this there is nothing,
perhaps, altogether new, but the striking and peculiar novelty
of the times seems to be, that all they write is received. Of the
three parties concerned in this business, the writers and the
managers seem the least culpable. If the town will have husks,
extraordinary pains need not be taken to find them any thing
more palatable. But what shall we say of the town itself!
The lower orders of the people are so brutified and besotted by
the lamentable follies of O'Keefe, and Cobbe, and Pilon, and I
know not who—*Sardi venales*, each worse than the other—that
they have lost all relish for simplicity and genuine humour;
nay, ignorance itself, unless it be gross and glaring, cannot
hope for ' their most sweet voices.' And the higher ranks are
so mawkishly mild, that they take with a placid simper whatever comes before them; or, if they now and then experience a
slight disgust, have not resolution enough to express it, but sit
yawning and gaping in each other's faces for a little encouragement in their pitiful forbearance."

* It is remarkable that the two keenest satyrists of the age
should have been born (out of the metropolis or any large
town) within fifteen miles of each other.

this attack, determined upon revenge. Instead, however, of applying in the first place to his most powerful weapon, "the grey goose quill," he assumed the *argumentum baculinum*, and sallied forth in quest of his adversary. Watching his opportunity, and seeing Mr. Gifford enter the shop of Mr. Wright, the bookseller, in Piccadilly, he rushed in after him, and aimed a blow at Mr. Gifford's head with the cudgel which he had provided for the occasion. Fortunately, a gentleman standing by saw the movement in time to seize the arm of the enraged Poet, who was then bundled out into the street, and rolled in the mud, to the great amusement of the gathered crowd. Nothing further took place at that time, but the disappointed satirist went home and penned one of his worst pieces, which he published with the title of " A Cut at a Cobbler." As, however, there was more passion than either poetry or wit in this performance, the only laugh which it provoked was against its author.

About this time, however, Mr. Gifford entered into a warfare of much greater moment. A number of men of brilliant talents and high connection, at the head of whom was Mr. Canning, the late Premier, having determined to establish a weekly paper, for the purpose of exposing to deserved ridicule and indignation the political agitators by whom the country was then inundated, had engaged as editor a Dr. Grant, well known as a writer in the reviews and other periodical works of that period. A few days before the intended publication of the first number of " The Anti-Jacobin " (which was the name given to the new paper), Dr. Grant being taken seriously ill, sent for Mr. Wright the bookseller, who was to be the publisher of it, told him of his utter inability to discharge the arduous and responsible duties of editor, and requested that he would communicate the

circumstance to some of the individuals by whom
the undertaking had been projected. Mr. Wright
accordingly waited upon Mr. Charles Long (now
Lord Farnborough), and informed him of what had
occurred. Mr. Long asked Mr. Wright if he knew
any one who was competent to the office. Mr.
Wright mentioned Mr. Gifford's name, and was
immediately commissioned to make Mr. Gifford
the offer, which that gentleman accepted without
hesitation. The first number appeared on the 20th
of November 1797, and the publication continued
until the 9th of July 1798. Some of the ablest
articles in this celebrated journal were written by
Mr. Gifford. A corner of the paper was expressly
reserved for the " misrepresentation" and " lies "
of the Opposition papers ; and these misrepresentations and lies it was especially Mr. Gifford's province to detect and expose. Mr. Gifford's connexion with the Anti-jacobin naturally led to a very
agreeable intimacy with a number of men of rank
and distinction, among whom were Mr. Canning,
Mr. Frere, Mr. Charles Long (now Lord Farnborough), Mr. Jenkinson (the present Earl of Liverpool), Lord Mornington (now Marquis Wellesley), Lord Clare, Mr. Pitt, &c. With one or other
of these eminent individuals Mr. Gifford dined twice
or thrice a week; and at these festive meetings many
of the most exquisite papers in the Anti-jacobin
were concocted. The value of Mr. Gifford's powerful assistance was acknowledged by every one; but
of all governments on the face of the globe, that of
England has invariably exhibited the most prudish
delicacy of finance in the recompense of literary
exertion. The ministerial recollection of Mr. Gifford's services was by no means a signal exception
to the rule, although he obtained the Paymastership
of the Band of Gentleman Pensioners. At a subsequent period he was made a double commissioner
of the lottery.

In 1802 Mr. Gifford published his Juvenal in quarto, under the title of, "The Satires of Decimus Junius Juvenalis; translated into English verse, with notes and illustrations." The translation was the first of the Roman satirist which had deserved that name*; and in the notes Mr. Gifford found opportunity to display a very extensive acquaintance with the early poetry of his own country. Throughout his life he prosecuted at his leisure hours this interesting study; and at intervals he published the results as a commentator. In 1805 an edition of the plays of Massinger, in four volumes octavo, was issued under his editorial care; and in 1816 appeared the Works of Ben Jonson, in nine octavo volumes. Of Jonson in particular, the most learned in the estimation of his contemporaries, the best poet of his age (although he who "exhausted worlds and then imagined new" is now, by the suffrage of posterity, preferred to a seat so vastly superior,) a standard edition was certainly a great desideratum. The impartial reader must peruse with delight and admiration the able and convincing vindication of the poet's personal character and disposition, which is contained in the 307 introductory pages. Jonson,

---

* The Monthly Reviewers thus expressed their opinion: "In the translation before us the Roman satirist appears with great advantage. Mr. Gifford has caught the spirit and style of his author; and he has in general accomplished his endeavour, which was to make Juvenal speak as he would probably have spoken if he had lived among us. Excepting Dr. Johnson's admirable imitations of the 3d and 10th Satires, we know not any prior version in our language which could convey to the English reader so complete an idea of the stateliness, force, and point, which are the prominent features of the compositions of this bard. It is needless to mention the translations of Stapleton, Holiday, Dryden and his coadjutors, and Owen, since they will not endure a comparison with that of Mr. Gifford, which conveys the sense and manner of the original in easy and flowing verse." Of some strictures on the Juvenal, which appeared in the Critical Review, Mr. Gifford published an "Examination," in 1803, and a "Supplement to that Examination in 1804." An octavo edition of the Juvenal was published in 1806.

though truly honest, sincere, and benevolent, had undeniably a somewhat rough and forbidding demeanour; this made enemies in his own time, and their aspersions were perpetuated by biographers who should have exercised more discrimination. The number was greatly increased by those, who to feed the popular deification of Shakspeare have attempted to immolate at his altar every author that could possibly be brought into comparison with him; as well as by those who in sacrificing to other authors of that period have so frequently made Jonson their victim; and all such Mr. Gifford has classed under the title of the " enemies" of Jonson. The folly, and in many instances the misrepresentations of these enemies, no writer could have proved so deeply, or cauterised so sharply, as the vigorous and undaunted author of the Baviad and Mæviad.

In 1821 appeared Mr. Gifford's translation of Persius, at the same time with another by that profound and elegant scholar, Sir William Drummond, author of " Academical Questions," &c.

At the time of his death Mr. Gifford left, in a complete state for publication, the Dramatic Works of Ford, in two volumes, which have since appeared *.

* " Of the text of this long-expected edition of Ford we shall merely say, that its correction and purification display in an uncommon degree, the extraordinary critical skill, sagacity, and perspicuity of the late William Gifford. His vast extent of reading and intimate acquaintance with our ancient dramatists, are signalised by a multitude of amendments; while his judgment and acumen are equally apparent in the great variety of new lights and able annotations dissipating almost all those corrections and mistakes with which careless typography and senseless commentaries had loaded the author. The prefatory matter, contained in an Introduction and Notes, and occupying nearly 200 pages, appears to have been written, or at least begun, about 1812-13, though not finished till very recently, as it alludes to the operas of Faust and the Freyschütz. Never did Mr. Gifford dip his pen in gall of deeper wormwood flavour than in his remarks on Steevens, Malone, Weber, (and, by implication with the latter, somewhat on Sir Walter Scott,) in these pages. He has cut, and spared not; and whether we

Those of Shirley, in six volumes, were also advanced towards the middle of the last volume; and whilst this page is printing they are still due to the world, although they may very probably be published before the present volume *.

Throughout the early part of these labours, the height of Mr. Gifford's ambition in this department of literature was to superintend an edition of Shakspeare : and in one passage of his Jonson in particular (perhaps in more than one) he particularly laments that his former prospects of the realisation of this wish were not likely to be gratified.

To proceed to speak of Mr. Gifford in the character in which he was most generally known,—that of editor of the Quarterly Review. On its establishment in 1809, he was, in a happy hour for the proprietor and for the public, appointed its conductor ; and it remained under his direction until about two years before his decease. Of the unwearied industry, extensive knowledge, varied talent, correct judgment, and sound principle, exhibited by Mr. Gifford in the management of this excellent and popular publication, during the long course of between fifteen and sixteen years, it is wholly unnecessary to speak. It must be acknowledged that at times his pen was at least sufficiently severe ; but it

acknowledge or deny the justice of all his lashes, we must, while we accuse them of being harsh and remorseless, confess that they bestow a discipline on the genius of lumbering and perplexing annotators, which may have a salutary effect in future times on worthies of that kind." Lit. Gaz. March 3, 1827.

* " The Plays and Poems of Shirley, which never had been previously collected and uniformly printed, Gifford lived to finish; and, it is said, the ' Life of Shirley,' which alone was incomplete at Mr. Gifford's death, was in a considerable state of advancement. The papers are, we understand, at present with the executor, Dr. Ireland, who laboured so hard upon his analysis of the Plays of Massinger, and had so long and intimate acquaintance with the views and literary opinion of Mr. Gifford; so that this most interesting work, which has been nearly eighteen years in the press, will probably soon be ready for publication." St. James's Chronicle, Oct. 1827.

merits observation, that none of the various parties, poetical, religious, or political, that occasionally felt the castigation bestowed upon their productions in the Quarterly Review, ever ventured to recriminate, by attacking the moral character of the editor. Even Lord Byron, who alternately praised and abused most of his contemporaries, professed great respect for Mr. Gifford, lauded the purity of his principles, and courted his friendship.

Mr. Gifford died at his house, No. 6, James-street, Buckingham-gate, on the 31st of December, 1826. It was his original wish to be buried in the burying-ground * attached to Grosvenor

* Where there is a tomb-stone displaying the following epitaph:

"Here lies the body of ANN DAVIES, for more than xx years servant to WILLIAM GIFFORD. She died February 6th, MDCCCXV, in the xxxxiii year of her age, of a tedious and painful malady, which she bore with exemplary patience and resignation. Her deeply afflicted master erected this stone to her memory, as a painful testimony of her uncommon worth, and of his perpetual gratitude, respect, and affection, for her long and meritorious services.

Though here unknown, dear Ann, thy ashes rest,
Still lives thy memory in one grateful breast,
That trac'd thy course through many a painful year,
And marked thy humble hope, thy pious fear.
O! when this frame, which yet, while life remain'd,
Thy duteous love with trembling hand sustain'd,
Dissolves (as soon it must), may that bless'd Power,
Who beam'd on thine, illume my parting hour!
So shall I greet thee, where no ills annoy,
And what was sown in grief, is reap'd in joy;
Where worth, obscur'd below, bursts into day,
And those are paid whom earth could never pay."

"His regard for this faithful attendant also manifested itself in the following simple, beautiful, and affecting stanzas; which rank with the best productions of our elegiac poetry:

" I wish I was where Anna lies,
    For I am sick of lingering here,
And every hour affection cries,
    ' Go and partake her humble bier.'

Chapel, South Audley-street; but his friend Dr.
Ireland* procured his consent to have his body

> I wish I could ; for when she died
>   I lost my all ; and life has proved,
> Since that sad hour, a dreary void—
>   A waste unlovely and unlov'd.
>
> But who, when I am turn'd to clay,
>   Shall duly to her grave repair,
> And pluck the rugged moss away,
>   And weeds that have no business there ?
>
> And who with pious hand shall bring
>   The flowers she cherish'd (snow-drop cold,
> And violets, that unheeded spring)
>   To scatter o'er her hallow'd mould ?
>
> And who, while memory loves to dwell
>   Upon her name, for ever dear,
> Shall feel his heart with passion swell,
>   And pour the bitter—bitter tear ?
>
> I did it ; and would Fate allow,
>   Should visit still—should still deplore ;
> But health and strength have left me now,
>   And I, alas ! can weep no more.
>
> Take then, sweet maid, this simple strain,
>   The last I offer at thy shrine ;
> Thy grave must then undeck'd remain,
>   And all thy memory fade with mine.
>
> And can thy soft persuasive look,
>   Thy voice that might with music vie,
> Thy air, that every gazer took,
>   Thy matchless eloquence of eye,
>
> Thy spirits, frolicsome as good,
>   Thy courage by no ills dismay'd,
> Thy patience by no wrongs subdued,
>   Thy gay good humour—can they fade ?
>
> Perhaps—but sorrow dims my eye—
>   Cold turf which I no more must view,
> Dear name, which I no more must sigh,
>   A long, a last,—a sad adieu ! "

* " With what feelings," says Mr. Gifford, in concluding the
preface to his Jonson, " do I trace the words—THE DEAN OF
WESTMINSTER ! Five-and-forty springs have now passed over
my head, since I first found Dr. Ireland, some years my junior,
in our little school, at his spelling-book. During this long
period, our friendship has been without a cloud ; my delight in

deposited in Westminster Abbey. Its interment took place on the 8th of January 1827, immediately below the monuments of Camden and Garrick. The first mourning coach contained Dr. Ireland, Dean of Westminster, General Grosvenor, Mr. Cookesley, senior, and Mr. Cookesley, jun.; the second, Mr. Croker, Mr. Barrow, Mr. Hay, and Mr. Backhouse: the third, Mr. Chantrey (the sculptor), Mr. Bedford, Mr. Lockhart, and Mr. Sergeant Rough; the fourth, Mr. Palgrave, Mr. Hoppner, Mr. Jacob, and Mr. Taylor (the late proprietor of the Sun newspaper); the fifth and last, Mr. Bandinell, Dr. Thompson, Mr. Parsloe, Mr. Cooper, and Mr. Murray, the bookseller. The deceased gentleman's carriage, with those of the

youth, my pride and consolation in old age!"—Mr. Gifford had before alluded to this faithful friendship, in the following beautiful lines of the " Baviad:"

> " Sure, if our fates hang on some hidden power,
> And take their colour from the natal hour;
> Then, IRELAND, the same planet on us rose,
> Such the strong sympathies our lives disclose.
> Thou know'st how soon we felt this influence bland,
> And sought the brook and coppice hand in hand,
> And shaped rude bows, and uncouth whistles blew,
> And paper kites (a last, great effort!) flew;
> And when the day was done, retired to rest,
> Sleep on our eyes, and sunshine on our breast.
> In riper years, again together thrown,
> Our studies, as our sports before, were one ;
> Together we explored the stoic page
> Of the Ligurian, stern though beardless sage !
> Together too, when Greece unlock'd her stores,
> We rov'd in thought o'er Troy's devoted shores,
> Or follow'd, while he sought his native soil,
> That " old man eloquent," from toil to toil ;
> Lingering with good Alcinoüs o'er the tale,
> Till the east redden'd and the stars grew pale.
> So past our life,—till Fate, severely kind,
> Tore us apart, and land and sea disjoin'd
> For many a year; now met, to part no more,
> The ascendant power, confess'd so strong of yore,
> Stronger by absence every thought controls,
> And knits in perfect unity our souls ! "

Dean of Westminster, Lord Grosvenor, Mr. Parsloe, Mr. Jacob, Lord Belgrave, Mr. Backhouse, Dr. Thompson, and Mr. Croker, closed the procession.

The probate of Mr. Gifford's will was taken out under £.25,000 personal property. He left the bulk of his fortune to the Rev. Mr. Cookesley, who was likewise appointed his residuary legatee. He left his house in James-street, for the remainder of the term, nearly thirty years, to Mrs. Hoppner, widow of the eminent portrait-painter, and legacies of a few hundreds to her children. He bequeathed a sum of money, the interest of which is to be distributed annually among the poor of Ashburton; and to Exeter-college another sum, the foundation of two scholarships. Three thousand pounds were left to the relatives of his beloved maid-servant. To Mr. Heber he bequeathed his edition of Maittaire's Classics, and any other books Mr. Heber might choose to select. To Mr. Murray, the bookseller, he left £.100 as a memorial; likewise five hundred guineas, to enable him to reimburse a military gentleman, to whom he appears to have become jointly bound for the advance of that sum for Mr. Cookesley, at a former period. To his executor, Dr. Ireland, he gave fifty guineas for a ring, and any of his books the Dean might select. He requested his executor to destroy all confidential papers, especially those relating to the Review, so that the illustrated Quarterly, in which the names of the authors, and the prices paid for each article, are said to have been inserted, will never see the light. There were also other legacies to individuals; and various codicils. The whole was in the hand-writing of Mr Gifford.

1. MR. GIFFORD'S AUTOBIOGRAPHICAL MEMOIR *.

" I know but little of my family, and that little is not very precise. My great-grandfather (the most remote of it that I ever recollect to have heard mentioned) possessed considerable property at Halsworthy, a parish in the neighbourhood of Ashburton; but whether acquired or inherited I never thought of asking, and do not know †.

" He was probably a native of Devonshire, for there he spent the last years of his life; spent them, too, in some sort of consideration, for Mr. T. a very respectable surgeon at Ashburton) loved to repeat to me, when I first grew into notice, that he had frequently hunted with his hounds.

" My grandfather was on ill terms with him; I believe not without sufficient reason, for he was extravagant and dissipated. My father never mentioned his name, but my mother would sometimes tell me that he had ruined the family. That he spent much I know; but I am inclined to think that his undutiful conduct occasioned my great-grandfather to bequeath a part of his property from him.

" My father, I fear, revenged, in some measure, the cause of my great-grandfather. He was, as I have heard my mother say, ' a very wild young man, who could be kept to nothing.' He was sent to the grammar-school at Exeter, from which he made his escape, and entered on board a man of war. He was soon reclaimed from his situation by my grandfather, and left his school a second time to wander in some vagabond society ‡. He

* Of the powerful impression which this narrative produced, at the time of its publication, on every candid and honourable mind, the following just and animated passages in a critique on Mr. Gifford's Translation of Juvenal, which appeared in the Monthly Review in 1803, will furnish a sufficient proof:

" Mr. Gifford has introduced this volume by a memoir of himself, which is written with so much ability and unaffected modesty, with so much ingenuousness and manly feeling, that it must secure to him universal regard and esteem. He may say with the admired author whom he translates, *Stemmata quid faciunt?* for he possesses what ancestry cannot bequeath, great talents and a noble mind; and while, without reserve, he discloses the obscurity of his origin, his struggles with poverty in the lowest situations, and his progress in mental improvement under the most sickening discouragements, he increases our respect for him, and prepares us to rejoice in those propitious circumstances which favoured the expansion of his mind, fostered his love of science, and raised him to a state of independence. Of such a life as that of Mr. Gifford, no man, who thinks and feels like a man, will be ashamed."

† " I have, however, some faint notion of hearing my mother say, that he, or his father, had been a china-merchant in London. By china-merchant, I always understood, and so perhaps did she, a dealer in china-ware."

‡ " He had gone with Bamfylde Moore Carew, then an old man."

was now probably given up, for he was, on his return from this notable adventure, reduced to article himself to a plumber and glazier, with whom he luckily staid long enough to learn the business. I suppose his father was now dead, for he became possessed of two small estates, married my mother * (the daughter of a carpenter at Ashburton), and thought himself rich enough to set up for himself, which he did with some credit at South Molton. Why he chose to fix there I never inquired; but I learned from my mother that, after a residence of four or five years, he was again thoughtless enough to engage in a dangerous frolic, which drove him once more to sea. This was an attempt to excite a riot in a Methodist chapel; for which his companions were prosecuted, and he fled, as I have mentioned.

" My father was a good seaman, and was soon made second in command in the Lyon, a large armed transport in the service of government; while my mother (then with child of me) returned to her native place, Ashburton, where I was born in April 1757.

" The resources of my mother were very scanty. They arose from the rent of three or four small fields, which yet remained unsold. With these, however, she did what she could for me ; and as soon as I was old enough to be trusted out of her sight, sent me to a schoolmistress of the name of Parret, from whom I learned in due time to read. I cannot boast much of my acquisitions at this school, they consisted merely of the contents of the ' Child's Spelling Book ; ' but from my mother, who had stored up the literature of a country town, which about half a century ago amounted to little more than what was disseminated by itinerant ballad-singers, or rather readers, I had acquired much curious knowledge of Catskin, and the Golden Bull, and the Bloody Gardener, and many other histories equally instructive and amusing.

" My father returned from sea in 1764. He had been at the siege of Havannah ; and though he received more than a hundred pounds for prize-money, and his wages were considerable, yet, as he had not acquired any strict habits of economy, he brought home but a trifling sum. The little property yet left was therefore turned into money ; a trifle more was got by agreeing to renounce all future pretensions to an estate at Totness †, and with this my father set up a second time as a glazier and house-painter. I was now about eight years old, and was put to the free-school (kept by Hugh Smerdon) to learn to

* " Her maiden name was Elizabeth Cain. My father's Christian name was Edward."

† " This was a lot of small houses, which had been thoughtlessly suffered to fall to decay, and of which the rents had been so long unclaimed, that they could not now be recovered, unless by an expensive litigation."

read, and write, and cypher. Here I continued about three years, making a most wretched progress, when my father fell sick and died. He had not acquired wisdom from his misfortunes, but continued wasting his time in unprofitable pursuits, to the great detriment of his business. He loved drink for the sake of society, and to this love he fell a martyr; dying of a decayed and ruined constitution before he was forty. The town's people thought him a shrewd and sensible man, and regretted his death. As for me, I never greatly loved him; I had not grown up with him; and he was too prone to repulse my little advances to familiarity with coldness and anger. He had certainly some reason to be displeased with me, for I learned little at school, and nothing at home, though he would now and then attempt to give me some insight into the business. As impressions of any kind are not very strong at the age of eleven or twelve, I did not long feel his loss; nor was it a subject of much sorrow to me that my mother was doubtful of her ability to continue me at school, though I had by this time acquired a love for reading.

" I never knew in what circumstances my mother was left; most probably they were inadequate to her support without some kind of exertion, especially as she was now burdened with a second child, about six or eight months old. Unfortunately she determined to prosecute my father's business; for which purpose she engaged a couple of journeymen, who finding her ignorant of every part of it, wasted her property and embezzled her money. What the consequence of this double fraud would have been there was no opportunity of knowing, as in somewhat less than a twelvemonth my poor mother followed my father to the grave. She was an excellent woman, bore my father's infirmities with patience and good humour, loved her children dearly, and died at last exhausted with anxiety and grief, more on their account than on her own.

" I was not quite thirteen when this happened; my little brother was hardly two; and we had not a relation nor a friend in the world. Every thing that was left was seized by a person of the name of C——, for money advanced to my mother It may be supposed that I could not dispute the justice of his claims, and as no one else interfered, he was suffered to do as he liked. My little brother was sent to the alms-house, whither his nurse followed him out of pure affection, and I was taken to the house of the person I have just mentioned, who was also my godfather. Respect for the opinion of the town (which, whether correct or not, was, that he had repaid himself by the sale of my mother's effects,) induced him to send me again to school, where I was more diligent than before, and more successful. I grew fond of arithmetic, and my master began to distinguish me; but these golden days were over in less than three months. C—— sickened at the expense; and as the people were now indifferent to my fate, he looked round for an opportunity of ridding himself of a useless charge. He had previously attempted to engage me in the drudgery of husbandry. I drove the plough for one day to gratify him, but I left it with a firm resolution to do so no more; and, in despite of his threats and promises, adhered to my determination. In this I was guided no less by necessity than will. During my father's life, in attempting to clamber up a table I had fallen backward and drawn it after me; its edge fell upon my breast, and I never recovered from the effects of the blow, of which I was made extremely sensible on any extraordinary exertion. Ploughing, therefore, was out of the question, and, as I have already said, I utterly refused to follow it.

" As I could write and cypher (as the phrase is), C—— next thought of sending me to Newfoundland to assist in a storehouse. For this purpose he negotiated with a Mr. Holdesworthy of Dartmouth, who agreed to fit me out. I left Ashburton with little expectation of seeing it again, and indeed with little care, and rode with my godfather to the dwelling of Mr. Holdesworthy. On seeing me, this great man observed, with a look of pity and contempt, that I was too small, and sent me away sufficiently mortified. I expected to be very ill received by my godfather, but he said nothing. He did not, however, choose to take me back himself, but sent me in the passage boat to Totness, from whence I was to walk home. On the passage the boat was driven by a midnight storm on the rocks, and I escaped with life almost by miracle.

" My godfather had now humbler views for me, and I had little heart to resist any thing. He proposed to send me on board one of the Torbay fishing boats; I ventured, however, to remonstrate against this, and the matter was compromised by my consenting to go on board a coaster. A coaster was speedily found for me at Brixham, and thither I went, when little more than thirteen.

" My master, whose name was Full, though a gross and ignorant, was not an ill-natured man, at least not to me; and my mistress used me with unvarying kindness, moved, perhaps, by my weakness and tender years. In return I did what I could to requite her, and my good-will was not overlooked.

" Our vessel was not very large, nor our crew very numerous. On ordinary occasions, such as short trips to Dartmouth, Plymouth, &c. it consisted only of my master, an apprentice nearly out of his time, and myself; when we had to go farther, to Portsmouth for example, an additional hand was hired for the voyage.

" In this vessel (the Two Brothers) I continued nearly a twelvemonth; and here I got acquainted with nautical terms, and contracted a love for the sea, which a lapse of thirty years has but little diminished.

" It will be easily conceived that my life was a life of hardship. I was not only a 'ship-boy on the high and giddy mast,' but also in the cabin, where every menial office fell to my lot; yet, if I was restless and discontented, I can safely say, it was not so much on account of this as of my being precluded from all possibility of reading; as my master did not possess, nor do I recollect seeing, during the whole time of my abode with him, a single book of any description, except the Coasting Pilot.

" As my lot seemed to be cast, however, I was not negligent in seeking such information as promised to be useful; and I therefore frequented, at my leisure hours, such vessels as dropt into Torbay. On attempting to get on board one of these, which I did at midnight, I missed my footing and fell into the sea. The floating away of the boat alarmed the man on deck, who came to the ship's side just in time to see me sink. He immediately threw out several ropes, one of which providentially (for I was unconscious of it) entangled itself about me, and I was drawn up to the surface till a boat could be got round. The usual methods were taken to recover me, and I awoke in bed the next morning, remembering nothing but the horror I felt when I first found myself unable to cry out for assistance.

" This was not my only escape, but I forbear to speak of them. An escape of another kind was now preparing for me, which deserves all my notice, as it was decisive of my future fate.

" On Christmas-day (1770) I was surprised by a message from my godfather, saying that he had sent a man and horse to bring me to Ashburton, and desiring me to set out without delay. My master, as well as myself, supposed it was to spend the holidays there; and he, therefore, made no objection to my going. We were, however, both mistaken.

" Since I had lived at Brixham, I had broken off all connection with Ashburton. I had no relation there but my poor brother *, who was yet too young for any kind of correspondence; and the conduct of my godfather towards me, did not entitle him to any portion of my gratitude or kind remembrance. I lived, therefore, in a sort of sullen independence on all I had formerly known, and thought, without regret, of being aban-

---

* " Of my brother, here introduced for the last time, I must yet say a few words. He was literally
' The child of misery baptised in tears ; '
and the short passage of his life did not belie the melancholy presage of his infancy. When he was seven years old, the parish bound him out to a husbandman of the name of Leman, with whom he endured incredible hardships, which I had it not in my power to alleviate. At nine years of age he broke his thigh, and I took that opportunity to teach him to read and write. When my own situation was improved, I persuaded him to try the sea ; he did so, and was taken on board the Egmont, on condition that his master should receive his wages. The time was now fast approaching when I could serve him, but he was doomed to know no favourable change of fortune ; he fell sick, and died at Cork."

doned by every one to my fate.   But I had not been overlooked.
The women of Brixham, who travelled to Ashburton twice a
week with fish, and who had known my parents, did not see me
without kind concern, running about the beach in a ragged
jacket and trowsers.   They mentioned this to the people of Ashburton, and never without commiserating my change of condition.   This tale often repeated, awakened at length the pity
of their auditors, and, as the next step, their resentment against
the man who had reduced me to such a state of wretchedness.
In a large town this would have had little effect, but in a place
like Ashburton, where every report speedily becomes the common property of all the inhabitants, it raised a murmur which
my godfather found himself either unable or unwilling to withstand; he therefore determined, as I have just observed, to recall me, which he could easily do, as I wanted some months of
fourteen, and, consequently, was not yet bound.

   " All this I learned on my arrival ; and my heart, which had
been cruelly shut up, now opened to kinder sentiments, and
fairer views.

   " After the holidays I returned to my darling pursuit, arithmetic; my progress was now so rapid, that in a few months I
was at the head of the school, and qualified to assist my master
(Mr. E. Furlong) on any extraordinary emergency.   As he
usually gave me a trifle on those occasions, it raised a thought in
me, that by engaging with him as a regular assistant, and undertaking the instruction of a few evening scholars, I might, with
a little additional aid, be enabled to support myself.   God
knows, my ideas of support at this time were of no very extravagant nature.   I had, besides, another object in view.   Mr.
Hugh Smerdon (my first master) was now grown old and infirm; it seemed unlikely that he should hold out above three or
four years ; and I fondly flattered myself that, notwithstanding
my youth, I might possibly be appointed to succeed him.   I was
in my fifteenth year when I built these castles; a storm, however, was collecting, which unexpectedly burst upon me, and
swept them all away.

   " On mentioning my little plan to C. he treated it with the
utmost contempt ; and told me, in my turn, that as I had learned
enough, and more than enough, at school, he must be considered as having fairly discharged his duty (so, indeed, he had) ;
he added that he had been negociating with his cousin, a shoe-
maker of some respectability, who had liberally agreed to take
me without a fee as an apprentice.   I was so shocked at this
intelligence, that I did not remonstrate, but went in sullenness
and silence to my new master, to whom I was soon after bound *,
till I should obtain the age of twenty-one.

   " The family consisted of four journeymen, two sons about

   * " My indenture, which now lies before me, is dated the 1st of
January 1772."

C 2

nly own age, and an apprentice somewhat older. In these there was nothing remarkable; but my master himself was the strangest creature! He was a Presbyterian, whose reading was entirely confined to the small tracts published on the Exeter controversy. As these (at least his portion of them) were all on one side, he entertained no doubt of their infallibility, and being noisy and disputatious, was sure to silence his opponents; and became, in consequence of it, intolerably arrogant and conceited. He was not, however, indebted solely to his knowledge of the subject for his triumph; he was possessed of Fenning's Dictionary, and he made a most singular use of it. His custom was to fix on any word in common use, and then to get by heart the synonym or periphrasis by which it was explained in the book; this he constantly substituted for the other, and as his opponents were commonly ignorant of his meaning, his victory was complete.

" With such a man I was not likely to add much to my stock of knowledge, small as it was; and, indeed, nothing could well be smaller. At this period I had read nothing but a black-letter romance, called Parismus and Parismenus, and a few loose Magazines which my mother had brought from South Molton. The Bible, indeed, I was well acquainted with; it was the favourite study of my grandmother, and reading it frequently with her had impressed it strongly on my mind; these then, with the imitation of Thomas à Kempis, which I used to read to my mother on her death-bed, constituted the whole of my literary acquisitions.

" As I hated my new profession with a perfect hatred, I made no progress in it; and was consequently little regarded in the family, of which I sunk by degrees into the common drudge. This did not much disquiet me, for my spirits were now humbled. I did not, however, quite resign the hope of one day succeeding Mr. Hugh Smerdon, and therefore secretly prosecuted my favourite study at every interval of leisure.

" These intervals were not very frequent, and when the use I made of them was found out, they were rendered still less so. I could not guess the motives for this at first; but at length I discovered that my master destined his youngest son for the situation to which I aspired.

" I possessed at this time but one book in the world; it was a Treatise on Algebra, given to me by a young woman, who had found it in a lodging-house. I considered it as a treasure, but it was a treasure locked up; for it supposed the reader to be well acquainted with simple equation, and I knew nothing of the matter. My master's son had purchased Fenning's Introduction; this was precisely what I wanted, but he carefully concealed it from me, and I was indebted to chance alone for stumbling upon his hiding-place. I sat up for the greatest part of several nights successively, and before he suspected that his treatise was discovered, had completely mastered it. I could now enter upon my own; and that carried me pretty far into the science.

"This was not done without difficulty; I had not a farthing on earth, nor a friend to give me one; pen, ink, and paper, therefore, (in despite of the flippant remark of Lord Orford,) were, for the most part, as completely out of my reach as a crown and sceptre. There was, indeed, a resource; but the utmost caution and secrecy were necessary in applying to it. I beat out pieces of leather as smooth as possible, and wrought my problems on them with a blunted awl; for the rest, my memory was tenacious, and I could multiply and divide by it to a great extent.

"Hitherto I had not so much as dreamt of poetry; indeed I scarce knew it by name, and whatever may be said of the force of nature, I certainly never ' lisped in numbers.' I recollect the occasion of my first attempt; it is like all the rest of my non-adventures, of so unimportant a nature, that I should blush to call the attention of the idlest reader to it, but for the reason alleged in the introductory paragraph. A person, whose name escapes me, had undertaken to paint a sign for an ale-house; it was to be a lion, but the unfortunate artist produced a dog. On this awkward affair, one of my acquaintance wrote a copy of what we called verses; I liked it, but fancied I could compose something more to the purpose; I tried, and by the unanimous suffrage of my shopmates was allowed to have succeeded. Notwithstanding this encouragement, I thought no more of verse, till another occurrence, as trifling as the former, furnished me with a fresh subject; and so I went on, till I had got together about a dozen of them. Certainly nothing on earth was ever so deplorable; such as they were, however, they were talked of in my little circle, and I was sometimes invited to repeat them, even out of it. I never committed a line to paper for two reasons; first, because I had no paper; and secondly—perhaps I might be excused from going farther—but in truth I was afraid, for my master had already threatened me for inadvertently hitching the name of one of his customers into a rhyme.

"The repetitions of which I speak were always attended with applause, and sometimes with favours more substantial; little collections were now and then made, and I have received sixpence in an evening. To one who had long lived in the absolute want of money, such a resource seemed like a Peruvian mine. I furnished myself by degrees with paper, &c. and, what was of more importance, with books of geometry, and of the higher branches of algebra, which I cautiously concealed. Poetry, even at this time, was no amusement of mine; it was subservient to other purposes; and I only had recourse to it when I wanted money for my mathematical pursuits.

" But the clouds were gathering fast. My master's anger was raised to a terrible pitch by my indifference to his concerns, and still more by the reports which were daily brought to him of my presumptuous attempts at versification. I was required to give up my papers, and when I refused, my garret was searched, my little hoard of books discovered and removed, and all future repetitions prohibited in the strictest manner.

" This was a very severe stroke, and I felt it most sensibly; it was followed by another severer still; a stroke which crushed the hopes I had so long and so fondly cherished, and resigned me at once to despair. Mr. Hugh Smerdon, on whose succession I had calculated, died, and was succeeded by a person not much older than myself, and certainly not so well qualified for the situation.

" I look back to that part of my life which immediately followed this event with little satisfaction; it was a period of gloom and savage unsociability: by degrees I sunk into a kind of corporeal torpor; or if roused into activity by the spirit of youth, wasted the exertion in splenetic and vexatious tricks, which alienated the few acquaintances compassion had yet left me. So I crept on in silent discontent; unfriendly and unpitied; indignant at the present, careless of the future, an object at once of apprehension and dislike.

" From this state of abjectness I was raised by a young woman of my own class. She was a neighbour; and whenever I took my solitary walk, with my Wolfius in my pocket, she usually came to the door, and by a smile, or a short question put in the friendliest manner, endeavoured to solicit my attention. My heart had been long shut to kindness, but the sentiment was not dead in me; it revived at the first encouraging word; and the gratitude I felt for it was the first pleasing sensation I had ventured to entertain for many dreary months.

" Together with gratitude, hope, and other passions still more enlivening, took place of that uncomfortable gloominess which so lately possessed me. I returned to my companions, and by every winning art in my power strove to make them forget my former repulsive ways. In this I was not unsuccessful; I recovered their good will, and came by degrees to be somewhat of a favourite.

" My master still murmured, for the business of the shop went on no better than before. I comforted myself, however, with the reflection that my apprenticeship was drawing to a conclusion, when I determined to renounce the employment for ever, and to open a private school.

" In this humble and obscure state, poor beyond the common lot, yet flattering my ambition with day-dreams, which, perhaps, would never have been realized, I was found in the twentieth year of my age by Mr. William Cookesley, a name never to be pronounced by me without veneration. The lamentable doggrel which I have already mentioned, and which had passed from mouth to mouth among people of my own degree, had by some accident or other reached his ear, and gave him a curiosity to inquire after the author.

" It was my good fortune to interest his benevolence. My little history was not untinctured with melancholy, and I laid it fairly before him; his first care was to console; his second, which he cherished to the last moment of his existence, was to relieve and support me.

" Mr. Cookesley was not rich; his eminence in his profession, which was that of a surgeon, procured him, indeed, much employment; but in a country town men of science are not the most liberally rewarded. He had, besides, a very numerous family, which left him little for the purposes of general benevolence; that little, however, was cheerfully bestowed, and his activity and zeal were always at hand to supply the deficiencies of his fortune.

" On examining into the nature of my literary attainments, he found them absolutely nothing. He heard, however, with equal surprise and pleasure, that, amidst the grossest ignorance of books, I had made a very considerable progress in the mathematics. He engaged me to enter into the details of this affair; and when he learned that I had made it in circumstances of discouragement and danger, he became more warmly interested in my favour, as he now saw a possibility of serving me.

" The plan that occurred to him was naturally that which had so often suggested itself to me. There were, indeed, several obstacles to be overcome. I had eighteen months yet to serve; my hand-writing was bad, and my language very incorrect; but nothing could slacken the zeal of this excellent man. He procured a few of my poor attempts at rhyme, dispersed them amongst his friends and acquaintance, and when my name was become somewhat familiar to them, set on foot a subscription for my relief. I still preserve the original paper; its title was not very magnificent, though it exceeded the most sanguine wishes of my heart; it ran thus: 'A subscription for purchasing the remainder of the time of William Gifford, and for enabling him to improve himself in writing and English grammar.' Few contributed more than five shillings, and none went beyond ten-shillings-and-sixpence; enough, however, was collected to free me from my apprenticeship (the sum my master received was six pounds), and to maintain me for a few months, during which I assiduously attended the Rev. Thomas Smerdon.

" At the expiration of this period, I found that my progress (for I will speak the truth in modesty) had been more considerable than my patrons expected. I had also written in the interim several little pieces of poetry, less rugged, I suppose, than my former ones, and certainly with fewer anomalies of language. My preceptor, too, spoke favourably of me and my benefactor, who was now become my father and my friend, had little difficulty in persuading my patrons to renew their donations, and continue me at school for another year. Such liberality was not lost upon me; I grew anxious to make the best return in my power, and I redoubled my diligence. Now, that I am sunk in indolence, I look back with some degree of scepticism to the exertions of that period.

"In two years and two months from the day of my emancipation, I was pronounced by Mr. Smerdon fit for the University. The plan of opening a writing-school had been abandoned almost from the first; and Mr. Cookesley looked round for some one who had interest enough to procure me some little office at Oxford. This person, who was soon found, was Thomas Taylor, Esq. of Denbury, a gentleman to whom I had already been indebted for much liberal and friendly support. He procured me the place of Bib. Lect. at Exeter-college ; and this, with such occasional assistance from the country as Mr. Cookesley undertook to provide, was thought sufficient to enable me to live, at least till I had taken a degree.

"During my attendance on Mr. Smerdon, I had written, as I observed before, several tuneful trifles, some as exercises, others voluntarily, (for poetry was now become my delight,) and not a few at the desire of my friends. When I became capable, however, of reading Latin and Greek with some degree of facility, that gentleman employed all my leisure hours in translations from the classics ; and indeed I do not know a single school-book, of which I did not render some portion into English verse. Among others, JUVENAL engaged my attention, or rather my master's, and I translated the tenth satire for a holiday task. Mr. Smerdon was much pleased with this, (I was not undelighted with it myself;) and as I was now become fond of the author, he easily persuaded me to proceed with him, and I translated in succession the third, the fourth, the twelfth, and I think the eighth satires. As I had no end in view but that of giving a temporary satisfaction to my benefactors, I thought little more of these, than of many other things of the same nature, which I wrote from time to time, and of which I never copied a single line.

"On my removing to Exeter-college, however, my friend, ever attentive to my concerns, advised me to copy my translation of the tenth satire, and present it, on my arrival, to the Rev. Dr. Stinton (afterwards Rector), to whom Mr. Taylor had given me an introductory letter: I did so, and it was kindly received. Thus encouraged, I took up the first and second satires (I mention them in the order in which they were translated), when my friend, who had sedulously watched my progress, first started the idea of my going through the whole, and publishing it by subscription, as a means of increasing my means of subsistence. To this I readily acceded, and finished the thirteenth, eleventh, and fifteenth, satires; the remainder were the work of a much later period.

"When I had got thus far, we thought it a fit time to mention our design: it was very generally approved of by my friends; and on the 1st of January 1781, the subscription was opened by Mr. Cookesley at Ashburton, and by myself at Exeter-college.

"So bold an undertaking, so precipitately announced, will give the reader, I fear, a higher opinion of my conceit than of my talents; neither the one nor the other, however, had the smallest concern with the business, which originated solely in ignorance. I wrote verses with great facility, and I was simple enough to imagine that little more was necessary for a translator of Juvenal! I was not, indeed, unconscious of my inaccuracies; I knew that they were numerous, and that I had need of some friendly eye to point them out, and some judicious hand to rectify or remove them; but for these, as well as for every thing else, I looked to Mr. Cookesley, and that worthy man, with his usual alacrity and kindness, undertook the laborious task of revising the whole translation. My friend was no great latinist, perhaps I was the better of the two; but he had taste and judgment, which I wanted. What advantages might have been ultimately derived from them, there was unhappily no opportunity of ascertaining, as it pleased the Almighty to call him to himself by a sudden death, before we had quite finished the First Satire. He died with a letter of mine unopened in his hands.

"This event, which took place on the 15th of January 1781, afflicted me beyond measure *. I was not only deprived of a most faithful and affectionate friend, but of a zealous and everactive protector, on whom I confidently relied for support; the sums that were still necessary for me, he always collected; and it was to be feared that the assistance which was not solicited with warmth would insensibly cease to be afforded.

"In many instances this was actually the case; the desertion, however, was not general; and I was encouraged to hope by the unexpected friendship of Servington Savery, a gentleman who voluntarily stood forth as my patron, and watched over my interests with kindness and attention.

"Some time before Mr. Cookesley's death, we had agreed that it would be proper to deliver out with the terms of the subscription, a specimen of the manner in which the translation was executed †. To obviate any idea of selection, a sheet was

* "I began this unadorned narrative on the 15th of January 1801; twenty years have therefore elapsed since I lost my benefactor and my friend. In the interval I have wept a thousand times at the recollection of his goodness; I yet cherish his memory with filial respect; and at this distant period my heart sinks within me at every repetition of his name.

† "Many of these papers were distributed; the terms which I extract

accordingly taken from the beginning of the First Satire. My friend died while it was in the press.

" After a few melancholy weeks, I resumed the translation; but found myself utterly incapable of proceeding. I had been so accustomed to connect Mr. Cookesley's name with every part of it, and I laboured with such delight in the hope of giving him pleasure, that now, when he appeared to have left me in the midst of my enterprise, and I was abandoned to my own efforts, I seemed to be engaged in a hopeless struggle, without motive or end; and this idea, which was perpetually recurring to me, brought such bitter anguish with it, that I shut up the work with feelings bordering on distraction.

" To relieve my mind, I had recourse to other pursuits. I endeavoured to become more intimately acquainted with the classics, and to acquire some of the modern languages; by permission, too, or rather recommendation, of the Rector and Fellows, I also undertook the care of a few pupils; this removed much of my anxiety respecting my future means of support. I have a heart-felt pleasure in mentioning this indulgence of my college: it could arise from nothing but the liberal desire inherent, I think, in the members of both our Universities, to encourage every thing that bears the most distant resemblance to talents; for I had no claims on them from any particular exertions.

" The lapse of many months had now soothed and tranquil-lized my mind, and I once more returned to the translation, to which a wish to serve a young man surrounded with difficulties, had induced a number of respectable characters to set their names; but, alas, what a mortification! I now discovered, for the first time, that my own inexperience, and the advice of my too, too partial friend, had engaged me in a work, for the due execution of which my literary attainments were by no means sufficient. Errors and misconceptions appeared in every page. I had, indeed, caught something of the spirit of Juvenal, but his meaning had frequently escaped me, and I saw the necessity of a long and painful revision, which would carry me far beyond the period fixed for the appearance of the work. Alarmed at the prospect, I instantly resolved (if not wisely, yet I trust honestly) to renounce the publication for the present.

" In pursuance of this resolution, I wrote to my friend in the country (the Rev. Servington Savery), requesting him to return the subscription money in his hands to the subscribers. He did not approve of my plan; nevertheless he promised, in

from one of them, were these. ' The work shall be printed in quarto (without notes), and be delivered to the Subscribers in the month of December next. The price will be sixteen shillings in boards; half to be paid at the time of subscribing, the remainder on delivery of the book'."

a letter which now lies before me, to comply with it ; and, in a subsequent one, added that he had already begun to do so.

"For myself, I also made several repayments ; and trusted a sum of money to make others with a fellow collegian, who, not long after, fell by his own hands in the presence of his father. But there were still some whose abode could not be discovered, and others on whom to press the taking back of eight shillings would neither be decent nor respectful: even from these I ventured to flatter myself that I should find pardon, when on some future day I presented them with the work (which I was still secretly determined to complete) rendered more worthy patronage, and increased by notes, which I now perceived to be absolutely necessary, to more than double its proposed size.

" In the leisure of a country residence, I fancied this might be done in two years: perhaps I was not too sanguine; the experiment, however, was not made, for about this time a circumstance happened which changed my views, and indeed my whole system of life.

"I had contracted an acquaintance with a person of the name of ——— *, recommended to my particular notice by a gentleman of Devonshire, whom I was proud of an opportunity to oblige. This person's residence at Oxford was not long, and when he returned to town, I maintained a correspondence with him by letters. At his particular request, these were inclosed in a cover, and sent to Lord Grosvenor; one day I inadvertently omitted the direction, and his lordship, necessarily supposing it to be meant for himself, opened and read it. There was something in it which attracted his notice ; and when he gave the letter to my friend, he had the curiosity to inquire about his correspondent at Oxford ; and, upon the answer he received, had the kindness to desire he might be brought to see him on his coming to town ; to this circumstance, purely accidental on all sides, and to this alone, I owe my introduction to this nobleman.

"On my first visit, he asked me what friends I had, and what were my prospects in life; and I told him that I had no friends, and no prospects of any kind. He said no more ; but when I called to take leave, previous to returning to college, I found that this simple exposure of my circumstances had sunk deep into his mind. At parting, he informed me that he charged himself with my present support and future establishment ; and that till this last could be effected to my wish, I should come and reside with him. These were not words of course; they were more than fulfilled in every point. I did go, and reside with him ; and I experienced a warm and cordial reception, a kind and affectionate esteem, that has known

* The Reverend William Peters, R. A.

neither diminution nor interruption, from that hour to this, a period of twenty years * !

" In his lordship's house I proceeded with Juvenal, till I was called upon to accompany his son (one of the most amiable and accomplished young noblemen that this country, fertile in such characters, could ever boast,) to the continent. With him, in two successive tours, I spent many years ; years of which the remembrance will always be dear to me, from the recollection that a friendship was then contracted, which time, and a more intimate knowledge of each other, have mellowed into a regard that forms at once the pride and happiness of my life.

" It is long since I have been returned and settled in the bosom of competence and peace. My translation frequently engaged my thoughts, but I had lost the ardour and the confidence of youth, and was seriously doubtful of my abilities to do it justice. I have wished a thousand times that I could decline it altogether; but the ever-recurring idea that there were people of the description I have already mentioned, who had just and forcible claims on me for the due performance of my engagement, forbade the thought ; and I slowly proceeded towards the completion of a work in which I should never have engaged, had my friend's inexperience, or my own, suffered us to suspect for a moment the labour, and the talents of more than one kind, absolutely necessary to its success in any tolerable degree. Such as I could make it, it is now before the public :

" ———————— Majora canamus."

2. ANECDOTES OF MR. GIFFORD †.

"The world has already been furnished with information relative to the life of Mr. Gifford, by his own pen, in the exquisite piece of autobiography prefixed to his Juvenal; and this is sufficient for the general purposes of history. But a simple knowledge of the succession and influence of events which befal men of eminence, is not all that a reasonable curiosity may

* To this passage Mr. Gifford, in the second edition of his Juvenal, appended the following note : " I have a melancholy satisfaction in recording, that this revered friend and patron lived to witness my grateful acknowledgment of his kindness. He survived the appearance of the translation but a very few days, and I paid the last sad duty to his memory by attending his remains to the grave. To me this laborious work has not been happy; the same disastrous event that marked its commencement has imbittered its conclusion, and frequently forced upon my recollection the calamity of the rebuilder of Jericho : ' He laid the foundation thereof in Abiram, his first born, and set up the gates thereof in his youngest son, Segub.'—1806."

† First published in the Literary Gazette.

require. We love to remove the veil which screens their domestic characters from our sight—to draw a chair round their fire-side—to listen to their conversation—to sympathise with their sorrows—to rejoice with their mirth. And thus circumstances, in themselves unimportant, become enrobed with a delight and an interest when associated with recollections of the good or the great. Impressed with the truth of these reflections, I shall throw together a few random anecdotes of the late Mr. Gifford. My family was intimate with him; and I had the honour of enjoying his acquaintance from my birth. One of his most remarkable talents, was the extraordinary rapidity with which he devoured knowledge; and the most remarkable proof of it, perhaps, was his having fitted himself for the University after being but two years at school. Very shortly after his arrival at Oxford he was informed that he need not trouble himself with any further attendance at the mathematical lectures, as he had already carried himself as far in the science as the University required. His sagacity and quickness of apprehension were indeed discoverable on all occasions; it was impossible to converse with him upon any subject, however trifling, without having this forcibly thrust on your notice; and it was considerably heightened in conversation by the peculiar animation and intelligence of his eye, an almost unfailing feature in a sensible face. His acquaintance with matters the most minute and insignificant was equally extraordinary:—as an instance, I remember a lady telling me, that having broken a valuable china basin, she accidentally mentioned the circumstance a short time after to Mr. Gifford; when he, to her great surprise, instantly gave her an excellent receipt for repairing it.

" One of his earliest serious attempts at poetry was an elegy on the death of his first friend and patron, Mr. Cookesley,— displaying a singularly classical correctness for one so slenderly acquainted with English literature as he then was, and occasionally equalling in pathos the most successful productions of the kind. I have subjoined it at the end of this article; though not so much for its intrinsic merits, which are, however, very considerable, as for the interest which necessarily attaches to his earliest productions. It was composed whilst he was at College. I have also before me five eclogues, written, probably, whilst he was at school; they are in the manner of Pope, and have much of his harmonious flow; probably Pope and Virgil were the only pastoral Poets with whom he was acquainted at the time of their composition.

" There is also among his early poems, though of considerably later date than his eclogues, an ode to the present Lord Grosvenor, then his pupil; and which is one of the happiest of his youthful efforts. In the exordium he obviates any objection that might be taken to his premature devotion to the Muses. In a correspondence with the daughter of his patron, he pre-

scribes for her a course of reading in English poetry; adding
occasional criticisms of his own, explanations of poetical figures,
&c. These letters are exceedingly curious; the criticisms, coming from one so young, are, of course, not very subtile or refined, but are distinguished by that elegance of taste and discrimination which characterised him to a remarkable degree.

"When abroad with his pupil, he kept his acquaintance well-
informed of his adventures, in a series of most entertaining
letters; his descriptions are exceedingly humourous — many
highly picturesque. Perhaps it may arise from unconscious
partiality—but I read his letters with as fresh a delight as if
they had been written yesterday, and were addressed to myself.
I wish to write the little I have to say in perfect good humour;
and, therefore, shall but incidentally hint at his political character; but his ' dearest foes' must acknowledge, that his integrity was unimpeachable, and his opinions honest. He disliked
incurring an obligation which might in any degree shackle the
expression of his free opinion. Agreeably to this, he laid down
a rule, from which he never departed—that every writer in the
Quarterly should receive so much money, at least, per sheet.
On one occasion (I dare say others occurred, but I only *know* of
one) a gentleman holding office under government, sent him an
article, which, after undergoing some serious mutilations at his
hands preparatory to being ushered into the world, was accepted. But the usual sum being sent to the author, he rejected it with disdain, conceiving it a high dishonour to be *paid*
for any thing—the independent placeman! Gifford, in answer,
informed him of the invariable rule of the Review, adding, that
he could send the money to any charitable institution, or dispose of it in any manner he should direct— but that the money
must be paid. The doughty official, convinced that the virtue of
his article would force it into the Review at all events, stood
firm in his refusal;—greatly to his dismay, the article was returned. He revenged himself by never sending another. Gifford, in relating this afterwards, observed with a smile, ' Poor
man! the truth was he didn't like *my* alterations; and, I'm
sure, I didn't like *his* articles : so there was soon an end of our
connexion.'

"His objection to asking a personal favour was, owing to
the same principle, exceedingly strong. If the united influence
of the Anti-jacobin and the Quarterly be considered, we may
probably be justified, in assigning to Gifford's literary support
of Government, a rank second only to Burke. His services, at
all events, formed a very powerful claim to any moderate favour
in the power of Ministers to bestow; and yet, though anxious
at all times to gratify the wants of his needier friends to his
utmost ability, his aversion to soliciting the bounty of Government was seldom overcome; on one occasion, indeed, in particular, he exerted his influence in favour of the son of a de-

ceased friend; but undoubtedly, not without being driven to it by such importunity as left an application to Ministers the less of two evils. About two years before his death, he wrote, I believe to the Chancellor, requesting a small living for a distressed relative of his first patron; his request was not complied with. But then it should be remembered, that at the time it was made, the Quarterly had passed into other hands. Othello's occupation was gone; and Gifford had to digest, as well as he could, the mortification which commonly awaits every political writer, of finding that the favour of a Government is self-interested, extorted, and ungrateful. It is true, his independence of opinion might seem to be interfered with by the situations he held; but they were bestowed on him unsolicited, and from motives of personal regard. I am sure every one acquainted with him will admit, that he would have rejected with scorn any kindness which could be considered as fettering the freedom of his conduct in the smallest degree. I am not more certain of many conjectures than I am that he never propagated a dishonest opinion, nor did a dishonest act. He enjoyed a very close intimacy with Mr. Pitt; he used to mention, that when he dined with the minister *téte-à-téte*, or with but a few chosen others, a servant was never permitted to remain in the room. The minister's ' dumb waiters' were as serviceable in his private as in any other house.

" Amongst other engaging talents, Gifford possessed that very agreeable one of telling a story well, in singular perfection. The gest of trifles of this kind depends principally on the *manner* in which they are told.' Many people acquire a *right* over particular stories, which, from their peculiar happiness in relating them, become exclusively their own; but Gifford had an inexhaustible supply, and his arch drollery rendered all almost equally good. I will merely mention one, the first that occurs, which has nothing particular in it, but which he contrived to render exceedingly entertaining.

" While at Ashburton, he contracted an acquaintance with a family of that place, consisting of females somewhat advanced in age. On one occasion he ventured on the perilous exploit of drinking tea with these elderly ladies. After having demolished his usual allowance of tea, he found, in spite of his remonstrances to the contrary, that his hostess would by no means suffer him to give up; but persisted in making him drink a most incredible quantity. ' At last,' said Gifford, in telling the story, ' being overflooded with tea, I put down my *fourteenth* cup, and exclaimed with an air of resolution, ' I neither can nor will drink any more.' The hostess then, seeing she had forced more down my throat than I liked, began to apologise, [and added, ' but, dear Mr. Gifford, as you did'nt *put your spoon across the cup,* I supposed your refusals were nothing but good manners!' He was a great tea-drinker himself, though not equal to the encounter of these Amazons. He generally had some brought to him between eleven and twelve at night, besides the regular meal which every one makes of tea who can afford it. I remember, when I complained once that I had met with some bad tea at a house where I had been dining, a friend observed, ' Your host has not enough of a gentleman's polish about him to set a right value on good tea. Estimated by this standard, Gifford was the very first of gentlemen—none of my acquaintance have such delicious tea as he used to give. The ladies used to complain of its being too strong; but they, seeing they have *nerves*, are quite out of the question.

" Gifford always—that is, for the last twenty years of his life—dined at four, drank tea at six, and for several years slept immediately after dinner till tea-time. *Then* he was always glad to see his private friends; it was at this meal that I saw him for the last time. He was for many years exceedingly feeble, and so dreadfully oppressed with asthma, as very often to be entirely deprived of speech. The fatigue of business entailed on him by the Review, and the various calls with which he was incessantly harassed during the morning, produced an overpowering exhaustion, which tends to sour the temper or excite irratibility. And if, when suffering under the complicated misery of distressing bodily disease and mental exhaustion, he occasionally became fretful or peevish, the most illiberal cannot withhold indulgence, nor the most malignant affect surprise. He continued the editorship of the Quarterly much longer than a just regard for his health authorized; but no successor that was proposed pleased him; and nothing but a bodily decay, little short of dissolution, compelled him to resign. He never stipulated for any salary as editor; at first he received £.200, and at last £.900 *per annum*, but never engaged for a particular sum. He several times returned money to Murray, saying, ' He had been too liberal.' Perhaps he was the only man on this side the Tweed who thought so! He was perfectly indifferent about wealth. I do not know a better proof of this than the fact that he was richer, by a very considerable sum, at the time of his death than he was at all aware of. In unison with his contempt of money was his disregard of any external distinction; he had a strong natural aversion to any thing like pomp or parade. A very intimate friend, who had risen like himself from small beginnings, having taken his doctor's degree, conceived his importance to be somewhat augmented by this new distinction. Having called on Gifford shortly after, he brought the subject on the *tapis*, and observed, with evident self-satisfaction, ' But I hope, Gifford, you wont *quiz* me, now I'm a Doctor?" " *Quiz* thee! God help thee! make what they will of thee I shall never call thee any thing but Jack.' Yet he was by no means insensible to an honourable distinction; and when the University of

Oxford, about two years before his death, offered to give him a doctor's degree, he observed, ' Twenty years ago it would have been gratifying, but *now* it would only be written on my coffin.' His disregard for external show was the more remarkable, as a contrary feeling is generally observable in persons who have risen from penury to wealth. But Gifford was a *gentleman* in feeling and in conduct: and you were never led to suspect he was sprung from an obscure origin, except when he reminded you of it by an anecdote relative to it. And this recalls one of the stories he used to tell with irresistible drollery, the merit of which entirely depended on his manner. I know an excellent mimic, who was immeasurably delighted with the story, but who never could produce more than a smile, with all his powers, by repeating it. It was simply this: At the cobbler's board, of which Gifford had been a member, there was but one candle allowed for the whole coterie of operatives. It was, of course, a matter of importance that this candle should give as much light as possible. This was only to be done by repeated snuffings; but snuffers being a piece of fantastic coxcombry they were not pampered with, the members of the board took it in turn to perform the office of the forbidden luxury with their finger and thumb. The candle was handed, therefore, to each in succession, with the word ' sneaf' (Anglicè ' snuff') bellowed in his ears. Gifford used to pronounce this word in the legitimate broad Devonshire dialect, and accompanied his story with expressive gestures.—Now, on paper this is absolutely nothing, but in Gifford's mouth it was exquisitely humourous. I should not, however, have mentioned it, were it not that it appears to me one of the best instances I could give of his humility in recurring to his former condition. He was equally free from personal vanity. A lady of his acquaintance once looked in upon him, and said she had a rout that evening, and endeavoured by every inducement to persuade him to join it. ' Now do, Mr. Gifford, come in; it will give such an *éclat*,' she added, patting him familiarly on the shoulder, to say, ' There is Mr. Gifford the poet!' ' Poet, indeed! and a pretty figure this poet,' he answered, looking demurely on his 'shrunk shanks,' ' would cut in a ball-room!' He was a man of very deep and warm affections. If I were desired to point out the distinguishing excellence of his private character, I should refer to his fervent sincerity of heart. He was particularly kind to children, and fond of their society. My sister, when young, used sometimes to go to spend a month with him, on which occasions he would hire a pianoforte, and once he actually had a *juvenile ball* at his house for her amusement. * * * He formed an attachment for his Pupil which no subsequent circumstances could abate. The change in his Lordship's political sentiments did not shake Gifford's unalterable affection for his character. He, on the other hand, met this attachment with an equal degree of warmth; their mutual respect was built on principle, and reflected equal honour on both. In Gifford's last protracted illness, when he was in bed, or asleep on the sofa, during the greater part of the day, Lord Grosvenor occasionally ventured on an infringement of his strict orders not to be disturbed, and walking on tiptoe to his side, used to gaze on his almost expiring instructor.

"Of Gifford's kindness to children I had numerous instances in myself. While at school I received more presents from him than from all my other acquaintance put together. Nor was his liberality confined to the importunities of a school-boy, as my more considerable prodigalities at College found in his bounty an unfailing remedy. The last time I heard from him he wrote to discharge a bill for me, and that, too, at a time when the labour requisite for writing a letter was such as to exhaust him. The reader will probably smile, but I wish to be understood literally. His debility for many months previous to his death was such as to incapacitate him for the smallest exertion—even that of writing! I called on him some little time ago, and learnt he was on the sofa; having undergone the fatigue of having one foot washed, which entailed an exhaustion requiring a glass of wine and an hour's sleep to restore him. He would sometimes take up a pen, and, after a vain attempt to write, throw it down, exclaiming, 'No! my work is done!' Excessive infirmity rendered existence a great burthen; the most common and involuntary thoughts, in their passage through his mind, seemed to leave pain behind them. He was once talking with perfect tranquillity, as indeed he always did, of the approaching termination of his life, when the friend with whom he was conversing expressed a hope that he might yet recover, and live several years; but he added, ' Oh! no! it has pleased God to grant me a much longer life than I had reason to expect, and I am thankful for it; but two years more is its utmost duration.' He died exactly two years after using these words. At my last interview with him, he spoke of Valpy's new edition of Stephens's Greek Thesaurus; he said, 'I only examined the former numbers, but finding it clumsily done, I left off.' I spoke of Ford, and observed that the public would be more gratified by an edition of that dramatist than of Shirley; adding, that it was a pity so noble a writer should have no worthier editor than Weber. At the mention of this man's name he seemed irritated, and said, rather angrily, 'He's a sad ignorant fellow.' The formal demolition of this poor man, to which he has condescended in his own edition of Ford, may seem like breaking a gnat on a wheel; and can only, indeed, be accounted for on the suspicion, which is, however, probably a correct one, that Weber was only the *ostensible*, and a much greater antagonist the *real*, editor.—Speaking of Dryden, whose genius he admired exceedingly, he observed, ' Dryden's Besetting Sin was a want of principles in every thing.' I used sometimes to send him the Etonian, which was published whilst I was at school; I found this no bad speculation. He had a great admiration of the poetical powers of the author of Godiva; he said, after reading that poem, ' If Moultrie writes prose as well as he does verse, I should be glad to *hear from him*'—meaning, he should be glad to receive an article from him. He once quoted to me, with great glee, the two lines in Godiva:

" Leofric thought he had perplex'd her quite,
And grinn'd immensely at his own sagacity;

adding, with a laugh, ' they are admirable.' I was at his house shortly after Sheridan's death. I took up a magazine which had for its frontispiece a head of that orator; Gifford, observing my attention to be directed to the picture, asked what it was? On my informing him, he stretched out his hand for it: ' Aye! it's very like him,' he said. He looked at it for some time with a melancholy air, and returned it, merely observing, ' Poor Sheridan!' In truth, his kindness of heart was universally warm and strong. He was greatly attached, amongst other domestics *, to a cat and a dog; which last was the most exquisitely proportioned spaniel I ever saw. These two used to take great liberties with him; but he never permitted them to remain in the room during dinner; and it was amusing to see this pair of domestics spontaneously walk out of the room together on the appearance of the first cover. He survived Tabby; and poor Fid is not likely to be long in following his master, for natural decay has entirely deprived him of locomotion; and he is at present sleeping away his existence in a lethargy few degrees removed from death. By the by, this little fellow showed one very remarkable piece of sagacity; he used to bark upon the arrival of any other carriage at the door, but never at his *master's.*

" Mr. Gifford was short in person, his hair was of a remarkably handsome brown colour, and was as glossy and full at the time of his death as at any previous period. He lost the use of his right eye, I believe, by gradual and natural decay; but the remaining one made ample amends for the absence of its fellow, having a remarkable quickness and brilliancy, and a power of expressing every variety of feeling. His head was of a very singular shape; being by no means high, if measured from the chin to the crown; but of a greater horizontal length from the forehead to the back of the head than any I remember to have seen. I believe he would have puzzled the phrenologists strangely, but that is an ordinary occurrence; and I, not being a disciple of these philosophers, shall not concern myself

* In speaking of Ann Davies it was omitted to be mentioned that Mr. Gifford had a portrait engraved of this faithful servant, copies of which he presented to a few of his intimate friends.

in their distress. His forehead projected at a right angle from his face, in a very uncommon manner. The portrait of him in his Juvenal, taken from a picture by his friend Hoppner, is a very good likeness; but there is a still better, painted by the same artist, which after his death came into the possession of his executor the Dean of Westminster *.

" A few days before his death he said, ' I shall not trouble myself with taking any more medicine—it's of no use—I shall not get up again.' As his last hour drew nearer, his mind occasionally wandered; he said once—' These books have driven me mad,—I must read my prayers'— singular words, as coming from a man deeply impressed with religious feeling. (By the by, I remember seeing in his library what appeared to be a paraphrase, or translation of the Book of Job, in his own handwriting.) Soon after, all power of motion failed him; he could not raise a tea-spoon to his mouth, nor stir in his bed. His breath became very low, and interrupted by long pauses; his pulse had ceased to beat five hours before his death. He was continually inquiring what time it was. He once faltered forth, ' When will this be over?' At last, on his nurse coming into the room, he said, ' Now I'm ready (words he generally used when he was ready to be moved); very well! — you may go.' These were his last words: on retiring, the nurse listened behind the door; she observed the intervals of his breathing to grow longer; she re-entered the room just in time to catch a breath that had a little of the strength of a sigh—it was his last! The few who saw him afterwards, agreed that the usual serenity of death was exceeded by the placid composure of *his* countenance.

'ΕΠΩΝΥΜΟΣ."

3. ANECDOTE RELATED BY MR. GIFFORD IN HIS PREFACE TO FORD.

" My friend, the late Lord Grosvenor, had a house at Salt Hill, where I usually spent a part of the summer, and thus became a neighbour of that great and good man, Jacob Bryant, who kindly encouraged me to visit him. Here the conversation turned one morning on a Greek criticism by Dr. Johnson, in some volume lying on the table, which I ventured (for I was then young) to deem incorrect, and pointed it out to him. I could not help thinking that he was somewhat of my opinion; but he was cautious and reserved. ' But, Sir,' said I, willing to overcome his scruples, ' Dr. Johnson himself (a fact which Mr. Bryant well knew) admitted that he was not a good Greek scholar.' ' Sir, he replied with a serious and impressive air, ' it is not easy for us to say what such a man as Johnson would call a good Greek scholar.' I hope that I profited by the lesson,— certainly I never forgot it ; and if but one of my readers do the same, I shall not repent placing it upon record."

* An engraving from this p' 'ure is prefixed to this article.

4. MR. GIFFORD AND MR. BULMER.

Shortly after the Right Honourable Lord Sidmouth was appointed Secretary of State for the Home Department, he very handsomely presented Mr. Gifford with the Paymastership of the Honourable Band of Gentlemen Pensioners, or Men at Arms,—a situation he enjoyed till the period of his death,—of which corps, Mr. Bulmer, his ancient typographer, had long been one of the oldest members. It was the practice of Mr. Gifford, whenever an Exchequer warrant was issued for the payment of the quarterly salaries of the Gentlemen of the Band, to inform its members, by a circular letter, that their salaries were in a course of payment; but on many of those occasions he was wont to depart from his usual routine, and indulge himself in a poetical notice to Mr. Bulmer. These notices were generally written on any blank or broken page he might accidentally find on the proof sheet of Shirley's Dramatic Works which he might be correcting at the instant,—a work he had long * been employed in conducting through the Shakspeare press. From a variety of those momentary effusions of the Satirist, the following have been selected :

" *Ad Cl. V. Gul. Bul. Gent. Pens. Epistola Hortatoria.*

" O qui, terribili Regem præstare securi
Securum gaudes, Βουλμηρων πιστατε παντων!
Nummorum (vox aurea) apud me jam stabat acervus
Ingens, officii merces lautissima fidi ;
Ad quem, si sapias, alato jam pede curras.
Nam, si quid veri veteres cecinere poetæ,
Ipsæ alas sibi opes faciunt, volitantque repentè.

TRANSLATION.

" *An Admonitory Epistle to the Right Worthy Gentleman,*
W. Bulmer, Gentleman Pensioner.

" O thou ! who safely claim'st the right to stand
Before thy King, with dreaded axe in hand,
My trustiest Bulmer ! know, upon my board
A mighty heap of *cash* (O golden word !)

---

* The work had commenced in 1816. — With respect to Mr. Gifford's intended Shakspeare (before noticed in p. 9) it may be added that so intent was he at one time on this project, that specimen pages had been prepared by his printer Mr. Bulmer. The edition was to have been in crown 8vo. with engravings from the designs of Gillray, produced by a new application of aquafortis to copper, which rendered the plates available, in the manner of wood engravings, to the operation of the letterpress. The design of his edition was to give a brief glossarial elucidation of the works of Shakspeare, and to expunge the absurdities which have too frequently been appended to the works of our immortal Bard.

Now lies,—for service done, the bounteous meed.
Haste then, in Wisdom's name, and hither speed :
For, if the truth old Poets sing or say,
Riches straight make them wings and fly away!"

" DEAR BULMER,   *May* 5, 1819.
  " Did but the proofs of Shirley's Plays
Return as quick as Quarter-days,
How would my friend Tom Turner * chuckle,
And you give thanks on either knuckle !
But, pardon! I will speed them faster ;
Meanwhile, to appease your wrath, my master,
You shall receive (before the others)
Your April salary and your Brother's."

" DEAR BULMER,   *Sept.* 21, 1820.
        " Why are you so late,
When all the Band, both small and great,
Are hourly pushing through the Gate,
            Hight Bucking-ham †,
To take their pay, before the mob
Of Wood have rifled every fob,
And made their " Waits " a paltry job
            Not worth a d—n."

" DEAR BULMER,
       Though your patriot brother
About Sir Francis keep a pother,
And hourly train his floor-cloth rabble
For Hunt and Liberty to squabble ;
Yet you are of a better feather—
(You could not, sure, be hatched together)
And love your Prince, and take his pay
Without a qualm, on Quarter-day ;
While he, who sniffs at kings and nobles,
And counts *e'en Pensioners* mere baubles,
Although the Salary make him itch,
Pockets it with an ugly twitch.—
But, leaving this—know I can pleasure ye,
Thanks to their Lordships of the Treasury,
With gold enough (unless it irk ye)
To purchase such a chine and turkey
As ne'er a city feast appear'd at,
Nor Coke of Norfolk wagg'd his beard at ;

---

* An assistant in Mr. Bulmer's office.
† Mr. Gifford's residence was in James-street, Buckingham-gate.

And—but alas ! my scrimp of paper
Is at a close—so is my taper—
And I can only add—come quickly,
For life is short, and I am sickly."

———

"To WILLIAM BULMER, Esq. brother to
Sir Fenwick Bulmer, Knt.*
                                    " Sept. 1821.
" Dread Sir, whose blood, to Knighthood near,
Is sixpence now an ounce more dear
      Than when my summons issued last ;
With cap in hand, I beg to say,
That I have money to defray
      The service of the Quarter past."

———

"To W. BULMER, Esq.
" I, who, like any pea-hen gay,
Cluck'd for my brood on Quarter-day,
And saw them, at the well-known sound,
Come waddling, gobbling, clustering round,
Now, thanks to your pernicious press
That robb'd the Forty, more or less,
Of all their ' Honour †'—find each note,
Stick like Grim-gribber in my throat.
      What imp of that Old Serpent's seed
Urg'd you to this felonious deed ?
Say, was it pride ?—that He, the Knight,
First of the name, Sir Fenwick hight,
Might shine ' in his new gloss,' and stand
Sole Honourable in the Band !
      Oh evil, evil have you done ;—
My letters now are spit upon ;
And though the Forty still repair
To James-street, humbled as they are,
Yet, blank of face and chill of heart,
They ' come like shadows, so depart ! '
      And come (for I would fain forget
My private wrongs, dear Bulmeret !)
You, too ; but not, as you were wont,
With careless air and open front,
But—lest the Band your steps should mark,—
Wrapt ' in the blanket of the dark ; '
Or you may witness to your cost,
What wrath can do, when Honour's lost ! "

* Mr. Bulmer's elder brother, as the Senior Member of the Band of
Gentlemen Pensioners, was knighted on occasion of the Coronation of
George the Fourth. He died May 7, 1824, aged 79.
      † In Mr. Gifford's first printed summons to the Band, the word
Honourable (a distinctive appellation to which the Members of the Band
are entitled) had been inadvertently omitted.

The Rev. JOHN HELLINS, F. R. S.

The preceding memoirs of a genius of Devonshire will be appropriately followed by some biographical notices of another native of that county, little
less remarkable for having risen from very similar
obscurity by the efforts of his own abilities and perseverance.

"That celebrated mathematician, the Rev. John
Hellins," says Mr. Polwhele in his History of Cornwall, " was born in or near North Tawton, of poor
but honest parents. I think he learned to write by
himself; but, be that as it may, his education at
best did not extend beyond the first four rules of
arithmetic. By occasionally looking on, he literally stole the art of a cooper, and worked at that
business for a livelihood, till about twenty years old.
Having in the mean time purchased Emerson, and
some other mathematical books, without the help
of a master, he made himself well acquainted with
algebra, &c. &c. Showing his books one day to a
school-master of the vicinity, the latter, on conversing with him, perceived more learning than generally falls to the lot of a maker of pails, and being
asked, soon after, whether he knew of any young
man fit to teach writing, &c. in a small neighbouring school then vacant, he recommended our cooper.
While a teacher at this little seminary, I fancy it was,
that he got acquainted with my friend, the Rev. Malachy Hitchins, of St. Hilary *, who introduced him,
I believe, into the Royal Observatory at Greenwich.
While his nights were engaged at this place in star-
gazing for Dr. Maskelyne, he was employed by day
in studying Latin and Greek, which at length enabled him to get into holy orders. He was for some
time Curate of Constantine in Cornwall, and either
after or before teacher of mathematics to the children of the late Lord Pomfret †."

* Of whom hereafter, p. 44.
† Polwhele's History of Cornwall, vol. V. p. 107.

The first paper by Mr. Hellins in the Philosophical Transactions appeared in 1780 *. In 1787 he edited "The Young Algebraist's Companion;" in 1788 published a quarto volume of " Mathematical Essays, on several subjects;" and in 1802, in two volumes quarto, " Analytical Institutions, originally written in Italian by Donna Maria Gaetana Agnesi. Translated into English by Professor Colson, Cambridge." He also from 1795 to 1814 occasionally furnished mathematical articles to the British Critic ‡.

* The following is a list of the essays by Mr. Hellins in that publication: " Two Theorems for computing Logarithms," 1780. Abr. xiii. p. 632.—" A new method of finding the Equal Roots of an Equation by Division," 1782. Ibid. xv. p. 317. — " Dr. Halley's method of computing the Quadrature of the Circle improved; being a transformation of his series for that purpose, to others which converge by the powers of 80," 1794. xvii. 414.—Mr. Jones' Computation of the Hyperbolic Logarithm of 10 compared," &c. 1796, ibid. p. 699. —" A new method of computing the value of a Slowly Converging Series, of which all the terms are affirmative, 1798. xviii. p. 312.—" An improved Solution of a Problem in Physical Astronomy, by which Swiftly Converging Series are obtained, which are useful in computing the perturbations of the Motions of the Earth, Mars, and Venus, by their mutual attraction." ib. p. 408.—" A Second Appendix to the Improved Solution of a Problem in Physical Astronomy," 1800. ibid. p. 599.—" Of the Rectification of the Conic Sections," 1802. ibid. p. 448.—" On the Rectification of the Hyperbola, by means of two Ellipses," of which latter treatise, and one on the same subject by Mr. Woodhouse, a discussion written by a very eminent mathematician and professor is printed in the Gentleman's Magazine, vol. LXXXV. i. pp. 18—22. The writer of this remarks that, the distinction between the two authors was very obvious, in respect that " Mr. Woodhouse borrows largely from books; Mr. Hellins takes from his own store. The former delights in gallicisms and is often obscure; the latter is plain and perspicuous."

‡ The most remarkable of these are the following: On Mr. Wales's Method of finding the Longitude, VI. 413; On Bishop Horsley's Mathematical Treatises, vol. XXI. p. 272; On Donna Agnesi's Analytical Institutions, of which he superintended the publication, vol. XXIII. p. 143, vol. XXIV. p. 653, and vol. XXV. p. 141; On Keith's Trigonometry, vol. XXXI. p. 489; On F. Baily's work, on the Doctrine of Interest and Annuities, vol.

After leaving Cornwall, Mr. Hellins became Curate of the parish of Greens' Norton near Towcester. This was either a cause or a consequence of his connexion with the Earl of Pomfret, whose seat of Easton Neston is in that neighbourhood. In 1790 he was presented by Earl Bathurst to the vicarage of Potterspury in Northamptonshire. He was elected a Fellow of the Royal Society in 1796; and in 1798 he obtained the Copley medal of that institution by his plan for computing planetary perturbations. In 1800 he took the degree of B. D. at Trinity-college, Cambridge. He died in March 1827; and at the Anniversary Meeting of the Royal Society on the following St. Andrew's-day, the President, Mr. Davies Gilbert, in noticing the losses sustained by the Society during the year then past, pronounced the following eulogium on the subject of this notice:

" The Rev. John Hellins was one of those extraordinary men, who, deprived of early advantages, have elevated themselves, by the force of genius and of industry, to a level above most persons blessed with regular education. Mr. Hellins at one time computed for the Nautical Almanac. He afterwards assisted at Greenwich. And, what is now perhaps almost unknown, he furnished the late Mr. Windham with all the calculations and tables on which that gentleman brought forward his new military system, as Minister. of War, in 1806. Mr. Hellins applied himself with great industry to some of the most useful branches of pure mathematics. No less than nine communications from him appear in our ' Transactions;'—' On the summation of series.'—' On the conversion of slowly-

XXXVIII. p. 622, and vol. XLIII. p. 502, when the first Series of the British Critic closed, and the connexion of Mr. Hellins with the work is supposed to have ceased. Several minor articles on scientific subjects were written by him, which are not here specified.

converging series into others of swifter convergency.' — ' On their application to computing of logarithms, and to the rectifying of circular arcs.' —'On the roots of equations.' And in 1798, ' On a method of computing with increased facility the planetary perturbations;' for the last he was honoured with your Copley medal.

" Retired to a small living in Northamptonshire, Mr. Hellins became a pattern of philosophical calmness and content.

> Far from the madding crowd's ignoble strife,
> His sober wishes never learn'd to stray.

He seems to have said—

> Curtatis decimis, modicoque beatus agello,
> Vitam secrete in rure quietus agam.

" I have known Mr. Hellins for above forty years, and I can testify to his virtues. It once happened that, through the late Dr. Maskelyne, I had nearly obtained for him the Observatory at Dublin. The failure cannot, however, be lamented, since Brinkley was appointed in his stead."

Mr. Hellins married, Nov. 10, 1794, Miss Anne Brock, of North Tawton, Devonshire, who survived him only a few months, and by whom he left one son.

PROFESSOR WOODHOUSE.

Robert Woodhouse, Esq. M. A. F. R. S. Plumian Professor of Mathematics at Cambridge, was of Caius College, where he took his Bachelor of Arts' degree in 1795, and was the Senior Wrangler and first Smith's prizeman of that year. He proceeded M. A. in 1798, and was elected a lay Fellow of Caius. Several papers from his pen appear in the Philosophical Transactions, beginning from 1801 *; and

------

* " On the necessary Truth of certain Conclusions obtained by means of imaginary quantities." Phil. Trans. 1801, p. 89.

in 1802 he became a Fellow of the Royal Society. In 1803 he printed, in 4to, "The Principles of Analytical Calculation;" in 1809, "A Treatise on Plane and Spherical Trigonometry," 8vo; in 1810, "A Treatise on Isoperimetrical Problems, and the Calculus of Variations," 8vo; in 1812, "An Elementary Treatise on Plane Astronomy," 8vo.; and in 1823, "A Treatise on Astronomy, theoretical and practical," 8vo.

In 1820 Mr. Woodhouse succeeded Dean Milner, as Lucasian Professor of Mathematics; and in 1822, on the death of Professor Vince, he was elected to the Plumian Professorship. In 1824 he was appointed by the University to conduct the Observatory then newly erected; and he died at Cambridge, after an illness of four months, Dec. 28, 1827.

The Rev. MALACHY HITCHINS

was of St. John's-college, Cambridge, M. A. 1785, and became Vicar of St. Hilary and Gwinnear in Cornwall, and principal calculator to the Board of Longitude. The Philosophical Transactions of 1801 contain from his pen an "Account of the Discovery of Silver in Herland Copper-mine;" and the Archæologia of 1803, an "Account of Roman Urns discovered in Cornwall; and of a Cromlech discovered in the parish of Madron in the same County." Mr. Polwhele has enrolled him among the Worthies

---

—"Demonstration of a Theorem, by which such portions of the solidity of a Sphere are assigned as admit of an Algebraic Expression." ib. 153.—" On the independence of the Analytical and Geometrical Methods of Investigation; and on the advantages to be derived from their separation." ib. 85.—" On the Integration of certain Differential Expressions, with which Problems in Physical Astronomy are connected." &c. 1804, 219, the last being the article by Mr. Woodhouse which has been already noticed in the note in p. 41.

of Cornwall in the following terms : " That the Rev. Malachy Hitchins, of St. Hilary, is a man of science is universally acknowleged; and my intimate acquaintance with him enables me to add, that the urbanity of his manners, his friendly disposition, his candour, and modest deportment, contribute not less to the comforts of private life, than his philosophical researches to the public instruction and entertainment. In the Annual Register for 1792 was published an account of a remarkable meteor, as communicated by Mr. Hitchins, who had seen it in the December of that year at Bideford. In the Philosophical Transactions we have several ingenious communications from Mr. Hitchins. And in the present Work I am indebted to him for much information *."

Mr. Hitchins died in 1809. He left a son, Fortescue, who was a solicitor, and author of " The Sea-shore, and other Poems, 1810," 8vo. He died in 1814, when a short biographical notice respecting him was published, stating that, " he had been long and well known as an author, possessing considerable judgment, vigour, and elegance. His lyre was generally attuned to the softer subjects, which he touched with a judicious hand ; and had he more sedulously cultivated the Muses, he would probably have risen to a high degree of eminence."—Ten years after the death of Mr. Fortescue Hitchins, was published, " The History of Cornwall, from the earliest records and traditions to the present time. Compiled by Fortescue Hitchins, Esq. and edited by Mr. Samuel Drew, of St. Austell," in two volumes quarto, 1824; but it would appear from the Preface that Mr. Hitchins's contribution to the work was little more than his name †.

* Polwhele's Cornwall, vol. V. p. 107.
† The statement alluded to is as follows : " As a friend of the Muses, whose favours he had frequently courted, and sometimes obtained, Mr. Hitchins was well known in his native county;

The Rev. MALACHY HITCHINS to Sir JOSEPH BANKS, Bart. K.B.
P. R. S. and F.S.A.

"SIR,   *St. Hilary, near Merazion, Feb.* 25, 1802.

"I take the liberty of transmitting to you a short account *
of three Roman urns found some years since in this neighbourhood, and mentioned briefly in a former letter which I did myself the honour of sending you, together with some notice of a
very curious cromlêh lately discovered by accident.

"I wish my knowledge of antiquities would enable me to
send you a more scientific statement of these facts; but as you
think that any record of them is worth preserving, I have done
the best in my power, and would rather expose my ignorance of
such subjects than appear ungrateful for the many favours you
have condescended to confer upon me.

"Conscious of the importance of your time to yourself and
to the world, I shall only add, that I remain, with the utmost
respect and with heartfelt gratitude, Sir, your most obliged and
very humble servant,   MALACHY HITCHINS."

* Printed, as before mentioned, in the Archæologia, XIV. 224—230.

----

and the celebrity which he had acquired as a Poet, and the
writer of some sprightly notes, procured for his projected History the confidence of many respectable subscribers, who expected to find in its pages new combinations of past events, connected with the information he might be able to derive from
actual observation, from local testimony, and from his own
resources. Scarcely, however, had Mr. Hitchins begun to make
his collections and arrangements, before he was arrested by the
hand of death. No part of the History was at this time printed;
but such of his papers as contained his compilation were put
into the hands of the printer, Mr. William Penaluna, of Helston,
with whom they remained several months, until an agreement
was made between him and the writer of this preface, to give
completion to the work thus begun by Mr. Hitchins. Such
were the circumstances under which it was announced to the
public, as a 'History of Cornwall compiled by Fortescue Hitchins, Esq. and edited by Mr. Samuel Drew.' To what extent
it was the intention of Mr. Hitchins to carry this work, the present editor has no means of knowing, as no plan had been made,
either for the extent of the work, or the arrangement of the
materials. He therefore found himself, on succeeding to the
arduous task, possessed of two sheets and a half of paper, from
which nothing has been taken; the name of Mr. Hitchins as a
compiler; and those resources which were yet unexplored."

The Rev. PETER CUNNINGHAM.

The ensuing letters were addressed by the Rev. Peter Cunningham, Curate of Eyam * near the Peak in Derbyshire, to the Rector of that place, the Rev. Thomas Seward, father of the Poetess.

I can add but few particulars of Mr. Cunningham to those which will be found in these letters. It will be perceived by them that he was the son of a naval officer, and, adopting the clerical profession rather from his own studious predilections than from his father's choice, had no University education; but, having been under the tuition of a respectable clergyman, was ordained in 1772 by Archbishop Drummond, and for the first two or three years after was Curate of Almondbury near Huddersfield, where he was honoured by the notice of the Earl of Dartmouth, who resided at Woodsome Hall in that populous parish.

In 1775 he became Mr. Seward's Curate at Eyam; and soon after addressed to him the letters now printed. How long he continued at Eyam I cannot say; but the eulogium pronounced on him from the pulpit by Mr. Seward, and printed hereafter, seems to have promised a long connexion †. It is surely a very singular document.

---

* Eyam is a retired parish, celebrated as the scene of Christian heroism displayed by the Rev. William Mompesson, a predecessor of Mr. Seward in the Rectory, during a great plague, which raged there in 1666, the year following that in London. See an account of the circumstances, composed by Miss Seward, in the Gentleman's Magazine, vol. LXXI. i. 300; and some letters written by Mr. Mompesson at the period, in " Anecdotes of distinguished Persons," by William Seward, Esq. A Poem has also been published on the subject, intituled : " The Desolation of Eyam; by William and Mary Hewitt, authors of the Forest Minstrel and other Poems."

† He was Curate in 1785 (see p. 52), and probably till Mr. Seward's death in 1790.

Mr. Cunningham's name does not occur in any of the editions of " Living Authors," but a poem intituled " Britannia's Naval Triumph " was the offspring of his pen *.

In the latter years of his life Mr. Cunningham was Curate of Chertsey in Surrey ; and he died there at his apartments in that town in July 1805, having been a few minutes before suddenly attacked with illness while dining with the Chertsey Friendly Society, to which he had been in the habit of delivering an annual discourse.

———

1. Rev. P. CUNNINGHAM to the Rev. THOMAS SEWARD.

" REVEREND SIR, *Deal, Sept.* 15, 1775.

" It is with particular satisfaction that I am immediately able to answer your favour of the 10th instant in the most explicit, and as I would hope, in the most satisfactory manner. Your own sentiments on the queries, that I confess every circumstance rendered peculiarly proper to be resolved, so perfectly correspond with my own, that I might spare you the trouble of dwelling longer upon this subject ; but as I am aspiring to your confidence, I am extremely anxious to convince you that it would not be placed in one that would deceive you by misrepresentations, or in any other manner forfeit a claim to your esteem.

" I was brought up from my earliest years in the strictest conformity to the established Church of England; nor have I since found, from pretty general reading, reflection, and greater maturity of years and experience, the least reason to deviate from my first ideas of her superior excellence, or depart from those doctrines by which she is particularly distinguished in opposition to all other Christian sects, whether of Calvinism, Methodism, or any other denomination, because I esteem the tenets I have imbibed in her Communion, to approach the nearest of all others to the pure religion of the Gospel, and her polity to be the best model of primitive Christianity. The intestine divisions, the illgrounded separations that have long, and particularly within these thirty years, perplexed and afflicted our Church, I have frequently and seriously lamented. My conduct, since I had the happiness and honour to be admitted to the priesthood, has been governed by those charitable maxims and lenient principles, with

* The only record I find of this production is in some lines extravagant in its praise, written by William Newton, of whom hereafter, p. 63. See them in the Gentleman's Magazine, vol. LV. p. 212.

respect to those dissensions, which I with great pleasure observe
you mention as the distinguishing measure of your own. This
I have on many occasions experienced to be attended with the
happiest effects; but I have ever been of opinion, that the acri-
monious oppositions which our Separatists, if I may be permitted the term, have not unfrequently met with from the ill-
timed zeal of some of our own communion, and which the
others never fail to dignify with the name of persecution, have
more contributed to accelerate the progress of enthusiasm and
strengthen the union of its members, than any other cause whatever. I would treat this religious evil as a physician would do
an inveterate disorder that has risen to too great a height, and
implanted itself too deeply in the constitution to be radically
cured. Its progress might surely be prevented, and many ill-
humours corrected, by opposing to both the true armour of the
Gospel; that gentle and benevolent spirit, which, when judiciously accompanied with the honest arts of persuasion, never
fails to disarm much rancour, and allay much of the ferment of
that turbulent spirit which so much distinguishes the lower
classes of our modern sectaries, who are led so much more by
their passions than by their reason. To eradicate this disorder
entirely, I dare say you will agree with me, is an event more to be
wished than ever likely to be fulfilled; and that what our most
excellent Hooker has observed in the beginning of his ' Ecclesiastical Polity' will apply extremely well in this case, and the
invariable truth of this maxim will remain a durable monument of his discernment and their propensities: ' That those
who go about to persuade a multitude they are not so well
governed as they ought to be, will never want attentive and
credulous hearers.' How far I have acted up in reality to the
principles I have mentioned, I can, with the greatest freedom
and consolation, refer to the whole body of the people, among
whom I have more or less resided as a minister, both here and
in the North of England; if they have not flattered me, they
have parted with me with a regret, the remembrance of which
still affects me both with pleasure and with pain.

"That I ever left any cure whatever on the least suspicion of
being a favourer of methodism, I may with the strictest honour
assure you, has by no means been the case. It has been a constant source of regret to me, that I ever relinquished the Curacy I served in his Grace of York's diocese. It was on no
motion of mine, but in consequence of an overture made me to
superintend the education of a young person, whose subsequent
conduct was a great disappointment to his friends, and great
vexation and trouble to me. It was with the sanction of his
Grace of York's approbation that I accepted the charge and
relinquished the cure; when I resigned the former I wished to
return to my late employment. It is with the greatest truth
that I can assure you, the desire of the numerous parishioners

to see this effected was not less than my own inclinations to reside again among them; whence, in all human probability, I should never after have been prevailed upon to remove during the incumbent's life. My Lord Dartmouth, as principal parishioner, most willingly concurred with the general wishes of my friends, and Mr. Smith, the Incumbent, who resides chiefly upon another living at Waddington, near Clitheroe, greatly lamented that he had it not in his power to oblige both parties; before whose application he had positively engaged with a relation to supply the Cure, whom he could not with honour and humanity disappoint. Your liberality of thinking, Sir, will easily and candidly conceive, that my Lord Dartmouth's kindness and condescension to me, might very well consist with a difference of opinion; and the instance may at the same time clearly convince you, whether the tenour of my conduct was sufficiently conciliating and uniform to make contending parties my friends.

" I had a difficult sphere of duty to move in; and, perhaps, am indebted for many happy events that occurred in it to a more extensive and various knowledge of the world than generally falls to the lot of a young clergyman of eight-and-twenty. This was consequent to many vicissitudes to which I was exposed in the very early part of my life, which has been chequered with incidents that fall indeed to the lot of many, but which I might with great propriety call severe trials in my own, if the ingratitude of friends and the disappointment of brilliant prospects in some part of my life, may be felt as such by a sensible heart. Religious persecution, I should imagine what I have already had the satisfaction to communicate to you of my sentiments will have convinced you, hath been no part of my trials, nor is ever likely to become so while our excellent Church continues on its present firm and uncorrupted establishment.

" That my education should have been different from the common forms adopted usually for the candidates for Holy Orders, proceeded from circumstances it was not in my power to remedy. My father, who has served the King with great honour and credit in the naval service the major part of his life, was possessed, and as you may imagine, Sir, prejudiced, more in favour of military than clerical ideas; mine, however, had always a cast of the latter, but I was not indulged at the usual time of life with an opportunity to pursue and improve them. The genius of the mind, however, though it may be oppressed, can never be totally changed or extinguished; and my father was too sensible to oppose my inclinations when my happiness and these were placed in the scale against his authority and different sentiments. I enjoyed the private tuition of a very respectable clergyman, and was ordained in the manner I have acquainted you. The Archbishop of York, whom you certainly will not suspect of enthusiasm, nor Mr. Marsden, his examining Chaplain, if you should be acquainted with either, were fully satisfied with the answers I gave them on the very interesting subjects you have glanced upon, and which so peculiarly distinguish the orthodox member of the Established Church from those of our fellow Christians called Methodists. I cannot explain my own sentiments on the principal one better than in your own very proper and comprehensive terms, ' interpreting the article of predestination by the doctrines of the Bible; not the Bible by the articles, for it certainly will bear the sense of conditional, as well as absolute, predestination.' Dr. Rotherham's * most elegant, and to me most satisfactory, Essay on Faith, leaves me nothing to add essential to this subject, when I acquaint you, that the sentiments and doctrines contained in that Essay, which so particularly relate to the principal points of dispute between us and the Methodists, entirely correspond with my own. I flatter myself much, this full and explicit account of myself will be sufficient proof to you, that I am incapable of any ungenerous reservations that might disappoint or deceive you. I could say more on the subject, but surely, good Sir, I need trouble you no further; yet there is one circumstance this observation reminds me to apprise you of at present, which I should have done before had I presumed you would have deemed it any material objection to my application. Perhaps the particular predilection I have ever had for my profession may have been increased by what to others may appear a personal misfortune, but which I have never yet felt the weight of myself; it is an infirmity of hardness of hearing, which, as I have executed every part of the ministerial duty since the year 1772 without any inconvenience or impediment, and in that time have so long had the care of one of the most considerable and populous parishes in the diocese of York, after Wakefield and Halifax, I presume you will not think a circumstance operating to my prejudice, as it has never been hitherto felt or mentioned as such by any one else. This you must be sensible is better to be explained by actual experiment than favourably described on paper. I would not however have had you in the least disappointed in your ideas on the supposition of my having the fortune of being any ways connected with you. If, after this full representation, your sentiments should be decided in my favour, I can only repeat the assurance, that you will have no reason to repent of your partiality in my behalf; and if it should not be my happiness to acquire the confidence, attention, and good-will of your parishioners, I beg you, Sir, to be equally assured that I will not stay at Eyam to their prejudice and our mutual pain.

" A state of suspense you are very sensible is the most painful of all others; and I would be very glad to receive your earliest determinations, both on that and other accounts. My acquaint-

* A memoir of Dr. Rotherham will be found in the " Literary Anecdotes," vol. VIII. p. 193, and in the same volume, p. 229, another testimonial to his work mentioned above.

ance is very general, and most of my friends know I am not actually in service. I receive frequent overtures of their readiness to inquire for, and establish me, agreeably in the Church, which is the only employment I truly relish and shall attend to; and I expect every day some particular applications to be made to me, which I would willingly preclude entirely, by devoting my best endeavours to serve and represent Mr. Seward. I shall in any case remain, with great truth and respect,

"Reverend Sir,

"Your most obedient humble servant, P. CUNNINGHAM."

2. Conclusion of a Sermon preached by Mr. Seward, at Eyam, on Sunday, Nov. 19, 1775 * :

"I hope and trust that I shall return to you, and frequently address you from this pulpit; but in the mean time I have the greatest consolation and joy that I leave you under the care of so excellent a preacher, whose piety to God, whose delight in the performance of the duties of his office, whose amiable, engaging, courteous, and affectionate behaviour to the richer, and condescending, affable, and charitable treatment of his poorer neighbours, is a continued living sermon to us all, and has so endeared him to us already, that he is become our general friend, our delight, and our joy. Like holy Job, 'when the ear heareth him, then it blesseth him; and when the eye seeth him, it giveth witness to him.' One hearer 'telleth another' how rational and clear he is in his arguments, how affecting and convincing he is in his persuasions, and how zealous and devout in his prayers; and one neighbour 'certifieth another' how cheerful and engaging he is in his common conversation, how candid and charitable in his opinions and characters of others, and how ready in shewing pity to all who are in the least distress. — Think not that I have put so much of the pulpit duty upon him, since we have been here together, through idleness and indolence; no, it was that I would not disappoint so many longing ears that wished to hear him; it was that I rejoiced at the occasion of really preferring his sermons to my own, and of giving so eminent and worthy, though so young, a man, 'the right hand of fellowship.' Grey hairs may receive instruction from *his lips*, and the aged bow down to him; and that because he keepeth the commandments of the Lord, and delighteth in the law of his God. O may he long continue amongst us our happiness and our crown! may his moving instructions sink deep into all your hearts, and spring up into a harvest of virtue, piety, and goodness! and may the fruits of it be a plentiful treasure of happiness to himself! may his eye see it, and rejoice in the success of

* Communicated to the Gentleman's Magazine in 1785, probably by Mr. Seward.

his pious and zealous labours! There is one thing indeed that I have reason to fear, which is, that his health and strength may not enable him to perform, so diligently as he wishes, the more laborious part of his office, the frequent visitation of the sick, of private baptism of infants, particularly in the more distant parts of the parish, during storms of violent winds, rain, and snow. His constitution is tender and delicate, and has been weakened by too sedentary an application to his studies. Let me therefore intreat you all not to press him to this without real necessity, but to be cautious of endangering his health and life, as he is desirous of continuing to do you all the good offices in his power, and of promoting at all times your eternal, external, and internal happiness. May long-continued health, prosperity, and, above all, the blessings of a good conscience, attend both him and you! may I find my parish, at my return, if it please God to grant me a return to it, a seminary of piety, sobriety, charity, and every moral and christian virtue! and may the good seed which he sows amongst you with so diligent, so judicious, and so bountiful a hand, spring up to eternal life in all your hearts!"

---

3. Rev. P. Cunningham to the Rev. Thomas Seward.

"My dear Sir,   *Eyam, Dec.* 21, 1775.
"Under what planetary auspices our correspondence first began I know not; to judge from its effects in general, I would hope, without imputing any thing to dreams or judicial astrology, that every circumstance of the benignant kind was combined in its commencement, and that its longer continuance will have no other than the happiest influence on every object within the sphere of our mutual concern. I have just been gazing at the stars with all the admiration of an *amatore* of the great works of nature; you will not therefore wonder at my beginning this letter in the style of an astronomer. The finest and most welcome frost imaginable has just succeeded the late most unwholesome weather. I always used to look up with fresh delight to the noblest 'declarations of the glory of God;' but here the Heavens seem to glow with uncommon splendour. Certainly this is not a mere vision of my romantic fancy, for Brydone, when he ascended Mount Ætna and slept in the Spelonca dei Capreoli,' which is far from being the highest region of the mountain, was struck much in the same manner that I am on these Ætnas of the North of England, I mean with respect to elevation. In return for the prospect from my windows at Deal, where I not unfrequently behold the sun rising from the bosom of the deep 'like a bridegroom coming out of his chamber,' &c. I have certainly gained a clearer view of the calm firmament,

——————— ' When it glows with living sapphires,
And where the River of Bliss, through 'midst of Heaven,
Rolls o'er elysian flowers her amber stream.'

" Nor is it merely from this occasional ocular demonstration
that I discover myself to be in a more elevated situation than of
late. My heart almost daily tells me so, for such is the true
language of its emotions on continually receiving from such
numbers of your parishioners the most affecting and expressive
demonstrations, that my continuance in my present station is
essential to their happiness and contentment. One grasps my
hands so vehemently, as a mark of cordiality, that it is a mercy
for me neither the gout nor the rheumatism are lodged there;
another takes them ' con amore religioso, alle labbre; ' a third
prays for a blessing on my head as I go along the street; a
fourth sends me a bottle of magnesia alba, expressing fears for
my studious life, and a fervent wish that it may in any measure
contribute to the preservation of the health of so, &c. &c.; a
fifth cries; a sixth offers me 40s. a year to teach his tenth or
eleventh son Latin for two hours in the day; a seventh,—but I
dare proceed no farther in this practical commentary on the elevation both of my situation and my feelings; however, these
simple instances may make my dear spiritual father smile; they
not unfrequently tempt me to the reverse. The conclusion that
I cannot help drawing from the whole is this: ' Inveni portum;
spes et fortuna, valete!' Would the acquisition of £.400
per annum, and every other splendid circumstance, have been
able to afford me the heart-felt joy I experience in my present
' Post of Honour,' though it is so private a ' station!' It is
very true, I am very few degrees richer than Aristides or Sir
Francis Walsingham were when they died. I do not believe
either had so much left, if as much, as was sufficient to defray
their funeral expences; but, ' there is that scattereth and yet
increaseth,' &c. and however differently more contracted and
sordid minds may think of the resolution I have taken, to bury
myself in the Peak of Derbyshire instead of ' rising to wealth
and splendour,' I am very certain that I am many degrees nearer
the summit of my best and ruling ambition where I am than I
should have been in any other sphere or situation of my life. I
know that when I die, my grave will be watered with many a
tear of grateful remembrance and affection; I know that my
memory will be blessed by those that survive me here; and the
thought that these will one day give a still brighter testimony
to my endeavours, to make them ' internally, externally, and
eternally happy,' enables me to look back on all my past misfortunes as ' blessings in disguise" that conducted me hither; to
look down with indifference on what the world calls fortune and
greatness, and to look forward with more serenity and consolation than ever to that reward that fadeth not. In the words

of the late Dr. Hough, Bishop of Worcester, I can very truly
say: ' I may not perhaps have chosen the most likely employment to thrive by, but I depend on a Master who never fails to
recompense those who trust in Him above their hopes.' These
being my unalterable sentiments, you may imagine, Sir, that
any difference between them and my father's will not make any
impression on me to the prejudice of what I see to be my duty,
a conduct perfectly in unison with my declarations. I have had
no tidings from Deal since those which were communicated to
you at Eyam. My time is so effectually engrossed by such a
variety of duties, engagements, and literary pursuits, that it is
impossible for me to be the regular correspondent to my family;
their entire leisure leaves them without excuse in failing to be
to me. Had any sinister incident happened, some of my friends
at Deal would most undoubtedly have apprized me of it. I
sent the extract of your Sermon, that did me such signal
honour to my father and sister for their perusal. I thought it
also the most explicit and expressive testimony of my gratitude
and lively sense of the Archbishop of York's former condescension and kindness to me that could possibly be presented to his
Grace; in this manner, therefore, I have made very lately my
acknowledgements to him, and taken my final leave. This, too,
will convince you, I have no intention to trouble his Grace for
any future favours that might effect my residence at Eyam.
    " I have been several times interrupted, and this is generally
the case when I am writing either letters or sermons, before I
could get thus far in my epistolary conversazione. In these intervals see the mutability of human things; the keen salutary
frost is already succeeded by the same drisling, dark, unwholesome weather, of which we have had our share, though not of
the electrified kind, as well as the inhabitants of Lichfield.
Both brick and stone walls, in every house in the country, have
been loaded with dew-drops, innumerable as those of the morning, ' which the sun

            " ' Impearls on every leaf and every flower.'

    " The old and young declare they never remember this to
have happened in their houses before. Colds, head-aches, and
pectoral complaints have been very general; but not so fatal as
the influenza has been at Derby, Sheffield, Bristol, and other
great cities, who cannot boast, amidst their various attractions
and advantages, of the pure ' marble air,' as Milton calls it, that
we breathe most generally at Eyam, who, like the Kenites of old,
have our nests and dwelling-places in the rocks. I thought myself invulnerable by escaping so long; but yesterday I was
taught, by a very severe cold in my head, to say: ' Let not him
that girdeth on his harness boast himself as he that putteth it
off.' However, by good care and precaution I am amazingly
better to day, and shall learn to be very heedful in future, as

you know how very ill I can afford to be an invalid. A few days
ago I was at Longsdon, and received every possible mark of
attention and affectionate respect that could possibly be paid to
the man you have delighted to honour. Master Wright was
my guide over the moors; and I am truly rejoiced to think that
this young gentleman, who bids fair to be a most amiable as
well as shining member of society, is likely, on some future day,
to have it in his power, by the possession of so fine a fortune, to
give a free scope to the exercise of the noblest virtues that can
adorn the man possessed of affluence and independence.   I
deem it not the least of my felicities, that my situation affords
me the opportunity, in some measure, to testify my grateful
sense of the numberless civilities and demonstrations of kindness I continue to receive from every individual of Major
Wright's family, with whom I am particularly acquainted.   I
have had daily opportunities, since your departure, to confirm
the truth of your observations on Master Wright's genius and
understanding.   In the instructions that he has occasionally
received from me in the Latin and the French languages, in
history, composition, geography, chronology, &c. &c. I have
been very agreeably surprised to find his comprehension, discernment, memory, and abilities in general, much superior to
his age and my sanguine expectations; and yet I must do him
the justice to say, that I have the strongest reasons to believe his
heart is by no means inferior to the goodness of his head.   I
shall extremely regret it, if such distinguished talents do not
receive every possible and advantageous cultivation, the more
especially as on this circumstance will depend much of the intrinsic lustre with which he may be enabled to distinguish himself in his future sphere of life.   Mrs. Trafford has been ill, and
is still confined to her room.   I hope, however, she is now on
the recovery.   With the Major she desires her compliments and
respects; so likewise do Mr. and Mrs. Simpson, who sent for
me the day before yesterday to dine on venison, &c. and would
not suffer me to return home like a primitive pilgrim, but sent
me back in the post-chaise.   I shewed them the extemporary
verses Miss Seward favoured me with; they pleased much, as
they did me and others that have seen them; but you, that are
so severe a critic, will not, I doubt, consider the rhymes ' mourn
and perform,' as admissible in golden letters.   I beg my best
respects and acknowledgements for this acceptable favour, which
I know not how to retaliate but with the verses that are inclosed.
One of the copies has already passed the ordeal of your criticisms; the other is not of dignity enough for your attention, as
it is only a sonnet; but I believe the air for which it is intended
will not be disagreeable to Miss Seward, as it has been so greatly
admired by the lovers of music.   You will observe, perhaps, the
Elegy on Mr. Roundell's death, which ought to have had the
seventeenth or eighteenth verses of the third of Habakkuk pre-

fixed to them, are not in my hand. I am absolutely obliged to employ frequently two copyists to answer the various claims of distant friends and correspondents, and leave me at some liberty to attend to my more immediate duties. One desires me to give them a directory for a morning and evening prayer; another requests copies of letters of consolation I wrote to some distinguished persons under deep affliction; a third, who has hung up his votive tablets in the Temple of Neptune, desires me to correspond with him on such duties and subjects as may enable him to depart in peace with his Maker; a fourth earnestly intreats me to continue a correspondence from which he derives so much profit and entertainment. Humbled to the dust with the conscious sense of my own manifold infirmities, and my inability to discharge the various duties and tasks imposed upon me, I have at the same time not a moment to spare as superfluous, after acquitting myself of those duties which no adventitious circumstance can excuse me from attending to. I mean not however to elude the promise you have obtained from me of some account of my own life; like other Biographers, I shall use my own pleasure as to epitomizing and dilating my adventures. As I am in the disposition to write them (and in this respect too I must claim the privilege of a Poet's fancy, not to be forced when the muse does not inspire it), you shall receive a very faithful account of the chequered scenes of my life. The conclusion that I flatter myself you will draw, after perusing the whole narrative, is, whenever you walk by my tomb, if you should happen to survive me, this concluding stanza to an epitaph, that always affects me extremely whenever I hear it sung by a feeling voice:

> Beneath yon stone the youth is laid;
>   O greet his ashes with a tear!
> May Heav'n with blessings crown his shade,
>   And grant that peace he wanted here.

" You will please to preserve the letters I write on this subject, as I made much the same kind of promise in one of my letters to the Earl of Dartmouth, and as I shall beg them awhile to transcribe, I shall be glad to know, while I am writing them, that I have no occasion to double my labour by copying them, as they go out of my hands to my dear and paternal friend. You see how my heart flows along with my pen to you. I know not when nor where to finish; and yet I must not finish without making you many acknowledgements for your anxiety and attention concerning my health. The galoches and shoes were brought to me a few days since; and I shall not fail to observe your injunctions. As indifferent as I really am to what relates merely to myself, I shall not suffer this disposition to degenerate into a delirium of sentiment, nor rush, like Curtius, in consequence of it, into the pit of destruction.

" Mr. Bird, jun. who desires his respects, told me a quarter's salary lay ready for me when I choose to receive it; it was not due till the 18th of next month, and I did not intend to have taken it before that time; however, as I wanted to pay some money before that time, and have had occasion for a variety of necessaries, that you may continue to ' have no occasion to be ashamed of my externals,' I have been obliged to do what the French very expressly call, *manger le bleden herbe.* After my year of probation is expired, I hope to be able to deserve the title of a better economist than to live by anticipation; before that time, I despair of arriving at any proficiency in the saving maxims that Shenstone dealt out very liberally to every one in the Muses' train, but never once put in practice himself. I am very sensible we must be just before we can be said to be liberal, and the former quality I trust no one shall find that I am defective in, whatever becomes of the latter.

" You entertain me with your resolution to make the Bishop of Bristol's franks serve as a practical commentary on this last mentioned subject. You are determined his Lordship shall lose no opportunity of doing good before he is translated; and I am willing to shew you what a good disciple I can be upon occasion, by sending this and the accompaniments in an envelope from a hand that I hope is very far from being likely, so soon as the Bishop's *, to swell the sound,

" ' Symphonious of ten thousand harps, that tune
Angelic harmonies.'

" For such I hope will be part of Dr. Newton's reward for many noble defences of his great master's honour and religion against the scorn of the libertine and the arrows of the infidel. You know my sentiments concerning the Priestleys, the Humes, &c. and will not, therefore, wonder that I should sensibly regret the probable loss of so distinguished a champion of Christianity.

" Dr. Rogers's † Sermons were particularly recommended to me by the Earl of Kinnoul; I have been greatly edified by them, but am very glad that the gentleman who lately put you upon the office of Inquisitor-general was not present when I preached one of them two years ago. My best and sincere respects attend Mr. and Mrs. Seward. That you may very long continue to be happy, and attain to a patriarchal, rather than an episcopal, age, is the cordial wishes of, my dear Sir,

" Your most affectionate and sincere, P. CUNNINGHAM."

* Bishop Newton's death, however, did not take place till seven years after this date.
† Of whom see the " Literary Anecdotes," vol I. p. 154 ; vol. II. p. 57.

4. " DEAR SIR,   *Eyam, March 28, 1776.*

"' Diffugêre nives, redeunt jam gramina campis,'—in a very few weeks I hope to add,

   " Arboribusque comæ.'

" The late fine weather that has been so genial as to produce these effects, and a variety of other instant avocations, have prevented me from an earlier acknowledgment of your favour containing the order for two guineas on the overseers; and of the Chinese column of writing you favoured me with in Miss Seward's very elegant letter of the beginning of this month. I call it a Chinese column because it was almost in the oriental style of writing from the top to the bottom, with no breadth for Ciceronian or Clarendonian periods; but in whatsoever form your letters greet me, I shall be happy to find, as I was then, that they contain accounts of your welfare and prosperity.

" I may in my turn greet you on the good accounts you must doubtless have had of the mine called Lady Wash, which as far as I am able to discover, from the overseers and other persons conversant in these things, will be an accession of better than £.200 *per annum* to your civil and ecclesiastical revenues at Eyam. I cordially congratulate you on the same * ; and I flatter myself when you hear on your next visit an account of my proceedings and the state of your parish in general, you will not think, when you take a retrospect from the beginning of our connection, that your evil genius came into the Peak of Derbyshire under my shape and character. On my part, ' I faint not, neither am weary;' but it is your misfortune that I shall certainly kill myself with exertions to please. So said C. Emanuel Bach, Director of the Concerts at Hamburgh; he said it however with the clause of being among such as deserved to be pleased. Now I am exactly in that predicament which he was not at Hamburgh, for I still continue to think that the singular regard and affection of your parishioners in general deserve to be repaid with equal fervour. But while I am endeavouring to give them continual evidence of this, I have but too much reason to apply to myself the motto of a Physician that I met in France, and which I was greatly charmed with: ' Consumo in aliis serviendo.' I have but one remedy to use, and on the supposition it is your general wish I should not in a hurry become ' Pulvis et Umbra' at Eyam, I shall not fail to use it, agreeably to the tenor of our first correspondence and agreement. While your health and inclinations may render the parochial duty

* Ten years after this, there had been a great failing in the lead mines. "Thank you," says Miss Seward to Mr. W. Newton, Dec. 17, 1786, "for your mineral intelligence, unwelcome as in itself it proves. The value of Eyam living to my father, once near £700 a year, is not now more than £150. So sink deeper and deeper, from year to year, our golden hopes in this watery mischief." Letters, vol. I. p. 223.

agreeable to you during your stay at Eyam, I shall beg leave to
use such kind reliefs on your part as opportunities of unbending
and recruiting myself among my friends. I can very safely
assure you, that no danger is to be apprehended of my listening
to overtures of any kind during my occasional absence; my
affections are now too firmly rivetted to Eyam and its environs to
give you a shadow of uneasiness on that account, but I very
plainly foresee, that without a few temporary relaxations of the
nature I have mentioned, my intense and continual application
to my parochial duties, and other literary and friendly engagements that will be coeval with myself, will in a very few years so
totally relax and destroy my health and spirits, as to render me
utterly unfit for any duties at all. When you are so good as to
acquaint me with the time you propose to set your face towards
Eyam, I shall be the better enabled to know how to shape my
intended course, and regulate the length of my little cruize.
Among the various claims that my friends have upon me, there
is one to which I must pay a particular attention, a Yorkshire
family, with whom I have been intimately connected above thirteen years, impatiently wish to see me. I have promised to take
the opportunity of your stay at Eyam, to come over to Eccles-
field, where part of them reside, and pay them the grateful
and affectionate acknowledgements that have always been due
to them on my part since the first hour of our acquaintance.
My friends at Almondbury are equally urgent with me; but I
believe I shall postpone my visit to that part of the county to
another season, and employ the remainder of the time I may
have to spare nearer home. The Squire of Longston, by whom
I have been received and entertained with particular marks of
respect and regard, expects that I should accompany his grandson thither some part of the season I have mentioned, as I have
no other time to spare for such excursions; indeed both himself, the Major, Mrs. Trafford, and the family in general, have
been so singularly kind and affectionate in every part of their
behaviour and notice of me, that I should be laid under obligations which I should never be able adequately to acknowledge,
if it was not to their grandson and nephew, whom they are
pleased to say, has done me and himself great honour by his
various improvements during the little time he has been with
me. I have no reason at present to doubt either his grateful
disposition or attention, and that gives me alacrity to proceed
with the pleasing task I have undertaken of his instruction. If
it should please God to spare my life, I expect to see this young
gentleman a great ornament to his family and country, and to
derive many future pleasing emotions and reflections from having been so instrumental ' in rearing his tender thoughts, in
teaching his young ideas how to shoot, and in fixing each generous purpose in his glowing breast.' The Major has been at a
great expense in altering and decorating my *Salon a manger*;

it is now, in consequence of his compliment, the prettiest room in Eyam. Nor has this been all; I am indebted to the care Major Wright has taken to prepare a very cordial reception for me at Hassop, for all the civilities and politeness I have received there from Mr. Eyre. My entertainments in the pleasure grounds, plantations, green-houses; and within doors with many fine paintings, and the uncommonly agreeable conversation of the owner, will not be the least pleasing circumstances of the intelligence I shall continue to send of my situation to the South of England. Mr. Eyre has given me a particular and general invitation to repeat my visits to Hassop; and he has also favoured me with some books to read.

"From Captain Bourne, of Rowsley, I have experienced, if I may so call it, an exuberance of hospitality and respect; he has also lent me Burgh's Political Disquisitions. When Mr. Parr, of Stanmore, who has my Lord Dartmouth's young sons under his care, and those of several other noblemen in administration, was asked whether he had read these Disquisitions; ' Have I read my Bible, Sir?' was the answer Mr. Parr gave to the question *. Captain Bourne moreover has presented me with a valuable pair of sleeve buttons, they are pebbles which he gathered himself in Martinico before that island surrendered to the English last war. Captain Bourne was then upon a reconnoitering party, and on his return had the pebbles set in gold. They are at length transferred from the torrid zone to the wrists of your humble servant; but I have had the misfortune yesterday to drop one of them in the dell that is now my favourite scene of meditation, and we have not yet recovered it. I mention these little particulars as a supplement to the other testimonies I gave you of your parishioners' affection to me; and I question not they will afford you on my account a kindred satisfaction. From the whole of my situation taken together, you may judge whether, when my parochial duties, correspondencies, and other similar employments and engagements are deducted, I have one spare moment remaining; indeed I never was less alone, or had less leisure in the whole course of my life. The new circle of connections in which my residence at Eyam has necessarily engaged me, has been a kind of vortex absorbing all remoter considerations; accordingly several of my southern friends complain heavily of my silence and apparent neglect of them. They have no real cause, for I purpose day after day to write to them, and employ my amanuensis to transcribe a variety of things to send them as a compliment of remembrance; in the mean time every succeeding day brings its full portion of employment, glides away like the last without the intended letter, and at length I find myself two, three, or four months after-

* " Political Disquisitions, or an Enquiry into Public Errors, Defects, and Abuses," by James Burgh, an eminent writer in his day, 3 vols. 8vo, 1774, have the epithet of " excellent" in the Bibliotheca Parriana.

wards surrounded with unanswered letters from my most respectable and worthy friends.

" Very lately I received a long letter from Sir Thomas Edwards, who is just recovered from a dangerous nervous fever. Sir Thomas acquaints me he was at a rout, and was playing cards with Lady Burland when the melancholy intelligence was brought of her husband's sudden death * ; they only told her in the rooms Sir John was extremely ill.   A very mournful transition indeed, from the card-table to a death-bed !   Sir Thomas, Lady Edwards, and all my London and Kentish friends, those of Almondbury, and many in Scotland, are truly rejoiced with the accounts I have sent them of my Derbyshire Curacy; and I am certain many of them will entertain a better opinion of the Peak from the colours with which I have endeavoured to soften and illuminate its most rugged and savage scenes.   My father and my sister, who have the least reason and excuse, are the most dilatory and negligent of all my correspondents.

" Tell Miss Seward, with my respects and acknowledgments for her last favour, that the Major has made ample atonement for sacrificing some of the beauties of the dell by creating others that bid fair to prosper, and in time to afford foliage and shade ample enough to fill the ears with harmony and the imagination with the most soothing corresponding pleasures.   I find it already extremely favourable to meditation and poetic dreams : and, in allusion to Petrarch's favourite retirement, have christened the whole scene of its romantic beauties by the name of Valclusa.

" I have still the inexpressible satisfaction to observe your Church more crowded than I am assured it has been ever remembered during this season of the year.   No more Methodist teachers appear at the Chapel at Eyam ; the few that resort to them at Grindleford-bridge are such as an angel from Heaven would have no influence with ; and as I suppose you do not expect me to work miracles, since nothing less will convince or convert them, they must even be left to prey upon garbage, 'and follow the wandering fires of their own vapourish imaginations.' However, we shall have no spiritual will-of-the-wisp to lead the inhabitants astray; for Justice, under the form of my good friend the Major, hath now fixed her seat among us, so you may judge whether one, who has used the sword so long and so honourably in the service of his country, is disposed ' to bear it in vain' in this case, so far as that of justice hath any concern in protecting the established religion of the country.   The very idea of the Major's justiciary powers hath already struck a terror into some of the few ' evil doers' in this neighbourhood ; and I persuade myself its influence will reach many little abuses against which a minister may argue, in his pastoral capacity, to the day of judgment in vain.

* Sir John Burland, Knt. died at Westminster March 28, 1776.

" 'The letter I wrote to the Archbishop of York did neither require an answer, nor did I expect one; however, a letter that I have just received informs me, that I am a favourite with the Archbishop, an honour for which I am greatly obliged to his Grace, but of which I never mean to avail myself any further.

" I shall begin a narrative * of my life in my next letter; in the mean time I remain with every good wish for your happiness and prosperity, dear Sir,

" Your very affectionate and humble servant,

" P. CUNNINGHAM.

" I have this moment brought to me your letter to the good and worthy Dolly. I thank you cordially for your kind remembrance in it; and you may observe I have anticipated, in the foregoing long letter, every thing you wished me to acquaint you with. I dined lately at Stoke; Mr. and Mrs. Simpson were both well, and received me and my young gentleman with their usual kindness and cordiality. Your donation of £.2. 2s. was distributed to forty-two poor persons, and came in a very seasonable time. All the persons that were relieved return their grateful thanks.

" Rejoice with me, for we have just found the golden ' Gage d'Amitié' that was lost. Adieu ! "

---

5. Miss SEWARD to Mr. URBAN.

" MR. URBAN, *March* 1785.

" Your Magazine is a proper and honourable repository for every thing curious in nature, in science, and in art. Therefore I transmit to it the ensuing account of a being in whom the lustre of native genius shines through the mists which were thrown around him by obscure birth, the total absence of all refined instruction, and by the daily necessity of manual labour.

" William Newton was born at Wardlow in Derbyshire, a small hamlet on Tideswell Moor, which extends along the tops of some of the Peak Mountains. This hamlet parishes to the village of Eyam, of which my father is Rector and Mr. Cunningham Curate. The inclosed specimen of William Newton's poetic talent is addressed to the last-named gentleman, whose poems are not unknown or unadmired. I give my word of honour that it has not received any correction from me. I send it in his own hand-writing. Mr. Cunningham assures me, that neither himself nor any other person has altered a single syllable of these verses; and indeed the style of their author's letters evinces that his imagination has no rude asperities which demand the critical chissel.

" William Newton's father was a carpenter, too ignorant to

---

* This narrative, if ever written, is not preserved with the letters here inserted.

give his son any literary advantages, and too indigent to procure them for him. A dame-school and a writing-master formed the boundaries of our Minstrel's education. He worked at his father's trade, and very early became so ingenious, skilful, and industrious as to be employed by some few genteel families of the neighbourhood. On these occasions, I have been told, he used to examine books which accident lay about in the apartments where he was at work. They awakened into sensibility and expansion the internal fires of his spirit. Every species of fine writing engaged his attention; but poetry enchanted him. From that period all the earnings of his ingenious industry, which he could prudently spare, were expended in books.

"Some five years since Mr. Cunningham by accident discovered this literary flower of the desert. A retired disposition, and the most unobtrusive modesty, had cast a veil over his talents, which few had possessed sagacity to pierce, though his inventive industry had raised his reputation as a workman. He was employed, I am told, not only to execute, but to construct, machines for the Derbyshire Cotton-mills, besides being one of the head carpenters at the Duke of Devonshire's splendid buildings at Buxton. He married early in life a young woman of his own rank, and is known to make a kind husband, a tender father, and to be in all respects a just and worthy man.

'When I was at Eyam with my father in the summer of 1783, Mr. Cunningham told me, that William Newton had a considerable number of well-chosen books on poetic, historic, philosophic, and religious subjects. That gentleman introduced him to me as a Minstrel of my native mountains. This self-taught Bard is rather handsome, but aims at nothing in his appearance beyond the clean and decent. When the first embarrassments were past, produced by a conscious want of the manners of the world, he conversed with perspicuity and taste upon the authors he had read, the striking scenery of the few countries he had beheld, and the nature of his own destiny, perceptions, and acquirements.

"The ease and elegance of his epistolary style are wonderful. I have extracted the following sentences from a letter of thanks which I received from him in the last autumn, upon my having presented him with the four Poems I have published, bound up together:

"'All that your pensive, your lonely friend can return for this unmerited kindness are the warm effusions of a grateful heart. My walk through the darkling vale of toilful life has not been through a wilderness of sweets. Your having scattered, in my solitary path, flowers of so agreeable an odour, culled from the bowers of the Muses, will lighten, in many an irksome hour, the iron weight of labour. Indeed, since I received this testimony of your amity, young Hope and Joy have aided the hands of the mechanic. Every sublime and beautiful object, which I used to view with a melancholy languor, have now acquired the most animating charms in my sight. As a warm sunbeam dispels the heavy dew, and raises the head of a drooping field-flower, so has your kind attention dispersed the clouds which were cast about me by adverse and wayward fortune.

"'I have lately added to my little poetical collection the works of that sublime Bard, and learned and judicious critic, Mr. Hayley; and I now live in the midst of that charming Monsaldale whose graces you have so faithfully described in the Poem which you are so good to address to me. Last week Mr. Cunningham found me in this lonely valley, surrounded by wheels, springs, and various mechanical operations. To his creative fancy they appeared as the effect of magic, and he called me Prospero *.'

"To have found, in the compositions of a laborious villager, some bright sparks of native genius, amidst the dross of prosaic vulgarity, had been pleasing, though perhaps not wonderful; but the elegance and harmony of William Newton's language, both in prose and verse, are miraculous, when it is remembered that, till Mr. Cunningham kindly distinguished him, he had associated only with the unlettered and inelegant vulgar. He is now only thirty years old.

"I have inclosed a little poem of my own, addressed to this creature of inspiration, chiefly because it describes Monsaldale, the loveliest among the vales of Derbyshire. If its features are not so sublime as those of Dovedale, they are more soft and smiling, and not less picturesque. Strange! that Monsaldale should seldom or ever be included in the chart laid down for the curious who mean to make the tour of that country.

"If you think my rhymes worth publishing, be so good as to insert them in the same Magazine with those of the Minstrel †.

"Yours, &c.   ANNA SEWARD."

---

6. As a proper continuation of the preceding narrative may be quoted the following extract from a letter of Miss SEWARD to the Lady ELEANOR BUTLER, dated Dec. 9, 1795:

"My Memoir of the Peak Minstrel ‡, and Poem addressed to him in the Gentleman's Magazine for March 1785, have had

* This is an excellent specimen of what Miss Seward considered, " an easy and elegant epistolary style!" In that lady's ideas, as appears by the next paragraph, prose and vulgarity were synonymous. The muse-stricken artisan deserves some credit for having so cleverly suited his patroness's taste.
† They are printed together ; see Gent. Mag. vol. LV. p. 212.
‡ Among Miss Seward's published letters are several to Mr. W. Newton. In August 1787 she writes to Mr. Hayley : " My poetic carpenter comes to see me soon. I had the pleasure of assisting to enable him to

the honour to interest you and your charming friend in his destiny, and suggested your inquiry into his present situation. At the time that memoir and poem were written, or very soon after, he was articled for seven years, upon a salary of £.50 *per annum*, as machinery-carpenter in a cotton-mill, in beauteous Monsaldale, Derbyshire. Two years after the mill was burnt, and he with difficulty escaped from its sudden and midnight conflagration. His tools, purchased gradually, and which cost him £.30, were consumed; he was refused any compensation for them; thus, with a wife and two children, he had the world to begin again. I procured a few guineas for their present support.

"That accident which seemed so ruinous, will, I trust, prove the means of making his fortune. His known ingenuity in mechanics, his industry and fair moral character, induced some monied people, who were going to erect a cotton-mill in that neighbourhood, but, alas! in a situation dreary as the former was Edenic, to offer to admit him third partner if he would undertake to construct its machinery, keep it in order, and could advance £.200 to the common stock. An old godmother of his, who had boarded with his wife some years, and experienced from him the kindness of filial attention, sold, for this purpose, houses which were her sole support, and which produced £.150. I lent him the remaining £.50, and he re-embarked in business, in the respectable station of cotton manu-

raise a sum sufficient to acquire his admission into partnership with an opulent cotton-spinner. He tells me he never made more than £50 *per annum* by his former business, and that his profits of the share in the mill were last year £150. This being has great merit in never having suffered the day-dreams of his imagination to lure him from the path of manual industry. Genius is to indigence a dangerous present. I shall rejoice his honest modest heart, by shewing him the high praise with which your last letter honours that poem of his that I inclosed."—In another letter to Mr. Hayley in April 1788: "That ingenious being, whom the muses condescended to visit in a saw-pit, the sometime-carpenter, now joint master of a cotton-mill, passed a week here lately; the mornings of which we devoted to poetic studies, and the evenings to the sublime muse of Handel, through the energetic tones of Giovanni, and the melting notes of his daughter. The mechanical genius and industry of this bard of the Peak mountain have procured him more of life's solid good than he was likely to have obtained from the nymphs who gilded his day-dreams. He lately wrote the inclosed verses (printed in the Sheffield newspapers) to promote the interest of a brother genius, now stricken in years, and whose ardent pursuit of the sciences cost him his eye-sight. An intention so benevolent, adorned with so pleasing an effluence of Aonian inspiration, will, I dare believe, make them acceptable to you."—In 1793 the same lady patroness thus writes from Buxton to Mr. Saville: "That being of true integrity, that prodigy of self-cultivated genius, Newton, the minstrel of my native mountains, walks over them from Tideswell, his humble home, to pass the day with me to-morrow. To preclude wonder and comments upon my attentions to such an apparent rustic at the public table, I have shewn two charming little poems of his, which are deservedly admired by every body here." Seward's Letters, vol. I. p. 318; vol. II. p. 98; vol. III. p. 262.

facturer. The mill to which he belongs stood, amidst the commercial wreck of so many great houses in Manchester, about two years ago. All the Peak-mills supply that town. A little before that dangerous crisis he wrote to me that he had realized a thousand pounds in the concern; a great sum for the short time he had been engaged in it. I find they are now going on very prosperously *."

THOMAS PITT, LORD CAMELFORD.

The family of Pitt was founded by John Pitt, Esq. who was Clerk of the Exchequer in the time of Queen Elizabeth †. From his eldest and his third sons the noble branches of Rivers and Chatham derive their descents; but each branch was principally established by a great-grandson of the above John,—the former by George Pitt, Esq. of Stratfield Say, who married into the Rivers family; and the latter by Thomas Pitt, Esq. Governor of Fort St. George, who obtained the famous Pitt diamond ‡.

Thomas, eldest son of Governor Pitt, having married Lady Frances Ridgeway, daughter and coheir

---

* Letters of Anna Seward, vol. IV. p. 134.

† A full pedigree of the family is given in Hutchins's Dorsetshire; second edition, vol. III. p. 361.

‡ Thomas Pitt, Esq. was born at St. Mary's, Blandford, 1653. He was in Queen Anne's reign appointed to the government of Fort St. George, in the East Indies, where he resided many years, and gained an immense fortune. In 1716 he was made Governor of Jamaica; but resigned that post in 1717. He was M. P. in the third, fourth, fifth, and sixth Parliaments of Great Britain, for Old Sarum and Thirsk. He repaired and beautified the Churches of Blandford St. Mary, Dorsetshire, Stratford in Wiltshire, and Abbot Inn, Hampshire. It having been reported that he gained his famous diamond by a stretch of power, he made the following solemn declaration (first communicated to the Gentleman's Magazine in 1825, by the Rev. William Meyrick, of Bath, an heir of some of the estates of the Pitts), that he purchased it fairly for 48,000 pagodas, or £.20,400. A

of Robert fourth and last Earl of Londonderry of that family, was created Baron Londonderry in 1719, and Earl of Londonderry in 1726. His sons Thomas and Ridgeway were successively Earls; and the title then expired.

Robert, second son of Governor Pitt, became seated at Boconnoc in Cornwall, which the Governor had purchased in 1718. His second son, William, was the first and immortal Earl of Chatham; his eldest, Thomas, succeeded him at Bo-

further vindication was thought necessary, in a Sermon preached at his funeral by the Rev. Richard Eyre, Canon of Sarum.

" Since my coming into this melancholy place of Bergen, I have been often thinking of the most unparalleled villainy of William Fraser, Thomas Frederick, and Smapa, a black merchant, who brought a paper before Governor Addison in Council, insinuating that I had unfairly got possession of a large Diamond, which tended so much to the prejudice of my reputation and the ruin of my estate, that I thought it necessary to keep by me the true relation how I purchased it in all respects, that so, in case of sudden mortality, my children and friends may be apprised of the whole matter, and so be enabled thereby to put to silence, and confound those and all other villains in their base attempts against either. Not having got my books by me at present, I cannot be positive as to the time, but for the manner of purchasing it I do here declare and assert, under my hand, in the presence of God Almighty, as I hope for salvation through the merits and intercession of our Saviour Jesus Christ, that this is the truth, and if it be not, let God deny it to me and my children for ever! which I would be so far from saying, much less leave it under my hand, that I would not be guilty of the least untruth in the relation of it for the riches and honour of the whole world.

" About two or three years after my arrival at Madras, which was in July 1698, I heard there were large Diamonds in the country to be sold, which I encouraged to be brought down, promising to be their chapman, if they would be reasonable therein; upon which Jaurchund, one of the most eminent diamond merchants in those parts, came down about December 1701, and brought with him a large rough stone, about 305 mangelius, and some small ones, which myself and others bought; but, he asking a very extravagant price for the great one, I did not think of meddling with it, when he left it with me for some days, and then came and took it away again; and did so several times, not insisting upon less than 200,000 pago-

connoc, and was Lord Warden of the Stannaries, and Steward to the Duchy of Cornwall. He married Christiana, sister to Lord Lyttelton, and had an only son, the subject of the present memoir.

Thomas Pitt, first Lord Camelford, was born on the third of March 1733. In 1751 he was placed as a Student at Clare Hall, Cambridge, where he continued until 1757, and was admitted to the degree of M. A. *(per literas Regias)* in 1759. It was during his residence at Cambridge that he was

das; and, as I best remember, I did not bid him above 30,000, and had little thoughts of buying it for that. I considered there were many and great risques to be run, not only in cutting it, but also whether it would prove foul or clear, or the water good; besides, I thought it too great an amount to be adventured home on one bottom. But Jaurchund resolved to return speedily to his own country; so that I best remember it was in February following he came again to me, (with Vincatee Chittee, who was always with him,) when I discoursed with him about it, and pressed me to know, whether I resolved to buy it, when he came down to 100,000 pagodas, and something under before we parted, when we agreed upon a day to meet, and make a final end thereof one way or other, which I believe was the latter end of the aforesaid month, or the beginning of March; when we accordingly met in the Consultation Room, where, after a great deal of talk I brought him down to 55,000 pagodas, and advanced to 45,000, resolving to give no more, and he likewise resolving not to abate, I delivered him up the stone, and we took a friendly leave of one another. Mr. Benyon was then writing in my closet, with whom I discoursed on what had passed, and told him now I was clear of it; when, about an hour after, my servant brought me word that Jaurchund and Vincatee Chittee were at the door, who being called in, they used a great many expressions in praise of the stone, and told me he had rather I should buy it than any body, and to give an instance thereof, offered it for 50,000; so, believing it must be a pennyworth, if it proved good, I offered to part the 5000 pagodas that was then between us, which he would not hearken to, and was going out of the room again, when he turned back and told me that I should have it for 49,000, but I still adhered to what I had before offered him, when presently he came to 48,000, and made a solemn vow he would not part with it a pagoda under, when I went again into the closet to Mr. Benyon, and told him what had passed, saying, that if it

favoured by his uncle the first and great Lord Chatham with a series of sensible, affectionate, and estimable letters, which in 1804 were given to the public by his son-in-law Lord Grenville, accompanied by an excellent Preface from the pen of that illustrious statesman. In 1761, on his father's death,

was worth 47,500, it was worth 48,000*; so I closed with him for that sum, when he delivered me the stone, for which I paid him very honourably, as by my books appear.   And I here further call God to witness, that I never used the least threatening word at any of our meetings to induce him to sell it me; and God himself knows it was never so much as in my thoughts so to do.   Since which, I have had frequent and considerable dealings with this man, and trusted him with several sums of money, and balanced several accounts with him, and left upwards of 2000 pagodas in his hands at my coming away.   So, had I used the least indirect means to have got it from him, would not he have made himself satisfaction when he has had money so often in his hands! Or would I have trusted him afterwards, as I did, preferably to all other diamond merchants?   As this is the truth, so I hope for God's blessing upon this and all my other affairs in this world, and eternal happiness hereafter. Written and signed by me, in Bergen, July 29th, 1710.

" THOMAS PITT."

The Diamond was brought over rough by Governor Pitt; and the following particulars, " copied from a memorandum made before it was disposed of," were given in the Gentleman's Magazine for 1776, vol. XLVI. p. 105.

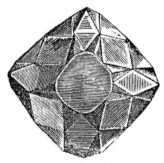

" Mr. Pitt's great diamond, when raw, weighed 410 carats; when brilliant cut, 135.

* £.20,400 sterling, at 8s. 6d. per pagoda.

he succeeded to the estate of Boconnoc; and also to the representation of the Borough of Old Sarum. He vacated his seat by accepting the post of a Commissioner of the Admiralty April 16, 1763; and was re-elected. At the next election in 1768 he was returned for Oakhampton, but at those in 1774 and 1780 again for New Sarum; and by patent dated the 5th of January 1784, he was called to the House of Peers by the title of Lord Camelford

" It cost £.5000 cutting in brilliant.

" The clips yielded £.8000.

" The diamond dust, to cut it, cost £.1400.

" It is about an inch and a quarter diamond diameter; and weighs about an ounce and the eighth part of an ounce."

The same memorandum states, that £.80,000 was bid for it by a private person. But it was finally sold, in 1717, to the Crown of France for £.200,000, and the state jewels, in sealed packets numbered, were pledged for the payment of that sum. The Governor delivered it himself at Calais, and his son-in-law, Charles Cholmondeley, Esq. of Vale Royal, who was for 42 years M. P. for the County of Chester, was accustomed at stated periods to take one of the packets of the French jewels to Dover, where he delivered his charge to a messenger of the King, and received from him an instalment of the purchase-money. " This property descended (says the Rev. Mr. Meyrick, in a letter in the Gentleman's Magazine,) principally in the other branches of Governor Pitt's family; but the estates I possess in Dorsetshire, Devon, and Wilts, were purchased with a part of this money on the marriage of his second son, Colonel Thomas Pitt, afterwards Earl of Londonderry, with Lady Frances, daughter of Robert Ridgeway, Earl of Londonderry. The ancient house at Woodlands, in the parish of Mere, Wilts, is a part of this property, which you will find amply described by our learned and indefatigable friend Sir R. Colt Hoare, in his elaborate and splendid History of the Hundred of Mere; and, as with his usual kindness he has given me the plate from which the print of Woodlands-house in that work is taken, I have sent it for insertion in your Magazine." See that Miscellany, vol. XCV. pt. ii. p. 105. Ridgeway, the last Earl of Londonderry of the Pitt family, having broken his leg in shooting, died at Woodyates Manor, a part also of this property, eleven miles from Blandford.

Governor Pitt died in 1726; and in Blandford St. Mary Church, Dorsetshire, is the following handsome memorial:

" To the Glory of God. Thomas Pitt, Esq. of this place, in the year of our Lord 1711, very much repaired and beautified

of Boccnnoc. In 1787 he visited several parts of
the continent, particularly Italy, where he continued to pass the greater part of the remainder of
his life, and he died at Florence, Jan. 19, 1793.

His Lordship married in July 1771, Ann, daughter and coheiress * of Pinkney Wilkinson of Burn-

this Church; dedicating his substance to his Maker, in that
place where he himself was first dedicated to his service. In
this pious action he is alone his own example and copy, this
being but one specimen of many of the like nature. Thus by
building God's houses, he has wisely laid a most sure foundation
for his own; and, by honouring the name of the Almighty, has
transmitted himself to posterity by such actions. He deserves
not only this perishing register, but also to be had in the everlasting remembrance."

On the north side is also a mural monument thus inscribed,
to the memory of his father, by Governor Pitt :

" H. S. E. vir reverendus Johannes Pitt, hujus ecclesiæ per
annos viginti octo Pastor fidelis, vitæ integritate, morum pro-
bitate, et doctrinæ puritate spectabilis. Duxit uxorem Saram,
Johannis Jay generosi filiam, ex eâque, Dei dono, suscepit
liberos novem. E quibus Johannes, Sara, Thomas, Georgius,
et Dorothea ipsi superstites.

"Obiit 25º Aprilis, anno { Dom. 1672º.
                          { ætatis suæ 62º.

" Hanc inscriptionem, postquam hanc sacram Ædem instau-
raverat, ornavit honoratus Thomas Pitt, armiger, defuncti filius
natu secundus, qui, post varias utriusque fortunæ vices, et multos
terrâ marique exantlatos labores, demum opibus et honoribus
auctus, et in hanc sedem natalem redux, erga Patrem cœlestem
et terrestrem pietatis suæ duplex erexit monumentum, anno
Domini, 1712."

The Pitt Diamond, after its arrival in France, was generally
called the Regency Diamond, from having been bought when
the Duke of Orleans was Regent of France during the minority
of Louis the Fourteenth. In 1776, a correspondent of the
Gentleman's Magazine testifies to having seen it sometimes
mentioned in the papers as worn by the French King for a
button to his hat on extraordinary occasions, and there is at
Boconnoc a portrait of Governor Pitt by Kneller, with the diamond in that situation. It is stated to have afterwards formed
the principal ornament of the Royal crown of France; but Buo-
naparte placed it in the hilt of his sword. It is still preserved
among the jewels of France.

* Mary, the other coheiress, was mother of Admiral Sir William Sydney Smith.

ham in Norfolk, Esq. and by her had issue one
son Thomas, who succeeded him in the title, but
was slain in a duel in 1804, not having been married; and one daughter, Anne, who was married
in 1792 to Lord Grenville *, and became heiress to
her brother.

That Lord Camelford was a sensible and an elegant writer, and possessed considerable talents, and
very elegant acquirements in the arts, the letters to
Mr. Hardinge, which accompany this brief sketch,
are a sufficient evidence. But his Lordship has
been honourably characterized by two Noble Peers;
in his early life, by the great Lord Chatham, for
being " one of the most amiable, valuable, and no-
ble-minded of youths;" and subsequently by Lord
Grenville †, as "combining a suavity of manners
with steadiness of principle, and a correctness of
judgment with integrity of heart; which produced
the affectionate attachment from those who knew
him, that has followed him beyond the grave."

The following inscription for a bust of Lord Camelford was written by his friend Mr. Hardinge:

" Farewell, accomplish'd mind, and worth rever'd!
In all 'the charities of life' ‡ endear'd,
The Arts in thee have lost their zealous guide,
And Senates heard thee with a Nation's pride,
A loyal subject—but the Regal trust
With spirit claiming, and severely just:—
How kind a Master let afflictions tell,
That rudely utter what they feel so well!
How generous a Parent who shall speak,
If Nature's eloquence itself is weak?

* The families were before connected by the marriage of Lord
Grenville s aunt, Lady Hesther Grenville, in 1754, with the first
and great Earl of Chatham.
† In the luminous preface to the Earl of Chatham's Letters,
p. xiv.   ‡ Milton.

If Imogen *, by love in vain caress'd,
Feeds the mute anguish of the filial breast ?
And bold Arviragus †, with heart sincere,
Abjures relief, nor hides the manly tear!
The Husband lives—in glowing thoughts enshrin'd,
The temple of a consecrating mind.
Whose cheering lamp forbids thee to expire,
And renovates to Love the deathless fire ;
But, oh! the hapless Friend ‡, whom thou hast left,
A pilgrim in the world—of thee bereft!
Above the converse of inferior souls,
He pants for thee, as Time's dull orbit rolls ;
Nor Liberty enjoys (though Britain's free),
Nor Life—but in the memory of thee."

Letters of Thomas Pitt, Lord Camelford, to Mr. Hardinge.

1.   *" Wednesday Morning* [1780.]
" We are all of a sudden just setting out for Norfolk. Will
you not write to us once or twice to cool the tip of our tongues,
for at a distance you know what a thirst there is for news ? we
shall be absent about a week, and the post goes every day. What
prodigies! Lord G. Gordon and Mr. Fox in coalition! aye, but
Lord George and the priest Arthur O'Leary in coalition, who
gives circular letters to his Catholic flock to tell them they may
safely take the oaths if they will vote for Mr. Fox. What the
devil will all this end in "

---

2.   [*Petersham Lodge*, 1780.]
" I do not wonder you snatch every moment you can to enjoy the banks of your sweet Thames ; if the weather would
promise to continue mild, we should follow your example, but a
sharp easterly wind or hail-storm chills me, and makes me cling
here to my fire-side. You do well to cultivate our neighbour
Cambridge § ; I do not know a man of more honour and worth,
and few men of so much general information. A character he
certainly is, but not a whit the worse for that, except when he
sometimes will persist in riding his own hobby-horse instead of

---

* His daughter, Lady Grenville, just married.
† The second Lord Camelford, at that time a naval officer.
‡ The writer of the inscription.
§ Richard Owen Cambridge, Esq. of Twickenham Meadows.

that of his company, which offends those who do not know how to make allowances. As for politics, the other party call it the Pittomania; and let them call it what they may please, so as it strengthen the faculties of government in honest and able hands, who mean sincerely by the country and the old constitution. Fox will run us hard at Westminster at last; but it is our own fault in suffering him to poll, not only all the legal votes his Dutchesses could seduce by every mode of application, but troops from Spital-fields, and any where else, which the indolence of the High Bailiff and the treachery of his Deputy have admitted. In spite of all this and the late creditable coalition with Lord G. Gordon, I think we shall gain upon the poll; but if not, a scrutiny will give it us all to nothing. There will, upon the whole, be such a majority as will give us permanency.

"Yours, adieu!"

3. "My dear Sir,   *Petersham Lodge, Dec. 2, 1781.*
"The approbation and confidence of the disinterested well-wishers to their country is, after the testimony of my own heart, the most ample, and the most honourable, recompence I can ever have for any exertions in the public cause. If I were ill understood in those exertions, I would still persevere in my attachment to that cause, from sentiments of duty; but, when I have the satisfaction to be credited as to my motives, and to be approved in my conduct, I am over paid in one of the most sensible pleasures the mind is capable of receiving. The proposition of last Friday*, though demonstrably the safest as well as the most efficacious measure for the public security, was certainly the strongest that has been offered to that House since the Revolution. Had there been more persons in it of your way of thinking, I am sanguine enough to believe, much might still have been expected; but, as I said the first day, ' there is no public, therefore there is no Parliament; there is no Parliament, therefore there is no Administration; there is no Administration, therefore there is no fatherly superintendance over our interests.'

"The person you mention † is certainly a most extraordinary youth; and I sincerely join with you in hoping such talents may be devoted to the good cause, instead of being perverted to the purposes of faction; he will then be as valuable an acquisition to his country as he will be an honourable one to his family.

"I am, my dear Sir, with great truth and regard, your most obliged and obedient servant,   Thomas Pitt."

* See the honourable gentleman's speech in Gent. Mag. LII. 101.
† The matchless son of the great Lord Chatham. See in Gent. Mag. vol. LII. p. 51, a very masterly speech of his delivered Nov. 28, 1781, a few days before the above letter was written.

4.   [1781.]
" You remember, when King William reproached the Duke of
Buckingham for having revealed a secret, instead of receiving
as an excuse that he had trusted it to his wife, the King replied,
' My Lord, I never trusted it to mine.' I cannot say as King
William did, for I have trusted it to mine, but you are almost
the only person else that has ever seen it; and though I have
no reason to suspect your good woman's weakness, I confess I
feel more easy that you have not mentioned it to her. At the
same time, however, that I cannot bring myself to indulge your
request, I am not a little flattered that you have made it. I
hope you will not be able to bring our amendments in the Irish
propositions to a dispute between the two Houses upon the
ground Fox seems to have laid in for them; that fiend will find
means to do the most effectual mischief to the country, whether
in or out of office. I wish he were with his father, wherever
that may be. Lord Camden would have been killed within one
week more; indeed, so should we all. Do you breakfast here on
Sunday?"

5.   [December 1782.]
" You say truly, the situation of the country leaves no room
for the concerns of the individual. When we meet we shall
have much to say; it is in vain now to look back at past errors,
and hopeless to look forward. I shall not, I believe, settle at
Petersham this Christmas; but whenever you and Mrs. Hardinge will dine with us here we shall be most happy to see you.
" After new year's-day we shall probably date from the first
year of the Republic; we may still date for a few days as usual,
vicesimo tertio G. III."

6. " MY DEAR SIR,   March 5, 1783.
" The strange unsettled way in which I now live, between
Petersham and London, keeps me in perpetual motion, without
giving me an opportunity of conversing with many of whose
opinions I should wish to avail myself in this very extraordinary
juncture. I have endeavoured to preserve my own consistency,
whilst every thing has been turning round me; which by those
who are carried on by the motion of others, is, I am told, deemed
inconsistent. I opposed my Lord North, because I thought he
availed himself of the influence of the Crown to its full extent,
in order to support a violent, absurd, and ruinous system of
war, which I trusted his successors meant to put an end to, after
the influence of corruption had met with some checks that might
bring it back again to certain bounds. Upon the death of Lord
Rockingham, all the strength and union of those who had promised us a better prospect was dissolved by that party, who,
thinking they have a right to the power of this kingdom jure
divino, could not bear to see the Treasury in hands they could

not trust, in other words, that they could not dispose of. I thought it my duty not to countenance so factious a proceeding, which could be capable of deserting the country at such a moment, because it was not surrendered up to them as their property.

"I was told, 'Lord Shelburne was deceitful—that he did not mean peace—that he would never grant America independence —that he would bring back Lord North, and betray the country.' I waited the event, to decide my conduct; I found the American independence granted, and the peace concluded. Was I inconsistent, in defending that unpopular peace, and those unpopular ministers, at the moment the declaimers had themselves made the league with Lord North, to overthrow the ministry, and bring themselves into power? Mankind can have but one opinion upon such a junction. I cannot be sorry for it, as it has pulled off the mask, and exposed them to the most unconscious. They will, I hope, be Ministers. The interested of their parties, especially of Lord North's, will revolt from disappointment; the men of principle will revolt from indignation; the people will despise them for their want of honesty, and hate them for the burthens it will be their lot to impose upon them;—it is then that others may come forward, who may unite the respect of their Sovereign, the confidence of the people, and the support of the respectable part of Parliament; this is the last hope of the country. Pray God it may not be defeated!

"I shall read with pleasure the Tract* you are so kind as to promise me, and with profit upon a subject so little generally understood.—I shall be always happy to see you; and shall think it hard if we cannot contrive to meet during the recess. Mrs. Pitt will certainly wait upon Mrs. Hardinge when she is settled in town; but at present her time is so much divided between her aged father † and her girl, who is just recovering from a long illness, that her attention and her time are almost wholly devoted to them. I am, dear Sir, your most obedient faithful humble servant,   Thomas Pitt."

---

7. "My dear Sir,   [Undated.]
"You shall have a fat slice of the inside, if you please, on Sunday, at four o'clock, and any slice excepting à la Bruce. You will find a parcel of schools-boys ‡; but that will only amuse you. We too are in our hay—but no Jupiter Pluvius."

* Probably the essay noticed by Mr. Hardinge in vol. V. p. 49.
† Pinkney Wilkinson, Esq. of Burnham, Norfolk.
‡ "The two schoolboys were the late and the present Lord Cowper."
                                                        G. H.

8. " MY DEAR SIR,   [*Undated.*]

" I hate your going away at this time, when we have not a law-yer to our back, and when your friend Scott * attacks our law. However, that question, I understand, will be decided the day after to-morrow. Pray take care that Sherwin goes on in your absence; I have almost lost all patience."

---

9.   [*November* 1783.]

" In the present state of things, one party meaning to obtain all possible evidence to ground their judgment upon, the other determined to decide upon public notoriety without evidence, it is impossible to know what turn things will take before hand; therefore you must, at all events, prepare yourself as well as you can. No specific charges, beyond what the Bill has stated in general terms, will be exhibited previous to the pleading, which is against the Bill. The task, therefore, hard as it is, must lie upon the advocates of proving, that there is no ground upon which to justify the measure. If I understand it right, your brief, at least that of the counsel for the Proprietors, which will be first heard, goes into that negative detail, which is to prove, that neither from the actual state of their finances, nor from the actual circumstances of their concerns in India, nor from any mismanagement either at home or abroad, can it be made to appear that the Company ought to lose its property and fran-chise; and to each of these circumstances evidence from au-thentic papers and from credible witnesses is to be brought and entered into at large. This will be brought forward by Bear-croft, as I conceive; and probably every head of evidence will produce a fresh debate and question. If the House refuses to receive the whole of the evidence offered on the part of the Pro-prietors, and there should be still time for you to enter upon the defence of your client, you will then have the same game to play over again step by step to find the justification of the conduct of the Director, as your brief will point out, and which will lead you into all the general matter, the whole history of Indian poli-tics, Mr. Hastings, &c. &c. Whether you are to undertake this before the second counsel for the Proprietors has been heard, you will be to settle to-morrow when you come down; but if they go into the evidence it will not be possible you should be heard to-morrow. If not, the four counsel may be heard as easily in one day as it was in the House of Commons. The Lords, you know, have scarce any evidence upon their table at present; and trust to the general notoriety of grievances and state necessity for their ground."

* Major Scott, a friend of Mr. Hardinge.

10.   " *Dec.* 27, 1783.

" Before you receive this you will have known that I had the honour to kiss the King's hand yesterday as Lord Camelford. My good woman is to be presented on the new year's-day, and has already engaged Lady Chatham to present her, which deprives her of the liberty of making another party ; any other day she will be happy to have the honour of waiting upon Mrs. Hardinge. Indeed, my good friend, I have been long enough in the House of Commons, through above twenty years' service, to be glad to be got into stiller water, at a time especially when what you say is true, it is become a Polish diet. If there was to be any moment, when with propriety I might secure this advantage to my family, it is when I am pursuing uniformly my own line of public conduct in conjunction with my own natural connections, and when it is bestowed upon me with every gracious mark of favour from the Prince who bestows it upon me. Letters are in these times so universally exposed to the curiosity of the post-office, that it is impossible for me to enter into the topics you touch upon further than saying, that both the persons you mention, having merits of different kinds to their party, certainly have strong claims to favour when opportunities should offer. *Au reste*—the system seems to gain strength every day since the banner has been fairly displayed. What will be the success, or what will be the event, or the succession of events, I am not bold enough to prophecy; and thank God neither you nor I are lookers out, for this is a time of all others which the knowing ones may be the most easily taken in. Lord Temple's going to Ireland is a mere newspaper idea ; I believe his Lordship would say as Lord Chesterfield did when they asked him to go a hunting, ' I have been.' The union is, however, most entire where you wish it, as sufficiently appears from his brother taking office, although he wisely in my opinion (not timidly) declined being the Lord Strafford of the day to stand as adviser of the Crown upon personal questions of crimination to be brought up directly or by implication against him to the foot of the Throne by an angry House of Commons governed by a desperate faction. The various comments that ignorance and malice have made upon this neither surprises nor deranges him. He is going to Stowe to enjoy a little quiet.

" Yours faithfully,   T. P."

---

11.   " *Jan.* 17, 1784.

" Many thanks to you for the very acceptable presents that accompanied your note, and which, if I had no partiality to the author would, as public tracts * as well as specimens of eloquence, deserve to be placed upon the most distinguished shelf in my library. William Pitt certainly gains ground ; and the splendid sacrifice he has just made of private emolument cannot

* A Speech in defence of Sir Thomas Rumbold, and another against Mr. Fox's East India Bill.

but have an effect upon the public. By what I have heard of
the House of Commons I cannot help thinking it looks somewhat like a leaning towards negotiation; although I think, if it
does, there are difficulties and obstacles without end. If it does
not, violence must beget violence to the end of the chapter.
Poor Lord Camelford can easily forgive the innocent wit of Mr.
Burke, were it even better attended to; but does not know by
what right he presumes to name him in a public assembly as
author of any thing to which he has not put his name. One of
the supposed authors of Junius should have known better what
belongs to matters of that kind.

" I will send the papers you desire the next time I go down
to Petersham. Yours,   CAMELFORD."

------

12. " MY DEAR HARDINGE,   *Oxford-street, Jan.* 28, 1785.

" A few words upon the last sentence in your note as to your
democratical principles of Reform, of which you say you gave
me early notice. The question now grows more serious, and
therefore let us understand one another. I never wished you
to vote against your opinion upon any subject, nor do I wish it
now *. Your principles, however, cannot be more decided upon
the business of Reform than mine; nor are they half so strongly
pledged to the public. Old Sarum has two representatives; upon
one of them I have not the smallest claim, because I never pretended any kindness to him in the seat I gave him. It is to be
sure, even in his instance, however, a whimsical thing, that
from his connection with Pitt he feels himself under a necessity
of subverting, as far as his vote goes, the seat he is entrusted
with by his constituents, or, if you chuse to call it so, by his
constituent   But were he to vote against what Pitt, to whom
he owes it, professes to have at heart, I am well aware it might
be interpreted by the enemies of his friend as inconsistency and
double dealing.   What is your case? the argument cuts exactly
the other way.   Who will believe, if they see you take a part in
direct opposition to what I have so often declared to be my deliberate opinion, that there is not a game played between us for
the sake of flattering the Minister's favourite object! My line
has been distinct, and I have never departed from it. I dread
every change; and at this moment in particular think it not only
unnecessary, but, considering the state of Scotland and Ireland,
I think such a measure madness and absurdity. If, however,
the circumstances were never so favourable, the utmost length
I can go to is the one additional County Member; but that I
consider as an experiment, and as a compounding to prevent
further mischief. This I shall certainly say in the House of
Lords, if ever it gets thither, and shall think (what I shall not

------

* This letter is endorsed by Mr. Hardinge: " A divine letter,—upon
the Reform of Parliament, for which Mr. Hardinge voted just after he
was chosen for Old Sarum! "

say) that he is an enemy to Parliament who goes further. If, from your general wish to support the Minister, or from your attachment to Lord Camden, or from a conscientious opinion upon the subject, you cannot think as I do, at least absent yourself upon this occasion, and do not distress me so far as to make me appear to hold two languages, at the same time that you oppose one of the most decided political tenets I can ever form, and oppose it with the weapon I have put into your hands.

" As to the democratical principle, how far that is likely to be gratified by enabling three or four great families in every county (generally Peers) to add to their influence in the House of Commons, or by rendering such additional influence still more powerful in extinguishing the balance of the open boroughs, I leave to your reflection. I profess to wish that power and property may go together, and am therefore not very anxious for the Plebeian system.

" All I shall add is, that, if I were to consider only my own emolument and that of my son (for I look no further), I should be happy that any scheme took place that would enable me to convert my privilege into an increase of income, which is a far more solid advantage than what is called importance and consideration. Weigh all this calmly in your own mind, and assure yourself that no difference of opinion will ever make an alteration in the affectionate regard with which I am faithfully
" Yours,   CAMELFORD."

13. " MY DEAR HARDINGE,   *Feb.* 19, 1785.
" Every day convinces me, that, as no man can think for another, so neither can one man feel for another. I perfectly acquit you upon the assurances you give me of any bias in your mind but what arises from your own judgment upon this occasion. I have only to lament that your judgment and your feeling are not the same with mine upon it. As I recollect, the reason why the delay in presenting your return was thought more delicate was, that you might not seem to take your seat with a view, one way or other, to such a question. When you offered to resign your seat to me, after having voted on Sawbridge's motion, I certainly should have thought myself much to blame to have accepted it; but so far was I from knowing your ideas upon the Reform, that I have not at this hour a conception either of the principles or the mode you would wish to adopt in that reformation.

" At this moment neither you nor I are acquainted with the plan Mr. Pitt has adopted ; all we know with certainty is, that any augmentation of County Members alone is quite unsatisfactory to the wishes of the reformers, and in the teeth of their professed principles, either of democracy or equality in proportion, or the right of actual representation; and that any extinction of boroughs, without proof of delinquency or forfeiture, is either an act of arbitrary violence, and therefore in every sense of the word unconstitutional, or it is liable to objections insuperable if it is attemped to be put into a shape that will make it optional without injustice.

" Do not imagine, however. my dear friend, that I wish to persuade you against your conviction; use your own discretion, act upon your own feelings in perfect freedom; all I have to beg of you is, that, if you apprehend your duty obliges you to take a part contrary to my opinions, you will at the same time find an opportunity of making it clearly understood, that it is so far from being in concert with me, that it is in direct opposition to those sentiments which I have so repeatedly declared, and which I shall entertain to my dying day.

" Having now explained our thoughts to each other freely on both sides, let us drop the subject, and hope that it will be the only important one upon which there will ever be such a difference of sentiment between you and your faithful and affectionate,   CAMELFORD."

----

14.   " *July* 8, 1787.
" A truce with your dragons, my good friend! Before your letter reached me they had, or ought to have had, a good sop. If you have not received a long letter from me, full of rocks and woods and watered valleys, and cloud-capped mountains, &c. &c. &c. it is not my fault; even my conscientious helpmate would not scruple to make her affidavit that I sent it; let the Duc de Polignac, who is Post-master-general of France, answer for the rest. I have been ill indeed, but it was before I left Montpellier, almost six weeks ago. I was seized with an alarming giddiness, which confined me to my room, and almost to my bed for a fortnight. They said it was a mixture of gout, nerves, and bile; they applied leeches, blisters, and sinapisms externally, and antimonial medicines internally, and I got well, though weakened most exceedingly. My head is at times weak, and my old head-ache goes on as usual; and I have lately had a slight touch of gout in my heel, and every body says I am in beauty, and that I am *si bien constitué,* that I ought to live to one hundred. If I lived here constantly, so I should, for it is a proverb in these mountains, that *qu'il faut apommer les viellards pour les faire mourir;* it is common to see people between eighty and ninety. We were talking upon this subject the other day, when a *vieux militaire,* who had served in the wars of Savoy and Piedmont, said a peasant of the Alps had told him, that thank God he could still walk well enough up and down the hills, but he was grown too old to walk upon plain ground without fatigue. I thought I had known understandings of

that kind in my life, who are equal to difficulties, but totally
unfit for the path of common life.

*   *   *   *   *   *   *

"I sent ——— some wretched puns some months ago, but
did not sign my name. I will tell you one that I thought perfect; the Bishop of Alais, visiting a Rector in this neighbourhood who was very rich and very avaricious, gave him some
gentle hint of the character he had heard of him, 'Mais Monsieur,' says the man, 'il faut garder une Poire pour la soif.'
'Vous avez bien raison,' replies the Bishop, 'prenez garde seule-
ment qu'elle soit du bon Chrêtien.'

"Is it not provoking to be laid by the heel in a country
where every step is a picture for Salvator Rosa, or at least for
a Poussin. What would I give to hire a pair of legs! I have
the plague also of weariness when I ride for above an hour,
which carries me to no great distance, and I want to explore
every thing. I rise between five and six, dine at two, and go
to bed very sleepy at ten. We have had two or three days of
sultry heat, but rains came to our assistance; and though my
good woman complains (for women, Lord North says, are always
hot or cold, and have no business to be either), in general the
weather has been very delightful, at least for those who can sit
still; the mornings and evenings charming to be sure. We
caught seven or eight scorpions in our rooms one day, but nobody yet has been stung by them; and it is not so painful or
so troublesome as the sting of a wasp when they happen to
sting, which must often happen. The quantities of flies are to
me a greater inconvenience; I hold the pen with one hand, at
this moment, and a fly-flapper in the other; there is no peace
for them but by living in utter darkness. My apartment opens
to a parterre, with shady bosquets and fountains of chrystal,
ending in a terrace, that, under the cover of lines of horse-
chesnuts, commands the valley beneath, with its rocky winding
channel of a river, over which are two bridges. The meadows
in the plain are just mown, and as green as Twickenham, dotted
with mulberries and fruit trees, and here and there an old
park-like chesnut-tree; the skirts of the hills verdant with
vines and copse chesnut-trees, which are used for cooperage,
and make a considerable branch of commerce where there
are no vines; and the bare bold cliffs of high mountains close
in the whole and form the frame of the picture. Two considerable villages are seen upon the sides of hills, and little buildings are scattered every where. There are goats upon every
rock, led always by Menalcas's and Thestylis's, and so tame that
my young people, who have made themselves peasants' dresses,
lead them about in the garden.

"Hic gelidi fontes, hic mollia prata Lycori.

G 2

" Virgil and Horace breathe in every scene ; and you, who
are classic all over, would recollect some favourite passage at
every step.   Adieu !"

———

15.   *" July* 10, 1787.
" You liked my pun, so I give you a better thing.   When the
Spanish Dauphine passed through France to Paris, Bourdeaux
received her and her suite with extraordinary magnificence.
The Duchesse de Caumont had a cabinet fitted up for her at the
house of a President, at God knows what expense, but she
tossed up her nose at it, and was seen by Montesquieu in the
anti-room of the Dauphine as he was going to pay his Court.
' Que faite vous, la Madame la Duchesse ?' ' Je m'échauffe, vous
sentez bien que je n'ai rien où je suis logé ; mais vous, President, comment pouvez vous abandonner Paris pour une Société
de Campagne ? que fait on ici de grace ? dites moi un peu,
et vos Presidentes, elles font ici les Duchesses je m'imagine.'
'Oh, non Madame ! pardonnez moi, elles ne sont pas assez im-
pertinentes.'
" And so our Montesquieu Thurlow does not forgive you,
and sits on your skirts, does he ? tu l'a voulu, George Dandin,
qu' aviez vous a faire dans cette galére.
" If Hastings is to be tried by our tribunal on his private
virtues of friendship and of gratitude, my vote would be ready.
He never made a better return to his friends for past services
than his country does to him for his; there is a poetical justice in the ingratitude that overtakes him.   Poor General Cowper * has good reason to hate him ; and so much part do I take
in my friend's resentment, that, though I have not been very
hostile to him as a public man, and should have more curiosity
to be acquainted with him than any man living, I have constantly refused to meet him, and have never seen his face.   Great
men are things to read about, and sometimes to admire, but
hardly ever to be loved : they have weaknesses ; but they soon
wear out affections, if indeed they are ever born with them.   Had
you been fortunate enough to have been Thurlow's brother, you
had been Bishop of Durham ; as you are, a Welsh judge must
serve your turn, and that is better than nothing to begin with.

* Spencer Cowper, Esq. a General in the army, was second cousin of
George third Earl Cowper, and first cousin of the Poet.   He was second
son of William Cowper, Esq. Clerk of the Parliaments, who died Feb. 22,
1739-40, by Joan, daughter of John Budget, Esq.   He attained the rank
of Lieut.-col. 1759, Colonel 1772, Major general 1779, and Lieut.-General
in 1787.   His regiment was the 1st Foot Guards and he was Lieut.-gover-
nor of Tynemouth.   He died at Ham Common, March 13, 1797, aged 73.
By Charlotte daughter of John Baker, Esq. who died at Ham Common before her husband, he had issue: 1. Spencer, who died an infant ; 2. William ; 3. Henry Cowper, of Tewin Water in Hertfordshire,
Esquire, late Assistant Clerk of the Parliaments, and who married his
first cousin Maria-Judith, daughter of Major William Cowper, but was
left without children on her death in 1815 ; and 4. a daughter, Jane.

As you say nothing of your re-election, I conclude you are tired of St. Stephen's Chapel, or disdain to represent the muttons, as Lord Mount Eliot calls the electors, with a bell-weather for the returning officer. I wish my good cousin would learn to add to his great talents and sterling virtues, ' the pretty and sweet manners ' which your friend Shakspeare says draws tears into one's eyes; but we are as it pleases God, and sometimes as it displeases him. Look, for example, in my face, and that of ――――, and say which is the jew. Because he persuaded me to let him my house at Petersham for nothing, he thinks I will sell it him at the same rate; but he is mistaken. If I get a fair price for it why so; if not, I will even live myself in it; and that I may not have the plague of three houses, which are more than I can live in, I will let my *palace* in Oxford-street till my son is old enough to marry and live in it. Thus I make my jewish calculation, and I care not who knows it; a place for which old Lord Harrington refused 20,000 guineas, I bought in the worst of times and in the worst condition, under £.8000; the first repairs cost me above £.2000 more; my purchase of the Crown to convert leasehold into freehold, brings it up to £.12,000; the alterations of the ground, additional repairs and improvements, considerably to above £.13,000; for my furniture, for the improved value of the premises above the money I actually paid the Crown, and for the increased value of all property between 1780, in Lord North's happy administration, and Mr. Pitt's 1787, whom God long preserve; for all these considerations, I say, put £.2,000, which brings it up to my selling price of £.15,000.

" To return to our General, whose idea is always connected in my mind with India, I do not wonder that you delight in him; he is of the true stuff; would to God his health did not keep his friends in a perpetual alarm for him. I conclude, as so many powers have armed, the Dutch will be made to keep the King's peace; *raccommodez vous, canaille*, is all that should be said to them, and if they do not instantly obey, the dykes should be cut and the frogs set a swimming."

―――――――

16.   " *Rome, Jan.* 12, 1788.

" This letter will be carried to England by Lord Belgrave, Lord Grosvenor's son, and delivered to you with a packet from hence, together with a letter from me to the Minister. The artists, fully persuaded of the influence I have with my relation, have employed me to get them released from the taxes they now pay upon the introduction of their own studies and performances, and the models which are necessary for the exercise of their professions. I am liberal enough to conceive, that the specimens of the fine arts are by no means objects of taxation, but

certainly the idea of taxing these poor young men at their
return to England for the means they have taken to improve
their industry and do honour to their country, is gothic to the
last degree; and is, in fact, considered so, as you will see, by
France, the States of Germany, the savage Russian, and even
the money-loving phlegmatic Dutchman; England is the only
country barbarous enough to set a fine upon improved talents,
and to tax the arts when they attempt to rise into perfection.
This is neither consistent with policy, nor humanity, nor justice;
the *materials* of industry cannot be an object of customs and
excise; it is inconsistent with the protection afforded to the arts
by the Prince upon the throne, it is inconsistent with the liberal
character of the nation, and with the character of genius which
distinguishes the minister. In a word, my credit is at stake, and
I know I need use no other argument with you to induce you
to back this application with all the zeal and activity which is
necessary to accomplish the purpose. The papers consist in a
memorial to the Treasury, a petition to the House of Commons
if a bill is necessary, and a blank paper signed in case any other
form be requisite, which you may fill up at your discretion. I have
added such other letters as may tend to give information and illustration as to matters of fact; and have referred Mr. Pitt to you as
being the soul of the business. If it can be done by an application to the Treasury only, it will be the easiest, provided it could
be a general standing order that every body may avail himself of;
but if it is to be a special indulgence shewn to each individual
upon application, it will extend itself only to those who have
good friends, who are usually the least aggrieved by the payment;
and will not be extended to those who have neither friends nor
money, who are more peculiarly the objects of such exemption.
If an act of Parliament is to be obtained, the expense of it need not
be a difficulty, as some how or other that shall be re-paid; but
then it should be carried to as large an extent as possible, and,
if possible, comprehend all moulds, plaister casts, and models,
whether imported by artists or others, as they are all acquisitions to the arts. If you succeed in your application, the least
they can do in return is, to erect a statue to your honour;
you have only to determine whether you prefer the bob or the
flowing dignity of the full bottom. Sir Joshua will be a useful
man to you both as to solicitation and information, being at
the head of the arts, and capable of instructing you in any
doubts that may occur; he will satisfy you that nobody can
assume the character of an artist who is not known to be one,
and that it is neither likely that an artist would consent, or a
gentleman propose, the covering property of others under the
solemn sanction of an oath; it is only in matters of trade where
people use themselves by degrees to kiss the thumb instead of
the bible, but few men are perjured who swear rarely, and who
are not induced to it by a very strong temptation of interest.

I will make no apology to you for addressing this business to you, because I know you are too liberal not to feel an interest in it upon its own account, as well as from the kindness you bear to your faithful and affectionate,   CAMELFORD."

---

17.   " *Rome, Jan.* 27, 1788.

" Here is a narrative of my poor Fabre*; a plain unvarnished tale. The Academie would say it was bad French; the *beaux esprits* that it was a bigot; the polite world that it was a bore. You will see throughout the history and sentiments of a virtuous man, to whom the bias of the world has been perverse from his early youth down to his present age of sixty years, when he is starving with his mother who is still alive at eighty-six; his *chère cousine*, who has been long enough his wife to have produced him a son and a daughter, both grown up and both without resource. I have just had a letter from him, by which I find his situation grows every day more and more critical to him. I have sent a copy, through Lord Harcourt, to the King and Queen; another through the channel of the Lady E. Forster to Devonshire-house; another to the Duke of Northumberland. The Duke of Montagu must be sounded, for he has a liberal hand and a feeling heart. Mrs. Montagu I mean to send a copy to, for she has often done noble things; as for you, your exertions will have their own reward in your own feelings.

" Whatever is collected should be paid into the shop of Messrs. Ransom, Hammersley, and Co. in Pall Mall, upon account of Jean Fabre le jeune, a Ganges, with orders to inform him by letter from time to time of the receipt, that he may give his directions."

---

19.   " *Rome, Feb.* 2. 1788.

" It shall never be said that I leave Rome, which I purpose to do the day after to-morrow for Naples, without first clearing my conscience and acknowledging a letter from you, which has lain by me, I am ashamed to say how long. It is in truth the more necessary, as there are now upon the road, by a private hand, two commissions for you, which will give you no small trouble, if you bestow upon them that zeal which I know animates you always in a good cause; the one is the cause of poor Fabre, the *honnette criminel*, whose narrative you will receive; the other is the cause of the artists of this place, who have put their trust in me, as I also put my trust in you. Their demand is just and reasonable, and such as even the boors of Russia and of Dutchland have long ago acquiesced in. England has the honour of being the last country in Europe that does not exempt

---

* The autobiography of a Protestant of Nismes, who had been persecuted on the score of religion, and for some time confined to the galleys.

the studies of her artists from the objects of her taxation. You, who are not insensible to the arts, hint to me as if you would trust me to lay out your money for you, and answer your bill at sight; you might as well order me to buy a horse or a mistress for you.   Here are, if you please, two sitting philosophical Greek Poets, a Menander and a Podisippos, cheap at £.2,000, to be bought; or a Demosthenes at £.500, all out of the Villa Negroni.   Here is a bust of Trajan, together with one of his wife Plotina, delicious morsels, at £.150.   I say nothing of the beautiful Paris at £.400, &c. &c.   As to pictures, you may have Guercinos, *soi-disant* Guidos, and Titians, for £.300, £.400, and £.500, particularly one of a Cornaro portrait by Titian, for which an impudent Venetian had the assurance to ask me the moderate price of £.600 or guineas.   Gems, if they are any thing remarkable, run up in the same manner; in a word, if you buy trash, it is not worth the carriage, and you can get it full as well at an auction at Christie's; and if you look out for things of real value, you pay for them *a poids d'or*. I am obliged to play the cat i'th'adage all day long, and should buy £.10,000 worth of virtu, if I bought any thing.   I content myself with a book or two of Piranesi, a few coloured drawings for Madame from the Raphael's Loggia, and such crumbs as fall from the table of taste to satisfy my longing.   What a place it is! here have we been these two months looking about us, and we have not yet gone once round all that is to be seen, and scarcely one of the fine things we have seen but should be visited ten times over.   What an enchanting cold did we all of us catch at the Vatican, in examining the dear Apollo by torch-light! what a miracle of human genius is that statue; it is so light it treads on air, whilst the spirit that it breathes and the dignity of its beauty strikes the imagination at the same time with awe and rapture; read Winkelman upon the subject, one can hardly think it possible that ever a German could have been warmed as he was with grace and elegance to such a pitch of enthusiasm.

"The country round Rome is unpleasant, but surrounded with a mountainous horizon that is beautiful in itself, and interesting from its classic recollections. The Soracte is in sight at this moment, covered with snow as when Horace described it; the Sabine-hills stretch forth in another district, and every spot like those which Gray alludes to in Greece is sacred to poetry or history: 'Where each old poetic mountain,' &c. The city contains little more than hints of its ancient grandeur; many magnificent melancholy palaces, built out of the *debris* of old structures, stand intermixed so whimsically with the wretched habitations of the inferior class, that the whole has an appearance of pride and misery.   Yet there are situations that overlook the town, and throw domes, and columns, and architecture into noble groupes with the most striking effects.   I take no notice of St. Peter's, as you know every thing of that already, except

what the sight alone can impress upon the mind. I know not
what to say of the climate; to me it is not unpleasant, though
not the best of all possible climates. When it is moist and rainy
it is mild at least, with intervals of sunny days that are perfect
summer; and when it is cold, it is that bright sky and bracing
weather that people are so fond of in our winters. The changes,
however, are extremely sudden, and subject people to colds more
than almost any country I have lived in. The people of all
ranks are quite mad during these last days of Carnival. It is
strange to see the streets filled with masks of all sorts, who,
though they have all of them their knives ready to revenge their
petty quarrels, never think of using them to rob, or to do any
unprovoked outrage; but are, upon the whole, a quiet and peaceable people, though it is computed, that, since the accession of
the present Pope, not less than 40,000 men have perished by
assassination in his dominions. Their operas are ridiculous
from the interdiction of women upon their theatres; some of
those dancers who represent their Theodores and Heinels jump
with so much force as to touch their chins with their knees.
The masked-balls have sometimes very good figures; though, as
they begin after one in the morning, I know them only by
report.   There was an Egyptian dressed after the Granite
statues, that was said to be the most perfect character, both in
manner and costume, that could be seen. This letter will probably recall to your mind those of the celebrated Lady Miller
to her dear mother Riggs; but I cannot help it. I give you of
what I have, to draw from you something better. Adieu!"

19.   " Rome, April 5, 1788.
" What, man! be not cast down with an Opposition flirt or
two, that is forgotten that day sevennight by him who spoke it
as by those who heard; be wiser for the future, and let this be
a lesson to you to know your beast before you ride him. Powys*
is, in the opinion of the country gentlemen, a great character,
an independent Knight of the Shire; in that of the Opposition
perhaps what you think of him, but he has been of singular use

* Thomas Powys, Esq. was Knight of the Shire of Northampton, in
five Parliaments, from 1774 to 1797, when he was created Lord Lilford.
In the House of Commons he was remarkable as a leader of the country
gentlemen. He was originally a supporter of Mr. Fox, but opposed
the Ministry with a degree of candour and discrimination which ever entitled him to respect, and gave him great consideration with all sides of
the House. Upon the breaking out, however, of the French Revolution,
Mr. Powys adopted that line of conduct which good sense and patriotism
pointed out, and became the firm and strenuous supporter of all the
measures of Government, reprobating, with all the energy of virtuous
feeling, the atrocious conduct of the French, and opposing his utmost
efforts against the prevalence of their detestable principles. His Lordship died at his house in Albemarle-street, Jan. 26, 1800, aged 56.

to them, and therefore they are obliged to flatter him and to
protect him. Could you therefore expect to attack him with
impunity? as little ought you to have supposed that a strain of
panegyric upon a first-rate Minister, however merited, could
escape the imputation of flattery from those who by the contrast
feel that his praise is their condemnation. Your feelings run
away with you; you must learn to praise sparingly, especially
those whose friendship may be useful to you; not only your
enviers will misinterpret you otherwise, but you may endanger
the diminishing the esteem of your friend himself by it. Nothing is in my opinion so nice as compliment. I never yet dared
to tell a woman she was handsome, but I found means to let her
find out that I thought so; in the one instance she gave me
credit for my taste, in the other she would, if she had any taste
herself, have laughed in my face. All this sermon applies to
the future; as to what is past, be persuaded that, as to the
satire, all the reasonable part of the House on both sides went
with you; and as to the eulogium, I should fear no consequence
from it if I could prevent its leaving an unfavourable impression upon the mind of the person commended, that is the only
danger. We rejoice in every testimony to the conduct of our
relation; who I really believe deserves immortality, if the purest
zeal and the most virtuous exertions for his country's welfare
can confer it. I did not, however, like the late debate, as far
as I collected it from the imperfect channel of the papers;
for, though he seems to have defended himself like an angel
against misrepresentation and petulance, yet it has drawn out
against him such beings as are caught with words more than
things, and whose vote counts for considerably more in their
counties than in St. Stephen's Chapel. I fear there has been
more consciousness of good intention, and being essentially in
the right in the question, than management and *savoir faire* in
the conduct of it. His power, as you and he say, is founded
alone upon the people; and without that confidence even his
abilities would be useless to himself, his King, and his country.
Popular clamour and captious questions, therefore, are the
things in the world he should the most avoid.

"Your business seems to go on successfully with you, and
keeps the wolf at a great distance from the door. You have
health, friends, domestic comfort, and, in spite of the Opposition,
who would not hate you if they despised you, a good reputation
which your own heart tells you you deserve; *ma foi, voila un
homme bien a plaindre !*

" Lord Belgrave, who carries you my packet, was to be in
England the beginning of this month; and was in such a hurry
that he very near broke his neck down a precipice in the Alps.
By this time you will feel the load I have put upon your back;
but I know it is strong enough to bear it, as you do not easily

sink under the burthen of doing good to those who cannot do without you.

" Do you know Sir Richard Worsley*, or do you know the Campbell Thane of Cawdor ? if not, you must know them as soon as you can; they are now both of them upon their return to England, fraught with all sorts of fine and curious things. The first is all drawings and antiquities in Greece, Asia Minor, and Egypt; the other pictures, marbles, and Etruscan vases collected in Italy, *Il faut voir tout cela.* Among the moderns I have here two living models, which, though French, are perfect and yet different. M. de Vaudreuil, who was in England with M. de Polignac. He has, with an agreeable figure and excellent address, all the politeness and varnish of Versailles, without the smallest affectation either in matter or in manner; he is neither important nor mysterious, nor *dédaigneux* nor *avantageux*; he is *sans pretensions*, as much as if he had never been a favourite; vacant and playful even with the children, full of vivacity, but without being noisy or petulant; gives his opinions frankly, commends with judgment, and criticises without ill nature; in a word, he is one of the most agreeable gentlemen I ever knew in my life. The Cardinal Bernis, well known in his younger days for his wit and elegance in the belles lettres, is now as conspicuous for his judgment and superior wisdom, which have been ripened by almost the experience and age of Nestor. He was himself in his day prime minister, having begun his career after forty. He knows mankind almost intuitively; but his good nature, that beams in his countenance, has never suffered his philanthropy to be impaired by his experience of the world. He is lively, and his wit cheers like the rays of the setting sun; whilst his knowledge and his wisdom afford an inexhaustible source of instruction to all those who converse with him. With all this, his house is the resort of strangers of all nations, and he alone does the honours of Rome with a magnificence that is beyond example. Why cannot such a man be immortal ? Let me hear from you as soon as you have received my commissions, and direct to me at Colmer en Alsace. The ladies desire their compliments. Yours faithfully, CAMELFORD."

---

20.   " *Venice, May* 27, 1788.

" I am now sitting in my balcony upon the great canal near the Rialto (you have heard of such a place), enjoying the fresco of the finest evening at about one hour of the night, which you vulgars call half after nine I believe. I have just got your letter, by which I find Lord Belgrave had acquitted himself of his commission, and delivered you your credentials. The zeal with which you take to it is just as I expected; so you see I knew how

* Who published the result of his collections abroad in the Museum Worsleyanum.

to rate you. I have been very unlucky about the other copies I sent to Lord Harcourt, the Duke of Northumberland, Mrs. Montagu, and Lady Elizabeth Forster, who is now in France; these, with letters to each person, were entrusted last Christmas at Rome to a gentleman who was returning with all speed to England, and who promised to deliver them according to their directions. I conclude he is drowned; and my papers long since at the bottom of the Channel, between Dover and Calais. In that case I wish you would supply the loss as well as you can, by getting three copies written immediately for the three first-mentioned persons; the last is out of the question, as she is abroad, and is to meet at Spa those for whom it was principally intended. I mean to subscribe £.250 myself; Sir Horace Mann, who is returning to England, (and who, by the bye, must have a copy,) has promised to put £.100 into the shop of Ransom; Lord Cowper will do as much; Colonel Campbell, the Thane of Cawdor, I have hopes from to some such amount; so you see of the £.1,000, which the poor man looked up to for his salvation, at least half is accomplished. I have some hopes from the Grand Duke and Duchess of Tuscany, through the Cowpers. Whatever your industry can add, or my machinations, will be all to the good; and I have the most sanguine expectations that I shall fill his heart at last with gladness, and give comfort to all that belong to him.

" There is no getting out of Italy; I ought to have been long ago on the other side the Alps, but every town I pass through has its claims upon me, and there is no refusing them. This is certainly the most wonderful novelty in the world. Lady Camelford seems very much struck with it; but it is the last place I should chuse as a residence. Canaletti gives a perfect idea of its canals and palaces upon them; but, as every house that is accessible by water has a door also to a street, which continues a communication on foot by means of innumerable bridges, this presents a scene of which the pictures give no idea; it is an immense labyrinth of Cranborne-alley, so intricate that it is astonishing that even the inhabitants themselves can unravel it. There is something in the air more debilitating than the greatest heats of Naples; indolence has fixed her empire here, and the lounge in the gondola is the utmost exertion of the day; towards evening they crowd upon the place of St. Marc, with all its casines and coffee-houses, till the hour of the theatre, which opens between ten and eleven, and lasts till three in the morning at this time of the year; I wonder any people can like it.

" We set forward to-morrow towards the Tirol, through Padua, Vicenza, and Verona, and hope in three weeks to reach the dear boy at Colmer en Alsace, who will by that time be a little settled to his collar. Write to me thither, as it is the only place that I can yet determine upon, and my letters will be forwarded to me from thence, wherever I may be through the summer.

I shall long to hear how you succeed with the Minister in the application from my Roman protegés.

"The ladies desire their compliments, and rejoice to have so good an account of your *chère moitié*, and of your own thriving prosperity. Adieu!"

---

21.   "*Lyons, Nov.* 2, 1788.

"I allow the force of what you say about poor Fabre. I do not think I should have been touched with reading his misfortunes as much as I was with hearing them from his own mouth; then the character impressed upon his countenance,—the scene of past persecutions, which recalled so forcibly every thing I had been reading in the war of the Camisards,—all the circumstances combined to make such a history doubly interesting to my feelings; however, I must observe, that what you felt upon simply reading his narrative was felt by others. Sir H. Mann, upon the bare recital, for I had not then the manuscript by me, offered instantly his £.100; and Lady Cowper, upon reading the narrative, was so much affected by it as to copy the material passages with her own hand, that she might read it to the Grand Duchess, who was moved by it to tears, and both she and the Grand Duke offered to interest themselves for the poor man in any way that could be the most advantageous to him. For all this I blame nobody for not being as much in earnest about him as you and I are; charity is one of the things that cannot be forced any more than the other affections of the mind. I wrote to beg you would lose no time in sending copies both to Lord Harcourt and to the Duke of Northumberland, to whom I have sent letters telling them they will receive them from you. It is a cruel effect of the *guignon* that attends my friend, that those letters and copies which I sent by a private hand last Christmas, have never been heard of. This has done much mischief, as the ground is now soiled; yet, if I can get the manuscript through that channel to find its way into the Queen's house, I have great hopes from the known benevolence and goodness of that quarter. What will you say to Fabre's luck when I tell you, that the bill of £.250 which I sent him lately to relieve his urgent distress, has never reached him; fortunately, as it was drawn at a month's date, I am in time to prevent the consequences, without loss either to him or to myself. Your £.100, though reduced by one cypher from what you had hoped, will be a very acceptable addition, which, together with what I count upon from others, will go a great way towards completing the £.1000 I engaged my credit for; alas, how frequently is that sum staked upon a card at Brookes's or upon a horse at Newmarket!

"You talk to me of Lord Clarendon's portrait of Lord Digby; it cannot be more resembling, or drawn with a bolder and happier pencil, than yours of my friend the philosopher at Ham*. I

---

* General Cowper; see p. 84.

am so struck with it that I shall copy it out of your letter, and am not sure you will not see it framed and glazed one day or other. Your rhapsodical vein was never luckier than in your last production; there were twenty passages in it that made me wish your three sheets six from the entertainment they afforded me. Your tour was a very agreeable one, and exhibited to you enough to admire and enough to laugh at. I once passed a week at Enmore with the noble builder; it was a comedy.

"You ask why the young Ascanius is left at Neufchatel? Because there is a very sensible man there to take care of him, and very excellent masters to teach him; the tutor I brought abroad with him lost his health, and has been returned to England sometime.

" I cannot be a Turk for my life; for I think it a scandal to humanity that such a nation has been suffered to subsist so long. At the same time I cannot wish well to the aggressors, for they are the *fleaux de la terre*, who undertake war for conquest.

" I am perfectly of your opinion, that the general idea of liberty is not the passive enjoyment of natural rights unmolested, but the active power of encroaching upon the liberties of others, for which reason I hate republics and republicans. I have no idea of freedom, neither is compatible with standing armies of one or two hundred thousand men to guard a frontier against arbitrary Princes, who have an equal force to bring against it; the army must subsist, must be governed by absolute authority, and must enslave whom they defend; as you say, *nous verrons.* Adieu!"

---

22.   " *Lyons, Nov.* 16, 1788.

" Yes, my dear Hardinge, I give you credit for all your exertions in favour of poor Fabre; and your own good heart will be your best reward for it. We can very well wait your leisure for the completing your collection, which if it attains to the sum of £.100, will be a very welcome succour to the poor man, from whom I have just had a letter, which tells me my supply has saved him in the present moment. He has in the world, *pour touts biens*, the house he lives in with his family, and a vineyard, which he bought for £.25; and which yields some fruit to eat in the season, and *un demi tonneau de vin.* He was upon the point of selling all this and his moveables when my bills arrived; he has no commerce, he says, and can have none, for he has neither funds nor credit. He has been living upon such small debts as from time to time can be brought in for a year or two, and he says he can neither throw his debtors into a jail nor seize their effects; he is not the man in the parable. I have a letter from Lord Harcourt, which destroys all the hopes I had conceived in a certain quarter; no matter,—the man whose ambition led him to be

Pope, attained to the being a Bishop; we must do the best we can. Sir H. Mann and Lord and Lady Cowper will not fail me, and perhaps something from the Duke of Northumberland, who has not yet answered my letter, but I conclude has received long since the packet I sent at Christmas, as I find Lord Harcourt's came safe to hand. The Duke of Montagu might perhaps contribute his ten guineas; we must take what we can get. Fabre forbad expressly the printing his narrative; and I much doubt whether the reading would awaken the feelings of those who can hear the tale unmoved. Be the event what it may, you and I shall have a source of satisfaction in reflecting that we were not insensible to the distress of a worthy being who must have perished but for our assistance. Adieu!"

23.   " *Lyons, Nov.* 19, 1788.

"Heavens! what a misfortune does your letter announce to me! I can think of nothing else. I loved him * as a man 'who bore his faculties so meekly.' I feel gratitude to him as one who so lately honoured me with proofs of his esteem and gracious distinction; but what are my private feelings to those of the public? I conclude, before this answer reaches you, our fate will have been decided; in truth I already look upon the stroke as past. I dare not look forward. What a revolution we are to expect; not only England, but all Europe, trembles at the expected change of men and measures! Our situation was too prosperous; happy in our interior government and respected abroad, every power looked up to us to restore and to preserve the peace of Europe. Young as our Minister is in years, the wisdom of experience seemed to be born with him, and he was regarded as a consummate statesman in the wisest cabinets. What will succeed him we are to see; but we know already that they are likely to be such as will be neither possessed of the confidence of the nation or the reverence of foreign princes. Pitt has shewn himself great in power, it remains for him to support when deprived of office the high opinion he has acquired. If he is betrayed into the petulance of opposition, and lends himself, as all have done before him, to be at the head of a faction, instead of consistently espousing the cause of his country, whether the proposition comes from one side of the House or the other, he will be no more in future than a common man with good parts; he will be tried with the touch-stone.

" In this state of things I must speak plainly to you, my dear friend. In the new Parliament, if he wishes to bring into Old Sarum *friends* of his, I have *friends* of my own to whom I will give the preference, and you are one of them; but if he calls upon me to place there two *public men*, who are necessary to him in Parliament, and for whom he can find room no where

* Our late gracious Sovereign, whose first illness took place at this time.

else, my private predilection will give way, because I think it
ought, and you will be the sacrifice, which would not have been
to a minister in place. I need not tell you this is a disinterested
determination on my part; that it proceeds from principle, and
from political motives, more than from the attachments of gratitude.
I do not recollect a single instance in which I have refused to
comply with any request of his; and I can scarcely recollect a
single instance through his whole administration where he has
had the means or the inclination to gratify any wish I have submitted to him. No matter; I love and respect him; I feel proud
of him, and think the safety and honour of the country depends
upon him; and in the moment of adversity I shall feel happy if
I can strengthen his hands by any means in my power. Do not
be angry with me; if we were to change situations I should
not be angry with you for it. I shall retain always a very sincere satisfaction in having had the opportunity of being useful
to you. Judge candidly of me; and believe me, whether you
are my representative or not, you have the sincere esteem of
yours faithfully,   CAMELFORD."

     24.   *" Lyons, Nov. 23, 1788.*
" No, my friend, I shall not set my face towards England; on
the contrary, I am going further off. I have not the heart to be
witness to the consternation of the times and the possible consequences, that it will not be in the power of those who wish
the best to the country to withstand. Mr. Fox passed through
this place, out of breath and ' stained with travel,' on his way to
England two or three days ago, leaving behind him his heavy
baggage and all incumbrances. He had not even Pistol nor
Bardolph with him; but pursued his journey night and day
to assist with his counsels and to support with his authority. *Fuimus!* There may be some difference in the mode,
but there can be but one thing to be done. Whilst there
is life there is a possibility of a recovery; and there can be
no other King it is true, the functions cannot cease for a
moment; and as it is not in this case possible that they can
be deposited any where by him, who alone has the constitutional right to appoint a Regency, the same authority which
gave the Crown must appoint those who shall exercise the temporary functions of it. Surely the two Houses of Parliament
sitting, are more competent to such extraordinary interference
than any other convention called together under any other
authority, which must consist of the Peers and the Representatives of the people, however called together. The natural Regent, where there is no incapacity in the person, must be the
same upon whom the Crown would of course devolve; if, instead
of a temporary suspension, it were an actual demise of the
Crown, may prudence and wisdom be his guide! I cannot my-

self imagine, that this situation can continue long ; some fresh
crisis will determine it either one way or other, either by placing
the Crown upon the head of the successor, or by restoring to
us the government of our poor King.   As there has been
nothing in the blood to give an hereditary cause for this malady,
it can be regarded only as accidental, and owing to some humour,
which, having manifested itself in the bowels and elsewhere, has
flown to the head, and causes appearances the most alarming.
This I should conceive, being no physician, must soon end in
death ; or by some effort of nature be diverted from the head
and be thrown into some other part of the body.   The stamina
are naturally strong, and have been never yet enfeebled either by
excess of any kind, or by distempers and severe illnesses.   What
a state for the Queen ! how I feel for her, and for all those
upon whom the goodness of his character has had the most constant influence.

> Cur invidendis postibus, et novo
> Sublime ritu moliar atrium ?

No; I will build no more upon political foundations ; I will, if
possible, harden my mind to all the revolutions of Courts and
Courtiers.   What a lesson to the successor ! what a mortification to the pride of monarchs ! what an humiliation !   call back
yesterday !'
   " Write to me frequently, I beseech you.   Though I try to
harden my feelings, though I would fly to the other hemisphere
rather than see what you will see, I shall be impatient for every
post to tell me events and speculations ; and there are few who
think enough of me, or care enough about me, not to refer me
to Say's Chronicle for my intelligence.
   " Defy the foul fiend ! you have too much feeling not to
suffer now and then the dragons ; but the reflections you justly
make upon your happiness ought to put them to flight.
   " We are going to comfort ourselves in the sunshine of Monaco, near Nice, where we shall live in perfect solitude : continue to direct your letters hither, and M. Coudere will take care
to forward them to me.   I know not whether I shall be able to
pity the modern Belisarius ; I shall think him so much the object
of virtuous envy. ' He is not covetous of gold ;' but, if it be a
sin to covet honour, he is the most offending man alive ! "

26.   " Carnolés, Dec. 27, 1788.
   " I am glad, my dear Hardinge, to find, by the letter I have
just received from you, that you see the explanation I made you,
with regard to Old Sarum, in the light I meant it.   The event
will probably soon take place ; as I conclude, if there is a new
Ministry, there must be a new Parliament, and the Ex-minister
will of course stand in need of every support that can be given

him. He will owe to both of us obligations for our disinterested way of thinking at such a moment, when I fear he will not be overpowered with testimonies of regard and attachment from the many. I am happy to hear the Chancellor* is staunch; he is himself a host in the House of Lords. I hear my old friend the Duke of Northumberland has done like himself in refusing to rank himself in the new Cabinet; and sacrificing some private resentment, which had influenced him upon the Westminster Election, to public principle. The restrictions you mention as likely to be imposed by Parliament as to Peerages and places for life, are extremely judicious; under such circumstances George the Fourth will be the fountain of honours in due time; alas, the fountain for the present flows no more! How I feel comfort from the probability of speedy recovery that Willis flatters us with; he will be deified by the nation if he succeeds. What you say of certain people makes me hate to be of the same species with them; ' is there cause for these hard hearts?' The papers are filled with eulogiums upon the Princes for their filial piety.

" I misunderstood your letter about Texier's advertisement upon first reading it; and expressed my alarm for the feelings of poor Fabre, who is sensible to humiliation, as dignified poverty never fails to be. I was afraid the story would be copied into the Courier de l'Europe, and thence would reach him even at Gauges; however, I was in time to write you a line when I discovered my error, and even to recover my first letter, which I have thrown into the fire. I should not be surprised if the epilogue should produce more profit than the piece, at least to Fabre; for as to Texier, he has made no bad bargain for himself, advertising the benefit of Fabre, whereas in fact it is Fabre for the benefit of Texier, who takes three-fourths to himself.

" Whilst they are skaiting upon the Seine, and for ought I know upon the Thames, we are basking by the sea-side in all the heat of May. We have had some days of what is called unusually severe weather, and the nights have been cold enough to cover the ground with hoar frost, and the water has been frozen in little puddles, as with us sometimes in October; but when the sun rises clear and bright in the horizon, all this melts away, and even when the wind is sharp a little exercise gives all the heat one can desire; when there is no wind it is the feel of summer, and the verdure of the evergreens all around might really deceive one. Every where you see rows of orange-trees, in many climates growing in the natural ground, but acres of them, woods of them, surround us here. It is is said to be two degrees warmer than at Nice, and would, I am persuaded, have greatly the preference if it were more accessible; the distance by sea from Antibes is equal to that between Dover and Calais,

---

* Lord Thurlow.

which is troublesome; we made the *trajet* with a very favourable wind in three hours and a half. From Nice it is about half as far; and there is a road which ladies have passed by land *en cnaise à porteur*, but it is a tremendous undertaking for such as are *frightful*; mules, however, pass every day. Monaco is the most romantic citadel imaginable, projecting forwards in the sea, and covering the whole little plain upon the top of a very high perpendicular rock, out of which grows in quantity the Indian fig, or prickly pear, which we have in our hot-houses; behind rises an immense bare mountain, which connects with the high ridge that reigns all along the coast. Nothing can exceed the beauty of a very good road, practised along the side of the hill, like Mount Edgecumbe terrace. For about two leagues to the place where we reside it is a constant succession of lovely pictures; the sea underneath, glittering through the shade of immense olive trees, which sometimes open, sometimes intercept the distant views of the bays inclosed with such rocks, and mountains, and promontories as painters only imagine; the skirts of which are clothed with plantations, and dotted with white buildings, villages, little towns, and castles *à fleur d'eau*. As yet I am the first Englishman who have thought of passing a winter here. In truth, there is not much resource of society; though the people of the little town of Manton, which contains from five to six thousand inhabitants, seem very civil, and desirous to draw to themselves the benefit of strangers. It would suit admirably small families, who seek only warmth and quiet, and to live cheap in their own way; but would not do as a place of amusement. Provisions, *i. e.* the necessaries of life, are in general good; but for the luxuries, they must be had from Nice or from Marseilles, with which there is a constant communication. I write you all this detail, in case at any time hereafter any friends of yours might wish to profit by our experience. We are, indeed, lodged in a country-house belonging to the Prince, which he has lent us; but there are small country-houses to be had, with gardens.'

27. " *Jan.* 23, 1789.

" I fancy my letters must have been lost in the snows, as you complain of not hearing from me. It is true I do not acknowledge punctually all those I receive from you, as I could do no more than thank you for the very interesting intelligence they contain; and any remarks I could make upon them would be so old before they would reach you that you would almost forget to what they alluded. I am not the less obliged to you for the hints and lively sketches you supply me with, which make me as much present as I wish to be. The triumph of Thurlow over the Scotch patriot, learned in the laws of the Constitution, is one of those *petites malices* that I allow myself to indulge in with a good conscience. I understand nothing of the protest. Let them speak out, and pledge themselves boldly to the indefeasible right of hereditary Regency, if they please, and stand to it. But if that point is given up, and they allow once for all, that the right is conferred upon the Regent by the two Houses, I do not see their distinction, whether it is conferred by an address without limitations, or by an act under commission with limitations; in either case it is an act of legislation equally, if it constitutes an authority that is obligatory upon the subject, and so far in the teeth of their maxim, that the two branches of the legislature can do nothing without the assent of the third. To my plain understanding, if the Parliament took the Regency under their plain address, I should conceive, upon their reasoning, the difficulty insurmountable. I should say to the Regent, 'You assumed the Government: upon what authority? you had no legal right in you, or you might have asserted it without the intervention of Parliament; and if you had not that right, nothing but the Legislature could give it you. And the two Houses inviting you to do what you had no right to do, and what they were incompetent to authorise you to do, only renders them accomplices with you in an illegal usurpation.'

"The difficulty about your Speaker seems of the same nature with the great difficulty above alluded to. The Constitution not foreseeing the cause, requires the approbation of the Speaker by the King; the case occurs, and there is for this purpose no King; then you must do without him. Elect your Speaker, remedy the defect in the Legislature, and then submit your choice to the approbation of the Regent. *Cela me paroit tout simple;* and whoever thinks otherwise would have hanged the man who released the foot of the Queen of Spain from the stirrup when she was in danger of being dragged to death, because that honour belonged properly only to the Cavallerizzo Mayor, who happened to be at home smoking a segar.'

"The comfortable news of the poor sufferer awakens all one's hopes. How I love Pitt for not permitting the crew to deprive him of his household! I rejoice in the lively part the public seem to take in the contest. John is after all an honester gentleman than I took him for, and has righter feelings about him than I gave him credit for.

"Why cannot you and your *chère moitié*, instead of going to your Castle on Saturday morning, flit away in spirit to this lovely shore. What a ride had we this morning along the clean beach, with a warm sun reflected from the clear sea, cheering and comforting us like the month of May! What olive trees feathering in terraces one above another, sometimes hiding, sometimes opening, the prospect partially in a succession of new landscapes! then the rich green of tufted oranges, with innumerable birds already singing under the shelter of their branches;

and, above all, the majestic craggs of rocky cliffs, that with a thousand tints of mellow colouring, tower into the skies, and teem to defend this little paradise from all invaders.

" Adieu! and do not reproach me if I prefer the peace and retirement of this enchanted scene to all the discordant brawlings of your debates,—the

" Res Romanæ perituraque regna."

28.   " *Monaco, Jan.* 30, 1789.

" This blessed 30th of January, and not before, do I receive your two letters of the 12th and 13th; not to mention one of the 8th, which came by the last post. No, I am liberal as the day; and if all the letters I receive were as interesting to me as yours are, I should not utter a pish in a twelvemonth; not but what I must say, that, when I have sometimes opened one of your dispatches with three lines and an envlop, I have made an ejaculation upon your extravagance, as you know we pay by weight; and all the post offices abroad are amazed at our large seals, thick paper, and dispatches like patents, when theirs are upon thin paper and of the size of three inches by two.

" Our correspondence resembles, at this distance, the two gentlemen who made the observation upon the weather at Hyde-park corner, and hatched the answer upon the same spot at their return. You will have forgotten the examination of the physicians; and will perhaps be congratulating upon the recovery by the time this comes to tell you, that this measure seems to me to verify an old adage of Fox the father, ' that nothing disconcerted an Opposition so much as yielding to their proposition.' It is one more indecency added to many, and ought to have been moved by Burke himself instead of having been supported by him. I thank you for the trait of Norfolk Windham; and for your lucky thought in calling him the illegitimate heir to Sir G. Saville's subtilties.

" I am sorry Pitt was provoked to a personality to Burke; the more obvious it was, the less it became Pitt to hint at it. Tell Lady Dacre * that she gives me a great deal more significance than I deserve, or than I really have, in either House of Parliament, if she thinks I could have made any difference by my presence. Were she now basking with us in orange-groves, or under the feathering boughs of our old olives, she would not think them well exchanged for your thrilling regions of thick-ribbed ice, and all the tumult of your violent politics.

" I have heard nothing from the Percy yet; but I shall have tidings anon. I can never persuade myself but that he is a true Percy. I am not surprised at the new Secretary; he has long looked for it, and has got it at last. Not so N———d; he has no place. I am delighted with your proof against my reasoning

* Anna Maria, at this time Dowager Lady Dacre, was sister to Lord Chancellor Camden.

as to Texier; we are odd animals. Surely Lord P—— will not take; and they would not think of him for Ireland. What are they reduced to! By the specimens you give me of the new Administration, we shall see rare times. If the two vacant Chief Justiceships in Eyre are refused to them by the Act, it will go much harder with them I believe than the restriction as to Peers, which will rid Fox of a great embarrassment, as it will keep him from the disgrace of breaking his word to all those he has promised without intending to perform, whilst it will hold them firm to his party. What could my friend Montagu mean by running Sir G. Elliot against Mr. Grenville? it was merely to expose him to the mortification of a defeat as a reward for his East Indian zeal, which has been defeated likewise.

"You talk of your cold, it is nothing to what I have heard of all around us. Officers in the garrisons living in the stables, soldiers frozen in sentry boxes, the port frozen at Marseilles, and women found frozen in their houses with their children at their breasts. Wolves in Switzerland attacking the doors of houses, and devouring all they meet; they carried off by night a dog at the door of the house we lodged at by the lake of Neufchatel. At Avignon all mills stopped, no bread; and almost every where the dread of famine. Here mild frost for a fortnight, with warm sunshine."

———

29.   *" Feb. 6, 1789.*

" It is very natural you should wish to be put out of suspense*, but here is the difficulty. When we ask the question, the answer will be, ' we do not know whether the event is to take place, or when; nor is it possible, therefore, to know in what circumstances we shall find ourselves when it does.' I never meant to wait till he knocked at my door, but only waited for the measure being determined upon to make him the offer through the person who is so good as to act for me in my absence. I have now written to have an explanation upon the subject, the result of which may perhaps put you at your ease. I have mentioned expressly that you joined in the offer, being willing to sacrifice your own satisfaction to the great object, if it was necessary; I do not think that sacrifice will be accepted, and you must prove that they will be no losers by your continuance, but that you can make yourself as useful and important as another man.

" I am ashamed of the disgraceful squabble among the Physicians, and of the much more disgraceful use that has been made of it. Public assemblies can preserve decorum for a short time only, but by degrees one sees that they are mere mob, *toute assemblée est peuple.* What grieves me the most is the cloud that is thrown over our fairest hopes; yet the accounts, such as they are, do not seem discouraging,—long and quiet sleeps, and long intervals of waking quiet. The majorities upon the questions

* Respecting his seat in Parliament.

of limitations are as great as under circumstances could be expected. I do not wonder you cast a longing wish towards these scenes of neutrality and sunshine. I have been longer a near witness to the revolutions of politics than you have, and have *vu le fond du sac*, as the Cardinal said, when he rejected the Sacrament upon his death-bed; it is a sad picture of the meanness and wickedness of the human heart, and I forgive Princes whose feelings are hardened by it. The sun shines bright, the sea is in beauty; let us go and enjoy the charms of nature, that never fail to make us feel our existence a blessing to us.

"Why Bedford-square, I pray? Could you not be contented with Ormond-street? I am afraid you are no better than an extravagant fellow."

---

30.   *" Monaco, Feb.* 14, 1789.

"I am thinking how you will be amazed at opening this letter to find one inclosed for Lord Malmesbury; it is still in the cause of poor Fabre. I have found a person who will pay eight hundred livres a year for two years to place his son in business; and I have found one of the first mercers in Lyons, who is willing to undertake to place him to advantage. So far so good; then your two hundred guineas in spite of the Percy; and I am still in hopes that Florence will do something considerable sooner or later, though I own it surprises me not a little to find no sign of life in that quarter, though I have written two letters, and thought, in the disposition I left them, they had the business as much at heart as I had. Now for Lord Malmesbury. Fabre has just written to tell me he has got the scent of a considerable fund in Holland, set apart by the good Queen Anne, and other pious English Protestants of that day, for the purpose of alleviating French persecuted Huguenots in the galleys. Fabre knows such fund actually existed, having partaken of it in his captivity, and having been trusted, before his release, in some share of the distribution of it. This fund has been accumulating now for twenty years without a claim upon it, since, from that time, nobody has been persecuted in France upon account of religion; and the late edict of toleration, supported by the enlightened and liberal spirit of the times, removes all apprehensions of the revival of such abominations. In this state of things our *honnéte galérien* is advised by a person who has got hold of this clue at Amsterdam, and who knows him only by story, to lay in his claim if he can get it properly backed by authority. I write then to the Ambassador, whose credit at this time I believe nobody will doubt, to try to interest him in this affair. I am not so sanguine about it as poor Fabre seems to be, but it is worth trying, and we must have nothing to reproach ourselves with. I refer his Lordship to you for the narrative, which you will leave at his door if he is in London; if he is gone back to the

Hague, which I do not believe, the Secretary's office will forward it to him by the first messenger.   In truth, my dear friend, I do give you full credit for all your zeal and activity in this good cause, and in every other in which the feelings of humanity are concerned.   Were others like you, we should see those who have better means vie with each other, and

> "———— make the rough paths of nature even,
> And waken in each breast a little Heaven.

" How lively and how descriptive are the short dashes of your pen as to what is passing in your busy scene !   Take care what you write ; for though I certainly shall not bring up your letters in judgment against you in a future day, I promise you I shall keep all those that relate to this interesting crisis with the greatest care; they will, in some distant day, be deciphered (not without trouble) as the most valuable documents to some Gibbon or Hume in the completing the history of the times.   How my indignation rises against the insinuations and unmanly attacks of the white-livered Chief Justice ! *   Is it possible to make such a person the butt of party malice, and in such an hour of distress !   How should I have been able to suppress the contempt such a conduct, inspired by such motives, must raise in every honest and liberal mind !   As to the apostacy of the proud Percy, I am sorry for it, as I am disappointed in an old friend.   *Au reste*, Landaff's disinterested prelate † is well known; and as for Lord Rawdon, I believe Thurlow did not obtain for him his Peerage for the purpose to which he has used it.   What truth and what pathos in the application of Dryden's lines !   Did the long-winded Viscount take nothing to himself !   I wonder they have given so much for their newspaper,—not that they do unwisely to stifle truth as far as they are able; but they will not succeed.   The virtues of our young hero are so luminous, and all Europe has borne so strong a testimony to them, that the confidence of the public will follow him, let them say what they will.   His father was vulnerable all over; yet his splendour could never be extinguished by all the dirt that party could fling upon him.   His son has not a spot upon him, or a weak place, and his public merits have been at least equally acknowledged; they cannot write him down.   The rashness of their cabal will draw them on from scrape to scrape, till the hour comes when he will be found necessary to others, who will not be able to do without him ; they are not necessary to his happiness or to his reputation, which can stand upon his own resources.

" I admire your delicacy about Old Sarum.   Make yourself easy; your offer, whether it be accepted or not, can never be made to reflect back any false colours upon your late conduct,

---

* Lord Loughborough, Chief Justice of the Court of Common Pleas.
† Dr. Watson.

although I think it very possible that the latter may have its
influence in the deciding upon the former.

"The person who gives the 800 livres *per annum* to the
young Fabre for two years is the Baron de Salis. It runs in
my head that I was told he had abandoned the young man after
having given him his education, and after having promised
to provide for him; if so, this act of kindness from him affords
sufficient proof of his sincerity."

---

31.   " *Monaco, Feb.* 25, 1789 ‡.

" I cannot say that what you tell me increases my ardour to
return to a country governed by such Ministers, whether it be
Mr. Fox or Mr. Sheridan that possesses the Royal ear.   Will
they allow Falstaff, Bardolph, and Peto, to appear upon the stage
during this administration ?   Your Welsh attorney is my delight,
and worth all of them put together.   I wish I could partake of
his hare, when it arrives, with a pudding in its belly.   I am persuaded Pitt will regale upon it with more appetite than upon
turtle and venison.   I thought Loughborough too wise to play
the dog in the fable ; Mansfield is the gainer by it, and will
hold fast I warrant him.   What indecent ribaldry and stuff do
they suffer Burke to insult the House with ! stop his mouth for
God's sake as soon as possible, and make him whatever he
pleases so as he will hold his Irish tongue for the future.   It is
high time for Mr. Fox to return, and put things a little in order
again.   Achilles is a more generous antagonist for the overthrow of our Hector, if he must fall.

" The samples of wit you send me out of the Morning Herald
are not without salt, but at this distance we lose a part of their
apropos; not but what Mr. Bradling's declaration is *de tout tems
et de tout pays.*   As I cannot write or speak Greek, I will send
you a Latin inscription I am putting upon a little monument by
the sea side; on the other side of the pedestal is a dedication
grato animo to the Prince, *cujus imperio hæc lætantur omnia.*
Towards the prospect, where you sit under the shade of pines,
with myrtle all around you, and the waves dashing against the
rocks under your feet, as follows :

Littora myrtilis lætissima,
fluctu levi percussa littora,
saxosum nemus,
aprici colles,
prærupti juga montis ;
et vos !
Alcinoi sylvæ,
vos et irriguæ valles ;

‡ Indorsed by Mr. Hardinge : " Feb. 25, 1789, from Monaco, with
two beautiful inscriptions written by himself."

> linquenda tandem
> amœna rura ;
> valete :
> Heu !
> quando revisurus ?'

" For the ladies I have translated it thus :

> Rivage de myrthes orné,
> Rivage par les flots doucement arrosé,
> Bois solitaires et sombres,
> Qui sous vos ombres
> Cachez vos rochers sourcilleux ;
> Cimes des monts, qui jusqu'au ciel
> Portez vos fronts majestueux ;
>   Et vous
>   Jardins de la fable,
> Vallons enchanteurs, toujours frais ;
>   Séjour aimable—
>   Adieu !
>   Peut-être à jamais.

" All that I describe is at the same moment under the eye of the spectator.

" We live upon your letters as our daily bread.   Adieu ! "

---

31.   " *Monaco, March* 1, 1789.

" The King is well, the King is well !   I can say nothing else to all I meet ; I say it in French, I say it in Italian, and should say it in Patois, if I knew how to express myself.   Your two letters were delivered to me in my walk before breakfast.   I first read Burke's affront, not to the House only, but to humanity. Gods, could he be suffered !   I had not digested the first movement of my choler when I opened your second letter ; my eyes swam with tears.   I was ready to fall upon my knees in the public walk.   I flew to my dear woman, transported, out of breath : 'The King is well, the King is well !   *Afflavit Deus, et dissipantur.*   Even Warren says he is well ; and that it will be a permanent recovery.'   How anxiously shall I expect the confirmation of these hopes !   How will it be possible to keep from the dear man the knowledge of such things as would overturn the calmest reason ?   I tremble for fear of a relapse ; may Providence protect us !   What must must be the feelings of our excellent Queen !   I envy Lady C—— her interview with her upon such an occasion.   A thousand thousand thoughts rush upon my mind at once ; it is like the waking from a feverish dream.

" Surely in this situation they will not dare to provoke the feelings of all mankind, by changing the government. I exult in all you say of our darling hero, in the testimony you bear as to his address his spirit, and his temper, in such trying times; his talents his enemies will not deny to him. The lines of your protegée are pretty. I could send you a part of a letter in prose which I received by this post, equally excellent and equally flattering to him; but you do not know the person, and every thing depends upon the character. You will have opportunities enough to distinguish yourself, my dear Hardinge, and you do well to choose with discernment; an angel would speak to no purpose, unless to those who wish to hear. Grey and Windham will couple together in the Opposition pack; they will be noisy and troublesome; but unimportant, and by degrees talk themselves out of favour. It is a thousand pities that the great qualities of our friend are not accompanied by every thing one could wish in the lesser ones; he is, as I said before, one of those peasants of the Alps who can walk well enough among precipices, but stumbles upon plain ground.

"I wrote to you by the last post, so will only end at present with what I began—the King is well! may the King live for ever!"

---

32.   "*Monaco, April* 5, 1789.
"——— Rege incolumi, mens omnibus una est:
Amisso, rupère fidem; constructaque mella
Diripuère ipsæ, et crates solvere favorum.

This would have been my device, if I had made an illumination. Were I to be admitted to an interview, I believe I should play Lady Effingham over again; the difference would be, that I should embrace him with all the zeal and affection as if we were still play-fellows together in the woods of Clefden. Do you know I have four letters from you altogether, besides one I received some time since. The new batch of Peers will occasion new clamour. I should say, why Lord Morton*? but as to Fife†,

---

* George, sixteenth Earl of Morton, K. T. was honoured with a British Peerage, but not until two years after the date of this letter. He was created Baron Douglas of Lochleven, Aug. 11, 1791, but the title expired on his death without issue, July 17, 1827. He had sat as a Representative Peer of Scotland from 1784 till 1790; and he was Lord Chamberlain of the Queen's Household from 1792 till her Majesty's death in 1818. His Lordship possessed a strong attachment to science, and had so frequently officiated as Vice-President at the Royal Society on the occasional absence of Sir Joseph Banks, that he was, on the death of that celebrated character, one of the persons who were mentioned as likely to succeed him. The Earl was not, however, put in nomination.

† James, second Earl of Fife, was created Baron Fife in the Peerage of the United Kingdom, Feb. 19, 1790. This Barony also expired on the death of the grantee, Jan. 24, 1809; but the same title was again bestowed on his nephew James, the present and fourth Earl, and K. T, April 25, 1827.

a man of £.20,000 a year, who brings four or five Members into the House of Commons, has as fair a claim methinks as another; moreover he is an old friend of mine, *de plus de trente ans*, which is a strong argument with me, whatever it may be with others. I am indeed stung to the heart with poor Cowper's disappointment, because I know it has inflicted upon him a wound that he will never probably recover. I have not been able to refrain from expressing my mind upon it to the Minister, but it will have no effect upon him; and then you talk of the use my credit might be of to my friends if I were present— *cela est plaisant!*

"As for my law suit, it must go on as it can. I expect the worst, and shall make up my back to it; but I know you will do the best that can be done for me, and that I am in good hands. If I have a chance, it will be, I am persuaded, from the colour of the cow, or whether her horns are long or short, or any thing in the world rather than the trifling circumstance of to whom the cow in common sense ought to belong. Your lines out of Tully are too agreeable to me to give the merit of them to any body but yourself. Pitt I dare say must have been flattered by the verses you addressed to him. I am a little angry with you for preferring my French translation to the Latin original, though I am well contented you should like them both. I send you them in print, that they may appear to the best advantage; and with them an English imitation rather than translation, which has the merit of more detail in the picture, and if I may say so, has here and there a good line in it *. Would to God you could see the spot! I am sure it would recall to you every beautiful classical idea you ever read. I shall leave it the day after Easter. Warren is a good Bishop, and so is Hallifax; *ils sont du bois dont on en fait.* The Right Reverend of Landaff is a good Bishop also; but not gifted with prophetic certainty in his speculations and leading principles.

"If Pitt has not the first Garter forced upon him, I shall say, kill the next Percy yourself! As to the Chief Justiceship in Eyre, it is enough to keep him from starving whenever the successor turns him a grazing, and I like it better than if it were greater, I mean richer; he wants no illustration but his virtues, and has no wants beyond his necessities. Why is he not to his friends all they could wish? Can there never be a perfect model? I suppose there will be a ball in opposition to White's all in black, with proper *enjolivemens* 'in jewels of sulphur and nitre.' I agree with you as to the pages. I am uneasy about Ireland; I wish their absurdity may not prove the bane of our tranquillity. Above all things I dread the most, the Coalition you talk of; avert it, Heaven! It would be the union of a moment only, and the discredit of ages; it would bring no strength with it, and leave a permanent weakness in altering the opinion of the

* This has been separated from this letter.

public, which is strength, safety, and honour under all possible circumstances. My Ambassador * is all politeness; and has written to his secretary to inquire and to forward the claim as far it is in his power. I intend to pass some days at Montpellier, and to get a sight of poor Fabre. I have got a situation for his son at Lyons that promises well ; the Baron de Salis, who gave him his education, pays £.30 *per annum* for two years for his pension, till he can stand upon his own legs.

"Rolle's motion was embarrassing; Pitt, who is *ferré à glace*, seems to have got out of the difficulty with admirable address. The doubt of Erskine about Burke's integrity and his principles is laughable,—*mutato nomine*, &c. Both madmen, and both 'the true Scotch interest working at the root;' and why not Burke's bankrupt-cousin on the same Treasury-bench with the great Sheridan?

"My ostensible letter that I wrote to Cowper came too late for the apropos; I have thought of a means of getting it shown to the Minister by a common friend, without imposing so painful a task as an interview between Cowper and him after what has passed. I should be sorry he should not know that, whilst my wishes have so little weight with him, his glory is the first object with me; perhaps when we meet I may shew you that in the very moment that he rejected my best friend I was offering him a very unequivocal proof of my personal regard.

"I believe for the future you had better write to me at Paris, *à la poste restante;* I shall be there about the middle of May. The ladies desire their compliments.

"Yours ever,   CAMELFORD."

33.   "*Lyons, May 6*, 1789.

"We envy you your St. Paul's, and your joyful countenances at every window, and your 6000 charity children joining their young voices in the sober melody of the 100th Psalm, and the gracious tears of sentiment that watered the cheeks of our good Sovereign! As to your club-balls, be they what they will, they may be repeated in every country, and perhaps with more gallantry by our unfeeling neighbours; but the procession was all English heart, and will probably be never seen again in any country. I wish to know whether the journey to Hanover takes place; if it does, please God I will turn my back upon Paris and its Etats to pay my duty to him there, that I may enjoy the satisfaction of seeing with my own eyes, that happiness which can alone compensate all the anxiety I have suffered. I have no recollection of the passage you shewed to Lord Ailesbury; but, as it was truth, and came from the abundance of the heart, I trust it can have given no offence.

"Your verses and your application from Tully's letter are very

* Lord Malmesbury.

flattering to me. Trust me, if I had at any moment conceived
my presence in England could have been of real use to the cause,
further than adding one more testimony to a decided majority,
where the argument stood as strong as the numbers, I should
not have hesitated one hour, whatever inconvenience it might
have put me to. I honour in Wilberforce the generous instinct
that animates his pursuit; but I hope the Legislature will have
sens froid enough to tread with caution in a path where prudence must go hand in hand with sentiment. Take care that
thousands of white men are not reduced to real misery to relieve
their brethren of another colour of imaginary evils. Lord
Westcote has often assured me that, from his own observations
in Jamaica, the slaves were in general in a happier state than his
labourers at Hagley.

"I embraced poor Fabre at Montpellier *en passant;* no,
there was no appearance of discontent upon his brow, but
tears of gratitude for what I had been able to do for him,
though far short of what I wished. My £.250 has not cleared
all his debts: he still owes £.100; but what he hopes to get
in of his own debts will more than replace it, so that £.220
remains entire in his hands. Lady Cowper gives no answer
to any of my letters from Florence; yet I hear from a bird in the
air that she gives £.100, and Lord Grosvenor, through Lord
Belgrave, another. Could we get together £.400 or £.500, it
would place the son as *associé* in business, and then we could
drive the world before us. It is a nice thing, and requires a
light hand; but, if in company with Lord Belgrave you could
touch upon the story of Fabre without directly applying it to
him, you might perhaps perceive whether there are any hopes in
that quarter. We are now trying a string of no small importance, no less than the mother of the Grand Duchess of Russia,
who is going on a visit to the Empress; she is one of the best
of women, and passes her life in acts of benevolence at her little
court at Monbelliard in Alsace.

" What a winter, or rather continuation of successive winters, we have had; snug in our little retreat we knew it
only by hearsay, but when we got into Provence it was
really horrible; not only all the orange and lemon trees cut
down to the root in the gardens, but scarce a single olive,
as we passed to Montpellier, with a green leaf upon it;
vines, capers, in a word, every thing has suffered more or
less, except corn, of which there is no great production. Add
to this, houses gutted by the insurgents in various places; and
in some, horrid massacres of the gentlemen who defended their
castles. Every town reduced to arm their own *bourgeoisie*
against the mob; Marseilles in arms, the whole road through
Dauphine covered with soldiers going to the support of Government; the wife of the Commandant travelling to join her husband at Aix, and concealing her name for fear of insult; in

short, the whole is a picture of confusion and desolation.   We
slept at Montelimart, in the full resolution of visiting the Cha-
teau de Grignau next morning.   How did you get hither? on
the outside of a horse?   They told us the roads were so bad
that our carriages would be broke to pieces, that it would
require five hours, and that we must come back the next day,
with our bones broken, in their cursed machines; all this
damped our courage.   I know you will despise us, but we set
forward on our journey; and contented ourselves with buying
Hermitage upon the spot at Tein, and got hither like incurious
Vandals as we were.   I expect my son here to-morrow; and,
after passing a few days with him, shall set forward to the great
city, where I shall hope for some of your letters.   I have written
to Cowper to persuade you to accept again the representation of
the ancient Borough * in case of a dissolution, which I take for
granted will take place after the rising of Parliament.   He writes
to me full of gratitude to you for your zeal in his son's business;
it has broken his heart, and his letters almost break mine.

   " Give the inclosed to some of the learned book-worms of the
British Museum; it is a publication by a famous Abbé Rives,
the Bentley of the age, who was librarian to the Duke de la
Valiere.   Vale."

                                           _____

   34.   " *Paris, May 22*, 1789.
   " I always knew I was a better lawyer than any of you.   The
Chancellor is a wise man, and is of *my* opinion; as Madame de
Sevigné used to say, M. de Turenne *est dans l'armée de mon fils*.
He may change you say, and leave the side of common sense to
reconcile himself with Westminster-hall.   I do not believe he
will; and I trust we shall have *gagné de cause*, and be never the
worse off for not having played the knave, which, however, will,
I confess, be a prodigy of the times worthy to be recorded among
the extraordinaries of Westminster-hall.   Well! be it as it may,
we are prepared for the best and for the worst that can befall.
I am surprised at what you tell me of the summons to the Members; and yet am so satisfied of the perfect rectitude and integrity of the summoner †, that, whatever appearance it may have
at the first sight, I am persuaded you will be convinced, when
he comes to explain it, that if he has not acted in it with his
usual judgment, he has at least preserved the consistency of his
character, which he has kept untainted when there was every
temptation to warp him, and now there is none.   Burke is a
fiend, as you call him, who scruples at no means that can contribute to the blind fanatical enthusiasm of the moment.   For
the dignity of both Houses, for the credit of the Nation, he
ought to be humbled, and never more than in this instance.
As to Hastings, I cannot reconcile any marks of ostentation with
his good sense and the system he had adopted.   I say nothing of

* Old Sarum.   † Mr. Pitt, the Prime Minister.

his wife and her diamonds; she is, I conclude, a vain silly woman, with her head turned by her elevation. But as for him, he has cautiously avoided, at the first setting out, all display of riches; and it would seem strange he should alter his plan just at the time that he is complaining that he is ruined by his persecutions.

" I have this instant a letter to tell me the Chancellor is to be President of the Council, and Lord Kenyon Chancellor *. What will become of me? Will Lord Kenyon adopt the opinions of Lord Thurlow, or shall we be all turned head over heels?

"I sincerely wish the waters of Spa, and the amusement of new things, may complete the recovery of your fair *moitié*; if she winters abroad, we will give her the best advice we can from our experience, but that goes no further than negative. As to the South of France, there is no mild situation but Hieres; all the rest of Provence and Languedoc is subject to the sudden vicissitudes of burning sun and dry piercing cold, which is certainly the reverse of what a delicate habit requires. They send all persons who have the least tendency of that kind to Lyons, *pour nourrir la poitrine*; but they had better send them to London, for all the winter long it is a thick cold fog, as dark as it would be with us, and as damp as in November. Upon the whole, there is nothing for her but Hieres or Nice, which is one degree less sheltered than Carnoles, but has the resources of amusement; and particularly the English colony, which to those who are not much used to foreigners and their ways, is a desirable thing, as it gives society upon easier terms.

"What a charming account you give of your audience at Windsor†; and how I envy you the pleasure it must have afforded you! There are ill-natured reports circulated here on purpose to plant thorns in the pillow of every one who loves good and eschews evil; but they are dissipated as soon as traced to their authors. I enter into all your feelings upon the junction at St. Paul's; what a moment! The sun should have accompanied the ceremony in all its splendour; and not a breath of air have presumed to disturb the decorations of such an evening. We got here three days ago; and find all minds in all classes in the fermentation of politics, animated with every sentiment of private interest and public enthusiasm. The first man named upon the committee of the *tiers état*, is the Huguenot Minister of Nismes, son of the famous Paul Rabot, who was the persecuted apostle of the times, and is still living to enjoy the triumphs of his son. What an important and imposing epocha for this country, when the whole assembly is met together without tumult, without arms, for the purpose of framing a constitution and establishing a legislation!

"I find Paris very much improved, and very inconveniently

* It need scarcely be remarked, that no such change took place.
† See Mr. Hardinge's own account of this interview in vol. III. of this Work, p. 15.

increased; it is a wonderful city. Every thing is ridiculously English. We are now near enough to correspond with a quick return. You will remember letters are opened on both sides the water."

———

35.   " *Paris, June* 3, 1789.

" There are persons on this side the water as well as on your side the water that make it their business to spread disagreable reports of our good King's health; though I am convinced they are groundless and malicious, I cannot help, whilst I contradict them, feeling at my heart a sort of unpleasant sensation that my reason disapproves. Lord Tichfield, who is just come to us; and the Devonshires that are expected, as well as the Spencers, *me rassurent,* as they certainly would not be absent if they foresaw a change. Write, however, and give me comfort, that I may speak positively when I hear what is disagreable to me.

" Poor General Cowper regrets extremely the loss of his neighbour Moses Franks*, who was one of the few he cultivated. It is a charming possession for those who acquire it; I do not wonder you lick your lips at it. I feel as you do about abolishing the trade of kidnapping; but I am not able to judge how far, in such a question of public and private interest, I ought to give way to feeling.

" When you are tired of representing Old Sarum, you may come here and represent either of the three orders; and be a bishop, a noble, or plebeian, as the Baliage or Senechaussée can settle it. The style is here avowedly to create a new Constitution, and to put the *noblesse* fairly out of the question. If Franklin is still alive, that great Solon, who lays out a plan for a government as easily as I should do for a seat in a garden, he is the only person to preside at their assembly; in the mean time there is somebody in London, a name that sounds like Bentham, that is kind enough, I hear †, to give them his ideas upon the subject. I dread the dissolution of their Assembly; and cannot conceive how it can be avoided. It is curious, indeed, to see how this nation is changed. I have not yet heard of a duel between one of the Royal party, however, with a Prince of the Blood. I will find you a keep-sake like that the Duchess of Kingston drew from the bottom of her capotte for the Consul at Genoa, who had lodged her, and cloathed her I believe, and caressed her for any thing I know. ' How do you like this diamond ring?' ' Very fine, my Lady.' ' This ruby?' ' Beautiful!' ' This snuff-box?' ' Superb!' &c. &c. &c. &c. ' Well, Mr. Consul, you see these spectacles (and here she sighed); these spectacles were worn twenty years by my dear Duke (here she

* Moses Franks, Esq. died at Teddington, April 2, 1789.
† The since well-known Jeremy Bentham, Esq.

opened the *etui* and dropped a tear), take them, Mr. Consul,
wear them for his sake and mine; I could not give you a
stronger proof of my infinite regard for you.' Sir Joshua was
willing to give as much of the natural as possible to his
story.

"Our poor General is better in health at present, because
he is better in hope and spirits. Your extracts from the
Patrician Shakspeare are delightful. There is a quarto volume
here that I have but just begun that has great vogue; it is
called Anacharsis; it is light pleasant reading for the ladies,
and yet full of Greek lore. It is a Scythian Coxe travelling
through Greece in the time of Philip; and relating in letters
to his friend every thing he meets with; I think it will entertain you. It is now out of print, but will soon be re-printed.

"Vale."

35.   "*Paris, June* 10, 1789.

"In this country we have nothing but mourning in our dress
and the dæmon of faction in our hearts, whilst the weather is
complete winter; *voilà où nous en sommes.* I went through the
ceremony of the presentation at Versailles yesterday, and was
trained along wet passages and open galleries up stairs and
down stairs to no less than ten Royalties, not one of whom
uttered a syllable or cast a look upon me, as is their custom;
but we have no such pleasant episodes as you mention in our
Court, I assure you.

"I never had the smallest doubt that the Opposition would
have cut their fetters with a new Parliament, if they could have
brought them up to it, but of that I have my doubts.

"You complain of want of common attentions; do you know
any body to whom he* has shewn them? I hear such stories of
him here as make me hang my head. I do not like the thoughts
of his being out-voted upon the abolition of slavery; not that I
am enough master of the question to decide whether it ought
or not to pass, but because I wish all his ideas to be so popular
as to carry all the world with him. Perhaps, however, it is the
best that could happen, if it displays the generosity of his character without hurting the public.

"The Parisian frolics, if they do not take a different turn very
soon, look like a civil war. It is astonishing *comme les tetes sont
montées de part et d'autres,* and the language they use. The *tiers*
seem determined to put the *noblesse* under their feet; and if they
suffer them to get up again, to let it be upon the condition of
an Eton boy, who says, I yield. The *noblesse* are equally determined, whatever sacrifices they may be inclined to make, to let
them be voluntary, as the deliberation of their order according
to the established usages since the time of Charlemagne; and

* Mr. Pitt.

have sworn to obey the instructions which were imposed upon them at their election. The numbers are with the *tiers* and the army with the *noblesse*. In the mean time all the pleasure of society is destroyed, and their pleasing amiable manners degenerate into those of our Westminster elections.

" I do not know whether I can bring the two Annes to execute your commission of the little barbett, unless an opportunity occurs of sending it away instantly to England. We are a good deal of Madame de Grignan's opinion as to those machines that are not *montées a la propreté*, and who are quite as troublesome, though not quite so interesting as children. Adieu ! "

37.   " *Paris, July 5,* 1789.
" I see at the top of your letter, ' When do you come to England ?' My answer is,

> ' When the hurly-burly 's done,
> When the battle's lost and won.'

I shall not come till Smith and I have settled accounts, till Burnham is sold, till I know what I have to trust to ; that will hardly be till next spring. At present I amuse myself with French politics, where the fine ladies pass their time in trying to *parfiler* the old constitution as out of fashion ; and where the beardless Solons in gillets and buck-skin breeches take upon them to weave new ones. There is a little pamphlet I send you that will give you some idea of the style of our society. In England we go on slowly ; but here I have seen, in less than a week, the transition made from the situation of the beginning of our Long Parliament to its Rump. Before the Assemblée des Etats, we were living in an absolute monarchy, under every abuse of monarchial power ; we are now under a democracy, the most complete that exists, without a King, without a nobility or clergy, without an army, a government, or police.

" It is the most curious and interesting moment that a foreigner could have chosen to have seen not only the humour of the nation, but to contemplate the follies of the creature man. I see no issue out of the difficulties they are involved in, but that which ends all disputes, the decision of *le plus fort*, which I cannot conceive to be at a great distance.

" They have here a perfect Abercorn *, called M. d'Escars, as

---

* The Earl of Abercorn, who died in the October of the year in which this letter was written, was remarkable for the stiffness and austerity of his manners. He is said to have made the tour of Europe in so *perpendicular* a style as never to have touched the back of his carriage. Though at one part of his life he was much about Court, he never *booed*. When Queen Charlotte landed from Germany, Lord Abercorn had the honour of receiving her at his house, where she and her suite slept. Soon after his Lordship went to St. James's, when his Majesty thanked him for his attention to the Queen, saying, he was afraid her visit had given him a

stiff, as proud, as lean, and as sententious. His coach was
stopped by the mob, and a parcel of dirty *polissons* opened the
door to demand money for bonfires, in honour of the immortal
Necker, *le père du peuple.* ' Allez-vous en,' says he gravely,
' dites de ma part a Monsieur votre père qu'il soigne très mal
ses enfans; vous êtes mal propres, mal habillés, mal nourris, et
surtout tres mal élevés. Allez-vous en et dites lui de ma part
qu'il prenne plus de soin de sa famille a l'avenir.' You must
observe that this sentence was interrupted at every phrase with
snuff, which added to the Spanish solemnity of his deportment.

  "My *sarvis* to your cousin of Londonderry, as he was so civil
to request it; I could not find in my heart to be the dog in the
manger, and to refuse him what he had set his heart upon, and
what could never be of use to me who have not a foot of property in Ireland*. I rejoice that we have taken Grenville out of
the chair†; he was too valuable to ring the dumb-bells in such
a situation now that things are set afloat again. I hold him in

good deal of trouble. "A good deal indeed;" replied his Lordship:
His brother, who was a churchman, once solicited him to apply for a living
which was vacant, and in the gift of the Crown. It was worth near
£.1000 a year. Lord A.'s answer was equally laconic and substantial:
" I never ask any favours; inclosed is a deed of annuity for £.1000."—
He generally visited his seat at Duddingstone, in the vicinity of Edinburgh, once a year, where he remained five or six weeks; but, contrary
to the maxims of Scots hospitality, he was highly offended if any person presumed to visit him without the formality of a card of invitation.
Dr. Robertson, the celebrated historian, not aware of this, went to pay
his respects to the noble Earl, and found him walking in a shrubbery
which had been lately planted. The Doctor, wishing to pay a compliment to the soil, observed the shrubs had grown considerably since his
Lordship's last visit: " They have nothing else to do," replied his Lordship; and immediately turning on his heel, left the Doctor without
uttering another word. These were the peculiarities of his character,
and they were such as made him very unpopular in his native country.
The *Castilian pomp* which he kept up, both at home and abroad, banished
all social intercourse with him; and of late years he was seldom visited
by any but the parson of the parish, who prudently followed the advice
of the Apostle, and became " all things to all men."
  * This alludes to the title of Londonderry. The Earldom having
become extinct in Lord Camelford's cousin Ridgeway Pitt in 1764, Mr.
Hardinge's cousin by marriage, Robert Stewart, Esq. was created Baron
Stewart of Londonderry in 1789. He was advanced to the Earldom in
1796, and to the Marquisate in 1816. His connexion with Mr. Hardinge
was by having married Lady Frances Pratt, niece to Mr. Hardinge's
mother. There has since been another matrimonial alliance between
the families, Alexander-Robert Stewart, Esq. the present Knight in Parliament for the county of Londonderry, and nephew to the first Marquis,
having married in 1825 Lady Caroline-Anne Pratt, niece to Lady Frances.
This union, however, was unhappily short, the lady dying in 1827.—
There has also recently been a more intimate connexion formed between
the Hardinge and the Stewart families, Mr. Hardinge's nephew, the present Sir Henry Hardinge, K.C.B. having married in 1821 his second
cousin, Lady Emily-Jane Stewart.
  † Of Speaker of the House of Commons.

the very highest estimation*; as to his successor † he is very young. What shall be done to the man that the King delighteth to honour? He shall be Secretary of State as long as he pleases, and then Chief Justice in Eyre ‡, with a provision for his son, Baron and Viscount, and what not. I am sorry your brother § falls a victim to the regulations of Lord Cornwallis; his intentions are good, but that is not enough in that station. I give you joy of your important acquisition of a trotting-horse; 'for riding is better than going on foot, which nobody can deny.' We cannot find a dog worthy your acceptance, or any one who will trouble himself with such a companion to bring him to you? What can you want it for? *gaudet equis canibusque.* Ladies desire their compliments."

---

38.   " *Dover, Sept.* 4, 1789.

" We landed here yesterday evening, I from Ostend and the ladies from Calais; but, alas, under what circumstances! The friend of my youth, the friend of forty years, who had at a moment's warning left every thing to accompany me ten years ago to Naples, and who had, though in an infirm state of health, taken the trouble to join us at Paris, was struck with palsy in the packet boats, taken out speechless and senseless, and is probably at this moment expiring. Whenever this melancholy scene is closed, I shall come on to Charles-street, Berkeley-square, to General Cowper's, where I shall be happy to see you; and to assure you of the truth, with which I am faithfully yours,   CAMELFORD."

---

39.   " *Boconnoc, Oct.* 11, 1789.

" ' Whoever has the smallest discernment cannot but perceive that the pamphlet attributed to Lord Camelford, from which an extract has been made in your Paper, must have been written by a Frenchman and a Parisian, not only from the style, but from the persons alluded to, and the local applications contained in it; but as this publication has been at last fixed upon, to give appearance of reality to a report originally propagated without the least foundation, and for purposes best known to those who invented it, you are authorised to assure the public, that Lord Camelford is not the author of this, or of any other publication upon the subject of French politics. This production was received with too general an applause at Paris, both from its wit and argument, not to have its real author suspected; it was

---

* This was written about three years before Lord Grenville became Lord Camelford's son-in-law.
† Mr. Addington, now Lord Viscount Sidmouth.
‡ Lord Sydney, on resigning the office of Secretary of State, was appointed Chief Justice in Eyre.
§ Sir Richard Hardinge, Bart.

118   ILLUSTRATIONS OF LITERATURE.

published before the Revolution, and before Lord Camelford came to Paris.'

" If you and the good General do not disapprove, let this be inserted in the Evening Post, and in any other papers you please; and the sooner the better. We got here yesterday and found your letter."

---

40.   " *Boconnoc, Nov.* 17, 1789.

" As to Johnson, I have often heard of a man writing and speaking himself down; but surely this is the first instance of a man so completely written down by his own friends. It is a pleasant trait of her Grace of Argyll; perhaps she would have said the same of Mrs. Belamy.

" Your character of E———— is like one of Titian's colouring; one knows it to be like, even though one had never known the original.

" I shall be glad to see the work of M. de Nivernois, if it answers at all to the specimen you have sent me. The truth is that, as Mr. Horace Walpole always thinks in French, he ought never to write in English; and I dare be sworn Nivernois' translation will appear much the more original work of the two *.

" I have been reading the account of the Island of Ceylon, only because you repeatedly asked to borrow it of me; it contains an account of kings with tails, and crocodiles with four eyes; and if you have not met with it, I will, upon the faith of Dr. Akenside, save you that trouble. I have read what is much more curious, but which also you need not read, the dialogues out of the Shanscrit, transmitted by Mr. Hastings. It is so obscure that I can believe its antiquity to be as remote as they please; yet in my opinion there are striking things in it, and, if nothing else, a *resemblance* to other things that is very surpris-

---

* Horace Walpole's " History of the Modern Taste in Gardening," was first printed at Strawberry Hill in 1771, attached to the fourth volume of the " Anecdotes of Painting," &c. It was re-printed, with a translation by the Duc de Nivernois, in 1785, at Strawberry Hill, in 4to.—The Duke had acquired a taste for English literature during an Embassy to this country in 1763. He collected many valuable books during his stay; and, besides translating Lord Orford's Essay, he wrote a Panegyrick upon Captain Cook. These and his other miscellaneous works (Ouvres Melées du Citoyen Mancini Nivernois, 1767) were printed at Paris in 4 vols. 8vo. His mission to England was to treat of peace in September 1763. " The first night of his arrival he slept at Canterbury, where his bills for twelve persons amounted to nearly £.45, and the wine to 11s. a bottle, for which extortion the innkeeper was deservedly reprobated by all his customers. When the Duke appeared on the Royal Exchange, he was attended by an amazing crowd, which he took as a compliment. Having executed his commission, his Excellency returned to Paris in May following, with his Majesty's picture set in diamonds." He died at Paris, at the age of 81, after only six days illness, Feb. 26, 1798. He retained his pleasant and amiable temper to the last, and on the very day he died made verses for his physician. Gent. Mag. vol. LXVIII. p. 355.

ing. Its purpose is evidently to correct the errors of previous revelation, and to do away the force of enjoined ceremonies by substituting real piety and morality to superstition and bigotry.

" I am sick in mind more than in body; and you will not wonder when I tell you that, for different reasons,—partly because he is rendered more independent by the death of a relation, partly because he is grown weary of the constraint of such a charge, my son's tutor is going to leave me. As it is a point decided with me, not to send him to school *, and as a tutor who is to have the charge not only of teaching him, but the far more important one of forming him, and who consequently must devote his whole time and attention to him, is not very easy to find, you will imagine I am under no small anxiety till I have been able to make my arrangements. I wish for this reason I could make it convenient to be in the land of the living, but know not how to compass it, as the plan is laid to remain here till towards the meeting of Parliament; and in truth the weeks pass so quickly by me that I only dread the time of my departure to the realms of sin and sea-coal.

" Lady Camelford joins in kind compliments to both of you. Write me of politics. We know nothing of what passes the other side the Tamur."

————

41.   " *Boconnoc, Nov.* 24, 1789.

" I will not venture to criticise any of your verses †, for fear you should say as the French do, *faites mieux.* 1 wait with impatience for the conclusion; in the mean time I will only say, that, though upon the whole I like your Latin better than your English, there are several excellent lines, and many very much in the manner of Dryden.

" In answer to the home question you put to me about Holwood ‡, I will put your heart at rest by saying, that your name did occur, and that there was a very honourable testimony both to your talents and to your personal qualities ; and you have no reason to think the wind blows cold from that quarter. You know, however, I have always told you, that you must depend upon yourself for the importance you may acquire in the public, which is the only sure way to obtain consideration with Ministers, such as tends to advancement in your profession. *Sis faber fortunæ tuæ.* Adieu ! "

---

* Will not many a reader be inclined to exclaim, on his thoughts being led to this youth's future fate, *Hinc fons et origo malorum !*

† An imitation of Ovid's Metamorphoses.

‡ The residence of Mr. Pitt, then Premier.

42.   *" Boconnoc, Dec. 5, 1789 *.*

"Why to be sure for a prudent *faber* I must own you did most cleverly in making at one stroke two powerful enemies where your interest was so much concerned to have made two friends. Do not call it frankness, but frank indiscretion, as you might have been silent, and contented yourself with the inferior triumph of knowing yourself in the right without insisting upon appearing so; there is the plague of it, because you disdain to be false as the new Baronet to court the smiles of fortune, you indulge yourself in spurning all access to her favours by a silence that prudence approves, and that the strictest morality cannot disapprove. Go to — be wiser another time, or you will marr all that good talents, a fair character, and professional merit may justly entitle you to. You must now wait for a new Chancellor for your preferment. Can you say, as my favourite Cardinal Bernis, when a young Abbé, said to the Cardinal Fleury octagenaire, or rather nonagenaire, who said he should never rise whilst he lived, ' Monsieur, je saurois attendre.'

"The trait of our lord and master is curious, and marks his information and sagacity. I am very much pleased with your silhouette of Calonne. I know him by your outline as well as by a finished miniature. I would not give you a farthing for a portrait of me that you intended I should see; but if I could intercept one that was intended only to be seen by Mrs. Hardinge, I should look into it as a mirror.

"None of your Whig nonsense to me about the French revolution; madness and knavery, fanaticism and cruelty, are the principles of them all, from the leaders in their Senate to their butchers in the streets. Let them not talk of liberty till they have learned the elements of justice, or of magnanimity till they are sensible to the dictates of humanity. They will go on from violence to violence, and from absurdity to absurdity, till common sense comes into fashion again at last, and things are brought back again into their old channel.

"If you will be a Whig, let it be in Brabant, where they have something to say for themselves. My heart bleeds for them, when tyranny drives them to the wall; and no alternative is left them for safety but the *ultima ratio*, with all its consequences. I hope the accounts are exaggerated from thence; but I know enough of the temper of both sides to believe in the most horrid carnage."

* Indorsed by Mr. Hardinge, " A good-humoured banter upon Mr. Hardinge's political indiscretion."

43.   " *Dec.* 17, 1789 *.

" Indeed, my dear friend, I feel a very sincere pleasure in
your having acquitted yourself so much to your satisfaction
upon so important an occasion.   It was just one of those opportunities which are the golden moments of reputation; and I
wish with all my heart I could have been present at your
triumph.   I return you Pitt's two letters, as I am persuaded
you will like to keep them.   If you follow my advice, you will
recollect the heads of your speech, and tie it up with them; and
by all means insert it truly in the Parliamentary Register, that
they may not spoil it and transmit your opinions falsely to posterity.   I do not wonder Pitt was happy to avail himself of
your talents at such a moment, or that he sets a proper value
upon the little mouse when all the rats are running away from
him.   What honour his conduct does him all over Europe!
In truth, whatever mischief may accrue to the country by this
resolution, his fame is carried to the pinnacle by the circumstances attending it, and which he has known so well how to
avail himself of.   If some rich Citizen or news-reading Squire
does not leave him an estate before the twelvemonth is over, I
shall say there is not a spark of public spirit left in the country.
Fox has been bewitched to play the game into his hands; and I
begin to agree with a wise by-stander in England, who asserted,
that with all his parts he has not sense, or he would never get
into the scrapes he does, and defeat himself for ever of his
own objects.   Pray Heaven what you hint at may prove true,
and the sooner the better!   You cannot think how much you
have made your court to the Baroness, as well as me, by the
intelligence you send us; she is politician, *dans les formes*, and
as a proof of it, sends you an extract from the Mercure de
France, which she wishes you to contrive to get inserted as an
extract in the English papers.   I want no argument to convince
me of the right of Parliament to appoint and to limit the Regency; and as to precedent, there can be no danger in establishing the power of doing or not doing, whatever the expediency of the times may render at the moment most advise-
able.   In this case, the expediency points out some limitations;
in another case, more or less power may be expedient; but we
may safely trust this to the discretion of future Parliaments, if
ever the melancholy case again occurs.   I wish the battle may
be as well fought by us in the other House; but cannot regret
that I shall have no share in it.   Let the Chancellor and the President try their strength with Lord Loughborough, I fancy
they will be a match for him; and as for Lord H——, who de-
claims by inch of candle, or rather till all the candles are burnt
out, I could not answer him without hearing him; and that
penance my friends, I am sure, will not impose upon me."

* Indorsed by Mr. Hardinge: " An affectionate letter to Mr. Hardinge
at the time of the Regency, commending him for the support he gave to
Mr. Pitt."

44.   " *July* 1, 1790.

" Thank you for your Eton Latinities. When we meet I will
tell you why I do not like them. The letter of which you would
have a copy is not mine to give, and my daughter would think I
used her very ill if I was capable of such a treachery; let it
live, however, in the tablet of your memory. We have had no
letter * since the arriving at the Cape; one came to me that gave
me a false hope, but it was an old one written when he was
going from the Cape towards Botany Bay.

" I have chosen you a bed-fellow that you did not expect; but
if you will come to me I will explain it to you. Nothing is so
easy and natural as a riddle when it is once unfolded.

" Sell your swan's nest if you will not come to it.

" The elections upon the whole are good, but it is no fault
of ours."

---

45.   " *Boconnoc, Nov.* 19, 1790.

" I have this moment finished the gospel of St. Edmund †,
which your enthusiastic encomium had given me additional
curiosity to read. As to style, he, like Shakspeare, touches the
double octave from the sublime to the bathos. In many passages he is divinely eloquent; in some his wit is clean and brilliant, and his quotations remarkably lucky. His argument, with
few exceptions, in my opinion, unanswerable. His work, with
all its faults, does him the highest honour as an author, as a
statesman, and as a moralist. It will do infinite good in France
if it were possible to get it read there; but what is of far
greater moment to us, it will do infinite service to us at home,
in shewing us the danger of metaphysical speculations, and
warning us not to go a-whoring after new inventions.

" It seems as if the world was always to go round in its circle,
least it should happen at any time to fix in a medium of common sense and common happiness. Ignorance and superstition produced the miseries of ages within our recollection; the
opposite extremes to which all Europe is tending, point to evils
full as great on the other hand, which I fear must afterwards
throw us back again into barbarism and its concomitant, ignorant superstition. We may reason and refine for our amusement, if we please in our closet, till we can distinguish no
longer between right and wrong, and at last doubt of our own
existence; but when once a people undertake to think for themselves, and to admit no principle they cannot prove logically and
mathematically, sense becomes nonsense, and all practical ideas
of social connection are at an end all together. Our religious
and our political opinions (prejudices, if you please to call them
so,) must be taken up and maintained upon trust by at least 999

---

* From his son.
† Burke's " Reflections on the Revolution in France."

in 1000, or the Lord have mercy upon us. Well, said the old French philosopher, that if he had all truths in his hand, he would die a thousand deaths before he would open it. The modern philosophers let out all, truth and falsehood together, to set mankind by the ears from one end of the globe to the other. I would tell them, that it requires but little genius to triumph over prejudices, but the proof of real understanding is shewn in respecting them, and directing them at the same time to the happiness of our fellow-creatures.

"Now you have read Burke's book you should read Calonne's *, if you have not already read it. It is not general, metaphysical, and entertaining like Edmund's, but it is the state of facts with very judicious reasonings upon them, a lively, and sometimes, eloquent style, and the advantage of one who treats his subject *en parfaite connoissance de cause.* I confess I am much staggered with regard to the author, whom I certainly was not taught to respect when I was in France, whilst I see him calling upon his enemies, who are in the situation to have every proof in their possession, and defying them to produce a single instance that would criminate his public gestion.

" I have run on till I have filled my paper. I have only to add, that we are expecting soon to part with our dear boy, and endeavouring to fortify our minds for the trial. Thank God the dangers of war are no longer to be superadded to those of the sea ; that is at least some consolation. The campaign at Westminster is soon to open. Scribble me now and then I pray, a few illegible lines in a committee-room, which I shall trust more in than in Woodfall's Diary."

---

46. *Answer from M. Dupont to Mr. Burke,*
By LORD CAMELFORD.

" My very good patron and friend Mr. Burke,
Give me leave to return you my thanks for the work;
Which in form of a letter to me † you address,
Though I'd rather it had not been sent to the press ;
For between you and me, I took it for granted,
When I ask'd your advice 't would be such as I wanted.
When I wrote I had made up my mind to a tittle,
But I fancied your credit would grace us a little ;
And having disjointed some parts of your speeches
In the senate, at table, under shade of your beeches ;
I ventur'd to answer for you in our party,
To the cause of mob-ocracy, zealous and hearty.
Oh could I have guess'd the advantage you 've taken,
You had saved yourself trouble, and we sav'd our bacon ;

* " Lettre sur l'Etat de la France, present et avenir."
† " Letter to M. Dupont, a Member of the National Assembly," 1791.

For tho' we'd fain put a good face on the matter,
You have dealt us a blow that still makes our teeth chatter.
Where argument fails you will not think it strange,
If we try in defence *de vous donner le change.*
Now here is our logic, short, pithy, and clear,
Which by help of the Lantern convinces all here—
" A King is a tyrant, who rules without law,
Ergo Kings should be nothing but robes stuff'd with straw;"
Who thinks that some medium might safely be hit on,
Is a slavish Aristocrat, Frenchman, or Briton.
And to raise the least hope that a King should have sway,
In whatever degrees, is no less than to say,
That all we have done is a mere usurpation,
And pray what becomes of the *crime de leze nation ?*
Again ; if in union strong counsels we see,
How should four of a trade e'er be made to agree?
By such balancing pow'rs we might be done,
So we voted to throw all the monsters in one.
Dukes, taylors, and bishops, Turks, Christians, and Jews,
The nightman, the hangman, (for none we refuse,)
May sit in one Senate, all equal in voice,
Whilst Mesdames de la Halle help to make up the noise.
This model so perfect of representation,
Express at one vote the whole sense of the nation.
Now consider, my friend, for I know you are good,
Could you change such a system, it must be by blood.
Sure the horrors we practice, whilst none dare oppose,
Might suffice without stirring contention or blows;
Who wishes for victims may glut his desire,
With " purifications by blood and by fire;"
But let us go on, and you'll find by degrees,
That all will slide back in their places with ease.
The æra we date from (we boast it with reason)
Was the day when first Paris broke out into treason;
When wild with alarms of ourselves knew not what,
Law and justice we banish'd, and pity forgot.
When our monarch, abandoned and led like a slave,
Was dragg'd forward to make his *amende* at the *gréve ;*
His arsenals plundered, his servants dismay'd,
His officers butcher'd, his fortress betray'd.
From that glorious epoch our happiness springs,
And blest Anarchy rules on the throne of our Kings.
   But be not imputed to us that are sober,
The scandalous scenes of the fifth of October;
That was all a mere mob of the fishwomen risen,
To send her to Heaven and her husband to prison
The nation is shock'd when such outrage they hear,
Tho' they think it as safe they should stay where they are;

And now to be frank at the risk of my fame,
I must own in some points we perhaps are to blame.
We have rescued the nation, but ruin'd the people,
And have left of the church little more than the steeple;
Nay, the fabrics have much useless cost still about them,
The primitive worship did better without them.
We melt down our bells, reams of paper we coin,
And use, as in desperate case, antimoine;
Yet all our expedients but add to the evil,
Our money and credit are gone to the devil.
What then? a portfolio is lighter than bags,
And the priests pray with ten times more fervour in rags;
Our multiplied wheels make a d——d constitution,
But that may be cured by some new revolution.
We've freedom; who doubts it? but then, to be sure,
Our lives and our goods there's no law to secure;
Or if there is law, *c'est la loi du plus fort*,
And the great *droits de l'homme* will admit of no more.
Europe laughs in her sleeve, and enjoys our disgraces,
Our troops and our seamen laugh out in our faces;
But our *national milice* need give no alarms,
For whenever we bid them they'll lay down their arms.
It is true we can't always enforce our decrees,
And the people obey them as much as they please;
But gar civil war, that would weaken us wholly,
And throw the whole state into madness and folly.
Besides, these are trifles scarce worthy to mention,
What system's complete *dans la première intention?*
Have patience, have patience, and give us fair play,
You all know that Rome was not built in a day.
    As for me, I confess it with joy and surprise,
I'm so dazzled with light that I shut both my eyes;
Such flashes of genius, such rapid decisions,
Such destruction of convents, of peers, and of pigeons!
The whole feudal rights, with poor old mother Church,
Out of breath we leave cold common sense in the lurch.
The sages of Greece should come hither to school,
What was Solon? a dotard! Lycurgus? a fool!
To pull to the ground the past wisdom of ages,
Was the work of a very few months to our sages;
Half that time, as you know, at the most it requires,
To build in its stead what their wisdom inspires.
Distant nations shall bear our establishments home,
And our Lantern shall shine to guide ages to come.
    But it's time to conclude, and I hope no offence,
For all I have said is by way of defence;
Tho' I fear we no longer are birds of a feather,
I trust we may still drink a bottle together.
Your wine's always good; I'll come over in spring,
And I'll pledge any toast—but the Church and the King."

47.   *" Boconnoc, Dec.* 25, 1790.

" I have read only half your speech in the Diary; and cannot help thinking, *que l'enfant dit vrai* as to the impeachment being abated.   It is a foolish scrape the House of Commons have got into only to give Burke the pleasure of hunting Hastings; there is but one way of getting out of it, which is an Act of Parliament to allow Burke to follow his diversion, whether Hastings is alive or dead, whether Parliament sits or not, as long as it is an amusement.   If, however, Hastings is at last to be hanged for *saving India,* I hope Lord Guilford * will be entitled to put the rope round his neck for having lost America.   The whole proceeding, from beginning to end, is a disgraceful business; and all Europe cries shame at it.   It is an unlucky thing that the Minister is the dupe of his feelings in all this, as he is in the Slave Trade and other instances; and it is unlucky for you that you are to stand forward to shew him that he is mistaken, which is a compliment never very ingratiating.   Nothing is more grand than to say, ' If the King can abate (for I like the word) an impeachment by a dissolution, there is an end of the great privilege of the House of Commons; the first authorities say it.' I am stupid enough not to understand it.   If one Parliament is dissolved, another must immediately succeed : if they think as the former one did, they impeach again, and with double violence; nothing is gained by it.   If they think differently, why then, whether it is continuing an old impeachment, or constituting a new one, it will be the same protection to the accused; in the one case they will drop the prosecution, in the other they will forbear from renewing it by a fresh impeachment ; I do not see, therefore, what difference it makes as to the responsibility of Ministers, or the privileges of the Commons.   It is true, if a prosecution has been malignantly turned into a persecution, through the course of seven years, it will be a little difficult to go on with it any longer if they are to begin again *de novo,* as the keenest sportsman will not bring himself to run so much ground again.   But, as I avow myself to be one of those who would rather give up the chace before half the disgrace of such a pursuit had stained the annals of my country, even though it should give impunity to the delinquent, I feel that argument the most powerful one in the world, to renounce the privilege, if you had it, of continuing such a vexation.

" What a sportsman are you,
With the game still in view,
　To be stopp'd by a mere legal cavil !
Burke, astride his great horse,
Scorns to check his free course,
　And will follow his game—to the devil."

* Lord North, having been Prime Minister for twelve years, resigned in 1782. He succeeded his father as Earl of Guilford in 1790, and survived him only two years.

46.   *" Boconnoc, Jan. 3, 1791.*

" I have read your speech more than once, and must confess your observations upon the only precedents that exist, and upon the opposite resolutions of the House of Lords, are conclusive with me, that impeachments do not revive again *in statu quo* after a dissolution. The more I have thought of the question the more I am persuaded that they ought not to do so. Had I been in the House of Commons, I should have given my voice with you, and all the great law authorities in that House; and, had the Minister lost the question, and attempted to alter the law, as I think it now stands, by a new Act of Parliament for that purpose, I should have voted to reject it upon the first reading, as disliking the principle of it. After all this you will be surprised to hear that, if you had consulted me, I should have dissuaded you from publishing any pamphlet * upon the subject now the Commons have pledged themselves to it; and that, if I were in the House of Lords at the time that matter is discussed, I should certainly vote against my opinion, and against what I believe to be the law, rather than tempt at this time a dispute between the two Houses upon a matter of privilege, which, to that extent, will, I trust, never be brought forward twice in a century. Peaceful and cordial union in all the branches of the legislature, forms, at all times, the strength of the empire; but at this crisis it is essential to its existence. This is no time for the Peers to oppose a claim, however mistaken, that is supposed to interest the liberty and privilege of the subject, or rather of the people; for in fact the question, well considered, does endanger the liberty and rights of the individual,—but then it is a great ministerial individual always, who is of course accounted in the opposite scale to that of the people. Send me, however, your pamphlet as soon as it comes abroad. You cannot have a better adviser than Scott †; and in truth you can walk alone in such a case as this without leading-strings.

" I am sorry our capricious Chancellor has turned short upon his own opinions, to send us to the devil ‡. As to right and wrong in matter of law, I have long known that it is a joke, and that Lord Mansfield's Governor of Barbadoes was the only judge that held to any system whatever, as long as he adhered to his Lordship's advice of ' heads or tails ? ' for the forming his decisions. I would rather trust to chance, for the security of my property, than to all the law of Westminster-hall put together.

" I must tell you, that Lady Camelford last night was reading your speech, and when she came to the Judges and Scroggs

---

* In 1791 Mr. Hardinge published "A Series of Letters to Mr. Burke, in which are contained inquiries into the Constitutional existence of an Impeachment against Mr. Hastings."

† Major Scott, M. P.

‡ In the law-suit in which Lord Camelford was engaged.

at the head of them, she exclaimed: 'I never heard of them before; what are the Scroggs?' concluding they were the Judges of some Court in Westminster-hall that she had never been told of. Vale."

———————

49   " 1791.

" *Ha sputata la sententia,* as the Italians say when a man has indulged himself in speaking what prudence would have bid him hold his tongue about. I have the satisfaction, however, to hear, that as Counsel for the Plaintiff you made an excellent speech, and was much admired; and as to the rest I have defended you the best I could when I have heard you attacked, by swearing myself black in the face, that I believed you spoke your own opinion. If you converted Wilberforce, you have no small glory to boast; but I, who converse as much with those who are out of Parliament as those who are in it, can assure you, that you are never more mistaken than in thinking that Hastings's cause is in the present moment (whatever it may be hereafter) unpopular, particularly in the article of the Rohilla war. A division of two to one, without the solicitations of the Minister, who I trust does not feel it a party question on his side, and if he did, would not dare to avow it, rather confirms my notion than yours; but in truth I have met with very few of the indifferent persons I converse with, who do not look upon the persecutions of Hastings in return for meritorious services with abhorrence.

" To come to something nearer home, and upon which we shall have no difference of opinion. My Bill is committed in the House of Commons for Wednesday; in the mean time Sargent * is slipped through our hands, and gone back to his wife at Abergavenny. We have sent a copy of the will after him, that he may sign it and send it back in time by some one who can attest the signature; he has signed the Petition to the House of Lords and has appeared there to give his consent in person; yet unless you can prevail with the Committee to dispense with his appearance, we must be put off till next Session. I must pay another £.200; and perhaps be brought back from the South of France, or from the other side the Alps to say, Aye.

My coach is finished. Petersham† is let to your friend J. J. Hamilton. Winterbottom tells me, he shall be ready with every thing for me in a very few days to sign. I know nothing that hangs, except that we cannot get the decree settled and enrolled. I understand there are some commas and colons, or semicolons, under your inspection; dispatch them, if you love me dispatch them !

"I hope your poor woman continues mending. Possibly we may meet in the hot caldron of St. James's to-morrow; in the mean time I send this by an opportunity to London."

———————

* John Sargent, Esq. was elected M. P. for Seaford in 1790, made Clerk of the Ordnance in 1794, and re-elected for Queenborough.
† Lord Camelford's house at that place.

30.   *" Brussels, Aug.* 12, 1791.

" You love news from the parts beyond the seas. What shall
I write to you ? the wild conjectures of the wretched fugitives,
who are under the sad alternative of starving here, or being
murdered in their own country ? Every hour begets some new
tale more improbable and ridiculous than the former. What *is*
but too probable because too true, is the sad catalogue of horrors committed and committing every day in that devoted kingdom. I live here with those who are the near kindred, or the
commensales, of those unhappy victims, who talk of their tragedies as of facts within their own knowledge, in which some
have borne a part. One of these gentlemen describes the sufferings of one of his neighbours, stifled in the cellar he had
retreated to with wet straw ; another the fate of a castle taken
by storm, where the owner had his eyes torn out, and was tor-
mented eleven hours before they finished him. Convents forced ;
and after having been given up to the brutal lust of the popu-
lace, scourged till the blood streamed from them, and then
dragged in derision by the hair of their heads, through the river
to wash them clean, and receiving such treatment as cost many
of them their lives. The gentry of Britanny hiding themselves
in the woods, and shot at by the peasants as wild beasts whenever they appear ; whilst their wives and children, together with
the nonjuring clergy, are thrown into the common jail at
Renne, whence they are taken out every evening, to afford
sport to their persecutors, set upon asses, and led in triumph
through the streets. There is no company you can go into,
where some such stories are not authenticated ; and these scenes
are acting more or less all over the extent of the empire. In
the mean time they talk of the assistance of Austria and of
Spain as of a thing at hand that is to work their deliverance ;
but you know how easily they run away with an idea, *et que le
cheval toujours les emporte.* It is said that, when the Royal
Family were brought back, the children were much affected ;
the daughter, who is *très hautaine,* was in despair, and when the
little Dauphin was separated from his mother, that his shrieks
and cries were dreadful. He sees her only once a day ; he said
to her the other day, ' Mais, maman, pourquoi ne venez vous
plus chez moi, vous qui veniez si souvent, qui m'aimiez tant ?
Je ne suis point méchant ; si je l'étois, je l'aurai merité ; mais je
suis bon. Venez de grace comme de coutume ; je n'ai d'autre
plaisir que de vous voir.' Both the children when they were
separated said, ' Grace pour papa, grace pour maman ! ne leurs
faites point de mal !' The whole scheme of the escape was frustrated by a delay of two hours. The aid-de-camp thought the
project had failed, quitted Chalons, where he was sent to wait
for them, did not give notice to the escort who were waiting
for that notice, by which means they were suffered to take some
repose after their fatigue, and could not be assembled in force

upon the King's arrival till it was too late. The King and
Queen thought themselves safe at Varennes, and told M. de Da-
mas, 'que le peuple etoit bon;' they were soon undeceived by
being told they must return to Paris, and that they were under
arrest. When the news of their flight was first announced to
La Fayette, he said coldly, drawing on his boots, ' Ce sera donc
un jour bien orageux.' The adventure of Madame de Coigny
is a comedy; *democrate enragée*, she chose to exhibit herself in
Carousal to see the triumph of the King's return. In the fulness
of her heart, ' Ce seroit bien hardi dans ce moment a quelqu'n
qui oseroit crier, Vive le Roi.' A lad near her hearing the last
words, turned round, and heard them repeated ; he immediately
gave the alarm, she was instantly hustled by the crowd. ' Moi,
messieurs, aristocrate ? mais j'ai toujours été le Chevalier de la
Democratic.' ' Chevalier! non, Madame, il n'y a plus de Che-
valiers en France! a la lantherne.' Rescued at last with her
clothes torn from her back, and some say, *fouttée d'importance*,
she found herself under the guard of the *soldats nationaux* in
the palace, where she gave vent to her tears. ' Comment, Madame, vous pleurez ! pourquoi pleurez-vous ? Croyez-vous que
nous sommes des barbares ?' ' Non, Messieurs, je ne pleure pas
du tout; non, Messieurs, je vous assure.' ' Tant pis, Madame,
il vous conviendrait mieux.' ' Eh bien! Messieurs, donc s'il faut
dire vrai, je pleurs de tout mon cœur.' ' Et comment donc,
Madame, qu'avez vous a craindre de nous ?' ' Oh, Messieurs,
rien du tout, rien du tout; c'est que je pleurs par reconnaissances
de toutes vos bontés.' You may believe that she is now become
aristocrate comme un diable.

" I think I told you, whenever you write, to send your letters
to Ransom, Morland, and Hammersley, who will always know
how to forward them. We shall leave this place in about a
week, and then remove to Spa for a few days; and after that,
pursue our route along the Rhine, *tout a notre aise*. The ladies
desire their compliments."

---

51.   " *Dusseldorff, Sept.* 4, 1791.
" Yesterday, where we changed horses, between this and
Juliers, there was a German boobyhutch which contained a
croix de St. Louis, an elderly, lean, ill-dressed lady, and a Curé,
whose wild and uncertain carriage soon announced a disordered
brain. We got acquainted in a moment, for where the heart is
full the mouth speaketh. ' My husband, whom you see there,
said she, ' is the Commandant at Calais, and that is my unfortunate brother. We are all ruined by the Revolution ; but my
poor brother, who has been stripped of every thing because his
conscience would not suffer him to swear against his opinion,
has been driven by his misfortunes into insanity. We have
fetched him from Hanover, to which place he had wandered on

foot in the utmost distress. We ourselves have scarce the means of subsistence, though we content ourselves for our provision in our journey with a loaf of bread, which we put into our basket, with a bottle of wine and water mixed. We are going on to Aix without stopping, that we may save the expence of a lodging on the road; and afterwards we know not whither, for we fear it will be impossible for us to get back to our own country; and indeed it will be the death of my poor brother if he should be witness to any further disturbances. As misfortunes multiply upon our heads, I have had the additional one of having had my leg broken by an overturn in this disastrous journey, and still suffer from the consequence of it.'

" The tears stood in our eyes, as she told her melancholy story with a feeling, and at the same time a simplicity, that gave force to every word. I followed the Commandant as soon as he left the room; and taking him aside, told him how much I was touched with so much complicated distress, and putting my purse into his hand, begged he would not refuse me the real pleasure I should feel if he would allow me to remove the inconvenience of the moment by facilitating their journey to Aix; that he need not have the smallest delicacy about it, as he might regard it as a debt which he should repay me one day or other when we might meet at Calais in happier times. His countenance glowed with the most generous expression of gratitude, and he thanked me over and over again, but it was impossible to make him accept my offer; on the contrary, he went back to the company to give vent to his feelings with a warmth, which he communicated to his fellow travellers, and which quite put me out of countenance. We took a kind leave of each other, and went our different ways; but the idea of that distressed family has haunted me ever since. What fruits of ' the most glorious fabric ever erected by human integrity !' The evening before we left Aix, the children of one of our friends had been walking out with their tutor, and had seen another instance of an expatriated Curé, who had fallen down exhausted with fatigue and famine, whom they were endeavouring to call back to life, but he was no longer able to receive the sustenance they fetched to him. When many of their proudest Prelates are reduced to an income of £.40 or £.50 per annum, what must be the subsistence of those whose state of prosperity was not more, and who are bereft even of that !

" You will see by the inclosed, that all this was predicted above two centuries ago by the prophet Nostradamus. The Bishop of Rennes, who gave me the paper, compared it with the three editions, and found it exact. Pray let Cambridge see it. I think it should be in the papers; it is really very extraordinary. If you know any body going to see the gallery here, tell them not to suffer the postilion to bring them the short way in open boats, but the longer way by the Pont volant."

" Rome, Nov. 5, 1791,
52.   *where we burn neither the Pope nor the Pretender.*

"Upon my word you have made a pretty tour upon the outside of your horse, and a very pretty sketch you have sent me of it.

"Other cares take hold of you by this time. Know ye by these presents, that I have read Mr. Long's promissory note to the artists upon my arrival, and that they are upon the tip-toe of expectation, and that I shall be the most disgraced and mortified of men if I do not receive from you the Act of Parliament, passed in due form for their relief, before I leave this place; *pensez y.* Whenever you come into fair Italy, be sure you take the route as I did, of Stutgard, Augsburgh, Munich, and the Tirol, to Bologna, when you may either pay your devotions to the Santacasa, or visit the lake of Thrasymene, as your choice directs you. Those who do the thing completely, take Saltzburgh in their way from Munich to Inspruck, which is, I am told, well worth while. What a succession of magnificent natural beauties have I passed through, with scarce any intermission, from Stutgard to within two posts of this interesting place, that stands in the most insipid of all possible campagnas. In the middle of the Tirol, at a little post, up comes the courier, ' It is impossible to dine here, there is nothing to be had, not even a room; we must go on—the whole house is taken up with a *fete de noce.*' ' So much the better,' said I. Up went we to the top of the house, following the noise of the fiddles and tabors. Such a ball, such dresses, such dances, such gold-laced jackets for the men, such piqued Queen Mary caps for the women; then the allemandes, the volses, the farlanas; it was a world to see! Presents were immediately found for the bride, and hung round her neck; the bridegroom took out my daughter, and twisted her round in an allemande. In the garden was a table spread for us in a kind of arbour, and served with *cocs de bruyere,* and I believe the Phenicopteras. Opposite our arbour a perpendicular rock, 500 feet high; at the bottom of which rolled the liquid chrystal of the Adige, overhung by steep shaggy mountains, richly clothed, and thrown into the boldest masses of light and shade, as the sun illumined one part or was intercepted by another. In the midst of our repast, came the bride and bridegroom, with the bride-cake, preceded by music, and followed by the guests in orderly procession. I never spent a pleasanter hour in five-and-fifty years, that I have been a seeker of adventures on this little globe. Why was you not with us!

"Far other were my feelings when about forty or fifty miles from hence. We passed in the evening, among a branch of the Appennines, a small village, that had but a few days before been overturned by an earthquake. The secret was kept from the ladies till the next day; but the clamourous importunity of the poor wretches that followed us, breaking out of their hiding places, where they had betaken themselves upon their houses threatening ruin, still rings in my ears. The Curé told me, whilst we were changing horses, there were but two habitations that were not in ruins ; and the people were totally left without resources, unless the Pope should send them some immediate relief.

"Rome is *tale quale* as it was, except that the society, which I formerly delighted in, is no longer to be found in it; even in my friend the good Cardinal Bernis, who is *cerasé* by the Revolution. The Mesdames are accompanied by a French colony, who are thrown into despair by the dereliction of those powers who are too politic to have generous feelings. In their policy they may be also mistaken; and in that case, if they should be the only sufferers, who would not say they deserve it ? If you are tempted to read any thing upon the subject, send for a very small tract addressed to the Corps Helvetique, attributed to the late Ambassador M. de Verac ; and for an Analyse of the Constitution, by M. de Clermont Tonnere. The first gives me a very true picture of the history of the Revolution ; the other, a very judicious criticism upon the ' noblest work of human integrity.'

" As to your friend Collins *, as long as our Constitution lasts, he has no chance of any preferment for his six children, till he becomes a *citoyen actif* in one of our *municipalities,* commonly called boroughs, which will be a better recommendation than all your nonsense of suffering merit and genius, which is nothing to the purpose *dans ce meilleur des mondes possibles.*

" We have had letters from the young Argonaut † at the Cape. ' Well and happy.' Adieu ! "

_____

53.　　　　　　　　　　　　*" Rome, Feb. 3, 1792.*

" Our dear General's partiality for every thing he loves can never be satisfied with any limit whilst there is a *plus ultra* to look forward to. His son does himself honour and his country service.

" You are kindly welcome to my ten guineas for your protegée; you have served mine too zealously not to have acquired that right over me. If I had £.60,000 upon the nail every year hard money, as the great B——— has, I would rather spend £.700 to make a near relation happy than £.7,000 upon a gold tea urn to make myself ridiculous; *mais c'est une affaire de gout.*

" If Pitt is abused for giving the parks to a brother Minister to keep him from starving whenever he shall be out of place, and that upon the resignation of a patent, which gave him the reversion of something of twice the value, I conclude the abuse hinges, as you call it, upon the moderate *quantum* of the pro-

_____

* The Rev. John Collins, of whom see a memoir in vol. III. p. 839.
† His Lordship's son.

vision, which, if I were Pitt, should be doubled some way or other, or I should think I had given scanty measure.

" Apropos to Ministers. I am all impatience to know that the Bill is brought in for my artists. I have read to them Mr. Long's promise, and they are all agog.

" I like your Indian war no better than you; God send us safe out. You will have a boisterous Session, but you have a strong vessel and a good crew; we shall weather that and others I trust before we put into harbour. The politics of our neighbours seem to be on the eve of some crisis. I have not read Burke's letter to the Emperor, nor the Empress of Russia's to the Pope, nor Burke's defence of the Papal rights, *sur le Comtat d'Avignon.* The wonders of the present times go on *crescendo.* Two stories I heard yesterday, which were new to me, perhaps will be so to you. Soon after the Revolution, a taciturn countryman of ours sitting at Paris at a great dinner next to an Abbé de Villeneuve, had long borne with all the impertinent nonsense of the day without a word, *en bon ou en mal.* At length the Abbé, determined to force his entrenchments, addressed himself directly to him : ' Monsieur, on dit que vous approuvez infinement chez vous tout ce que nous venons de faire;' a nod of the head ; ' et que vous commencez a croire que quelque changement pourroit se faire en Angleterre pour vous approcher en peu plus de notre constitution;' a silent stare; ' enfin on dit que vous vous etes determiné a declarer l'égalitié parfaite et d'abolir votre chambre des Pairs.' John immediately seized the arms of the democrat with a hard gripe, and looking him full in the face, and with a loud voice that all the ladies might hear, ' Monsieur l'Abbé, l'Anglois qui vous a dit tout cela se foutoit de vous.'

" Another being pressed by the ladies, and forced to declare what sort of Constitution he thought would be the fittest for France under the present circumstances, answered very composedly, ' Celle de Constantinople pendant six mois.'

" We are going this May-day to the Villa Borghese. Adieu!"

---

54.   " *Rome, March* 21, 1792.

" You are a simpleton to *bouder* and to take it ill that I am a bad correspondent, instead of my writing to every body but you; the fact is, that to some of my friends, whom I do not love the less for all that, I have not written since I left England, whereas to you I have written oftener than you have received my letters. It is so difficult for me to write; for example, yesterday was the first day for many days that my head would suffer me to hold a pen ; my daughter was forced to be my secretary for every note I was obliged to answer. All yesterday, till four o'clock, was taken up at some distance (forty stades from Rome) with a learned antiquary : and the evening at a delicious concert, consisting of two sweet English girls who sing, and of the pleasantest youths I ever saw, who play their brothers; they are all of Kent, and are returning to England, and you must be acquainted with them, and you will love them all as we do, and the father into the bargain. Taylor is the first letter of his name, a clergyman. I never saw such a family. But to return to my morning. What think you of treading the very steps of the Horatii and Curiatii; here stood the altar between the two little camps, upon which the parties swore, the troops ranged on each side—here the friendly warriors took their last embrace—here fell the first of the Horatii, and here the second; their tombs still witnessing the spot which was stained with their blood—here passed the remaining brother, goaded with the reproaches of his despairing countrymen in his wary flight—here the foremost of his adversaries met his fate near the Roman camp, and here the brother at a little distance, and at a still less the third, too much exhausted with fatigue and loss of blood to make his defence. On every spot, a tomb similar in its shape, consisting of a subterraneous vault, with the traces only of the superstructure above ground, ruined by time and the sacrileges of barbarous ignorance. All this is a discovery made by the gentleman who showed it me, who proves his hypothesis beyond a doubt. At a little distance is the proud camp, another discovery of his, where Coriolanus bent his angry brow upon the ungrateful city, marked out as his victim. Here along that path passed the Latian way,—along which came and returned the rejected embassies of pacification—here stood, upon this projecting angle of his Prætorium, where was his Tribune, the inexorable exile, when slowly advanced towards him the female procession—here he rose towards his aged mother; and here, with that imposing dignity which overawed even his haughty spirit, she rejected his tendered homage till he ceased to be the enemy to his country. Here was erected the statue of the Fortuna Muliebris, which answered, 'She was contented with the honours done her by the Roman ladies;' and here (who would believe it?) still exists the pipe from a souterain, where the voice was conveyed to favour the miracles. Close by still exists, in curious workmanship of brick, the very temple dedicated to the Goddess, of which Valeria was made the priestess, in reward for the salutary counsel that had saved her country; and that building which you see about three hundred yards further, of the same architecture, was the tomb of the family of Coriolanus, as appears by the sculpture upon an urn not long since taken from thence, and deposited in the Pope's Musæum. Not one word of all this interesting detail was known when I was last at Rome, nor is now known but to a few friends that M. d'Ancarville takes the trouble to shew it to.

" This letter was begun at six o'clock this morning; it is now near eight in the evening, and I have but just time to close my letter for the post, having not been one moment alone; this is the life we lead. Press the Bill for the Artists, I beseech you; they depend upon it. Adieu! the ladies desire their compliments; and I beg you that, when you do not hear from me, you will not believe me less sincerely and faithfully

"Yours,   CAMELFORD."

55.   "*Brussels, June* 14, 1792.

"I am not at all satisfied with excluding drawings; sculptors, as well as painters, cannot exist without them. Architects have no other studies, and would be excluded from all benefit from the indulgence. Finished drawings stand upon the same footing as paintings; they are the fruits of industrious labour, and the stock in trade for future profit. Is that an object of taxation? Models are in the same description; and more bulky, more expensive, and more necessary for sculptors and architects than even drawings, though both are indispensable. For God's sake why are we to be the only nation in Europe barbarous enough to levy money upon the arts? Let them do the thing handsomely; and not cling to a six and nine-penny profit in an instance where premium should be given instead of discouragement.

"The levellers are known, thank God, and therefore less to be feared; yet we must be vigilant and decisive. I cannot conceive how they can let the Session rise without giving to the Secretaries of State the power of excluding such foreigners as they may judge proper. It is madness to let thieves into your house in order to turn them out afterwards when you catch them with the forks and spoons in their pockets. West wind prevails; no getting over. *Au plaisir de vous revoir.*"

57.   "1792.

"They dare not try the Queen of France, because there is no *corpus delicti*; in the next place, because she is sister to the Emperor. Her defence upon her examination is concise,—*teres atque rotunda*; there is no taking hold of it.

"Te seguitai felice quand era il ciel sereno,
Alle tempeste in seno voglio seguirti encor.

"'I scorned to fly from my husband; it was my duty to fly with him; I obeyed *mon mari et mon souverain.*' 'But the Dauphin?' 'Well; where can the children be but with their father?' This is all they can get from her.

"As to the King, he says, 'I was in prison; and had a right to seek my liberty when I had given it to all my subjects. I was not suffered even to change the air for my health.' 'But who were the advisers?' 'I wanted no adviser to break my prison when I had the opportunity.' 'Who contrived your escape?' 'Those who acted by my order.' 'Who were they?' 'I wont tell you.'

" Stick to that, Louis, and none can hurt you ! The Duke of
Clarence says, he understands they are to send the Queen to
Havre de Grace."

---

57.   " *Florence, Jan.* 8, 1793.

" Here am I reduced to the being *citoyen passif et meme en
etat d'arrestation depuis* 5 *semaines.* Gout in both feet, and all
the miseries that attend it. I am, however, getting better; and
hope soon to get to Pisa, and from thence to Rome. Your letters
found me here. I know not what to say; I trust to the good
sense, or, if you will, to the prejudices of our countrymen, that
the tree of liberty will not easily strike root with us. Ministers
are hereby truly in a whimsical situation; if they do nothing
in such times, and mischief overtakes us, they will be stoned
in the streets; and, what is more, they will deserve it ! If they
interfere, whatever precaution they take is a cause of clamour.
Every body can find fault; but I suppose of all the niceties of
the Cabinet, the most delicate in such a nation as ours is to
know, how far to yield and where to check the humours that
arise amongst us.

" I shall not say all I think on a letter that is to be opened in
every municipality; but I will own I am not without my doubts
as to the institution of certain clubs, especially the last, which
professes to be upon a more extended plan, and to give its *profession de foi,* which is such as for the world I would not set
my hand to. Fox's speech is that of a Cataline; and proves that
his part is taken. He is to be the Mirabeau of the country;
may he meet the fate whilst living that the other has done when
he was insensible to it ! By the bye, have you read the letters
Mirabeau wrote when in the dungeon of Vincennes to Madame
Monnier, whom he had stolen from her husband ? such a rhap-
sody of sublime indecency, sublime ethics, and determined
atheism, was never I believe thrown together upon paper. It
is really curious to see how a man can at once avow himself
the apostle of the two extremes of both virtue and vice, justify-
ing every excess that his own passions prompt him to, and at the
same time dictating to others moral precepts, and fulminating
his censures upon his neighbours like a Cato. What a time we
live in ! I have just heard here a report of a Gun-powder plot
at Vienna that is so shocking that I tell every body I will not
believe it till I am absolutely obliged to it. Poor Louis Capet !
he has shewn two things at his first appearance at the bar, first,
that he is no coward, for a brave man might well have lost his
presence of mind under such circumstances; the second, that
he is no fool, for his attorney could not have answered more to
the purpose; but, alas ! he has answered like an attorney, not
like a King. Is it not a lion in the toils ? but is it his fault that
he was born without a kingly spirit ? Poor man ! his death will
be the corner-stone of the counter-revolution. He will be

known then only by his virtues and his sufferings; his weaknesses and his awkward person will be forgotten. I wish to
God I could shew you a Ciceronian speech that has been read to
me, as if it had been spoken upon his first appearance; it is a
fine canvass, ' voila tous mes forfaits en voici le salaire.'
Necker has made little or nothing of it. Apropos, read his
work *sur le Pouvoir Executif*; it is far the best of his productions. The conspiracy at the King's Bench was *dans le vrai
genre.* I tremble at every possibility; and wish, with a friend of
mine here, that I was four-score. In return for Lucy's prophecy, I pray you to hunt for an old book printed in or near
the time, which I have never seen, containing *le reve de Catherine de Medicis.* I am told it sets forth the league, the murder
of Henri Quatre, Cardinal Richelieu, Louis XIV., and every
thing down to the present reign, when nothing presented itself
but a black veil, and rats and cats eating one another. This
I will believe when I see it.

" I am glad you was so well pleased with your Irish tour ;
but I am disappointed in what you tell me of the head of the
law there. I never should expect to find there either elegance
of manners or sound judgments; but handsome women in
plenty for those who are a match for them, which, alas! I am
not. My journey has been trist enough; and where I now am
it is as cold as Christmas, and I have been shut up in a room
where no glean of sun ever enters. Italy is quiet since the dis-
persion of the French fleet, which was owing to the relics of two
Saints exposed on the beach at Cagliari. In every capital resides a little Minister, who gives law to the Sovereign as the Russian Ambassador does to the poor King of Poland at Warsaw."

---

58. LADY CAMELFORD to Mr. HARDINGE.

" MY DEAR SIR,   *Feb.* 19, 1794.
" As it is impossible for me either to speak or write upon the
subject that wholly occupies my mind, I will not attempt to
make a reply to the kind letter I have received from you; but
I can thank you for it, which I now do most sincerely. Indeed
I should have conveyed those thanks sooner but for a little inflammation in my eyes, which made writing troublesome to me.

" I hope it will not be long before I shall be able to see you,
without distressing your feelings more than may naturally be
expected, on your entering this melancholy house.

" I cannot close this short note without assuring you that
both General Cowper and Sir W———— did justice upon a late
occasion, not only to your talents, but to that zeal of friendship
which prompted their exertion.

" I better know how to value such friendship than by words
to express my sense of it I beg you to present my compli-

ments to Mrs. Hardinge; and to believe me, dear Sir, your faithful and obliged friend and servant, A. CAMELFORD *."

[*The following letter should have been inserted before; but the year is uncertain.*]

59.   " *Brussels, June* 27, 178–.

" I am not sure I should have been so good a boy as to have written before I got to Spa, but for the anxiety I feel for the precarious state of health of your poor woman. We hope to have a letter from you at Spa, to tell us the Bristol waters have removed all your apprehensions. I fear I cannot comply with your request as to Journal, which I am too lazy to undertake; and, in truth, the road to Spa is too hackneyed to require it. Rich cultivation in an endless extent of flat territory; fortifications, wet ditches, and lines of shady trees upon old ruinous ramparts, with frogs croaking under them; large venerable cities of antient commerce; gothic piles of devotion filled with pictures, and deformed at the same time by the most stupid superstitions; clean well-paved spacious streets with few inhabitants; unsocial nobility in coaches of the last century; soldiers, monks, and merchants mixed together; these are all the ideas that have presented themselves to me since I left England, or rather since I left M. Dessein, which, however, are entertaining enough to me, though not descriptive to others. This day, in a real deluge of rain, and amidst the crackling of a most violent thunder-storm, we reached the beautiful scene from whence I write this. From my window I look directly upon the verdure of trees, richly clothing a large garden, with some inequality of ground mixed with statues and ornaments, the extent at least equal to Lincoln's-inn-fields, surrounded with palaces, one line of which, of the noblest architecture, and all of stone, is fore-shortened to the eye, whilst at the same time, through a break over a theatrical wall of ballustrades and vases, I command the distant view of an extensive country over the roofs of the old city, which lies directly under our view.

" We are all well; and have slept in our coach but one night. We shall proceed in a few days for Spa, where, thank God, there is yet nobody; but the Archduke of Milan and his Consort, who are now here, will be there in a fortnight; if it were her grand-father he would be an acquaintance of mine. Take care of all my worldly concerns; and believe me ever

" Yours,   CAMELFORD."

---

* This Lady, as before noticed in p. 72, was Anne, daughter and co-heir of Pinkney Wilkinson, of Burnham, co. Norfolk, Esq. In the constant exercise of the most amiable qualities of the heart, she lived universally beloved, and died as universally lamented, May 5, 1805, aged 65, and was interred in the family vault at Boconnoc, attended by her son and daughter.

Rev. B. N. TURNER.

The Rev. Baptist-Noel Turner, M. A. Rector of Denton, co. Lincoln, and of Wing, co. Rutland, was the eldest son of the Rev. James Turner, his predecessor in the Rectory of Wing *; and grandson of the Rev. James Turner, Vicar of Garthorpe, Leicestershire, whose elder brother, William, Master of the Grammar School of Stamford (then one of the most flourishing schools in the kingdom), was a man of great erudition, and in his time, a celebrated grammarian. He was author of " Turner's Exercises," and other school books, once famous, but now out of date. He published also an elegant piece of classical humour, intituled, " Bellum Grammaticale," which is well worth the perusal of the curious.

The subject of our biography was born at the close of the year 1739, and baptized on New-year's day 1740; Baptist Noel, Earl of Gainsborough, after whom he was named, being one of his godfathers. He received the first rudiments of his education at the Grammar School of Oakham in Rutland, and completed it at Emanuel-college, Cambridge, where he was about two years senior to Dr. William Bennet, the Bishop of Cloyne, with whom, on his first arrival at College, he instantly cultivated such an intimacy as proved most happy and honourable to both parties. He was under the tuition of Mr. Hubbard, and took his degree of B. A. 1762; M. A.

* Mr. Turner never spoke of his father without feelings of the highest affection and veneration. In a short sketch of his life, which he has left behind him, he writes of his father thus : " My father's passing through Clare Hall, Cambridge, was with the same blameless and noiseless tenour of his way, for which he was conspicuous in after life. His acquirements were of the most solid and useful kind; not evincing any ambition of acquiring academical honours, but aiming to support the truly estimable character of a good parish priest."

REV.ᴰ BAPTIST NOEL TURNER M.A.

Born 1739. _ Died 1826,

Engraved from a Painting by his friend the
Rev.ᵈ W.ᵐ Peters. M.A. by H. Meyer.

1765. He was then elected a Fellow of his College, which, however, he soon after vacated by his marriage with Sarah, the eldest daughter of the Rev. Richard Easton, Prebendary of North Grantham in the Church of Salisbury *. On taking his degree of B. A. he was the seventh Wrangler, and at the same time obtained a silver prize-cup for the best classical exercises.

Early in life, whilst still a student at Emanuel, he undertook, in conjunction with his friend Mr. Lettice, of Sidney †, a new translation of Plutarch's

* Of his father-in-law Mr. Turner has recorded the following character: "Another affectionate, though far later, connection has a claim to be noticed. A little before this time, there arrived from Salisbury a new Vicar of Grantham, the Rev. Richard Easton; of whom Bishop Hoadly was the patron. Of this active and most warm friend of mine, as well as near relative, I must take the liberty of being a little more particular. With a fine figure, and a set of features as grand and dignified as I ever beheld, his manner was popular and attractive, and he was consequently a much admired preacher. Dr. Trevor, then Bishop of Durham, a man also of handsome form, and dignified deportment—so much so as to have acquired for himself the appellation of the Beauty of Holiness—was a great admirer of Mr. Easton; and, in passing between London and Durham, he would generally contrive to attend the Church at Grantham on a Sunday. On such occasions the Vicar, in his full canonicals, always waited upon the Bishop at the inn; and to see these two reverend personages (the Bishop being also in his robes) walking side by side to the Church, was a spectacle which is said to have struck the beholders with awe and reverence. Mr. Easton was also exceedingly well seconded by his clerk, a person of the name of Hutchinson, who had been of long standing in the town as a musician, then filling that station; who not only made the responses, but gave out and lead the psalms with becoming propriety and grace."—The conclusion of this anecdote might furnish a useful hint to some of our clergy, who are not so attentive, in the selection of a parish clerk, to his qualifications for the office, as they ought to be!

† Mr. Lettice accepted the Vicarage of Peasmarsh in Sussex, from his College, and subsequently took the degree of D.D. The intimacy between these two friends commenced in early youth, for they were at school together; and it continued, without the slightest interruption, up to Mr. Turner's death. Dr. Lettice still survives. During this long period they kept up a constant correspondence (a considerable portion of which was in Latin)

Lives. In this undertaking he was encouraged by
Dr. Johnson, to whom he had the good fortune to
be, about that time, introduced; but, after working
at it for a few months, the project was relinquished.
Of his interviews on this and several other occasions with the Colossus of Literature, Mr. Turner
gave the public an account, in the New Monthly
Magazine for 1818 and 1819, in which several interesting anecdotes of this extraordinary man, either
wholly new, or previously imperfectly related, are
detailed *. This was a subject on which, in a private circle of friends, Mr. Turner was delighted to
dwell. His lively and animated description of the
several conversations which passed between them,
and his close imitations of Dr. Johnson's peculiar
manner and diction, placed the very man before the
eyes of his hearers.

In 1769 he was presented by his father-in-law
to the Rectory of Denton, and two years after, by
the Crown, to that of Wing.

After giving up the translation of Plutarch, Mr.
Turner amused himself by modernising, in familiar
English verse, "The Characters of Theophrastus,"
which were printed for Leacroft in 1774. In 1782,
after some strictures on the loose notions of Soame
Jenyns, in eight letters to him, called, " Candid
Suggestions,"—he made an attack on the political
infallibility of Mr. Locke, in a little work called,
" The true Alarm." On the occasion of the inclo-
sure of one of his livings in the year 1788, he threw
out a pamphlet, intituled, "An Argumentative Appeal," in which he endeavoured to call the atten-

replete with learning, vivacity, and humour. Dr. Lettice is the
author of a Poem on the Conversion of St. Paul, which gained
him the Seatonian Prize at Cambridge about the time of his
taking his M. A. degree; of " Travels in Scotland ;" a " Translation of Isaac Hawkins Browne's Poem on the Immortality of
the Soul ;" " Fables for the Fire-side ;" " Suggestions on Clerical Elocution ; " and other literary productions.

* See these hereafter, pp. 147 *et seq.*

REV. B. N. TURNER. 143

tion of the heads of the Church and the public, to various instances of injustice done to the Church revenues, by the manner in which inclosures were managed.

In 1791 he published a political satire, called, "Infant Institutes," " fraught," he observes, " with matter so eccentric and laughable as might chance to arrest the attention, and raise the spirit of the public."

For a few years, in the early period of his life, Mr. Turner filled the station of Head-master of the Grammar School at Oakham, where the foundation of his own classical education had been previously laid. This office, however, was not congenial to his habits and disposition, and on taking possession of the living of Wing he relinquished it. Amongst other pupils, he had under his care the son of Dr. Percy, Bishop of Dromore, the celebrated editor of the " Ancient Ballads," with whom he was on terms of intimacy.

After Mr. Turner retired from Oakham, he resided for several years on his living at Wing, until a spirit of perverseness and opposition, on the part of his parishioners, manifested in their persisting to put up a new and additional peal of bells in a decayed and tottering steeple, overhanging the parsonage-house, compelled him to remove to his other living of Denton. Here he continued a constant resident till within a few years of his death; when attention to his health required him to spend the winter months in London. But during the long period of half a century, this truly pious Clergyman discharged all his sacred functions in person; and few men can be found who have more zealously, faithfully, and conscientiously performed these important duties. As he administered to the spiritual wants of his poorer neighbours, his wife was always ready, with a tenderness and care peculiar to her disposition, to lend her aid in affording them comfort and succour in their temporal necessities. The door of his mansion was ever open to their applications, and no one but the idle and worthless applied in vain.

In 1824 he published, " Songs of Solyma; or a new Version of the Psalms of David, the long ones being compressed, in general, into two parts or portions of Psalmody, comprising their prophetic evidences and principal beauties." These translations are highly respectable in point of literary merit (simplicity and unaffected piety being their chief characteristic); particularly when it is considered that they were the amusements of the evening of a literary life, the author having attained his eightieth year when he began the task *.

In his younger days, Mr. Turner was remarkable for a fine elocution. His manner of reading our beautiful liturgy was dignified and impressive, without any mixture of affectation. A fine melodious voice, clear articulation, and strict attention to propriety of emphasis, rendered his reading so natural, distinct, and intelligible, that the most ignorant could scarcely fail to be edified, as the better educated were charmed and gratified. By his spirited manner, in lighter reading, by his ready imitation of character, and by his turn for mimickry, when the occasion called for it, he would fascinate his auditors;—he was, indeed, fully qualified to have

* He communicated specimens of the translations to the Gentleman's Magazine; see vol. XC. part i. pp. 259, 395 ; see also vol. XCIV. part ii. p. 64. Several of them have been adopted in the elegant volume of Sacred Music published under the direction of Montagu Burgoyne, Esq. with a view to promote congregational Psalmody.—In a letter of that truly amiable, pious, and excellent authoress, Mrs. Cornwallis, to a friend, she remarked, " 1 had not heard of Mr. Turner's departure to a better world. His ' Songs of Solyma' lie upon my couch with me at this instant; I only put them out of my hands to write to you. How soothing to his relations it must be, to think how delightfully his thoughts were employed during his closing years, and how pleasantly to himself!"

sought his fortune on a different arena, had fate so
ordained it.   In conversation he was full of anecdote and humour; he delighted in society, and was
the life of it.   But on grave occasions, Mr. Turner
could be grave.   He never forgot the dignity of the
clerical character, and the duties which his sacred
office imposed upon him; and in maintaining the
integrity and purity of the Established Church, or
in opposing any innovations upon it, no man was
more zealous.   Nor was his zeal less conspicuous
in his loyalty to his Sovereign, and his attachment to the glorious Constitution under which
we live, and which he never failed, when the
opportunity presented itself, to defend, both in
conversation and in writing, with an earnestness
and uncompromising spirit, which proved how
much his heart and soul were devoted to the
subject.   His literary attainments were considerable.   Besides a thorough knowledge of the Latin
and Greek classics, his reading was extensive;
and being blessed with a remarkably retentive memory, he acquired very general information on all
subjects connected with literature.   Though unacquainted with the Hebrew (which he often lamented) yet when engaged on the "Songs of Solyma," he would, by the aid of dictionaries and
commentaries, and through the assistance of literary friends, dive into biblical learning, and examine
difficult passages, even in the original language, with
much critical acumen.   In the retirement which the
seclusion of a country life imposed upon him, he
relieved many a heavy hour by his literary pursuits;
and the volumes of manuscripts he left behind him,
besides his few published works, attest how much
of his time and attention was devoted to these
subjects.

Mr. Turner died in Dorset-place, Mary-le-bone,
May 18, 1826, in his 87th year, leaving a son and
daughter, three grandchildren, and two great-grand-

children surviving him.   His eldest son, William, who had embraced the military profession, and was a Captain in the 81st regiment, sacrificed his life in the cause of his country, early in the war.

---

1. Rev. B. N. Turner to Mr. Nichols.

" Denton, near Grantham, July 11, 1799.

" I have taken the liberty of sending the inclosed for the reason which is there expressed.   I thought it might as well be addressed in the third person; and I have signed it 'an old Correspondent,' which indeed I am.   But as this signature may perhaps belong to some known correspondent of yours, you may alter it to any initials, such as ' A. B.' &c. or, if you please, to ' Anti-jacobin,' a title perhaps not yet used in your Miscellany, and to which I have some right, as I believe I was one of the first, if not the very first, Anti-jacobin in the kingdom, as might perhaps be proved by Essays in the Gentleman's Magazine so far back as the years 1776 and 1777, long before the name had a meaning.   If you approve of the article I now send, I should be obliged to you to insert it in the present month *, or at least in the next; and I may have an opportunity of pointing it out to my old friend the Bishop of Cloyne, to whom I have already written something on the subject.   Should you have any objection to publishing it, I will thank you to return it to my son, J. Turner, Esq. No. 3, Essex-court, Temple.

" I am still in a state of uncertainty with respect to the Second Part of the Infant Institutes; I should be glad, therefore, if your Reviewer could make it convenient to notice the First Part soon.   I am afraid that from the title, some have been led to fancy it only a book for children, though it is in fact a political satire; and was meant, I am sure, not merely to amuse, but to do good, if it should succeed.

" I find you have been engraving for your History of Leicestershire, some of the Fossil-fish belonging to my brother-in-law William Easton, of Barrow.   If I could have the pleasure of seeing either yourself or Mr. Pridden here, I have a little Museum in which are some things that might be worth engraving, though not for the History of Leicestershire, yet for the Gentleman's Magazine.   Amongst others I have a petrefaction of a skeleton of probably some quadruped, about three feet and a half long and two feet broad, which I believe cannot any where be matched.   Your obedient servant,   B. N. Turner."

---

* The article appears not to have been inserted.

2. Johnsonian Letter the First, addressed to the Editor of the New Monthly Magaziue.

" Mr. Editor,   *Denton, Lincolnshire, Oct.* 17, 1818.

" To specify the reasons why the following communication has been so long delayed, might be difficult in itself, and certainly is not of the smallest importance. Suffice it to own myself in your debt ever since the year 1814, for an elucidation of a note to one of the Letters on Etymology in your two first volumes, of which 1 acknowledge myself the author, under the assumed name of Humfree Tellfair. The note in question (see vol. II. p. 525) is as follows : ' Johnson—Farmer. Though liberties have been here taken with the former of these great men, yet the writer of these papers knew him well, which is the same thing as saying, loved and revered him. Early in 1765 he had the singular happiness of introducing these two literary luminaries, to their first personal interview, at Emanuel-college, Cambridge, and of enjoying the intellectual banquets that ensued, especially that attempted to be described by Dr. Sharp, of Bene't, in the Gentleman's Magazine for March of that year *.' After almost despairing for some time of being able to send you a narrative of Johnson's journey to Cambridge, worthy of your acceptance, I now hope, through the assistance of a dear and very old friend, to transmit you something not derogatory to its illustrious subject. The gentleman here alluded to is the Rev. J. Lettice, then Fellow of Sidney-college, (since Rector of Peasmarsh, Sussex,) of whose merits, as a writer, the public is already well apprized, and whom, in the following narrative, I shall always mention as *my friend.*

" My first introduction to Dr. Johnson was owing to the following circumstance. My friend and I had agreed upon attempting a new taanslation of Plutarch's Lives ; but previously, as I was just then going to town, my friend wished me to consult Johnson about it, with whom he himself was well acquainted. In consequence, when in town, I procured an interview with Levett †, who willingly next morning introduced

* It was certainly written to some friend at that time, but it appears not to have found its way into the Gentleman's Magazine until twenty years afterwards, *viz.* in March 1785.

† Dr. Levett, as he was called, was a native of Hull, and in early life became a waiter in a coffee-house at Paris. The surgeons who frequented it, finding him attentive to their conversation, raised a subscription for him among themselves, and gave him some instructions in anatomy. He also obtained by the same means admission to the lectures on medicine, and thus was enabled to set up for himself; but whether he ever took any degree is uncertain. The rest of his life also is unknown, till he became acquainted with Johnson, who made him his domestic physician, gave him apartments in his house, and treated him with great kindness. After breakfasting with the Doctor, he usually went round among his patients, then attended Hunter's lectures, and returned at night. " All his physical knowledge," said Johnson, " and it is not

me to breakfast with the great man. His residence was then in
some old fashioned rooms called, I think, Inner Temple-lane,
No. 1. At the top of a few steps the door opened into a dark
and dingy looking old wainscotted anti-room, through which
was the study, and into which, a little before noon, came rolling,
as if just roused from his cabin, the truly uncouth figure of our
literary Colossus, in a strange black wig, too little for him by
half, but which, before our next interview, was exchanged for
that very respectable brown one in which his friend, Sir Joshua,
so faithfully depicted him. I am glad, however, I saw the queer
black bob, as his biographers have noticed it, and as it proved
that the lustre of native genius can break through the most dis-
figuring habiliments. He seemed pleased to see a young Cantab in his rooms, and on my acquainting him with the business
on which I had taken the liberty of consulting him, he rather
encouraged our undertaking than otherwise; though after working at it for a few months we found the work too tedious and
incompatible with other pursuits, and were obliged to relinquish
it. After this, the great man questioned me about Cambridge,
and whatever regarded literature, and attended to my answers
with great complacency. The situation of these apartments I
well remember. I called once more before I left town, but the
Doctor was absent, and when Francis Barber, his black servant,
opened the door to tell me so, a group of his African countrymen were sitting round a fire in the gloomy anti-room; and on
their all turning their sooty faces at once to stare at me, they
presented a curious spectacle. I repeatedly afterwards visited
him, both in Johnson's-court and Bolt-court.

"Though I meant at first to confine myself solely to his Cambridge excursion, yet, that we may not lose, as Garrick says,
' one drop of this immortal man,' permit me to say a few words
respecting these different calls. When alone he sometimes asked
me to take tea with him; and I can truly say, that I never
found him morose or overbearing, though I freely contradicted
him, with which he seemed pleased, and in order to lead a
young man into a sort of controversy or discussion, he would
now and then advance what he did not think. He has been
aptly compared to a ghost, as he would seldom speak first, but
would sit liberating in his chair till a question was asked, upon
which he would promptly and fluently dilate. The reason for
this seems, as a first-rate genius, who feels himself equally pre-

inconsiderable, was obtained through the ear. Though he buys books,
he seldom looks into them, or discovers any power by which he can be
supposed to judge of an author's merit." Before he became an inmate
of the Doctor's, he married a common strumpet, who passed herself off
upon him as a heiress, while he did the same upon her as a physician of
great practice. They were separated by the intervention of Johnson, with
whom Levett resided above twenty years, and died at his house, January
1782. His memory was honoured by his old patron, with a poetical tribute of affection.

pared to discuss whatever subject may be started, must deem it
more to his own honour that he should not chuse the topic himself. When I saw the Doctor again, after we had given up Plutarch, I told him that my friend and Professor Martyn * had
undertaken to give an edition in English, with the plates, of the
Herculaneum Antiquities. Johnson. ' They don't know what
they have undertaken ; the engravers will drive them mad, Sir.'
And this, perhaps, with other reasons, might prevent their executing more than one volume. At another time he said, ' That
Mr. Farmer, of your College, is a very clever man indeed, Sir.'
And on my asking him whether he knew the fact with respect to
the learning of Shakspeare, before that gentleman's publication ? Johnson. ' Why, yes, Sir, I knew in general that the
fact was as he represents it ; but I did not know it, as Mr. Farmer has now taught it me, by *detail*, Sir.' I was several times
the bearer of messages between them ; and my suggesting and
expressing a hope that we should some time or other have the
pleasure of seeing him at Cambridge, when I should be most
happy to introduce them to each other, might somewhat conduce to his taking the journey I am about to describe.

" The last time I called upon him was long after the Cambridge visit, and I found with him Mr. Strahan, his son the
Vicar of Islington †, and two or three other gentlemen, one of

---

* The Rev. Thomas Martyn, Fellow of Sidney-college, and Botanical Professor at Cambridge. See vol. V. of this Work, p. 752.

† George Strahan, D. D. was the second of the three sons of
the eminent printer, William Strahan, Esq. M. P. and elder
brother to Andrew Strahan, Esq. M. P. Printer to the King ;
see the " Literary Anecdotes," vol. III. p. 397.
He was educated at University-college, Oxford, where he was
contemporary with the two celebrated brothers, Lord Stowell
and Lord Chancellor Eldon ; and through a long life enjoyed
the honour of their friendship. He took the degree of M. A.
April 17, 1771 ; and the degrees of B. and D. D. as a Grand
Compounder, June 18, 1807. He was presented to the Vicarage
of Islington in 1772 ; to the Rectory of Little Thurrock in
Essex in 1783 (which he afterwards resigned) ; and of Cranham in the same county, by dispensation, in 1786 (also afterwards resigned). In 1805 he was elected one of the Prebendaries of Rochester ; and by the Dean and Chapter of that
Cathedral was presented, in 1820, to the Rectory of Kingsdown
in Kent.—The most interesting feature in Dr. Strahan's life,
was his close intimacy with Dr. Samuel Johnson. Between the
father of Dr. Strahan and Dr. Johnson, there existed a long and
sincere friendship, which was extended by the good Doctor to
the young divine, to whom in early life he shewed the strongest
mark of affection, and who was, during Dr. Johnson's last ill-

whom was upon his legs taking leave, and saying, ' Well, Doctor, as you know I shall set off to-morrow, what shall I say for
you to Mrs. Thrale, when I see her?' Johnson. ' Why, Sir, you
may tell her how I am; but, noa, Sir, noa, she knows that
already; and so when you see Mrs. Thrale, you will say to her,
what it is predestined that you are to say to her, Sir.' Amidst
the general laugh occasioned by this sally, the gentleman retired;

---

ness, his daily attendant. Of the Doctor's visits at Islington,
Mr. Boswell thus speaks :

"On Wednesday, May 5, 1784, I arrived in London; and next
morning had the pleasure to find Dr. Johnson greatly recovered.
I but just saw him; for a coach was waiting to carry him to
Islington, to the house of his friend the Rev. Mr. Strahan, where
he went sometimes for the benefit of good air, which, notwithstanding his having formerly laughed at the general opinion
upon the subject, he now acknowledged was conducive to
health."

" The Rev. Mr. Strahan, who had been always one of his
great favourites, had, during his last illness, the satisfaction of
contributing to sooth and comfort him.   That gentleman's
house at Islington afforded Johnson occasionally and easily an
agreeable change of place and fresh air; and he also attended
on him in town in the discharge of the sacred offices of his profession."

" Various prayers had been composed by Dr. Johnson at different periods, which, intermingled with pious reflections and
some short notes of his life, were entitled by him ' Prayers and
Meditations *.'   These were, in pursuance of Dr. Johnson's
earnest requisition, in the hopes of doing good, published in
1785 by Mr. Strahan, to whom he delivered them.   This admirable collection evinces, beyond all his compositions for the
public, and all the eulogies of his friends and admirers, the sincere virtue and piety of Dr. Johnson."

Dr. Bray's associates were to receive the profits of the first
edition, by the author's appointment; and any further advantages that might accrue, were to be distributed among Dr. Johnson's relations.

Mr. Strahan was a witness to Dr. Johnson's will; and in a
codicil to the same he bequeathed to him, " Mill's Greek Testament, Beza's Greek Testament by Stephens, and all his Latin
Bibles, and his Greek Bible by Wechelius." Dr. Strahan died
at Islington, May 18, 1824, aged 80. His remains were
interred on the 24th of May, in Islington Church, with the
respect which was justly due to the exemplary discharge of his
sacred duty for more than half a century. The funeral cere-

---

* To authenticate the work, Mr. Strahan deposited the original manuscript in the library of Pembroke-college, Oxford.

and the Doctor, joining in the merriment, proceeded, 'For you know, Sir, when a person has said or done any thing, it was plainly predestinated that he was to say or do that particular thing, Sir.' I recollect but one more interview with him in

---

mony was solemn and impressive. The hearse, drawn by six horses, was followed by five mourning coaches, and the carriages of the Lord Chancellor and several private friends, anxious to shew their esteem for so worthy a man.

On the following Sunday a funeral sermon was preached in Islington Church by his old and highly-respected friend, Dr. Philip Fisher, Master of the Charter-house and Precentor of Salisbury, to a most crowded and attentive congregation, from Chron. xix. 15. Dr. Fisher discoursed in a perspicuous and masterly manner on death; and concluded with an elegant eulogium on the character of Dr. Strahan, of which the following will give but a very faint outline:

"If he regarded his youth, a time of life too often devoted to levity and dissipation, he (Dr. Fisher) could, from an intimacy of more than 50 years, bear witness to his excellencies. At that period he was the admiration of the society he adorned, a society which he enlivened by his wit, benefited by his advice, and instructed by his example. From this society he was early removed, having been appointed to an office of the highest importance—that of Pastor to this extensive and populous parish. The manner in which he discharged this arduous duty was best known to those present, to those who had heard, known, and lived with him. The congregation could remember the clearness of his pronunciation, the melodious accents of his voice, and the excellence of his discourses, clothed in language neither rendered unintelligible by too flowery ornaments, nor burthened with metaphors, nor yet disgraced by mean and low expressions. Most would recollect his assiduous attention in the care of the poor, the visitation of the sick, and the establishment of schools; his private charities were known only to his own breast, and to those who had experienced their benefit. He could not omit to notice one most honourable attestation of the worth of the deceased; this was, that in early life he had been encouraged by the notice, and honoured by the friendship, of the greatest Moralist of the age. By the express desire of that truly pious philosopher, he had given to the world those prayers which will ever be a memorial of the sincere piety of their author, and which ought to be preserved in the closet, and cherished in the bosom, of every devout Christian."

Dr. Strahan married, June 25, 1778, Miss Robertson of Richmond; and by that accomplished lady, who survived him, had two daughters, both married on the same day, July 23, 1812. Margaret to Freeman W. Eliot, Esq. and Maria-Isabella to W. Rose Rose, Esq.

town, but to describe that would lead me so far out of my way at present, that I believe I must defer this to some future communication.

"Of the journey I principally intended to describe, there is, as I observed, a short account by Dr. Sharp in the Gentleman's Magazine for March 1785, in which he there addresses his friend, ' I have had Johnson in the chair in which I am now writing. He came down on Saturday with a Mr. Beauclerk, who was a friend at Trinity (a Mr. Lester, or Leicester). Caliban, you may be sure, was not roused from his lair till next day noon. He was not heard of till Monday afternoon, when I was sent for home to two gentlemen unknown. He drank his large potations of tea with me, interrupted by many an indignant contradiction and many a noble sentiment, &c. He had a better wig than usual, but one whose curls were not, like Sir Cloudesley's, formed for ' eternal buckle.' He went to town next morning; but as it began to be known that he was in the University, several persons got into his company the last evening at Trinity.' And then his conclusion is equally foolish and indecent; ' Where about twelve he began to be very great, stripped poor Mrs. Macauley to the skin, then gave her for a toast, and drank her in two bumpers.' Who these several persons were will appear in the sequel.

"When I mentioned a wish to introduce him to our common friend Farmer, the Doctor did not seem disinclined to the proposal; and it was on Saturday in the beginning of March 1765, that having accepted the offer of Topham Beauclerk, Esq. to drive him down in his phæton, they arrived at the Rose Inn, Cambridge. My friend *, of Sidney, had the honour to be the only gownsman sent for by the great man to spend the first evening with him, though Mr. Beauclerk had probably also his friend from Trinity. Next morning, though Caliban, as Sharp saucily calls him, might have been time enough out of his lair, yet I admire his prudence and good sense in not appearing that day at St. Mary's, to be the general gaze during the whole service. Such an appearance at such a time and place might have turned, as it were, a Christian Church into an idol temple ; but vanity consorts not with real excellence. He was, however, heard of that day, for he was with the above party, with the addition perhaps of another friend of his, our respectable Greek Professor, Dr. Lort; but whether or not, I was myself of my friend's Sunday party, we can neither of us recollect. To my inquiries concerning this Sidney symposium, my friend has returned the following short, but lively description of it: ' Our distinguished visitor shone gloriously in his style of dissertation on a great variety of subjects. I recollect his condescending to as earnest a care of the animal as of the intellectual man, and after doing all the justice to my College bill of fare, and without

* Mr. Lettice.

neglecting the glass after dinner, he drank sixteen dishes of tea. I was idly curious enough to count them, from what I had remarked, and heard Levett mention of his extraordinary devotion to the tea-pot.'

" On this subject Boswell observes (vol. I. p. 286), that 'Johnson's nerves must have been uncommonly strong, not to have been extremely relaxed by such an intemperate use of the infusion of this fragrant leaf. He assured me that he never felt the least inconvenience from it.' It is remarkable that the only controversy Johnson ever was engaged in, was with the truly amiable Jonas Hanway, about his Essay on Tea. I have several times met with that eminently *good*, which is better than *great*, man Mr. Hanway, at the house of Mrs. Penny, or Penné, in Bloomsbury-square, a lady, who in 1771, dedicated to him a volume of poetry, calling him 'The Second Man of Ross.' Once he was unluckily introduced in the very midst of a large tea-drinking party, which made the Philanthropist look grave, and rather disconcerted our elegant and accomplished hostess. At the same house too, I once heard him mention Johnson and his criticism with a warmth that I did not expect from the meek and gentle Hanway. ' The man,' said he, ' abuses my work upon tea; and he sits in this manner,' mimicking the shaking of the Doctor's hands and head, ' and then he wonders what I can mean by writing against so wholesome a beverage; while, as he is unable to keep a nerve of him still, he is all the while slopping half of it upon his breeches knees.' When I told this anecdote to Dr. Percy *, he was much diverted, and observed, ' Aye, aye; and yet, in spite of all his tea-bibbing, the gigantic Johnson could have seized with both hands upon the puny Hanway, and *discerped* him.'

" Before I close my account of the Sidney dinner, let me observe, that though my friend could not recollect any of the Doctor's bon-mots at the time, yet the inquiry brought to his mind a former one of our literary hero, so well authenticated and perhaps so little known, that though it has no reference to our present story, I shall take this opportunity of recording it. From the year 1768 to 1771, my friend was Chaplain to his Majesty's Minister at the Court of Denmark, Sir R. Gunning, and tutor to his children. One of the latter, a very accomplished young lady, became in process of time the Hon. Mrs. Digby, who related to her former tutor the following anecdote. This lady was present at the introduction of Dr. Johnson at one of the late Mrs. Montague's literary parties, when Mrs. Digby herself, with several still younger ladies, almost immediately surrounded our Colossus of literature (an odd figure sure enough) with more wonder than politeness, and while contemplating him, as if he had been some monster from the deserts of Africa, Johnson said to them, ' Ladies, I am tame;

* The late learned and amiable Bishop of Dromore.

you may stroke me.'—' A happier, or more deserved reproof,'
Mrs. Digby said, ' could not have been given!'

" I now hasten to redeem my pledge by describing the first
meeting of our two great luminaries, Johnson and Farmer,
referred to in your second volume, p. 525. On Monday morning I met the former at Sidney with the view of conducting him
to the latter at Emanuel. As the Doctor was a stranger at
Cambridge, we took a circuitous rout to give him a cursory
glimpse of some of the colleges. We passed through Trinity,
which he admired in course, and then said to me, ' And what
is this next?' ' Trinity-hall.' ' I like that College.' ' Why so,
Doctor?' ' Because I like the science that they study there.'
Hence he walked, or rather, perhaps rolled or waddled, in a manner not much unlike Pope's idea of

> "A dab chick waddling through the copse,

Either by or through Clare-hall, King's-college, Catherine-hall,
Queen's, Pembroke, and Peterhouse, to the place of our destination.

" The long-wished-for interview of these unknown friends
was uncommonly joyous on both sides. After the salutations,
said Johnson, ' Mr. Farmer, I understand you have a large collection of very rare and curious books.' Farmer. ' Why yes,
Sir, to be sure I have plenty of all such reading as was never
read.' Johnson. ' Will you favour me with a specimen, Sir?'
Farmer, considering for a moment, reached down ' Markham's
Booke of Armorie,' and turning to a particular page, presented
it to the Doctor, who, with rolling head, attentively perused it.
The passage having been previously pointed out to myself, I
am luckily enabled to lay it before the reader, because I find it
quoted, *totidem verbis*, as a great curiosity, which it certainly is,
at line 101 of the first part of the ' The Pursuits of Literature.'
The words in question are said to be the conclusion of the first
chapter of ' Markham's Booke,' intituled, ' The difference between Charles and Gentleman,' and is as follows: ' From the
offspring of gentlemanly Japhet came Abraham, Moses, Aaron,
and the Prophets, &c. &c. — and also the king of the right line
of Mary, of whom that only absolute gentleman, Jesus, gentleman by his mother Mary, Princesse of Coat Armorie,' &c.
Towards the conclusion of which unaccountable and almost incredible folly, the Doctor's features began most forcibly to
remind me of Homer's μειδιαων βαοφυροισι προσωπασι; and if
you can conceive a cast of countenance expressive at once of
both pleasantry and horror, that was the one which our sage
assumed when he exclaimed, ' Now I am shocked, Sir—now I
am shocked!' which was only answered by Farmer with his
usual ha! ha! ha! for even blasphemy, where it is unintentional, may be so thoroughly ridiculous as merely to excite the
laugh of pity!

"What I have next to relate occurred during the visit, but at what period of it is uncertain. If the great man left us on Tuesday morning, as Sharp asserts, and I think correctly, then it must have been on Sunday afternoon, which will prove that I *was* of the Sidney party, and went with the rest, conducted by Mr. Leicester, into Trinity library. On our first entering, Johnson took up, on the right-hand side, not far from the door, a folio, which proved to be the Polyhistor of Morhof, a German genius of great celebrity in the 17th century. On opening this he exclaimed, 'Here is the book upon which all my fame was originally founded; when I had read this book I could teach my tutors!' 'And now that you have acquired such fame, Doctor,' said Mr. Leicester, 'you must feel exquisite delight in your own mind.' Johnson. 'Why noa, Sir, noa, I have no such feeling on that account, as you have attributed to me, Sir.' Whether the sincerity of Johnson's declaration be allowed or not, the anecdote may perhaps supply a useful hint to future aspiring geniuses ambitious of emulating so great a man.

"Monday, then, we may say, was probably that *last evening* on which the symposium took place, of which Sharp has attempted to give so ridiculous an account. That some strangers crowded about him was the absurd notion of Sharp; but the plain truth is, that on this *last evening* there was assembled at the chambers of Mr. Leicester, in Neville's-court, Trinity-college, the very same company as before, viz. Mr. L. the entertainer, Mr. Beauclerk, Drs. Johnson and Lort, my friend, and myself, with the addition only of Farmer, on whose account principally the journey was undertaken.

"During our conviviality nothing occurred that was at all like an *indignant contradiction*, though the Doctor was himself sometimes purposely contradicted to elicit the sparks of his genius by collision. There was, however, no lack of *noble sentiments;* and on any subject being started, he would instantly give a sort of treatise upon it in miniature. Long before twelve o'clock our hero *began to be very great;* for, on his entering the room, having a pain in his face, he bent it down to the fire, archly observing, with a smile, 'This minority cheek of mine is warring against the general constitution.' 'Nay, Doctor,' said Beauclerk, who well knew how to manage him, 'you musn't talk against the minority, for they tell you, you know, that they are your friends, and wish to support your *liberties,* and save you from oppression.' Johnson. 'Why yes, Sir, just as wisely, and just as necessarily as if they were to build up the interstices of the cloisters at the bottom of this court, for fear the library should fall upon our heads, Sir.' He was brilliant, therefore, from the very first; and might not the above be accepted as a lively and decisive answer to minority politics in general, during the whole of the present reign?

"Kit Smart happening to be mentioned, and that he had

broken out of a house of confinement: ' He was a fool for that,' said Beauclerk, ' for within two days they meant to have released him.' Johnson. ' Whenever poor Kit could make his escape, Sir, it would always have been within two days of his intended liberation.' He then proceeded to speak highly of the parts and scholarship of poor Kit; and to our great surprise, recited a number of lines out of one of Smart's Latin Triposes; and added, ' Kit Smart was mad, Sir.' Beauclerk. ' What do you mean by mad, Doctor ? ' Johnson. ' Why, Sir, he could not walk the streets without the boys running after him.' Soon after this, on Johnson's leaving the room, Beauclerk said to us, ' What he says of Smart is true of himself; ' which well agrees with my observations during the walk I took with him that very morning. Beauclerk also took the same opportunity to tell us of that most astonishing, and scarcely credible effort of genius, his writing Rasselas in two days and a night, and then travelling down with the price to support his sick mother ! But Boswell says this was done after her decease, to pay her debts and funeral expenses. (Vol. I. p. 306.) In either case, what parts! what piety !

" On the Doctor's return, Beauclerk said to him, ' Doctor, why do you keep that blind woman in your house ?' Johnson. ' Why, Sir, she was a friend to my poor wife, and was in the house with her when she died. And so, Sir, as I could not find in my heart to desire her to quit my house, poor thing ! she has remained in it ever since, Sir.' It appears, however, that the friendship and conversation of the intelligent Anna Williams, proved in general highly gratifying to him, and he feelingly lamented her loss, in 1783. (See Boswell, vol. III. p. 494.)

" A question was then asked him respecting Sterne. Johnson. ' In a company where I lately was, Tristram Shandy introduced himself; and Tristram Shandy had scarcely sat down, when he informed us that he had been writing a Dedication to Lord Spencer ; and *sponte sud* he pulled it out of his pocket; and *sponte sud* for nobody desired him, he began to read it ; and before he had read half a dozen lines, *sponte med*, Sir, I told him it was not English, Sir.' This trifle is prefixed to vol. V. and may be fairly said to justify the censure of the critic, even supposing it contained no other error previously to the giving of the above broad hint. It will scarcely be regarded as a forced digression, if I here relate what Farmer observed to me a year or two before this period, respecting the ill-judging Sterne. ' My good friend,' said he one day in the parlour at Emanuel, ' you young men seem very fond of this Tristram Shandy ; but mark my words, and remember what I say to you; however much it may be talked about at present, yet, depend upon it, in the course of twenty years, should any one wish to refer to the book in question, he will be obliged to go to an antiquary to inquire for it.' This has proved truly prophetic ; and it affords a strong confirmation of that poetical adage, generally, though falsely, attributed to Pope, while it belongs to Lord Roscommon, *viz.*

That want of decency is want of sense.

" In the height of our convivial hilarity, our great man exclaimed : ' Come, now, I'll give you a test; now I'll try who is a true antiquary amongst you.   Has any one of this company ever met with the History of Glorianus and Gloriana ?'   Farmer, drawing the pipe out of his mouth, followed by a cloud of smoke, instantly said, 'I've got the book.'   ' Gi' me your hand, gi'me your hand,' said Johnson, ' you are the man after my own heart.'   And the shaking of two such hands, with two such happy faces attached to them, could hardly, I think, be matched in the whole annals of literature !

" As to politics, it is well known that the Doctor was a firm and strenuous defender of the monarchial form of government, as approaching the nearest, that human wisdom is capable of doing, to the Divine model, by placing over the nation a Prince who shall be clearly above, and unconnected with the very highest ranks of his subjects.   This must be the most natural form of a community, the safest and the freest, because the most impartial.   Why then should mortals wish for a different one ? why covet the rule of factious nobles or burgomasters? or destroy millions of their fellow-creatures, to establish that most horrible of all tyrannies, the power of La Peuple Souverain, or a lawless and infuriate mob ?   Being, therefore, himself a true patriot, he was naturally much amused by facetiously exposing and ridiculing sham-patriots or reformers; and on being asked for a toast, his answer was, ' If you wish for a gentleman, I shall always give you Mr. Hollis; if for a lady, Mrs. Macaulay, Sir.' This Mr. Hollis, it may be proper to say, was a bigotted Whig, or Republican ; one who mis-spent an ample fortune in paving the way for sedition and revolt in this and the neighbouring kingdoms, by dispersing democratical works, and sometimes highly ornamented with daggers, caps of liberty, &c.   His favourite author was Milton, though I fear he respected the rebel rather than the bard.   And here I am tempted to observe, that England and her newly recovered monarchy acquired immortal honour, by so far paying homage to the genius of Milton, as to exempt him from the list of the regicides!   This Hollis, indeed, might be said even to have laid the first train of combustibles for the American explosion ; he having long ago sent a present of some elegant book or books, to Harvard-college, in New Cambridge, accompanied by the following curious document : ' People of Massachussets ! when your country shall be cultivated, adorned like this country, and ye shall become elegant, refined in all civil life, then—if not before—'ware to your liberties !'   Well, and might we not, with the same kind of old-goat-like elocution, say to every loyal, peaceable, and conscientious man in the kingdom — ' Should democracy too much

abound, then— ware your liberties and properties!—or even—
'ware your lives; or at least — ware those rights and privileges, without which social life cannot either be comfortable or
secure!'*

"It seemed requisite to record thus much of this almost
unknown simpleton, of whom not a word more was said on the
present occasion. As for the female politician, her notions about
government have been sufficiently trumpeted by herself. It has
been reported, but whether in print or no I cannot tell, that in
a dispute with this political lady, Johnson once said, 'You are to
recollect, Madam, that there is a monarchy in Heaven.' Mrs.
Macaulay. 'If I thought so, Sir, I should never wish to go
there.' True it is, that our philosopher's exhibition of this
lady's principles and conduct was a rich classical treat, of which
I much regret that I can present to my readers nothing more
than the concluding circumstance, with which it now appears to
be high time that this narrative also should be brought to a conclusion.

"After much of the Doctor's sportiveness and play of wit, at
the lady's expense, it must be owned, Beauclerk called out,
'Come, come, Doctor, take care what you say, and don't be too
saucy about Mrs. Macaulay; for, if you do, I shall find means of
setting her upon you as soon as we return, and she will comb
your wig for you pretty handsomely.' Johnson. 'Well, Sir, and
pray by what means do you propose to achieve this notable exploit of yours, Mr. Beauclerk?' Beauclerk. 'Oh! I'll soon tell
you that, Doctor. You can't deny that it's now a full fortnight
since Mrs. M. made you a present of her history; and to my
certain knowledge it still remains in your study without one of
the leaves being cut open; which is such a contempt of the
lady's genius and abilities, that, should I acquaint her with it,
as perhaps I shall, I wouldn't be in your place, Doctor, for a
good deal, I assure you.' Johnson, sub-laughing all the while
at this threat, 'Why, in the first place, Sir, I am so far from
denying your allegations, that I freely confess, before this company, that they are perfectly true and correct. The work of
Mrs. Macaulay is indeed in the situation that you have described.
But in the second place, Sir, I may safely, I believe, defy all
your oratorical powers so far to work upon that lady's vanity as
to induce her to believe it possible, that I could have suffered
her writings to lie by me so long, without once gratifying myself by a perusal of them. However, pray try, Mr. Beauclerk,
I beg you will try, Sir, as soon as you think proper, and then
we shall see whether you will soonest bring the lady about my
ears, or about your own, Sir.'

---

* Thomas Hollis was born in London in 1720, and died suddenly while
walking in his grounds at Corscombe, in Dorsetshire, in 1774. He re-
printed many of the political works of Milton, Algernon Sidney, Harrington, and other republican writers, at a great expense.

"Such was the rapid appearance and disappearance, the very transient visit of this great man, to an University super-eminently famous in itself for the production of great men. It was a visit, however, of which he spoke afterwards in town, to the writer of this account, with very pleasing recollections. Though he must have been well known to many of the Heads and Doctors at this seat of learning, yet he seemed studious to preserve a strict incognito; his only aim being an introduction to his favourite scholar, his brother patriot and antiquary, who was then Mr. but afterwards Dr. Farmer, and master of his college, and who finally declined episcopacy. Merit like Johnson's seeks not publicity; it follows not fame, but leaves fame to follow it. Had he visited Cambridge at the Commencement, or on some public occasion, he would doubtless have met with the honours due to the bright luminary of a sister University; and yet, even these honours, however genuine and desirable, the modesty of conscious excellence seems rather to have prompted him to avoid.   B. N. TURNER."

3. Rev. Mr. Turner's Second Johnsonian Letter.

"MR. EDITOR,   *Denton, Lincolnshire, July* 20, 1819.

"Having, rather incautiously perhaps, made you a sort of a promise of adding something to the account I before transmitted, respecting the intercourse I once enjoyed with the late Dr. Johnson, I have been rather checked, *in limine,* by the consideration of the comparative unimportance of what remains to be told. And yet, since it may be desirable to contemplate such a man in various moods and under different circumstances, and since he himself has directed that biography should not consist wholly of panegyric, the objection may not be material. In consequence, therefore, of my first letters having been honoured by the attention of more than one gentleman of eminence, I am encouraged to proceed; and I shall, at the same time, introduce to the reader's notice another literary friend, whose character may form no unfit accompaniment, even to that of the incomparable Johnson. Yet still what I am the most apprehensive of is, lest in the sequel I should be almost inevitably led into such a strain of egotism as the reader, however indulgently disposed, might find it difficult to excuse.

" In my present essay, my late dear friend Dr. Percy, afterwards Bishop of Dromore, will necessarily be as conspicuous as Dr. Johnson himself. Dr. Percy, besides his apartments in Northumberland-house, had a residence for his lady and family in Half-moon-street, Piccadilly, and there it was that I dined on the day of the Johnsonian visit, which I before left undescribed. The company, besides the Doctor and his ' Nanny, the fairest of the fair,' whose appearance and manners did no discredit to the charming song, consisted of the blind poetess, Anna Williams, from Dr. Johnson's, a Mr. Percy, a relation of the Doctor's, and myself. Dr. Percy had just before published his 'Hermit of Warksworth,' and when the ladies were withdrawn, he began to tell us that he had consulted Johnson on that publication, and appeared very much dissatisfied with his behaviour on the occasion. Having been for some time prevented by lameness from seeing Dr. Johnson, I proposed escorting Mrs. Williams home in a coach that evening, and paying my compliments to her patron, to which Dr. Percy consented, on my promising to return to Half-moon-street.

   " At Bolt-court (I think it was) I found the great man in an upper-room, not quite alone to be sure, for at an humble distance sat a little, shrivelled, greasy-looking old fellow, whom I took for a printer's devil, though something was said about his being an amanuensis. As I was come directly from Dr. Percy, the conversation turned naturally upon him and his new Poem. Here it should be premised, that our sage had, some how or other, acquired a sort of distaste or contempt for the minstrelsy of the dark ages. Should this be wondered at, we may recollect, that the brightest geniuses are not exempt from whims or imperfections; nay, rather, we cannot fail to remark, that the greatest strength of mind has ordinarily been attended by some such weaknesses, as might prevent its too great preponderancy.

   " The substance of the conversation which then ensued, as far as it can now be recollected, was as follows :

   " Johnson. 'Why, yes, Sir, he showed me his Poem, but I could give him no great encouragement.' 'No!' I answered, affecting a surprise, 'why, surely, Doctor, it is a pleasing and very creditable imitation of those ancient bards and minstrels who formerly charmed and refined our too rude and unpolished ancestors.' Johnson. 'Aye, Sir, but were they worth imitating?' I professed that I had often been charmed myself with their lyric strains, and knew of many others who had been so too. I urged that this kind of poetry was to my friend, as it were, *hereditary ;* observing, that he had so intensely studied their composition, he might well be expected to have caught their manner of writing; and I well remember mentioning the now-forgotten name of some ancient scholar, who is recorded to have read Virgil till he acquired a style perfectly Virgilian. Johnson. 'Why, yes, Sir, and that was something worth acquiring, which cannot be said of the sing-song of your bards.' I still, however, advocated the minstrel cause, alleging that I could see no reason why the manners and poetry attending the revival of literature might not be as worthy of observation as those which rendered Homer, &c. so illustrious at the first dawnings of it. I even suspected that the latter era was the more curious of the two, from its striking singularities—its gallantry tempered with gentleness, whence our word *gentleman*—its mixture of pathos with simplicity, and its rich machinery of witch-ladies, enchanters, giants, and dwarfs.

Johnson. ' Such trifles, indeed, might amuse us during the nonage of science; but the world has now outgrown them, Sir.' I respectfully suggested, however, that there were things which the world might fancy it had outgrown, while the more proper account might be, that it had lost them by the way, and would be very happy to recover them; and I instanced gothic architecture and painted glass, as sciences coeval with our bards. In short, the great man's complacency and appearance of being amused by my loquacity, encouraged me to rattle on at such a rate, that, whenever I casually glanced at our greasy listener in the corner, I saw him with his hands and eyes lifted up, in utter astonishment at my inconceivable audacity! While the Doctor, in perfect good humour and glee, crowned the whole by the following ludicrous impromptu : ' Sir, it is an infantine style, which any man may imitate who thinks proper to try. As, for instance,

> ' I put my hat upon my head,
> And walked into the Strand ;
> And there I met another man
> With his hat in his hand.'

" On my return to Half-moon-street, I found that Dr. Percy had just heard from his publisher; and with great agitation, and in no very gentle terms, was inveighing to his cousin and namesake, against the then object of his resentment, whom I had just parted from.—' Fool that I was,' said he, ' to trust such a fellow. He has persuaded me to print but 500 copies, and now the public calls for a second edition, before I have any means of judging how it has received the first.' I never saw his aristocratic spirit so ruffled and disturbed before; and, indeed, on the present occasion his anger was not without a cause; since to this discouragement it was probably owing, that the success of a very meritorious poetical effort was defeated, and its amateur author disheartened from trying his talents again in his favourite and bewitching pursuits.

" Meanwhile our sage himself, the unconscious and unintentional cause of all the mischief, still indulging the same playful humour, and thinking the joke too good an one to be lost, seems to have been making the most of it in different companies, and especially at Sir Joshua Reynolds's; for we read in Northcote's Life of Sir Joshua, vol. I. p. 81, every reader will recollect the *so often told* anecdote of Johnson's versification at Mr. Reynolds's tea-table, when criticising Percy's Reliques, and imitating the ballad style—

> ' O hear it then, my Renny dear,
> Nor hear it with a frown,
> You cannot make the tea so fast
> As I can gulp it down.'

And another account I have somewhere seen of the same joke, and at the same place, but somewhat varied, for it began with the exact words originally elicited, no doubt, by my defence of Percy. After these came one or two more such burlesque stanzas, which ended, Miss Renny being the tea-maker, with—

> ' Then give to me, my Renny dear,
>   Another cup of tea.'

" I was extremely desirous, on the first occurrence of this curious sally, that, if possible, it should not transpire so as to cause irritation betwixt two such estimable friends. But my precaution was nearly frustrated, since in the papers the very next morning, a most clumsy and blundering attempt was made to report this sarcasm of Johnson, which evidently must have proceeded from our oily companion in the corner; and the only wonder was, that a person in any degree connected with the typography of the journals should have produced so absurd and puzzled an account. Hence, however, I was consoled by the hope, that the matter would remain unintelligible to either party, and therefore no mischief would ensue. For myself, I never suffered the scene I had witnessed to escape my lips, until I returned, two or three months afterwards, to a truly revered and excellent father in the country, constrained by the renewal, through incautiously walking in town, of an unfortunate lameness of old standing, caused ten years before by a violent scald at College, and which had been nearly cured.

" But here the most powerful of all gratitudes lays a sacred obligation upon me, to stop and to correct the word *unfortunate*, with a heartful acknowledgement that my forced retreat at that particular juncture, was eventually the cause of all my future success in life. So true is it that, through the unmerited bounty of Providence, our greatest seeming misfortunes prove frequently in the end no other than blessings in disguise.

" Hastening now towards the conclusion of a detail, which even a great name can scarcely render important, I have only to add that, on my coming to town a year or two afterwards, (which, having some relief from my lameness, I frequently did,) Dr. Percy said to me, ' I have been told that Johnson once spoke very disrespectfully of my Northumbrian ballad, but, on my charging him with it, he remembered nothing at all about it.' Being, I acknowledge, rather off my guard at the moment, my looks betrayed a consciousness which could not escape the penetrating glance of such a critic, nor did he ever cease his solicitations and promises of forbearance, till he had extorted from me all the truth. Some ebullitions of passion were the consequences; but, soon after, I had the happiness to hear him promise a total oblivion of the business. And, having thus promised, it pretty plainly appears that our ducal Doctor was true to his word, since a subsequent sharp contest is recorded by Boswell, in which latent resentment would probably have been aroused, had there been any remaining. Boswell gives this as an instance of Johnson's placability; and it seems to me at least as much so of Percy's. The story is told in vol. III. p. 55. ' Johnson was praising Pennant's Tour in Northumberland, Percy resented the account there given of *his* family. Words ran high. Percy talked about *rudeness*—and Johnson said, that ' civility was now at an end,' when Dr. Percy rose, and taking him by the hand, assured him affectionately that his meaning had been misunderstood. Johnson. ' Dear Sir, I am willing that you shall hang Pennant — hang him up, hang him up.' Which surely was equally honourable to both.

" But what I chiefly wished was to introduce the following extract of a letter from Johnson to Boswell in consequence of the above dispute: ' If Percy is really offended, I am sorry, for he is a man whom I never knew to offend any one. He is a man willing to learn and very able to teach; a man out of whose company I never go without having learned something. *Percy's attention to poetry has given grace and splendour to his studies of antiquity.* A meer antiquarian (so spelt here) is a rugged being. Upon the whole, you see that what I might say in sport or petulance to him, is very consistent with a full conviction of his merit.' P. 62.

" Thus an *amende honorable* was made to my friend, though his beautiful Poem seems to have been nipped in the bud. On this I shall here add a few words. It is on a subject happily chosen and sufficiently authentic, and is elegantly written in three fits or cantos. It treats of the return of young Hotspur from Scotland, where he had been educated, under the Regent, ever since his father's defeat and death at Shrewsbury. On his passage he has the happy chance of delivering from banditti Eleanor, daughter of Ralph Neville, Earl of Westmoreland, and receives her hand as his reward. Her mother, Johanna, who was half-sister to Henry IV. now applied to Henry V., in their behalf.

' She suppliant at her nephew's throne
    The royal grace implor'd ;
To all the honours of his race
    The Percy was restor'd.'

" I cannot help noticing in this place the comparative mildness and clemency of the two first Lancastrian Princes, considering the age in which they lived. Yet were they obliged to submit entirely to the Pope, from their consciousness of being usurpers. Kennet speaks in the highest terms of both these kings, especially the last. (See his History, vol. I. pp. 305—339.) And yet Sawtre, Bayley, and Cobham, the three protomartyrs of England, were immolated during their reigns; the statute ' de heretico comburendo' being actually passed by the father in

1401; and the son, when only ' My royal Hal,' was an eye-witness to the second of these tragedies.

" I cannot conclude without noticing a late speech of Lord Grey, in which he reminds us that even under Popish monarchs, who were, in general, abjectly submissive to the Pope, because they knew of no other religion, the encroachments of papal ambition frequently became so intolerable as to require being repelled by force. Yet unhappily his Lordship's politics did not permit him to draw the obvious corollary, by observing, ' What madness then would it be were we ever again to associate a necessary-intolerant Pope of Rome with our *heretic* kings, in the government of a *heretic* kingdom ! '

" Having acquired a little addition to my Johnsoniana, should the present letter be approved, I might be tempted, Mr. Editor, once more to address you under the sanction of this great name.
B. N. Turner."

---

4. Johnsonian Letter the Third.

" *No. 30, York-buildings, New-road, Nov.* 15, 1819.
" On introducing to the reader's notice a friend of whom I cannot but be proud, I shall chuse, as an Octogenarian, to adopt the just character given of him by the Sexagenarian, vol. II. p. 175 : " The excellent and very learned Bishop of Cloyne was the tutor of Emanuel-college, and private tutor there to Lord Westmoreland, &c.' To whom, as this writer might have added, he became a most useful chaplain and confident, when that nobleman was Lord Lieutenant of Ireland, executing, in person sometimes, the most hazardous public services, which required consummate prudence, secrecy, and address; together with that cool fortitude, by which one who is *integer vitæ scelerisque purus* can alone be actuated.

" The author then proceeds, p. 176, ' Whoever knew this amiable prelate in his early life, or have been honoured by his friendship in his progress to his present dignity, cannot but experience the truest satisfaction from seeing the benefits of fortune so honourably bestowed and so discreetly enjoyed.' That the present writer can advance a very superior claim to such satisfaction will be readily admitted, if he can but be pardoned the vanity of the following extract from a letter of his lordship's, dated November 1814: ' Though you are hindered from walking much yourself, yet I find your pen moves as actively as ever, and is not likely to stand still, while atheists, or jacobins, or Catholics are to be exposed or corrected. I am grown old and idle, and can only behold with sincere regret the evils which I cannot cure; while you, my earliest friend and instructor, are upon the alert as much as ever, and, as Johnson said of Priestley, are ready, like the porcupine, with a quill pointed against every opponent.' In truth, I was so struck with the amiable qualities of this young friend, on his first arrival at Emanuel-college, two years later than myself, that I instantly cultivated such an intimacy with him, as has proved most happy and honourable to myself ever since.

"At the time of Johnson's arrival at Cambridge, this dignified friend was still an Under-graduate; and he says himself, 'I perfectly well remember Johnson's journey in 1765; I was in the organ gallery when you all went to look at Emanuel Chapel. I scudded away in a fright the moment my curiosity (which for the time overcame my shyness) had subsided, as you may remember I did, to your great amusement, on finding myself accidentally seated in a coffee-house close by Martyn, when he was proctor.' Here his lordship forgets himself a little. Seeing Professor Martyn, then proctor, approaching, he rushed out of the coffee-room, in spite of my efforts to prevent it, and hurried by him in the passage, to *avoid* being seated near so great a man. This we both regretted; and Martyn said, 'That is a very valuable young friend of yours. I am very sorry that he was so scared at my horns and hoofs.' In allusion to which, when my friend, in process of time, became Proctor himself, he pleasantly wrote me word, 'That he was almost afraid of looking into a glass, for fear he should see his own horns and hoofs.

"The same communication assures me also, that I *was* at Johnson's classical symposium, on the Sunday, (see Letter 1,) at the rooms of my dear friend Dr. Lettice, then of Sidney, but now of Peasmarsh; that we kept it up till day-light, and that the great man was in high glee; for my then juvenile friend informs me that I delighted him by relating a profusion of wit next morning. All this being unluckily forgotten, I shall take the liberty of mentioning his own amusing account of my return home, though he seems in it to attribute to myself somewhat of his own avowed and amiable timidity *. 'You returned,' he says, 'agitated with apprehensions of being seen and known in the streets at so improper an hour; and of the porter's astonishment at opening the College-gate to a fellow at such a time. Nothing, however, of this happened. Apollo threw a cloud about you. The morning was so far advanced that the porter had set the gate open, and retired to rest. Not a bed-maker was stirring, and you passed the butteries delighted, and surprised, when an unexpected sight stopped your course! The court was paving, and a dozen lusty fellows were scattered in every part of it, hard at work with their spades and wheel-barrows. The very path to your staircase was blockaded by men astonished at seeing amongst them a grave fellow of the College in his gown, who was retiring to sleep just as they rose to work. In the midst of your distress, the ludicrous idea of their being the

* " Isaac Walton records the same *amiable infirmity*, as he calls it, to have been equally conspicuous in the good Bishop Sanderson."

Antipodes struck you, and you could not help quoting to your-
self, from Fielding's comical play, ' What shall I do with these
Tippodians ?' adding, by way of comment, when you told it me,
' You know they do work with their lower parts uppermost.'

" The same amiable prelate has supplied me also with another
Johnsonian reminiscence on the following occasion : Having executed a little poetical undertaking for my own amusement, I
had submitted it to his lordship's critical judgment; and though
he honours it with his own unqualified approbation, yet he warns
me that should I dare to publish it, no apologies of mine could
stop the roar of criticism which would echo against me from
Edinburgh to Charing-cross ! of which more bye-and-bye.   I
am then reminded of what he calls ' another daring and original
work of mine, the Imitations of Theophrastus; which Johnson
himself was startled at, but from which he could not withhold
applause.'   This account, indeed, honours me too much, yet as
I am undertaking to record Johnsoniana, I shall endeavour to
relate the circumstance, trifling as it is, just as it occurred.

" After giving up the translation of Plutarch, as mentioned
in my first letter, I had amused myself by modernizing, in familiar English verse, ' The Characters of Theophrastus.'   Having
been told that Dr. Johnson was fond of encouraging young candidates for literary reputation, it was not without some ambitious thoughts as well as tremours, that I one day put a number
of these detached characters into my pocket, for the purpose of
laying them before this now-first-dreaded censor.   Soon after
my arrival there came also the well-known Tom Davies, introducing Moody, the player, with ' Here's Mr. Moody to pay his
respects to you, Doctor.'   A gracious reception and pleasant
party were the consequences.   When they had retired, with
considerable palpitations, no doubt, and a proper preface, I ventured to present my manuscripts.   The first he silently received,
and as silently perused, his head rolling, as usual, all the while;
a second, ditto; then a third, &c.; till, a little piqued myself,
I must own, I began something like, ' I'll not trouble you any
further, Doctor;' when, relaxing into a smile, with his hand
still stretched out, he just articulated, ' No, no; another.'   Thus
was the dumb shew carried on till I had no more; and yet, as
the great man appeared satisfied, or even pleased, no wonder if
a juvenile scribbler was willing to construe it into something
like approbation.   And certainly he was not in the same humour
as when he is reported to have said of some one else, ' Why yes,
Sir, I have read the gentleman's poems, but I have *no comfort
in them*.'   I made, however, one more effort to elicit some sentiment pro or con, by saying, ' Supposing, Doctor, I should
ever be induced to print what I have taken the liberty, &c.
would you be so good as to recommend me a publisher?'
Johnson. ' Why, Sir, I don't know any one who would suit you
better than that Mr. Davies who has just left us, and who is,

&c.' From this, however, Dr. Percy dehorted me, alleging that
D. was not easily brought to account with his authors. ' I have
charged him with it ; said he, ' and I 'll shew you his answer.'
The answer denied the charge, appealing, as witnesses, to about
a score of names, not only unknown, in course, to me, but
which.Dr. P. himself declared he had never heard of as writers
before ! When, after a hearty laugh at ' every nameless name,'
he recommended Leacroft, who had just then set up, and who
afterwards became the publisher of my work in 1774 *.

"Though the above odd and eccentric version was approved
by some friends, besides the Bishop, yet, as it ended merely in
amusement, I never could prize it much myself. But when, as
his Lordship hints of me, I was roused to exertion by my
country's danger and my sovereign's wrongs—after some strictures in 1782, on the loose notions of that philosophical wag,
Soame Jenyns, in eight letters to him, intituled, ' Candid Suggestions,' I made, what I then supposed, the first regular attack
on the political infallibility of Mr. Locke, though I soon found
that he had been encountered in the preceding year, with a much
stronger lance I must own, by the excellent Dean Tucker. This
last little work, which I called, ' The True Alarm,' was elicited
by the too great reason there was to fear that something which
had unwarily dropped from the pen of the great and good, but
rather too whigified, philosopher, Mr. Locke, had been so perverted, through the arts of wicked men, as to have occasioned
all the evils with which England, America, and France, were
subsequently afflicted. I wish to be concise. Mr. L.'s book on
Government seems greatly to lessen, instead of enhancing, his
former fame. What is his state of nature but the baseless
fabric of a vision ?† And while he intended nothing but to
stigmatize a popish tyrant, James II., he seems not to have been
aware that he was in danger of rendering the kingly office still
more and more difficult, if not almost impracticable, by his own
friend William III. by a George III. or any future sovereign
who might be eminently just and merciful ‡.

---

* " On the failure of this little publication, as any one may banter himself, I hitched it into a ballad ; and should the Nugæ Canoræ (some of
which have been *kept* above five times *nine years)* ever be committed to
press, this would appear amongst the rest." See hereafter, pp. 186, 187.

† " I can scarcely conceive a stronger refutation of the position that
' all government originates from the people,' than this very book
affords; for had there been any truth in it, how is it possible that no
convincing arguments should be brought in its favour by such a reasoner
as Mr. Locke ? "

‡ "This last epithet would scarcely be accorded by our northern brethren to our great deliverer William III. Two ladies of quality, the one
English and the other Scotch, were conversing when his death was
announced: ' Aye,' said the former, ' he 's gone to Heaven, if ever a
man did.' ' Nae dout, nae dout,' replied the latter, ' but he may gae
ni to ca' in his way at Darien and Glenco.' "

" Yet, alas! it is, I fear, too true, that Mr. Locke did once
give a slight hint which seems to favour that most destructive
of all measures, universal suffrage! Mr. Locke, considering
when he wrote, is easily excusable; but what excuse can be
made for those wicked men, who, on no better grounds than
these, would overthrow this glorious constitution? Our dis-
turbers now say, ' The people of England must all have votes,
or else be *slaves,* and therefore *we* will defend their *liberties!*'
Luckily, however, they have made it plain that they do not
mean the liberties of men, but of devils, *i. e.* just such liberties
as were so lately *enjoyed* in France; for no sooner did they arrive
at the Crown and Anchor, after the Manchester business, than
they sang ' Ca Ira and the Marsellois hymn ! ' ' Let no man vote,'
says the Constitution, ' who possesses less than *£.2 per annum,*
as valued in the time of Henry VI.' thus providing that the
Lower House should be chosen by the most competent electors,
and therefore with the truest wisdom.—' No,' says Faction, ' let
them be chosen by everybody; ' and then, as the great majority
of the common people neither ever can rightly, nor ever ought
to understand politics, and are naturally led astray by artful
knaves, Parliament would soon abound with those, who, as
Cobbett * says, are doubly despicable, (though he is one of them
now himself,) *i. e.* the people's parasites. Indulge me a moment
longer, that I may make this important subject still more plain.
Universal suffrage would take the lower ranks out of the sphere
where nature and nature's God has placed them, and where
alone they can benefit themselves and others, and place them
where they would do the greatest mischief; for the inevitable
consequences would be, that, on every election, some democrat
would constantly march in with thousands, tens of thousands,
or hundreds of thousands, as occasion required, of these folly-
made voters, so as to overwhelm and nullify the true ones, and
would choose no one who is untinctured with their own detestable principles. Thus the elective franchises, the undoubted
rights of numbers of Englishmen, would be all swept away by
people bragging about *rights!* and thus the King, Lords, and
legal Commons, the three Estates of this Realm, would be thence-
forth subjected to the no-mercy of their avowed enemies, the
republican democrats.

" But to return. These two tracts, ' The Candid Suggestions' and ' True Alarm,' having been sent to our patriotic
sage, it seemed not to be his turn of mind to foster incipient

---

* "This person, who from a good man has been *reformed* into an infa-
mously bad one, thus speaks on the subject : " On all hands it is allowed
that the parasite of a prince is a most despicable character ; a people's
parasite, then, must be doubly despicable. The courtier may find some
apology, &c. but what must be the man (if, indeed, he is worthy of the
name), that can crouch to the dregs of mankind ? " &c. See Porcupine's Works, part ii. p. 283.

literature; for, though the principles were the same as his own,
yet he never took any notice at all of them. For this I might
have naturally reflected upon myself, did I not possess testimo-
nials from other men of eminence, too flattering to be here
inserted, which fairly rescue me from such humiliation. And
yet I must, in a great measure, attribute my want of success to
my own folly and inexperience, since, Leacroft having failed
in business, through neglect or forgetfulness no other publisher was appointed. Hence the country printer substituted
the name of his own correspondent who sent him magazines,
&c.; upon which some one afterwards very justly observed that,
I had published my works at the bottom of a well!

" In short, disappointment, expenditure, and want of all support, completely discouraged me from all further literary attempts, until the doubly-gloomy period of December 1797,
when our jacobin neighbours franticly vowed and decreed ' the
total extirpation of the British people, excepting only, first,
the mutineers at the Nore; secondly, the Defenders in Ireland
and Scotland; and, thirdly, those *generous* members of Opposition, who unceasingly demand peace with France, and a Re-
FORM in the English government.' (See the *Redacteur* of the
above date.) Nearly at the same time, a letter was handed
about in the House of Lords, from Condorcet to some one of
our self-called patriots, in which it was said, ' Get REFORM, RE-
FORM by all possible means; for if you once bring about RE-
FORM, REVOLUTION must inevitably follow *.' On the spur of
such an occasion, being tempted to try whether broad humour
might not help a little to dissipate the gloom, I threw out a
political satire, called ' Infant Institutes' (printed for Riving-
tons), and fraught with matter so eccentric and laughable as
might chance to arrest the attention, and raise the spirits of the
public. Yet again I was unlucky. A gentleman setting off for
Bath, ordered a parcel of them, which, through a mistake, were
not sent. Some loyal and friendly Reviewers, especially the
British Critic, failed me; for, though Mr. Nares had once by
letter invited me to join his corps, yet, not knowing this to be
mine, as he afterwards explained, he left it to some assistant, and

---

* " *Fas est ab hoste doceri.* Yet I am sorry to find that a certain
law lord still talks about *reform*, and fancies faction would be silenced if
the right of voting could be extended fairly and judiciously, *without
violating the Constitution!* Can we do a thing and not do it, both at the
same time? Would the millions who must still be left out be persuaded
that it was *fair* and *judicious* to break the constitution for others, but
not for them? The elective franchise would indeed be a very great
curse to the lower ranks; but they will never believe this, for they are
blinded by their demagogues, as papists are by their priests. But in
some places there are far too many voters already. A Westminster
election always shows what the people would do could they ever get the
upper hand; and an election should surely be rather set aside for brutal
outrages than for peaceable bribing."

that assistant, plainly appearing to have seen but a single page, treated the whole with contempt. Hostile critics, however, seemed to have conned it thoroughly, and even to have been constrained to praise. One set represented the author just as he would have wished, as a sort of mystagogue extracting recondite wisdom from the lullabies, or childish sing-songs that used to be learned in our nurseries; and another set (the Analytical), called him ' A wag of the first water; ' but all agreed that he was sadly *illiberal !*

" Thus far, though it has led me into too great egotism, I have ventured to explain; and yet, having always been anxious to raise my voice, however feeble, in my country's cause, and being ready, in the same glorious cause, to do so again on any future emergency, 1 am not indubitably convinced that any apology is necessary.

" All 1 can do further at present is, to account for his Lordship's alarm respecting my danger from irascible critics. The case is this : having always particularly admired, and frequently recited that capital work of Dryden's, his Alexander's Feast, I discovered in it défects, perhaps unnoticed before. The Poet's noble plan clearly was, to represent six different passions as successively awakened in the royal breast by the varied strains of the skilful musician. These passions are ambition, fondness for wine, martial ardour, pity, love, and revenge. Yet from some unhappy cause, such as the *res angusta domi*, a pressure for time, &c. he was prevented from writing, even upon such a subject, *con amore*, or finishing it satisfactorily. In fact, the second incitement is left without its corresponding passion or effect, and the third passion or effect is without an incitement. Hence I have long amused myself by an humble attempt to fill up the outline of the Poet's grand idea, as I had successfully done to some inferior authors. To aim at rivalling the *spirit* of Dryden would indeed have been a vain presumption*; but all I wanted was, to see how the bard's great work would appear, if finished in the best manner it could be *now*, and in the form intended, had its admirable author been blessed with the *otium literarium*. Having also by me, as I said, some scribblings of my own, which, to use an expression of Sterne's, have long ' looked up to me for light,' I had pleased myself with the project of trying to dignify these by introducing, at their conclusion, a piece, decidedly excellent in itself, and not, it is hoped, unpardonably disgraced by the new supplementary matter. But this, I own, is treading on dangerous ground; for, too true it is I fear, that

---

* " Speaking of coining and forging, Dr. Johnson once said to me, ' Why, Sir, what one man can do, another man can do.' This is true with respect to the arts, but men cannot counterfeit works of genius. It is one thing to have mechanical skill, but quite another thing to have ' the poet's eye in a fine frenzy rolling,' &c. And this shows the folly of those who say, ' all men are equal.' "

in these times, as Hayley, I think, somewhere suggests, with regard to the Epic and the Pindaric, *The table is full!*

" It might indeed be said, that the principal manuscript from which Dr. Percy extracted his Reliques, was so mutilated and defaced, that the world is indebted for that charming work to the Doctor's judicious and tasteful additions. Yet I call not this a case in point, since the splendour of Dryden's sun has always concealed its spots from common eyes. But had not these better be removed, if possible? If so, then alterations are allowable. As a better illustration, let me observe, that, at Bottesford in Leicestershire, there are many beautiful monuments of the Rutland family, the present Head of which displays the principles of the ancient peerage in its genuine lustre, untainted by the sophisms of modern times. Now these monumental figures having been much impaired by time, one perhaps having lost a finger, and another a toe, or some of their appropriate ornaments, my late worthy and learned friend and neighbour, the Rev. William Mounsey, on taking that curacy some years ago, for his own amusement set himself to work, and most ingeniously restored them to their original elegance and beauty *. At first, then, I had no apprehension that I should be more liable to censure for my own undertaking than my ingenious neighbour was for his. Reflection, however, soon pointed out the difference. Alarmed at my own seeming success, what I asked my estimable friend was, whether I should not appear, on such an attempt, like one who had stretched out an adventurous hand to shoot with the bow of Ulysses? His answer assures me that ' the defects I have mentioned in Dryden's poem do certainly exist;' ' that he really thinks the whole has been better executed than could possibly have been expected; and that, should I persevere in the resolution of bending the bow of Ulysses, he shall stand in the circle of applauding critics.' Yet he finally warns me, with great pleasantry, ' not to think of escaping from the host of bawling adversaries I shall have to encounter, unless I can transfix them in the same part where Ulysses hit Antinous, *viz.* in the throat.' As, however, I am far from being so dextrous a marksman as to execute such a plan of defence, the only prudent way will be, to lay aside all thoughts of the hazardous attempt, unless some such arguments should appear as might tend to remove, or greatly to diminish, the above scruples and apprehensions.   B. N. Turner."

* For that matchless industry Mr. Mounsey was rewarded in 1792 with the two small vicarages of Saltby and Sproxton, at which latter place he afterwards resided, and in 1811 presented to his noble patron an urn found there, containing 100 silver coins. Mr. Mounsey gave Mr. Nichols great assistance in the description of his two parishes; and also contributed to the History of Leicestershire a scientific account of the petrifactions, strata of stone, and fossil bodies, found in the Vale of Belvoir. As a parish priest he exhibited the character of a conscientious pastor and an Israelite without guile. He died at Sproxton, April 30, 1811, leaving a widow and one daughter.

5. Rev. B. N. Turner to Mr. J. B. Nichols.

" Dear Sir,   13, *Dorset-place, April* 5, 1826.

" It being now your leisure time at the beginning of a month, I take the liberty of saying, that I should be happy to see you could you take your tea with me any afternoon at my old-fashioned and countryfied hour of six; and indeed it is rather too much to expect you to come so far to visit a man so inefficient and useless in point of literature as myself. I am now too a trifle further off than I was, having purchased what I now occupy, a new house, No. 13, in Dorset-place, just beyond the square.

" My motive for addressing you at this particular time is, my seeing in this month's Magazine in the extract from Mr. Polwhele's Traditions and Recollections, a surprise expressed at Mason's finding many faults in Dryden's celebrated Ode *. This has strongly engaged my attention for a long time together some years ago (no sign of disapprobation) : in short, I was so charmed with its beauties, and disgusted by the blemishes with which they are disgraced ; I was so delighted with the grandeur of the plan, and disappointed at the listlessness with which the great Poet executed it himself at last, that I could not help thinking, however rash it may now appear, that it was possible for a modern to improve it even now, by filling out the grand idea, as manifestly intended by the Bard himself, *i. e.* to render every passion regularly excited by Timotheus, and the corresponding effects as regularly produced on the Monarch. This, however charming and fascinating, notwithstanding, as the Poem is in reality, is far from being the case ; and, could it be effected, the lighter blemishes might perhaps be easily removed at the same time : but you may have some time foreseen that this opening leads only to a confession that I was once so adventurous, or rather perhaps so simple, as to have executed the plan myself. This, however, I once submitted to Bishop Bennet, who returned it with his own unqualified approbation, yet warned me by no means to print it, for, if you do, said he, you can expect nothing but abuses thrown out against you all the

---

* " We conversed much upon poetry ; and particularly upon Dryden. Would you conceive it, that he (Mr. Mason) disapproves of many parts of the celebrated Ode on St. Cecilia's-day. He objected, in some respects, against the measure, as partaking too much of the ballad species ; and as being too remote from the lyric genius ; such as

" War, he sung, is toil and trouble;
Honour but an empty bubble," &c.
" With ravish'd ears
The monarch hears," &c.
The repetition of
" Fall'n, fall'n, fall'n, fall'n," &c.
he said was devoid of all meaning ; and that it rather tended to excite something bordering on the ludicrous, than to add to the pathetic impressions already excited." Rev. R. Greville to Rev. R. Polwhele, July 28, 1788.

way from Edinburgh to Charing-cross. This advice is too good I fear, and it is what I have since acted upon; yet, as my friend Bennet was constitutionally timid, I have thought there would be no harm in handing you a copy, to show to your venerable father, or any friend who may condescend to notice it, so it may at least afford a little temporary amusement. If the time of your coming be a matter of indifference, I might point out some time when I was likely to be alone, and we might converse more freely.

" I received a most polite and friendly note, with a respectable dramatic piece, from my old friend Mr. Cradock, whom I should be exceedingly happy to see again, and who am glad to find by his writing appears to have retained his faculties better than myself. He has done himself great honour too by his ' Memoirs.' He says he has imitations of mine, Theophrastus I know; but I doubt he has nothing of mine in manuscript. If he has, I shall be obliged by the sight of them, for I have been bringing together my own scribblings. I am, dear Sir, your sincere friend and obedient servant, B. N. TURNER."

———

6. After the diffidence expressed in the preceding letters, it is conjectured that the reader can scarcely attribute to presumption Mr. Turner's alteration of Dryden's Ode; nor will its production be otherwise than satisfactory to the curiosity which may probably have been excited.

Prolegomena to the Alexander's Feast.

" This Ode," Johnson tells us, " perhaps the last (he might have added, perhaps the happiest) effort of Dryden's poetry, has always been considered as exhibiting the highest flight of fancy, and the exactest nicety of art. This is allowed to stand without a rival." Yet the same great Critic observes, " It is said to have cost Dryden a fortnight's labour; but it does not want its negligences." How the acknowledgement of negligences is consistent with what was just before said about possessing "the exactest nicety of art," I do not clearly comprehend, unless the nicety of art could be supposed to refer not to correctness of composition, but to a peculiar felicity and excellency of plan. Since, however, these negligences will be found, I fear more considerable than the great Critic was aware of, it is a pity that the Poet did not employ more labour and attention upon it; or at least afterwards give it the finishing touches of his own masterly hand. Some I have met with are so offended at its defects as to depress the piece itself even below mediocrity; I am by no means of this opinion, but think that its general effect is exquisite, and that its faults or negligences might be literally compared to solar spots, since the general effulgence of beauties is capable of concealing them until they are deliberately and critically examined.

One of these faults, evidently the effect of haste and inattention, is thus pointed out by the Doctor himself. " Some of the lines," says he, " are without corresponding rhyme,—a defect which I never detected till after an acquaintance of many years." The case was the same with myself, and probably with most other readers. This fault occurs in the passage respecting the amour of Jupiter and Olympias. Here the Critic rightly observes that, " the enthusiasm of the writer might have prevented his observing the deficiency;" and it appears that he must have imparted his own enthusiasm to his readers, since they also are equally apt to overlook it.

But besides the above, there are, I doubt, several other imperfections in this divine Poem, arising from similar causes, which the author would have done well had he " discreetly blotted." No reader of taste can be much charmed, for instance, with the idea of " ordaining drinking joys," ——

> Drinking joys did first ordain.

And, whatever defence may be set up for the drums, trumpets, and hautboys in the march of Bacchus, or whatever similarity to them may be discovered among the ancients, I must own it rather too forcibly reminds me of the dramatist who introduced Demetrius, the son of Antigonus, with a brace of pistols. In the line,

> Soothed with the sound the king grew vain,

the word soothed, compared with the context, which relates to exciting martial ardour, is surely one of the most unhappy that could have been chosen. The word " vain " seems to be but a creature of the rhyme—music's " winning a cause " is not a whit more tolerable than " ordaining drinking joys;" and I must own the following passage:

> The Prince, unable to conceal his pain,
> Gazed on the fair
> That caused his care, &c.

is surely too much like turning the world's great conqueror into a whining and desponding lover !

True it is, that I feel myself, as it were, blushing at my own presumption in producing the faults of such a Poem as this before the chancery of public taste; and yet the spirit of the great Bard, could it be conscious of the attempt, would surely pardon it in one, who censures only from the hope of being able to ameliorate, and whose ambition (a daring one it must be owned) is to try whether this divine Ode be not capable of being rendered, by proper management, much more incontestably than it now is, the sublimest composition to be met with, either in its own or in any other language.

After the above apology, it will scarcely perhaps be expected that my principal purpose is to bring forward a new and more formidable objection than ever was produced before against this most celebrated Ode, an objection which I may truly say, " I never detected till after an acquaintance of many years ; " and which others are so far from having detected at all, that I can scarcely find any one, who, on the first mention of it, will be convinced of its reality ; hence it becomes necessary to defend the criticism before any proposed alterations can be established upon the basis of it. Well, then, my objection is this,—a want of correspondence between the cause and effect in that passage, where, as soon as " the sweet musician " had sung the praise of Bacchus and " drinking joys," as he is pleased to call them ; the King is thereby inspired with a martial ardour, and falls to fighting and killing his foes ! "—" Aye," every one is ready to exclaim, with a stare of surprise at my ignorance, ' but you do not consider that Bacchus was a Warrior as well as the God of Wine ; and it was from the first of these characters that the hero caught his martial enthusiasm." Let me now produce my own plain and unsophisticated idea on the subject.

My idea then is, that the prototype or model, as formed in the Poet's own fancy, was complete and astonishingly grand and beautiful. We have no adequate conception of the wonderful power that ancient music possessed over the passions, any more than we could have judged of their sculpture, had none of their statues come down to us. When, therefore, our Bard was required to write in praise of music, what more glorious subject could he have chosen than that of the first of minstrels, at a royal banquet, working alternately and irresistibly upon the passions of the first of heroes ? The perfection of design must have required, and his genius have intended, that the six passions he has selected should each have their regular incitement, and each incitement its correspondent effect. Thus, in the first instance,—ambition, the song regularly excites the passion, and the proper emotion follows it. In the second instance the song excites to love of wine without any corresponding effect being produced ; and thirdly, the King is inflamed with martial ardour, without there being any previous music adopted to inspire him with it. With respect to the three last passions, pity, love, and revenge, all is regular. Notwithstanding, then, the great fame that this Ode has always possessed, the symmetry of it must have been in some manner strangely impaired.

But let us hear the plea of the Poet's apologists. " Bacchus either was, or was said to be, a warrior, and therefore, at the mention of his name, the hero is naturally excited to martial fury." Is one then, of the above passions, to be omitted ? If so, which is it, the second or third ? Alexander, I grant, might have such a notion of Bacchus. His flatterers had made him into a sort of god, and he effected a similarity with other gods, by imitating the march of Bacchus in his eastern expedition, and drinking out of the cup of Hercules. There may, indeed, be historical doubts whether Bacchus was really a warrior or not. We might be led to suspect that, instead of leading an army, he might have overrun and frightened some savage nations into a belief of his divinity by the clangour of strange instruments, accompanying the yells of his followers, the dancing of satyrs, and a drunken masquerade procession of antics, frantics, and bacchanalian mad-women; or, if he took amongst them his new-invented juice of the grape, they might, like so many Calibans, willingly bow the neck, and cry out,

" That's a brave god, and bears celestial liquor ! "

But we need not trouble ourselves to inquire whether or not Bacchus was a fighter, if Timotheus did not actually describe him as such. He comes indeed in triumph; but this does not necessarily imply previous victory, for Berecynthia, &c. might be said to come in triumph when attended by her devotees. But, supposing it did imply previous victory, Bacchus is not here either fighting, or preparing for fight, but for the festal carousal. There is, indeed, in the original, martial music, which I have ventured to omit, but it seems rather prepared to wait for, or receive the approaching hero or deity, than accompanying his march; rather welcoming to festivity than animating to conflict. There are also soldiers mentioned, but not either fighting or preparing to fight; no, on the contrary, they are enjoying the rich meed or reward of all their labours and pains; —

Sweet is pleasure after pain.

And the King is surely hereby called upon to partake of the pleasure, and not the pain alluded to. But let us see how this deity himself appears; he is fair and young, and well fitted to " lead each pleasure in his train."

Flushed with a purple grace,
He shews his honest face.

The ancients painted him with a beautiful and rather feminine complexion, with an honest, open, and ingenuous countenance; mantling with smiles like his own rosy liquor, much rather than lowring like a warrior breathing nothing but blood and slaughter. How could it be then that such a man as Alexander, when called upon by such powerful melody to sacrifice to Bacchus, should instantly and completely exhibit himself as the votary of Mars? They who can think this possible must suppose that, though the passion excited in all the other instances was direct and natural, and, from the master's skill, inevitable; yet here the hero must have acquired his emotions in the most awkward, oblique, and zigzag manner imaginable; for, while the grand interest of the piece is successfully going on, whew! there comes across him a side wind, that whispers Bacchus's being a warrior; and away it hurries all his ideas into the midst of arms and battles!

Oh! far, far be it from me to detract from the fame of the great and immortal author! I would guard his fame as if it were that of a father; I only wish to defend it against those ill-judging advocates who wish to cover an imperfection by fixing upon him an absurdity. But, when it is once seen and owned that there is some omission or deficiency, that there is a chasm, or rather two chasms, left in this immortal poem, (for both the symposium of the chiefs, and the martial strains of the bard, are wanting,) then many and sufficient reasons will appear to account and apologize for this defect. Among these we may reckon his advanced age, the *res angusta domi*, or a distress of circumstances that must have quenched the poetic fire, or clipped the wings of any fancy less powerful than his own; in consequence of this, the precipitation with which he was generally necessitated to compose, and in the present case his being obliged to finish his task before a given day. Add to all this, that Johnson has given us a curious letter from the Poet, telling his son in Italy that he was then altering a play of Sir Robert Howard's, by which he was in hopes that he should gain a hundred pounds; and adding, " In the mean time I am writing a song for St. Cecilia's feast. This is troublesome, and no way beneficial; but I could not deny the stewards of the feast, who came to me in a body to desire that kindness," &c. Here we cannot but be surprised to observe, that this work, admirable as it is, seems not to have been executed *con amore* by its illustrious author; that what has since filled the minds of its readers with rapture and enthusiasm, was regarded by himself as an irksome and laborious task! Hence it is more than probable that, when the particular purpose was served and the compliment paid, he scarcely ever afterwards reverted to this divine Poem; nor ever gave himself any further trouble about it. So true it is, however strange, that the world's greatest Poets have been incapable of appreciating their own excellencies, and are seldom sensible which are the most brilliant of their own productions! Such being the case, what wonder if our Bard, fatigued by his fortnight's labour, and seduced by the golden prospect from Sir R. Howard's play, might become insensibly duped by that idea, which even some of his critics have admitted, *viz.* that by naming Bacchus, and the word soldiers, &c. he had already said enough about war, so that he might here close the business, and console himself with being prepared before the appointed day.

The certainty and nature of the above deficiency being thus settled, apparently beyond the danger of any further doubt or quibble, this necessarily induces a strong desire of seeing this noble Poem revised and completed, if possible, that the public might have a chance of judging how the Poet's charming design would appear when fully carried into effect. But who shall undertake to supply a deficiency of this sort? The great Bard himself, who alone was adequate, did not do it, because, as we have seen, he looked upon it as a labour, and had not time enough allowed to complete that labour; which was his misfortune, and not his fault. Afterwards a reluctance to the work, together with a strange and unnatural insensibility to those astonishing beauties it really does possess, and which, notwithstanding its imperfections, have triumphantly borne it above censure, and stuck it in the very galaxy of fame. This want of self-applause, if I may so call it, or rather, we may say, the urgency of his own necessities and a provident care for his family, which rivetted all his attention to the play that he had then in hand. These causes conjointly brought about so very extraordinary a poetical dereliction, that no further recurrence was thought of; not the least ulterior regard is known to have been paid to one of the most brilliant productions of the human intellect that ever astonished the world by its appearance.

An Answer to the Criticism of Dr. Knox,
on Dryden's Feast.

It was not till after I had finished my supplementary expansion of Alexander's Feast, and sketched out the Prolegomena, that I first heard of Dr. Knox's criticism on this celebrated Ode. The circumstance of my having taken great liberties with this Poem myself, though not more, I hope, than was necessary, seemed, however, to lay me under a sort of obligation to defend the Bard, now no longer able to defend myself, against all such censures as might appear unnecessary, and were far from tending to increase his celebrity.

The exordium is in a high strain of compliment. " If a foreigner were to ask an Englishman for the best specimen of lyric poetry in the English language, I have no doubt but that he would be presented with Dryden's Ode on St. Cecilia's-day. This celebrated piece is supposed to have reached the pinnacle of excellence; to have surpassed Horace and rivalled Pindar. The critic then rightly observes, that, " an Ode could never have been so universally renowned without intrinsic and extraordinary merits ; " but then he directly tells us that, these extraordinary merits have been over-rated, and that this is not the best Ode in the language. Now my own ambition (a very daring one, I acknowledge) was, not to inquire whether it is the best, but, rather, by removing its accidental defects, to render it more worthy of comparison with the noblest Odes in this, or any other language. The critic " admires its excellences," yet finds out blemishes, lownesses, and vulgarities; while I, the Poet's advocate, have brought even more objections, though in general very different ones; having, at the same time shown, as

I hope, that these were not in consequence of any fault, but of
the misfortunes of the great Bard. Still further, he owns that,
" the plan is excellent and the spirit noble, and his chief objection is to the choice of words; " however, it so happens, that
with respect to the words he first objects to; and, I believe may
add, with respect to all the rest, I scarcely think I shall feel myself at all justified in agreeing with the critic.

His first objection is to the line,

" A dragon's fiery form belied the god;"

as being " beneath the dignity of the serious lyric." All, however, whom I have consulted, are as unable as myself to find any
want of dignity in the line at all. To me it rather appears to
possess an elegance similar to that of the *mentitaque tela*, of
Virgil, which seems to have been a favourite expression even
with Virgil himself. The story is this : at the taking of Troy,
Chorebus, with a company of Trojans, having cut off a party
of the enemy, proposes that they should assume the spoils of
the Greeks to attack the rest of the Greeks with most security; but, behold the folly of disguise and the danger of fighting under false colours! Their own friends are first deceived,
armorum specie Grajarum errore jubarum, and kill them from
the tops of the temples ; while the Grecians, having had time
to rally, discover the cheat, *clypeos mentitaque tela agnoscunt*,
(Æn. II. v. 542) ; and soon complete their destruction. Here
then I cannot but suspect that the epithet *mentita* was a
favourite one with Virgil himself. Correct and accurate as he
is, he seems to have admitted an impropriety of expression for
the sake of retaining it. The substantive here should have
been *arma*, *quasi ex armis pendentia*, and not *tela*, which is from
τηλε *procul*, i. e. missile weapons; yet the Poet submitted to use
the improper word *tela*, because the proper one *arma* would not
scan in this place with his elegant epithet *mentita*. But further
in Pope's Odyssey, l. xxiii. v. 116, when Ulysses, in mean attire,
is unknown to Penelope, he says to his son Telemachus,

" This garb of poverty belies the king."

If then the expression in question be sanctioned by the approbation of Pope and Dryden in English and Virgil in Latin, how
can it be in any respect inelegant, undignified, or at all inconsistent with the serious lyric ?

But there is another most strange objection to this line, so
unaccountable indeed, that it affected me only with astonishment. " It is inconsistent," he says, " with the sublime idea of
the God of Heaven and Earth metamorphosed to (into) the
fiery form of a dragon!" I shall not trust myself to analyse
such words as these ; I wish not to offend, and therefore I shall
leave them to the author's own cool and sober consideration, to
judge for himself how they ought to be appreciated.

In the next objection the critic is sufficiently tangible. He thinks, " the stamping an image of himself, as he was then in the image of a dragon, conveys to a careless reader the idea of his having stamped a dragon." What careless readers may chuse to fancy is far beneath the notice either of authors or their commentators. Fools, if they will meddle with classical works, ought to be left to find out their own folly for themselves; but since in this case a classical critic, by guessing at the above objection, may seem to have made it in some measure his own, we might ask him on what grounds, on what analogy, does such a notion rest? Did Leda bring forth cygnets, or Europa calves? But may we not suspect that even the critic must have been a little careless too himself in not seeing that in such a case the Poet must have written, not, " *He* stamped an image of *himself*," but that, " *It* stamped an image of *itself*." But here the critic could not surely have meant to disparage or burlesque the heathen mythology, that fertile source of the most charming poetry of the ancients. He could not but know that by the amours of Jupiter the ancients intended in general to shadow *vis naturæ generativæ universalis;* though, as to the particular transformation of Jupiter now in question, it was the invention, no doubt, of Alexander's flatterers, readily sanctioned by the politic priests of Ammon, and the use here made of it is excellent. Nothing more appropriate could have been pitched upon by the heathen Minstrel for the commencement of his poetical eulogies. It seemed unavoidable; and the behaviour of Alexander is perfectly in character.

But it was the next suggestion of the critic that chiefly provoked me to answer his criticism, alarmed as I was lest, through his imprudence, the credit of this Poem, or its illustrious author, might be seriously injured. Every one, since the days of Locke, must be aware of the danger arising from the concatenation of low or disgraceful ideas to an elegant composition ; what, therefore, I must think the critic was highly blameable in suggesting, it would be unpardonable in me fully to repeat. This, then, in course I must touch as lightly as possible, and bring forward no more than is barely necessary to render myself intelligible. The passage found fault with by the critic is the following couplet:

> " Flush'd with a purple grace,
> He shews his honest face."

But principally the latter of these two lines, for he tells us that, though " honest " in its classical sense means " beautiful," yet not one English reader in a hundred understands the epithet any otherwise than as applied to a drunkard or *bon vivant.* Alas, poor England ! all thy inhabitants then, male and female, must have been alehouse-goers to have heard of so vile a slang. I for one was fortunately never in such company; but I may have heard that it was once the custom for sots to call their brother topers (generally with an oath) "honest cocks" or "honest fellows;" but we surely may presume that it is obsolete by this time, even in sots'-holes.   Who, then, would wish to revive and perpetuate defunct blackguardism merely to obliterate the graces of a beautiful Poem?   I cannot, indeed, myself conceive, that a Poet "with his eye in frenzy rolling," would ever turn to the very sink and kennel of society in search of appropriate phraseology for a lofty Ode!   Nor will it, I apprehend, be difficult to demonstrate, that Dryden did not do this.   The "shewing an honest face," is surely too respectable an expression to be intelligible amongst low-lived or depraved companions; he could not then have borrowed it from a place where it never was used, because it would not have been understood if it had been used.

But the critic soon contradicts himself by saying that, "it is probable," nay, "there is every reason to think, that Dryden used honest in its classical sense of beautiful, intending to display his classical knowledge of taste; and had he written to none but classical scholars, his epithet would have been applauded without one dissenting voice."   Had he written!   To whom else could he write?   Should common, careless, or low-lived readers, and alehouse-goers, ever chance to stumble upon what they cannot understand, what they might think is nothing to the purpose.   Strange, however, it is to tell, but so far from there being not one dissentient voice, let the Poet have written to whom he would, the critic's own voice would have been dissentient; for he says also that, "as honest in this classical sense is not yet naturalised in England (English), it was injudicious in Dryden so to use it."   This is a civil expression of the critic; *O si sic omnia!* but if Dryden should not appear to use the word in this sense at all, there is an end of his injudiciousness. Let us then endeavour to ascertain the true meaning, without obliquity or sophistication.

Honestus in Latin does mean beautiful.   Terence frequently so uses it; as for instance, when Thraso sees Chærea dressed for the eunuch, he says, "Ita me D'i amant, honestus est." "Bless me, he's a fine handsome fellow!" (Eun. act iii. sc. 2).   Thus in the line quoted by the critic, "Et quocunque deus circum caput egit honestum." (Georg. ii. v. 392).   This Dryden renders, "On whate'er side he turns his honest face." (v. 540).   And yet he need not mean beautiful, for honest has a good, plain, downright English sense of its own, in which the Bard himself uses it.   This passage I allude to is in Georg. iv. where the Poet is describing the battle of the bees. The king or leader of one army is a noble generous animal; and that of the other army is just the reverse.   Of the first then he says,

———— " hic melior, insignis et ore ; "

which Dryden thus freely renders by an expression entirely his own,

"One monarch wears an honest open face."

Virg. v. 92, Trans. 138.

Thus also, "He shews his honest face," may have the same force without the smallest reference to the Latin meaning, supposing this to be not yet naturalised in English, which I cannot say it is, though I have met with its opposite, dishonest, used to signify ugly. Thus, when Ulysses beheld his companions turned by Circe into swine, they are called,

"Enormous beasts dishonest to the eye."

And what can this mean but ugly or disgusting? (See Pope's Odyss. l. x. v. 462). But as for sots and blockheads,

"Procul o procul este profani!

"Hence avaunt—'tis holy ground!

Could we allow, even in imagination, the existence of a muse of criticism, she also, whenever necessary, ought to support a matron-like dignity and decorum, in imitation of her poetical mistresses.

ALEXANDER'S FEAST.

An Ode altered from Dryden.

'Twas at the Royal Feast for Persia won
  By Philip's warlike son,
   Aloft in awful state
   The god-like hero sate
    On his imperial throne.
His valiant Peers were placed around,
Their brows with roses and with myrtles bound,
 So should desert in arms be crown'd;
  The lovely Thais by his side
  Sate like a blooming eastern bride,
 In flower of youth and beauty's pride.
  Happy, happy, happy pair!
   None but the brave,
   None but the brave,
None but the brave deserves the fair.

  Timotheus, placed on high,
   Amid the tuneful quire,
 With flying fingers touch'd the lyre;
 The trembling notes ascend the sky,
   And heavenly joys inspire!
 The song began from Jove,
 Who left his blissful seats above
 (Such is the power of mighty love);
A dragon's fiery form the god belied,
 Onward he moved in radiant volumes curled;
When fondly pressing to th' imperial bride,

He stamp'd an image of himself, a Sov'reign of the world.
  The list'ning crowd admire the lofty sound;
    A present deity! they shout around,
  A present deity! the vaulted roofs abound.
        With ravish'd ears
        The Monarch hears,
        Assumes the God,
        Affects to nod,
    And seems to shake the spheres!

The praise of Bacchus then the sweet musician sung,
  Of Bacchus ever fair and ever young;
    Flush'd with a maiden grace,
    He shews his blooming face,
  And while the many in his gifts rejoice,
The brave have made him their peculiar choice,
And sing his praises in melodious strain:
    Bacchus' blessings are a treasure,
    Drinking is the soldier's pleasure;
      Rich the treasure,
      Sweet the pleasure,
    Sweet is pleasure after pain!
Great Ammon's son delighted hears
      The festive lay,
    A massy goblet rears—
A goblet erst by fam'd Alcides borne,
Whose sides the triumphs of the rosy God adorn;
  With copious draughts he greets the pow'r,
    Sovereign of the genial hour;
    Bacchus, of each martial deed
    At once the pattern and the meed.
The accordant train with mingled shouts approve;
    And 'mid their wine the notes of praise,
    To Bacchus and Alcides raise,
And hail the kindred gifts of either son of Jove.

  Straight as they quaff'd the purple stream,
  The sapient artist caught a nobler theme,
           The theme of war's alarms.
    The neighing steed, the clanging shield,
    The martial shout, the glittering field,
           And dauntless feats of arms!
  Now in loud Doric or Orphean strain,
  He paints the hero on the embattled plain;
    Swift as the lightning of his sire,
    Piercing thro' adverse ranks amain,
    While vanquished foes expire;
      The notes inflame
  With ardour all his martial frame.
  See! wildly starting on his throne,

The monarch grasps a ponderous spear ;
And sword in many a battle known,
That like a gleaming meteor shone,
And warring worlds had learned to fear.
  He, sternly frowning as he rose,
  Fought all his battles o'er again,
And thrice he routed all his foes,
    And thrice he slew the slain.

The master saw the madness rise,
The hero's glowing cheeks, his ardent eyes;
  And while he earth and heav'n defies,
Chang'd the song and check'd his pride.
  He chose a mournful muse,
  Soft pity to infuse.
He sung Darius great and good ;
  By too severe a fate,
Fall'n, fall'n, fall'n, fall'n,
  Fall'n from his high estate,
    And weltering in his blood.
On the bare earth exposed he lies,
With not a friend to close his eyes ;
By those deserted at his utmost need,
Whom his own bounteous hand was wont to feed.
  With downcast looks the joyless victor sate,
    Revolving in his altered soul,
    The prevalence of human woe
      And sad vicissitudes of fate,
Which spares not mightiest monarchs here below;
    And now and then a sigh he stole,
    And tears began to flow.

The tuneful lyrist smiled to see
That love was in the next degree;
'Twas but a kindred sense to move,
For pity melts the heart to love.
Softly sweet in Lydian measures,
Thus he soothed his soul to pleasures.
" What is honour ? 'tis a bubble ;
What is war ? 'tis toil and trouble,
Never ending, still beginning,
  Fighting still, and still destroying.
If the world be worth thy winning,
  Think, O think, it worth enjoying !
See fair Thais sit beside thee,
Take the good the Gods provide thee ;
Joys descend from pow'rs above,
And their choicest gift is love ! "
The chiefs with rapture eyed the matchless dame,

Beauty lift up, and music fanned the flame,
And Love's unbounded empire all proclaim.
    The monarch melted by the strain,
     Felt in his breast the pleasing pain,
And hence convinced that love possessed a throne,
    Of power superior to his own,
       Gaz'd on the fair
       With tenderest care,
And sigh'd and look'd, sigh'd and look'd,
    Sigh'd and look'd and sigh'd again,
   At length with love and wine oppressed,
The vanquish'd victor sunk upon her breast.

    Now strike the golden lyre again,
A louder yet, and yet a louder strain:
    Break his bonds of sleep asunder,
And rouse him like a rattling peal of thunder.
      Hark! hark! the horrid sound
       Has raised up his head,
       As awak'd from the dead,
      And amaz'd he stares around.
Revenge! revenge! Timotheus cries,
      See the furies arise!
     See the snakes that they rear,
     How they hiss on their hair,
And the sparkles that flash from their eyes!
      Behold a ghastly band,
      Each a torch in his hand.
These are Grecian ghosts that in battle were slain,
     And unburied remain,
     Inglorious on the plain;
       Give the vengeance due
       To the valiant crew.
Behold how they toss their torches on high,
    How they point to the Persian abodes,
      Where frantic they espy
The glittering temples of their hostile Gods!
   Ere well the master's voice the lay could close,
      Shouts of vengeance arose;
     Thro' the host all around,
     Shouts of vengeance resound,
And the princes applaud with a furious joy;
     But before all the rest,
     With new frenzy possessed.
The King seized a flambeau with zeal to destroy,
      Thais led the way,
     To light him to his prey,
And, like another Helen, fired another Troy.

7. Rev. B. N. TURNER to Mr. J. B. NICHOLS.

" DEAR SIR,   *May* 8, 1826.

" As I had but little opportunity of speaking to you when here, I sit down to make a few hasty observations on the too daring liberty I have taken with Dryden, while thinking to do him honour.

" You know, perhaps, the line ending, ' sovereign of the world,' was carelessly left by the author without a corresponding rhime; I supplied the defect, though the critics, unknown to me, had done so in another way before. I mentioned the liberty I had taken of omitting the march of Bacchus, because it excites to no passion, as it rather should have done, and brings in unnecessarily drums, trumpets, and hautboys, which too much remind one of, ' Enter Prince Demetrius with a brace of pistols.'

" However, I cannot explain every thing thoroughly, as I thought to do when I begun. But, as I am in no hurry for its return, I should wish it to be shown to a few good judges before it comes back, though it must not I fear be openly acknowledged.

" It might be added that the Poem has nothing to do with sing-song; but seems meant purely for recitation, to which it appears excellently adapted.

" I find I am not like to leave this place at soonest before this day month; so, if in the little leisure after next publication you should go to Hampstead again, I shall be very glad if you will take your tea with me as before, and bring your son, or any friend with you; we can then sit any where without a fire, and have a little conversation.

" I am, dear Sir, very truly yours,   B. N. TURNER.

" P. S. I only meant that this would be time enough for return of papers, and I should be glad to see you; not that I would encroach on your valuable time, or well-applied abilities; and then I could show you a few scraps that I have now and then thought of sending to you, and perhaps with the signature ' Strephon,' which word in English will produce my own name."

———

8. Extracts from a Manuscript volume, intended for publication *, intituled, " Nugæ Canoræ, or amusements of Scribblethorpe-hall; a Miscellany of Metrical Effusions, the produce of upwards of Half a Century. With an adventurous attempt to elevate, if possible, into its own proper sphere of nearly unrivalled excellence, Dryden's Alexander's Feast. By an Octogenarian."

* See before, pp. 167, 170.

A PARODY.

Καλεπον το μη φιλησαι,
Καλεπον και το φιλησαι·
Καλεπωτερον δε παντων
Αποτυγχανειν φιλουντα.

Hard, ye critics, 'tis to print,
Hard one's hope of praise to stint;
But to print and lie on stall,
Critics, this is worst of all!

To Mrs. PENNE *, *Bloomsbury-square.*

Yes, I scribble, tis true—if I 'm tempted sometimes,
To set up for a small haberdasher of rhymes;
Have not you, my dear Mistress, yourself been the cause,
Since whatever I 've scribbled you crown with applause;
So that hence I might haply be led to conceive,
That a pittance of fame I could this way achieve;
And so fortunate prove (tho' you 'd think it in me droll)
To string up a new sort of "Poetical Bead-roll!"
  Yet what claims on the Muse can that scribbler advance,
Who, no Poet by birth, proves a rhymer by chance?
He might serve, thro' good humour or innocent frolic,
To dispel the blue vapours, or mists melancholic;
But whatever, if tried, his exertions might end in,
Rest assur'd to the bays he 'd be far from pretending.

---

* This beautiful and accomplished lady was of Welsh extraction, the daughter of a clergyman of the name of Hughes. By her first husband, Captain Christian, R. N. she had one son, the late Admiral Sir Hugh Clohery Christian, K. B. Her second husband, Mr. Peter Pennè, or Penny, a gentleman of the Custom-house, was said by his extreme good-nature, for which he was ever remarkable, to have overcome her strong resolutions against a second marriage. Being by descent a Frenchman, his real name was Pennè; but, he having been left an orphan, a stupid schoolmaster forced him to spell it Penny. The above lady, who was the admiration and delight of all who knew her, published in 1771 an elegant volume of Poems, dedicated to her intimate friend Jonas Hanway, Esq. whom she aptly intituled, "A Second Man of Ross," in a neat dedication. The frontispiece represented her offering her book at the shrine of Virtue, with this inscription:

  O Nymph divine! wilt thou one smile diffuse?
  One smile from thee will cheer the trembling Muse,
  Who at thy sacred shrine submissive pays
  The truest homage in the humblest days.

ANTI-PASTORAL.

To the same.

In a rural retreat,
Tho' in truth very neat,
With a garden, and paddock, and serpentine river;
With a bank in full sight,
That with shrubs is bedight,
Whose names, if I knew them, would sound very clever.
O Muse, or O Goddess, or O Common Sense!
O tell a poor Bard what's the reason or whence,
That in these rural scenes he can find no delight,
But droops all the day and is vapour'd at night?
Can it be that the plains have no charms for a mind,
To the Muses attuned, and by letters refined?
We were made to believe, mighty maidens, that ye
Of the lawns and the meads were as fond as could be;
That your groves were all music, your vallies all sweet,
And that flowers sprung at once beneath Phillis's feet.
Not a tree nor a bush,
But it harbours a thrush,
And he warbles no doubt o'er the lass and her swain;
And the nightingale's note,
When he stretches his throat,
Oh it's oft thrown away on the sons of the plain!
But if these be your choice, oh! why are they not mine?
Much I fear 'tis a sign,
Ye most tunable Nine,
That a brain so indocile ye ne'er could refine.
Then resound, hills and vallies, and thou cooling breeze,
Take my murmurs, and bear—to themselves, if you please,
My complaints that the Muses so long could surround me,
And yet leave me at last just as dense as they found me.
Yet why should I say,
That the Muses here stray,
Enchanting each rural retreat with her lays?
I was born a poor swain,
And was nurs'd on the plain,
Yet I never once saw them in all my born days.
Nor at last should have known how engaging they are,
But that lately I found one in Bloomsbury-square.

THE BODY POLITIC.

When rightly scann'd, each human frame,
Of wondrous conformation;
Appears to differ but in name
From each well-order'd nation.

The King we' ll call its head in course,
  The shoulders are each Parliament;
By arms the military force,
  By legs the mob are fairly meant.

The learned we may call its heart,
  Its paunch the corporations;
And thus we 've each material part
  That form the plan of nations.

Intestine wars bring on its doom,
  As said the sage Menenius,
Who quell'd a mutiny at Rome,
  By fable most ingenious.

Then let each rank, with true good-will
  And patriotic junction,
In body politic fulfil
  Its own peculiar function.

Thus might its Constitution thrive,
  Uninjured and entire;
And bless'd and blessing still survive
  'Till time itself expire.

TIME.

'Ο γαρ Κρονος μ' εχαμψε τεκτων ου σοφος·
Απαντα δ' εργαζομενος ασθενεστερα. WINTERTON

Time in our youth we fail to prize,
  Ah fools so lightly to esteem it!
Since, when at length we grow more wise,
  The task how arduous to redeem it.

Time all agree that we should seize,
  For he 's a runaway confest;
Or you may call him, if you please,
  A thief that all men should arrest.

But of all thoughts on Gaffer Time,
  Inscribed on monument or grotto,
In prose, or verse, or blank, or rhyme,
  I like th' old Grecian's in my motto :—

" How Time unmakes us all at will!
  We bend beneath his stern command,
Who, like a vile mechanic still,
  Spoils every work he takes in hand."

INSCRIPTIONS *for two new Rectorial-houses.*

Quemcunque his cellis donavero parjetis auctor,
    Is, precor, assiduè pascat ovile Dei.
Usque domum hanc fugient rixæ, mentisque furores,
    Et quodvis, valeant si mea vota, nefas.
Parva licet, Pater Alme, tuo consurgat honori,
    Parva licet, parvo sit modo fausta gregi.
Tuque O! cui condo, domibus cælestibus olim
    (Quàm tamen indignum) me, Deus, accipias!

> May they who to these walls succeed,
> Th' intrusted flock sincerely feed.
> From ev'ry crime, from ev'ry ill,
> Be this abode protected still.
> Let strifes be far away, and peace
> Abound, and more and more increase!
> And here while humble pastors dwell,
> To the small flock high truths to tell,
> To me, its Founder, may a rest,
> Amid the mansions of the blest;
> A place (how undeserv'd!) in Heav'n,
> Thro' stretch of mercy, Lord, be giv'n!

PUBLIC GRIEFS.

MARTIAL LITERALLY RENDERED.

Ille dolet vere qui sine teste dolet.

Mere public griefs might make beholders doubt one;
He with a witness grieves who grieves without one.

TOM TIPPLER.

As Tom like his father the liquor would tip,
He was commonly call'd of the old block a chip;
But, as this was not quite the right phrase, by-the-bye,
For your chips are poor drinkers, tho' apt to be dry;
So Miss Chloe desired, as the merry thought struck her,
That Tom might henceforward be call'd "a young sucker."

THE MODERN SAINT.

> His curses o'er the wall-eyed crew,
> As if such only were their due,
>   The Modern Saint lets fall,

And scarcely blesses them at all—
That 's hard, since his attention 's such,
'Tis thought he seldom leaves them much
    To bless themselves withall.

Soon after going to Emanuel-college, Cambridge, the author
was taken aside by a Fellow, and asked whether he could not
strike off something a little epigrammatic in vindication of a
young lady he was engaged to, and who had been slandered by
some old gossip. This was most flattering to a young Under-
graduate; and the following was the result:

PATTILINDA.

——— *" Vexat censura Columbas."*   Juv.

When will Belisa's envious tongue
    The charming Pattilinda spare?
When will she cease th'insidious wrong,
    Nor sneer at gifts she cannot share?
'T will be—you need not doubt how long—
    'T will be as soon as she 's as fair,
    As good, as happy, and as young!

---

*Ad Amic. opt. dilectiss. W. B. Episcop. Cluniensem,
        vacante jam Sede Tuamensi.* 1795.

Quandoquidem celebris viduata præsule sedes,
    Sanciat hanc fatum, mi Benedicte, Tuam!

THE UNCANONICAL NATURE OF POETRY.

Alas! we rectors must resign
    All claims upon the Muses blithe;
The blithesome Muses are but nine,
    And so we 've none you see for tithe.

Exceptio confirmat regulam.

To the Rev. George Crabbe, *on the general failure of the
        laurel-tree in* 1814.

In you, my dear friend, we 've a proof that the Nine
May propitiously smile on the soundest divine;
And as now in these plains you no longer will stay,
See the laurels, alas! are all fading away.

RENUNCIATION OF POETIC FAME.

No, to fame I aspire not, for what can it boot,
That I loiter sometimes at Parnassus's foot;
Since e'en there I 'm a mere accidental sojourner,
Scarce worthy the name of an epigram—Turner.

THE HAPPY BARD.

*A Self-satire on the Failure of a Metrical Translation of
Theophrastus*.—To the tune of Gossip Joan.*

How happy is the Bard,
  Whose book no man peruses;
Thus free from all regard,
  He thinks on 't what he chuses. Happy Bard!

No tongue will censure raise,
  Since none may chance to have it;
But friends who needs must praise,
  Because to them he gave it.   Happy Bard!

No fears to lose a friend,
  Can cause its author sorrow,
Since he need never lend
  What no one wants to borrow. Happy Bard!

He rest secure from such,
  As spite of prohibitions,
Or Irish, Scotch, or Dutch,
  Still pirate false editions.   Happy Bard!

No thumbs its leaves debase,
  All hands to it are kinder;
His shelf it still may grace,
  An honour to the binder.   Happy Bard!

AN ÆNIGMA OF ANAGRAMS.

A famous city's name there is,
  The Latin tongue must show it;
Whose syllables transposed will give
  A no less famous Poet.

This Poet's name, if backwards read,
  As witches' prayers are patter'd,
Leads to a coast, as he once led,
  His hero soused and batter'd.

* See p. 167.

Now take again this City's name,
    And read this also backwards ;
What have we here? 't is Love itself!
    And thus we quibblers rack words.

But put first letter last ; when, ah !
    Instead of Love—O cruel!
You 'll meet with nothing but delay,
    'That wastes its choicest fuel.

Once more these syllables transpose,
    The poor conceit will gang on ;
Whence you might aptly be supplied,
    With what ?—a branch to hang on.

Next two first letters shift, and here,
    So pliant is the Latin,
Against all ills myself I arm,
    And still this word comes pat in.

This branch too you might backwards read,
    A thought I 'd almost lost, Sir,
And here you 'll find a successor
    Of Mecca's famed impostor.

But stop ; nor let us roam too far,
    Nor words too idly squander,
While in plain English this poor word
    Means nothing but—to wander *.

Epistle to J. B. a young friend and pupil, who, being newly at Trinity-college, Cambridge, and not having had time for graduation, was one of those called Non Enses, i. e. having not yet acquired any academical existence.

So you will have a letter, good Mr. Non Ens,
Then take one that is more for the jingle than sense ;
Tho' the letter, if once it could find you and reach you,
Might a lesson, dear Joe, of humility teach you ;
By expressing our doubts as to whether you 've got
Any being as yet to be proud of or not.
If you claim it, still may we not fairly insist on 't,
That such being belongs to a state pre-existent ?
    Impressed with this notion, pray think me to be as
Amus'd when I see you as erst was Æneas,
When by Lethe he stood all amazement at seeing
Each hopeful young sprout shooting up into being,

---

* Roma—Maro—oram—amor—mora—ramo—armo—Omar—roam.

And to think as their spirits new bodies were sheathing,
What courses they'd run when they once got a-breathing.
Not that our classic stream I could mean to asperse,
For of Lethe we 're certain it 's just the reverse ;
So we trust we shall see you both happy and famous,
When you rise into life from the banks of old Camus!
   Ulysses, that other far-famed navigator,
(As great as Æneas, I wont say a greater)
When seiz'd and shut up by the giant, from thence
Escap'd by pretending to be a Non Ens ;
So he found it of use, and it may so befall,
To pass off now and then for nobody at all.
Now we know your existence is still but in *posse,*
(And *teipsum* we know should be matched with its *nosce,*)
Of no use, though perhaps it might serve to define,
A mere form evanescent, a point, or a line.
Yet e'en try to refute by the force of your wit,
That old axiom that *nihil ex nihilo fit.*
   Now pray what will you say for your intimate Priestley,
Who a system maintains both disgraceful and beastly ;
For they beastify men who perversely bespatter
Their souls by declaring they 're nothing but matter ?
There 's another great man, whose system as odd is,
For if yours steals our souls, so does Berkeley our bodies* ;
Should then both these philosophers' notions be true,
Why we 're all as completely Non Enses as you !
   Yet in spite of all this, let us hope that you 'll find
Many means of improving both body and mind.
But, as first to be born you must need have the honour†,
And your dear Alma Mater (my blessings upon her !)
Will so soon set you free, as her time is so near,
(For she reckons, it seems, at the end of the year,)
So I mean by poetical anticipation,
Thus to send you beforehand our congratulation ;
And, well knowing, like Maia's right eloquent chit,
That you 're doom'd to be born ready furnish'd with wit ;
I advise you to rival the freaks of young Hermes,
And to steal yourself hither when ended the term is.

---

* Whether Dr. Priestley, who denies the existence of soul, or Bishop Berkeley, who denies that of body, be the ablest philosopher, I shall not pretend to guess; but the latter was by far the most worthy and amiable man.

† A young senator, wishing to speak in the house, is said to have been able to get no further than, "I had the honour to be born, Mr. Speaker,—hem—I had the honour, Sir, to be born, &c.——" "And pray, Mr. Speaker," said a rough old Member (supposed to he Sir J. H. Cotton), "I wish to know which of us all has not had the honour to be born as well as the honourable gentleman ? "

Rev. WILLIAM CHAFIN, M.A.

The following lively piece of Autobiography was written purposely with the view to its posthumous publication in this Work * by a highly respectable old gentleman of Dorsetshire, who, although a clergyman by profession, perhaps partook more of the character of a country squire.

" A Short and Imperfect Sketch of the Life of William Chafin, Clerk, written by himself from memory alone in the year 1816."

I was born, as appeareth by the Parish-register of Chettle (which is as old, I believe, as any register can be, having its beginning in the year 1538, and in good preservation) on the first day of February 1732-3, and was the eleventh child which my mother had borne, three of whom only were alive at the time of my birth, one son and two daughters, the youngest of which was nine years old. My father †, who attributed the loss of so many children to the too tender nursing of them in their infancy, was determined that a different course should be taken with me; and I was baptised the day after my birth by the Rev. William Box, Rector of Cheselbourne in the county of Dorset, who happened to be on a visit to my father at that time ‡, and after

* The circumstances will be learned from the Correspondence, printed hereafter.

† To his parents and elder brother Mr. Chafin erected a mural monument in Chettle Church in 1777, bearing the following inscription : " In memory of George Chafin, Esq. who, for his great popularity, had the honour of representing the County of Dorset in Parliament forty years. He died September 7, 1766, aged 77. And of Elizabeth his wife, daughter of Sir Anthony Sturt, by whom he had eleven children. She died Aug. 23, 1762, aged 72. And also of George their eldest son, Lieut.-Colonel of the Dorsetshire regiment, who died much lamented, June 30, 1776, aged 59."

‡ William Box, M. A. was instituted to Cheselbourne in 1733

the ceremony, I was immediately conveyed to the
cottage of my father's shepherd in the village, to
be nurtured by his wife, who, fortunately for me,
was in the same situation as my mother.   The
sponsors at my baptism (represented by proxies),
were Mr. Banks, of Milton Abbas, Sir William
Napier, of Critchill in the county of Dorset, and
Miss Penruddock, of Compton Chamberlain in the
county of Wilts, who was afterward married to
Henry Wyndham, Esq. of the Close, Sarum, and
she was the mother of the present Penruddock
Wyndham, Esq. of that place, who was many
years Representative of the county of Wilts, and
an author of great celebrity.   She was also the mother of Lady A'Court, a descendant, as well as myself, of Colonel John Penruddock, who was beheaded; and who was my great-grandfather.   I
remained in this cottage under the care of the good
inhabitants, and was fed with their fare, until I was
nearly five years of age, without once sleeping in
my father's house.   As soon as I was able to crawl
about, I was carried to the sheep-fold by the shepherd every morning even in the depth of winter,
by which a foundation was laid for that strength of
constitution which has carried me through eighty-
five summers and winters without being in any way
greatly impaired.

When nearly five years old, I was taken from the
shepherd's cottage to a small school at Blandford,
two years after the dreadful fire which consumed
the greater part of the town.   The school was at
that time kept by the Rev. Mr. Hare, who, before
one year, was elected Master of a well-endowed
school at Crewkerne in Somersetshire, and left
Blandford.   He translated the Odes of Horace;
and his version, I believe, was received with merited applause *.

by George Chafin and Morton Pleydell, Esqs. and died Dec. 28,
1749.

* In the Gentleman's Magazine for 1755, p. 9, is a letter from

As my parents were unwilling to have me so far from them, I was, by the desire of Mr. Banks, my godfather, removed to Abbey Milton school; but, unfortunately, not only for me (who was insensible to such a loss) but to the whole county of Dorset, this most amiable, popular, and accomplished gentleman, in his very prime, beloved by every one who knew him, lost his life before I was admitted at the school.

He went to London to attend Parliament; called in his way on his most intimate friends, my father and mother, and slept at Chettle in perfect health. When he arrived in London, he found himself a little indisposed from his journey, in very severe weather, and sent for a surgeon of his acquaintance to take a little blood from him, who was adverse to the operation at so late an hour, but, at the most earnest desire of the patient, it was performed, the arm bound up, and he went immediately to his bed, but the next morning his servant found him dead in the bed; the bandage had got loose in the night, the orifice opened, and he had bled to death; probably it was an easy one, and only a prolongation of a gentle sleep. The account given of this fatal event in the History of the County of Dorset, that he died from a polypus of the heart, is certainly erroneous. I was at that time about four years of age; and my mother had taken me in the coach with her on a short visit to her sister, the wife of Mr. Sergeant Hussey, at Edmondesham, about six miles from Chettle, who was afterward appointed a Judge, but died before he possessed that dignity.

this Gentleman, whose Christian name was Thomas, and who then dated from Crewkerne. The subject of his communication was to point out the probability of the Chinese Empire being Antichrist; and this strange hypothesis is rebutted by two answers at pp. 71, 72; the writer of the latter of which humourously and ingeniously shows, that the flexible " number of the beast" might be found both in the name of " Thomas Hare," and that of his residence " Crewkerne," when they were spelt in Hebrew letters!

On our return home, before we had quitted the coach, a servant of Mr. Banks, who had come express from London, delivered the melancholy tidings of his master's death, exactly in the manner I have mentioned. My mother was taken from the carriage in a fainting fit, and carried into the house, and I was conveyed to the shepherd's cottage; but it made such an impression on my tender mind as never to be forgotten.

I remained at Abbey Milton-school, which was then kept by the Rev. James Martin*, for nine years. In the fifteenth year of my age, I was taken home to my father's house, a poor, raw, ignorant youth, not having acquired any classical knowledge whatever, whether owing to dullness of parts, or want of a proper mode of instruction, I know not, but such was the fact; and, to add to these deficiencies, I was kept at home one whole year, which was spent in following sports of the field, and no school-book was looked into the whole time; thus a year was lost at the most critical time of my life. I was then sent to Emanuel-college, Cambridge, at the recommendation of Sir John Cotton, of Madingley, near Cambridge, an intimate friend of my father, and a near relation of mine by my mother's side, Sir John and my mother being grandchildren of Alderman Parsons, the greatest brewer of porter in London in those days; who, when he was Lord Mayor, at his great City feast had twenty sons and daughters grown up, sitting at the table with him, of which no doubt he was not a little proud. But such is the mutability of human affairs, that not one male heir of the family of the name of Parsons is now in existence.

When I came to Emanuel-college, I was the most fortunate of all youths that ever entered College, for I fell into the very best of hands. Dr. Richardson

* He was appointed Master by Sir William Napier and other feoffees in 1737; and died in 1757.

was the Master, the good and worthy Mr. Hubbard
first College-tutor, Mr. Bickham second, and the
most amiable of all men, Mr. Hurd, was the Dean,
and it was my happy fate to come under his examination for admittance into the College books. He
immediately discovered my insufficiencies, and took
compassion upon me, and made the most favourable
report he could possibly do to the Society, and I
was admitted; at the same time he desired me to
come to his rooms every morning for half an hour
after breakfast until Mr. Hubbard's public Lectures
began. What the good Mr. Hurd discerned in me
I know not, but I was countenanced by him in the
kindest manner during the whole time of my residence in College, which was seven years. By his
kind assistance, which I diligently attended to both
from gratitude as well as inclination, I was enabled
to attend Mr. Hubbard's Lectures without cutting
any despicable figure in the lecture-room; and in
course of a short time I was frequently called upon
by my good tutor to construe some book in the
classical order when my companions could not. But
besides these great helps, I had the advantage of
being known to Mr. Barford, then a Fellow of
King's-college, a friend of my father, of a Dorsetshire family, and who had known me from my infancy. Mr. Barford was afterward Chaplain of
the House of Commons, Rector of Fordingbridge,
Hants, and a dignitary in the Church *. He introduced me to the good and learned Dr. Glynn, an
eminent physician, a Fellow of King's also †. These
gentlemen were very indulgent to me; I was invited to their rooms two or three times each week
to an afternoon tea-drinking, when they examined
me respecting my College exercises, and gave me, in

---

* See an ample memoir of William Barford, D.D. who
died a Prebendary of Canterbury, in the " Literary Anecdotes,"
vol. IX. p. 576.
† Of Dr. Glynn Clobery see the " Literary Anecdotes," VIII. 211.

the most pleasing manner, such instructions as were of the most essential benefit to me through all my exercises in the University.

To enhance my good fortune, my friend Mr. Barford was chosen one of the Moderators for the very year when it came to my turn to keep exercises in the schools. The other Moderator was Mr. Eliot, I believe of Queen's-college. When Mr. Barford presided, I was generally classed with some of the best scholars of the year, particularly when the questions for disputation were such as he deemed to be within the compass of my abilities; and sometimes I received a compliment from him a little beyond the usual one of *bene fecisti.* In the course of these exercises I had the honour of being concerned in them with Mr. Bell of Magdalen, Disney of Trinity, Craven of St. John's, Denne of Peterhouse; Preston, who was afterwards Bishop of Leighlin; and other eminent scholars. I must here mention an extraordinary occurrence which happened whilst I was keeping an Act as Respondent under Mr. Eliot, when Mr. Craven, who was many years Master of St. John's, was my second Opponent. I had gone through all the syllogisms of my first Opponent, who was Disney, tolerably well. One of the questions was a mathematical one from Newton's Principia; and Mr. Craven brought an argument against me, fraught with fluxions, which overwhelmed me entirely, for I was totally ignorant of the science, and therefore at the greatest *non plus ;* and should, in one minute, inevitably have been brought to shame, had not at that instant the Esquire Beadle, with the insignia of his office, entered the schools, and demanded the book which the Moderator carries with him, and is the badge of his authority. A convocation was that day held in the Senate-house, and some demur having happened, it was found requisite to inspect this book, which was immediately delivered, and the Moderator's

authority put an end to for that day, and the school
dismissed. The relief to my feelings was beyond
expression; it was the happiest moment of my life,
and the more so as it was the last exercise I had to
perform in the schools.

By the perseverance of my good friends in their
instructions, I was enabled to take my Bachelor
of Art's degree with the highest honour I could at
that time acquire. I was prevented from attending
and being examined in the Senate-house at the
regular time on account of the small-pox. I could
not, therefore, obtain the honour of being a Wrangler; but that of first Senior Optime was reserved
and conferred upon me, as will appear by reference
to the Tripos of 1753. I was also presented with
a piece of plate by my own College, which is
annually given to the best proficient in Arts of the
College for that year, in case he obtained an honour
in the University; a donation bequeathed by a
Dean of Durham, arising from lands left to the
College for that purpose. It so happened that no
honour had been obtained for three years, so that
the fund had accumulated. I had also held a Greek
scholarship for some years, and there was an arrear
due to me from it, about four pounds, which was
added to the cup, and made it much larger than
usual; the value of the silver is, I believe, about
twenty pounds—the cup to me invaluable. The
like circumstance happened to the celebrated Dr.
Farmer, who was admitted into Emanuel-college in
the year that I was a Questionist; he kept (the cant
word in those days for lodged) in Bungay-court.
He succeeded me in gaining the cup, which had
been unclaimed for two or three years, therefore it
was much larger than it otherwise would have been;
and the Doctor prided himself much in the possession of it, and it is preserved with the greatest care
by the Doctor's family; and I hope mine will in
like manner be so by mine. Nothing material oc-

curred to me after that time. I continued to reside in College until I obtained my Master of Arts degree. I soon after entered into Holy Orders; I was ordained Deacon at Oxford by Dr. Secker, then Bishop of that Diocese, afterward Archbishop of Canterbury, and two years after I was ordained Priest in London by Dr. Egerton, Bishop of Bangor, afterward of Durham, by letters dimissory from Dr. Newton, Bishop of Bristol, and I was soon after presented by Henry William Portman, Esq. grandfather of the present Member for the county of Dorset, to the Vicarage of St. Mary Magdalen in Taunton, Somersetshire, which I held by dispensation with the Rectory of Lidlinch in the county of Dorset, the gift of my own father, more than forty years; the former I resigned in the year 1803, for reasons which I shall hereafter mention; the latter I still hold. The parish of Lidlinch is fourteen miles from Chettle, where I resided with my father, who had no other of his family with him; and, knowing that it was his wish and desire that I should never sleep from home, or leave him alone at night, I rode every Sunday morning to Lidlinch, did the duty of my church twice, both the morning and evening service, and returned to my father before he retired to rest; and this I continued to do for the space of seven years without intermission, without any assistance, and without any let or hindrance of any kind. I had a sister a widow with one daughter residing in my parsonage-house, and servants of my own, so that I was well accommodated when there. It seems rather a remarkable incident, that my father should also have been the youngest of eleven children; he had two brothers grown up to manhood, and the elder was member for Shaftesbury, but both died before my father became of age. At the age of twenty-two he married my mother, the daughter of Sir Anthony Sturt, of Horton in Dorset, and of Heckfield in Hants. In the same year he was chosen member for the county of Dorset, which he represented forty years, in three Sovereigns' reigns. He was first elected at the latter end of the reign of Queen Anne, and on being introduced to her presence on some particular occasion, she honoured him by calling him Cousin; he was indeed allied to the Hyde family, at the head of which was the great Lord Clarendon. My father at the time was afflicted with a bad cold, sore throat, and hoarseness, which her Majesty perceiving, drew a blue and white silk handkerchief from her pocket, and desired him to put it round his neck before he left the room, which handkerchief he constantly wore to the day of his death, and died with it on his neck, with my hand in his. A broken blood-vessel was the cause of his death in the seventy-seventh year of his age, in the year 1766. He outlived my mother only four years.

At the time of my father's death, my brother was on duty as commanding officer of the Dorsetshire regiment of militia, at that time stationed at Chatham. At the first raising of that regiment, under the command of Lord Shaftesbury, Lord-lieutenant of the County, my brother was a Captain of a company of grenadiers, and in course of time became Lieutenant-Colonel, and the late Lord Rivers the Colonel. My brother was seldom absent from his corps. When the regiment was first raised, it was sent to Exeter to guard the French prisoners. The summer following it was encamped, with several other regiments of militia, at Winchester, where I officiated as Chaplain, deputed by the Rev. Dr. St. Loe, Rector of Stourminster Newton, whose health would not permit him to attend in person; and I held forth every Sunday to two regiments, the Wiltshire and Dorsetshire, from a rostrum formed by the drums, which answered the purpose of a pulpit, with a small carpet thrown over them. However, I spent a very comfortable summer in camp, having a convenient tent; and was soon reconciled to the beat of the revelle in the morning.   At the breaking up of the camp, the regiment marched to Chatham Barracks, and I returned home to my domestic pursuits, and never joined it afterward. My brother, as soon as he was at liberty, hastened home to his own house, and settled his household nearly on the same establishment as my father left it.   Our younger sister and elder niéce presided; and I spent as much of my time there as my clerical duties would permit.   Our elder sister and her younger daughter were still resident at my parsonage-house at Lidlinch.   When my brother was disengaged from his military duty, he settled entirely at his house at Chettle, and I took up my abode with him; and I believe no two brothers ever lived more happily together, or with more fraternal love than we did for many years.   Our pursuits were congenial; they were sports of the field, which we followed with great ardour, and were perfect adepts in the science of hunting, shooting, and fishing.   My brother was the best huntsman I ever knew, and very seldom missed any thing he shot at; in proof of which I will mention one occurrence. He went out in the month of October after breakfast, about ten o'clock, with one pointer only, and a single attendant to hold his horse when his dog made a point, and about half after three o'clock he returned, and placed on a table about thirty fine fat quails, which he had killed at as many single shots without missing one bird; and this was performed with a regimental fusee, which cost three guineas, and I do not believe more can ever be done by the various new improvements of fire-locks, some of which cannot be bought for less than sixty pounds.   Such a number of quails, too, will never, in all likelihood, be killed by any sportsman in one day in this country, for that species of birds are now nearly extinct here, though plentiful in France, bordering on our shores. I do not find that any naturalist has ever discovered the cause for their deserting our fields, for I remember them equally as plentiful here as they are now across the water. It was somewhat singular that my brother and I should mutually delight in following the same diversions, when there was so great a disparity in our ages and professions, that of a soldier and parish priest, and my brother was eighteen years older than me.

He was a Gentleman Commoner of Oriel-college, Oxford, at the time when I was born, under the tuition of Dr. Bentham, who sent him home, after three years residence, a complete scholar in classical learning, and well versed in natural philosophy, in so much that he outshone his contemporaries of the same rank and standing. He spent his younger days in general at home with his parents, but joined his associates in London for a month or two every year, and also visited France, Scotland, and Ireland. In the latter country he had a very intimate friend, Lord Kenmare, at whose hospitable mansion he spent some months at different times, near the Lake of Killarney in the county of Kerry, where my brother was indulged in his propensities for field sports, both shooting and fishing, in the highest perfection. After our father's death, my brother, as I have before mentioned, lived at Chettle in a very hospitable manner, respected and beloved, and was an acting and very active magistrate for the county. He lost his life in the fifty-ninth year of his age. He was returning from a morning visit which he had made to the Honourable Everard Arundell, the father of the present Lord, when his horse, by treading on a loose stone, fell on his knees, and in his exertion to rise my brother received an internal bruise, (though he never quitted the saddle till he got home,) which put an end to his valuable life on the ninth day after the accident happened. On the death of my brother I quitted Lidlinch entirely, and removed my household to Chettle, where I resided with my younger sister and two nieces very happily many years, acting as a Justice of the Peace and Pastor of two neighbouring parishes, amusing myself at intervals in agriculture and sports of the field, to which I have been perhaps too much addicted. At this time, could I have obtained the height of my ambition, I should rather have been master of his Majesty's fox-hounds or harriers than Archbishop of Canterbury, being competent for the one and very unfit for the other, for I hunted a pack of fox-hounds for nearly twenty years with the greatest success; but during the whole time I never neglected my pastoral duties one moment to the best of my knowledge. My life has, therefore, been an active one; but took a wrong bias in the beginning, owing to the rural life that I was trained up in from infancy.

My younger sister, who resided with me, had been an invalid and infirm for many years, and was obliged to have recourse very frequently to the warm baths at the city of Bath. Her complaints were caused by unskilful inoculation for the small-pox when she was a very fine girl of fifteen years of age. It was long before that art was brought to perfection by the celebrated Mr. Daniel Sutton, who was my operator; and before the now fashionable substitute was discovered, politely nominated vaccination. But of this I know too much to dare say any thing more. My sister, notwithstanding her infirmities, lived to the advanced age of seventy-two.

Before her death, an occurrence happened which occasioned some little alteration in our domestic concerns. A boy about nine years old, the youngest son of a clergyman with a very large family of the name of Napier, one of the oldest families in the county of Dorset, residing near Chettle, brought me a letter from his father respecting some justice business of little consequence. The day was a very rainy one, and the boy was thoroughly wet and uncomfortable. I therefore introduced him to my sister and nieces, who took compassion on him and supplied him with dry habiliments as well as they could; and, as the weather continued wet, he stayed with us two days, during which time he so ingratiated himself that he was invited to repeat his visit, which he did not neglect doing; and, after a few had been paid, he was taken into the family, and took up his abode with us entirely. My nieces, who were competent to the task, instructed him in English grammar, writing, and arithmetic; and by the kind assistance of a clergyman, a worthy friend, he was enabled to make some proficiency in the Latin and Greek languages, without ever being at any regular school, so that I deemed him not unqualified for one of our Universities, and I entered him as a Pensioner at Emanuel-college, Cambridge, under the present worthy master, Dr. Cory, where he went through his college exercises with credit to himself and satisfaction of his College, and took the degree of Bachelor of Arts, and soon after was ordained both Deacon and Priest by the present Lord Bishop of Salisbury. He has now some preferment in the Church *, is happily married, and comfortably settled. Nearly about the time that Mr. Napier was entered at Cambridge, my younger niece was married to a worthy gentleman, with whom she is now living very happily. My elder niece and I accompanied Mr. Napier to College at his first admittance, and finding that Mr. Pemberton's house at Trumpington was to be let ready furnished, I took it for the term of three years, to be near our favourite companion, who had not, for seven years,

---

* The Rev. John Tregonwell Lewis Napier, B. A. 1806, was instituted to the Rectory of Chettle, on the presentation of Mr. Chafin, in 1810; but resigned, it is believed, in 1820.

ever before been absent.   I let my house at Chettle
to a good tenant, Mr. Radclyffe, and resided the
three years at Trumpington; and I have reason to
believe that my presence so near answered every
end at which I aimed.

But these pleasing expectations were in some
measure discomfited by a letter which I received,
quite unexpectedly, from Dr. Pelham, who had lately
been preferred to the Bishopric of Bristol, admo-
nishing and accusing me of neglect of duty, in ab-
senting myself from his diocese without leave; and
desiring to know my reasons for so doing.   In my
answer to his Lordship's letter, I gave him a true
account of my inducements for residing at Trumpington; but chiefly dwelt on that of superintend-
ing the education of a pupil at Cambridge, in whose
welfare I was much interested; and, as he was intended for Holy Orders, I thought he required
more of my attention than he would otherwise have
done.   But his Lordship would not admit of any
of my idle excuses, as he was pleased to call them;
and, as I held two Benefices, he insisted upon my
residing on one of them.   Several letters passed
between us; and finding that epistolary correspondence would not avail, I determined to take a journey into Dorset, and to pay my duty to his Lordship at his primary visitation at Blandford.   I
found a greater assemblage of clergy than I ever
saw there before.   After divine service had been
performed, and the Bishop's excellent charge delivered, and all the regular forms gone through, his
Lordship with about forty of his clergy sat down
to a sumptuous dinner at the greyhound inn.   When
the dinner was removed, and the customary toasts
of Church and King, &c. had passed merrily round,
Mr. Archdeacon Hall, who sat on the right hand
of his Lordship, rose from his seat, and walked
down the room with all eyes upon him until he

came to me, to inform me that the Bishop desired
to speak to me. I found myself in a very awkward
situation, as being about to do penance in public. I
was ushered up the room by the good Archdeacon
in great form, and was placed in his seat, and he
took his station, standing behind his Lordship's
chair whilst I received a severe lecture; to which all
ears were open. His Lordship at first received me
kindly; and said he was glad to see me so readily
return to my duty. I replied that, " I deemed it
my duty to attend his Lordship's visitation, and
had taken a long journey to do it;" he immediately
rejoined, " And your parochial duty also." I assured his Lordship that, " I had taken particular
care in respect to that matter; and had entrusted
my cure, during my absence, to a relation and
friend, who was much more competent than myself." " But you have two benefices," his Lordship
said, " and I am informed good ones; and I shall
insist that you reside on one of them. The excuses you make for not doing it, I cannot admit of;
and that of overlooking the education of a young
man at college is the most futile; for it is not so
long that I left Cambridge myself but that I know
how lax the discipline of that University now is,
and that the young men do as they please, and
that your residing two miles from the place can be
no check to the young person you allude to; and
I do insist on your returning to my diocese immediately."

I informed his Lordship that I had left his diocese before he became the diocesan, that I had taken
a house at Trumpington on a lease for three years,
that I had a family in it, and could not remove
them until my lease expired without sustaining
much damage and great inconvenience. " You are
resolved then," says his Lordship, " not to reside
in my diocese?" " I am, my Lord, at this present

time." "That is your final resolution?" "It is, my Lord." "Then," says he, " you must abide the consequence ;" and I immediately got up, made obeisance, and walked down to my seat at the bottom of the room, when for a few minutes there was a total silence; and then his Lordship, accompanied by the Archdeacon, the Chaplain, and other attendants, left the room, the remainder of the company ceremoniously standing up until the door was closed. They then took their seats, put about the bottle, drank many loyal toasts, and we spent, between twenty and thirty of us, as cheerful an afternoon as I ever passed in my life. The Bishop's assertion respecting the laxity of discipline at Cambridge soon reached that University, by what means I know not, but it gave umbrage to the Heads of many Colleges, and was a subject of converse for some time.

For the three years that I resided at Trumpington, I was not so idle and neglectful of my professional duties as Bishop Pelham deemed me to be; for very few Sundays passed but I lent my assistance to some one or other of the clergymen of the neighbourhood, not only in performing the service of the Church on that day, but often the weekly duty also, particularly to the worthy Vicar of Trumpington, Mr. Heckford, who had two Churches of his own, and was very frequently engaged as preacher at Great St. Mary's Church, Cambridge *. This is well known to our good Bishop of Bristol, Dr. Mansell, who has always been very kind and indulgent to me.

Some few years before I retired to Trumpington, his Royal Highness the Prince of Wales occupied Mr. Sturt's superb mansion and large domains at Critchill, about three miles from Chettle. I was

---

* The Rev. Thomas Heckford, of Trinity-college, B. A. 1776, being the eighth Senior Optime of that year; M. A. 1779. He is still living.

introduced to his Royal Highness's notice by Mr. Churchill of Hanbury, a confidant of his Royal Highness, and I believe chief manager of his Household at Critchill; and I was recommended by him as a proper person to execute a commission for his Royal Highness, no way political, but merely relative to fox-hunting. His Royal Highness wished to extend his hunting country, but was unwilling to do so without the consent of some gentlemen, who were confederates in keeping another pack of fox-hounds, and hunted in the country which his Royal Highness wished to add to the Critchill Hunt. I was honoured and entrusted by his Royal Highness with a commission to negotiate this important business, in which I used my best endeavours, but I had persons to deal with of tempers not very compliant; and, although they were all intimate acquaintances, I could not prevail upon them to grant my suit in full. During this negotiation, which lasted some time, I had several private conferences with his Royal Highness; and when he was absent from Critchill for a short time he condescended to write several letters to me on the subject; and, although I could not succeed so well in my embassy as I wished, and the Prince expected, yet he never laid any blame on me, but I was taken more into favour than before, and was invited to attend his Royal Highness in his field sports, both in hunting and shooting; and to enable me to attend him in the former, he made me a present of a very fine hunter. At that time, Mr. Napier, whom I have before mentioned, was taken much notice of by his Royal Highness. He was a spirited lad, and rode a very fleet poney of his own, of the New Forest breed, which cost him four guineas; and he was in at the death of many foxes after fine runs with the Prince's hounds.

About this time, a very remarkable circumstance

took place.   One morning his Royal Highness
called upon me alone, without any attendant, not
even one servant, and desired me to take his information for a robbery, and to grant him a search warrant.   He insisted on my administering the oath to
him, which I reluctantly did ; and he informed me,
that the head groom of his stables had his trunk
broken open in the night, and a watch and many
valuable articles stolen and carried away ; and that
it was suspected that they were concealed in such
and such places, and that he chose to come himself,
lest an alarm may be given and the goods removed.
His Royal Highness sat by my side, while I filled
up a search warrant, which his Royal Highness
hastened home with, and saw the execution of it
himself; the goods were found in the suspected
places, a nest of thieves were detected, and all
brought to condign punishment.   Should his Royal
Highness become Sovereign, as by the grace of God
he may soon be, what a strange story it will be to
tell, that a King of Great Britain did apply to a
poor country justice to grant him a search warrant
for stolen goods !   But this would be a real fact.

A few days before I left Chettle for Trumpington,
our good King made his second excursion from
Weymouth, to visit Lord Dorchester at his magnificent seat at Milton Abbey, where he spent some
days, and took a critical view of all the fine paintings, pictures, and family portraits in the various
apartments ; and in the library he saw the portraits
of all the officers of the Dorsetshire Yeoman Ca-
valry, painted by Beach *, an old school-fellow of

* Thomas Beach was for many years a well-known portrait-
painter at Bath.   He was a native of Milton Abbas ; and having,
from his earliest years, evinced a strong desire to become an artist,
was patronized by the family of the Earl of Dorchester, and
became a pupil of Sir Joshua Reynolds in 1760.   His works are
very numerous in the neighbourhood of Bath ; but the picture
by which he obtained most credit, was one of the domestics of
H. H. Coxe, Esq. of Penmore.   This was in the possession of

mine at Milton school, and afterward a pupil of Sir
Joshua Reynolds. Among them was my portrait
as Chaplain to the corps, under his Lordship's command; it was drawn dressed in a canonical form,
sitting on an armed chair, leaning one hand on an
arm and holding a book in the other. His Majesty
took much notice of this portrait; and inquired of
Lord Dorchester whether he thought it a good likeness, to which his Lordship answered that he did,
and that it was generally deemed to be so; and that
it was probable his Majesty may see the original
soon, and be a more competent judge. Either on
the next day or the day following, his Majesty made
a morning visit (which is omitted in Mr. Hutchins's
History) to Lord Rivers, at his grand lodge at Rush-
more, situate in the centre of his extensive Chase,
called Cranbourne Chase. The road to it was the
great western turnpike, until they came to a direction post near my house, where a private road
branches off leading to the lodge; but my house
was in view for near a mile before the carriages
came to that spot; and I believe his Majesty had
noticed it, and had made some inquiries about it.
His Majesty's journey being made known, many
persons went out of curiosity to see the cavalcade
pass by; and, among others, my two nieces and I
were standing near the place where the road turned,
when his Majesty's carriage suddenly stopped, and

the late Sir J. C. Hippisley, of Stone Easton. An excellent
mezzotinto engraving of Dr. Harington is from one of his
paintings; as is the portrait of Dr. Cuming, given in volume IX.
of the "Literary Anecdotes," p. 589. "To Mr. Beach's professional excellence we must add, that no man ever possessed a
more friendly and benevolent disposition. He was a good scholar, and exemplary in the exercises of religion and charity; yet
no man more enjoyed the social circle, or more contributed to
its mirth:

> Happy life's duties with its joys to blend,
> Reynolds his master, Henderson his friend.

Beach died at Dorchester, Dec. 17, 1806, aged 68. Gent. Mag.
vol. LXXVI. p. 1252.

a horseman rode up to us, whom I immediately
knew to be Lord Walsingham, and he knew me;
for, some time before, I had a Bill pending in the
House of Lords, and his Lordship was at that time
Chairman of the Committee, and in the process
of the business (in which I did not succeed) I had
the honour of having several conferences with his
Lordship, which I gratefully acknowledge. His
Lordship, addressing me with a smile on his countenance, said, " His Majesty wants to speak to you;
he wants to see whether your picture at Lord Dorchester's is a good likeness."   I was much confused
at this notice; and was hastening towards his Majesty's carriage, when I observed a favourite little
dog of my nieces' running under the wheels of
another carriage, and in great danger, which with
some difficulty I released, and took it up in my
arms, and in that situation presented myself at the
side of his Majesty's chaise.

His Majesty very graciously begun a conversation
with me, by asking me, if that house, pointing to
it, was not mine.   I answered his Majesty, that it
was.   He observed, that it was pleasantly situate,
and appeared a good old mansion; I informed his
Majesty, that it was built by my father; he said,
that he thought it must have been much older; and
then very quickly added, " Walsingham tells me,
that you are about to leave this fine healthy country
for the foggy one of Cambridgeshire."   I answered,
" Yes; and please your Majesty I do it for reasons, with which, if your Majesty was acquainted,
I think you would not much blame me."   He instantly said, " I know, I know all."   And then,
looking earnestly at me, he said to Lord Walsingham, " Beach has done justice; it is a good likeness, a good picture."   Then looking at me again,
with a smile on his countenance, said, " In your
picture you are drawn with a book in your hand,
but now you have a dog, a pleasanter companion, I

suppose; for Walsingham has informed me that you are a sportsman; all in character I find." And immediately the glass was drawn up, and the cavalcade passed on. Now it is my most sincere wish and daily prayer, that his Majesty was capable of making so shrewd a remark at this time.

As my father and many of my ancestors were conversant in every thing relating to Cranbourne Chase, and I have myself borne a considerable share in it, I think it incumbent upon me to say something on that subject; but as there are litigations at this time pending, and much hath lately appeared in several public prints concerning it, I am precluded from expatiating on the subject at present, although a very interesting one to me, and in which many events to be mentioned in my simple History are interwoven. I shall, therefore, stop short now, and defer what I have further to communicate to a more appropriate time.

---

1. Rev. WILLIAM CHAFIN to Messrs. NICHOLS.

"SIRS,   *Chettle, Dec.* 20, 1814.

"I have taken the liberty of troubling you with some particular occurrences respecting Mr. Hutchins's History of Dorset. I was a subscriber to the two volumes published during his life; and fully intended to continue being so to those which were to be published under the direction of General Bellasis, but, being called away from home into Cambridgeshire, I unfortunately neglected it. I had the honour of a short correspondence with the greatly lamented Mr. Gough, to whom, by his particular desire, I sent some old letters, written by my grandfather to his wife, at the time of Monmouth's rebellion, both before and after the battle of Sedgemoor, which letters Mr. Gough returned to me, together with a proof sheet of the third volume, to show me what use he had made of them; and requesting me to send any other old records relating to my family in the county of Dorset, if I had any. And I had collected a few old papers, such as pardons, &c. to my ancestors, one under the Great Seal of England in the reign of Queen Elizabeth, and some other matters, which would have been sent, had I not seen the melancholy account of Mr. Gough's death announced in the papers, and I was then at a loss where to send them, and I suppose it

is too late for them to be of any use now. I am very desirous
of procuring the third volume of the History, which is my
principal reason for addressing myself to you at this time; and
shall be very greatly obliged if you can supply me with it. Mr.
Hutchins, the original author, was well known to me, and
longer, I believe, than to any other person now alive; and I shall,
perhaps, surprise you when I inform you that I knew him well
in the year 1744. He at that time resided at Milton Abbey,
where, as a school-boy, I have many times said my lessons to
him; but I will no longer trouble you with the garrulity of a
very old man. If you favour me with a letter, please to direct
to Rev. William Chafin, Chettle-house, Sarum, which will oblige
"Your humble servant,   Wm. Chafin."

2. Mr. Nichols to Mr. Chafin.

"Rev. Sir,

"I am truly obliged by your very kind letter; and much
regret I had not the pleasure of hearing from you in time to
insert any other communications you might have to send, in the
account of Chettle in vol. III. of Dorsetshire History. If, however, you think fit, I would add them in an Appendix of Additions which I am now printing. In Feb. 1811, I announced my
intention of publishing vols. III. and IV. in the Dorset and Salisbury papers; and in June 1813, I published vol. III.; and since
I received your favour have published the fourth volume also.
It contains a portrait of Mr. Hutchins, with a Memoir by the
late Rev. Mr. Bingham; a curious Essay on British Antiquities,
by Sir R. C. Hoare, with many very beautiful plates. I am myself a Septuagenarian; and was employed on the History of Dorset as the printer more than forty years ago; but you must be
some years older."

3. Mr. Chafin to Messrs. Nichols.

"Sirs,   Chettle, March 23, 1816.

"I have taken the liberty of writing to say that, in case the
Appendix to Mr. Hutchins's History of Dorset is published, or
whenever it may be, I shall be glad to have it to bind up with
the volume which you sent last; and shall be obliged if you will
inform me of the price of the first and second volumes of the
new edition. I was a subscriber to the original publication; but
left both volumes at Cambridge many years ago. There are
some little publications, which I often wish to have, but cannot
get from the booksellers in the country without long delay; and,
reading being my only amusement, if such a trifling matter be
not beneath your notice, your indulgence in admitting me to a
correspondence will greatly oblige
"Your humble servant,   Wm. Chafin."

4. " SIRS, *Chettle, Cashmoor-inn, July* 30, 1816.
" I have herein sent a draft for the Appendix to Mr. Hutchins' History of Dorset, and other books. Had I rightly comprehended the scope and design of that Appendix, I think I could have added some few trifling matters to it, for, having in my younger days, almost from childhood, lived nine years in the same place (Milton Abbey) with Mr. Hutchins the author, many little occurrences happened which made an impression on a juvenile mind not to be obliterated even in extreme old age. They were too trifling indeed to engage the notice of the Rev. Mr. Bingham, when he wrote the short history of Mr. Hutchins' life. In the Appendix I meet with a very melancholy story which I never before heard of, I mean the wilful and premeditated murder of a Mr. Fussell, of Blandford, by a Mr. George Strangeways, which seems to have cast a blot on the escutcheon of the noble family of Ilchester. What induces me to mention this matter is this. A coincidence hath fallen in my way which corroborates the truth of that tragical event. The murdered man was agent and steward to my great-grandmother, Amphillis Chafin, then a widow; she was an heiress of the Tichborne family in Hampshire, and I have letters in my possession written by her to Mr. Fussell at Blandford just before he took his fatal journey to London, which letters are at your service whenever you may wish to see them. I had once the honour of having a short correspondence with the much lamented Mr. Gough, and I sent to him some letters which were written by my grandfather to his wife at the time of Monmouth's rebellion, and he inserted as many as he thought proper in the History of Dorset, and returned the whole to me. I now regret that I did not at that time send other old letters which I now have relating to persons of old families in the county of Dorset; but as they are chiefly on sporting subjects, I thought them of no use, but I now think some of them may have had a place in the Appendix.

" It is my wish, if it should be agreeable to you, to keep up an occasional correspondence with you; and at some future time, if I should be capable of doing it, I should be glad to commit to your custody a short sketch of my own life, which, although a domestic one (for I have never been more than one hundred and sixty miles from my birth place in the course of a very long life), has been attended with peculiarities somewhat uncommon, and the situation I at this time stand in is so very particular, that it is impossible for any other person to be in the same, for I believe that I am the oldest Member of the University of Cambridge, the oldest clergyman in the diocese of Bristol, and the oldest magistrate in the county of Dorset; of the two latter I am certain, but out of so many thousands there possibly may be a senior Member of the University, but on the strictest inquiry I can hear of no one. You may depend upon my veracity in every thing which I may communicate to you, and you are welcome to make what use you please of my communications; and I am your obliged humble servant,

" Wm. Chafin."

---

5. Mr. J. B. Nichols to Mr. Chafin.

" Rev. Sir,   *Red Lion-passage, July* 31, 1816.
" I beg to return you my very grateful thanks for your kind and agreeable letter. To my father especially, *who is no modern*, your letter will be particularly interesting. Allow me to take the liberty of asking whether you happen to have met with his work, intituled, ' Literary Anecdotes of the Eighteenth Century;' if not, I think it would interest you, as it contains a multitude of anecdotes of learned Cambridge men, who must have been your contemporaries. I doubt not it is in your power to add to the interest of such a work from the early recollections of your well stored mind. If this would be agreeable to you, any such communications would be highly acceptable, either relating to yourself or others, accompanied with any original letters that might be worth printing.
" The tragical event in the Strangeways family is, I doubt not, correct; as I perceive Mr. Gough has stated it shortly in the first volume of Dorset, and given a fuller account of it in the Appendix. Whence he derived his information I know not. At all events, I hope you will find leisure to favour us with the sketch you so kindly promised us of your own life, embracing such a long series of eventful years; and which I hope may be prolonged to as distant a day as you can possibly enjoy existence. I am, Reverend Sir, yours very respectfully and faithfully,   J. B. Nichols."

---

6. Rev. Mr. Chafin to Messrs. Nichols.

" Sirs,   *Chettle, Aug.* 5, 1816.
"I have received your kind letter, and I shall be much obliged if you will send me the ' Literary Anecdotes' which you mention, for I have never seen them, and they will certainly be entertaining to me, and perhaps instructive, should I be capable of accomplishing my present design.
" I am your sincere humble servant,   Wm. Chafin."

---

7. " Sirs,   *Chettle, Aug.* 26, 1816.
" I received the ' Literary Anecdotes' quite safe, and I have no doubt but I shall derive much amusement from them when I can find time to peruse them. I herewith send a first assay of the sketch which I proposed, and it rests with you whether I shall make a full stop at once, or endeavour to go on a few sheets

further. If I can give the elder Mr. Nichols a few minutes entertainment I shall be content. I find it a more arduous task than I was aware of; I have no amanuensis, no diary, no memorandums to help, and have nothing to depend on but mere dint of memory, which, among all the infirmities incident to old age, I thank God has not as yet failed me, especially in events long past.

" I have very little time to spare; I have many avocations which take up the greatest part of it, as a farmer having a small farm in my hands, as a justice of the peace, which occupies much of my time, although I have never attended the assizes or quarter sessions, but left that to my lay brethren, as more proper for them, and have never acted but at home, and that only on emergencies, and yet it is a restraint on my domestic habits. My chief business in this way is the hearing complaints of paupers, and ordering them relief according to the best of my judgment; a very unpleasant and distressing employment it is, and multiplies daily. I have but little leisure in the day-time for writing; and can only get a spare hour or two at night to do it by candle-light. If I should continue the sketch proposed, I shall relate some trifling anecdotes of the two greatest personages in the kingdom; no female, for that would be too delicate a subject for such a pen as mine, nor shall what I say give offence to any one; God forbid it should! Salisbury is my post-town, sixteen miles from my habitation; I cannot, therefore, conveniently pay postage.

" I am your obliged humble servant,   Wm. Chafin."

8. " Sirs,   *Chettle, Sunday-night.*
" I was very sorry to find by your last letter that the elder Mr. Nichols was much indisposed; but I hope and trust he is at this time in a state of convalescence. As you gave me some encouragement to continue my trifling little sketch, I have herewith sent you a sheet or two more. I represented to you in my last the predicament I labour under; my avocations in the day-time are such that I have only time to write by candle-light. You must therefore make allowance for blunders * and false orthography; and I must leave it to you to correct all deficiencies, if you think it worth your while. I have communicated the chief incidents of my life, on the truth of which you may depend; but I have many extraneous matters still to send, some of them of a ludicrous kind; but whatever I communicate I leave entirely to your disposal, to throw into the fire or to make any use of that you please. I keep no copy, I have no helper, and only scribble just what occurs to my memory at the time; therefore I shall go on or leave off just as you think most advisable;

---

* Mr. Chafin's hand-writing, so far from needing an apology, is beautifully clear and legible.

it is a matter between ourselves, and the result of no consequence to any one.

"I am your obliged humble servant, WM. CHAFIN."

---

9. Mr. J. B. NICHOLS to Mr. CHAFIN.

"REV. SIR, *Sept.* 24, 1816.

"I have the double satisfaction of assuring you that my father is considerably better in his health, and that he is delighted with your kind and instructive communication. He desires me to return his best thanks, and heartily wishes that you may have health and spirits to continue so agreeable a narrative of passing events, which otherwise might be entirely lost. Permit me also, Sir, to add my own acknowledgments for your repeated marks of friendly attention to, Sir,

"Your much obliged humble servant, J. B. NICHOLS."

---

10. "SIRS, *Chettle, Sept.* 26, 1816.

"Your letter, which I received yesterday, gives me much satisfaction in hearing that Mr. Nichols is so much better in health, and somewhat amused with my scribble; I should have continued it, but for the reason which I mentioned to you. Lord Rivers is my relation and friend; his rights of Chase have lately been invaded, and a kind of conspiracy formed against them, and a cause was tried at the last Salisbury assize, and a very unjust verdict given against his Lordship. This event has ever since been the general topic of conversation in all companies, even at ladies tea-tables, and among all sorts of persons. And as I have been more conversant with the rights of the Chase, and for a much longer time than any other person living, I have thought it my bounden duty to collect from memory as many circumstances as possible relating to this matter, and to make them public; for I am convinced that, if this had been done before the trial, it would have turned the scale in his Lordship's favour. My task is finished, and only wants publication; and that is the business on which I wish for your advice. It consists of two sheets written exactly in the same manner as those I sent last, and would form a very small pamphlet, which, if circulated in the counties of Wilts and Dorset, would be in high request, and not one would remain on hand; for, even if they contained nonsense, with any thing relating to the Chase attached to it, such is the rage at this present time, that they would be all bought up immediately. I shall impatiently await your sentiments, for no time is to be lost; and we must strike while the iron is hot. There will be some anecdotes in this little performance that I flatter myself will be amusing to Mr. Nichols; and I am

"Your obliged humble servant, WM. CHAFIN."

11. Mr. J. B. Nichols to Mr. Chafin.

" Rev. Sir,

" We are much obliged by your favour of the 26th instant; and shall be very happy in being instrumental in assisting you in the publication of your proposed pamphlet on the subject of Cranbourne Chase, either on your own account, or in any way you may please to point out. Of course, it is your intention to affix your own name to the pamphlet. It is, we doubt not, needless for us to hint, that it is a delicate task to differ from the decisions of judges and juries; you will doubtless be on your guard, so to express yourself as to avoid any ground for litigation. If you print the pamphlet, what booksellers at Salisbury, Blandford, and any other towns, would you recommend should sell it ? "

----

12. Mr. Chafin to Mr. J. B. Nichols.

" Sir,   *Chettle, Oct. 8,* 1816.

" Since I received your last letter, with a postscript in your good father's own hand-writing, which gave me much satisfaction, I have had communication with Lord Rivers respecting the little performance which I mentioned to you, and I have good reason to believe that Mr. Farrer, my Lord's principal steward, will call on you to consult on the readiest means of making my little History of the Chase public. You may assure yourself that I have taken the utmost precaution not to commit either printer or myself, for there is nothing personal in it, nor any thing inserted that any person living can gainsay or contradict. In regard to this matter I am quite easy; but I am doubtful about the orthography, for I was obliged to send it away unfinished, and before I had time to revise it. You know the disadvantages I labour under, and I hope will correct all errors, should my little account of Cranbourne Chase come to the press. It is matter of no concern to the world in general, but not so to Lord Rivers; his Chase rights rest much upon it, for I have communicated facts unknown to any other person, and unsuspected; and, should we be successful in assisting his Lordship in the recovery of his rights, it will be no bad thing to oblige a Lord of his Majesty's Bed-chamber; and I think we shall be fairly entitled to some of the good things which the Chase will produce in season, as fees justly due for our trouble, and I flatter myself you will receive a sample of it ere long; and I am your obliged humble servant,   Wm. Chafin."

13. Mr. J. B. Nichols to Rev. W. Chafin.

" Rev. Sir,   *Oct.* 11, 1816.
" Your favour of the 8th came duly to hand; and I assure
you it will give my father and myself much pleasure, if we can
co-operate with you in establishing your noble Patron's Rights
of Chase, in any way you and Mr. Farrer may think best.   There
could be no apprehension of your prudence in avoiding per-
sonalities; and I am glad that you excuse the liberty I took in
hinting that judges and juries are tenacious respecting their
determinations.   With great regard and true respect, I am, Sir,
your obliged and humble servant,   J. B. Nichols."

14. Mr. Chafin to Messrs. Nichols.

" Sirs,   *Chettle, Oct.* 16, 1816.
" I have not heard any thing from Lord Rivers since I wrote
last.   I believe he is at Windsor in waiting; but I have good
reason to think that the papers which his Lordship sent to me
for will be lodged in your hands.   My motive for troubling you
with this is to say, that those papers were sent away in a hurry,
and there are omissions in them that must be rectified; and
some additions also, which will be submitted to you to insert or
not, as you may think proper.   If any communication be made
to you by any agent of Lord Rivers, a line from you will greatly
oblige your humble servant,   Wm. Chafin."

15. " Sirs,   *Chettle, Salisbury, Dec.* 30, 1816.
" I know that you must be surprised at not hearing from me
for so long a time; but when you are informed of the reason of
my breaking off our correspondence so abruptly, I am confident
you will acquit me of any neglect.   In the first place I have
been labouring under a very severe domestic affliction in the
loss of a worthy friend and relative, the good husband of one
of my nieces, after a long and painful illness.   This melancholy event had such an effect on both my nieces, that their
lives were in great danger for many days, and at this time they
are scarcely in a state of convalescence.   My own health has
also suffered much, and I am now very unwell, and have been
confined to the house more than a month.
" So much respecting my own private concerns; but there
is one in regard to Lord Rivers, which gives me much uneasiness, and lies heavy on my mind, and I do strongly suspect,
that both his Lordship and myself have been unfairly dealt with.
It is a very serious matter, and a complicated one, and requires
much explanation, which I am at present incapable of giving,
for I have a complaint in my hand, and use a pen with difficulty,
as you may perceive, and I have no scribe nor assistant what-

ever; but it is my intention, within the course of a few days, to transmit to you all the letters which I have received from Lord Rivers and his agents, from which you will, in a great measure, be enabled to form a judgment of the case. And I hope and trust that you will indulge me in a renewal of our correspondence, that we may consult together in what manner it will be best to proceed in this arduous business, for such it is, though unknown to Lord Rivers; and I am not at liberty to withdraw the veil from his eyes. When you have read the letters, you will understand what I mean; and I flatter myself your opinion and mine will coincide. I shall be much obliged if you will favour me with a line as soon as you receive this, and inform me how your good father has stood this sickly time, for I have a fellow feeling for all my contemporaries, but more particularly Mr. Nichols; and let me know if Messrs. Farrers have ever had any communication with you on Lord Rivers's account. When I hear from you, I hope to be able to expatiate more on this affair of Lord Rivers's, which is a very interesting one to me. The present is the most melancholy Christmas that I ever experienced in the course of my very long life, I hope it has not been so with you; and I am

" Your sincere humble servant,   WM. CHAFIN."

---

16. Mr. J. B. NICHOLS to Mr. CHAFIN.

" REV. SIR,   *Red Lion-passage, Jan.* 2, 1817.

" Truly sorry am I to hear of your domestic affliction. It has been a very sickly time in town; but, I thank God, my dear father has passed thus far through the winter tolerably well, which I attribute partly to his not so frequently leaving his own comfortable library at Highbury.

" We were rather surprised not to have heard further of Lord Rivers's case. Messrs. Farrers have never communicated with us on the subject. To ourselves, my dear Sir, it is a matter of little moment, except inasmuch as we are likely to contribute to your gratification, and to Lord Rivers's interest. I am truly grieved the matter should have given uneasiness to yourself.

" Your previous communications to my father afforded him so much pleasure that I earnestly hope your health and strength will enable you to renew your correspondence. Most heartily wishing you the compliments of the season, I am, dear Sir, your very obedient humble servant,   J. B. NICHOLS."

---

17. Mr. CHAFIN to Mr. J. B. NICHOLS.

" DEAR SIR,   *Chettle, Jan.* 5, 1817.

" It gave me much pleasure to hear that Mr. Nichols had weathered the dreadful season so well. It has not been so with

me; but I am a much older man than your good father. I have
taken the earliest opportunity of transmitting to you all the
letters which passed between Lord Rivers and his agents, which
I hope you will receive safe, for I have no copies.   When you
have perused them, I think you will be perfectly informed how
matters stand; and the more so as I have herewith sent (as a
sort of preface) my motives for writing the little matter I have
done, which was the work alone of ten hours in five evenings
by candle-light.   You will find that Messrs. Farrers and Mr. Serjeant Lens approve of my performance; but they have made a
different use of it from what was intended by me.   On the
strength of my evidence you will find that they have obtained
a rule for a new trial, which is directly contrary to my wishes
and design; my aim was to set forth Lord Rivers's claims in a
clearer light, and to prevent future law suits instead of encouraging them.   Between ourselves, I cannot help saying that I
feel myself as having been made a tool of by the lawyers; they
seem to have taken the advantage of my communication to
Lord Rivers only to draw his Lordship into great expence, and
to empower the learned Serjeant to make another fine florid
oration in the Court, with no better success than before.   Had
Lord Rivers taken his own course, and not have consulted lawyers, many distressing events, which have since happened, would
certainly have been averted.   The delay of six weeks in not
returning my papers (which they acknowledge) has been very
injurious to Lord Rivers, as you will find in the sequel.   In the
night of the seventh of December, some deluded persons, led
astray by notions instilled into their minds, particularly by the
little pamphlet which I shall send you, that Lord Rivers had no
right to the deer in Wiltshire, and that any person may kill
them with impunity; four men, not of the lowest class, but
mechanics, came armed with fire arms into the Chase to destroy
the deer; but they were met by two resolute young keepers belonging to Burseystool-lodge, when a very severe conflict ensued,
and many serious wounds were given on both sides; but in
the end the keepers gained the victory.   They took one prisoner,
and the others ran away without attempting to rescue him; in
revenge for which, he impeached his companions, who were
apprehended and committed to Dorchester gaol for felony.
The scene of action was in Dorset; the very unpleasant act of
commitment fell upon me, and that at a time when I was
assured that it was a measure that would be very hostile to
Lord Rivers's Chase rights, and which would not have happened
if those rights had been made generally known.   The imprison-
ment of the people has brought a burden on the county; and
also to the parishes on whom the families of the criminals are
become chargeable.   This unlucky affair has thrown an odium
on his Lordship's rights, and made them very unpopular; and
I know that Mr. Serjeant Best, who has considerable property

in Dorset, and is Member of a county borough, will make himself well acquainted with all these unhappy circumstances, and will be an overmatch for Mr. Serjeant Lens, being retained on the other side.   In my last letter to Messrs. Farrers, I requested them not to build any thing on my evidence in regard to a new trial, for that nothing should induce me (even if I was able to travel) to expose myself in a court of judicature, where I could not hear one word that was said.   I made a proposal to have my evidence taken by a commission; but you will find by Messrs. Farrers's letter, that it may be done in the Court of Chancery, but not elsewhere.   If, as the lawyers are pleased to say, my little performance 'contains a mass of evidence, and is written with great perspicuity,' why then should not Lord Rivers avail himself of that evidence when he can ?   Why should it not be secured to him immediately; and not suffer it, as must soon happen, to die with me ?   It is very certain that my evidence cannot be received in any court, and therefore of no service to Lord Rivers unless made public; and I am clearly convinced in my own mind it would be doing Lord Rivers a most essential service at this time.   But how it is to be done is the question, and which I submit to your consideration; and if your opinion of the matters agrees with mine, as soon as I hear from you, I will transmit to you the whole performance, for until you have read it, it will be impossible for you to judge of the propriety or impropriety of publishing such an incongruous a performance.   Yet at the same time I do flatter myself that your father, should he be pleased to peruse it, will not be displeased with it, to whom I beg leave to present my respects; and I am,

" Your sincere humble servant,   Wm. Chafin.

" I have herewith sent an account of my motives for writing at all concerning the Chase."

Rev. W. Chafin's Motives for Writing concerning Cranbourne Chase.

" That what I have written respecting Cranbourne Chase may be rightly understood, I think it necessary for me to declare my motives, which were various, for writing on the subject at all.   Some short time after the decease of the late Lord Rivers, Mr. Beckford, of Stapleton, on whose son the title is entailed, and who is interested in reversion in the rights of the Chase, requested of me (knowing that I had been conversant with the affairs of the Chase longer than any other person then living) to sit down at any leisure time, and recollect all the incidents and occurrences that had happened respecting the Chase within my memory, and to commit them to paper.   This injunction I obeyed; and with some difficulty wrote several sheets of paper, which I formed into a little packet, and which I put into my pocket with intent to deliver it into Mr. Beckford's own hands, whom I was engaged to meet on that day with

his son. Mr. Horace Beckford was there, and I delivered my
packet to him, who promised that his father should have it the
night, but owing to some woeful mischance, I know not what, the
papers never reached the father's hands to his dying day. After
the late trial at Salisbury, in which a verdict was given against
Lord Rivers, I did presume to say to his Lordship, that I was
well convinced that, if the contents of my lost papers had
been known to the Court, a different decision might probably
have been the consequence. Lord Rivers desired me to endeavour to recollect as much of the purport of those papers as I
could, and send it to him. To execute this task was the first
and principal motive for writing what I did, but from a great
lapse of time, and many occurrences intervening, I could not
write in the same form as before, but was obliged to conform
to the taste of the times. Another motive for writing thus was
this: An honest quaker, a schoolmaster at Salisbury, was induced, by the dictates of some persons unfriendly to Lord Rivers's
rights, to publish, some little before the aforesaid trial, a small
pamphlet *, in order to prejudice the minds of some people, and
to persuade them that Lord Rivers had no Chase rights in Wiltshire. It has been my aim, therefore, to contravene many
assertions in this little book, and to expose the fallacy of them.
Within a few years last past, there has been a great change
of landed property in the Chase; and the present possessors are,
I believe, not perfectly informed of Lord Rivers's rights and
claims. Another motive, therefore, for my writing was, to set
these rights and claims before them in a clearer light, in hopes
of preventing vexatious contests in future. How far I have
been successful, I must leave to all those who are concerned
impartially to judge."

<hr />

18. Mr. J. B. Nichols to Mr. Chafin.

"Dear Sir,   *Red Lion-passage, Fleet-st. Jan.* 8, 1817.
" I have read over to my father with great interest your
correspondence with Lord Rivers and his agents; and hasten to
express my father's and my sincere concern that matters should
have turned out so unfortunately. It was polite and correct in
you to submit your manuscript to Lord Rivers previous to publication, as you had his Lordship's interest mainly at view; but
the consequences make me regret you did not surprise Lord
Rivers with your printed defence of his rights. It would, how-

<hr />

* "A History of the Forest or Chace, known by the name of Cran-
born Chace, collected from authentic early records, and continued to a
late period; with a brief description of its present state. By William
West. Gillingham, printed by E. Neave, 1816." 8vo, pp. 132. It appears
to have been chiefly compiled from the History of Dorsetshire. The same
author afterwards published another pamphlet on the subject, which
is noticed hereafter, p. 242.

ever, we humbly conceive, be improper now to print the statements, after what has passed between Lord Rivers and you,
whilst the litigation is going forward; but I sincerely hope so
important a document will not be wholly lost; and that you
may live to see the time when it may be published with propriety. Your motives for writing it might be easily converted
into a good prefatory introduction. I wish your health and
strength would have conveniently borne a journey to London,
as it would have given me great pleasure to have paid my respects
to you at your hotel or lodgings; and still greater to have seen
you at my humble abode. I fear, however, by what you say, this
is not likely to be the case; and without it how can Lord Rivers
be benefited by a new trial?

"If you intrust us with your manuscript, we doubt not to be
amused and instructed by it; and it shall be carefully returned.

"I now send back the letters; and remain, dear Sir,

"Your obliged and faithful servant,   J. B. NICHOLS."

---

19. Mr. CHAFIN to Mr. J. B. NICHOLS.

"DEAR SIR,   *Chettle, Jan. 12, 1817.*

"I received your packet safe. As Lord Rivers can have no
such evidence as mine to support his Chase claims, from lapse
of time and other casualties, I cannot but think that, if my
manuscript documents should die with me, it would be an
irretrievable loss to Lord Rivers. I have, therefore, sent you
the whole of my simple performance, which I wish you to keep;
but, as I have no copy, I should be obliged if you will have it
transcribed, and return a copy to me instead of the original.
You will find it very different from what you expect; there are
many anecdotes and little stories related in it, which will appear
very trifling, but you, who are acquainted with my design, will
clearly perceive the intent of them; and that they tend to establish rights of great value, which could not have been done in
a serious way without giving offence, which I have carefully
avoided. I have also sent the Quaker's book which I mentioned
to you, which has done mischief; and which it has been my aim
to prevent. I have the presumption to flatter myself that your
good father will find some minutes' amusement from my performance; and he may assure himself that all the facts are true.

"Your sincere and obliged humble servant, WM. CHAFIN."

---

20. "DEAR SIRS,   *Feb. 5, 1817.*

"Not having heard from you for some time makes me apprehensive that you may have sent a parcel, which I have not
received, and that is the reason of my troubling you now. If
no transcript of my papers hath been taken, I think, upon due
consideration of the matter, that it will be a useless trouble to

do it, as you have got the original in your keeping. As to the renewal of Lord Rivers's Chase cause, I have not heard any thing concerning it, nor have I had any communication with any of his Lordship's agents, which I suppose I should have had if a new trial was to take place; but I am at present quite in the dark respecting that matter. I was pleased to see, in the Gentleman's Magazine, a proper notice * of that insidious publication which I sent you; and that your opinion of it exactly coincides with mine. It has already done much mischief, which will be made manifest to the world at the ensuing assizes at Dorchester, where several poor criminals will be tried for capital offences, committed in consequence of having been seduced by the dictates of that book. As I have mentioned the Gentleman's Magazine, I take the liberty of giving you an account of an uncommon appearance (as I believe it to be) which has lately been observed here; and if you can spare a little room for it in your next Magazine, I think it would be interesting to Ornithologists. A pair of swallows, the *arundo rustica*, Lin. Syst. having bred up a nest of young ones the last summer in a hovel adjoining a dwelling-house in this village without being disturbed, came on the eleventh day of January last and visited their nest, and one of them was seen in it, busily employed either in pulling it down or repairing it, the other sitting on a rafter near. They both flew in and out many times in the course of the day, and appeared strong on the wing. It was a warm day for the season, and some gnats were perceived in the air; they departed about one o'clock. In about ten days after they re-visited their nest, but made a much shorter stay, the weather not being so favourable, and have not been seen since. A line from you will greatly oblige your sincere humble servant,   WM. CHAFIN."

---

21. Mr. J. B. NICHOLS to Mr. CHAFIN.

"REV. SIR,   *Feb.* 6, 1817.

" On the receipt of your parcel, which was truly acceptable, the papers were given to Mr. Nichols senior to peruse, which afforded him very considerable satisfaction. They were sent to a confidential scribe to be copied fair, as you desired. This person, I am sorry to say, has detained them much longer than I imagined.

" I am glad the slight notice in the Magazine of the Cran-

---

* " By what authority the misnomer of *Forest* has crept into this pamphlet, we are at a loss to comprehend, as in sober truth it never was a *Forest;* nor is it *Chace* but a *Chase.* The plan of the publication is evidently to insinuate that Lord Rivers has no Rights of Chase within the County of Wilts. The subject, however, being still *sub lite,* we shall leave the further notice of this pamphlet to that upright and very able Critic, the Lord Chief Justice of the Court of King's Bench."
Gent. Mag. Jan. 1817, p, 54.

bourne pamphlet was to your satisfaction. I doubt not my
father will avail himself of your notice of swallows *,—a subject which a few years ago was frequently agitated by the correspondents of Mr. Urban.

" Yours, &c.   J. B. NICHOLS."

22. Mr. CHAFIN to Messrs. NICHOLS.

" SIRS,   *Chettle, Oct.* 15, 1817.

" I should not have so long delayed having communications
with you if I had been capable of writing; and I have no
helper. I had the misfortune, in the course of the summer (if
it may be called so), to be struck with a flash of lightning as I
was sitting in a window, attended with tremendous thunder and
hail-storm, which did not extend half a mile either way. It
hath deprived me of the sight of my left eye, and the use of
two fingers of my right hand, and greatly affected the muscles
of my breast, which I at this time very severely feel; but it
does not seem to have injured any inward vital part. The hail
did great damage in gardens, and where glasses were used; but
spared the produce of the fields, which were never known to be
more plentiful or of finer quality. My principal motive for
writing to you now is, to inform you that I have very lately been
honoured with three visits by Lord Rivers, and we have had long
conversations relating to his Chase; and I find that all the
Judges are unanimously adverse to the granting a fresh trial on
the former plea, of claim of the great boundaries of the Chase
in former days, and that his Lordship must be content with the
smaller inbounds, which I have set forth in my little manuscript; but it is doubtful whether or no his Lordship will, after
so long a delay, be able to obtain even those. His Lordship
seems to regret he did not follow his first intention of making
my little manuscript public; and I verily believe that, though
very trifling and imperfect as it was, it would in some measure
have prevented some very distressful occurrences, which have
since happened, and which oblige me to add much to that manuscript, and to relate some unpleasant transactions which I
wished to avoid. And as I am now in for it, and have some very
old letters in my possession, giving an account of the field
sports with which our ancestors were amused, it is my present
intention, if my health will permit, to introduce these subjects
into my narrative, with transcripts of the letters, without interfering in the least with Lord Rivers's concerns, but to catch the
attention of some readers, and to keep up good humour and
create a laugh, which is all I aim at. The difficulty will be, how
to form a connexion in regard to these discordant matters, but
I must do the best I can; and if I can get on, I shall swell my

* See the Gentleman's Magazine for March 1817, p. 221.

humble performance to a considerable size. I think I shall get
it ready before the end of November; and, as Lord Rivers is
not now adverse to a publication, I will, if you approve of it,
transmit the manuscript for your perusal, and then consider
what will be best to do. My fingers give in, and I must conclude, hoping that Mr. Nichols (much my junior) hath been
blessed with as good health as myself; and I am your sincere
and obliged humble servant,   Wm. Chafin."

23. Mr. J. B. Nichols to Mr. Chafin.

"Dear Sir,
  " Both my father and myself seriously regret, that your long
silence should have been occasioned by so untoward an accident.
Yet we rejoice that it did not prove more fatal; and we are
happy to perceive that your mental faculties retain their wonted
vigour.
  " The publication you mention will be interesting in no small
degree; and we shall be happy to print it either on your account
or at our own risk. Whichever you may prefer will be perfectly
agreeable to, dear Sir, &c.   J. B. Nichols."

24. Mr. Chafin to Messrs. Nichols.

"Dear Sirs,   Chettle, Oct. 24, 1817.
  " I believe I shall be able to finish what I am about before the
time I mentioned. It will come in as addenda to my manuscript
of the Chase; and it will be a medley of various anecdotes,
manners, and customs of all sorts of sporting, as practised two
centuries ago, collected from old letters in my possession, transcripts of which will be inserted, and I think may be pleasing
to smatterers of antiquity. The letters were written by persons
well known in their days, and are curiosities in their way. My
performance will be entirely harmless and inoffensive; and I
verily believe no objection can be made to it but its simplicity, of
which you will be the best judge when you have seen it. I must
be obliged to send it in an imperfect state of calligraphy, for I
write by candle-light, and have no help; and there is no person in my family that knows that I write at all. If you should
think it worthy of publication, the sooner it is done the better,
on the Chase account, for things are going on very bad there.
I am your very sincere and obliged humble servant,
                                     Wm. Chafin."

  25. "Dear Sirs,   Oct. 29, 1817.
  " I shall transmit with this my manuscript, which I have hurried through, fearing my health would not suffer me to finish it.
You know that my aim and design through the whole has been
to serve Lord Rivers; and if my short account of the Chase

had been known at the proper time, it would have prevented several unhappy occurrences. But there hath been such a lapse of time, that the little performance alone, if published, would be nearly obsolete; and very few persons would look into it except those who were personally interested. Upon due consideration of this therefore, and not wholly to abandon the first design, I thought it might answer my purpose, if I added to the little manuscript a mass of extraneous matters, and to show in what manner our ancestors amused themselves in the sports of the field in former days; which I was enabled to do by having old letters treating of those subjects. And I have, as you will see, gathered together a great number of anecdotes and simple stories, and some of them entertaining ones, in hopes that some of them may catch the attention of some knowing person who is looked up to, and whose aye or nay may raise curiosity in others, which may cause a demand for the book, and be the furtherance of my only design, that of causing Lord Rivers's claims to be more widely diffused and more generally made known; for, if a person is induced to read any one remarkable story in a book, he will generally be tempted to read the whole. If, on the perusal of my performance, you should think it worth printing, which I am apt to think you will, we must consider in what manner it is to be done. I am quite ignorant of the mystery, and never saw the operation of printing a sheet of paper in my life. I must, therefore, submit the whole to you, and it must be at your own risk; but if it should succeed beyond our expectations, and there is no knowing how novelties may take, and this is a novelty I believe, and the sale of it be a rapid one, as possibly it may be, I shall then rely on your liberality for some recompense for the hours idly spent and for damages done to my eyes.

"I have no copy nor single scrap of paper left; you have it all, and you must make allowance for my candle-light scribble, with very weak eyes. I hope and trust your good father will not disapprove of my simple lucubrations, as he knows my sole aim and design in writing such a medley of, I will not say nonsense, for it is not so; and I am, with my respects to him,

"Your sincere humble servant,   Wm. Chafin."

"I forgot to mention that, if we have any publication, the preface which we once proposed * must not be thought of. If there is any preface at all, it must be an apology for the folly of a man, in the eighty-fifth year of his age, engaging in such a simple business as it must appear to be to those who do not know the drift of it."

---

* That printed before, in p. 225.

26. Messrs. Nichols to Mr. Chafin.

" Rev. Sir, *Nov.* 1, 1817.

" We will immediately set about printing the little pamphlet at our own risk; although we think it best at once to suggest to you, that it is a great doubt whether it will repay our expences. As to the prospect of much profit from it, that is entirely out of the question. You will, we trust, excuse our saying thus much; but it may prevent future disappointment. We fear it will not excite that general interest you seem to apprehend; but should it succeed to the extent of your ideas, and the sale be great and rapid, we should be very much pleased to be enabled to present you with a portion of the unexpected profits. With sincere esteem we are, dear Sir,

" Your faithful humble servants, Nichols and Son."

---

27. Mr. Chafin to Messrs. Nichols.

" Dear Sirs, *Nov.* 5, 1817.

" I find by your letter that what I said in jest you have taken in earnest; and I do not like to leave any one in an error. I never had the vanity to expect that my little performance would, if printed, bring any emolument to me; and when I mentioned a recompense for loss of time and eye-sight it was a mere joke, and nothing more. All I wish and expect in the printing is this, that you may not be losers, and that Lord Rivers may gain some advantage from it in the support of his Chase rights, which has been my sole aim and design; and I have set forth those rights as claimed and exercised by his ancestors, which I verily believe are unknown to the present generation. My statement of them is taken from ancient letters alone, which I apprehend would not be admitted as evidence in Westminster-hall, but would be convincing proof to the public in general. If you send me a proof sheet, I will take care to follow your directions; and we must not regard the expense of postage. What is incurred by my letters you will place to the account of

" Your sincere and obliged humble servant, Wm. Chafin."

---

28. Dear Sirs, *Nov.* 11, 1817.

" It is my wish that the title should be as I have stated in the copy, or something like it; because what I have added does not affect Lord Rivers's concerns, but written at random, merely to induce readers from curiosity.

" What I have said in the addenda respecting the cruelty of horse-racing, I wish, in some measure, mitigated, if possible, otherwise I may get into a scrape, as the diversion is now so universally in fashion. But I submit these matters to your own discretion, and leave it entirely to you, to alter or suppress whatever you may think proper. The copy is your own, to do with

as you please; and if you print it, I hope, and am confident, you will not be a loser by it, for it will be well-timed, as matters now stand; and I am
            "Your sincere humble servant,   WM. CHAFIN."

---

29. "DEAR SIRS,   *Chettle, Nov.* 13, 1817.
    "I received the second proof sheet yesterday; but it had been opened and read before it came to my hands, and the subject of it made known and publicly talked of. My newspapers and letters are left at an inn about a mile from my house; and many persons assemble there who, out of curiosity, take the liberty of reading any thing in print, and I cannot fix on any particular delinquent, but must caution you not to send any thing in that manner to save nine pence. I much approve of the sheet; I have carefully perused it, and find not the least error in it; and as you are much better able to revise the whole than I am, I hope there will be no occasion of sending any more sheets to me, but I shall be at all times ready to follow your directions. I shall return the sheet with this in a basket, accompanied with a hare, which I hope will pay the carriage.
    "A little occurrence hath lately happened, on which I wish to have your opinion. In conversation respecting Cambridge with some Cantabs, I happened to mention the circumstance of what happened to me so many years ago in the schools, of the Moderator being called away to my great relief, which I find has been since much talked of, and no one will believe the fact. I wish, therefore, to convince them of the truth of it under my own hand; and if you should have no objection, I wish to have a very short account of my life, to the time of my taking an A. M.'s degree, and no further, inserted in the Gentleman's Magazine, which would also be of service to me in some other respects. If this should be approved of, I will draw up a very short sketch, to take up as little room as possible in that valuable publication *; but if you think there will be the least impropriety in so doing, I will desist, and will let the matter rest. A line from you will oblige
            "Your sincere humble servant,   WM. CHAFIN."

---

30. "DEAR SIRS,   *Chettle, Nov.* 27, 1817.
    "I received the little pamphlet last night, and I take the earliest opportunity of acknowledging it. I have carefully looked it over, and I find some few errors in it, which must be rectified.

---

* A small portion of the preceding autobiographical memoir was printed, in compliance with this request of Mr. Chafin, in the Gentleman's Magazine for January 1818; see that Miscellany, vol. LXXXVIII. i. p. 8.

" I do not think it proper for me to add any thing more; for, although I could bring forward a great number more of anecdotes and transactions respecting the Chase, which would enlarge the pamphlet, yet from what you know was intimated to me in Messrs. Farrers' letter, I think it best to stop short, and go no further. The gentleman deer-hunter, whom Mr. Hutchins has described, and whose print is inserted in the History of Dorset, was a very intimate friend of my father's, and spent much of his time with him, and has taken me out with him many times in his field sports when I was a boy. I could mention numerous entertaining anecdotes of that gentleman, who was much esteemed by all who knew him. He has descendants high in the world at this time; it would be improper therefore for me to say any thing concerning his few eccentricities.

" Messrs. Brodie and Co. at Sarum, are the properest persons to employ; they are the publishers of the Salisbury newspaper, which has the largest circulation of any paper in the west of England. At Blandford are two booksellers, Mr. Shipp and Mr. Simmonds, both eminent men in great business. You are welcome to use my name as you please in any advertisement. I write in pain; and can only add, that I am

" Your sincere humble servant, WM. CHAFIN."

31. " DEAR SIRS, *Chettle, Dec.* 4, 1817.
" I this evening received your letter containing the title-page of the little pamphlet, in which I wish to have a little alteration made, *viz.* Rev. W. Chafin, and nothing further, or, rather, William Chafin, Clerk, which is my usual signature in all matters as a magistrate, by which I am best known; my reason for wishing this alteration I think you will coincide in. There are a great number of new clergymen come into this neighbourhood, to whom I am entirely unknown, and they quite unacquainted with any concerns between Lord Rivers and me. It would appear, therefore, very strange to them, that a Rector of a parish in the diocese should demean himself so much as to write any thing on so trifling a subject. Another thing I beg leave to hint to you is this. It is my opinion that you have set too small a price on the little pamphlet, trifling as it is; and I am very confident that, if you double the price, or set it at five shillings at least, it will have a better sale than at the very low price of three shillings; for many persons judging, from the lowness of the price, that it is a catchpenny trifle, will think it below their notice. If, amongst the booksellers mentioned, you add the library at Weymouth, I know not the name of the person who keeps it, but I believe there may be a considerable call for it there. It is my bed-time; and I have nothing more to add than that I am,

" Your sincere humble servant, WM. CHAFIN."

32. " DEAR SIRS,   *Jan.* 10, 1818.

" I have taken this method of conveying to you some papers; and I hope the contents of the basket will indemnify the charges. I am entirely recluse, and see little of what passes, and my infirmities will not permit me to enter into conversation; but from what intelligence I can pick up, I have the pleasure to find for your sakes, that my little performance hath been favourably received, and the only fault of it was, its being too short. I certainly could have prolonged it. I sent to you some time ago, at the request of a friend at Blandford, the copy of an old letter, giving an account of some occurrences which happened at Blandford in former days; and I find that he expected to have seen it inserted in the last Magazine, and that it has been a disappointment to several of his friends. If you should think it worthy of insertion at any time, it is my wish to add a little to it to satisfy my own curiosity *. Where the gaming matters are mentioned †, there is no name given to the game at which so much money passed; it could not be an out-of-door game, because it was in the winter, and I cannot guess what game it could be. I know that, at the time when Prince Ferdinand of Brunswick commanded the British army before the battle of Minden, there was much gaming in the camp; and much money won and lost at a game called pass-dice; then succeeded Pharaoh, E. O., rouge et noir, and many others of the kind; but they must have been unknown in those days, and chess, draughts, backgammon, &c. must have required much more thought and attention than the persons in question could have been endowed with; I wish, therefore, to know what game it could be. If you can find room for the little sketch of my life, and see no impropriety in the insertion of it in your Magazine, I think it will be of great benefit to me at this time, under the circumstances which I have mentioned in the paper herewith sent; and will greatly oblige

         " Your sincere humble servant,   WM. CHAFIN.

" A line from you at the receipt of this will be acceptable.

" This instant, whilst the basket was packing up, I received the favour of your letter, to which I will pay due attention; and

---

* This article, an amusing letter from Mrs. Chafin (our author's grandmother, and the daughter of the martyred loyalist Col. Penruddock) to her husband Thomas Chafin, Esq. in 1688, was printed in the Supplement to the LXXXVIIth volume of Gent. Mag. pt. ii. p. 603.

† "Saturday was a se'nnight there was lost at Blandford Ornary a thousand pounds, by one Mr. Clark, a parson's son; Sir George Savage woon six score pounds back that he had lost to him the Saterday before, and five hundred more on tick; and Sir Simon Leek woon three hundred pounds; but afterwards there was a great quarrel, which have caused great disturbance. My brother Ryves is weary of going, for now he says it is not an Ornary for bisness but for play; but for all what he says they were all there again a Saterday, and a great deall of money lost. Mr. Ogden have the devill on his side still."

should it happen that another edition be required, I will endeavour to be prepared for it.   It gives me much satisfaction to
find that Mr. Nichols is well, whom I have known, though not
personally, many years, and highly esteemed ; and I thank God
I am much better than I could reasonably expect at my very
great age."

33. DEAR SIRS,   *Chettle, Feb.* 11, 1818.
    " I yesterday perused the reviewing part of your Magazine,
and I was sorry to see so much notice taken of the little pamphlet. It is overstrained ; and, should any thing else come forward,
it will fare the worse, for it will be expected to keep up to the
same mark * ; but I have much to say on that subject.   When I
last heard from you, a hint was given me that in all likelihood a
second edition of the pamphlet would be called for.   I took the
hint; and, as I have been blessed with an interval of better
health than I could have reason to expect, I have taken the
opportunity of continuing on the History of Cranbourne Chase
to a much greater extent, with some strange stories and tales.
And I take the liberty of advising you not to wait for a call for
a second edition, but to proceed immediately, for it never can
be so well timed as now, and many things have lately occurred
which make it particularly so at this instant, and you will find
calls enough for it.   I shall herewith send all that I have prepared,
which I hope will come safe, for I have no copy ; and, should it
be favoured by the approbation of Mr. Nichols senior in the
slightest degree, I shall be encouraged to go on with alacrity
somewhat further.   I have sent an explanatory paper, and an
old letter to be inserted in the former edition, and marked the
pages where; and I do not think it will be necessary to add any
thing more to it, for you will find a minute account of every
particular respecting the Chase which can be given with propriety, and I have most carefully avoided giving offence or an unpleasant feeling to any one ; and I am confident that the only
objection that can be made to my new performance is the lowness of the subjects.   My tales are rather antique, but founded
on truth.   I shall be anxious to hear from you ; for, if the papers
should be lost, they can never be recovered, for my memory

* The commendation of Sylvanus Urban was thus supported by a publication more immediately dedicated to the subject of the little volume :
" We take the earliest opportunity of paying attention to this interesting publication.   It contains much important information on the question now pending in regard to Lord Rivers's rights over Cranbourne Chase ;
and will be found highly agreeable and amusing to sportsmen in general,
both with respect to the sporting habits of their ancestors, and the present state of affairs in the district described, that ancient theatre of field
sports.   The pleasure of reading these clear-headed and spirited pages
is greatly enhanced by the consideration that they were penned by a
gentleman so far advanced in life, as actually to have followed the buck-
hounds *seventy years!* " *Sporting Magazine, Jan.* 1818.

never will bear such a stretch again.   I hope, therefore, to hear from you as soon as possible ; and I am,
" Your sincere humble servant,   Wм. Chafin."

34. " Dear Sirs,   *Chettle, March* 10, 1818.
   " I have been confined to my room the last seven weeks, and I am so now, and I have not been able to attend to any thing but for a few short intervals at a time when pain abated ; and I took every opportunity I could to scribble something towards your proposed publication, but I can go no further. What I have written I shall send to you; it has cost me much pains, more than all I have before written.   Of the way in which you propose printing and publishing I can form no judgment; but I am confident that the higher the price you set upon the books, the more demand you will have for them.   If you should think proper to add to the foregoing what I have now sent, it will be advisable in the title-page to say, ' with some scenes in, and anecdotes of, Windsor Forest.'   You will find much novelty and extraordinary circumstances, but all founded on truth, and can give no offence to any one ; and I flatter myself that I have kept up my character, and ended in the same sporting way that I began.
   " I have received your parcel, and have read your letter, and I do not think a frontispiece to be of any consequence.   There are more material matters to be considered, in which I totally differ from you.
   " You may assure yourself that, if you go on to publish in two separate parts, such patch-work will never go down, but will be scouted, and will lie on your hands ; and I do most strongly advise you not to do it, but, as you have materials sufficient to print the whole in one handsome volume, with a better type and at a price according, it will be of ten times the advantage to you.   Those who have got the first edition will not, for the sake of a few shillings, be deterred from buying the second, but it will be rather a motive for doing it.   After what I am about to mention, I think you will agree to what I have proposed.   The Rev. Mr. Rackett, that worthy ingenious gentleman who was such an assistant in Hutchins's History, and who cannot be unknown to you, expecting that a second edition of the Chase would be published in the manner I have mentioned, hath been preparing prints for the work, which would be presented to you ; one of them, that of deer-stealers with the swindgels, as I have described in my narrative.   Your plan, if pursued, will put a stop to Mr. Rackett's assistance, as well as several others whom I know, and it will throw a damp upon the whole business; and you will have no demand for your two separate volumes, but one large one complete will be called for from all quarters.   I am certain of what I say; and I hope you will consider it well.   I am faithfully yours,   Wм. Chafin."

35. Messrs. Nichols to Mr. Chafin.

" Dear Sir,   *March* 12, 1818.

" Many thanks for your advice, which we mean to follow, in
so far as to publish the whole in one continued handsome
volume, placing the article on Alarm-gate in its proper situation.
We will endeavour to communicate with Mr. Rackett, who is
a most kind friend to us on all occasions; and it shall be our
study to publish the work so that it shall be agreeable to yourself. As the frontispiece is engraved, we think it a pity not
to use it; but will consult Mr. Rackett on the subject. It
grieves us to have so indifferent an account of your own health.

" With our sincere wishes for its amendment, we are, dear
Sir, your obliged humble servants,   Nichols and Son."

---

36. Mr. J. B. Nichols to Rev. T. Rackett.

" Dear Sir,   *March* 12, 1818.

" Our kind old friend Mr. Chafin is about to publish a new
edition of his account of Cranbourne Chase, with considerable
additions; including an account of a gentleman whose portrait
is in Hutchins, vol. III. under the title of a deer-hunter. Of
this character we had a very neat engraving made in a reduced
8vo. size by way of frontispiece. On consulting Mr. Chafin,
however, he seems not much to approve of this plate; but
alludes in his letter to some kind intentions you entertained, of
presenting to us some prints for the work, one of them that of
deer-stealers with the swindgels, such as Mr. Chafin has described. This information has stopped our progress, as we
thought to have published the second volume immediately.

" I am, dear Sir, yours very truly,   J. B. Nichols."

---

37. Mr. Chafin to Messrs. Nichols.

" Dear Sirs,   *Chettle, March* 22, 1818.

" I should have acknowledged your last letter before, had I
been able. My health is now somewhat better; and, as the
weather seems to be getting more favourable, I am in hopes of
getting about again. I have the very great pleasure and satisfaction of informing you that the last little publication hath
answered all my ends and purposes far beyond my most ardent
expectations. If the lawyers had permitted the publication of
it at the proper time, there would have been no occasion for an
application for a new trial, and Lord Rivers's purse would not
have been emptied into that of the lawyers; but thank God my
feeble endeavours have been successful, and have set the matter
at rest; and I have the vanity to think that the next publication
will be more beneficial to Lord Rivers's interests even than the
last. As I am at this time capable of using my pen, though

badly, I will take the advantage, for fear of what may happen, to mention to you two or three things, which I wish to have added in the next publication *.

"I have not heard any thing from Mr. Rackett, but I have no doubt he will supply you with a drawing I mentioned, a group of deer-stealers with swindgels. I hope there will be no delay in the intended publication, for it would be now well-timed; and it is my earnest wish and desire that you would send the earliest impression you can to Lord Rivers; and I am faithfully yours,   WM. CHAFIN."

38. Messrs. NICHOLS to Mr. CHAFIN.

" DEAR SIR,   *March 25, 1818.*

"We have heard from our friend Mr. Rackett, and he has mentioned to us a sketch by Byng †, in the possession of Mr. Wray, a barrister in Chancery-lane, representing Mr. Good and a group of hunters with their swindgels, which perhaps we might obtain leave to copy. We will endeavour to procure a sight of the picture. Mr. Rackett does not mention any other embellishments.

"If you have nothing further to add, we will proceed to print the second edition immediately. We are, dear Sir,

"Your faithful humble servants,   NICHOLS and SON."

39. Mr. CHAFIN to Messrs. NICHOLS.

" DEAR SIRS,   *Chettle, March 26, 1818.*

"The sketch Mr. Rackett mentions by Byng, of Mr. Good, is the self same as is exhibited in Mr. Hutchins's History of Dorset, nor is there any other. I have been as cautious as possible in not mentioning the name of Good in my long narrative of the exploits of that gentleman; nor would I have the name in print on any account. I was informed that Mr. Rackett had made a sketch of deer-stealers with swindgels, which was intended for you; but the scene was that which I described in the battle at Rushmore-lodge.

"The last sheet which I sent was written at a time when I was very ill (and I am still much indisposed); I fear it will require a great deal of revising, and I have no copy of any thing. Believe me to be

"Your faithful humble servant,   WM. CHAFIN."

* They were inserted in the second edition.
† Byng was a friend of Sir Godfrey Kneller, and his assistant in painting back-grounds and draperies. He was much at Salisbury and in the Chase, near which in Wiltshire Sir Godfrey resided.

40. Mr. J. B. Nichols to Mr. Chafin.

" My dear Sir,   *March* 28, 1818.
" With regard to the frontispiece, I wish to consult your own wishes (as well as in every thing else). Mr. Wray having given permission, I have had a little drawing made from his sketch, which I thought of engraving instead of the single figure. This I send herewith for you to look at; and pray favour me with your early reply, whether you prefer the group of hunters, as in the drawing, or the single figure, as already engraved.

" I am, dear Sir, &c.   J. B. Nichols."

41. Mr. Chafin to Messrs. Nichols.

" Dear Sirs,   *Chettle, March* 30, 1818.
" I received the packet of books very safe yesterday, and your kind letter; and as you desire an early reply, I write to inform you that I very much approve of the drawing which you have sent. It is beyond my expectation, and I think you could not have a better frontispiece, for all the figures are excellent. But I can see no reason why the first engraved little figure should be neglected; I think it may be placed with great advantage at the little interval where the deer-hunter in cap and jack is first introduced by me from Mr. Hutchins's History; it will serve to elucidate the particulars of the dress more than those of the group *. I advise you to make as little delay as possible in the publication, for several occurrences have lately happened which will cause it to be well-timed. How it will be received I know not; but I am self-confident that I have not, in the whole performance, advanced a single syllable that can give offence to any person whatever.

" I cannot help thinking but that the scenes which I have described in Windsor Forest will be noticed by some of the Royal Family, who may not be indifferent to the amusements of their ancient relatives. I am, dear Sir,

" Your sincere and faithful humble servant, Wm. Chafin."

42. " Dear Sirs,   *Chettle, April* 19, 1818.
" I entirely object to the title-page, as the word concise cannot be proper in the second edition; and I recommend it to be worded in this manner, or somewhat like it:

" A Second Edition of the Anecdotes and History of Cranbourne Chase, by William Chafin, Clerk. With additions; and a continuation of the said History to some extent. To which are added, some Scenes in, and Anecdotes of, Windsor Forest, by the same Author.'

* This plate was not used in the pamphlet; but was inserted in the Gentleman's Magazine, vol. LXXXVIII. part ii. p. 118.

" Many occurrences have lately happened, which makes the second edition desirable at this time ; and I am
" Your sincere humble servant,   WM. CHAFIN."

---

43. DEAR SIRS,   *April* 1818.
" I have received the books ; and according to your desire I have returned both the drawings. Engraving is a matter I know nothing of ; and as to the frontispiece, it is of little consequence, and I wish it had never been thought of, for it has been the cause of much uneasiness to me. The application made to Mr. Rackett caused the name of Good to be mentioned, which will unavoidably give umbrage ; and I now sincerely regret that I ever took up the story of the deer-hunters, and related the foolish tales, for I find that I shall incur great censure for doing it, which would not have happened if the drawings had never been thought of. There are persons ready to catch at any thing which can be objected against my writings concerning the Chase ; and a reply to what I have already made public is now advertised from Shaftesbury. A speedy publication of the second edition may perhaps put a stop to their proceedings ; but it is a matter of indifference to me. I am
" Your sincere humble servant,   WM. CHAFIN."

---

44. " DEAR SIRS,   *Chettle, May* 12, 1818.
" Since I heard from you last, a pamphlet hath been published in review of my Anecdotes of Cranbourne Chase, as abusive as possible, accusing me as a busybody interfering in matters in which I had no concern ; and aspersing and casting reflections on the characters of some of the principal gentlemen in the county of Wilts. This simple publication, at two shillings price, hath met with a very rapid sale. Not a person of any denomination who attends Shaftesbury markets but what hath been supplied with it ; and every thing which has the least appearance of hostility to Lord Rivers's Chase rights is greedily caught at by such people. The performance in itself is the most absurd, futile, and contradictory production that I believe was ever published, and far beneath my notice ; but at the same time I must labour under the aspersions which have been cast upon me, and are still dwelling in the minds of those deluded persons who are not capable of judging for themselves. An earlier publication of the second edition, with the additions of the anecdotes, would have prevented all this ; but it is now too late. The author of the pamphlet is the same person who published a History of the Chase prior to the trial at Salisbury, the greater part of which I afterwards confuted in my Anecdotes. For this, as well as for many other reasons, I wish the second

edition of the Anecdotes could have been brought forward in
the month of March. It would at that time have been much
called for; but those persons most interested have left the
country, and are gone, some to France, and others on summer
tours, and few are left who will give themselves any concern
about the Chase; and I fear the second edition will not have
that demand for it that it would have had a month or two ago.
I have underneath sent you a copy of the title-page of the
pamphlet, which you can easily get; and form your own opinion
of its merits:

" A Review of the Statements contained in a Treatise, enti-
tled, ' Anecdotes respecting Cranbourn Chase.' By William
West. Shaftesbury: printed by John Rutter; sold also by
Longman and Co. London; Brodie and Dowding, Salisbury;
Shipp, Blandford; and by all other booksellers. 1818.

" Please to favour me with a line, for I am in suspense, which
will oblige your sincere and faithful humble servant,

" WM. CHAFIN."

45. Mr. J. B. NICHOLS to Mr. CHAFIN.

" MY DEAR SIR,   May 15, 1818.

" I am sorry that the second edition of your pamphlet should
have been so long in the press; but ill health on my part, and
pressure of other business, has unavoidably delayed it. A very few
days, however, will completely finish it, and the plate will be
also ready; so that we hope to send you copies by the end of
next week.

" I was very anxious to peruse the answer to it, but repeated
inquiries in town have failed in procuring a copy. The circulation of it must therefore be very confined. The first communi-
tion I have with either Brodie or Shipp, I will order a copy of
be sent me. I send you another volume of my father's " Literary Illustrations," which I hope will entertain you. He desires
me to present his best respects and good wishes.

" I am, dear Sir, yours, &c.   J. B. NICHOLS.

" P. S. I have now the pleasure to send a complete copy of
the second edition; and, if you approve it, will publish it directly."

46. Mr. CHAFIN to Messrs. NICHOLS.

" DEAR SIRS,   " Chettle, May 19, 1818.

" I have duly received the books; and I have no doubt but
I shall be much entertained with the ' Literary Illustrations,'
should I ever be able to peruse them; but at present I am not,
nor capable of attending to any thing serious, for I have been
very unwell for some weeks past; and at my very advanced
period of life I cannot expect amendment, but rather increase

of the malady, though my complaint at present is not the effect of old age alone, but from a stroke of lightning, which penetrated and discomposed my whole frame both of body and mind, my eyesight greatly injured, and hearing totally lost, so that I am in a melancholy condition. I have no objection whatever to the printed pamphlet you have sent; and I think the sooner you publish it the better; and as there is certainly more than as much again letter-press contained in it than in the last, I think you ought to have more than a double price. And I am confident if you add a few shillings, and make it eight, or even ten, it will be rather an excitement for the demand and call for the book than otherwise; and I am

   " Your sincere humble servant, WM. CHAFIN."

   47. " DEAR SIRS,   Chettle, June 6, 1818.

 " From your last letter I did expect to have seen my little pamphlet published ere this, for I fear it will come out much too late, either to answer my purpose, or be of that advantage to you as it would have been had it made its appearance at the latter end of March or beginning of April. Those who would readily have called for it at that time have left the country, and very few remain who are at all interested in such matters. I was exceedingly ill used in the publication of the Anecdotes as well as yourself; many copies of my manuscript, which was sent to Lord Rivers at Amesbury, were, by the connivance of some of his agents, suffered to be taken, and were dispersed in Wiltshire, and the contents well known exactly one year before the book was published. This fact hath been lately made known to me by a letter from Mr. West, the very man who has been writing against it, a harmless inoffensive quaker of Shaftesbury, whose only view was to put a few shillings into his pocket, which I hope he has done. The premature knowledge of the contents of the Anecdotes, thus fraudulently obtained, may have been of service to the gentlemen of Wilts, and certainly was so, as they were by it perfectly acquainted with the nature of my evidence, and had time allowed them what measures to follow. They found, on investigation, that my evidence was incontrovertible, and therefore gave up the cause, and proposed an amicable compromise with Lord Rivers for his rights of Chase. My point was gained a full year before my Anecdotes were published; and all law process hath ceased. The whole drift and plan of this second edition of the Anecdotes is to establish Lord Rivers's rights of Chase for ever; and to oppose, with all my might, all offers of compromise, which I flatter myself I have effectually done.

 " I have for some time past had a correspondence with John Laurence, Esq of Somers Town, a great author on sporting

matters; and many letters have passed between us. He has
lately published a work, intituled, ' British Field Sports,' but
under the feigned name of W. H. Scott. In one of his letters
to me he acknowledges that he has borrowed much from my
Anecdotes, particularly in regard to buck-hunting; and I have
reason to believe he will do the same to the second edition
respecting the species of deer. I have a wish to peruse the
British Sports. It is so filled with prints that I am certain the
price of it is much above its value; but I shall be obliged if
you will make inquiry in what manner it is generally received,
for I cannot think that much of consequence can have been
written on the subject after the perfect work of the Rev. Mr.
Daniel s ' Rural Sports.' I have had much literary intercourse
with Mr. Laurence, and have a very high opinion of him in
every respect.

" Let me hear from you as soon as possible; and believe me
to be your faithful and obliged humble servant, WM. CHAPIN."

---

48. " DEAR SIRS,   *Chettle, June* 20, 1818.
" I must beg leave to observe to you, that the painter or engraver hath made a sad omission or mistake in the figures in
the frontispiece; their legs are all left naked; as they are supposed to be in the field of action, their legs surely should have
been guarded and covered with the same materials, or somewhat
of the kind, as the caps and jacks.

" I have a great desire, for particular reasons, to see Scott's
British Field Sports, lately published; and I must not regard the
price, which is &.1. 18s. and I shall be much obliged if you will
get it for me, and send it as soon as you can.

" The author of the British Field Sports, which I have desired
you to get for me, is John Laurence, Esq. of Somers Town,
with whom I have had some communications. He is a friend of
Mr. Wheble's; and as I find that Mr. Wheble is an old and
respectable friend * of Mr. Nichols senior, I shall endeavour
to contribute my mite as far as it will go, in aiding and assisting in the establishment of the Sporting Magazine. I am not
unknown, to Mr. Wheble. I have been lately very ill, but I

---

* Mr. Wheble was a much respected printer and bookseller in War-
wick-square; and for sixteen years a representative of the Ward of Farringdon Within in the Court of Common Council. He figured away
as far back as the days of " Wilkes and Liberty," having been in 1771
committed by the House of Commons, but discharged by Wilkes, as
Sitting Alderman. Mr. Wheble was the projector of " The County Chronicle," a very successful weekly newspaper, as well as of " The Sporting
Magazine." He died at Bromley, Kent, (where he had repaired for the
medical aid of the eminent Surgeon Scott,) in his 75th year, Sept. 22,
1820.

am now somewhat better; although not capable of attending
any length of time to either business or amusement *.

" I am your faithful and humble servant,   WM. CHAFIN."

* Our venerable old friend survived the writing of this his last letter
to his printers about seven weeks. He died at Chettle, in the mansion
of his ancestors, at the age of 86, Aug. 14, 1818. He was the last heir
male of his family. In July 1826 the whole parish of Chettle, with the
manor, advowson, and mansion-house were advertised for auction, by
Mr. Robins of Regent-street. The latter was on this occasion described
as " a substantial uniform edifice of brick, with handsome stone dress-
ings, built in the style of Sir John Vanbrugh, on a fine eminence commanding views of great extent." The whole estate was calculated as
comprising rather more than 1100 acres.

SAMUEL GOODENOUGH, D. C. L.

BISHOP OF CARLISLE.

This learned, pious, examplary, and venerable
Prelate was the third son of the Rev. William
Goodenough, Rector of Broughton Pogges in the
county of Oxford * ; and was born at Kimpton
near Weyhill in Hampshire, on the 29th of April,
O. S. 1743. His father was then holding the Rec-
tory of Kimpton, for a minor and distant relation,
Mr. Edward Foyle † ; and in 1750, upon Mr.

* Rev. William Goodenough was of Pembroke-college, Oxford, M. A. 1732. He died Nov. 10, 1768.

† The Rev. Edward Foyle was of Merton-college, Oxford, a
grand compounder for the degree of M. A. in 1749. In 1753,
according to the will of Mrs. Frances Harris, widow of his
uncle John Foyle, of Chute in Wiltshire, Esq. (afterwards
re-married to William Harris, of Salisbury, Esq.) he succeeded
with his elder brother Gorges Foyle, Esq. to several estates in the
counties of Wilts and Dorset. He married Jan. 12, 1755, Miss
Hayter, with a fortune, according to the announcement of the
day, of £.10,000 (see Gent. Mag. vol. XXV. p. 42); and,
secondly, August 24, 1773, Miss Thomas, of Southampton. He
died May 7, 1784, being then styled of West Chelderton, Wilts,
Rector of Kimpton, and Prebendary of Minor Pars Altaris in
the Cathedral of Bath. His daughter, Miss Foyle, was married
June 11, 1790, to John Maurice Eyre, of Botley Grange in
Hampshire, Esq.; and his son, the Rev. Edward Foyle, is still
living. He was of Queen's-college, Oxford; M. A. 1780; was
instituted in the Rectory of Chilcombe in Dorsetshire in 1785,
on his own presentation; and was presented to that of Kimpton

Foyle's being of age to take the living, returned to his residence at Broughton, where his family had been settled for nearly two centuries, in possession not only of the advowson of that Rectory, but of very considerable landed property; which had then, however, passed into other hands, through the improvidence of some of its hereditary possessors *.

A school of good repute being at that time established at Witney, under the direction of a most excellent man, the Rev. Benjamin Gutteridge †, Mr. Goodenough placed his sons there ‡; from whence, in 1765, the future Bishop was removed to Westminster-school, where, under the kind and able instruction of the late venerable Archbishop Markham, he succeeded in becoming a King's Scholar, and was elected in 1760 to a Studentship of Christ Church, Oxford. He proceeded M. A. 1767; D. C. L. 1772.

at the same period by his uncle Gorges Foyle, Esq. Further particulars of this family may be found in Hutchins's History of Dorsetshire, vol. I. pp. 90, 466; vol. II. pp. 294, 423, 436, 438, (in which last page for *George* read *Gorges);* vol. IV. p. 95.

* Mr. Skelton, in his Antiquities of Oxfordshire, has the following paragraghs under Broughton Pogges: "This estate was, for nearly 300 years, in the Goodenough family, who yet present to the living. The church is a small but ancient structure, composed of one aisle. In the chancel, which is one of the neatest in the county, are numerous memorials of the Goodenough family. The principal one of them is over the communiontable, and is to the memory of William Goodenough, who died on the 18th of March, 1673. On this monument is recorded, in a long Latin inscription, several interesting particulars connected with the history of the family."

† The Rev. Benjamin Gutteridge was of Emanuel-college, Cambridge, M. A. 1748.

‡ Mr. Carlisle, in his "Endowed Grammar-schools," states of Witney, that, "The present Head-master, the Rev. Thomas Cripps, and three other gentlemen his contemporaries, and now in the Church, received their education in this school." Mr. Cripps took the degree of M. A. at Oxford in 1790, so that his school-days were doubtless long subsequent to those of Dr. Goodenough. It is, however, a honour well worthy of remembrance at Witney, that the late Bishop of Carlisle received his early education there.

In 1766 he returned to Westminster-school in the capacity of Usher, and filled that honourable station with much diligence and ability for four years; when, having inherited from his father the advowson of Broughton, and obtained also from his College the Vicarage of Brizenorton, one of the adjoining parishes, he married, April 17, 1770, Elizabeth, eldest daughter of Dr. James Ford *, one of the most eminent medical professors of that time in London, and retired to his living of Broughton. But he was speedily called from this retirement by applications which were made to him to take charge of the education of various young noblemen and gentlemen of high condition. This led, in 1772, to the formation of his establishment at Ealing, and laid the foundation of his future advancement in his profession. During six-and-twenty years that he continued to reside there, he had successively the charge of the children of Lord Willoughby de Broke, Lady Albemarle, Lord George Cavendish, the Earl of Northampton, the Marquis of Bute, the Duchess of Rutland, the Duke of Beaufort, and the Duke of Portland; together with many others of high distinction, among whom may be specified Henry Addington, Esq. created in 1805 Viscount Sidmouth. While ardently devoted to the improvement of these chosen pupils, he still found time to gratify his own peculiar taste and inclination, by the study of theology and the cultivation of science. The retirement of his own closet, and the meetings of the Royal and Linnæan Societies, (of the latter of which he was one of the original framers †,) were his chief recreation after the fatigues of teaching. This procured for him the friendship of Sir Joseph

* He was Physician to the Middlesex Hospital; see the " Literary Anecdotes," vol. IX. pp. 2, 372.

† Dr. Goodenough had been a member of the parent Natural History Society. At the formation of the Linnæan Society in 1788 he was named for Treasurer. Gent. Mag. XCVIII. i. 416.

Banks, and of nearly every individual eminent in
science; and on so solid a foundation were their
friendships laid, that it may be truly said they only
ceased with the lives of the respective parties.   His
own personal proficiency in the department of
science, may best be shown by referring to his
various papers in the Transactions of the Linnæan
Society, particularly those upon the genus Carex *.
It is certain that they have, amidst all the subsequent improvements in botanical knowledge, continued to be the text-book of all who would wish
to master the difficulties of that genus ; and how
great was his success in horticulture, a pursuit
which had not then been advanced to the degree of
fashion which it has since attained, has been sung
by the author of the Pursuits of Literature †.   He
was, at the period of his death, Vice-president of
the Royal and Antiquarian Societies, and a Fellow
of the Society of Antiquaries.

Professional advancement, founded upon knowledge of a higher cast, now, however, called him to
other scenes ‡.   In 1797 he was presented by Dr.

* " Observations on the British Species of Carex," printed
in the Transactions, vol. II. p. 126 ; vol. III. p. 76; " Of the
Porbeagle Shark, the Squalus Cornubicus of Gmelin," vol. III.
p. 80; " On the British Fuci," ibid. p. 84; " On the Wheat
Insect," ibid. p. 224.

      † " Or good Palæmon, worn with classic toil,
         Complain of plants ungrateful to the soil."
" I allude to a learned, modest, ingenious, and laborious gentleman, who has educated many of the *first* sons of the first
nobility and gentry of this country, between twenty and thirty
years, with unremitting *personal* diligence and ability.   He is
but *just* § promoted, to the satisfaction of all who know him,
and to the shame of those who so long neglected him.
      " Quis gremio Enceladi doctique PALÆMONIS affert
QUANTUM GRAMMATICUS MERUIT LABOR ? "
                    Pursuits of Literature, 8vo, 1808, *p.* 332.
    Dr. Goodenough is generally supposed to have been the first
cultivator who succeeded in bringing to its present state of per-
ection the favourite vegetable sea-kale.
    ‡ In a letter of Mr. Tyson in 1799 (see " Literary Anec-
      " § Feb. 1798.   Need I name the Rev. Dr. Goodenough ? "

Smallwell, then Bishop of Oxford, to the Vicarage of Cropredy in Oxfordshire. In 1798 he was appointed to a Canonry of Windsor; in 1802 removed from thence to the Deanery of Rochester *; from that station † advanced in 1808 to the Bishopric of Carlisle. His own merits were in these several steps aided by the warm attachment of his pupil the present Viscount Sidmouth (whose sister was married to the Bishop's brother ‡), and especially by the generous condescension, it may be said the strong friendship, evinced by the late Duke of

dotes," vol. VIII. p. 642) he says: "Dr. Goodenough is preparing a very learned work, called Botanica Metrica, containing the etymology of all botanical names, both technical and also of the plants." See a letter respecting this undertaking in the Gentleman's Magazine, vol. LXXXIV. ii. 205.

* The single decease of Dr. Bagot, Bishop of St. Asaph, occasioned at this period a remarkably long series of changes. Dr. Horsley was promoted to St. Asaph, Dr. Dampier to Rochester, Dr. Goodenough to the Deanery of Rochester, as above stated, Mr. Busby, it is believed, to the Canonry of Windsor. Then, Dr. Vincent succeeded Dr. Horsley as Dean of Westminster, and to him Dr. Ireland as Prebendary. Again, Dr. Wingfield succeeded Dr. Vincent as Head-master of Westminster-school; and not to pursue the transition further in that establishment, to him Mr. Page as Second-master.

† In the "Literary Anecdotes," vol. IX. p. 714, in a letter from the learned Jacob Bryant to Edward Roberts, Esq. of Ealing, it will be perceived how much Dr. Goodenough's departure from a place he had enlivened and instructed by his society, was regretted by his circle of friends.

‡ William Goodenough, of Merton-college, Oxford, A.M. 1764; M.B. 1767; M.D. 17... He married Jan. 2, 1770, Anne, eldest daughter of Anthony Addington, M.D.; but died on the 8th of the following August, at Paddington. His lady's decease occurred at the White-lodge, Richmond-park, June 12, 1806.—The Rev. Edmund Goodenough, another brother of the Bishop, was educated with him at Westminster and at Christ Church, and attained the degree of M. A. in 1769. In 17.. he was presented by the King to the Vicarage of Swindon, Wilts. and afterwards, in 17.., by the Dean and Canons of Christ Church, to the Rectory of Littleton in Worcestershire. He died at Bath, Nov. 8, 1807, aged 62, leaving a widow, sister to Sir William-Elias Taunton, of Oxford, and who died in that City, April 11, 1815. Their second daughter, the wife of William Farmer, Esq. of Swindon, died June 23, 1809.

Portland for the tutor of all his sons. His unaffected piety, punctuality, high integrity, and inflexible adherence to his duty are as amply attested
by all who acted with him, or lived under his government. He tranquilly expired at Worthing in
Sussex, on the 12th of August 1827, full of years
and honours, having survived her who was the wife
of his youth and the partner of his age only eleven
weeks *; and having lived to see his children and
his grandchildren prospering in their generation.

His remains were interred on the following Satur-
day, August 18, in the north cloister of Westminster
Abbey, near those of his revered master and friend
Dr. Markham, the late Archbishop of York.

At the Anniversary Meeting of the Royal Society
on the 30th of November following, the President,
Mr. Davies Gilbert, in noticing the Members deceased during the preceding year, thus noticed the
loss of this much lamented Prelate:

" Dr. Samuel Goodenough, late Bishop of Carlisle, has ever sustained the character of a sound
and elegant scholar. Entrusted with the education
of distinguished personages, and having qualified
them for the first situations in the state, he fairly
and honourably ascended to the summit of ecclesiastical preferment. To classical and theological
learning, Dr. Goodenough added a very intimate
knowledge of natural history, as is manifested by a
communication to the Linnæan Society, where his
labours have thrown a steady light over an extensive genus of aquatic plants, left by all former botanists in obscurity and confusion. The memory of
Dr. Goodenough will long be cherished with affection and with esteem by all who had the honour
of his acquaintance, either in his public or in his
private life."

Except his papers in the Linnæan Society's
Transactions, Dr. Goodenough's printed works were

* Mrs. Goodenough died in Berners-street, May 26, 1827.

confined to three Sermons, delivered on occasions when publication is generally expected. They were, one on the Fast, preached before the House of Commons *, 1795; another before the Lords in Westminster Abbey, on the Fast-day, 1809 †; and the third, "before the Society for Promoting the Gospel in the East, and other parts, 1812."

Dr. Goodenough had three sons, all in the church.

1. The Rev. Samuel-James Goodenough, of Wadham-college, Oxford, M. A. 1797; presented by his father in 1798 to the Rectory of Broughton Pogges; in 1803 to the Vicarage of Hampton in Middlesex by the King; and in 1810 to a Prebendal Stall in the Cathedral of Carlisle.

2. The Rev. Robert-Philip Goodenough, who was brought up at Westminster, was admitted a Student at Christ Church, Oxford, in 1792,. and proceeded M. A. in 1799. He arrived at the University in the time of the celebrated and never to be equalled Dean Cyril Jackson, and had for his contemporaries some of the most eminent scholars of the present day, among whom are to be numbered Mr. C. Williams Wynn, Dr. Phillimore, Lord

* " We do not recollect a discourse of this kind better adapted to the occasion, and to the audience before whom it was delivered. It breathes the genuine spirit of piety; and it is rational, patriotic, and manly. Whilst the preacher earnestly exhorts us to endeavour to avert the judgments of God, by reforming our lives, our manners, and our morals; while he would have us devoutly pray to Heaven to aid our laudable exertions in defence of the religion, the laws, and the liberties of our country; we meet with nothing of the unchristian language (too frequently heard!) of intolerance and extermination. Although an air of primitive plainness and of the evangelical piety ' of other times' prevails through this discourse, unaffected strokes of eloquence are occasionally interspersed." Monthly Review, N. O. vol. XVI. p. 355.

† It was on one of these occasions, that the following lines were penned :
      'Tis well enough that Goodenough
      Before the House should preach,—
      For sure-enough full bad-enough
      Are those he has to teach.

Kenyon, Mr. W. E. Taunton, Hon. W. Herbert, Dr. Lushington, Dr. Elmsley, Mr. Gaisford, &c.

Under the encouragement which Mr. G. in common with all other young men of talents and diligence, received from Dr. Jackson, he was soon distinguished as a sound and good scholar. In 1797, while a Bachelor of Arts, he gained the University prize for an English essay on "The Influence of Climate on National Manners and Character," and for some years after he had taken his degree of M. A. he officiated as one of the public tutors of the College. In this department he at once preserved the dignity of his station, and the affections of his pupils; and, like a true disciple of the Dean, never forgot that, if they were to be scholars while at Christ Church, they were to be gentlemen through life *.

In 1805 he was presented by his father's old friend, Archbishop Markham, to the Prebend of Fenton in the Cathedral of York; and in 1806, by the same patron, to the Vicarage of Carlton in Lindrick, Nottinghamshire, and to the Prebend of Halloughton, in the collegiate Church of Southwell. On the

---

* In a letter of Barrè Charles Roberts (one of Mr. Goodenough's pupils) to his father Edward Roberts, Esq. of Ealing, March 4, 1806, is the following affectionate passage: " I am made very melancholy about my tutor; he told me to-day of his having the offer of a living, and his accepting it. I am most excessively sorry for it, on many general accounts; but, considering him as the tutor and friend he is to me, it is an irreparable loss, by far the most unfortunate circumstance that could have happened for me here. The greatest pleasure I have, is in receiving his instruction, and being with him. This can be the case with no other man. I shall find in my next tutor, perhaps, as good a scholar and as good a man, but the best qualities of all other tutors united, cannot form what he was to me, nothing but friendship continued from the earliest date can form such an one. I looked forward with pleasure to the time, when taking my degree would lessen the distance he is obliged to preserve, and would allow me more of his company. That academic distance will be removed, but for no advantage to me, as by chance alone we shall meet."

6th of December 1808 (after his Grace's decease) he married the Archbishop's fifth daughter, Cecilia*. In 1811 he was presented by his father to a Prebendal Stall in the Church of Carlisle; in 1819 by Southwell-college to the Rectory of Beasby in Lincolnshire; and in 18... to a Prebend of Ripon. He was also one of his father's Chaplains. Mr. Goodenough resided principally on his living of Carlton, and left behind him the character of an excellent parish priest (the most valuable member of society which can exist), of an affectionate husband, a good father, a dutiful son, and a faithful friend. He had long laboured under a mesentric complaint, and in 1825 received much benefit from the advice of London Physicians while resident at Caen Wood, the seat of his brother-in-law, the Earl of Mansfield. But his constitution was entirely worn out, and he sunk at last in the prime of life, after a few days illness, April 20, 1826, in the 51st year of his age.

Mr. Goodenough left a numerous family; one of

* Archbishop Markham had seven daughters: 1. Henrietta-Sarah, married by Archbishop Moore at Lambeth Palace, June 28, 1784, to Ewan Law, Esq. son of the Bishop of Carlisle, and brother to the late Lord Ellenborough and the present Bishop of Bath and Wells; 2. Elizabeth-Catharine, married April 13, 1793, to William Barnett, Esq. of York, son of the Rev. William Barnett, of Jamaica; 3. Alicia, married Nov. 27, 1794, to the Rev. Henry-Forster Mills †; 4. Frederica, married Sept. 1, 1797, to William third and present Earl of Mansfield; 5. Cecilia, married Dec. 6, 1808, to Mr. Goodenough, as above stated; 6. Anne-Catherine, who died unmarried at Roehampton, Oct. 3, 1808; and the seventh was married August 20, 1815, to Major-General Sir Rufane Shaw Donkin, K. C. B. This statement will correct some errors in the Gentleman's Magazine, vol. XCII. ii. 374; where it is believed the sons of the Archbishop are rightly stated. A memoir of George, the Dean of York, is there given; and one of the Admiral was published in the Magazine for April 1827, vol. XCVII. i. p. 363.

† The Rev. Henry-Forster Mills was of Trinity-college, Cambridge, B.A. 1790, M.A. 1793. In 1802 his father-in-law, the Archbishop, presented him to the Chancellorship of York Cathedral; and in the following year to the Rectory of Gawsworth in Cheshire. In 1804 he was presented by the Hon. R. Lumley Savile to the Rectory of Emley in Yorkshire; and he died at Bath, April 27, 1827, aged 58.

whom, shortly before his father's death, was elected
from Westminster-school a Student of Christ Church.

3. Rev. Edmund Goodenough was of Christ Church,
Oxford, M. A. 1807 ; D. D. 181..; and was Proctor
of the University in 1816. He was elected Master
of Westminster-school in 1819, and resigned in
1828. He succeeded his brother Robert as Prebendary of Carlisle in 1826; and was elected on the
Council of the Royal Society in 1828. He married May 31, 1821, Frances*, daughter of Samuel
Pepys Cockerell, Esq. of Westbourne-house, Middlesex, and first cousin to the lady of Dr. How-
ley, Archbishop of Canterbury. Dr. Goodneough
has a numerous family ; of whom his eldest daughter Frances died in Dean's-yard, Westminster, April
25, 1828.

Bishop Goodenough's eldest and second daughters
were both married at Ealing, on one day, May 25,
1797. The eldest was united to her first cousin, the
Rev. William Goodenough. He was of Christ
Church-college, Oxford, M. A. 1797. He succeeded his uncle and father-in-law in his school at
Ealing†; and was, in 1811, presented by him to
the Rectory of Mareham-le-Fen in Lincolnshire
in 1818, and to the Archdeaconry of Carlisle before 1826. An infant son of this gentleman died
at Ealing, April 22, 1804; and his eldest daughter,
Mary-Anne, in Curzon-street, London, April 3, 1823.

* These ladies are descended from a sister of the celebrated
Samuel Pepys, Esq. Secretary of the Admiralty.

† Barrè Chas. Roberts, Esq. " was in June 1799 placed under the
care of the Rev. William Goodenough at Ealing, between whose
family and that of his pupil a long course of intimacy and esteem
had existed. Here, as there was only a small limited number
of boys to divide the attention of the master, Barrè experienced
all that friendship could contribute to his comfort, and all that
the abilities of scholarship could bring to the cultivation of his
talents. The preceptor had leisure to discover the characters
of those under his care, and to direct towards each the particular mode of treatment which might best conduce to its formation and developement." Memoirs of B. C. Roberts.

2. The second daughter, Henrietta, married on the same day as her elder sister, was wedded to the Rev. Francis Minshull, Rector of Nunney in Somersetshire. She died early, April 4, 1802; and Mr. Minshull survived only to 1817, when his decease occurred at Nunney, June 28, in his 48th year. He was of Jesus-college, Oxford, M. A. 1793.

3. The third daughter was married in January 1805 to the Rev. James Lynn. He was of Wadham-college, Oxford, M. A. 1803; and is now Minor Canon of Rochester and Rector of Stroud, to which living he was presented by the Dean and Chapter of that Cathedral.

4. Maria, the Bishop's fourth daughter, died unmarried, Feb. 12, 1813.

In the third and fourth generation, the Bishop had also, at the time of his death, forty grandchildren and three great-grandchildren.

---

1. Dr. GOODENOUGH to Mr. NICHOLS.

" Ealing, June 9, 1794.

" Dr. Goodenough presents his best compliments to Mr. Deputy Nichols, and takes the liberty of sending him a hasty sketch of something which ought to be said of his most worthy friend the Duchess of Portland *. Having had the honour of her acquaintance for more than twenty years, he can vouch for the truth of what he has written."

---

2. " DEAR SIR, *Ealing, Dec. 6, 1796.*

" I am much obliged to you for sending me the papers of your excellent Natural History of Leicestershire, containing the lists of plants, &c. &c. I wish I may be able to make any corrections or additions. Master Shallow † and I drank your health in the hospitable Vicarage of Melton. May I beg you to insert the inclosed. I am, dear Sir,

" Your obliged and obedient servant, SAM. GOODENOUGH."

---

* Printed in the Gentleman's Magazine, vol. LXIV. p. 579.
† Dr. Ford; see vol. V. of this Work, p. 221.

3. " Dear Sir,   *Windsor, Aug.* 11, 1799.
" I send you herewith a sketch of the life of a very valuable
man *; which you would oblige me much by inserting in your
next Magazine.

" If you ever come to Windsor, you will find Dr. Goodenough,
Canon of Windsor, will be as glad to take you by the hand as
he was when he was plain Dr. Goodenough, of Ealing.

" I have been writing to Master Shallow ; and telling him that
there is no necessity for his total silence. I am, dear Sir, your
much obliged and most obedient servant, Sam. Goodenough."

GERRARD ANDREWES, D. D.
DEAN OF CANTERBURY.

This distinguished divine was the male representative of a family, whose pedigree will be found
under the parish of Syston in the History of Leicestershire.   At the head of that pedigree stands
the name of Thomas Andrewes, of Weston Bag-
gard in Herefordshire, who died in 1615, at the
age of 114 ; and had, only six years before, appeared
at some races at Hereford, and officiated as one of
the four " Marshalls of the Field," who were all upwards of 100 years old, whilst six couple, who also
averaged nearly a century, performed a morris-dance
for the entertainment of the gentry assembled †.
Of his father, a clergyman and schoolmaster at Leicester, the Dean communicated to the same work
the following brief memoir:

" Gerrard Andrewes, born June 27, 1704, son of
John Andrewes, Esq. a solicitor in London, was
admitted in 1719 a King's Scholar at Westminster-
school, which he left in 1725 ; and, though elected
from the foundation there to Trinity-college, Cambridge, he entered of Baliol-college, Oxford, where

* An interesting memoir of Mr. William Curtis, Editor of
the Botanical Magazine.   It is the first article in the Magazine
for August 1799 in the form of a letter, and is signed Kewensis.

† It was erroneously supposed, from the authority of Fuller's
Worthies and the Baronetages, that this morris-dance took place
before the King; but see this explained in the " Progresses of
James the First," vol. I. p. xx.

he became M. A. Dec. 5, 1738; was presented in
1744, by the University of Oxford, to the Vicarage
of Syston; and by the Lord Chancellor to the Vicarage of St. Nicholas, Leicester, in 1757. He
died Feb. 29, 1764, in his 60th year, and was buried
in the Church of St. Nicholas. As a divine he
alike captivated in the desk and pulpit. Possessing
a very harmonious voice, he read with an energy
just and influencing; taught with conciseness per-
tinently persuasive, and intelligible to a general
auditory; and was long considered as one of the
brightest ornaments of the clerical profession. He
also filled, with distinguished credit, the office of
the master of the free-school of the town of Leicester; which, under his superintendance, was a
seminary of great repute; not only the sons of the
first families * in those parts were placed under his
care, but numbers from much greater distances also
received the rudiments of education."

Mr. Andrewes married Isabella, daughter of John
Ludlam, Esq. of Leicester, niece to Sir George
Ludlam, Chamberlain of London from 1718 to
1727, and sister to the Rev. Peter and Rev. Thomas
Ludlam. She died in her 70th year, March 10, 1788.

The Dean of Canterbury was their only surviving child. He was born at Leicester, April 3,
1750; and was educated, as his father had been, at
Westminster-school, where he was elected a scholar

* In the Literary Memoirs of Joseph Cradock, Esq. M.A. F.S.A.
vol. I. p. 3, is the following passage: "At the age of nine I was
sent to the endowed school at Leicester, and was placed under the
care of the Rev. Gerrard Andrewes. There were about thirty
boarders; the Earl of Stamford's three sons adding no small
celebrity. Under that most excellent preceptor I remained till
about the age of seventeen."—" Mr. Andrewes was an elegant
classic; and, by constantly attending Garrick, read better than
almost any man. He was the supposed heir to a great fortune;
the matter was litigated; he was tendered half, and he lost all."
Ibid. vol. IV. p. 90. This latter anecdote must apply to the
period when the male line of an elder branch of the family expired, as is shown in the pedigree.

in 1764, and whence he was elected a fellow of Trinity-college, Cambridge, in 1769.   He proceeded
B. A. 1773, being the ninth Junior Optime of that
year; M. A. 1779; S. T. P. 1807.   In 1772 he
returned to Westminster as an assistant-master, and
such he continued till 1784.   One of his first clerical duties was that of an occasional Assistant Preacher
at St. Bride's, Fleet-street; he was afterwards engaged at St. James's Chapel in the Hampstead-road.
In 1780, when his friend Sir Edmund Cradock Har-
topp served High Sheriff of Leicestershire, Mr.
Andrewes acted as his Chaplain.   In 1788 he was
presented by Lord Borringdon, whose tutor he had
been, to the Rectory of Zeal Monachorum in Devonshire.   On the 1st of December in the same
year, he was united to Elizabeth Maria, daughter
of the Rev. Thomas Ball, Rector of Wymondham
in Leicestershire, and Curate of Bloomsbury *; by

* He was son of the Rev. Thomas Ball, of Kingsclere, Hants,
at which place he was born, May 25, 1721; being descended
from the ancient family of the Balls, originally of Axminster,
and afterwards of Mamhead in Devonshire; one of whom, Sir
Peter Ball, was Recorder of Exeter before the Usurpation.   He
received his education on the foundation at Winchester, and in
the year 1740 proceeded thence to New-college, Oxford.   He
married a daughter of Richard Palfreyman, of Boston, co. Lincoln, by whom he had a daughter, who was married to Dean
Andrewes, as above stated.   In 1751 he went to reside at
Oakham, in Rutlandshire, as assistant to Mr. Adcock, then
master of the school there; in November 1752 was chosen
warden of the hospital in that place; and on the death of Mr.
Adcock in 1753, was a candidate for the mastership of the
school, which was obtained by Mr. Powell.   In March 1753 he
was presented by Sir John Danvers, Bart. and Thomas Noel,
Esq. trustees named in the will of Bennett Earl of Harborough,
to the living of Whissendine in the same county.   In 1756 he
was master of the free-school at Melton Mowbray, which he
resigned in 1757.   In July 1761 he was presented to the living
of Burley-on-the-Hill; and in the October following to the
Rectory of Wymondham in Leicestershire; where, having done
much for himself and successors, by setting aside a pretended
modus, and raising the value of the living by no means beyond
what was just and equitable, he could scarcely ever appear without receiving those insults which the clergy too often experience
on similar occasions.   (See the History of Leicestershire, vol. II.

this marriage he had three daughters, the eldest of whom, Mary-Anne, was married May 12, 1812, to G. Baker, Esq. son of John Baker, Esq. formerly M. P. for Canterbury; the second, Elizabeth, died an infant; and the third died unmarried; his youngest child and only son is the Rev. Gerrard-Thomas Andrewes. He was of Trinity-college, Cambridge, B.A. 1817, M. A. 1820: and was presented to the Rectory of Allhallows, Bread-street, by the Dean and Chapter of Canterbury in 1819. He married June 10 that year, Elizabeth Catherine, only daughter of William Heberden, M. D. F. R. S.

In 1791 he was chosen alternate Evening Preacher at the Magdalen; and in 1799 at the Foundling Hospital. In the latter year he preached in St. Paul's, at the anniversary meeting of the Sons of the Clergy, a Sermon which he afterwards published*. His efforts in the pulpit having excited the admiration of Lady Talbot, and obtained her

pp. 258, 405, 406). In 1766 he was installed a Prebendary in the Collegiate Church of Brecon. This preferment is in the gift of the Bishop of St. David's, but by lapse then fell to the Lord Chancellor Northington. Mr. Ball made application for it through the Earl of Winchelsea, who (on Mr. Ball's waiting on him to know the success of his visit to the Chancellor) told him that he had done all in his power for him, but had received a denial, the Prebend being engaged. About two months after, when the Earl of Northington was about to be succeeded by Earl Camden, and the Prebend was still undisposed of, Mr. Ball waited in person on Lord Northington, and expressed his hope that it might still be his; adding that, he trusted the recommendation of Lord Winchelsea would entitle him to notice. "His recommendation!" said Lord Northington, "he has never said a syllable to me either about you or the Prebend, but, as I cannot now give it you myself, I will hand you over to Pratt; apply to him, and I will lend you my assistance." He did so; and Mr. Ball succeeded. Soon after, Lord Winchelsea met him, and, expressing his surprise at his appointment, asked him, in a tone not very expressive of friendship, how he could possibly have obtained it? "I got it," replied Mr. Ball, "by really asking, and not receiving a denial." In 1771 he was chosen Lecturer of St. George's, Bloomsbury, which, with the Curacy, he held to the day of his death, which occurred in Great Russell-street, May 18, 1796.

* See the Gentleman's Magazine, vol. LXXIII. p. 255.

esteem, she presented him, in 1800, to the Rectory
of Mickleham in Surrey. He was offered the Rectory of Wormley, Herts, by Sir Abraham Hume,
Bart. but the kind proffer was declined. He was
most unexpectedly collated to St. James's, Aug. 10,
1802, by Bishop Porteus, who, though personally
unacquainted with Mr. Andrewes, had the uncommon fortitude to advance merit in opposition to the
concerted intrigues of interest, and the formidable
demands of power. His Rectory of Mickleham
having become vacant on his preferment, he was
again presented to it, and instituted Sept. 7, 1802.

In 1804 he published a plain energetic " Sermon, preached at St. Nicholas, Deptford, June 6,
1803, before the Trinity Brethren." The substance of seven Lectures on the Liturgy, which he
delivered at St. James's, in February and March
1809, occupies thirty-four pages of " The Pulpit,
by Onesimus," vol. I. 8vo, 1809. In that year,
through the influence of Mr. Perceval, then Prime
Minister, he was elected Dean of Canterbury ; and
he thereupon finally left Mickleham. In 1812, on
the translation of Bishop Sparke, he was offered,·
by Lord Liverpool, the Bishoprick of Chester, but
declined on the plea of his advancing years.

Dean Andrewes died at the Rectory-house, Piccadilly, June 2, 1825, aged 75. His remains were
interred in a vault he had prepared at Great Book-
ham in Surrey ; those of his wife, daughter, and
granddaughter were removed thither from St. James's
early on the day of his funeral.

Enjoying vigour of talent and maturity of experience, alike estimable for soundness of doctrine and
purity of living, Dean Andrewes was justly considered one of the most eminent members of our
ecclesiastical establishment. " In the pulpit he was
argumentative but not impassioned, conclusive but
not eloquent, a good rather than a great preacher.
He was often striking, but seldom moving. All
that human information suggests, or human inge-

nuity can devise, in aid of truth, elucidatory or confirmatory, presented itself ready to his mind, and was impressed by him on the minds of his hearers. He was, therefore, fond of illustrating the evidences of religion; and of enforcing, from motives of propriety or expediency, the practice of the moral duties. Sometimes he rose into considerable animation; and he uniformly secured attention."

Such is the opinion given by "Onesimus" in the work before quoted, vol. I. p. 26. The following is the Dean's character as delineated in a Sermon preached after his funeral by the Rev. Edward Repton, A. M. at St. Philip's Chapel, Regent-street, on Sunday, June 12, 1825:

" In manners gentle and conciliating; in temper cheerful, equal; in domestic life a *practical* exhortation to his children, a living pattern to his dependants. To all men kind and considerate; ever ready to listen to the tale of sorrow, prompt and unhesitating to relieve it; liberal without ostentation; charitable without reproof. Strict and uncompromising in his sense of religious duties, though a stranger to the unnatural gloom of fanaticism; shunning the dissipations and vanities of the world, but ever rejoicing in the joy of others, and sharing with cheerfulness the rational amusements of society.

" Such was this good man in private life, and they who knew him best, will know that I have not passed the boundaries of truth. But his public life is known to all. His zeal—his earnestness—his simplicity — his unaffected and peculiarly impressive manner need no comment.

" In *doctrine* as in *life*, he was the same—followed, courted, praised to a degree almost unprecedented and unequalled, he seemed, as it were, unconscious of the voice of flattery; aiming solely to impress upon his hearers those great truths, which formed the basis of his own belief and practice. For a long period his effective powers were exerted

in behalf of two * public institutions, which, for
the benevolence of their design, and the extensive-
ness of their benefit, rank amongst the foremost in
this great centre of national philanthrophy. They
who had no earthly parent to nourish and protect
them, found in him a spiritual father, who conducted them to the knowledge of their God.   And
she who had sought refuge from the perfidy and
scorn of man, in the retreat of penitence and reformation, was encouraged by his soothing assurances of reconciliation with her God, and confirmed
in the renewal of her soul.

"Called by a discerning patron from these and
other duties still more arduous, to the charge of this
extensive parish, his ministry among you was conspicuous, from its commencement to its close, for
the strict discharge of all its various duties   No *one*
was left unfulfilled, and each was conscientiously
performed as it became a faithful minister of Christ."

Dean ANDREWES to Mr. NICHOLS †.

"DEAR SIR,   *April* 14, 1800.

"I return you the sheet ‡, with no material alterations, except the addition of some descendants of Robert, born in the
year 1608, of the name of Charlton, who lived at or near Hexham.   I have made a note of my grandfather John having
twelve other children besides Elizabeth-Fenn, John born 1702,
and my father; because it is remarkable that my father was
one of fifteen children, and my mother one of seventeen, and
I am the only male remaining from both grandfathers, the present Mr. Ludlam being a descendant of my great-uncle.   I
have taken the liberty of noticing a date or two, which I conclude are errors of the press.   My father was admitted on the
foundation at Westminster in 1719.

"As I came to the Magdalen contrary to the wishes of many,
I had rather it was said, 'chosen in the year 1791 and 1799 by
the governors,' &c. adding nothing after the words, 'excellent
institutions,' respecting any of my other chapels.   Your in-

---

* The Foundling and Magdalen charities.
† A letter of the Dean to the late Mr. Cradock is printed in that Gen-
tleman's Memoirs, vol. IV. p. 91.
‡ Of the Andrewes pedigree in the History of Leicestershire.

sertion of any thing belonging to me in your excellent work gives me, I must confess, a kind of consequence to which I have little pretension; and I can only say, and that with great truth, what Ovid has said before me, that in this instance at least, *Materiem superavit Opus.* I am, my dear Sir,
  " Your much obliged servant, &c.   GERR. ANDREWES."

JOHN EARDLEY-WILMOT, Esq.

John Eardley-Wilmot, F.S.A. Esq. was second son of the Right Hon. Sir John Eardley-Wilmot, Knt. Lord Chief Justice of the Court of Common Pleas.

He received the first rudiments of education at Derby and at Westminster schools, at both which places he remained but a very short time. From thence he was placed at the Academy at Brunswick; and having remained there till he was seventeen, he went to University-college, Oxford, where he was contemporary with many men who afterwards distinguished themselves in public and private life. He was at first intended for the Church; and it was for his use that the Bishop of Gloucester, Dr. Warburton, wrote the Directions for a Young Clergyman, since published in his posthumous Works; but, upon the death of his elder brother in the East Indies, and upon the elevation of his father to one of the highest judicial situations, his intended pursuits were changed, and the profession of the law was ultimately fixed upon. From All Souls'-college, of which he had been elected a Fellow, he removed to the Temple, and studied the law under the superintendance of Sir Eardley. He was at the usual time called to the Bar, and went the Midland Circuit.

He soon after married, April 20, 1776, the only daughter of Samuel Sainthill, Esq. by whom he had four daughters and one son, now Sir Robert Eardley-Wilmot, Bart. all of whom survived him.

In 1776 he was chosen M. P. for Tiverton in Devonshire, and he was re-elected in 1780. Though seldom taking an active part in the debates of those times, he was always attentive to the important duties of a Member of Parliament, and constant in his attendance in the House. He uniformly opposed the American war, from the purest principles of liberty, justice, and benevolence ; and, though at the termination of that disgraceful contest, when the claims of the American loyalists were to be inquired into and satisfied, it was most natural to suppose that some gentleman on the other side of the House, who had, as it were, drawn the sword in their cause, would have been appointed Commissioner for that purpose; yet Mr. Wilmot's known abilities, integrity, and benevolence, were so universally acknowledged, that his nomination to that arduous office gave perfect satisfaction. How far the labours of himself and colleagues were crowned with success, the universal approbation of this country, and of America, sufficiently testify.

In 1783 he was made a Master in Chancery ; and in 1784 he was elected, with Lord Eardley his brother-in-law, Member for Coventry, in opposition to Lord Sheffield and Mr. Conway, afterwards Marquis of Hertford, whither they had gone to add to the triumphant majority, which ultimately secured Mr. Pitt in his situation as Prime Minister, and consequently this country from ruin.

It was in the summer of 1790, that the Revolutionary storm, so long collecting in France, suddenly discharged itself; and an immense number of French clergy and laity took refuge in this country. The subject of these memoirs was then in town ; and the continual scenes of distress he was daily witnessing in the streets, added to particular instances of misery which came under his own immediate observation, induced him alone, without previous communication with any one, to advertise for a meeting of the gentlemen then in town, at the Freemasons' Tavern, to take into consideration some means of affording relief to their Christian brethren. The meeting was most numerous and respectable; the Archbishop of Canterbury, many Bishops, and most of the nobility then in London, attending; and Mr. Wilmot being called to the chair, and having stated his object in calling them together, subscriptions to a large amount were immediately entered into; and a fund created, which, with the assistance of Parliament, and the contributions of every parish in the kingdom, relieved, and continued to relieve, until the return of peace rendered a continuance unnecessary, those unhappy exiles from their native shores. Mr. Wilmot continued, till he retired into the country a few years ago, to dispense under government this national bounty;— a task well suited to that universal benevolence and kindness of heart which so eminently distinguished him, and in which he had few equals, and none superior.

In 1793 he married a second wife, Sarah-Anne, daughter of Colonel Haslam; by this lady he had a son and a daughter, both of whom died in their infancy.

It was in the spring of 1804, that, finding himself ill able, from bodily infirmity, to continue the various employments he had so long zealously fulfilled, as also from an innate and hereditary love of retirement and study, he resolved to quit London entirely, and live in the country. He accordingly resigned his Mastership in Chancery, his situation as Distributor of Relief to the French Refugees, and some of the many important trusts which his own kindness and the importunity of friends had induced him to accept. He bought Bruce Castle, formerly the seat of the Coleraine family, situated at Tottenham, about five miles from London; near enough to town to continue what remained of the duty of Commissioner of the American Claims, and to discharge several trusts which were of a family nature.

He passed his time in his favourite employments, reading and study; to which may be added, active benevolence; and having been one of the best of sons as well as the best of fathers, he employed himself in writing the Life of Sir Eardley, whose memory he revered to adoration; and published with it several letters from that great man to different members of his family, which are universally acknowledged to be some of the finest models of sound morality and nervous composition that were ever edited for the training up of youth in virtue and honour. He also printed with his Life several Opinions and Judgments of Sir Eardley, abridged indeed in the Law Reports of the day, but copied more at large from the manuscript papers of that great Judge.

He soon after engaged again in biography, of which he was always remarkably fond, and published a Life, with original Letters, of Bishop Hough, a character not unlike Sir Eardley's, for benevolence, learning, and a love of independence.

Besides the above publications, Mr. Wilmot published in 1779, " A Short Defence of the Opposition," in answer to a pamphlet intituled, " A Short History of the Opposition." He also published in 1780 a re-publication, in duodecimo, of Glanville, which he had carefully collated from the Harl. Cott. Bodl. and Mill. MSS.

The last publication which his labours bestowed on the public, was a History of the Commission of American Claims, printed in the beginning of 1815, and which gives a luminous and concise account of that noble monument of national gratitude.

Being repeatedly attacked by a paralytic affection, which undermined his health and strength, his constitution, never strong, gradually gave way;

and for the last two or three years of his life he was not equal to much exertion. It was in the beginning of June 1815 that he was attacked by a bilious complaint, which greatly debilitated him; but, having in some measure recovered, he carried into effect a resolution he had much at heart, of visiting his son and grandchildren in Warwickshire. This journey much weakened him; but the cause of his death was a disease' which must have been some time increasing, water in the chest. On the day of his death, which occurred at Tottenham, June 23, 1815, in his 67th year, he was apparently in better health than he had been for years; his countenance had resumed the benevolent mildness which characterised it, less tinctured by disease, and more animated; his spirits were excellent, even joyous; and his family anticipated with delight a return of health and happiness. But these symptoms were a presage of that eternal happiness, which, we trust, through the mercy of God, awaited him; for, after passing the evening in mirth and gaiety in the bosom of his family, as he was stepping into bed, without a sigh or murmur, or any external sign of dissolution, he suddenly breathed his last, and seemed to fall asleep rather than to die.

After the preceding account, it is almost unnecessary to write the character of so good a man. As a son, father, husband, and brother, he was most tender and most affectionate; as a friend, unremittingly zealous, sincere, and benevolent; as a master, liberal and kind; to all most courteous and attentive; in every thing preferring the happiness of others to his own, and suffering no obstacle, however difficult, nor any repulse, however ungrateful, to overcome his exertions to do good. To the poor he was a liberal, and often an unknown, benefactor; and always increased the obligation of his charitable beneficence, by the affectionate sympathy with which he bestowed it. As long as humility and benevolence shall be esteemed two of the greatest as well as rarest of human virtues, the name of Mr. Wilmot will be endeared to posterity, and his example looked up to by the followers of true Christianity.

---

1. John Wilmot, Esq. to Richard Gough, Esq.

" Sir, *Bedford-row, June* 14, 1798.

" I waited a few days to answer your obliging letters, in hopes of being able to do it more satisfactorily. Upon inquiry I find there are not many of the French Clergy who are conversant in the particular branches that you mention, and fortunately few of them are in a situation of need and distress ; in fact, not above one half of the French Clergy refugees in these dominions are upon our relief list. There are two now employed at the Museum ; and one ecclesiastic, very well versed in antiquities, Mons. Bevy, is lately returned to Brabant. At the same time there are undoubtedly many who might be employed, and are qualified, as transcribers; and I have already got some of them to teach French in private families. These of course are few in comparison of the great number who are in want ; but still every thing of this sort is both a benefit and an amusement to the individual, and a source to the general fund. If, therefore, you should know of any opportunity of employing one or more in any line whatever, I have no doubt of finding persons qualified in the capacity you may have occasion for.

" I have the honour to be, Sir, with great respect, your most faithful and obedient servant, John Wilmot.

" I think it will give you pleasure to hear that we have already received above £.15,000 for the use of the French Clergy."

---

2. J. E. Wilmot, Esq. to Mr. Nichols.

" *Tottenham, April* 15, 1807.

" Mr. Wilmot's compliments to Messrs. Nichols and Son, and sends them the remainder of his Biographical Sketch *, which he is afraid cannot be got into the next Magazine. He has sent also a plate of a head, which he has had altered, &c. It has cost more than he expected. He wishes to have the plate again when quite done with.

" Messrs. Nichols may use the plate either next month or the ensuing, as they think best. Mr. Wilmot would be glad to see the proofs."

* This was a memoir of the Bishop of St. Pol de Leon, which extended through several numbers of the Gentleman's Magazine, and was accompanied by a portrait of that benevolent Prelate.

3. Dear Sir,   *Sept.* 1, 1812.

" I would with pleasure send you a copy of the letter you allude to of Bishop of Warburton, had not a particular friend of his desired me not to print the whole of it, which I presume is what you wish ; but any others I have shall be at your service.

" We got home safe (as I hope you did) after seeing Althorpe, Woburn, and Luton-park, with all which, particularly the latter, and indeed all the rest, we were much gratified.

" Yours very sincerely,   J. E. Wilmot."

---

4. " Dear Sir,   *Tottenham, Jan.* 16, 1813.

" I have been very ill, which will account to you for my using another hand. I am preparing a letter for your Magazine of next month, which I hope to send you in a few days at furthest. It is an answer to a letter signed N. S. in your December Magazine, p. 499 *. I know I can depend upon your taciturnity during my life at least, though I shall say nothing in it I shall be ashamed to avow. I am an old Correspondent.

" When I get better, V. Deo, I will send one or two original letters.
J. E. W."

---

5. " Dear Sir,   *Tottenham, Jan.* 19, 1813.

" I was struck with the first letter, signed N. S. in your last Magazine, p. 499; and it occurred to me, ill as I was, to answer the substance of it. At the same time I had not then read, as I since have done, more than one volume of Woodfall's late edition of Junius's Letters, which would have afforded many other, and still stronger reasons, against N. S.'s conjecture. I do not see, however, any thing to retract in my observations ; but as I used another hand, and have not been well, I beg you to exercise your judgment as to the substance and inditing of it, as well as to any other errata you may perceive. I wish you to insert or not, in your next number, as you think proper.

" If you have marked any of the many errata in the Life of Bishop Hough, I should be obliged to you for them. I received lately some prints from Dr. Disney from Bath ; if you ever write to him, please to say my illness has prevented my sending him thanks sooner. I am glad you are pretty well. Mine and the ladies' respects to you and your daughters.

" Yours very faithfully,   J. E. W."

---

* It is an article, by Mr. Nichols, suggesting that Junius was the Earl of Shelburne, afterwards Marquis of Lansdowne. Mr. Wilmot's answer was signed JUNIOR in the January Magazine, p. 3.

6. " DEAR SIR,   *Tottenham, Feb.* 8, 1813.

" I am obliged to you for the loan of the first volume of the Sepulchral Monuments, which I shall return the first time my carriage comes to town. You know I have got the second volume; what must I give to add the first to it?

" As to JUNIOR *, I could have added another reason if the letter CORREGIO † be, as said by Woodfall to be, a true Junius; but query? proofs are numerous. I have inclosed a copy of the letter you wished to be possessed of, which I had rather you or your son should defer the making use of for a few years. But hope, though ill at present, to see you here at Tottenham in a smaller house; this being too large now I have married three out of five children since I came here.

    " Yours very sincerely, J. E. WILMOT.

" Do you wish for any autographs? Come and see the letters."

---

7. " DEAR SIR,   *Tottenham, March* 17, 1813.

" I send a very rough draft of two articles for the Obituary of next month, if you think them worthy of it, and would be so good as to correct or shorten them if too long. I am so lame, hand and foot, I cannot copy them over again.

" We leave this house the 2d of April; and expect to have a wedding the 29th of March ‡.

" Have you noticed any more of the many errata of Bishop Hough's Life?   Yours, &c. J. E. WILMOT.

" P. S. The worthy and respectable quaker, of whom I bought my new abode only a few weeks ago, is dead, after four days' illness."

---

8. " DEAR SIR,   *Tottenham, May* 2, 1813.

" I intend to call upon you on Tuesday, as I think you are generally in town, by half past ten; and should be obliged to you to let me see, if you have got, Lysons's Environs of London. I want to look for an Abbey at West Ham, from the ruins of which a friend has lent me an old seal (agate or onyx), the impression an animal like a dragon §.

" I am told there is an account of the ruins at West Ham in a periodical, or occasional publication, called the Ambulator, or some such name. I have got into a snug house here in White Hart-lane.

" Have you ever met with some Lectures on the Miracles of the Old and New Testament, by Bengo Collyer? I should like

---

* The letter in the Gentleman's Magazine, vol. LXXXIII. i. p. 1.
† A letter supposed to be by the author of Junius had that signature.
‡ The marriage of his daughter Jemima-Arabella to John Holt, jun. esq.
§ This is engraved in Ogborne's Essex

to look at then if you have got them ; and perhaps I may bring a volume of my manuscript letters with me.

" I hope your daughters and son are well ; and desire my compliments, being yours, &c.   J. E. WILMOT."

9. "DEAR SIR,   *White Hart-lane, Tottenham, May* 1813.

" I am really so ashamed of the errata in the second volume of Bishop Hough's Memoirs, some of the printer, but mostly of the author, that I have taken some pains to correct them, with a view both to print them on a separate sheet, and to print a cheaper edition, but principally the latter, concerning both which I wish to ask your opinion ; and as to the expence of the latter, without engravings, except perhaps that of the alliances of the Bishop, in order to make the letters more intelligible. But, as I wish to make it a cheap book to the purchaser, let me know the difference of two different papers, and what should be the price in each case.

"Yours very faithfully,   J. E. WILMOT."

10. " DEAR SIR,   *June* 10, 1813.

" I have torn out three or four leaves of a little account I inclose, which I intended to leave my son or executors, to print or not ; but I have some thoughts, if I live so long, that I may print it myself next spring. I believe the first part of it would contain from thirty to forty of the inclosed sheets ; the next reports, &c.

" I wish, if this allowable imperial and royal phrensy will permit, that you would look it over at your leisure ; and if you think it is fit for publication, and tolerably correct, I wish you would let me have a sheet of it in print (but not the title-page, which perhaps I might alter). A handsome quarto I think would be the best size ; and a proof on such paper as one could write upon. By a sheet I mean two letter-press pages, as a specimen ; and I might be tempted to go on with it in the autumn, when I return from Worcestershire, whither I go in July.

"Yours sincerely,   J. E. WILMOT."

11. " DEAR SIRS,   *Tottenham, Jan.* 11, 1814.

" If I were not so lame, I should call upon you both, to wish you many returns of the year, *multos et felices.*

" I cannot help expressing my thanks for the entertainment I frequently received this Christmas from your ' Literary Anecdotes.'

" I have been amusing myself likewise with corrections ; and adding to the many errors and omissions in the printed pedigrees of the Wilmots *, which I will one of these days show you, please God I live. Best compliments to all your amiable family from your faithful servant,   J. E. WILMOT."

_____

12. "DEAR SIR,   *March* 30, 1814.
" I wish to print two or three epitaphs in the Church of South Normanton in the county of Derby, which might be bound in octavo size; and accompany, or not, the pedigree of which I sent you a copy. I have marked them progressively in the inclosed, according to the dates. Something of this might be the title: ' A few Epitaphs relating to the Pedigree of the Wilmots of Derbyshire.'
    " Yours very sincerely,   J. E. WILMOT."

_____

13.   " *April* 2, 1814.
" Mr. Wilmot's compliments to Messrs. Nichols and Co. and begs to know whether they received his account of the National Debt † ; and what Mr. Nichols senior thinks of it ?   J. E. W."

_____

14.   " *April* 5, 1814.
" As my brother-in-law Lord Eardley has desired me to draw up an account of him and his descendants, and I have sent my copy of the Gentleman's Magazine to my son in the country, and Longmate is very erroneous, I wish you would let me know from your accurate Magazine when he took (which he does not recollect) the name of Eardley, and when created an Irish Peer.
    " Yours, &c.   J. E. WILMOT."

_____

15.   " *April* 1814.
"I received yours; and I think of having a few more family epitaphs printed in the same form, *viz.* a large octavo, best paper, to bind up with the Life of my Father, or not, though I have given some of them in that volume already; and would wish them to be in order of their dates, except that the Revells had better be all, or nearly, together; but the most modern, (that to Col. Revell,) had better be the last.
" I should be glad likewise to have another sheet, or half sheet, of the same size and paper, containing the inclosed letter from the Rev. J. H. Michell, now Rector of Buckland, Herts, to J. Eardley-Wilmot, which, if I should ever re-print it again, but I do not think it likely (even if life would permit), I should add to the Appendix.
" I have added one epitaph, but two or three others you might

_____

* See Nichols's History of Leicestershire, vol. IV. pp. 344, 937.
† "Account of the National Debt, and the Public Funds or Stocks," printed in Gent. Mag. vol. LXXXIV. i. p. 339.

take from the volume, which I believe you have, *viz.* Lady
Marow, Bishop Hough (which notice), Elizabeth Eardley, and
my sister Lady Eardley.   J. E. W.
  " P. S. Write to me if you want further particulars ; and you
may put it to press, and send me a proof when you please."

———

[*As probably few copies of Mr. Michell's excellent letter, mentioned in the preceding note, have been preserved, and as it affords
some interesting details of the life of Sir Eardley Wilmot in
his retirement at Wickham, it is here appended. It refers to
p. 197 of the " Life of Sir Eardley Wilmot," l. 15.—Of the
worthy writer see in the " Literary Anecdotes," vol. VIII.
p. 213 ; and vol. IV. of the present Work, p. 866.*]

16. The Rev. J. H. MICHELL to J. EARDLEY-WILMOT, Esq.

                          Buckland, near Buntingford,
     " MY DEAR FRIEND,   *Dec. 23, 1813.*
  " Your request that I should endeavour to communicate to
you the manner in which your dear father passed his retirement
at Wickham during my residence with him, conveys a kind of
obligation on my part, which I feel myself bound to fulfil,
though not without some reluctance. We are both arrived at
that period of life, when the recollection of past scenes, in
which we have spent the cheerful season of youth with those
whom we loved, and from whom death has long separated us,
must be accompanied with some painful retrospects. But I will
not give way to such melancholy ideas, though I cannot suppress
them at the present moment.
  " At this distance of time, after a lapse of more than thirty
years, it may be difficult to recall many of those images which
once interested and delighted me, in the character, manners, and
habits of Sir Eardley, while I had the happiness of being the
witness and the partaker of his domestic society. But some of
those scenes can never be effaced as long as I have power to
think upon his name and memory. His life, however, was so
uniform and regular, that the detail of a few days may present
a pretty accurate outline of his general employment.
  " In summer he rose about seven, when I often accompanied
him in his walks into the garden and grounds. There he
amused himself with giving directions, which equally shewed
his taste and judgment. While his strength permitted, and the
weather was favourable, he often exercised himself in the morning in sawing small logs of wood, an exercise, which, I believe,
was recommended to him by a medical friend. Immediately
after breakfast, which was precisely at nine o'clock, we retired
to the library. This was well furnished with books, chiefly from
the collection of Lord Eardley, previous to their removal to his
lordship's noble mansion at Belvidere. Our first employment

was the perusal of a chapter in the Greek Testament, which Sir Eardley studied with all the accuracy of a scholar and divine, and often with expressions of regret that his professional engagements had precluded him from the enjoyment of sacred literature. This was followed by his kind indulgence to myself in permitting me to read Coke on Littleton, and occasionally parts of Coke's Reports, with a view to my particular instruction, as I was at that period designed for the law. Here I had frequent opportunities to admire his uncommon powers of retention and judgment; any mistake in reading was instantly corrected by him. His observations in elucidating difficult passages and intricate arguments astonished me. He often expatiated on the excellence of the English law, as a system of the finest reasoning in its principles, tracing its origin from the feudal establishments, and shewing in what manner the legal terms, forms of conveyance, and juridical proceedings, were derived from this source. Sometimes he relaxed from this study by substituting some treatise on modern law. Astronomy, too, formed part of our mornings' reading, as far as Ferguson's book on that subject could afford any instruction.

" About one o'clock, unless interrupted by visitors or the weather, he rode on horseback, until the chronic complaint on his loins compelled him to exchange this exercise for a carriage. In accompanying him in his little excursions, I was repeatedly gratified with his conversation with the farmers, workmen, and villagers. His inquiries after their mode of managing their farms, or employing their labour, always ended in gaining from them such knowledge as he could not easily obtain by any other means; while his engaging manner of asking them questions made them anxious to communicate whatever they knew, without reserve or dissimulation. This was a talent which he possessed in a remarkable degree, and served to render our ride an object of information to himself and of interest to them. It was one of his maxims on these occasions, always to level his discourse to the capacity or experience of the inferior ranks, and by this mode of conversation with them on what they knew better than himself, to enlarge his own knowledge.

" In the course of our morning rambles we often called upon some of the neighbouring gentlemen. The urbanity of Sir E.'s manners, and the enlivening powers of his conversation, invariably made him a very welcome visitor.

" Belvidere, the country residence of his beloved daughter Lady Eardley, and within a few miles of Wickham, was one of the favourite places for our excursion. You know the reciprocal enjoyment that must have arisen from such interviews, in which it was difficult to discern, in the scale of affection, whether parental or filial love had the preponderance.

" About three o'clock, the fixed hour for the family dinner, we returned; and, if no company were present, the rest of the day in summer was divided between walking, music, and conversation. In the winter evenings, two or three hours were principally engaged in reading. Sir E.'s taste for music was highly gratified by your dear sister, Lady Blomefield, who often filled up the vacant intervals by charming us with various pieces from the most celebrated masters.

"If I were writing to a stranger, I should with difficulty restrain myself from enlarging on the manner in which Sir E. occasionally read Milton, Pope, and Shakspeare, his three favourite Poets. Nothing, I think, could excel the *silver* tones of his voice, its variation, cadence, accents, and modulation. How often has he received the book from my hand; and in repeating what I had perused with propriety in my own opinion, has given to the passages a force, beauty, and effect, to which I was before a stranger!

" Though he had many resources within himself for retirement, yet his disposition was social. While his health continued, he could enjoy his select parties at his table, where, with unaffected simplicity, he communicated ease and cheerfulness to all his guests. Indeed the sweetness of his temper was remarkably captivating, accompanied with an indescribable manner of engaging the attention both of young and old. I never witnessed but one instance of the least inequality in his temper; but it was only momentary, and the provocation might have ruffled the mildest breast.

" His benevolent visits to the cottagers sometimes occupied part of his morning or evening walks. His knowledge of medicine was not inconsiderable, and he had a little dispensary in his house. If he heard of the illness of any poor neighbour, after having ascertained the disorder, he would direct me to mix and administer what he prescribed, and which seldom failed of success. His patients also, during their convalescence, partook of some strengthening food from his kitchen.

"There was a school about a mile from his house, at which Sir Eardley sometimes stopped, in order to inquire into the state of the little seminary. Every thing that related to the moral and literary improvement of the mind, was an object of attention to Sir Eardley. He was anxious to give some importance to the master, who was an industrious and intelligent man. In the summer, when the fruit was sufficiently ripe, I was deputed to select, according to the master's nomination, two of his best boys. They were desired to come with baskets to the house, where they were regaled; and then dispatched into the garden, with permission to eat whatever it produced, and to fill their baskets and pockets for the use of their school-fellows. This little trait of kindness became, I understood, a great incitement to the boys to deserve the good will of their instructor.

" I should have taken notice of his devoting many of his hours at Wickham to the formation of a plan for Rugby-school.

But you have so amply explained this part of his employment in your very interesting Memoirs, that I find myself completely anticipated. Indeed, whoever possesses those Memoirs, and reads them with that attention which they deserve, may easily conceive that the retirement of Sir Eardley was marked with the exercise of many amiable and useful virtues, consistently with every other part of his public and private life.

" I should be very unjust to his memory, if I concluded this sketch of his residence at Wickham without being reminded of the exemplary manner in which he passed the Sunday. His attendance at public worship was constant. He would permit nothing to interfere with this duty, except actual sickness; and the close of the day was engaged in the perusal of some serious or devotional book.

" Thus have I endeavoured to comply with your request, with a consciousness of my inability to satisfy either you or myself by this imperfect review of scenes which I can never recall without regret.

" In January 1782, at the age of 73, Sir Eardley left that sweet spot, where he enjoyed, with such dignity and comfort,

" Sollicitæ jucunda oblivia vitæ.

"Adieu! my dear friend, and while I feel how much your heart has sympathised with mine in the remembrance of your dear and venerable father, let us be thankful that he terminated this life, ' full of days and full of honour.'

" ' Gentle to me and affable hath been
His condescension, and shall be honoured ever
With grateful memory.'

With my fervent prayers that *your* retirement from the active scenes of public life, in which you were so long and so usefully engaged, may be attended with health of body, tranquillity of mind, and the prospect of everlasting blessings, believe me to be, my dear friend,
" Your affectionate and obliged,   J. H. MICHELL."

---

17. J. E. WILMOT, Esq. to Messrs. NICHOLS.
" May 25, 1814.
" Mr. E. Wilmot's compliments to Messrs. Nichols and Co. and sends them the manuscript, which Lord Eardley desires they will print on the best paper in an octavo size, and which Mr. Wilmot has since corrected and added to."

---

18.   " Tottenham, June 16, 1814.
" Mr. Eardley-Wilmot's compliments to Messrs. Nichols and Co. and as he is going out of town early on Monday morning,

he sends them a short account of Caroline Watson, who died the 10th of June*; but has not been able to learn any exact account of her father."

---

19. *Memoir of the Life of Sampson Gideon, Esq. of Spalding, co. Lincoln, and Belvedere, Kent, by J. E. Wilmot, Esq.*

Sampson Gideon, Esq. was the son of Mr. Rowland Gideon, a considerable West India merchant, who purchased his freedom of the City of London by redemption, and was admitted a Liveryman of the Painter-Stainers' Company the 17th Feb. 1697.

Mr. Gideon was born in the year 1699. His father died in 1720. His accounts shew that he was in business for himself in the year 1719, and that in July of that year he was worth £.1500. His father left him a handsome provision, the amount of his fortune in April 1720 being £.7901. From this time he carried on the business of a general merchant, establishing a character for skill and punctuality, gradually increasing his capital every half year, as appears from his own accounts; having struck a balance every six months, and sometimes oftener, from that period for near forty years, *viz.* to the year 1759; when he retired in great measure from business, and lived chiefly at his house at Belvedere in Kent till his death.

In the year 1727 he paid the portions of two of his sisters, about £.2000 each, and in September 1729 he was admitted a sworn broker for the sum of three hundred guineas. His balance on the 9th of September 1729 was £.25,000.

Notwithstanding Mr. Gideon carried on the business of a broker from this period, he continued his concerns as a general merchant. He had transactions with the East India and South Sea Companies, in the Dutch and French funds, in Bottomree and Respondentia Bonds and Insurances, and had frequently large ventures himself to all parts of the world, which were generally †, if not always, successful, and proved his skill and integrity in every thing that related to trade and commerce.

The rapid and progressive increase of Mr. Gideon's fortune appears from his accounts and the balances which he struck two or three times a year, against which he always wrote these words in large characters, " WHICH GOD PRESERVE."

Extracts from some of these Accounts.

1735. June 1st	£.40,800	1745. December	81,000
1740. June	44,000	Long Annuities	1,188
besides Long Annuities	650	1748. August	156,000

---

* This amiable woman and accomplished engraver died in her 54th year. See Mr. Wilmot's account of her in Gent. Mag. LXXXIII. i. 700.

† There is only one instance in the accounts of a loss, of about £.2000, against which is written "imposed upon."

1750. December .. £.180,000	1757. July * 283,000
1755. July 4th 279,000	1758. Ditto 296,000
1756. July 8th 285,000	1759. Ditto † 297,000

When the war with Spain was declared in 1742, it appears, from his correspondence, that he was consulted by the Ministers of that day, and that he delivered a scheme for raising three millions, making himself answerable for a considerable portion of it.

In 1743 he presented a scheme to Mr. Pelham for raising supplies, and another also in 1744, when the French fleet was in the Channel and the funds daily falling. This appears from letters to Mr. Pelham and Mr. West.

At the time of the Rebellion in 1745, and just before the battle of Culloden, he gave his note to make good his first payment on £.1,700,000; which was dispersed in the city.

At this time he proposed the subscription for circulating bank notes, and got in one day 1300 signatures to this plan, which immediately stopped the run on the Bank. — He regularly attended the Committee for supplying the soldiers in the north.

In 1749, being employed by Mr. Pelham to assist in bringing about the reduction of interest in the funds, he subscribed *all his own*; he convinced the proprietors at their General Court, that it was prudent to consent to such reduction, though they had resolved to the contrary a month before ‡.

In the year 1750, Mr. Pelham proposed to raise a million at £.3 *per cent.*; but the person who undertook it not succeeding, Mr. Gideon was sent for, and in three days the whole was raised; Mr. Gideon taking £.100,000 on his own account, though at that time it bore a discount at market. This transaction brought the foreigners and outstanders into the second reduction.

He was concerned in the year 1753, together with two other eminent merchants, Messrs. Bristow and Boehm, in advancing the sum of £.90,000 sterling to the Citizens of Dantzic on their bond at common interest, to extricate them from some difficulties the City was in at that time. A licence dated 13th Feb. 1753, was obtained from his Majesty for that purpose. This was a noble spirited act, and worthy of the merchants of a great commercial nation.

At the breaking out of the war in 1756, he was the first private person, who, with leave, advertised on his estate in Lincolnshire (which he had purchased a few years before), to pay a bounty for recruiting his Majesty's army; an example after-

---

* He observes that he this year married his daughter to Lord Gage with a portion of £.40,000.

† He mentions the reason of his balance being this year so little more than the last, *viz.* the great fall of Stock, he having valued it at the market price.

‡ This was known to Lord Winchelsea, who was present, and has often noticed it since.

wards followed by many, and persevered in by himself with great success.

The same year he subscribed on his own account £.107,000 to the loan, though the supplies were raised with great difficulty that year.

In 1758 he was very instrumental in completing the first and second payment of the Hanover loan. He took an equally active part with regard to raising the supplies of 1759.

It appears from the various letters which passed in the years 1758 and 1759, between Mr. Gideon and the Dukes of Newcastle and Devonshire, Mr. Legge, Mr. Martin, and Mr. West, that he was consulted and almost wholly relied on for raising the supplies of those years, and the disinterestedness, as well as the ability, of his conduct appears from this correspondence.

" His accounts shew that he added less to his fortune in those years than in any preceding, and very little more than the natural accummulation of his capital. His fortune indeed had been long made to the utmost extent of his wishes. In the year 1750 he had realized a considerable part of his property in the counties of Lincolnshire and Bucks ; his public spirit had been long distinguished, and in fact the interest of himself and his family was now strongly cemented with that of the public. He seems to have been very anxious at this period, and since the commencement of the war, for the prosperity of his country and for the support of public credit ; and it appears from his letters that, in more than one instance, he advised giving less advantageous terms in the loans, then negociated, than the ministers had proposed to grant, though himself would have been equally benefited with others, if such terms had been granted.

The principal object of his ambition for some years, seems to have been the rank of a Baronet, first for himself and afterwards for his son, founded on his known services to the public, from the time of Pelham in 1743 and 1744, and which was obtained for his son in the year 1759.

———

Letters from the Dukes of DEVONSHIRE and NEWCASTLE.

"SIR, *Devonshire-house, June* 13, 1757.

" I this morning mentioned to his Majesty what you desired about the Baronetage, and acquainted him with the service you had been of in relation to raising the supplies, and particularly how much obliged I thought myself to you, and urged the zeal you had shewn on all occasions to serve the public. The King seemed very well disposed, spoke very handsomely of you, and said he should have no objection himself to oblige you, but was afraid it would make a noise at this time, and therefore desired I would inform you in the civilest manner, that it was not convenient for him to comply with your request.

" I flatter myself that you will be persuaded I have done my best to serve you on this occasion ; for I do assure you that nothing would have given me greater pleasure than an opportunity of convincing you of the regard with which,
" I am, Sir, yours, &c.   DEVONSHIRE."

" DEAR SIR,   Newcastle-house, Sept. 26, 1758.
" I am much obliged to you for your goodness to me, particularly upon our new Hanover loan.   I have told the King how good you have been in it, and I am sure I shall soon have the satisfaction to acquaint his Majesty, that through your means and the rest of my friends the business is done.   I am, dear Sir, ever most sincerely yours, &c.   HOLLES NEWCASTLE."

In 1759 he in great measure retired from public business, but gave his opinion and advice in the year 1760, 1761, and 1762, to the Duke of Newcastle and Lord Mansfield, who consulted him on subjects of finance, as appears from their letters.

It has been seen that Mr. Gideon made his balance in July 1759, amount to £.297,000; but this was in a time of war, when the funds were low, and he always valued them at the market price ; and he observes many articles were undervalued, so that upon the whole his property at that time may be considered near £.350,000, and as he lived about three years longer, the natural accumulation of such a capital, deducting perhaps 3 or £.4000 *per annum* for his expenditure, would, with the peace which soon followed, have considerably increased it.

Mr. Gideon's private life and character were no less respectable than his public and commercial.   He had not only strong abilities and great judgment in business, but was very correct in all the various relations of private life.   He had a happy talent of expressing himself both in writing and conversation ; and was famed for wit and pleasantry in his social hours.   He had married Elizabeth, daughter of Charles Ermell, Esq. of the Protestant religion and of the Established Church, and brought up all his children in that persuasion.   He proved himself an excellent husband, father, and master, of which many proofs might be derived from his letters and papers.

" DEAR SON, (æt. 13.)   Belvedere, Feb. 16, 1758.
" I received your letter, and think to have discovered in it a dutiful mind, a good heart, and a distant prospect of understanding ; be steady with the former, to God, to your parents, and to your King; extend the second to those who shall deserve your esteem; the latter will improve as you advance in learning, which may be acquired by application; cherish and

cultivate commendable talents as your friends, and let impiety, pride, malice, and folly, remain always strangers to your breast.

"Doubtless, by the many Gazettes published since November last, you are acquainted with the many exploits of the Great King of Prussia in Germany. The inclosed (Gazette) will inform you of those, not less glorious, performed by the brave Col. Clive in India; compare their feats with those of old, and conclude that miracles have not ceased; and that constancy and resolution in an honest cause may still relieve the oppressed. Rome had its Cæsars, and Macedon an Alexander; Prussia gave birth to a Frederick, and England sent forth her Clive.

"In whatever station Providence may hereafter place you, act with spirit and honour, that you may be acceptable to the people and dear to your father,   SAMPSON GIDEON."

S. G. jun. Eton.

———

He had shewn himself from the very first to be a man of the strictest integrity and punctuality in all his dealings. This was his philosopher's stone, which had procured him such rapid and progressive success in all his pursuits and undertakings; nor was he less distinguished for his great liberality and humanity, than for his observance of the rules of the strictest justice and honour. His lenity and forbearance were experienced by many, his severity by none. It does not appear that he was engaged either as plaintiff or defendant in any law suit. The utmost resentment he ever shewed to any person was to cease to deal or have any connexions with him, and this appears to have happened only once, or at most twice, in the course of a long life. He was very open on such occasions, and always declared to the party the cause of his disapprobation; but whenever he thought himself unjustly accused or attacked, he repelled the accusation with great spirit and vigour, and seems always to have had the best of the argument, enforcing it with such reasons as carried conviction with them.

The instances of his humanity were numerous; the writer will only mention two: the first of which was related to him by the person on whom it was conferred; and the other is upon record, the original paper having been deposited by him in the archives of the Foundling Hospital.

Mr. Boulton, of Lincolnshire, was in the early part of his life engaged as an Underwriter, and had almost his whole fortune depending on one venture, which was so circumstanced, that, though he could not gain much, there was hardly a possibility of loss. However, by an unfortunate and almost miraculous coincidence of circumstances, which sometimes happens in this eventful life, accidents happened which were least probable, and Mr. B. was apparently involved in irretrievable ruin. He did not at that time know Mr. Gideon, or the principal parties in this commercial concern ; but he attended a meeting of all of them at Garraway's, when he expected his final doom to be pronounced. Instead of which, to his great surprise, Mr. Gideon addressed the company; and after explaining to them the nature of the business, the extreme improbability there was of the events that had happened, and that there had been no want of discretion or prudence on the part of Mr. B. ; and after reminding them that he was himself much more interested in the venture than any one else, he proposed that they should all respectively bear their proportion of the loss, and that none of it should fall on the unfortunate sufferer. The whole company immediately consented to his proposal, and Mr. B. declared to the writer, with tears of gratitude in his eyes, that he was so much surprised and affected with this unexpected generosity, that for some time he could hardly give credit to what he heard and saw.

Another instance of his active humanity was in favour of Captain Coram, the venerable Founder of the Foundling Hospital, who having successfully made the most laudable exertions in behalf of exposed and deserted young children, was at last in his old age reduced himself to extreme poverty and distress. Mr. Gideon took up the cause of this worthy veteran, and beside much private charity and assistance, he promoted in the year 1749 a subscription amongst his brother merchants, which he headed himself, and procured the names of 160 of the merchants in London, which subscription he collected himself, and paid to this respectable old man one guinea a year each for the remainder of his life. The original agreement on parchment signed by 160 persons, is in possession of the Governors of the Foundling Hospital.

His name generally appeared one of the first in all public subscriptions; and for many successive years he contributed one hundred guineas to the Sons of the Clergy.

Though Mr. Gideon never lived at any period of his life to the extent of his income, yet he lived creditably and genteelly, having an elegant Villa at Belvedere near Erith in Kent, where he had built a noble Saloon, and fitted it up with pictures of the first masters, Murillo, Rubens, Paul Veronese, Claude de Lorrain, and others. He appears to have had a very superior taste for painting. The collection is not a large one, consisting of between thirty and forty pictures ; but there is not one indifferent painting among them *. He lived here chiefly the last years of his life, employing himself in the improvement of his gardens and grounds ; he had been for some time afflicted with the dropsy, which at last carried him off in October 1762, at the age of sixty-three.

* He says in one of his letters, "I would not give a single shilling for the best *copy* in the universe. As to myself, I had rather throw the money into the sea than employ it in such baubles."

He expressed a desire in his will to be buried in the Jew's burial-ground at Mile End, a wish not unnatural, as, whatever his opinion might have been concerning Christianity, yet he had never been baptised, nor had formally abjured the religion of his forefathers.

It has been observed, however, that he married a Protestant of the Church of England, and had bred up all his children to the Established Religion. He took no part in the year 1750, in the Bill for naturalizing the Jews. He was much offended with that body for making use of his name and influence in soliciting and procuring that measure, and wrote a letter addressed to the Wardens or Elders of the Portuguese Jews, dated in 1750, to withdraw himself from that communion, assuring them at the same time, " that he did not by this step intend to discontinue his charity, and that he should in his life-time, and at his death, convince them of the great regard he had for the necessities of his fellow creatures."

In another letter he says, " the affair you mention does not in the least concern me, having always declared my sentiments against any innovation ; but contrary to my wishes and opinions, it was solicited in folly, and want of knowledge, granted in lenity and good nature as a matter of no consequence, and now prosecuted with malice to serve a political purpose. It would give me concern as an Englishman, if I apprehended any danger to my country; but, as I look upon it in a trifling light, I am perfectly easy, and shall not choose to meddle either way."

His will was dated 17th April 1760 ; and after having made most ample provision for all his family and relations, he gave

To the Portuguese Synagogue..............£.1000
To the Corporation of the Sons of the Clergy .. 2000
To the London Hospital. 1000
To the Lying-in Hospital in Brownlow-street.... 500
To the Jew Orphans........................ 200
To the Portuguese Jews' Hospital. 100

besides many other charities.

He left the reversion of his estates, if his children died without issue, to the Duke of Devonshire, whom, together with Lord Besborough, Beeston Long, Esq. Sir Francis and Robert Gosling, Esq. he made his executors, with a legacy of £.1000 each.

On the whole, it appears, that Mr. Gideon was a man of great natural abilities, of unremitting industry in his profession, and of the highest integrity and honour in all his concerns, public and private ; that he had an enlarged mind, capable of overlooking the prejudices, but justly estimating the advantages, of birth and education ; that he had great generosity and benevolence of heart, the effects of which were frequently experienced by his friends, and even by strangers ; that his country likewise partook of the benefit of his abilities, experience, and public spirit, and that he highly deserved the fortune and rank which he acquired in the state for himself and his family.

His son, Sir Sampson Gideon, Bart. changed his name to Eardley in 1789 by licence, and was created a Peer of Ireland, in November 1789, by his Majesty George the Third, and in the administration of Mr. Pitt, for his distinguished loyalty, patriotism, and other virtues, by the name and title of Baron Eardley of Spalding, in the county of Lincoln.

[This short sketch is drawn up from the numerous books and papers, in the possession of the Right Hon. Lord Eardley.

J. E. W.]

Mr. JAMES ESSEX, F. S. A.

One of Mr. Gough's most voluminous correspondents, was Mr. James Essex, an intelligent surveyor at Cambridge. A memoir of him has been published in the "Literary Anecdotes*;" and there are numerous allusions to him interspersed in the several volumes of that work †. Some extracts from his Correspondence shall here be appended.

1. Mr. Essex to Mr. Gough.

" Dear Sir,   *Cambridge, July 30, 1772.*

" I received yours; but Mr. Tyson is not in College. Before he went out, we had fixed on Monday next to meet you and Mr. Haistwell at St. Alban's, at which place and its neighbourhood we intend to spend two or three days; but, as Mr. Tyson cannot be out after Friday or Saturday at furthest, we proposed to return by way of London. We intended going from hence to St. Alban's in post-chaises, from thence in the coach to London, and from London to Cambridge in the Fly.

" A horse is of no use to a man who cannot ride; I never was able to ride much, and, as riding never agreed with me, I was obliged to give it up two or three years ago, and since that time I have not been on horseback.

" It would have given me great pleasure to accompany you and Mr. Tyson on this journey, or any other of the same sort, and I would have contrived to meet you at the principal places by means of coaches or chaises; for though I have seen the

* Vol. VI. p. 624.
† See the various references in vol. VII. pp. 128, 562.

principal places you intended to visit, I should be glad to see them again, with the additional pleasure which your joint remarks on them would give me.

" I am, dear Sir, your humble servant,   JAMES ESSEX."

2. " SIR,   *Cambridge, March* 18, 1774.
" I take the liberty of troubling you with the remarks which accompany this, and should be glad if you will give them a reading; you will find in them some observations on a subject which the late Bishop of Carlisle * thought worthy his notice. But as these remarks are extended to Masonry in general, and consequently include the necessary observations on brick-buildings, to which his Lordship's remarks are particularly confined, they may perhaps afford some amusement to those gentlemen who entertain themselves in surveying the remains of ancient buildings; and if, after reading them, you should think them worth communicating to the Society of Antiquaries, you have my permission to read them there †; but if you find upon examination that they are not worth their notice, I shall esteem it as an act of kindness if you will return them with any corrections you may think proper to make; not that I have any thoughts of publishing them, they being written for my amusement only, while I entertained myself with endeavouring to trace the origin and principles of the several modes of architecture which have been used by the antients since the time of the Romans. For want of time to transcribe these remarks I was obliged to employ a young lad, who may have committed some errors, which I hope you will correct and excuse ; and am, Sir, your very humble servant,   JAMES ESSEX."

3. " DEAR SIR,   *Cambridge, April* 12, 1774.
" I received yours by means of Mr. Beecroft, with the account of Lincoln Cathedral, which I have read; and believe it was written by the Rev. Dr. Robert Richardson (who is now in London). He was with me the greatest part of the time I was making the survey he mentions; and after I had sent an account of the state of the Church to the Dean and Chapter, he showed me an account which he had drawn up, and I believe it was the same which was found among Bishop Lyttelton's notes.

" As there were some defects in the fabric, which could not be properly accounted for without inquiring into the ages of the different parts of it, and having neither time nor opportunity of consulting any account of the Church but Mr. Willis's, which I

* Dr. Lyttelton, Pres. S. A.
† Mr. Essex's "Remarks on the Antiquity and the different Modes of Brick and Stone Buildings in England," were read at the Society of Antiquaries, Dec. 8, 1774, and are printed in the Archæologia, IV. 73.

could not reconcile with my observations of the building, I drew up such an account as I could collect from these observations, only without regarding what Mr. Willis had said on the subject; and fixed the several æras of the building to the times of such Bishops as the different parts of it pointed out, rather than depend on more uncertain accounts. I would have sent you an extract of my account *, but could not get it transcribed in time, but will send it the first opportunity ; in the meantime I have sent the paper of Dr. Richardson's, and think, as he is now in London, it will be proper to consult him before it is published. I showed it to Dr. Richardson, Master of Emanuel-college, who tells me he may be found in Madox-street. I hope to be in town sometime next month, and will do myself the pleasure of calling upon you; and am, Sir, your obliged humble servant,   JAMES ESSEX."

---

4. " DEAR SIR,   *Paternoster-row, London, Aug.* 15, 1775.
" I am satisfied that my papers relating to the antiquity of brick and stone-buildings in England were too imperfect for publication, unless they have received your kind correction ; but I shall be glad of an opportunity of looking them over before they are worked off; and likewise to have a few copies to dispose of to some of my friends, who may not have an opportunity of seeing them in the next volume of the Society's papers.
" As I have been from home full a month, and obliged to stay in town a few days, I cannot accept your kind invitation at this time; but I will take the first convenient opportunity of waiting on you at Enfield; and am, Sir, your obliged humble servant,
                                JAMES ESSEX."

---

5. " DEAR SIR,   *Cambridge, Oct.* 16, 1775.
" I was favoured with yours by Mr. Tyson, with the paper on brick-buildings, which I have compared with my own copy, and find the compositor has made a few omissions.
" Though Mr. Grose, in the explanation of his print of the gate at Lincoln, says no part of the impost now remains, I have said in page 83, that part of it is remaining, having seen it since this paper was read. In line 17, same page, I say eleven feet of this gate are buried under the road. I have since examined what remains of the south gate, where the ground is not much raised, and find it answers very nearly to the measures I have given to the north; and from the manner of building conclude they were built at the same time. I wish Mr. Basire had sent a proof of the plate, that there may be no mistake in the references; if he has one taken off, he can send it any time by means of Mr. Beecroft. I am, Sir, your very much obliged humble servant,   JAMES ESSEX."

* Mr. Essex's " Observations on Lincoln Cathedral " will be found in Archæologia, vol. IV. p. 149.

6. " Dear Sir,   *London, Oct.* 30, 1776.
" I have left at Mr. Beecroft's two impressions of a plate which the late Sir James Burrough had engraved from his design for the public library at Cambridge, which I formerly mentioned to you was in his niece's possession ; a few impressions have been taken off by my desire.
            " Your obliged humble servant,   JAMES ESSEX."

---

7. " Sir,   *Cambridge, Sept.* 11, 1778.
" You are very welcome to the sketch of Ampthill Cross *.   I did not send the verses on the pedestal, concluding you had them before ; and am, Sir, your most humble servant.
                              JAMES ESSEX."

---

8. " Dear Sir,   *Cambridge, Sept.* 27, 1778.
" It is impossible to make a window to suit the painted-glass, unless the form and dimensions of the principal pieces are known ; but the annexed sketch is made for a Gothic window † of three days, such as was used in the time of Henry the Sixth, and suitable to a room twelve or fourteen feet high.   I have instructed a man here, to paint upon glass, so as to equal the modern stained-glass in beauty and transparency ; and am persuaded it will stand many years.   He can paint arms or copy any figures, fit for windows of any form or dimensions, and imitate any stained-glass, with good effect, at much less expence than can be done in stained-glass.
" Dr. Barnardiston's books were bought by J. Deighton, successor to Mr. Mathews, bookseller in Cambridge.   I called upon him, and he says you may have any particular books ; they are all in his shop, but did not say that a catalogue of them would be published.   I am, Sir, your humble servant,   JAMES ESSEX."

* Engraved in Mr. Gough's edition of Camden's Britannia.   The Cross was designed by Mr. Essex.   It bears the arms of Catharine of Arragon, wife of Henry VIII. who resided at Ampthill at the time of her divorce.   The Cross is inscribed with the following lines by Horace Walpole :

"In days of old, here Ampthill's towers were seen,
The mournful refuge of an injur'd Queen ;
Here flow'd her pure, her unavailing tears,
Here blinded Zeal sustain'd her sinking years.
Yet Freedom hence her radiant banners wav'd,
And Love aveng'd a realm by Priests enslav'd ;
From Catherine's wrongs a nation's bliss was spread,
And Luther's light from Harry's lawless bed."

† Several of Mr. Essex's letters are respecting this window, which was erected in the library which Mr. Gough was at that period building at Enfield.

9. Mr. Gough to Mr. Essex.

9. "Dear Sir,   *Jan.* 9, 1779.

"In Mon. Ang. vol. I. p. 582, are certain charters granting lands in Okeburn, Wilts, to Bec abbey, with seals appended, said to be in the archives of King's-college, Cambridge, to which these lands were given. If you have interest with the Provost and Fellows to procure drawings of the seals, I will gladly pay the artist you employ, and you will confer a favour on self and friend. What would your glass-stainer charge for a single pane of single and impaled arms ?

" Mr. Tyson is at length in quiet possession of Lamborne. I wish you and yours the felicities of the season; and am
                    " Yours sincerely,   R. Gough."

———

10. "Dear Sir,   *Cambridge, Jan.* 17, 1779.

" There is no one in King's-college at this time to whom I can apply for a sight of the charters you mention; and I believe it will be difficult to get leave for taking them out of their treasury to copy the seals, nor do I apprehend they will suffer any one to do it there. In all Colleges writings of consequence are kept with the same care as their common seals; and two or three of the Society must be present when taken out. If there is a probability of obtaining leave I will do my endeavour to get them, but I doubt there is little room to expect it; and am your humble servant,   James Essex."

———

11. "Dear Sir,   *Cambridge, Jan.* 9, 1780.

" I have been taking some pains to get Mrs. Chettow to agree with Mr. Elstobb, an ingenious land-surveyor, to finish Dr. Mason's Map of Cambridgeshire. He has been many years employed in surveying the rivers, cuts, &c. and making large maps of particular districts in the fenny parts of the county, which have furnished him with many correct materials towards filling up what is not taken by Dr. Mason, who has nothing more in his than the situations of many churches, but they are accurately laid down, and corrected by trigonometrical calculations; and if the whole is completed, as it may be by Mr. Elstobb, I have not a doubt of its being one of the most accurate maps hitherto published.

" If the project takes place, I wish Mr. Elstobb may be instructed to insert all the ancient camps, ditches, barrows, and Roman roads, &c. of which there are many in this county, though omitted in the old maps, or not truly placed; and I think by your instructions and Dr. Lort's, Mr. Elstobb may make it more useful and agreeable to the curious than maps are in general; and if it should be taken in hand, I shall willingly give any assistance in my power, being well assured if Dr. Mason's materials and Mr. Elstobb's are not used now, there never

will be another opportunity of getting so correct a map of this
county as may be made from their materials. Mrs. Chettow
has promised to write to Dr. Lort upon the business; and of
him you may be better informed of her intentions. I wish you
all the pleasures of this season, and many returns ; and am
" Yours affectionately,   JAMES ESSEX."

---

12. " DEAR SIR,   *Cambridge, March* 5, 1780.
" Your window and chimney-piece, being finished, are now
packed up, and ready to be sent by the first waggon. I have
returned all the glass not used in the window; but of the last
parcel I could not introduce more than the boar, which Freeman has properly matched with a talbot. As to the initials, we
could not bring them in without more work than making new,
which Freeman has done very well.
" I think Mr. Tyson must be mistaken about Elstobb's Map
of the Fens. I fancy the map he means was published in 1750;
and contains only Sutton and Mepall levels, on six sheets, dedicated to the Duke of Manchester; whether it is to be sold or
not I cannot say. Dr. Colman saw this map at my house; I
had it to show what Mr. Elstobb could do, and as a specimen
of the materials he has by him towards finishing the map of
this county, begun by Dr. Mason.
" Yours sincerely,   JAMES ESSEX."

---

13. " DEAR SIR,   *Cambridge, April* 23, 1780.
" Agreeably to my promise to Dr. Lort, I have made a fair
drawing of our Round Church, restored to its primitive state.
I have likewise put together a few ' Observations on the origin
and antiquity of Round Churches in general, and of this at
Cambridge in particular,' which I fear are not worthy notice,
but such as they are I will send them to you for correction ; and
if you can collect any thing from them worthy the notice of the
Society of Antiquaries *, they and the drawing shall be at their
service ; but I fear some parts will be found trifling, and others
merely local, which being struck out will reduce them to a more
reasonable compass, and you have my permission to suppress
any part of them, or the whole if you think proper.
" I am, yours sincerely,   JAMES ESSEX."

---

14. " DEAR SIR,   *June* 18, 1780.
" Mr. Cole has sent the manuscript to me; and it shall be
transmitted to you as soon as I receive Mr. Ashby's parcel.
" I thank God the disturbances, which have been so fatal to

* These Observations were read before the Society May 24, 1781, and
are printed in Archæologia, vol. VI p. 163.

many innocent people in London and other places, have not reached us; though I believe it was not the want of inclination in many to promote it, but the lucky check that was given to their associates in London that prevented it. I assure you we have people here who talked with seeming pleasure of an approaching Civil War, before the capital was in flames; and when the rioters were suppressed, lamented that they did not do ten times more mischief. The minds of the people about this place were poisoned at the county meeting in April, by the artful harangues of Wilkes, and one day assisted by the Duke of Manchester, who, finding the majority of the meeting consisted of the lower class of people, addressed them in such a speech as has not been delivered in any public assembly since the insurrection under Wat Tyler; in short, he used every means to encourage them to rise, except offering to be their leader. And had he not declared the whole of the nobility were without virtue, honour, or understanding, I could not have supposed it possible that any man would dare to say what he did to an ignorant multitude; to many who heard him it gave great concern, and to no one more than to, yours affectionately,   JAMES ESSEX."

15. " DEAR SIR,   Cambridge, July 8, 1780.
" The pamphlets inclosed I think are not mentioned in your Topography; and it is probable you have not seen them, or several others which were published about the same time relating to the Fens. Among others was a small octavo, supposed to be written by S. Jennings, 1777 : ' Remarks on a Bill presented to Parliament in the last Session, for preserving the Drainage of the Middle and South Levels, and the several Navigations through the same; the Bedford Level Petition, and Report of the Committee,' octavo, 1777.

" ' Observations relative to a Bill intended to have been presented to Parliament this Session, for the better Draining,' &c. This is a small octavo pamphlet, supposed to be written by Mr. Palmer, 1778.

" ' Observations on the means of better Draining the Middle and South Levels of the Fens, by two Gentlemen who have taken a view thereof, addressed to the Landed and Commercial Interests affected by the Bill proposed to be brought into Parliament.' This is a thin quarto, with two plates, 1777.

" ' The Case of T. Jones, Clerk, &c. with some introductory Remarks on the General State of the Bedford Level, particularly the South part of it; ' quarto, 1777.

" ' Considerations and Reflections on the Present State of the Fens near Ely, with a proposal for inclosing and dividing the Common called Gruntifen ;' a small octavo, 1778. Mr. J. Bentham *, the author, luckily escaped being killed by the mob,

* The Historian of Ely Cathedral. See Literary Anecdotes, vol. VII. pp. 28, 513.

which, amounting to four or five hundred men and women, collected from Hadenham, Wilburton, and other villages, marched to Ely, and would have pulled down his house had not Mr. Keen promised that no such Bill should be proposed to Parliament without their consent.   They then went away without doing any other mischief than frightening our friend Bentham, who, I am told, hid himself in the cellar.

" There were some other small pamphlets published about the years 1777 and 1778, upon the subject of Draining and Navigation, which I have read, but could not get them, and have forgot the titles.   I am, yours affectionately,   JAMES ESSEX."

16. " DEAR SIR,   *March* 29, 1781.
" I beg the favour of you to strike out what you find amiss, and add what you think proper to my account of Round Churches. Since I wrote, the Town-hall in this place has been taken down, and is to be re-built. In clearing away the old buildings, I think I have discovered the Jews' house, which was bought for a prison; and part of the synagogue, in which about the same time a cell of Mendicant Friars were placed. In my paper I referred to Tanner's Notitia; but in Leland's Collectanea, last edition, vol. III. pp. 341 and 342, is a more particular account of their being placed there, which it may be proper to add in a note, as it corresponds with that above from Mr. Baker's manuscript, and confirms that in the Notitia."

17. " DEAR SIR,   *Cambridge, Sept.* 22, 1781.
" Since my return from Margate, which was a few days ago, I called upon Mr. Cole at Milton, when, inquiring after you, he informed me he had a letter from you some days before, and that you intended spending a week at Oxford. I since recollected that, in the Life of Anthony a Wood, mention is made of a curious manuscript, but unfinished, among the manuscripts of Mr. Aubrey in the Ashmolean Museum, intituled, ' Architectonica Sacra.' If this is an antient manuscript, it may possibly contain something relating to Gothic Architecture; and, if it does, it may be worthy your perusal. I shall be very glad, if your time will permit, to have some account of what it contains; for the title is remarkable, and corresponds with the ideas I have long entertained that Gothic Architecture is better adapted to sacred buildings than any other.   I am, Sir,
                " Yours affectionately,   JAMES ESSEX."

18. " DEAR SIR,   *Cambridge, Oct.* 14, 1781.
" If the specimens of Gothic windows, engraved by Perry, are part of the contents of Aubrey's Architectonica Sacra, it must contain a very imperfect account of Gothic Architecture.

I am persuaded something better might be done, which would be useful and entertaining ; and, if it could be managed, I should gladly assist in forwarding it.

" I have not had an opportunity of seeing Mr. Cole since I received yours; but I have found the two volumes of tracts you mentioned * in the Royal Library. The first volume, marked No. 72 in the Catalogus Manuscriptorum Angliæ et Hiberniæ, is in class D. 5, 11, in this Library ; it contains ten tracts only. The titles answer to those in the printed catalogue; and the dates of them, as there numbered, are as follow :

" No. 1, 1521 ; 4, 1521 ; 5, Nov. 20, 1520; 6, 1514; the 2d, 3d, 7th, 8th, and 9th, are without dates; the 10th is imperfect. These tracts are all by Wynken de Worde, unless the 10th is by another hand, it being imperfect. Somebody has written in the 4th tract, ' I have seen another nearly the same as this by Peter Traueris in Southwark, without date.'

" No. 73, the second volume, is in class D. 5, 2. The dates of the several numbers in the printed catalogue, are as follow :

" No. 1, 1506 ; 6, 1506 ; 7, at Westminster, March 9, 1496; 9, 1509; 19, 1508; 20, 1511 ; the 2d, 3d, 4th, 5th, 8th, 10th, 11th, 13th, 14th, 15th, 17th, 18th, 21st, 22d, 23d, 24th, and 25th, are without date; the 12th has neither date or printer's mark, all the rest by Wynken de Worde. The 16th is printed by Richard Pynson, without date.

" There is a tract in this volume, called, ' Nichodemus' Gospell; printed by Wynken de Worde, March the 23d, 1509.' The 5th number in this volume seems to be the 11th of the first volume, as in the printed catalogue.

" Nobody can have a book out of this class except the Vice-chancellor, or Dr. Farmer, librarian ; but, if you want an account of the contents of each tract, Mr. Cole can have the perusal of both volumes by means of Dr. Farmer, and I dare say will make any extracts you desire.

" I am, yours sincerely,   JAMES ESSEX."

---

19. " DEAR SIR,   Cambridge, Jan. 31, 1782.
" Some time ago I received by Mr. Merrill's parcel, a proof of the plate of St. Sepulchre's Church †. I think Mr. Basire has executed the engraving very well; and there are but few corrections necessary, and those very inconsiderable.

" I believe you will find I have mentioned, in my account of Round Churches, that at Maplested in Essex.

" I hope, when I see you again, to have some drawings made of Gothic Architecture, which I shall be glad to talk with Mr. Basire about engraving, if I live to be in town in the spring.

" Sir H. Englefield called upon me some time before Christ-

* This inquiry was for Mr. Herbert.
† See Archæologia, vol. VI. pl. xx. p. 173.

mas, and pressed me much to publish my Drawings and Observations on King's Chapel. I think they may make a part of a general account of Gothic Architecture, as specimens of the style of the age it was built in ; and I hope the College will promote the design, as some of the Fellows have expressed a desire of having some of the plates engraved at the expence of the Society. Though I would willingly do all in my power to forward the work, I am afraid it is too late for me to undertake it, considering the time required to complete it ; I will, however, do as much as I can in preparing it, but I see little probability of its being published. Works of this kind are calculated for men of taste only ; but of these very few can be found in this place, and these not likely to encourage it.

"When I was last at Mr. Cole's, I found him with the gout in one hand, but he was rather better than he had been, though I think he is very much broken and far from well. He much approves what he has seen of your Account of Monuments, and so does Dr. Colman. Yours affectionately,

JAMES ESSEX."

20. "DEAR SIR,   *Cambridge, Feb. . . . 1782.*
"Since my last I called upon Mr. Cole, and delivered his prints with Mr. Masters's. The second volume of Wynken de Worde's works were taken out of the library since Mr. Cole returned it, by Dr. Farmer, who is now in London or Canterbury, and it cannot be come at before he returns.

"Mr. Masters has been greatly disappointed by the Fellows of Corpus Christi-college, who at a late election of Fellows unanimously refused to elect his son ; the case is very singular, as no objection was made to his abilities or sobriety of behaviour, but they seem to have taken a dislike to the father and son *. I am sorry for the young man, who is in a bad state of health, and the disappointment may make him worse.

"I have inclosed the proof of the plate of St. Sepulchre's Church, having added a scale, and pointed to the places where the corrections are wanting.

"I am glad to hear you have been with Mr. Walpole; I dare say you will find his collections useful and entertaining. I am sorry to say I have not seen him since he removed from Arlington-street ; and, having omitted waiting on him so long, I am almost ashamed to call, considering how many civilities I have received from him.

"I beg my respects to the ladies, and compliments to Mr. Herbert ; and am, yours affectionately,   JAMES ESSEX."

* The Rev. Wm. Masters, on being refused this fellowship, removed to Emanuel-college ; and, on the resignation of his father in 1784, was instituted Vicar of Waterbeach, where he died in 1794.

21. " Dear Sir,   *Cambridge, April* 7, 1782.
" I received a proof sheet from Mr. Nichols; and in consequence of the hint you think I might give of my intentions of publishing some Observations on Gothic Architecture, I have drawn up the inclosed paper, which may be added at the end of the account of Round Churches, if you think it a proper conclusion to it *; if you think it will do, I shall be glad if you will correct it, and order it to be added. I think I cannot say more, least it should be thought I intended it as an advertisement.

" The reference in p. 172 may be omitted, if you think it is not necessary; that in p. 175 refers to the place where the Franciscans first settled in Cambridge, near which, yesterday, I saw the workmen dig up the cover of a stone-coffin, ten feet below the surface of the ground; on it was carved in a rude manner, the figure of a cross, but it was too dirty to be exactly copied; when it is washed I will make a drawing of it.

" I hope the tracings from Wynken de Worde came safe. I sent them as soon as I could; if any others are wanting, I will borrow the book again of Dr. Farmer. I am, with best respects to your family, yours affectionately,   James Essex."

——————

22. " Dear Sir,   *Cambridge, Oct.* 31, 1782.
" I was much disappointed by missing you at Lincoln, and not meeting you here. I stayed at Lincoln two days; and would with pleasure have stayed as many more had you been there. Dr. Gordon, to whose civility I am greatly obliged, pressed me much to stay some days longer; but I left it sooner, hoping I might find you at Cambridge or its neighbourhood. Dr. Gordon told me he had opened Bishop Grosseteste's tomb †for you, but could not prevail on you to stay so long as he wished; and believed the races drove you from Lincoln sooner than you intended.

" It is now five or six-and-twenty years since I first saw York Cathedral; it was then kept in better order than at present. It is a very fine building, and on the outside superior to Lincoln, but inferior to it within, especially since the nave and aisles of the latter have been new paved; and if the consistory and morning prayer chapel were laid open to the nave, and the choir properly managed when they come to work on it, it will be much superior to any Cathedral in England. There are greater variety of styles in the Church at York than in Lincoln,

* " It is not my design to enter upon a minute description of this building, because I may hereafter have occasion to take notice of it, in a work purposely intended to explain what relates to the various styles of architecture which comes under the general name of Gothic;—if I should live to compleat it." Archæologia, vol. VI. p. 178.
† The opening of this tomb is described by Mr. Gough, in " Sepulchral Monuments," vol. I. p. 47.

and those badly connected. I observed the undercroft or crypt is more antient than the Church, being of Norman work.

" Dr. Gordon told me you did not choose to visit the subterraneous building lately discovered at Lincoln ; nor did I find the least inclination to creep into a common sewer in search of it. I am perfectly satisfied with the plan and section, and am convinced that it was made for a hypocaustum, though some gentlemen are of a different opinion ; but if it was not made for that purpose, I should be glad to know to what use it could be applied.

" The antient state of Granta and Cambridge, from Dr. Mason's manuscript, is, I conceive, irregular or imperfect ; and the account of colleges, religious-houses, and hostles in Cambridge, incorrect. I will read them again with more attention, and mark the places of which I have any doubts ; but I cannot pretend to so much knowledge as Mr. Cole, whose life has been spent in collecting whatever relates to this University and County.

" From the account of Croyland, that Church must be compounded of various styles. The plate sent with the sheets I suppose is intended to represent part of the west end of the south aisle ; but I may be mistaken, as it is very different from what it appears to be in Carter's print, and in the description. The interlaced arches on little pillars are not so antient as the round arches, but were often used in the same building ; and it is not probable that they should have been added as a casing to older work, though they may by time and frost be separated from the inner parts of the walls, of which they were at first an outer casing. The arch-work, in pannels and small mouldings, as in the sketch, was the last improvement in that branch of masonry ; and was most used after the time of Henry VI.

" I fear the plan of the east end of the Church, made from my sketch, will not be understood without the references ; and before they are finished, I should like to compare them with the description in page 45 (said in the proof) misprinted.

" Query. What sort of bricks were used in Saint Guthlac's original cell and chapel, on which Dr. Stukeley supposes the buttress was built A. D. 716 ? I think there is little probability that what he supposes is true ; but if it is, those bricks are in the shape of Roman wall tile ; and, if not Roman, show that bricks were used very early by the Saxons. If the bricks are of the common form, the buttress, &c. are more modern than the Doctor supposes ; and I think it very certain not built on any part of Guthlac's cell (page 83).

" When you see Mr. Herbert, pray present my compliments to him, and tell him his papers are still in Dr. Farmer's hands, who has had Mr. Steevens with him several weeks, and I have not been able to speak with him about them ; but I hope while they are together Mr. Steevens will take notes of all the black letter, or other books, in Dr. Farmer's collection, that may be useful to him. I am, yours sincerely, JAMES ESSEX."

23. " DEAR SIR, *Cambridge, Nov. 7,* 1782.
" Having an opportunity of sending a small parcel to town, I have taken advantage of it to send these sheets to be left for you at Mr. Nichols's. I have read over the whole, and have made some alterations, which you will see in the margins; those, against which I have made a Q, are such as I believe want rectifying. Mr. Cole, who knows much better than I do, I dare say will correct all that he finds amiss; but, if he cannot give the sites of the hostles, &c. will it not be better to give a list of them in general, without naming their sites, than to place them where they were not? I am by no means satisfied with the account of the antient state of Cambridgeshire, its rivers, camps, and ditches, which would require a map drawn on purpose to describe them; but as yet no correct map of the county has been made, consequently nothing correct can be laid down from what we have. I wish to see a good map of the county, with every thing of this sort ·truly drawn upon it; but, as Cambridgeshire is the least civilised part of the kingdom, it is not probable it will be done very soon. The late Dr. Mason did much towards it; but what he has done, though mathematically correct, is consigned to the worms, who in a short time will destroy the labour of years, and deprive the curious of a work, which would do honour to his memory, if preserved.
" In my last I mentioned the lid of a small stone coffin, which I saw in my way to York; it is fixed in the wall of a cottage at Milforth in Yorkshire. You will see the form of it by the sketch below*; it is 1 foot 8 inches long, 11 inches wide at top, and 8 inches at bottom. The letters T A seem to be modern. There are some scratches, which seem intended for a date, but seem unintelligible, being only rude scratches made with a nail or point of a knife.
" I saw another stone of this sort about the same bigness, worked into the walls of the tower of a Church at York; I think it is St. Mary the Elder.
" I am, yours sincerely, JAMES ESSEX."

24. Mr. GOUGH to Mr. ESSEX.
" DEAR SIR, *Nov.* 30, 1782.
"Turning the map of Cambridgeshire in my mind, if Mrs. Chettow could be prevailed on to trust me with a sight of it, I could

---

* Mr. Essex has represented a cross flory of a form not uncommon on ancient grave-stones, particularly in the North of England. Several are engraved in Whitaker's Richmondshire.

at least give some advice as to the use that might be made of it, or price given for it. It seems to be given up by the Cambridgeshire people and Mr. Elstobb, and is open ; and, if you have interest enough with her, it might at least pay her better than by being worm-eaten. You need not mention my name; but that you would show it to a friend. Yours, R. GOUGH."

25. Mr. ESSEX to Mr. GOUGH.

" DEAR SIR, *Cambridge, Dec.* 18, 1782.

" It is with much concern I now write to acquaint you, that our old friend Mr. Cole is no more. He was confined to his bed, for the first time, last Thursday se'nnight. On Tuesday the 10th he sent for me and Mr. Lombe the attorney, having, as he said, no time to lose, and gave directions about his will, which he had written himself; but desired him to put it into proper form, with some few alterations.

" His manuscripts, consisting of about 100 volumes, he has given to the British Museum ; likewise a large collection of loose letters and papers of antiquities, which he has directed to be sorted and coarsely bound, and deposited with the manuscripts in a large strong box, not to be opened until twenty years after his death; he likewise desires, that no person, except his executors, may be admitted into his study until all his letters and loose papers are sorted and locked up with the manuscripts.

" All his printed books are to be sold with the house and furniture, painted-glass, &c. &c. and has appointed me and his old servant Tom executors *, with Mr. Lombe as overseer of his

* Mr. Essex's name was apparently not inserted as executor in 1779, when Mr. Cole wrote him the following letter, of which he has preserved a transcript in vol. XLI. of his MSS. at the British Museum, p. 344 :

" *For Mr. Essex, opposite Catharine-hall in Cambridge.*

" DEAR SIR, *Milton, Sat. July* 24, 1779.

" I hope you and the ladies got safe home on Thursday, and are well. I wish you a good journey to Margate, and all the good effects of it. I I was not well enough yesterday to be a venison eater, and thought it best to be quiet at home.

" Dr. Gooch called here yesterday in his way to Ely, and said he would call on his return to-day. He is not much to be depended on; yet, if he does not call, I will send this and the inclosed on purpose early to-morrow, and before you set out. They are for Mr. Tyson (to whom, with Mrs. Tyson, pray make my best respects), to Mr. Walpole, and to Mr. Gough. I will beg you to put them into the general post at Lamborne, if you call not in Arlington-street, or do not mean to see Mr. Gough.

" I am not well to-day. Perhaps I may not see you again. If I am under ground at your return (for I expect to go off suddenly, and wish for it), as a friend look at the spot; and, as you contrived me a neat place here for a temporary dwelling, so I beg you to recommend it to my executor to desire you to ornament my longest home.

" Adieu ! WM. COLE."

will. He died on Monday the 16th instant, about half after five
in the afternoon, perfectly resigned, and sensible to the last
moment, without a sigh or groan. He took a very affectionate
leave of me, for the last time, about three hours before he died;
he was in his sixty eighth year. He desired to be buried under
the old wooden belfry in St. Clement's parish, Cambridge, in a
vault; and, after the death of his sister Jane *, a tower to be built
over it by way of monument. He has likewise left £.10 for a
black marble stone, to be laid in St. John's-college Chapel, over
the place where Mr. Baker was buried †.

"He told me you had one of his manuscripts; and I must
beg the favour of you to return it as soon as you can collect what
you want from it, as he has ordered it to be put with the others.
I received yours of the 30th last, but have not had an opportunity
of seeing Mrs. Chettow, and am well satisfied she will not suffer the map to go out of her own hands; she is even afraid that
any one should see it. I am, with compliments to the ladies,
    "Yours affectionately,   JAMES ESSEX."

26. Mr. GOUGH to Mr. ESSEX.
"DEAR SIR,   *Jan.* 10, 1783.
"I am in hope still not to be thought to trangress the will of
our deceased friend, if compelled, by delay of the press, to detain
his manuscript a week or ten days longer; you have the keys
of the rest in your hands, and I suppose are not obliged to
lodge them in the Museum by a limited time.

"When I return this we may exchange manuscripts, for there
is one which he lent Mr. Tyson and had back on his death, and
always intended for me; I saw it when I dined at Milton last
September. It had been new written; and there was a particular direction in the first leaf that it should be delivered to me
after his decease. It is a thin quarto; and contains memorandums of the antiquities of Bene't."

27. Mr. ESSEX to Mr. GOUGH.
"DEAR SIR,   *Cambridge, Feb.* 7, 1783.
"Yours of the 10th last I ought to have answered before now,
but have been so much engaged in Mr. Cole's business that my
time is almost equally divided between Cambridge and Milton.
Several persons have been desirous of purchasing the remainder
of the lease of Mr. Cole's house; among them Mr. Masters was
the most pressing, wanting to take the house and furniture,

* This lady is mentioned in the "Literary Anecdotes," vol. I. pp. 651,
663.
† See the inscription in the "Literary Anecdotes," vol. IX. p. 602;
see also what is said in a note written by the Rev. George Ashby, ibid.
vol. V. p. 663.

books, farming utensils, horses, cows, pigs, and poultry, all in a lump; but Mrs. Cole has consented that her brother's servant, T. Wood, shall have the lease of the farm and the stock by private contract, and that the furniture should be sold by auction, which will be in about three weeks' time. Among them I believe there is nothing worthy your notice except the stained-glass, which Mr. Cole ordered in his will to be sold, and plain-glass put in its place. When a catalogue is printed, I will send it to you.

" As Cambridge is not a place for the sale of books, I have, by desire of Dr. Lort and Mr. G. Steevens, sent the catalogue (made by Mr. Cole of his books) to them, directed for the latter, at Mr. Nichols's, they having obligingly offered to treat with Mr. White, or some other bookseller, for the disposal of them all; the catalogue was sent about a fortnight ago, but I have had no answer concerning them.

" The manuscripts are all locked up in a large chest, which is not yet brought from Milton, or examined. I mentioned the manuscript you inquired for to T. Wood, who tells me that his master wrote in the beginning of it (since you saw it) ' That he would have it go with his other manuscripts *.' When I find it, if it is directed as you say, you shall have it; but, as our old friend often changed his mind, I shall not wonder if he has done it in this particular instance, as his servant seems very certain about it.

" The manuscript volume XLIV. I received last night very safe; and will take care to put it among the rest. No time is fixed for delivering them to the Museum, as they cannot be sent until the loose letters and papers are sorted, and packed up with them, which will take up some considerable time, though I have separated and destroyed a great many, which have no relation to history or antiquities. Yours sincerely,   JAMES ESSEX."

---

28. " DEAR SIR,   *Cambridge, Feb. 23, 1783.*
" With this I have inclosed the catalogue of Mr. Cole's goods to be sold by auction, in which I believe you will not find any thing worth your notice besides the glass, which, if you wish to have, I will get somebody to bid for it. There are no rings or seals, except those he has given away by his will; nor any prints of value.

" Mr. White has agreed for the books, which will be sent to town this week.

" I am glad Dr. Mason's map is likely to be saved; and hope Dr. Lort will give Faden† instructions to insert the ditches,

---

* See this particularly explained in " Literary Anecdotes," I. 694.
† After all the Map was not engraved by Faden. It was first published in 1808 by Mr. Lysons in his Magna Britannia, by the favour of Mr. Thomas Fisher, banker, of Cambridge.

Roman roads, and encampments, wherever pointed out by Dr. Mason in his manuscripts.

"Yours to command,   JAMES ESSEX."

---

29. " DEAR SIR,   *Cambridge; March 2,* 1783.

" On Sunday last I wrote to you, and sent my letter inclosed in a parcel, with a letter in answer to Mr. Herbert's query concerning Hall's Chronicle, and two catalogues of Mr. Cole's furniture. I said in my letter, I expected to hear within a week, who serve the Churches of Raveley and Upwood; I have since been informed, that the Rev. Mr. Wadeson serves Raveley, and lives at Harford; and the Rev. Mr. Cooper, who lives at Wistow, serves Upwood.

" Mr. Cole's books are gone to White's; I think you will find some curious notes in many of them, particularly in the History of Corpus Christi College, Cambridge, by R. Masters, a specimen of which you saw in the manuscript volume he lent you. Bentham's History of Ely is full of notes; so are many others, perhaps more singular than useful.

" I am, yours sincerely,   JAMES ESSEX."

---

30. " DEAR SIR,   *Cambridge, March 18,* 1783.

" Our auction ended the week before last; but, the assizes coming on, and I being obliged to attend, I had no opportunity of writing to you sooner. I endeavoured to execute your commissions at the auction; but, notwithstanding the severity of the weather, it is amazing how many people attended the sale, and the prices they bid for every lot. Mr. Masters attended every day; and bought two cart-loads of rubbish, besides what he carried home in his coach.

" The first lot of glass, which was in the two bow-windows of the study, I bought for you, but could get no more; those in the parlour were sold for near £.4, and the odd pieces, lot 3, which altogether were not worth 5s. sold for nearly £.6 to a person who came more than thirty miles in the snow and rain to buy them.

" Mr. Tysons's drawing of St. Etheldreda was sold for near £.1; other things in proportion. The lot of antiquarian prints, No. 9, contained some of those monuments (published by the Society) in Westminster Abbey, with three or four of your monuments; they sold for £.1. 8s. 6d. The Plan of London, in Elizabeth's time, by Vertue, sold for 8s. 6d. to a Fellow of Trinity-college; the other lots you marked sold for double their value. Among the plate was a large silver skewer, put in by the auctioneer, which sold for 8s. 11d. *per oz.* the buyer supposing it had been Mr. Cole's. The map No. 9 was a map of England of no value, put in by the auctioneer.

" I saw Mrs. Chettow at the sale, and inquired after the Map of Cambridgeshire, but she had not heard about the agreement you mentioned; and am, yours truly, JAMES ESSEX."

31. " DEAR SIR, *Cambridge, June 7, 1783.*
" I deferred writing an answer to yours until Dr. Smith's return from Lincoln, by whom I received another letter from Dr. Gordon; and I having now determined upon my journey to Lincoln, I hope it will suit your convenience to go with me. I intend to go through with my own horses, and make two days of it. You talked of meeting me at Lincoln; but if you can come to Cambridge, we may go from hence together, and return by Croyland. Dr. Gordon and Mr. Simpson * will entertain you at Lincoln, while I am engaged in taking necessary measures in the church; and I shall find time, during two or three days we are there, to examine whatever you may discover worthy notice. I cannot conveniently go until the first week in July, and wish not to defer it longer, because it will interfere with my journey to Margate.
" I am, dear Sir, yours affectionately, JAMES ESSEX."

32. " DEAR SIR, *Cambridge, July 28, 1783.*
" I take the opportunity of Dr. Colman's passing through London to acknowledge the receipt of your parcel, and a copy of the History of Croyland; I wish I had read it before I went there, as it would have assisted very much in directing my attention to many things worthy notice. I intend to send you a plan of the Church in its original form, with a description of it, and such remarks as I have been able to make (upon the present remains) on the spot. I wish we could have spent more time there, particularly about the Bridge, of which much is said in the History. Upon this I have made a few remarks †, which, with those about the Church, will require some time to put together; but they shall be done as soon as I can conveniently do it, and submitted to your better judgment. As the two plates of Guthlac's Cross in your preface are very far from the truth, and that of Governor Pownall's not quite correct, if you will send the sketch and measures we took, or a copy of them, I will draw one more correct, and send with the other remarks; and am, yours sincerely, JAMES ESSEX."

33. " DEAR SIR, *Cambridge, August 11, 1783.*
" I have read the sheet of Camden relating to Croyland, and think it wants no addition. The plate of Guthlac's Cross wants some amendment; I have touched up the proof with Indian ink.

* See " Literary Anecdotes," vol. VII. p. 382.   † See p. 304.

If the engraver had observed the plan, he would have shaded the staves on the angles properly. I have not the measures of the letters, but you can examine their heights and distances of the lines by the scale I have added at the bottom of it.

" I should have no objection to visiting Croyland again, but cannot this year; I shall, however, make as many notes as I can recollect before we make another visit.

" Mylne has added little to the strength, and nothing to the beauty of Rochester Cathedral; I saw it two years ago with some concern.

" The Rector of Landbeach* is not married, as said in the papers, to Miss F——. She is a fine tall girl under twenty, but her fortune I believe not worth his notice. They talk of an agreeable widow with a large fortune, and an ancient abbey at her disposal. I dined with him at a Justices' meeting on Saturday fortnight, where they rallied him upon the occasion, which he seemed not displeased at.

"I am, dear Sir, yours sincerely,   JAMES ESSEX."

———

34. " DEAR SIR,   *Lowestoffe, Aug.* 27, 1783.
" I received your letter last night; and, supposing you wish for a speedy answer, have returned one as soon as I could. I do not understand why the Doctor† should be out of temper with you about a matter which seems not to affect him ; why should he be offended at your saying the West-gate did not stand in a direct line with the East-gate, unless he told you he had got it measured, and found they were directly opposite each other ? The difference between you seems to arise from a mistake, neither of you being certain where the West-gate stood. If I mistake not, you suppose it was pulled down about sixty years ago; if so, it must have stood between the north-west angle of the Castle and the north-west angle of the town-wall, and consequently could not be opposite to the East-gate. Part of the East-gate was taken down within my memory, but I never heard where the West-gate stood. Mr. Lumby may remember it, and consequently where to measure from, and it appears by his measure that the two gates were nearly opposite each other.

" I think it is somewhere said, that the four Roman roads met at Lincoln. One runs through it from north to south ; if the other can be traced from east to west, the situations of the two gates may be discovered, as it is probable the Roman town had four gates, leading to the four principal roads. Sir H. Englefield, I think, takes the West-gate of the Castle to be Roman; but I saw it last year, and concluding it was Saxon or Norman, of the same age with the Castle, I did not think of examining

———

* Rev. Robert Masters. See " Literary Anecdotes," vol. III. p. 480.
† Dr. Gordon, Dean of Lincoln.

its situation with respect to the place where the East-gate stood;
but if Mr. Lumby took his measures from this gate, there must
be a mistake about the West-gate being taken down sixty years
ago; and we may conclude that the Castle gate was built on the
site of the Roman gate when the Castle was built by the Saxons
or Normans.

" I do not recollect that any thing was said upon the subject
when we were at Lincoln; and if it had, I was so much taken up
with the Church that I had no time to examine it.   It is a pity
we have not a good plan of the City.   Dr. Stukeley has made one.
How has he placed the gates? are they in a line with each other?
If the Roman road cannot be traced through the place from
east to west, how do we know whether there was a gate to the
west?

" The Doctor consulted Mr. Simpson, who refers to his
father's papers about the East and West-gates; but how could
his father determine the site of the West-gate unless it was
taken down in his time?   He might perhaps have measured, and
found the Castle gate was opposite the east, and from thence
conclude it was the West-gate of the Roman town, or that it
was built upon the site of it, as we may do from the measure
lately taken; but I should be glad to know what Mr. Simpson
has written about.   I hope you will excuse this hasty letter; and
believe me, yours to command,   JAMES ESSEX."

---

35. " DEAR SIR,   *Cambridge, Sept.* 22, 1783.
" I received yours with Mr. Herbert's sheets by Mr. Nichols.   I
have examined Lambarde's account of Rochester-bridge, but find
a difficulty in understanding him.   The manuscript from which
he has taken the account is curious, but does not contain particulars sufficient to give an idea of the structure of the bridge;
it only mentions the works that were to be done by particular
people.   All I can collect from it is, that the bridge consisted
of nine piers, which I suppose were built with timber (but of
this I cannot be certain); it had eight arches or passages, over
which the sylls were laid from pier to pier, and on them the
planks which formed the floor of the bridge.   The whole length
was 26 yards, or rather poles, equal to 429 feet, including the
abutments; these, I suppose, were about 10 feet each, the seven
piers about 16 feet each, and the arches about 32 feet each, the
breadth of the bridge about 17 feet clear, except over the two
middle arches, which I believe were wider by three or four feet.
The number of sylls or beams, which were about 40 feet long,
was 97 or upwards; 28 of these, with about 26 rods of planking,
belonged to those who built or repaired the nine piers, the rest
to those who made or repaired the railing on both sides.   I

would have explained all this by a plan * ; but, Mr. Nichols leaving Cambridge so soon, I had not time. If you think it necessary I will send it with my Observations on Croyland-bridge, &c. which I fear you will think too long, if not impertinent, though not yet complete. I am, yours affectionately, JAMES ESSEX."

36. "DEAR SIR,   *Cambridge, Oct. 23, 1783.*

" I take the opportunity of sending this to Mr. Nichols by a friend, imagining you have been some time expecting from me a plan of Croyland Church, according to my promise; but my eyes being very weak, occasioned by a cold I got since I came home, prevented my doing it. I have indeed made a longer and more trifling account of it than was necessary; but am not yet quite satisfied with some particulars in the printed account. When we were there, I had no opportunity of measuring the height of the ruins; but in page 85 it is said, the height to the roof is 25 yards; should not this be 22 yards?

" In page 94 it is said, the monastic apartments ranged on the south side of the Church, and were bounded on the south by a rill of water, whose obstructed channel is scarcely to be seen. I shall be glad to know whether the rill there mentioned

* The subject of this letter will be illustrated by the following from the Rev. Owen Manning to Mr. Gough :

" DEAR SIR,   *Godalming, Sept. 18, 1783.*

" As I never heard of the small History of Rochester you speak of, or ever looked into Lambarde before, I was consequently a perfect stranger to the Bridge in question.

" The first thing observable in respect to this bridge is, that the floor of it consisted of nine unequal portions of planking, to be kept in repair by nine different sets of persons; whence it is plain that what the author of the Text. Roff. calls piers, were not what we call such, *viz.* the supporters, but the intervals between, or what in stone-work we call the arches.

" As 26½ of our rods are equal to 437¼ feet, there can be no doubt but that the word ᵹypᵭ was our rod. The river, you say, was but 431 feet wide; but they might think proper to extend the floor a yard at each end into the bank, in which case the bridge would be 437 feet long, and require so many feet, or 26½ rods of planking.

" Sẏll was a large piece of timber hewn square, and applied either perpendicularly or horizontally; in the former case it was a column or supporter, in the latter it answered to our ground-sill, plate, or joist, according to the different places it occupied. In the present instance I take the sẏlles to have been the joists which lay across the bridge from side to side, to which the planking was nailed.

" You complain that you cannot find lẏccan in the Saxon dictionary. You must not expect to find, in a dictionary where the orthography is preserved as much as possible, the false or degraded manner of spelling words, in a century or two after the language ceased to be properly Saxon; but though you do not find the word lẏccan there, you will find Lecᵹan, *ponere,* as well as *jacere.* I am yours, &c.   O. MANNING."

is not the entrenchment with two small bastions, which we observed about 30 yards to the south of the Church; if it is not, what is the distance of the rill from the south wall of the Church? My design being to give a plan of the Church built by Ethelbald, in its primitive state, and a general plan of the monastic apartments and offices as far as can be collected from the History *, the measures of their boundary will be useful.

"In Hayward's Map of the Fens, made 1604, four or five crosses are inserted about Croyland; were not those some of the stones which marked their bounds? How do they agree with those lately found? May not a map of the ancient bounds be traced from the great Map of the Fens, which would explain the old map, page 84, and determine some points relating to the several crosses still remaining in those fens? I have lent Mr. Nichols a plan of Sturbridge Fair to engrave; when the outline is done, I wish he would send a proof and my plan, and I will add the references and a sketch of the old Chapel. I am, with best respects to the ladies, yours affectionately, JAMES ESSEX."

---

37. " DEAR SIR,   *Cambridge, Nov.* 8, 1783.
" The inclosed Observations on Croyland Abbey† were the amusement of my leisure hours at Lowestoffe. I have not had time to correct nor copy them, or the drawing; but if you find any thing in them worthy being inserted in a future edition of Croyland, you are welcome to extract what you like, but I shall be glad to have the manuscript and drawings returned, as I have no copy of them.

" I will take an early opportunity to make a plan of Rochester bridge ‡; but, as my last observations were made in haste, I will examine the account of it in Lambarde with more attention. When I have made that clear to myself, I will send you my thoughts upon it; until then I wish Mr. Denne not to make any use of what I sent before.

" I received a letter from Dr. Gordon, written the day after Dr. Cust § died; it was written in the same genteel style as usual, and nothing mentioned about his differing with you.

" I have no acquaintance in Clare-hall likely to give any account of Abraham Wheelock. The Master of Clare is Vice-chancellor.

" I received last night, by Mr. Wimbolt, three sheets of Mr. Herbert's book. Mr. Steevens being still at Emanuel, I have not

---

* This Plan will be found in Bibl. Top. Brit. vol. III. No. XXII. p. 202.

† Mr. Essex's Observations on Croyland Abbey and Bridge, were afterwards printed as an Appendix to Mr. Gough's History of Croyland, and form the XXIId number of the Bibl. Top. Britannica.

‡ A Description and Plan of Rochester Bridge by Mr. Essex, is printed in Archæologia, vol. VII. p. 395.

§ Richard Cust, D. D. uncle to the first Lord Brownlow, and the predecessor of Dr. Gordon in the Deanery of Lincoln, died Oct. 16, 1783.

found Dr. Farmer enough disengaged to put them into his hands. I hope Mr. Herbert is well, and desire my respects to him.

" Mr. Whisson, Public Librarian, was buried on Thursday last. I hear there are seven candidates for the place *.

" I am, yours affectionately,   James Essex."

---

38. " Dear Sir,   *Cambridge, Nov.* 29, 1783.

" I write with difficulty in consequence of your last letter relating to Croyland. I had no idea that you would think of publishing the whole, though you might, upon some future occasion, have picked out a few hints which might serve to explain some parts of what you have already published; but if you mean to publish the whole, I hope you will first model and correct it. You must observe some parts, which appear as notes, should be inserted in the text, and are referred to with a letter as thus a; I believe there are two or three of this sort. In one place I mentioned the old Church at Hexham; I think the description should be added in a note at bottom. Any other additions or alterations you may make which you find necessary. The first page is wrote over a geometrical plan of the bridge; the measures are taken from the plan in your book, but without the wings. I am, Sir, yours affectionately,   James Essex."

---

39. " Dear Sir,   *Cambridge, Dec.* 19. 1783.

" Mr. Masters is printing the Life of Mr. Baker; in which, I hear, you and Mr. Cole are to be roughly treated; Mr. Cole for stealing it, you for publishing it knowing it to be stolen. I do not know whether Mr. Nichols may not get a side blow for printing it. Mr. M. called on me yesterday for the clause in Mr. Cole's will, relating to Mr. Baker's monument, and told me he had given you both a dressing; he said the work is printed, and will soon be published †.

" Yours affectionately,   James Essex."

---

40. " Dear Sir,   *Cambridge, Jan.* 13, 1784.

" I received, by favour of Mr. Cox, your letter and two proofs, both very neatly executed. That of Croyland wants no addition. To the plan of Sturbridge Fair I will add (when my eyes will permit me), a drawing of the old Chapel, and the names of the several parts of the fair. I wish Mr. Nichols not to be in haste to publish it, as I hope to collect some materials from the Corporation Book of Orders relating to the fair, and other

---

* Of the Rev. Stephen Whisson, and the election for Public Librarian at Cambridge consequent on his decease, see the " Literary Anecdotes," vol. III. p. 657; see also vol. VIII. pp. 349, 520.

† See p. 308.

things, if I can find any worthy notice, which may add to those
I suppose he has alredy; and am, yours affectionately,
J AMES ÉSSEX."

---

41. "DEAR SIR,   *Cambridge, Feb.* 12, 1784.

" I have added the names of places in the plan of Sturbridge
Fair; and have sent a small drawing of the Chapel of St. Mary
Magdalen, belonging to the Hospital of Lepers, to whom the
fair was first granted.   If I knew what Mr. Nichols intended
to print, I would endeavour to assist, having leave from the
Mayor to examine the book in which all orders relating to the
fair are entered.

" A few days ago I was looking over a letter of yours, dated
the 15th of August last, which I received at Lowestoffe; in it
you mention Dr. Gordon's angry letter concerning the correspondence of the East-gate of Old Lincoln with the West, in point
of situation.   Since my answer to that letter, I looked into Sir
H. Englefield's account of the Castle gate, in which he tells us,
' Dr. Gordon says that, as near as the eye can judge, this arch is
directly opposite to the site of the eastern Roman gate, which
was only destroyed about twenty years ago;' and Sir H. adds,
' that the Normans and Saxons both found this great arch built
to their hands.'   Hence it appears that the Doctor and Sir H.
concluded, that this arch was the West-gate of the Roman city;
to confirm this opinion Sir H. has given measures which prove
this arch is within 24 yards, or 72 feet, of the middle of the
west wall; and the Doctor by other measures shows, that it is
exactly opposite to the place where the East-gate stood, being
the same distance from the north-west corner of the old Roman
wall as the East-gate was from the north-east corner.   Neither
of these measures prove that the west gate of the Castle was the
West-gate of Old Lincoln; but that it was not is evident, for
Leland, in his Itinerary, vol. I. speaking of the gates of Lincoln
says, ' Barre-gate at the south ende of the toune; Baile-gate by
south, a little on this side the Minstre; Newport-gate, flat north;
East-gate and West-gate toward the Castle.'

" Thus it appears that the West-gate was standing in Leland's
time; consequently, although the Castle gate is near the middle
of the west wall, and exactly opposite to the site of the East-gate,
the old West-gate could not be so, but must have stood near
the north-west angle of the Castle walls.

" It is probable the great roads which passed through Lincoln in the time of the Romans, were made before the gates
or walls were built, and that the gates were placed to suit the
direction of the roads; but, if they were not at right angles to
each other, the gates could not be in the middle of their respective walls, nor at equal distances from the angles, unless
the walls were built parallel to the roads, and inclosed a rhom-
boid instead of a parallelogram, which was the most common

X 2

figure of the Roman camps; such as this, probably, was before
it was walled about. I am, with compliments to the ladies,
"Yours affectionately,   JAMES ESSEX."

---

42. " DEAR SIR,   *Cambridge, Feb.* 19, 1784.
" Mr. Nichols wishes to oblige the public with some History
of Barnwell Abbey *. I believe Mr. Peck can furnish him with
one which he has in manuscript, but I cannot say by whom;
but it is the only one I have seen. If Mr. Peck will undertake
to complete it, nobody can do it better. Mr. Peck is now in
London, and Mr. Nichols has an opportunity of mentioning it
to him. I desire my compliments to Mr. Nichols; and am,
"Yours sincerely,   JAMES ESSEX."

---

43. " DEAR SIR,   *Cambridge, March* 14, 1784.
" Agreeably to your desire, I have paid Mr. Merrill the half
guinea for the second subscription for Dr. Glynn's portrait †;
and have put down your name for Sir J. Newton and Mr. Whisson's prints ‡.
" I suppose you have seen the Life of Mr. Baker; it was published last week. Mr. Masters is in London; I met him at Dr.
Farmer's the day before he went. He told me he had given
you and Mr. Cole a dressing; and mentioned his intention of
publishing a History of his two parishes with Denney Abbey §,
and at the same time asked me for my plan and description of
it to insert in the work; and, as he told me he intended it
for Mr. Nichols to publish in the Bibliotheca Topographica, I
told him Mr. Nichols should have it; and if you think it will
be proper to add the foundress's cup, I will get leave to make
a drawing of it, which may be put on the same plate if
necessary.
" I have not seen Mr. Nasmith very lately, but Mr. Colman
tells me he talks of putting Tanner to press very soon.
" I imagine your meeting on St. George's-day will be more
than commonly splendid. I hope the great reformations will
be useful; but do not see what a draftsman can do more than
Mr. Basire might do, if he attends every evening.
"Yours affectionately,   JAMES ESSEX."

* A History of Barnwell Abbey, by Mr. Thomas Rutherforth, was
communicated by Mr. Peck, and together with an Account of Sturbridge Fair, forms the XXXIIId number of the Bibliotheca Topographica
Britannica.

† By Facius, from a drawing by the Rev. T. Kerrich; see Dr. Glynn's
memoir in the "Literary Anecdotes," vol. VIII. p. 216.

‡ Mr. Whisson's portrait, by Mijn, was engraved in folio by J. Trotter,
1784.

§ See a letter of Mr. Masters to Mr. Nichols, respecting both these
subjects, in the "Literary Anecdotes," vol. IX. p. 596. The History of
Landbeach and Waterbeach was probably never published.

44. "DEAR SIR, *Cambridge, May 3, 1784.*

" Since my last I received two letters from you, one of which was written before you received mine. I am not yet in a condition to consider your queies relating to Rochester bridge. As soon as I am permitted to amuse myself with things of that kind, I will consider them; but I have been too ill to apply to any thing since I received them. This is the first day for some time that I have been able to ride for an airing, being confined with a blister on my head, which is not yet healed, though laid on this day was se'nnight.

"I hope I may be able to get to town on this day three weeks, though my stay will be short. If I can call on you in my way home, I will; and am, with best respects to Mrs. Gough and all friends, yours affectionately, JAMES ESSEX."

---

45. Miss ESSEX to Mr. GOUGH.

" SIR, *Cambridge, June 13, 1784.*

" I am desired by my father to acknowledge the receipt of a parcel from you or Mr. Nichols, by means of Mr. Merrill, last night. He had promised himself the pleasure of seeing you at Enfield some day this week, and had taken a place in the Fly on Wednesday last for London; but the night before he was to have set out, he was seized with a paralytic fit, and fell from his chair in his study, which has deprived him of the use of one side. By timely assistance he soon recovered his senses; and we hope, by proper application of blisters, will recover the use of his limbs. This accident has prevented his looking over those papers; but he hopes, in a little time, he will not only be able to read them, but to take a journey to Margate in the course of this summer; and hopes, if it should be convenient, to meet you somewhere in his way to town.

" My father and mother join with me in compliments to yourself and family. I am, Sir, your humble servant, M. ESSEX."

---

46. Mrs. ESSEX to Mr. GOUGH.

" SIR, *Cambridge, Oct. 4, 1784.*

" I received your kind letter on Saturday; we are much obliged to you for it, and your friendly offers of service to us. Mr. Essex died without a will, therefore we can know nothing how he would have liked to have had the manuscripts, &c. disposed, except by the information of our friends, for which we shall think ourselves greatly obliged, as we would wish to have every thing done that he would have ordered himself. The manuscript you mention, with some drawings we were informed by a friend here he meant to give to the Society, has not yet fallen into our hands; when we have found it, I will trouble you with a line to consult with you what is proper to be done. If there

is any other observation, or anything else that you can recollect, that you should like to have in memory of your old friend,
it shall be entirely at your service. I will not dispose of any of
his papers till I hear from you. You, I imagine, was not much
surprised at hearing of his death, considering the state he has
been so long in. We were never much encouraged to hope,
from the beginning of his illness; but it came on very sudden
at the last. He was down stairs two days before he died, and as
well, and better in appearance, than he had been for some
months. My daughter joins with me in respectful compliments
to Mrs. Gough and yourself; and I am, Sir, your much obliged
humble servant,   E. Essex."

In the 41st volume of Mr. Cole's MSS. (at the British Museum) are transcribed some of Mr. Essex's reports on Surveys of
Lincoln and Ely Cathedrals. He is thus complimented in an
introductory memorandum: " In December 1770, Mr. Essex, of
Cambridge, lending me his MS. Surveys of the Cathedral of Lincoln *, on Bishop Thomas and the Dean and Chapter generously
appropriating a tenth part of their income from the Church to
the repairs and ornaments of it, about ten years ago, when his
judgment was thought necessary to take a general view and
survey of it, I thought them so curious and judicious that, with
his leave, I took a copy of them. The first was made in 1761;
the latter in 1764. Since which times he has built them a new
altar-piece, from a design of his own which is universally
approved of; he knowing more of Gothic architecture than any
one I have heard talk of it; and by his works of this sort will
convince the world that many people who have written on the
subject are but dabblers in the science, and know not what they
are about. His altar-piece for King's-college Chapel, now going
to be erected within these two or three months, will satisfy the
curious that what I have advanced is no mistake. Wm. Cole."

The Rev. T. Kerrich, in his communication on Gothic Architecture, addressed in 1809 to the Society of Antiquaries, says, " No
man had explained and compared more buildings of all the different ages of Gothic Architecture than the late Mr. Essex, of
Cambridge. He had also studied regular architecture with great
attention, under Sir James Burrough; and must be considered
as a good judge in this matter †."

* His Survey of Lincoln Cathedral is the subject of his letter to Mr.
Gough in p. 285. Following the articles above-named is a letter of Mr.
Essex to the Dean and Prebendaries of Ely, concerning the removal of
the choir in Ely Cathedral from its situation under the dome into the
Presbytery; and also some correspondence between Mr. Essex and Mr.
Gostling concerning the Cathedral of Canterbury, which is printed in the
" Literary Anecdotes," vol. IX. p. 341.   † Archæologia, vol. XVI. p. 306.

Wivel. Del.   B.Reading Sculp.

Theophilus Buckeridge,M.A.

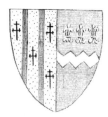

Published April 1820, by J.Nichols & Son.

Rev. THEOPHILUS BUCKERIDGE, M.A.

Theophilus Buckeridge, son of Wild Buckeridge, Gent. and Theophila, daughter of Mr. George
Hand, of Lichfield, was born in that city, July 22,
and baptised at the cathedral, Aug. 1, 1724.

He was educated at the Grammar-school of Lichfield, under the Rev. John Hunter *. From thence

* Under the same Master, Thomas Newton, Bishop of Bris-
tol, Lord Chief Justice Willes, Lord Chief Baron Parker, Mr.
Justice Noel, Lord Chief Justice Wilmot, Sir Richard Lloyd,
Baron of the Exchequer, Robert James, M.D. well known for
his Medical Dictionary, and as the inventor of the Fever Powder,
Isaac-Hawkins Browne, an ingenious and elegant Poet, David
Garrick, and Dr. Samuel Johnson, received the rudiments of
their education. It is said of Mr. Hunter in Boswell's Life of
Johnson, that, " though he might err in being too severe, the
school of Lichfield was very respectable in his time. The late
Dr. Taylor, Prebendary of Westminster, who was educated under
him, told me ' that he was an excellent master, and that his
ushers were most of them men of eminence; that Holbrook, one
of the most ingenious men, best scholars, and best preachers of
his age, was usher during the greatest part of the time that
Johnson was at school. Then came Hague, of whom as much
might be said, with the addition that he was an elegant poet.
Hague was succeeded by Green, afterwards Bishop of Lincoln,
whose character in the learned world is well known. In the
same form with Johnson was Congreve, who afterwards became
Chaplain to Archbishop Boulter, and by that connexion obtained good preferment in Ireland. He was a younger son of
the ancient family of Congreve in Staffordshire, of which the
poet was a branch. His brother sold the estate. There was also
Lowe, afterwards Canon of Windsor.' Indeed Johnson was very
sensible how much he owed to Mr. Hunter. Mr. Langton one
day asked him how he had acquired so accurate a knowledge of
Latin, in which, I believe, he was exceeded by no man of his
time; he said, ' My master whipt me very well. Without that,
Sir, I should have done nothing.' He told Mr. Langton, that,
while Hunter was flogging his boys unmercifully, he used to say,
' And this I do to save you from the gallows.' Johnson, upon
all occasions, expressed his approbation of enforcing instruction
by means of the rod."—The poetess, Anna Seward, was Mr.
Hunter's granddaughter; and has often been heard to relate
that he was found in a field, soon after his birth, by some gen-

he became a Member of St. Mary-hall, Oxford,
where he took his degrees in arts. Having entered
into Holy Orders, he obtained in 1748 the Perpetual Curacy of Edingale; and, at an early period
of life, married Margaret, daughter of the Rev.
Josiah Durant, Rector of Hagley in Worcestershire*, the husband of his father's sister. At Hagley he had frequent invitations to the mansion of
the accomplished Lord Lyttelton, where were occasionally assembled the most eminent statesmen and
wits of the age; and to the hours passed in this elegant and classical society he was accustomed to
recur with peculiar delight. During his residence
at Edingale he devoted much of his time to the
study of the antiquities of his native county. He
was one of the earliest correspondents of the Gentleman's Magazine. In 1746 he corrected and explained an inscription in marble, then recently discovered among the ruins of the Friary in Lichfield,

tlemen who were pursuing the chase, near Solihull in Warwickshire; one of whom took care of him, was at the charge of his
education, and gave him, in consequence of the singularity of
his discovery, the name of Hunter.

* Robert, Josiah, and John Durant were successively presented by the Lyttelton family to the Rectory of Hagley, in
1706, 1732, and 1764. They were descended from George
Durant, Clerk, 1627, Vicar of Blockley, co. Worcester, who was
dispossessed of his living during the Civil War. His children
(ten then living, and most of them very young) were dragged
from their home; and the neighbours charitably placed them in
a poor cottage in the same village and relieved them, where a
sister of George Durant was put to nurse them, their own
mother being lately dead. It is supposed he died before the
Restoration. Walker's Sufferings of the Clergy, p. 224.
Josiah, the Rector of Hagley, is said to have assisted in the
work, (if he did not in the most part write it,) which Lord
Lyttelton published, on the "Conversion of St. Paul,"—"a
treatise," says Dr. Johnson, "to which infidelity has never been
able to fabricate a specious answer." He died March 30, 1764.
His son, the Rev. John Durant, was of St. Edmund-hall,
Oxford, B. C. L. 1753. He had a brother, George Durant, Esq.
who was of Tong Castle in Shropshire; and M. P. for Evesham
from 1768 to 1774.

which was engraved in vol. XVI. of that publca-
tion, and which is now placed against the wal of
the remaining buildings of the house*. In 1751 he
contributed to the same Miscellany a short account
of the bridge at Burton-upon-Trent. In a letter from

* The trouble taken by Mr. Buckeridge on this subject is evident from the following letter of Mr. Greene of Lichfield to Mr.
Gough, Dec. 31, 1777 : "The tomb-stone, with the epitaph you
mention, was discovered in the year 1746, in digging for the foundation of a wall at the Grey Friars in this city. I took an exact
drawing of it upon the spot where it was found, which my friend
Mr. Buckeridge inclosed, with a particular account of its discovery, and the true reading of the monkish verses, to the
Editors of the Gentleman's Magazine, which were unnoticed by
them for some months, when a wood-cut, from my drawing,
very faithfully executed, appeared in the Magazine of September, p. 465, accompanied with an explanation by a George
Smith, who, as you will perceive by his letter, conjectured, from
the Noverca, which he read Norica, it was found at Norwich.
Mr. Buckeridge's letter, which ascertained the legend, was, as
they afterwards confessed, mislaid by the Editors, and certainly
lost. You will find the shape of the letters, cross, size of the
stone, &c. so very exact, that I cannot send you a more accurate fac-simile. Mr. Smith having so egregiously mistaken the
true reading, it was no wonder his translation of it, as well as
the subjoined account of its discovery, was erroneous. You
will see it was animadverted upon by Mr. Pegge, under the signature of PAUL GEMSEGE, in the October Magazine, p. 546;
but, as neither he nor Mr. Smith could possibly know from
whom the drawing was sent, Mr. Buckeridge wrote a second
information of the discovery of the stone, with a further illustration, and some pretty severe reflections upon Mr. Smith's
great ignorance in matters of antiquity, published in the December Magazine, p. 646. To this, which was signed J. B., Mr.
Smith thought proper to reply, in January 1747, p. 36; and in
the next succeeding month Mr. Buckeridge closed the correspondence, as you will find, p. 62. Before I conclude this long
letter, permit me to add, that I think my friend Buckeridge was
unpolitely treated by Messieurs of the Magazine. His first
letter, giving an account of the stone, was irrecoverably lost;
and the two letters he afterwards wrote were so garbled and cur-
tailed by them, as scarcely to be known when they appeared in
print."—This statement has been transcribed from the hand-writing of Mr. Buckeridge, who evidently prepared it for Mr. Greene ;
and has been communicated by the Rev. Thomas Harwood, of
Lichfield, to which this and the following article are in other
respects greatly indebted.

Dean (afterwards Bishop) Lyttelton, to Dr. Wilkes, dated Hagley, Oct. 3, 1753, he says: "I have wrote to Mr. Buckeridge at Lichfield (to whom I have sent my folio Staffordshire manuscript), and desired him to send it to the George at Wolverhampton, directed to you; it contains several miscellaneous matters relating to the county at large, and particularly the arms in church-windows before the year 1600." In another letter, dated Hagley-hall, Aug. 9, 1755, he says: "Mr. Buckeridge of Edinghall has made several collections from the registers at Lichfield, &c. which, I believe, he would gladly put into your hands." He employed himself about this time in correcting the innumerable errors in Erdeswick's "Survey of Staffordshire," printed in 1723. He compared it with many copies in public and private libraries; with some papers of Erdeswick in his own handwriting; with the collections of Wyrley, who was the amanuensis of Erdeswick; and with many other manuscripts and printed authorities, from which he extracted some charters to which Erdeswick refers, and he compared the names of places with the Conqueror's survey in Domesday-book. He thus laid the foundation for the much improved edition of the work of that celebrated antiquary, which was published in 1820 under the superintendance of the Reverend Thomas Harwood, B. D. F. S. A.

In 1760 Mr. Buckeridge was presented, by Lord Anson, to the consolidated rectories of Gresham and Barsingham in Norfolk. In 1769 he was collated by Bishop Egerton to the Mastership of St. John's Hospital in Lichfield, in which he succeeded the learned and amiable Dr. Sneyd Davies *. Of that building he contributed an engraving to the "History of Staffordshire" by Mr. Shaw, who acknowledged also the value of his communications. For

---

* The interesting subject of the extended memoir by Mr. Justice Hardinge, in the first volume of this Work.

Churton's " Life of Bishop Smith," the Founder
of the Hospital, he presented another view of it,
and communicated a list of the Masters; and from
his papers, extracted from the episcopal registers,
Mr. Harwood was enabled to give a more accurate
account of the institution in his " History of Lichfield."

In 1779 Mr. Buckeridge was presented to the
Perpetual Curacy of Tong in Shropshire; and in
1771, by Thomas Anson, Esq. to the Rectory of
Mautby in Norfolk ; but he made the house belonging to his Mastership his constant residence for
the remainder of his life. In 1784 he was appointed by Dr. Smalbroke, the Chancellor of the
Diocese of Lichfield, to be his principal Surrogate,
the duties of which office he performed with remarkable regularity and ability, and in which he was succeeded by his eldest son. Mr. Buckeridge died at
Lichfield, in his 80th year, Dec. 23, 1803, and was
buried on the 29th of the same month at Edingale,
near the remains of his wife, who, after a union of
forty years, had left him a widower, Feb. 4, 1793.
They had thirteen children; but lost many of them
in their childhood. The following epitaph is in the
Church of St. Chad, Lichfield :

M. S.

Mariæ,			Aug. 1775.
Georgii,	} ob. {		Jun. 1779.
Thomæ,			Mar. 1786.
Frederici *,			Mar. 1789.

fil. Theoph. Buckeridge, (Hosp. Sant. Johis Bapt. Magri) et
Margaretæ uxoris ejus.

---

* His death, which took place at Lichfield, March 13, 1789,
when at the age of twenty, is recorded in the Gentleman's
Magazine, with the following affectionate memorial by his father:
" Frederick Buckeridge, of St. John's-college, Oxford, a youth
of extraordinary endowment. Intense application to study impaired a constitution, weakened in his infancy by a rapid succession of infantile diseases. Incapable of sustaining the constant drudgery of a school, where much attendance is required

Three sons only survived:—

1. The Ven. Charles Buckeridge, Archdeacon of Coventry. He was of St. John's-college, Oxford, M. A. 1781; B. D. 1791; D. D. 1807. In 1789 he was presented by the Crown to the Rectory of Pulchrohon in Pembrokeshire, and the Vicarage of Lancarvan in Glamorganshire; in 1790, also by the King, to the Vicarage of Newport in Shropshire; in 1804, by the Chancellor of Lichfield Cathedral (Dr. Vyse) to the Perpetual Curacy of King's Bromley in Staffordshire; in the same year, he was collated by Bishop Cornwallis, to the Prebend of Wolvey in the Church of Lichfield; in 1807, to the Precentorship, the first of the six Residentiary Canonries; and in 1816, by the same Prelate, to the Archdeaconry of Coventry. With the exception of the Prebend of Wolvey, he enjoyed all these preferments, together with the office of Principal Surrogate, at the period of his death. Early in life he had been one of the Priest-Vicars of Lichfield Cathedral, but resigned it on succeeding his father in the Perpetual Curacy of Tong; which latter he also resigned on his collation to the Residentiaryship of Lichfield. He died at his residentiary-house, September 28, 1827, aged 74. He had been twice married. To his first wife, Miss

for little instruction, he learned to read, write, and the first rules of arithmetic, without a master. In the acquirement of Latin and Greek he had little assistance; as little, perhaps, as the learned Scaliger, who called himself an autodidact. His amusements were music and drawing, in the latter of which he excelled; but his favourite studies were experimental philosophy and mechanics. A wheel of his contrivance, intended as a model of a perpetual motion, had he lived to complete it, would have borne ample testimony of his ingenuity. His disorder, which was a pulmonary phthisis, resisted every medical application, and the waters at Bristol. A sweetness of temper, a constitutional politeness, and gentleness of manners, endeared him to all those who knew him; and it can be truly said, he never grieved his parents but when he was sick, and when he died. As his life was all innocence and piety, his death was without a groan and without a sigh; and he literally fell asleep."

Hussey, there is an elegant marble monument, by Richard Westmacott, in the north transept of Lichfield Cathedral in a false window. A female figure, with her left arm leaning upon an urn, points with her right-hand to the inscription :

"Obiit 7 Januarii 1787, æt. 25."

And underneath :

"M. S.
Catherinæ Ceciliæ,
Caroli Buckeridge
uxoris dilectissimæ,
amplexu ejus ah ! nimium beati
mense consortii septimo
direptæ."

ARMS. Or, two pallets between five cross-crosslets fitchee in saltire Sable, Buckeridge; impaling, 1st and 4th, Barry of six, Ermine and Gules; 2d and 3d, Or, a cross Vert, Hussey. — The arms of Dr. Buckeridge also occur in the Prebendaries' window, placed in the choir between 1806 and 1808.

Archdeacon Buckeridge married, secondly, Miss Elizabeth Slaney, by whom he had two children, who both died before him, Mary-Elizabeth, in 1810, at the age of thirteen; and Charles-Lewis, in 1812. Mrs. Buckeridge is now living, Jan. 1829.

2. The Rev. Richard Buckeridge. He was also of St. John's-college, Oxford, where he took his degree of B.C.L. June 22, 1791. In the same year his father resigned to him the Curacy of Edingale; in 1802 he was presented by the Lord Chancellor to the Perpetual Curacy of Stone in Staffordshire; and in 1790 he was presented by Viscount Anson to the Rectory of Beighton in Norfolk. He was also Dean's Vicar in the Cathedral of Lichfield. He was married at Lichfield, January 5, 1792, to the eldest daughter of Mr. William Wright, and granddaughter of Richard Greene, Esq. the Collector of the Lichfield Museum. He died at Stone in June 1824, at the age of 59; leaving two sons and three daughters.

3. Lewis Buckeridge, Esq. He died at Lichfield, Nov. 23, 1821.

RICHARD GREENE, Esq. M. D.

This intelligent Collector of Curiosities was a respectable Surgeon and Apothecary at Lichfield, and one of the Aldermen of that City.

He was proprietor of a Museum which attracted and merited the notice of the antiquary and the curious of every denomination; to the formation of which he dedicated the principal part of his life; and which was open, free from expense, to all scientific and inquiring individuals. In 1776 it was visited by Dr. Samuel Johnson, a circumstance thus recorded by Mr. Boswell: " We went and viewed the Museum of Mr. Richard Greene, apothecary here, who told me he was proud of being a relation of Dr. Johnson's. It was truly a wonderful collection, both of antiquities and natural curiosities, and ingenious works of art. He had all the articles accurately arranged, with the names of the contributors upon labels, printed at his own little press; and on the stair-case leading to it was a board, with the names of the contributors marked in gold letters. A printed Catalogue of the collection was to be had at the bookseller's *. Johnson expressed his

* There were two or three editions of the " New and Accurate Survey of the Lichfield Museum, in which every article is particularly described. Printed by J. Jackson, bookseller in Lichfield." It is now very scarce. Several of the more curious articles, particularly those of local interest, are described in Shaw's Staffordshire, vol. I. p. 331. A view of the apartment was published in 1788 in the Gentleman's Magazine, vol. LVIII. p. 847, accompanied by a letter which is re-printed hereafter, p. 325. He had previously, at various times, had several of his curiosities engraved in that publication. One of the several urns found in the wall of Fairwell Church, Staffordshire, was represented in vol. XLI. p. 59; a chalice, found in Lichfield Cathedral, vol. XLII. p. 168; a Roman pig of lead found on Hints Common, ibid. p. 558 (on which see also vol. XLIII. p. 61; LV. p. 693); a sepulchral urn found at Yoxall in vol. XLIV. p. 358; a celt and spear-head found

admiration of the activity, and diligence, and good
fortune of Mr. Greene, in getting together, in his
situation, so great a variety of things; and Mr.
Greene told me that Johnson once said to him, 'Sir,
I should as soon have thought of building a man of
war, as of collecting such a museum.' Mr. Greene's
obliging alacrity in showing it was very pleasing.
His engraved portrait has a motto truly characteristic of his disposition, NEMO SIBI VIVAT *."
In 1784 Dr. Johnson consigned to Mr. Greene
the task of inscribing a grave-stone to his father,
mother, and brother, in St. Michael's, Lichfield†.
The following brief notice of Mr. Greene is from
an unpublished manuscript of the late Rev. Mark
Noble, F.S.A. written in 1808: "A more inoffensive character I never knew. We were well
acquainted; and many interchanges took place between us. He visited us in Birmingham and I him
in Lichfield. He collected a Museum, perhaps the
finest that was ever formed in a provincial City, and
he was so generally beloved that the neighbouring
Nobility, Gentlemen, and Clergy were constantly
adding to it, often presents of no small value. I
have myself been a contributor, and when I have

in Staffordshire in vol. LII. p. 281; a painted altar-piece
in vol. LV. p. 25 (before described in vol. LIV. p. 396);
another chalice, and a crucifix, also found in Lichfield Cathedral, in vol. LV. p. 332; a medal and seal in vol. LVI. p. 632;
an ivory carving of the Nativity, ibid. p. 925. All these were
in Mr. Greene's Museum, and most of the engravings are accompanied by letters of Mr. Greene. Among his other communications were, an interesting letter on Dr. Johnson's willow at Lichfield, and other localities, in vol. LV. p. 495; one on the death
of the Parliamentarian general Lord Brook, ibid. p. 943; on
the opening of the grave of Adam de Stanford in Lichfield
Cathedral (who died Precentor in 1278) vol. LVII. p. 461.
    * This was a private plate, but was lent by his son to the His-
tory of Staffordshire, where it may be seen, representing a pleasing elderly countenance, vol. I. p. 308. The original painting
is now in the possession of his son.
    † See the Doctor's letter in Boswell, vol. I. p. 566; or in
Shaw's Staffordshire, I. 327.

gone to London he has commissioned me to purchase rarities for him, depending a good deal upon
my judgment. He laid out, however, no very large
sums; the whole, though at his death sold for a considerable amount, had been of little expense, comparatively speaking, to himself. He was religious,
strictly just, diligent in business, and very moderate in his charges. A Scottish University, without
any solicitation of his own, sent him the degree of
M. D. He was gratified by it; but never assumed
the title of Doctor. As a husband, father, neighbour, and master he was most estimable; I think
he could not have had an enemy in the world. It
must be remarked that he was the first who brought
a printing-press to Lichfield, as he informed me;
so we see Dr. Johnson's father and brother were
only booksellers."

Mr. Greene died at Lichfield, June 4, 1793, in
his 78th year; and his widow on the first of August
following. He had been twice married. By his
first wife, whose name was Dawson, he had a
daughter, who was married to Mr. William Wright,
of Lichfield *. One of her daughters became the
wife of the Rev. Richard Buckeridge (of whom in
p. 316); and another of her daughters is yet alive.
Richard Wright, M. D. (mentioned in p. 321,) was
her son.

Mr. Greene's second wife was Theodosia Webb, of
Croxall in Derbyshire. "Mrs. Greene," adds Mr. Noble, " was plain in her person, manner, and dress;
but a very valuable woman, being strictly attentive
to her duty. By her Mr. Greene had an only son,
Thomas, a Lieutenant and Surgeon in the Staffordshire Militia. He was educated in the Free Gram-

* The wife of William Mott, Esq. a proctor at Lichfield, and
for many years Secretary, Registrar, and Chapter-clerk to the
See, was a daughter of Mr. Richard Greene,—not the collector,
but a relation, whose family resided at Brewood at Staffordshire.
Mr. Mott died at Lichfield, May 13, 1826, aged 71.

mar School of King Edward the Sixth in Birmingham, where I often invited him at that time to dine
with me. He seemed to have none of his father's
Thoresbeian taste *; and he sold the Museum soon
after it had passed into his hands." Some part of
it came, whether by sale or otherwise, into the possession of Richard Wright, M. D. the grandson of
Dr. Greene, who greatly increased it. It was afterwards removed to Bath, where it was sold, with
the exception of a small portion of it, also dispersed by auction after his death.

-----

1. Mr. GREENE to Mr. BOWEN.

"DEAR MR. BOWEN,   *Lichfield, April* 17, 1769.

"By favour of my friend Mr. Buckeridge †, I send you an
impression in plaster, taken from a brass seal; which, by very
good luck, has fallen into my hands. I am so much of an antiquary that I can perceive it is the Great Seal of Henry Prince
of Wales, son of Henry IV. Duke of Aquitaine, Lancaster, and
Earl of Chester. My dear friend, shall I entreat an explanation
by the return of Mr. Buckeridge? I shall be glad of the cir-
cumscription in the old character, with the abbreviations, and an
explanation in your own hand; and, if not too much trouble,
your sentiments upon this curious piece of antiquity. I am
amazed how it chanced to be in private hands. There are four
holes in the same number of ears, which, I suppose, were to
receive four pins, to keep the other part steady. I am in pursuit of that part; but as yet cannot find it.

"An antiquarian acquaintance, the Rev. Mr. Percy ‡, a relation of the Duke of Northumberland, is now collecting materials for a History of the Battle of Shrewsbury, temp. Henry IV.
I have furnished him with a print of the Battle-field Church,
with which he seems greatly pleased, as I find it is re-built.

"Do not give yourself the trouble to send back the casts, as
I can coin more. I have some thoughts, if I could get a draw-

-----

* A letter of Miss Seward, to Captain Seward, Sept. 2, 1787, contains
the following anecdote connected with young Greene. Lord Heathfield
had paid a flying visit to Lichfield, and, we are told, " had he passed only
one night, the compliment of a general illumination through our little
city had been paid. The words Elliot, Gibraltar, Victory, enwreathed
with flowers, were to have shone in phosphorus upon the walls of our
town-hall, and over the arms of our city. It was the contrivance of an
ingenious young surgeon, of the name of Greene, who prepared it when
you taught me to expect one of the most flattering distinctions of my
life; but his Lordship arriving on a Sunday morning, and departing in
the afternoon, he frustrated the wish of our inhabitants to have wel-
comed, with public eclat, the restorer of the nation's glory." Seward's
Letters, vol. i. p. 322.

† The Rev. Theophilus Buckeridge, the subject of the preceding
memoir.   ‡ Afterwards Bishop of Dromore.

ing, to have a copper-plate of it engraved; or to publish it in
the Gentleman's Magazine *. I send two casts, as they are not
cleverly taken off, that you may make out its legend.

" Were you to see my Museolum, it would surprise you. My
collections of antiquities, animals, fossils, shells, coins, woods,
&c. are vaſtly great. I wish very much to see you in Lichfield.
I wish you and yours all health and happiness; and am, with
great truth, my dear Sir, your sincere friend and obliged humble
servant,   RICHARD GREENE."

2. *In* 1782 *Mr. Greene circulated a general Invitation in the form
of a hand-bill, and, as a curiosity, a copy is here inserted:*

Lichfield Museum.

Mr. GREENE, deeply impressed with a sense of the favours of
his numerous *Benefactors,* to whose kind Contributions he is
indebted, in a great measure, for a valuable Collection of *Curiosities;* begs leave to desire their acceptance of a general Syllabus of his *Museum;* and takes this opportunity of acquainting
them, that they, and as many of their friends as they please to
recommend, will be entitled to visit the *Museum,* at all times,
except *Sundays.*

ANIMALS preserved; *viz.* Birds, Fishes, Snakes, Lizards, Insects, Moths, and Butterflies.

SHELLS; Corals, Coralines, Sea-plants, Sponges, and other
Marine productions.

STONES; Fossils, Minerals, Ores, Crystals, Spars, Marbles,
Fluors, Incrustations, and Petrefactions.

WOODS; Seeds and Fruits.

ROMAN, and other Coins, Casts, and Medals.

DRESSES, and Ornaments of the Natives of *Otaheite;* their
Cloth, Weapons, Fish-Hooks, Nets, Tools, &c. presented for the
most part by the Rt. Honourable the Earl of DONEGALL, Lord
PAGET, and Sir ASHTON LEVER †: *Cherokee-Indian* Pouches,
Mawcassons, Scalping Knives, Scratcher, Spoon, Tomahawke,
Wampum, &c.

ENGLISH and Foreign Weapons, Arms and Armour; This

* See in vol. XXXIX. of that Miscellany, pp. 277, 377, an engraving
of the seal, and a description by Dr. Pegge.

† In a letter to David Samwell, Esq. May 15, 1791, Miss Seward says :
" Your bounty to me enabled Mr. Greene to display in his Museum, those
Otaheitean curiosities whose exhibition prócured him one of the medals
struck by the Royal Society in honour of Captain Cook. I presented
him with a part of your present [the reader will observe Mr. Greene had
some such curiosities before this generous piece of liberality], and was
doubly glad that I had done so when I found his displaying them
rewarded by a distinction which cheered and delighted his honest benevolent heart. If there is aught of estimable in my composition, it consists in an utter exemption from envy, which even my enemies confess,"
&c. &c.—The fair scribbler had written a poem on Captain Cook, but
had not been " rewarded."   " I own," she says, " the *neglect of the
Royal Society* hurt me !"   Seward's Letters, vol. III. p. 60.

Collection exhibits the gradual improvements in the Gun and Fire-lock.

REMAINS OF ANTIQUITY; *viz.* Urns, Vases, Patera, Sepulchral Relics, and a Roman Monument of Lead, cast in the time of the Emperor VESPASIAN.

ROMAN Missals wrote on Vellum, decorated with a variety of Paintings, and the Initial Letters finely illuminated: Crucifixes, Images, Thurible, Rosaries of Beads, &c.

An uncommon Musical Altar Clock: Model of *Lichfield* Cathedral, &c. JANUARY 22d, 1782.

---

3. Mr. GREENE to Mr. NICHOLS.

" MY DEAR SIR, *Lichfield, March 6, 1785.*

" As my worthy friend Mr. White is writing to you, I beg leave to add a few lines, to inform you, that the chalice and crucifix, mentioned in your late publication, page 158, are in my Museum; a neat drawing of each shall, in a very little time, be sent for your Magazine*. I often lament my infelicity in not having more of your company when you visited Lichfield; but am somewhat consoled with the thoughts, that Mr. White had explained every article in my collection. If ever you again visit Staffordshire, I hope my patients will contrive to be free from complaints, or excuse my frequent visits, that I may enjoy more of your company.

" I have requested my friend Mr. White to beg the favour of an impression of your portrait; on which I shall set the highest value. I am, dear Sir, your much obliged and affectionate humble servant, RICHARD GREENE."

---

4. " DEAR MR. NICHOLS, *Lichfield, April 8, 1785.*

" I received from my worthy friend Mr. White two prints, one a neat and just representation of yourself, the other a perspective view of our late friend Dr. Johnson's house †, &c. I beg leave to return you my sincere thanks for them, as well as for former favours. On the first I shall set a just value; and, with proper decorations, place it in my Museum, among some others of my worthy friends.

" I was sorry to hear of your late illness: but am comforted with the thoughts of your recovery. I hope you exactly conform to the directions of the medical gentlemen, in order to preserve a life so useful to the public in general, and to your friends in particular.

" I received the manuscript relative to the Committee at Stafford; and could wish to see some of the most interesting parts in your monthly publications, as it displays a true picture of those arbitrary saints. If you have not taken a copy of it I will send you some extracts. I am, dear Sir, your much obliged, &c. RICHARD GREENE."

* See before in the note, p. 319.
† Engraved in the Gentleman's Magazine, vol. LV. p. 100.

5. The Rev. HENRY WHITE to Mr. NICHOLS.

" DEAR SIR,   *Lichfield, Sept.* 13, 1785.

" I am as sincerely concerned at your last illness as rejoiced
that your Suffolk journey has so well answered. I now write,
at the request of Mr. Greene, who, reading in the last Magazine that the original picture of poor indefatigable Martin would
be given to the Curators of any public Repository*, is very
desirous of placing it in his Museum, as he thinks it well worthy preservation *.

" You must not think of coming this year into Leicestershire
without taking a bird's-eye view of Lichfield. We all long to
see you†.

" Mr. Pegge, sen. supped with me on Monday evening in perfect health and spirits. I lent him Carter's Numbers ‡, which
he had never before seen. He sends you his best compliments.

" Mr. Greene joins his friendly compliments with, dear Sir,
yours most truly,   H. WHITE."

———

6. Mr. GREENE to RICHARD GOUGH, Esq.

" DEAR SIR,   *Lichfield, Oct.* 17, 1786.

" On the receipt of yours of the 14th, I immediately applied
to Mr. Stringer, a very ingenious painter of this place, and have
given him full instructions relative to your request concerning
the Chapel at Barton-under-Needwood. He sets out to-morrow; and I make no doubt will be able to produce a correct
drawing of the Chapel, as well as a fac-simile of the inscription
within the same.

" Mayfield is within one mile of Ashbourn, about twenty-
three miles distant from this city. I shall take care that he
fulfils your desire in getting a correct copy of the inscription.

" I had last night the pleasure of spending the evening with
my good old friend Mr. Pegge, who told me he was possessed of a
copy of the Mayfield inscription, but that it was not correct.

" I am happy to tell you, that I have just received a valuable
present from Mr. Grose, *viz.* his Treatise on Armour; it is the
more acceptable, as he gives a pleasing account of many antient
pieces of armour now in my possession, particularly the coats of
mail, cuirasses, &c. With much regard, I remain, dear Sir,

          " Yours faithfully,   RICHARD GREENE."

———

* This request was granted by the proprietor of the Portrait,—that
of Mr. Benjamin Martin, the optician and philosopher, which had been
published in Gent. Mag. LV. p. 583.

† I had paid a delightful visit at Lichfield in the autumn of the preceding year, where I had the gratification of witnessing the filial affection
of the dutiful, though vain, Anna Seward, in administering to the comforts of her aged father, at that time almost unconscious of her tender care.
The kindness of Mr. White, and the introduction he gave me to the
most distinguished characters then resident in Lichfield, I can never
forget. See the " Literary Anecdotes," vol. II. p. 551.

‡ The valuable " Antiquarian Researches" of honest John Carter.

7. " Sir,   *Lichfield, Dec. 3, 1786.*
" I am happy to find by yours of the 23d of last month, that
Mr. Stringer's performance meets your approbation. I know of
no one I can so warmly recommend to your notice as that artist;
whose diligence, and moderation in respect to charge, equals his
ingenuity. As you seemed desirous to know his charge, I called
on him for that purpose. One guinea only for the whole, which
I dare say you will not think unreasonable, when I inform you
that Mayfield is twenty-five miles and Barton eight miles distant from this city. The inscription at the former place could
not be copied perfectly without the assistance of a long ladder.
    " I am much pleased that I have had it in my power to serve
you in this affair; being with the greatest respect your most
obedient humble servant,   Richard Greene."

8. " Dear Sir,   *Lichfield, July 9, 1787.*
" Mr. Stringer having finished the drawings of the tombs in
Bromsgrove Church, I yesterday carefully packed them, and
delivered the parcel to Mr. Butler, of the George, saw them
booked, and hope, by the mail-coach, they will be with Mr.
Nichols by to-morrow morning. They are neatly, and, I hope,
accurately taken; and am only sorry you have waited so long
for them, owing to the hurry of business in which Mr. Stringer
is constantly engaged. I inquired of the price, which he said
is one guinea and a half; which I believe you will not dispute
when you are informed that Bromsgrove is thirty-two miles
from this place.
    " Any odd prints relating to antiquities you may please to
bestow on me, will come safe if left with Messrs. Wilson and
Hodgkinson, druggists, Red Cross, on Snow-hill.
    " I am very respectfully, dear Sir, your most obliged humble
servant,   Richard Greene."

9. Rev. Henry White to Mr. Urban *.

" Mr. Urban,   *Lichfield, Sept. 9, 1788.*
" Inclosed you receive an internal view of one side of the
room which contains the Museum of your old and worthy correspondent Mr. Greene. It will form, I hope, both an useful
and ornamental embellishment to your Magazine. The Catalogues of this Museum not having found their way to the London booksellers, many ingenious travellers pass through this
city, unapprised of that source of information and amusement
which the sight of this great and valuable collection of the
wonders of Art and Nature would afford them. To the Collector of them too much praise cannot be given. ' I should as
soon have thought, Sir, of building a first-rate man of war,'
said the great author of the Rambler. And well does this

* From the Gentleman's Magazine;—see note in p. 318.

encomium seem to be merited, when we consider the disadvantages of an inland situation, the want of fortune to make valuable and expensive purchases, the want of connexions with men of science in other countries, and the constant and laudable attention to the duties of his profession.

" The view meets the eye of the spectator when he stands with his back to the organ * ; the scale is rather too small to do sufficient justice to the articles, nor does it include the most rare or valuable. It consists of two rooms, communicating with each other by an opening crowned by a large elliptical arch, from whose centre depends, by brass chains, a buffalo's horn, mounted, and neatly painted with the arms and crest of the late Sir Thomas Aston, of Aston in Cheshire. It was used for a drinking-cup, bearing the motto, *Prest complere.* Also, the tusk of an elephant, dug out of a gravel pit near Stratford-upon-Avon, six feet beneath the surface of the ground ; when taken up, it measured near a yard and three-quarters in length ; the ivory, by long continuance in the earth, was rendered as soft as chalk.

" A collection of South-sea rarities, brought over by Capt. Cook and other navigators, fills the glass-case on the left hand. The opposite one, on the right hand, contains a collection of fire-arms, among which are the match-lock, wheel-lock, and snaphance ; Turkish, Spanish, Italian, and old English muskets. —Pistols, of almost all kinds, occupy the lower part of the case.

" In the centre of the inner room appears an uncommon musical altar-clock, whose outer case represents a Gothic church-tower, adorned with pinnacles, battlement, images, &c. and crowned with an octagonal lantern of open work.

" For a more particular description of these articles, and for a general account of the Museum, reference must be made to the printed Catalogue, sold in Lichfield, the last edition of which appeared in December 1786, dedicated to Sir Ashton Lever and Mr. Pennant.

" It is but justice to the public-spirited Collector to record, that the Museum is constantly open for the inspection of the curious, except on Sundays, *gratis.* The drawing was made August 1788, by Mr. Stringer, painter, of this city.

" Yours, &c.   H. W."

* The following lines by Anna Seward were in gold letters on the front of the organ, and a few copies were printed for distribution among her friends :

> " The docile gales which here imprisoned dwell,
> Do thou release from every hollow cell ;
> They for their freedom shall the gift repay,
> With sounds respondent to thy dulcet lay.
>   ANNA SEWARD."

GEORGE RICHARD SAVAGE NASSAU, Esq.

The subject of the following biographical notice was descended from the noble and illustrious house of Nassau, a family which has produced heroes allied to the greatest Princes of Europe, and renowned both in the cabinet and in the field.

Henry Frederic de Nassau, Prince of Orange, and grandfather to William the Third, of glorious memory, Stadtholder of the United Provinces and King of Great Britain, had a natural son, Frederic de Nassau, whom he endowed with the Lordship of Zulestein, in the Province of Utrecht, and who thereupon assumed that name. By his wife, Mary, the daughter of Sir William Killigrew, of the county of Cornwall, Bart. and Chamberlain to Queen Catherine the consort of King Charles the Second, he had issue a son and heir, William Henry de Zulestein, a person high in favour with King William the Third, and whom, in consideration of his faithful services and eminent abilities, as well as of his near alliance to him in blood, that Monarch was pleased to create, by letters patent bearing date on the 10th of May 1695, Baron of Enfield in the county of Middlesex, Viscount Tunbridge in Kent, and Earl of Rochford in the county of Essex. His Lordship purchased of Sir Henry Wingfield, Bart. a branch of a very antient and widely-extended family in Suffolk, the manor of Easton in that county, with the remainder of his estates in the neighbourhood; and made that place his occasional residence.

From this illustrious personage was descended the late George Richard Savage Nassau, Esq.

His father, the Hon. Richard Savage Nassau, was the second son of Frederic, the third Earl of Rochford, by Bessey, the eldest daughter of Richard Savage, the fourth Earl Rivers, and was born on

the 1st of June 1723. On the 24th of December
1751, he married Anne, the sole daughter and heir
of Edward Spencer, of Rendlesham in the county
of Suffolk, Esq. and the widow of James, the third
Duke of Hamilton. By this lady he had issue
Lucy, who was born on the 3d of November 1752,
and who died unmarried; William Henry, born
June the 28th, 1754, and who, on the decease of
his uncle William Henry the fourth Earl of Rochford, succeeded him in his honours; and George
Richard Savage, the subject of the present notice.
Mr. R. Nassau purchased Easton of the Earl, his
elder brother, and made it for several years his constant residence. He was likewise one of the Clerks
of the Board of Green Cloth, and a Representative
in Parliament for the borough of Maldon; and departed this life in May 1780, the year previous to
the decease of his brother. Her Grace died on the
10th of March 1771.

George Richard Savage Nassau was born on the
5th of September 1756; and inherited from the
will of Sir John Fitch Barker (who died Jan. 3,
1766), of Grimston-hall in the parish of Trimley
St. Martin in Suffolk, Bart. considerable possessions. In 1805 he served the office of High Sheriff
of the County, although he had no regular establishment except in London, which was his place
of residence during the greater part of his life.
On the 12th of August 1823, he was seized with a
paralytic affection, under the effects of which he
lingered until the 18th following, when he expired
at his house in Charles-street, Berkeley-square,
to the inexpressible grief of his numerous friends
and acquaintance. His remains were conveyed
from London, and interred in the family vault in
the Church of Easton, where a very handsome
monument is erected to his memory, on the north
wall of the chancel, with the following elegant and
appropriate inscription from the pen of his afflicted
brother the Earl of Rochford:

" Sacred
to the memory of
George Richard Savage Nassau, Esq.
brother to William-Henry fifth Earl of Rochford,
and second son of
the Honourable Richard-Savage Nassau,
by Anne *
Duchess of Hamilton and Brandon;
he died the 18th of August 1823,
aged 66 years.

Here lies a NASSAU—Honour owns the name,
And GEORGE prefix'd awakens friendship's claim;
Affection, springing from a brother's breast,
Rais'd to his worth this tributary test.
A polish'd mind, rul'd by a generous heart,
Form'd of his character the leading part;
Integrity, candour, benevolence, and love,
Vied in their turns ascendancy to prove.
On duty's course he won the glorious race,
And crown'd morality with Christian grace.
Vain is the poet's art and sculptor's plan,
Truth of herself best celebrates the man;
Religion guards his ashes as a prize,
And wafts his soul immortal to the skies."

Throughout life, Mr. Nassau was an universal favourite, inasmuch as he possessed those qualities, of which mankind are seldom jealous, and which they are ever ready to recommend; but his real personal character could only be justly appreciated by those who witnessed him in his domestic circle. With a suavity and urbanity of manners peculiarly attractive, he united an ardour and activity of benevolence to a temper liberal, disinterested, and humane. Adorned with the graces of external accomplishments, acquired at a period when independence and politeness, not servility and adulation, were the characteristics of a gentleman, his easy condescension endeared him not only to the circle in which he moved, but also to those with whom the forms and fashion of the world rendered it neces-

* In most of the Peerages there is an error in the Christian name of the Duchess. It is in them stated to be Elizabeth.

sary that he should associate.   He possessed in perfection the

> " Morum dulce melos, et agendi semita simplex."

Though he lived much with the great, his manners were not proud or arrogant, they were the pure
and simple courtesies of life,—the courtesies, which
proceed from Christian benevolence and a lively
apprehension of the feelings of others.   His piety
to his Maker was ardent; his faith in his Redeemer
unshaken; his affection to his friends consistent;
and his charity to those around him judicious and
unostentatious.   Beloved, respected, and admired
by all who knew him; he will live, as long as ever
man lived, in the memory and affection of his
acquaintance.

While, therefore, they deeply lament the too
sudden termination of such exalted virtues, they
will console themselves with the reflection (to use
the words of an eminent writer in the delineation of
his own character) that, "if he relieved the wants
and distresses of the unhappy without ostentation,
did justice without interest, maintained his own
independence without pride or insolence, moderated
his attachment to external objects, and placed his
affections on those above; trusting to have so passed
through things temporal, as finally to lose not the
things that are eternal, he will be found by them to
have — lived enough."

Attached, at an early period of life, to the arts
and literature of his country, as well as to the investigation of its antiquities, Mr. Nassau long held a
distinguished rank among the collectors of rare and
curious works.   Possessed of an ample fortune, by
which he was enabled to gratify his love of literature, and which he did without regard to expense, he spared no pains in the formation and ex-
tension of his library.   In this honourable and
praiseworthy pursuit, his taste in selecting was no
less conspicuous than his zeal in acquiring what-

ever was scarce and valuable in the various branches of literature, from the earliest period to his own time. His favourite classes, however, were early English poetry, the drama, topography, and history. In the two latter departments his collection comprised the best and most valuable works, many of which were on large paper, and illustrated with a profusion of drawings, prints, and portraits; and was further enriched by an extensive series of the rarest historical tracts. His tomes of old English poetry and of the drama were numerous; his works on emblems unique; and in the miscellaneous productions of the English press, during the reigns of Queen Elizabeth and King James the First, most extensive. Surrounded by his favourite books, and in the *Otium literarium cum dignitate,* to him, as Prospero says,

—————————————— " His library
Was dukedom large enough; " ————

and even to the close of his life few days passed which did not witness some choice and valuable addition to his rich and curious treasures *.

To the elucidation of the History and Antiquities of Suffolk his attention was early directed; and his collections in this, his favourite department, most ample; and profusely enriched with accurate drawings of views, churches, monuments, seats, buildings, &c. &c. His series of engravings, both of portraits and of other subjects, in illustration of Suffolk, were very extensive; and were only exceeded, perhaps, by those of Mr. James Conder†,

---

* A few of the most remarkable articles of Mr. Nassau's Library are noticed in Clarke's " Repertorium Bibliographicum," in his " Select List of some rare books in minor Sales, or in Private Collections."

† This worthy and respectable man was the youngest son of the Rev. John Conder, D. D. Pastor of the Congregational Meeting of Protestant Dissenters on the Pavement, Moorfields, London, and Divinity Tutor in the Dissenting Academy at Homerton, by Miss Flindell, of Ipswich. He was born at Mile-

of Ipswich, another eminent collector in this department.   Mr. Nassau's collection of productions

end, and educated at an eminent dissenting academy at Ware in Hertfordshire, then under the superintendence of the Rev. Mr. French, a Minister of the Unitarian persuasion; and married Miss Mary Notcutt, the third daughter of Mr. George Notcutt, of Ipswich, by whom he had two sons and one daughter.

The character of Mr. Conder exhibited many amiable traits; and without any violation of truth it may be said, that as a father, a husband, and a friend, he was indulgent, kind, and affectionate; and throughout life adorned these situations by the uniform practice of every virtue.   Of integrity unimpeached, and of a life and conversation that became the Gospel of Christ, he studied to approve himself to God, and to evince his love to his Redeemer, by a rigid attention to every relative duty, and by a calm but persevering course of unaffected piety.   His benevolence, founded on principle and corroborated by habit, was not active at intervals, and at other times torpid and inert; but his efforts to do good to every one around him were constant and uninterrupted.   The idea of the establishment of a Society in the town of Ipswich, which is designated by the name of " The Friendly Society," from the benevolent nature of its object, was no sooner suggested to him, than it instantly engaged his services; and to him, beyond any other individual member, it is mainly indebted for that support and patronage which it has so deservedly obtained.

His death was sudden and awful, and accompanied with severe bodily suffering; but, under the providence of God, he was prepared for its approach.   The manly fortitude and Christian resignation with which he met this agonizing event, was indeed highly commendable.   The hope of the Gospel supported him under the trial; and by his firm reliance on the merits and mediation of a Saviour, his end was peace and joy.   He departed this life on the 22d of March 1823, in the 61st year of his age; and his remains were deposited in the cemetery of the Meeting-house in Tacket-street, Ipswich, amidst a mournful and attentive crowd of spectators, where a just and well-drawn eulogium on the character and virtues of the deceased was pronounced by the Rev. Charles Atkinson.

Mr. Conder was much attached to the study of antiquities; and eager in their investigation and pursuit.   He was in possession of an extensive numismatic collection; and his series of Provincial Tokens was most probably unique.   His collections, likewise, relative to the History and Antiquities of the County of Suffolk, were considerable; and in the department of Pictorial Illustrations, most ample.   This, indeed, was his favourite pursuit; and in the prosecution of it he spared no pains to bring it to complete perfection.

from the pencils of Rooker, Hearne, and Byrne;
and those he possessed of Suffolk artists, particu-

He published a work of great utility to the Provincial Jetton
Collector, under the title of, " An Arrangement of Provincial
Coins, Tokens, and Medalets, issued in Great Britain, Ireland,
and the Colonies, within the last twenty years; from the Farthing to the Penny size," 1799, 8vo, and in two volumes, small
quarto; a work, in which considerable attention was bestowed to
render it acceptable, and which the author's own extensive collection could alone have enabled him to complete.

His knowledge of the dissenting history and interests in the
county of Suffolk was likewise deep and extensive, and enriched
with a variety of anecdote well calculated both for amusement
and instruction. He had meditated, for some years previous to
his decease, on the suggestion of the writer of this brief Memoir,
a "History of the Dissenting Establishments in the County of
Suffolk, including Biographical Notices of their respective
Founders and Pastors," on the plan of that well-written
work of Mr. Wilson's, intituled, " The History and Antiquities
of Dissenting Churches and Meeting-houses in London, Westminster, and Southwark." To the Protestant Dissenter such
a work has long been a *desideratum;* and would prove most
highly valuable. It is, indeed, a matter of surprise, that while
the parochial churches, and the lives of their respective incumbents, have received ample illustration from the pen of the
antiquary and historical churchman, the sanctuaries of the Dissenters have been hitherto neglected, and the biography of their
respective Pastors unrecorded, with the exception of the late
laborious Historian of Leicestershire; and the intelligent modern
Historians of Northamptonshire and South Yorkshire.

Mr. Conder was a frequent contributor to many periodical
publications; and his name is honourably recorded, for assistance received, in the preface to Wilson's " History and Antiquities of Dissenting Churches," and Brookes's " Lives of the
Puritans."

The memory of those private individuals, indeed, who,

" Along the cool sequester'd vale of life,
Have kept the noiseless tenour of their way,"

is too frequently doomed, after their short existence is terminated, to survive only in the recollection of their more immediate acquaintance; but the writer of this short biographical
notice, who admired the virtues of Mr. Conder, and was gratified by his friendship, is anxious that the quiet excellencies of
one, who had deservedly conciliated the esteem of his neighbours and acquaintance, and who, amid the cares of life and the
toils of business, had been ever attached to literature and mind-
ful of eternity, should not pass away unnoticed, but be recorded

larly Gainsborough, Frost *, and Johnson †, were

for the imitation of others ; and has, therefore, paid this humble,
but well-merited tribute of respect, to the memory of a much-
respected friend, a sincere Christian, and a truly virtuous and
honest man.

    * Mr. George Frost, whose peculiar merits as a painter were
well known to the discerning few in the county of Suffolk, was
a native of Barrow, where his father was a builder, and to
which business the son was brought up. He soon, however,
relinquished this, on being appointed to a confidential situation
in the Blue Coach Office at Ipswich, which situation he retained
                                            for

---

    † Mr. Isaac Johnson, an artist of considerable eminence, and
whose productions are deservedly esteemed for their neatness
and fidelity of execution, is a resident at Woodbridge in Suffolk.
Throughout a long life, his accurate pencil has been employed
on almost every curious article in architectural antiquity existing in the county. The late Mr. Nichols, the Editor of these
" Illustrations," states, that he was proud of possessing views of
nearly every Church in Suffolk, taken uniformly by this excellent draughtsman ‡.' This very beautiful volume is now in the
possession of Mr. J. B. Nichols. It is intituled, " Ecclesiastical
Antiquities of the County of Suffolk, being Original Views of
all the Churches and Parochial Chapels in the County. Taken
on the spot, and drawn by Isaac Johnson, Land Surveyor,
Woodbridge, in the years 1799—1816." Prefixed is a Map of
the County, accurately laid down by Mr. Johnson from the
latest surveys. The whole volume contains more than 500
views,_ and each of the twenty-two hundreds has a separate
Map prefixed to it. — Mr. Nassau's collection was enriched
with many of Johnson's drawings, and contained highly-finished
sketches of the churches, monuments, fonts, as well as every
curious remnant of antiquity which are comprised within the
Hundred of Loes, in illustration of Hawes's Manuscript History
of that Hundred. The large sheet engraving of the " Church
of Woodbridge," published by Mr. Loder in 1788, together with
the views of Seckford-hall and Alms-houses, and the portrait of
their Founder, were executed from the designs of this pleasing
artist. The engravings, likewise, which illustrate that gentleman's " History of Framlingham," are from his pencil ; as are
those of the monuments and figures of the Wingfield family,
formerly in the Church of Letheringham, which were engraved
for Mr. Gough's " Sepulchral Monuments," and given also, by
his permission, in vol. III. of the " History of Leicestershire,"
p. 513.

    ‡ Fuller's Worthies, by Nichols, vol. II. p. 351.

numerous and highly valuable; and selected with
the nicest taste and most accurate discrimination.
The many small articles of unfrequent occurrence,

for many years, and from which he retired about eight years previously to his decease, after having acquired a comfortable com-
petency with the greatest credit to himself, and the most perfect
satisfaction to his employers.

At a very early age Mr. Frost evinced a strong inclination for
drawing; and in this pleasing pursuit he freely indulged at such
intervals as his necessary avocations would allow. With no
assistance whatever, either from the advice or the instruction
of others, but by the powers of his own native genius and talents
alone, exercised with the most steady and persevering application, he raised himself to distinguished excellence as a most spirited and delightful artist.

His drawings exhibited abundant proofs of the touch and handling of a master. He studied nature with the closest attention;
and in his attempts to delineate her beauties, was remarkably
successful. He was a most accurate observer of her in all her
appearances, and possessed a characteristic touch for all her
forms. The subjects, which he selected, were such as did credit
to his taste and judgment; and whatever came from his pencil
bore the lively impress of originality and truth; and evinced, in
a bold and masterly manner, the local character and features of
the county, out of which he had scarcely ever moved. Of him,
indeed, it may be truly said,

> "His genius lov'd his County's native views,
> Its taper spires, green lawns, and shelter'd farms;
> He mark'd each scene with Nature's genuine hues,
> And gave the Suffolk Landscape all its charms."

"The pleasing scenery around the town of Ipswich,—its hol-
low and tortuous lanes, with broken sand-banks,—its copse-
grown dells,—and, above all, the richly-wooded acclivities of its
winding river,—were his perpetual haunts *."

> ———— "Here I've mark'd the Artist stray,
> Here linger out the summer day;
> And with enthusiast pencil trace
> Or storm, or sun-shine's varied grace.
> But chief, when golden lights relieve
> The dark and giant shades of eve,
> He felt his soul to transport warm,
> And fixed every fleeting charm."

"These were his academy; and the many beautiful specimens
which he has left of his successful treatment of such subjects

* Reveley's Notices, p. 260.

of prophecies, of wonderful relations, and of witch-
craft; of prodigies, of stories, and of murders, which
enriched this department, were well worthy of at-

sufficiently attest with what diligence he studied in this school
of Nature *." Every part, indeed, in his productions, was closely
copied from her details, with artless description and with simple
effect; but at the same time executed with the utmost freedom of
expression and a peculiar felicity of handling. Every object of
nature, — "weeds, docks, leaves, ferns, stumps of trees, &c.
were marked with firmness and precision; while the cattle and
figures, with which he embellished his landscapes, were always
disposed with judgment, and added life and animation to the
scene. His trees, distinctly marked as they are by the specific
character of each species—the oak, the ash, the elm, the willow
—have particular claims to excellence. The boles, with all their
richly varied hues, are touched with characteristic beauty and
spirit; the ramification is easy, natural, and flowing; and by a
peculiarly dexterous and rapid stroke, is so happily connected
with the leafiage as to produce a waving appearance in the
branches, a pliant susceptibility of motion, uncommonly light
and airy in its effect. In seizing the picturesque features and
accidents of nature, Mr. Frost was very happy. The old grey
cart-horse, the rough-coated ass, the ivy-mantled pollard, the
lowly cottage with its weather-stained walls, moss-grown thatch,
and quarry-window, bright with reflected sun-beams, were exhibited with an air of pure and exquisite truth, which showed
how deeply he was imbued with a genuine feeling for such beauties †."

Mr. Frost was a most ardent admirer, and a close and correct imitator, of the productions of his countryman, the celebrated Gainsborough; and in "his own admirable sketches
from nature evinced, with what a congenial ardour, and with
how keen a relish, he had imbibed the genius and the spirit of
his adopted master ‡."

He possessed a pleasing collection of paintings; and many
valuable original drawings of his favourite Gainsborough, executed in different ways, but principally with black chalk and
lead pencil, in the neat style of his earlier manner—an inestimable treasure to one who almost idolized the hand that sketched
them.

The work which closed the career of Mr. Frost's labours,
was an excellent copy of Gainsborough's large view of the Mall
in St. James's-park, of which he possessed the original. It was
painted in the 77th year of his age, and must, therefore, be
considered an extraordinary performance.

The following lines, written in a room filled with paintings

---

* Reveley's Notices, p. 260.   † Ibid. p. 262.   ‡ Ibid. p. 266.

tention; and fully evince with what a keen relish
and ardour he sought for

"The small rare volume, black with tarnish'd gold."

Indeed, a more choice or valuable treasure of Suf-

by Gainsborough, may, with the strictest justice, be applied to
the ingenious subject of this memoir:

" How close yon imitative tablet treads
    On Nature!—Mark! with what enchanting grace
    On the rich canvas is her mirror'd face
Reflected. How the artist's pencil sheds
Its vernal light on yon tall mountain heads;
    Then sinks into its loveliest tints, to trace
    Low copse, or loamy bank, or sheltering place,
Where, through wild flowers and weeds, the brooklet spreads.
Thou hast not Titian s colours; nor is thine,
    Ingenious artist! the great Tuscan's throne,
    On which he sate gigantic and alone;
But loveliest graces in thy tablet shine,—
    The soft, the pensive scene is all thine own,
That soothes full many a heart, and chiefly mine *."

During the last few months of this worthy man's career, he
suffered the most excruciating torments, occasioned by a mortification in his foot, which he bore with the greatest fortitude.
Throughout a long life, his conduct was truly virtuous, exemplary, and irreproachable; his religious sentiments pure, and his
morality perfect. The possession, therefore, of these virtues
left him nothing to reflect on, which could tend, in the slightest
degree, to embitter his declining hours. To strangers his manners appeared shy and reserved; but to those who were intimately
acquainted with him they assumed a very different aspect. Possessed of true independence (a quality, alas! but rarely found
amongst those who presumed to call themselves his betters), he
scorned to solicit the approbation of others by mean compliance
or servile adulation. His reading had been extensive, and he
had profited much by it; for the information, which he had thus
acquired, was applied to the promotion of his favourite, his
beloved pursuit.

Mr. Frost was relieved from his sufferings on the 28th of
June 1821, in the 78th year of his age; and his remains were
interred in the church-yard of St. Matthew's, Ipswich, over
which is placed the following simple inscription:

" IN MEMORY OF
GEORGE FROST,
WHO DIED JUNE 28, 1821,
AGED 77 YEARS."

* From the elegant muse of that accomplished scholar, the Rev. John
Mitford, Vicar of Benhall, Suffolk.

folk History and Topography, and works in illustration of them, has been seldom or ever collected.

His manuscript collection was extensive and
highly valuable; and profusely enriched with works
pertaining to his more favourite pursuit.

This " choice, curious, and extensive library" was
dispersed by Mr. Evans, at two several periods in
1824. The first Part on Feb. 16, and eleven following days; and the Second Part on March 8, and
seven following days. These catalogues contained
4264 lots; and the whole collection realised the
sum of £.8,500.

The following enumeration of transcripts from Mr.
Nassau's MSS. illustrative of the History and Antiquities of Suffolk, (the originals of which, amounting to thirty volumes, were not exposed to sale, but
were reserved for the library of the family mansion
at Easton,) with the sums they sold at, and the names
of the purchasers, may not be uninteresting to
inquirers into the topography of that county :—

" The History or Memoirs of Framlingham and
Loes Hundred in Suffolk. Containing an Account
of the Lords and Ladies thereof, with the most
Remarkable Occurrences in Church and State,
wherein they were concerned. Of Framlingham
Town, Castle, Church, and Manor, with their re-
spective Revenues. Of the Hundred of Loes, the
Churches, Monasteries, Nobility, Clergy, and Gen-
try thereof, as well ancient as modern. With the
Pretences of the Dean and Chapter of Ely to some
Royal Privileges thereto belonging. Framlingham,
An. Dom. 1712 *." £.35. 10s. Thorpe.

The writer of this brief sketch, who has pored over the productions of his pencil again and again with renewed delight,
and in whose society he has spent many an agreeable hour, pays
this last humble, but well-merited tribute of respect, to the
memory of a most ingenious artist and an honest man.

* Robert Hawes, Gent. the compiler of this valuable and
highly-interesting MS. was the eldest son of Henry Hawes,
Gent. (a family which had been long seated at Brandeston in

A volume of MS. Collections relative to Suffolk. Transcripts of Old Charters and Curious Materials illustrative of the History of that County."

£.18. 7*s.* 6*d.* Thorpe.

" Liber Primus Curiæ Hundredi de Loes in Suff. incipit anno 9, desinit anno Jac. I. Regis." *£*.2. 2*s.* Thorpe. This manuscript is a Minute-book of the Steward of the Hundred of Loes.

" Transcript of the Charter granted to Ipswich in 1634." *£*.2. Thorpe.

Suffolk,) by Mary, one of the daughters and co-heirs of John Smith, of Pyshalls, in the parish of Dennington in the same county. He was born in 1665, and brought up to the practice of the law; and in 1712 was appointed Steward to the Lordship or Manor of Framlingham by the Master and Fellows of Pembroke-hall, Cambridge. He married Sarah, the youngest daughter of George Sterling, of Charsfield, Esq. and, dying at Framlingham, was interred in the south aisle of the chancel of that Church, under a plain grey stone, on which is the following inscription :

" Under this stone lies interr'd ye bodies of Robt Hawes, Attorney-at-Law, Gent. and Sarah his wife, both of this Parish.

He } dyed { August ye 26, 1731, aged 66.
She } dyed { October ye 11, 1731, aged 63."

Mr. Hawes's History of the Hundred of Loes is a MS. of upwards of seven hundred pages, very neatly written ; and illustrated in the body and the margin of the work with numerous drawings of Churches, Seats, Miniature Portraits, Ancient Seals, and of the Arms of the Nobility, Gentry, and Clergy of the Hundred, blazoned in their proper colours. It is dedicated to the Master and Fellows of Pembroke-hall, in the University of Cambridge, Lords of Framlingham and Loes Hundred, in the following words :

" Gentlemen ; My only design at first was to reduce your Lordships or Manors of Framlingham and Saxted, according to the trust reposed in me, out of those confusions, wherein I found them, to a better order and method ; but when once entered upon this work, curiosity soon led me further, and time and opportunity encouraged me to search into the antiquities of your whole Hundred of Loes.

" As to what concerns the Churches and Clergy. I am equally indebted to the generous assistance of those two worthy gentlemen, the Rev. Dr. Tanner *, Chancellor of Norwich, and Mr.

* For an account of this learned man, see the " Literary Anecdotes," vol. VIII. p. 402.

"A Volume of MS. Collections relative to the Counties of Suffolk and Norfolk, with the Pedigrees." *£*.64. 1*s*. Carpenter.

"Visitation of Suffolk in 1562, with Drawings." *£*.8. Thorpe.

"Antiquitates Suffolcienses; or, Essay towards recovering some Account of the ancient Families of Suffolk, very fairly and legibly written." *£*.11. 0*s*. 6*d*. Thorpe.

"Heraldic MS. with Drawings of Arms of Suffolk Families." *£*.7. 7*s*. Triphook.

John Revet *, of Brandeston-hall in this Hundred; and in all other parts of this History or Memoirs, I was abundantly supplied with the materials from your own records and other manuscripts, as well as from Historians antient and modern.

"Out of all which it hath been my endeavour to collect, and (as far as in me lies) retrieve from oblivion, many considerable actions of your reverend and illustrious predecessors, both at Pembroke-hall and Framlingham Castle; the one being *Domus Episcopum*, and the other *Sedes Principum*, as well as of those persons who moved in a lower orb, the Gentry of this Hundred.

"But with some digressions from the subject matter, about the growth of schism and heresy in their days, and the consequences thereof,—rebellion and sacrilege, originally sown in this kingdom by Papists and Puritans, which tares have taken such deep root, and thriven so much, as ill weeds generally do, that they are likely to grow up with the wheat, until (if the former choke not the latter before) the general harvest.

"I am sensible that a collection of this nature cannot but be liable, not only to some censures, for *Obsequium amicos, veritas odium parit*, but also to many, though no wilful errors; and, therefore, my vouchers are all placed in the margin, that the credit of any story by me related may stand upon the authority of its author, and that by having a recourse to those authors themselves, it might be in your power more easily to correct any mistake of your steward and servant,   ROBERT HAWES.

"*Framlingham, August* 1, 1712."

A copy of this work was presented by the author to Pembroke-hall, which in return gave him a silver cup and cover, adorned with the arms of the Society; not, says the Latin inscription upon it, as an adequate reward of his merits, but as a memorial of their grateful acceptance of his favour. The inscription is as follows:

* The father of that eminent architect Nicholas Revet, Esq.

"MS. containing Pedigrees of eminent Families."
£.5. 15s. 6d. Triphook.

" A Breviary of Suffolk, or a Plain and Familiar Description of the County, the Fruits, the Buildings, the People, and Inhabitants; the Customs, the Division Political and Ecclesiastical, Houses of Religion, with all their several valuations; the chiefest men of learning, as of Divines, Privy-counsellors, Marshal-men, and Navigators of former times; with several other things of note and

" Seneschallo suo
ROBERTO HAWES,
viro integerrimo,
antiquitatum
investigatori diligentissimo,
ob navatam
in Historia FRAMLINGHAMIENSI
conscribenda
egregiè ab eo operam,
Hoc Poculum
non quod meritis sit dignum satis præmium,
sed beneficij gratanter accepti μνημόσυνον,
donat
COMMUNITAS PEMBROCHIANA.
MDCCXXIV *."

A copy of this work was likewise presented by the author to his friend, John Revet, of Brandeston-hall, Esq. It was sold at the sale of his books by Mr. Saunders in April 1821, and was purchased for £.40 by Mr. Rodwell, bookseller in New Bond-street, for Mr. Nassau. Mr. Revet's copy is now probably in the possession of the Earl of Rochford, as it was not the same as that sold at Mr. Nassau's sale.

Another copy of this work is said to be in the Public Library at Cambridge; a fourth in the collection of the Marquis of Hertford; a fifth in the possession of Mr. John King, of Ipswich, the respectable Editor of the Suffolk Chronicle, from the collection of Henry Jermyn, of Sibton, Esq. †; and a sixth is in the collection of the Writer of this notice.

* Loder's Framlingham, p. 396.

† This gentleman was descended from a branch of the very antient family of Jermyn, of Rushbrooke-hall in Suffolk. He was a Barrister-at-law, and resided at Sibton in that county, where he deceased on the 27th of November 1820, in the 53d year of his age.

In conjunction with David Elisha Davy, Esq. he had amassed considerable collections in illustration of the History, Topography, and Antiquities of Suffolk. His valuable library was dispersed by public auction; and the following is the title of the catalogue:

" A Catalogue of the valuable Library, containing upwards of 2000 Books, and also of a curious Collection of Engravings and Drawings

observation within this County of Suffolk. By
Robert Ryece *." £.14. 3s. 6d. Thorpe.

* Robert Ryece was born in ......, and was resident at Preston in Suffolk. He was placed for some years in the house of
the celebrated Theodore Beza, at Geneva, for the completion
of his education, and is described as "an accomplished gentleman, and a great preserver of the antiquities of the County
of Suffolk †." He set up in the Church of Preston the Royal
Arms of England on a fair table; and in glass those of many of
the most eminent Knights and Esquires of the county, most of
which are still remaining. He deceased on the 15th of September 1638, and was interred in the chancel of the Church of
Preston, but without any inscription to his memory.

made and designed for the Illustration of a County History, of the late
Henry Jermyn, Esq. of Sibton Abbey in Suffolk; together with numerous
Manuscripts, and various Miscellaneous Articles, to be sold by Auction,
by Mr. King, on Monday, the 25th day of June 1821, and Three follow-
ing days," 8vo.
   The following is a list of the MSS. and Drawings which relate to Suffolk:
   Drawings of the fourteen Churches in the Town of Ipswich, by Johnson.
   Twenty-eight Churches of the Hundred of Samford, by the same.
   Eight Churches of the Hundred of Colneis.
   Twenty Churches of the Hundred of Carlford.
   Nineteen Churches of the Hundred of Loes.
   Fifteen Churches of the Hundred of Wilford.
   History of Framlingham and four quarto MSS. comprising, with the
printed work, a complete copy of Hawes's entire Collections for Suffolk
History, with his notes and additions. Illustrated with many Drawings
of Arms and Antiquities.
   Twenty-three Churches of the Hundred of Plomesgate, by Johnson.
   Twenty-seven Churches of the Hundred of Blything, by the same.
   Eight Churches of the Hundred of Mutford.
   Sixteen Churches of the Hundred of Lothingland.
   Twenty-six Churches of the Hundred of Wangford.
   Twenty-eight Churches of the Hundred of Hoxne.
   Two quarto MSS. of Pedigrees of some Suffolk Families, with Draw-
ings of their Arms.—MS. of the Lords of the Manor of Benhall, from the
Conquest to 1803.
   The Plan of the Remains of the antient City of Dunwich in 1587,
published by Gardner in 1754, with an Original of that Plan of older
date and on a larger scale, and some fine MS. and topographical notices.
   Drawings of Monuments in Letheringham Church, previous to their
demolition in 1789—when the Church was taken down—with a View of
the present edifice.
   Copy of the ancient Plan of Aldeburgh, made by Appleton in 1588;
and of another made in 1594, with a modern Account of that Town.
   Copy of a very antient Plan of the Town and Parish of Gorleston in
the County of Suffolk, and Lands therein.
   Original Maps or Plans of the several Parishes of Kessingland, Carlton Coleville, Kirkley, Reyden, Frostenden, South Cove, Wrentham, Sot-
terley, Halverstreet, and Uggeshall, in three lots, with MS. references.
   Mr. Jermyn's MS. Collections for a History of the County of Suffolk
were not offered for sale.
   † "MS. Collections for Suffolk," in the possession of the Writer of
this Memoir.

This MS. is dedicated to Sir Robert Crane, Knt. in a letter signed Ryece, and dated Feb. 9, 1618.

In the "Repertorium Bibliographicum," are enumerated several choice articles in Mr. Nassau's library. J. F.

He married Mary, the daughter of Thomas Appleton, of Waldingfield Magna, Esq. who dying on the 29th of February 1629, was interred in the same place; with the following inscription on a brass plate:

" Maria uxor Roberti Ryece patroni hujus
Ecclesiæ et filia Thomæ Appleton de
Waldingfelde Armigeri obiit xxix die
Februarii A° MDCXXIX.
Ut Tipula, Ut Papilio,
Sic vita hominis.

In cinere' cuncti redeunt, primæq. parenti
Quod tulit assignat mortua facta caro ;
Tunc aurum, stultos tunc quisq. relinquit honores,
Et quos in toto tempore junxit opes.
Ergo animis mansura piis cœloq. petamus;
Mentibus ex nostris sit procul omne fugax.

Mr. Anstis possessed a copy of Ryece's " Description of Suffolk," Cat. 545 †. This was most probably the MS. which was communicated by Mr. New to the Compilers of the Magna Britannia, and which is alluded to in the following terms : " We have in our hands a MS. containing an account of all the Hundreds, Towns, and Villages, with the Names of the Lords of them at that time, viz. temp. Edward I. returned by the Sheriffs into the Exchequer, according to a special writ to them directed, Reg. 9, by that Prince; which, being both curious and useful, we have inserted great parts of it in the body of our History ; and when we have no other helps shall add the rest at the end of each Hundred ‡."

Mr. Ryece " left by deed, dated 1622, £.5 per ann. for ever, charged on the great tithes of Preston for the binding out of two sons of poor men of that parish; and, for want of such there, of Lavenham, to such masters as the Justices of Peace should approve of §."

† Nichols's " Literary Anecdotes," vol. II. p. 707 ; vol. IX. p. 413.
‡ Mag. Brit. vol. V. p. 175, note.
§ M'Keon's Inquiry into the Charities of Lavenham, p. 20.

TREADWAY RUSSELL NASH, D.D. F.S.A.

A biographical memoir of Dr. Nash, and an extended bibliographical review of his *magnum opus*—the History of Worcestershire, were given in the Eighth Volume of the "Literary Anecdotes *." The subject will be further illustrated by the following extracts from his Correspondence.

---

1. Dr. Nash to Richard Gough, Esq.

"Dear Sir, .   *Bevere, Sept. 26, 1774.*

" If I had not been on a tour in the West, I should before this have thanked you for your History of Dorsetshire, and congratulated you on your nuptials, to which I wish all success in every respect.

" I should esteem it as a particular favour, if you would freely give me your opinion of the History of Worcestershire; and collect for me such matters as in your various reading comes to hand. I shall have a fac-simile engraving of Domesday, so far as relates to Worcestershire; and, besides the views of antiquities and modern seats, I propose portraits of such eminent men as were either born in Worcestershire, or adopted by being made Bishops, or the like; I should, therefore, be much obliged to you if you would note down the names of such eminent persons, and where is the best engraving or picture of them. I looked for the MSS. in Jesus-college, Oxford; some are lost, others are the same with what I have already.

" If I did not know how ready you are to assist in any of these works, I should make a thousand excuses for the liberty I take; but I hope you will forgive me, and believe me to be your most obedient and obliged humble servant,   T. Nash."

---

2. Mr. Gough to Dr. Nash.

"Sir,   *Enfield, Feb. 11, 1775.*

"I ought to make many apologies for having so long deferred answering your obliging letter which inclosed the printed proposal; but, at once to confess the truth, it has not been, nor yet is, in my power to give you the assistance you desire. As I understand by Mr. Vernon, who will convey this to you, that

* Pp. 103 *et seq.;* see also the various references in vol. VII. p. 282.

S. Gardner pinx *P. Audinet sc*

Rev. T. Nash. D.D. F.S.A.

Born 1725.— Died 1811.

T. Maynard pinx *P. Audinet sc*

J. C. Brooke, Som.^t F.S.A

Born 1748.— Died 1794.

you have engaged with Mr. Bonner for your plates, I congratulate you on your choice of so able an artist; whose drawings of churches and monuments in his native County of Gloucester do him so much honour whenever they appear. I foresee by this choice, that the public will be indulged with many curious remains in Worcestershire. If you are not provided with a person to trace and engrave Domesday, which I understand you likewise intend, (and which, considering the inadequate method of publication now carrying into execution by Government, but not likely to be finished these four years, will be a very valuable acquisition,) I would take the liberty of recommending to you Mr. Pouncy, of May's-buildings, who has just finished Surrey Domesday for a particular friend of mine. He has great merit in this art; and will, I dare say, be as reasonable for you as for Mr. Manning; and I shall be very glad to bring you together whenever you are in town. I will bear in mind your desire of what assistance I can afford you; and it will be a real pleasure to me. I am, Sir, your obedient servant,   R. GOUGH."

---

3. Dr. NASH to Mr. GOUGH.

" DEAR SIR,   *Bevere, Nov. 23, 1775.*

" I should be highly wanting to my own interest, as well as to good manners, if I did not return you my heartiest thanks for your obliging offers of assistance, an assistance which has been highly serviceable to many men much more capable than myself.

" I have taken the liberty of desiring Mr. Rose to leave for you, with Messrs. Bowyer and Nichols, Printers in Red Lion-court, Fleet-street, the first complete impression that is taken off of Domesday; and should esteem it a particular favour if you would give me your opinion upon the difficult words, &c. I have heard much of Dean Milles's Dissertation on Domesday; doubtless you have seen it; would he care to communicate? As it is the first County printed in his favourite manner, perhaps he would assist.

" I had originally an intention of printing, in short, with a broad margin, the substance of Abingdon's papers, and giving them away to such persons as would be likely to communicate further information; but upon more careful examination of the papers, I found it would be attended with a great deal of trouble, and perhaps not answer much purpose.

" My design at present is, if you approve it, to publish next spring, a specimen of two or three parishes, an impression of the Worcestershire Domesday, and some of those plates which the engravers may be alert enough to supply me with. This, perhaps, may bring assistance better than any other way, when the reader sees how much I want it. I am very much out of humour with engravers; they are so little to be depended upon, and yet one cannot do without them.

" Lady Elizabeth Windsor spent a day here last week. She is a most amiable young woman; and I much wish her married to your cousin Sir Harry Gough *. She performs, I suppose, next Monday, in a play which Lord Plymouth exhibits at his house; but, as we all are affected with the influenza, I fear we cannot go. I am, Sir, your most obedient and obliged humble servant, T. NASH."

---

4. " DEAR SIR, *Ham Court, near Upton, June 7, 1777.*

" I beg leave to trouble you to ask your opinion of the two parishes I left, and trust your friendship will give it freely. I assure you I am by no means prejudiced in favour of this, or any other part of the work; and if you advise me to throw it in the fire, you shall be obeyed, and it will save me a great deal of trouble and expense. If you think it worth going on with, and will give me your advice and assistance, I will acquiesce.

" I should esteem it a particular favour if you would give me your advice ; and, if I proceed, what method I had best pursue.

" Mr. Martin (from whose house I write this) desires his compliments to you ; and was very sorry he did not see you last winter in town, to thank you for the books you re-published, and were so obliging as to send him. I am, dear Sir, your most obedient and obliged humble servant, T. NASH."

---

5. " DEAR SIR, *Near Worcester, July 26, 1777.*

" I am much obliged to you for the favour of your letter dated June 23; and through your solicitation and encouragement am determined to proceed. I hope you have made many alterations in the two books you were so kind to look over. I have not yet been able to receive them, having sent several times to Mr. Martin's house in Dover-street, but can get no tidings of them. I should be much obliged to you to inquire what is become of them ; and if you can recover them, pray send them to Mr. Brooke at the Heralds' Office, who has some other books of mine, and will send them altogether.

" I am very sensible the papers are ill arranged; and wish to know in what manner you think it best to sort them. I propose to call the book, not a History of Worcestershire, but, ' Parochial Collections towards a History of Worcestershire.' What think you of that ?

" In the Account of Droitwich, I find I am mistaken about Serjeant Wylde; it was not the Serjeant Wylde that lived in

* Lady Elizabeth married, in the June following the date of this letter, Gore Townsend, of Honington-hall, Warwickshire, Esq. She died April 2, 1821, aged 63.

Oliver Cromwell's time, and is mentioned in Whitlocke, but a Serjeant Wylde that died about the year 1616.

" I have employed Mr. Paine, that is in White's shop, to get the copper-plate rolled off for me, and to get a sheet printed on such paper and with such a type as may be a good sample. I should be much obliged to you if you would see him, and give me your advice, and favour me with a line. Believe me to be, dear Sir, your much obliged and obedient humble servant,

T. Nash."

6. Mr. Gough to Dr. Nash.

" Dear Sir, *Enfield, March 8, 1778.*

" I have carefully perused the printed sheet of your History, which Mr. Brooke put into my hands; and I cannot see any reason why you should not go on as you have begun at the Bowyer press, and be your own master.

" Nobody can so well superintend any publication as the author; and in a work of this nature it is essential to correctness that the corrector should have the materials before him; and who can have them but yourself? This appears to me the strongest of all reasons for this mode of proceeding, and the press is at no inconvenient distance from you.

" As you propose printing the inscriptions under their respective Churches, you need not refer to them from Abingdon as you go on; but, if they are destroyed since his time, I would in the proper place refer to them from him. I would avoid Latin terms, as *jure uxoris*, &c. in the text, and as much as possible in pedigrees ; except *ob.* and *s. p.*

" What else struck me I have mentioned on the sheet; and am, Sir, your obedient humble servant, Richard Gough."

7. Dr. Nash to Mr. Gough.

" Dear Sir, *April 30, 1778.*

" I am much obliged to you for the honour of your letter, which I received yesterday; and shall, with the greatest pleasure, obey your commands with regard to the Topographical Anecdotes of Worcestershire, or any thing else in my power. I should be much obliged likewise, if you would take the sheets of Worcestershire as they come from Mr. Nichols, and make in them what alterations you think proper. Mr. Nichols has franks, which you will be pleased to make use of.

" Poor Granger and I talked over the portraits. He said the head of Tenure Lyttelton was very scarce, and ought to be engraved; accordingly I have put my drawing of him in the hands of a very good artist. He will not engrave the whole-length, which adds so much to the expense, but will make it a three-quarters. I am, Sir, your most obedient and obliged humble servant,   T. NASH."

---

8. Dr. NASH to Mr. NICHOLS.

"SIR,   *June* 24, 1778.

" In the first place give me leave to wish you joy of a wife. I should have been happy to have met you at Hinckley, which town I passed through in my way to Burghley the day you were married, but did not know of it till I saw the Leicester paper. Your engagements are a sufficient excuse for not thinking of my paper. I do not care to begin till the whole is in your hands, examined, counted, and weighed, according to the sample. I entirely trust to you that it is of equal goodness in every respect ; and when you tell me the whole is in your possession, I will send some copy to proceed with.

" Pray let me hear from you soon ; and believe me to be,
                    " Yours most faithfully,   T. NASH."

---

9. Dr. NASH to Mr. GOUGH.

"DEAR SIR,   *Oct.* 5, 1778.

" I take the first opportunity of obeying your commands ; and have sent * the account of the death of Thomas Abingdon, who died October 8, 1647, aged 87, and is buried at Hindlip in Worcestershire. If you can recollect where you saw Cromwell's letter about the battle and taking of Worcester, September 1651, I should be very glad to see it, as I doubt not it would be curious ; and, as it is scarce, your readers would be glad to know where to turn to it.

" I begin now to think in earnest of printing my Collections ; I have bought paper, and shall proceed directly. Inclosed is a letter, which, when you have an opportunity, I wish you would give to Mr. Brooke; it contains a continuation of the Sheldon family. If I thought he was in town, I would trouble him with a line ; but in your former letter you said I should soon hear from him, which not having happened, I conclude he is not yet arrived in winter quarters. I wish I could persuade him to look over my pedigrees before they are printed. I am, dear Sir, yours most sincerely,   T. NASH."

---

10. "DEAR SIR,   *Oct.* 22, 1778.

" I was last night favoured with your letter ; and return you many thanks for the trouble you have had, and the obliging offers you make me of your assistance, which I thankfully accept. I have written to Mr. Nichols ; and mentioned some things which I thought wanted altering.

---

* For Mr. Gough's " British Topography."

"I agree with you entirely, that the word Worcestershire should not be at the head of every page, but rather the parish described. The hundreds of our county are so irregular and disjointed, that I found it impossible to walk in that path; I shall, therefore, place the parishes alphabetically.

"I am, dear Sir, your most obedient and obliged humble servant,   T. NASH."

———

11. "DEAR SIR,   *Bevere, Nov. 8, 1778.*
"I expected before now to have received a third, fourth, or, perhaps, fifth sheet, as I wish Mr. Nichols to go on with all convenient speed. As you are so obliging as to offer me your kind assistance, if any errors occur, I trust you will be so good as to correct them.

"I have no other particulars of poet Walsh but what are mentioned in Abberley. The inscription on his tomb, I believe, shows his age. He died March 16, 1707, aged 46, was chosen three times for the county, stood a strong contest upon the Whig interest, and carried it. I have been told by people that knew him, that my sketch of him is as like as so free and loose an engraving can be. I spoke to one of the Prebendaries this day, who promises me to make a thorough search for King John's will; and will do every thing in his power not to incur your displeasure. I am, dear Sir,
"Your most obliged and faithful,   T. NASH."

———

12. Dr. NASH to Mr. NICHOLS.

"SIR,   *Worcester, Nov. 30, 1778.*
"I believe this is the fourth letter I have troubled you with, and received no answer. A fatality seems to attend the History of Worcestershire; this is the third time a volume has begun to be printed on that subject, twice death has surprised the editor before they were all printed, and the sheets wrap up pies and tarts; the third time I believe death will come before the work is at all advanced, unless you hasten your steps and break the charm. Pray write immediately; I am quite tired of waiting, and am ready to throw it all in the fire.
"Yours most sincerely,   T. NASH."

———

13. Dr. NASH to Mr. GOUGH.

"DEAR SIR,   *Bevere, Dec. 6, 1778.*
"I received this day your very obliging letter, and return you my best thanks for your corrections. I doubt not but they will be perfectly satisfactory, though I have never seen what you added about Mr. Walsh. I entirely approve of striking out Mr. Abingdon's tautology on heraldical descriptions, &c. It is what

I always wished to do, in many places have done, but some may escape me; and I shall think myself much obliged to you if you would do it wherever you meet with it.

" Before I was favoured with yours, I had altered the word Counsellors into Radmen, not at all approving of the translation; but my clerk, who transcribed the account of Allchurch, turning (unknown to me) for the word *Radmannus* in Jacob's Law Dictionary, and finding it Counsellors, put it down, thinking I had forgotten to translate it.

" I have written to Mr. Brooke by this post, to beg his assistance in the heraldical part; and that he would permit Mr. Nichols to send him the sheets for correction. When you see him, I wish you would forward my request.

" There has been, and in some degree continues, a very fatal disorder in Birmingham, and many parts of Warwickshire; it is a putrid sore throat, of which the patients die in a few days. I have heard, but do not speak from authority, that forty have been buried of a night for several nights together. The clergyman is dead, and many grown people; but it chiefly attacks children. Lord Willoughby had sixteen ill of it at one time in his house; one or two died. Some relations of yours have been attacked by it, but all recovered. I am, dear Sir, your most obedient and obliged humble servant,   T. NASH."

---

14. " DEAR SIR,   *Bevere, Feb. 21, 1779.*
" I was sorry it was not in my power to see you when I was last in London; I stayed but a few days, and went to Chancery-lane * on Thursday, in hopes of meeting you. Mr. Brooke was there, and we had some distant conversation on the subject of remuneration; I said I should be happy to make him a proper acknowledgment; that as to the mode and quantum I left it to you. I suppose, therefore, all the sheets where there is any heraldry have been sent to him, especially all relating to Beoly, which is his own drawing up.

" In your Topographical Antiquities, art. Worcestershire, you mention a letter from Oliver Cromwell, giving an account of the battle of Worcester; I quite forgot to ask you for it when at Enfield. Pray is it print or manuscript? If it be short, I wish you would employ somebody to copy it for me. Your drawing of Bordesley Abbey I will take care of, and return very safe.

" I am, dear Sir, your most obedient and obliged humble servant,   T. NASH."

---

15. " DEAR SIR,   *April 10, 1779.*
" I am much obliged to you for your letter began Feb. 18, and ended April 2d. You are so fully engaged for the public and your friends, that no one has the least right to complain.

---

* The chambers of the Society of Antiquaries.

" I think Mr. Brooke's corrections of great use, though I have not yet seen any pedigrees printed perfect.

" I thank you for your hint respecting Alsborough and Austin's Ac or Oak ; the former is a farm and small manor in the parish of Pershore, and the latter I suppose to be in Gloucestershire, and shall notice them both in proper place.

" Taylor's Maps of Gloucestershire and Worcestershire I have procured for you, and they wait your orders.

" What think you of the Charters published as Appendix to each parish ? are not some of them needless, and do they not tend to swell the work too much ? would it be better to leave them out, or print them in a smaller type ?

" I beg my compliments to all your family ; and am, dear Sir, your most obedient and obliged humble servant,   T. NASH.

" The Map of Birmingham is published."

---

16. " DEAR SIR,   *Aug. 6*, 1779.

" Yesterday I received a letter from our friend Mr. Brooke, the contents of which I beg leave to lay before you, and request your opinion. After some preamble he says : ' You must be very sensible how much of my time will be employed in this work ; nor can I estimate it, including the fees paid to the office for copying out pedigrees, without disadvantage to myself, at a less sum than *£*.100 ; and I must also beg leave to assure you, that I do not look upon this as a full indemnification for my loss of time, was it not that I shall in some measure be recompensed by the pleasure I receive from such works. Should you not choose to comply with these terms, what I have already done for you is much at your service ; and I wish it may be a means of enabling you and the printer to proceed with the remainder on the like plan.'

" If you remember, you and I had some conversation upon this subject before Mr. Brooke was applied to ; and believe our ideas differed somewhat from the proposal above-mentioned. I had no intention of employing him to draw up the History, as he calls his employment in another part of his letter, but only to examine the heraldical part, and see there was no false *Latin*, —I mean false heraldry. I beg pardon for giving you this additional trouble ; but should be much obliged to you for your opinion before I give Mr. Brooke any answer.

" A very exact Map of Worcester City is now engraving ; I will take care to secure you a copy. The Map of the County shall be sent up with the next parcel that is sent to Mr. Nichols.

" I am, dear Sir, your most obedient and obliged humble servant,   T. NASH."

17. " DEAR SIR,   *Bevere, Aug. 22, 1779.*

" I am very sorry you have had so much trouble about the Claines Charters; I will again look over the original, and make it as correct as I can.

" I have written a general civil letter to Mr. Brooke, without entering into any particulars. What I wished of him was only to see that there was no false heraldry; I did not wish him to arrange and write the book, as he seems to intimate, or to insert all his own MSS. which would be a great trouble indeed, and more than I could make him any satisfaction for. Copy is sent under the letters D, E, F, and G. Droitwich is not quite completed, but shall be soon. I waited in expectation of hearing from Mr. Lort, in answer to what I assert, that Lady Pakington was the supposed author of ' The Whole Duty of Man.' I often reflect how I can possibly make you satisfaction for the trouble you take, tenfold more than Mr. Brooke.

" Inclosed in Nichols's box is a parcel for you containing the Map of Worcestershire, some views of Worcester and Hereford; if there is any thing more you think of, pray command me.

" Bishop Warburton's library is on sale; it is not choice, but an awkward farrago in middling condition.

" I believe the Bushels of Cleve were all gentlemen farmers, and seldom stirred out of the Vale of Evesham till lately, when the great Fettiplace estate in Oxfordshire came to them.

" My house is at present full of company, and they are all talking around me; hope, therefore, you will excuse it, if this letter be unintelligible; and that you will always know me to be your most obedient and obliged humble servant,   T. NASH."

---

18. GEORGE ROSE, Esq.* to Mr. NICHOLS.

" DEAR SIR,

" I will be obliged to you if you will let me have your printed copy of Domesday, which I understand you have in boards, as I want to look through the book for Mr. Bryant, respecting a matter of curiosity, which will enable me to do it at home instead of being confined to the office hours for the original. Doctor Nash will tell you I hope to give you the explanation of such words in Worcestershire Domesday as I can make any thing of by the end of next week. Pray beg he will be so good as let me see the sheet, in which he mentions the explanation, before it is worked off. I am, dear Sir,

" Your faithful humble servant,   GEORGE ROSE."

* Afterwards Clerk of the Parliament, Treasurer of the Navy, and a Privy-councillor.

19. " DEAR SIR, *March* 24, 1781.
" I do assure you I have bestowed every hour I could spare this week on Dr. Nash's Domesday. There are so many things to refer to, it is inconceivable how slow I go on; but I will let you have the notes as soon as I possibly can. I shall not be easy till I have done them. I am, dear Sir,
" Your faithful humble servant, GEORGE ROSE."

20. " DEAR SIR, *Duke-st. Westminster, April* 12, 1781.
" I have got through the explanation of Dr. Nash's Domesday; but I really wish to revise it before I part with it. What I have done may appear trifling; though I have been kept many days at the Chapter-house till three o'clock in referring to records, &c. for it. I am going out of town for four or five days these holidays, and return on Wednesday or Thursday; and will then put the finishing hand to the copy. If you write to the Doctor, pray tell him so. I am, dear Sir,
" Your faithful humble servant, GEORGE ROSE."

The Right Hon. GEORGE ROSE to Mr. NICHOLS*.

" DEAR SIR, *Old Palace-yard, Jan.* 6, 1812.
" I was not aware of an intention to publish a new edition of Pope's Works till I saw an advertisement in the Courier a few days ago. I wish you had mentioned it to me. You probably know that the late Earl of Marchmont was not only one of his most intimate and confidential friends, but his acting executor, and that I was sole executor to his lordship; in which situation I became possessed of all Mr. Pope's unpublished writings—few in number, and of no value; but I have letters of his on various subjects; notes respecting his quarrel with Lord Bolingbroke, in which Lord Marchmont was the mediator; the best portraits of Mr. Pope, of Sir William Wyndham, and Lord Bolingbroke, each of whom sat for my Lord. It must, however, be too late now to make use of any of these. I am, dear Sir, your very faithful humble servant, G. ROSE."

ANSWER.
" DEAR SIR, *Jan.* 9, 1813.
" I am very much obliged by your kind favour of the 6th; and for the mention you are pleased to make of Mr. Pope's MSS. I was well aware that Lord Marchmont possessed such treasures; and that they were now your property. But the

---

* This letter, although originating in a mistake, is considered well worthy of preservation, not only as containing some interesting information respecting very eminent individuals, but also as an instance of the considerate kind-heartedness for which Mr. Rose was distinguished, and of which Mr. Nichols received very numerous proofs.

354   ILLUSTRATIONS OF LITERATURE.

fact is, that I have never had any concern in editing Pope's
Works, though I have published several editions of Swift and
of Atterbury. And the edition of Pope, recently advertised, is
rather an abridgement of the former ones than an improvement. My name to it is merely that of a bookseller, possessing
a share in the Works of Pope.

" But your letter, Sir, has suggested a new idea to me; and,
if you had no material objection, I should be both glad and
proud to present to the public a new volume of Pope's Correspondence and Works, as a companion to the editions of Warton
and Bowles, with Engravings of the Portraits. Such a volume,
or two if the materials are sufficient, if published under your
sanction, could not fail of being acceptable to the public, and
would be afterwards incorporated in any subsequent edition of
Pope's Works. With true respect, 1 am, Sir,

" Your much obliged and faithful servant,   J. NICHOLS."

JOHN CHARLES BROOKE, Esq. F.S.A.

This amiable and accomplished man, and skilful
herald and antiquary, was of a Yorkshire family,
and was born in 1748 at Fieldhead in the parish
of Silkstone near Sheffield. His father William
was a Doctor of Medicine, and his mother was
Alice, the eldest daughter and co-heir of William
Mawhood, of Doncaster *.

John Charles Brooke was their second son; and
was sent to the metropolis, to be apprenticed to Mr.
James Kirkby, a chemist, in Bartlet's-buildings,
Holborn. But he had already acquired, perhaps
inherited, a taste for historical and genealogical
research; and having drawn a genealogy of the
Howard family in a most masterly manner, it
deservedly procured him the notice of the Duke of
Norfolk, and he thus obtained an entrance into the
College of Arms. He was appointed Rouge-croix
Pursuivant in 1773, and promoted to be Somerset
Herald in 1777; was Secretary to the Earl Mar-
shal; and, also through the patronage of the Duke

* For further particulars of his family the reader is referred
to Noble's " History of the College of Arms," p. 428.

of Norfolk, a Lieutenant in the Militia of the West
Riding of Yorkshire.

Mr. Brooke made many collections, chiefly relative to the County of York. His father had inherited the MSS. of his great uncle the Rev. John
Brooke, Rector of High Hoyland in Yorkshire,
which had been formed as a foundation for the
topography of that great division of the kingdom.
These came into the hands of our industrious
herald; and in the course of a few years he had
greatly enlarged them by his own assiduity, and by
copying the manuscripts of Jenyngs and Tilleyson,
which relate to the same district *.

Having been elected a Fellow of the Society of
Antiquaries, April 6, 1775, he became an active
contributor to the Archæologia. His first communication was intituled, "Conjectures on a Seal
of Sir Richard Worsley†." His next was, "The
Ceremonial of making the King's Bed‡;" his
others, "Illustration of a Saxon inscription on
the Church of Kirkdale, in the North Riding of
Yorkshire §;" "Account of an Antient Seal of
Robert Baron Fitzwalter ‖;" "Description of the
Great Seals of Queen Catharine Parr and Mary
d'Este, second wife of James II. ¶;" "Illustration
of a Saxon inscription in Aldbrough Church in
Holderness **;" "A Deed of the Manor of Nether
Sittlington, co York ††." Mr. Brooke was a con-
stant attendant on the meetings of the Society of
Antiquaries, as will appear by his reports to Mr.
Gough in the ensuing correspondence ‡‡.

* See a Catalogue of them in Gough's "British Topography,"
vol. II. pp. 397, 401.
† Vol. IV. p. 192.   ‡ Ibid. p. 311.   § Vol. V. p. 188.
‖ Ibid. p. 211.   ¶ Ibid. pp. 232, 367.
** Vol. VI. p. 39.   †† Vol. VII. p. 416.
‡‡ It is remarkable that Mr. Gough, although holding the
office of Director, seldom attended the Society's weekly meetings.
This arose from his residence so far from London as Enfield.
For the meetings of the Council he purposely came to London.

To the Gentleman's Magazine Mr. Brooke was a Correspondent, under the signature of J. B.; and the principal authors of his day in genealogy and topography, were indebted to him. He assisted Dr. Nash in the early part of his Worcestershire Collections; Mr. Gough in many of his works, especially in the account of Yorkshire, in the new edition of Camden's "Britannia;" and was the coadjutor of the Rev. Mr. Watson in his Memoirs of the Earls of Warren and Surrey *. He also contributed to Bigland's Gloucestershire, Worsley's Isle of Wight, and King's Castles. He furnished the memoirs of the Nevills to Pegge's "Forme of Cury;" and several of the descriptions in Hearne and Byrne's Views.

Besides a History of Yorkshire, Mr. Brooke also contemplated a new edition of Sandford's Genealogical History†; a Baronage after Dugdale's method‡; and a History of all Tenants in Capite to accompany Domesday §.

This talented and amiable man had fair prospects of rising to the highest rank in his profession, when, by a melancholy and peculiarly calamitous accident, he was prematurely taken from the scene of his industrious exertions. With Mr. Pingo, York Herald ‖, and fourteen other persons, he

---

* It is well known that the object of this volume was to prove the legitimate descent of the Warrens of Poynton from an early Earl of Warren. The subject has been recently elucidated and set to rest by the Rev. Joseph Hunter, F.S.A. the historian of South Yorkshire. By the production of an abstract by Dodsworth of the will of the last Earl, that erudite and scientific antiquary has proved the Warrens of Poynton to have actually derived their descent from Edward de Warren, one of the *illegitimate* sons of that Earl by Maud de Neirford. See the "History of the Deanery of Doncaster," vol. I. p. 110; or the "Retrospective Review," Second Series, vol. II. p. 527.

† See hereafter, p. 366.   ‡ See p. 410.   § See pp. 370, 382.

‖ Benjamin Pingo, Esq. the fifth son of Thomas Pingo, an eminent engraver of seals, and assistant engraver of the Mint, was born in the parish of St. Andrew, Holborn, and baptised at that Church, July 8, 1749. Led to the College of Arms by a taste for heraldry, he was appointed Rouge-dragon Pursuivant in 1780, and York Herald in 1786. At the calamitous accident

perished in the fatal catastrophe of the 3d of February 1794, in attempting to get into the pit at the Little Theatre in the Haymarket. It did not appear that he had been thrown down, but was suffocated as he stood, as were several others. His countenance had the appearance of sleep, not death; and even the colour of his cheeks remained. His body was three days after interred in a vault under the Heralds' seat in the Church of St. Bennet, Paul's Wharf, where several of the College

which occasioned his death with Mr. Brooke, he was thrown down, and being corpulent, was much disfigured. His remains, attended by the Members of the College, were interred in the Chapel belonging to the Tower of London. He possessed high esteem with his heraldic brethren, to which his merit, as a good and amiable man, justly entitled him ; Mr. Brooke's opinion of him will be found hereafter in p. 415. He bequeathed his MSS. to the library of the College; his books were sold with Mr. Brooke's by Leigh and Sotheby in 1794. His father, Mr. Thomas Pingo, is mentioned by Lord Orford, as having engraved a plate of arms in Thoresby's Leeds. He died in December 1776; and his widow, who was Mary, daughter of Benjamin Goldwire, of Romsey in Hampshire, died in Gray's-inn-lane, April 17, 1790, aged 76. The herald's brothers, Lewis and John, were both eminent in their father's profession, as engravers to the Mint, and executed several excellent medals.

The following are two notes of the herald:

1.   *" Heralds'-college, Dec. 3, 1791.*
" Mr. Pingo presents his compliments to Mr. Nichols; and, agreeably to his promise, has sent him a List of the Mayors, &c. of Leicester, which he copied some years ago from a manuscript of the late Mr. Alderman Gamble, of that town. Mr. Pingo would have sent it before, but waited for an opportunity to add a few trifling inscriptions not published, and which are not to be found in Leicestershire Churches, but in other counties, for persons connected with that county."

2.   *Heralds'-college, April 2, 1792.*
" Mr. Pingo presents his compliments to Mr. Nichols, should be much obliged if he can inform him in what parish in Leicestershire the Brentnals are to be found, as he wants to obtain a testimonial of the baptism of Mary Brentnal, the daughter of John Brentnal and Rachael Cockran his wife, who died in March 1765, in Spain, aged 72, but who was born in Leicestershire. Mr. Pingo has inclosed a few inscriptions of Leicestershire families."

have been deposited.   His funeral, attended by the
Heralds and his own relations, was also accompanied by his Grace the Duke of Norfolk, Earl Marshal of England, the Earl of Leicester, President of
the Society of Antiquaries, Sir Joseph Banks, President of the Royal Society, John Topham, Craven
Ord, and Edmund Turnor, Esqs. FF.A. and R.SS.
Rev. Mr. Brand, Secretary of the Antiquarian Society, John Caley, James Moore, and John Lambert, Esqs. FF.A.S. who voluntarily paid this last
tribute of regard to their deceased friend.

The circumstances of Mr. Brooke's death heightened the general regret felt at his loss; and few men
have been so much deplored.   His elegant and
refined manners had obtained him admission to the
drawing rooms of the great; and in every circle his
society was courted and esteemed.   A monumental
tablet was erected over his remains, with the following epitaph by Edmund Lodge, Esq. F.S.A. then
Lancaster Herald, and now Norroy King at Arms:

Sacred to the Memory of
JOHN-CHARLES BROOKE, ESQ.
SOMERSET HERALD,
SECRETARY TO THE EARL MARSHAL OF ENGLAND,
AND FELLOW OF THE SOCIETY OF ANTIQUARIES;
descended from the respectable Family of
Brooke, of Dodworth in the County of York,
and a person of unrivalled eminence
in his antient and useful profession.
When we are told that this valuable man,
to a moral and pious disposition,
united a most cheerful and lively humour;
that with a mind to comprehend, a judgment to select,
and a memory to retain,
every sort of useful and agreeable information,
he was blessed with a temper
calm, unassuming, and inoffensive;
that he lived in a strict intimacy
with persons of the highest rank
and of the first literary character,
without the smallest tincture of vanity;
above all, that he enjoyed,
with a happy constitution of body,

an uncommon prosperity in worldly affairs;
let us, instead of envying the possession,
reflect on the awful uncertainty
of these sublunary blessings.
For, alas!
he was in a moment deprived of them,
in the dreadful calamity
which happened at the Theatre in the
Haymarket,
on the third of February 1794.

ARMS. Within a collar of SS, Ermine, on a bend Sable a hawk's lure Or, the line and ring Argent; a crescent in chief for the difference of a second son. Crest, a goat's head erased Sable, horned and bearded Or.

Mr. Brooke, who was a well-regulated economist, had acquired about £.14,000. By his will he appointed his two sisters executrixes and residuary legatees, although his elder brother, an attorney, survived him. He bequeathed his MSS. to the College of Arms, with a legacy of £.100 to arrange, and £.10 to bind them. He left rings to all the members of the College. His books, with those of his fellow-sufferer Mr. Pingo, were sold by Leigh and Sotheby in 1794.

A portrait of Mr. Brooke is honoured with a place in the Gallery at Arundel Castle. A quarto plate by T. Milton from a painting by T. Maynard, is the frontispiece to Noble's " History of the College of Arms."

_____

1. J. C. BROOKE, Esq. to RICHARD GOUGH, Esq.
" SIR,   Heralds'-college, Jan. 8, 1776.
" I should be much obliged to you to inform me if you know any thing of a Sir Samuel Bickley, a clergyman, who assumed the title of Baronet; and is said to have died at the post-house at Enfield about four years ago*. He is said to have left behind

* The death of this person is thus recorded in the Gentleman's Magazine for 1773: " July 27. At the King's head Inn, Enfield, the Rev. Samuel Bickley, who came thither the Saturday before in great distress. In his pockets were found three manuscript sermons and a petition to the Archbishop of Canterbury, dated February 18, 1773. The prayer of the petition was as follows: 'Your petitioner, therefore, most humbly prays, that, if an audience from your Grace should be deemed too great a

him a Manuscript Survey of Kent, with drawings of the various Churches; which was to be sold at Wagstaff's in Spitalfields in 1773.

" The antient coat on glass you showed me of the cross quartering barry, and on an escutcheon pretence on a chief two mullets, which you say came from Edmonton, belonged to William Hussey, second son of Sir William Hussey, Knt. Lord Chief Justice of England, temp. Edward IV. and younger brother of John Lord Hussey. He married Anne, daughter and heir of Sir John Salvin, Knt. of North Duffield in Yorkshire, who bore, Argent, on a chief Sable two mullets Or, by whom he had a good estate in the East Riding; and from that marriage descended the family of Hussey, of Hareswell and North Duffield (2 D 5, fol. 62, in Coll. Armor.)

" The other arms, of the bend between martlets, and chevron between eagles, impaling unicorns' heads, being a modern affair, I cannot so well decypher. In former times, when the science of heraldry was much attended to, nobody presumed to fix up any arms in churches, houses, &c. but what were allowed by the Earl Marshal, so that any such before the time of Charles I. we are almost certain of finding out in our records; since that time it is more difficult. Staverden bears, Argent, a bend ingrailed between two martlets Gules; but yours, I think, were Sable. Dynge bears, Sable, a chevron between three eagles displayed Argent. As to the coat on the woman's side of the escutcheon, of party per chevron Gules and Sable, three unicorns' heads couped Or, it was granted by Sir Edward Bysshe, Clarencieux, November 30, 1670, to Philip Jemmet, Esq. of London, who fined for Alderman of the said City.

" The other coats, with the dragon holding a sword, I think I explained to you before.

" I beg my compliments to Mrs. Gough; and am, Sir, your most obedient humble servant,   J. C. BROOKE, R.C."

favour, you will, at the least, grant him some relief, though it be only a temporary one, in his deplorable necessity and distress; and let *your Grace's charity cover the multitude of his sins.* There never yet was any one in England doomed to starve; but I am nearly, if not altogether so: denied the sacred function wherein I was educated, driven from the doors of the rich laymen to the clergy for relief, by the clergy denied, so that I may justly take up the speech of the Gospel Prodigal, and say, ' How many hired servants of my father have bread enough, and to spare, while I perish with hunger!' "—Respecting this clergyman's right to the title of Baronet, it may be remarked that he had assumed it as long back as 1759, when he was presented to the Vicarage of Bapchild in Kent; and that he may have been nephew and heir to the Rev. Sir Humphrey Bickley, Bart. who died Rector of Attleborough in Norfolk, Sept. 18, 1754, and which Sir Humphrey, being unmarried himself, had a brother Joseph, who had children. See the descent of the Baronetcy to Sir Francis Bickley, father of Sir Humphrey, in Blomefield's Norfolk (edit. 1805) vol. I. p. 520. The surname is one of uncommon occurrence. EDIT.

2. "Dear Sir, *Heralds'-college, Jan. 12, 1777.*

"I have addressed to you some conjectures on the Kirkdale inscription, which, if you think proper, may be read at the next meeting of the Society *; in which case please to make what alterations or corrections you think proper. I have made exact drawings of the Church, and the inscription with part of the porch, which should have been sent to you along with this, but for fear of folding in the letter; they shall be delivered to you on Thursday night; on which day, if agreeable to you, I shall be glad to see you to tea between five and six in the afternoon, and we will adjourn to the Society together. From

"Yours sincerely,   J. C. Brooke, R. C."

3. "Dear Sir, *Heralds'-college, April 12, 1777.*

"I spent yesterday at Mr. Brander's with Mr. Pegge, Sir Joseph Ayloffe, Grose, &c. and he produced two beautiful impressions of Royal seals, *viz.* of Queen Catherine Parr, wife to Henry VIII. and Catherine of Portugal, Queen to Charles II. which he desires I would have drawn for him, and write upon them, that they may be produced at the Society and engraved †.

"Dr. Nash is in town; he spent the evening with us on Thursday, and inquired much after you; he stays about a month. He does not seem to have the least design of laying aside his work ‡, but appears very sanguine about it.

"Sir Edward Blackett was at the Society on Thursday; and I spoke to him about the Durham sword, which is now in his possession as Lord of the Manor of Sockburne §. He says that, when the present Bishop took possession of his diocese, his steward, who performed the ceremony, imprudently cleaned it up, and had the blade new ground.

"Mr. Bigland desires his compliments to you, with many thanks for the prints of the Duke of Clarence's tomb at Tewkesbury, which he had not got; but he has a very elegant drawing of it. He has a private plate of Arundel Castle, quarto, engraved at his expence; an impression of which he desires you to accept. He would be infinitely obliged to you for the loan of those books which contain the Gloucestershire drawings.

"Yours sincerely,   J. C. Brooke."

* Read before the Society of Antiquaries, Jan. 16, 1777, and printed in the Archæologia, vol. V. p. 188.

† The former was engraved and described by Mr. Brooke in Archæologia, vol. V. p 232. The latter had already been published among the works of Simon.

‡ The History of Worcestershire; see before, pp. 344 *et seq.*

§ See it engraved in Surtees's Durham, vol. III. p. 243; and copied in the Gentleman's Magazine, vol. XCIII. ii. p. 612.

4. " DEAR SIR,   *Heralds'-college, Friday, May* 2, 1777.

" I received the favour of your letter; but, being not determined till this day whether it would be in my power to accompany you to Cambridge or not, did not take the places, and find they were all engaged for Monday; I have, therefore, taken them for Tuesday, and will take you up at the Wash.

" I was at the Society last night, where, to use Mr. Grose's droll expression, the last hind-quarter of St. George * was dished up to a numerous and tired audience. I had sent Mr. Brander the drawings of his seals, and a paper upon them; but Mr. Norris is so good an economist in doling out the proper portion of weekly literature, that he desired they might not be produced, as, it being so near St. George's-day, he thought that Saint might serve for the evenings repast.

" Yours sincerely,   J. C. BROOKE."

---

5. " DEAR SIR,   *Heralds'-college, June* 27, 1777.

" I have, according to your desire, procured the drawings of Kirkdale Church from Mr. Norris, and delivered them to Mr. Basire, who will soon put them in hand; but I have desired him to omit for the present that part of the inscription which runs round the dial, *viz.* that which Mr. Manning has treated upon, as I am dubious that I might not take it right, being the most defaced; I have, therefore, written to Dr. Comber on the occasion, desiring that he will make a fac-simile copy of that part with black lead, and will have it completed when I receive his answer. I hope you have received my letter to you concerning Kirkdale from Mr. Norris; for I have happily collected various additions to the historical part, which I wish to have inserted before printed, and will finish it before I go into Yorkshire.

" I spent the evening with Mr. Russell at Mr. Topham s yesterday. Sir Joseph Ayloffe is still jollifying at Brander's at Christchurch. He writes to Mr. Topham most florid accounts of their elysian manner of living; and I can believe it true.

" In looking over some old registers of funerals in our records, written in the time of Henry VIII. I find a very curious one of ' that Honourable Knight Sir Thomas Lovell, Bannerett, who departed out of this transitorye lyef at his place at Enfylde, in the year of our Lord God 1523, in the 16th yere of the Raigne of our Soveraigne Lord King Hen. VIII. the dominical lettre being B, the 25th day of the month of May, being Wensday and Corpus Christi Eve, betwene 6 and 7 of the cloke at afternone,' &c. It relates all the jolly feastings that were used on the occasion, with the ceremonial of the procession to London; and

---

* Mr. Pegge's " Observations on the History of St. George," occupy the first 32 pages of the fifth volume of the Archæologia.

how the crafts of London, and the Gentlemen of Armes at
Court, in good order, drank wine, bere, ale, and ypocras, and
ate comfyttes and spyce bred in great abundance in the nonnes'
parlours at Hallywell.' Pray have you got it * ?

" I expected we should have had a council before the Society
was adjourned. I intended to have moved for the two other
Royal female seals, in the possession of Messrs. Bartlett and
More, of the Queens of Charles I. and James II. to have been
drawn to accompany Mr. Brander s.

" From yours sincerely, J. C. BROOKE."

---

6. " DEAR SIR,
" I spent the evening with Mr. Topham at Mr. Russell's last
Monday ; and he expresses a desire of being introduced to you,
and also of making you acquainted with his brother. He
drinks tea with me to-morrow, and goes to the Society; and
I shall be glad to see you to meet him, if agreeable. We expect
great opposition to the new regulations to-morrow evening.
The Dean † and none of the Vice-presidents will attend, being
prevented by various accidents, as Mr. Lort informs me, whom I
saw at Court to-day. From yours sincerely, J. C. BROOKE."

---

7. " DEAR SIR, *Heralds'-college, July 17, 1777.*
" I will answer the queries in your letter when I see you. I
never saw such a coat as that you mention of the star supported by horses or bulls.

" If you correspond with Sir John Cullum, please to inform
him that Mr. Howard, having heard much of his antiquarian
fame as a Suffolk collector, is desirous of being acquainted with
him; and, if Sir John has no objection, I will endeavour to
bring them together sometime next winter.

" From yours sincerely, J. C. BROOKE."

---

8. " DEAR SIR, *Heralds'-college, Aug. 4, 1777.*
" I received your letter with Dr. Comber's inclosed, and think
it will be attended with much inconvenience to trouble him with
taking an impression of the inscription ; but, as the chief matter
in dispute is whether there is room to insert the letters PIN
between the M and T, which certainly a person may be trusted
to discover with his naked eye, I will write to him by this day's
post to examine that, and desire him to return an immediate
answer, with the result of which I will acquaint you.

" Upon mentioning the Aldbrough inscription ‡ to a friend in
town, I heard a fac-simile copy was taken of it in 1772, which

---

* It is printed in Robinson's " History of Enfield," vol. I. 129—137.
† Dr. Milles, President of the Society of Antiquaries.
‡ See hereafter, pp. 365, 369, 370.

upon inquiring after I have discovered, and it is now in my possession; it differs not materially from yours, but, as I have made many curious discoveries relative to the parties mentioned in it, I propose writing to my correspondent in the East Riding, to take another, that in this instance we may have no deception, as likewise a view of the Church; and then I will arrange my materials for the Society.

"Pray let me know what you have done about Dr. Nash? I am working up the History of Beoley for him.

"Yours sincerely,   J. C. Brooke."

---

9. "Dear Sir,   *Heralds'-college, Aug.* 20, 1777.

"I received the favour of your letter; and was very sorry you was prevented going to St. Alban's last Sunday. Mr. Brander has been in town for a fortnight; and had proposed accompanying us, and taking Topham and me in his chariot; and desires now that the scheme may be put off till he returns to town. He goes to Christchurch on Friday, and takes Mr. Topham with him. Mr. Currer has also intimated how agreeable such a party would be to him; so that I imagine, by the time we go, our journey of business will terminate in a jolly bout.

"I am much distressed about the Kirkdale inscription. Dr. Comber is at Scarborough; and I am afraid will not return in time enough to return an answer before I go into the country. As there are two copies to justify Mr. Manning's conjectures, I think there can be no impropriety in publishing his first letter to you on the subject. He need not be afraid of a new fac-simile starting forth; and you know all these things are con-jecture at best. I am much at a loss how to proceed about Mr. Pegge's paper on the subject. When these matters are laid before the Society for publication, they are supposed to select what will be most interesting to the public, and compose a palatable dish out of all the ingredients; and not to give such seasoning as suits only particular appetites. It cannot be very entertaining to the public to have Mr. Pegge's interpretation of an inscription, which was imperfectly taken, however ingenious at that time; or to read his conjectures on the identity of per-sons, who by a subsequent paper are proved from records. As his paper was written so long ago, pray would there be any impropriety in weaving the most material parts of his letter into mine (quoting his authority) and then omitting it? in which case I would say nothing of the disputable part of the inscription; but leave that entirely to Mr. Manning, which might then follow in his admirable letter addressed to you. Mr. Pegge is extremely clever, and the learned world are under infinite obligations to him; but he has one fault, which hurts him even as an antiquary, and that is, writing too much, and upon every thing.

" I have quite settled with Basire respecting the Fitz-Walter
seal, which I have put into his hands to engrave; and have also
left with him the impression I had taken for you, fixed in a
curious box, which, when he has done with, you will please to
receive from him. I have also corrected and altered my paper
on the subject, which I will either leave at Nichols's for you,
or where you may appoint; but I desire, when printed, you will
correct it as your better judgment shall think proper *.

" Mr. Bigland is soon going into Gloucestershire. He has
had all the monuments in your book copied most elegantly, as
well as the plan of Tewkesbury, which he proposes taking with
him; and he desires that you will put down, and send to me,
what observations you would have him make concerning the
monuments there.

" I am quite in raptures with the Aldbrough inscription. I
have found so much curious matter relating to it, as I hope will
make it a most interesting dish for the Society. If Mr. Dade's
letter to me on the subject is not sufficiently satisfactory, I do
not know but what I may go seventy miles, when in Yorkshire,
on purpose to see it.

" Messrs. Brander, Topham, Currer, and self, rise at six to-
morrow morning, breakfast at Highbury-barn, and go to survey
Jack Straw's Castle, dine together, and finish the day at the
Museum. You think, while basking on the sunny banks of
Forty-hill, that we Cits can have no pleasures in town in sum-
mer, but you are much mistaken; we have many agreeable anti-
quarian parties, and manage to pass our time extremely well.
We have already passed judgment on the fortification near
Copenhagen-house; and have unanimously exploded your con-
jecture, which I hinted to them, that it was raised in the Civil
Wars. I have had a letter lately from Mr. Manning, who is
very well. From yours sincerely,   J. C. BROOKE."

---

10. " DEAR SIR,   *Heralds'-college, Sept.* 19, 1777.
" According to your desire, I called on Dr. Ducarel, who was
extremely civil; and begged his most respectful compliments to
you. He says, that formerly he took a Catalogue of the Royal
Society's Library, but all his notes were left there; and would
recommend that you apply at the house for the MSS. of Aubrey's
Wiltshire. He desires I would inform you that, by letter from
Brand, he understands that Ellison's MSS. relating to Newcastle
are lately come into his possession, which is the reason that
induces him to go on with his History, having once dropped the
design for want of materials.

" I have done all I can now to Kirkdale, and will leave it at
Nichols's. I have also corrected the plate; and given it to Basire
to put the finishing stroke to it; after which will inclose it to Dr.

* See it printed in Archæologia, vol. V. p. 211.

Comber for his correction.   Having taken leave of all my friends
for my intended Yorkshire journey, I have been little interrupted
of late, which has enabled me to do much business; and I have
particularly employed myself about Sandford's Genealogical History, a new edition of which I much wish to see, and find, that
I have near twenty ceremonials (funerals, baptisms, &c.) as
many monuments, and near as many Royal seals, besides other
curious anecdotes, not inserted in that work.   I have lately discovered the procession to the funeral of Anne of Cleves, which
I think would do well to accompany her monument when produced at the Society *.

" Mr. Topham is still carousing at Christchurch.   I have
received a letter from Sir Richard Worsley this week, with thanks
for a pedigree of the Redvers's, formerly Lords of the Isle of
Wight, which I sent him.   He says he looks upon himself but as
an agent for the public in his work, and shall spare no pains to
render it complete.   I have collected for him above a dozen seals
of the antient lords, which are to be engraved, as well as other
monuments.

" The town is now quite empty and deserted,—not one solitary
antiquary to be found !   We had a venison feast at Mr. Pegge's
last week ; and he could muster only five, of which Astle was
one, who has given me a draught upon Topham for all his private publications, prints, &c. when I demand which, I will remind
him of Astle's former promise to you.

" I can find no memorial of Lady Lucy Gates at Scarborough.
When I was there, I carefully examined the Church, but found
nothing in the least interesting ; but the chancel was demolished in the Civil Wars, and probably it might be there.   I find
mention of her in the Gates' pedigree, viz. that she was daughter
of Charles Knevit, and first wife of Sir Henry Gates, of Sey-
mer, near Scarborough, Knight, living 1584.   My brother Comber has the matrix of an antient seal of these Gates's, of which
an impression is in my collection.

" I should wish much to have a drawing of the seal of
Charles 1. from the Society's Minutes, which you showed me,
before returned, for my Sandford.

" From yours sincerely,   J. C. BROOKE."

---

11. " DEAR SIR,   Heralds'-college, Oct. 14, 1777.
" As we have now deposited the Earl Marshal in the chantry,
founded by his ancestors, in the Church at Arundel †, I shall be
soon more at liberty ; and propose, before the expiration of the
month, spending a few days with you.

* An engraving of the altar-tomb of Queen Anne of Cleves in Westminster Abbey was published in the Vetusta Monumenta, vol. II. plate
xxxv; but the ceremonial of her funeral was not appended to it.

† The funeral of the late Edward Duke of Norfolk had taken place
on the first of the month.

" Are the two Royal seals to be in the next volume of Archæologia? because I shall make some additions to the account of Queen Katherine Parr. I have found the ceremonial of her funeral at Sudley, not yet printed that I can find, with an abstract of the Protestant Sermon preached by Dr. Coverdale on the occasion, ' which was verie goode and godlie, and did much proffite the auditours, tho' not the dede.'

" I have begun arranging my *Sigilla Magnatum* in portfolios; where I propose giving some account of the parties, with reference to Dugdale's Baronage, and numbered. It is my intention of collecting drawings of seals, so as to prove the arms of every family treated on in Dugdale, thereby. If you have any duplicates which are engraved, I make no scruple of asking you for them, because I shall give you other prints in return; and I propose collecting all that are published before I have any drawn.

" I have compliments to you in a letter this week from Mr. Frampton, of Moreton. Pray have you the Saxon Gospels and the Saxon version of Bede, in the original?

" From yours sincerely,   J. C. BROOKE."

12.   *" Friday, Dec. .., 1777.*

" We had a very agreeable meeting last night; present, the Dean, King, Bartlett, Brander, Topham, Barrington, Drs. Hunter, Layard, d'Argent, &c. and much entertaining matter. A curious MS. on vellum, communicated by Sir John Hawkins, containing curses pronounced by some religious house against delinquents, and some antient music. Mr. King produced a most exquisite drawing of the elevation of the East end of Henry the Seventh's Chapel; Mr. Strong a fine seal; read a paper from Pegge to Brander on stone-coffins found at Christchurch; a Roman inscription found at Whitby, likewise produced, with an explanation in a letter from Dr. Percy. Bartlett will subscribe to Thetford; or, as he says, anything you are concerned in. Brander says he is desirous of being sociable these dark days before Christmas; and therefore the Crown and Anchor Club will soon meet.

" From yours sincerely,   J. C. BROOKE."

13. " DEAR SIR,   *Heralds'-college, Dec.* 12, 1777.

" I do not know of any person who has a right to the Earldom of Rivers; if there had, I imagine it would have been claimed. Richard, the last Earl, had by his wife a daughter Elizabeth, married to James Earl of Barrymore, of Ireland, who had by her a daughter, Lady Penelope Barry, married to General James Cholmondeley, brother of George, late Earl Cholmondeley; and, I believe, died s. p. He had also, by Mrs. Elizabeth Colleton, a natural daughter, called Bessy Savage, married to Frederick Nassau, Earl of Rochford, father of the present Earl, who in her right is now possessed of St. Osyth's Priory in Essex, the seat of Earl Rivers, who by will left her all his estate that he could.

" We had a very full meeting on Thursday night, but nothing interesting. I hear that Grose is gone with you to Thetford, which gave me pleasure. Next Thursday will be read a paper from Bowle to confute Drake on the word Romance *. He can prove, from various Spanish authors, that the word Romance has been used for Scripture History, which could not be considered as fable.

" Mr. Walmsley, Mrs. Braddyll's executor, did not choose to bear Mr. K——'s expenses down with the funeral, so he would not go. She has left him £.200; his brother James £.100.

" Brander has had an offer of the original matrix of Richard Cromwell's Great-seal as Protector†, price £.50; and is wavering whether he shall accept it or not.

" From yours sincerely,   J. C. BROOKE."

---

14. " DEAR SIR,   Heralds'-college, Jan. 12, 1778.
" According to my promise, I send you an account of the result of Mr. Topham's expedition with me to Jack Straw's Castle. We set out on Saturday, being a fine frosty morning, and was but in time to see the remains of the Mount, which is now nearly levelled by order of the owner, Dawes, formerly a stock-broker, and broker to Hoares' house, the bankers, who purchased the Manor of Highbury a few years since, for a considerable sum of money, of the assignees of Sir George Cole-brooke, Bart. The said Dawes is about to build himself a house on the site of Jack Straw's Castle; and has paled round a considerable space of ground for a park, which will have a delightful view of the Essex hills, the vale below Hornsey, Highgate and Hampstead, and Islington. He has also built that large pile of building which extends from Islington to his estate, called Highbury-row. It appears very plain, from the materials of which the hill has been composed, that it is artificial, there being large layers of rubbish about a yard from the surface, consisting of mortar, brick, stone, tiles, &c. which served to prove that Jack Straw raised it, and that some building was destroyed for the materials for that purpose; and probably the house of the Knights Templars, who then owned the manor of Highbury. Some of the tiles have been for pavements, which seem as if the house had been erased to the ground; a few of these are glazed and ornamented with figures, of which both Topham and self found each a fragment; but some they said had been dug up whole, and one with a date on it, which the labourers said Harris of Islington, the overseer of the work, had got, but when we saw him he denied it; they likewise said two coins had been found, one

* Printed in the Archæologia, vol. V. pp. 267—271.
† Engraved in Simon's " Medals, Coins, Great Seals," &c. by Vertue, plate XXIII.

copper, with a cock on it, the other silver about 400 years old
i. e. I suppose circ. temp. Richard II. ; but of these we could
procure no certain intelligence. I brought away with me many
fragments of the covering tiles, which have two holes for the
use of slating ; a piece of figured pavement tile, ornamented
with leopards' heads and tracery ; a large square pavement tile,
glazed but with no figures ; and a rusty nail, all which I dug up
myself. A fragment of pan-tile, the point of the rusty nail,
which unfortunately broke off in bringing home, and some
scrapings of mortar from the figured tiles, carefully preserved
in a vial, shall be reserved for you against Thursday, to add to
your Museum!

" Mr. Dade, my worthy Yorkshire correspondent *, called up
to London by the sudden and melancholy death of his patron Sir
Griffith Boynton, visited me this morning, but leaves town to-
morrow with the funeral. He desires to be proposed at the
Society. He brought the agreeable news that another Saxon
inscription has been discovered in a church in Yorkshire.

" From yours sincerely,   J. C. BROOKE."

———

15. " DEAR SIR,   *Heralds'-college, April* 21, 1778.
" I will certainly, *Deo volente*, attend the dinner on St.
George's-day, and likewise help to devour the fragments in the
evening ; but I am afraid I cannot attend the business in the
morning, as I believe we are to have a creation of a Herald-
extraordinary by the Earl Marshal, with the ceremonial according to the antient custom on that day.

" I shall give my paper on Aldborough to Mr. Norris to be
read at next meeting. Shall send Mary d'Este's seal to Basire to
make a drawing of it to-morrow; and will work up a paper to
accompany it soon. Do you take in the Morning Post? A few
days since were inserted sketches of episcopal characters from
Shakspeare ; and the following was given to a friend of yours,
which I dare say you will think exceedingly applicable :

" D—n of Ex——r†.

" ' Why thus it is. See! see!
I have been begging sixteen years in court,
(Am yet a Courtier beggarly) nor could
Come pat betwixt too early and too late.'

" I received a letter to-day with the account of the death of
my brother Dr. Comber, at Buckworth, of a paralytic stroke.
He was a man of much learning and industry, but too fond of
the things of this world. He wrote several things, but nothing
of any consequence. I shall send a small account of him ‡ to
Dr. Kippis, which may do for a note in his grandfather's article
in the Biographica Britannica.

---

* Of whom see the " Literary Anecdotes," vol. VII. p. 474.
† Dr. Milles.   ‡ See the " Literary Anecdotes," vol. I. p. 600.

" I bought the Pembroke family, and some other things for you, at Granger's sale, which I have sent in a parcel sealed up to Nichols.

" I have this week begun making collections for a new work, which I propose shall accompany Domesday when published, *viz.* a History of all the Tenants, *in capite,* mentioned therein, with their Pedigrees, and account of their families as long as the estates continued in possession of the male line, and to notice those families who as heirs general still inherit property by descent from them. To be illustrated by deeds in the time of the Conqueror; seals, and other monuments. Likewise an account of such Saxons as held under them as Valvasors, and to notice their descendants where I can meet with them. To notice such Churches as are mentioned in Domesday; and which, by their present remains, evince their existence in the time of the Saxons (on this head I shall hope for much assistance from you), with views of such Saxon fragments, &c. I think such a work will throw much greater light upon the state of the Saxons at the Conquest, than has hitherto appeared.

" From yours sincerely,   J. C. BROOKE."

---

16. " DEAR SIR,   *Heralds'-college, May* 9, 1778.
" Last Thursday se'nnight my Aldborough paper was read, and last Thursday ditto, and Mr. Pegge to Mr. Brander, accounting for the number of monastic seals, which yet remain in England, very ingenious *. Mr. Pegge looks extremely well; and I hope will long continue to entertain us.

" Catherine Parr has passed the press, and only waits to receive the last finishing of your able hand. I shall receive the rough letter-press from Mr. Currer to-morrow, and will leave it at Nichols's on Monday for you. Basire has made a beautiful drawing of Mary d'Este s seal, which may be produced with the impression, when I write upon it, at the Society.

" Yours sincerely,   J. C. BROOKE."

---

17. Mr. GOUGH to Mr. BROOKE.

" DEAR SIR,   *May* 18, 1778.
" My attempt on Weston House was crowned with success, though I stormed it while the family were at dinner, and consequently was obliged to quit the family pictures; but had the gallery all to myself; and the Maps of Oxfordshire, Worcestershire, and Warwickshire, are glorious things. You see there, pourtrayed in tapestry, every minute object, even to windmills, (except hundreds and roads,) that was to be noticed at the time, which, by the arms, could not be later than Elizabeth; great part of the bordering counties are included; and there is a piece about

---

* Printed in the Archæologia, vol. V. pp. 346—356.

seven feet square, shown as a sample of fresher and more beautiful work, which takes in the south part of Surrey, and which
I wish to borrow; the others are of an immense size *.

" I am not without hopes of having one more interview with
my friends in Chancery-lane next Thursday; if I do not,
Nichols will send any thing you leave with him.

" Yours sincerely,   R. Gough."

---

18. Mr. Brooke to Mr. Gough.

"Dear Sir,   *Heralds'-college, May 22, 1778.*

" I received your letter at the Society, and will certainly write
upon Mary d'Este's seal before the recess, probably against next
Thursday. We had a very agreeable meeting at Claxton's †,
Astle, Lort, Butler, Topham, and self; from thence adjourned
to the Society, which was very full, considering the season. My
swan-roll was produced, with a short note, which seemed to give
great satisfaction ‡. I have sent you the Prior of Thetford's
swan mark. A long letter was read from Mr. Wyndham, of
Salisbury, who attended, describing, as he supposes, an antient
Saxon Church, built by Wilfrid, before the seventh century, at
Warnford in Hampshire, accompanied with three beautiful drawings § ; the whole curious, but entirely conjecture. Mr. Essex
says it is nothing but an old barn. Mr. Wyndham seems a
valuable acquisition to the Society.

" Dr. Kippis has written in the book he sent me, from the
author;' am I to consider it as a present?

" In pursuance of a note from the Lord Chamberlain, we had
yesterday a Chapter at the office to consider of a proper ceremonial for Lord Chatham's funeral; to-day our report was made to
him, and to-morrow is to be laid before the King in Council for
his approbation or alteration. It will be chiefly the same as that
of Monk, Duke of Albemarle, with the omission of military
trophies, to which Lord Chatham can have no right.

" I am glad to hear you have got some plates of seals for me;
please to send them by the first convenient opportunity. I shall
be glad also of a few more of those you formerly favoured me
with, the last having been all begged from me.

" I called upon Hearne to day, in company with Lord Surrey;
his first number comes out to-morrow.

" Yours sincerely,   J. C. Brooke."

---

* The subsequent history of these very curious maps will be found in
the " Literary Anecdotes," vol. VI. pp. 325 *et seq.*

† John Claxton, Esq. elected F.S.A. in 1772. See the " Literary Anecdotes," vol. VII. pp. 83, 537.

‡ This was an antient vellum roll representing swan-marks; and was
in the possession of Edwin Francis Stanhope, Esq. It does not appear
to have been noticed in the Archæologia. Five different swan-marks are
engraved in the History of Thetford, p. 293.

§ Printed in the Archæologia, vol. V. pp. 357—366.

2 B 2

19. Mr. Gough to Mr. Brooke.

"Dear Sir, *Enfield, May 24, 1778.*

"I presume Mr. Essex was at the Society last Thursday. What pity to overturn so fair a vision; I hope it will not be suppressed. I have seen a Barn Church, or Church Barn, which you please, near Romsey in Hants, said to have been removed thence on building the present Church, itself of very early date.

"I expect a long account of Lord Chatham's funeral, if you are not smothered in the crowd, or a screen or half an aile pulled on your head.

"Nichols has sent me a half sheet of Brute's Morton in Worcestershire, from Dr. Nash's book. It wants some correction, or rather typographical forming.

"Pray let me know by return of post, where Lord Chatham is at last to be buried, and at what time of day?

"Yours truly, R. Gough."

20. Mr. Brooke to Mr. Gough.

"Dear Sir, *Heralds'-college, May 25, 1778.*

"It is quite undetermined as yet, when or where Lord Chatham is to be buried; I will give you the earliest notice.

"Dr. Ducarel called to-day, and sat an hour. He told some droll tales; and desires I would hint to you, that there is a peculiar mode of behaviour between gentleman and gentleman, the decorum of which ought never to be deviated from; and he cannot think of delivering up Tanner's Catalogue until he receives a card from you on the occasion; pray write one, and put him to the expense of a double post letter! He sets out on his visitation of Sussex 5th June, and will let you have it while absent. Mr. Pegge called and took leave to-day, desired his kind respects to you, and many apologies that he has had this time so little the pleasure of your company; he goes on Thursday.

"A letter from Dr. Nash to-day, by way of White, so I suppose he has sent up some MSS. It contains nothing new. Brute's Morton received many additions and corrections by me; if, therefore, it wants topographical * forming, what must we think of the rest of his History?

"Mr. Bartlett is got abroad again. He called on Saturday; is very busy in drawing up a History of Manceter †, and the parts adjacent to his estate in Warwickshire.

"Yours sincerely, J. C. Brooke."

21 "Dear Sir, *Heralds'-college, June 5, 1778.*

"Dr. Ducarel has put into my hand the Catalogue of Tanner's MSS. and I have carried it to Nichols's. Mr. Price has given

* Mr. Gough said, "typographical forming." See the preceding letter.
† Bartlett's "History of Manceter" was printed in 1791, as Part I. of "Miscellaneous Antiquities," in continuation of the "Bibliotheca Topographica Britannica."

it to the Lambeth Library; and the Doctor made me give a receipt for it, and that it should be returned in twenty-one days from this day.

"I was obliged to you for the play-tickets, but my sisters had left town long before, and I seldom go to plays *; I carried them to Billy Kirkby, but he could not go, so I presented them to two of my friends, who were well entertained.

"I saw Lort at the drawing-room yesterday; he informed me that the Dean of Exeter has put his other knee out of joint, in coming down the old tower at Bristol, where the MSS. of Rowlie's Poems were deposited; his foot slipped, and the accident happened.

"We had a thin meeting of Antiquaries last night; many members are gone into the country. My paper on Mary d'Este's seal was read, and the drawing much approved. I suppose there will be another council, before the recess, to vote more papers for the volume. Some prints of Persian inscriptions at Persepolis, with an account of them, by Forster. A paper from Mr. Pegge to Banks-Hodgekinson, with an account of a pig of lead with an inscription, found in Derbyshire †. A further account of the Roman pavement found in Wales, with another drawing of it, by Wyndham; he esteems it the finest thing of the kind yet discovered, either in this kingdom or on this side the Alps.

"I am very much obliged to you for the seals, &c.; such additions to my collection are extremely acceptable to me. Lord Exeter called on me this week; has promised me drawings of several Abbey seals in his possession, belonging to dissolved houses, of which he is owner, as likewise to bring up several ancient deeds, &c. for my inspection. What treasures may we not expect from the archives of a family which began to flourish so soon after the dissolution! I took an opportunity of throwing in a word for poor Tattershall ‡; he said he knew nothing about it, but would inquire into the premises; and, if true, have the windows repaired.

"Old Mr. Pegge left town last Thursday se'nnight. I spent the preceding evening with him and Dr. Percy at his son's, and he was in admirable spirits; the son has much his father's turn, and I dare say will be a valuable phœnix to the Society. I was this week on a visit with Dr. Kaye and Mr. Topham at Mr. Payne's the architect, near Chertsey, for two days, a most agreeable jaunt; he showed us the finest collection of drawings in his way, I ever beheld.

---

* This passage in a letter of a person who me this death when going to a play, cannot be passed without remark.

† "Remarks on an antient Pig of Lead discovered on Cromford-nethe-Moor in the County of Derby," is printed in the Archæologia, vol. V. pp. 369—378.

‡ An engraving of Tattershall Castle was afterwards published by Mr. Gough, in vol. II. of his Sepulchral Monuments.

" Lord Chatham is to be buried on Tuesday morning at twelve
o clock in Westminster Abbey, Whit-tuesday; think what a
crowd! From yours sincerely,　　　　　J. C. BROOKE."

---

22. Mr. Gough to Mr. Brooke.

" DEAR SIR,　　　　　　　　*Enfield, June* 10, 1778.
" I was in town yesterday, but can forgive your not meeting
me in person or by representative, when you composed a court
of claims the night before, and were to bury the great patriot
next day. While you were in the midst of pomp and bustle
(of which pray give me an account at your first leisure, and
how many limbs of effigies and spectators were broke), I
calmly surveyed the picture and cork exhibitions, and after a
snug dinner in an empty coffee-house, retired hither in the
evening.

" To-day I have been to look after a shield removed from an
old chimney, which by a sixpence of Elizabeth and James, and
a copper piece of Charles I. was built either in 1572 or 1607.
The arms are, paly of seven Or and Gules, in chief Sable or
Gules three martlets; impaling, Azure, a cross Gules, in the
first quarter a fleur-de-lis Or. I am not positive as to the
colours, for the material is stucco, which has stood its time.
Tradition calls the alehouse the King's Mews, and says it
belonged to King Bruce's Castle, now Mr. Townshend's, at
Tottenham.

" By Mr. Norris's intelligence, the Dean's accident seems as
problematical as Rowlie's Poems. He could learn nothing of
it at his son's chambers.

" Dr. Kippis has made me a present of his book; and made
much more honourable mention of me in its preface than I am
entitled to. It is at least encouragement to write great men's
lives.

" I had all the papers voted at the last council except your
Aldborough; of which in due time. If you will call on a Mr.
Hunter, No. 13, St. Thomas Apostle, in mine or Mr. Herbert's
name, he will furnish you with as many proposals for Mr. Herbert's edition of Ames's History of Printing, as you please to
circulate. You may venture to recommend it.
　　　　　　　" Yours truly,　　　R. GOUGH."

---

23. Mr. Brooke to Mr. Gough.

" DEAR SIR,　　　　　　*Heralds'-college, June* 11, 1778.
" I have reserved a printed ceremonial of the funeral for you;
but a more particular and exact account will be in the Gazette on Saturday night. I am glad it is over, for we had a
most tiresome piece of work of it; it was hurried over in such
a manner that I had not time to inform you that, had you chose
it, you might have walked in the procession.

" The chief reason of my writing to you at this time is, to inform you that Mr. O'Halloran called on me this morning, and shall be glad to see you, if you come to town, during his stay in London, which will be till Tuesday or Wednesday next. He lodges at Davison's, Parliament-street, Westminster.

" From yours sincerely,   J. C. BROOKE."

---

24. Mr. GOUGH to Mr. BROOKE.

" *Friday, June* 12, 1778.

" I am not certain of being in town next week ; but if you will put the inclosed into Mr. O'Halloran's hands, with my compliments, and desire him to write as much on it as he pleases, and return it to me from London or Ireland at his earliest leisure, I shall be much obliged to you. I am at present in too much litter and bustle to ask him or you hither.

" I am credibly informed that you attended an empty coffin to the ground last Tuesday, and that the real Lord Chatham has been disposed of quietly at Hayes long since. This is of a piece with burying the Duke of Marlborough pompously, and the taking him up again. Whose ashes have been disturbed on the occasion ? I am yours truly,   R. GOUGH."

---

25. Mr. BROOKE to Mr. GOUGH.

" We had a very pleasant ride home on Monday. Mr. O'Halloran called yesterday, and will be at the Society on Thursday night ; if you are there I will introduce you to him.

" The prints I bought for you at Granger's sale came to £.1. 11s. as by the following lots, if you have kept the catalogue: 34, 5s.; 51, 4s. 6d.; 53, 4s. 6d.; 80, 12s.; 86, 2s. 6d.; 31, 2s. 6d.;—£.1. 11s.

" I am afraid you will think lot 80 dear. We happened to attend the King to Parliament House that day, and I could not go myself, but employed a friend to bid for me, without seeing them ; and the fifty antiquities turned out to be prints of Strutt's. I am sorry for it ; but it was no fault of mine.

" From yours sincerely,   J. C. BROOKE."

---

26. " DEAR SIR,   *Heralds'-college, June* 19, 1778.

" We had a good meeting last night at the Society, considering the time of year. A curious sword of the Marquis de Spinola produced, engraved in the manner of Brander's chair. A curious paper, produced by Mr. Barrington, from the Abbé Mann at Brussells, concerning Cæsar's voyage from Gaul to Britain ; he conjectures he landed at Deal *. The Prince of

---

* Not printed in the Archæologia. There are two papers in that work

Hesse elected an Honorary Member because he has established an Antiquary Society in his dominions in Germany; the motion made by Lort, seconded by Dr. Kaye. I introduced Mr. O'Halloran to the Society, who presented an elegant copy of his work *; and afterwards spent the evening with him and two of his Irish friends at the Crown and Rolls, where we were exceeding joyous. The Irish are vastly lively and entertaining! I have the pleasure to inform you, from the Bishop of Rochester himself, that no more banners, or other temporary trophies, are to be fixed up in the Abbey, as every stroke given to the walls, in some measure damages the building; and Lord Chatham's are to be carried to Hayes. At his funeral, as well as all others for the future, the twelve poor almsmen of Westminster are to be stationed at the monuments most likely to be damaged by the procession. Mr. Brander has left town above a fortnight ago. Other matters when I see you.

" I have given your Irish anecdotes to Mr. O'Halloran, who will make what additions he can, and return them. He was quite astonished where you could have met with your information, as you mention books that he had the utmost difficulty in obtaining. He gives a melancholy picture of the state of antiquarian research in Ireland.

" From yours sincerely, J. C. BROOKE."

---

27. Mr. GOUGH to Mr. BROOKE.

" DEAR SIR, *Enfield, June 27, 1778.*

" I return you the Tanner Catalogue, that you may deliver the precious deposit into the Lambeth Librarian's hands, with my thanks.

" It was not in my power to attend you and Mr. O'Halloran last Thursday; and to see the wonderful circle of stones at Grinstead, which I wonder how they escaped Sir Joseph, their neighbour, so long.

" I propose, at present, calling on you next Tuesday, about twelve, to prowl and dine at the first chop-house that comes in our way. I must call at the British Museum to see if the table is spread with Salisbury missals for me; and on Mr. Bartlett, before he goes out of town, which from his not answering my letter, I fear is the case. I want his paper on Prelatical Coins †.

" Yours truly, R. GOUGH."

---

by the Abbé Mann, as noticed in the copious memoirs of that able antiquary in vol. VIII. of the " Literary Anecdotes," p. 45.
* " A General History of Ireland, from the earliest accounts to the close of the Twelfth Century, 1778," two volumes, quarto.
† Printed in the Archæologia, vol. V. pp. 335—339.

28. Mr. Brooke to Mr. Gough.

" Dear Sir,   *Heralds'-college, June 29,* 1778.
" I received your letter and the Catalogue this morning, and will deliver it to Dr. Ducarel. I shall be glad to see you to-morrow at the hour you mention.

" Mr. Bartlett is in town. I spent yesterday afternoon with him, Combe, and Southgate, at Dr. Hunter's Museum, and was most agreeably entertained; but am afraid you will not meet with him to-morrow, as on Tuesdays he is generally engaged. Besides the circle of stones you mention, we had a paper from Pegge to Dr. Hunter, confuting Colebrooke on the Coin in the fourth volume of the Archæologia, which was so long as to be but half read through *.

" I have corrected the paper on Thetford Monuments; and sent it to Nichols some days since, with a desire that the corrected sheet may be returned to me. I have furnished Warren seals enough for a new plate for Watson's book.

" From yours sincerely,   J. C. Brooke."

29. Mr. Gough to Mr. Brooke.

" Dear Sir,   *Enfield, July* 14, 1778.
" What Millar is made a Baronet? Is it Mr. Millar, of Bath Easton, the chief of modern *beaux esprits,* who certainly should have the famous urn for an augmentation; or Sir John Millar, of Sussex, my *quondam* proud fellow-collegian; or some unpresuming Hibernian of Ballicasey? for all these are competitors for the bloody hand, if we believe the newspapers.

" Yours truly,   R. Gough."

30. Mr. Brooke to Mr. Gough.

" Dear Sir,   *Heralds'-college, July* 16, 1778.
" The Millar created an Irish Baronet is, I believe, of that kingdom; the docket of his patent has not yet been brought here to be registered, and therefore I can give you no further information. Your fellow-collegian was a Baronet by birth, and of course could have no reason to accept another title.

" I have received from Mr. Dade a drawing of Aldborough Church, with sketches of different Saxon fragments in the building; may I venture to have them engraved without a further order of Council?

" I shall be going into Yorkshire in about a month's time or

---

* Mr. Colebrooke's " Observations on a Coin of Robert Earl of Gloucester" occur in vol. IV. of the Archæologia, pp. 132—141; Mr. Pegge's paper was inserted in vol. V. pp. 390—415, under the title of, " The Penny with the name of Rodbertus IV. asserted to Robert Duke of Normandy; and other matters relative to the English Coinage occasionally discussed."

less. An aunt of mine is on a visit at Crowland in Lincolnshire, and I shall call upon her there in my way, and shall have
a good opportunity of seeing the place. Mr. Scribo, the Rector,
at whose house my aunt is, says he has a large collection of
curiosities, which have been dug up there of late years.

" From yours sincerely,   J. C. BROOKE."

---

31. " DEAR SIR,   *Heralds'-college, Aug.* 5, 1778.
" On Saturday morning, six o'clock, King Bigland, with
three heralds and two antient damsels of Mr. Dore's acquaintance, set out for his seat at Badgemore, where we shall stay
till Wednesday. We shall arrive there by dinner time. On
Sunday morning go to Henley Church ; in the afternoon to
Sir Thomas Stapleton's, at Rotherfield Greys, to see his antient
house, and the monument of the old Earl of Banbury and his
Countess, of infamous memory, in the Church, which I am told
is one of the finest in England, but going to ruin. On Monday to Ewelme, where several of the Delapoles are buried ; a
seat they acquired by marriage with the granddaughter and
heir of Chaucer the Poet. (Vincent on Brooke, p. 503.)

" Yours sincerely,   J. C. BROOKE."

---

32. Mr. GOUGH to Mr. BROOKE.

" DEAR SIR,   *Enfield, Aug.* 20, 1778.
" Many thanks for your circumstantial account of your Tour.
I long to discourse with you about it, and to see your notes, &c.
for which purpose I invite you to spend a long day here, either
next Sunday, or any other day that suits you.
" I propose a jaunt into Bedfordshire for a day or two, as
usual, in a week or a fortnight's time ; and if you give me your
company, we may take some church notes at least.
" I am greatly disappointed in Hasted's book, both history and
prints ; the latter are dreadful. What says Dr. Ducarel to it ?
" We had some of his colleagues here yesterday with Robert
Bishop of London, to consecrate our new church-yard. They
took Shoreditch in their way ; and did the like good office there.

" Yours, &c.   R. GOUGH."

---

33. Mr. BROOKE to Mr. GOUGH.

" DEAR SIR,   *Heralds'-college, Sept.* 15, 1778.
" I returned from Christchurch on Monday, after a most
delightful journey through Hampshire to Winchester, Christchurch, Merley, Standlinch, Salisbury, Stonehenge, Old Sarum,
&c. and of course could not meet you at Forster's I intend
setting out for Yorkshire in a week's time ; but will spend a day
with you before I go, in order to compare my collections while
fresh in my memory. Yours sincerely,   J. C. BROOKE."

34. " DEAR SIR, *Heralds'-college, Sept.* 21, 1778.

" I received your letter; but as I shall leave town on Wednesday or Thursday for Yorkshire, I cannot possibly do myself the pleasure of waiting on you before I go. I shall take the rough copy of your Yorkshire with me, together with my papers, and will finish what I can of it there, and send it up in franks to Mr. Harrison; and at the same time will write to you when to send for it to the office. A packet will be sent to me by him every week; if you want to send me a single letter, please to direct at Mrs. Brooke's, Silver-street, Wakefield, Yorkshire.

" Yours, &c.   J. C. BROOKE."

---

35. Mr. GOUGH to Mr. BROOKE.

" DEAR SIR, *Enfield, Oct.* 21, 1778.

" When you consider that upwards of eight sheets of Topography (for so much does Yorkshire take up) are waiting your corrections, you will not think me importunate in soliciting their release from a confinement of now almost a month. I suppose you have received most of them; though, when I called on Mr. Harrison, with a packet for you from Dr. Nash, a fortnight ago, he was out of town. The first sheet of Worcestershire was sent me last Saturday; and I am in great hopes so fair a beginning will have a good end. The Doctor earnestly entreats your aid in the pedigrees *. Yours, &c. R. GOUGH."

---

36. Mr. BROOKE to Mr. GOUGH.

" DEAR SIR, *Northgate, Wakefield, Oct.* 31, 1778.

" I received the favour of your letter; and am extremely sorry it has not been in my power to finish your Yorkshire Topography, nor can I till my return to town, which I hope will be within a fortnight, and then it shall be my first business.

" I have been extremely happy in making antiquarian surveys of this county since my arrival, and have collected large materials. The Churches in these parts afford many more curiosities than those in the southern counties, which may be accounted for from the more people of wealth, which, by reason of the manufactories, have resided here. I have collected such a variety of crosses, that I propose having a portfolio on purpose for them; and I think such a collection may hereafter be of much use. Crosses are often found over incumbents in churches, where there is nothing else worth observation; and by comparing the form of those without dates with those that have them, their ages may be nearly ascertained; and then the dates of the erection of Churches, and different parts of them, may be the better discovered. From yours sincerely,   J. C. BROOKE."

* See before, p. 348.

37. " Dear Sir,   *Heralds'-college, Nov.* 20, 1778.

" I am returned from the country, after one of the most agreeable tours I ever yet had, loaded with antiquities ; and (to use Christie's expressive phrase) ready to burst with health. I shall be glad to know what you have done with your Yorkshire Topography; whether the press is yet standing, or you defer my observations till the Appendix, as I am ready to give you any assistance. I am, yours sincerely,   J. C. Brooke."

---

38. Mr. Gough to Mr. Brooke.

" Dear Sir,   *Enfield, Nov.* 21, 1778.

" I am glad to find you are at last returned so able and willing to assist your friends. I was going to have renewed my expostulations, but you have disarmed me. The Topography is all in your room; and you will oblige me by dispatching it altogether to Mr. Nichols as soon as you have done with it; you have full power over it.

" Dr. Nash has a demand on you for pedigrees. Walsh's has waited your return; and if not on your table, may be had at Nichols's. Pray God send that neither war nor installation may interrupt your lucubrations on this side Christmas.

" Whenever you want a mouthful of country air, you will find a well-aired bed here. Yours truly,   R. Gough."

---

39. Mr. Brooke to Mr. Gough.

" Dear Sir,   *Heralds'-college, Nov.* 25, 1778.

" I have nearly finished all your Topography in my hands; and have sent the paper on Mary d'Este's seal corrected, and directed to you at Nichols's. I have written to Mr. Neate to inform him you will call on him about the papers on Fitz-Walter's seal.

" I dine in company with Mr. Currer to-day; and will, with your permission, leave the Topography in his hands for a day, in order for him to look it over.

" Mr. Bartlett called this morning; I have settled with him about his Prelatical Coins. He desires you would look in your copy of Warwickshire, by Thomas, to see if any additions there in MSS. to the articles of Manceter, Hartishill, Oldbury, and Atherston.

" *Nov.* 26. I deferred sending this last night, to give you an account of the Society. A full meeting; no Vice-president; Sir John Cope in the chair; a Survey of the Palace of Nonsuch, anno 1650 *, read; and a paper (I think, for I only heard a part) proving that Bulls were sacrificed in Wales in the sixteenth

---

* Printed in the Archæologia, vol. V. pp. 429—439.

century; something from Sir William Hamilton at Naples. Attended the King to the House to-day; approaching wars and tumults; dine with a large antiquarian party at Brander's to-morrow. Yours, &c.   J. C. BROOKE."

40. Mr. GOUGH to Mr. BROOKE.

" DEAR SIR,   *Enfield, Nov.* 26, 1778.

" If I should come to town (as I probably may) next Monday, ot elect a new President in Crane-court, can I meet you at Mr. Nichols's, rather before eleven ; or, if I get away in time from the anniversary dinner, will you spend the evening with me at Mr. Pugh's, or any half-way place that you may fix upon? I wish to see you; but know not how it will be in my power to call on you without this sort of appointment.

" I delivered six of Fitz-Walter's seal and your paper, to Mr. Neate this morning, by favour of an exceedingly fine day.

" This being delayed, in expectation of hearing from you, which I did to-day, I write to authorise you to take from Mr. Nichols the remainder of Yorkshire; I have no other objection to your laying it before Mr. Currer than that it is not in a fit condition to be seen by him, and I must beg he will not keep it long. Yours truly,   R. GOUGH."

41. Mr. BROOKE to Mr. GOUGH.

" DEAR SIR,   *Heralds'-college, Dec.* 7, 1778.

" I have finished the remainder of your Topography, but shall be glad to see the revise. I also send you the pedigree of Walsh corrected, but cannot say I approve Dr. Nash's plan; the introducing the Stonor pedigree, an Oxfordshire family, merely because a daughter and heir was married to the Walsh's, is unnecessary; and the connecting the Blount family thereto, because they married a daughter, who was no heiress, more so. The Blounts are an antient family in the county; and their pedigree should be introduced at large under their estate at Sod-dington, which they still possess, and not in this place. As Sheldesley-Walsh was the antient seat of the family, I should have recommended the former part of the pedigree to have been placed there ; and speaking of Walter, fourth son of John, ancestor of the Abberley line, said, ' Walter Walsh, fourth son, ancestor of the Abberley line, which see,' — then, under Abberley, introduce the pedigree from Walter to Bromley; by this means the pedigree would be quite complete, the descent of the estates shown under their different heads, and the pedigrees might have been introduced in the common folio size of the book, without folding sheets, which I imagine would save expense.

" Pray have you got a spare copy of Domesday Book for Dor-

setshire? I am collecting all the Domesdays I can, as I propose
gathering anecdotes for a history of the Normans, mentioned
therein, and the Saxons, their under-tenants, as far as they can
be obtained; which, I think, will elucidate the Conquest, and
the state of the Anglo-Saxons before that event.

" Mr. Bowle called upon me this morning; is come to town
for a fortnight. He will be at the Society on Thursday night;
and has got some anecdotes of Wiltshire Topography for you,
if the press is not yet broken up. Yours, &c. J. C. Brooke."

---

42. " Dear Sir,   *Heralds'-college, Dec.* 9, 1778.
" I have received a letter from Dr. Nash, requesting I would
draw out his pedigrees, for which he shall be obliged to me *,
&c. and propose returning him for answer, that it is quite inconsistent for me to keep employing myself for other people's
advantage, and neglecting my own; and that I cannot possibly
think of engaging in such a troublesome undertaking.

" On Thursday the 3d, nothing new was produced at the
Society but instructions to Clarencieux King of Arms, temp.
Henry VIII. when sent Ambassador to Scotland; and four large
prints lately published by Green, *viz.* views of Ragland, Ludlow,
Wigmore, and Brampton-Bryan Castles, in aquatinta.

" I called on Hearne this week, who showed me all the views
he took in his late tour, which are numerous and very beautiful; chiefly of ruins in Scotland. I find he travels with Sir
George Beaumont, a young Leicestershire Baronet, who has a
great taste for drawing; last year they went with themselves,
but this year Sir George took his lady; they travel in his post-
coach and four, her maid and one footman, and were out two
months. I have promised to draw out an account of Lumley
Castle for him in his next number.

" *Dec.* 14. On Thursday the 10th, a tolerably good meeting;
read Pegge's letter to you on a Danish instrument, and a
curious paper relative to an antient Vicar of Warfield, Berks.
Mr. Brooke, of Colney Hatch, was there; he and Mr. Neate propose giving you a morning call. After the Society broke up,
he, Bowle, Topham, and self, retired to Richards's coffee-house,
and had an agreeable evening. Bowle has given me his notes
on Wiltshire Topography for you.

" Mr. Norris complains that the Society was never at so low
an ebb for matter as at present; he is nearly a perfect bankrupt. Pray can you furnish anything? I am too much engaged to attend to such matters at this time. I have the pleasure to inform you, that Evans is going to re-publish Tanner's
Notitia Monastica, price £.1. 10s. Peck's Desiderata has answered to him very well †. Yours sincerely, J. C. Brooke."

43. Mr. Gough to Mr. Brooke.

" Dear Sir,   *Enfield, Dec. 11, 1778.*

" I received your remaining additions to the Topography, for which I am obliged to you: but they are so numerous that types can hardly be found to compose those in the two first sheets. As soon as the revises are finished you shall see them.

" The following is an extract of a letter from Dr. Nash, December 6:

" ' I have written to Mr. Brooke by this post, to beg his assist-ance in the heraldical part; and that he would permit Mr. Nichols to send him the sheets for correction. When you see him, 1 wish you would forward my request.'

" I suppose you will answer for yourself, whether you will undertake the heraldical part; I assure you I will not. I be-lieve the pedigrees were drawn by Abingdon; but such altera-tions as you recommend should be made in the MS. and you should tell Dr. Nash so. Pray let me hear what passes in Chan-cery-lane, if not too much trouble for you to make minutes.

         " Yours truly,   R. Gough."

---

44. " Dear Sir,   *Enfield, Dec. 18, 1778.*

" I think your answer to Dr. Nash a very proper one; and if you will allow me to second you, I would advise him to apply to you officially, or on such reasonable terms as you are enti-titled to for your trouble, for I should be sorry his book should want any of the improvements that you, or any other antiquary, can furnish.

" I understood my name was given in to Peck; but I have heard nothing of the book. If these kind of things answer to booksellers, they will not to the public. Few people will give their notes to booksellers; and Tanner is capable of a great many. And yet, on the other hand, who will undertake re-pub-lications without a bookseller? Yours truly,   R. Gough."

---

45. " Dear Sir,   *Enfield, Jan. 3, 1779.*

" I forego my twelfth-cake to dine with the Dean* next Wed-nesday. If you are not better engaged, will you come and eat your supper with me at nine.

" Thank you for the revisal of Yorkshire hitherto. You will soon receive your last notes.

" Does the College of Arms survive the storm which ushered in the present year? and is not one Sibylline leaf of Vincent, Glover, Dugdale, and a long &c. blown out of the library into the Thames?

" Many returns to you of the present season. May you con-tinue and improve the labours of your predecessors with hap-

* Jeremiah Milles, D. D. Dean of Exeter.

pier prospects; and may you reign a King in the bright fields
of blazonry, and, when you eat viands, not deny them to your
officers!   Yours truly,   R. GOUGH."

46. " DEAR SIR,   *Enfield, Jan.* 8, 1779.
" I saw the Exeter Penates at the Dean's; a very pretty
desert, to be dished up ere long for an evening entertainment *.
" When was Queen Catharine Parr born, and married to her
first and fourth husbands? and when did her second, John
Nevill, Lord Latimer, die?   R. GOUGH."

47. Mr. BROOKE to Mr. GOUGH.
" DEAR SIR,   *Heralds'-college, Jan.* 11, 1779.
" A thin meeting of the Society on Thursday; read a paper
concerning the Picts Wall; and Barrington to Blackstone on
the Antiquity of Clocks and Watches†.   Brander produced a
silver vessel found in cleansing his river at Christ Church.
" I have no particulars relating to Catharine Parr but what
are in my paper on her seal; though at that time I took much
pains to collect fresh matter concerning her, but without success. In Vincent 31, in Coll. Arm. is a copy at large of the
will of John Lord Latimer, her second husband, dated Sept. 12,
1542, proved 11th March following, whereby it should seem he
died between those periods.   See my paper on Kirkdale.
" I wish you joy of your new relation at Perry-hall; as I
know it will give you pleasure to be informed, that your cousin
has not degraded the blood of the Goughs by an inferior alliance ‡.
I must tell you the lady is of a very antient house.   Her ancestor,
Henry Mytton, of Shipton, Esq. registered his pedigree at the
Visitation of Salop, 1623, and a descendant again at that in
1663.   Nineteen generations of the male line are entered.
" I shall spend the day to-morrow with the old party at Mr.
Brander's, who has promised to put into my hands all his cop-
per-plates to have impressions taken of them; and I shall save
you a set.   Yours, &c.   J. C. BROOKE."

48. " DEAR SIR,   *Heralds'-college, Jan.* 29, 1779.
" A prodigiously full meeting at the Society on Thursday;
nothing new but a letter from Strange relative to Pavements,
and other Roman remains, found in Wales §.   Forster produced

* An Account of some Roman Penates discovered at Exeter, by Dean
Milles, Pres. A. S. are printed in Archæologia, vol. VI. p. 1.
† Printed in the Archæologia, vol. V. pp. 416—428.
‡ Mr. Brooke was not aware that Miss Mytton's grandmother had been
a Gough, her husband's own aunt.   There were three marriages between
the Goughs and Myttons; see the pedigree in the History of Staffordshire,
vol. II. p. 188.
§ Printed in the Archæologia, vol. VI. pp. 6—38.   It was in addition
to some former papers by Mr. Strange on the same subjects; see the
memoir of him in the " Literary Anecdotes," vol. VIII. p. 10.

an elegant gold snuff-box, a present to him from the King of Spain, with his own ugly Royal phiz set with brilliants at the top.

" I have finished the Walsh pedigree; and desire you will give Nichols directions to let me see as much of Worcestershire as is printed. I propose writing soon to Dr. Nash.

" We dine a large party at Claxton's on Thursday; cannot you come and meet us? Excuse haste, for I am going to spend the evening at Topham's chambers, to meet Russell and Parson Brooke, to hear strictures on the conduct of Henry III. and encomiums on Montfort, whom he, Russell, doubts not he shall prove the greatest patriot that ever this nation produced*.

" Yours, &c.   J. C. BROOKE."

49. " DEAR SIR.   *Heralds'-college, Feb.* 13, 1779.

" Adam Cleypole, of Narborough in Northamptonshire, grand-father of John who married Oliver's daughter, had a fifth son, called Henry, who I suppose was the person you inquire after. Narborough lies between Peterborough and Deeping; the family had a fine old house there, now belonging to Earl Fitzwilliam, which I saw in 1774.

" At the Society on Thursday was read a further portion of Strange's paper; and Dean Milles produced the Exeter Penates and read a paper on them.

" Dr. Nash has been in town a day or two on some family business, but leaves it to-day. We had some conversation on our affair, which you shall know when we meet.

" From yours sincerely,   J. C. BROOKE."

50. " DEAR SIR,   *April* 15, 1779.

" The inclosed petition has been put into my hands by our porter's son for my interest, for his being a settled man, or pen-sioner, of the Goldsmiths' Company. In a list of the Court of Assistants I observe your friend Mr. Thorne is one; can you with propriety mention the name to him?

" Old Mr. Pegge is in town; I met him to dinner at Mr. Brander's yesterday, and he is in perfect health. He set out for Canterbury for ten days this morning, and on his return will be a fortnight at Lambeth. He has brought up a most elaborate and entertaining account of antient Cookery, including William the Conqueror's boxing Fitz-Osborne's ears for sending up a crane half roasted, and other curious matters.

" From yours sincerely,   J. C. BROOKE."

51. " DEAR SIR,   *Heralds'-college, April* 26, 1779.

" After I left you on Saturday, I went to Lord de Ferrars, and was shewn by him one of the most magnificent works that I

---

* Mr. Russell's memoirs were afterwards inserted in the History of Leicestershire; see vol. III. of this Work, p. 748.

Imagine was ever executed in this kingdom, a History and Pedigree of the Howard Family, in a large folio volume, containing
near 600 folios of vellum, elegantly written and most beautifully
illuminated, which seems to have been done for the Earl of
Northampton temp. Car. I., and is said then to have cost
upwards of £.1000, bound in crimson velvet richly embossed
with silver gilt. It contains all the family monuments painted
in their proper colours in so highly a finished manner that each
figure might deserve a frame, particularly those at Framlingham;
all those engraved in Weever, and a fine collection of portraits
of the Mowbrays and Howards from the windows of Long Melford Church in Suffolk, and many others which I never heard
of before, and too numerous to recite to you; but what occasions my informing you of this is, to acquaint you that there
is a representation of the tomb of the second Duke of Norfolk,
who died in 1524, and of whose funeral I see you take particular notice in Thetford *, set up at that place, and which was
brought to Lambeth, and laid in Howards' Chapel when Thetford Abbey was destroyed; it represents his effigy in brass cumbent, with the arms, but no inscription. If you choose to have
this engraved, it will not only do for Thetford, but, on being
retouched, for your Monum. Angl. also; and his Lordship commissioned me to inform you, that you should be welcome to send
any person to make draughts from it.   There are also two other
brasses for Duchesses of Norfolk at Lambeth, now destroyed;
so rich and sumptuous, that your Joyce Tiptoft at Enfield will
appear an orange-wench to them. The brasses are done with
gold, lackered over in such a manner that they appear exactly
like the real metal, and then the lines in black are traced
upon it †.
  " The book was done by Henry Lilly, Rouge-dragon Pursuivant, who died 1638, (and lies buried in Farnham Church near
Bishop Stortford, Herts, where is his monument,) and seems never
to have been in possession of the Howard family, for by a note
it appears, that it was bought of Lilly's heirs for £.100 by
Compton, Earl of Northampton, temp. Car. II. merely because
it had been done for an Earl of Northampton, and it now belongs to the present Earl, but they have thoughts of offering
it to the Norfolk family for their purchase.
  " The late Duke of Norfolk is said to have employed Vertue
to copy the effigies, &c. but what became of his drawings I have
not heard.
  " Lord de Ferrars, who is a most ingenious young man, of
his own motion lamented the want we have of a history of
monuments in this kingdom; and upon my mentioning your
collections to him, was quite charmed with the idea ‡.   When

* History of Thetford, p. 122.
† None of these monuments, it is believed, have ever been engraved.
‡ This passage is interesting as being an early notice of a nobleman,

you next come to town, I will introduce you to him, and you may then see this book, with which I conclude you will be much delighted. From yours sincerely,   J. C. BROOKE."

52. Mr. GOUGH to Mr. BROOKE.

" DEAR SIR,   *Enfield, July* 28, 1779.

" Mr. Cole has sent me an introduction to Dr. Bernard at Wethersfield, whom he says we must visit in our way into Suffolk ; and we must also dine with a party of Cambridge antiquaries at his (Mr. C.'s) house.

" I really hardly know how to engage myself to either. I would compound for an Essex tour round from Dunmow, &c. to Colchester, doubting your possibility of compassing a Suffolk one this season any more than the last, though I hope and trust you will try for it. Yours, &c.   R. GOUGH."

53. Mr. BROOKE to Mr. GOUGH.

" DEAR SIR,   *Heralds'-college, Aug.* 9, 1779.

" I congratulate you on having got Claines * through the press, of which I have been most heartily tired. I have received no more copy from Dr. Nash. Nichols has got all under the letter C. I lately wrote to the Doctor, to inform him of the terms upon which he must expect me to proceed in his work, but hitherto have had no answer. I should be glad to have two impressions of your plate of Crosses for Thetford, one for myself, the other for the young man that engraves them for me, that he may endeavour to imitate Basire's antique style.

" A letter lately from Dr. Kaye at Brighthelmstone, who has had the misfortune again to lame himself, and is confined, but will be in Nottinghamshire in September, and I shall stay a day or two with him in my way into Yorkshire ; and hope to see Hardwick, Welbeck, &c.

" By a letter from the Rev. Mr. Dade, of Barmeston, co. Eb. he says, he shall shortly have in the press a History of Bridlington and the adjacent country ; and talks of sending up drawings for me to give Basire to engrave †. Mrs. Jenkins, of Yorkshire, heir to the estate of the late Sir Job Brooke, Bart. the lunatic, lately died, and has made Mr. Dade one of her executors and residuary legatee, by which he gets a considerable fortune. I see in the Cumberland papers that my old friend Mr. West, author of the History of Furness, died last month.

who afterwards became, when Earl of Leicester, President of the Society of Antiquaries.
   * In the History of Worcestershire.
   † This work was not completed ; see the memoir of Mr. Dade in the " Literary Anecdotes," vol. VIII. pp. 474.

" One of the old women, who I told you had their life-estates
in that which lately fell to me, is dead since I saw you, by which
I now enter into her moiety of it.

" From yours, &c.   J. C. Brooke."

---

54. " Dear Sir,   *Heralds'-college, Sept.* 6, 1779.

" I propose setting out on my northern tour on Thursday
morning early, and shall be absent till the middle of November.

" I have promised Dr. Nash to go on with his book to the
end of letter C; and have desired him to furnish Nichols with
covers for me for that purpose. The remainder of his copy I
have returned to Nichols, as likewise two engraved plates of
Droitwich seals and Dudley Priory, and two impressions of seals
in sulphur, which I suppose the Doctor means to have engraved;
and I have referred him to you for instructions on that head.
By letter from Dr. Percy on Friday, I find he is going this week
on a visit to Dr. Nash.

" I shall go first into Huntingdonshire, and, after staying
a day or two, shall proceed to my relation Dr. Disney, at Flintham near Newark, from whence I hope to make an excursion
to Bottesford, where the Rutland family bury, which Sir John
Cullum speaks so highly of. From Flintham Dr. Disney is to
escort me across Nottingham Forest to Dr. Kaye's at Kirkby (see
the Doctor's map); and by the way I shall hope to pay my
respects to a Duchess of Norfolk, who lies buried under a fine
tomb in Hoveringham Church; and from Kirkby into Yorkshire.

" When you come to Hill Cromb, please to insert that
George-William, Earl of Coventry, is the present Lord; and, if
I have time, will copy out some inquisitions, and other charters
relating to Cotheridge, which you will please to interweave into
the history of that manor.

" I remain, yours sincerely,   J. C. Brooke."

---

55. " Dear Sir,   *Heralds'-college, Dec.* 12, 1779.

" I returned to town last week, after one of the most agreeable excursions I have ever yet had. I left London the beginning of September for Huntingdonshire, where I stayed a week
with my sister; but I have already, in various journeys, so
thoroughly surveyed that neighbourhood, that nothing in the
topographical way occurred new to me there. From Buckworth I went to Flintham-hall, near Newark, to visit Dr. Disney, who is married to a relation of mine *. Here I staid a week,
and spent it very agreeably; during that time we made several
excursions into Nottinghamshire, Lincolnshire, and Leicestershire. In the second county I was much pleased with Norton

---

* Jane, daughter of Rev. Archdeacon Blackburne.

Disney Church, the ancient burial place of the Doctor's family, where are several curious monuments for them, I think six in different styles. You will find the inscriptions, but they are erroneously taken, in your quarto book of Lincolnshire Church-notes *.

" From Flintham I also went to visit Belvoir Castle and Bottesford. I took an account of all the antique arms in the former, which has nearly been stripped of all its furniture and pictures ; but, though the Rutland family are now so poorly lodged when living, the state and magnificence of their habitation when dead will amply compensate for it, for at Bottesford is the finest collection of monuments for one family that I ever saw in England : two tombs for the Albinis, two for the Lords Roos, and eight magnificent monuments for the eight first Earls of Rutland, with the effigies of themselves and wives cumbent, all in good repair, and some of them of fine sculpture. Two are in the centre and three against each wall, the two Rooses on each side the altar, which entirely fill up the chancel, on the floor of which are two brasses of priests †.

" From Flintham I crossed the Trent ; saw Hoveringham Church, where is an altar tomb with their effigies for Sir Robert Gousill and a Duchess of Norfolk, his wife (see Thoroton, Dugdale under the Earls of Arundel, Sandford, &c.) and a Saxon porch with a curious bas-relief of St. Michael and the dragon ; and crossed Nottingham Forest to Dr. Kaye's at Kirkby, where I stayed a fortnight. The Doctor had unfortunately lamed himself, and could not stir out ; but Grimm, who was with him some months, the Doctor's butler, who is very intelligent, and myself, made an expedition out every morning to survey the country, and either returned to a late dinner, or took provisions with us, and Grimm made drawings of every thing curious ; in these rides we saw Newstead Abbey, Felley and Beauvalle Priories, Hardwick House, Wingfield and Bolsover Castles in Derbyshire, another Hardwick, an antient seat of the Talbots Earls of Salop, where Wolsey was confined, in Nottinghamshire, and all the neighbouring churches within a day's ride. I must in this place inform you, that Dr. Kaye has by Grimm a most invaluable collection of elegant drawings, to the amount, I dare say, of upwards of 1200, of ruins, monuments, curious trees, churches, views, &c. in the counties of Nottingham, Derby, Durham, York, and Northumberland, all taken under his own inspection.

* An ample pedigree of the Disney family, with the epitaphs, &c. illustrative of it, were communicated by Dr. Disney, to the new edition of Hutchins's Dorsetshire, see vol. IV. p. 389—398. See also Gough's Sepulchral Monuments, vol. I. pp. cix, cxxii.

† All the *early* monuments to the memory of these distinguished families were engraved in Mr. Nichols's " History of Leicestershire ; " who expected that the later monuments would have been presented to that work by the Rutland family, but the minority of the present Duke, at that time, prevented it.

I mention this that you may record it; few people in these days having spirit sufficient to be at the expense of such works. I mentioned to the Doctor how happy it would make you to survey them; but he said that could only be done by your visiting him in Nottinghamshire, where he should be glad to see you, but never thought of removing them from thence. Major Rooke, who lives at Mansfield, was much with us at Kirkby, and in some of our tours. The Doctor lives in an elegant style, and keeps a most hospitable house.

" From Kirkby I went to Mansfield, and so into Yorkshire, where I found all my friends well, and stayed seven weeks. I could do but little in the antiquarian way there, my time being much taken up with regulating my affairs, occasioned by my late accession of property. I have got an excellent old stone house, built by my great-great-great-grandfather Brooke, in the year 1648, as by the date and his initials over the door, who gave it with the estate to a younger son, the last of whose branch entailed it upon me, in failure of issue of his heir-at-law, who died in May last, 1766.

" From Wakefield I came to Southwell, co. Nottinghamshire, to visit Dr. Kaye again, who is now keeping his three months' Prebendal residence there. Here I staid a fortnight; but the severity of the weather prevented any longer expeditions than to the neighbouring churches; however, I have taken a complete survey of the antient collegiate Church at Southwell, which is a fine pile of Saxon architecture in excellent preservation; and I must observe, that I never saw so many remains of antient buildings as are retained in the churches in Nottingham and Derbyshires, which I fancy is owing to the goodness of the stone. There is scarce a church but has either a Saxon porch or other tracery; and in three or four I discovered curious bas-reliefs, which I have drawn.

" From the residence I have made in Nottinghamshire this summer, I have obtained so much information relative to families, descent of property, &c. that I could, with little trouble, continue Thoroton to the present time; but, as it would answer no end to communicate such notes to a printer, I must reserve them in MSS. for my own copy of that work. I must observe that we took the book with us in our expeditions; and, by comparing the plates with the originals, find them all incorrect, and some flagrantly different.

" Yours sincerely,   J. C. Brooke."

---

56. Mr. Gough to Mr. Brooke.

" Dear Sir,   *Enfield, Dec.* 20, 1779.
" I received your letter from the country, and should have answered had any thing occurred worth troubling you with; and had your last come to hand before last Thursday, I should

have answered that sooner, though not by meeting you at the Society, where I shall hardly be this year.

" I accompanied Mr. and Mrs. Tyson to Earls Colne, and he went on to Sir John Cullum's, and to Wingfield, where, and on his route, he has made some admirable drawings of monuments, &c. of which hereafter.

" I intended calling on you yesterday, or asking you to meet me in Ivy-lane, but I had hardly time to take care of myself, and must therefore take my chance of calling on you some morning about eleven, to gratify my impatience to see your three field books. I hope you have materials to furnish several papers on Saxon antiquities, to feed the famished flock in Chancery-lane, who will go with hungry bellies into their new fold *.

" The room over the lantern at Ely was found on fire by a carpenter passing through the church late. He gave the alarm, tore up the flaming boards, and threw them down into the church, and so saved the whole. Yours, &c.   R. GOUGH."

---

57. Mr. BROOKE to Mr. GOUGH.

" DEAR SIR,   *Heralds'-college, Dec. 22, 1779.*
" The eight views for Hearne's two next numbers are, Hospital of St. Cross near Winchester, two of Malmesbury Abbey, two of Melrose Abbey, Lanercost Priory, Kelso Monastery, and Edinburgh Castle. Lanercost I have drawn up for him. Can you point out to him authorities from whence he can extract little histories of the rest? it will be a kind act to an ingenious man. Yours sincerely,   J. C. BROOKE."

---

58. Mr. GOUGH to Mr. BROOKE.

" DEAR SIR,   *Enfield, Feb. 12, 1780.*
" I have assisted Mr. Hearne, as far as I can, by the loan of the History of Winchester and Melrose Abbey; but, touching Malmesbury, I have nothing new to say. Yours truly, R. G."

---

59. " DEAR SIR,   *Enfield, March 9, 1780.*
" I beg your pardon for so long detaining your MSS. The Neville paper would make an excellent supplement to Mr. Pegge's Cookery Book, which is still open to receive it. If you give it to the Society, there is a chance whether they print it; they certainly will not make up another volume soon. Let me advise you, therefore, to draw up an introduction, and send it to Mr. Nichols, or reserve it till Mr. Pegge comes to town at Easter †. Yours truly,   R. GOUGH."

* The Society of Antiquaries was about to move into Somerset House.
† See hereafter, p. 393.

60. Mr. Brooke to Mr. Gough.

" Dear Sir,   Heralds'-college, March 14, 1780.

" By Mr. Browne's death we all mount a step higher; Mr.
Dore, as Senior Herald, succeeds to the vacant kingdom. I hear
Browne has died extremely rich *.

" A monument has been put up lately in the cloister of Christ's
Hospital for your friend Mr. Misenor, thus inscribed :

" Here lies
Thomas Misenor, Esq.
He died May the 28th, 1779,
Aged 51.

" It is against the wall, east cloister, plain white marble, no
arms. From yours sincerely,   J. C. Brooke."

---

61. Mr. Gough to Mr. Brooke.

" Dear Sir,   Enfield, March 26, 1780.

" At Patterson's, Tuesday noon, will be sold sundry papers
relating to Norfolk and Suffolk, deeds with seals, a Howard pedigree, *cum multis aliis.* If you are not better employed, I shall be
obliged to you to look at them; and, if not wanted by yourself,
buy them for me at what you think they are worth, within reasonable bounds. Just call on Nichols in your way about them,
that he may attend if you cannot.

" I understand the last Boteler of the Woodhall family is the
incumbent of Wotton; or, if he has any elder brother, I think
he is a fox-hunting 'squire, and not in a military or naval
department; but more of both questions hereafter.

" How is the Society fallen! for want of a Parker, or a Whit-
gift, or some *mere* (for which we should read *rare*) antiquary to
patronise it. Of all my expected party only Dr. Lort adjourned
to Dick's; and he run away to Lambeth at ten.

" Marriage of Henry V. and Catharine of France, by Diepenbeck ? if fantastic, or of the time ? Yours truly,   R. G."

---

62. Mr. Brooke to Mr. Gough.

" Dear Sir,   Heralds'-college, March 29, 1780.

" Agreeably to your desire, I called at Patterson's; but only
receiving your letter on Monday night, I had not time to look
over half the things you mentioned, and therefore left it to Mr.
Nichols's judgment to buy for you as he saw the lots cheap.
Mr. Bartlett wanted some of the lots of deeds. The three lots
of Norfolk and Suffolk papers consisted of so large a number
of papers each, that it would have taken a day to have examined them. The marriage of Henry V. and Catharine, by

* See the particulars in Noble's "History of the College of Arms."

Diepenbeck, was a very beautiful drawing, in the dresses of the time. Mr. Bartlett thought it would go dear; have you got it?

" I spent Saturday morning with Mr. Ord, to look over his impressions from brasses, which are curiously done; and he has a large collection. The manner in which he does them is this: He has French paper damped, and kept in a tincase made on purpose to keep it so, printer's ink in a bottle, and a quantity of rags; he inks the brass, and then wipes it very clean, lays on the paper, covers it with a cloth, and treads upon it, and takes the impression; and he has a man at home to finish them up with printer's ink where the lines have failed; he then cuts out the figure, and pastes them into a large portfolio, with blue paper leaves, large enough to contain a figure six feet high; and you cannot imagine how beautiful they appear. He has lately been a tour into Oxfordshire, and has taken the Chaucers, of which I gave you a slight sketch; and several priests at Ewelme, Lord Grey of Rotherfield at Greys, others at Dorchester, Henley, Marlow, Hambledon, &c. I think he talked of having some duplicates for you and Sir John Cullum. He met with one Richards, an ingenious man, a coach-painter at Ewelme, who has drawn him all the stone effigies at Dorchester, and offered to make a complete drawing of Alice de la Pole's fine monument at Ewelme for £.10. 10s. If you will appoint some morning I will accompany you to look over his collections.

" I suppose you have seen the various paragraphs of newspaper wit which have been thrown out for this week past upon the great loss of the Dean of Carlisle's library *.

"Captain Boteler, of the Ardent, I am told, is a younger brother of the vendor of Woodhall.

" From yours sincerely,   J. C. BROOKE."

---

63. " DEAR SIR,   *Heralds'-college, April 22,* 1780.

" By a letter from Mr. Manning yesterday, I find he is well, and far advanced in his History of Surrey.

" Mr. Pegge senior called on Friday, and stayed with me some time. He is by all allowed to be in much better health and spirits than for many years past; we dine together to-morrow at Mr. Brander's. He has got Sir John Nevill's accounts to look over; both Mr. Brander and Dr. Kaye wish them to be printed; and I have drawn up a long history of the parties to accompany it. The book I find is printed; but it is to be in an appendix †. Mr. Pegge thinks them very curious.

" Dr. Nash called on Friday, and has of late been much indisposed; he seems resolved now not to publish the first volume till the whole is completed.

" Yours sincerely,   J. C. BROOKE."

* Dr. Percy's library was damaged by a fire at Northumberland House.
† This was done accordingly; see Pegge's " Forme of Cury," 163—188.

64. " Dear Sir,   Heralds'-college, May 30, 1780.

" I herewith send you my book of Crosses, of which you may make what use you please, so you return it to me safe. I likewise inclose you drawings of three escutcheons for the centre of your chimney-piece * ; if you will inform me of the names of the other eight worthies who you intend to honour by placing their insignia thereon, they shall be drawn for you. No. 1 is your own arms quartering Hynde. As you inherited landed property from your mother, I think it will be but a proper mark of respect to her memory to quarter her arms somewhere; and I think you have never hitherto done it. The Littletons of Pillaton quarter the Royal arms, through the match of an ancestor with the co-heir of Devereux, who had married the co-heir of Bourchier Earl of Essex, who had married the co-heir of Thomas of Woodstock, Duke of Gloucester, son of Edward III. Sir Edward Littleton bears his arms in this manner on his coach, which I have seen several times this winter in town; and would advise you to have them painted in the same way, as it will thereby denote your descent from the blood Royal, some few drops of which may yet flow in your veins. How happy would it have made Woodstock and his wife, and her ancestors the Bohuns, could they have known, that from their loins a descendant should spring who would take such pains to preserve their seals, the remains of their Castle at Pleshey, and other memorials concerning them !

" Query the right of your mother's family to the arms they bear ? Their coat and crest were granted in 1583 by Robert Cooke, Clarencieux, to Rowland Hynde, of Hedsor, co. Bucks, and of the Inner Temple, London, Esq. son of Austen Hynde, Alderman of London ; unless your Hyndes descended from him, they assume the arms without right.

" Dr. Watson, of Stockport, called upon me this morning; he has brought the Warren book up with him, having had about a dozen copies printed to distribute about among the genealogical literati, that they may make notes on it, and then it is to be re-printed a third time. He desires I will ask your permission to have one sent to you, that the type, manner, vignettes, &c. may receive your approbation, as I told him you was well-skilled in these matters, and please to give an answer on this head; it will be a good introduction to your having a copy of this pompous book when printed. He talks of having several more plates engraved for it.

" They have lately pulled down the last remains of the Priory of St. John at Clerkenwell; two antient circular arches in the passage, leading from St. John's-square to Clerkenwell-green, were demolished last week. It was said in the papers, that an inscription has been found, which I have been to inquire after; it was a round piece of copper much defaced, inscribed, ' Johannes,' &c.

* See before, p. 289.

it is in the possession of —— Wallis, surveyor of the new building, and I have been promised a sight of it, but fear it will
only prove a coin.

" I have made out the chief of the arms in your window,
which shall be sent hereafter. Yours, &c.   J. C. Brooke."

---

65. Mr. Gough to Mr. Brooke.

"Dear Sir,   *June 8, 1780.*

" I have heard and seen such doings as makes me shudder at
this distance from the scene of action. Heaven knows where
these disturbances may end, or to what lengths they may proceed,
or whom they may involve in them. I have spent this day in
town inquiring after distressed friends. I hope you are not of
the number. It will be a satisfaction to hear, by return of post,
how you fare, and how friends in general fare. I conclude
neither Society will meet to-night.

" Yours, in haste as ever,   R. Gough."

---

66. Mr. Brooke to Mr. Gough.

"Dear Sir,   *Heralds'-college, June 9, 1780.*

" I return you thanks for the favour of your kind letter of
inquiries, and answer it by return of post to inform you that
we are here, thank God! all safe, which in some measure has
been owing to a party of Guards placed in St. Paul's Church,
sent there upon the joint petition of our Body and the Commons,
both places having been threatened with destruction for no
other reason but that they contained records of value The
choicest of our books we piled up in an arched vault in the building, and covered them over with stones and tiles, as the safest
defence against fire, not knowing of any place of security to
which to send them. Since martial law has been proclaimed,
we have been pretty quiet; but people are so terrified that few
stir abroad. It is said preparation is making on Tower-hill for
the execution this evening of a number of the ring-leaders.

" The Kirkbys called upon me this morning, having suffered
nothing on the occasion. I had the good fortune to save the
house of my relation Mr. Mawhood, an eminent woollen-draper
in Smithfield, from ruin. He was among the proscribed; and
with all his family had secreted themselves in town, having
removed the most valuable of his goods. A party was detached
from Holborn-bridge on purpose to destroy his house; but by
expostulation, intreaty, producing an old prayer-book, and a
gratuity to a man who seemed to be a ring-leader, they were
diverted from their purpose till some guards arrived, and he has
hitherto escaped; but his house at Finchley is said to have suffered severely.

" I pity Mr. Langdale exceedingly, as he is a most worthy
and respectable character, and has twelve or thirteen children.
He is the greatest sufferer of any individual, and his loss irreparable ; for his ingenious and large apparatus for his business had
been the work of years at an immense expense; nor can again be
erected till his extensive business is diverted into other channels.
I hope Government will make him some compensation; some
estimate his loss at £.70,000.

" This will be attended with worse consequences than we are
at present aware of; many of the principal Catholics have been
so terrified that they talk of disposing of all their property and
leaving the kingdom, which will much impoverish us. Among
these is my friend above-mentioned, who hopes to have no concern in this kingdom two months hence.

" And now I have been relating our misfortunes to you,
which I hope are pretty well over, let me advise you to take
good care of yourselves, for it is thought that yours are to come.
The culprits let out of the prisons, finding no refuge here, by
reason of our force, will fly into the country and commit their
depredations; and I fear the villages about town will suffer
severely from them. From yours sincerely,   J. C. Brooke."

67. Mr. Gough to Mr. Brooke.

" Dear Sir,   *June* 18, 1780.
" Will you, if it is not too long, oblige Dr. Nash with a
transcript of the funeral of Mrs. Abingdon, a gentlewoman of
the Privy-chamber to Queen Elizabeth, and a great favourite
with her Majesty, who buried her at her own expense ? It is
said to be in your office; and if you can send it to Mr. Nichols
the first opportunity, he has a sheet waiting for it.
                    " Yours truly,   R. Gough."

68. Mr. Brooke to Mr. Gough.

" Dear Sir,   *Heralds'-college, June* 21, 1780.
" I have looked over the index of Funeral Certificates, but
can find none for Mrs. Abingdon, whom you inquire after; if I
could you should be welcome to it. The authority which informs Dr. Nash such a funeral is entered here, probably directs
where it is to be found; I will send a note of inquiry to him on
the occasion.

" John Robartes, the last Earl of Radnor, died at Twickenham, July 15, 1757, æt. 71, s. p. and the title became extinct.
He left a considerable part of his fortune, and his fine seat and
furniture at Twickenham, to John Atherton Hindly, his steward,
who, having imprudently engaged himself in large sums of money
with one Ca—r, an East India captain, hath thereby ruined him-

self, and his seat at Twickenham, pictures, &c. are now upon sale; but the antient Robartes' estate in Cornwall went to Mary Vere, sister and heir of Henry Earl of Radnor, who married Thomas Hunt, of Mollington in Cheshire, Esq. Feb. 4, 1720, and died Oct. 23, 1758, leaving George Hunt, now of Lanhydroch, and Member for Bodmyn, her eldest son and heir; and Thomas of Mollington, by purchase from his brother, who is married to a co-heir of the family of Bold, of Bold, co. Lancaster. The said George is seised of the remains of the Radnor estate in Cornwall.

"With this letter you will receive a manuscript History of the Devereux Family, put into my hands by an Irish gentleman, now in France, for my opinion whether it would sell well if printed, or so that he might not be above £.100 out of pocket by it; the drawings in it to be engraved, &c. As you are a much better judge of these matters than I am, I shall be obliged to you to look it over, and give me your opinion; but pray take care of it. From yours sincerely,   J. C. BROOKE."

69. Mr. GOUGH to Mr. BROOKE.

"DEAR SIR,   Enfield, July 1, 1780.
"I thank you for your several answers to my queries; and if it suits you to call at Mr. Nichols's next Wednesday about noon, will give you my opinion about the Devereux manuscript.

"By the copy of the Rowe Mores' pedigree, which Mr. Nichols, with the Rowe monuments in Hackney Church, will send you, you will see some confusion about Henry, younger son of Sir Henry Rowe, and Lord of the Manor of Shacklewell. I wish to continue the Rowes to Lord Hillsborough.

"The Bromley pedigree is also to be submitted to your revision.

"Atkins's Gloucestershire has just been re-published by Rudder, printer, at Cirencester, with additions, I think for £.3. 3s. to non-subscribers. I gave the full price for both editions, and am not satisfied with either.

"John English Dolben, Esq. is to be introduced here to-day.
"Yours truly.   R. GOUGH."

70. DEAR SIR,   Enfield, July 6, 1780.
"I am sorry you would not let Mr. Nichols send for me from Chancery-lane yesterday, where I was employed with the Committee in taking the stock of the Society previously to their removal to their new apartments.

"I shall resume this business on Saturday next; and if you will give me the same chance of seeing you (for I shall hardly have time to call on you) I have much to say to you, of which I can only tell you thus much, that Mr. Nichols will print and find paper for the Devereux manuscript for forty pounds.
"Yours truly,   R. GOUGH."

71. Mr. Brooke to Mr. Gough.

" Dear Sir,   *Heralds'-college, July* 15, 1780.

" I set out on Wednesday next with Mr. Mawhood's family for Flanders. We shall go by the way of Margate to Ostend, and shall be six in party, *viz.* Mr. and Mrs. Mawhood, their eldest daughter, a younger daughter going to school at Bruges, and a Mr. Montford, Procurator to the English Convents at Bruges. I have got notes of every thing curious to be seen in our tour, which will be to Ostend, Bruges, Ghent, Brussells, Antwerp, Lisle, St. Omer's, &c.

" I think I told you that I was to spend a day with Mr. Burrell, to see his new addition of Sussex drawings by Grimm, which consist of about sixty, and are very beautiful; many views, and, in the monumental way, all the tombs at Arundel, particularly two elegant drawings of the rich sides of the chapel, monuments of the Lords Delawarr at Broadwater, &c. all highly-finished. He has a prodigious collection of materials for that county *.

" I this week took a thorough survey of Hallywell precincts, Shoreditch; the gate of the Nunnery is pretty intire, but where the Nunnery stood is a perfect jakes; nor can one possibly conceive where the body of the pious Sir Thomas Lovell now lies. Neither could I discover any traces of his house there, which afterwards became the town house of the Earls of Rutland; and there died the Countesses of that family, buried in Shoreditch Church, of whose monuments you have drawings †. Did I ever give you a copy of Sir Thomas Lovell's will? He died possessed of vast property.

" By a letter from Mr. T. Gery Cullum, of Bury, this week, I find Sir John is at Hardwick, and proposes staying there all the summer. From yours sincerely,   J. C. Brooke."

---

72. Mr. Gough to Mr. Brooke.

" *Enfield, July* 24, 1780.

" I should have been glad to have seen you here last week since your voyage is postponed.

" The Berkeley pedigree is, or shall be, sent you to finish before you go, and I will return the Devereux History, which I hope to see in print in the course of this year ‡.

" Yours truly,   R. Gough."

---

* They were bequeathed by him to the British Museum; and have since been employed in the History of Sussex, commenced under the patronage of the late Duke of Norfolk, of which two volumes have been published by the Rev. James Dallaway, F.S.A. and a third by the Rev. Edmund Cartwright, F.S.A. is now (1829) in the press.

† Engraved in Nichols's Leicestershire, vol. II. p. 29.

‡ This, it is believed, was never brought to pass. Memoirs of the family are now being collected by a gentleman who bears the name.

73. Mr. Brooke to Mr. Gough.

" Dear Sir,   *Heralds'-college, July 26, 1780.*

" I received your letter, and have corrected and sent to Nichols the pedigrees of Bromley and Berkeley. I can do nothing more to Rowe, which is now very correct. I took a walk to Hackney, and was much disappointed with the Church, as it has been much modernised. The arms on the Rowe monuments, as far as I could observe, are right, but night came on so quickly that I had but an imperfect survey of them.

" To-morrow we set out on our tour. After having been at Bruges long enough to have made observations worth sending to you, I may probably write; the direction to me will be, ' A Monsieur Monsieur le Chevalier Brooke, chez les Dames Augustines, Rue des Carmes, Bruges, Flanders, per Ostende.'

" I hope Mr. Devereux will print his book; I do not think it is ill drawn up. I will write to him to let him know Nichols's proposals; and, as he is a man of fortune, do imagine he will not grudge a little expense. I suppose, if dressed up with prints, some copies may sell, though probably not enough to bear his charges.

" Dr. Kaye is made Archdeacon of Nottingham, *loco* Dean of Ely deceased. Yours sincerely,   J. C. Brooke."

---

74. " Dear Sir,   *Heralds'-college, Sept. 7, 1780.*

" I arrived from my tour to the continent yesterday, after a most agreeable excursion of six weeks. I have reason to apologise that I did not write to you agreeably to my promise; but we were in such a continual hurry all the time that I really could find no leisure, and must therefore make it up to you with shewing you my journal, and describing things to you by word of mouth. We started for Margate on the 27th of July, being nine in party, and joined another there; just before our arrival the wind chopped to the north-east, directly contrary to Ostend, where it has continued with little variation to this day. We waited a week at Margate, in hopes it would alter; but that not being the case, we were tempted on a fine afternoon to set sail, having engaged a vessel to ourselves, and had a most turbulent voyage over.

" The delay at Margate was not disagreeable to me, as it gave me an opportunity of making a thorough survey of the Isle of Thanet. We every day made parties out, one day to Deal, where we dined; and Sandown Castle, Sandwich, Ramsgate, Richborough Castle, Minster, Dandelion, &c. The Catholics are not disagreeable for an antiquary to travel with, for they exceedingly enjoy the sight of ruined abbeys and churches, as the devastation reformation has made in ours gives them an opportunity of exalting their own pure religion, which has not

suffered such ravages; though by-the-bye we no where see so
many grave-stones stripped of their brasses as in Flanders.

" As in the space of a small letter it will be impossible to
inform you of all I have seen, I shall only say that we were
every where treated with the greatest civility. Though Mr. Mawhood's extensive acquaintance with the English settled abroad,
and with the religious of various Monasteries, we had access to
the inmost recesses of their houses. At the Nunnery where his
daughter is at Bruges, the Bishop of Bruges gave us leave of
admittance for a whole day; and we supped with the Lady Abbess
at her own table, the nuns being arranged on each side, the lay-
sisters at a table at the bottom, and waited on by the novices;
after which we went in procession to the church, and had grace
sung with music. I only lamented you was not of the party;
you would, I am sure, so much have enjoyed it. Both at the
Augustine Convent and the other Franciscan Order called Prin-
cen-hoff, the Abbesses gave me leave to copy their registers; and
every thing else I chose relative to their houses.

" I have made two very agreeable acquaintances abroad, with
whom I shall correspond, Mr. Mumford, Procurator to the
English College at St. Omer's, and Mr. Wilkes, a Benedictine
Monk at Paris; the latter you may probably have heard of, as
he is in some estimation among the learned world.

" We got to Margate on Tuesday morning five o'clock; and
after breakfast set out for Canterbury, where we spent the day,
in order to see the place. I there met by accident with Mr.
Essex, of Cambridge, and his family, who introduced us to Mr.
Gostling, with whom we spent the afternoon, and he perambu-
lated his father's History of Canterbury with us. I am quite
charmed with the place, and could have spent a week there.

" I shall set out for Yorkshire in a fortnight or three weeks'
time. Yours sincerely,   J. C. BROOKE."

───────

75. " DEAR SIR,   *Wakefield, Yorkshire, Oct. 27,* 1780.
" I left London on the 29th of last month, and had a very
agreeable journey down in the Diligence with two clergymen
who had been to Cambridge to vote at the late election. At
Sheffield I met with Mr. and Mrs. Frampton and their family,
going on a visit to a gentleman's house in the north, and spent
some agreeable time with them there.

" A few days ago I paid a visit to Mr. Waterton, of Walton-
hall, nephew to my good friend Mrs. Mary-Augustina More,
Prioress of the Convent of Augustine Dames at Bruges, and
delivered to him and his lady the presents I brought from Mrs.
More to them. I mention this visit to you on two accounts,
first, to describe to you the beautiful situation of Walton-hall,
which is extremely romantic and singular; though I think

hitherto unnoticed except by Leland, who in his Itinerary mentions Maister Waterton, of Walton, as an antient gentleman of fair lands, or the like. His house is built on a rock in a large lake, near a mile over, and of considerable depth, to which you have admittance over a draw-bridge, leading into an exceedingly antient postern. Having passed this gate, you enter a court, one square of which is a modern house, elegantly fitted up, where the family reside, another the offices, and a third is open to the lake, and beautifully laid out in walks, the whole surface of the rock having been levelled for the convenience of the house. The lake is surrounded with hills, laid out in pasture and woods, the whole forming a view most agreeably striking. Such objects we often see in Italian and Dutch pictures, but are rarely met with in this country. Mr. Waterton is a Catholic, of antient family and good estate.

" I mention this visit to you, secondly, to inform you that the owner is one of the heirs-general of the Burghs, of Burghgreen in Cambridgeshire, a family you are well acquainted with; and the contemplation of whose effigies in the church of that place, I think I have heard you say, gave you the first gust for the ravishing delights of antiquity. The Burghs had large possessions in this county by marriage with an heiress of the Nevills, and some time resided at Walton-hall, in the parish church of which village, Sandal Magna, some of them were buried, and their arms still remain in the windows. The family expired in co-heiresses, one of which married Assenhull, and the heiress of Assenhull married Waterton, temp. Henry VI. who on the division of the Burgh property had the manor of Walton, where they have ever since continued. You may see much concerning these Burghs in Philpot's Cambridgeshire in Coll. Armor. and drawings of their tombs at Burgh-green in the last Visitation of that county, but they are poorly done.

" I have collected for you since my arrival some beautiful crosses from tomb-stones with inscriptions and dates, and for people of note, of whom I can furnish some little history, which will render them more interesting than mere blanks, if hereafter you choose to send them forth into the world.

" Yours sincerely,   J. C. BROOKE."

---

76. Mr. GOUGH to Mr. BROOKE.

" DEAR SIR,   *Enfield, Dec.* 10, 1790.

" I was glad to hear of your arrival in the capital, which ought to have been announced by the discharge of all the cannon on the College ramparts.

" I have made my selection from your book of Crosses to the amount of forty; and shall, with your leave, shew them to an engraver when I come next to town. If he and I can agree

I shall then ask your further permission to let him copy them, either by intrusting the book in his hands, or tracing them here or at your room. Yours truly, R. GOUGH."

77. Mr. BROOKE to Mr. GOUGH.

"DEAR SIR, *Heralds'-college, Dec.* 14, 1780.

" You may make what use you please of my Crosses so you return them to me safe. If the engraving from my drawings will save you any expense, and can be done without materially injuring them, you may so copy them. I must inform you that none of my three last years' collection ,of Crosses are entered in the book you have got, and some of them, with dates, arms, and inscriptions, are more curious than any of those in the book.

" On Tuesday last I dined at the Duke of Norfolk's; and your Topographical Anecdotes made a part of the conversation. Lord Surrey had seen it; and pronounces it one of the most laborious, curious, and useful works the English press has produced of late years. He recommended it to the Duke, who sent for it while I was there from Payne, and is now busy going through it. Lord Surrey has given me an invitation to spend a few days with him these Christmas holidays at Arundel Castle, which I probably may accept; and in that case shall also see Cowdray, Lord Montagu having given me a like invitation. I expect much pleasure from visiting those two Peers in the houses which have so long been the seats of their noble families.

" Mr. Bowle called this morning; and writes the title of a book on the other side, which he recommends to you as containing much local history*. He has brought up a beautiful antique ivory chest, richly carved with deeds of chivalry, which he proposes producing at the Society of Antiquaries this evening. He wrote to me in Yorkshire concerning some arms upon it; and I have given him all the information in my power.

" Mr. Watson has put into my hands his History of the Warren Family, which is now finished; but is to go through another edition previous to its being ushered to the public. Would you wish to see it? From yours sincerely, J. C. BROOKE."

78. Mr. GOUGH to Mr. BROOKE.

"DEAR SIR, *Enfield, Dec.* 19, 1780.

" I shall make use of your Crosses; and undertake to return them to you safe and unsullied. I shall unglue them, and sort them into plates; and shall be glad to add any more to them as fast as you have leisure to draw them. I divide them into six classes—plain, ornamented, with a sword, with arms, with arms and sword, *en dos d'ane.*

* Joannes Capgrave, Nova legenda Angliæ. Lond. 1516, fol.

"I envy you the invitations to Arundel and Cowdray. I never saw the inside of the first, but the latter often. Can you contrive to take in Petworth, and to sketch an old knight in its church? My compliments to Mr. Bowle; ask him about the Hungerford bodies found when the tomb was removed at Salisbury. He does well to furnish matter to the Society, who are very hungry; and will meet in their new room next month with gaping mouths if some one does not feed them. It would be an ill omen to have Mr. Gale's, and other discoveries sixty years ago, chewed and re-chewed for want of fresher meat. I long to see the Warren book; pray send it to Nichols's care. Cannot one make a copy of the first edition one's own?

"Yours truly,   R. GOUGH."

---

79. Mr. BROOKE to Mr. GOUGH.

"DEAR SIR,   *Heralds'-college, Dec.* 21, 1780.
" I herewith send you Watson's History of the Warrens; but you must not keep it long, as he wants it to be sent down to him in order to begin printing the last edition. I wish when you read it over you can make any notes in it, as it would thereby intitle you to expect a copy; even literary corrections will do better than nothing, and I will magnify your labour and pains in my next letter to him. Yours,   J. C. BROOKE."

---

80. Mr. GOUGH to Mr. BROOKE.

"DEAR SIR,   *Enfield, Dec.* 27, 1780.
" I have gone through Mr. Watson's splendid book with as much attention as the Christmas week and visitors allowed; and with a cautious hand have hazarded a few notes and corrections which I wish may be of use. I am concerned to see Monast. Collect. Antiq. and such half words in so well printed and so well written a work. Yours truly,   R. GOUGH."

---

81. Mr. BROOKE to Mr. GOUGH.

"DEAR SIR,   *Heralds'-college, June* 16, 1781.
" Having a little leisure, I sit me down to inform you of Thursday evening's transactions. The reading of Essex on Round Churches in England was finished. There was produced a ring, which the family to whom it belongs have always understood was the identical one which Queen Elizabeth gave to the Earl of Essex, and he to the Countess of Nottingham *; it was brought in a crimson velvet bag, ornamented with gold lace and bugles. Many of the members, who doubt its authenticity, were for publicly declaring the same, lest it should be thought

* Related in Sir Robert Carey's " Memoirs," published by Lord Corke.

the Society gave a sanction to it, by tacitly receiving it as such. There was also produced a good drawing of a corpse in a stone coffin, found in Lincoln Cathedral in April last, when repairing the pavement, together with some part of the shroud, which appeared of diapered linen of a coffee colour.

" Colonel Twisleton's claim to the Barony of Say and Sele was put off till Thursday next; a great hardship upon him, as every meeting in the House on the occasion costs him £.100. I hope he will succeed.   I have got his two cases for you.

" I have in my possession a beautiful pedigree of Lord Teynham's family, compiled in James the First's time, which is to be continued to the present; in it are some curious paintings of effigies in windows and antient tombs.   Remember that you ask to see it the next time you call upon me.

" Sir Richard Worsley sent his " Isle of Wight " on Thursday to the Society, and me a copy yesterday.   How do you like it?
                    " From yours sincerely,   J. C. BROOKE."

---

82. Mr. GOUGH to Mr. BROOKE.

" DEAR SIR,   Enfield, June 20, 1781.
" It is nearly four years ago since I was introduced to the ring you mention at a mercer's in King-street, Covent-garden, whom I then solicited to let it be shewn to the Society; but he seemed very shy of making it public.

" If I have time on Friday, I will pay my respects to the Teynham pedigree without fear of Jack Roper; but I doubt the Council and the Dean together will take up my time.
                    " Yours, &c.   R. GOUGH."

---

83. Mr. BROOKE to Mr. GOUGH.

" DEAR SIR,   Heralds'-college, July 18, 1781.
" I have had a long letter from reverend mother Mary-Austin at Bruges, full of news, together with a postscript from my cousin, sister Louisa the choir nun.   They give me a parti-cular account of the Emperor's reception at Bruges, and the affectionate meeting between him and the Duke of Gloucester; the latter was twice at their Convent, and had a permission from the Bishop to go within the inclosure, who accompanied him. The Duke was with them near two hours, and examined every part of the Convent minutely; they say he was quite charmed with the order and regularity within their house, and hinted to the Bishop that it was to be lamented such excellent institu-tions for piety and chastity were not established in this kingdom.

" I am this month engaged in the office ; the beginning of the next am going to Nottingham to attend the assizes, with some of our books to prove pedigrees in a great cause, to prove the heirs-at-law to a gentleman, who died not long ago, and so devised an estate of near *£*.3000 *per annum*, when such heirs could be found; but this jaunt will not take up much time. In August I may probably be in Herefordshire with Lord Surrey.

" I have received a very polite invitation to Christchurch along with Topham, and propose accepting it the beginning of September; and upon my return from thence shall immediately go into Yorkshire.

" Garter King of Arms and Norroy King of Arms *, in consequence of invitations which they say you have often given them, propose, in the course of the summer, spending a day with you; and I shall attend them as their Marshal and Deputy. We shall come in a chaise, and partake of your family dinner; so when it will be agreeable to you to receive so much royalty let me know. Norroy is at present in Wiltshire.

" When you next write to Mr. Cole, of Milton, I wish you would ask him if he can give me any account of the family of Walsingham, of Chesterford in Cambridgeshire.

" By letter from young Mr. Turnor, of Lincolnshire (the editor of the Lincolnshire Sheriffs, &c.)† he desires to know if your Camden for Lincolnshire is printed, as he will add to it. He tells me he hears Sir William Musgrave intends printing a Catalogue of English Portraits; do you know anything of such a work? Mr. Turnor is just returned from his travels.

" I shall see old Pegge, at Nottingham; he is a witness for one of the claimants, who is his relation.

" Yours sincerely,   J. C. BROOKE."

---

84. " DEAR SIR,   *Heralds'-college, July* 23, 1781.

" By letter from Lord de Ferrars, he informs us that Chartley Castle was an extremely old wooden building, much decayed and rotten, and hardly habitable. There was a good deal of painted-glass in the windows of the alliances and badges of the Lord Ferrars of Chartley, which Earl Ferrars, the proprietor, had promised to him (Lord de Ferrars), but which is all destroyed, as are all the antient Ferrars' and Devereux writings down to the marriage of Lady Dorothy Devereux with Sir Henry Shirley, which were kept there. His lordship laments the loss of these exceedingly, as they would have been of much use in a History of the Ferrars Family, which he-is now compiling. He says Earl Ferrars has little to lament at its destruction, as his seat at Staunton in Leicestershire is already much too large for his estate.

" I lately did the business respecting Lord Teynham's proving his pedigree previously to his taking his seat in the House of Peers,

---

* Ralph Bigland, Esq. and Peter Dore, Esq.

† Edmund Turnor, of Stoke Rochford, Esq. F. R. S. and F. S. A. author of the History of Grantham.

his lordship having conformed to the Established Church. In the course of my acquaintance with him, he informed me that he has such quantities of grapes at his seat at Linsted-lodge in Kent, that some years they have made two three tuns of white wine, little, if any, inferior to Lisbon—an anecdote for the vineyard controversy. Yours sincerely, J. C. BROOKE, Somt."

---

85. " DEAR SIR, *Heralds'-college, Aug. 6,* 1781.

" I have the pleasure to inform you, that the two parties, on whose account I went to Nottingham, gained their cause; and that our books were admitted in evidence with great *eclat,* the Judge receiving a pedigree in one of them as sufficient, without any other proof. The successful claimants owe the first knowledge of their affinity, as well as some other circumstances which enabled them to gain their cause, entirely to my information, of which they express themselves very sensible. I lived with old Pegge all the time I was there, who was all life and spirits, and looks as well as ever I remember him; he desired to be particularly remembered to you. Dr. Kaye came to the assizes one day, and is very well. He gave me the pleasing information that, when he had Grimm at Oxford, he drew the Duchess of Suffolk at Ewelme, and Lady Harcourt at Stanton, the two monuments where ladies wear the Garter; and I intend next winter producing a paper at the Society on that subject, which these effigies will much serve to elucidate. Anstis mentions another, a Countess of Tankerville; can you find out where she was buried? While at Nottingham I saw the Castle, Lenton-abbey, and Wollaton-hall, Lord Middleton's, of which there is an engraving in Thoroton; but it falls far short of the beauty of the building, which is in excellent repair, and the stone as perfect as when first built. I saw some copy at Nottingham of Whittingham's Thoroton, and some of the prints; and was glad to find it is going on with.

" I purpose being with Lord Surrey at Home Lacey by the 14th or 15th; can you point out anything in Herefordshire particularly worth seeing? Yours sincerely, J. C. BROOKE."

---

86. " DEAR SIR, *Home Lacey, Aug.* 25, 1781.

" I left London for this place on Wednesday the 15th, and arrived at Hereford the following evening. The next morning I took a survey of the Cathedral; but as you have been over it yourself, it is needless to say anything to you about it. I intend taking drawings of the Bohun tombs and of Sir Richard Pembridge in the nave. Did you observe that the latter, who was K. G., has a Garter about each leg * ? The Denton tomb I

---

* Engraved in the " Sepulchral Monuments," from a drawing by Carter, vol. I. p. 135.

think is in your series; there is another extremely like it for a Scudemore in Home Lacey Church.

" On Monday last we paid a visit to Mr. Scudemore at Kent-church; and from thence made a tour in Monmouthshire. Was you ever at Grosmont Castle? there is a beautiful Chimney in it in a singular style, which terminates in a coronet of fleurs-de-lis; I have taken a drawing of it. In Kentchurch Church is a magnificent monument of the Scudemores, temp. James I. which is placed behind the altar; the only instance of the kind I ever met with in a parish church.

" On Thursday last we dined and stayed the night at Mr. Walwyn's at Longford, who shewed me all his MSS. relating to the antiquities of this county; they were chiefly collected by his father, who wrote an excellent hand, and seems to have had a good method; but died a young man, before he had made any great progress. Mr. Walwyn says he will put them into any person's hands who will seriously set about writing a History of the County.

" On Friday we dined at Mr. Foley's at Stoke Edith, a very fine house, the first in the county; a magnificent hall and stair-case painted by Sir James Thornhill, little inferior to his works at Greenwich Hospital. In the house here are some good Van-dycks; and a profusion of elegant carving by Gibbons.

" On Wednesday next we set out to the Music Meeting at Gloucester, and from thence to Bristol; so that I shall have the satisfaction of seeing four Cathedrals in this expedition, for I purpose staying at Worcester in my way to town, which will be the middle of next month; and shall from thence take a trip for a day to Dr. Nash, if he will receive me.

" Among the family papers here, are many letters from Guil-lim the Herald, who was related to the Scudemores; and in a MS. of his presented to the family is an article intituled, ' Or-dinaunces made by Charles the Great in 700, appointing in what manner the Effigy or Representation of every Man of Noble and Vallerous Courage should be placed upon his Sepulchre,' &c. Are these printed in Weever or elsewhere? they will be of good use to you. Yours sincerely,   J. C. BROOKE."

---

87. Mr. GOUGH to Mr. BROOKE.

" DEAR SIR,   *Enfield, Sept.* 1, 1781.

" Though I am more than two letters in your debt, I shall at present acknowledge only the last, as I hope to avail myself of some opportunities which present themselves during your stay in Herefordshire.

" My first object is, that you would find out some skilful artist, capable of making a sketch of Cantelupe's shrine and Aquablanc's monument in Hereford Cathedral. I shall wait for your sketches of the others which you mention. There is

a singular tomb, or inscription on a tomb, dirty and ill kept, in
a vault at the east end, to which you approach from a door
without on the north side. I doubt not your notes will much
assist mine. You should see the old parchment-framed Altar-
piece, or Map of the World, in the library, from whence I made
my sketch of old Britain; and, if you have time, take a sketch.

" I hope you saw the Grey Friars in the north-west end of
the City, and their beautiful stone cross. Do you not mean to
survey Kentchester, the antient Ariconium?

" At Worcester pray examine the tombs ascribed to Bishops
Gifford and de Constantiis; and sketch them as the oldest in
the church.

" I wish you could call on the Berkeleys at Berkeley Castle;
they have some beautiful monuments. Will Sudeley and its
venerable chapel fall in your way?

" At Gloucester you will admire Edward II. Abbot Parker, Osric,
and the Lady Chapel. Look at the Pilgrim's staff, and initials of
Seabroke on the south side of the altar, and his neglected chapel
behind. Examine Robert Curthois with particular attention;
and inquire for the arches of the old church, behind the cloisters
of the present, which few know of. Look over the south transept and the altar, &c. pavement; nor let the whispering-gal-
lery and the larger cloister-roof escape you. See the Black-
friars, a complete religious house, at the bottom of the town.

" At Bristol see some monuments of the Fitz Hardings; but
do not put out your knee-pan in Rowley's tower. See Canning's
two tombs in Radcliffe Church.

" I shall be glad of Guillim's Ordinaunces, and any thing
else you can pick up. Yours sincerely,   R. GOUGH."

* * *

88. Mr. BROOKE to Mr. GOUGH.

" DEAR SIR,   *Heralds'-college, Sept. 24, 1781.*
" I am returned from Herefordshire, having seen all things
you was so good as to point out to me. I shall go into Yorkshire for the remainder of the autumn in about a fortnight's
time, but will spend a day or two with you to communicate my
collections before I go, if you will inform me when agreeable
to you. I inclose a copy of Charlemaine's orders for tombs,
which I must have returned, and, with regard to other matters,
more when we meet. Yours, &c.   J. C. BROOKE."

* * *

89. " DEAR SIR,   *Heralds'-college, Oct. 17, 1781.*
" I inclose you part of a letter, which I have received from
Mr. Turnor, of Lincolnshire, containing new matter for your
Camden. He seems very desirous of assisting you therein; and
therefore when you come to that county, I would advise you to
send to him, directed to Edmund Turnor, jun. Esq. Panton-
house, near Lincoln.

" I have corrected all the Camden that has been sent to me since my return from Enfield, and sent it to Nichols. I must be sincere with you in telling you, that I think that much of the new information you have added is erroneous.

" Yours, &c.   J. C. Brooke."

---

90. " Dear Sir,   *Heralds'-college, July 22, 1782.*

"Inclosed I return your pedigree of Wrighte * with some additions, which shew how the Lord Keeper was related to those of Cranham and Kelvedon. Your authority was erroneous, which states him to have been of a mean family; we have a pedigree here signed by himself in the year 1681, from whence what I send you is extracted. The pedigree you have drawn out of the other branches from Morant is also erroneous.

" The arms in glass in the south-west window of your library, *viz* the cross and bordure engrailed, quartering the squirrel and eagle and child, are those of the family of Holcroft, of Holcroft, co. Lancaster; a branch of which were seated at East Ham in Essex, from whence it is probable the Whitechapel glazier had the shield now in your possession.

" The other coat in a small lozenge in the same window, the three fleurs-de-lis between two bends, impaling four quarterings, belongs to the family of Hacket.

" From yours sincerely,   J. C. Brooke."

---

91. " Dear Sir,   *Heralds'-college, Sept. 23, 1782.*

" I had a letter from Mr. King yesterday; we are grown wonderfully gracious since the assistance I gave him in his Castles. He is at present at Norwich, but will be in town in November, if the great metropolis can possibly be made a place of comfort or safety to him.

" I have seen much of the Bishop of Dromore of late; he has been very busy in collecting anecdotes, &c. of the Grenville and Temple families, in order to prattle and ingratiate himself with the new Lord Lieutenant of Ireland upon his return. He gives a most curious and entertaining account of Ireland and its inhabitants.

" Is it not very odd that your friend Dr. Nash should send me the first volume of his work and not the second?

" In our office we have a copy of the accord made at Berwick, Feb. 27, 1559, between the Scottish nobility and Queen Elizabeth, for expelling the French out of that kingdom, with an account of their families, estates, &c. and drawings of their seals, &c. Do consult your library and your friend Mr. Paton, if necessary, and inform me if the original is in being and

---

* For the History of Hinckley, 4to, 1782, p. 151; enlarged in the History of Leicestershire, vol. III. p. 219.

printed; if not I may probably in the winter produce it at the
Society of Antiquaries, as I do not see why a public record of
that nature is not as well worth engraving as the Barons' Letter
to the Pope, though not quite of such antiquity.

    "Yours sincerely,   J. C. Brooke."

92. Mr. Gough to Mr. Brooke.

"Dear Sir,   *Enfield, Oct.* 18, 1782.

"The original accord between Elizabeth and the Scottish
nobles, Feb. 27, 1559, at Berwick, seems to be printed at large
in Keith's History of Scotland, pp. 117—119, but subscribed,
and having the seals only of the six Commissioners from the
Cotton Library; it is likewise in Rymer's Fœdera, vol. XV.
p. 569, dated Feb. 27, 1560, but whether it has the seals you
mention I know not.

"You cannot wonder Dr. Nash did not send you his second
volume when his first was stolen upon you by him in such a
manner that you were not to know whence it came, and I suppose he thinks that a sufficient equivalent for your share of the
trouble; but I really know nothing of his thoughts.

    "Yours sincerely,   R. Gough."

93. "Dear Sir,   *Enfield, Dec.* 22, 1782.

"Can you inform me what relation John Dudley, whose
widow married Sutton, Founder of the Charter-house, was to
the Leicester and Warwick family, whose arms appear on her
tomb at Newington? Yours truly,   R. Gough."

94. Mr. Brooke to Mr. Gough.

"Dear Sir,   *Heralds'-college, Dec.* 25, 1782.

"John Dudley, of Newington, who married Elizabeth, daughter of John Gardiner, of Crome, co. Bucks, afterwards the wife
of Sutton, was second son of Thomas Dudley, of Yeanwith in
Westmoreland, Esq. by Sarah his wife, daughter and co-heir of
Lancelot Thirkeld, of Yeanwith, Esq. which Thomas Dudley
was seventh son of Edmund Lord Dudley, by Maud his second
wife, daughter of Thomas Lord Clifford. The said John Dudley died Dec. 27, 1580, and lies buried at Newington. The
Mr. Robert Dudley, to whom Sutton by will leaves a legacy of
£.20, was his nephew, viz. second son of his elder brother
Richard Dudley, of Yeanwith, Esq. If ever I live to publish
my Baronage after Dugdale's method, you will have all these
younger branches of our antient nobility fully treated on.

"My aunt Gough has considerable property in the Fens in
Lincolnshire, but I do not know she has any in Crowland. It
was a mistake of mine with regard to Scribo's treasures found

at Crowland; I understood my aunt he had many. I suppose he showed you the History of Crowland which he has written.

"We are in Christmas time so much engaged with Collar days at Court and heraldic feasts, that I cannot possibly yet awhile come to see you, though I wish it much, as I long to hear what has passed in the antiquarian world in my long absence. To-day we jollify in a body with Master Garter.

"By letter from Burrell yesterday, I find he has had Cowdray, and almost all its contents, beautifully painted this summer. Bowle called upon me a day or two ago, and is much broken. His nephew, a young man who married his only daughter, died last summer, to the great affliction of all the family. A John Bowle, his grandson, is now almost his sole joy; and is so fine a child that he can already almost lisp, *alcança quien no causa.*

"From yours sincerely,   J. C. BROOKE."

95. "DEAR SIR,   *Heralds'-college, Dec.* 27, 1782.

"In addition to what I formerly told you about John Dudley, it is my opinion that the marrying Elizabeth, his widow, was Sutton's rise. I think it is somewhere said, that that man chiefly acquired his wealth by being Secretary to the two Dudleys, Earls of Warwick and Leicester, in which office, I take it, he succeeded John Dudley.

"Have you seen Dade's proposals for his History of Holdernesse? I have a high opinion of the work, as I know the pains he has taken and his liberality. He told me he would bestow all the subscriptions upon the work. Pray obtain some for him if you can. We should encourage such works.

"Yours sincerely,   J. C. BROOKE, Somt."

"*Feb.* 1, 1783. I send you a pedigree of the Fleetwoods, which will clear up most of your queries; I believe it is pretty correct. I beg you will take care of it, and let me have it safe again, as it belongs to a collection of pedigrees of the Regicides. In the course of last summer I collected a quarto volume of their descents, anecdotes of them, &c. together with drawings of their arms, serving to explain their seals on Charles's death warrant, published by the Society of Antiquaries, from whence what I send you is in a great measure extracted."

96. Mr. GOUGH to Mr. BROOKE.

"DEAR SIR,   *Enfield, Feb.* 7, 1783.

"I am much obliged to you for your letter with the pedigree of Fleetwood, which being intended for a number of the Bibliotheca Topographica *, you will not be displeased that I have forwarded a copy of it to Mr. Nichols.

* See the pedigree of Fleetwood in Brown's "History of Stoke Newington," No. IX. of "Bibliotheca Topographica Britannica."

" There is such a dearth of provision at Somerset-place, that Mr. Norris was glad there was such an anniversary as King Charles's martyrdom to conceal it ; it is exceeded only by the dearth of corn in Scotland, which in the northern parts I am assured is dreadful. I dined with the Dean lately ; and Dr. Lort threw out a challenge, which only Mr. King accepted, that if six more of the company present would furnish a paper he would. Now then is your time to throw in comments on Regicides and the Scottish Association with Elizabeth.

" Pray send me every proposal for the furtherance of the study of antiquity. Yours truly,   R. Gough."

---

97. Mr. Brooke to Mr. Gough.

" Dear Sir,   *Heralds'-college, March* 13, 1783.

" Agreeably to your desire I called yesterday at Mr. White's, and saw Hall's Chronicle ; the arms in the vignette are the Hall arms, and probably were meant for his own ; they are the same as are in several places in the north window of your library, and are numbered in the account I took of them, beginning at the top and taking them in rows, 6, 9, 11, and 12. You told me the three last were given you by young Kirkby, and brought by him from Ratcliffe ; and query did he not give you the sixth, as it belonged to the same family ? The coat I mean is that of the dragon within a bordure, which quarters three others, Aubemond, Mortimer, and Antingham, both in the Chronicle and your windows. In the Chronicle is also the crest a dragon standing on a castle, which is painted No. 11 in your window, together with the supporters, which we have curiously drawn here in a book marked Vinc^t, 134, fol. 478^b. These Halls were of Kinnersley and Northall, co. Salop, and descended from Sir Francis Hall, Knt. of the Garter, temp. Edward III. who was son of Frederick de Halle, a natural son of Albert Archduke of Austria and King of the Romans, so called from being born at the city of Halle in Tyrol, as appears by a curious pedigree of the family in the book quoted above, which I will show you when you are next here.

" No. 6 in your window, Hall with quarterings, impaling three lions rampant, are the arms of William Halle, of Kinersley, with those of his wife Joan, daughter of Walter Limbeake, of Stow, co. Gloucester.

" No. 9, in the same window, arms of John Halle, of Northall, co. Salop, his son, who died Feb. 22, 16 Henry VIII. impaling those of his wife Katharine, daughter and heir of Thomas Gedding, who bore gules, a chevron between three griffins' heads erased or.

" Did I never give you the arms in your window ? I have them all explained ; and, if I did not, will bring them with me when I see you at Easter.

" With regard to Segar, you will find a tolerable good account of him in Anstis's Garter, vol. II. p. 398; if you want his life, compile it from thence, leave margins, and I will correct it.

" In a letter I had from old Pegge to-day, is the following: ' As to the Society, nobody will send them any thing, for they give no encouragement. Their counter-ordering the printing eight or ten supernumerary copies of gentlemen's papers for their own use was such a mean and scurvy act that no wonder they should resent it.' Yours truly, SOMERSET."

----

98. " DEAR SIR, *Heralds'-college, April* 14, 1783.

" The arms you gave me from Herbert on Thursday are those of Queen Katherine Parr; and you will find them described in her seal, Archæologia, vol. V. p. *233, only they are differently arranged in your account, *viz.* 1, Roos of Kendal; 2, Parr; 3, Augmentation granted to this Queen by Henry the Eighth; 4, Green; 4, Fitzhugh; 6, Marmion. With regard to Roos being the first coat, you know, I conclude, that it was usual formerly for families, who in a manner had made themselves by any great heiress, to bear her arms in the first place before the paternal coat. I wish to know in what book these arms are, and how they come there, as I shall quote it in Sandford as an unnoticed mode of this Queen's bearing her arms.

" Grose, I am told, is soliciting to be dubbed a divine; he will be a curious orthodox priest! Yours, &c. SOMERSET."

----

99. " DEAR SIR, *Heralds'-college, June* 4, 1783.

" There was a board of Treasury on Tuesday last to consider about Domesday Book; and Lord Surrey was so obliging as to mention me as a proper person to be consulted about a preface, which is to be in Latin. I told him I was incompetent to the business, but pointed out you as the most proper person either to do it, or recommend those who could, and likewise to give directions about it; they are to have an answer in a week. Some of them mentioned that to Gale's Richmond as a proper model. Do consider the business, and either let me see you or hear from you soon on the occasion.

" My friend Dade tells me that a family in the East Riding of Yorkshire are in possession of a collection of letters written from Cheshunt by a woman who lived as mistress to Richard Cromwell, which gives a particular account of his death, and of the most material transactions of the latter part of his life.
" Yours, &c. J. C. BROOKE, Somt."

100. Mr. Gough to Mr. Brooke.

" Dear Sir, *Enfield, June* 5, 1783.

" Latin prefaces to English records appear to me quite out of fashion ; and, if they were not, I know not how to rub up my old Latin on this occasion. An English preface may be written by many abler hands.

" I thank you for the offer of the drawings at Ewelme, &c. which I shall be glad first to look at. Yours, &c. R. Gough."

---

101. Mr. Brooke to Mr. Gough.

" Dear Sir, *Heralds'-college, Aug.* 23, 1783.

" I herewith return your Camden for Nottinghamshire, with some notes by myself and Dr. Disney. Dr. Kaye called upon me the day before you sent it, and inquired after it ; it was unlucky, but probably you can find some means of sending it to him at Kirkby near Mansfield. Yours, &c. J. C. Brooke, Somt."

---

102. " Dear Sir, *Heralds'-college, Sept.* 23, 1783.

" Mr. Turnor called on me on his way to Lincolnshire from Normandy, but I did not see him ; but have had a letter from him since, by which I find he has had some drawings made of anti-quities in that country, which he will bring to town to show us next year. He is much delighted with his expedition.

" Yours, &c. J. C. Brooke, Somt."

---

103. " Dear Sir, *Heralds'-college, Jan.* 7, 1784.

" I suppose Mr. Nichols would tell you, as I desired him, that I could not venture to alter the Bensted pedigree in the sheet of Monuments ; and that, as I had my doubts about your copy of it, it would be better omitted.

" You have, I presume, heard of the dreadful commotions that agitate the Royal Society at present ; and threaten, for a time, destruction to all science. I expect you will be in town to-morrow to throw your interest into the scale of one of the par-ties ; for it is said such interest has been made on the occasion, that there will be 200 people present. I believe you have never yet seen Mr. Pingo, who corrected the Cromwell pedigree for you ; sometime when you are in town I will introduce him to you. He is a very ingenious, sensible, well-behaved young man, and may hereafter be of service to you as an heraldic acquaint-ance when I am in the country. I have a very magnificent pedigree, lately finished, to go to Germany for Sir John Webb, to show you when I next see you. It goes the first week in February. Yours, &c. J. C. Brooke, Somt."

104. " DEAR SIR, *Heralds'-college, March* 17, 1784.
" I cannot find the arms of Prior Bolton, of St. Bartholomew's, though I doubt not we have them somewhere; his
device, the bolt and tun, I find in many places. I must observe
to you, that in monuments which have been repaired, there is
no judging of the arms, they are so apt to be mistaken by unskilful painters. I have of late taken much pains to attribute
to their proper owners Symonds's drawings of the Monuments
at Pleshey, and think I have succeeded. Pray let me have
your notes upon them, and an account of their present state ;
and then you shall have drawings of them. Symonds's three
volumes abound with curious matter relative to the antiquities
of Essex.

" I spent the day with Lord de Ferrars yesterday, who gives
a curious and ludicrous account of the behaviour of a certain
friend of ours, lately advanced to high honours, in his late transactions with him ; it was with great difficulty he could prevent
his making an elegant speech of considerable length in praise
of antiquity to a great personage upon his introduction; but
this *entre nous.* I think, rather than otherwise, Lord de Ferrars
seems pleased with the prospect of his new office * ; and, as he
appears to have no vice or other amusement than heraldry and
genealogy, I hope he will make a good President. His toast is
Mr. Pitt, whom he calls our first antiquary, because he has
taken such care of that good old piece of antiquity, the English Constitution. Yours, &c. J. C. BROOKE, Somt."

---

105. Mr. GOUGH to Mr. BROOKE.

" DEAR SIR, *Enfield, April* 5, 1781.
" If, amidst the late revolutions in the College, you have
leisure to look over two counties at once, I shall be obliged to
you for corrections of Stafford and Shropshires; to be returned
as early as convenient to Mr. Nichols.

" I thought I had before told you there is not a fragment of
a monument at Pleshey ; and the church itself is so reduced
that scarcely any part of the old walls remain. I shall, however, be obliged to you for any drawings of what monuments
were there.

" Pray assure Mr. Pingo that I do not forget him or any of
my friends ; but the Cromwell pedigree is not yet worked off.

" All things being now ready, even to the glasses in the ink-
stands, for the advancement of Lord de Ferrars to the Presidency, I hope to meet him and you and the rest of our friends
in the Hall of Apollo, at the Devil Tavern on St. George's-day,
by which time our present President may, perhaps, have a seat
in St. Stephen's Chapel.

" Till then, unless you will pass a few of the ensuing holidays
here, I bid you adieu ! Yours, R. GOUGH."

* President of the Society of Antiquaries.

106. Mr. Brooke to Mr. Gough.

" Dear Sir,   Heralds'-college, April 10, 1784.

" I herewith return your Staffordshire. I am not much acquainted with the two counties you sent me, and cannot therefore be expected to make many additions to them.

" Mr. Bigland was buried with great funeral pomp on Thursday last in Gloucester Cathedral, agreeably to his will, which is a very strange one. He makes no mention therein of his books and manuscripts, which of course go to his son.

" Yours sincerely,   J. C. Brooke."

107. " Dear Sir,   Heralds'-college, April 23, 1784.

" It gives me much concern to be deprived of meeting you at Somerset House to-day, which has not happened to me before since I have been a member; but Lord Surrey, having a mind to retire to Greystock Castle, after the hurry of electioneering business, to enjoy the country till the meeting of Parliament, has invited me to accompany him; and, as so good an opportunity of seeing that part of the world may not again happen, I could not resist accepting it.

" Yours sincerely,   J. C. Brooke."

108. " Dear Sir,   Heralds'-college, July 13, 1784.

" I have received a letter from Topham to acquaint me that a party, of which you are one, is formed for Knole, Penshurst, &c. to set out about the 23d of this month; but the day to be left to you. If you could defer it till the first week in August, I would endeavour to accompany you; but am this month engaged in waiting in the office, and the 20th am engaged to attend the House of Lords, to give evidence in Sir John Griffin's claim to the Barony of Howard of Walden, which business I am afraid will not be so far completed that I can be disengaged on the 23d. Pray consider this, for I shall like much to be of the party.

" Can you inform me of the Christian, sirname, and profession of the gentleman who married Lady dowager Napier, and lived sometime at Enfield. From yours, &c. J. C. Brooke."

109. Mr. Brooke to Mr. Gough.

" Dear Sir,   Enfield, July 18, 1784.

" I hope the excursion will be settled to the satisfaction of all parties at Mr. Bray's, where it seems we are to dine on Wednesday next.

" Mr. Webb, who married Lady Napier, was, or had been, a Colonel, I believe in the Guards; his Christian name was James. They had a son born here, christened Daniel.

" Yours,   R. Gough."

110. Mr. Brooke to Mr. Gough.

" Dear Sir,   *Heralds'-college, Sept.* 13, 1784.

"I hope this letter will find you well, and that you have so been since our Kentish expedition. It is my intention, either in this month or the beginning of the next, to pay a visit for a few days to Mr. Frampton at Moreton ; and, as you formerly threw out hints as if such an expedition would not be disagreeable to you, I inform you thereof, in hopes that you will give me the pleasure of your company. The following is my plan : to go in the coach to Salisbury, and spend a whole day there, or more as agreeable, to make a thorough heraldic survey of the Cathedral, &c.; then to take the same coach on to Blandford; and from thence chaise it to Moreton, where we shall have a hearty welcome; to come back in a chaise by Wimborne, to call on Mr. Willett, at Merley, if agreeable to you, survey Wimborne, call upon Mr. Brander at Christchurch, and take the Poole coach to Winchester, stay there a day or more as at Sarum, and then to town *.

" I have been for a month past with Lord Surrey at Home Lacey in Herefordshire ; and while there made an expedition into South Wales, to Brecon, Abergavenny, Trecastle, &c. &c. &c. In the Priory Church, Abergavenny, are a number of fine tombs for the Herberts Earls of Pembroke, of which I have taken a particular account : pray have you seen them ? I also spent a day at Hampton Court, the Coningsby seat ; and have taken a very particular account of the pictures and other curiosities †. In this tour I have adopted two plans, which I think will prove very useful in our pursuits; one is to draw the ichnograpy of churches, where the tombs are sufficiently numerous to deserve it, and number them with references; the other, to number the pictures in large houses.

" At Home Lacey is a head of Vandyke, drawn by Pope, in black and red chalk, finely executed. Have you heard of any other of his works in that way extant, since his portrait of Betterton was burnt at Lord Mansfield's ?

" I have got some beautiful crosses with inscriptions from Acornbury Priory, co. Hereford. Lord Surrey caused several tombs and the Chandos vault to be opened there ; but the space of a letter will not admit of my informing you of the discoveries.

" The King has refused granting the Baronets a badge.

" From yours sincerely,   J. C. Brooke, Somt."

---

111. Mr. Gough to Mr. Brooke.

" Dear Sir,   *Enfield, Sept.* 14, 1784.

"I have this moment received yours ; and have just time to acquaint you that I set off to-morrow early for Suffolk, to meet

* In a subsequent letter Mr. Brooke mentions that he was not able to accomplish this tour.
† A somewhat full account of them was printed in the Gentleman's Magazine, vol. XCV. ii. pp. 18—21.

Mr. Ord ; and am so little certain how long I shall stay there that I cannot engage for a Dorsetshire journey.

" I am much pleased with your account of your excursion into Herefordshire and South Wales. I have notes of the Abergavenny monuments ; but presume yours to be much correcter. I should have called on you before, but heard you were with Lord Surrey. I will take an early opportunity of seeing you and your crosses on my return ; meantime am

" Yours,   R. GOUGH."

---

112. Mr. BROOKE to Mr. GOUGH.

"DEAR SIR,   *Heralds'-college, Dec.* 8, 1784.

" I am but lately returned from the country, where, except about a week in September, I have been for near four months past. I have not had an opportunity of attending the Society since my return, and therefore know little of what is going forwards in the antiquarian world; indeed at present the various occupations in which I am employed so much engage my time, that I have not an opportunity of keeping up my acquaintance with people in that line of study as formerly, which gives me much concern.

" When in Yorkshire I found myself inclined very much to arrange my collections ; and copied fair all my this year's drawings. I should be glad if you would return the book of Crosses of mine you have, as I wish to fix in all my late additions, now scattered loose, and you shall then have it again, I shall then see what are missing ; and hope to replace some of them from the rough draughts, some of which I have happily discovered. I shall be glad also to have at the same time such plates of them as you have engraved.

" In Pangbourne Church, Berks, is a monument for Sir John Davis, who died in 1625, with effigies of himself and two wives, all carved out of chalk.

" In Methley Church, Yorkshire, is a beautiful monument, with effigies cumbent, for Sir Robert Waterton and his lady, temp. Henry IV. rings on every finger and several on some, and on every joint. She wears the same collar of SS about her neck as her husband. Have you met with that before * ?

" Bigland, our late Garter's son, when in town, had a number of impressions from his father's Gloucestershire plates taken, and has hawked them about the County at one shilling each, and I am told meets with bad success in the sale You know how to procure a set if you choose it ; probably for one complete he may abate.

* Mr. Gough has put a note : " Dudley at Dudley. Nash's Worcestershire, vol. I. p. 361." See also hereafter, p. 424. — The Collar of SS has been recently elucidated by G. F. Beltz, Esq. Lancaster Herald, in an article in the Retrospective Review, New Series; see also Gent. Mag. vol. XCVIII. ii. p. 602.

" Since my return to town, I have arranged all my topographical prints and drawings; and if you have any duplicates, I will exchange with you ?

" I beg my compliments to the ladies; and am, dear Sir,
        " Yours sincerely,   J. C. BROOKE, Somt."

---

113. Mr. GOUGH to Mr. BROOKE.

" DEAR SIR,   *Enfield, Feb.* 15, 1785.
" I now send you two plates of the Crosses from your own collection, and hope shortly to be able to send you a third. You will oblige me making up a fourth of the richest and most ornamented you have met with in stone or brass, with figures and inscriptions, or without either.

" I wish for some information touching the monument inclosed, which is in Gloucester Cathedral, and commonly ascribed to a Bohun Earl of Hereford and Gloucester, 1371. There is nothing to ascertain it more than appears in the print; and I find no Earl of the Bohun family who died about that time, or was buried there, unless one could suppose the tomb to have been removed thither from Lantony Abbey, in the neighbourhood, where so many of the Bohuns were buried.

" Accept the remains of Dore for yourself; and present the three others in my name to Messrs. Heard, Harrison, and Pingo.
        " Yours, &c.   R. GOUGH."

---

114. Mr. BROOKE to Mr. GOUGH.

" DEAR SIR,   *Heralds'-college, Feb.* 28, 1785.
" I received your letter with the Crosses, and the copies of Dore's pedigree, which I distributed with compliments as you desired. With regard to the monument at Gloucester, I never could attribute it to my satisfaction, no more than those said to be Bohuns in the Lady Chapel, Hereford Cathedral, though I think the arms of Bohun are painted on one of the latter. The family seem entirely to have been buried at Lantony, and that at Lantony seems the likeliest to be one of them from its proximity to Gloucester; but on the reverse, from the whole style of the monument, in an arch, &c. it has not the appearance of having been placed there so late as the dissolution; besides, I imagine there were many other fine monuments at Lantony; if so, what became of the rest? In short, I have my doubts as to its being a Bohun, and always had. Bigland had it engraved by Bonner *.

" Mr. Pennant is in town, and spent Saturday evening with me here; he talks of publishing another Tour. Can we contrive to meet him at a tavern dinner party ?
        " From yours sincerely,   J. C. BROOKE."

* See Bigland's History of Gloucester City, p. 128.

2 E 2

115. Mr. Gough to Mr. Brooke.

" Dear Sir,   *March 3, 1785.*

" I thank you for your letter of Monday, which I received yesterday; and happening to meet with Dr. Lort, who had just parted with Mr. Pennant, he undertook to engage him to dine at the Devil on Monday next at four, with Messrs. Topham, Ord, Claxton, and your humble servant, to which party I hope you will add yourself.

" We hold the same opinion about the Bohun monument at Gloucester; but having engraved it *, it must answer for itself as an example of the fourteenth century.

" Will Dr. Nash be of the Monday party?

" Yours truly,   R. Gough."

---

116. " Dear Sir,   *Enfield, March 15, 1785.*

" I return Mr. Pugh's MS. account of Delwin, which, as far as it goes, I am much pleased with; but it is only an outline, and wants filling up. Is it drawn from some older accounts, or are the church notes of later dates? I heartily wish success to it.

" Yours truly,   R. Gough."

---

117. Mr. Brooke to Mr. Gough.

" Dear Sir,   *Heralds'-college, March 19, 1785.*

" I am glad you approve of Pugh's plan; I shall see Lord Surrey to-morrow, and will shew him your letter. He seems to have much zeal in the business; and if there is a probability he will go through with it. I will give him myself some assistance in the work †.

" I had a very pleasant journey to Nottingham, which was made the more agreeable by the company of your friend Mr. Forster, of Threadneedle-street; but the ill-success of the gentleman, on whose account we went, who was non-suited, in some measure damped our pleasure. One morning we made a tour to Wollaton, having previously obtained permission of Lord Middleton to see the house, and both Forster and myself were much delighted with it; it is a magnificent old mansion in excellent repair. I took a particular account of all the pictures, arms, &c. which I will hereafter shew you; and was much pleased with a beautiful portrait of a Lady Willoughby, of the Lyttelton family, who has a rich jewel on her left breast, on which is a Neptune, the antient badge of that family. Young Turnor gave me a letter of introduction to his sister, married to Mr. Smith, Member for Nottingham; and I was very politely treated by them while there.

" A Mr. Thomas Brian Richards, an Oxford antiquary, who

---

* See Gough's Sepulchral Monuments, vol. I. pl. LXV. p. 195.

† A projected History of Herefordshire, which was unfortunately stopped on Pugh's leaving Hereford a disgraced man in 1786.

lives at Benson, was here to-day, and tells me (see the drawing) that on the slab on which the effigy of the Duchess of Suffolk lies at Ewelme, on the lower part over the skeleton, are painted two pieces, the Salutation and the Apotheosis of the Duchess, in water colours and well preserved ; did you know this ? The former is over the head, the latter the feet, of the skeleton.

" Have you a pedigree of the Raintons ? Were any of them ever seated at Shelton, Berks ? By letter from Dr. Nash, I find his daughter is soon to be married to Mr. Cocks, eldest son of Lord Sommers. I have this day put the finishing hand to all that is necessary in our way for plate, seals, coach, &c. The Doctor seems very happy on the occasion.

" Yours sincerely, J. C. BROOKE, Som^t."

---

118. Mr. GOUGH to Mr. BROOKE.

" DEAR SIR,   March 22, 1785.

" I am glad to hear so good an account of your late excursion ; and that the walk of antiquity afforded more satisfaction than that of law. Has Mr. Pegge's kinsman lost his estate ?

" Neither of the drawings mentioned by Mr. Richards appear in Grimm's drawing of the Duchess of Suffolk's tomb at Ewelme, which is no great proof of his accuracy.

" Yours truly, R. GOUGH."

---

119. Mr. BROOKE to Mr. GOUGH.

" DEAR SIR,   Heralds'-college, May 29, 1785.

" The arms Mr. Herbert mentions as so frequently used by Christian Barker, the Queen's printer, were those of Sir Francis Walsingham, the Secretary of State ; and probably were inserted out of compliment for his kindness in licensing Barker's books. We have a pedigree of the Barkers entered here by Matthew Barker, his grandson, in 1634, whereby it appears that the printer bore, Or, on a fess dancettè Vert three fleurs-de-lis Argent. He was printer both to Elizabeth and James ; and had a son, Robert Barker, of Southfee, Bucks, Esq. father of Matthew above-mentioned.

" When you go your Yorkshire tour, please to let me know, and I will give you letters to some of my friends most likely to give you information and a kind reception. I had a letter from Mr. Tunstall last week, which I intend answering on Tuesday, and shall inform him of your intended expedition ; and shall desire him to signify the same to his brother Constable, at Burton-Constable, whose magnificent house and valuable library I hope you will endeavour to see, being the first in its way in the East Riding, if not in the county *.

* See vol. V. of this Work, pp. 509 et seq.

" Turnor, Ord, Topham, and self, went our City rout yesterday, and spent the whole day, from nine in the morning to eight
at night, much to our satisfaction; but our discoveries, notes of
what should be drawn, &c. &c. must be reserved till we meet.

" You was so much engaged on Thursday I had not time to
tell you what an agreeable week's expedition I had to Arundel
at Whitsuntide, and how much I saw, as we every morning
made little tours, viz. to Michelgrove, Sir John Shelley's; Bram-
ber and Knap Castles; Goodwood, Duke of Richmond's; Petworth; Slindon, Lord Newburgh's; Chichester; Halnaker House,
late the Morley's, but formerly Lord Delawar's; in the latter is
an old hall, fitted up with wainscot carved with arms, mottoes,
and devices before 1525, for in that year Thomas Lord Delawar,
whose arms are on it, died.

" Mr. Humphry Senhouse, of Nether-hall in Cumberland, the
heir of Camden's friend, was with me here some time on Friday;
and seemed to have all the regard for antiquity possessed by his
ancestor, whose Roman collection he preserves with religious
care.   He is nearly related to the Kirkbys.

" Yours sincerely,   J. C. BROOKE, Somt."

120. Mr. GOUGH to Mr. BROOKE.

" DEAR SIR,   June 16, 1785.
" I mean this should be accompanied with eleven sheets of
Yorkshire * for your examination, which being a great number to
stand at one press, you will give them due dispatch. Some
arrangement of religious houses will be wanting, besides other
corrections, for which I trust to your candour.

" Yours truly,   R. GOUGH.'

121. Mr. BROOKE to Mr. GOUGH.

" DEAR SIR,   Heralds'-college, June 19, 1786.
" I had a letter from Mr. Chadwick the 8th ult. wherein he
desires that, if you made any application respecting the drawings, I would write to his father in Lancashire, by which I suppose he has returned them to him. He took leave of me the
6th, being then going with a friend to Brighthelmstone, from
whence they cross to Dieppe, and make the tour of Normandy,
to collect antiquities relative to his ancestors the Malvesyns, in
order to illustrate a copious pedigree I am compiling for him.
He talks of returning in six weeks, when I shall see him, and
will introduce him to you. He had a book of drawings, viz.
external and internal views of the Church of Malvesyn Ridware,
two cross-legged tombs of the Malvesyns under arches, views of
the bodies in the same tombs when opened, five tombs with effigies for the Carwardens, who were heirs to the Malvesyns, traced

* In Mr. Gough's edition of Camden's Britannia.

with black on white marble, arms in windows, &c. &c. He talks of having them engraved; and desired I would ask Basire his prices *.

" By letter from Mr. Tunstall, he informs me his brother has refused Beckwith's MSS. in the gross, as so many would be useless to him. I wish you would buy them.

" Yours sincerely,   J. C. BROOKE, Somt."

---

122. "DEAR SIR,   *Northgate, Wakefield, Sept.* 10, 1787.

" Being now quietly settled here for a few weeks after the hurry of travelling, I sit me down to inform you of my late excursions. I left London the 18th of July, and went into Cumberland, by the way of Staffordshire and Lancashire. At Manchester I met with Sir Thomas Cullum and his family going to the Lakes. In the old Church there, the brackets which support the roof represent the angels playing on various music, seven on one side on stringed instruments, the seven on the other side on wind instruments, which give the antient forms of such; are these any where noticed or drawn?

" At Greystoke Castle I found Mr. Hiorne, of Warwick, the gothic architect, whom the Duke of Norfolk had invited there to consult with relative to his intended repairs at Arundel Castle; and we made a party to see Alnwick Castle, &c. in Northumberland, for Mr. Hiorne's information. This gave me an opportunity of surveying the Roman wall, which I was much surprised to find so perfect, being discernible for more than nine miles, from Glenwelt to Chollerford; and likewise to find the number of unnoticed sculptures and inscriptions which are to be seen in the houses near the wall, some of which I drew. The wall is now no where above seven feet and a half high and eight broad; and I am sorry to tell you, considerable inclosures are now in agitation by the Blackett family, which, in all probability, will entirely destroy the remains, as the Ashler stone, with which it is faced, is very valuable for building. It is to be wished that the Society of Antiquaries would liberally enable Mr. Brand to publish his account of it in an elegant manner, with better plates of such of Warburton's Antiquities as now remain, and those since discovered; views of the wall where most perfect, stations, &c. &c. While in Cumberland we had parties to see most part of the county worth observation; to Mr. Senhouse's at Elnebrough, where I drew many of his altars, &c.; to Whitehaven, Workington, up Skiddow, the Lakes, &c. &c. Saw at Carlisle several Roman antiquities dug up this summer, amongst which, two beautiful altars, very perfect, but without inscriptions; on one the figure of Hercules in bas

---

* The plates, six in number, were published in the first volume of Shaw's History of Staffordshire.

relief in the front; on the other, a figure of Victory on one side, and a woman sitting in a chair on the other, nothing in front. On the effigy of the lady on the Salkeld tomb at Wetherall, see Burn, vol. II. p. 336. She has a collar of SS, like her husband, about her neck. On the Ratcliffe tomb at Crossthwaite, see Burn, vol. II. p. 78; both the effigies are brass, in dress of the times, and have both Knight and Lady, the cross of Malta or Jerusalem appendant to chains about their necks. The effigy of a Knight of which order, in his proper habit, remains in one of the windows, of which Sir Thomas Cullum has a good drawing. Have you met with instances of this sort in your monumental researches? I shall stay here till the latter end of October, being busily employed in copying my Cumberland collections into Burn, and itinerating this neighbourhood; but hope to meet you in town the beginning of November.

" In Wetheral Church, Cumberland, is much painted-glass preserved and brought by Lord William Howard from Lanercost Priory, when the Church there was dismantled; and much of the furniture in the Church was brought from Wetheral Priory Church at the dissolution; *inter alia*, a curious antique wooden wardrobe, now used for the like purpose in the present Church. Lord Carlisle has lately had Lanercost ruined Church cleaned out, the Dacre tombs repaired, doors and windows secured, &c. &c. He has lately done much also at Naworth Castle and the grounds; the former is now in excellent repair.

" Yours sincerely,   J. C. BROOKE."

123. " DEAR SIR,   *Heralds'-college, April 6,* 1789.
" I had last week a visit from Mr. Champion Dymoke, who has commissioned me to do some genealogical business for him. I think I have seen in your library a volume of Lincolnshire Church notes; if there is any thing therein concerning Scrivelsby, I wish you would copy it for me, or lend me the book so to do. From yours sincerely,   J. C. BROOKE, Somt."

124. " DEAR SIR,   *Heralds'-college, Jan. 16,* 1790.
" I yesterday sent to Nichols a parcel of the Shrewsbury papers to be sent to you; and request you will look them over, and give your candid opinion whether you think them worth publication. Part of them are papers in Henry the Eighth's reign with notes, ready for the press, and part are ten years of Elizabeth, from 1560 to 1570, the notes to which are written, but not copied fair; there are as many as will make three volumes in quarto *. Mr. Lodge comes to town to go with me

* They were so arranged, and published in the year following the date of this letter, under the title of, " Illustrations of British History, Biography, and Manners."

to the drawing-room on Monday; and on Wednesday, if you will be at home, we will take a ride over, and give you a morning call; if then you can give him any information relative to the best mode of ushering this work into the world, it will be a favour.

" We have lately had an official letter sent here from Le Chevalier de la Haye Chérin, Roi d'Armes de France, requesting a particular account of our office in every respect, as to our fees, powers, mode of transacting business, &c. &c. to lay before the national assembly, with a view of regulating these matters in France something after our model. Is not this rather paying us a compliment?

    " From yours sincerely,   J. C. BROOKE, Somᵗ."

---

125. Mr. GOUGH to Mr. BROOKE.

   " DEAR SIR,   *Enfield, June* 17, 1790.

" I received the two parcels of the Shrewsbury letters safe from Mr. Nichols, and shall be glad to see you and Mr. Lodge on Wednesday as early as you please, to breakfast at nine, if you can mount your horses so soon; for, whatever it may be in London, it is light here by six.

" I am much pleased with the intended publication as far as I have gone, and shall be ready to give the editor any information in my power. Yours very truly,   R. GOUGH."

---

126. Mr. BROOKE to Mr. GOUGH.

   " DEAR SIR,   *Heralds'-college, March* 10, 1790.

" I herewith send you Mr. Duncombe's MS. History of the Hundred of Wormelow, co. Hereford, which I request you will look over, and give me your opinion of.

    " From yours sincerely, &c.   J. C. BROOKE, Somᵗ."

---

   127. " DEAR SIR,   *Heralds'-college, Sept.* 6, 1790.

" I herewith return the Bourchier Monument corrected; shall be glad of an impression when engraved, as also an impression of the Disney monument from the drawing I furnished you with; and another print you promised me, have forgot what, but my letters will show you. I set out for Lincolnshire on Thursday or Friday, whence, after staying a short time on visits to the Dean and Mr. Turnor, I shall go forward into Yorkshire, and stay till November. On my return shall be glad to see your notes at Wingfield Church, to examine how they correspond with mine.

" Have you drawings of the Duke and Duchess of Suffolk at Wingfield? If you do not engrave them, I think the Society of Antiquaries should, for she being a Royal personage has as good a title as her aunt the Countess of Essex at Easton. I was disappointed at finding the Sussex tomb at Boreham in so ruinous a condition *; the arms are all gone, but drawings of them, as well as the inscriptions on the coffins in the vault, are luckily preserved in a MS. here.   Yours, &c.   J. C. BROOKE."

---

128. Mr. BROOKE to Mr. NICHOLS.

" DEAR SIR,   *Heralds'-college, Jan.* 8, 1791.
" I should not have been so long in answering your favour, but having spent the holidays with Lord Leicester in Hertfordshire, I only lately arrived from thence.   I am glad to hear you are engaged in so laudable an undertaking as the History of Leicestershire, in which I wish you all success.   I have an idea that the arms in our book are the same as are already printed in Burton's Leicestershire, except that ours are drawn; but, being in waiting this month, I will compare them in the course of it, and let you know.
" From your obedient humble servant, J. C. BROOKE, Somt."

---

129. Mr. BROOKE to Mr. GOUGH.

" DEAR SIR,   *Heralds'-college, March* 11, 1791.
" I thank you for the plates.   Mr. Basire by mistake sent me plate four of your second volume, Grevile and his wife at Cambden; it is beautifully executed.   I suppose you know he was ancestor to the Earl of Warwick, though the Peerages notice not this tomb.   I think you have not done Lady Disney justice; the tomb is curious, *alto relievo* in good preservation, like Queen Eleanor's at Westminster.   My drawing is not extraordinary; but the engraving has not done that justice.
" I find they are selling all their painted-glass in the Churches in France.   Young Mr. Howard, of Corby Castle in Cumberland, who is re-building his family chancel in Wetherall Church in a gothic style, has sent over a commission for the History of the League, painted in the windows of a Convent in Paris.
" Mr. Basire is engraving Arabella Stewart (from Mr. Walpole's) for Mr. Lodge; and has obtained, by means of the Gentleman's Magazine, a fine original of old George Earl of Salop from Chester, for the like purpose.   He has a very good subscription.   From yours, &c.   J. C. BROOKE, Somt."

---

130. Mr. BROOKE to Mr. NICHOLS.

" DEAR SIR,   *Heralds'-college, March* 12, 1791.
" If you think the paper that accompanies this worth printing in this month's Gentleman's Magazine, it is much at your

---

* This fine monument is rapidly falling to decay; but might still, at some expense, be restored.   It represents whole-length figures in armour of three Ratcliffes, Earls of Sussex, and Knights of the Garter.

service for the purpose, in which case pray correct it, if you see meet. I have a drawing of the seal mentioned in it, which, with the drawing I send, would together make a plate proper for the Magazine size. If you think this worth while, let me know, and I will send it you *.

"I have to apologise for not sooner writing to you about Leicestershire matters, but will not forget that business.

"From yours, &c.   J. C. BROOKE, Somt."

---

131. "DEAR SIR,   *Heralds'-college, Dec.* 15, 1791.

"I return your printed paper, which seems to me sufficiently correct, and requires no assistance from me. I never before heard of Dugdale's drawings of the Bottesford Monuments; they are certainly not with us. Query if not in possession of his heir, Mr. Guest, of Blyth-hall in Warwickshire? but all his drawings that I have seen are most miserably incorrect, in comparison of those of our time. I have a description of them taken by myself at Bottesford a few years ago, and sincerely wish both the elevation and figures were engraved; for, according to my observation, they are the finest collection together for one family in the kingdom. I congratulate the public on your labours for Leicestershire, and heartily wish you success; and am sincerely sorry to be so much involved in business at present as to prevent me lending you that assistance to which otherwise my inclination would strongly lead me. If by subscription, pray put my name down; and if you engrave the Bottesford Monuments, I will overlook the letter-press.

"From yours sincerely,   J. C. BROOKE, Somt."

---

132. Mr. BROOKE to Mr. GOUGH.

"DEAR SIR,   *Heralds'-college, Jan.* 3, 1792.

"Mr. Burton Conyngham, the Teller of the Exchequer in Ireland, and uncle to Viscount Conyngham, and an eminent patron of Irish literature, is now in England. He says you have had some correspondence with him, and he wishes to pay his respects to you before he returns. If agreeable to you, and you will give me a line when you are disengaged, we will give you a morning call before he leaves town. He mentioned Sunday next, if that day will be convenient, and will bring with him all his drawings of Irish antiquities to show you, of which he has a numerous and beautiful collection.

"From yours sincerely,   J. C. BROOKE, Somt."

* This article, consisting of "Anecdotes of Philip Howard Earl of Arundel," with a plate of an inscription in the Tower of London, and the Earl's seal, were inserted in the Magazine for March 1791, p. 218.

133. " DEAR SIR, *Heralds'-college, Jan.* 23, 1792.
" Mr. Conyngham sent this morning this letter to you open.
If you cannot go with him to Lady Lucan's to-morrow or Wednesday morning, you may suit your own convenience for that
purpose, as I often see her, and will appoint any morning that
may be agreeable to you both, and will accompany you.
" From yours sincerely, J. C. BROOKE, Somt."

Mr. Conyngham to Mr. Gough.
" DEAR SIR, *Jermyn Street.*
" I am mortified at being obliged to leave London so suddenly, which will prevent my cultivating the acquaintance I was
so fortunate to make by the means of Mr. Brooke. I shall certainly be obliged to leave this either Wednesday or Thursday;
but Lady Lucan will, I am sure, be much flattered by a visit
from you, which will be fixed by Mr. Brooke.
" The drawings I must necessarily take back with me to
arrange for publication, at least such as you shall think worthy;
but you may rest assured that, if you will do me the honour to
point out any worthy of being placed in your collection, I will
send you copies on my return to Ireland. I will send to-morrow
evening for the boxes. I have the honour to be, dear Sir, with
much respect, your most obedient and very humble servant,
" WILL. CONYNGHAM."

---

134. " DEAR SIR, *Heralds'-college, Feb.* 25, 1792.
" Mr. Constable, of Burton Constable, who inherits something
of the taste of his family for antiquity *, lately brought me a
pretty drawing of an old tomb in Winchester Cathedral with
the figure of a Knight cumbent, on his shield two cows in pale,
quartering three garbs †; do you recollect it, or know for whom
it was erected ?
" Mr. Bigland desires I will give his compliments to you. He
is making a fine pedigree in a book for the family of de la
Beech, and they wish to have the monuments of de la Beech at
Aldworth elegantly drawn in it; we have bad drawings here
of them taken by Ashmole at his visitation of the county of
Berks, which, I think, I once had copied for you, but have you
not since had better drawings made ? If you have and will lend
them, or an engraving of them, to Mr. Bigland, to copy, he
will be much obliged to you.
" From yours sincerely, J. C. BROOKE, Somt."

* See vol. V. p. 510.
† It is engraved in Britton's Cathedral Antiquities.

Audinet. sc.

The Right Hon. *Wm. Conyngham*

born 1733.___ died 1796.

David Earl of *Buchan* F.R.S. & S.A.

born 1742.___ died 1829.

135. " DEAR SIR, *Heralds'-college, March 20, 1793.*

" Mr. Duncombe has lately put into my hands another volume of his intended History of Herefordshire to look over; but, being shortly going to join the Yorkshire Militia at Durham for about three weeks, and being otherwise so much engaged in business that I have not leisure to pay that attention to these matters that my inclination leads me to, I send it to you as he desires. From the slight view I have had of it, I think, if it was properly dressed up, and made the most of, it would not rank in the lowest order of such publications.

" I am going on Friday to Penshurst to be present at the ceremony of young Sidney's taking possession of the estate on his coming of age, and expect much pleasure from the hospitality which will be exhibited in the old hall on the occasion. His affairs have been so well managed in his minority, that I am told his estate will be between 4 and £.5000 *per annum* clear, after paying all Mrs. Perry's debts.

" From yours sincerely,   J. C. BROOKE, Som^t."

The Rt. Hon. WM. BURTON CONYNGHAM.

This gentleman was born in 1733, the younger son of the Right Hon. Francis Burton, Esq. M.P. for Coleraine and the County of Clare, by Mary, third daughter of Lieut.-Gen. Henry Conyngham, and niece to the first Earl Conyngham. He was returned to the Parliament of Ireland in 1761 for Newton Limavady, and in two subsequent Parliaments for Kellybeggs; was Lieutenant-Colonel of the 12th regiment of dragoons, which he resigned in 1775, and the same year took his place as Comptroller and Commissioner of the Barrack Board; and in 1777 was appointed Cashier or Teller of the Exchequer in Ireland, and a Member of his Majesty's Privy Council. On the decease of his uncle Henry Earl Conyngham in 1781 he became possessed of the family estates in the county of Donegal, and of Slane in the County of Meath; and, together with his elder brother, who then succeeded

to the title of Baron Conyngham, had his Majesty's
license to assume the name and arms of that family.

In 1789 he was Vice-Admiral of Ulster and a
Governor of the county of Donegal. When the
office of Vice-Treasurer in Ireland was suppressed in
1793, Mr. Conyngham was appointed one of the
First Commissioners of the Board of Treasury, and
he so continued to his death, which took place at
Dublin, May 31, 1796, when, as he had never married, his estates devolved on his nephew, the present Marquis.

As a patron of antiquarian literature Mr. Conyngham was very conspicuous. In 1780 he was
the principal founder of a Society of Antiquaries
at Dublin, consisting of himself as President, the
Rev. Mr. Archdall, author of the Irish Monasticon
and Peerage, Mr. O'Connor the dissertator, Colonel
(afterwards General) Valancey the amazing etymo-
logist, Dr. Ellis, a physician, who created a Society
of Natural History, Dr. Ledwich, and Mr. Beau-
ford, of Athy. Matters went on very well until
Governor Pownall addressed a letter to them, which
Mr. Ledwich answered in the "Collectanea Hi-
bernica," No. XI.; and by the lively jocular way
in which he wrote, offended Colonel Valancey, who
expatriated him from his Collectanea, and from a
Society which immediately ceased *. On the form-

* Gent. Mag. vol. LXVI. p. 528. In Whitelaw's and Walsh's
" History of Dublin," under the account of the Royal Irish
Academy, is the following passage: " The first society of this
kind established in the University about the year 1782, was
called the Palœosophers. Their object was the investigation of
antient learning, particularly the fathers of the Church. Dr. Percival had just returned from the Continent, and introduced the
new system of chemistry, then almost totally unknown, and
little attended to in this country. The investigation of this had
excited a kindred zeal in pursuit of other sciences, and Dr. Percival proposed to Dr. Usher to establish a new society to promote
it. In the year 1785, therefore, another association was formed;
their object was the investigation of science and modern literature, and they denominated themselves Neosophers; into this

ation of the Royal Irish Academy, Mr. Conyngham was appointed Treasurer.

In 1786 Mr. Archdall dedicated his Monasticon Hibernicum to Mr. Conyngham, " as a testimony of respect for his many public and private virtues *."

Mr. Conyngham was the originator and patron of Murphy's magnificent work on the great monastic establishment of Batalha in Portugal †. Mr. Conyngham had himself visited that structure in 1783;

the Palæosophers in a short time merged. They met at each others' houses, dined together once every fortnight, read essays and debated ; they kept regular journals of their proceedings, but published no transactions. From these emanated the Royal Irish Academy, combining and enlarging the objects of both the former, and having distinct Committees for the investigation of Science, Antiquities, and Polite Literature."—"The Committee of Science meets on the first Monday of every month, that of Polite Literature on the second, that of Antiquities on the third, and the Academy at large on the fourth, at eight o'clock in the evening."

* Mr. Archdall was at that period Chaplain to Francis Lord Conyngham, Mr. C.'s brother. In 1789, when he published his Peerage, the seventh volume of which is dedicated to Henry Lord Conyngham, he was, through Mr. Conyngham's patronage, Rector of Slane.

† " Plans, Elevations, Sections, and Views of the Church and Royal Monastery of Batalha, situated in the Province of Estremadura in Portugal ; with the History and Description, by Fr. Louis de Sousa, with remarks. To which is prefixed an Introductory Discourse on the Principles of Gothic Architecture, by James Murphy, Architect. Illustrated with 27 plates. Lond. 1792—1796." Five Numbers, imperial folio, 15s. each. Mr. Murphy also published in quarto, 1795, " Travels in Portugal, through the Provinces of Entre Douro e Minho, Beira, Estremadura, and Aleintejo, in the years 1789 and 1790, consisting of Observations on the Manners, Customs, Trade, Public Buildings, Arts, Antiquities, &c. of that Kingdom." 24 plates. This was reviewed at some length in the Gentleman's Magazine, vol. LXV. pp. 848—855. Mr. Murphy also added in 1798 a second volume, intituled, " A General View of the State of Portugal, containing a Topographical Description thereof. In which is included, an account of the Physical and Moral State of the Kingdom; together with Observations on the Animal, Vegetable, and Mineral Productions of its Colonies. The whole compiled from the best Portuguese Writers, and from Notices obtained in the Country. Illustrated with 16 plates." Reviewed in Gent. Mag. vol. LXVIII. 960—963.

and, with two other gentlemen who accompanied
him in his travels through Portugal, had made some
sketches of it. " These sketches, which are very
correct representations of the original, gave Mr.
Murphy so high an idea of that building as to excite in him an earnest desire to visit it; and Mr.
Conyngham having generously offered his patronage
and support, he set out for Dublin in a trading vessel, and arrived at Oporto in January 1789." Mr.
Murphy concludes his preface with " acknowledging his obligations to this gentleman, by whose
munificence he was enabled to carry on his work.
The Portuguese have too much gratitude not
to add their acknowledgments to him also for
having made known the merits of this inimitable structure. Till now no part of it, as far
as I could learn, has ever been published. The
honour of presenting it to the world was reserved
for a private gentleman, a native of Ireland, who,
induced by no other motive than a love of the fine
arts and a wish for the advancement of science, has
expended upwards of £.1000 in rescuing this noble
edifice from the obscurity in which it has lain concealed for ages. I have taken the liberty to dedicate this work to him, in consideration of his exemplary liberality, and as an humble testimony of
my everlasting gratitude and respect." Above the
dedication is placed a portrait of Mr. Conyngham,
painted by Stuart and engraved by Schiavonetti.
Mr. Conyngham subscribed for ten copies of the
work.

Mr. Conyngham's large collection of drawings of
Irish antiquities, " from the time of the Druids to
the Reformation," (mentioned before in p. 428) comprised views of almost every relic of antiquity in
the country, with the plans of the most remarkable
castles and abbeys. They were drawn by J. J. Bar-
ralet, Michael-Angelo Bigari, G. Beranger, John
Fisher, Col. Valancey, Henry Pelham, Lord Car-
low, J. G. Bliers, R. Kendrick, Samuel Hayes, Esq.

Thomas French, and J. Ralton. Many of them
were engraved, and published in 1794 in the work
intituled, " Grose's Antiquities of Ireland," in two
volumes quarto. The Editor, Dr. Sedgwick, thus
acknowledges the obligation : " To conclude, I beg
leave to join my most grateful acknowledgements,
with those of the Publisher, to the Right Honourable William Conyngham, who, with unexampled
munificence, generosity, and patriotism, bestowed
his noble collection of drawings for the use of this
work, and at the same time indulged me with free
access to his magnificent library, abounding in valuable MSS. and books on this subject. The following
beautiful views are the truest panegyric on his taste
and love of the arts."

The work is dedicated in the following terms:

" To the Right Honourable William Conyngham, one of his
Majesty's most honourable Privy Council, and a Lord of the
Treasury in Ireland, the munificent Patron of whatever can promote the honour and happiness of that Kingdom, this volume *,
formed, for the most part, from his noble collection of Drawings, is, with the most respectful gratitude, humbly inscribed
by the Publisher,   M. HOOPER."

Mr. Conyngham was elected a Fellow of the
Society of Antiquaries of London in 1790. His
death occurred in Harcourt-place, Dublin, May 31,
1796. It was supposed that he had died intestate ;
and his property consequently devolved on his
nephew the Viscount (now Marquis of) Conyngham; but some time after a will was found †, which
divided his estates between his Lordship and his
mother the Baroness dowager.

---

* The second volume, published in 1795, has no preface or
dedication.

† The remarkable manner in which it came to light was found
related in the following memorandum of Gen. Valancey, made in his
" Green Book," which contained an historical account of manuscript and printed documents relative to Ireland, and was sold
at the sale of the General's library. " Mr. Burton Conyngham
had free access to my library in my absence, leaving a receipt for
such books as he took out. I was absent six years on duty in

The Right Hon. W. B. Conyngham to Mr. Nichols.

"Sir,   Dublin, July 7, 1791.

"I had the honour of receiving your letter inclosing to me the copy of a letter to Mr. Burton, of Leicestershire, relative to Sir William de Burton mentioned in Camden's Annals. His inquiries probably tended to find out whether that Sir William was of the Yorkshire or Leicestershire Burtons; and, though it gives no light upon the subject, I feel myself under obligations to you for taking the trouble to satisfy my curiosity. I wish I could in any shape be of service to you in this country; in which case I hope you will be as ready to apply to me as I was to you, through Sir Joseph Banks.

"I find this William de Burton was very confidentially employed by Edward the Third as early as his 9th year in Ireland, by a Liberate in the Rolls Office here, "pro victualibus providendis in Guerram Scotiæ." In 1345 he was employed by Sir R. de Ufford to seize the Earl of Kildare; and, from the connection with Lionel Duke of Clarence, probably attended him to France, where he appears to be one of Commissioners for treating of peace in 1360 (Rymer). In 1349 Sir William Burton (probably the same person) was appointed Ambassador to treat of peace with Lewis Count of Flanders, and in 1375 with the Pope. I have not been able to trace him further. But William Burton, author of the Commentaries on Antoninus, (descended from the Yorkshire Burtons,) mentions some particular circumstances of the family which I wished to have from his papers, said to have been in the possession of the Chetwynd family. To them I applied without success; and I am lately informed that the papers, &c. belonging to the Chetwynds, of Ingatestre in Staffordshire, are in the possession of Lord Talbot.

"I have the honour to be, your much obliged and obedient humble servant,   WILL. BURTON CONYNGHAM."

Cork harbour, leaving the care of my house in Dublin to a servant maid; this book was taken by Mr. C., and a receipt on a slip of paper given, which the servant put into a book on the shelf. She was some time after discharged, and another hired. On my return, at the expiration of six years, I missed this book. In about two years, taking down the octavo in which Mr. B.'s note had been carefully deposited, the receipt fell out. Mr. Conyngham was dead, and died, as was supposed, intestate; and his great estate devolved upon Lord Conyngham his nephew! I produced the receipt, and demanded the book or the payment of £.200. The book was not to be found; with others it had been packed in boxes, and sent to an auction; not sold, and brought back. At length Mr. A. Cooper, of the Treasury, who had the care of Mr. C.'s affairs, by long search discovered the book, when, on opening it, Mr. C.'s will fell out, by which it appeared that the estate was divided between Lord C. and his mother."

The Rev. THOMAS LEMAN, F. S. A.

This eminent antiquary, the oracle of his day on the subject of Roman Antiquities in Britain, was of a highly respectable Suffolk family*; and son

* Mr. Leman traced his descent from —— Leman, who in the reign of Henry VII. came into England, "flying from the Netherlands;" on what account is not said. His son, Thomas Leman, was Rector of Southam; and his grandson, Sir John Leman, died in 1632, and was buried at St. Michael's, Crooked-lane, London, having been an Alderman of that City, Sheriff 1606, and Lord Mayor 1616.

William, the brother of Sir John, had five sons, each of whom was the progenitor of a family bearing the name.

1. John; he was seated at Beccles and Otley. He had two sons, William and Thomas. From the latter descended the Lemans of Wenhaston, the last of whom, Mrs. Philippa Leman, died in 1757, leaving her Wenhaston estate to her cousin the Rev. John Leman, who was great-grandson to William, the eldest son of John, and father to the subject of this memoir. On Mr. Leman's death, the male issue of the first-named John became exhausted.

2. Robert, who was buried at Ipswich, 1637. He had two daughters, Mary, married to Richard Bennet; and Alice to Charles Goring, Earl of Norwich.

3. Thomas, of Bruenshall in Hetheringset, and of Brampton. This branch became extinct in Mrs. Mary Leman, daughter of Robert Leman, of Brampton, Esq. who died in 1807, at the age of 84, leaving a large fortune to the Rev. Naunton Orgill, grandson of her aunt Sarah Leman, which Sarah was the wife of her kinsman William Leman, of Beccles, Esq. elder brother to the Rev. John Leman, of Wenhaston, the father of the antiquary.

4. William, of Warboys in Huntingdonshire, Rampton in Cambridgeshire, and Northaw in Herts, whose son William Leman, Esq. was created a Baronet in 1665. The title became extinct on the death of William Leman, grandson to the first Baronet, in 1742. The name of Leman was assumed by Richard Allic, of Northaw, Esq. cousin to the last Baronet; and after his death by John Grainger, also of Northaw, Esq. See their pedigree in Clutterbuck's Hertfordshire, vol. II. p. 44.

5. Philip, of Herefordshire, and also of Thames Ditton in Surrey, died in 1679, aged 89; and had a son named John.

The above is taken from Mr. Leman's own account of his family in one of the genealogical volumes bequeathed by him to the Bath Institution Library.

of the Rev. John Leman, of Wenhaston in that
county, by Anne his wife, daughter of Clement
Reynolds, of Cambridge. He was born at Kir-
stead in Norfolk, March 29, 1751; and went to
school at Uggeshall in Suffolk in 1758.

He was afterwards of Emanuel-college, Cambridge,
where, from congenial pursuits, he formed a strict
friendship with his fellow collegian, the Rev. Dr.
Bennet, subsequently Bishop of Cloyne. He took
the degree of B. A. 1775; was elected a Fellow of
Clare-hall, and proceeded to the degree of M. A.
1778. He never held any other ecclesiastical preferment but the Chancellorship of Cloyne, to which
he was presented before 1796 by Bishop Bennet.
It was a perfect sinecure, being called £.500, but
never brought Mr. Leman in £.200. Through the
favour of Bishop Bennet, and his interest with his
successors, Mr. Leman was some time excused residence, on the score of ill health; but a succeeding
Archbishop (Brodrick), insisting on Mr. Leman's
residence, compelled him to resign it*. In 1788
he was elected a Fellow of the Society of Antiquaries; and he proved himself worthy of that honour
by his attention to the history of his Country, particularly during the period of its occupation by the
Romans. In conjunction with his friend Dr. Bennet †, he traversed nearly every remain of British
trackway or Roman road ‡, and liberally contri-

* See a letter from Bp. Bennet to Dr. Parr, in Parr's Works,
vol. VII. p. 110
† See vol. IV. of this Work, p. 703.
‡ Mr. Leman thus notices those who have trod in the same
paths. " Lord Arundell in the time of Charles I. endeavoured
to have surveys and plans made of the roads and stations on
them; but all these curious memorandums were lost to the
world by a fire at Worksop in 1761; as indeed would soon have
been the knowledge of these antiquities themselves, had it not
been for the feeble efforts of Leland, who first casually noticed
them in his useful journies; of Aubrey, though he had indeed
more zeal than knowledge in the pursuit; of the active but
visionary Stukeley, who, by examining the remains on the spot,
has been of incalculable service; of Horsley, perhaps the best

REV. THOMAS LEMAN, F. S. A.   437

buted the result of his investigations, wherever they
could be appropriately bestowed. *Volens semper-
que juvare paratus* was his family motto, and suited
him well.

To Mr. Nichols he communicated an Essay " on
the Roman Roads and Stations in Leicestershire,"
printed in the History of that County, vol. I.
p. clxvii.; to Mr. Clutterbuck, he contributed a
very learned and ingenious Memoir concerning
" the primæval inhabitants in Hertfordshire, and
the roads and earthworks which formerly existed
in it, whether of British or Roman origin," printed
in vol. I. of the " History of Herts," pp. vi—xvii.;
to Mr. Surtees he presented some interesting observations on the Roman and British state of
Durham, accompanied by plans of Roman and
British roads and stations; and to Mrs. Ogborne
" a slight sketch of the Antiquities of Essex," prefixed to that lady's History of the County, pp. i—iv.
To his friend Sir Richard Hoare he supplied some
maps for his " History of Giraldus Cambrensis * ;"
to the Magna Britannia of Messrs. Lysons, Bishop
Bennet and Mr. Leman contributed much † ; and

of writers on the subject; of Roy, whose character has given
credit to this line of study, and whose professional abilities have
illustrated and improved it; of the ingenious Mr. Reynolds,
who, without seeing them, has thrown light on many of the
obscurer parts by his labours; and still more by the unwearied
exertions of Dr. Mason, of Cambridge, who, at a time when
this part of our early history was sinking into neglect, and the
knowledge of it even disfigured and disgraced by the reveries of
Salmon, employed no small part of his life in visiting the roads
and stations with the active spirit of Stukeley; in which he has
been imitated of late by my respected friend the Bishop of
Cloyne, the late General Simcoe, Sir Richard Hoare, and others,
to which list I am proud to add my own name." History of
Hertfordshire, vol. I. p. xv.

* In the dedication of the second volume of his Ancient History of Wiltshire, to Archdeacon Coxe, Sir Richard remarks,
(in 1822), " Twenty years have elapsed since, in concert with
our mutual friend Mr. Leman, we projected the History of
Ancient Wiltshire, which has at length been accomplished."

† In the preface to his Devonshire the Rev. Daniel Lysons
says, " The late learned Bishop of Cloyne obligingly transmitted

to Mr. Brewer's "Introduction to the original Delineations, topographical, historical, and descriptive,
intituled, The Beauties of England and Wales,"
Mr. Leman furnished much intelligence in regard
to British and Roman Antiquities*. Doubtless
other authors have been equally indebted.

Of the Itinerary of Richard of Cirencester, he
had a very high opinion; and the edition of that
work, published in 1809, with a translation and
extensive commentaries †, was chiefly prepared by

his paper on the Roman Roads and Stations not long before his
death; and on the subject of Ancient Encampments, I have been
kindly assisted by his friend and fellow-traveller the Rev. T. Leman."

* "It is with sincere pleasure that the Editor acknowledges
the assistance of the Rev. T. Leman, of Bath, since the name of
this gentleman must necessarily bestow importance on those
pages which underwent his revision. To Mr. Leman this Work
is indebted for the drawings of the two Maps by which it is
illustrated; the first exhibiting the different tribes of Britain,
with their towns and trackways as they existed at the first invasion of Cæsar, and the second containing a display of Roman
stations and roads.—It is here necessary to explain that the
latter map is formed on one, from a drawing by the Rev. T.
Leman, inserted in Mr. Hatcher's edition of Richard of Cirencester; to which are added, in the present publication, numerous
discoveries made since the appearance of that work. — That
part of the letter-press which relates to the geography of antient
Britain, is chiefly formed on intelligence conveyed by Mr. Leman; and it is to be regretted that the limits of the Introduction prevented the Editor from availing himself more largely of
the rich stores of information unreservedly laid open by so profound and judicious an antiquary. All that is of principal value
in the remarks on the construction and characteristical features
of Roman roads, likewise proceeded from information and corrections afforded by the same gentleman." Mr. Brewer's preface to " Beauties of England and Wales," p. xxviii.

† "This valuable treatise was discovered by Charles Julius
Bertram, a professor residing at Copenhagen; who transmitted
it to Dr. Stukeley, our celebrated British antiquary, who re-published [an abstract of] it in his Itinerarium Curiosum. The
original edition was published, together with other works, in a
thin octavo volume, at Copenhagen, in 1757, and became so very
scarce, as seldom to be met with. In the year 1808 my friend
Archdeacon Coxe, assisted by our joint friend the Rev. Thomas
Leman, supplied notes illustrating the History of Richard; the
original text was translated into English; and the whole was
published in the following year in one volume octavo." Hoare's

him. His own copy, with many notes, is left to the Bath Institution. He could scarcely hear with patience any hint of suspicion that Richard is not what he pretends to be *. The late Rev. J. J. Cony-

Ancient Wiltshire, vol. II. part ii. p. 16 —It is intituled, "The Description of Britain, translated from Richard of Cirencester; with the original Treatise de Situ Britanniæ, and a Commentary on the Itinerary, illustrated with Maps." 8vo, pp. 320. The editor, Mr. Henry Hatcher, the friend and amanuensis of Mr. Archdeacon Coxe, acknowledges his obligations "to the Right Rev. the Lord Bishop of Cloyne, for his remarks on the Roman roads and stations; to the Rev. Thomas Leman for the valuable Commentary on the Itinerary [this occupies 66 pages of smaller type], the result of his long and successful investigation of British antiquities. and for many remarks and corrections, of which I have been happy to avail myself; to the Rev. William Coxe, Archdeacon of Wilts, for the original treatise, for various interesting communications, and for his kind advice and inspection during the progress of this work; to Sir Richard Colt Hoare, Bart. for some information relative to the Welsh Iters; and to William Owen Pughe, Esq. for his communications relative to the manners, customs, and language of the ancient Britons." —In 1814 Mr. G. Dyer, bookseller, of Exeter, published "A Commentary on Richard of Cirencester, and Antoninus's Itineraries of Britain; containing the *usual* explanations of itinerary names — their *long-lost* imports — sites of *doubtful* stations — places of supposed *lost* ones—and proofs of *imaginary* ones. This Work also contains, the *common* expositions, and the *genuine* imports, of the principal names of the world; remarks on our history and description, depending on fiction; with Richard's Original Work," 8vo, pp. 230. In 1816 the same author re-published the same, with some further results of his lucubrations, intituled, "Vulgar Errors, ancient and modern, attributed as imports *to the proper names of the globe*, clearly ascertained, with *approximations* to their rational descents. Investigating the *origin* and *uses* of letters—Moses's (hitherto misunderstood) account of Eden—Biblical *long-lost* names— *unknown* names of Heathen gods, of nations, provinces, towns, &c. With a Critical Disquisition on every Station of Richard of Cirencester and Antoninus in Britain, exhibiting our fables concerning it, and showing from names, distances, &c. its *certain*, *doubtful*, or *imaginary* situation. To which is added Richard's Original Work." These match in size with the volume first-named.

* " It has been the fashion, and even amongst distinguished authors, to accuse Richard of Cirencester of incorrectness; but his authenticity becomes more established every year, by the discovery of Stations recorded by him in his Itinerary, and omitted in that of Antonine." Hoare's Ancient Wiltshire, II. pt. ii. 29.

beare *, on the other hand, was confident that the work was a modern forgery, and meditated a paper on the subject for the Archæologia.   He considered the Latinity of Richard as not that of the fourteenth or fifteenth century, but of the preface-writers of the eighteenth.

Mr. Leman had a good collection of historical and topographical works.   He had several volumes of genealogy written by himself, which he left with some of his annotated books to the library of the Bath Institution†.

* Of this talented gentleman some ample memoirs are preserved in the Gentleman's Magazine, XCIV. ii. 187, 376, 482.

† In a paper " On the Connection of Bath with the Literature and Science of England; by the Rev. Joseph Hunter, F. A. S." read before the Literary and Philosophical Association of Bath in the spring of 1827, Mr. Leman was thus appropriately noticed : " Last only because he was the last who ceased to pour upon the world the lights of his antiquarian and historical knowledge, must be named that careful investigator of one very important branch of our national antiquities, the early roads and other earthworks, which are scattered in such abundance over the surface of this Island,—the Rev. Mr. LEMAN, a Founder and original Trustee of this Institution, who has marked his sense of its usefulness and permanence by making its library the depository of many volumes of Genealogical Collections in his own neat and beautiful hand, and many scattered but precious notices of various English antiquities.   Few are the works of English topography that have appeared in his time that have not owed something to the assistance, ever so kindly rendered, of Mr. Leman."

The following are the books left by Mr. Leman to the Library of the Bath Institution :

Carey's County Maps, interleaved.   An Epitome of the British and Roman Topography of each County, as far as Norfolk, in the alphabetical order, and of the County of Suffolk, is written on the inserted leaves, with other topographical remarks.

Carrington Bowles's Maps of the Counties, interleaved, full of manuscript notes, historical and topographical.   This book appears to have been taken by Mr. Leman in his journeys.

Horsley's Britannia Romana, with many valuable notes and additions.

Stukeley's Itinerarium Curiosum, vol. I. with many notes.

Reynolds's Iter Britanniarum, with a few notes.

The Description of Britain, translated from Richard of Ciren-

There was an elegance running through every thing about Mr. Leman. His hand-writing was correct and beautiful, his mode of expressing himself, in conversation or in writing, appropriate and happy, without being either adorned or having the appearance of an intention to convey more than he felt. His house (one of the best in the Royal Crescent, Bath,) was furnished in excellent taste; his study retired and quiet, an irregular room, or rather two rooms thrown into one, the inner separated from the other by a slight paling in which was a sort of door. He had some good paintings, amongst them a full-length of Sir Robert Naunton *; and

cester, 8vo, 1809. This is enriched with very numerous and important notes.

General Roy's Work on the Roman Antiquities of Britain.

Genealogical Collections from printed books, the visitations, previous collections, with some original pedigrees, 13 vols. folio; arranged in counties, viz. Yorkshire; Cambridgeshire; Norfolk and Suffolk, 2 vols.; Bucks; Berks, 2 vols.; Warwick; Gloucester; Somerset; Devon and Cornwall, 3 vols.

Two volumes of Wiltshire Pedigrees, and a volume of Notes on Roman and British Roads and Stations, were left by Mr. Leman to Sir Richard Colt Hoare, Bart. who had long been his intimate friend, and are now in the library at Stourhead.

* Mr. Leman was descended from the family of Naunton; but not from Sir Robert, whose issue became extinct in the second generation. It has been suggested that a memoir of Sir Robert Naunton was published, or privately printed, by Mr. Leman. There was a thin volume published in 1814, intituled, " Memoirs of Sir Robert Naunton, Knt. author of the Fragmenta Regalia; with some of his posthumous Works from Manuscripts in his own hand, never before printed ;" but it is presumed Mr. Leman was not concerned in its compilation. Perhaps the following note to Mr. Nichols may tend to explain the circumstance :

" St. Martin's-lane, Oct. 17, 1814.

" J. Caulfield and G. Smeeton respectfully beg Mr. Nichols's acceptance of the present copy of Sir Robert Naunton's Memoirs; the bulk of which, Mr. N. will perceive, is taken from his own indefatigable work, the History of Leicestershire. The Publishers were led to expect more manuscript materials; but, in consequence of the gentleman who promised them being for a long time indisposed, they are under the necessity of putting forth the volume in its present state."

his drawing-room was painted *en fresco* with the
scenery around Lake *Leman*.   In his latter years
he was quite celebrated for his agreeable and splendid parties, and he received all strangers of eminence.   His house was open one evening in the
week to all who were introduced to him, and in
the other evenings to some.   He usually rode out
in a morning on horseback.

Mr. Leman was twice married,—first, at Bath,
Jan. 4, 1796, to Frances, daughter and heiress of
William Nind, Esq. Barrister-at-law, of Beaufort-
buildings, Strand, and widow of Colonel Alexander
Champion, of Bath.   This lady died Jan. 15, 1818;
and was buried in the burying-ground of Walcot,—
the parish at Bath in which Mr. Leman resided.
His second lady, to whom he was married about
January 1819, was Frances, daughter of the Right
Hon. Sir Robert Deane, Bart. and aunt to the pre-
sent Lord Muskerry, widow when married to Mr.
Leman of Colonel John Hodges, only son of Sir
James Hodges.   This lady survives him.   Mr. Leman had no children by either marriage.   He had
three sisters; Philippa, married to John Ewen, Lucy
to Richard Purvis, Capt. R. N. and Lætitia to the
Rev. Thomas Purvis, cousin-german of Richard.

Mr. Leman was buried in Walcot burying-ground,
where his first wife lies interred; but a cenotaph to
his memory has been erected in the chancel of
Wenhaston Church, Suffolk.   He left very explicit
directions respecting it, and especially its heraldric
ornaments.   It is in good taste,—an altar-tomb of
the old fashion, six feet long by three wide, with
shields within quatrefoils on the sides and ends.
An inscription on the upper surface was written by
Bishop Bennet :

Sacred to the memory
of the Rev. Thomas Leman, of Wenhaston-hall
in this parish,
who died on the 17th day of March 1826;

the last male descendant of his ancient name.
He added to the feelings of a Gentleman,
Talents and Learning without Ostentation,
and Christian Piety without Austerity.
In a curious line of antiquarian research
(the knowledge of Romain remains in Britain)
he had few superiors;
but in the nobler and more amiable merit
of domestic life,
as a husband, a son, a brother, a friend, and a master,
he never was exceeded.
We flatter not in the grave:
" He that saw it bears record, and his record is true."
John, xix. 25.

Six brass plates are affixed to the monument, namely, three in front, one at each end, and one on the upper surface (it stands against a wall), each having engraved upon it a shield of arms. At the head the arms, crest, and motto of Leman; at the foot, sixty-four quarterings, most of which were brought in by the marriage of John Leman, Esq. (Mr. Leman's great-grandfather) with Theophila Naunton, daughter of Robert Naunton, nephew of Sir Robert Naunton, the Secretary, and eventually in her issue heiress to the Nauntons, Mr. Leman conceiving that the descendants of this lady were entitled to the quarterings of Wingfield and Vere. The three front shields contain the achievements of the marriages of his ancestors with heiresses of Sherwood, Naunton, and Sterling; and that on the upper surface, Leman impaling Deane or Nind, for these two families (it is remarkable as a coincidence) use the same figure.

———

1. Rev. T. Leman to Mr. Nichols.

" Sir,   18, *Margaret-buildings, Bath, Jan.* 1792.

" As I find that you intend publishing soon a History of Leicestershire, in case any information that I can give you about the Roman Roads or Stations in that county may be thought useful to you, I shall be ready and willing to contribute my mite towards so useful an undertaking.

" My friend Dr. Farmer spoke to me about it when I was last at Cambridge; and I fully intended calling on you as I passed through London for that purpose, but was prevented by indisposition. My fellow traveller (the present Bishop of Cork) Dr. Bennet, who attended me several summers in riding about England, informed me he had sent you some extracts for this purpose; but, lest he should not have done it, I would readily look over my papers again, and think it no trouble to collect together every thing I can recollect of having observed in passing sometimes through your county.

" I am your very humble servant, THOMAS LEMAN."

2. " SIR, 46, *Rivers-street, Bath, Nov.* 5, 1793.

" On my arrival here yesterday from Ireland, I found a parcel from you, which I am sorry to say has been at Bath for these last eighteen months; but you may rest assured that, had I known of its having been here, I would have ordered it to have been forwarded immediately to Dublin, and would have returned you directly an answer to it.

" I saw, whilst I was with the Bishop of Cork in the year 1792, the paper which you sent to him for his inspection, which I had slightly drawn up about the Roman Roads in Leicestershire, and we both thought that it would be better not to alter it; nor indeed, on looking it over now, do I see any correction I could make except in page 2, where Godmanchester is mentioned. I wish the words, ' the supposed,' to be inserted before Durolepens; for, though almost all the antiquaries, except Horsley, gave it that name, I have strong reasons to think it is not so.

" In sending me Mr. Throsby's Excursion, I suppose you wish I should give you my opinion about it; and I will not scruple to say that it appears to me infinitely too trifling to be inserted in any book in the eighteenth century. Mr. Throsby appears to me totally unacquainted with the antiquities of all other counties as well as his own; and, if it appears surprising that any one at this time of day should insert even the errors of the great and venerable Camden, surely it is much more so that a person should copy the known mistakes of other ignorant and ill-informed authors (as in the note to page 11 of his History of Leicester). In the " Leicestershire Collections" also, (Bibl. Top. Brit. vol. VII. p. 289,) is an extract in a note even from Salmon.

" Mr. Bartlett, in his History of Manceter, has been misled by Baxter (p. 6), into an error in regard to Ostorius's line of fortifications. Camden, who possessed the greatest talents, supposed them to have existed on the Nen; he is complimented by the great Lipsius on this observation. And the discovery of Richard of Cirencester's book on the Itineraries has confirmed the judicious observation both of the antiquary and the critic.

" This line of fortifications exists almost at this hour; and I once intended, with my friend Colonel Simcoe, to have given an explanation of the celebrated passage of Tacitus which alludes.

to it, together with a map drawn by him. They are now both by me *; and show, in the strongest manner, his profound learning, and his intimate acquaintance with the tactics of the Romans.

" The paper I sent you I wished might be of some use to you, in the manner you should find most convenient to yourself; but I own that both myself and the Bishop of Cork would find ourselves hurt in case any observations that either he or I had communicated to you were at all mixed with those of Mr. Throsby.

" I am, with the greatest respect, your very humble servant,
THOMAS LEMAN.

" In case I can give you any other information, I shall be very ready to do it."

———

3. " SIR,   46, Rivers-street, Nov. 24, 1793.

" The infinite pains you seem to be taking in your History of Leicestershire makes me almost wish that I had drawn out more fully the paper I sent you ; and indeed, had the Bishop of Cork or myself found time when I was with him in Ireland, I believe we should have been almost tempted to do it. I can only answer for the great correctness of the trifle I gave you.

" As you have desired me to make any little alterations I think necessary, I have taken the liberty of marking with my pen, in one or two places, such as I think would be better left out. Such is the whole note of Salmon's page cl. ; and a few incorrections in Mr. Gale's account of the Watling-street, which may be better corrected from the map †.

" I make no apologies for these observations, as they are meant to serve you ; and I leave you at perfect liberty to take notice of them or not, as you think best.

" I know not whether I mentioned before, that, in case subscriptions are taken in for your work, I should think myself honoured in having my name inserted as a subscriber.

" I am yours, &c. &c. &c.   THOMAS LEMAN."

———

4. " SIR,   Stoke-park, Aug. 13, 1795.

" Seeing in your Gentleman's Magazine of last month that the first parts of your History of Leicestershire are ready for delivery, I will be obliged to you to pack up carefully for me a copy of the small paper, and have it sent by Wiltshire's Bath waggon, directed to Mrs. Hodges, No. 11, Brock-street, Bath ; and Mr. Penn, with whom I am at present, desires that his copy of the small paper also may be sent to his house in Spring-gardens.

* Qu. was this ever printed?
† Mr. Leman added several other corrections, which were properly attended to.

" We intend both being in London the latter end of next week, when I will wait upon you, and pay for them.

" I am yours, &c. &c. &c. THOMAS LEMAN."

---

5. " SIR,   *Crescent, Bath, Oct.* 24, 1801.

" In regard to Bigland's Collections for Gloucestershire, I have looked it over, and find no part of the least use to me except the twenty-second number of the first volume ; I shall, therefore, return the work to you, and you will inform me if I may keep this at the original price. The only thing which could have been interesting to me would have been, if Mr. Bigland had given the genealogies of the different families.

" I am yours, &c. &c. &c. THOMAS LEMAN.

" Have you, among your papers, any account of the last three or four generations of the Waldgraves, who resided at Smallbridge in Suffolk ? Or can you tell me anything of the Chauncys who lately lived in Hertfordshire, more particularly such part of them as are descended from the family of John Leman of Nuttam *, who lived about the beginning of last century."

---

6. " SIR,   *Crescent, Bath, Nov.* 18, 1801.

" I return you my thanks for the Waldgrave pedigree you sent me ; unfortunately it is not so full, or continued so long, as the one at present in my possession. You mention a pedigree of the Chauncys already printed ; pray in what work is it to be found † ? for I should like to see it. And in case you can, from any of your acquaintance, find out how the Strodes of Hertfordshire were descended from the Strodes of Somersetshire, I shall be obliged to you for the information.

" I remain yours, &c. &c. THOS. LEMAN."

---

7. " SIR,   *Crescent, Bath, Feb.* 3, 1807.

" As I have a friend now in London, who will return to Bath in the course of a few days, I shall think myself much obliged to you if you will have the kindness to take out, from the Antiquarian Society, such books and papers as may be due to me, and send them, directed to me, to the Right Honourable Isaac Corry's, No 38, St. James's-street, to the care of his sister Mrs. Browne, who will convey them to Bath.

" I most earnestly hope that, when you have completed your very valuable History of Leicestershire, you will add to it a full index, which is absolutely necessary ; but as I know that such an

---

* On this letter being shown to Mr. Gough, he remarked to Mr. Nichols: "The Chauncy pedigree you gave me has no Lemans in it."
† In Chauncy's Hertfordshire, must have been the answer.

undertaking is attended with not only great trouble, but also considerable expense, I shall be happy to contribute my share towards it, exclusive of the work itself, which will then be a model for the collection to be made for all other counties.

"I remain, Sir, your very humble servant, THOS. LEMAN."

---

8. " SIR,   *Crescent, Bath, Jan.* 1, 1812.

"I received very safe the last volume of the History of Leicestershire. I observe, however, that you have not charged the engraving of the plate of Elmsthorpe*; will you, therefore, when you send me the Antiquarian Society papers, inform me what I am indebted to you for it, that I may pay it also.

"I am yours, &c. &c.   THOMAS LEMAN."

---

9. " SIR,   *March* 13, 1814.

"Having observed in one of the Magazines a proposal for giving to the world an account of the Antiquities of the County of Hertford, I desired my bookseller here (Barrett) to put my name down as a subscriber to it; and, as I wish well to a literary work of this kind, and am a great favourer of County Histories in general, if the author be a friend or an acquaintance of yours, you may say that I will send him (in case he stands in need of it) a short memoir of the county while possessed by the primeval inhabitants, down to the time of the Romans, as the Bishop of Cloyne and myself have taken some pains about it; and are certainly better informed, relative to this æra, than most other antiquaries. The same also may be offered to the gentleman who has undertaken Cheshire, if you know him.

"I am yours, &c. &c.   THOMAS LEMAN."

---

10. R. CLUTTERBUCK, Esq. to Mr. NICHOLS.

" DEAR SIR,   *Watford, March* 16, 1814.

"I received your note last night, and am much flattered by the contents. I shall be very happy to avail myself of Mr. Leman's offer, and will write to him to-day. I have fully stated to him that, had his offer come a short time hence, it would have been out of my power to have accepted it; and, from what I have said respecting my order of arrangement, he will see that I am desirous of being favoured with his communication immediately.

"Upon considering the nature of the memoir, I think, in the order of arrangement with respect to time, that it should form the very first part of my work, and come in under the title of ' Aboriginal or Ancient Inhabitants;' after which may

* Which was dedicated to Mr. Leman.

follow the description of the Roman Roads, which I have at present annexed to the geographical description. As I had not intended to introduce such an account as I am now likely to receive, for this reason it will be desirable to stop the press for a few days, in the course of which I hope to receive Mr. Leman's communication. Believe me to be, dear Sir,

"Very faithfully yours, ROBERT CLUTTERBUCK."

---

11. Mr. LEMAN to Messrs. NICHOLS.

"SIRS, *March* 1814.

"This morning I have had a letter from Mr. Clutterbuck in consequence of what I mentioned to you, and feel myself a good deal puzzled to know what to do, as I find he had sent the first portion of his History of Herts to the press, and has stopped the printing of it till he receives the memoir I mentioned. Now you must know that such a memoir requires some little time to digest; and that such is my state of health at present, that I cannot turn my attention, or give up my time always when I wish to do it. It would take me probably a month to compose and to correct it; nor would I wish it even then to go out of my hands without its being first revised by my old friend the Bishop of Cloyne, for to give to the world a crude and indigested work, would mortify me as much as it would disappoint the encouragers of his History.

"In regard to the History of Durham, I had some time since an application from the author for assistance; and I have sketched already for him a memoir, which I have not been able to complete, on account of my health not permitting me to apply, for any length of time, to any object.

"In regard to Cheshire, I drew up last year for a friend of mine, a memoir for Cheshire, which, if it will be of use to Mr. Ormerod, I will endeavour to procure for him, as I sent it into that county to my friend Mr. Leycester, and since to a Mr. Pyke (the brother of the Member for Wicklow), who was coming to reside at Shrewsbury.

"You will mention this circumstance to Mr. Clutterbuck immediately; and let me know his answer.

"I am yours, &c. THOS. LEMAN.

"On second thoughts I think it better to write to Mr. Clutterbuck myself."

---

12. "SIRS, *Royal Crescent, Bath, June* 21, 1816.

"With this you receive the eight parts of the History of Leicestershire, which I would have whole-bound in calf, lettered and gilt. I beg great care may be taken, lest the plates, *which are emblazoned*, should be beaten with the letter-press, and deface the opposite side. I am yours, &c. THOS. LEMAN."

The following character of Mr. Conyngham appeared (together with a bad copy of his portrait) in the European Magazine in 1794:

"The abilities of Mr. Conyngham have been particularly applied to objects of national utility and convenience. He often speaks in the Irish Senate upon matters of trade and policy; and, as few men possess more information on these subjects, he is always heard with the greatest attention. He is a very excellent engineer. The road that leads to Dublin from the Phœnix-park bears his name; an honour bestowed upon him for planning it, and the exertion and talents he displayed in its fabrication. And also one of the finest roads in Ireland, extending upwards of sixty miles, from Rutland to Donegal, was planned by him; a work which for ages had been considered as impracticable by all the gentlemen of that country. But the subject which mostly engages his liberal leisure is antiquity. The collection of drawings relating to Irish churches, abbeys, and castles, in his possession, is esteemed the most valuable extant; and there are but few objects of antiquity in Spain or in Portugal of which he has not drawings, as he travelled through those countries accompanied by three ingenious artists he employed for that purpose. One of these artists relates, that three score workmen were employed by him in digging and clearing away the rubbish which concealed a great part of the Theatre of Saguntum in Spain. The novelty of this sight gave rise to a report among the people of that town, that Mr. Conyngham was digging for the gold bells, valued at one hundred thousand pounds sterling, which tradition reported to have been concealed in this place. The fable obtained credit so far that the Prime Minister of the day thought it expedient to dispatch one of his Majesty's engineers from Madrid to inspect these operations; the workmen notwithstanding proceeded, and discovered the treasures which Mr. Conyngham sought for; they consisted of a number of ancient inscriptions, bases, and capitals of columns, and a curious Roman altar. As soon as drawings were taken of these antique fragments, the originals were presented to the engineer as a reward for his trouble."

Mr. Conyngham's "Observations on the description of the Theatre of Saguntum, as given by Emanuel Marte, Dean of Alicant, in a letter addressed to D. Antonio Felix Zondadario; and a "Letter to Joseph C. Walker, Esq. being an Appendix to the same memoir," appeared in the Transactions of the Royal Irish Academy, vol. III. pp. 21—50, with eight plates.

---

1. Mr. JAMES MURPHY to the Rt. Hon. W. B. CONYNGHAM.

"DEAR SIR,   *Royal Convent of Batalha, March* 1789.

"Since I had the pleasure of seeing you last, Providence has favoured me with a safe voyage and an agreeable journey to

Batalha, where I was kindly received by the Prior and all the
Convent; they remember you perfectly well, and often speak
of you with the highest respect. Your elegant sketches of this
fine building often led me to think on the grandeur of the original; which I think is one of the finest pieces of Gothic architecture in Europe. If the distance were three times as far I would
most cheerfully undertake the journey without repining at the
length of the way to contemplate such inimitable beauty.

" I have finished all the sketches of the Church and Monastery,
Capellas imperfectus, &c. with the doors, windows, columns,
bases, capitals, and mouldings on a large scale accurately figured,
together with the tombs, pataras of the groins, figures, groups,
ornamental pieces and inscriptions throughout the whole building, the manner of uniting the stone in the fleur de luce ornament, roof, spire, pinnacle, &c. Where any part is executed
with uncommon judgment, difficulty, or elegance, I have drawn
it with the minuteness of a Degodetz. As the most correct
sketches that can be taken of a complicated building like this
cannot be compiled at a distance without a great part being
supplied from recollection, many traces of which are liable to
be worn out by length of time, therefore I thought it better to
make the finished drawings on the spot. The following are
finished nearly on the same scale with the large plan I made for
you in Dublin: A general plan of the Church and Monastery—
plan of the second story—plan of the second story of *Capellas
imperfectas*—plan of the roof of Church—elevation of the south
front—elevation of the north front—elevation of the west front,
including the refectory, kitchen, &c. being the extent of the
ancient building—a general section from east to west, through
Church, Chapel, and *Capellas imperfectas*—section of *Capellas
imperfectas* (large).

" I have some views of the building yet to complete before
I go to Alcobaça, where I hope to be well received, as the
good Prior of this Convent has given me a letter to that of Alcobaça, and another to the Dominican Convent at Lisbon. I
have endeavoured to penetrate into every part of the building
from the foundation to the top. The elevation of the spire is
equal to the height of a cone, whose base and angle of inclination of the side is given to find the altitude. The rest down-
wards can be measured with a line; this method has proved
two other modes of calculation which I tried.

" In the ancient building alone are eight staircases constructed within the walls, winding round a column, which with
the steps are cut out of the solid stone. To perfect the whole,
I have a complete description of the building, monuments, &c.
by Father Lewis de Sousa, a Portuguese fiedalgo, transcribed
from forty-five pages of large quarto, which I esteem the more
as you charged me to collect as much of the history of this Convent as possible. Some of the Friars were apprehensive at first

2 F 3*

that I did not come to Batalha for the sake of making drawings of the building, but for some other purpose. Lest they should take it in their heads to prevent me, I applied so close to the drawings day and night as to make all the sketches with a finished plan and elevation in twenty-two days. After all they often put me to the blush in relating the abilities of Manuel Caetano, and other celebrated Portuguese architects, who took off the whole building in a few minutes at one glance of an eye. My application threw me into a fever, which took its leave of me in one-and-twenty days, during which time I had no one near me to whom I could tell my sad story, not being able to speak ten words of the language, and none of the fathers could speak any language but Portuguese. The ignorance of the physician only helped to increase the evil; he was one of those wretches who carried fate and physic in his face, commissioned by that seminary of dunces at Coimbra to dispatch the unfortunate candidates for the grave! He knew no other remedy but bleeding, which he performed till he almost left me a bloodless corpse; hope was my last medicine, and that I should live one day to see all the drawings of Batalha in your possession, and prove my grateful recollection of your past friendship. The Consul of Treguria hearing that some one belonging to you was sick at Batalha, sent a messenger with a letter to me offering to have me brought to his own place; and another to the Prior charging him to let me want for nothing. If I could spare time, I would most cheerfully accept of his repeated visits, not so much for my own indulgence as to see the man whom Heaven has blessed with so large a portion of tenderness and humanity; he has just now sent me a letter recommending me to his best friend, Richard Sealy, Esq. Lisbon. Such is the case in every part through which you passed; the very whisper of your name is sufficient to make a friend.

" I was visited a few days ago by Marshal Valera, who has given me an invitation to his house at Coimbra; and promised to have me introduced to the Viscount Mormode Mor, the Prime Minister at Lisbon. He told the Prior that he thought it impossible to complete so large a work in the time, and expressed a great desire to see it published, which, if it ever is the case, the world will have a right to thank your penetration in bringing to light such a master-piece of hidden Gothic elegance, formed from the produce of the simple quarry alone without the least aid from those train of mouldering materials as timber, iron, copper, &c. to which our modern architects are obliged to have recourse. It is strange that amongst all the travellers that passed by Batalha none give us either drawing or satisfactory description of this Church. Mr. Twiss, who could so minutely describe the wretchedness of an Irish hamlet on the bleak mountains of Tipperary, could see nothing in this venerable pile, with its numerous pinnacles, mouldering minerets, and lofty spire, but the letters *lays* which I find at the entrance to the *Capellas imperfectas.*

" Inclosed is a sketch of the Viscount Clarard, the French pilgrim, who visited our Convent a few days ago in his journey to Rome.   He was dressed in a long grey coat and laced waistcoat, a black half mantlet of varnished oil cloth set with variegated shells, a broad hat and cockade, three long rosaries of different size and colour suspended from his neck and girdle, with a paper tin case, calabash, and pouch ; round his waist was a thick cord of St. Francis set with many knots, which he very devoutly applied to the shoulders of his servant, a huge fellow just deserted from the French service, and often experiencing his master's abilities in discipline.   The Count's whole retinue consisted of this single servant, who carried his baggage in a sheepskin wallet, suspended from his shoulders in an inclined direction across his back.   His age, as near as I can judge, is about twenty-eight, of a middle stature, with short black hair, and a countenance betraying some sentiments of sorrow for his youthful folly.   His story is rather too long for the few remaining lines of this letter.

" I shall not trouble you with a description of Oporto, which you know very well already.   The twentieth day I arrived there from Dublin, and made only a short stay, when I got letters from the Dominican Convent to Batalha ; the Consul, Mr. Whitbread, showed me many civilities, and put a letter into my hand on coming away, strongly recommending my knowledge of architecture to Mr. Stephens.   He has almost finished a large building there for the British factory, for which very little can be said, being in the anti-Moorish style, like all the modern works of architecture in this country.

" It distresses me I have not been able to write you before, though I prepared four letters to send you at different times, which my ignorance of the language rendered impossible to have forwarded. With this I am obliged to take a guide to Marinha, in order to have it sent to Lisbon.   Mr. Stephens, I understand, is expected there every day ; but I shall not make myself known to him without he has received your letter concerning me.   Let me intreat you, dear Sir, to favour with a few lines one who is poor and friendless in a foreign land, for be assured that among all who are attached to you by the ties of obligation and friendship, none wish you better, or would serve you with more zeal, than he who has the honour to be, dear Sir,

" Your very much obliged humble servant, JAMES MURPHY."

2. " DEAR SIR,   *Marinha Grande, Portugal, May* 1789.
" Having finished all the drawings of Batalha, I received a very friendly invitation from Mr. Stephens to spend a few days with him at Marinha Grande, which I readily accepted ; as being

in my way to Alcoboça. He informs me that the greatest confusion reigns in that Convent at present, the Queen having put a stop to their election of a new General, which causes some serious apprehension among them; the consequence they suppose at least will be an abridgement of their present unlimited power. He advises me not to set out for thence till something be determined on, when it will be in his power to obtain there an agreeable reception for me.

"The connoisseurs at Lisbon are in great expectation of shortly seeing the drawings of Batalha, which I do not purpose to submit to their inspection; but in this respect I will be entirely guided by your instructions.

"This day I received a letter from Mr. Skies, who begs me to assure you of his attachment; and informs me, that he has lately got three medals of great antiquity, which he wishes to send you by me if I should go to Feguiera, but as my circumstances will not admit of taking that journey at present, I must beg of him to forward them to me at Lisbon.

"Mr. Stephens, who is just returned from Lisbon, presents his compliments to you; likewise the Prior and all the Friars at Batalha. In a country like this, which is incessantly visited by strollers from all parts of Europe, every one who is not well recommended is set down at first sight as an impostor; and as I brought no letters from you, I must submit to be ranked under that name till time or your letter to Mr. Stephens, and your other friends here, convinces to the contrary.

"In a few days I set out for Alcobaca, where I purpose staying a few weeks, or according as I find any thing worth observation; from thence I will go to Lisbon by way of Mafra and Cintra, where I expect to receive your directions. A few lines from you will set me in an enviable situation; and make me forget the remembrance of many a painful feeling excited by the sorrowful reflections of being forsaken and friendless in this solitary country. I remain, dear Sir, with particular attachment, your faithful and obliged humble servant, JAS. MURPHY."

---

3. " DEAR SIR,   *Lisbon, June 28, 1789.*

" From Marinha Grande I proceeded to Alcobaça, as soon as the General was elected; and was kindly received by the Friars, to whom I was strongly recommended by Mr. Stephens. It is unnecessary for me to give you a description of a place which you know so well already; there is very little architecture worth a traveller's notice. I gleaned it of every thing remarkable, and took my leave of the Friars after a stay of nearly three weeks, who parted with me with great reluctance, as they expected that I would stay there to complete drawings of the Church and Monastery similar to those which I made of Batalha; so that it was with difficulty I could get away from them. The manners

of the people are deserving of a stranger's notice. There are
here at present one hundred and fifteen Friars, who, with their
attendants, occupy a building containing an area of four hundred and eighty-four thousand and fifty-six square feet. Computing it at three stories high, it would be sufficiently large to
contain four thousand five hundred families; which, if industriously employed in directing the plough or the loom, would
contribute more to the real advantage of Portugal than their
vast conquests in the Brazils.

"I have copied an inscription from the base and neck of an
antique chalice here, of which Mr. Bluteau, as I am informed,
has written a great deal. Last night I arrived in Lisbon, when
my best friends here, Messrs. Stephens, informed me that a few
days ago they received two letters from you, wherein you recommend me to their protection. Yours, JAMES MURPHY."

4. "DEAR SIR, Lisbon, July 18, 1789.
"In my last I informed you that I intended making drawings
of some things about Lisbon till such time as I received your
answer; but, being informed that it was necessary first to obtain
permission from the Court before any thing of the kind could
be done, on that I applied to Mr. Seabra, the Minister for the
Home Department, to whom Mr. Stephens showed your letter;
he immediately granted leave, saying that he would be very
happy in having an opportunity of obliging any one belonging
to Mr. Conyngham. I showed him the drawings of Batalha,
with which he was highly pleased, and took them to show the
Queen, who had them in her possession for three days; they are
just returned without receiving scarcely any damage; with a letter, which Mr. Stephens has in his possession, of which the following is a literal translation:

"'Her Majesty and his Royal Highness the Prince have seen
the drawings of Batalha, with which they were greatly pleased;
they now return them, requesting that, as soon as they are engraved, the artist will remember to send them some copies to
renew the pleasure they had in seeing the original drawings.
(Signed) SEABRA.'

"The people here did not imagine that the Queen would
receive a production of art with so much pleasure until they
saw this letter. It was then they began to know the value of
the work; and the next day I fortunately discovered the intention of some people here, whom I will not mention, who are
determined to have drawings of Batalha made at any expense,
when they found that all other solicitations were ineffectual to
obtain them, in order to have them presented to the Queen, with
a view to insinuate themselves into her good graces. This I will
endeavour to prevent if possible; I have therefore got my friend

the Rector of Corpo Sancto to write to Batalha, requesting that they will let him know if any one should come there with an intent to make drawings of the Church; in the mean time I intend going some distance into the country as being cheaper and less subject to the intrusion of people than this place, there to make another set of the drawings of Batalha, and to have them presented to the Queen in your name if you will permit me; and to open a subscription for the work to prevent others from undertaking it. As I have not been so fortunate as to receive your answer to any of my former letters, I am obliged to act in the best manner I can. However, what I state here I humbly submit to your consideration, pledging myself to follow strictly whatever advice you send me, as I do not propose to take a single step in this affair until such time as I receive your answer. I am, &c. JAMES MURPHY."

5. " DEAR SIR, *Lisbon, Aug.* 10, 1789.
" The particulars of what I mentioned to you in my letter of the 18th of July I communicated to your friend, the Rev. Mr. Hill, who recommends to me not to present any copy of the work to the Queen, as the people about her, he thinks, might take advantage of the opportunity, and have them engraved before mine would be published. He thinks it would be advisable to open a subscription for the work here as soon as convenient: and that many of the natives, taking example by her Majesty and the Prince, would become subscribers; I have, therefore, given up the idea of going to the country, or doing any thing further with respect to the Batalha drawings until such time as I receive your directions how to proceed. Since the date of my last, I waited on his Grace the Duke de la Toens and his Excellency Mr. Pinto, the Secretary, who from the friendship they have for you have offered me their protection whilst I remain in this country. A gentleman here, whose name is Verdié, informs me, that on looking over some ancient records he found the architect of Batalha mentioned, and that his name was Stephen Stephenson, a native of England, who together with the master stone-cutter and gate-keeper is mentioned among the list of pensioners of King John the First.

" There lives in Lisbon a man who possesses the secret of making Marseilles soap, who begged I would inform you, as he wishes to know whether the Dublin Society would encourage him to carry on a manufactory of said article in Ireland.

" Mr. Stephens has drawn bills on you for £.50 sterling, the amount of which I have received agreeably to your orders, for which I return you my most sincere thanks. I remain, dear Sir, with my best wishes for your long life, your grateful and obliged humble servant, JAMES MURPHY."

THE preceding letters have been copied from a small quarto copy-book which Mr. Murphy used in Portugal; and which is now in the possession of T. Crofton Croker, Esq. F. S. A. To that gentleman, who has recently presented to the Society of Antiquaries of London the original drawings of Mr. Murphy's magnificent work on Batalha, the Editor is indebted for these pleasing illustrations of Mr. Conyngham's liberal patronage of rising merit; and of the earliest efforts and adventures of a man who afterwards attained considerable reputation both as a traveller and an architect.

James Cavanah Murphy was a native of Blackrock near Cork, and originally a bricklayer in that city, where his talents for drawing—it is said in caricaturing his master with a burnt stick upon the wall — attracted the notice and procured the patronage of the late Sir James Chatterton, Bart. He was thus enabled to visit the Irish metropolis, and there introduced to Mr. Conyngham, by whose encouragement he proceeded to Portugal. Whilst abroad he acquired a competent knowledge of the Portuguese and Spanish languages, and held for a short time a diplomatic situation of importance from the Court of Portugal to that of Spain. During a residence of some years in the Peninsula, he pursued his professional studies with the most devoted and persevering attention, of which his works afford abundant testimony. The titles of three of these have been given in p. 431; but there was besides a posthumous publication (in 1816) entitled, " Arabian Antiquities in Spain *," which exceeds in magnificence his previous works, and indeed is equalled by few architectural publications which this country has produced. It contains 98 plates, on a very large folio. On this work Mr. Murphy was employed for the last fourteen years of his life; the former seven of which were spent in Spain, and the latter at home. This appears from the preface; which, as the work is necessarily of rare occurrence, shall be here quoted at length :

"The Antiquities of the Spanish Arabs have, for many ages, continued unheeded or unknown. The annals of past centuries scarcely deign to mention them: and the descriptions of modern pens but imperfectly supply the place of the pencil. Accurate delineations, so essential to render them intelligible, might have been expected from the enlightened nations of the Peninsula, whose artists and antiquaries have vied with the most celebrated of other countries. The task, however, was supinely deferred, or feebly attempted, while prejudice, the sad inheritance of nations, was actively employed in demolishing the works of infidels, whom it was accounted both pious and popular to divide.

"The suffrages of the discerning few, and especially of Bayer and Casiri, at length contributed to remove, or at least to miti-

* It is in the title of this work that Mr. Murphy's name of Cavanah first appears.

gate, this prejudice, and to arrest the progress of destruction. In consequence of the representations made by those profoundly learned and virtuous men, the Royal Academy of St. Ferdinand was commissioned by the Spanish Government to send two Architects under the direction of a Captain of Engineers, with instructions to make drawings of the Palace of Alhamrā, and of the Mosque of Cordova. After a lapse of several years, the joint labours of the three Academicians were published at Madrid, in the year 1780, in a folio volume, intituled, Antiguedadas Arabes de España; containing about sixteen plates of Arabic designs together with a few pages of letter-press. Some of the inscriptions in this publication were translated by the accurate Casiri. Such was the greatest progress made, to the end of the eighteenth century, in exploring the antiquities of the polished and enlightened people, who occupied the Peninsula during a period of nearly eight hundred years.

"The interesting but imperfect description of the remains of Arabian art, exhibited in the volumes of some modern travellers, as existing in the once renowned Mohammedan cities of Granada, Cordova, and Seville, excited in the author an ardent desire to visit them. He accordingly embarked for Spain, and arrived at Cadiz in May in the year 1802; whence he proceeded to Granada, through Lower Andalusia. The Governor of the Alhamrā, desirous that the knowledge of its splendid remains should be accurately transmitted to posterity, obligingly facilitated the author's access to that royal palace, at all hours of the day, while he was employed in the agreeable task of measuring and delineating its interior works. Equal facilities were offered at Cordova, the remains of whose celebrated Mosque and Bridge are delineated in the former part of the present volume. Seven years were unremittingly devoted to these delightful pursuits; and since the author's return to England in 1809, nearly seven years more have been wholly given to preparing for publication the present work. The Admirers of the Arts are here presented with the result of fourteen years' continued labour, executed at an expence of many thousand pounds;—in the hope that, by the union of the graphic art with the descriptions of the engravings annexed, such facilities will be afforded, as shall enable the reader to form an accurate estimate of the very high state of excellence to which the Spanish Arabs attained in the Fine Arts, while the rest of Europe was overwhelmed with ignorance and barbarism *."

* "In justice to the memory of an eminent and noble patron of the Arts, the late Earl of Bristol, the author with pleasure records that his Lordship had it in contemplation to send two Roman artists to Granada to make designs of the Palace of Alhamra, and to publish them at his own expense. The Earl of Bristol relinquished the idea only on being informed by the letter of a friend who was visiting that city, that the author had anticipated his munificent intention."

In illustration of Mr. Murphy's work, the same booksellers (Messrs. Cadell and Davies) published a quarto volume entitled: " The History of the Mahometan Empire in Spain; containing a general History of the Arabs, their institutions, conquests, literature, arts, sciences, and manners, to the expulsion of the Moors. Designed as an Introduction to The Arabian Antiquities of Spain, by James Cavanah Murphy, Architect." 1816.

The authorship of this volume is thus, in the Preface, assigned to its rightful owners: " For the Introduction, which presents a concise account of the early history of the Arabs previously to their conquest of Spain, the publishers are indebted to the kindness and liberality of the acute and learned HISTORIAN OF ANCIENT GREECE*. Part I. containing the Political and Military History of the Mohametan Empire in Spain, together with the description of Cordova, and the translation of the Arabic inscriptions in the Appendix, are due to Mr. John Shakespear †, Professor of Oriental Languges to the Hon. East India Company's Military Seminary. The remainder of Part I. comprising a topographical account of the principal seats of the Mahometan Empire in Spain, and the whole of Part II. which treats on the literature, sciences, arts, manufactures, and commerce, as well as on the civil and military institutions of the Arabs, were composed by Mr. Thomas Hartwell Horne, Sub-Librarian of the Surrey Institution ‡."

After his return to England, Mr. Murphy was engaged with the Admiralty in a correspondence respecting the Dry Rot ; and that Board appears to have paid particular attention to his proposition; but the exorbitant terms which he demanded delayed the experiments, and the disclosure of his plans was frustrated by his death, which took place in Edward-street, Cavendish-square, Sept. 12, 1814. From some of Mr. Murphy's memoranda it appears that when in Portugal he had his attention drawn to the circumstance that those vessels which had received their first cargo *of salt*, were free from the destructive disease which was the object of his researches; and it is probable his ideas were derived from this circumstance.

An accumulation of notes and drawings which Mr. Murphy left behind him, are in the possession of Thomas Deane, Esq. now Sheriff of Cork ; and, notwithstanding the labour bestowed on his publications, it is only by inspecting these remains, that an adequate idea can be formed of his industry, and of the minute and careful manner in which every object is detailed.

* Of William Mitford, Esq. F.S.A. (elder brother to Lord Redesdale) memoirs will be found in the Gentleman's Magazine, vol. XCVII. i. 368, 386. He died Feb. 10, 1827, aged 83.

† Author of a Grammar of the Hindustanè Language, 1813. 4to. A Dictionary Hindustani and English, 1817. 4to.; and Muntakhabat-i-Hindi ; or selections in Hindustani, for students in that language; with a verbal translation and grammatical analysis. Vol. I. 1817 ; II. 1825, 4to.

‡ The Rev. Thomas Hartwell Horne, M. A. who has been an author on various subjects, and is particularly distinguished for his works in Bibliography and Theology, is now engaged in compiling a classed Catalogue of the Books at the British Museum.

13. Mr. Leman to James Norris Brewer, Esq.*

" Sir,   *Crescent, Bath, Aug. 26, 1816.*

" I yesterday received your parcel very safe, containing three dissertations; one on the British Trackways, a second on the Roman Stations, and a third on the Roman Roads.

" The sources from which you have been obliged to draw your information have been so various, and so totally disageeing all of them with each other, that it is no wonder, n spite of all your uncommon ingenuity to reconcile them, hat some confusion has occurred.

" For everything which regards the construction of Roman Roads, you may refer safely to Bergier's Histoire des grands Chemins; for what regards their Camps partly to King's Munimenta and a good deal to General Roy: As to British Trackways, I must refer you, unwillingly, to the slight and hasty Commentary I drew up, some little time since, for Mr. Hatcher; for his translation of Richard of Cirencester, and to which I added notes on the different Iters. The Map which is inserted in my friend Sir Richard Hoare's Giraldus I gave him; but it is rendered undesirable by a heap of strange names which he unfortunately added to the different roads. The only person who knew any thing about Roman roads was Dr. Mason.

" I have completed two Maps of antient Britain, the one with the British towns and trackways, as at the time of Cæsar's invasion, as far as I have been able to discover them; the other showing all the Roman Stations and Camps hitherto discovered. Were you here for a few days I would lend them to you; and point out, as far as I am able, what I think still wanting to complete them. I remain, &c. &c.   Tho. Leman."

---

14. " Sir,   *Crescent, Bath, Feb. 11, 1817.*

" Do not fail to recollect that before the time of Claudius the Belgæ had extended their conquests northwards; and continued doing so until they were finally subdued by the Romans. Hence arises the difference between the accounts given us by Richard and Ptolemy; for the latter describes the site of their tribes as they were in Claudius's time. Thus the Hedui, who existed in Richard's account as possessors of Somersetshire, had been expelled by the Belgæ in the time of Ptolemy.

" In the Map you have sent me are the following omissions: the tribes Ottadini, Gadeni, the town of Bremenium or Reichester; of Deva, Chester; of Regentium, Chichester. I have made great additions to the one I return you. I have added on the sides all the towns mentioned by Richard of Cirencester; I have corrected the Trackways carefully; I have given lists of

* This and the two following letters have been obligingly communicated by that gentleman.

all the Celtic as well as Belgic tribes, and numbered them as I would advise you to describe them in the text.

" You will observe, and will see faithfully corrected in the engraving, the number placed before each Celtic and Belgic tribe; and you will observe that, to distinguish the one from the other, the Celtic tribes are written in black, with a blue line drawn underneath them (to prevent their being confused with the names of places), and that the Belgic tribes are in red.

" I do not know any means of marking accurately the limits of each tribe, either Celtic or Belgic, better than I have done in my manuscript Richard of Cirencester, of which I believe you have a copy. An attempt to do so on the Map would confound such boundaries with the trackways, and make the whole a mass of confusion. Were you here you might form another Map of the Roman roads, which would make your work more complete. Yours, &c. Tho. Leman."

---

15. " Dear Sir, *Crescent, Bath, Feb.* 14, 1819.
" I have been so thoroughly occupied with some family business, which has taken up the whole of my time, that I have not had it in my power to answer sooner your letter relating to the antiquities of Berks*. There can be no person who wishes better to your work than I do, nor who would be more ready at all times to afford you all the information in my power; but as to undertaking to write a memoir for this county as I did for Herts, it is totally out of my power, as I grow very old, and have so many other occupations which fill up the whole of my time that I really have scarcely a moment to myself.

" When Mr. Lysons was going to publish his short account of the County, I gave then to the Bishop of Cloyne the notes from which he drew up the statement published in it; since which I certainly have collected a good deal of additional information, which, if you pass through Bath, shall be at your service.

" I hope that you will not neglect what is so much wanted, the genealogies of the families as far as you are able to collect them from the heraldic visitations of the county, for there is only at present the miserable work of Ashmole. I remain, your faithful humble servant, Thomas Leman."

---

16. *Recollections of the Rev. T. Leman by J. N. Brewer, Esq.*

" *Pillerton-house, Warwickshire, Dec.* 20, 1828.
" I was introduced to Mr. Leman in the year 1816; and from that date until the time of his decease, was favoured with his

---

* This alludes to a work on the History of Berkshire, which was projected by Mr. Brewer, but not executed.

occasional correspondence. In the year above-mentioned, I passed with him, at Bath, the greater part of a week, and received from him much valuable information in arranging the materials for my brief disquisitions on British and Roman-British Antiquities, forming parts of the ' Introduction to the Beauties of England and Wales;' which assistance I have duly acknowledged in the preface to that work. I have two maps chiefly drawn by himself, and both engraved for my ' Introduction;' the first shewing the situations of the different tribes of Britain, with their towns and trackways, as they existed at the first invasion under Cæsar; the second presenting a display of Roman stations and roads.

" The contributor to ' Parriana' justly remarks, that Mr. Leman's ' hand-writing was correct and beautiful.' It was, indeed, eminently so, as is sufficiently proved to me by numerous letters in my possession. One, alas! forms an exception. It was the last I received from him, and is dated Aug. 26, 1825. It is in some places nearly illegible, and the news of his decease too quickly followed. In it he writes, ' A most dreadful illness, which has confined me to my house, and I may almost say to my bed, for these last ten months, put it out of my power to reply more speedily. Besides the weakness consequent on such a lengthened illness, I have to add the irreparable and total *loss of an eye*, which precludes my reading and writing, except for matters of absolute necessity.'

" Mr. Hunter is equally faithful in asserting that, ' an elegance ran through every thing about Mr. Leman.' He was rather above the middle height; of a spare habit and genteel form. His features were handsome and pleasing, and his address that of an accomplished man of the world. Mr. Hunter observes, that ' he usually rode out in a morning on horseback.' If Boswell were collecting anecdotes concerning the deceased, it might not be superfluous to mention that he was rendered conspicuous (eleven years ago) in these rides, by a white hat, and the display of a pendent eye-glass in a golden frame much ornamented.

" It has been remarked, with some justice, that his manners, on a first acquaintance, would often too plainly insinuate, that he knew himself to be a rich as well as a talented man, and that he was disposed to admit to a freedom of association such only as were equally fortunate with himself. Thus, every person of title, or distinction for affluence, whom he named, was ' his friend.' The untitled, or moderate in circumstances, whom he was obliged to mention, however great their worth or talent, were merely persons of whom he had heard, or of whom he might chance to know something, — at a distance. It was curious to observe how this fantastical humour spread itself amongst his servants,—almost invariably the apes of their masters. I recollect calling once in the Crescent, and on inquiring if Mr. Leman were at home? was thus answered by his man: 'No, Sir! Mr. Leman is out, and I do not exactly know where. But he is gone either to call on my Lord ——, or my Lord ——, *or some other Nobleman.*'

"But littlenesses, like that above-noticed, were mere specks in the sun, and were speedily relinquished when he found that they obtained for him no advantage over his companion.

"Mr. Leman was, undoubtedly, an elegant scholar, and a man of great antiquarian research. He is, also, entitled to more estimable commendation. When the frivolity of his habit, as related to an affectation of grandeur, was overcome, he evinced a friendly ardour of feeling that could spring only from a heart intrinsically good.

"As regarded his literary capacity and attainments, he was shrewd and ingenious rather than profound and philosophic. His quickness of perception, and art of disentangling and simplifying abstruse subjects, cannot be readily understood by those who have not passed days with him in his library. I will venture to say, without hesitation, that no man had formed correct ideas respecting the early periods of British History until Mr. Leman directed to that subject his penetrating and ingenious mind. I have heard him speak with great praise of Mr. Whitaker of Manchester; but himself possessed all the masculine acuteness of Whitaker, without the fervour of imagination, which perhaps betrayed that writer, upon some occasions, into too great a boldness of hypothesis.

"Mr. Leman's inquiries respecting the roads and stations of the Romans, in their occupation of this island, were not less satisfactory than his disquisitions on British history. But here his considerable powers had, perhaps, a less genial direction. The patient investigations of the antiquary were sufficient for this topic, with little call upon the vigour and perspicacity of the historian. Himself and the Bishop of Cloyne personally inspected the whole line of the principal Roman roads in Britain; and their writings upon those remains are, consequently, invaluable favours to the antiquary. But they lived at too late a date for satisfactory remarks on many of the *stations*. I have heard him (half-jocosely) lament that they were not in being to lend a helping hand to Leland and Camden, whose opportunities were so much greater than we possess in these 'laggard days.'

"I cannot advert to the name of Mr. Leman's distinguished 'friend,' Dr. Bennet, Bishop of Cloyne, without paying the humble tribute of my admiration to that excellent prelate and amiable man. I was honoured with his assistance, in the same work of literary amusement that caused me to become acquainted with Mr. Leman. Possibly without so penetrating an activity of mind, he possessed a sounder, if not a finer degree of understanding; whilst he could not be approached without a conviction of his profound learning, reverence for his virtues as a man, and applause of his accomplishments as a gentleman."

17. Mr. Leman to the Rev. Samuel Parr, LL. D. *

"My dear Sir,   *Crescent, Bath, Feb.* 13, 1820.

" I have the great satisfaction of being able to contradict the cruel report of the death of my beloved friend the Bishop of Cloyne; for at the very time the account of his loss appeared in the public papers, I received a letter from him on the morning of the 9th instant, and, as you are equally interested with myself in his welfare, I send you his own account of his situation at that time.

" 'The gout (he says) has been more tedious, as well as more severe this winter than I ever experienced. It is now ten weeks since I have ventured to cross the threshold, once excepted, when I drove out in the carriage, and was so much shaken that it did me more harm than good; and these constant attacks of pain depriving me of sleep and exercise, and coming upon me when I was beginning to recover a little my loss of appetite, and of flesh, has been very hard upon me. I literally do not think that I could have stood it if my niece had not been with me; and women, I have always agreed with you, are so careful and tender, and such excellent nurses, and so anxious to amuse one, as well as capable of doing it, that one of them is worth a host of male creatures.'

" Such, my dear Sir, is the private and confidential account I have received from my dearest friend; and, although it still leaves me greatly uneasy about him, yet I hope that the change of air, and a milder climate, may thereby restore him to his former health. As soon as he can travel with comfort to himself, I shall press upon him his coming down to this place, where I know that he will have every comfort and attention which I can give him.

" It is with great pain that I read the unpleasant account you give of yourself; and the influenza which has been laying waste all around me, has fallen upon me also with a very heavy hand; for I have been almost confined for nearly three weeks; I hope, however, I shall get over it, and nothing would give me greater pleasure then to have the satisfaction of seeing you quite well at Bath. I scarce know what I write, but I remain very faithfully your very obedient humble servant,   Thomas Leman."

───────────

18. " My dear Sir,   *Crescent, Bath, July* 18, 1820.

" The loss of my dearest friend has so overpowered me that I can scarce see to write to you. By a letter I have this moment received from his excellent niece, I find he has appointed me his sole executor in England, which will oblige me to be in town

* This and the two following letters are extracted from the Memoirs of Dr. Parr by Dr. John Johnstone, p. 486. They are particularly interesting as exhibiting Mr. Leman's affectionate attachment to his old friend Bishop Bennet, to whom he was sole executor.

the beginning of next week. This painful office, which millions
would not have tempted me to accept, he pressed upon me so
urgently when I last saw him, that I could not refuse him. He
is to be buried in Plumstead Church, somewhere near London.
Should you like to attend the funeral, you have nothing to do
but to send word to Montagu-square. I trust to your friendship to mention his death in the public papers. Alas! I am
incapable of doing any thing but to lament the irreparable loss
I have sustained. Yours most truly,   THOMAS LEMAN."

19. " MY DEAR SIR,   *Crescent, Bath, Dec.* 1, 1820.
" Being now able to read your letter, I can return you specific
answers to all your queries. The monument, or tablet, is directed in his will; and in a private paper, left me as his executor, he adds, ' I hope the Master and Fellows of Emanuel-
college will let my monument be (after the design, and with
the inscription affixed to my will,) placed at the north end of
the cloisters.' As to any alterations that you may think necessary, I leave them entirely to your pure taste and sound critical
judgment; and I add only, that I shall readily pay any expense
relative to the having it written by your schoolmaster. I never
saw Mr. Shout, nor do I know any thing of him; but I suppose,
of course, that he will rigidly follow any orders you are so good
as to give him.
" You cannot conceive what a weight you have taken off my
mind by employing an amanuensis; for since I received the
stone from Rosetta, and the brick from Babel, I have never
been so completely puzzled. Your writing certainly is more
mysterious than the former, and more inexplicable than the
latter.
" Sir William Scott has written to me to inquire if I had found
among my friend's papers some letters relating to the late Dr.
Goldsmith, and which had passed between him and Burke, and
Johnson and Marley, and were supposed to be in the Bishop's
possession. There are none such in England, and I do not
recollect ever having heard of such having been in his possession. Can you, who lived in such intimacy with the Bishop,
recollect any thing about them?
" I do hope, and even entreat you to pay some attention to
your health, and not to neglect the trifling complaint in your
leg; for your life is of consequence to the world, and more
particularly to your friends. I remain with great respect, my
dear Sir, yours very faithfully,   THOMAS LEMAN."

Rev. JAMES DOUGLAS, F. S. A.

The Rev. James Douglas, author of the Nænia Britannica, was originally of the military profession. In January 1780 he married Margaret, daughter of John Oldershaw, Esq. of Rochester (who had previously been an eminent surgeon at Leicester); and in the same year he was elected F. S. A. being then styled of Stratton-street, Piccadilly, and entered into holy orders. For some time he was a member of Peter-house, Cambridge. He afterwards settled in Sussex, where, after serving several Curacies, and having for some years been a Chaplain in Ordinary to the Prince of Wales, he was in 1799 presented by the King to the Rectory of Middleton. In 180.. he was presented by Lord Henniker to the Vicarage of Kenton in Suffolk.

His first publication was in the line of his original profession, "Essay on Tactics, from the French of Guibert, 1781," 2 vols. 8vo.

In 1782 he published, but without his name, one volume of "Travelling Anecdotes, through various Parts of Europe," and promised a second. This work was a mixture of description and anecdote, and was written somewhat in the manner of Sterne. It attracted considerable notice *; and a second edition, with the author's name, appeared in 1785. In the Preface to this, he "made an apology for declining to give the promised second volume of these Anecdotes, hinting very properly that more serious avocations are better suited to his present engagements in the solemn duties of the Church †."

In 1785 he contributed to the Bibliotheca Topographica Britannica, "Two Dissertations on the brass instruments called Celts, and other arms of

* See the "Literary Anecdotes," vol. VIII. p. 685. There is a critique upon it, with extracts, in the Monthly Review, vol. LXVII. pp. 93—100. † Ibid. vol. LXXIV. p. 235.

the Antients, found in this Island *." The dedication to Lieut.-General Melville, F.R.S. F.A.S.
&c. is dated from Chiddingfold in Sussex.

The same friend having addressed to him some
observations on an ancient sword †, supposed to be
Roman, Mr. Douglas returned him a reply; and
both letters were read before the Society of Antiquaries, Jan. 27, 1785, and are printed in the Archæologia, vol. VII. pp. 374—378. On the same
day also was read to the Society, and will be found
in the pages following those named, a letter addressed to Mr. Douglas by the Rev. Mr. Mutlow,
containing an "Account of some Antiquities found
in Gloucestershire."

About the same time he sketched the well-known
whole-length portrait of Captain Grose, whom he
caught napping; it was "cordially inscribed to
those Members of the Antiquarian Society who adjourn to the Somerset, by one of their devoted
brethren ‡."

Also in 1785 he published in 4to, "A Dissertation on the Antiquity of the Earth;" read at the
Royal Society, 12th of May that year §. This was

* The first of these had been read before the Society of Antiquaries, June 17, 1784, but not printed in the Archæologia, the
Council fearing that so doing might "invade on Mr. Douglas's
materials for the work he was then writing on the sepulchres of
the ancients found in this island." His plan, however, being
somewhat altered, and having perceived himself obliged to discard such observations as did not immediately relate to his subject, communicated his papers on Celts to Mr. Nichols; and
they formed the Thirty-third Number of the Bibliotheca Topographica Britannica, but are bound in the first volume.—
This pamphlet has two masterly aquatint engravings by the
author. To these in a review in the Gentleman's Magazine due
commendation was given, whilst the Critic (Mr. Gough) found
many holes to pick in the dissertation. See vol. LVI. of that
work, p. 150. Mr. Douglas wrote a letter in reply, which will
be found, ibid. p. 245.

† Engraved in the Nænia Britannica, plate xxvi.
‡ This plate is particularly noticed with the Captain's other
portraits, in the "Literary Anecdotes," vol. III. p. 659.
§ Noticed by the Monthly Reviewer, vol. LXXV. p. 457 —

an early essay on those diluvian remains, the study
of which has been recently renewed with such increased ardour.

In 1786 appeared in folio, the first number of Mr.
Douglas's greatest undertaking, intituled, " Nænia
Britannica; or, a Sepulchral History of Great Britain, from the earliest period to its general conversion to Christianity. Including a complete series
of the British, Roman, and Saxon Sepulchral
Rites and Ceremonies, with the contents of several hundred Burial-places, opened under a careful
inspection of the Author; tending to illustrate the
early part of, and to fix on a more unquestionable
criterion for the study of antiquity. To which are
added, Observations on the Celtic, British, Roman,
and Danish barrows discovered in Britain." In
this work every circumstance relative to the tombs
is particularly described, and the tombs themselves,
with all their contents, are represented on aquatinta plates, executed by Mr. Douglas, and admirably adapted for conveying an accurate idea of the
decayed relics *.

In the Forty-second Number of the Bibliotheca
Topographica Britannica, which was published in
1787, was another article by Mr. Douglas. This
was " On the Urbs Rutupiæ of Ptolemy, and the
Lundenwic of the Saxons †."

Mr. Douglas's excellent specimens of amateur engravings were
thus applauded: " The plates in aquatinta, which we find to be
the author's own performance, are neatly executed, and are good
representations of the originals, particularly those of the coins,
which we cannot help commending as engravings, although they
are totally foreign to the main subject of his book."

* See the criticism of the Monthly Reviewer quoted in the
" Literary Anecdotes," vol. IX. p. 8.

† Mr. Douglas maintained that Rutupiæ was not Richborough, but Canterbury; that "the Lunden-wic, where Mellitus
was Bishop, was London; the Londen-wic, cited from the Textus Roffensis, concerning commerce in that place, was Canterbury; and the Lunden-wic, so called in Ethelbert's grant, Re-
culver."

In 1791 Mr. Douglas published "Twelve Discourses on the Influence of the Christian Religion on Civil Society," 8vo *.

In 1793 he completed his Nænia Britannica in one folio volume, containing nearly forty plates, besides vignettes; and dedicated it to the Prince of Wales, to whom he had previously been appointed a Chaplain in Ordinary.

In 1795 he contributed to the History of Leicestershire a delicate plate of Coston Church, accompanied by the representation of a perfect fossil oyster, found in that parish. This plate was by his own masterly hand, in that species of engraving in which he so much excelled.

In 1818 Mr. Douglas communicated to the Gentleman's Magazine, a letter on some Roman Antiquities discovered at Blatchington in Sussex, with notices of other remains in that county †.

Mr. Douglas died at Preston in Sussex, Nov. 5, 1819, leaving a widow, three sons, and one daugther.

---

1. Rev. James Douglas to Mr. Urban ‡.

"Mr. Urban,   Sept. 28, 1793.

"It was a remark of Dr. Johnson, that the duty of criticism is neither to depreciate nor dignify by partial representations, but to hold out the light of reason, whatever it may discover; and to promulgate the determinations of Truth, whatever she shall dictate. The justness of this aphorism is universally received.

"On the publication of the Nænia Britannica, as the author had spoken freely, though not unhandsomely, of modern antiquaries, it was natural to suppose he would meet with various opinions, and encounter the occasional attacks of those who differed from him. The work became the property of the public, and praise or censure the public had a right to bestow; but, in the promulgation of critique, how far the dictates of truth

---

* See the " Literary Anecdotes," vol. IX. p. 88.
† See Gent. Mag. vol. LXXXVIII. ii. 107. In a note Mr. Douglas mentions having been favoured by " a correspondence with the Rev. Thomas Leman, of Bath, one of the able Editors and Commentators of the new edition of the Itinerary of Richard of Cirencester."
‡ From the Gentleman's Magazine, vol. LXIII. ii. p. 881.

have been considered, the readers of this work have now an opportunity of judging. The Critical Review for August 1793 has observed, that Nænia is a funeral song, and the name of the work inept to the subject. However dull and malignant a Reviewer may be, he should not be either ignorant or unlearned. The authority of Festus will prove Nænia a Goddess, to whom a temple was dedicated; a circumstance which certainly had escaped the Reviewer's reading: ' Næniæ deæ sacellum extra portam Viminalem nunc tantum habet ædiculam *.' The spot being here mentioned where the temple was dedicated, there is consequently the same authority for Nænia Britannica as Flora Britannica †. St. Augustin has also prefixed the name of Nænia to a goddess: ' Et deos clausit ad Næniam Deam quæ in fune- ribus fenum cantantur ‡.' Also Arnobius : ' In tutelâ sunt Or- bonæ orbati liberis parentes, in Næniæ quibus extrema sunt tempora §.   J. Douglas."

---

2. Mr. Douglas to Mr. Nichols.

" Dear Sir,   *March* 7, 1799.
" I have just thrown these cursory remarks ‖ together in reading your page, without an idea of making any correction, in which opinion may be urged on either side. Your request was, to add some further remarks on the relics discovered at Bagrave; and I have given you all I received on the subject. If it is your desire that I should give you a digested remark on the subject of our antient sepulchres, more than I have published, I will with pleasure throw the papers together which I have on the subject; and I shall feel myself very pleasingly employed to add anything in my power to the arduous and extensive task which you have undertaken, to the perfect satisfaction of every friend to a good county history.
" Mr. King, I understand, is about to give us a learned work on the subject of mounds and tumuli. As I live entirely out of the world, I wish you would give me a line when his work makes its appearance.
" I sincerely wish you every gratification in fame, and pro-

---

* L. F. Festi, lib. XII. p. 26; Amstel. 1699.
† These were the words of that great champion of virtue, the late Dr. Johnson, to the author of this work, a short time before his death. On a visit to the Doctor, at his house in Bolt-court, after his return from Derbyshire, to inquire after his health, the author questioned the Doctor on the propriety of the title for his book. " Why not, Sir," says he, " Nænia Britannica, as well as Flora Britannica?" But, without the shield of this great literary character, the above authority may be deemed a sufficient reply.
‡ Aug. de Civit. Dei, lib. V. 9.   § Arnob. lib. I.
‖ Some additions, for the History of Leicestershire, to his description of antiquities found at Bagrave in that county, extracted from his Nænia Britannica. They were printed in the History of Leicestershire, III. 289.

per remuneration, for the great undertaking which you have so
eminently advanced towards a completion; and believe me, as
far as my ability, dear Sir, your faithful and much obliged friend
and servant, J. Douglas.

" P. S. If you have any further commands, please to direct to
me at Petworth, where I now reside, in the discharge of my
clerical duty."

———

3. " Dear Sir, *Barnham near Arundel, March* 19, 1810.

" Having received a letter from my nephew, J. Douglas, of
Old-hall, Pendleton, near Manchester, expressing his anxiety of
an error of your press, which in your Obituary announced the
death of his father, under the name of Alexander instead of
William *, he has requested me to beg you will have the goodness to correct the same.

" I am much obliged by your polite mention of my name. I
do assure you that your kind considerations have been always
commensurate with that respect I have ever entertained for

———

* William Douglas, Esq. of the Old-hall, near Manchester, died highly
respected, Jan. 30, 1810. " His ancestor was Alexander Douglas of Reeth
in Yorkshire, whose possessions in that county were granted to him by
James the First, on his coming into England. He raised and equipped,
at his own expence, a troop of horsemen for the service of King Charles
the First. On his march to join the Royal forces, he was intercepted,
by a detachment of Cromwell's army, and made prisoner. Having
effected his escape into one of his own woods, he was there, for a long
time, concealed and supported by a faithful servant. After the Restoration of Charles the Second, many repeated but fruitless applications were
made to that ungrateful Monarch for the recovery of his confiscated
estates.—Mr. Douglas, on the female side, was descended from Stephen
Gardiner, Bishop of Winchester and Lord Chancellor of England. [It
may, however, be remarked by the way, that Gardiner is supposed to
have been a natural son of Bishop Lionel Widvile; and, being a Popish
Prelate, was not himself married]. His mother, the last surviving relative of his blood, was daughter of Mr. Gardiner, of Haling near Croydon in Surrey, which mansion was originally built by the Bishop, and to
which Queen Elizabeth, in one of her Progresses, on a visit to that place,
gave the name of Healing, or All-heal, from the salubrity of the spot.
[On the absurdity of this no other remark need be made than that on
reference to the History of Surrey, vol. II. p. 554, its incorrectness will
be directly shown, Haling being a name much anterior to Elizabeth's
reign.] Sand-place, near Dorking, was also a mansion of the above gentleman's, whose sister was married to the Right Hon. Arthur Onslow,
Speaker of the House of Commons." [This does not appear in the
Peerages.] " The late Mr. William Douglas, conjointly with his brother
Mr. Douglas of Grantham in Lincolnshire, were the persons who tried
the celebrated cause with Sir Richard Arkwright, on the specification of
his patent for the Spinning Machines; by which means a great national
benefit was obtained, by liberating all these machines throughout the
kingdom from the overbearing monopoly of his patent, and which the
Court of King's Bench, by this cause, set aside."—On the death of this
gentleman, our author, the Rev. James Douglas, was his only surviving
brother. Gent. Mag. vol. LXXX. i. 185, 489.

your own personal worth and your most laborious literary productions, for which I trust your remuneration will be still ample, and in every degree gratifying to your feelings ; not always the case in this country, where national favour is more liberally bestowed through party and family interest, than real merit.

" On Lady-day I remove to Arundel, where I have taken a house as more convenient for my Churches of Middleton and Tortington. I have received an invitation from the Duke of Norfolk, and have dined with his Grace at his Castle ; and should you wish for any of the archives of the Howard family in the course of your historical inquiries, I make no doubt of having an opportunity of being accessory to any assistance you might wish for in this quarter. I have been consulted about the history of this county ; the compilation has been offered to me. Much assistance can be had from the manuscripts of the late Sir W. Burrell in the Museum ; but the work being under the auspices of a nobleman of the highest consequence, who wishes it to be got up on the most elegant scale, I am afraid the expence will exceed all profit ; what say you, my dear Sir ? Is it likely for an individual, to obtain from the public, a recompence equal to the labour ?   I am afraid not.

" I have serious thoughts of re-publishing Stukeley's Abury and Stonehenge, with notes. The latter I have ; the former, with the Stonehenge bound together, some years ago I parted with to White, for some other books, and now I want the Abury. Could you procure me the loan of it ? it shall be most faithfully returned on any set time. I want it immediately for an extract, being in correspondence with Sir R. Hoare and Mr. Cunnington, of Heytesbury, who are indefatigable in the work of Antient Wiltshire ; a *livraison* of which will be published in April next. I wish to forward this curious and fine publication, with some hints for further elucidations of the history of our celebrated national temple of Stonehenge. The plates of Abury and Stonehenge, with others, I should execute myself, for my own edition. If in any of your literary engagements I can be in any way useful, you may now command me, as I shall have leisure on my removal. And if you could propose to me any emolument from any labour of mine, to help me in the education of two fine boys, who are at two expensive schools, I should readily embrace the offer in these times of great national pressure.

" With every earnest good wish for the continuance of your health, and the most satisfactory completion of your literary engagements, I have the pleasure to be, with kind regards of Mrs. Douglas, dear Sir, your faithful and much obliged servant,
JAMES DOUGLAS."

The Rev. WILLIAM CLUBBE, LL. B. *

AND

JOHN CLUBBE, M. D. †

The Rev. William Clubbe was the second son of the Rev. John Clubbe ‡, A. B. Rector of Whatfield and Vicar of Debenham in Suffolk; and was born in 1745. He received his academical education at Caius-college, Cambridge, where he proceeded to the degree of LL. B. in 1769. In the same year he was presented to the Rectory of Flowton and to the Vicarage of Brandeston, both in that county. He deceased at Framlingham, where he had resided for some years previous to his death, on the 16th of October 1814, and was interred in the church-yard of Brandeston, where, on a coffin-shaped stone, is the following inscription to his memory:

> The Rev. WILLIAM CLUBBE,
> Forty-five years
> Vicar of this Parish,
> Died Octr ye 16th 1814.
> Aged 69.

Mr. Clubbe was a person of considerable literary attainments, and, like his facetious father, possessed of a rich fund of natural humour. In his Vicarial-garden at Brandeston, he had collected together many fragments from the antient Church of Letheringham, its brasses and monuments; and of these a pyramid was erected by him, with the following inscriptions:

> · Fuimus.
> Indignant Reader!
> These Monumental Remains
> are not
> (as Thou mayest suppose)
> The Ruins of Time,

---

* See the "Literary Anecdotes," vol. II. p. 378. † Ibid. pp. 378, 723.
‡ For a Biographical Notice of whom see "Literary Anecdotes," vol. II. p. 377: and vol. VIII. p. 410.

but
were destroyed in an irruption of the Goths
so late in the Christian Æra
as the year 1789.
Credite, Posteri ! ! !

———

Undique collectis membris,
Abi Lector !
et, si nomen perenne cures,
quæras aliunde ;
Marmori famam credere
quàm fallax vanumque sit
hinc collige !

———

Who sees with equal eye, as God of all,
The hero perish or the sparrow fall.

M. S.
Antiquiss^mae Familæ
Restitum
(quoad restitui potuit)
A° Dom. 1789.
Quicunque sis,
hos hortos post hâc coliturus,
vive memor mortuorum ;
neu sinas
hasce Reliquias
iterum in ruinam labi ;
Hâc conditione, Valeas !

Mr. Clubbe was the author of the following
works, *viz.* " Six Satires of Horace, in a style between Free Imitation and Literal Version. 1795,"
4to ; " The Epistle of Horace to the Pisos, on the
Art of Poetry, translated into English Verse. 1797,"
4to ; " The Omnium, containing the Journal of a
late three days' Tour into France ; curious and
extraordinary Anecdotes, Critical Remarks, and
other Miscellaneous Pieces in Prose and Verse.
1798," 8vo ; " Ver ; de Agricolæ Puero, Anglicano
Poemate celeberrimo excerptum, et in morem Latini
Georgici redditum. 1804," 8vo ; " A Letter to a
Country Gentleman on the subject of Methodism,
confined chiefly to its Causes, Progress, and Consequences. 1805," 8vo ; " Three Lyric Odes on
late celebrated occasions. 1806," 4to ; " An Ad-

dress to the Lower Classes of his Parishioners, on
the Subject of Methodism, from the Minister of
their Parish, by the Author of a Letter to a Country
Gentleman on the same subject. 1806," 8vo: "A
Plain Discourse on the Subject of National Education, written and intended chiefly for the information of the Lower Classes of his own Parishioners.
1812," 12mo; "Parallel between the Characters
and Conduct of Oliver Cromwell and Bonaparte,
addressed to the French Nation, at this inviting and
momentous crisis, by a British Officer." 8vo.

In the "Six Satyrs of Horace," p. 3, Mr. Clubbe
draws the following humourous character of himself:

> Amongst the gaping crowd, should one desire
> To know your AUTHOR, or his NAME enquire,
> Say, in few words, his Father was a Priest,
> And of the Reverend Order not the least.
> A Bishop? no; a Canon? not so high,
> A Country Parson on a Rectory;
> A Country Parson? but his children's pride,
> That in his virtues he was dignified.
> With income for his notions much too small,
> His·SON makes out to live, and that is all;
> Inclin'd to soar, he chance a dinner gives,
> That only leads to question how he lives.
> Acquaintance rather large, but nothing higher,
> Nor does he court it, than the Country Squire;
> Unfit for deeper studies, pleas'd with rhyme,
> And, from late illness, *grey* before his time;
> Of middle stature, fond to bask away
> In sun and indolence the summer day;
> Prone to dispute, if chance he takes a cup,
> But never known to keep resentment up.
>   Should one more curious teaze you to be told,
> Exactly to a year or month how old,
> Fifteen when George the Third his reign begun,
> And now just entering upon Fifty-one.

Dr. JOHN CLUBBE was an elder brother of the
subject of the above notice; and was born in 1741.
He was brought up to the medical profession, and
practised for many years in Ipswich, both as a surgeon and physician, with well-merited reputation
and great success, where, after a long and painful

illness, he departed this life on the 25th of April 1811.

Of the Doctor, who, like his father and brother, was a man of considerable humour and of a most cheerful disposition, many lively and pleasant anecdotes are still in the recollection of his friends. To a pun, or a facetious story, he was no enemy. His medical acquirements had deservedly obtained for him the highest esteem of the public; while the suavity of his manners and the sociability of his character had justly endeared him to a large circle of admirers. He was the author of the following professional works, *viz.* " A Treatise on the Inflammation in the Breasts of Lying-in Women, 1779," 8vo; and " On the Venereal Poison, 1782," 8vo.

He lies buried in the Church-yard of St. Stephen in Ipswich; and in the Church a neat mural tablet is erected, with the following inscription:

" To the Memory of JOHN CLUBBE, late a very eminent Physician in this place, who died 25th April 1811, aged 70 years. His well-known probity, universal benevolence, friendly disposition, obliging temper, and engaging manners, during a long residence in this town, endeared him to all who sought either his acquaintance as a friend or his assistance as a Physician, and his loss is as generally lamented."

His last surviving brother, Nathaniel Clubbe, Gent. was a solicitor at Framlingham, and died April 13, 1829, in his 83d year.

The REV. SAMUEL DARBY, A. M.

This learned and amiable divine * received his academical education at Jesus-college, Cambridge, of which Society he became both a Fellow and a Tutor. He proceeded to the degree of A. B. in 1743, and to that of A. M. in 1749. In 1773 he

* See the " Literary Anecdotes," vol. II. p. 571; VIII. 410.

was presented by his College to the Rectory of
Whatfield*; and in 1788, by the Crown, to that
of Bredfield, both in the county of Suffolk. He
died at his house in Ipswich on the 31st of March,
1794, in the 72d year of his age, and his remains

* Mr. Darby succeeded Mr. Clubbe, the ingenious author of
an admirable piece of irony at the expense of modern antiquaries, " The History and Antiquities of the antient Villa of
Wheatfield in the County of Suffolk," and of whom see " Literary Anecdotes," vol. II. pp. 377—379; vol. VIII. p. 410. He
was in turn succeeded by Mr. Plampin. The latter respectable
divine received his academical education at Jesus-college, Cambridge, where he proceeded to the degree of A. B. in 1776; and,
being classed the Twelfth Wrangler on the Tripos, was, in consequence thereof, elected Fellow. In 1779 he proceeded to the
degree of A. M. In 1794, on the decease of Mr. Darby, he was
presented by his College to the Rectory of Whatfield, and in
1800 to that of Stanstead. In the garden at Whatfield Mr.
Plampin placed an elegant inscription to the memory of his
facetious predecessor, Mr. Clubbe. See " Literary Anecd." II. 378.

He deceased on the 30th of May 1823, at Chadacre-hall, and
was interred in the Church of Stanstead. The following chaste
and elegant inscription from the pen of that pleasing writer and
ingenious moralist Dr. Drake, of Hadleigh, who " had known
the deceased for more than a quarter of a century, and known
only to esteem and love," is placed by his sorrowing widow over
his beloved remains :

" Near this tablet are deposited the remains of the Rev. John
Plampin, M. A. of Chadacre-hall in this parish, Rector of
Whatfield and Stanstead, in the County of Suffolk, a Magistrate
for the district in which he resided, and formerly Fellow and
Tutor of Jesus-college, Cambridge. He died May 30, 1823, in
the 69th year of his age.

> If taste, if learning, if the love of art,
> What schools can give, or foreign realms impart,
> May claim a tribute from the polished few,
> Here might it flow, as not unjustly due;
> But in the fane to pure devotion given,
> Can these light graces point the path to Heaven ?
> Then be it added, as in truth it can,
> Here sleeps, what all should prize, an honest man !
> Who taught unerring, to his faithful flock,
> Christ as their hope, their living stay and rock;
> Who loved through life, whate'er the vale he trod,
> His kind, his King, his Country, and his God."
>
> Noontide Leisure, vol. II. p. 30.

were interred in the Church-yard of St. Stephen
in that town, where, on a table-monument, is the
following inscription to his memory, from the pen
of his intimate friend the Rev. Thomas Cobbold * :

M. S.
Reverendi Sam. Darby, A. M.
Coll. Jes. apud Cantab. olim Socii,
at postea de Whatfield et Bredfield
in hocce comitatu Rectoris ;
viri docti et integerrimi,
sine ostentatione liberalis,
sine fuco pii ;
Qui carissimus conjugi et amicis,
multis bonis flebilis,
sæva paralysi fractus
decessit pridie cal. April.
MDCCXCIV. Æt. LXXII.

Mr. Darby was a man of a most social and
friendly disposition, strict integrity, distinguished
abilities and extensive literary attainment ; but, to
the inexpressible grief of his dearest friends, and
of all who had the happiness of knowing him, he
was deprived of these valuable endowments by a
paralytic affection, which gradually undermined
his health and mental faculties, and some time previous to his death entirely destroyed them †.

* This worthy divine is a native of Harwich in Essex, and
received the early part of his education at the Free Grammar
School of Bury St. Edmund ; from whence he was entered of
Trinity-college, Cambridge, where he proceeded to the degree
of A. B. in 1765, and to that of A. M. in 1773. In 1767 he
was presented to the Rectory of Wilby, and in 1781 to that of
Woolpit, both in the County of Suffolk. In 1779 he was
licensed, on the nomination of the parishioners, to the Perpetual Curacy of St. Mary at Tower in Ipswich. This gentleman,
who was on terms of the strictest intimacy with Mr. Darby, has
published " A Sermon, preached at St. Mary Tower Church,
Ipswich, for the Benefit of the Schools of Grey-coat Boys and
Blue-coat Girls, on Thursday, October 12, 1809 ; a day observed
as a Jubilee by the Friends of the said Schools, it being the
close of a Century from their first Institution. Ipswich," 8vo ;
and, " A Justificatory Reply to an Article inserted in the Suffolk Chronicle, in a Letter addressed to his Parishioners, assembled in Vestry Meeting, June 24. 1818," 4to.

† The late Lord Chedworth, in a letter to Mr. Crompton,

Mr. Darby married Martha, the only daughter of the Venerable John Jortin, D. D. Vicar of Kensington and Archdeacon of London, a learned divine and a celebrated writer.   It is a sufficient eulogium on her character to say, that she inherited her father's candid and benevolent mind; that she was highly esteemed by a most respectable acquaintance; and that in her the poor lost a valuable friend and benefactor.   She died at her house in Uxbridge on the 20th of March 1817, in the 86th year of her age, after having survived her husband for the space of twenty-three years.

Mr. Darby is known to the literary world as the author of the following works: *viz.* " A Sermon, preached at the Primary Visitation of the Right Reverend Lewis, Lord Bishop of Norwich, holden at Bury St. Edmund's, on Monday, May 17, for the Deanery of Sudbury.   London, 1784," 4to; " A Letter to the Rev. T. Warton, on his late Edition of Milton's Juvenile Poems.   London, 1785," 8vo, a just and very elegant piece of criticism *; and " A Sermon preached at the Visitation of the Reverend Thomas Knowles, D. D. Official of the Archdeaconry of Sudbury, holden at Lavenham, on Thursday, Sept. 28, 1786.   Ipswich, 1786," 4to †.

On the publication of Bishop Watson's " Letter

---

thus feelingly describes Mr. Darby's situation : " I am sorry to tell you that Mr. Darby is gone to London to consult Dr. Warren.   He sometimes loses his recollection suddenly, and sometimes his sight is imperfect; he is very low, and fears he shall be bereft of his faculties.   From what Clubbe says, I have a hope that this will not be the case; if it should, I shall feelingly exclaim : ' O what a noble mind is here o'erthrown ! ' "
Letters from the late Lord Chedworth, p. 69.

* Green's Diary of a Lover of Literature, p. 235.

† Lord Chedworth thus notices this Discourse in a letter to Mr. Compton : " You will see that the emendation in Mr. Darby's Sermon, Mark, ix. 49, 50, is Jortin's.   This Mr. Darby told me soon after the Sermon was published; however, the defence and illustration of the proposed correction are Mr. Darby's own."   Letters from the late Lord Chedworth, p. 196.

to the Archbishop of Canterbury," Mr. Darby sent
his Lordship the following letter, which does such
infinite honour to his memory, that the reader cannot but be gratified by its perusal:

" MY LORD,   *Ipswich, April 9,* 1793.
" I have been content hitherto to observe your progress in
reputation and honours with a silent satisfaction.   I was pleased
with your answer to Mr. Gibbon, and entertained by your Chemi-
cal Essays, which brought an abstract subject nearer to the level
of such understandings as mine; and I sincerely rejoiced to
hear of your advancement to the purple.   Yet, on these occasions, I did not think myself warranted to break in upon you,
either with my acknowledgments or solicitations.   You owe the
present trouble I give you to the recent publication of your
Letter to the Archbishop of Canterbury.   I cannot resist the
impulse which I feel to return you, my thanks for this Letter,
especially for your defence of the second consequence (the independence of the Bishops in the House of Lords) of your plan,
which, in my opinion, entitles you to the thanks of every honest
man in England.   It is the privilege of your situation, my Lord,
to speak words that will be heard in high places; and it cannot
be indifferent to the community whether they be words of truth
and soberness, or of self-interest and adulation.   I have my
fears, indeed,—my fears not for you, my Lord, but for my
country,—that you will reap no other fruit from your proposal
than the applause of the public and the approbation of your
own heart.   A contrary doctrine prevails, and is disseminated,
with some caution indeed, but much industry, even among the
lower ranks of courtly politicans, so far as to reaching my ears,
—*the doctrine of the necessity of corruption to our welfare.*   I
remember two or three years ago to have seen a well-written
letter to Dr. Watson, under the character of a Country Curate,
(it proceeded from the pensioned pen of Cumberland,) in which
the writer pleasantly enough contends for some influence of the
Crown to counteract the effects of republican principles, pride,
envy, disappointment, and revenge.   Unluckily, in a postscript
to this letter, the cloven-foot peeps out from under the cassock,
and the writer has added to his opponents two others, wisdom
and virtue.   'Suppose,' says he, 'for a moment, (some, perhaps,
may think it a violent supposition,) the Members of the House
of Commons to be all honest, intelligent, and uncorrupt; that
no minister could prevail upon them by place, pension, or arti-
fice.   What is the consequence?   Why the constitution is overturned; that constitution which the wisdom and blood of our
ancestors was exhausted in establishing;' that is, which wisely
established a balance to counterpoise the effects of wisdom and
honesty, and provided an antidote against the poison of virtue.

The writer may quibble, but I defy him to get fairly off from this consequence of his own words.

" A true description of the present system might, perhaps, be given in the words of an old Briton, which, though immediately applied to Roman tyranny, might, in a secondary sense,be considered as prophetic of a modern British House of Commons : ' Nata servituti mancipia semel veneunt, atque ultro a dominis aluntur; Britannia servitutem suam quotidie emit, quotidie pascit.' Galgacus in Tacit. But I have rambled too far, and must only add, that I am, with great truth and regard, your Lordship's much obliged and most obedient servant,   S. Darby*."

To this Letter the Bishop transmitted the following reply :

" Dear Sir,

" I return you a thousand thanks for your kind letter. The approbation of one good and liberal-minded man is dearer to me than the highest honours of the church ; the puff of lawn was never any object of my ambition ; but I ever have been ambitious of being thought well of by men of virtue and understanding, and you must allow me to say, that in that light I am proud of your letter. I have great hopes that my plan will be effectuated, but I mean not to bring it forward till men's minds, the minds especially of the church dignitaries, are recovered from their idle apprehensions of danger from innovation.
" I am, &c.   R. Landaff†."

" Mr. Darby," says the Bishop, " was a most respectable character, highly esteemed by all who knew him for his integrity and abilities; and had formerly been an eminent Tutor in Jesus-college, Cambridge ‡."

The Rev. JOHN PRICE, B. D.

KEEPER OF THE BODLEIAN LIBRARY, OXFORD.

This gentleman, who for nearly half a century eminently promoted the interests of literature, by the ready, liberal, and intelligent aid which he afforded to the researches of scholars and antiqua-

* Anecdotes of the Life of Richard Watson, 4to, p. 108.
† Ibid. p. 110.   ‡ Ibid.

ries *, was a native of South Wales, and was born
in March 1734-5, at Tuer, near Llangollen, in
Brecknockshire. After receiving the rudiments of
his education in his native country, he was entered
at an early age of Jesus-college, Oxford, where he
proceeded to the degree of M. A. on the 4th of
June 1760, and to that of B. D. on the 15th of
Jan. 1768, in which latter year he was elected, after
a very strong contest, Keeper of the Bodleian Library. His opponent on this occasion was, I believe, Mr. William Cleaver, then Fellow of Brasennose-college, but afterwards its Principal, and successively Bishop of Bangor and St. Asaph.

In 1782 he was presented to the Rectory of
Woolaston, with Alvington annexed, in Gloucestershire, and in 1798 to that of Llangattock in Brecon, both by the kindness of his noble and generous
patron Henry, the fifth Duke of Beaufort, from
whose family he ever received the most friendly
and polite attentions; and in 1774 to the Rectory
of Wilcote in Oxfordshire, by Mrs. Elizabeth Wel-
lington.

Mr. Price was elected a Fellow of the Society
of Antiquaries about 1797.

From his situation in the Bodleian Library, Mr.
Price was a constant resident in the University,
with the exception of his occasional visits to his
native county, and to Badminton, the seat of his
munificent patron. To his Rectory of Wilcote,
the duties of which he regularly performed, he was
much attached; and there, in the society of his
friends and the company of an occasional visitor,
he solaced himself whenever his Bodleian avocations would permit. In private life Mr. Price was
hospitable, friendly, and liberal; of the strictest
integrity and of the warmest attachments. In the
faithful discharge of his public duties in the Uni-

* Chalmers's History of the University of Oxford, p. 464.

versity, he acquitted himself with the highest credit,
and deservedly conciliated the esteem of others by
his readiness to communicate information from the
rich literary stores over which he presided, and of
which he was a most jealous and watchful guardian.
He was from long habit so completely attached to
the Library, that he considered every acquisition
made to its contents as a personal favour conferred
upon himself. The writer of a biographical notice*
in the Gentleman's Magazine, from which this is
partly extracted, states, that he is in possession of
many of his friendly letters, acknowledging the
receipt of publications occasionally sent as presents
to the Bodleian; and adds that, when such communications were delayed longer than usual, Mr.
Price would now and then send a reminder, or, to
use the expression of an old Oxford friend, "John
Price would growl."

His duties as a Librarian naturally introduced
him to the acquaintance of many eminent literary
characters; and his promptitude in assisting their
inquiries and guiding their researches gained him
from amongst them many friends. With Mr. William Huddesford †, of Trinity, he was well ac-

* Gentleman's Magazine, vol. LXXXIII. part ii. p. 400.
Monthly Magazine, vol. XXXVI. p. 179.

† This gentleman was the eldest son by the first wife of the
Rev. George Huddesford, D.D. sometime Keeper of the Ashmolean Museum, President of Trinity-college, Oxford, and Rector of Glympton in that county, a divine of the highest respectability, and the writer of the following pamphlets, viz. "A proper Reply to a Pamphlet intituled, a Defence of the Rector
and Fellows of Exeter-college, &c. 1755," 4to; and " Observations relating to the Delegates of the Press; with an Account
of their Secession from their original Appointment, 1756," 4to.
He deceased on the 21st of April 1776, and was interred in the
Anti-chapel of the College, where, on a flat-stone, is this inscription to his memory:

Depositum
GEORGII HUDDESFORD,
S. T. P.
Hujus Collegii Præsidis,

quainted ; and with the Laureate Warton, whose
death prematurely for the interests of classical taste
and elegant literature no one more sincerely regretted or more keenly felt than Mr. Price, he was

necnon Eccles. de Glympton
in com. Oxon. Rectoris.
Obiit 21mo die Aprilis,
Anno Dom. 1776,
ætat. 80.

His son, Mr. William Huddesford, was born on the 15th of
August 1732, and received his academical education at Trinity-
college, Oxford. He was elected a Scholar of that Society in
1750, and Fellow in 1757. On the 20th of October 1756, he
proceeded to the degree of M. A. and on the 7th of December
1767 to that of B. D. In 1755 he was appointed Keeper of the
Ashmolean Museum, which highly disgusted Dr. Rawlinson.
("Literary Anecdotes," vol. V. p. 495.)—In 1765 he served the
office of Senior Proctor of the University. To the inexpressible
grief of his numerous friends and acquaintance he deceased on
the 6th of October 1772. See " Literary Anecdotes," vol. I.
p. 166; vol. II. p. 622 ; vol. III. p. 677, 683, 684 ; vol. V. p.
291, 296, 495; vol. VIII. 595, 597, 600.

This melancholy event is feelingly alluded to in the following
letter from Mrs. Cox to Mr. Granger:

" REV. AND WORTHY SIR,   St. Giles's, Oct. 19, 1772.

" I have the honour to address you, by the desire of Mr. Cox,
who is prevented (by being out of town) answering your letter,
though he has taken care of the request contained in it, which
will be fully complied with (if such prints are to be found) as
soon as the executor arrives. He has commissioned me likewise
to thank you very kindly for your sympathising letter, which
so exactly suits our sentiments and affection for our beloved and
ever to be lamented friend, that it both soothes and nourishes
our grief. You justly observe, that he was never in better
health and spirits than when you saw him last. The few days
he passed at Oxford, in his way to Warwickshire, he spent chiefly
with us, when he was remarkably well and cheerful, which rendered the melancholy news of his death still more afflicting to
us, who had conceived great hopes of his perfect recovery ; but
he is called to the reward of those virtues and excellencies which
he has left us to admire, and happy for us if we endeavour to
imitate.

" You are very obliging in transmitting to us his lively verses,
which are so exactly like him, that, without his name, we had
known the author. The prompt reply, with your characteristical distich, do honour to the poetical genius of the Biogra-

on the most intimate terms of friendship. At the suggestion of the latter it was that Mr. Price removed
from Jesus to Trinity-college, of which society he ever
after continued a member, and to which, on various

phical Historian. I am, Reverend Sir, with great respect,
"Your obedient humble servant, JANE COX.
" P. S. The President and Mrs. Huddesford are as well as can
be expected after so severe a shock." Letters to and from Gran-
ger, by Malcolm, p. 426.
Mr. Tyson, in a letter to Mr. Gough, thus mentions Mr. Hud-
desford's death : " Poor Huddesford! he is a loss indeed! with
what accuracy has he made indexes to those four volumes of
Original Correspondence of Lister, given to the Ashmolean
Library in 1769 by Dr. Fothergill. He had many works in eye ;
a collection of curiosities from those 160 MS. Pocket-books of
Tom Hearne in Bodley." Literary Anecdotes, vol. VIII. 600.
Mr. Gough, in his "British Topography," observes that Mr.
" William Huddesford, whose immature death * every one who
had the pleasure of his acquaintance must join with me in de-
ploring, had collected materials for the Lives of Humphrey
Lluyd, a Physician of Denbigh, and in Mr. Camden's opinion
one of the best antiquaries of his time, and author of ' Com-
mentarioli Britanniæ Descriptionis fragmentum, auctore Hum-
fred Lloyd, Denbyghiense, Cambro-Eritanno, 1572,' 12mo, and
of Edward Llwyd, Keeper of the Ashmolean Museum and Author
of ' Archæologia Britannica. Oxon. 1707.' fol." British Topog.
vol. II. p. 486.
Mr. Huddesford was the editor of the following works, viz.
" Catalogus Librorum Manuscriptorum Viri clarissimi Antonii
à Wood, being a minute Catalogue of each particular contained
in the Manuscript Collections of Anthony a Wood, deposited in
the Ashmolean Museum at Oxford, 1761," 8vo, a publication of
very unfrequent occurrence ; " Martini Lister, M.D. Historiæ,
sive Synopsis Methodicæ Conchyliorum et Tabularum Anatomi-
carum, Editio altera, &c. 1770," folio ; " The Lives of those
eminent Antiquaries John Leland, Thomas Hearne, and Anthony à Wood, with an authentic Account of their respective
Writings and Publications from Original Papers ; in which are

* In a note from the family at Caversham to Mr. Granger, it is said,
Mr. Byrne "is greatly distressed at the loss of that truly worthy and
ever to be lamented man Mr. Huddesford, with whom he had been
acquainted more than seven-and-twenty years ; who knows, but that if
he had been under the hands of the faculty at Oxford, he might still have
continued here a blessing to mankind! From the scorbutic humour
which Mr. Cox mentioned to Mr. Granger as having fallen upon his
brain, it is much to be feared that unskilful management might be the
occasion of this disaster." Letters to and from Granger, by Malcolm,
p. 151.

occasions, he proved himself a liberal benefactor. To his assiduous applications and marked attention to Mr. Gough, with whom he was a frequent correspondent and by whom he was greatly respected, it is in a great measure owing that the Bodleian can boast of the most extensive and perfect collection of British Topography* that any library can produce.

occasionally inserted memoirs relating to many eminent Persons and various Parts of Literature. Also several Engravings of Antiquity, never before published. In two volumes, 1772," 8vo. In the " Literary Anecdotes," vol. V. p. 291, is a letter to Mr. Huddesford from Dr. William Borlase, detailing many particulars of his life.

In 1764 Mr. Huddesford published anonymously, " An Address to the Fremen and other Inhabitants of the City of Oxford. Lucern, printed for Abraham Lightholder."

Mr. Malcolm, in " Letters to and from Granger," has inserted " A Parody on Cato's Soliloquy, occasioned by being sick with drinking Punch over-night at a Club in Oxford ; and drinking a glass of water and reading Dr. Cheyne's Essay the next morning," p. 11, which he conceives to be Mr. Huddesford's production ; as well as a whimsical effusion, which he considers to be from the same pen, p. 150. In the same work likewise are inserted nine letters from Mr. Huddesford to Mr. Granger, pp. 136—150.

His library was dispersed in a Sale Catalogue of Messrs. Fletchers, Oxford, 1771.

In Kett's "Flowers of Wit" vol. II. p. 180, is an anecdote relating to Mr. Huddesford.

In the Fourth Volume of this Work, pp. 456—476, are fourteen letters from Mr. Huddesford to Mr. Da Costa; p. 466 a letter to Dr. Wright ; pp. 476—478 three letters to Mr. Gough; and p. 479 Memoirs of the Rev. Francis Wise, B. D. F.S.A. and a letter to Dr. Ducarel.

Mr. Huddesford contributed to the Gentleman's Magazine, in 1771, " A Description of Oseney Abbey," printed in vol. XLI. pp. 153, 204 ; and in a Description and History of the Nunnery at Godstow near Oxford, vol. LIII. pt. ii. p. 462. In Wood's " Athenæ Oxonienses," ed. Bliss, is a character of the author by the same pen. Life, vol. I. p. cxxxiv.

* Dr. Bandinel, the present Keeper of Bodley's Library, arranged this munificent bequest on the plan adopted by Mr. Gough himself in his British Topography, and edited it under the following title: " A Catalogue of the Books relating to British Topography and Saxon and Northern Literature, bequeathed to the Bodleian Library in the year MDCCXCIX, by Richard Gough, Esq. F.S.A. Oxford, MDCCCXIV." 4to.

With the ingenious Mr. Astle also, and many other
gentlemen eminent for their talents and literary
worth, Mr. Price was in habits of the strictest intimacy and regular correspondence.

A few years previous to his death, Mr. Price
resided in a small house in St. Giles's, adjoining the
back gate of the College, where he breathed his
last on the 12th of August 1813, in the 79th year
of his age.

> " His saltem accumulem donis, et fungar inani
> Munere."

His remains were conveyed to his favourite Wilcote ; and, at his particular request, interred in the
Church-yard of that parish. In the Chancel a
mural-tablet is erected to his memory, on which is
sculptured the following just and appropriate inscription :

> Juxta conditus est
> Johannes Price, S. T. B.
> Hujusce Parochiæ nuper Vicarius *,
> Primum in Collegium Jesu,
> Deinde S. S. Trinitatis
> apud Oxonienses
> admissus,
> Bibliothecæ Bodleianæ
> Præfecturam
> per quinquaginta fere annos
> sedulo et fideliter administravit.
> Vir
> Literarum amans,
> earum vero
> Antiquitates patrias illustrantium,
> quas præcipuè coluit,
> amantissimus.
> Vixit annos LXXVIII,
> Decessit die Augusti XII,
> anno Christi MDCCCXIII.

Mr. Price† never, I believe, published anything
of his own, with the exception of a communication

---

* This is an error. It should be Rector.

† Mrs. Serres, in her " Life of Wilmot," p. 153, in enume-
rating her uncle's friends, thus characterises the subject of this

to the Society of Antiquaries, which was inserted in the Archæologia, under the following title: "Account of a Bronze Image of Roman Workmanship, and other Antiquities, discovered at Cirencester," vol. VII. pp. 405—407, with a plate.

He assisted in the publication of the "Lives of Leland, Wood, and Hearne, 1772;" and few works appeared during the long period in which he was the Bodleian Librarian, the nature of which required deep, extensive, and laborious research, in the prefaces to which his essential services were not gratefully acknowledged.

In "Letters to and from Granger," by Mr. Malcolm, pp. 312—315, are inserted three letters from Mr. Price to that gentleman.

In the present Work, vol. III. pp. 506,507, are two letters to Dr. Ducarel; and in vol. V. pp. 514—558, is a series of epistolary correspondence between Mr. Price and many of his intelligent friends on interesting subjects of literary inquiry.

In Mant's edition of "the Poetical Works of Warton" is the following acknowledgment: "To Mr. Price, of the Bodleian Library, I return my hearty thanks, not only for the zeal which he shewed in giving me such oral intelligence as might be serviceable, but also for favouring me with what he possessed of Mr. Warton's correspondence *." And in that gentleman's Life of the Laureate, prefixed to his works, are inserted four letters from Mr. Warton to Mr. Price †.

Memoir: "Mr. Price, usually called 'Honest Johnny Price, Keeper of the Bodleian Library, who was patronised and respected by the late Duke of Beaufort, Dr. Wilmot was wont to describe as one of the worthiest characters he had ever known. At the house of Dr. Chapman, President of Trinity, the editor had the pleasure of being introduced to Mr. Price, and several other dignified members of the University, who were her uncle's friends."

* Preface, p. iv.   † Life, pp. lxxiv—lxxix.

In that entertaining work the " Bibliomania,"
Dr. Dibdin, whilst expressing an earnest wish for
the publication of a " Catalogue Raisonnè of the
MSS. and printed Books in the Bodleian Library,"
thus notices Mr. Price: " I am aware that the aged
hands of the present venerable Librarian of the
Bodleian Library can do little more than lay the
foundation-stone of such a massive superstructure;
but even that would be sufficient to enrol his name
with the Magliabeechis and Baillets of former times,
to entitle him to be classed among the best benefactors to the Library, and to shake hands with its
immortal Founder in that place were are

——————— et amœna vireta
Fortunatorum nemorum, sedesque beatæ *."

JOHN DISNEY, D.D. F.S.A.

John Disney, D. D. F.S.A. was born at Lincoln,
Sept. 17, 1746, the third and youngest surviving son
of John Disney, Esq. of Swinderby (descended
from a family of high antiquity † at Norton Disney)

* Bibliomania, p. 100.
† See a particularly full pedigree of the family, compiled by
John Charles Brooke, Somerset Herald, printed in the History
of Dorsetshire, vol. IV. pp. 389—398. At Swinderby is the following epitaph to Dr. Disney's father: "In memory of John
Disney, of Lincoln, Esq. High Sheriff of the County of Nottingham (7th Geo. II. 1733) and in the Commission of the Peace
for the Counties of Lincoln and Nottingham, who died Nov. 26,
1771, aged 71 years. He married, Dec. 29th, 1730, Frances,
youngest daughter of George Cartwright, of Ossington, in the
County of Nottingham, Esq. by whom he had three surviving
sons: 1. Lewis Disney Ffytche, of Danbury-place, in the county
of Essex, Esq. who married Elizabeth, only daughter of William
Ffytche, Esq. Governor of Bengal in the East Indies, and heir
of her uncle Thomas Ffytche, of Danbury-place, Esq.; 2.

in Lincolnshire, by Frances, daughter of George Cartwright, of Ossington in Nottinghamshire, Esq. His grandfather, the Rev. John Disney, Vicar of St. Mary's, Nottingham, was the author of an " Essay on the Laws against Immorality and Profaneness," and several other works *.

Dr. Disney was educated at Peter-house, Cambridge, where he took the degree of LL.B. in 1770. He was presented by his family to the Vicarage of Swinderby, and by his brother-in-law Edmund Turnor, Esq. to the Rectory of Panton in Lincolnshire; and was Chaplain to Dr. Edmund Law, Bishop of Carlisle (who had been Master of Peterhouse). But these preferments he relinquished in 1782 †, having adopted the opinions of the Unitarian dissenters. He became assistant minister to the Rev. Theophilus Lindsey at the Unitarian Chapel in Essex-street, London; and in 1793 his successor.

In September 1804, Dr. Disney, on the death of Thomas Brand Hollis, Esq. unexpectedly found himself in possession of the large property of that gentleman; who bequeathed, without annexing any condition, all his real and personal estates, as well those in Essex, which he inherited from his father, as those in Dorsetshire, which he received from his friend Thomas Hollis, Esq. " to Dr. John Disney, of Sloane-street, Knightsbridge, near London, his

Frederick Disney, Esq. Major in the army, who died June 15th, 1788, aged 16 years; and 3. John Disney, D.D. F.S.A. some time Vicar of this parish, who married Jane, eldest daughter of the Rev. Francis Blackburne, M.A. Rector of Richmond, and Archdeacon of Cleveland in the county of York; also one surviving daughter, Mary, who married Edmund Turnor, of Panton in the county of Lincoln, Esq. Frances Disney, widow of the said John Disney, Esq. died at Lincoln January 5, 1791, aged 81 years."

* See a list of them, with memoir of him, in Malcolm's " Letters to and from Granger;" with other communications of Dr. Disney, they occupy pp. 195—210 of that work.

† See a particular account of this change in the " Literary Anecdotes," vol. III. p. 19.

heirs, executors, and administrators, to his and their sole use and benefit *." Dr. Disney soon after removed to Mr. Hollis's mansion, the Hyde, in the parish of Ingatestone, Essex, where he died, aged 70, Dec. 26, 1816.

The following is a list of Dr. Disney's numerous publications:

" Animadversions on Dr. Rutherforth," an octavo tract, 1768.

" Four Sermons, on Christmas Day. 1771," 8vo (afterwards re-published in his two volumes of Sermons).

" Sermon on Psalm xcvi. 9. 1773."

" Loose Hints on Nonconformity, 1773."

" Letter to the Archbishop of Canterbury, 1774."

" Rational Christian's Assistant, 1774."

" Remarks on Dr. Balguy's Consecration Sermon, 1775."

" Short View of Confessional and Clerical Petition Controversies, 1775."

" Thoughts on Licensing Alehouses, 1776."

" Visitation Sermon, on Romans, ch. xiv. 5. 1777," 4to.

* " In the disposition of his fortune," remarks Dr. Disney in his Memoirs of his benefactor, " Mr. Brand Hollis might seem, as it were, to have adopted the precedent of his friend Thomas Hollis, Esq. The date of his will (Nov. 2, 1792) was nearly twelve years before his decease. On no one occasion, and in no one instance of our confidential or familiar conversation, either in London or at the Hyde, during my repeated visits there, did he give the slightest intimation of his partial intention, or drop one unguarded expression leading that way. So lately as September 1802, he presented to me a sleeping cupid, by Algardi, upon his indirectly learning from another person that I much admired it; but this marble was the only memorial that he had given me in his life-time. Since his death, I have sometimes thought that I could call to my remembrance some faint traces of his great watchfulness over himself in this practised reserve; and I can with pleasure bring to my recollection some marked evidences of his regard : but these in no degree amounted to tokens of friendship so unbounded; and which he intended to confirm by so magnificent and splendid a bequest."

" Remarks on Bishop Hurd's Charge, 1777."

" Considerations on the Clergy acting in the Commission of the Peace, 1781."

" A Spirit of Industry Recommended; a Sermon on 2 Thess. iii. 10, 1781," 12mo.

" Reasons for quitting the Church of England, 1783," 8vo *.

" Dialogue between a common Unitarian Christian and an Athanasian, 1784," 12mo.

" Memoirs of the Life and Writings of Arthur Ashley Sykes, D.D. 1785 †," 8vo.

" The Works, Theological, Medical, Political, and Miscellaneous, of John Jebb, M.D. F.R.S. with Memoirs of the Life of the Author, 1787." 3 vols. 8vo ‡.

" Discourses on various Subjects, to which are added, Considerations on Pluralities, by the Rev. Sam. Disney §, LL.D. late Vicar of Halstead, Essex, 1788," 8vo.

" A Friendly Dialogue, between a common Unitarian Christian and an Athanasian; occasioned by the former's behaviour during some part of the Public Service; or, an attempt to restore Scripture forms of Worship. To which is added, a Second

* There was published in animadversion of this : " Socinian Integrity Examined ; in Reply to a Pamphlet, intituled, ' Reasons for gutting the Church of England, Lond. 1783," 8vo.

† See hereafter, p. 485.

‡ See the " Literary Anecdotes," vol. I. p. 572.

§ The Rev. Samuel Disney was Dr. Disney's first cousin, being the only surviving son of the Rev. Samuel Disney, Fellow of Corpus Christi college, Cambridge, (where he proceeded B.A. 1727, M.A. 1731, and who died Lecturer of Wakefield in Yorkshire, July 22, 1741,) by Margery, youngest daughter of Francis Procter, Esq. of Thorpe-on-the-Hill, co. York. The son was of Clare hall, Cambridge, LL.B. 1761, and was presented to the Vicarage of Halstead in Essex in 1768. He died at Halstead July 10, 1786, aged 48 ; he having married August 1, 1767, Anne, eldest daughter of the Right Rev. Christopher Wilson, D.D. Bishop of Bristol, by Anne, youngest daughter of the Right Rev. Edmund Gibson, Bishop of London. She was born in Fulham Palace, Sept. 14, 1745, and dying May 8, 1785, was buried in Bishop Gibson's vault there. They had no family.

Dialogue, between Eugenius and Theophilus, on the same subject, 1788," 8vo.*

" Address to the Bishops, 1790."

" Observations on the Homilies, 1790."

" Arranged Catalogue of Publications on Toleration, Corporation, and Test Acts, 1790," 8vo.

" Letters to the Students of Divinity in the Diocese of Chester, 1790," 8vo.

" A Defence of Public or Social Worship, in Answer to Gilbert Wakefield and Paine's Age of Reason, a Sermon, 1792 †," 8vo.

"Memoirs of the Life and Writings of John Jortin, D.D. 1792 ‡," 8vo.

" A Vindication of the Apostle Paul from the charge of Sedition ; a Sermon, 1792," 8vo.

" The Book of Common Prayer Reformed, for the Use of Unitarian Congregations, 1792 ;" second edition, with a Collection of Hymns, 1802.

" Letters to Vicesimus Knox, D.D. occasioned by his Reflections on Unitarian Christians, in his Advertisement to a volume of Sermons, 1792," 8vo.

"The Progressive Improvement of Civil Liberty; a Sermon preached in Essex-street, on Sunday, Nov. 4, 1792, the Anniversary of the Revolution 1688 ‖."

"Sermons, 1793," 2 vols. 8vo. and two more, 1816.

" The Reciprocal Duty of a Christian Minister and a Christian Congregation ; a Sermon, 1793," 8vo.

" A Caution to Young Persons against Infidelity ; a Sermon, 1796," 8vo.

" The Duty of Perseverance in Well-doing, 1796," 8vo.

* This publication is reviewed in the Gentleman's Magazine, vol. LVIII. p. 620.—The first dialogue was by the Rev. Dr. Hopkins, the second by Dr. Disney.

† See the Gentleman's Magazine, vol. LXII. p. 242.

‡ See the " Literary Anecdotes," vol. II. p. 575; and Gent. Mag vol. LXII. p. 935.

§ In reply was published, " Free Remarks occasioned by the Letters of John Disney, D.D. to Vicesimus Knox, D.D. By Henry Barry Peacock." See Gent. Mag. vol. LXII. p. 933.

‖ Reviewed in the Gentleman's Magazine, vol. LXIII. p. 546.

" A Sermon preached at the Unitarian Chapel, Essex-street, on the death of the Rev. Dr. Priestley, 1804," 8vo.

"Memoirs of Thos. Brand Hollis, Esq. 1808," 4to. [Not published].

" The Life of Sir Michael Foster, by Michael Dodson, Esq. his nephew, republished from the Biographia Britannica. 1811 *." 8vo.

" Remarks on the Bishop of Lincoln's Charge to the Clergy of his Diocese in 1812," 8vo.

" Six Letters occasioned by the institution of an Auxiliary British and Foreign Bible Society, 1812," octavo.

"Short Memoir of the late Rev. R. E. Garnham, 1814."

" Short Memoirs of late William Hopkins, B. A. Vicar of Bolney, Sussex, 1815."

The following character of Dr. Disney was written by a surviving friend † :

" He sustained a painful and lingering illness with a fortitude and dignified composure, founded on the principles of that system of Christianity which he had adopted upon deliberate investigation and mature conviction, with the manly decision and disinterestedness which strongly marked his character. Of those principles he was an able, strenuous, powerful advocate, as his writings, various, useful, and important, abundantly testify. A native energy of sentiment and vivacity of manner, gave an unusual interest and spirit to his conversation, which animated all around him. Distinguished by his rank in society, and adorned by the nobler distinction of his virtues, he was justly eminent in the several departments of

---

* Michael Dodson, Esq. who led for many years a retired life in Boswell-court, Chancery-lane, left a considerable property between his executors, Mr. Serjeant Praed and Dr. Disney. — See hereafter, p. 486.

† His son-in-law the Rev. Thomas Jervis, who published a funeral sermon on Dr. Disney's death, intituled, " The Memorial of the Just," preached at Mill-hill Chapel, Leeds,

Theology and Literature, and highly esteemed and
respected in the neighbourhood in which he was
resident, in the circle of his numerous and respectable friends, and by all who were competent to
judge of the strict honour, purity, consistency, and
integrity, which governed all his actions; who knew
how to appreciate the ingenuousness, the dignity,
and elevation of his mind, the characteristic candour, sincerity, and benevolence of his heart."

The united Libraries, antient Coins, and collection of Medals, Bronzes, and Terra-cottas, of the
celebrated Thomas Hollis and T. Brand Hollis, including the Theological and Political Library of the
late Dr. Disney, were sold by auction in the spring
of 1817, by Mr. Sotheby.   A bust of Dr. Disney
by J. Cockaine, was in the same season exhibited in
the model-room of the Royal Academy.

Dr. Disney married, at Richmond in Yorkshire,
Nov. 17, 1774, Jane, eldest daughter of the Rev.
Francis Blackburne, Rector of Richmond, and Arch-
deacon of Cleveland.   By this lady, who was a few
months older than himself, and died Oct. 2, 1809,
he had issue two sons and five daughters: 1. John
Disney, Esq. of the Inner Temple, Barrister-at-
law, and Recorder of Bridport, and High Sheriff of
Dorsetshire in 1818; he married in 1802 his first
cousin Sophia, second daughter of Lewis Disney
Ffytche, of Swinderby, Esq. (who assumed the
latter name in 1775), and has a family; 2. Frances-
Mary, married May 29, 1818, to the Rev. Thomas
Jervis; 3. Elizabeth-Jane, and 4. Catherine-Dorothy,
who both died infants; 5. Algernon, of Peter-house,
Cambridge, B. A. 1801, M. A. 1804, and afterwards
a Major in the army; 6. Elizabeth-Collyer, and 7.
Jane, who both died young.

---

1. Dr. DISNEY to Mr. NICHOLS.

" SIR,   *Swinderby, near Newark, Feb.* 11, 1782.
" I inclose to you a true return of the baptisms and burials
within a certain district and during certain periods, for admis-

sion into the Gentleman's Magazine.   The letter accompanying the table will explain the rest *.

" The Visitation Sermon, which makes up the packet, is at your service, as a present from the author; it was very sufficiently noticed in your Magazine at the time of its publication.

" I have occasionally contributed to the Gentleman's Magazine.   Of late you may know me by the two final letters of my name, and I give you this information in confidence †.

" Of Dr. Twells (of whom you tell an affecting truth in a note in No. 2, pt. ii. of your Bibliotheca Topographica Britannica, p. 182), you are, I believe, under a mistake in his Christian name, which was Leonard and not Matthew.   You will excuse this correction.

" I have wished to be able to send you some memoirs of Dr. Arthur Ashley Sykes, but I cannot meet with materials or information beyond a list of his publications, which I believe I could make out with tolerable exactness; but I could not go much beyond it.   He was an able writer in his day, and deserves to be held in remembrance ‡.

" If you think good to let me hear from you, be pleased to direct to me as above; and if you will accept of my correspondence (subject to the plan of your Magazine), I shall very willingly contribute some little matter occasionally.   If you accept of the papers sent herewith, I wish them to be authenticated with my name as I have written them.   I am, Sir,
" Your humble servant,   JOHN DISNEY."

2. " SIR,   Swinderby, Aug. 7, 1782.
" I return you many thanks for the information you have been so kind as to send to me of some papers in the British Museum relating to Dr. Sykes.   I wish it were in my power to examine them myself, but many circumstances conspire to prevent me. I have a pretty accurate list of Dr. Sykes's works, first formed with the assistance I found in Masters's History of Corpus Christi College, Cambridge, where also is a short account of his life. Dr. Birch's opportunity of information and assiduity in biographical collections may probably afford much more matter than the short article in Mr. Masters's book.   Dr. Sykes's letters may require selection; and yet it is not improbable but something may be gleaned from each which may be of use in the proposed Account of his Writings as well as of his Life.

" In short, your obliging notification of the materials in the Museum may lead you into some inconvenience, as it tempts me to desire you to employ a careful person to copy the whole of

* See the Gentleman's Magazine, vol. LII. p. 74.   The district is the Hundred of Boothby Graffoe in Lincolnshire.
† With this signature appears some corrections to Warton's English Poetry in June 1781, and a short memoir of Sir Michael Foster in November.
‡ Dr. Disney's materials subsequently swelled into an octavo volume.

what is there relating to Dr. Sykes, with all proper and accurate references to the place of their deposit.

" Mr. Johnson, of St. Paul's Church-yard, is now looking out for several of Dr. Sykes's works for me, that I may be better able to be thoroughly acquainted with my author.

" Your biographical anecdotes of your late worthy and learned predecessor and valued friend are now before me; and I must confess myself at a loss which to admire most, your gratitude and diligence, or Mr. Bowyer's many excellent and amiable qualifications.

" If you can give me the address of Mr. Robertson *, the editor of Sidney's Works, and who, as I take it, is the same gentleman who is mentioned in p. 477, note † of the Biographical Anecdotes, I shall be obliged to you for it. I think he was once Curate to Dr. Sykes, and consequently may be able to give me some information in regard to him. I am, Sir,

" Your obliged and obedient humble servant, JOHN DISNEY."

---

3. Dr. DISNEY to RICHARD GOUGH, Esq.

" Sloane-street, Knightsbridge, Oct. 19, 1784.

" Dr. Disney presents his compliments to Mr. Gough. He has left the engraved plate of the Brass Monument at Norton-Disney in Lincolnshire with Mr. Cook; and desires Mr. Gough will, at his own time, take any number of impressions he may choose for his work, or, if Mr. Gough should particularly desire it, the plate itself shall be at his service. Dr. Disney will send Mr. Gough a printed explanation of the plate, as far as concerns the personal history of the parties, as soon as he has leisure to get his paper through the press."

---

4. Dr. DISNEY to GEORGE ALLAN, Esq.

" Sloane-street, Knightsbridge, Dec. 27, 1792.

" Dr. Disney returns his compliments to Mr. Allan, and is much obliged to him for the portraits and the note, forwarded to him so long ago as the 12th of last month, but which he did not receive till the 22d instant. Those of Mr. Allan's family he shall preserve with particular pleasure ; and should Dr. Disney hereafter become possessed of any more private plates, he will not fail to send some good impressions to the Grange."

---

5. Dr. DISNEY to Mr. NICHOLS.

" DEAR SIR,   *The Hyde, near Ingatestone, Aug. 23, 1810.*

" The life of Mr. Justice Foster, written by my late friend Mr. Dodson †, was, as you well know, printed for the intended

---

* The Rev. Joseph Robertson, of whom see memoirs by himself in " Literary Anecdotes," vol. III. pp. 500—506. See also VII. 354, 664.
† See p. 483.

sixth volume of the Biog. Brit. Some copies were presented by you to Mr. Dodson.

" It is proposed by some immediate friends of the Judge's family, to re-print his nephew's account of him from one of those copies, and to prefix a well engraved portrait, from an original painting, when he was advanced in years.

" But we jointly thought it most correct to mention the scheme to you, though we are not aware of any objection to our pro-ceeding. It is proposed to print the work in octavo, and in the same sized page as his ' Crown Law,' and to have it done with great care and correctness, with a good letter, and on good paper. Trifling as the work is in quantity, it is the desire of the parties concerned, to offer the re-printing this Memoir to your office; and, as soon as I receive your answer, I will again write to you upon the subject. I am, dear Sir,

" Your sincere friend,   JOHN DISNEY."

7. " SIR,   *The Hyde, near Ingatestone, Sept. 26, 1810.*

" I inclose the Life of Mr. Justice Foster, and wish you to proceed in the re-printing of it as early as may be, agreeably to the instructions inclosed.

" I am now on the eve of a journey into the north. This circumstance will prevent my seeing any thing of the work as it passes through the press; but it is with entire confidence that I commit it to your attention and superintendance, wishing, at the same time, to be understood that I do not desire any proper expense to be spared that shall tend to produce the work with any advantage in its execution. I will furnish you on a future day with the title and a short preface. I also intend to engage Mr. Basire to engrave a portrait of the Judge from an original painting in his advanced age. I am, Sir,

" Your sincere friend,   JOHN DISNEY."

8. " DEAR SIR,   *The Hyde, May 24, 1813.*

" I thank you for the early transmission of your Leicestershire Index, and congratulate you having satisfactorily gotten through so laborious and useful an undertaking. The insignificant inclo-sure in my last letter was in no other way entitled to your acknowledgment, but as it was intended as a token of good-will in return for your very liberal conduct to the public, of which I could not think of availing myself.

" The Index to the Memoirs of Mr. Thomas Hollis is much at your service; and I am gratified that I have it in my power to desire your acceptance of a copy, and also a print of the writer of that work.

" I have also inclosed a few insignificant errata, which occurred to me in the course of my reading the " Literary Anecdotes" last summer. I am, dear Sir, very sincerely yours, JOHN DISNEY."

8. " DEAR SIR,   *The Hyde, Jan. 6,* 1815.
" I inclose the pedigree*, in which you will recognise the hand-
writing of the late J. C. Brooke, Somerset.   The fairer copy is
transcribed into a large volume. I fear you will find it unwieldly.
I should be obliged to you for half a dozen extra impressions of
the revised copy on paper that will take ink, by the Chelmsford
coach from Gracechurch-street.
" I will have a packing-case made forthwith for the view by
Peter Andreas Rysbrach, taken 1741, (elder brother of the
statuary,) and desire, once for all, that you will place all inci-
dental expenses to my account, and I will readily discharge them
whenever you will transmit them to me.
" Some supplementary notes, or illustrations of the pedigree,
shall be forwarded in as few days as may be, in the box with the
painting ; and also a continuation of my own descent.
" I have added a couple of my book plates, if you should have
occasion for them.
" I thank you for a sight of two pages of the additions and
corrections of volume one.
" I am, dear Sir, very sincerely yours,   JOHN DISNEY."

9. " DEAR SIR,   *The Hyde, Jan. 9,* 1815.
" The illustrative notes I have inclosed in the box, which conveys ' A View of part of Urless Farm in Corscombe,' which will
be taken to morrow by the Blackmore van to the Talbot inn,
Whitechapel ; and the best way of conveying it to your house,
or Mr. Basire's, will be to send on Wednesday morning some
person to move it in a coach ; it is more cumbersome than heavy.
" The copy of a monument in Norton Disney Church, and
some account of it, is sent without meaning it to be used, as it
has no appropriation in Dorset ; but is at your service. I gave
the plate to Mr. Gough. I am, dear Sir,
          " Very sincerely yours,   JOHN DISNEY."

10. " GENTLEMEN,   *The Hyde, March 23,* 1815.
" A plate of my arms, with the quarterings on the dexter side
of the shield to affix to the pedigree, shall be much at your service ; and I will with pleasure, at any moment, reimburse you
the expense of engraving it, in the same kind of shield, crest,
and motto as my present book-plate, omitting the arms of my
late wife, as they should not be in the situation you intend for
them ; the present plate is also almost worn out.
" I know not what to reply as to an engraving of Thomas
Hollis ; I have no good painting. I have, indeed, a fine bust by
Wilton, which the Society of Arts engraved and prefixed to one

* For the History of Dorsetshire.

of their volumes in 1806; but the draftsman and engraver
entirely failed of any likeness. The engraving of a profile likeness fronting the 'Hollis' Memoirs,' is, I understand, a fair
resemblance of him; and the copper-plate should be at your
service, but I fear it would not suit for your history, having been
placed in another and immediately appropriate work. But do
as you please. I remain, Gentlemen,

"Your obedient humble servant,   JOHN DISNEY."

DAVID EARL OF BUCHAN.

The Right Hon. David Steuart Erskine, eleventh
Earl of Buchan and sixth Lord Cardross, was born
June 1, 1742 (O.S.), the second but eldest surviving
son of Henry David the tenth Earl, by Agnes,
second daughter of Sir James Steuart, of Good-
trees, Bart. his Majesty's Solicitor for Scotland;
and was the elder half-brother of Thomas Lord
Erskine, for a short time Lord High Chancellor of
England.

From an account communicated by himself to Mr.
Wood's edition of Douglas's "Peerage of Scotland,"
we learn that he "was educated by James Buchanan,
of the family of the memorable poet and historian,
under the immediate direction of his excellent
parents. He was founded in the elements of the
mathematics by his mother, who was a scholar of
the great Maclaurin; by his father in history and
politics; and by his preceptor in all manner of useful learning, and in the habits of rigid honour and
virtue." By a memoir in the "Public Characters of
1798," to which also it is probable that his Lordship
contributed, we are further informed that, "at the
University of Glasgow, in early youth, he applied
with ardent and successful diligence to every ingenious and liberal study. His hours of relaxation
from science and literature were frequently passed
in endeavours to acquire the arts of design, etching*,

* A specimen of his abilities in etching (a view of Icolmkill

engraving, and drawing, in the academy which the excellent, but ill-requited, Robert Foulis for some time laboured to support in that western metropolis of Scotland."

Having completed his education, Lord Cardross was probably at first intended for the military profession, as he held a half-pay lieutenancy of the 32d foot even to the period of his decease. It has been said, however, that he repaired to London, to pursue the study of diplomacy under the patronage of the Earl of Chatham. Whilst resident in the metropolis, he was elected a Fellow of the Royal and Antiquarian Societies in 1765. Of the latter, and perhaps of the former, he would, for some years before his decease, have been the senior Member, had he not resigned the honour a few years after returning to Scotland.

His Lordship was appointed Secretary to the British Embassy in Spain in November 1766; but, losing his father Dec. 1, 1767, " withdrew from public life at a very early period after his succession to the title, and dedicated himself to the duties of a private station, the advancement of science and literature, and the improvement of his native country by the arts of peace." Such is his Lordship's own account. His political feelings, however, were strong; and several occasional manifestations of them are on record.

One is thus noticed in the " Public Characters:" " The King's Ministers had been long accustomed, at each new election, to transmit to every Peer a list of the names of sixteen of his fellow-Peers, for whom he was required to give his vote, in the choice of the Members who should represent the nobles of Scotland in the British Parliament; and to this humiliating usurpation the descendants of the most illustrious names had accustomed themselves tamely to submit! The Earl of Buchan, with the spirit

Abbey), was published in the first volume of the Transactions of the Scottish Antiquaries, as noticed hereafter.

of an antient Baron, took an early opportunity of declaring, that he would oblige the Secretary of State,
who should insult him with such an application, to
wash away the affront with his blood. The practice
from that time ceased; and Ministers were obliged
to adopt some other less offensive mode of exercis-
ing their electioneering influence over the Caledonian
Peerage." Lord Buchan's "Speech, intended to
have been spoken at the Meeting of the Peers of
Scotland, for the General Election of their Representatives; in which a plan is proposed for the better Representation of the Peerage of Scotland,"
was published in 4to, 1780. His Lordship never
voted at subsequent elections of Representative Peers.

To revert from these political efforts to those
scenes where his zealous enthusiasm was more successfully and beneficially exerted, the " Public Characters" shall be again quoted: "The Earl had two
very promising brothers [the Chancellor and the
witty Henry Erskine]; and on their education he earnestly bestowed that care which was to be expected
from the kindness and vigilance, not merely of a
near relation, but of a prudent and affectionate parent. The fortunes of his family had been, from
different causes, not dishonoured indeed, but impaired so considerably that they could no longer
afford an annual income sufficiently ample to support its dignities with due splendour, and to enable
him to gratify all the generous wishes of a munificent spirit. Struck with this, he resolutely adopted
a plan of economy, admirably fitted to retrieve and
re-establish those falling fortunes; and his endeavours (perhaps the most honourable and difficult
which a young and liberal-minded nobleman could
resolve upon), without subjecting him to the imputation of parsimony, were crowned and rewarded
with opulence.

" The High School of Edinburgh is confessedly
one of the best seminaries in the kingdom for the
initiation of youth in the first principles of the

Latin language. By frequent visits to this seminary, the Earl of Buchan has sought every opportunity of recommending to public notice the skill and attention of the teachers, as well as the happy proficiency of their pupils; and a premium, his gift, is annually bestowed at the University of Aberdeen, upon the successful competitor in a trial of excellence among the Students."

Of a school for Students of more advanced years, the Society of Antiquaries of Scotland, the Earl of Buchan may justly be styled the Founder. The first meeting, preparatory to its formation, was held at his house, Nov. 14, 1780; when he explained, in a pertinent discourse, (printed that year in octavo,) the general plan and intention of the proposed Association. A second meeting assembled at the same place a fortnight after; and at a third, on the 18th of October, the Society was instituted, when the Earl of Bute was elected President, and the Earl of Buchan the first of the five Vice-Presidents. A few weeks after it was annouced that " the Earl of Buchan has presented to the newly-instituted Society of Antiquaries of Scotland, a correct Life of the admirable Chrichton, written by the Earl himself, in which many falsities relative to this prodigy of human nature are detailed. [This was afterwards employed in the Biographica Britannica.] His Lordship has likewise deposited with the Society some valuable literary productions of Chrichton." His subsequent exertions will be considerably illustrated by the correspondence appended to this article.

In December 1784 the Earl communicated to Mr. Nichols, two letters containing some " Remarks on the Progress of the Roman Arms in Scotland, during the Sixth Campaign of Agricola," which, with a third by the Rev. Mr. Jamieson, and six plates, were published in 1786 as the XXXVIth number of the Bibliotheca Topographica Britannica. The first letter begins in this singular manner, the quotation of which will impart some further idea of his Lordship's political sentiments : " Sir, Next to the united loss of health and character, accompanied by the gnawing torments of an evil conscience, is the misfortune to a good man of surviving the virtue, the glory, and the happiness of his native country. This misfortune is ours; and such has been the accumulation of disgrace and discomfiture that has fallen on us as a people, since the last wretched twenty-four years of the British annals, that I turn with aversion from the filthy picture that is before my eyes, and look back for consolation to the times which are past. It was in seeking, Sir, for such opiates to the watchful care of a good citizen in a falling empire, that I fell into antiquarian research, and shall give you from time to time the results of it."

On reviewing the memorials of the Scottish nobility, Lord Buchan felt his enthusiastic veneration in a particular manner excited by the science and virtues of the illustrious Napier, the inventor of logarithms, and the most eminent discoverer in philosophy which Scotland could boast. With a generous hand he aspired to crown the memory of his illustrious countryman with due honours, and, in conjunction with Walter Minto, LL. D. published at Edinburgh in quarto, in 1787, " An Account of the Life, Writings, and Inventions of Napier of Merchiston ; " as a specimen of biography on a new plan *.

In 1787, Lord Buchan, from regard to his health, left Edinburgh and went to reside at his country mansion of Dryburgh Abbey. The circular Latin epistle, which he addressed to his learned friends on this occasion, will be found in a subsequent page. His Lordship then applied his energies to the improvement of his ancestral seat ; and no tourist who has visited the south of Scotland will forget the beauties of Dryburgh. The Earl himself commu-

* See the Monthly Review, vol. LXXX. pp. 232—237.

nicated to Grose's Antiquities of Scotland a description of the place *, with two views taken in 1787
and 1789; and another description to "The Bee."
In 1814 he erected in his grounds a statue of
Wallace†; and a chain bridge of his formation
crosses the Tweed at Dryburgh.

The enthusiasm of Lord Buchan led him in 1791
to institute an annual festive commemoration of
Thomson, at Ednam, the scene of that poet's birth.
In the Gentleman's Magazine ‡ will be found an
" Eulogy of Thomson the Poet delivered by the
Earl of Buchan, on Ednam-hill, when he crowned
the first edition of the Seasons with a wreath of
Bays, on the 22d of September, 1791." This con-
tains some strong reflections on Dr. Johnson, for his

* Printed in vol. I. pp. 101—109.

† " This colossal statue is 21½ feet in height, and was designed
by Mr. John Smith, sculptor, exactly from the authentic portrait of Wallace in water colours, painted during his residence in
France, which was purchased by the father of the late Sir Philip
Ainslie, of Pilton, Knt. The hero is represented in the antient
Scottish dress and armour, with a shield hanging from his left
hand, and leaning lightly on his spear with his right. On the
summit of the natural rock adjoining to the statue is a colossal
urn, on which is inscribed the very appropriate speech made at
the dedication of the statue, by the public-spirited nobleman
who erected it." Gent. Mag. vol. LXXXVII. i. 621.

" On Thursday the 22d of September, 1814, being the Anniversary of the Victory obtained by the brave Sir William Wallace,
at Stirling-bridge in 1297, the Earl of Buchan dedicated the
Colossal Statue of that Hero, on a rock at Dryburgh, in the following very laconic and impressive manner:

" In the name of my brave and worthy Country I dedicate this
Monument as sacred to the memory of Wallace,

       ' The peerless Knight of Ellerslie,
       Who wav'd on Ayr's romantic shore
       The beamy torch of liberty!
       And roaming round from sea to sea,
       From glade obscure, or gloomy rock,
       His bold compatriots call'd, to free
       The realm from Edward's iron yoke.'

" The situation of this monumental statue is truly striking,
and commands a lovely view." Ibid. LXXXIV. ii. 631.

‡ Vol. LXI. pp. 1019, 1083.

" profane" criticisms on the Scottish bard ; and in
the following year the Earl pursued the subject in an
" Essay on the Lives and Writings of Fletcher of
Saltoun, and the Poet Thomson, biographical, critical, and political ; with some pieces of Thomson's
never before published." 8vo. In this are found
some further specimens of his Lordship's political
feelings *. He says himself, in the notice in the
Peerage which has been twice before quoted : " In
his Essay on the Lives of Thomson the Poet, and
Fletcher of Saltoun, and in his correspondence with
Christopher Wyvill, as Chairman of the Yorkshire
Committee, he has sufficiently explained the political motives by which he has been guided ; and his
public acts, which have been few, will speak for
themselves. *Est quodam ire tenus si non datur
ultra.*"

In the Gentleman's Magazine for March 1792†,
the Earl of Buchan published proposals for editing
the voluminous manuscripts left by the celebrated
Peiresc ; but the plan does not appear to have led to
any result.

It was not till the same year that the first volume
of the "Transactions of the Society of the Antiquaries of Scotland," was completed at the press.
It contained the following articles by the Earl of
Buchan : " Memoirs of the Life of Sir James Steuart
Denham, Baronet," (pp. 129—139) ; " Account of
the Parish of Uphall" (pp. 139—155). This begins thus : " Some time ago I threw into a weekly
paper, published by Messrs. Ruddiman, some anonymous hints for giving accounts of country parishes
in Scotland, suited to the various objects of our
institution, and pointed out a few of the many
advantages which might arise from the promotion
of such communications. Having been lately in a
very indifferent state of health, and finding my

* See the Gentleman's Magazine, vol. LXII. p. 52 ; Monthly
Review, N. S. vol. VI. pp. 425—428.   † Vol. LXII. p. 258.

mind unable to invent, or to range in my favourite
fields of science, or of the fine arts, I thought my
time could not be better employed than in compiling the notes I had formerly made, with respect to
the country parish where I reside."—His " Account
of the Island of Icolmkill," in pp. 234—241, is
accompanied by the before-mentioned etching executed by himself when at the University of Glasgow, and dedicated to his mother Isabella the Countess dowager; and in pp. 251—256 is a " Life of
Mr. James Short, Optician," by his Lordship.

Lord Buchan was an occasional contributor to
various periodical publications. His favourite signature was Albanicus; under which, in a letter to
his friend Hortus, he describes his own delightful
residence of Dryburgh Abbey in the fourth volume
of " The Bee." In some letters (where printed we
are not informed) he warmly embraced the cause of
Mary Queen of Scots against Dr. Robertson. To
the Gentleman's Magazine he communicated in
1784 a description of the Grave of Ossian, with an
epitaph in blank verse *; and a letter on the Antiquities of Scotland †; and in 1785 a fragment of
Petronius, received from Constantinople ‡.

The mind of this indefatigable nobleman was, as
we have seen, almost continually devoted, through a
long series of years, to the pursuits of literature.
His correspondence with scholars and men of science,
both at home and abroad, was almost unbounded;
and he numbered among his friends many of the
most distinguished characters of his period, — a
period which may almost be said to comprise the
Nestorian age of three generations. In Scotland
patronage can rarely afford to take a very munificent form, nor did Lord Buchan's circumstances
enable him to become an exception to the general
order. But in kind offices, in recommendations,

* Vol. LIV. p. 404.   † Signed with his own name, ibid. 674.
‡ Signed A. B. vol. LV. p. 105.

in introductions, in suggestions, and in warmly interesting himself and others within his sphere for the promotion of deserving efforts, and youthful or lowly aspirants to fame, he well merited the name of a zealous patron. The poet Burns, Tytler the translator of Callimachus, and Pinkerton the historian and antiquary, were, amongst others, fostered by his countenance and friendship.

Lord Buchan married at Aberdeen, Oct. 15, 1771, Margaret, eldest daughter of his cousin-german, William Fraser, of Fraser-field, co. Aberdeen, Esq. The Countess, who died May 12, 1819, never had any family. The Earl died April 16, 1829, when the titles devolved on his Lordship's nephew, Henry-David Erskine, Esq. elder son of the Hon. Henry Erskine, who died in 1817.

A portrait of the Earl of Buchan, when Lord Cardross, was painted by Reynolds in a Van Dyck dress, and engraved in mezzotinto by J. Finlayson in 1765. A profile taken by Tassie in 1783 was published in 1797 at the head of the dedication to his Lordship of Herbert's Iconographia Scotica *; and is copied in the present volume. Among the etchings of the clever self-taught artist Kay, is also a small whole-length of the Earl in 1784, in the same plate with the Marquis of Graham (the present Duke of Montrose). They stand *dos-a-dos* in the Highland military costume.

* " To the Right Honourable the Earl of Buchan, by whose aid, and numerous communications, the following work has been chiefly promoted and enriched, the first volume of the Iconographia Scotica is respectfully dedicated by his Lordship's most devoted humble servant, ISAAC HERBERT." In the similar work, intituled, Pinkerton's Scottish Gallery, printed in 1800, we find a long list of the works of Jameson, " communicated by the Earl of Buchan, whose many services to this publication cannot be too highly estimated."

1. Lord Cardross to Mr. Da Costa.

" My dear Sir,   *December* 1765.

" I shall have the pleasure of meeting you at the Royal Society
to-night; but, as I may not find a proper opportunity of speaking to you aside, I write this to mention a favour I have to ask
of you which I forgot to take notice of the other day.   You
must know I have taken it into my head to gather duplicates
from my obliging friends to erect a little Museum in Scotland.
If you, my good Sir, do me the favour to set apart such specimens from your collection as may be easiest spared, I in return,
from the pretty general correspondence I have formed, will give
you specimens from time to time which may be new to you,
and to the Royal Society.   I intend to beat about for recruits in
this service; and hope you will be serjeant to my recruiting
party.   Doctor Walker is to leave London in a fortnight; and
I could be glad to send by sea in his baggage such things as I
have already collected and such things as I may be able to procure.   I am, dear Sir, with sincere regard,

        " Your most obliged humble servant,   CARDROSS."

---

2. " My dear Sir,   *Monday, Dec.* 1765.

" I do myself the favour of calling to acquaint you that on
recollection I shall not send down to Scotland the specimens till
the middle of January, so I need not be in such haste; but any
day you please to appoint shall be happy to accompany you, when
you are setting apart the specimens you are so good as to promise me, in addition to what I have already, for I will not dispatch my collections till they amount to somewhat more considerable.   Adieu !   CARDROSS."

---

3. Lord Cardross to Dr. Birch *.

        " *George-street, Hanover-square, Dec.* 3, 1765.

" Lord Cardross's best compliments to Dr. Birch, and begs he
will be so kind as to assist Mr. Lind, the bearer of this, a most
ingenious gentleman who is going to Canton in China, and Lord
Cardross knows Dr. Birch corresponds with some of the Jesuits
there.   Mr. Lind wants to go up the Country that he may bring
home to Europe some useful drawings."

---

4. Lord Cardross to Mr. Da Costa.

        " *Walcot, near Bath, June* 14, 1766.

" Lord Cardross's best compliments to Mr. Da Costa, and
hopes that during the vacation of the Royal Society he will
arrange some of the fossils, &c. for the Museum Cardrossianum
in Caledonia, as he is to send off a large pacquet to that part
of the world in autumn.   Also begs Mr. Da Costa would tell
my Lord how the Conspectus, &c. goes on, and would tell Mr.
Magellan that his Lordship expects and wishes to hear from him
soon.   Compliments to his son David Riz."

* From the British Museum, Addit. MSS. 4302.

5. "My dear Sir,   *Walcot, near Bath, Oct. 22, 1766.*

" As I shall be in London very soon, may I beg you will have the goodness to set apart for me such specimens of your collection of ores and fossils, &c. as you can spare, and depend upon my giving you in return many things that are new and curious to you, making up the deficiency freely in any manner you please.

" 1 have collected a good many things of late ; and in particular the bones of an immense elephant, found in a bed of ochre in Somersetshire at a great depth.   If you have interest enough with your natural history friends to get me some of their duplicates, I would make it up to them.   I ever am, my dear Sir,
                    " Yours affectionately,   Cardross."

---

6. The Earl of Buchan to Mr. Nichols.

" Sir,   *Edinburgh, Feb. 13, 1782.*

" Your attention to the infant Society of the Antiquaries of Scotland is a proof of that liberality of sentiment which distinguishes the legitimate members of the great republic of letters. To a fond father this attention must be particularly pleasing ; and I do most cordially thank you in my own name and in that of the Society for your fostering and generous care of our interests and reputation.

" Poor as we are in Scotland in the magnificent remains of a classic age, there are many things worthy of attention which may employ our researches.

" The account of the institution and progress of the Society, together with a list of the discourses which have been read at the meetings, a list of the donations received, and of the members, is now in the press, compiled and printed by Mr. William Smellie, printer to the Society, and will be ready (as I suppose to be delivered) about the 12th of March, price 2s. 6d. 4to. Messrs. Cumyng and Paton will take care to transmit a copy to you in course.   I am, Sir, with real esteem,
                    " Your obliged humble servant,   Buchan."

---

7. " Sir,   *Edinburgh, July 8, 1782.*

" Your repeated attentions to the infant Society lately established in Scotland for exploring the antiquities of nations, and of this country in particular, together with numerous objects connected with such pursuits, give me great satisfaction, and demand my warmest acknowledgments.

" No doubt I am very anxious to see my child past the age of helplessness, and the risk of being lost or neglected when I am gone ; and the kindness of such zealous friends as you have been, will, I hope, soon make me easy about a body of men whom I strove successfully to bring together for the good of my country and the promotion of useful learning.   I am, Sir, with regard, your obliged humble servant,   Buchan."

8. "Sir,   *Edinburgh, Aug.* 8, 1782.

" I have snatched this opportunity of Dr. Aitken, a Member of our Society, going to town, to return you my sincere and warm thanks for your attention to my child the Scottish Antiquarian Society; it grows, and will I hope soon be a chopping boy. Your kindness to it, when it was as it were hanging at its mother's breast, will all find a place in the breast of, Sir,
    " Your obliged servant,   BUCHAN."

---

9. The EARL of BUCHAN to Mr. GOUGH.

" Sir,   *Edinburgh, Aug.* 9, 1782.

" I take the opportunity of Dr. Aitken, a Member of the Antiquarian Society of Scotland, his going to London, to convey a letter of thanks to you for your attention to my favourite literary child.

" It grows apace, and, if properly cherished, will be soon able to shift for itself. An account of its progress, published by Mr. Smellie, the translator of Buffon, accompanies this as a present from the Society to you in token of respect. By a strange blunder of the press, I look in vain for your name among the lists of the Society; this is corrected indeed among the errata, but ought especially not to have been there. Interesting communications are daily received ; and, by a resolution of the members to present copies of their books when authors, a little nucleus of a library is already formed. The Society having no funds as yet for purchase, makes this an important and flattering circumstance. Your worthy correspondent George Paton informs me frequently of your welfare and useful employment, which gives me pleasure.

" I do hope that I shall be the happy instrument of exciting a spirit in this country to dig up, examine, and explain the monuments of its antient story,—a spirit of general literature, in addition to that polished taste for historical composition and for more abstruse inquiry which has made Scotland known in the republic of letters. I am Sir, with regard,
    " Your obedient humble servant,   BUCHAN."

---

10. The EARL of BUCHAN to Mr. NICHOLS.

" Sir,   *Edinburgh, March* 15, 1783.

" I return you many thanks for your acceptable letter of the 15th of February, which I only received a few days ago, together with the following books for the Society, which is much indebted: 1. The History, &c. of Hinckley, 4to ; 2. Proofs, &c. 4to; 3. Statesman's Remembrancer ; 4. Collatio Codicis Cotton. Gen. 8vo; 5. Consiglio, &c. Sig. Sherlock, 8vo.

" These tracts, particularly that of Hinckley, have furnished

me with agreeable entertainment, and are an acceptable donation to the library of our infant institution. I had, and still
have, much to struggle with * in promoting the interests of
erudition in this country; and the illiberal opposition made to
the charter of the Society by the College of Edinburgh, the
lawyers, or faculty of Advocates, and the Society calling itself
the Philosophical, prove very glaringly that it is no easy matter to
copy the institutions of more polished nations in a country where
a sordid monopolising spirit, engrafted on the remains of antient
barbarity, checks the progress of every thing that can tend to
take the people out of their trammels. In about a fortnight
after you have received this letter, the caveats and answers of our
Society will reach you, and you will then see how ungenerously
I have been requited by my countrymen for endeavouring to
make them happier and more respectable.

" This is the common lot of men who have a spirit above
that of the country and age in which they act, and I appeal to
posterity for my vindication.

" I could have passed my time much more agreeably among
Englishmen, whose character I preferred to that of my own
countrymen, in a charming country too, where my alliances with
the noblest and best families in it, and my political sentiments,
would have added much to my domestic as well as civil enjoyment; but I chose rather to forego my own happiness for the
improvement of my native country, and I expect hereafter, that
the children of those who have not known me, or received me
as they ought to have done, will express their concern, and blush
on account of the conduct of their parents.

" ' Præclara conscientia igitur sustentor cùm cogito me de
Republica aut meruisse quum potuerim aut certè nunquam nisi
divinè cogitasse.' I am, Sir, with esteem,
                " Your obliged humble servant,   BUCHAN.
" P. S. Your portrait will be most cordially received as that
of a generous friend to our Institution. The portrait of your
worthy partner will be most acceptable also."

———

11. " SIR,   *Kirkhill, June* 8, 1783.
" I have had the pleasure to receive your letter of the 29th of
May, informing me of the fortunate purchase you have made of

* "The Society of Antiquaries (of which the Earl of Buchan is Præses)
have at last succeeded, after some opposition from the University, in
obtaining a royal charter. This excellent Institution has for its object
the investigation of natural and civil history in general, and the antiquities of Scotland in particular. The University of Edinburgh, dreading
a rivalship in this Society in the branch of natural history, warmly
opposed the charter, and proposed the establishment of a society upon
a more extensive plan, to be called, The Royal Society of Scotland.
The dispute was referred to the Lord Advocate of Scotland, and it has
been decided that the Society of Antiquaries should have their charter."
Gent. Mag. 1783, vol. LIII. p. 440.

the rare book of Bellenden. The price you paid for it is much less than I expected; and I return you, in my own name and that of our Curators, hearty thanks for the trouble you have taken on this occasion.

" The book you kindly present to our library shall be carefully deposited as soon as it shall come to my hand; and I desire you to be persuaded that you do not bestow your favours on the ungrateful.

" I expect soon to see the fruits of my circular letters to ingenious persons in different parts of Scotland relating to local histories; several I know are now at work. Macfarlane's collections contain accounts of many parishes which are mentioned by Mr. Gough in his great topographical work. I made an attempt lately to purchase them, but was foiled by higher hopes of sale at London. They ought to be in our library; and I have still hopes of seeing them there, because I know that I could make them subservient to more accurate and useful details. I have seen a very good specimen of parochial history by Mr. Warton in that of Kiddington. I wrote one of my parish (I mean that in which I reside) which is a very small and uninteresting one, as an encouragement to others to proceed on a plan of that sort; and I am glad to find the example has been useful. It is amazing the effect a pioneering genius has in exciting the curiosity of mankind to explore new paths and unbeaten regions. Mr. Pennant found us very inattentive but a few years ago; but now men think their time better employed in innocent researches of that sort, when they find leisure from more important pursuits, than in penny quadrille, backgammon, or spitting into a stream from the parapets of a neighbouring bridge. If I had had better health, and a little more money, I could have done more; but I have had much greater success under all my obstacles than my most sanguine expectations gave me to suppose some years ago.

" My insatiable thirst of knowledge, and a genius prone to the splendid sciences and the fine arts, has distracted my attention so much that the candid must make ample allowances for me in any one department; but considering myself as a nobleman, and not a Peer of Parliament, a piece of ornamental china as it were, I have been obliged to avail myself of my situation to do as much good as I possibly could without acting in a professional line, which my rank and my fate excluded me from. Our annual publication is gone to press. The first volume of our Transactions will appear about the 14th of November.

" The Biographical part of my plan, which I know will be very agreeable to you, goes on briskly. Some whom I have set to work will no doubt be tempted to sell their works to the booksellers rather than print them in our Transactions; but it matters not how knowledge is disseminated if truth be the object, and it be faithfully and carefully pursued. It is the

improvement and happiness of society at large which are the final objects I have in view. I am, Sir, with great regard,
"Your obliged humble servant,   BUCHAN."

_____

12. "SIR,   *Great Cumberland-street, March* 12, 1784.
" I have received by the hands of the learned and worthy Dr. Ducarel, two copies of your excellent master and friend the late Mr. Bowyer's portrait engraved by Basire, and three copies of Mr. Rogers's engraved by Cook. I believe it is unnecessary for me to assure you that I feel very sensibly the advantage I have in enjoying the correspondence and aid of the real friends of useful learning in promoting the advancement of it in my country; and that I think myself particularly fortunate in having your extensive influence engaged to remove the obstacles which have hitherto stood in the way of our communicating effectually with the English Antiquaries.

" Poor Scotland has no Bowyer or Nichols; and it has cost me no small trouble to stir the dry bones, and it will cost much more to embody them.

" Your portrait I accept as a mark of your personal attention; and shall place it in my little cabinet in what I am persuaded you will reckon very good company.

" My friends are the friends of humanity, religion, good government, and learning; my spirit is public and my views are not sordid. I am, Sir, with great regard,
"Your obliged humble servant,   BUCHAN."

_____

13. "SIR,   *Edinburgh, June* 15, 1784.
" It gave me great pleasure to hear that you had perfectly recovered from your late indisposition, and to observe public marks of your having returned to those exercises of your function, which are, and always have been, so interesting to society.

" You, my learned friend, and your indefatigable predecessor Mr. Bowyer, have kept up the succession of our British Aldi in an age remarkable (in the midst of information) for the rarity of learned editors and typographers; and I hope some future Bowyer or Nichols will be brought up at your feet to vindicate our British press from the sneer of erudition, and the chastisement of the envious continent.

" Since the death of Robert Foulis, of Glasgow, and Thomas Ruddiman his predecessor, we have had only one learned printer in Scotland, William Smellie, whose fort is Natural History, and whose press groans under the weight of Edinburgh theses and lawyers' briefs. When I founded the Society of Antiquaries, and laid the platform of the new Royal Society of Edinburgh on the same foundations by emulation, there was hardly an individual in Scotland who had any notion of writing but for a bookseller; and gentlemen commonly withdrew any paper of merit from the old Philosophical Society soon after it was read, and prepared it for the press, and at the dissolution of that Society all the papers were withdrawn. At present I have the pleasure to find that several gentlemen addict themselves to literary pursuits, and communicate to both Societies with a view to enrich their Transactions, exclusive of any views of separate publication.

" Some papers, indeed, I have recommended to be enlarged and published separately, where I thought they might be professionally beneficial to the country, or interesting to the public at large, independent of our Societies and those attentive to the objects of their pursuits. Among these are Mr. Tytler's publication of the Works of our King James the First of Scotland, with a Sketch of his Life, and a Discourse on our Antient Melodies; and Mr. Wight, the late Solicitor-general for Scotland, his Discourse on the Parliaments of Scotland, which last is now in the press, and is a work of great merit.

" We are now preparing for the press the first number of Transactions of the Scotch Society of Antiquaries; and there is established a branch of the Society at Perth for exploring Gaëlic antiquities, and making a Parochial Survey of the Highlands, the MS. communications to be regularly transmitted to the Mother Society, and to pass the review of the Committee at Edinburgh for publication. A library for the Classics, Antiquities, and Natural History, has been begun in Perth; and it is proposed, that all the Clergy of the Synod and Freeholders of Perthshire should give a small annual contribution for the purchase of books in these departments. The first meeting of the Society was held at Perth on the 12th of June, which day the gentlemen politely chose as being the birth-day of the Founder of the Society of Antiquaries of Scotland.

" They have received lately from Mr. Thorkelin, Secretary of the Royal Society of the Danish Antiquaries, some very curious books relating to Danish and Icelandic antiquities, and expect the great publication of the Edda in August next. Mr. Johnstone, Chaplain of our Embassy, promises copies of several MSS. relating to Scotch connections with Norway and Denmark, and a copy of Coryneus, by the next ships.

" We are very lame in books relating to Northern antiquities; and our public libraries in Scotland do not buy many books in our line, which makes it of great consequence to us to receive communications of that sort, our funds being yet very inconsiderable.

" My own pursuits of late have, in the way of collecting, been confined to curious missive letters elucidatory of Scottish Biography; and in general characteristic letters of illustrious or learned persons. When you can pick up any thing in this line for me, you will do me a particular favour. In every other line of collecting I have uniformly made myself no more than a channel for the public.

" The Bodleian, Cotton, and King's libraries, the British Museum in general, Lord Shelburne's library, the Paper Office, the Tower Records, the Vatican, the Scots-college at Paris, have many thousand letters worthy of preserving yet untranscribed or unprinted; and selection is the object which my provincial situation excludes me from, and wherein I must be dependant on my literary friends.

" My objects are, first, as leading to a Biographica Scotica; secondly, Biography in general; and thirdly, the printing of Characteristic Letters by Centuries of the most Eminent Characters in the State or in Literature since the restoration of letters in Europe.

" I send inclosed a copy of the Highland Address to George the First at his accession, which was delivered to me last summer by a gentleman, who had it from the Earl of Mar at Antwerp a little before his death, with an injunction to deliver it as a *pièce justificatif* to such of his family as should seem most likely to make a proper use of it at a proper time *. I am, Sir, with regard,
" Your obedient humble servant, BUCHAN."

---

14. " SIR, *Kirkhill by Edinburgh, Aug.* 3, 1784.
" Literary correspondence being about to receive a heavy blow by a law relating to the privileges of Members of Parliament, which ought to have made an exception in favour of all Societies instituted for the purposes of science, literature, arts, and manufactures, I cannot think of allowing the few covers I have addressed to my learned friends, and to you, good Sir, in particular, to become waste paper, and have therefore made use of a leisure half hour to send you some of our Scottish news in the republic to which we belong, and which consoles us in some measure for the distractions and the misfortunes of the political.

" The Scottish Society of Antiquaries have not yet thought it prudent to hazard their infant reputation by the publication of any of the valuable papers which have been communicated since their institution, but are now preparing for a specimen of their budget in the course of next winter. They propose to publish in quarto numbers, selecting only the most choice and interesting communications, and printing at the same time such state papers and letters as shall by the Censors be judged sufficiently valuable, and keeping them *in retentis* until they shall become sufficiently numerous to form a separate volume; by this means they will avoid that farrago which too often appears in Antiquarian Transactions, and which renders them less useful to the public.

" The Biographical Numbers will be published also without any admixture of matter that does not tend to elucidate the

* It was printed in the Gentleman's Magazine, vol. LIV. p. 503.

lives of those illustrious or learned persons which compose the
numbers so published; and it is thought that this mode of publication will enable the Society to satisfy the taste of their
learned friends without loading them with the expense of purchasing what may not be to their palate or their purpose. These
are my hints to the learned body, and will, I hope, meet with
your approbation. I propose further, that the Chartularies of
our religious foundations, with a copious index and glossary to
each, shall be published in the same manner; and that a specimen of a short one shall be given in the course of the ensuing
spring.

"These Chartularies I propose to accompany with judicious
extracts from the Bullarium Romanum, for a copy of which I
intend to apply to my ecclesiastical friends in the Rota at Rome.
Forty volumes of this great work, begun by order of Pope Benedict XIV. have been already printed; and, as I believe it has
already reached the middle of the sixteenth century, no more
will be required for the purpose of our ecclesiastical antiquities.

"Parochial histories in Scotland, Gaelic topography, with
maps, charts, and views of places, will form another separate
department, and will have a more extensive demand in the literary market.

"To this last part of my plan I propose to dedicate a room
in our Musæum, fitted with a separate repository for each of the
parishes in Scotland, in which are meant to be deposited a survey of each parish, accompanied with specimens of mines,
minerals, and every thing that is politically useful to the community; and from whence future proprietors of the soil may
be able to draw every information that can tend to their profit
or local curiosity. I am proud of this adject; and, if it is executed, I flatter myself it will preserve me from the common consequences of the four grey stones covered with moss, and from
the accusation of having had too little of the useful in the scope
of my amusing research! *Valeat quantum valere potest.*

"As a specimen of what may be done even in this barren
and neglected field of antiquarian research, I shall mention,
that in this parish, where I occasionally reside during the summer, I found lately, in digging a foundation for a pillar in the
body of the parish church *(Uphall in vicecomitat. de Linlithgo)*,
the font and *Lapis fidei*, Stane of Faith, of a very antient chapel
dedicated to Saint Katherine and the blessed Nicholas de Strath-
broke, which stood formerly near this house, where I now write,
which font has the date of the Millenium, when reigned in Scotland the Grüm, King of the Scots, whose Christian appellation is, I believe, no where to be found, he having had a name
like Caligula, Caracalla, Severus, and other Roman princes, which
had well nigh obliterated all others, and certainly would but for
their being masters of the civilised world and the objects of
universal attention.

"I suppose this Font of mine is the most antient remain of

antiquity in Scotland which has a date; and from the inscription bearing the appellative of the reigning King (at least so far as can be judged by the initials *) on one side of the Font, which is octagonal, fixes the æra of that King of the Scots, foolishly latinised by George Buchanan from Joannes Fordun, Grimus.

" The Stane of Faith is an octagonal stone perforated, of a size fitted to the reception of the hands and cubits of those who were sworn at the altar on covenants of all sorts among the antient Gaëls and Scots, a custom coeval with the Druidical rites, and, from the Scriptures of the Jews, probably a primæval ceremony. This Stane of Faith is probably of the most remote antiquity, and had been handed down from the earliest ages in this neighbourhood.

" There is a Stane of Faith resembling this in the islands of Orkney; if elsewhere I know not; but the most antient covenants for the payments of money were formerly in this country prescribed, ' solutionem pecuniæ super lapidem in quasdam Ecclesias nominatas,' after the manner of the Jews above-mentioned.

" Of these remains I propose to have an engraving for our antiquaries; and it may excite others to explore such antiquities as may verify the race of our fabulously mangled Kings of the Scots and the Picts.

" A group of our Antiquaries have undertaken to print a Catalogue Raisonnée of the series of our Scottish money; and to accompany it with accurate plates, executed from the originals, and original deeds of the Mint Acts of Parliament relating thereto, &c. and tables of weight, alloy, and comparative value with foreign money. This will be curious, as it will relate to an extinct kingdom which grows every day more obsolete.

" When I was in London last winter I put into the hands of Joseph Edmondson, Esquire, Herald, a catalogue of our little assortment of Scots money, which he will communicate to you, and perhaps you may lead us to new acquisitions.

" I formerly mentioned to you my little department of personal collection, viz. copies or originals of characteristic missive letters of illustrious or learned persons. When you can lay hold of any such you will oblige me by procuring them for me.

" I mean, when my collection swells to a sufficient size for a choice selection, to publish a century or two of the most interesting which are not too close to the present times. In this collection I do not limit myself to British or Irish; taking such as occur, and separating them afterwards for the use I intend to make of them, as an adject to this department. I am glad to collect catalogues of the portraits of illustrious and learned persons, which specify the names of the painters, the times when probably painted, the names of the persons, and of those in whose custody the pictures are; in this line perhaps you may be

* See the engraving in Gent. Mag. vol. LIV. p. 671.

able to do me some good.   Dr. Ducarel was so good as to send
me a list of his choice little collection very lately; and I expect
one from my friend Mr. Horace Walpole, who is, I believe, still
adding to his noble collection at Strawberry-hill.   I am, Sir,
with great regard, your obliged humble servant,   BUCHAN."

---

15. " SIR,   1784.
" To-morrow I shall send you the continuation of Albanicus's Remarks on the progress of the Roman arms in Scotland
during the sixth campaign of Agricola, accompanied by a
sketch of Richard of Cirencester's Itinerary, and a Topographical
Map of the country adjacent to the remains of encampments at
the north-eastern pass of the Grampian hills.

" Lieutenant-General Melville I find is possessed of a drawing
of the Camp at Rea-Dykes or Garnacahill, described in the
account given of it by Albanicus in his second letter to the
printer of the Gentleman's Magazine, and I have written the
inclosed letter to that brave, humane, and learned General, the
rival of the Marquis de Bouillé, who will probably permit you
to use it for the purpose of rendering Albanicus's communication more satisfactory. How fortunate it is for learning and
for learned men, when there are Bowyers, Nichols's, and Rud-
dimans, not to mention Aldus's, and many antient apothecaries
of literature, who, like those I have mentioned, have shared
the glory of the physicians of the great republic! I am, Sir,
with regard, your obedient humble servant,   BUCHAN.

" With a view to Biography, I have been for some years
collecting characteristic missive letters of familiar correspondence of the most eminent and learned persons, particularly of
the last and present ages; if you can assist me at any time in
this research it will be very agreeable to me. From the Marquis of Lansdowne's collection I hope to have considerable aid;
and I intend to make a selection from the mass in the Bodleian,
Cotton, and King's libraries, as well as from the Museum at
large, and the Scots-college at Paris."

---

16. " SIR,   Edinburgh, April 11, 1785.
" Not having learnt by any direct or authentic information of
the safety of my commentaries on the account given by Tacitus
of the progress of the Roman arms in Scotland, I am in some
doubt with respect to the safety of those papers ; and should be
glad if you would take the trouble to let me know if they have
come safely to your hands, and how you mean to dispose of
them, whether to the publication of Local Antiquities, the Magazine, or to the new edition of Camden's Britannia.

" I expect every day accurate drawings of the different Camps
and Fortresses from Perth to Ross-shire; and intend, some time

hence, to have them engraved, and to accompany the whole disquisition, when completed, with these plates and an itinerary, together with engravings of the warlike instruments and tools of the Romans and Caledonians dug up on the fields of battle and in the Stations.

" I am just now engaged in preparing for publication an account of the Life and discovery of the great logarithmic Napier, which, as well as the former, I intend to print at London.

" Mr. Adam Cardonnel has already furnished five plates of his series of the Numismata Scotiæ; and imagines the whole may be comprised, including the few medals we have, in twenty plates. These will be accompanied with very accurate descriptions in letter-press; and to the whole an appendix will be required to contain such additions as may come to hand too late to enter the principal work. I have advised him to dispose of this work to a bookseller; and, as Snelling is far inferior in all respects to this new work, and is besides out of print, I should think he ought to meet with encouragement, especially if by its being announced to the public collectors and antiquaries they were to have an opportunity of coming forward to declare their approbation of the undertaking. Your advice is desired on this head. I am, Sir, with regard,

"Your obedient humble servant, Buchan."

---

17. " Sir, *Edinburgh, April 28, 1785.*
" On the 26th current I transmitted, by the favour of Lord Dacre's inclosure, an account of the two Roman Camps in the county of Forfar, referred to in my Commentaries on the progress of the arms of Agricola; and this account (written by the Rev. Mr. Jamieson, of Forfar) was accompanied by plans of the Camps, and of the military way of connecting them together. I expect soon to have plans and descriptions of all the other Roman Camps and Forts in Strathmore, &c. on the route of Agricola and in the seat of the war, which, being hereafter presented to the public at one view, will enable us to read the Life of Agricola by Tacitus with more relish than ever, the account given in his nervous and rapid narration being inadequate to instruct us without the aids I have now had the good fortune to procure.

" I mentioned formerly my *experimentum crucis* with respect to the exploration of the remains of antiquity as looked for to support an hypothesis, and arguments drawn from the internal evidences of an antient text.

" I write my Commentary on the latter, and put it into the hands of those who may discover the adaption of local circumstances by actual survey; and I write to others to survey local remains without my Commentary and without any hypothesis of their own, and from the result of the whole I draw my *q. e. d.*

" Mr. Jamieson, without having been distracted by the respect which my judgment might have raised in him, set himself, at my desire, to examine the camps and grounds in his neighbourhood; and you see the result has led him to draw the same inferences I had done long before relating to the third and fourth campaigns of Agricola.

" One remark I will add, and no more, that it appears evident from Tacitus that these Camps of Battle Dykes and Haer Dykes * (or the inclosures of the stranger) connected by a military causeway, were the winter quarters of Agricola's army *in Horestiam,* whither he led back his troops after the decisive campaign, and, receiving hostages, sent in the following spring his fleet round the coast, and scouring the country by an awful march under its terror, gave the Admiral orders to circumnavigate the northern extremity of the island.

" I forward to you a packet from the modest and industrious George Paton, who is one of a little flock in Scotland, who resemble learned men in England.. I am, Sir, with regard,
" Your obedient humble servant,   BUCHAN."

---

18. " SIR,   *Kirkhill, Sept.* 22, 1785.
" Mr. Adam Cardonnel being now far advanced in his plates and History of our Series of Scottish Money, I expect he will be ready for the press in the beginning of next winter; and I believe he intends to accompany me to town with a view to have it printed and published under our joint inspection, together with the advice of the learned in the metropolis. It has been a work of much trouble, but will, I hope, defray the expense and labour of the worthy undertaker.

" I have now nearly prepared my account of the invention of Logarithms, by John Napier, of Marchieston, to which I propose to add memoirs of his life,—short, as must always be those of a man of letters in a remote situation ; and those of his son the first Lord Napier, who was Lord Treasurer depute of the Kingdom of Scotland.

" An Appendix to this biographical tract will contain the unpublished works of the father and the son ; and such letters as may be found in the repositories of the learned relating to the lives and inventions of either. Some time ago I wrote to Dr. Ducarel, begging him to cause a transcript to be made from John Napier's letter to Anthony Bacon, touching secret inventions, profitable and necessary in these days for the defence of this island,' &c. June 7, 1596, preserved in the Archbishop's library at Lambeth, and which, together with others, having been copied for Dr. Birch, was by him deposited in the British Museum. See Ayscough's Catalogue, vol. I. pp. 155, 376. Whether my letter

---

* Haer, an old British name signifying *Hostis Peregrinus.*

miscarried I know not; but, having had no return, I beg you will procure this transcript either from the Doctor or from the British Museum, as it is one of the unpublished tracts to which I allude, and which I mean to have annexed to my publication.

" Whatever profit I can draw from this number of the Biographica Scotica I mean to apply to the service of a very deserving countryman of mine, Mr. Walter Minto, who has assisted me in the mathematical and arithmetical part of this work. Mr. Minto was a scholar of Professor Slops at Pisa in Italy, and has given to the public the Elements of the Planet Herschel.

" I have lately excerpted from the Orkneyinga Saga of Jonas Joneus, printed at Copenhagen by him, at the expense of the learned Lord Suhm, from a MS. of the beginning of the thirteenth century, the History of the Dominion of the Normans in the Isles of Scotland, from the reign of Harold Harfagr, of Norway, to the death of Thorfinn Earl of Orkney, anno 1064, wherein there are some curious notices of our Scottish Kings Indulphus, Malcolm II. and Culenus, and interesting specimens of the manners of those times.

" From Rome I am given to expect transcripts from the parchments and papers relating to Scotland, which are in the secret archives of the Vatican; and of such I have already received the titles of a considerable number.

" About a year ago there was presented to our Antiquaries at Edinburgh, a MS. which bears the mark on the first leaf of having been in the library of Icolmkill; it is of the end of the thirteenth century. As it is known that there were in that collection many valuable books, and particularly copies of the Classics, the stragglers may perhaps be found in some corner of Europe where they were carried at the Reformation. If I could once present to the world perfect copies of Livy, Tacitus, and Tully, I would expect to be drawn with a classic nimbus about my head ; but I fear the battle-doors or rackets for shuttlecock, and the rasure of parchments for legends, have come in the way to disappoint my hopes.

" Nevertheless the research is plausible, and shall be made. Neither do I altogether despair that some nook of the unexplored library of the Vatican may be found to contain these dainty morsels of antiquity; or, if his sublime Highness of the Porte should bring this peace-offering to the Christian world, ' Body of me,' as Don Quixote said to the Bachelor Carrasco, ' for I 'll curse nobody but myself,' I think the whole republic of letters should rise to a man to guard the Thracian Bosphorus and defend the Tower of Leander. I am, dear Sir, with regard,

" Your obliged humble servant,   BUCHAN."

19. " Sir, *Edinburgh, Oct. 6,* 1785.

" I expect to be in London about the 21st of November, and shall have my Biographical Tract at that time ready for the press. In my last I mentioned my desire to have the letter of John Napier to Anthony Bacon transcribed, either from the original in Lambeth Library, or from the copy by Dr. Birch in the British Museum. See Ayscough's Catalogue, vol. I. p. 389, for the title ; it is No. 4405, 8, of the MSS. Pray be so good (if Lieutenant-General Melville, to whom also I wrote on this subject, has not already complied with my wish,) as to cause this transcript to be made ; and if you examine the MSS. of Gresham-college, where you can discover them, with a view to find letters from Napier to Dr. Briggs, you will add a singular favour, and enrich the Appendix to our publication.

" Of Archibald first Lord Napier, the son of the Inventor of Logarithms, I have also for the press a curious tract on the sub-ject of manuring land with salt, for which he had a patent ; and the memoirs of that Lord, written by himself, from which I in-tend to draw a short account of his life. The whole tract may, I think, require twenty sheets in quarto; perhaps it may extend to twenty-five, so you can judge of the price that ought to be affixed to the publication ; and, as I do not wish to disappoint any of the learned, to whom such a book must be particularly interesting, I wish gentlemen in London belonging to the lite-rary societies to be informed of the intended publication, that no greater impression may be made than is necessary, and yet enough to supply the demand.

" It is probable that some of the learned members of the Royal and Antiquarian Societies at London, or some of your learned acquaintance, may know where Napier's correspondence with Briggs and Oughtred, &c. may be found, and if so you will be good enough to procure transcripts of the letters.

" If I had intended to publish this work on my own account, I should have been very indifferent about receiving any profit from it ; but I intend to dedicate any that may arise from it to Mr. Minto, a scholar of Professor Slops at Pisa, to whom I am indebted for his assistance in the scientific part of my under-taking.

" I imagine Mr. Adam Cardonnel will be of my party to London ; and will be then ready for putting his History of Scot-tish Money and Coinage to the press.

" Your obliged humble servant, Buchan."

---

20. Mr. Gough to the Earl of Buchan.
" My Lord,

" I am honoured with your Lordship's favour of ——, accom-panying the drawing of the Earl of Buchan's monument; and am happy in thinking that I can be instrumental to the pre-servation of such monuments, or to the perpetuating of them by drawings, and that artists may be led to subjects in which I have found so very few initiated. If the present has adhered strictly to his subject, the monuments in North Britain differ materially from those of the South. This will be seen at one view by examining the armed figures at the sides, whose attitudes as well as proportions, and the articles in their hands, differ greatly from those among us. It is however very fortunate to be provided with exemplifications of such differences; and I think myself particularly obliged to your Lordship for the trouble you take in procuring them.

" Give me leave to address to you, as Founder and President of the Society of Antiquaries of Scotland, my concern how ill your animated exertions have been imitated, and how faint a flame has been kindled at the altar erected by the *Genio Caledoniæ.*

" It has not been unknown how long I have been meditating a new edition of Mr. Camden's description of Scotland; and yet, to pass over the silence with which such a design has been received there, it is now just four months since ten sheets of my work have been in circulation in Edinburgh and the environs, and ten more have followed those as fast as the press could emit them; not a single sheet can I get back with corrections, additions, or improvements. The sheet which contains the Law Courts, and which one would think might have been re-written in a fortnight in the capital, is not yet returned. No inclination has been wanting in my worthy friend Paton, to whom they were consigned, nor I have reason to think in Lord Hailes, but still a want of time and leisure is pleaded; and I am referred back to the best maps and books, which is but sitting me down where I was taken up. The Society of Antiquaries, if they would fulfil the ends of their Institution, ought to have so much regard to the honour of the nation as not to let an imperfect account of it go abroad in this enlightened age. Should my papers be detained any longer, and it is not without great inconvenience to me and my printer that they have been detained so long, I must enter my protest against all future complaints of incorrectness on my part as totally involuntary.

"On whom, my Lord, is the reproach to fall, that such a treasure of a man in his favourite line as G. Paton is not patronised and promoted in his several departments; and that the plan of Thomas Philipe * to procure such capital drawings of the antient buildings in Scotland as I bought of him, was so entirely neglected? I am, my Lord, with respect;
" Your obedient humble servant,   R. GOUGH.

" *Perlustras uno oculo Scotos,* was the charge brought against Mr. Camden; and will you not join in an endeavour to explore every part of your Topography with the keenest view ? "

* See the " Literary Anecdotes," vol. III. p. 693.

20. The EARL of BUCHAN to Mr. GOUGH.

"SIR,   *Jan.* 10, 1786.

" I am favoured with your letter of the 1st current, and am
but too sensible of the force of your strictures, which would not
have been applicable to Scotland if my fortune had enabled me
to make up for the deficiencies of others; but, though I have
been disappointed in the expectation I had formed of exciting a
spirit of literary inquiry in this country with respect to our
Laws, History, and Manners, I feel myself happily conscious of
having used my utmost endeavours to that end; and that, as my
very small fortune rendered it impossible for me to give pecuniary aid, I have done all that was practicable in my circumstances to do respecting the subject of our regret.

" The *noblesse* in Scotland have no school for laudable ambition, and are careless of every thing that does not tend to enrich
their families, or to indulge their passion for social intercourse;
and the middling class of people here are either too poor or too
much occupied in professional engagements to prosecute any
inquiry that does not promise them a pecuniary reward. These
unhappy circumstances would long ago have put an end to my
troubling my countrymen on the subjects for which neither their
genius nor their spirit seems to be adapted, if I had not been
rather of a sanguine disposition when the honour of my country
is at stake, and unwilling to let so proper an undertaking drop
without the fairest trial.

" I now begin with you to be convinced that it is fruitless to
cultivate any thing in this country that is not attended with
profit to the undertakers; and to think of satisfying myself with
affording every aid in my power as an individual, to those who,
like you, Sir, are the beneficial depositories of useful knowledge
for the public. You may believe, from what you know of my
disposition, that the loss of T. Philipe and his drawings to Scotland, but still more the national disgrace of letting drop his
undertaking, was the subject of chagrin to me, and a very ill
omen for my success in promoting the study of the History and
Antiquities of Scotland; but a discarded Courtier with a little
estate does not find it easy to make his voice be heard in any
country, and least of all in Scotland. This will sufficiently
account for honest George Paton continuing to fag in the Custom-house, since I have not a single coadjutor except Lord
Hailes to help me forward in any thing relating to literature, or
the patronage of men of real erudition, whilst all the patronage
of the Crown is at the disposal of those who deal it out according to their political services or connexions.

" I am glad to have had this opportunity of explaining myself thus freely, and particularly on a subject that seems to touch
my reputation, and I am glad to do it to a person whose good
opinion I desire to possess; being, with great consideration,

" Your obedient humble servant,   BUCHAN."

21.   *" Edinburgh, Jan. 5, 1787.*

" Lord Buchan's compliments to Mr. Gough; he omitted in the account of Alexander Earl of Buchan's tomb, that the height of it is two feet four inches.

" My Lord has applied to Mr. Charteris, of Annesfield, for a fine drawing of the monuments of the Maitlands at Haddington, and to another gentleman for those at St. Andrew's of Archbishops Kennedy and Shairp; hoping to procure still more in that department to enrich Mr. Gough's noble undertaking, which does honour to the editor and to the country."

22. " LEARNED SIR,   *Edinburgh, March 9, 1787.*

" I had gone so far in correcting the sheets herein returned, when I found that the whole was so incorrect that to render them fit to inform those who knew any thing about the country, it would be more to the purpose to cancel the whole ; and delay troubling the public with any survey of Scotland till something can be done to give satisfaction on the subject.

" Selfish sordid views on the one hand, and a rage for idle shows and sports on the other, have rendered this country so inattentive to grave pursuits, that I despair of any thing being done to answer your design but in a long course of time ; which, by the institution of the Society of Antiquaries here, and the collections I am making, and causing to be made, will, in spite of every adverse circumstance, produce at last a complete and accurate survey of the country, political as well as geographical and antiquarian.

" General Melville will very soon deliver to you a drawing of the monument of Archbishop Kennedy at St. Andrew's; and Mr. Charteris, of Annesfield, has promised me elegant drawings of the tombs of the Maitlands at Haddington.

" I wish I could do anything to assist your noble undertakings that was of greater consequence; but when you consider the many avocations to which a man of my rank is exposed, and how little encouragement I have received from my country or my countrymen, you will rather give me credit for having made a platform for the raising of future monuments to the honour of my province. I am, learned Sir, with great regard,

" Your obedient humble servant,   BUCHAN."

23. The EARL of BUCHAN to Mr. NICHOLS.

" March 10, 1787.

" Mr. Nichols; I have sent you inclosed an address to my learned correspondents, which will sufficiently explain the intention of it, and wish it to be inserted in the foreign Journals, and in the most respectable periodical publications at home. I

consider the Gentleman's Magazine, under your direction, as one
of them ; and there it may appear when you think proper *, and
thence it will readily be copied by the printers of the foreign
journals at Paris, &c. &c. &c. I am, Sir, with great regard,
your obedient humble servant, Buchan.

"Omnibus Literatis et domi et foris qui Epistolas ad me
transmittere haud dedignati sunt,
Buchaniæ Comes, S.P.D.

"Viginti abhinc annis me Literis penitus dedi, et post moram
forsan nimis diuturnam in Edinburgo Scotiæ Urbe primaria, ut
veri investigandi et cum Doctioribus colloquendi mihi esset
facultas, valetudinis cura mihi suadet rusticari.

"Non me latent tamen commoda et voluptas, quæ ab hoc
literarum jucundo commercio accepi ; et in hoc secessu vivere
vellem, nec oblitus meorum nec illis obliviscendus, quorum ope
et auxilio Reipublicæ, quantum in me fuit, inservire a prima
adolescentia conatus sum.

"Ita natura comparatum est, ut qui siliunt, ad eos potis-
simum confugiant, qui sitim relevare possunt, ideoque vos obse-
crare mihi liceat ut scribendi labor delectabilis permaneat, et
ut lux illa quæ florem ætatis meæ illustravit usque ad ætatis
flexum sit splendidior, in gratiam Terræ hujus quam incolimus,
et cujus summa est et erit ambitio me Civem fuisse non prorsum
inutilem.

"Non mihi sed toti genitum me credere Mundo.

"Ad impensas vestras minuendas a tributo Literario, et ne
nugis meis plus onerati quàm honorati sitis, hanc supplicationem
meam in Actis Publicis inserendam curavi Linguâ Latinâ, (ser-
mone Eruditorum peculiari, Præscriptionis jure,) ut cum Juris-
consultis loquar, quo profanum arcemus vulgus.

"Historia, Philosophia, et Artes Humaniores mihi præcipue
arrident, in quibus progressus qualescunque facere cupio sub
auspiciis vestris.

"Prelum Typographicum in animo est rus mecum portare.
Nihil inde emittetur quod non spectat ad Reipublicæ emolu-
mentum et Civium veram felicitatem; superstitioni et rebus
politicis, ut in hac Insula vocantur sub prætextu Libertatis,
catenas injicere infra prelum, fixum et ratum est.

"Multi Libri MSS. pretiosi, blattarum et tinearum epulæ, in
doctorum et indoctorum scriniis jacent sepulti. Ea nunquam
compilabit Bibliopolarum Societas, quos non Scientiæ ardor sed
lucrum semper sollicitabat.

"Multæ etiam Epistolæ gravissimæ a Viris Doctis scriptæ
post literas xv Sæculo instauratas in eodem sunt statu mox
periturо.

"Tullii et Plinii Epistolæ injuriam temporis et superstitionis
feliciter evaserunt, quarum præstantia et utilitas causa est cur

* It was printed in the Gentleman's Magazine, for March 1787, p. 193.

alias antiquorum desideremus, quibus certiores facti essemus
non tantum de vita privata Græcorum et Romanorum, sed de
irradiantibus ingenii scintillis, quæ melius splendore extem-
porali illustrantur, quàm ponderosis voluminibus quæ pretium
unicum debent industriæ et labori.

"Sed ad rem redeamus—Pergite, Amici Honoratissimi, mecum sententias vestras communicare.   Me nec ingratum nec
immemorem unquam invenietis.   Benevolentia vestra, quam
expertus sum, mihi iterum roganti, ut spero, non deerit.

"Epistolæ quæ a regionibus exteris veniunt, more solito mit-
tendæ sunt ad Georgium Dempsterum virum dignissumum, unum
ex Senatu Inferiori in publicis regni Comitiis, libertatis et virtutis vindicem strenuum, vel ad meipsum in Scotia.   Denique
promitto et spondeo me eâ amicitia, quæ omnes in studiis Hu-
manitatis ac Literarum versantes, qui ubique sunt, connectere
et conjungere debet, fore vobis devinctum.   Apud Cænobium de
Dryburgh vi. ante Kal. Februarii Anno S. MDCCLXXXVII."

---

24. The Earl of Buchan to Mr. Nichols.

"SIR,   *Edinburgh, April* 10, 1787.

"Some time ago I sent for insertion in your excellent Magazine my letter to my learned correspondents abroad, which I
hope you caused to be printed; as my retirement to the country,
or at least my meditated retirement thither, might affect that
flow of literary intelligence which, affording me much pleasure,
may hereafter produce effects not altogether uninteresting to
literature.

"My account of the Life, writings, and inventions of Napier
(given as a specimen of Biography on a new plan) is just now
publishing at Edinburgh, and will reach London I suppose in a
fortnight or three weeks.   I propose sending author's copies to
the libraries abroad, particularly to Paris, Berlin, and Copenhagen; and, for the honour of Scotland and the illustration of the
good effects of my establishments here, have had this tract printed
at Perth.   I wish to make my country as famous for erudition as
it has been formerly for gallant soldiers, and for the Belles
Lettres.   I am, Sir, with regard,

"Your obliged humble servant,   BUCHAN."

---

25. The Earl of Buchan to Mr. Gough.

"SIR,   *Edinburgh, June* 10, 1787.

"I am glad to be informed that my excellent friend General
Melville has a good drawing, executed from the monument
of Bishop Kennedy at St. Andrew's, for the continuation of your
noble undertaking of our British funeral memorials.

"I have been lately to view three very respectable subjects in
the Church of Costorphin near Edinburgh, which are as follow:

"The tomb of Bernard Stuart, Seigneur d'Aubigny, who was

general of the French army under Charles VIII. and Louis the XIIth, and who being sent on an Embassy to Scotland, fell sick, and died at a place called East Craigs near Costorphin, being then on his journey from Edinburgh to the Court at Stirling, and was interred in the chancel of Costorphin Church. There appears no inscription on the monument; but from history I learn that he died in the year 1508. Bernard Stuart, of an heroic family, was the great-grand-uncle of the Lord Bernard Stuart, the intended Earl of Lichfield, who fell gloriously during the Civil Wars of the last century in the year 1642; and I have the honour, by descent from Esme Duke of Lennox, to stand in the same relation to this illustrious person. This funeral monument is of a bastard marble, and represents the General in full armour at length, on a sarcophagus lodged in a niche, with two escutcheons, which are defaced.

" Secondly, the tomb of Sir John Forrester, of Costorphin, and the Lady Jean Sinclair his wife, daughter of Henry Earl of Orkney. Sir John was Lord High Chamberlain of Scotland, anno 1425, temp. Jac. I. and Master of his Household, and was employed in several embassies to England. He died anno 1440. The figures are *ad longum* in prayer; and are pretty much in the style of the former.

" Thirdly, the tomb of Sir John Forrester, of Costorphin, son of the preceding, who married the widow of Sir John Stuart, Knight, of Dalswinton, ancestor of the Earl of Galloway. Sir John and his wife are represented *ad longum* in prayer; and it would seem that both monuments had been erected at the same time.

" I propose going out to Costorphin on Wednesday next the 13th, to begin drawings of these three monuments for your book; and remain, Sir, with great regard,

" Your obedient humble servant,　　Buchan."

———

26.　　　　　　　　　　　　　　*Edinburgh, Oct. 20, 1787.*
" Lord Buchan presents his compliments to Mr. Gough, informing him that he sent about a fortnight ago by favour of Mr. Maxwell, of Camden, a parcel containing his drawings of the funeral monuments of the great Lord d'Aubigny, and the Lord Chamberlain Forrester at Costorphin, which he hopes have come safe to hand, and have given satisfaction.

" There is yet another tomb at Costorphin; but the principal figure is headless, so that, without deviation from truth, it could not be made a proper subject for engraving. It is the tomb of the son of the Chamberlain and his wife recumbent, under a niche and canopy, which is more in the modern gothic style than the other."

27. Mr. Gough to the Earl of Buchan.

" My Lord,   *Enfield, Oct.* 22, 1787.

" A packet from my printer this evening conveyed to me your present of the drawings of the monuments at Costorphin, for which, as well as for that of Bishop Kennedy, which I ought to have acknowledged sooner, you will accept my thanks.

" I am happy in having excited a spirit in your countrymen of preserving the monuments of their ancestors, as well as being instrumental in giving the public representations, which differ so materially in shape and proportion from the like figures in England. I will take care that the drawings be restored to your apartment in the state in which I received them *

" My Lord, I confess my vanity is hurt in seeing my name mentioned in the Gazetteer of the 4th instant, in the way of an announcement of my second volume, which is yet young in preparation. Nothing but the giving a spur to the national taste for antiquarian research could justify such an announcement. I am sure your Lordship will feel the justness of my complaint. I am, my Lord, your obliged humble servant, R. Gough."

28. The Earl of Buchan to Mr. Nichols.

" Sir,   *Jan.* 5, 1793.

" Lord Bute will probably communicate to you the particulars of a valuable discovery I have made of a choice collection of the *chef-d'œuvres* of Peiresc's correspondence in Italy †, prepared for the press, the publication of which at London would do honour to Britain and to the republic of letters.

" My notion is, that Lord Bute will patronize the edition, and that you and Mr. George Nicol will be chosen to be the editors. I am, Sir, with regard, your obedient humble servant, Buchan."

29. " Dear Sir,

" I have read with great pleasure that excellent part of our friend Thomas Search's Journal which is addressed to you, and was not the less charmed with those addressed to Dr. Simmons and myself, the last of which was very useful to me in preparing my literary report to my Society of Antiquaries when my health happened to be so infirm that I was unable to draw much from my own resources.

" The inclosed copy of Latin verses came anonymously to my hand sometime ago ; and as the hand-writing of the original is unknown to me, I am unable to guess to whom I am indebted for the very partial compliments contained in it, so partial that I was at first tempted to destroy the original, but on a second thought resolved to send a copy of it to you as curious in collecting literary pieces of that sort ; and supposing that it was

---

* The drawings were never engraved.   † See before, p. 495.

possible my friend Search, who had seen my letter to Lord Kaimes, transformed into a discourse delivered to the Literary and Antiquarian Society at Perth, which is alluded to in the Ode, ' Stabilemque legem injecit amni materia ; ut tumet,' &c. might have permitted his friendship to riot in such a way at the expense of the blushes of, dear Sir,

" Your obedient humble servant,   BUCHAN."

---

30. Mr. WASHINGTON to the EARL of BUCHAN.

" MY LORD,   *Philadelphia, May* 1, 1792.

" I should have had the honour of acknowledging sooner the receipt of your letter of the 28th of June last, had I not concluded to defer doing it till I could announce to you the transmission of my portrait, which has been just finished by Mr. Robinson, of New York, who has also undertaken to forward it. The manner of the execution of it does no discredit, I am told, to the artist. of whose skill favourable mention had been made to me. I was further induced to intrust the execution to Mr. Robinson, from his having informed me that he had drawn others for your Lordship, and knew the size which would best suit your collection.

" I accept with sensibility and satisfaction the significant present of the box * which accompanied your Lordship's letter. In yielding the tribute due from every lover of mankind to the patriotic and heroic virtues of which it is commemorative, I estimate, as I ought, the additional value which it derives from the hand that sent it, and my obligation for the sentiments that induced the transfer.

" I will, however, ask that you will exempt me from compliance with the request relating to its eventual destination. In an attempt to execute your wish in this particular, I should feel embarrassment from a just comparison of relative pretensions, and should fear to risk in justice by so marked a preference. With sentiments of the truest esteem and consideration, I remain your Lordship's most obedient servant,   G. WASHINGTON."

---

31. " MY LORD,   *Philadelphia, April* 22, 1793.

" The favourable wishes which your Lordship has expressed for the prosperity of this young and rising country, cannot but be gratefully received by all citizens, and every lover of it ; one mean to the contribution of which, and its happiness, is very judiciously pourtrayed in the following words of your letter, ' to be little heard of in the great world of politics.' These words, I can assure your Lordship, are expressive of my sentiments on

---

* A box made of the oak that afforded shelter to Wallace after the battle of Falkirk.

this head; and I believe it is the sincere wish of United America to have nothing to do with the political intrigues or the squabbles of European nations, but, on the contrary, to exchange commodities, and live in peace and amity with all the inhabitants of the earth; and this I am persuaded they will do if rightfully it can be done. To administer justice to, and receive it from every Power they are connected with, will, I hope, be always found the most prominent feature in the administration of this country; and I flatter myself that nothing short of imperious necessity can occasion a breach with any of them. Under such a system, if we are allowed to pursue it, the agriculture and mechanical arts—the wealth and population of these States will increase with that degree of rapidity as to baffle all calculation, and must surpass any idea your Lordship can hitherto have entertained on the occasion. To evince that our views (whether realized or not) are expanded, I take the liberty of sending you the plan of a new city, situated about the centre of the union of these States, which is designed for the permanent seat of the government; and we are at this moment deeply engaged, and far advanced, in extending the inland navigation of the river Potomac, on which it stands, and the branches thereof, through a tract of as rich country for hundreds of miles as any in the world. Nor is this a solitary instance of attempts of the kind, although it is the only one which is near completion and in partial use. Several other very important ones are commenced; and little doubt is entertained that in ten years, if left undisturbed, we shall open a communication by water with all the lakes northward and westward of us, with which we have territorial connections; and an inland, in a few years more, from Rhode Island to Georgia inclusively, partly by cuts between the great bays and sounds, and partly between the islands and sand-banks, and the main from Albemarle sound to the river St. Mary's. To these may also be added the erection of bridges over considerable rivers, and the commencement of turnpike-roads, as further indications of the improvement in hand."

In the preface to the " Picturesque Antiquities of Scotland, etched by Adam de Cardonnel," 8vo, 1788, is this paragraph: " In providing materials for this little work, I am under great obligations to the noble founder of the Society of Scottish Antiquaries, who generously gave me every assistance in his power."

In 1794 the Earl of Buchan, under his favourite signature of ALBANICUS, communicated to the Gentleman's Magazine an Essay by the Rev. Donald Macqueen; his letter introductory of which was re-printed in vol. V. of this Work, p. 402.

RICHARD BEATNIFFE,

THE AUTHOR OF "THE NORFOLK TOUR."

This eminent bookseller and worthy man was a native of Louth in Lincolnshire, and was born in 1740. He was brought up by an uncle, the Rev. Samuel Beatniffe*, Rector of Gaywood and Bawsey, in the county of Norfolk, whose kindness and attention he thus gratefully acknowledged in a note appended to "The Norfolk Tour." "If fastidious criticism should discover that too much is here said of an obscure village (Gaywood) and an obscure man, let gratitude be permitted to make the following reply. The compiler of this humble performance here spent great part of his early years, and, being the adopted son of this worthy man, pays this small tribute to his memory †."

* This gentleman was born in 1702, and received his academical education at St. John's-college, Cambridge, where he proceeded to the degree of A.B. in 1724. In 1728 he was presented to the Rectory of Bawsey; and in 17.. to that of Gaywood. He deceased on the 10th of August 1781, and was interred in the chancel of the latter church, with the following inscription to his memory:

In Memory of
The Rev. SAMUEL BEATNIFFE, M.A.
who died at Lynn, August 10, 1781,
in the 79th year of his age,
having been Curate and Rector of this parish
and Bawsey 55 years.
He was benevolent and charitable;
his mind was cheerful, easy, and unsuspicious;
to all mankind he was just and friendly
and to his relations generous.
He lived respected, and died lamented.

There is an error in this inscription, as Mr. Beatniffe appears never to have proceeded to the degree of A.M.

† Norfolk Tour, p. 282.

At an early age he was placed with Mr. Hollingworth, a bookseller at Lynn, when becoming, after having completed two years of his apprenticeship, dissatisfied with his situation, he waited on his uncle at Gaywood, to complain of the harsh treatment of his master. His uncle, after eying him attentively, said, " Richard, you look well; " to which Richard immediately replied, " Yes, Sir, I am perfectly well in health." " Then go back to your master," said his uncle, "and serve out your apprenticeship; and never come again to me with your complaints." This advice of the uncle was implicitly obeyed; and Mr. Beatniffe completed his term of servitude to the complete satisfaction of his master. He was, however, the only apprentice that ever did; for, although Mr. Hollingworth was in business for more than forty years, and always had four apprentices at a time, they all, with the exception of Mr. Beatniffe, either ran away, went to sea, or enlisted into some regiment. Nor will this occasion any surprise, when it is known that they were all compelled to sleep in the same bed, had clean sheets but once a year, and were dieted in the most *economical manner*.

At the expiration of his apprenticeship Mr. Hollingworth offered him the hand of his daughter, accompanied with the tempting lure of a share in his business; but the lady being very deformed, and not according with Mr. Beatniffe's taste, he declined the offer, and repaired to Norwich. Here he worked for some years as a journeyman bookbinder, and was in the constant habit of frequenting the theatre at half-price on every Saturday night, arrayed in his best suit, and decorated with ruffles.

On the failure of Mr. Jonathan Gleed, a bookseller in London-lane, in the parish of St. Andrew, Mr. Beatniffe, with the assistance of his old master, who generously lent him five hundred pounds, pur-

chased the stock, and commenced business on his
own account. After having been settled here a
short time, a Dignitary of the Cathedral stopped at
the door, and inquired who had taken the concern?
On being told that it was a Mr. Beatniffe, he replied, " Then I give him half a year." This anecdote Mr. Beatniffe used to narrate with infinite
pleasure.

Mr. Beatniffe's first Catalogue was published in
1779, and his last in 1803, to which an Appendix
appeared in 1808 ; but in these no particular libraries are specified.   He had the good fortune to purchase the principal part of the very valuable collection of books which was made by the Rev. Dr. Cox
Macro *, of Little Haugh, in the parish of Norton
in Suffolk, and which had remained undisposed of,
and scarcely been looked into, since the death of the
doctor, a period of nearly forty years.   This rich
treasure of black-letter and early printed books, old
poetry, and original letters and autographs of eminent
persons, Mr. Beatniffe bought for the sum of £.150
or £.160 ; and the purchase, of course, proved by
no means unproductive †.   Such, indeed, was the
rarity of the poesy of the " olden time" that he is
said to have realised upwards of a thousand pounds
by its sale,—some volumes having produced from
fifty to a hundred pounds each ‡.   Throughout life
he was a large purchaser of libraries and of second-
hand books; and his Catalogues were in general
well-stored with valuable articles, for which he
always knew how to ask a good price.

To his customers Mr. Beatniffe was peculiarly
blunt in his manners; and many anecdotes of his
singularity in this respect are well remembered.   A

* A memoir of this divine, with many of his letters, is inserted
n the " Literary Anecdotes," vol. IX. p. 359.

† Ibid. vol. VIII. p. 467.

‡ " Concise Description of Bury," p. 247.

Scotch nobleman once called to purchase a Bible;
Mr. Beatniffe took an Edinburgh one down, and
named his price. "O mon!" said his Lordship,
"I could buy it for much less at Edinburgh."
"Then, my Lord," replied Mr. Beatniffe, calmly
re-placing the volume on the shelf, and abruptly
quitting his noble customer, "You must go to
Edinburgh for it."

In politics Mr. Beatniffe was a very warm and
decided Tory; and on one of his workmen once
voting against that interest at a general election, was
observed to shed tears. At the commencement of
the French revolution he sided with the alarmists;
and one day hearing an apprentice of his exclaim
inadvertently, that he did not blame the French, as
they had so long lived under a tyrannical government; he replied with much warmth, "What is
that you say, boy? I tell you what, young man,
if you go on this way, you will soon spit at me and
kick your father."

For many years Mr. Beatniffe was supposed to
possess as large and as valuable a stock of old books
as any provincial bookseller in the kingdom. On
the publication and distribution of his Catalogues,
the trade in London were in the constant habit of
sending him extensive orders, which he very rarely
executed. "They want all my good books," was
his reply, "but I will take special care they shall
not have them." Indeed his great pride was to sell
his books to gentlemen; and, not wanting money,
his greatest pride was to have good books around
him, which he used facetiously to call "his jewels."
On looking over these valuables, his customers would
often remark, "I think this book is dear, Mr. Beatniffe." "You do, do you?" was his reply; "there
it is; if you don't like it, leave it."

In that amusive work, "The Sexagenarian, or the
Recollections of a Literary Life," Mr. Beatniffe's
character is thus delineated:

" In the provincial town where our friend in early
life resided, there were three booksellers of very
different characters and attainments. *One* was a
shrewd, cold, inflexible fellow, who traded principally in old books, and held out but little encouragement to a youth, who rarely had money to expend,
to become a frequenter of his shop. Of course frequent visits were not paid by our Sexagenarian to
him. The principal feature of this man's character
was suspicion of strangers, and a constant apprehension lest he should dispose of any of his *libri
rarissimi* to some cunning wight or professed collector. If any customer was announced as coming
from the metropolis, he immediately added at least
one third to his price." But notwithstanding these
eccentricities, Mr. Beatniffe was much respected by
those who knew him most intimately. By his knowledge of books, which was considerable, and his skill
as a bookbinder, which was excellent; as well as by
his strict attention to business, he amassed a large
fortune, and retired from his favourite and lucrative
pursuit a short time previous to his decease, which
took place at Norwich on the 9th of July 1818, in
the 79th year of his age. His very valuable stock
of books was disposed of by public auction.

His remains were deposited in the nave of the
Church of St. Peter at Mancroft, in Norwich, where,
on a flat-stone, is the following inscription to his
memory :

To the memory of
RICHARD BEATNIFFE,
who died July the 9th, 1818,
aged 78.
Also
MARTHA DINAH, wife of
RICHARD BEATNIFFE,
who died June the 6th, 1816,
aged 69.

Mr. Beatniffe married Miss M. D. Hart, the
daughter of Mr. Hart, an eminent writing-master,

and an Alderman of Bury St. Edmund's, by whom
he had issue a son, who died an infant, and a daughter Catherine, who was twice married, *viz.* firstly, to
Mr. Cook, of the City of Norwich, by whom she
had no issue: and, secondly, to Mr. Austin Palgrave Manclarke, of Yarmouth, by whom she had
issue two sons and two daughters, of whom, Ri-
chard-Beatniffe was married to Eliza-Marian-Elea-
nor, the daughter of Major John Carige; and Jane-
Elizabeth, to John Herbert Carige, Esq. both on
the 1st of January 1824.

Mr. Beatniffe was author of that useful and highly
entertaining little work, "The Norfolk Tour," which
he lived long enough to see pass through six editions,
and which, it must be fairly confessed, well merited
that favourable reception which it has so amply experienced.   The first edition of this work was published in 1772, and the last in 1808, under the following title, "The Norfolk Tour; or, Traveller's
Pocket Companion, being a concise Description of
all the Principal Towns, Noblemen's and Gentlemen's Seats, and other remarkable Places in the
County of Norfolk, compiled from the most authentic Historians and modern Travellers, corrected
to the present time.   To which is added an Index
Villaris for the County.   The Sixth Edition, greatly
enlarged and improved.   Norwich," 12mo.   Prefixed is the following advertisement: "Having carefully revised every page of the Norfolk Tour, and
by the friendly communications of several gentlemen in the county, and my own observations during
the last ten years, greatly enlarged, and, I hope, improved it, with much deference this Sixth Edition is
offered for public approbation by R. Beatniffe *."

* Norfolk Tour, advertisement. — For some slight notices of,
and allusions to, Mr. Beatniffe, see the " Literary Anecdotes,"
vol. III. p. 672; vol. VIII. p. 467; vol. IX. 365; Gent. Mag.
vol. LXXXVIII. pt. ii. pp. 93, 286.

The book, in this last edition, was amplified to 399 pages.

This well-digested and instructive Compendium of the History and Antiquities of Norfolk is one of those useful compilations which are commonly known under the name of Guides ; and is highly creditable to the talents and research of the author. It contains a luminous account of the state of the manufactures of Norwich at the period of its compilation ; and the pages which relate to this subject, are, perhaps, the best in the volume.   Its ingenious author, it is said, received much valuable information on this point from a gentleman of undoubted ability, who was intimately connected with the manufactures.

The " Norfolk Tour" is now, and has been for some years, out of print.

Rev. JOHN BRAND, A. M.

This profound mathematician and eminent political economist, whose peculiarities were of the most singular and striking kind, was a native of Norwich, in which city his father followed the occupation of a sadler.   The family consisted of a son and two daughters, who on their father's decease found themselves left with a very scanty provision.   The son, having a taste and turn for science and literature, went for some years to the continent for improvement, where, among other attainments, he so acquired the manners, singularity, and even grimace of the people among whom he sojourned, that on his return the agnomen of Abbè was spontaneously and universally given him.

Mr. Brand now entered himself a Member of

Caius-college, Cambridge, where he was invariably respected for his talents, his diligence, and his learning; and as constantly laughed at for his eccentricities and whimsicalities of manners. In 1766 he proceeded to the degree of A. B. with distinguished honour, being classed the Fifth Wrangler on the tripos; and to that of A. M. in 1772. On his attainment of the latter degree, he wrote an ethical essay, intituled, "Conscience," for Seaton's prize; but an accidental delay which it met with on the road occasioned its being presented to the Vice-chancellor two days after the appointed time, and on that account it could not be admitted to the competition. Mr. Brand, however, published his Poem in a quarto pamphlet in 1772, and it was allowed to possess considerable merit, but not enough to procure it a place among the favourite poems of the day.

He now took orders with very little prospect of preferment; but by a rigid economy, added to some trifling literary employments, managed to make a respectable appearance. At a very early period he distinguished himself for his profound and accurate knowledge as a Cambist, and became an avowed opponent of the celebrated Dr. Price, and others of that class. A nephew of the doctor's, who was a dissenting minister, and of considerable abilities, resided in the neighbourhood of our Abbè; and similar pursuits and propensities had introduced a familiar acquaintance between them. At this period Dr. Price's nephew was well known to be a writer in the Monthly Review; and in a country town this was a circumstance which conferred a sort of local dignity and importance.

Mr. Brand having published a tract on his favourite topic, in which Price and his friends were not mentioned in the terms of respect to which this relative of one of them thought they were entitled, the consequence was, that in a subsequent Review the publication above alluded to was handled with no

common severity. There was no difficulty in imagining the author, or if there had, this was removed
by Mr. Brand, who found an opportunity of seeing
the MS. of the offensive article. This he thought
was a grievous and unpardonable violation of the
laws of confidence and honour, and the consequences which ensued, though somewhat serious,
border on the ludicrous.

Mr. Brand called as usual on his quondam friend,
and requested his company to take a walk. This
was complied with without hesitation. When they
had proceeded to some distance, and come to a
retired spot, the critic was not a little astonished at
seeing his companion strip to his shirt, and, with
many and bitter reproaches, insist upon satisfaction
for the baseness and treachery with which he had
been treated.

Remonstrance and expostulation were in vain,
and there was no alternative between submitting
to a hearty drubbing or standing upon the defen-
sive. The result was, what not unfrequently happens in similar cases, that the offending person, who
was the more athletic of the two, proved the conqueror, and the mortified and discomfited Abbè
retired from the contest with one of his ribs broken.

Another adventure in which he was engaged, and
from which he did not escape with much brighter
laurels, seems worthy of being recorded in this place.
A family of rank and opulence had their villa at
a short distance from the Abbè's residence. They
had a taste for learning, and were remarkable for the
distinction which they paid to literary characters.
They were seldom without some more or less eminent individuals in their house, and among others
they always treated the Abbè with particular kindness. The lady, however, of the mansion had
rather a propensity to what she considered an innocent mischief, and would often amuse herself at the
expense of her guests.

One evening the party was kept up till a very late

hour by the recital of ghost-stories, to which Mr. Brand had listened with extraordinary attention. On returning to his apartment, and ruminating upon what he had recently heard, he thought he perceived something like motion in the countenance of an old family picture. He was a little startled, but on looking more attentively, he evidently saw the eyes of the picture open and shut, and at last a loud groan was uttered. He could bear it no longer, but rang his bell, and, running out of his room, made the old staircase reverberate with the cries of thieves and murder. The family, who were prepared for the event, all assembled with well-feigned astonishment and sympathy to hear the cause of his alarm, and to search his apartment. When an *eclaircissement* took place; it appeared that the head had been taken out of an old picture, and a groom, properly instructed to act his part, was placed behind the tapestry.

After a tedious apprenticeship as a Curate, and after having been for some years the Reader at St. Peter's Mancroft, in Norwich, he obtained the patronage of the father of the present Lord Stafford; and in 1775 was presented by John Wodehouse, Esq. to the Vicarage of Wickham Skeith, in Suffolk, a small living on which he proceeded to reside. What often happens in similar circumstances happened also in this. His establishment consisted of one female, a servant of all work, plain, ignorant, and of the meanest extraction; her, however, he thought proper to marry. The consequence was a numerous family and the most deplorable poverty. This latter evil he attempted in some degree to palliate by the exercise of his pen in those particular branches of science, for which he had long been so justly eminent; nor was it wholly without success. Fortunately for him he had some connection with the conductor of a literary journal of extensive circulation, who knew his merits, and availed himself of

his talents and industry. The particular proofs in
this way, and through this channel, which were
exhibited of his knowledge as a Cambist, attracted
the notice of a very distinguished individual, the
Lord Chancellor Loughborough, who had the disposition as well as the opportunity of rewarding literary merit. He was accordingly introduced to his
Lordship; and in 1797 presented by him to the
Rectory of St. George's in Southwark, then vacant
by the death of the Rev. Joseph Pote, the value of
which Mr. Brand procured to be so considerably
increased, by an Act of Parliament in 1807, as to
hold out to him the hope of passing the remainder
of his life in ease and tranquillity; but death deprived him and his family of this advantage, as he
deceased on the 23d of December in the following
year. By this event a numerous family, consisting
of eight orphan children, were left totally unpro-
vided for. The active benevolence of a friend, however, promoted a subscription for them; the amount
of which was expended in their education, and in
placing them in such situations as to enable them
to obtain a future support.

Throughout life Mr. Brand was distinguished for
his profound knowledge of mathematics, as well as
for his intimate acquaintance with political economy. There were, indeed, few topics in these
departments of science that have of late years excited the public attention, in which his pen was not
employed. In matters of commerce, exchanges,
and specie, his skill was admirable, as may be sufficiently proved by some very valuable articles written
by him in the British Critic; more particularly by
a very able review of a financial pamphlet from the
pen of Mr. W. Morgan.

Mr. Brand's publications are as follow: " Conscience, an Ethical Essay, 1772," 4to.; " Observations on some of the probable effects of Mr. Gilbert's Bill, with remarks deduced from Dr. Price's

Account of the National Debt, 1776," 8vo.; "Select Dissertations from the Amœnitates Academicæ,
a Supplement to Mr. Stillingfleet's Tracts relating
to Natural History. In two volumes. London, 1781,"
8vo.; "The Alteration of the Constitution of the House
of Commons, and the Inequality of the Land Tax,
considered conjointly, 1793," 8vo. a most able and
profound tract; "A Sermon on the Fast-day, 1794,"
4to.; " A Defence of the Pamphlet ascribed to
John Reeves, Esq. and intituled, ' Thoughts on
the English Government,' addressed to the Members of the Loyal Associations against Republicans
and Levellers, 1796," 8vo. a clear and methodical
treatise, but exceeded in general utility by his " Historical Essay on the Principles of Political Associations in a State; chiefly deduced from the French,
English, and Jewish Histories; with an application
of those principles in a comparative view of the
Associations of the year 1792, and that recently instituted by the Whig Club, 1796," 8vo.; " Considerations on the Depression of the Funds, and the
present Embarrassments of Circulation, 1797," 8vo.;
" A Determination of the Average Depression of
the Price of Wheat in War, below that of the preceding Peace, and of its re-advance in the following, according to its yearly rules, from the Revolution to the end of the last Peace; with remarks
on their greater variations in that entire period,
1800," 8vo. a treatise in the highest degree perspicuous and conclusive; " A Letter to —— ——,
Esq. on Bonaparte's Proposals for opening a Negociation for Peace; in which the British guarantee
of the Crown of France to the House of Bourbon,
contained in the triple and quadruple alliances, and
renewed by the treaty of 1783, is considered; together with the conduct of our national parties
relating to it, 1800," 8vo. an argument more ingenious than satisfactory, and unfortunately leading
to an impracticable conclusion; " A Visitation Ser-

mon, 1800;" " A Letter to the Bishops of the
United Church of England and Ireland ; containing
a Counter Representation to the Statement laid before their Lordships, in a Letter from the Committee
of the Philanthropic Society, relating to their intended Chapel (which he considered as interfering
with his parochial rights), 1806;" and " A Refutation of the Charge brought against the Marquis
Wellesley, on account of his conduct to the Nabob
of Oude.   From authentic documents, 1807," 8vo.

Miss HANNAH BRAND, the younger sister of the
Rev. John Brand, was possessed of a considerable
share of learning and talents.   In conjunction with
her elder sister she conducted a very respectable
seminary for French education at No. 18, St. Giles's
Broad-street, Norwich ; and as they both were clever
and accomplished, and promised something of re-
finement beyond the ordinary level of provincial
schools, they were for a time very successful ; but it
is more than probable that this success was interrupted and finally destroyed by the wayward and
very eccentric character and conduct of this younger
sister. Miss H. Brand now commenced authoress and
actress ; and exhibited the remarkable phenomenon
of representing on the stage the principal character
in a tragedy written by herself, which nevertheless
was damned.   The editor of the "Biographia Dramatica," however, remarks, that as an actress he
" remembers her performance of Agmunda in her
own Huniades to have been marked by force and
discrimination, though with the drawbacks of a provincial pronunciation, and a deportment not greatly
to be admired."   She died in March 1821.
Miss H. Brand was certainly a very extraordinary
lady, and endowed with considerable talents; but
she was vain, conceited, and pragmatical ; a worthy
disciple of the Wolstoncraftian school, and consequently a great stickler for the dignity of the sex,

and the rights of woman. Having failed as a teacher, as an authoress, and above all as an actress, she offered herself, and was accepted, as a governess in the family of a lady, who had formerly been brought up by her sister and herself. The lady was of an old and considerable family, and heiress to a large property; her husband was the elder son of a Baronet, of no great pretensions on the score of intellect, but a well-meaning, good sort of man. Until the governess came among them, they had lived tranquilly together, with no other or greater interruptions than are found to occur in all families. No sooner had the poetess entered upon her office, than she took it into her head that delicacy was offended by the familiarity and unconcealed affection with which her quondam pupil outwardly treated her husband. She endeavoured to persuade the wife that this was highly indecorous, and, unhappily, she but too well succeeded. Her familiarity was turned into cold civility, her affection changed into a reserved demeanour, and the whole character of her behaviour assumed a new form.

The husband was not insensible of the alteration, which at first excited his astonishment and afterwards his indignation. On discovering the cause, he very naturally insisted that the governess should be dismissed. The foolish wife, however, resisted this; and so implicated her own case with that of her counsellor, that she declared one would not go without the other. The husband was firm, and the result was that the indiscreet wife sacrificed three young children and the society of her husband, with whom she had hitherto lived happily, to share with her female friend the disgrace, contempt, and privations which accompanied their departure.

The husband instituted different suits in Doctors' Commons for the establishment of his just rights, in every one of which, the decisions, as might be expected, were in his favour; and in the printed proceedings of the Consistorial Court Miss Brand's conduct was most severely animadverted upon by the presiding Judge. The fugitives at length found it expedient to retire from Great Britain to a remote island in its dependencies, where they lived victims of self-reproach, of the greatest folly, and of the most unjustifiable perverseness.

Mr. Tate Wilkinson, in his "Wandering Patentee," a really amusing, though very quaintly written book, has some entertaining anecdotes and characteristic traits of this most extraordinary lady.

Miss H. Brand was the authoress of the following dramatic pieces, viz. "Adelinda, a Comedy;" "The Conflict, an Heroic Comedy;" "Huniades, a Tragedy;" and "Agmunda, a Tragedy," never printed. The last was the preceding piece altered, with the omission of the character of Huniades. These were collected and published by subscription in one volume octavo, under the title of "Plays and Poems, 1798;" and her conduct with respect to the printer is thus detailed by Mr. Beloe:

On giving the MS. of her Poems to the printer, she desired him to strike off a thousand copies. The MS. contained enough for a tolerable thick volume of royal octavo. The printer himself represents the following dialogue to have taken place:

"Have you made any estimate of the expense?"

"No; but I must have a thousand copies."

"How many subscribers have you?"

"About two hundred; but I know, indeed I have no doubt, of an extensive sale. I must have a thousand copies."

"Perhaps, Madam, you may not be aware that of your two hundred subscribers all will not send for their copies, and of those who do, some will not send the money; that the expense is immediate, as no long credit can be given; so that after the first advertisements the poems of an unknown author are generally considered as waste paper."

" It does not signify, Sir, I must and will have a thousand copies."

The result may easily be anticipated; a thousand copies were actually printed, but after a lapse of several years, no less than seven hundred and fifty still groaned upon the shelves of the printer's warehouse *.

Miss MARY BRAND, the elder sister, was a woman of considerable attainments; and, after leaving Norwich, conducted, with reputation and success, a seminary for young ladies at Woodbridge. She died at Ipswich, where she had resided a few years previous to her decease, with a limited number of pupils under her care and tuition, on the 12th of July 1826, and her remains were interred in the Churchyard of Sproughton, where, on a head-stone, is the following inscription to her memory, as well as to that of her niece:

SACRED
To the Memory of
HANNAH BRAND,
Daughter of the Reverend
JOHN BRAND, A. M.
late Rector of St. George
the Martyr in Southwark.
She departed this life
6th April 1822, aged 18.
Likewise to MARY BRAND,
Aunt of the above,
who departed this life
12th July 1826,
in her 76th year.

---

* The above particulars are collected from Beloe's " Sexagenarian;" Chalmers's " Biographical Dictionary;" " The Censura Literaria;" "The Biographia Dramatica;" " The Gentleman's Magazine;" "The General History of the County of Norfolk;" and "The Bibliotheca Britannica." In the Biographical Dictionary it is stated, that Mr. Brand's name does not occur among the Cambridge Graduates; this, however, is incorrect. He is there called FITZ-JOHN BRAND.

The Rev. RICHARD CANNING *, A. M.

THE EDITOR OF THE SECOND EDITION OF
THE " SUFFOLK TRAVELLER."

Richard Canning, Esq. the father of this learned and highly-respectable divine, was bred to the navy, and in that profession attained the rank of Post Captain. On retiring from active service, he settled at Ipswich, in which town he ended his days in 1726, and was interred in the Church of St. Helen, where, on a mural-tablet, is this inscription to his memory :

Underneath are deposited the remains of
RICHARD CANNING, ESQ.
an active and experienced Commander in the Royal Navy,
who having served his country with unexceptionable
courage and conduct during the wars of K. William and Q. Anne,
retired to this town, A. D. 1712,
and through resentment of party,
founded on misreported facts,
died a private Captain, anno $\begin{cases} \text{Dom. 1726,} \\ \text{æt. 57.} \end{cases}$
Also of MARGARET CANNING, relict of the
said Richard, who for her piety, benevolence,
and conjugal as well as maternal affection,
was an example worthy of imitation.
She died anno $\begin{cases} \text{Dom. 1734,} \\ \text{æt. 67.} \end{cases}$
And of ALICE CANNING, mother of the said Richard,
who died in a good old age, anno $\begin{cases} \text{Dom. 1716,} \\ \text{æt. 88.} \end{cases}$
With them lieth intombed the body of
CORDELIA, wife of RICHARD CANNING, Clerk.
She was possessed of many amiable qualities,
which greatly endeared her to her friends,
by whom her loss was the more regretted,
as she was taken from them before
the usual decline of life,
anno $\begin{cases} \text{Dom. 1751,} \\ \text{æt. 36.} \end{cases}$

His only son, Richard Canning, the subject of

* See " Literary Anecdotes," vol. II. p. 274; VIII. p. 488.

this brief notice, was born on the 30th of September 1708, and received his academical education at Catherine-hall Cambridge, where he proceeded to the degree of A. B. in 1728, and to that of A. M. in 1735. In 1737 he was licensed to the Perpetual Curacy of St. Lawrence, in Ipswich; in 1738 he was presented to the Rectory of Harkstead, which he relinquished to his son in 1769; in 1755 to that of Freston, and the Vicarage of Rushmere St. Andrew, all in Suffolk, which latter he resigned in 1756. He died on the 8th of June 1775, and was interred in the Church of St. Helen, where, on a mural-tablet, is this inscription to his memory:

Arms: Argent, three Moors' heads, side-faced, couped at the neck Proper, wreathed about the temples, Or and Azure, impaling, within a bordure engrailed, two chevronels.

Near this place are interred
the remains of
RICHARD CANNING, M. A.
many years Minister of
the parish of St. Lawrence,
in this town,
a man
of unblemished honour and integrity,
and of taste and erudition
superior to most of his cotemporaries,
but ever considering
all human knowledge and learning
of no other use or service
than as they might tend to advance the interests,
and promote the influence
of religion and virtue.
His preaching was recommended by his practice,
and the doctrines he delivered
enforced by his own example.
How well and how successfully
he imitated his Divine Master
in carrying on the great business
of universal benevolence,
the several charitable institutions
of this town,
which his indefatigable zeal and industry
placed at last on the most solid foundation,

will abundantly testify.
Born Sept. 30th, 1708 ; died June 8th, 1775.
This monument was erected
by his only surviving daughter,
CORDELIA CANNING,
whose unaffected simplicity
and gentleness of manners,
joined to that filial piety
for which she was eminently distinguished,
rendered her universally amiable.
She was cut off
in the thirty-sixth year of her age,
to the inexpressible grief
of all who knew her.

Mr. Canning was a gentleman of very considerable literary attainments, an elegant and accomplished scholar, and a learned and most judicious divine. With the History and Antiquities of the County of Suffolk he was intimately acquainted, and in a thorough knowledge of the descent of property, and the connection of families, was well and accurately versed. His edition of " The Suffolk Traveller" confirms this remark ; a work which is highly creditable to his talents and research, and which evinces a most intimate acquaintance with the manorial as well as topographical history of the county. It was, indeed, for many years after its appearance, the only distinct publication which had been attempted in illustration of its history ; and it has been one too from which all succeeding writers have most largely borrowed.

Mr. Canning's literary productions are as follow:
" A Short Answer to a Pamphlet, called Plain Reasons for Dissenting from the Church of England, &c. By a Clergyman. Ipswich, 1740," 8vo.; " A Sermon preached Dec. 18, 1745, on occasion of the present Rebellion. Ipswich, 1746," 8vo. ; " A Sermon preached at the Ordinary Visitation of the Right Reverend Father in God Thomas Lord Bishop of Norwich, in Ipswich, June 17, 1747; occasioned by a Pamphlet, called ' Christianity not founded

on Argument.' Published at the request of his
Lordship. Ipswich, 1747," 8vo.; "An Account of
the Gifts and Legacies that have been given and
bequeathed to Charitable Uses in the Town of Ipswich; with some Account of the present State and
Management, and some Proposals for the future
Regulation of them *. Ipswich, 1747," 8vo. " Remarks on a Pamphlet intituled, 'A Vindication of
the Principles and Practice of Protestant Dissenters,
&c. By the Author of the Short Answer to the
Plain Reasons for Dissenting, &c. London, 1749,"
8vo.; "The Principal Charters which have been
granted to the Corporation of Ipswich in Suffolk,
translated. London, 1754," 8vo. This useful work
was published for the benefit of the Free Burgesses.
"The Suffolk Traveller. First published by Mr.
John Kirby †, of Wickham-market, who took an

* This publication " was occasioned by an Order of Great Court
that was luckily obtained Oct. 16, 1743, by which a Committee
was appointed to inquire what donations have from time to time
been given to the town of Ipswich, or to any particular Burgesses as such; and under whose direction and management the
same now are or ought to be, by the wills or appointments of
the donors; and also to inquire into whose hands, as trustees,
the pecuniary donations, or any part thereof, were respectively
last paid, and who have received the rent and profits of the real
donations for thirty years last past, and how the same have been
paid or applied." From the papers of some of the Members of
this Committee the above account is drawn, with the laudable
intention of preventing any future mismanagement or misap-
plication.

† Mr. John Kirby was originally a schoolmaster at Orford, and
afterwards occupied a mill at Wickham-market, and is well
known to topographers by his " Map of Suffolk," as well as by
" The Suffolk Traveller," the result of an actual survey which
he took of the whole county. He afterwards resided at Ipswich,
and is called a " Painter" there by Mr. Grove in his " Dialogue between Wolsey and Ximenes," p. 124. In 1735 he published in 12mo, " The Suffolk Traveller; or a Journey through
Suffolk. In which is inserted the true Distance in the Roads
from Ipswich to every Market-town in Suffolk, and the same from
Bury St. Edmund's. Likewise the Distance in the Roads from
one Village to another; with notes of Direction for Travellers,
as what Churches and Gentlemen's Seats are passed by, and on

actual Survey of the whole County, in the years

which side of the Road, and the distance they are at from either of the said Towns. With a short Historical Account of the Antiquities of every Market-town, Monasteries, Castles, &c. that were in former Times. By John Kirby, who took an Actual Survey of the whole County in the Years 1732, 1733, and 1734. Ipswich. Printed by John Bagnall."

In 1736 he published " A Map of the County of Suffolk ; " dedicated to his Grace the Duke of Grafton, and illustrated with 124 Arms of the Nobility, Gentry, and Clergy of the County ; and with views of the following buildings, *viz.* Burgh Castle, Bungay Castle, Blithburgh Priory, Butley Priory, the Gateway to Bury Abbey, Covehithe Church, St. James's Church at Dunwich, Framlingham Castle, Leiston Abbey, Mettingham Castle, Orford Castle, and Wingfield Castle. An improved edition of this Map, on a larger scale, was published in 1766, under the following title : " A New Map of the County of Suffolk, taken from the original Map published by Mr. John Kirby in 1736, who took an actual and accurate survey of the whole County, now re-published with corrections and additions. By John and William Kirby, sons of the author, and engraved by John Ryland.

In the " Ipswich Journal " for Nov. 13, 1732, No. 587, are the following announcements respecting this publication :

" Proposals for Surveying the County of Suffolk, by Nathaniel Bacon, jun. and John Kirby. In which Map shall be described all the rivers, (and where navigable,) brooks, bridges, locks, &c. roads, (and the true distance from town to town,) the ground plots of all market and other considerable towns, parish churches, castles, demolished in whole or in part, monasteries, and other religious houses, and what order they formerly were of, the names of their founders, when founded, with their antient revenues, division of hundreds, antient Kings' seats, and fields of battle, the seats and parks of all the nobility and gentry residing in the said county, with their arms on the sides of the Map, latitude and longitude, with whatever else remarkable that may offer itself to view in surveying the same.

" This Map shall be protracted from a scale of one mile to an inch, and is proposed by subscription at ten shillings a Map ; the one half paid in hand, the other on delivery ; they who have their arms half a guinea more towards the engraving, the one half paid in hand the other on delivery ; they who subscribe for six shall have a seventh gratis."

In the same paper, for Jan. 29, 1732, No. 598, is the following notice :

" Whereas Nathaniel Bacon, jun. and John Kirby did lately publicly advertise their design of taking an actual Survey of the County of Suffolk ; these are therefore to certify, that the said surveyors do design to begin the said survey of the County of

1732, 1733, and 1734.   The Second Edition, with

Suffolk as soon as the roads are fit for a perambulation to travel in, which will be in March or April next at longest.

"The authors propose to begin at Ipswich, and first to take a true and actual survey of the said town, and from thence to proceed in a trigonometrical method to find the true bearings and distances of every parish church in the said county from the said town of Ipswich; the bearings and distances in the roads shall be taken by a perambulator; and in the said Map shall be inserted the true distances not only between market, but all other towns of any traffic in the said county. The rivers and brooks shall be traced up to their fountains' heads, and the coast from Harwich to Yarmouth; all woods that are remarkable shall be taken notice of; as also all monasteries, religious houses, gentlemen's seats and parks, antient Kings' seats, &c. as before proposed. And the whole work shall be performed with that care and industry as shall render it useful, pleasing, and intelligible, and so as to stand the test of a mathematical demonstration."

And again on the 5th of August 1732, No. 625:

"Whereas Nathaniel Bacon, jun. and John Kirby have formerly advertised their designs of taking a true and actual Survey of the County of Suffolk, the proposals for doing thereof, and in what manner they proposed to do the same, need not to be here mentioned, as being before made public in taverns and other public places. This is therefore to give notice, that the said surveyors have begun the said survey, and made a considerable progress in the same, having now surveyed the coast from Dunwich to Harwich, and up into the country, so as the Hundreds of Colnes, Wilford, Loes, Plomesgate, and Carlsford, are very near finished, with part of some other Hundreds, in respect of the true bearings and distances of the parish Churches situate in the said Hundreds. The beginning of the said Survey was on Tunstall-heath, by taking (on a plain parcel of land) a measured distance of fifty chains, or five furlongs, by help of which the true distance was found between Tunstall Church and Wantisden Church; and likewise between the said churches and that of Wickham-market, having thus completed a triangle by gaining all its sides and angles, (which upon proof was true, according to the rules of geometry, having its three angles equal to 180 degrees,) from thence the calculations have been carried on hitherto (and it may be said without boasting) with great exactness, for as it is undeniably true, that, if two or three lines concur in one point, the work cannot be erroneous, so in the perambulation that has been taken, the object for proof was Stoke windmill in Ipswich (being all that could be discerned of Ipswich town from off Rushmere steeple); then taking another perambulation from Baudsey through the Hundred of Wilford, Colnes, and part of Samford, at Woolverston the angle was taken from

many Alterations and large Additions, by Several
Hands. London, 1764 *," 8vo. This work con-

Nacton to the said wind-mill at Stoke in Ipswich ; also again at
Freston another observation was made of the quantity of the
angle from Nacton to the said wind-mill at Stoke in Ipswich ;
and by drawing two lines from Woolverston and Freston (according to the quantity of their respective angles observed from Nacton) they concurred in the point before assigned for the said
wind-mill, so that, although we dare not say it is mathematically
true (for if so it must not vary the thousandth part of an inch)
yet we dare take the liberty to say, it will stand the test of a
mathematical demonstration, and be useful, pleasing, and intelligible.   And as such an undertaking is too great and expensive
to be perfected by private persons, without encouragement, it
is hoped that, as several gentlemen have already subscribed,
others will follow the examples, for the promoting so useful an
undertaking.   There shall be no more printed than are subscribed for, nor sold for any other or lower price."
    And lastly in the same paper of Dec. 23, 1732, No. 645:
    " The Survey of the County of Suffolk, as before proposed to
be undertaken by Nathaniel Bacon and John Kirby, has been,
and now is, attended on by the said John Kirby ; the coast being
now truly surveyed from Harwich to Yarmouth, and the river
Waveney from Yarmouth to Diss in Norfolk.   The authors
hope it will not be unacceptable to the readers to give an account
of the true horizontal distances of the several towns under-
named, from the Market Cross of the town of Ipswich, viz.
from the Market Cross in Ipswich the horizontal distance to
Diss, 17 m. 5 f.; Eye, 15 m. 3 f.; Debenham, 10 m. 6 f.; Harlston, 22 m. 1 f.; Yarmouth, 43 m. 7 f.; Halesworth, 22 m. 1 f.;
Framlingham, 13 m. 1 f.; Lowestoft, 38 m. 2 f.; Southwold,
27 m. 2 f.; Dunwich, 23 m. 3 f.; Saxmundham, 16 m. 7 f.;
Wickham-market, 10 m. 3 f.; Woodbridge, 7 m.; Aldeburgh,
18 m. 6 f.; Orford, 15 m. 4 f.; Harwich, 9 m. 3 f."
    Mr. Kirby deceased on the .. of Dec. 1753, and his remains
were interred in the church-yard of St. Mary at Tower, in Ipswich.
    In vol. I. p. 5, of " Some Account of the Life and Writings
of Mrs. Trimmer," is a letter from Mr. Kirby to his son, dated
from Wickham-market, Jan. 17, 1741.
    Mr. Joshua Kirby, eminent for his talent in perspective, was
his son ; the celebrated entomologist, the Rev. William Kirby,
his grandson ; and the ingenious Mrs. Trimmer, his granddaughter.
    * Among the many collections for the History of Suffolk,
which occur in the " Catalogue of the curious and valuable
Library of Craven Ord, Esq." sold by Mr. Evans in Pall Mall
in June 1829, is " Kirby's Suffolk Traveller, interleaved in two
folio volumes, with additions in print and manuscript, and a

tains a Map of the County and four Plates of Roads. In 1755 Mr. Bowyer printed for him on a half sheet folio, " An Address to the Freemen of Ipswich."

Mr. Canning left issue by Cordelia his wife a son and a daughter, *viz.* Richard, who received his academical education at Emanuel-college, Cambridge, where he proceeded to the degree of A. B. in 1763. In 1769 he was presented by his father to the Rectory of Harkstead, and in 1785, by Edmund Tyrell, Esq. to that of Weston-market, both in the county of Suffolk. He married Miss Tyrell, by whom he had no issue; and dying at Ipswich on the 17th of January 1789, was interred in the Church of St. Helen, but without any inscription to his memory. He bequeathed to the Society for Promoting Christian Knowledge the sum of £.9,946. 4s. 11d. invested in the following stocks, *viz.* Long Annuities, £.76. 5s.; Reduced ditto, £.1,200; Four per cent. £.710. 9s. 8d.; Three per cent. Consols, £.7,959. 10s. 3d. The daughter, Cordelia, died unmarried, in the thirty-sixth year of her age.

———

EDMUND GILLINGWATER *,
THE HISTORIAN OF " LOWESTOFT,"
AND " ST. EDMUND'S BURY."

Edmund Gillingwater, the subject of this notice, was the second son of Edmund Gillingwater and Alice his wife, and was born at Lowestoft in 1736. There he carried on for some years the trade of a barber, the profession of which, of all others, approaches that of an antiquary; witness our old acquaintance, " The Barber of Bagdad " in the Ara-

few ancient deeds;" it was purchased for the British Museum, at the price of £.6. 12s. In the Antiquaries' Closet, in the Bodleian Library, Oxford, is another copy illustrated with MS notes by Scott.

* " Literary Anecdotes," vol. III. p. 200.

bian Nights' Entertainments. From Lowestoft he removed to Harleston in Norfolk, where he continued in the same occupation, and where he ended his days with the well-earned character of an ingenious, upright, and inoffensive man.

He deceased on the 13th of March, 1813, and was interred in the Church-yard of Redenhall in Norfolk, where, on two stones, are the following inscriptions to his memory, as well as to that of his wife:

Sacred
to the memory of
EDM. GILLINGWATER,
who died March 13th, 1813,
aged 77 years.

———

Sacred
to the memory of
MARY, the wife of
EDM. GILLINGWATER,
who died May 18th,
1802,
aged 65 years.

In 1786 Mr. Gillingwater, as overseer of the poor at Harleston, published " An Essay on Parish Workhouses; with some regulations proposed for their improvement," 8vo.; an useful and well-written pamphlet.

In 1790 he published by subscription, " An Historical Account of the antient Town of Lowestoft, in the County of Suffolk, to which is added some Cursory Remarks on the adjoining Parishes, and a General Account of the Island of Lothingland." 4to. In the preface Mr. Gillingwater states, that " the principal motives which excited him to engage in this work were a regard to the place of his nativity; the information and amusement of the merchants, and other inhabitants of the town of Lowestoft; and a desire of recovering from the hands of all-devouring Time, and transmitting them to posterity, the best accounts of the antient and modern state of the town that he was able to procure.

"In the prosecution of this design, the amusement of the inhabitants of Lowestoft has been only a secondary motive in his undertaking; the primary object which he had in view was, an ardent desire of being useful to them; and in pursuance of this plan he has endeavoured to give every information in his power respecting the herring fishery, so as to prevent, he hopes, any disputes arising in future concerning it. The several charitable donations given to the town he has fully described; and extracts from wills, relating thereto, he has been as careful in collecting and transcribing as possibly he could. He has also industriously endeavoured to do justice to the memories of those worthy characters, either born in Lowestoft, or connected with it, who have distinguished themselves either by their regard to the welfare of the town or their country, their zeal for religion or their love of humanity; these amiable friends of mankind he has particularly attended to, by rescuing them from that oblivion in which they were almost wholly absorbed, and placing them in those advantageous points of view to which they were so justly entitled."

Mr. Gillingwater modestly concludes his Preface in these words: "The author of this publication is perfectly sensible of his want of those necessary materials which are requisite for rendering his work so complete as he could wish; the deficiency of remaining evidence compels him frequently to listen to the doubtful voice of tradition, and sometimes to tread the dubious paths of probable conjecture. It is likewise unnecessary to observe, how inadequate he is to an undertaking of this nature, as too evident proofs of it will present themselves in almost every page; these considerations oblige him to apologize for his presumption, and to submit himself to the candour and indulgence of his readers."

The following notice respecting this work appears
in the Literary Anecdotes * : "I have his (Ives's) beginning of the History of Lothingland in eight pages
only of large quarto.   I voluntarily lent it to Gillingwater, who has printed it without the least mention of either of us.   I think Mr. Stevenson of
Norwich, doth not allow him to be the writer of the
books he publishes, but that they are done by a
poor person of Lowestoft; and his so readily adopting Ives's looks like it.   This I know, that Mrs.
Harmer told me that her husband †, to whom he
communicated some observations, had a good opinion of him.   T. F. ‡ "

Whatever assistance Mr. Gillingwater might have
received, or whatever he may have borrowed from
others without a due and proper acknowledgment,
there is little doubt, I believe, but that he was the
real author.   I have heard, indeed, his brother,
who resided at Lowestoft in very humble circumstances, remark, that the work in question was compiled from his collections; but from the conversation I then had with him, and from a slight and
cursory inspection of these " Collections," I can
see no just reason to controvert his brother's right
to be considered as the legitimate proprietor of the
" Historical Account of Lowestoft."

In 1804 appeared his "Historical and Descriptive Account of St. Edmund's Bury, in the County of
Suffolk; comprising an ample Detail of the Origin,
Dissolution, and Venerable Remains of the Abbey,
and other Places of Antiquity in that ancient Town
of St Edmund's Bury," small 8vo.   A second edition of this work was published in 1811.

This volume contains engravings of the Abbey-
gate, St. James's Church, Ruins of the Abbey, and

* Vol. III. p. 200.
† The learned and ingenious author of " Observations on
divers passages of Scripture."
‡ Taylor's Friend, i. e. Rev. George Ashby.

the Angel-hill, and displays greater industry in the collection of materials than skill or judgment in their arrangement.   It is on the whole, however, highly creditable to the talents of the pains-taking writer; and provides the curious traveller with a very useful guide to those venerable remains of architectural beauty, which at almost every step arrest the attention of the admirer of antiquity.

Isaac Gillingwater, the elder brother above alluded to, resided in Lowestoft, and for many years carried on the trade of a barber.   In the latter part of his life he was in very distressed circumstances, and indebted to many of his friends for occasional assistance.   Here he ended his days on the 14th of May 1813, and his " Collections," which appeared to me but of little value, and which were in a very dirty state, came into the possession of Mr. Robert Reeve, an attorney of that town *.

His remains were interred in the Church-yard of Lowestoft, with the following inscription to his memory, as well as to that of his parents:

In
memory of
Edm. Gillingwater,
who died Sept. 23, 1772,
aged 79 years.
Also of
Alice, his wife,
who died Feb. 17, 1784,
aged 78 years.
Also of
Isaac Gillingwater,
their son,
who died May 14, 1813,
aged 81 years.

* " This gentleman is possessed of a great variety of scarce prints, drawings, and papers, illustrative of the History of Lowestoft and its neighbourhood.   This selection must have been attended with perseverance and industry, and is highly creditable to the taste and talents of its possessor." Druery's History and Topographical Notices of Great Yarmouth, &c. p. 281.

550

Rev. THOMAS BISHOP, D. D.

Thomas Bishop was a native of Lincolnshire, and received his academical education at Sidney Sussex-college, Cambridge, where he proceeded to the degree of A.B. in 1700; to that of A.M. in 1704; and to that of S.T.P. in 1725. In 1706 he was presented to the consolidated Rectories of Creeting All Saints and Creeting St. Olave; in 1707 he was licensed to the Perpetual Curacy of St. Mary at Tower in Ipswich; and in 1720 was instituted to the Rectory of Gosbeck, all in Suffolk.

He married Elizabeth, the daughter of the Rev. John Fowle, Rector of Creeting St. Peter, in that county, by whom he left issue two sons, Thomas and Richard, and one or more daughters. He deceased on the 29th of June 1737, in the 56th year of his age, and his remains were interred in the south aisle of St. Mary at Tower, where, on a mural tablet, is the following inscription to his memory:

Arms: Argent, on a bend, cotised Gules, three bezants.
Crest: On a wreath a griffin sejant Argent, resting the dexter claw on a bezant.

M. S.
Thomæ Bishop, S. T. P.
honesto loco Lincolniæ nati,
et hujus Ecclesiæ
triginta fere annos Ministri.
Uxorem duxit Elizabetham,
Joannis Fowle, Cl. filiam
de Creeting St. Pet.
in comitatu Suffolciensi.
Hic procul sub arâ, ubi filios duos
et quatuor filias jam antea composuerant,
ambo requiescunt in pace
et spe certâ felicis resurrectionis.
Mortem obierunt
ille die xxixo Junii, A.D. 1737,
ætatis anno 56o;
hæc die iiio Junii, A. D. 1749,
ætatis anno 62o.
Nihil opus est

ut hoc marmor virtutes testetur viri,
seu concionatoris, seu scriptoris
merito insignis;
qualis vixit
testentur Parochiani qui uno ore filium
grati ergo animi
in patris locum eligebant.
Quale vero et quantum
in Scholarum severioribus disciplinis
ingenii acumen ostentabat
testetur clara illa Vox Academiæ Cantabrigiensis
quum S. T. P. gradum solicitaret.
Sic virtute adornatus, doctrinâ celebris,
et vitâ quasi cœlo maturus,
placidè decessit.

Mr. Bishop was the author of the following
works, viz. "The Errors and Absurdities of the
Arian and semi-Arian Schemes, and especially the
Politheism and Idolatry by which they have cor-
rupted the Christian Faith; represented in Eight
Sermons preached at the Cathedral of St. Paul in
London, in the years 1724 and 1725. At the Lecture founded by the worthy Lady Moyer. To which
is added, Concio ad Clerum in Ecclesia Beatæ Mariæ Cantabrigiensis habita quinto nonas Julii, anno
Salutis humanæ 1725. London, 1726," 8vo.; "An
Abridgement of the Exposition of the Creed; written
by the Right Reverend Dr. John Pearson, late Lord
Bishop of Chester. More especially designed for
the Use of English Readers. London, 1729," 8vo.;
"A Plain and Practical Exposition of the Catechism
of the Church of England. London, 1736," 8vo.

His creation to the degree of a Doctor in Divinity at Cambridge was attended with this singular
circumstance, which is alluded to in his monumental inscription, — that there were six others
who were created with him, viz. Ellis* and Maw-
son†, of Corpus Christi; Waterland‡, of Magda-
lene; and Mangey §, Newcome ‖, and Palmer,
of St. John's-college. It formed the opening of the

* See "Literary Anecdotes," vol. III. p. 668.
† Ibid. vol. IV. p. 459.   ‡ Ibid. vol. I. p. 215.
§ Ibid. p. 136.   ‖ Ibid. pp. 186, 222.

Speech of the then Regius Professor, the celebrated
Dr. Bentley, which is prefixed to his edition of
Terence, under the following title, *viz.* " Ricardi
Bentleii, cum septem in Theologiâ Doctores crearet,
Oratiuncula; Cantabrigiæ in Comitiis habita, Julii 6,
1725."

" D^{nus} Procurator, Venerande Pater, ad Creationem. Ad Creationem vocas? Ego vero, dig-
nissime Procurator, volens obtempero; eo minus
gravate hoc Creandi munus obiturus, quod tot et tales
hos filios meos almæ Matri Academiæ sisto. Nam
superioribus quidem temporibus, prope summa vo-
torum decessori meo erat, ut singulis apud vos annis
jus trium liberorum obtinere posset. Mihi vero
felicitas illa perpetuo obtingat, ut septem pluribus-
ve liberis quotannis fiam auctior."

The Rev. John King, a short memoir of whom
is given in the fifth volume, p. 125, of this Work,
was married to the Doctor's granddaughter.

══════

The Right Rev. THOMAS PERCY, D.D.
Lord Bishop of Dromore.

This learned and venerable Prelate has been frequently noticed in the " Literary Anecdotes *."
He was descended from a family which had been
for several generations resident at Worcester; and
which it was his ambition to connect with that of
his illustrious patron and namesake, the Duke of
Northumberland †.

He received the rudiments of his education at
the Grammar-school of Bridgnorth, his native town;

* See memoirs of Bishop Percy in that work, vol. III. pp. 160,
752; and various notices referred to in vol. VII. pp. 317, 649.

The portrait now engraved is from a very interesting whole-
length in Dibdin's Decameron, representing the Bishop when an
old man, and nearly deprived of sight, walking in his garden,
and about to feed his swans.

† Dr. Percy took great pains in the investigation of his descent, a pedigree of which he communicated to Dr. Nash (see

Audinet sculp.

Thō: Dromore

Born 1729 — Died 1811.

H.P. Briggs pinx.   *P. Audinet sculp.*

Rev. T. Kerrich M.A. F.S.A.

Principal Librarian of the University of Cambridge.

Born 1748. — Died 1828.

and thence removed to Christ Church, Oxford, with one of three exhibitions on the foundation of Mr. Careswell, with which that school is endowed.

He proceeded to the degree of M. A. at Oxford in 1753; but, at the close of 1769 *, having in that year been appointed one of the King's Chaplains †, he repaired to Cambridge for that of D. D. to which he was admitted as a Member of Emanuel-college, early in 1770. His first fortunate introduction to the Northumberland family had taken place in 1765 ‡.

the History of Worcestershire, vol. II. p. 318. It will there be perceived that it was his aim to identify his family with that of the descendants of Ralph, younger brother to the third Earl of Northumberland; and about 1795 he printed on a broadside a pedigree of the Earls of Northumberland, in which he introduced " the Worcester branch," as his own family is styled, taking for granted the connection presumed in the History of Worcestershire. Supposing the descent capable of proof, the Bishop was decidedly Earl of Northumberland; but he left no relation to inherit his claims.

* In a letter dated Dec. 11, 1769, addressed by the Rev. William Cole to Mr. Granger, is this passage: " I design calling to-day on Mr. Percy, formerly of Oxford, and editor of the old English Ballads, who is now at Cambridge for his D. D. degree; he preached yesterday afternoon at St. Mary's on that account. He is a collector of heads, and formerly I had some correspondence with him." Malcolm's Letters of Granger, p. 330.

† " Dr. Percy not unfrequently introduced me at the Chaplains' table at St. James's, where I met with some of the first literary characters of the age. I must own, though some compensation was made, I have always regretted the loss of that table. Each Chaplain for his month admitted his select friends; the company was miscellaneous but always instructive; and I was never witness to any altercation in that lettered society. Dr. Percy introduced Mr. Hume, and all the company were highly gratified with his conversation."

" Dr. Percy was a most pleasing companion, and to me a steady friend; there was a violence in his temper which could not always be controlled; but he had a wife,

——— " Without one jarring atom form'd,
And gentleness and joy made up her being."

" She was wet-nurse at Buckingham House to the infant Prince Edward, afterwards Duke of Kent." Cradock's Literary and Miscellaneous Memoirs, vol. I. p. 239; vol. IV. p. 292.

‡ See in vol. IV. of the present Work, p. 643, a congratulatory letter of his friend the Rev. Edward Blakeway.

The Bishop's lady was Anne, daughter of Barten Goodriche, of Desborough in Northamptonshire, Esq. She died at Dromore-house, Dec. 30, 1806, aged 75.

The following warm eulogy upon Bishop Percy's most popular literary pursuit, is from Dibdin's Bibliographical Decameron. " The name of Thomas Percy, Bishop of Dromore, is consecrated in the annals of black-letter learning, dear to every man who has the curiosity and the sense to listen to the rude songs of his ancestors, and to catch a portion of the energetic simplicity which they impart. The flowers which Percy gathered from the 𝖇𝖆𝖑𝖑𝖆𝖉-𝖕𝖔𝖊𝖙𝖗𝖞 of our fore-fathers, have served, ever since their appearance, to regale and refresh us. Within the cups of these flowers, Scott, Campbell, Moore, like poetic bees, have ' lurked,' and sipped, and enriched their own delightful stores. The late Bishop of Dromore is entitled to the proud praise of being the *Father of poetical taste* in that department of literature which he has the exclusive merit of having first brought into public notice. His ' Reliques of Ancient English Poetry' is a publication that reflects lasting honour upon his name; and it has proved the germ of a rich harvest in the same field of the Muses."—" In his latter years (adds Dr. Dibdin) Bishop Percy almost wished to *forget* that he had published the Reliques of Ancient English Poetry; but the wish was both vain and injudicious: for his memory will live, and gloriously live, upon the strength of THAT WORK ALONE, when his professional publications (few, and comparatively unimportant, undoubtedly,) may possibly be forgotten. The truth is, the leading feature, or bias (call it as you will) of Bishop Percy's mind, was philological taste ; and, I had almost said, poetical as well as philological. He had the eye and the hand of a master in this study. He was the first, ' among the sons of Britain,' who may be said

to have truly felt, and exactly appreciated, the force
and beauty of our earlier ballad-poetry ; and, transformed by his talismanic touch, the sombre-seeming
productions of our typographical forefathers—the
De Wordes, Pynsons, and Copelands, of the sixteenth century—started up into shapes and appearances the most inviting, or curious, or beautiful, or
interesting. From him Tom Warton might have
caught or increased the glow of poetical inspiration;
and Shenstone hastened to pour the tributary waters
of his urn into the reservoir before-named, which
has so long continued to refresh and delight the
' thirsty in poetical love.' Formed and fashioned
upon the ' Reliques' of our old poetry, the Ellises,
Ritsons, and Southeys of the day have put forth a
series of volumes, without which no library, which
aspires to elegance and utility, can be said to be
complete. The Bishop's emendations and supply
of *lacunæ*, in the defective copies of the more
ancient ballads, equally showed the felicity of his
conception and execution; while, in prose matters,
his publications of the 'Northumberland Household Book,' 1770, 8vo.; and ' Mallet's Northern
Antiquities,' with notes, maintained his reputation
with undiminished splendor *."

* Dr. Dibdin describes, in a note, the manuscript from which
many of the Ancient Ballads were selected, which is represented
in Sir Joshua Reynolds's portrait of Dr. Percy, and which is
still in the possession of the Bishop's daughter Mrs. Isted, at Ecton, in Northamptonshire :
" The MS. in question is a narrow, half-bound book, with
blue-paper sides and brown leather back. It is fifteen inches and
five-eighths in length, by about five and six-eighths in width.
Every page has a margin to the left of about an inch and a half
in width, marked by a perpendicular line ; the poetry uniformly
occupying the right side of the margin.   The book may be about
an inch in thickness. We have the following introductory prefix in an antient hand : ' Curious Old Ballads, which occasionally
I have met with. N.B. This volume contains near 40,000
verses, reckoning 520 pages, and about 75 lines to a page ;
which, however, makes it 39,000.' A little further the Bishop
has written as follows : ' N. B. When I first got possession of

1. *Agreement between the Rev. Mr. Percy and Mr. Tonson.*

" Whereas the Rev. Thomas Percy, of Easton Mauduit in Northamptonshire, clerk, is preparing for the press a collection

---

this MS. I was very young, and being in no degree an antiquary, I had not then learnt to reverence it; which must be my excuse for the scribble which I then spread over some parts of its margin; and in one or two instances for even taking out the leaves to save the trouble of transcribing. I have since been more careful. T. P.'—This is followed by a memorandum of great interest, signed by the Bishop himself: 'Memorandum. Northumberland-house, Nov. 7, 1769. This very curious old manuscript in its mutilated state, but unbound, and sadly torn, I rescued from destruction; and begged at the hands of my worthy friend Humphrey Pitt, Esq. then living at Shiffnall in Shropshire, afterwards of Prior Lee, near that town, who died very lately at Bath, in summer, 1769. I saw it lying dirty on the floor under a bureau in the parlour; being used by the maids to light the fire. It was afterwards sent most unfortunately to an ignorant bookbinder, who pared the margin, when I put it into boards in order to lend it to Dr. Johnson. Mr. Pitt has since told me, that he believes the transcripts in this volume, &c. were made by that Blount, who was author of Jocular Tenures, &c. who he thought was of Lancashire or Cheshire, and had a remarkable fondness for these old things. He believed him to be the same person with that Mr. Thomas Blount, who published the curious account of King Charles the Second's Escape, intituled, Boscobel, &c. Lond. 1660, 12mo. which has been so often reprinted; as also the Law Dictionary, 1671, folio, and many other books, which may be seen in Wood's Athenæ, vol. II. p. 73, &c. A descendant or relation of that Mr. Blount was an apothecary at Shiffnall, whom I remember myself, named also Blount. He (if I mistake not) sold the library of his said predecessor, Thomas Blount, to the above-mentioned Mr. Humphrey Pitt, who bought it for his nephew, my ever-valued friend, the Rev. Robert Binnel. Mrs. Binnel accordingly had all the printed books; but this MS. which was among them, was neglected, and left behind at Mr. Pitt's house, where it lay for many years. N. B. Upon looking into Wood's Athenæ, I find that Thomas Blount, the author of the Jocular Tenures, was a Herefordshire man. He may, however, have spent much of his time in Cheshire or Lancashire; or, after all, this collection may have been made by a relation of his of the same name." Dr. Dibdin then proceeds with a list of the poetical pieces contained in the volume, with the Bishop's marginal remarks, and gives some fac-similes of the hand-writing. See the Bibliographical Decameron, vol. III. pp. 340—344.

of the Works of George Villiers, Duke of Buckingham*, with an
account of his Life prefixed thereto, and a new key to the Re-
hearsal; Now it is hereby agreed between the said Thomas
Percy and Jacob Tonson, Esq. of London, that the said book
shall forthwith be printed in two volumes octavo; and the said
Jacob Tonson doth hereby agree to pay the said Thomas Percy,
or his executors, the sum of £.52. 10s. for his trouble in preparing the said work for the press, which is to be paid in manner following: viz. thirty guineas on putting it to the press, and
twenty guineas more when the printing of it is finished. And
the same Jacob Tonson doth further promise and agree to pay
the said Thomas Percy, or his executors, a further consideration,
as shall be agreed upon between them, when the said work
comes to a second, and all future editions. In witness whereof
the parties above mentioned have hereunto set their hands this
12th day of June 1761.

" JACOB TONSON.   THOMAS PERCY.

" Witness Joseph Wall, living with Mr. Tonson."

------

2. Rev. Mr. PERCY to Mr. TONSON.

" SIR,   *Easton Mauduit, April 26, 1764.*

" Before I received the favour of your letter, I had intended to
write this week to inform you, that I have gone through the two
first volumes of the Spectator with the most minute attention,
and have compared them with the original papers, by which
means I have corrected innumerable mistakes which had crept
into the latter editions. I have also added explanatory notes,
as far as my materials would enable me, but these are rather
too scanty; and I must beg you to furnish me with some other
books which I shall mention hereafter.

" But, as this survey has given me a further insight into the
subject than I could possibly have before I entered upon it, I
have some further improvements to propose, which I think will
make it worth your while to defer the printing for a month or
two longer, while I go over the volumes a second time upon a
more enlarged plan. For now I have taken the work in hand I
would do my business effectually; and I doubt not but you will
be repaid any expense it may occasion tenfold, for the world is
glutted with the former editions, and fresh inducements should
be given to invite all readers of taste to throw away their former
books and furnish themselves with new copies.

" Permit me then to lay a kind of plan of the improvements
I propose to make, in which, if some of the articles appear trivial, be pleased to attribute it to my desire of being exact, and
of omitting nothing, however minute, that may tend to render
this a standard book.

* Printed in two octavo volumes by Mr. Reeves in the Savoy; see
hereafter, p. 571.

" 1. I would throw out all italics, except in quotations from
other languages. I would have no capitals retained at the beginning of unimportant words. Where any thing is emphatical
it should be distinguished by inverted commas. In short, I
would have the text given according to the neatest manner of
the improved modern printing. I would also have the ornamental frontispieces prefixed to this edition, &c.

" 2. Besides correcting typographical errors, I shall rectify
whatever is faulty in the orthography and pointing. This may
seem a trifling labour; but the neglect of it is the source of
almost all the obscurity and confusion which is found in bad
editions of good authors.

" 3. I propose, wherever I can, to give the names of concealed writers. Many of these I have already recovered; and I
have written to many men of eminence in the republic of letters
for further information. I shall also rectify the initial letters
denoting the respective authors which are subjoined to the several papers; but this properly belongs to the former article.

" 4. To each volume I will prefix a table of contents, in the
same manner as hath been done of late in the Ramblers, Adven-
turers, &c. The reader will thus, with one glance of his eye,
run over a list of the several subjects handled in each volume,
without being bewildered in tumbling over the index; yet, as
this will still have its use, I shall endeavour to correct and enlarge it.

" 5. The mottoes ought generally to be translated anew.
Since your translations of the mottoes first appeared, many new
and more elegant versions of the Classics have been published;
these ought now to take place of the old ones. Since Francis's
Horace has appeared, who can bear to read a quotation from
Creech? I must add further, that it will be sometimes necessary
to give a new translation of the motto particularly adapted to
the subject of the paper to which it is prefixed, because it often
happens that the whole application depends upon some nice turn
of the original phrase, which does not hold in the received versions, even the best of them.

" 6. It is proposed to give short notes wherever they are
wanted, or can be had; never unnecessarily or for ostentation;
but only where a passage is, through length of time, become
obscure. Those admirable essays contained in the Spectators
are generally so clear as to need no comment; yet, as they frequently allude to facts which are no longer known, and reprove
follies and vices which no longer exist, now and then a marginal
note may be needful; yet, because one would not incumber the
pages with a large farrago of annotations, one would give the
notes as sparingly as possible, and always in as few words as may
be. To do this will cost an editor more pains and labour than
to run out into a great prolixity of ostentatious enlargement.
This part of the work will also be the more difficult to execute,

because the things that want explaining are the allusions to popular fashions, modes, and follies, but these are seldom recorded in any books; and all one can hope to learn must be for the most part from personal information. Something, indeed, may be gained from the advertisements and newspapers of those times; and this source of information shall not be neglected.

" Thus, Sir, have I laid before you some of the most important heads of improvement which will give this new edition the advantage of all others. In the course of the work many other smaller improvements will occur which are not here enumerated, and which will all of them contribute to help off a numerous sale. As you are in haste to begin the printing, I could get ready the first volume by Whitsuntide with all these improvements, though possibly the notes may not be so satisfactory or numerous as if I had more time to make inquiry; but as a good deal may be hoped from future discoveries, any posterior ones may be thrown to the end of the volume by way of supplement.

" You have acted by me upon all occasions with so much honour that I can refer very safely the consideration of copy-money to yourself. I shall enter upon the inquiry with great diligence, and give a great portion of my time to it; and I doubt not but you will make it worth my while. When you have seen a volume you will be better able to judge of the value of my labours, though indeed they will be often most exerted where they least appear.

" As I have filled the margin of the Spectators you sent me down before, with all my hints, queries, and private memorandums, I could wish you would send me another copy of the same edition [1753, 12mo] to transcribe my notes fair into for the press; and at the same time accompany them with the several books mentioned in the inclosed list, all of which will be more or less needful for me to have recourse to.

" I have already applied to several men of letters for all the information they can furnish me with. I am ransacking all the books likely to afford it. What if we were to print a modest advertisement to inform the public, that a new edition of this valuable work is intended with notes, &c. and that the proprietor would be extremely obliged to any gentleman that could furnish him with illustrations of any particular passages, or could discover to him the concealed writers of any occasional essays, letters, &c. Something of this kind might be of use; and if you approve of it I will send you up a form of an advertisement.

" I beg your opinion of the foregoing plan. I have described it in too prolix a manner, but I had not time to transcribe or shorten it; therefore excuse any inaccuracies in, Sir,

" Your most obedient servant, THOS. PERCY."

3. *Agreement between Rev. Mr. Percy and Messrs. Tonson.*

"*May* 1764.

" Whereas an edition of the Spectator and Guardian is preparing for the press with explanatory notes on many passages that by length of time are become obscure, and also an account of the names of some of the occasional writers in those books not mentioned in any of the former editions, together with a table of contents to be prefixed to each volume, and new-translations of several of the mottces, by the Rev. Mr. Thomas Percy, of Easton Mauduit, in the county of Northampton.

" Now it is hereby agreed by Jacob and Richard Tonson, Citizens and Stationers of London, of the first part, and the said Mr. Percy on the second part, That, in consideration of the care and trouble the said Mr. Percy will have in preparing the above edition for the press, that the said Jacob and Richard Tonson shall and do hereby agree to pay him the sum of £ 105 in manner following, *viz.* one half part thereof on putting the said work to the press, and the other half when the whole is finished.

" And the said Mr. Percy doth hereby agree with the said Jacob and Richard Tonson, that he will deliver one volume of the Spectator so prepared for the press within one month from the date hereof, and the other seven volumes of the Spectator on or before Christmas next.

" In witness whereof the parties above-named have hereunto set their hands this 25th day of May 1764.

" JACOB TONSON, for self and brother.
" THOMAS PERCY."

Indorsed.

" Received, May 31, 1764, ten guineas in part of payment.
" THO. PERCY.

" Received, June . . . . , ten guineas more in part of payment.
" Drew for ten guineas in favour of Mr. Haslewood.
" Drew for ten guineas in favour of my brother.
" Drew for twelve pounds in favour of Mr. Apperley.

"Agreement with Mr. Tonson for Spectator and Guardian, May 25, 1764, £.105."

---

4. *Account between Rev. Mr. Percy and Messrs. Tonson.*

" J. and R. Tonson, Drs.

To the Rev. Mr. Percy.

		£.	s.	d.
1761, June 12.	By agreement for an edition of the Duke of Buckingham's Works..	52	10	0
1763, March 24.	By an agreement for an edition of Lord Surrey's Poems *	21	0	0
1764, May 5.	By agreement for Notes to Spectator and Guardian.	105	0	0
		£.178	10	0

* Printed in one volume octavo by Mr. Reeves of the Savoy.

Creditors.

		£.	s.	d.
1761, Aug. 15.	Paid you by my notes..........	10	10	0
——— 27.	Paid your draught to Mr. Bateman	21	0	0
Jan. 7.	Paid Mr. Apperley, as by his receipt	6	10	0
1762, Nov. 15.	Paid your draught to ditto........	16	0	0
1763, March 24.	Paid you as by receipt..........	10	10	0
,——— 25.	Paid you by my note payable to Mr. Apperley...................	10	10	
June 1.	Paid your draught to Mr. Thomas Haslewood.................	16	0	0
Oct. 29.	Paid ditto to John Orlebar, Esq...	12	0	0
Dec. 15.	Paid ditto to Mr. Douglas Steer. ..	12	0	0
1764, May 31.	Paid you as by your receipt.......	10	10	0
June 11.	Paid your draught to Mr. George Haslewood · · · ·..............	10	10	0
——— 12.	Paid you as by your receipt.......	10	10	0
——— 15.	Paid your draught to Mr. A. Percy	10	0	0
————	Paid ditto to T. Apperley, Esq.....	12	0	0
July 31.	Paid your draught to Mr. Thomas Haslewood · ·...............	10	10	0
		£.179	0	0

5. *Agreement between Rev. Mr. Percy and Mr. Tonson.*

" Whereas Thomas Percy, clerk, of Easton Mauduit, in the county of Northampton, is preparing for the press a new edition of the Tatler, with explanatory notes, after the manner of his new edition of the Spectator and Guardian now printing; It is hereby agreed between Jacob Tonson, Citizen and Stationer of London, for himself and partners on the one part, and the said Thomas Percy on the other part; that, in consideration of the care and trouble the said Thomas Percy will have in preparing the said edition of the Tatler for the press, the said Mr. Tonson shall, and doth hereby agree to pay him, the sum of £.52. 10s. in manner following, viz. one half part thereof on demand, and the other half when the work is finished.

" In witness whereof the parties above-mentioned have hereunto set their hands this 16th day of March 1765.

" THOMAS PERCY.

" JACOB TONSON, for self and partners."

6. Rev. Mr. PERCY to Rev. WILLIAM COLE.

" SIR, *Easton Mauduit, Northamptonshire, March 9, 1767.*

' Having retired for a few days to my living in the country, your obliging letter followed me down. My new edition of the antient English Poems was nearly printed off before I received your judicious remarks; however, they will add greatly to the value of some Supplemental Notes which I shall throw to the end of each volume.

" What you mention about the pictures of Jane Shore, still preserved at Eton and King's colleges, is curious; and to me entirely new. The first time I go to either of those places I shall not fail to give them an inspection. In the meantime, Sir, I should take it as a favour if you would give me a particular account of the mezzotinto print of her.

" With regard to the poem attributed to Sir Walter Raleigh, and entitled the Lyre, I am still inclined to ascribe it to that great man rather than to the Earl of Essex; though, when it was first written and handed about in manuscript, we may suppose various reports and conjectures would travel about concerning the author, who at first would not be generally known. As Sir Walter survived the Earl so many years, and as the world at last generally agreed in ascribing these verses to the former, I think it may be presumed that he publicly owned them. The open and avowed enmity that was between Sir Walter and the Earl of Essex, I think renders it rather unlikely that there should be any poetical correspondence between them, and therefore I rather suppose the erasure, &c. which you mention in your MS. to be owing to misinformation. Of the two additional stanzas, which you have favoured me with, one, (viz. the last) I have already seen in a MS. copy of this Poem preserved in the British Museum, but from the levity of it I then judged it to be an interpolation; the other is much better. I believe I shall mention them in my supplemental note; but, be that as it may, I am much obliged to you, Sir, for the information, and should be extremely so for a sight of the antient poems of Sir J. Crew, which greatly pique my curiosity, because I have strong reason to believe that my antient folio manuscript, so often quoted in my book, was the work of a Cheshire man, and once belonged to some antiquary of that county. Should you come to town this spring, if you would not think it too much trouble to bring these Poems with you, I should be extremely happy to be indulged with a sight of them, under whatever restrictions, and should gratefully acknowledge the favour.

" Your two other notes, about the ' Hue and Cry after Cupid, and the ' Introduction of Dramatic Writing into Germany, would be curious additions to my book, and, with the former, lay me under great obligation. In return, I beg you will do me the favour to accept of a copy of my new edition, when published, for the improvement of which I hope you will be so good as to transmit me any other remarks that may occur. Any line to me may be inclosed under cover to his Grace the Duke of Northumberland, at Northumberland House, London, where

I should be glad to pay my respects to you in person. I am, with compliments to Mr. Knapp, when you see him, your most obedient humble servant,   T. PERCY *."

7. "DEAR SIR,   *Northumberland House, March* 28, 1767.

" I have received the obliging favour of your letter and the packet you were so good as to send, containing innumerable curiosities, which merit my best thanks. The head of Jane Shore I had never before, and wish you could procure from Mr. Gray the anecdotes you mention about her; but then I must beg the favour not to have my name used to him, as I do not chuse to apply to him for any favour of any kind.

" I should also be glad to see the pedigree you mention of the Percies of Cambridge; and, whenever you come to town, hope you will afford me an opportunity of thanking you in person for all your obliging favours to, dear Sir,

                     " Your most faithful servant,   THOS. PERCY.

" P. S. My friend Mr. Astle (S. S. A.), who was with me when your curious parcel arrived, desires me to inquire whether you had among John Crew's MSS. any papers relating to Staffordshire, particularly any Registers of Religious Houses. He is collecting materials for a History of that County, and would thankfully acknowledge any assistance you would please to give him."

8. Dr. PERCY to RICHARD GOUGH, Esq.

" *Northumberland House, March* 3, 1774.

" Dr. Percy presents his compliments to Mr. Gough; he is just come to town, and finds a very obliging card from Mr. Gough, informing him that he has sent him the copy of Vincent on Brooke, with Sir William Dugdale's manuscript notes; but, as Dr. Percy does not find the book here, he hopes that Mr. Gough has it still in his possession, in which case he earnestly solicits the favour to have it lent him, which will oblige him exceedingly. The inclosed letter followed Dr. Percy into the country; and, as Mr. Paton informed him that it required no haste, he has ventured to keep it till he came to town. He begs the favour of Mr. Gough to let him have Sir David Lindsey's Satirical Play as soon as possible, as he wants to perfect it by a Scottish manuscript lent him out of the Advocates' Library, which he has been called upon to return. Dr. Percy will with pleasure pay the porter that brings Vincent on Brooke and this fragment of Sir D. Lindsey, whenever Mr. Gough pleases to send them. Capt. Grose having given me a small impression of the description of the Hermitage of Warkworth, be pleased to accept of it as it is very exact."

* From the British Museum, Additional MSS. 6401.

9. Dr. Percy to Mr. Nichols.

"Sir, *Northumberland House, Feb.* 11, 1779.

" You flatter me exceedingly by your very obliging present *, which does equal honour to the subject and the author, for I presume they are the same anecdotes which I have been reading with great pleasure in the Gentleman's Magazine. I should be very happy if you would allow me to give you a dish of chocolate when you come this way; and I should be exceedingly glad to see Mr. Iliffe, of Hinckley, should he ever come to town, as I believe he and I are both descended from a sister and a brother of John Cleiveland the Poet, concerning whom I want to pick up some anecdotes to insert in the new edition of the Biographia Britannica. In the mean time pray give my respects to Mr. Iliffe; and desire him to recollect any thing he has heard concerning the Cleiveland family, which I believe came from York into Leicestershire.

" I have lately received a letter from Dr. Nash, who has desired me to inspect the proof of his History, so far as relates to the family and genealogy of Meysey. I can make some improvements there; and am, Sir,

" Your much obliged humble servant, Thos. Percy."

Easton Mauduit (near Bozeate),
10. " Sir, *Northamptonshire, March* 28, 1779.
" A multiplicity of business, in which I was very much engaged before I left town, prevented me from waiting upon you as I intended, which I hope you will have the goodness to excuse; and allow me to request the favour of you to send me the sheet of the History of Worcestershire which contains the account of Bayton (page 54), in order that I may properly connect my genealogy of the Meysey family with the preceding and subsequent page.

" In the cover of this letter you will see directions how you may forward it to me by the post. I should be also much obliged to you for a line to inform me how far the said History is advanced; and pray remember to give me timely notice before you come to those parishes which begin with the letter L, that I may prepare some communications I have to send for Lindridge parish One of the most antient families in that parish, Lowe of the Lowe, is at present represented by the Rev. Mr. Cleiveland (the only male descendant of the Hinckley family), whose mother was a Lowe, and through whom he inherits the estate above-mentioned; this will give me an opportunity of introducing a very curious and full account of the family of Cleiveland of Hinckley, in which you and your relations there are interested as well as myself. I have got large collections relating

---

* An octavo pamphlet, containing memoirs of Mr. Bowyer.

to this subject; and if any further points of inquiry should arise, I will trouble you with my queries, to which you will have the goodness to procure me answers from your friends at Hinckley. Since I had the pleasure of seeing you, I have had occasion to write to my friend and relation Mr. Cleiveland above-mentioned, and he has desired to join with me in compliments to yourself, Mr. Green, and Mr. Iliffe and his family. In looking over my collections, I find that Elizabeth Cleiveland (daughter of the Rev. Thomas Cleiveland, Vicar of Hinckley), who was born in 1626, was married in 1649 to William Iliffe. I presume this couple were the lineal ancestors of your relation the present Mr. Iliffe, of Hinckley. I should be glad if you could procure from him an exact account of the names of all the intermediate generations between him and his said ancestors William Iliffe and Elizabeth Cleiveland. Desire him to set down upon paper the names of his father and mother, grandfather and grandmother, great-grandfather and great-grandmother, with the dates of the year when they died, as also their trades or professions, where they lived and where buried. If you will be so good as to transmit the same to me, I shall then perhaps trouble him with further queries. Inclosed I send a short sketch of Mr. Cleiveland's descent, which may be a sort of direction to Mr. Iliffe.

" Since I saw you, I have read with pleasure your History of Mr. William Bowyer; and the only criticism which occurs at present to me is, that Ichabod Dawkes (whom you mention in p. 1) did not, I apprehend, print a newspaper; but both he and Dyer sent written letters of intelligence all over the kingdom, which was the custom at that time. I remain, Sir,

" Your very obedient humble servant,   THO. PERCY."

---

11. DEAN PERCY to the Rev. THOMAS MAURICE *.

" DEAR SIR,   *Easton Mauduit, Sept.* 5, 1779.

" Upon returning a few days ago from Carlisle, where I have spent all the summer, I received a parcel from Northumberland-house, the packet containing all the copies of your new publication †, together with your very obliging letter. I was quite concerned that it has not been in my power to acknowledge it before, more especially as you have laid me under particular obligation by the honour you have done me in your Poem. As soon as I come to town I will endeavour to collect the several subscriptions for the said books, and, together with my own, pay the same to your order, though I fear it will not be till the end of the year at soonest. I was not long since at Netherby, where I was most hospitably entertained by Dr. Graham; and with plea-

---

* Author of the Indian Antiquities, and of some autobiographical Memoirs, from which this letter is extracted.

† " Poems and Miscellaneous Pieces."

sure talked of you *. We expect the Doctor will attain the
lawn, when I hope he will, by a good benefice, reward the celebrity you have conferred on his villa; this and every other good
that shall befall you will give sincere pleasure to, dear Sir, your
very faithful and most obliged humble servant, THOS. PERCY."

---

12. Dr. PERCY to Mr. NICHOLS.

" DEAR SIR,   *Feb.* 10, 1780.

" Accept a few remarks on the ' Ode to Solitude, by Bevil
Higgins,' in the first volume of your 'Select Collection of Poems.'

" Page 133, stanza ix, the sense, I think, requires to be read
thus :

> ' The raven with his dismal cries
>   (That mortal augury of fate)
> *Those ghastly goblins* † gratifies,
>   Which in these gloomy places wait, &c.

" Page 134, stanza xi, l. 1, ' antick' is a common word to
express gambols, rude sports, plays, awkward motions, &c. Dr.
Johnson's explanation is ' bold, ridiculously wild, buffoon in
gesticulation.' 'Antick marble' signifies marble exhibiting, in
its clouded veins, strange fanciful appearances, to which a
fruitful imagination annexes the resemblance of birds, beasts,
trees, &c.

" Page 136, stanza xvi, *Lege, meo periculo*,

> ' Sometimes the sea *the sand dispels*,
>   Trembling and murmuring in the bay,
> And rolls itself upon the shells
>   Which it,' &c.

" Page 137, stanza xix; l. ult. does not the measure require,

> ' As the flame which *transports* me.'

---

* Mr. Maurice had printed in 1777, " Netherby, a Poem." Dr. Graham was never raised to any dignity in the Church; nor could any
professional income be an object of desire with his great private property, which is prominently noticed in his epitaph, in the Church of
Arthuret, Cumberland: " Near this place are interred the remains of
the Rev. Robert Graham, D.D. the owner and improver of this large
territory, who died February 2, 1782, ætat. 72. Blest with an ample fortune, he regarded not the gifts of Providence in a selfish view, but as
the means of dispensing blessings and happiness to others. He was,
indeed, of a disposition truly kind and beneficent; and the affectionate
family he left, and those who were honoured with his acquaintance, must
long lament the loss of the best of fathers and of friends.

" Here likewise rest the remains of his eldest son Charles Graham,
Esq. who survived his father only a few days."

Dr. Graham's next son was created a Baronet in the following year,
and was father of the present Sir James Graham, of Netherby.

† " Which had been mentioned in the preceding stanza."

"Your engraved heads are neat; but the first of Dryden differs from all the usual representations of that Poet's features, and the last of Steele, I fear, does not represent that author's own face, but a fancied head imagined for Isaac Bickerstaff, the supposed author of the Tatler, being certainly very different from the larger engraving of Steele's countenance, which appears elegant and sensible, whereas this coarse vulgar phiz was prefixed to some editions of the Tatler (if I remember right) as an idea of this gruff old lucubrator. All this I mention to you under the rose, with the utmost freedom of friendship; and to convince you what an anxious interest I take in this your literary offspring, to which you made me sponsor.

" My wife and family join in kind compliments to yourself and spouse, with, dear Sir,

" Your most obliged servant,   THO. PERCY."

13. " DEAR SIR,   *Carlisle, Nov. 24, 1781.*

" The scurrilous attacks that have been made upon me, render it necessary that I should publish a circumstantial relation of what passed with regard to the Earse Poetry in my presence. I could wish to have my inclosed narrative inserted in the Gentleman's Magazine for this month, for which I hope it will not come too late, as you will receive it on the 27th. If it should come time enough, it were to be wished that you would accompany it with the other two advertisements signed Adam Ferguson and W. Shaw ; and that they could all three be arranged in the following order, viz. 1. the advertisement signed Adam Ferguson ; 2. the advertisement signed W. Shaw ; 3. the advertisement signed Thomas Percy. To the whole may be prefixed a short introduction to this effect, or something like it, very short and simple :

" 'The following papers, having been addressed to the public, seem deserving of a place here.'

" As soon as you can get my paper composed correctly in letter-press for the Gentleman's Magazine, I should be much obliged to you if you would be pleased to take off a dozen or score copies of my narrative separately; and get the same inserted, as soon as possible, in each of the following newspapers: the Public Advertiser, Morning Chronicle, St. James's Chronicle, General Evening Post, Whitehall Evening Post, Middlesex Journal, and London Chronicle.

" The three first I would pay any sum to have my narrative inserted in, as Mr. Ferguson's advertisement appeared in them ; but the four others I am less anxious about, though I could wish it inserted in them all as soon as might be convenient.

" Above all, I could wish my narrative and the two others could all appear, conspicuously printed, in the Gentleman's Magazine for this present month ; but, if that is now impossible, then be pleased to have them ready for the Magazine of next month, of which you will be so good as to give me notice as soon as possible, sending me several printed copies of my narrative for me to disperse among my friends.

" As I have preserved no other copy of Shaw's advertisement, &c. I hope you will take particular care of this inclosed. Your obliging services in this affair I shall ever consider as a most important act of friendship to, dear Sir,

" Your faithful servant and kinsman, Tho. Percy.

" P. S. All our compliments to cousin Nichols. I have received the sheets of St. Martin, &c. but cannot inspect them time enough for to-night's post."

I. *Mr. Ferguson's Advertisement.*

" *Edinburgh, July* 21, 1781.

" In a pamphlet intituled, 'An Enquiry into the Authenticity of the Poems ascribed to Ossian,' having read the following passage, p. 45, ' Mr. Smith mentions Dr. Percy's Reliques of Ancient Poetry, in which he says, the Doctor confesseth, that he himself heard pieces of it recited; and being compared with the translation, exactly corresponded. Dr. Percy does not understand a syllable of the Earse, and therefore could be no judge. The truth is, Dr. Blair and Professor Ferguson, when Dr. Percy was at Edinburgh, took care to introduce a young student from the Highlands, who repeated some verses, of which Professor Ferguson said such and such sentences in Fingal were the translation.' To prevent any inferences which might be drawn from my silence, I think it material to declare that the above passage, so far as it relates to me, is altogether false; and that I never was present at the repetition of verses to Dr. Percy by a young student from the Highlands. Adam Ferguson."

II. *Mr. Shaw's Advertisement.*

" *Aug.* 31.

" Having no interest to gratify but the love of truth, I have no reason to be sorry when any falsehood is detected. Mr. Ferguson has denied that he was present when the attempt was made to convince Dr. Percy of the genuineness of Ossian. My relation was not from my own knowledge. I desire to acquit Mr. Ferguson, whose presence or absence makes no difference in the question; and I am too well supported by truth to need, or to wish, the help of falsehood. The attempt was really made, and Dr. Percy was for a while credulous, with which I do not mean to reproach him, for I have confessed that I once was credulous myself; but I shall be credulous no more till the works of Ossian are produced. W. Shaw."

III. *Dr. Percy's Reply.*

" *Carlisle, Nov.* 10, 1781.

" In one or two pamphlets lately published, concerning the authenticity of Ossian's Poems, great liberties have been taken with my name, and two advertisements on the same subject, signed Adam Ferguson and W. Shaw, have appeared in the newspapers; one of which only came to my notice very lately. It is with the greatest reluctance I enter at all into a controversy, of which I am so incompetent a judge, from my utter ignorance of the Earse language; but regard to truth compels me to give the following relation of a fact respecting it, which has been greatly misrepresented.

"On October 8, 1765, I arrived at Edinburgh, where I passed five days with the Rev. Dr. Blair, who, among many learned and ingenious men, introduced me to Dr. Ferguson, Professor of Moral Philosophy. To this gentleman he mentioned some doubts I had entertained concerning the genuineness of Ossian's Poems; and he, in the evening before I left Edinburgh (*viz.* October 13), invited us to drink tea at his house, where he produced a student, a native of the Highlands, who recited several passages or verses, in Earse (some of which he afterwards sung to me) as what he had heard in his own country; and I perfectly remember, that when he interpreted the verses to me, some of them appeared to contain part of the description of Fingal's chariot. Dr. Ferguson also gave me, in his own hand-writing, some specimens of Earse poetry in the original. Dr. Blair afterwards desired me to mention the recital I had heard, in the next edition of the Reliques of Ancient Poetry; and, in compliance with his request, I gave a short account of what had passed in a note to the first volume of my second edition, 1767, (p. xlv). Some years after, on discussing this subject with a very judicious friend, a native of Scotland also, who knew much more of the grounds of the Earse poetry than I did, he made it credible to me, that there might be some deception in the case, and advised me to suppress the passage in question; which I did, soon after, in my third edition, in 1775. But as I never believed Dr. Blair to have been conscious of any deception in what passed between the student and me, so the same may have been the case with Dr. Ferguson also, as he now appears so entirely to have forgot the whole transaction.

"THOMAS PERCY."

———

14 "DEAR SIR,   *Carlisle, Jan.* 10, 1782.

"Your more than filial regard for the Cleiveland family makes me believe you will not dislike any additional information respecting that great ornament of this family the Poet Cleiveland. To the collections you have made on this subject may be added the following note, which was entered by the antiquarian Oldys in a copy of Fuller's Worthies that belonged to him, *viz.*

"[Upon Cleiveland's Poem called the 'Mixed Assembly,' see William Lilly's Merlin for 1654, in which he sets it flying most extensively abroad; whereupon Tho. Gataker, one of that Assembly of Divines, in his Discourse Apologetical, 4to, 1654, has made some animadversions, both on Lilly and Cleiveland, the author of the Satire.] So the MS. note.

" Now I apprehend that an application to your *multiscient* correspondent Mr. Cole may be very likely to procure you a sight or extract, if not from Lilly's Merlin for 1654, which is not so likely to be preserved, yet, from Tho. Gataker's Discourse Apologetical, 4to, 1654, so far at least as he (Gataker) has animadverted on our Poet; and though the animadversions of so rigid a Presbyterian as Gataker on the cavalier Bard must be expected to be very severe and caustic, yet they may give us some new information relating to him, especially at this period of his life (1654) when we know little of him.

" I need not renew to you the information of my having long intended to draw up a Life of him very minute and particular, for the new improved Biographia Britannica, in which I shall probably take the epitome you have printed for my text, and then add all my additional collectanea by way of annotations. Any information you can procure on the above subject will be of great use to me in this scheme, &c. and by the bye I will beg you to inform me, when you think the editors of the new improved Biographica Britannica will get to CLE in their alphabetical arrangement, that I may not be too late for them."

---

15. Mr. Nichols to Bishop Percy.

" MY GOOD LORD,   *April* 24, 1782.

" By some conversation I have had with a few of the principal proprietors in the Spectator, I find there will be no difficulty in the arrangements your Lordship proposes, unless some should arise on determining what were the original terms. The particulars of what was to be paid, and of what has been paid, cannot be obtained for some days.

" If I understand your Lordship right, there is still £.180 to be received, of which Dr. Calder is to have £.100, and myself £.80. If this agrees with the statement of the booksellers, I shall think myself paid, and honoured by being your Lordship's representative in this business; but, if it should turn out that there is not so much as £.80 for me to receive after Dr. Calder's £.100 is paid, it will scarcely be an object of attention to one immersed in business as is your Lordship's most obliged and very faithful servant,   J. NICHOLS."

---

16. Bishop Percy to Mr. Nichols.

" DEAR SIR,   *Northumberland House, April* 24, 1782.

" As I have the several agreements by me, I can tell what has been stipulated, and, I believe, what has been received. I believe there are £.200 still to be paid, of which £.100 to Dr. Calder, the other to you; only of this last £.20 is to be de-

ducted to a Mr. Turner, who assisted me. I mean you shall at
least have £.80, otherwise I should not think of troubling you
about it. If it should not amount to that, as it now it stands, I
must make such a new disposition as that it may; and am sincerely yours,   T. D.
    " N. B. Call on me any morning before ten, and I will show
you my counterparts of the agreement, and other interesting
particulars.

---

    17. " Dear Sir,   *Carlisle, April* 12, 1783.
    " You and Dr. Kippis will, I am sure, with great candour, ex-
cuse the delay of Cleiveland's article for the Biographica Britannica (the text of which has been finished some time, and the
notes only remain to be completed) when you know the distress
in which I and my family have been for near six weeks past
involved, by the unhappy accounts I have received every post of
my son's declining health, who now lies at the point of death at
Marseilles, all hope of his recovery having long been lost. He
received at first great benefit from his voyage to Italy; but the
air at Leghorn and Pisa disagreed with him, and he removed to
the south of France, when, alas! the disease had taken root too
deep to be eradicated, and we hourly expect to hear of its fatal
termination. This has almost reduced his poor mother and sisters here to the same state; and I have had my attention too
much distracted to be able to pursue literary subjects. We are
endeavouring to fortify ourselves to receive the last melancholy
account with all possible resignation; and to submit, as we
ought, to the will of God.
    " I cannot, however, delay my acknowledgement for your last
obliging letter about the Spectators, &c. which mentions the
satisfactory circumstance of your having at last brought the
booksellers to a final agreement on the terms proposed some
time since. Two preliminaries of which were, that they were
to deliver up to you all the sheets of two former works, formerly
projected by the late Jacob Tonson, *viz.* The Works of Villiers
Duke of Buckingham, and the Works of Lord Surrey and Sir
Thomas Wyat, &c. The delivery of all the sheets of both these
publications, so far as they go, into your care, *bona fide* and
without reservation, must be performed without delay; and by
that time you are able to inform me that you have received
them (mentioning the number of copies of each work, and
how far in the alphabet the sheet of each work extend to), I
hope I shall be able to collect my spirits sufficiently to give you
all possible information about the plan, execution, materials,
and assistances for completing the new edition of the Tatlers,
Spectators, and Guardians, according to what is already executed in the second volume of the Spectator, which has been
long ago printed off.
    " Had I consulted only my own interest (who was under no

obligations at Mr. Tonson's death to carry on my scheme with these new proprietors), I might have paid back to his family what money had been advanced by Mr. Tonson, and begun myself a superb edition by private subscription ; which my numerous friends and acquaintance, among people of rank, would have made extremely profitable to me and my family. But I have been content to forego this advantage, and to give it up to the booksellers, with no other reservation than their resigning the sheets of the two petty incomplete works above-mentioned; and therefore I hope they will be sensible of the value of my concession, and without delay deliver up all the sheets to you for my use, to be disposed of as I shall think proper. In your friendship and attachment to me, I place an implicit confidence; and therefore hope soon to hear that you have received them.

" In the mean time, with what application I can bring my mind to give, I will proceed to finish the article of Cleiveland, and send it up to you as soon as finished.

" We all join in kind respects to cousin Nichols and yourself; beseeching the Almighty that you may never like us experience the loss of an only son, when, with fondest hopes, we had seen him ripen into perfect manhood.

" I remain, dear Sir, very truly yours,   Tho. Dromore."

---

18. Bishop Percy to Mr. Allen *.

" My good Mr. Allen,   Carlisle, April 26, 1783.

" You will I know be much concerned to hear that a fatal consumptive complaint hath deprived me of my son, whom I sent last autumn to try the effect of a warmer climate, but in vain; for, after lingering through the winter, he deceased at Marseilles in the south of France about the beginning of this month, though we did not receive the account till lately. Our sorrow, though great, is alleviated by the assurance we have received from the clergyman that attended him, that his reflections in his last illness were proper and devout, and that he appeared deeply affected with those religious impressions which give us a comfortable hope that he has only been removed from youthful temptations to a blessed immortality.

" If you mention our loss to your good neighbours Dr. Johnson and Mrs. Williams, I know they will kindly sympathise with us.

" Will you now allow me to trouble you to call in Serjeant's-inn, and pay my assurance for the last quarter, £.1. 5s. before the 3d of May. I have given a draught on the other side. The other 10s. be pleased to give to poor Mrs. Rolt at Mr. Townsend's, tallow-chandler, No. 396, facing Cecil-street, Strand, merely to remind her that I do not forget her (this small sum

---

* Dr. Johnson's neighbour, landlord, and " dear friend." See a notice of him in the " Literary Anecdotes," vol. IX. p. 417 ; but his name was Edmund not Edward.

is a balance of an account with Messrs. Gosling, or I should make it more, as I shall hereafter). Tell her I received her letter, but am too full of trouble at present to write, and I have not the least acquaintance with Mr. Wallis, about whom she writes to me, or I would apply to him to pay her what is due for her attendance at the Opera-house. Perhaps if she relates her tale to you, you can put her in way to be paid, or perhaps Dr. Johnson would generously serve her in it; she is really a great object of compassion. Excuse all this trouble. Mrs. Percy joins in compliments, with, dear Mr. Allen,

"Your obliged servant, THO. DROMORE."

------

19. BISHOP PERCY to Mr. NICHOLS.

"DEAR SIR, *Carlisle, May* 16, 1783.

" I have duly received your obliging letters in succession, and shall now endeavour to give you a sketch of the original plan for the improved edition of the Spectators, &c. as settled between Mr. Tonson and myself, near twenty years ago, at least I think in 1764, but which my becoming Domestic Chaplain and Secretary to the present Duke of Northumberland prevented me from executing, as my time became appropriated, and his Grace's employment left me not sufficient leisure for so voluminous a piece of editorship.

" Mr. Tonson's intention was not to exceed the original number of volumes. The Spectators were still to be confined to eight, the Tatlers to four, and the Guardians to two. For this reason the notes were to be short as possible, and to be confined merely to necessary explanation or illustration. It was intended that these should principally relate to manners and customs, give concealed names and characters, and point out hidden allusions and less obvious references.

" How this was performed and executed you will see in those sheets of the second volume, 12mo, which were then printed, of this intended edition. There you will see a specimen of this work, the aim of which was to give,

" 1. A correct text, chiefly printed from the first octavo edition, which was published under Steele's own inspection, and received from his pen, or that of Addison, while it went through the press, innumerable alterations and improvements, as may be seen by comparing this octavo edition with the original papers; and among your materials you will find one 12mo copy, collated throughout, with the original papers; and you have also the said original papers bound up in volumes, as also complete copies of the octavo editions, which ought generally to be your text, except in such numbers of the Spectator, Tatler, and Guardian as were republished by Tickel in the four volumes of Addison's Works, 4to, where it may be supposed the latest improvements of Addison's pen are correctly given. These four volumes, therefore, will give you a standard text for all Addison's papers; and will clearly point out what parts of the Tatler were written by him, which otherwise would not have been so well ascertained. For all the other papers you should follow the first octavo edition, and where any oversight appears consult the original papers, and the next edition after the first octavo.

" 2. Notes; these I said were principally to illustrate and explain forgotten customs and manners, obscure references, and local and temporary or personal allusions. Among the notes sometimes it would be curious and entertaining to give some of the original passages as they stood in first fugitive publication in the separate papers, and to show how they were altered when they were collected into volumes. In one or two instances you will find the papers has been new written for the 8vo edition, and frequently paragraphs omitted or inserted ; these may properly be thrown into the notes. The advertisements, &c. at the end of the original papers will frequently illustrate passages in the papers themselves, pointing out the reigning amusements, follies, and topics of conversation alluded to in the text.

" 3. To give the names of the concealed authors, wherever they can be recovered. Bishop Pearce wrote some numbers ; so did Lord Chancellor Hardwicke and Mr. Hughes, besides several others, who were more or less occasional correspondents. Some of these are recovered, and perhaps others may be communicated to you for a subsequent edition when once the public hath seen the attempt.

" 4. To give more elegant translations of all the mottoes and classical quotations, from the latest and best versions of the classics. The common current editions give the mottoes as translated by Creech for Horace and Theocritus, those of Virgil from Dryden (which, though perhaps more elegant and spirited than that of Pitt, is frequently more remote from the original, and often gives quite a different idea from that alluded to in the Spectator,) &c. Of late years we have had all the classics re-translated; and most of them far better than they had been done when the mottoes were first published. Sometimes, however, no printed version will quite give the turn or peculiar phraseology which is alluded to; there a new translation should be attempted, or that of any printed version altered or adapted to the particular purpose. You will see some instances in the specimen given in the second volume.

" 5. A table of contents to each volume, in the manner of the Rambler, Adventurer, &c. giving, in a concise manner, the subject of each paper, and the name of the author, as for instance,

" Volume I. No. 7. On Vulgar Superstition.   Addison.
" No. 8. On the Masquerade.   Ditto (or, The same).
" No. 19. On Envy.   Steele.
" No. 24. On Impertinence.   Ditto.

" If this is done properly to each volume, then one general Index will do for the whole. Where the author is not known, then say anonymous, and sometimes, various writers.

" And here I think the original single letters should still be kept subscribed at the end of each paper as Addison and Steele fixed them in the Spectators, *viz.* CLIO for Addison and R. S. T. for Steele, except in the Tatlers, &c. where Addison's name may be given at length; but wherever in the Spectators any concealed occasional writers are recovered, there you may mention it in a note.

" This is the general outline ; and the specimen of the execution may be seen in the sheets of the second volume, which you must examine, as far as it goes. I know not also but there were some sheets of the third volume also printed. These sheets you must get and gather them into a volume ; though when you re-print them you will probably much enlarge the notes if you increase the size and number of volumes. In which, however, I question but you will injure the sale, as the former size will be the object of cheaper purchase, and probably occasion a preference to be given to printed editions. This at least was Mr. Tonson's opinion, and for this reason he meant to contract the notes, &c. as above-mentioned ; however, all this I leave to you and the booksellers.

" I at first thought only of publishing the Spectators; then Mr. Tonson persuaded me to take in the Tatlers and Guardians also, and I made collections for them all, which you have in your possession. Being obliged to decline the work, Dr. Calder took it up; and he can give you further information, and assist you in executing it, I doubt not, sufficiently well. He had written in interleaved volumes notes, &c. which should, however, be carefully revised before they are committed to press. This revisal I should have performed myself for him last year if Mr. Rivington had readily closed with the business, but he made it so disagreeable, that I had no pleasure in thinking any more of the subject at that time, and I cannot be answerable for any part of the work but those sheets of the second volume, which near twenty years ago were printed under my own inspection. Ever since I have collected all the books and papers that I thought might be of use; and with their assistance and your own great fund of this sort of knowledge and happy skill at illustration and biographical commentary (as displayed in Dr. King's Works, your Supplement to Swift, and Life of Bowyer), you will, I am persuaded, give such an edition of the Tatlers, Spectators, and Guardians as will render those useful and entertaining volumes new favourites with the public, and renew the property to the booksellers.

" Whether Dr. Calder has the interleaved volumes by him, or whether they are amidst the great mass of materials and collections delivered last year to you, you will soon see, and by applying to him will have ready assistance and full information in many particulars which may have escaped my recollection.

"I must apprize you that I am not sure that in the sheets of my said second volume the text was correctly printed from the octavo edition, nor from Tickel's Works, as to Addison's Papers; nor are the variations from the fugitive original papers noted, for I think these and other improvements occurred after those sheets were printed off. When you re-print those sheets make all these improvements in the text and notes; but you must by all means get those sheets from Rivington the printer.

"One part of our plan I have omitted above, which was to mention in a short note at the end of any paper (when the subject was left unfinished) in what succeeding number it would be found resumed; and so at the beginning of that succeeding number the reader was to be informed where he would find what had been premised.

"This at present is all I recollect of the general plan; if any thing material should occur hereafter, I will mention it in a future letter; and if you wish to ask any questions I will answer them to the best of my power; and I shall send you some notes, particularly some from a MS. of Dean Swift.

"You will, I presume, begin with the Tatlers*. If you think Harrison's fifth volume has merit enough to deserve to be revived, you will, I suppose add it. I do not sufficiently remember what its merit is, but I fear below par; and care I think should be taken not to add too much to the work, perhaps sinking into oblivion from its present exuberance. A good deal of the Tatler is taken up with mere articles of news now uninteresting. Do not think it necessary to enlarge this useless part by any notes.

"You have, I presume, Dr. Calder's address; if not, only send to Mr. Elmsly (his intimate friend) and he will give you a direction to him, which just this moment I cannot recollect.

"We are all still drooping with our sad loss; but much obliged to you both for your very kind inquiries, and wishing you all health and happiness.

"I remain, dear Sir, truly yours,   T. DROMORE."

"P. S. I do not use the franks for this, which is only a double sheet, because when I get to Ireland I shall find it difficult to get franks to you, and thence the postage will be very heavy.

"I must now desire you immediately to get all the books and papers, &c. which relate to the two publications of Buckingham and Surrey, carefully packed up in a box, and add thereto any thing else you may have for me, well secured by close and neat

---

* This annotated edition consisted chiefly in the publication of the Tatlers, in six volumes 8vo. 1786. The principal merit of the edition is due to Dr. Calder. Mr. Nichols wrote the preface, and contributed several notes. The edition was commented on by Lord Hailes, in Gent. Mag. vol. LX. See Index to "Literary Anecdotes," vol; VII. pp. 411, 687.

package from rubbing and shuffling about, and send the said box by the very first Carlisle waggon."

20. " DEAR SIR,   [*Undated.*]
" Whilst you are at Hinckley, pray endeavour to obtain answers to the following queries :
" 1. To see if there are any monuments or epitaphs relating to the Cleivelands of Hinckley, and to copy them, if there are ; and the same of any of the families descended from them.—2. To note, if there any where preserved, portraits of any of the above.—3. To inquire if there is any traditional remembrance, what was the family-name of Elizabeth, the wife of the Rev. Thomas Cleiveland, Vicar of Hinckley; who was father of John Cleiveland the Poet, and of Elizabeth, wife of William Iliffe. (N. B. Thomas Cleiveland was married to her before he removed from Loughborough to Hinckley in the reign of King James I.) —4. Joseph Cleiveland, an attorney, one of the sons of the Rev. Thomas Cleiveland, Vicar of Hinckley, lived at Hinckley, where he had estate ; he had two wives. The first wife brought him a son and several daughters. The son was John Cleiveland, who removed to Liverpool, where he was a merchant, and acquired a very great fortune ; so that in Queen Anne's reign he was a Member of Parliament for Liverpool. The second wife of Joseph Cleiveland was a very severe step-mother to his first children, and spent all their fortune, as also the family estate. She had only a daughter. But afterwards, on her death-bed, she had such remorse for her ill treatment of her husband's children, that she sent to Liverpool to ask forgiveness of her son-in-law John Cleiveland aforesaid; and he either went to her, or sent her the most ample tokens of friendship,—Query, if the names of the said wives of Joseph Cleiveland can be recovered, or any remembrance what the estate was, or any account of the above particulars?"

21. " DEAR SIR,   *June* 19, 1783.
" I received safe the box of books ; and have been reading with great pleasure the History of Hinckley, which, contrary to all my expectation from the subject, you have made extremely entertaining and interesting. Before the next edition I shall propose a few corrections or remarks ; and the same to your Memoirs of Bowyer, which I also read over with great pleasure. I have received safe all the pamphlets sent me by post ; and am now going to Ireland, where I hope to be settled next week at Segoe, near Lough-Brickland, north of Ireland. Hereafter I shall desire to have the Magazines and Pamphlets, &c. sent me thither by the post, the same as hither; but our Irish Parliament is going to be dissolved, when all franking will cease for some time, and every letter will be three times the expense it is to

Carlisle. So only send me single letters till I give notice ; after-wards all letters and packets will come free to me. With your leave I shall order my poor son's books, &c. to be sent from Cambridge to your house, to be kept till further orders ; and I shall also send a small parcel from hence to your friendly man-sion, with proper directions therein what to have done with the contents. I am,

"Dear Sir, sincerely yours, &c.   T. DROMORE.

"P. S. I hope you will find in this Life of Cleiveland, though so often sifted before, some things rather new to you. We have now pinned up the basket."

22. BISHOP PERCY to Mr. ALLEN.

"DEAR MR. ALLEN,   *Dromore, Dec.* 28, 1783.

" You may do good by stealth, and hope it will be concealed, but it will get vent in spite of all your attempts at conceal-ment. Poor Mrs. Rolt's gratitude would not let her obey your instructions of keeping secret your kind donations to her. It grieves me that she should be more indebted to you, a mere stranger, than to me her relation, in a situation of such appa-rent splendour; but, I assure you, my good friend, I never knew what it was to want money like what I have done since my great preferment. The laity little knew the heavy burdens that over-whelm us ecclesiastics. The moment I entered on my Bishopric, I became debtor to my predecessor in the sum of three thousand two hundred pounds for a new episcopal house, which, by the laws of Ireland, is charged upon the successor, and must be paid out of the first receipts of the See. In consequence of this I had £.1,200 to pay at the end of the first year (besides £.200 for my patent) when I had only received £.900. To add to my burdens, my brother, whose unprosperous affairs had long been a great drawback from my revenue, is now this month become a bankrupt, and has involved me in losses occasioned by my being security for him; and is moreover with his family to be maintained by me into the bargain. So you see that all is not gold that glistens,—that under a mitre there may be heavy cares and grievous disappointments. But of all that I have suffered in consequence of these distresses, none have given me more concern than that I have been prevented by them from fulfilling my kind intentions to poor Mrs. Williams. I had engaged to add £.10 *per annum* to her little annuities, of which I had only been able to advance her five guineas before she was snatched away from me; and all my intentions of making it up to her by greater kindness in future, rendered abortive. I wish you would mention this to Dr. Johnson, lest I should have suffered in his opinion from what may have appeared a wanton breach of my engagement, which I believe I entered into with his pri-vity, as indeed it was he that kindly suggested it ; but before I

could be charitable it was my duty to be just; and to this hour
I have never been able to pay your bill, but I do not forget it;
and I even rely so far on your candour and generosity as to
request a further favour, which is this. Poor Mrs. Rolt has written to request I would assist her with a little money to pay the
arrears of rent. Though I am at this time involved with the
troubles of my brother's bankruptcy, I am unwilling the poor
woman should sink under her distresses, and if you will, with
your wonted goodness, call on her and learn what sum will
do; if it does not exceed five guineas I will advance it, or repay
it to you, if you dare give me credit for so much till I can remit
it you. I have also written to Mr. Stirling (agent to the Duke,
at Northumberland-house) to desire that when his Grace's
annual benefactions are distributed, he will remind the almoner
(who is this year a new one) of the old pensioners to whom you
have usually conveyed his Grace's annual charity; so that, if you
will be so kind as to call on him with the wonted list, I trust their
donations will be continued. I could only recollect the names
of Mrs. Rolt and Mrs. M'Mullein. Mrs. Percy and my family
desire to join with me in kind respects to you, and in begging
you will present the same to our good friend Dr. Johnson, concerning whose health any intelligence will be gratefully received
by, dear Sir, your faithful humble servant, Tho. Dromore."

---

23. Bp. Percy to Dr. Douglas, Bishop of Carlisle *.
"*Dromore House*, 1787.
"Having accidentally heard that your Lordship was about to
pay a visit to Rose Castle, and make some stay there, I could not
resist the inclination I had to present my compliments, on your
connection with a country where I spent some time agreeably,
and where I should have probably been now waiting to receive
your Lordship as Dean of your Cathedral, if you had not yourself kindly interposed and sent me hither. * * * * In troubling your Lordship with this detail, I presume on your benevolence, and that it is possible you may not be altogether unin-
terested concerning the lot which you were the means of procuring me."

---

24. Bishop Percy to Mr. Nichols.
"Dear Sir,   *Dromore House, May 6,* 1788.
"It was but lately that in this remote region I heard of your
very great loss by the death of my cousin, which gave me very
sincere concern, as she seemed a most amiable young woman;
and I cannot but sympathise with you in your affliction. To

* From the Biographical Memoir prefixed to the Select Works of
Bishop Douglas, by the Rev. William Macdonald, now Archdeacon of
Wilts.

urge the common topics of comfort to a mind so well informed as yours, is, I am persuaded, unnecessary, and would appear impertinent ; but I have never myself, under severe trials of that kind, found any so efficacious as those suggested by religion, and the well-grounded hope which it inspires of a future re-union.

" I have been myself this winter very near experiencing a similar loss. Mrs. Percy was seized at the beginning of December with a bilious fever which held her confined more or less for near three months, under which she had several relapses of so dangerous a kind that more than once we despaired of her life ; she is now, thank God, pretty well recovered, and joins with me in compliments of condolence.

" I have been long intending you a remittance; and only wait for some payments to be made into the hands of my banker, which have been long due, when you shall hear again from, dear Sir, your very obedient humble servant, Tho. Dromore.

" Allow me to inquire what young family you have surviving from my late amiable relation."

---

25. " Dear Sir,   *April* 10, 1790.
" I have seen your Magazine for March *, and in your account of our great philanthrope Howard, you say no attempt ever succeeded to catch his likeness, &c. I hope you will find yourself agreeably disappointed by the inclosed †, which was published by Mr. Allen, a printseller in Dublin, some time since ; and is at your service to be re-engraved if you think proper.
                    " Yours truly,   Tho. Dromore."

---

26. " Dear Sir,   *March* 10, 1794.
" I so much approve of your account ‡ of our poor friend and relation Mr. Cleiveland, that I shall be glad to find that

* Vol. LX. p. 279.
† See the Magazine for August 1790, vol. LX. p. 685.
‡ The Rev. William Cleiveland, M.A. was Rector of All Saints parish in Worcester, of which he had been incumbent near thirty-seven years, having, Feb. 8, 1758, succeeded his father, the Rev. William Cleiveland, M. A. who had been presented to the same by that excellent prelate Bishop Hough, and instituted by him June 10, 1731. So that the father and son had held this benefice upwards of sixty-three years, even from the very birth of the latter, who may be said to have spent his whole life, from his cradle to his death-bed, in the parsonage-house at All Saints; for which he had such a predilection, and such an attachment to this his first and only church (although attended with very severe duty, which he continued to the last to discharge himself), that no desire or prospect of preferment could tempt him to forsake it ; for, the person who favoured us with this account hath assured us, that, to his knowledge, he once refused the offer of a considerable benefice, which would have required him to abandon his beloved parishioners at All Saints. This conscientious worthy clergyman (who has died without issue) was the last of the

mine came too late, in which case do not insert mine in the
next month, but let your own close the subject."

---

27. BISHOP PERCY to Mr. NICHOLS.

" DEAR SIR, *Worcester, June* 12, 1795.
" By favour of Dr. Nash I yesterday received the parcel you
were so good as to send, accompanied with your obliging letter.
I arrived here a few days since, and am busy settling the affairs
of our poor deceased relation Mr. Cleiveland, who, through his
want of health and spirits, poor good man, left them in much
confusion; and the personal estate barely sufficient to pay his
debts, if so much. I shall reserve further particulars till I see
you, which I hope to do next week without fail. This being the
case, I will beg you to defer printing off the odd leaf (vol. I.
p. 4) till I see you. I am sorry to hear of the death of so
respectable a relation as Mr. Iliffe*; on his account I shall resume
black wax, which I had laid aside; and am, with sincere compliments of condolence, dear Sir,
    " Your very faithful servant,   THO. DROMORE."

---

28. " DEAR SIR, *Near Northampton, June* 22, 1797.
" I received yesterday the packet containing the requested
volumes of Leland's Itinerary and your obliging letter, in which
your very reasonable request to be accommodated with the payment of *£.*100, so long promised you, ought to be immediately
complied with; and should have been followed by this post by a
draught on my bankers if you had not kindly suggested the hint
of drawing on Messrs. Rivington, who have never yet accounted
for one shilling of the receipts on the Reliques, &c. I have, there-

name of Cleiveland, of the family at Hinckley, which produced the celebrated Royalist, John Cleiveland the Poet, to whom this Mr. Cleiveland's
grandfather was nephew; as may be seen in the History of Hinckley,
1782, 4to, pp. 134 et seq.; in Dr. Nash's History of Worcestershire,
vol. II. p. 95; and in Biographia Britannica, vol. III. art. Cleiveland.—
He was born June 27, 1731; educated at Magdalen-hall, Oxford, where
he proceeded B. A. 1754; M. A. 1757. He married in 1767 Mary, daughter of James Jones, Esq. of Stadhampton in Oxfordshire, an amiable
lady, whom he had the misfortune to lose in 1777, six days after the birth
of a daughter, an only child, who lived but two days. He was a most
exemplary parish priest, a man of benevolence, and blended with the
strictest purity of manners a cheerful conviviality, which rendered his
company and conversation peculiarly desirable.—He died Oct. 28, 1794,
aged 63.
 * Mr. Joseph Iliffe was a respectable hosier at Hinckley. After having
lived within a week of 76 years in the same house in which he was born,
he died March 5, 1795, universally respected. He was a strenuous supporter of the Church, a loyal subject to his Sovereign, and to his friends
unboundedly benevolent. A pedigree of the family of Iliffe may be seen
in the History of Leicestershire, vol. IV. p. 708.

fore, by this post written to them, to desire they will accept my bills in your favour to that amount, which for their own convenience I have told them shall be drawn in such proportions, and payable at such times, as will suit them best, &c. Should they evade compliance, or propose distant times inconvenient for you, I will then send you a draught for £.100, payable by Messrs. Goslings to you or your order, at one month after date, by which time I hope to have remittances from Ireland to meet the same.

" And though I do not mention it as even wishing to delay my payment to you, I shall inform you as my friend, that in the troubled state of our part of Ireland, not only our rents are not well paid, but of even what is received for me I am obliged to allow my steward to advance the greater part for the present payment of the Yeomen Infantry, which we have been raising in Dromore for the protection of the vicinage ; this I expect will, at some future time, be re-paid by the Treasury of Ireland, but in the present exigence it has no money, and I am advancing between £.60 and £.70 a month of that very money which should be remitted for me and my family (after having given £.100 donation towards their original equipment). Of £.400, which had been received for me of the last March rents, &c. I could only have £.100 remitted me for my own use. This is a situation of a country, of which my English brethren have no experience, and I trust in Heaven they never will, nor any of their flocks. At the same time I have very good hope of the final issue, from the very proper exertions of Government, for the deluded are now coming in and submitting, and their seducers are flying away that can, to which the happy and providential restoration of our navy must exceedingly contribute.

" The constant interruption of our Irish disturbances, and some other domestic avocations, have so exceedingly engaged me, that I have not lately been able to attend to your business so much as I now hope to do, and thereby release you from tedious delays, which you have borne with a friendly patience, which I ought to acknowledge ; and for which I must ever consider myself, dear Sir, your obliged and faithful servant, Thos. Dromore.

" P. S. I thank you for your kind congratulations on the birth of a fine healthy grandson. I hope my young relations and all the rest of your family are well as possible."

---

29. " Dear Sir,   Dromore, March 29, 1799.
" The Gentleman's Magazine reaches this remote part but slowly, so that I did not see till lately your queries, &c. relating to Rev. Martin Hill, of Asserby, &c. vol. LXVIII. pp. 372, 570. I suppose you know that Geo. Hill, Esq. the King's Ancient Serjeant, is the lineal descendant of the said Martin Hill, because I believe it is so recorded by Bridges ; but perhaps you do not know that my wife is a descendant, her mother being Anne

Hill, daughter of Joseph Hill, Gent. great-uncle of the Serjeant. I have some curious particulars relating to that family, but they are with my other papers at Ecton, the seat of Mr. Isted, near Northampton; if I go there this summer I will rummage among them for you, but I know not of any writings published by Martin Hill.

" You have been very good to bear with the delays about Surrey, &c. which our troubles in Ireland have occasioned, but I hope ere long to finish all.

" What an illiberal charge of Mr. Ashby, that they got the Roman mile stone* to repair the roads! whereas Mr. Pochin removed it to the turnpike-house, to preserve it for the inspection of the curious; but I have more to tell upon that subject than I have room for here."

30. " Dear Sir, *Ecton, near Northampton, Sept.* 13, 1800.

" I have been inquiring of the editors of the British Critic, when justice would be done to your highly-meritorious labours; and am concerned to find that, although the review of your third volume was finished before the end of August, it cannot appear earlier than in the British Critic for October; but Mr. Nares has expressed so much respect for you, and has assigned such reasons for the delay, that I believe we must excuse it. The interest I take, as a Leicestershire freeholder, in your valuable work, and my personal regard for the public-spirited author, must be my excuse for giving you this trouble; who, I hope, will believe me to be very truly, dear Sir,

" Your faithful and obedient servant, Thos. Dromore.

" P. S. My kind respects to my kinsman your son.

" Should you see Mr. Rivington, be pleased to inform him, that on account of some particular interruptions, which I will explain hereafter, the fourth volume of the Reliques (as proposed) by my nephew, is obliged to be postponed."

31. " Dear Sir, *Dromore House, May* 19, 1802.

" On the 13th I transmitted some Memoirs†, &c. for your next month's Magazine, which I hope will come safe to hand. I have just seen the new edition of Goldsmith's Miscellaneous Works ‡ in four volumes octavo, the press-work of which does honour to your printing-office, and, as I conceive, to my kinsman your son, who I presume superintended it; but the proprietors would have done well to have consulted me in the selection and

* The Roman Miliary, now at Leicester. See Hist. of Leic. I. p. cliv.
† A Memoir, it is believed, of Dr. James Johnstone, of Galabank, eminent for his skill and humanity during a practice of more than fifty years in the city and county of Worcester. See Gent. Mag. vol. LXXII. p. 473.
‡ This edition of Goldsmith's works was edited in 1801, by Samuel Rose, Esq. barrister-at-law. See " Literary Anecdotes," vol. III. p. 387.

arrangement, for they have omitted one of the very best productions of Goldsmith, although it had been particularly pointed out in the account of his Life,—his ' Introduction to Brooke's Natural History,' and have only given his ' Preface ' to that work, far inferior to the former.   This is what they got by quarrelling with me for only supplicating a little assistance in advance to Goldsmith's poor niece, who was starving, for I would have given them every advice and direction gratis; but they carried their ill-humour so far as to refuse to let me see and make some corrections in the MS. Life of Goldsmith, which had been compiled under my direction.   They have also omitted noticing, that the Epilogue, now first printed in vol. II. p. 82, is given from a MS. in Dr. Goldsmith's own hand-writing, which he had given to me as well as the other, which they have noticed in the note p. 88.   I have only just looked into vols. II. and IV. and immediately stumbled upon these defects ; I fear I shall find others.

" I gave them the foregoing original unedited Poems of Goldsmith in consideration of their delivering 250 copies for me to dispose of for the benefit of Goldsmith's poor relations, of which 125 might be sold in England, the remainder in Ireland. The former are delivered to Mr. White, to whom I offered 100 copies for 100 guineas to be paid in six months ; but he utterly refuses to take them on those terms, although the price to the trade in sheets he says is twenty-six shillings each copy, but he says he can have as many as he pleases at twenty-two shillings, and have a twelvemonth's credit.   Indeed he offers me no terms at all, so that I am at a loss how to proceed, and am sorry I sent them to him.   Having no interest in it myself, and wishing only to serve the poor woman, pray favour me with your advice ; and (as far only as may be proper without giving offence to any of the trade) your assistance how to dispose of them to the best advantage for their benefit.   Whatever you suggest shall be in perfect confidence.   I am distressed for the poor niece, who is in want ; and the more concerned at this refusal of Mr. White, as I am unexpectedly prevented from being in London at this time, where upon the spot I would have struggled for them.   But Parliament will now be ended before I can come over, and therefore I shall defer my visit to England ; and, as my privilege of franking will cease the day Parliament is dissolved, I must beg your answer, and the copies of the memoir before that takes place.   With kind respects to your son, I am, dear Sir,

" Yours sincerely,   Tho. Dromore."

---

32. " Dear Sir,   *Dromore House, May* 14, 1803.
" This day's post brought me your most obliging letter, which is so expressive of sincere regard that I cannot allow it to remain unacknowledged, if but by a single line.   Permit me at

the same time to request that you will take off two dozen of
copies of the two Poems I sent you. This will extremely oblige
me, who desire you will present my kind respects to my young
kinsman your son, and all your family; being, with every good
wish for you and yours, dear Sir,

       "Your faithful servant,   THO. DROMORE."

33. "DEAR SIR,   *Dromore House, Jan.* 11, 1805.

    " With my best wishes and compliments of the season to you
and all your family, I inclose a little packet, which I hope will
come time enough for your next Magazine.

    " My eyes are declining so fast that, although I sketched out
part of the notes, which I could scarce read when I had written
them, yet the rest being committed to a secretary, I must recommend them, as well as what I had written myself, to a careful
examination.

    "Our Infant Bard * continues to make a wonderful progress, as
you will see by the inclosed; and will, if he lives, I doubt not
verify the most sanguine hopes of his friends. As you will have
had the merit of first announcing his genius to the world, the
inclosed will, I am persuaded, give you pleasure. Believe me to
be very truly, dear Sir,

    "Your obliged and faithful servant,   THO. DROMORE †."

34. "DEAR SIR,   *Dromore House, April* 11, 1805.

    " I send you the inclosed ‡ to be inserted in the Gentleman's
Magazine for this month, which you may announce to the world
as written by Thomas Romney Robinson, the Infant Bard of
Belfast, who is not yet twelve years of age, though he will have
completed his twelfth year on the 23d of this month. See the
account of him in the Gentleman's Magazine for January, p. 64.

    Although the failure of my sight prevents me from coming to
England, and completing there some literary plans I had formed,
yet I will soon endeavour to ease you of some of the sheets with
which you have been so long incumbered; and for your patiently
submitting to the same I cannot sufficiently express my obligation. It is also my intention to make a complete settlement with
you, and pay whatever is due to you for paper, press-work, and
every other demand. In the mean time I beg you will be assured
of my kind regards for you, and all your family, who will ever
have the best wishes of, dear Sir,

    "Your faithful servant and kinsman,   THO. DROMORE."

* Named in the next letter.
† This signature is that engraved under the Bishop's portrait, p. 552.
‡ An Elegy on the death of Clotworthy Earl of Massareene; see Gent.
Mag. vol. LXXV. p. 359.

35.   *" Dromore House, July* 18, 1805.

" The Bishop of Dromore presents his compliments to Mr. Nichols, and has now the pleasure to inform him, that he hopes soon to bring the publication of Lord Surrey's Poems, &c. to a conclusion, which the gradual failure of his sight has for a considerable time prevented. A son of the Rev. Mr. Boyd, the ingenious translator of Dante, has been appointed Curate of Dromore. He was lately a student of Trinity-college, Dublin; and has genius and learning which fully qualify him for any literary undertaking. To him the Bishop will now assign the completion of that work, and he is already engaged in examining the sheets heretofore published; and also preparing a glossary of the obsolete words. As Mr. Nichols will in due time hear from him, it may be necessary to mention, that his contracted signature is H. E. Boyd, but his names at length are Hannington Elgee Boyd."

---

36. " DEAR SIR,   *Dromore House, Dec.* 11, 1805.

" It is so long since I informed you that a Glossary was preparing for Surrey's Poems, that, not having heard of it since, you have doubtless concluded that it was wholly neglected and the subject forgotten, nor could I blame you for entertaining such an opinion; but the truth is, it has both been undertaken and finished by young Mr. Boyd, son of the translator of Dante, whom I have engaged to complete the publication of Surrey's Works, and he would before this have proceeded to the conclusion of it, but it has necessarily been delayed while he waited for some materials for the lives of the authors, and to add to the specimens of blank verse; but we now hope every difficulty will be removed before the conclusion of this Session of Parliament, at the end of which my power of franking will commence, and then I can both receive and transmit proof sheets, &c. free of postage. The failure of my sight, which is nearly approaching to total blindness, and it is with difficulty I subscribe my name, will prevent me from attending Parliament in person.

" Whatever profits may arise from this publication, after all expenses of printing, &c. and your long arrears have been discharged, I shall desire may be divided between Mr. Boyd, the editor, and your son my young kinsman, whom I shall request to accept the same as a small token of my regard.

" I know not whether you are a subscriber to Mr. Manning's History of Surrey, but if you are not I shall desire you to accept the copy for which I have subscribed, for I am incapable of reading a word of it myself. You will inform me if my offer does not come too late; and with my compliments to your son, his spouse, and sisters, and every good wish for you and your family, I remain, dear Sir,

" Your faithful and obedient servant,   THO. DROMORE."

37.   " *Dromore House, Feb.* 10, 1807.

" The Bishop of Dromore presents his kind respects to Mr. Nichols. He has heard with great concern from the Rev. Mr. Meen of the very afflicting accident which befel him, but hopes he is fast recovering, and that his health will be fully restored.

" The very obliging manner in which the Bishop's severe loss is recorded in the Gentleman's Magazine of last month, and the verses of Mr. Stott, signed Hafiz, will probably induce the editor to accept and insert the inclosed tribute of respect from the translator of Dante in the next number."

---

38. Mr. H. E. Boyd to Mr. Nichols.

" *Nov.* 3, 1807.

" Mr. H. E. Boyd presents his respects to Mr. Nichols, and sends herewith some additional copy of poems to be added at the end of the second volume of Surrey's Works, &c. but before the same are committed to his compositor, he requests that Mr. Park may be allowed to examine them, and make whatever corrections therein he may think proper; and the same worthy gentleman has kindly promised to correct the press, and a letter is addressed to him by this post to give him notice of their being transmitted to Red Lion Court. Mr. Boyd has long had the Glossary to the above work ready for the press, but defers sending the same until he is able to accompany it with some account of the respective authors, which he is preparing. The Bishop of Dromore desires Mr. Boyd to add his best compliments; his Lordship is in excellent health, but his sight has long since totally failed him. He hopes Mr. Nichols is recovered from his late fatal accident, which he heard with sincere concern. He and all his family will ever have the Bishop's best wishes.

" P. S. Mr. Park's address is Church-row, Hampstead, Middlesex; and the Bishop requests that a copy of every sheet of the two volumes of Surrey may be sent him."

---

39. Bishop Percy to Mr. Nichols.

" *Dromore, Feb.* 20, 1808.

" The Bishop of Dromore presents his kind respects to Mr. Nichols. Although his failure of sight prevented him from reading it, he heard with great concern the article in the papers which described the dreadful fire that consumed his house, &c. and begs he will be assured that none of his friends more truly sympathize with him on this melancholy occasion; yet he hopes the premises were insured, and a considerable part of the stock rescued from the flames.

" It affords no small consolation to find that no lives were lost; and he sincerely hopes none of the family received any personal injury, although the alarm must have been highly distressing.

" The urgent demand for every moment of Mr. Nichols's time and attention at this interesting period would make it very unreasonable to expect any portion of it should be spent in writing long letters, but one line to an absent friend to relieve his anxiety on the above subjects would be extremely obliging, and also to mention what has been the fate of those sheets which Mr. Nichols has so long most kindly allowed to incumber his warehouse. Should Mr. Nichols be too much engaged, or otherwise indisposed to write himself, the Bishop hopes his son, or some one of the family, will indulgently grant this request, however briefly, and accept the assurance that they have all his best wishes for their health and happiness."

---

40. Mr. NICHOLS to the BISHOP of DROMORE.

" MY KIND AND GOOD LORD,   Feb. 25, 1808.

" When called on by the inquiries of friendship so long and so happily enjoyed, it would be cruel to delay for a moment the returning my hearty thanks, and state briefly the outline of a melancholy event, which I feel it a public duty to state as distinctly as I can in the Magazine for the present month.

" I am happy to say, that no personal injury has been sustained by any individual; and that, great as my own loss is, the injury has not affected a single neighbouring house.

" My own health too (truly thankful am I to the Almighty) is as good as I could reasonably expect when turned of sixty-three; and my fractured thigh so far strengthened that I can walk a mile or two with little inconvenience.

" For the last six years, though I have been daily in business, my residence has been at Islington, where five of my daughters are my housekeepers and my consolation; a circumstance which prevented my being a witness to the dismal scene of the 8th of February. My son, who is the housekeeper in Red Lion Passage, was that evening with us at Islington. His wife and only child were at home, and of course were dreadfully alarmed, but escaped unhurt. For further particulars I refer to the Magazine; and shall only add, that not one article that was lodged in my warehouses was preserved. Providentially the dwelling-house was saved, in which was a single copy of most of the works that were printing; amongst which I hope to meet with one copy both of Surrey and Buckingham.

" The MS. lately sent by Mr. Boyd is in the hands of Mr. Park, who waited the receipt of more before he chose to begin the small parcel that was received.

" Of Leicestershire, I had just finished a sixth part, of which only about 120 copies have been called for. The rest of the impression, with all the stock of the former volumes, is consumed.

The MS. of the concluding volume is fortunately preserved at Islington.

" Though I have to lament the dreadful accident which has occasioned the present correspondence, it is at all times a pride and a comfort to me to hear of your Lordship's welfare; and it is a little singular that within half an hour after the receipt of your last kind letter, I was favoured with a call by Mr. Meen, with a commission from Mrs. Isted to inquire into the particulars of my distressful situation.

" My son and six daughters request to have the honour of joining in dutiful respects with, my Lord, your Lordship's much obliged and faithful servant,   J. NICHOLS."

---

41. BISHOP PERCY to Mr. NICHOLS.

" *Dromore, Ireland, May* 20, 1808.

" The Bishop of Dromore presents his kind respects to Mr. Nichols, and requests the favour of him to admit the article sent herewith into the Obituary of the Gentleman's Magazine for the present month *.

" The Bishop has hitherto forborne troubling him on the subject of Surrey's Works, but would be glad to know what he would propose concerning them. The Bishop had formerly offered to give up the profits to be divided between his kinsman Mr. Nichols, jun. and Mr. Boyd, a young clergyman, who has composed a Glossary for this edition, and has taken some pains in preparing an Account of the Lives of the several Authors, whose works are there printed; but his materials here fall so short, that it was proposed to call in the assistance of Mr. Park, editor of the Royal and Noble Authors, and to offer him a third share of the profits, if any should remain, after Mr. Nichols's debt is discharged, whose opinion on this subject is requested; and the Bishop begs he will be assured of his sincere regard and constant good wishes for him and his family."

---

42. Mr. NICHOLS to BISHOP PERCY.

" MY DEAR AND KIND LORD,   *July* 12, 1808.

" Overwhelmed as I have been for the last eighteen months by a complication of terrible misfortunes; not yet recovered from the effects of a sadly fractured thigh in January 1807; and deprived in one fatal hour of nearly £.10,000 *beyond my insurance*, the produce of a long and laborious life, I yet sympathize most sincerely with your Lordship in the loss, which I, in common with all who knew and valued Dr. Percy, have sus-

* This was an account of the death of his nephew, the Rev. Thomas Percy, LL. D. inserted in the Gent. Mag. vol. LXXVIII. p. 470; and copied, with additions, into the " Literary Anecdotes," vol. VIII. p. 148.

tained, but which to you must have been most poignantly afflicting * !

"Very sincerely do I thank your Lordship for your generous intentions towards my son in the proposed division of profits from Surrey's Poems, but, alas! they are all (with the exception of a single copy) consumed in the dreadful conflagration! And much, very much, have I to lament the cruel delays which have attended this ill-starred publication, which on my own account I shall never have the courage to resume. What may be the wishes of Mr. Boyd and Mr. Park (than whom no worthier coadjutors could have been found) must be determined by themselves. At present my finances are too reduced to enter into any scheme of publication on my own account that I can possibly avoid. By the ' History of Leicestershire ' alone (which in honour I am bound to complete) I have lost at least £.5000.

"Once more I thank your Lordship for all your kind favours, and implore your blessing and protection; being, with all possible regard and respect, my Lord,

"Your Lordship's very dutiful humble servant, J. NICHOLS."

---

43. BISHOP PERCY to Mr. NICHOLS.

" Dromore, Ireland, Oct. 19, 1808.

"The Bishop of Dromore presents his kind respects to Mr. Nichols. The Gentleman's Magazine for September arrived here so late that it was not till yesterday that the quotation from Dr. Scully concerning Vaccination was read to the Bishop, and he cannot sufficiently express his surprise at the bold and unqualified manner in which that gentleman has asserted the universal success of vaccination as if the practise of the whole world had been within his own immediate observation. Under his direction, and in his neighbourhood, it may have been attended with great success, and he may have met with no instances of its failure, but that has not been the case every where. Two eminent physicians in this district have found it in several instances to fail of prevention, when they have afterwards applied variolous inoculation. One of these is the Bishop's particular friend, and was much prejudiced in its favour; yet after the most correct application of vaccination, more than one instance of its failure has occurred to him, and even in the Bishop's family; but under his present deprivation of sight, and the infirmities to be expected at the age of eighty, the Bishop must beg to be excused from engaging in the controversy, and therefore must desire his name may no way be mentioned respecting it. And, although the physicians will doubtless at some future period transmit their observations to the proper judges, they cannot at present be expected, amidst their great practise, and at this remote distance, to engage in so warm a controversy as this

* The loss of the Bishop's nephew.

would probably occasion if they were to enter into it in the Gentleman's Magazine.

" As therefore a fair and full discussion of the subject cannot therein be given, the Bishop, from the truest sense of duty and from the influence of conscience, requests his good friend to make a handsome apology to Cosmopolitos for declining to proceed in it any further, for which he may have a sufficient excuse in urging, ' that, if particular cases are produced, as they must be *pro* and *con* in doing justice to the subject, it would occupy more space than could be allowed it in this periodical work. Such more properly belong to medical publications, to which, therefore, the writers on both sides are respectfully referred.'

" Mr. Nichols and all his family have the Bishop's constant good wishes for their health and happiness."

---

44. Mrs. ISTED to Mr. NICHOLS.

" DEAR SIR,   *Ecton, near Northampton, Nov.* 19, 1811.

" The distress of mind occasioned by the death of my beloved and revered father (the late Bishop of Dromore) prevented his family's sending any particulars respecting him for insertion in your Magazine for October; and the press of business that devolved upon us in consequence of that afflicting event for a time obliterated all recollection that a future number would supply the deficiency, until, on my return home yesterday, after a long and tedious journey from Ireland, a letter from my honoured father's confidential secretary was put into my hands, reminding me of the subject; and, in consequence of your desire that his family should send you materials for insertion in the Obituary, I lose not a moment in assuring you that such particulars as I am able to collect I will transmit by to-morrow's post. My father's secretary, Mr. Meredith Darley, by living so much with his Lord, and enjoying his full confidence, is better enabled to furnish you with the circumstantial parts of his life than myself or sister, as he could accurately transmit dates, &c. But I am fearful lest the delay of writing his answer from Ireland to my inquiries may be too late for insertion in your next number.

" With compliments and best wishes to yourself and family, I beg to subscribe myself, dear Sir,

" Your sincere humble servant,   BARBARA ISTED."

EDMUND TURNOR, Esq. M.A. F.R.S. & S.A.

The family of this excellent English gentleman and antiquary is supposed to have come over to this country at the time of the Norman Conquest; their name was originally spelt Tournour, afterwards Turnour.

Edmund Turnor, Esq. of Stoke Rochford and Panton, in the County of Lincoln, was descended from a younger branch of the Turnours of Haverhill in Suffolk, whose representative is the Earl of Wintertoun. His ancestor, Christopher Turnor, became seated at Milton Erneys in Bedfordshire, in the reign of Henry the Eighth, by marriage with Isabel, daughter and heiress of Sir Walter Erneys. Their grandson Christopher had two sons, who rose to considerable eminence. Sir Christopher, the elder, was appointed one of the Barons of the Exchequer in 1660, and at his death left as his widow a sister of the celebrated Sir Philip Warwick, a lady who lived to the age of 101. From that marriage the families of Byng and Pocock are descended. The younger brother, Edmund, was one of the Farmers of the Customs, and was likewise knighted in 1633 *

---

* There is a portrait of Sir Edmund in the house at Stoke Rochford, painted by Verelst; and a print of it in Mr. Turnor's History of Grantham, engraved by Fitler. In the same place is also a portrait of John Turnor, Esq. (son of Sir Edmund) and of Diana Cecil, his wife, both by Sir Godfrey Kneller; the latter is engraved in mezzotinto by Beckett. The portrait of Sir Christopher Turnor, at the same place, painted in his Judge's robes, by Sir P. Lely, as one of the Barons of the Exchequer, was purchased at Lord Torrington's sale, many years since, by Mr. Turnor; and was considered by Sir Joshua Reynolds one of the finest pictures of that master. It is due to Sir J. Reynolds to record the following circumstance, which is one of the many proofs of his obliging disposition. At the above-mentioned sale, Sir Joshua had intended purchasing this picture as a rare example of Sir P. Lely's pencil; but when it was made

By marriage with Margaret, daughter of Sir John
Harrison, of Balls, near Hertford, Knt. he became
possessed of the manor of Stoke Rochford, and
from that alliance the subject of this memoir was
fourth in descent.   His great-grandmother was
Diana Cecil, a granddaughter of the second Earl of
Salisbury *.   His father was Edmund Turnor, Esq.
who died at Panton-house, Jan. 22, 1805, at the
age of eighty-nine †, and his mother was Mary,

known to him by William Seward, Esq. that the subject of
the picture was a member of the family of his friend Mr. Turnor, who much wished to possess it, Sir Joshua most obligingly
declined bidding for it, and it was purchased by Mr. Turnor.

* In the house at Stoke Rochford is a fine painting by Zuc-
chero of Robert the first Earl, the Treasurer and Prime Minister of King James the First.

† He left, besides the subject of this memoir, three other sons:
The Rev. George Turnor, of Trinity-college, Cambridge,
LL.B. 1783; and presented by his father in that year to the
Rectory of Panton and Vicarage of Milton Erneys.   In 1822
he was collated by Bishop Pelham to the Prebend of Lafford in
the Cathedral Church of Lincoln ; and he died in 1824.

John Turnor, Esq. also of Trinity-college, Cambridge, B.A.1788,
M.A. 1793, Barrister-at-law of the Inner Temple, and living 1829.
This gentleman, with motives purely benevolent, has greatly
exerted himself to recommend to the public the White Mustard
Seed as an efficacious medicine.   In this object he has spared
neither expense nor trouble, having published his " Observations" on the subject in various forms; and made an extensive
tour on the continent (from which he returned in the spring of
1829 after two years' absence) solely to spread its fame in foreign
countries.

The Rev. Charles Turnor, as his three elder brothers, of
Trinity-college, Cambridge; B A. 1791, M. A. 1794; F.S.A.
1791.   He was presented to the Vicarage of Wendover in Buckinghamshire by the Crown in 1802.   In 1811, when his brother was High Sheriff of Lincolnshire, he preached an Assize
Sermon in Lincoln Cathedral, which was afterwards printed.
In 1818 he was collated by Bishop Tomline to the Prebend
of Sutton in Marisco in the Cathedral Church of Lincoln;
and in 1825 he succeeded his brother George as Vicar of Milton
Erneys.   Mr. Turnor is also a Justice of the Peace for Buckinghamshire; and author of " Thoughts on the present state
of the Poor; with hints for the improvement of their condition;
in a Letter addressed to the Archdeacon of Lincoln," 1818.

There were also four daughters: Elizabeth-Frances, the wife

only daughter* of John Disney, of Lincoln, Esq.
by Frances, daughter of George Cartwright, of
Ossington in Nottinghamshire, Esq.

Mr. Turnor was a Fellow Commoner of Trinity-
college, Cambridge, where he proceeded B. A. 1777,
M. A. 1781. On quitting the University, he took
a tour in France, Switzerland, and Italy. He early
acquired a taste for topography and antiquities, and
was elected a Fellow of the Society of Antiquaries in 1778. In 1779 he printed in 4to, "Chronological Tables of the High Sheriffs of the County
of Lincoln, and of the Knights of the Shire, Citizens, and Burgesses in Parliament within the same,
from the earliest accounts to the present time. London, printed by Joseph White." In 1781, Mr. Turnor is mentioned in a letter of Mr. Brooke, Somerset
Herald, to Mr. Gough, as desirous "to know whether
your Camden for Lincolnshire is printed, as he will
add to it;" which from a subsequent letter it appears
he did†.

In 1783 he compiled and printed a neat little
pamphlet, intituled, "London's Gratitude; or, an
Account of such pieces of Sculpture and Painting
as have been placed in Guildhall at the expense of
the City of London. To which is added a List of
those distinguished persons to whom the Freedom
of the City has been presented since the year MDCCLVIII.
With Engravings of the Sculptures, &c." small 8vo.

Again, in 1783, Mr. Brooke mentions a tour
which Mr. Turnor had made in Normandy, and
adds, that " he has had some drawings made of

of Samuel Smith, Esq. of Woodhall-park, co. Hertford (next
brother to Lord Carrington); Mary-Anne, of Sir William Foulis,
Bart.; Diana, of Sir Thomas Whichcote, Bart.; and Frances,
unmarried.

* And sister to Dr. Disney, the subject of a previous memoir
in the present volume.

† See before, pp. 405, 408; and also other allusions to Mr.
Turnor in Mr. Brooke's letters to Mr. Gough, pp. 420, 425, &c.
Mr. Turnor was one of those intimate friends of Mr. Brooke,
who attended his funeral (see p. 358).

antiquities in that country, which he will bring to town to show us next year. He is much delighted with his expedition *." In pursuance of this promise, Mr. Turnor communicated to the Society of Antiquaries in the following spring, a " Description of an ancient Castle at Rouen in Normandy, called Le Château du Vieux Palais, built by Henry V. King of England †." Mr. Turnor, it thence appears, had been elected a Fellow of the Royal Academy of Rouen.

In 1792 Mr. Turnor communicated to the Society, as a supplement to the volume of Household Accounts which they had published, " Extracts from the Household Book of Thomas Cony, of Bassingthorpe, co. Lincoln ‡," a MS. in his own possession.

In the Royal Society Mr. Turnor was associated in 1786, and in 1792 he communicated to that body " A narrative of the Earthquake felt in Lincolnshire, and the neighbouring Counties, on the 25th of February 1792. In a letter to Sir Joseph Banks §."

In 1793 Mr. Turnor communicated to Dr. Kippis, for his edition of the " Biographia Britannica," then in progress, a memoir of Sir Richard Fanshawe, the eminent statesman, negotiator, and poet, in the reign of Charles the First ||. He had been led to this subject by a perusal of the interesting memoirs left in MS. by Lady Fanshawe ¶,

---

* See p. 414.

† This was read before the Society, April 1, 1784, and, with a folding plate of two views and a plan of the castle, is printed in the Archæologia, vol. VII. pp. 232—235. Mr. Turnor also furnished the Society with a drawing of a Fountain (since removed) in the Place de la Pucelle at Rouen, which was engraved in the Vetusta Monumenta, vol. II., plate xxxviii.

‡ These were read, Jan. 19, 1792, and are printed in the Archæologia, vol. XI., pp. 22—33.

§ Read May 10, 1792, and printed in the Philosophical Transactions, vol. LXXXII. pp. 283—288.

|| Printed in the fifth volume of that biographical collection, pp. 661—664.

¶ They were first published complete in 1829, with an appendix of correspondence, edited by N. H. Nicolas, Esq.; see the Gentleman's Magazine, vol. XCIX. pt. ii. p. 238.

who was Anne, daughter of Sir John Harrison, and elder sister to Margaret, the wife of Sir Edmund Turnor, before-mentioned. From the same source Mr. Turnor communicated some extensive extracts to Mr. Seward's collection of Anecdotes.

In the same year he printed, in an elegant little volume, "Characters of Eminent Men in the Reigns of Charles I. and II. including the Rebellion. From the Works of Lord Chancellor Clarendon."

In 1801 Mr. Turnor furnished the Society of Antiquaries with some "Remarks on the Military History of Bristol in the Seventeenth Century *," where his ancestor, afterwards Sir Edmund Turnor, was treasurer of the garrison for Charles the First; and in 1802 with "A Declaration of the Diet and Particular Fare of King Charles the First, when Duke of York," from a manuscript in vellum, in the possession of his brother-in-law Sir William Foulis, the descendant and representative of Sir David Foulis, the Prince's Cofferer†.

At the close of the year 1802 Mr. Turnor was elected to Parliament for the borough of Midhurst; but he sat only until the dissolution in 1806. He served the office of High Sheriff for Lincolnshire in 1810-11; and for a long period acted in the commission of the peace for that county. As he was well versed in the laws of his country, and was cool, judicious, and accessible, his retirement, some years before his death, from the duties of a magistrate, was a matter of regret to his neighbourhood. He has been known to express his dislike of the character of an over-zealous magistrate, but no one more exhibited in his own person the just and useful one.

Having for a considerable time made the topography of his neighbourhood his study, in 1806 Mr. Turnor published the result of his researches in a

---

* These were read June 11 and 18 that year, and, with a plate giving a plan of the Outworks, were printed in the Archæologia, vol. XIV. pp. 119—131.

† It is printed in the Archæologia, vol. XV. pp. 1—12.

handsome quarto volume, under the title of "Col-
lections for the History of the Town and Soke of
Grantham; containing authentic Memoirs of Sir
Isaac Newton, now first published from the original
MSS. in the possession of the Earl of Portsmouth *."

Mr. Turnor is believed to have been the editor of
" A Short View of the Proceedings in the County of
Lincoln, for a limited exportation of Wool," printed
in 4to, 1824.

In 1825 he furnished the Antiquaries with an
" Account of the Remains of a Roman Bath near
Stoke in Lincolnshire †;" and only a fortnight before his death he announced some further discoveries of a similar nature in the same neighbourhood, which had been investigated by his brother-
in-law Sir Philip Vere Broke.

Mr. Turnor was twice married, firstly, to Elizabeth, eldest daughter of Philip Broke, Esq. of Nacton, Suffolk, and sister to Captain Sir Philip Bowes
Vere Broke, Bart. K.C.B.‡ and to Lieut.-Colonel
Sir Charles Broke Vere, K.C.B. By this lady,
who died Jan. 21, 1801, he had one daughter, Eli-
zabeth-Edmunda, the wife of Frederick Manning,
Esq. His second marriage, March 22, 1803, was
with Dorothea, third daughter of Lieut.-Colonel
Tucker, and sister to Captain Sir Edward Tucker,
K.C.B. by whom he had: Mary-Henrietta, who
died in 1815 at the age of eleven; Edmund, who
died at Eton-school in 1821, at the age of fourteen §; Algernon and Sophia, who died infants in

* This work has a long review in the Gentleman's Magazine,
vol. LXXVI. pp. 529—535, and in the Monthly Review, vol. LVI.
pp. 396—407.
† Printed, with three plates, in the Archæologia, XXII. 26—32.
‡ Sir Philip's fourth son was named Edmund-Turnor; he
died July 12, 1829, in his ninth year.
§ His epitaph and character by his tutor the Rev. C. S. Haw-
trey, were printed as a leaf to be inserted in the History of Grantham, pp. 135*, 136*. See also the Gentleman's Magazine,
vol. XCI. i. 283, 549. — Another addition which Mr. Turnor
made to the copies of his History in the libraries of his friends,
was a plate of the tomb of Henry Rocheford, Esq.

598   ILLUSTRATIONS OF LITERATURE.

1807 and 1818; and five sons and two daughters, who survive, Christopher, a Fellow-commoner
of Trinity-college, Cambridge; Cecil, a Commoner
of Brasennose-college, Oxford; Algernon, Henry-
Martin, Philip-Broke, Charlotte, and Harriet.

Mr. Turnor died at Stoke Rochford, March 19,
1829, aged 74; and his remains were there interred
in the family vault, which was erected in 1801.
He had also built for himself an altar-tomb in the
wall of the chancel, decorated in front with angels,
and divided by Gothic compartments; and over it
a Gothic arch, ornamented with foliage, roses, &c.

The following character of Mr. Turnor is from
the pen of a near relation:

"To form a distinguished character two things are
requisite, talent and mental exertion; Mr. Turnor
was certainly blessed with the former. His mind
was comprehensive, his judgment discriminating and
accurate, and to these advantages he added a just and
well-cultivated taste. His favourite pursuits were antiquarian research and the fine arts; and, had his diligence been commensurate with the powers of his
mind, he might have ranked very high among the
votaries of those refined and elegant studies. He
possessed, however, a considerable share of knowledge on these and other subjects of inquiry, derived
from books and frequent intercourse with men of
taste and learning, in whose society he took particular pleasure. Amongst his numerous friends and
associates were Gough, Grose, the Lysons', Seward,
Bennet Langton, Dr. Kippis, and Sir Joseph Banks,
with the last of whom he lived for many years in
habits of close friendship and intimacy. Though
he inherited a considerable patrimony, he did not,
like many others in a similar situation, indulge in
gay, fashionable, and frivolous pursuits. His leisure hours were generally employed in reading, and
in conversation and correspondence with learned
friends. In proof of his attachment to the fine arts,
Stoke Rochford, his favourite residence, and which

he greatly improved, will long remain a monument of his taste for landscape. He looked at Nature with a picturesque eye, instantly discovering her beauties and defects; the former he knew how to heighten and improve, the latter how to remedy and conceal. Refined and rational, however, as his pursuits were, they did not wholly engross his thoughts. His mind was very susceptible of benevolent impressions. In the relations of husband and father his conduct was exemplary; and, though he is now, by the course of nature, separated from his family, he still lives in their affection and esteem. He was also a kind and considerate landlord; but his benevolence was not confined to his family and tenants; he took an interest in the public good. In the year 1824 he founded a national school on the system of the celebrated Dr. Bell, at Colsterworth in the county of Lincoln, for the religious education of poor children in that parish, and the adjoining hamlet of Woolsthorpe, and the parishes of North Stoke and South Stoke, generally called Stoke Rochford, and Skillington, in the same county. This foundation (the particulars of which are detailed in the endowment made by a codicil to his will) consists of an excellent school-room newly built, and a very commodious house and garden for the school-master adjoining it. The advantages derivable from this valuable institution he anticipated with the greatest satisfaction; may his anticipations be realized! may the present and future generations evince their gratitude to their benefactor, by their advancement in religious knowledge and a corresponding improvement in life and conduct!"

----

1. Mr. TURNOR to Mr. NICHOLS.

" SIR,   *Stoke Rochford, April* 15, 1803.
" I return you thanks for your obliging congratulations, and for the perusal of the proof sheets respecting Gaddesby*. I have

* In the History of Leicestershire.

made a few corrections to the pedigree of Smith ; and have sent the sheets to Mr. Samuel Smith *, requesting him to forward them to you.   The Smith property, not having been the manor, is not mentioned; but, as it was in consequence of that property that Thomas Smith was High Sheriff of Leicestershire in 1717, the pedigree of the family seems to come in with propriety.   I suspect it went to the daughters of Thomas Smith by his first wife, but am not certain.

" I have not an accurate description of the arms and crest of Smith, but it may be seen in the Peerage.   I am. Sir,

" Your obliged and obedient servant,   EDM. TURNOR, Jun."

---

2. " SIR,   *Stoke Rochford, July* 5, 1804.

" Inclosed you will receive payment for the History of Leicestershire.   Like a giant refreshed, you renew the attack with redoubled ardour ; the last volume appears to me to yield to none of the former in interest and information.

" I am, Sir, your obedient servant,   EDM. TURNOR."

---

3. Mr. TURNOR to RICHARD GOUGH, Esq.

" DEAR SIR,   *Clea, near Grimsby, Sept.* 20, 1804.

" Having succeeded in my application for copies and extracts of certain papers respecting Sir Isaac Newton, from Hertsborne-park, I have began to print my Collections for the Soke of Grantham.   Your additions to Camden have furnished me with much information; and, although my book will profess to be only Collections, yet in the progress of it one cannot help feeling a desire to make it as complete as possible.   With a view, therefore, to its further improvement, I hope you will allow me to inclose a few queries, which, it is very probable, you may have the goodness to answer at your leisure.   If it be convenient to let me hear from you in the course of this month, I will beg of you to direct to Panton, near Lincoln; if after that time, to Stoke, near Colsterworth.   I am, dear Sir,

" Your very obedient servant,   EDM. TURNOR, Jun."

---

4. " DEAR SIR,   *Stoke, June* 30, 1805.

" Having a spare sheet of Dr. Stukeley's letter to Dr. Mead (of part of which you have a transcript) I venture to send it to you, though dirty from the press.   My book, slim and meagre as it will be, will not be out till October; if you will deign to look at it, I must, in a particular manner, crave your candour.

" I am going to-morrow to Panton, near Lincoln, where it will be a pleasure to me to hear that you are in good health.   I am, dear Sir, your very obedient servant,   EDM. TURNOR."

* Mr. Turnor's brother-in-law ; see p. 594.

5. Mr. Turnor to Mr. Nichols.

" Dear Sir,   *Panton-house, near Lincoln, July* 8, 1812.

" I thank you for remembering to send me your last portion of Leicestershire, accompanied with an impression of Lubenham Manor-house.

" The Church of St. Peter's, Paul's-wharf, was not re-built after the Fire of London; but the parish was annexed to the Church of St. Bennet's, Paul's-wharf, of which the Rev. John Owen is Rector. If there be in existence the parish register of St. Peter's, Paul's-wharf, before the fire, I should be curious to know whether there is an entry of the marriage of Edmund Turnor and Margaret Harrison in September 1654, or thereabouts; and, subsequently, whether any christenings of their issue occur, I mean between 1654 and 1660. This is a mere matter of curiosity, which I should like to have gratified if it can be done with little trouble and trifling expense. In a Diary of my ancestor Sir Edmund Turnor, mention is frequently made of Robert Mossom, Minister of St. Peter's, Paul's-wharf. He was the author of two single Sermons printed at the Restoration of Charles the Second ; but not the same Dr. Mossom who was at that time made a Doctor in Divinity, and afterwards an Irish Bishop.

" I cannot close this without thanking you as the means of my being possessed of the most comprehensive County History ever published. I am, dear Sir,

" Your very obedient servant,   Edm. Turnor."

---

6. " Dear Sir,   *Stoke, near Colsterworth, May* 23, 1814.

" If the new edition of the Biographical Dictionary by Mr. Chalmers embraces characters eminent for piety and charity, I may be induced, under the letter T, to offer a short memoir of my ancestor Sir Edmund Turnor *; and I am the more inclined to do it, because in the additions to Granger by Mr. Noble, an erroneous notice is there taken of him.

" I have been to-day to take leave of our friend Mr. Crabbe †, who sets out immediately for his living at Trowbridge; this neighbourhood will be very sorry to lose him. Mounsey I have not seen very lately; he now does not go much from home.

" When you have leisure to write, it will give me much pleasure to hear that you are in good health. I am, dear Sir,

" Yours truly,   Edm. Turnor."

---

7. Dear Sir,   *Stoke, near Colsterworth, June* 8, 1825.

" My curiosity has been awakened by the very curious assemblage of particulars contained in the prospectus of King James's

---

* This offer probably arrived too late.   † The Poet.

Progresses now printing by you; and when I consider that the author is my old acquaintance, who has the rare felicity, at his very advanced age, of offering such a treat to his antiquarian friends, I cannot repress my inclination to become a subscriber, and to have my name enrolled in the list of his friends and admirers.

" I can make inquiry at Grantham if there be any entry in the Corporation Books respecting King James when he passed through the town. I observe in my book that there is an account of fees paid when the Corporation received Charles I. in 1633; and it is possible there may be entries of a similar nature previous to that time. Some notices I may be able to give you of Knights made by James; Sir Sutton Cony in particular, whose marriage settlement I have, which was made long before the ceremony took place. I believe it was not unusual in those days to affiance the parties.

" I will thank you to point out, if you write in the parcel, any particulars in which I may be able to contribute to your work.

" I am, dear Sir, yours very truly,   EDM. TURNOR."

---

8. " DEAR SIR,   *Stoke Rochford, Oct.* 18, 1825.
" I have had a visit from our old friend Mr. Leman, who, notwithstanding his severe illness last year, and his age of seventy-five, is as eager after his favourite pursuit, the Roman roads, as ever. Seeing your numbers of King James's Progresses upon my table, he desired me to request, in his name, that you would send to him at Bath as usual the numbers which are out; and such publications of the Society of Antiquaries as may be due.

" If it be your intention to make any addenda et corrigenda by way of appendix, I might perhaps furnish you with a few before the Progresses are finally printed off.

" I am, dear Sir, yours truly,   EDM. TURNOR."

---

9. " DEAR SIR,   *Stoke, March* 1, 1826.
" Since the receipt of your note I went to Belton to inquire if more information than my book afforded could be obtained. Lord Brownlow was kind enough to look up all the papers he could find on the subject; but nothing more could be made out.

" I wrote to the Town-clerk at Grantham to require that he would search the Corporation Books for the year 1617; his answer was that they begin in 1633, which I find I had noted in my book, p. 52.

" I am rejoiced to find that you can write in such spirits; and am yours truly,   EDM. TURNOR."

ROBERT DARLEY WADDILOVE, D.D. F.S.A.

The long life of this very respectable divine was distinguished throughout its course by a steady attachment to the regular duties of his sacred profession, whilst his classical attainments and taste in the polite arts found many occasions of exertion in his progress.

He was son of Robert Waddilove, Esq. of Bartlet's-buildings, Holborn, who died at Cheshunt, Nov. 10, 1762; was educated at Westminster-school, and afterwards at Clare-hall, Cambridge, where he proceeded B. A. 1759, being the sixth Junior Optime of that year; M. A. 1762. For some years in early life he was resident as Curate at Wotton in Surrey. In 1771 he became Chaplain to Thomas second Lord Grantham, when Ambassador at the Court of Madrid. Here he appears to have formed an intimate friendship with the Abbè Bayer, the Preceptor to the young Prince or Infant of Spain; and, a Spanish translation of Sallust being formed and published by the Prince in a very superior style of elegance, two copies of this work were in the Dean's possession, having been presented to him by his friend the Abbè.

Whilst thus engaged at Madrid, he was apprised of a remarkable MS. of Strabo in the library of the Escurial. The Oxford edition of that author being then in preparation by Mr. Falconer, Mr. Waddilove, at the request of Archbishop Markham, undertook, with the assistance of a learned Spaniard, probably the Abbè Bayer, to collate the MS. For his attention to this business the delegates of the Clarendon press presented him in 1808 with a copy of their two magnificent folios of the Strabo. These volumes the Dean in his will bequeathed to the library of York Cathedral, together with another very curious and recondite work in two volumes folio, " Bibliotheca Arab. del Escurial."

Other notices occur of his willing exertions to promote the cause of literature.   Dr. Robertson, in his
History of America, particularly acknowledges the
very great assistance he had received from Mr. Waddilove *.

* Dr. Robertson's thanks are thus warmly expressed: " In
describing the atchievements and institutions of the Spaniards
in the new world, I have departed, in many instances, from the
accounts of preceding historians, and have often related facts
which seem to have been unknown to them.   It is a duty I owe
the public to mention the sources from which I have derived
such intelligence, as justifies me either in placing transactions
in a new light, or in forming any new opinion with respect to
their causes and effects.   This duty I perform with greater satisfaction, as it will afford an opportunity of expressing my gratitude to those benefactors who have honoured me with their
countenance and aid in my researches.

" As it was from Spain that I had to expect the most important information, with regard to this part of my work, I considered it a very fortunate circumstance for me when Lord Grantham, to whom I had the honour of being personally known,
and with whose liberality of sentiment and disposition to oblige
I was well acquainted, was appointed Ambassador to the Court
of Madrid.   Upon applying to him, I met with such a reception
as satisfied me that his endeavours would be employed in the
most proper manner, in order to obtain the gratification of my
wishes; and I am perfectly sensible that what progress I have
made in my inquiries among the Spaniards ought to be ascribed
chiefly to their knowing how much his Lordship interested himself in my success.

" But did I owe nothing more to Lord Grantham than the
advantages which I have derived from his attention in engaging
Mr. Waddilove, the Chaplain of his Embassy, to take the conduct of my literary inquiries in Spain, the obligation I lie under
to him would be very great.   During five years that gentleman
has carried on researches for my behalf with such activity, perseverance, and knowledge of the subject, to which his attention
was turned, as have filled me with no less astonishment than
satisfaction.   He procured for me the greater part of the Spanish
books which I have consulted; and, as many of them were printed
early in the sixteenth century, and are become extremely rare,
the collecting of these was such an occupation as alone required
much time and assiduity.   To his friendly attention I am n-
debted for copies of several valuable manuscripts, containing
facts and details which I might have searched for in vain in
works that have been made public.   Encouraged by the inviting
good-will with which Mr. Waddilove conferred his favours, I

Mr. Waddilove became Chaplain to Archbishop Drummond; and, after that prelate's death in 1776, to Archbishop Markham. He was presented to Topcliffe in 1774 by the Dean and Chapter of York, and collated by the Archbishop to Cherry Burton in 1775.

In 1775 he was elected a Fellow of the Society of Antiquaries; and at the beginning of 1779 we find the Rev. Michael Tyson thus writing to Mr. Gough: " Waddilove, Chaplain to the Embassy at Madrid, has himself translated the Essay on Painting by Mengs, and seems to desire I should hold my hand. Without doubt I shall; he is too great a knight for me to enter the lists with. He promises great assistance if I will undertake Don Ulloa *." And again at the same period Mr. Tyson writes, " Lort tells me that Waddilove has sent him a sheet of remarks on Charles the First's Catalogue, compared with the pictures at the Escurial. You remember the King of Spain is supposed to have purchased great part of the Royal Collection †."

In 1780 Mr. Waddilove was admitted by Archbishop Markham to a Prebend in the Collegiate Church at Ripon; and on the 3d of April 1781, he married Miss Anne Hope Grant, daughter of Sir Frederick, and sister to Sir James Grant, of Grant, Bart. Mrs. Waddilove died at the age of fifty,

transmitted to him a set of queries with respect both to the customs and policy of the native Americans, and the nature of several institutions in the Spanish settlements, framed in such a manner that a Spaniard might answer them without disclosing any thing that was improper to be communicated to a foreigner. He translated these into Spanish, and obtained, from various persons who had resided in most of the Spanish colonies, such replies as have afforded me much instruction.

" Notwithstanding those peculiar advantages with which my inquiries were carried on in Spain, it is with regret I am obliged to add, that their success must be ascribed to the beneficence of individuals, not to any communication by public authority."

* See the " Literary Anecdotes," vol. VIII. p. 638.

† Ibid.; and see also p. 650.

May 21, 1797, and has a monument by Bacon in the Church of Ripon.

In 1783 the Prebend of Wistow in the Cathedral Church of York was conferred on Mr. Waddilove by Archbishop Markham; in 1786 the same patron advanced him to the Archdeaconry of the East Riding of Yorkshire; and in 1791 he was nominated by the Crown to the Deanery of Ripon. He subsequently proceeded B. and D. D.

In 1806 Dr. Waddilove communicated to Mr. Gough some corrections for the new edition of Camden's Britannia then in progress *.

* The following is his letter to Mr. Gough :
  " SIR,   Ripon, April 7, 1806.
  " I observe that a re-publication of your Camden's Britannia is in hand; and, though the booksellers do not solicit any corrections (as they do in a trifling Guide to Watering Places), and though perhaps you may have no concern in it, yet I trust you will excuse the liberty I take in pointing out two or three errors which may have accidentally escaped your accurate searches.
  " Vol. III. p. 88. Henry Jenkins is said to have been born and lived at Bolton, near Bolton Castle, instead of Bolton-upon-Swale, near Catterick. There is a good account of him in the History of Knaresborough, art. Fountains Abbey; and also in the London Magazine, 1753, with a good portrait.
  " P. 57. Newby-hall, late Weddell's, now Lord Grantham's.
  " P. 84. This Newby, late the seat of Sir Edward Blacket, is erroneously stated to be near Yarm. Newby, near Ripon, was purchased by the late Mr. Weddell's father, of the father of the late Sir Edward Blacket, about sixty or seventy years since.
  " In the same page, Mount St. John, Feliskirk, and Kerby Knowle, are stated to be in Cleveland, instead of near Thirsk, in the Hundred of Birdforth.
  " I hope you will excuse the liberty, which I, perhaps erroneously, take ; if I was sure that I was not doing so, I might, perhaps, look over this neighbourhood in the Britannia with a little more attention ; as I have the honour to be, with much respect, Sir, your faithful and obedient servant,
                            " ROB. DARLEY WADDILOVE."

In the preface to " The Topographical Dictionary of Yorkshire," edited by Mr. Thomas Langdale, bookseller, of Ripon, in 1822, is the following acknowledgment : " To the Very Rev. the Dean of Ripon he has to express his obligations for the use of several papers belonging to his archdeaconry ; as well as for his readiness, at all times, in furnishing him with information which might in the least tend to render the work correct."

The editor of the Beauties of England and Wales, in his

In 1808 Dr. Waddilove communicated to the Society of Antiquaries "A Description of a Font in the Church of South Kilvington in Yorkshire *."

In 1810 he sent to the same learned body "An Historical and Descriptive Account of Ripon Minster †."

On the Dean's nomination to the Church of Ripon his active disposition showed itself in an undeviating attention to every circumstance that might promote its welfare. He regulated the public service of the Minster, and enforced it by his own constant attendance. He also much improved the fabric by various alterations—by ornamenting the west towers with a range of Gothic battlements of corresponding style; and by attention to the embellishment of the whole structure.

At the same time he was active in all public and private charities; and especially as President of the Society for the Relief of the North Riding Clergy his kindness was shown in unremitting endeavours towards its prosperity. In the East Riding his humane and useful exertions as the Archdeacon were equally valued and esteemed; and no life extended to such a period can be shown as exhibiting a more continued and valuable application of the best principles to the best objects of piety and religion. He died at Ripon Deanery, August 18, 1828, in his 92d year.

Dr. Waddilove had three sons, of whom one only survived him. Thomas, the eldest, died in 1799, at the age of seventeen, when a King's scholar at Westminster. The second, the Rev. William James Darley Waddilove, was of St. John's-college, Cambridge, B.A. 1807, M.A. 1810, and was

description of Ripon, also "acknowledges himself greatly indebted to the judicious remarks of the Rev. Dr. Waddilove."

* Printed in the Archæologia, vol. XVI. pp. 341—345, with a plate of the font, which is remarkable for its heraldic ornaments. See also some additions to the communication in vol. XVII. of Archæologia, p. 334.

† This is printed in Archæologia, vol. XVII. pp. 128—137; and, revised and corrected, was re-printed at Ripon, in 8vo. 1827.

preferred to a Prebend of Ripon in 1811, and presented by his father,—as Prebendary of Wistow in
the Cathedral of York,—to the Vicarage of that
parish in 1818. He married in 1816, Elizabeth-
Anne, sister to Sir James Graham, of Netherby,
Bart. Robert, the third son, was also of St. John's-
college, Cambridge, B. A. 1811, and had taken holy
orders, when he died at Penzance, July 3, 1813,
aged 23. Dr. Waddilove had also three daughters,
of whom he lost Mary-Catherine in her infancy;
another became the wife of Charles Oxley, Esq. of
Ripon; and one resided with him, unmarried, at
the Deanery.

Dr. Dibdin, in his " Bibliographical Decameron,"
  thus described a visit to " the worthy Dr. Waddilove, Dean of Ripon : "

" A letter from Mr. Eyre secured me the most favourable
reception. ' Good Mister Dean, my object is the Minster Library ; ' ' Here,' quoth the Dean, ' is the catalogue, peruse this
while I attend three-o'clock prayers.' I perused with avidity,
and made a tick or mark against two articles, in especial, which
appeared to require explanation, ' English Chronicle, Antw.
1493 ; ' ' Boetius, old Engl.' Upon conclusion of the service I
ascended a small flight of stone steps with the Dean, and found
myself in a narrow modernised old room with books on all sides,
in a somewhat littered condition ; but, as the references in the
catalogue were correct, I quickly discovered what I wished to
examine. The Old English Chronicle was, as I suspected, Gerard de Læen's re-print of Caxton's text ; but where was ' Boetius,
old Engl. in folio ? ' High and low, among octavos and folios,
amidst dust, cobwebs, and perished wooden book-covers, and
with a thermometer hard upon eighty-one, did I resolutely continue the search for the said ' Boetius, old Engl. in fol.' not
doubting that it would turn out to be a quarto, and the poetical
version printed at the ' exempt Monastery at Tavistock ! ' The
catalogue, however, had placed it among the folios ; when, as
the last desperate effort, I drew out a melancholy-looking ' for-
rel,' or white sheep-skin covered folio volume ; opened it, saw,
and what should it prove to be but Caxton's own prose imprint
of the Boethius,—large, clean, and perfect, save one leaf ! Yet
the book is unusually thick ; I persevere, and find at the end of
it nothing more or less than a beautiful and perfect copy of
Caxton's ' Book for Travellers,' of which Lord Spencer's copy
had been considered unique. The ' worthy Dean' wonders and
miles ; and smiles and wonders again. In due time these pre-

cious tomes are consigned to Charles Lewis, who returned them
with many other small, and rather scarce and curious volumes,
from the same Minster Library, decorated in morocco, or russia,
or calf, according to their supposed rarity or worth. May this
fashion of decoration obtain quickly throughout all the Cathedral libraries in the realm! for good sense and good taste equally
impose the necessity of such a measure. Before I dismiss the
notice of Dean Waddilove, let me add, that the Dean's own
library is rather rich in Spanish lore ; and that I obtained intelligence from him upon this subject worthy of being recorded in
a basil-red-covered travelling memorandum book, measuring
seven inches by four and a half. The evening of this visit to the
Deanery of Ripon was delightfully concluded by a trip to Fountains Abbey, in company with the said Dean, from which we
returned by the lustre of a full moon."

Rev. SAMUEL DENNE, F.S.A.

Of this intelligent and industrious Antiquary a
memoir has been given in the Literary Anecdotes *,
and his works have frequently come under notice †.
He was one of Mr. Gough's most voluminous correspondents; and the following are the most important of a long series of letters.

1. The Rev. Samuel Denne to Richard Gough, Esq.

" Dear Sir,   *Wilmington, Aug. 23, 1783.*
" A very bad state of health some time since made it necessary for Mr. Podmore, the Vicar of Cranbrooke, to absent himself from that place. I have a notion he may be returned home,
and when assured he is, I will not fail to communicate to him
yours and Mr. Nichols's application respecting some curious
entries in the Register-book of that parish, supposed to have
been inserted by his predecessor Mr. Johnson, for I shall be
always ready to contribute the little in my power in assisting
both of you in your intelligent and entertaining pursuits.
" It was a mortification to me to find that you had passed so
near my house without giving me the pleasure of conversing
with you; had I had the least hint what route you was taking

* Vol. III. pp. 528—531.
† See the various references in " Literary Anecdotes," vol. VII.
pp. 108, 550.

this should not have happened, for, my house being only a mile from Dartford, you could, with little loss of time, have had your refreshment at Wilmington Vicarage. Mr. Thorpe will, I know, be equally disappointed at not having seen you and your fellow-traveller. He called on Thursday afternoon, and missed me; but I propose to return the visit early in the next week, and acquaint him with your excuse.

" Possibly when you was at Rochester you saw Mr. Fisher, and if you did he doubtless told you of his intention to publish a new edition of the History and Antiquities of that place, &c. My partiality for a place where I so long lived has drawn me in to promise to revise and enlarge the work; but I find myself engaged in a more arduous task than I expected, especially as I cannot in my country retirement have several books I wish to consult. The description given of the old timber bridge in the present edition does not by any means satisfy me. After a careful perusal of the MSS. in the Textus Roffensis, relative to the repair of it, I am clear that the person whom Fisher employed to write that chapter was mistaken in his idea of the piers being placed at equal distances from one another; and, if the distance between some piers was not less than sixty-six feet, I cannot conceive how sylle (rendered by the writer beams) could be found of a sufficient length and bulk to support the weight of the planks, and of the heavy burdens which were to be carried over the bridge *.   Your faithful humble servant, S. Denne."

2. " Dear Sir,   *Wilmington, Sept.* 15, 1783.
" Upon my return on Saturday from a visit of almost a fort-night to my friend Dr. Milner, formerly of Bene't-college, but now of Preston Hall, I was favoured with your letter; and am much obliged to you for your researches after the meaning of the term sylle.

" Mr. Clark will not probably find any employment for his pencil at the mills which antiently belonged to Spilman, there being not, as I suspect, any part of them remaining; and as to the two lime trees said to have been planted by him, they are no more, the last of them having been blown down about three years ago.   Your faithful and humble servant,   S. Denne."

3. " Dear Sir,   *Wilmington, April* 16, 1784.
" In your favour of the 26th of December last, which was accompanied with Mr. Essex's scientific and very curious remarks upon the old wooden bridge at Rochester, you was pleased to permit me to use them at my full leisure. Of this indulgence I have so freely availed myself that I should be inexcusable did I not account for not having sooner returned the MS. with my

* On this subject see in Mr. Essex's correspondence, before, p. 304.

sincere thanks for the loan of it. The fact was, that I wished a few of the leading members of the Bridge Corporation to have the perusal of it, in hopes of inducing them to contribute to the engraving of a well delineated plan.

" Mr. Essex's MS. I have read with close attention, and am perfectly satisfied of the justness of the greater part of his observations. It is most likely that such doubts as I may have remaining proceed from my having no skill in architecture.

" Since I wrote last, I discovered in Tanner's Bibliotheca Britannica, p. 294, that Bartholomew Fowle, Prior of St. Mary Overy, wrote a book upon London Bridge. Tanner does not mention the MS. being extant, but refers to Pitt's Appendix, p. 839, for his authority. If the MS. be preserved, I however question its giving any description of the original Bridge, as Fowl was, comparatively, a very late writer, being the last Prior of his monastery *.

" The inclosed memoir on Hokeday I will trouble you to communicate to the Society of Antiquaries, should you be of opinion it will afford them an evening's amusement †.

"   I remain, dear Sir, yours faithfully,   S. DENNE."

---

4. Mr. DENNE to Mr. NICHOLS.

" DEAR SIR,   *Wilmington, March 3, 1788.*

" Obliged am I to you for looking upon the returned sheets of Mr. Thorpe's Antiquities as a waste copy. The use I shall ere long make of them will be to select such parts as I think will be an amusement to my distressed brother, whose mind can bear but little reading, and that of a peculiar kind ‡.

" The cover of the last Gentleman's Magazine encouraged me to hope, that the Rochester Thorpe § would soon be under sail; may it have fair weather, and be the voyage advantageous as well as honourable to the owner! At Rochester, unfortunately, there is not one F.S.A.; nor are there many who have a bent to antiquities. I trust, however, that four or five, perhaps six, bales of the cargo will be delivered at that port.

" It appears from Mr. Urban's last review you have publicly laid at my door the account of Archiepiscopal Manerial Houses ||; but qu. *quo jure?* Are you aware of what may be the consequence of my being known to have insinuated that no Primate or Prelate can be considered as living in a Palace, unless he resides in his Cathedral City? Master Berington, I observe, has, with reluctance, given up a part of his plan ¶. Sure I am that,

---

* Stowe quotes Fowle's authority; but it does not appear that the latter wrote a book on the subject.
† It is printed in the Archæologia, vol. VII. p. 244.
‡ See the " Literary Anecdotes," vol. III. p. 528.
§ The Custumale Roffense, published by John Thorpe, Esq.
|| In Bibl. Top. Brit. No. XLVI.
¶ That all communications should be signed by a real name.

if adopted, the number of correspondents would have been soon diminished. In particular the highly laughable anecdotes of Dr. Battie would not have appeared *, for unless I am much mistaken you had them from one of the most learned men of the age, who would have been averse to the subscribing of his name to them. It is an *absq. sign.* paper, but I think I have heard the writer relate them. The hand-writing of my serious and funny friend is well known to me; but I conclude the MS. has been committed to the flames weeks ago.

"My father having left a note of reference to the seal and arms of Bishop Wellys at the beginning of his Register, I searched for it whilst I was at Rochester; and it appearing to me to be very curious, though perhaps not singular as to the arrangement of the several bearings, I desired Mr. Fountaine to ask Mr. Tracy to favour me with a delineation; he readily complied with the request, and to his accurate drawing has subjoined a description of the arms of other persons of the name of Welles. The original is, you observe, within the initial letter of Registrum, and the illumination is neatly executed. From the form of the cross it may be inferred that St. Andrew is the Saint to whom the episcopal portrait beneath is represented as offering his devotion. If you turn to the memorials you will find that Brown, the predecessor of Wellys, was extremely solicitous to have his name and arms perpetuated in the Cathedrals of Rochester and Norwich, and that no traces of them are discernible in either of the Churches. His successor has been more fortunate, by taking care to have them delineated in a register, though fabricated of materials less durable than stone or brass. I am, Sir,

"Your faithful and humble servant,   S. Denne."

5. Mr. Denne to Mr. Gough.

"Dear Sir,   *Wilmington, Dec.* 15, 1789.

" The public prints must have apprised you of the death of George Lynch, the oldest friend I had†. With anxiety I have observed for two or three years that he did not wear well, being subject to fits of the gout that were not of a salutary kind; and I am apt to believe that during the summer he felt such a change in himself as portended a suspicion that his days would be soon numbered. This I collect from his solicitude to have a monument finished which he was preparing as a memorial of the departed branches of the family; but this satisfaction was denied him, and his intention must be executed by his two surviving sisters, my sister Denne and Mrs. Herring.

" Pleased was I to find that Bishop Yorke had complimented

---

* See Gent. Mag. vol. LVIII. p. 4.

† See a biographical notice of the Rev. George Lynch in the "Literary Anecdotes," vol. IX. p. 558.

Fisher* with the Vicarage of Linton, which, from its nearness to Duxford, must be a desirable living to him. What may be the situation of Duxford, and the sort of house appertaining to it, I am not aware; but Linton in my eye was the prettiest village I ever saw in Cambridgeshire.

" It had almost escaped my memory to apprise you that Delineator Clarke† is a clerk in the Ordnance-office at Chatham, and an occasional contributor to Mr. Urban's Miscellany. He is Indagator Roffensis, who subscribed the description of Woldham Church in the Magazine for July ‡; and in the next letter offered his conjectures touching the ' No Chalice ' on the monument in the Chapel at Greatham, co. Durham. I remain,
" Dear Sir, yours truly,   S. Denne."

————

6. " Dear Sir,   *Wilmington, Dec.* 3, 1790.
" Inclosed is a revised and enlarged edition of my Remarks on Stone Seats or Stalls §; whether the additions will entitle this paper to a second reading at a meeting of our brethren at Somerset-place Mr. Director is a competent judge. There is an inaccuracy of expression in Mr. Wells's ‖ observations, which, as it did not affect the principal question, I have not noticed; it occurs in the passages cited below ¶, where he repeatedly styles the Deacon and Subdeacon Priests. At this impropriety I am the more surprised, because I understood from you that our departed member was of the Romish persuasion; but I conclude from this instance, and from the errors into which he had fallen in his illustration drawn from Westminster Abbey, that he wrote his letter in haste, and that he did not examine with attention the canopies, bench, and royal monuments in the Confessor's Chapel. At page 6 he has referred in a note to the Gentleman's Magazine, vol. LVI. p. 649, for a short description of the triple seat in the Church of Hastings; but he has not referred to p. 751, where the subject is further considered, and from which paper he has copied several sentences. This inclines me to believe that he was the communicator of it under the signature of O, though he might have his reasons for not acknowledging it.

" Mr. Boys's Collections for the History of Sandwich, part ii. will ere long make their appearance, every sheet being worked off except what Mr. Latham, of Dartford, terms the Fauna; and

* The Rev. Edmund Fisher, M. A.
† Charles Clarke, Esq. F.S. A.   See Index to Archæologia, p. 15.
‡ See Gent. Mag. vol. LIX. p. 589.
§ See the Archæologia, vol. X. pp. 298—324.
‖ David Wells, Esq. F. S. A. of Burbach.
¶ " It is clear stone seats were originally designed for the three officiating Priests at the solemn Mass and Vespers, and these Priests were of three different dignities, to wit, the Celebrant, Deacon, and Subdeacon, p. 5; which remark serves further to confirm what has been advanced concerning the office of the three Priests, p. 6."

he being a very intelligent naturalist, this was submitted to his
correction, and he has, I think, returned it.   The delay has been
owing to Mr. Boys's choosing the book should pass under a press
that was near him rather than send it to a London printer, because he could upon more easy terms have the proof sheets;
and as often as Messrs. Simmons and Kirby were busy about
newspapers and catalogues, the Kentish Almanack Companion,
and Lady's Diary, Sandwich was dispatched to Coventry.

" The next time I write to Master Colman *, I shall hint to
him that he is not the first man of his county who has governed
the old House, having discovered, what had escaped the researches
of the indefatigable historian thereof, that Dr. John Porie, who
was said to be of Norfolk, was really a native of Thrapston in
Northamptonshire, and that he did not allow Archbishop Parker
the option of a legacy.   He appears, however, to have been a
benefactor to the church and poor of the parish where he was
born; and his Grace was not mistaken in his opinion that his
friend was not in affluent circumstances, though the world
reputed him to be rich.

" In a catalogue of books as advertised for sale by Bristow,
a bookseller at Canterbury, there is notice of there being among
them the valuable library of a gentleman who lately left this
county; for county perhaps might be read with propriety country, as I rather suspect the valuable library of the Historian of
Kent is alluded to, and to him the motto in his third volume is
truly applicable, ' Quo me cunque rapit tempestas, deferor
hospes.' A stranger in a foreign land is he, as it is generally believed, likely to remain for ever and aye, because he has deviated from the Poet's rule in the preceding verse, ' Quod verum
atque decens curo et rogo, et omnis in hoc sum.'

" I am, dear Sir, yours sincerely,   S. DENNE."

7. " DEAR SIR,   *Wilmington, Feb.* 24, 1791.
" Should the surmises concerning the figures in the window
of Brereton chancel † be novel at Somerset-place, the recital of
them may afford a quarter of an hour's amusement to the
Society; but if any other F. A. S. has anticipated them, the
encoring them even with variations may be rather tiresome, St.
Thomas à Becket and his Prince being a very hackneyed theme.

" With regard to the conjectures about the coat of arms of
an unknown Knight of the Garter, after consulting Ashmole
and Anstis, you may be competent to decide upon their validity;
and if any doubts still remain with you, I am persuaded that
our intelligent and communicative brother of the Heralds'-office ‡,
who is eke one of your fellow-council, will at once obviate them.
Much do I wish to discover whom the figure alluded to was
designed to represent.   Mr. Walpole, in Anecdotes of Painting,

* Dr. Colman, Master of Bene't-college, Cambridge.
† Printed in the Archæologia, vol. X. p. 334—344.   ‡ Mr. Brooke.

does not notice the portrait of any Talbot; and if this should be
a portrait of the renowned Sir John Talbot, it may be an unique.
It is well executed; and of the group of numberless heads of persons supposed to be spectators of the ceremony of the inaugu-
ration of the Virgin Mary, there are four beautiful faces just
behind the chairs of state in which are seated the Father and
Son; and at the footstool of the throne, on the left side, is a
man kneeling, with his arms and legs bare, and in tattered garments. For whom it was meant I have not the faintest idea."

" Your sincere friend,   S. DENNE."

---

8. " DEAR SIR,   *Wilmington, July 26, 1792.*
" At our last interview you hinted that there was not now so
many papers as heretofore for communication to our brethren
in Somerset-place; and you expressed a wish to receive assistance from myself and friends. By the favour of Mr. Clarke,
of Gravesend, a letter from whom was inserted in the last volume
of Archæologia, I send you a drawing of a single stone seat with
a piscina in the chancel of Chalk Church; and the latter object
is the more curious and interesting because it is in such a state
of preservation as to point out clearly the purpose for which it
was constructed. Mr. Clarke has also promised to illustrate it
by proper authorities, and to thus effectually subvert the general
idea hitherto prevailing of these being a receptacle for holy
water in the chancel. It is to be presumed that he will at the
same time take an opportunity to support the opinion he first
suggested in the Gentleman's Magazine, under the signature of
Indagator, concerning the original use of stone stalls, in which
I do not yet see sufficient grounds to concur with him; and it
is in consequence of a description of the stalls in Cotterstock
Church in Northamptonshire, in Bridges's History, vol. II.
p. 435, which seems to add weight to the notion I have formed,
that I give you the trouble of a few lines, apprehending that you
may be able to procure from one of your many correspondents
a drawing of these four seats, which according to Bridges rise
one above the other.
" Mr. Clarke is desired by me to make use of his pencil should
he discover in Chalk Church any other striking objects. The
front of the porch is indeed remarkable for its capricious and
ludicrous embellishments; but there being an engraving of
them in the Bibliotheca Britannica, No. VI. part I. I have hinted
my doubt, whether a new drawing would meet with the Society's
particular attention. His delineation of the Stall and Piscina,
or, to write more correctly, Fenestella with a Piscina, is fit for
a quarto volume; and I have recommended to him to let that
be the size of any other drawing he may consent to have exhibited, as thinking you are more in want of pieces for Archæologia than for Vetusta Monumenta.

" In a dearth of papers for the amusement of F. S. A. further remarks on Fonts may not be unacceptable; and I have it therefore in my thoughts to transmit some when the meetings of the Society shall be renewed. I have applied for a description of the Font in Canterbury Cathedral, and by means of that compared with the engraving of that in the original edition of Somner's Antiquities, as eke with Richard Culmer's, alias Blue Dick, the Iconoclast's 'Dean and Chapter news from Canterbury,' I am persuaded I shall clearly show that Batteley was mistaken in his averment, that after the Restoration ' Bishop Warner caused a new Font, more costly and beautiful than the former, to be set up at his own charge.' As Batteley did not choose to be at the expense of a plate, he ought certainly to have favoured his readers with a circumstantial detail of the figures exhibited; and indeed this is wanting, notwithstanding the plates given by Somner and by Gostling in the 'Walk about Canterbury,' they presenting the same view of the Font, and but a little more than a fourth part of it.

" The chancel of Maidstone Church is repairing. It has been covered with a new roof; and, should a new pavement be laid, I hope that accidentally by design an opportunity will be taken to discover whether the ashes of old Courtenay are deposited under the stone laid there for a memorial of him. On the digging for a vault in March last in the Church-yard very near to the east end of the chancel, some massy foundations were removed; and it is reasonably supposed that they were a part of those of the old Church, which it was not necessary to take away on the erection of the present building, supposing it to be placed upon a different site. And in the Church-yard of Bromley, on opening the ground to lay a foundation for a north aile, just below the surface was found a stone coffin; but whether there was an antiquary present to examine it with attention I have not heard.

" Mr. Tracy, of Brompton, near Chatham, whose name, as delineator, is subscribed to several plates in Mr. Thorpe's Antiquities, in acknowledging the receipt of my articles in the last volume of Archæologia, which I had transmitted to him as a small recompense for civilities he had showed me, thus expresses himself:

" ' The accounts hitherto published of William de Tracy, whom you mention in your remarks on the portraits at Brereton, are very erroneous (see note t). That Baron was living 6 Richard I. and died before the first of John, from whom Henry de Tracy, nick-named Le Bossu, his son, through the interest of Geffery Fitz-Piers, Earl of Essex, obtained possession of his land, and paid a relief for fifty Knights' fees.' — From a paragraph in Mr. Thorpe's Antiquities, p. 131, it appears that my correspondent is well versed in the genealogy of a family to which he bears a relationship by consanguinity. I am, dear Sir,

" Your faithful and obliged servant,   S. DENNE.

" William Parslow, M. A. whose promotion to the Vicarage of
Yardley, Herts, is announced in the newspapers, is, 1 conclude,
the son of my contemporary Thomas Parslow, of Bene't-college,
of snuff-taking memory. To whom of the Chapter, if not to
the Right Rev. the Dean of St. Paul's, is the young man indebted for this presentation? It is not mentioned that he is a Fellow of the old House, and it may therefore be presumed that he
has not a title to this appellation *."

———

9. " DEAR SIR,   *Wilmington, Feb.* 11, 1793.
" The names of the benefactors to Lambeth parish, with
numerous references to vouchers, not legible without some difficulty, were among my father's papers, and a fair transcript
thereof into a book was sent by me to Dr. Porteus. From my
father's notes the tables of benefactions were formed, which are
mentioned in the History of Lambeth in Bibliotheca Topographica Britannica; and I conclude that the tables in Shoreditch
Church were compiled from my father's MS. which has fallen
into your hands.

" Partly from my wishing to minute divers passages in Mr.
Clarke's observations on stone seats, and partly from my waiting
for some additional remarks which he had promised, a delay has
ensued in transmitting to you the book and drawings; but I am
now prepared to catch the first safe conveyance that shall offer.
Not a doubt have 1 of your concurring in opinion with me, that
thankful acknowledgments are due to Mr. Clarke for his valuable
communications.

" Is it new to you that Mr. Thorpe has left to Mr. Meggison's
eldest son all his books, prints, drawings, and papers? flattering
himself, it may be presumed, that the stripling would have the
like bent to antiquities as had his grandsire and great-grandsire.
In consequence of such a bequest it is probable that the collection will be locked up for years in cases and boxes †.

" 1 remain, dear Sir, yours sincerely,   S. DENNE."

———

10. " DEAR SIR,   *Wilmington, Nov.* 15, 1793.
" Most willingly do I consent to Mr. Carter's taking a copy of
the Talbot portrait, in the MS. Collection of Devotions which
possibly belonged to the nobleman represented; and you are
welcome to review, at your leisure, the contents of that book.
The drawings on the margins of the Calendar are certainly
curious and very amusing; and often have 1 regretted that one
month should be missing.

" The Dean of Rochester ‡ being elected F.A.S. will not, I

———

* Mr. Parslow was of Corpus Christi-college, Cambridge, B.A. 1788,
M.A. 1791; he died at Yardley, July 22, 1827, aged 61.
† This library was sold by auction, by Leigh and Sotheby, in the
year 1811.   ‡ Thomas Dampier, D. D.

trust, be what the mercantile folks term a sleeping partner. In his letter to me dated, Durham, October 14, are some inuendos which show he has a strong bent to antique lore.

" ' Since I wrote last (he says) I have been employed for some days in our treasury with a gentleman from the Register-office at Edinburgh, in searching for Scotch records, some of which he supposed might be found among the many belonging to that Kingdom, which he had heard were in our possession. Though he was disappointed in his main object, his trouble was fully repaid by the sight of the greatest number of old charters and records that are any where deposited. Our Scotch MSS. are those of the Abbey of Coldingham in Berwickshire, heretofore dependent on this; and contain charters of the Kings of Scotland, from Duncan to the Reformation, in general very well preserved, particularly as to their seals, some of which were not noticed by Anderson. If the Diplomata was in our library, I would see what was wanting there, and get drawings made of the most curious; nor are the records of our own Church less numerous, they begin with the Conqueror. The contents of the first are rather curious. In a small strip of parchment he confirms to the Prior his privileges, and particularly that of sitting *in sinistrâ parte chori.* This is the Dean's seat at present, the Bishop sitting, when at Church, on the right, till the second service on Sunday mornings, when he goes up to the throne. The seals here too are most perfect; one of a late comparative date is a most beautiful specimen, it is appendant to a grant of Henry Earl of Northumberland (temp. H. IV.), and shows his greatness and pretensions in assuming a broad seal. As the place where these valuables are kept is inconvenient, we talk of having them removed and newly arranged, which will enable me to see every one of them. You know that we have originals of Magna Charta and de Foresta.'

" I am, dear Sir, truly yours,   S. DENNE."

---

11. " DEAR SIR,   *Jan.* 10, 1794.

" After you moved from Wilmington Vicarage, often did I regret that the sinking of the quicksilver in my antique barometer did not discourage you from mounting your steed, for a deplorable day it was for that exposed method of travelling. I trust, however, that pleasure will ensue from mortification; because, as the weather did not admit of your visiting Lullingstone, I am willing to flatter myself that you will, in a more propitious season, take another trip to satisfy your curiosity, and that I shall then be favoured with a longer visit.

" In answer to your inquiry about the successors in the manor of Famingham since the publication of Mr. Hasted's first volume, I am somewhat inclined to believe that it may not yet have been alienated by Lord Coleraine. With the great house near the bridge I am apt to suspect no more land was parted with than was requisite to encourage bidders for that mansion. It is now vested in Mr. Fuller, a substantial yeoman of that parish; and Mr. Warre is only sub-tenant under a lease granted to the late Henry Thoyts, a corn-factor and under-writer, who acquired more money than discretion, and agreed to pay a most enormous rent for it; but the rent is lowered to Mrs. Warre, and a nephew of Henry Thoyts is answerable to the landlord for the difference. That is not, however, the manor-house, for this was taken down some years ago; it stood on the opposite side of the road, and some part of the wall which inclosed the court, &c. are remaining. The present shewy building was begun (for there have been sundry additions to it) and first inhabited by a man of the name of Crakelt. He dealt largely in wool, and was growing rich apace; but being detected in clandestinely running that staple commodity, the Court of Exchequer squeezed him so hard, that at his death this ill-gotten pelf was very much decreased.

" Sir Thomas Hyde Page, with his many rolls and books, was doubtless the gentleman who apprised you of his having printed, in 1784, Considerations on the State of Dover Harbour, a tract I have seen. As the History of Dover Castle, published in 1788, and compiled by Mr. Lyon, may be new to you, I have inclosed it for your perusal. It was, you see, dedicated to the Rev. Mr. Byrche, F.S.A. and no F.S.A.

" With thanks I return ' Objections to the War examined and refuted,' a title which promised much more than is to be found in the pamphlet. And the writer has clearly shown in the last four pages how lamentably he was mistaken as to the glory, and the lustre, and the numberless advantages that were to accrue from that superlatively impolitic plan, the acquisition of Toulon.

" Concerned am I to find, that the Society of Antiquaries are in so craving a way. I now transmit to Mr. Director a morsel, with Mr. Clarke's drawing of the grotesque relief on the porch of Chalk Church. Not discovering in the indexes to the volumes of Archæologia the word *giveale*, I thought it expedient to offer copious authorities for the surmise I have suggested; but I have entered them in a separate paper, that Secretary Wright may or may not, as he finds most convenient, read the notes with the text.

" Decisive, in my opinion, are the evidence and the arguments offered in your memoir of Sir John Fastolff, to show that Shakspeare had not any intention of calumniating that brave warrior, by assuming the name of Falstaff when he found it requisite to drop that of Oldcastle in his Plays of Henry IV.; and on the perusal of that part of your note in p. 4, in which you observe, that the Poet might mean to express a trait in the character of the lying Knight by styling him Falstaff, it occurred to me that in the Merry Wives of Windsor the like notion is implied.

The passage I mean is at the conclusion of Act. I. sc. 1, when to the question asked by Shallow, ' Let us see, honest Page, is Falstaff there ?' the answer of Sir Hugh Evans is, ' Shall I tell you a lie ? I despise a liar as I despise one that is false; the Knight Sir John is there.' Qu. Is there not here an indirect allusion to the first syllable in Falstaff?

" I am, truly yours,   S. Denne."

12. "Dear Sir,   *Wilmington, Feb.* 10, 1794.

" Mr. Todd's publication has not been yet seen in Dartford, which, though a market town in which an abundance of grain is vended every Saturday, has not in it a shop that can be called a Bibliopolium ; and as by master Gillman's figuring in the Gazette, with a Whereas prefixed to his name, the elder Fisher, who was his principal assistant in the book way, has left Rochester, I cannot, with the same ease as I was wont to do, obtain tracts and papers from the eastern part of our county ; however, I shall make it my business to inquire after a volume that has your approbation. Of Mr. Todd I have no other knowledge * than what I learnt from Mr. Wall, who was the friend I applied to for information concerning Bishop Warner's Font; and, if I did not mishear Mr. Wall, he was chiefly indebted to Mr. Todd for the description of it. He was a Minor Canon of Canterbury Cathedral, through the interest of Dean Horne, afterwards Bishop of Norwich; and I have understood that he is the descendant of a Dr. Todd, who was a great Canon at Carlisle. Mr. Wall had told me of its being Mr. Todd's purpose to publish some memorials of the Deans of Canterbury; but I hardly thought of his having had sufficient time to collect materials.

" Mortified am I with your report of the antiquarian corps being, in one instant, so extremely necessitous ; and I fear it will not be in my power this Session to contribute another mite towards their relief, being much engrossed in winding up the Addenda to the Histories of Lambeth Palace and Lambeth Parish †. Notwithstanding Dr. Ducarel's too free correction of Parkinson, I have not a doubt in my mind of old Tradescant's having lived at Canterbury before he settled at South Lambeth ; and I think I can trace by whom, and in what spot, he was employed as a gardener in the vicinage of that city.

" That there were two Spring Gardens in Lambeth is also clear to me ; I do not, however, mean the two so denominated by the inaccurate Maitland, but I am guided by a passage in Aubrey's Surrey, which evidently alludes to two. When Dr.

---

* The Rev. Henry John Todd is now universally known from his numerous highly important publications, and as universally respected.

† " Historical Particulars of Lambeth Parish and Lambeth Palace," were published by Mr. Denne in 1795. This is a most accurate and curious book ; and, from the greater part of the impression having been destroyed by fire, has become remarkably scarce.

Ducarel noticed the grant of Copthall-house (improperly called Vaux-hall) I wonder he did not apprise the reader, that Samuel Moreland most probably had it from Charles the Second, as a reward for his services on the eve of the Restoration.

"It is mentioned by Mr. Lysons that Archbishop Abbot was the preacher at the funeral of Sir Noel Caron. If the Sermon was printed (which probably it was not) the perusal of it would afford some occurrences in the life, and traits in the character, of a man of rank, concerning whom very little is known, though he was a resident in England upward of twenty-eight years, and, as it were, naturalized himself to the country; for that he was ever naturalised by an Act of the Legislature I am not aware.

"When I had the pleasure of seeing you, I hinted to you that a Kentish Monthly Register had been started by the printers of the Kentish Gazette; for a reason already assigned not a single number of it has yet travelled to Dartford, but I find by that newspaper and by the Maidstone Journal, that it continues upon what the editors deem an improved plan. A copy of the advertisement I have inclosed for your amusement *; and shall only remark upon the first plate with which they have favoured the public, that, unless there be a surprising alteration in Dene, they exhibited the view of a mansion that has nothing in it picturesque or striking.

"The proofs of Mr. Clarke's paper on Episcopal Chairs and Stone Seats † may as well be submitted to the correction of the writer, as I have not some of the books he has cited. There has

* Advertisement copied from the Maidstone Journal, Jan. 18, 1794.

"The Kentish Register, improved and embellished with engravings for January 1794; embellished with a very elegant view of Dene in East Kent, one of the seats of Sir Henry Oxenden, Bart.

"In the design of embellishing the Kentish Register with engravings, the object is not merely ornament, but information. Whatever, therefore, in particular belongs to an historical repository of the County seems to form the most desirable series of plates; on this account a draughtsman and engraver, peculiarly conversant and well known in this line, is employed, by which we shall, in a course of time, introduce such a collection of Seats, Towns, Ruins, Religious Buildings, Remarkable Scenes, and other local subjects hitherto unengraved, as will render our publication as it advances not only more valuable, but we hope of no small estimation to Persons of Curiosity in Topography, Antiquities, and History, throughout the Kingdom; subjects, indeed, of general and interesting curiosity, which one circumstance of the times may point out, will by no means be excluded, whilst that which is peculiar to the County of Kent must be the leading feature of the work.

"One engraving at least will be given with every subsequent number, and without any advance in the price of the work. *Our sale hitherto, and without plates, has extended to* 750 *copies.* The proposed embellishment will be a heavy and continued expense; but we are confident that the public patronage will keep pace with our exertions to deserve it. Printed by Simmons, Kirkby, and Jones."

It was observable that the words in italics, noticing the number of copies sold, were omitted in the Kentish Gazette of the same date.

† In Archæologia, vol. XI. pp. 317—374.

not been any correspondence between us since October last; but I shall soon dispatch a letter to him, and may he in return advise me that his pencil has been employed on some object that will be worthy the notice of our brethren in Somerset-place! He has promised to let me have a drawing of an Archiepiscopal Portrait in good preservation in a window in Mepham Church; but he is, I know, a valetudinarian, and not very willing to pass an hour or two in a cold damp place, and such is a country church in a winter month.

"I am, dear Sir, yours sincerely,   S. DENNE."

13. "DEAR SIR,   *Wilmington, Feb.* 26, 1794.
"It was not my intention to make any report of the discovery of Primate Courtenay's bones till I had had an opportunity of conversing with some of the party present at the opening of his grave; but your letter has quickened my movements, and a letter has been dispatched to Mr. Cherry *, the school-master,

* The Rev. Thomas Cherry, for twenty-four years the highly-respected Master of Merchant-taylors' School, was himself educated at that foundation, where we find him in 1763, in some dramatical exhibitions, performing the part of Pyrrhus in the Troades of Seneca, and that of Trico in Ruggle's Latin Comedy of Ignoramus. On the following St. Bartholomew's day (June 11) he was elected Fellow of St. John's-college, Oxford; where he proceeded B. A. 1767; M. A. 1771; B. D. 1776. His first clerical employment was the Curacy and Lectureship of St. Anne's, Limehouse; to which was subsequently added an alternate Lectureship at Christ Church, Spitalfields. In 1777 he was appointed Master of the Grammar-school at Maidstone, in which office, and as Curate to Mr. Denne as above noticed, he continued for eighteen years. He also held for some time the Vicarage of Leckford in Hampshire, and that of Loose in Kent. At the close of 1795 he was elected Head-master of Merchant-taylors' School on the death of the learned Rev. Samuel Bishop. "Excellence like Bishop's," says Dr. Wilson in his History of the Institution, "had the effect of rendering the Company somewhat fastidious in the choice of a successor. Impressed with the simplicity of manners, the strength of penetration, the integrity of conduct, the depth of learning, and the brilliancy of imagination, which characterised their departed friend, they overlooked every other consideration in their wish to see 'his like again;' and, thinking that more of these estimable qualifications were united in the Master of Maidstone School than in any other of the candidates, they elected him on the 16th of December. How far the choice was justified by experience, the flourishing state of the school for nearly a quarter of a century, bears ample testimony. He uniformly inculcated that principle of disinterested loyalty, which has in every age been the distinguishing characteristic of Merchant-taylors." In another division of his volume Dr. Wilson paid Mr. Cherry the following deserved compliment: "Of this amiable man it may be truly said, (and what can be greater praise?) that in taste and talents he yields to none of his predecessors. Placed as he is between the dead and the living, he forms one of the links that unite the scholars of the present day with those of former times. And when, at last, his honourable career of usefulness is closed, his literary companions will long remember him for his intimate, yet unostentatious, acquaintance with the treasures of antiquity." Mr. Cherry combined with his scho-

and my poor brother's morning Preacher Assistant, desiring the favour of him to communicate to me his remarks, he having been an attentive observer. My motive for applying to him for information is, that I cannot at present find the brief notes I took, and am unwilling wholly to trust to memory.

" The death of our worthy brother, Mr. Brooke, must be regretted by every one who had the pleasure of his acquaintance, and the more so from the dreadful manner in which he passed out of the world *. Always did I find him ready to impart his knowledge in the heraldic, antiquarian, and biographical line; and it was within a week of the terrible catastrophe that I had solicited some information touching the Slingsby family, having some reason to believe that one of them might have for his sponsors Archbishop Abbot and the Duke of Buckingham, who appeared in person at the font in Lambeth Church, after having heard a suitable sermon by Dr. Featley, the then Rector of the parish. The difficulty of ascertaining who the bairn thus highly honoured might be, has proceeded from the carelessness of the person who had the charge of the register-book, there not being any entry of a christening on the day the Sermon is mentioned to have been preached. The Sermon is printed in Clavis Mystica; and sundry quaint expressions there are in it which you will probably read, though I know not how soon, in the types of Mr. Deputy Nichols.

" Sir John Fenn's decease cannot be a very novel matter to you †. He had, it seems, a mother very far advanced in years, to whom he daily paid a visit, and dropped down in apoplexy whilst he was in her apartment. I understand that he survived the fatal stroke only two days; and if I am not mistaken he had

lastic occupations the Curacy of St. Mary Abchurch and St. Lawrence Pountney, and in 1813 was Chaplain to George Scholey, Esq. when Lord Mayor of London. He resigned the Mastership in 1819, and was succeeded by his son-in law, the Rev. James William Bellamy, B.D. the present Head-master. On his retirement he had the pleasing satisfaction of receiving from his grateful scholars a silver urn, inscribed on one side with the following lines : " Thomæ Cherry, S. T. B. qui Scholæ Mercatorum Sciss. annos viginti quatuor felicissimè præfuit, Alumni superiorum ordinum hoc pietatis monumentum consecravêre A. D. MDCCCXIX ; " and on the other his arms, Argent, a fess indented between three annulets Gules ; and crest, a demi-lion rampant, in the dexter paw an annulet.

Mr. Cherry passed his latter days at his Vicarage of Sellinge in Kent, to which he had been presented by the Lord Chancellor in 1817, on the resignation of his son-in-law Mr. Bellamy. He died at Merchant-taylors' School, March 10, 1822, aged 75, and was interred on the 16th, in Poplar Chapel, where the remains of his wife, who died at Hertford in 1810, had been deposited. There is a portrait of Mr. Cherry in Wilson's "History of Merchant-taylors' School," engraved by H. D. Thielcke from a painting by Drummond.

* See before, p. 356.

† Of Sir John Fenn memoirs are given in the "Literary Anecdotes," vol. VIII. p. 139, and a series of his letters in the present Work, vol. V. pp. 167—180.

about two years ago a paralytic stroke, which has been properly termed a first warning of the human clock. He was interred in the family vault of the Freres in a Church on the borders of Suffolk. To the Society in Somerset-place he was not so good a contributor in the correspondent way as the F. S. A. had reason to expect from a brother who was certainly possessed of some choice MSS. The first and second volumes of Original Letters certainly yielded a considerable profit to him and his bookseller; whether they might be equally well satisfied with the sale of the third volume I doubt from this circumstance, — Sir John not having made a present of it to Mr. Currey, though he had given him the former volumes. Mr. Currey became Vicar of Dartford in exchange for Dereham.

　　　　" I remain, dear Sir, truly yours,　　　S. Denne."

14. " Dear Sir,　　　　　　　　*March* 25, 1794.

" The inclosed additional epistle * touching that often mooted case, the place of burial of Archbishop Courtenay, awaits your acceptance; and I trust that no great inconvenience has arisen from my not having sooner dispatched it to you.

" In answer to your inquiry after the paternal lineage of the late Countess Digby, I will refer you to the account given by Mr. Hasted of the Knowler race. Her ladyship's father was Recorder of Canterbury, Faversham, and of sundry other places where there are Corporations; but as Counsellor Knowler, or the Plowden of Kent, as he was sometimes called, was a native of Faversham, I am inclined to believe you will find the most copious detail of the family in our historian's description of that town.

" Mr. Lysons has a happy conjecture of Vauxhall having acquired that appellation from Fulk, alias Foukes de Brent (Environs, p. 321). Not a doubt can be entertained of the probability of the surmise, if it be considered that this ignoble foreigner is thrice styled Faukisius by a monkish writer ;—a circumstance which strongly implies that Fauks or Faukis was his name in the vulgar tongue. He was a seditious fellow, and bore a character as notoriously infamous, as did in a later age his namesake Gunpowder Guido.

" Some remarks on the first two volumes of Original Letters were transmitted to the late Sir John Fenn from myself; one of them is noticed in the Memorials of Rochester Cathedral in Thorpe's Antiquities, p. 217.

　　　　" I remain, yours sincerely,　　　S. Denne."

---

* Introduced by Mr. Gough into his Sepulchral Monuments; Mr. Denne had previously discussed the subject in the tenth volume of Archæologia.

15. " DEAR SIR, *Devereux-court, April* 25, 1794.

" From Mr. Deputy I had, in pursuance of your intimation, a proof of that sheet of your Introduction to Sepulchral Monuments, in which you have condescended to insert my letter on the discovery of the bones of Archbishop Courtenay ; and it shall be forthwith revised and delivered at the Cicero's Head.

" Many thanks to you for your kind present of the description of the most curious Roman Missal *, or collection of devotions, perhaps extant. I was disappointed in not having the opportunity of making my grateful acknowledgments in person at the Antiquarian Anniversary on St. George's-day. One loss you certainly sustained by your absence, for had we met at the Somerset Coffee-house there would have been exhibited to you a curious sepulchral relic, *viz.* the tooth of a Metropolitan that had been dispossessed nearly two centuries. It was shown to Mr. Deputy, who will not, however, admit my Courtenay's fang to be so precious a treasure as his bone of Sir Hugh of Lincoln. De gustibus non est disputandum !

" I have procured ' Some Account of the Deans of Canterbury,' and am satisfied with my purchase, though still of opinion Mr. Todd might as well have waited till he had compiled a few more materials. Should I hear of a likelihood of a second edition, I may be induced to transmit to him references to books to increase his collection. I remain, truly yours, S. DENNE."

16. " DEAR SIR, *Wilmington, May* 9, 1794.

" When I was compiling Memoirs of Lambeth Chaplains for Addenda to Dr. Ducarel's History of that Palace, I did not meet with any particular of consequence relative to Chapman that was not noticed in the Obituary of the Gentleman's Magazine ; and the same observation will apply to Bishop Lisle, who was Chaplain to Archbishop Wake. As to this Prelate, whose father and himself were natives of Dorsetshire, and buried at Blandford, I take for granted you have biographical anecdotes more than *quantum sufficit* for a County History. There are, however, some original *notitiæ* of him and his family, written by his Grace himself, still extant, and as I conclude in the safe custody of his grandson the Archdeacon of Canterbury. With the perusal of them my father was favoured by the late Dean Lynch ; and I have now transcribed a long extract relative to his father †, who was gathered to his ancestors in the Church of Blandford Forum. You will find also in the same paper two transcripts in which the County of Dorset is noticed. And observing that, from rather strange inadvertency, the dedication of Archbishop Wake's Sermon was omitted when the Sermon itself was re-printed, this is tacked to my epistle ; but for the explanatory

* Mr. Gough's Account of the Bedford Missal.

† This was printed in the new edition of the History of Dorsetshire, vol. I. pp. 140—143.

MS. it might have remained a matter of doubt who was the Prelate, a native of Dorsetshire, that had engaged to preach the Sermon on the revival of the county feast; and it is left to you to trace whether any of the stewards of the feast enacted any other deeds worthy of being recorded in the History of their County.

" Messrs. Todd and Gutch will engage * in an arduous, extensive, and hazardous work if they do resolve to publish a new edition of Le Neve's Fasti. It was a subject of correspondence between my father and the Historian of Bene't; for my tutor, well knowing that his coadjutor had an interleaved copy with copious references, could not avoid expressing a wish that the alterations and additions might appear in print, owning, however, at the same time, he had his apprehensions that the sale would not pay costs.

" An opportunity of reading the Analytical Review, in which, as you suggest, Todd's Deans are too severely criticised, has not offered. I am, dear Sir, very truly yours,   S. DENNE."

17. " DEAR SIR,   *Wilmington, July 9,* 1794.
" Having prepared for insertion in the Miscellany of Sylvanus Urban some notes of Monuments in Wilmington church-yard, I am unwilling to miss the opportunity of putting into the packet a few lines to you, expressing my thanks to you for apprising me of the day fixed for the delivery of Archæologia, vol. XI. which many F. S. A.'s have long expected.

" Whether it may be in my power to figure in vol. XII. must be a matter of doubt. In my situation means are wanting to pursue rsearches to any extent; and besides, when a man has passed his grand climacteric, other difficulties may be expected yearly to arise. All that I have promised to Secretary Wrighte is a narrative, with remarks, of the trial of Phineas Pette, on a charge of ignorance in constructing the famous ship the Prince, at which King James the First presided, he being, in his conceit, as well versed in naval architecture as in controversial divinity. I shall offer this only as a readable paper when there is scarcity at Somerset-place of antiquarian food for the entertainment of the evening, being at present not a little dubious whether it will be of sufficient consequence to appear in the Archæologia. Mr. Latham, on a late visit to his son at Romsey, amused himself in drawing some parts of their antient Monastic Church, which he has promised to show me. I wish I could prevail on him to employ both pen and pencil for the information and amusement of our fraternity; and I do not despair of succeeding in my attempt, because he will in future be more at liberty than he has hitherto been, having taken a partner into his shop. That

* See vol. V. of the present Work, pp. 342 *et seq.*

he is not disposed to be idle is clear from what he has published on birds and other parts of Natural History.

" This paper will be closed with black wax in consequence of my having had the honour to be a second cousin to the late heroic Captain of the Brunswick *, whose departure out of life must be regretted by every true Englishman. It was not without surprise as well as concern that I heard of his danger, having been told, and as I thought on good authority, he was not likely to suffer any other loss than that of his arm, which was amputated beneath the elbow; but I now understand that owing partly to the great effusion of blood, because he refused for a long time to leave the quarter-deck, and partly to the fatigue of the action and the wind of the balls, his whole bodily frame had received such a concussion that it was soon apprehended to be a desperate case. He has left a large number of very near relations to lament his loss, viz. a wife and several children, the eldest of whom, Captain William Harvey, is a master and commander, and the youngest under four years of age; a father, mother, four brothers, and four sisters. Richard Harvey, a contemporary of yours, is the eldest brother; Henry, of the Ramilies, now an Admiral, the next. The parents are both stricken, but the father very hearty and active. On the 20th of February last they completed the sixtieth year of their matrimonial connexion. The Admiral, there is much reason to fear, has lost his son, who was a Lieutenant of the Ardent, said to be shipwrecked near Corsica; a stroke which must be the more affecting to his father, who in the summer of 1788 was unfortunately deprived of his eldest son, a fine youth between nineteen and twenty. Henry Harvey was at that time Captain of the Convert on the Newfoundland station; and of fifteen who fell overboard when the ship was under sail, young Harvey was the only person drowned, and that in the presence of his father, after many unavailing attempts to save him.

" Room only is left for wishing a pleasant tour into Derbyshire to yourself and Mr. Deputy; and for a tender of best respects to the worthy Patriarch of Antiquaries, from his and your faithful and humble servant,   S. DENNE."

---

18. " DEAR SIR,   *Wilmington, Aug.* 27, 1794.

" It was with greater satisfaction I read your favourable account of the venerable Rector of Whittington, because from your former report there was ground to apprehend that the days were come in which he was not likely to have much pleasure in them. His precaution and admonition to one who was born when he was in the prime of life, merits regard; but at the same time has not a man as little reason to flatter himself that he shall

* Capt. J. Harvey fell in Lord Howe's glorious naval victory of the 1st of June 1794. See Gent. Mag. vol. LXIV. p. 673.   † Rev. Dr. Pegge.

attain to the age of fourscore years and twelve, with a full possession of his intellectual powers, as he has that he shall gain a
prize of £.20,000 in the lottery?

" When you see Mr. Ord I will trouble you with my thanks to
him for his extracts relative to a Font in Christ Church, Canterbury. Mr. Gostling had had an intimation of it, but was doubtful whether it belonged to that Cathedral or to the Abbey of St.
Austin. 'I find,' writes he, (Gent. Mag. vol. XLV. p. 13,) 'in
vol. IV. of Leland, p. 180, edit. 1771, in Margaret Countess
of Richmond's orders for preparations against the delivery of a
pregnant Queen, that the Font of Silver at Canterbury was to be
sent for, or another made like it.' This, however, does not
controvert the truth of Somner's observation, of there not
having been a fixed Stone Font in Canterbury Cathedral prior to
that which was given by Bishop Warner.

" To the few Fonts of Lead as yet noticed may be added one
standing at the west end of the middle aile of St. Peter's Church
in Thanet. It is by Mr. Lewis (Hist. p. 161) described to be a
large leaden basin placed on a pedestal of brick plastered over;
and so ingeniously done as to look like hewn stone. Broad-
stairs, a place much frequented by sea-bathers and sea air-
breathers, is in that parish; but there may not, I trow, be an
antiquary among them to whom the Font may appear so striking
an object as to occasion its being delineated.

" As it has happened, you might again have kept the august
gala in the hall of the old House * with the master thereof, Dr.
Colman not being able to migrate to Stalbridge at the time he
had proposed. The illness of his servant was one of the incidents which delayed his journey, as I am told by Fellow James
Currey, who is at present visiting his father the Vicar of Dartford.

" Mr. Currey informs me that his co-Fellow Owen s Sermon at
the Summer Assizes was more to the zest of the University than
that delivered by him in March on the like occasion, because he
was less diffuse and flowery in his language; and, notwithstanding the copious eulogies scattered by Reviewers on the Sermon
which he published, I must own that many of the passages
appeared to me to be filled with what in our time would have
been styled 'white bears.' But Fellow Dixon †, who was
in St. Mary's pulpit on Whitsunday in the afternoon, made
his hearers of both sexes stare and smile at his suggesting,
among other curious remarks, that the gift of tongues was not
conferred on a woman on the day of Pentecost.

" Young Masters ‡, as I understand, died consumptive. He
was offended by the old man's desiring two of the Cambridge
physicians to go to Waterbeach to consult upon his dangerous
case; father and son, however, seldom conversed together in a

---

* Bene't-college.
† Rev. Francis Dixon, A.B. 1777; A.M. 1780; S.T.B. 1788.
‡ See before, p. 293.

friendly and affectionate manner, probably from their both having
a perversity of temper, though once the former hinted to Dr.
Colman he was greatly astonished where his son could acquire
such a degree of obstinacy as was discernible in him. Till it
was mentioned to me by Mr. James Currey, I was not apprised
that *tenacem propositi* was the motto to Mr. Masters's arms.
Qu. was it chosen by the bearer as characteristic of himself, or
did it devolve to him with a devise of a red lion rampant with a
brace of long tails erect, by hereditary right?

" By favour of the Bishop of Ely, Mr. Masters resigned Waterbeach to his son; and by favour of the same Prelate he may be
again incumbent thereof; or, it is said, his Lordship has offered
to collate to it a son-in-law there now is, or a clergyman who
is thought to be a son-in-law elect. But Mr. Sprowle, it seems,
has his doubts, whether it may be worth his while to cede for
Waterbeach, the parish he has in Appleby; and it is only from
report that Mr. B——— is an humble servant of the daughter.
The young man is of Trinity-hall *. I was for giving his Lordship full credit for the generosity of these several acts of
indulgence towards his *quondam quasi* tutor, for I have a notion
James Yorke might be now and then of the party when we sat
at the feet of Gamaliel, to hear in his apartment a learned lecture on $a+b-c$, or on a proposition in Euclid's Elements, or
when we descended with him into the cellar to see the experiments of an axis in peritrochio; but it has been suggested to
me that Mr. Masters has some well-founded pretensions to these
marks of regard, from his having, at a considerable expense,
re-built the Vicarage, and from his having with spirit, and at
no small charge, set aside a modus. He must, indeed, have
greatly improved the Vicarage, if it really be of the reputed
value of £.200 a year, because in the King's books it is rated
at no more than £.5. 15s. $7\frac{1}{2}d$.

" Perhaps you observed in Lloyd's Evening Post a paragraph
which announced the taking down of the tower of the steeple
of St. George's Church in Canterbury; it was thus more circumstantially related in The Kentish Gazette, of August 8:
'The workmen on Monday began to throw down the antient
round tower, attached to the south-east corner of the steeple of
St. George's Church. It contained a flight of stone steps to its
top, crowned with a spire and handsome weathercock, useful
and ornamental to the City; but in consequence of the new
pavement in 1788, an arched passage was opened through its bottom for foot passengers †, which was supposed to have weakened
the building so much that it was judged necessary to be removed.'
Is there not reason to conclude that there might be want of
skill in the surveyor employed to turn the arch? for, was not

the experiment made with success under the tower of the much
more lofty steeple of the Church of St. Magnus, near London-
bridge * ? I remain, dear Sir, truly yours,   S. DENNE."

---

19. " DEAR SIR,   *Wilmington, Sept.* 24, 1794.
" Since I was favoured with your letter I have endeavoured in
vain to find any other Sermons in print preached at the anniversary meetings of the natives of Dorsetshire than those by
Wake and Spratt; but, whilst searching through the many
volumes of single Sermons (nearly 150) of which I am possessed, I discovered three that were preached in the county,
and a summary of the contents, with a few extracts, are transmitted to you, notwithstanding I have my doubts as to the
expediency of mentioning in a County History any part of my
scroll except that which gives a curious trait of the character
of Sa. Bolde, the zealous Vicar of Shapwick. There shall be
also inclosed a paper with a few notes concerning the Archdea-
cons of Dorset.
" Among the desiderata in antiquities not likely to be
answered, one is evidence to ascertain what might be the
height of the spring-tides in the Thames about London and
Thorney Isle, in the times of the Romans, Saxons, and Norman
Kings; because it might enable us to form a judgment of the
state of the land opposite during that period. The surmise I
entertained is, that till the marshes of Kent and Essex were
inned, the flow of the tide above London was weak in comparison, and not high. The earliest mention of the tide that
has occurred in my reading is in Simeon Dunelm. X. S. col. 186,
31, &c. where he is relating the passage of Harold with his
ships through London-bridge, anno 1052; and of the preparations made by him to attack King Edward's fleet, it should
seem, near the Royal Palace at Westminster. On turning to
Fitz-Stephen, I perceive he notices the flux and reflux of the
tide, ' sed fluvius maximus piscosus, Thamesis, mari influo
refluoque, qui illac allabitur, mœnia illa (ab austro) tractu temporis abluit, labefactavit, dejecit.' Can you recollect any other
antient Historian than Fitz-Stephen who asserts the ruin of
this supposed south wall by the washing of the river? to me it
appears not very improbable that the river in front was considered as a sufficient defence; and the wall, if there were one,
must have been interrupted by the river.
" What an egregious blunder is committed by Pennant in
London, p. 294, where he suggests, that Unlaf the Dane sailed
up the river as high as Staines! Saxon Chronicle, p. 145 (error
of MS. or press for 127), is the authority cited ; and if you turn
to that page you will at once be satisfied that Stane there men-

---

* In this instance Sir C. Wren is said to have provided for the improvement, in his original construction of the Tower.

tioned must mean some place on the eastern coast of Kent, either Stonar in Thanet, or, as I rather believe, Stone in the Isle of Oxney. Harris, in Kent, p. 302, relates that this place was terribly spoilt and burnt by the Danes, A. D. 990, a mistake only as to the year when this evil befell it. As to Staines in Middlesex, there is not any reason to imagine that the river was navigable for ships so high in the tenth century; at present, as Pennant writes, p. 424, just above Kingston the Thames feels the last feeble efforts of a tide. Does the word *æstus*, or *rheuma*, applied to tide on the river Thames, occur in the History by Matthew Paris within the period above stated?

" I remain, dear Sir, yours truly,   S. DENNE."

---

20. " DEAR SIR,   *Wilmington, Oct.* 29, 1794.

" Dr. Gale, in his Iter Antonini, has certainly taken no notice of Canute's Dyke, as hastily suggested in the History of Lambeth Palace, p. 157; and when in p. 86 he thus writes, ' atque inde ut prius monui transmisso fluvio, alterum ejus aggerem,' I am not clear to what page he alludes for his prior hint of turning the course of the river, unless it be to p. 66, where he cites the long controverted passage from Dion Cassius, which he seems to have left as obscure as he found it. The meaning of the author being doubtful, and the expression unquestionably confused, I believe I shall be tempted to sport a surmise whilst surveying Lambeth Marsh and St. George's fields.

"The Dean has, I perceive, adopted the mistaken notion, that the Romans passed the river where the Horseferry was, for which I do not believe there was any other ground than its having been the common transitus after the Archbishops of Canterbury were settled at Lambeth-house. How early or how late they provided this ferry-boat, it is to be regretted that Dr. Ducarel did not discover from the Lambeth Registers. My opinion is, that we are to look for the Roman Ferry at Stangate; and I think I shall be able to support it by somewhat more than plausible reasons.

" As to Mr. Lysons's conjecture (and indeed the conjecture of others) that the course of the Thames was turned when London-bridge was built in 1173, Sir Christopher Wren (according to Hawksmoor, in his Historical Account of the Bridge, p. 8,) was of opinion that it was not turned; and I perceive by Hawksmoor, that I am not by any means singular in my opinion that in the twelfth century the æstuary was not so rapid, and did not rise so high in this part of the river as it now does. Concerning the state of the tide near the metropolis during the time of the Romans, I have stated a query in a letter addressed to Mr. Urban, which will be conveyed to him with this letter; and I wish it may cause the subject to be fully discussed by some correspondents in the Gentleman's Magazine, who enjoy the

opportunity which I want of consulting a variety of books.
What I have to offer upon the question is designed for Addenda
to Histories of Lambeth Palace and Lambeth Parish; and when
I shall transmit the sheet or sheets to Mr. Nichols, I shall desire
him to show you the MS. before it passes under his press. Has
Horsley, in Britannia Romana, on the authority of Dion Cassius, mentioned St. George's fields as being the spot where
Aulus Plautius encamped his army, and waited for the arrival of
Claudius? My father had Horsley upon his shelves; but it was
one of the books of which my poor brother made choice, and
unhappily it has not been of any use to him for upwards of
seventeen years. If you turn to Tindal's translation of Rapin's
History, folio edition, vol. I p. 13, note ³, (under the year 43,)
you will find that the editor has attempted to explain a passage
in Dion Cassius in a sense different from that put upon it by the
Historian, and by Gale, who has thus rendered the words I
allude to: ' ad fluvium Thamesin, quâ is se in oceanum exo-
nerat, *eoque affluente stagnat*, se receperunt. Is this passage
fully considered by Horsley, or does he abide by the common
acceptation of it?

"Ere long Mr. Thomas Fisher will transmit to you two not
very long letters, addressed by me to Mr. Director. One of
them will have for its subject a drawing of a Triple Stone Seat
in the chancel of the Church of Upchurch *, not far from Rain-
ham in Kent, a topic that I should not have renewed had not I
considered this Triple Seat to be an unique as to its form; and
had it not served for an introduction to the copy of a somewhat
curious and superstitious letter penned by Bishop Buckeridge in
1625. The other letter will contain remarks cursory on sixty
and more Paper-marks, delineated by Mr. Fisher from writings
deposited in a room over the Court-hall in Rochester; and there
will be subjoined to it six or seven letters which he copied from
those writings, together with autographs of the writers and a
drawing of a significant Seal, which was the signet of Dr. Walter Balcanquall, first Dean of Rochester, and afterwards removed
to the far more profitable decanal Stall of Durham.

"I am, dear Sir, sincerely yours,   S. DENNE."

---

21. " DEAR SIR,   *Wilmington, Nov.* 14, 1794.
" Obliged am I by your extracts from Horsley's Britannia
Romana respecting the controverted passage in Dio. I do not
quite agree in opinion with either Gale, Horsley, Ward, or Tindal; and this want of coincidence partly arises, as I hinted in
my last letter, from their not seeming to have duly weighed the
difference there certainly is between the operation of the tide in
antient and modern times; but, after all, the early transactions
of the Romans in England will, I suspect, be ever involved in

* Printed in Archæologia, vol. XII. p. 101.

obscurity. Considering when Dio wrote, and that he probably trusted in great measure to traditional report, it is the less to be expected that he should be accurate in his detail of the marches and countermarches of the army led by A. Plautius; for, though Cæsar penned the Commentaries on his own deeds, what confusion has he occasioned by calling the Medway the Thames! But it was also clearly from the Medway that the Britons fled, according to Dio, towards the mouth of the Thames, after being routed by A. Plautius; nor can I devise on what grounds Dean Gale conceived that the Severn was the river meant (*Sabrina relicto*).

"By letter dated Somerset-place, Nov. 4, 1794, I had this intelligence and request from Secretary Wrighte: 'Dear Sir, Mr. Fisher desires me to inform you, that he has left in my possession three drawings of paintings in Maidstone Church, Kent, which I have at his request added to three others of the same kind, executed by him, and before deposited in the library of the Society. Allow me to add, that I hope the Society will be favoured with your observations on them.' And two days after I received from Mr. Fisher duplicates of the drawings, with a reserve of one that he could not finish to his satisfaction without another survey of the monument represented, which he hoped he should soon have. The monument he alludes to is that in memory of Wotton, the first Master of the College founded by Archbishop Courtenay, and is placed on the back of the stalls on the south side of the chancel. Mr. Fisher was but just in time in delineating the figures and armorial bearings on the Corboyl stones, and in some other places; for on a late repair of the Church and chancel, when both were covered with roofs entirely new, those remains of antiquity were destroyed.

"Mr. Clarke, in a letter I lately received from him, acquainted me with what cannot be unknown to you, Mr. Carter's having published proposals for a work on early English Architecture, in which the error of supposing it of Gothic origin is by apt specimens, and other authorities, to be refuted. If this ingenious artist can use his pen as well as he can his pencil, this will be a valuable work; and, if he cannot, I trust he will procure an able coadjutor in collecting and adjusting the historical part. Often have I regretted that the late Mr. Warton was too indolent to complete his proposed History; for you may remember that in the second dissertation prefixed to his History of English Poetry, he announced that there were preparing for the press, 'Observations, Critical and Historical, on Castles, Churches, Monasteries, and other Monuments of Antiquity in various parts of England.' My Gravesend * correspondent's intelligence is followed by this pertinent remark, 'There are many noble remains in England in which Gothic Architecture may be said to exist in its purest model, unmixed with the Morisco as in Spain, Por-

* Mr. Clarke.

tugal, and, as I think, parts of France. Mr. Murphy's History
of the Monastery of Batalha, with sumptuous plates, and an
annexed History of Gothic Architecture, seems not well calculated for this country. He supposes, however, from the relationship
between John of Gaunt and the Crown of Portugal,
that English artists were employed for its construction. This is
but merely supposing, whilst the style itself of the building
points out a taste very different from that in use at home.
From Mr. Carter I am led to expect great things; and wish the
remote and poor parish Churches were thought worthy of attention. Many are the curious specimens to be found in those
neglected buildings which are necessary as good authorities for
fixing the different mouldings and carvings, &c.

"In the Kentish Gazette of Friday November 7, now lying
before me, is an advertisement which begins thus, ' This day is
published, Hacton, Marrable, and Claris's Catalogue, 1795, containing the Library of Edward Hasted, Esq. Author of the History and Topographical Survey of the County of Kent; also a
considerable part of the Library of the late learned and Reverend
Dr. Backhouse, Archdeacon of Canterbury, deceased,' &c. &c.

"I remain, dear Sir, truly yours, S. DENNE."

22. "DEAR SIR, *Wilmington, Nov.* 29, 1794.
"Remarks and surmises touching the passage of Plautius
through the Thames, and concerning the state of the æstuary
in that river some centuries ago, will soon be submitted to your
revisal and correction. Proof positive is not to be expected on
topics which I have discussed; but my conjectures are not, I
apprehend, destitute of plausibility, and they may serve as
innuendoes to those who have it in their power to pursue the
inquiry.

"The report you make of the late Mr. Warton's small progress in architectural researches somewhat surprises me, though
I have always understood that he wanted a spur to take a pen
in hand. I concluded that he must at least have arranged his
work, from the following expression with which he concluded his
concise account of the use of coloured glass, in his dissertation
on the Gesta Romanorum, p. xxi: ' I could give very early anecdotes of this art in England; but with the careless haste of a
lover, I am anticipating what I have to say of it in my History
of Gothic Architecture in England.'

"Mr. Carter's plan is not upon the whole the most eligible;
and I trust that the Baronet you mention * is not to be his only
coadjutor, because the closest application will be requisite; however, the specimens to be given must render it a work of merit.

"From Mr. Clarke I have obtained satisfactory information,
that there was one St. Margaret who had a title to a regal

* Sir John Ayloffe.

crown; and, as I apprehend, there was another to whom a
coronet of martyrdom was an appropriated symbol. The use
I intend to make of this discovery is to illustrate a figure upon
the font in the Church of St. Margaret's, Rochester, delineated
by Mr. T. Fisher, and which he wishes to have exhibited in
Somerset-place, together with a drawing of Shorne Font upon a
much larger scale than that engraved for Custumale Roffense.

"A letter which I received from Mr. Fisher yesterday, apprises
me of his intention to transmit to you a drawing of a Triple
Seat in the Church of Sutton Valence, with the drawing of that
in the chancel of Upchurch Church. He likewise promises to
communicate to me some notes of what he had observed in a
late excursion in the Churches of Stone, Northfleet, Gillingham,
Milton near Sittingbourne, Maidstone, Loose, and Linton.

"Since there is, as you tell me, so little Kentish in the
Kentish Register, I am very glad that I did not become a purchaser for it. Not having any correspondent in that part of the
county, I am not aware who are the assistants to the editors; but
surely in and near Canterbury there must be a choice of persons
well qualified for such an employment, and sure I am there are
many objects of antiquity that ought to be brought forward.

"Tutor Masters has met with a disappointment, Bishop Yorke
having collated I know not whom to the Vicarage of Waterbeach, doubtless from a lapse of memory that he had encouraged
Mr. Masters to believe that a son-in-law elect should be the successor of his son in that living*. The Fellows expectant of the
old House will have that such a severe stroke will shorten the
days of the Rector of Landbeach, and be of course in their
favour; but probably you and I may concur in opinions that the
heart-strings of the veteran incumbent are not of that tender
delicate fabric as to be easily cracked. The mortification will
unquestionably occasion, or, rather, has more than once occasioned, an effort of the lungs in a person who has always been
in the habit of speaking his mind in a Stentorian style; but I
will venture to affirm that he has not lost an hour's rest by it.
The Prelate, to make him amends, should seat Robert Masters,
A.M. F.A.S. in the Prebendal Stall in Ely, vacant by the death
of Mr. Bentham, a more eminent antiquary; but, alas! the
Bishop, though he was a Member of the College which boasts
of the number trained within its walls in the study of antiquity,
is not of that respectable corps.

"By the demise of Dr. Dowbiggin†, nephew-in-law of Bishop
Green, the Prelate of Lincoln has more valuable preferments in
his disposal, though I rather suspect that the Stall of Subdean in

* To his son-in-law, the Rev. T. C. Burroughs, Mr. Masters afterwards
obtained permission to resign his other living, the Rectory of Landbeach.
† Robert Dowbiggin, D.D. Sub-Dean of Lincoln. See Gent. Mag.
vol. LXIV. p. 1063.

that Cathedral was the option of his Lordship.   It is not within
my recollection that I ever saw the deceased; and I have my
doubts whether he ever distinguished himself by any literary
publication.   Qu. was not his being possessed of a considerable
private fortune the circumstance which recommended him to
the notice of his right reverend uncle?
"I am, dear Sir, yours truly,   S. DENNE."

23. Mr. DENNE to Mr. NICHOLS.

"SIR,   *Wilmington, Nov.* 29, 1794.
" Before the conjectures and remarks on Lambeth, Stangate,
Lambeth Marsh, &c. pass under your press, they are, as you
have been apprised, to be perused by our friend at Enfield; and,
should you have acquired any information from your antiquarian
correspondents respecting the tracts of the Roman Roads in
St. George's fields, and the vicinity thereof, you will be pleased
to incorporate it where most proper.   As far as appears to me,
the Addenda should commence with the inclosed section ; and
by way of splicing it to what is now the leading section, I have,
towards the conclusion of my observations, introduced Lambeth
Palace ; not but that I think the author of London was open to
a gentle stricture for editing so glaring an anachronism as is
discernible in his plan of 1563.
"I am, Sir, truly yours,   S. DENNE."

24. Mr. DENNE to Mr. GOUGH.

"DEAR SIR,   *Wilmington, Jan.* 6, 1795.
" Perhaps before this letter reaches Enfield, you will have
received in its way to Somerset-place a packet containing drawings of Paper-marks and autographs by Mr. T. Fisher, and my
copies of original papers, with remarks concerning the progress
of King Charles the First through Kent, when he wedded Henrietta Maria of France.   The communication of these to the
Society will not be unseasonable at a time when the arrival of
a Royal Bride will have been a frequent topic of chit-chat;
though in suggesting that the Princess of Wales will be arrived,
I may probably have anticipated the event, it being the report
at Dartford, that she has, for reasons only surmised, deferred
her journey and voyage; and to be sure it must be admitted,
that neither the time of year, nor the weather, nor the state of
affairs in and near Holland, is of the most favourable kind for a
lady's taking such a trip, though a husband *in præsenti,* and a
crown *in futuro,* be the prize in view.
" Young Fisher, I agree with you, is much improved as a
delineator, and he has also a strong bent to subjects of antiquity; but the appointment he has luckily for himself obtained
will not allow of his giving so many specimens of it as he might
otherwise do.   He, however, informs me that, as he is removed

from the Secretary's office to the Examiner's office, he hopes to have more time for pursuing what is a very agreeable employment. I understand that his pencil has been of service to him in his department in the India-house, by recommending him to the notice of persons of influence there; and he has occasionally used it for the President of the Royal Society.

"Among the Church notes which he sent to me since his late excursion, there is one I shall mention to you, though the circumstance in it which struck me as a peculiarity may not be novel to you. Linton Church, near Coxheath, is the place of sepulture of the Mann family; and on a monument is 'a tree painted in a large tablet, displaying a long pedigree, but now almost defaced.' Fisher imagines this to be of the age of Elizabeth.

"Too true it is, that on the eve of the departed year there was a terrible and woeful catastrophe at Dartford powder-mills, nor have the newspapers increased the number of persons to whom it was fatal. Nine fragments of skulls, and other scattered relics, were collected, and being placed in five coffins, were interred in the upper burial-ground at Dartford on Saturday evening; and I understood that the trunk of another body has since been discovered at a greater distance from the mill than could have been expected, as also a part of a foot suspended on a tree. Of the eleven men, which are five more than were blown up by the explosion in October 1790, the body of one only could be ascertained. As the corning mill in which it happened was nearer to my house than the mills destroyed at that time, it was more felt by my servants (for I was sitting at Dartford), and on examining I find that it cracked one sash pane; but three panes were driven in at Mr. Tasker's house, which is close by Wilmington Church, an incident that rather surprised me, because it is situated so high above the level of the mill. The immediate cause of it will ever remain unknown, but the concussion was certainly the greater from the cakes being under the press; and but a short time previous to the blow upwards of forty-five barrels of powder had been removed. This manufacture is, alas! a most lucrative business to the proprietors, who cannot answer as speedily as they could wish the demands of their customers; and while the Christian rulers of so many European countries (our own not excepted) are averse to the taking one step towards a pacificatory negotiation, this abominable infernal composition must be in great request.

"No other account have I had of the decease of our old friend Dr. Colman than from the public prints; but I am inclined to think it was rather unexpected, because Mr. George Currey, of Trinity-college, whose eldest brother is Fellow of Bene't, left Cambridge early on Tuesday morning, and had not heard of Dr. Colman's being indisposed; he on the contrary says, that he understood from his brother, that the Master was under an engagement to pass Friday evening with him, and according to the newspapers, he died that afternoon. From what Mr. James Currey intimated to his father, with whom he was at Dartford during the summer recess, Mr. Bradford, the senior Fellow and Tutor, will prefer the Rectory of Stalbridge to the Headship; and I conclude you are aware that, should he be elected Master, he is by Archbishop Tenison's will precluded from that living; and whether Mr. Douglas, who is the subtutor, and a very respectable man, will think the Mastership an object worthy his attention without being possessed of an additional benefice is rather doubtful. The revenue of the Mastership is not adequate to a post of that pre-eminence; and it may be some time before a living may fall, or the Premier have it in his power to make a suitable provision for him. Somewhat solicitous am I to know how this vacancy in the old House will be supplied, and I was in hopes that ere this Mr. James Currey would have apprised his father of what must be of consequence to the son; but perhaps he conceives it to be expedient to be upon the reserve while the affair is in suspense. For the credit of the Society the Fellows will not, I trust, elect an alien, as they did when Dr. Green, that Yorkshire tike, was brought from St. John's, and the Benedictines acquired the denomination of Cappadocians.

" Since I wrote the above, a newspaper and a letter have been brought me. The former announces the Rev. Philip Douglas, B. D. to have been unanimously elected Master of the old House; and on the receipt of the latter I am become indebted to you for three unanswered epistles.

" Till I read the second paragraph in p. 1148 of the Magazine for December, I was not aware that the late Mr. Knight * was possessed of a choice collection of medals and a series of English coins; nor does the article mention whether it was made by himself, or devolved to him from his father. If the latter were the case, Dr. Pegge, whilst Vicar of Godmersham, must have often examined this antique treasure. Mr. Austen, who, by the will of Mr. Knight, is to have the reversion of all his estates, and is to take the name of Knight, is a very distant cousin †. The two seats, viz. that of Godmersham-park and that of Chawton in Hampshire, are, however, devised to the widow for life, with, as it is said, a net £.4000 a year.

" I am, dear Sir, yours sincerely,   S. DENNE."

* Thomas Knight, Esq. of Godmersham-park, Kent; M. P. for that county in the Parliament which sat 1774—1780.

† Mr. Knight was descended from the Austen family, but entirely through females; which of course made the connection obscure, and gave rise to groundless surmises, Mr. Denne's hints of which the editor has suppressed. It was Mr. Knight's mother's maternal grandmother that was by birth an Austen; she was great-grand-aunt to Mr. Knight's legatee, who was consequently his third cousin. His sister was the author of " Pride and Prejudice ;" see Gent. Mag. C. ii. 596.

25. "DEAR SIR,   *Wilmington, March 2,* 1795.

" I have been apprised by Secretary Wrighte of his having exhibited the Upchurch Font, &c.; and as the Paper-marks are to precede the drawings of the other Fonts, you will have time to be rather more explicit touching the veil you wish to have drawn over the blessed Margaret in tenderness to my antiquarian reputation,—a friendly innuendo that satisfies me of your thinking that my surmises concerning her are of too light and ludicrous a cast for a grave F.A.S. This being the case I am willing to accede to any alterations and omissions that you shall recommend; and for this purpose you will be pleased to return that part of the paper in which St. Margaret is noticed, and to subjoin to it your remarks. My real opinion is, that the Font is decorated with the bust of her as the tutelary saint of the Church, and on discovering that in a Cathedral the huge effigies of a Bishop had for years passed for an image of the Virgin Mary, it did not appear to me to be a very extravagant conceit, that in an age of collusion and ignorance the figure of a Prince or an Earl should have been metamorphosed into the portrait of a female saint. As to the coronet dug up in the Church-yard, I might have added, by way of illustration of my conjecture, from Archæologia, vol. V. p. 442, ' that an engraving of an elegant little crown of gold, found on new paving the Tower of London in 1772, was supposed by the President, who communicated it to the Society, to have been intended to adorn the head of a small statue of the Virgin Mary, or some other Saint which had been placed in an oratory or private Chapel.' I am not, however, at all partial to my surmise, and shall readily acquiesce in any change that you shall suggest.

" The late Alderman Sawbridge was my school-fellow and co-boarder in the Master's house at Canterbury. I wish that his family may not have cause to regret that from a country gentleman he would become a citizen and eke Parliament man. So many contested elections as he was obliged to fight his way through must have been attended with a very heavy expense; and report says, that his alliance with an Alderman's daughter * was not much to his pecuniary interest. No notice was taken in the paper of his age, but I judge him to have entered into his grand climacteric.

" It is a heavy imposition on the Chaplain of the House of Commons to be obliged to publish three Sermons on January the 30th. He merits for his task a decanal stall, though it is likely a Prebend of Canterbury will be his portion. You must have noticed that the Archbishop has collated his son to the stall vacant by the decease of Dr. Berkeley; and I understand that the young dignitary is soon to be married to a daughter of Lord Errol †, though among the many accomplishments of which it

* Sir William Stevenson.

† The Rev. Geo. Moore married Lady Maria-Elizabeth Hay, June 29, 1795.

may be presumed she is possessed of, she is in want of one that many judge requisite to render the marriage state happy, *viz.* a fortune. Since the demise of Archdeacon Balguy, Bishop Hurd, I suspect, may be the only disciple remaining of the Warburtonian school; and he, according to an account which a friend of mine received of him in May last, is in a very tottering state.

" The Bishop of Bristol very kindly admitted Bishop Stuart's plea of residence at Windsor, and out of course preached before the House of Peers on the Fast-day. Bishop Buller's recent loss of a son, killed in one of the late unfortunate engagements, disqualified him from undertaking an employment which necessarily would have obtruded on his mind distressful reflections.

" When you return the sheet in which the marvellous feats of St. Margaret are displayed by Vida the immortal, and others, in order to guard against mistakes, may it not be as well for you to draw your pen through the passages that are exceptionable ? I have not the least objection to omitting the whole I have written from the account of St. Margaret's Font to the description of the Font in Gillingham. The intermediate paragraphs were considered by me as episodical ; and added from a suspicion that our brethren might complain they had had *quantum sufficit* of Fonts as well as of Stone Seats ; and I was at the same time unwilling to disappoint Fisher, who is improving as a delineator.

" I am just returned from my morning walk to Dartford with my great coat covered with snow. At Dartford I heard that the remains of Alderman Sawbridge were conveyed with pomp through that town yesterday afternoon.

" I remain, truly yours,   S. Denne."

---

26. " Dear Sir,   *Wilmington, March* 12, 1795.
" The morning after I was favoured with yours of the 6th current, I had a few minutes' chat with brother Latham, (for an F. A. S. is one of the many appendages to his name,) who expressed his satisfaction at your having acceded to the proposal of a change of his Synopsis of Birds for your Sepulchral Monuments ; and as his is a very curious work, though not in your line of pursuit, and well executed, I am persuaded you will not have cause to regret a compliance with his offer. In the new list of the Members of Society of Antiquaries, John Latham's name will be dignified and distinguished with a variety of abbreviations pursuant to a hint suggested to Mr. Deputy at the Cicero's Head ; and my friend having shown me the instrument of his association to one of the honourable fraternities alluded to, I was at the trouble of transcribing it because it was new to me ; I have also under a notion that it may be novel to you.

Imperialis Academiæ Leopoldino-Carolinæ Naturæ Curiosorum
Præses, viro doctissimo atque experientissimo
Joanni Latham,
Pharmaciæ, Chirurgiæ, et artis obstetriciæ Practico
Dartfordiensi celeberrimo,
Reg. Soc. Scient. Lond., Soc. Antiquar., ac Linnean. Londin.
Sod., Societat. Chirurgor. Londin. Soc. Incorporat., et Societ.
Naturæ Scructator. Beroliens. Sodali Honorario.
S. P. D.

Quod statim a primordiis suis symbolum elegit Academia
nostra NUNQUAM OTIOSUS, hoc ipsum ut cuncti in eamdem
recepti vel recipiendi, sedulo observarint, et perpetuo observent,
vehementer exoptat, atque illud quoque de iis quos noviter ad
collegium suum invitat, aut qui generoso instinctu ad societatem
feruntur, aut qui a collegis commendati sunt, subsumit. Sunt
enim inexhaustæ rerum naturæ, et medicæ scientiæ, et artis
divitiæ, ut cuilibet prostet aliquid, in quo industria sua se exer-
cent. Atque cum unius hominis, aut paucorum, non sit in tantum tamque amplissimum campum excurrere, et cuncta in eo
perscrutari, et sint mille species, et rerum diacolor usus; utique
complurium bonarum mentium inclinatione, labore strenuo, et
consociatione opus est. Quapropter non poterit non exoptatus
gratusque evenire nobis accessus tuus, vir doctissime atque ex-
perientissime! Quo magis eruditio tua, et in perscrutandis
naturæ operibus admirandis, præcipue vero in indagandis avium
insectorumque speciebus, studium, non nobis solum, sed toto
orbi literario cognita perspectaque jam exsistunt. Esto igitur
ex merito nunc quoque noster! Esto Academiæ Cæsareæ Naturæ
Curiosorum decus et augmentum, macte virtute tua et industria,
et accipe in signum nostri ordinis, cui te nunc adscribo, ex anti-
qua nostra consuetudine, cognomen ARISTOPHILI, quo collegâm
amicissimum te hodie primum salutamus. Salve in consortio
nostro! Salve inquam, et effice ut in posterum tua, nunquam
otiosa, suavi doctaque sodalitate læti frui diu queamus. Vale.
Dabam Erlangæ d. vi Octobris A. R. S. cɪɔɪɔCCLXXXXIIII,

D. Io. Christianus Daniel Schreber, S. R. I. Nobilis, Acad.
Imper. Nat. Cur. Præses, Consiliarius Archiater. et Comes Pala-
tinus Cæsareus rel.

"Non Otiosus is, I think, a well adapted motto for a scientific society ; and suitable would it be were it subjoined to the
armorial shield of Mr. Latham, who is always busy. In giving
him the name of Aristophilus, Præses Schreber and Co. do not
appear to me to have been peculiarly fortunate, it not being a
denomination so appropriate as it ought. Surely Ornithophilus,
or Ornithologus, would have been more characteristic for a
naturalist who was remarkably assiduous in the collecting of
birds, judicious in his mode of preserving them, and skilful in
his representation of them. The British Critic, in the review

of the Linnean Transactions, have, I observe, noticed his having communicated a good and solid paper, which will not detract from his well-earned fame.

" Bishop Horsley has lately inquired after the Charter of Foundation of the Dean and Chapter of Rochester, with a view to the instituting of a suit in the Ecclesiastical Court against culprit Cooper, Lady Cadogan's paramour, whom he is determined, if within his power, to eject from his Prebendal Stall. His Lordship, I understand, conceives that Mr. Cooper is absolutely subject to him as ordinary by virtue of the declaration of canonical obedience, but some doubt whether the Bishop can thereby derive a power of removal from a freehold; and if he cannot, I am not aware of there being any statute of the Dean and Chapter that will confer this ability; and the creditors of the delinquent will, for their own sakes, keep him if possible in possession of a preferment of the yearly value of £.200. The Bishop waits for the decision in Doctors' Commons on the suit commenced by Lord Cadogan before he begins his vigorous attack. He means to prosecute in his own Court, though it is a method of proceeding contrary to the opinion of the civilians. His Lordship has, however, intimated that he was sanctioned by the highest authority, and it is supposed that Lord Thurlow is his adviser; but it may be questioned whether it may not be more prudent to be guided by the practitioners in the Commons than by the private conversation of a common lawyer, however respectable he may have been in Westminster-hall.

" The Kentish Register for February 1795 is, according to the advertisement, embellished with an elegant view of Denne Hill, the seat of Hardinge Stracy, Esq. Did it exhibit a true representation of the mansion when inhabited by Alured de Denne, the engraving would be far more acceptable to,

" Dear Sir, yours very truly,   S. Denne."

----

27. " Dear Sir,   *Wilmington, April* 29, 1795.
" Mr. Hasted probably did not notice the Mompessons * in his account of Sundridge because he had not traced their being possessed of any considerable estate in that parish. It appears, however, from the poll-book for Knights of the Shire in 1754, that Thomas Mompesson voted for lands in Sundridge; and as his name does not occur in the poll at the election in 1734, the presumption is that he might not then be a freeholder of Kent. The inscriptions annexed to Registrum Roffense by Mr. Thorpe, are taken from monuments and grave-stones within the Churches; but if you turn to the Gentleman's Magazine of the year 1767, p. 280, you will find that the monument of the Mompesson family is in the church-yard.

" On the day before Ascension-Thursday, I am, as Vicar of

* See the History of Dorsetshire.

Darenth, to make my visitation bow at Sevenoaks to the Dean of the Arches; and, as Sundridge is in the peculiar Deanery of Shoreham, it is not unlikely that I may have an interview with the Rector, Dr. Vyse. Should this be the case, and he have it in his power to collect from the parish register, or by tradition, any anecdotes of the Mompessons, he shall be solicited to favour me with a few lines, which shall be forthwith communicated to you.

" Between the time of concluding the business at Somerset-place on St. George's-day and the assembling of half a score of us at the Crown and Anchor to celebrate the feast of the tutelary saint of the antiquaries, I passed a pleasing hour in viewing the curious and choice library of the late Mr. Southgate, who, by-the-bye, is styled only A. B.* in the title-page to the Catalogue, and M. A. in the last year's list of the Members of our Society. Whilst at the Crown and Anchor, I remember I hinted to Archdeacon Hamilton that I thought it strange that the Rector of a valuable benefice, and a librarian of the British Museum, had acquired no higher degree than that of Bachelor of Arts; and he seemed to attribute it to the economy of the deceased, who was never willing to open his purse but to buy a book or a coin.

" In a former letter I believe I mentioned that Dr. Hey, Prebendary of Rochester, who was of Bene't-college, was most dangerously ill at Bath. He is now, however, a convalescent; and his brother, the Commissioner of the Customs, makes a favourable report of it to the Archdeacon †.

" Dame Mosyer, the veteran widow, whose departure will, I imagine, be announced in Master Urban's Obituary of the current month ‡, had exactly completed her 90th year; and I was told by the undertaker that she had repeatedly prognosticated that she should die on the anniversary of her birth-day.

" I remain, dear Sir, yours sincerely,   S. DENNE."

---

28. " DEAR SIR,   *Wilmington, June 2, 1795.*
" Soon after Mr. Hayward§ became Incumbent of Harrietsham, which was in 1773, I met him at my late worthy friend's Mr. Milner, but I have not kept up any acquaintance with him, as we live many miles from each other. Since he

---

* Mr. Southgate never took his Master's degree. On this subject see " Literary Anecdotes," vol. VI. p. 373.

† The Commissioner died first, in 1797, the divine not till 1807. They will both be further noticed in a subsequent page.

‡ " April 24. At Darenth, aged 90, Jane Mosyer. She was a native of that parish, Munn her maiden name, and two of her sisters survive her, the elder born in 1702, the younger in 1717." Gent. Mag.

§ Rev. James Robinson Hayward, of All Souls College, Oxford, M.A. 1765, presented to St. Mary-le-Strand in 1781. He died at Harrietsham, Oct. 6, 1812, aged 73.

married I understand he has almost always resided at Harrietsham ; of his movements, however, to town, I should suppose
you may be duly apprised from his assistant at his parish in
Westminster, or from the clerk.   Perhaps it may be new to you,
that Mr. Hayward was for several years a practitioner at the
Bar; but that, being a Fellow of All Souls'-college in Oxford, he
judged it expedient to change the cut of his gown for the
Vicarage of Harrietsham.   The Rectory of the New Church in
the Strand was given to him by Lord Chancellor Thurlow ; and
it is surmised that his having been of the honourable fraternity
of lawyers was a circumstance in his favour.

     " Have you heard of some sepulchral relics that were very
lately discovered near the Priory of Cerne in Dorsetshire ?   Mr.
Peete, my friend Mr. Latham's galenical partner, from whom I
have just received this piece of intelligence, says that they much
resemble the figure, &c. of Bishop Rogers in Salisbury Cathedral.
                         " Yours truly,   S DENNE."

                    ─────────

        29. " DEAR SIR,   Wilmington, July 20, 1795.
    " I will dispatch the engraving of the brass in Cranbrook
Church to Mr. Jefferys, of Maidstone, with a request that he will
show it to Mr. May, the Mayor of that town ; and should it be
in their power to collect any circumstances that will illustrate
the figures exhibited, I doubt not of their readiness to communicate them to me.   Mr. Jefferys was noticed by S. D. in Gent.
Mag. vol. LXIV. p. 201, as eke in my letter concerning Archbishop Courtenay's grave; and Mr. May is the gentleman who,
in the same letter, I mentioned as being a spectator of the discoveries we made on opening it.   They have both a propensity
to antique lore.
    " When I was at Maidstone in June, Mr. May showed me a
drawing of a brass plate fixed upon a pillar in the south aisle of
the chancel in memory of the family of Beale, the inscription
upon which is imperfectly printed in Newton's Antiquities of
Maidstone, p. 90.   There are upon it many figures of the Tri-
tavus and his descendants; but I conclude you must, in your
monumental pursuits, have met with several brass plates of the
same kind.   I remain, dear Sir, truly yours,   S. DENNE."

                    ─────────

        30. " DEAR SIR,   Wilmington, July 27, 1795.
    " At the conclusion of your letter of June 2 ult. was this
passage : ' I shall write after the Cerne discoveries.   Can Mr.
Peete procure sketches ? '   The hint has answered, for I have the
satisfaction of transmitting to you the inclosed drawing, which
Mr. Peete has procured from Mr. John Williams, who is Vicar
of Marston Magna, alias Brode, co. Somerset, (but Sherborne is
the nearest post town,) and he permitted me to make the follow-

ing extract from the letter of his intelligent and communicative correspondent:

" ' Has Mr. Gough any drawing of the gateway to the Old Abbey of Cerne, that which now remains, or any copy of the pavement discovered last summer in a mead called Nunnery Mead, near Mr. Browne's at Frampton ? Should he wish to have them, the former would be in my power to send; and I have no doubt but Mr. Browne would permit any of Mr. Gough's friends to take a copy of the latter. On what terms does Mr. Gough mean to publish his new edition co. Dorset ? ` It may be proper to acquaint you that, when Mr. Peete saw the stones, of which you now receive the sketches, they were cast aside as lumber in a farm-yard.

" The drawings of the Stone Seats and Piscinas were given to me by Mr. Peete; but, as they represent objects in Churches co. Dorset, I thought you had a better pretension to them, and shall therefore put them into the packet, though it is likely that you may have already delineations of the same. If I did not mishear Mr. Peete, the shield of arms in the Winborne Stalls was so defaced that he could not distinguish the bearings. The opening, or the fenestella at the west end of the lowest seat, was novel to me.

" Knowing that Mr. Tracy, who was a fellow-labourer in Mr. Thorpe's antiquarian pursuits, is always pleased with any particulars concerning the family whose name he bears, I sent him a long extract from Sepulchral Monuments; and in his letter of acknowledgment of it he thus expresses himself: ' Yours of the 18th of June I received by the favour of Mr. Fountaine; and I consider myself as particularly obliged to you for the contents. The work from which you kindly made the extract is truly valuable; but in the account of William de Traci, &c. there is much error respecting both the Baron and the Minister. I possess many authentic documents, and have been some time digesting a short memoir illustrative of the early part of the Tracy history, but know not when I shall find time to finish it. Had I any interest with Mr. Gough, I would solicit a sketch of the Tracy monument at Morthoe, but, having no personal knowledge of that gentleman, I dare not ask it; and the place is too remote to make a flying trip thither, so must be content without it. Any notes, or references to any particulars of the Tracys will at all times merit my best thanks.'

" In my answer, Mr. Tracy was apprised that I did not think you had any sketch of the monument at Morthoe from the late Dean of Exeter, who was your informant, but that I would not fail to make an inquiry.

" Your query concerning the Cranbrook Parsonage inscription shall be conveyed to Mr. Jefferys this week; and I wish he may be able to gratify your curiosity. As to the Alkham inscription, I know not at present to whom to apply, not having any correspondent at Dover, or in its vicinage; but should an opportunity offer, I trust I shall not forget to avail myself of it.

" The day was so wet when I was at Aylesford, that I could not with any degree of comfort, examine for any length of time the numerals on the barn, but from what I did see, and from the conversation I have more than once had with my late worthy friend Milner upon the subject, I am of opinion that the engraving in Hasted's History is a fac-simile. However, before what is improperly termed a summer shall be ended, it is my purpose to pass four or five days at Preston-hall; and while there I will revise the figures in question.

"I remain, dear Sir, truly yours,   S. Denne."

---

31. Mr. Jefferys to Mr. Denne.

"Sir,   *Maidstone, Aug.* 3, 1795.

" From the best information I can get respecting Mr. Gough's inquiry, it appears that the antient grave-stone referred to belongs to the Weller family, who for a long time back resided in or near Cranbrook, where there still lives one of that name. He is the son of a breeches-maker; and on some of the same family coming to Cranbrook to make inquiries concerning their ancestors, they there found this young man, his father being then living. They agreed to take his son, whom they educated and treated well; they afterwards sent him to Jamaica to other relations, but from some dislike (or, perhaps, from his own misconduct) he left them, and is now some where about Cranbrook, rather in a state of indigence. It is said they meant to have adopted him. There are two maiden women (Miss Sharpeys) now living in Maidstone, with whom I have had some conversation respecting their ancestors. They told me their family generally were buried at Benenden, where, for some centuries, they had resided. They showed me a very antient Bible, printed in the year 1566, in several parts of which was written a kind of register of births, christenings, marriages, &c.; but only relating to deaths, which were of a Thomas Sharpey, who died April 17, 1643, and of Thomas Sharpey, who died the 5th of September, and was buried the 8th day of the same month in the church-yard of Benenden, 1651. Miss Sharpey said, only her grandfather, his wife, an uncle, and aunt, ever lived at Cranbrook, and supposes might be buried there; her grandfather about the latter end of the last century, or beginning of the present; so I think it is beyond doubt that this grave-stone could not ever belong to their family, as it must be many years antecedent to the burial of her grandfather. Miss Sharpeys are now the only remains of two antient families. I hope these crude and incorrect remarks may be sufficient to gratify the curiosity of Mr. Gough. I am, Sir,

"Your most humble servant,   William Jefferys.

" N. B. This grave-stone lies in the isle near the chancel. There are traces of the Sharpeys in Maidstone Church of three hundred years back, as I am told.

" The Parsonage-house at Cranbrook is now totally re-built. The Rev. Mr. Disney, of Pluckley, the son of the late Mr. Disney, of Cranbrook, may probably give you some light respecting the antient letters delineated in Mr. Gough's letter of July 25."

32. Mr. DENNE to Mr. GOUGH.

" DEAR SIR,   *Wilmington, Aug.* 10, 1795

" It is to be regretted that my correspondent, Mr. Jefferys, has not been more explicit, touching ' the best information he had got,' that the grave-stone in question belonged to the Weller family; for I must own I a little suspect it may be founded on traditional report, and that owing to the recent interment of some of the name beneath that stone.

" The N. B. respecting the part of the Church where the stone remains, was occasioned by a question I put to Mr. J. in my second letter ; and my reason for making the inquiry was, that, supposing the stone to have been in a private Chantry Chapel that had appertained to the owners of Pleckinghurst (the estate in Cranbrook, according to Philipott, possessed by the Sharpeighs) it would have added weight to your surmise, that the brass figures were memorials of a man and a woman of that family.

" By Mr. Disney, of Pluckley, Mr. Jefferys means Dr. Disney *, Rector of that parish, who was of Trinity-college in Cambridge, and Regius Professor of Hebrew in that University. He was the Senior Wrangler of my year, and of course eminent as a mathematician and philosopher ; but I do not recollect the having heard of his being inclined to antiquarian researches. Has Mr. Deputy of the Ward of Farringdon extra any acquaintance with him ? Bishop Hinchcliffe collated his fellow-collegian and friend, Dr. Disney, to the Rectory of Paston in Northamptonshire ; and he in 1777 changed it with Mr. Jones, now of Nayland in Suffolk, for Pluckley.

" I remain, dear Sir, truly yours,   S. DENNE."

33. " DEAR SIR,   *Wilmington, Aug.* 24, 1795.

" The report you made of the health, vigour, and spirits of the worthy Rector of Whittington, was pleasing, though mingled with a regret at his being not always able to employ himself in reading, and of a want of power to inform and entertain the world antique with his pen. When you write to him, I will trouble you to tender my grateful acknowledgments of his favourable attention towards me ; oh that I could satisfy myself that I was entitled to a long slip of the veteran's mantle ! In

---

* See the pedigree of the Disney family in Hutchins's Dorsetshire, vol. IV. p. 396.

my retired situation I am precluded from having an access to
the number of books necessary for making any considerable
progress in what is certainly to me an agreeable pursuit; and
unfortunately there are not more than two of my neighbours
who have the least bias to the same researches; Mr. Latham is
one of the number. He is now peregrinating in Hampshire on
a visit to his son at Romsey, whose immediate predecessors on
the spot inhabited by him, turned an abbey into a brewery; and
from thence Mr. Latham will remove to Winchester, to make a
short tarrying with a daughter not long since wedded to a Mr.
Wickham, an apothecary of that city, who conceives himself,
and I believe upon good grounds, to be a kinsman to the illustrious Founder of Winton and New Colleges.

" Whilst on his journey, Mr. Latham had an opportunity of
sketching the Church of Scures, alias Nately Scures, Hants,
and was so obliging as to forward it to me; and as it is in my
opinion a Saxon edifice, I shall, when he returns, desire him
to finish the drawing, and to convey it, as shall best please him,
to Somerset-place, or to Cicero's Head in Red Lion-passage. The
chancel is at the east end semicircular; and two of its windows,
viz. that in the east wall and that in the north wall, of the lancet
kind. In the north wall, and not far from the west end, there
is a door-way with Saxon ornaments in good preservation.

" I am, dear Sir, yours truly,   S. Denne."

34. " Dear Sir,   Wilmington, Sept. 12, 1795.
" There does not seem to be much difficulty in pointing out
the original uses of the three little niches in the south wall of
Hadham Church chancel. The western niche was the credentia
or buffet, within which were placed the holy sacramental vessels
before it was proper to remove them to the altar; the almost
contiguous piscina was to receive the rincings of the calix that
had held the consecrated wine; and the upper piscina was
for taking the water in which the officiating priest had washed
his fingers. If you turn to Mr. Clarke's Observations on Stone
Seats, Piscinas, &c. in Archæologia, vol. XI. pp. 347—350, you
will, I believe, readily concur in opinion with me respecting this
appropriation of those arched recesses.

" On several Sundays in the current year, I have had for one
of my auditors in Darenth Church a young gentleman of the
name of Daniel, in consequence of his marrying in January a
Miss Hodges, a grand-daughter of Town-clerk Sir James Hodges,
and niece to Mrs. Hodges, who is one of my parishioners. Qu.
Is this Mr. Daniel related to Mr. Daniel, whose prints of antient
and modern buildings you so much admire? The young gentleman was of Harrow-school; and I have a notion one of the
stewards of the last anniversary feast of that corps.

" A second letter from the author and editor of the Annual

Register is promised in Index Indicat. Qu. his name? For
many years it was surmised that Mr. Burke took the lead in that
miscellaneous work, which has unquestionably suffered in character from the extreme dilatoriness of the conductor, whoever
he may be. An Annual Register ought unquestionably to make
its appearance before the close of the succeeding year.

"Yours truly,   S. DENNE."

———

35. "DEAR SIR,   *Wilmington, Oct.* 24, 1795.

"On my return from Preston Hall last Saturday, my sister
delivered to me your letter, in which you express the joint
wishes of yourself and Mr. Ord, that I would investigate the
chapel of our lady in the Piers, which is now the kitchen of
Speaker Addington, as also the chapel of Scala Cœli in Norwich.
My answer is, that I am not at present possessed of a note concerning one or other of those antient edifices, and that I fear
my shelves will not furnish me with many steps towards them.

"While at Preston Hall, I again, again, and again examined
the inscription on the window case of the Old Barn; and could
not perceive any other difference between the original and the
engraving in Hasted's Kent than that in the latter the 0 is placed
rather too high, it being on the stone nearly on a line with the
curve of the figure 2. There cannot, however, be a doubt, as
Hasted has suggested, that 1102 is the date meant; and as a
proof of it, the same numerals are still in full preservation on
the original door-case of another building converted into an
oast-house. Not a little surprised am I that neither Harris nor
Hasted should have given a fac-simile of the inscription alluded
to, the characters being more accurately cut than are those of
the inscription they have exhibited. I have desired Mr. Peter
Rashleigh (Rector of Southfleet and Vicar of Barking, and
brother to Philip Rashleigh, F. A. S.) to favour me with drawings of both; and I am satisfied he will use his pencil upon
them the first time he pays Mrs. Milner a visit. When I get
them they shall be forthwith transmitted to you; and I have
it in contemplation to subjoin to them a few remarks *.

"Will not the death of Dr. Kippis be regretted by the proprietors of the Biographia Britannica; and occasion a further
delay in the publication of that voluminous work, the second
edition of which has already met with too many obstacles? The
Doctor had certainly a talent for biography; and I have imagined, but without competent authority, that he might be one
of the conductors of the Monthly Review. What was the
remark of the venerable Patriarch at Whittington on the suggestion that the less that was said the better about St. George
and his Dragon? By-the-bye, this Dissertation by Mr. Milner
had been published two years before it was noticed by the
Reviewers; and they have slumbered for a long as period over

* See the Archæologia, vol. XIII. pp. 107--168.

Archæologia, vol. XI.   Can you account for this neglect, while they have speedily made their report of the Proceedings of the Societies, Royal, Medical, and Linnæan in England, and of the Literary and Philosophical in North Britain and Ireland ?

" It had almost escaped my memory to acquaint you, that when Mr. Pegge was Vicar of Godmersham, and had in some degree under his tuition the present Sir Edward Dering, he, with his pupil, visited Sir Roger Twisden ; and that while at Bradbourn he went over to Preston-hall to examine the inscription on the barn.   From Mr. Bartholomew, of Addington-place, who accompanied Mr. Pegge, I had this anecdote ; but as my friend is not of the antiquary cast, he will not think it of consequence to regard what might be the observations made by an F. S. A. whose curiosity was doubtless awake at the time, though perhaps he might not commit his thoughts to paper.

" From a kinsman who lives at Littlebourne in East Kent, which is a parish adjoining to Wickham Breaux, I have a very unfavourable account of my old schoolfellow and fellow-collegian Dr. Hey.   It is in these few words: ' Dr. Hey and his lady called on me the other day to see my India pinks.   He says that he is much better; but he is a mere skeleton.   I find he is going again to Bristol next month.'   The Bishop of Bristol, who is a brother Prebendary of Rochester, has offered the Doctor the use of his Episcopal Palace for the winter.

" The Archbishop of Canterbury has collated Dr. Radcliffe, Vicar of Gillingham, who was his Chaplain, to a Prebendal Stall in the Cathedral*, vacant by the resignation of Dr. King, who succeeds the late Master of Keys in the Chancellorship of Lincoln, which was the option on the consecration of Bishop Pretyman; and I understand that the Bishop of Ely has consented to Dr. Radcliffe's resigning his Stall in Ely Cathedral in favour of Dr. Griffith, Rector of St. Mary-le-Bow.

" I remain, dear Sir, yours truly,   S. DENNE."

---

36. " DEAR SIR,   *Wilmington, Nov. 28, 1795.*
" Thanks to you for your hint that you shall probably transmit to Somerset-place the fruit of my researches on the Preston-

* The Rev. Houstonne Radcliffe was a native of Lancashire, and an eminent tutor of Brasenose, where Lord Ribblesdale, Lord Viscount Sidmouth, his brother the Right Hon. Hiley Addington, and many other men of eminence were his pupils. He proceeded M. A. 1764, B. and D. D. 1784.   He was presented to the Vicarage of Gillingham by his college in 1779; to the Rectory of Ickham, also in Kent, in 1778, by Archbishop Moore; by the same patron to a Prebend of Canterbury in 1795, and the Archdeaconry in 1803; and in 18.. to the Subdeanery of Wells by Bishop Beadon, whose wife was a sister of Mrs. Radcliffe, those two ladies being the daughters and co-heiresses of John Gooch, D. D. the younger son of Sir Thomas Gooch, Bart. Bishop of Ely (see the " Literary Anecdotes," vol. IX. p. 582).   Archdeacon Radcliffe died at Gillingham, April 8, 1822, aged 83.   He published one excellent Sermon, preached in 1787 at the consecration of Bishop Cleaver, his contemporary and fellow-collegian.

hall barn date; for, though it may perhaps induce me to extend my disquisition further than I had proposed, it will likewise make me more wary in my remarks than I might be were the paper to pass under your inspection only.

" An attempt to illustrate the heretofore much agitated Helmdon date shall be adjoined by me; and unless my spectacles and my nonce deceive me, I shall controvert with success the explanation of it maintained by Dr. Willis, as eke the amendment by Professor Ward, being clearly of Mr. North's opinion that their reveries concerning it are very questionable, nay unaccountable. (Archæologia, vol. X. p. 370.)

" Having thus revived the topic of the introduction of Arabic numerals, I may be prompted to scribble a little, and but little, upon that subject; and somewhat more copiously on the time when they generally were first used in arithmetical computations, and in marking the dates of years. As to the introduction into England, that is a point not likely to be ever fully ascertained, though I am apt to suspect that it might not be till centuries after the ages so zealously contended for by the two eminently learned men I have named. Concerning the common use of them in the ways I have mentioned, I have it in my thoughts to suggest queries, remarks, and surmises, that may place the matter in a different point of view from what, as far as I know, it has yet appeared in. The leading question which I shall propose is, which is the oldest authentic MS. account of receipts and disbursements, in which all the sums of money are minuted in Arabic figures; and shall I be judged to be egregiously mistaken, should I express a doubt whether a single account under this description is known to be extant previous to the sixteenth century? As far as my confined research has been pursued, not one specimen can I show.

" The question concerning annual dates (and why not apply it to days of the month?) will be, where are the earliest inscriptions on stone, wood, or brass, (or fac-similes of them,) to be found in which the whole date of the year is carved, punched, or stamped in these figures? The conjecture I am prompted to hazard is, that not a single instance is to be traced in the fourteenth century, and perhaps very, very few instances in the fifteenth, and these towards the conclusion of it. In order to lessen your amazement at the venturousness of my surmise, I will remark, that in the plates in Dugdale's History of St. Paul's, there is not an epitaph within those centuries that exhibits an Arabic numeral; and, as I believe, only two inscriptions occur in Sepulchral Monuments, respecting the originality of which I have my doubts, that you, I am persuaded, can remove, if they are not well founded. The former is in plate xlvii. p. 123, whereon it is mentioned, ' Dnus Ludovicus Charlton, Ep'us Heref. obiit A. D. 1369;' and your observation is that ' within the wall is painted this inscription,' implying, as I understand the

term painted to be of a later date than the erection of the
monument. The latter instance is in plate liv. p. 135, on which
it is recorded, that Sir Richard Pembridge died 1375, being the
33d Knight of the Garter. But query are 1375 and 33 coeval
with this monument?

" Whether Dr. Pegge's Sylloge will furnish a specimen of an
inscription with Arabic figures before the year 1500 I cannot
recollect; and shall be obliged to you to examine. An intelligent member of our corps, who was apprised of my present pursuit, communicated this inuendo in a letter written to Mr.
Latham: ' I need not point out to Mr. Denne how very unhappy
Mr. Pegge is in reading the dates, page 73, plate xvii. [1420
for 1520], and page 74, plate xiv. fig. 4, [1424 for 1525] of his
Sylloge, both which are evidently of the sixteenth century.

" The commission of inquiry after the Preston-hall date has,
you see, indirectly imposed on me a long task. The field,
indeed, affords a wide scope for a wanderer in antiquities: and
I trust that I shall not quite lose my way whilst rambling over
it. For, whatever may be ultimately decided respecting the surmises started of the æra of the common use of Arabic figures,
I am very sanguine in my belief that I shall find myself upon
firm ground as to the Helmdon inscription, which has hitherto
been considered by almost all antiquaries as a secure base of the
hypothesis of an earlier introduction of those characters into
England than can be supported by substantial proofs.

" In a newspaper, but under what denomination I do not
remember, was the underwritten paragraph: ' The Earl of Leicester is printing a book upon Heraldry, which will disgrace
many antient families in the kingdom. His lordship's accuracy
in this nice and useful science will in return, it is waggishly said,
immortalise a great many footmen and Chaplains.' Of this sarcastic article is any part strictly true? And if his lordship has
sent to press any of his investigations in what is deemed to be
his forte, and to have in some degree contributed to his being
placed in the chair of F. S. A. what will be the contents of the
volume? I remain, very truly yours, S. DENNE."

37. " DEAR SIR, *Wilmington, Dec. 10, 1795.*
"Obliged am I for your information touching the inscription
in Ware Church; it is probably as early a specimen of the Arabic
numerals in brass as any that will be found; and perhaps it
might not be carved immediately after the decease of the person commemorated. I was somewhat inclined to surmise, that
a date in those characters might not be discovered before the
expiration of three fourths of the fifteenth century.

" Under the print of Caxton, prefixed to his Life, by Lewis,
and between the initial letters of his names, are the same figures
crosswise that are at the end of many of his books. I had

thought that it might denote the year of his age, nor does his visage discountenance such a conjecture; but yours may be a more lucky guess, that it alludes to the time when he began printing in England. Judging from the list of the books he printed, as enumerated in Tanner's Bibliotheca Britannica, there is ground for believing that not one is dated in Arabic numerals, and most probably for this reason, that in the MSS. the dates of years and months were expressed in Roman characters. In the first and second volume of the Paston Correspondence, not an Arabic numeral occurs in any date.

" Yours truly,   S. Denne."

---

38. " Dear Sir,   *Wilmington, St. Thomas's-day,* 1795.

" In my last letter I hinted, upon the authority of Tanner's Bibliotheca Britannica, that not a book printed by Caxton has a date of the year in Arabic numerals. What I wish to learn is, whether there may be any numerals of that class in any book that passed under his press, and if there are, whether they are frequently to be met with. The surmise I somewhat lean to is, that neither Caxton, nor any contemporary printer, thought it necessary to have their boxes supplied with many types of Arabic numerals, well knowing that the MSS. they should be employed to print would be in the other characters. The characters which formed the cypher used by Caxton himself must have been cut for the purpose; and, as he applied these figures unquestionably to the date of a year, it is somewhat strange that he should not have ascertained the dates of many others in a manner as concise, instead of having recourse to that far greater number of characters which the Latin letters required, for instance, MCCCCLXXXIII. *i. e.* a thousand CCCCLXXXIII. (See p. 80, note ².) In truth, the very slow progress made in the use of these most convenient, nay, now almost necessary characters, the Arabic numerals, is astonishing; and perhaps I may be prompted towards the end of my designed remarks on the Preston-hall and Helmdon parsonage inscription, to risk two or three plausible conjectures on the cause of this tardiness.

" Mr. Boys has sent me the fac-simile of a Conventual Seal, which, as I believe, I mentioned in a former letter, as being the earliest he had with a date inscribed in Arabic numerals. The figures are indisputably 1484, with the 4 formed out of the half 8; but neither Mr. Boys, nor Mr. Latham, nor your humble servant, can appropriate the Seal, though so far I soon perceived that it belonged to a Priory of the Order of St. Austin, but whether it may be a foreign Monastery I have some doubt *.

---

* This seal was engraved in the Gentleman's Magazine, vol. LXVII. p. 201; and some years after, in vol. LXXII. p. 615, was noticed by Mr. Gough as having been assigned by Mr. Tyssen to Brentford Priory; but that appropriation appears doubtful.

" Which may have been the most antient seal examined by
you that had insculped on it the date of the year in Arabic
numerals? According to the venerable Patriarch of Whittington, the late Mr. Gustavus Brander had a very large collection
of matrices of Conventual Seals. (Archæologia, vol. V. p. 346.)
Is it dispersed? or, if remaining with his heir, is there an opportunity of inspecting them?

" Sir Joseph Ayloffe, in ' Description of a Picture in Windsor
Castle,' (Archæologia, vol. III. p. 222,) observes, ' that Henry
VIII. chose the aubepine, or hawthorn, as his badge or cognizance,
in imitation of his father Henry VII. who bore the same inclosing a crown, in allusion to his being crowned in Bosworth Field
with the diadem of Richard III. which after the battle was found
there concealed in a hawthorn-bush. Query the form in which
the Heralds displayed the device of the hawthorn (without the
crown)? And I beg leave to remind you, that you have not
apprised me, who might be the Rouge Dragon Pursuivants in the
reign of Henry VIII.? Yours truly,   S. DENNE."

---

39. " DEAR SIR,   *Wilmington, Jan.* 13, 1796.
" Much obliged am I to you for gratifying me with the perusal of Dr. Lort's Miscellaneous Collections concerning Arabic
numerals, and of your curious and copious discoveries and
observations in the same line. Such of the former papers as I
have an opportunity of examining, shall be returned with the
proof sheets of the preface to Sepulchral Monuments, and the
plate of fac-similes.

" Respecting the no early general use of these numerals, (and
by no early I mean centuries when they were probably not even
known to one person in ten thousand,) we concur in our sentiments, though we may differ in opinion touching some of the
instances you have specified   On the inscription placed in the
out-buildings at Preston-hall, 1102 are obviously the figures displayed * ; and, considered as the date of the year, they must,
in my apprehension, be retrospective to some memorable æra in
the Colepeper family ; because, before my late all-worthy friend
(who, alas! was for a very short time a Pilgrim at Preston)
altered and improved that mansion and its premises, there
were no fewer than four inscriptions bearing the same date.
Had Mr. Hasted paid a due attention to the genealogies and other
documents which he has cited, he would have found that there
was not before the sixteenth century, any Colepeper of Preston who had any right to the arms of Hadreshull; and that about
the close of that century and the beginning of the seventeenth,
there were two Thomas Colepepers, father and son, one of whom
might empale, and the other quarter, that coat with their paternal bearings ; and that the buildings in question were erected by

* Probably 1502.

one or the other of these Thomas's (or perhaps they were the joint work of both), the style of structure shows.

" In examining the inscriptions that have been brought forward in this controversy, too little notice has been taken of the buildings from which they were delineated. Of Helmdon Parsonage, in particular, Dr. Wallis did not communicate any information; if he had, I am inclined to believe he would at once have exposed the futility of his mode of decyphering this mantle-piece. Of the age of the house or parlour not a word is mentioned. Supposing either to be coetaneous with the reputed date of 1133, the room was built and fitted up before the Royal-hall of the Westminster Palace; and the house, on the score of antiquity, ought to be held in as high veneration by F. S. A.'s as the Santa Casa at Loretto by the Papists. 3, 3, are manifestly two of the figures; but query as to the æra of figures thus formed? If I do not mistake Wallis, these figures in the 12th century were very differently written (see his Planud. Cyphers); and are there any authentic MSS. extant on mathematical or astronomical subjects in which the figure designed for 3 corresponds to the Helmdon date?

" Mr. Boys's Seal is very curious; though if it appertained to a foreign Priory, and we are of opinion it did, it be not directly within our scope of investigation. To the best of my recollection there is not a date to any one of the Seals in Scotland engraved at the expense of the Society.

" At p. cclxvi you have noticed the Testoons coined at Tournay in 1513, from Simons's Irish Coins, p. 5. Folkes, in his Table of Silver Coins, p. 27, describes the groat of Henry VIII. of the same date. He also mentions at p. 19, a very uncommon singular coin, of which the inscription is, ' Mani Tekel Pharer, 1494;' and he supposes it to have been coined by the Duchess of Burgundy for Perkin Warbeck, when he set out to invade England in that year.

" Snelling expresses a belief that the penny of Edward VI. A. D. 1547, is the first English coin that bears the date of the year; and Folkes describes a piece somewhat broader than a groat of the same year in which the date is thus marked, M.D.xl.7. (Page 28). A reference is made by me to this coin on account of the Arabic numeral 7 being added to Latin numerals. There is the like mixture of characters in the Helmdon date. Dr. Wallis and Professor Ward admit this mixture not to have been uncommon; but query can any fac-simile instance be shown in the twelfth, thirteenth, or even fifteenth century *? A specimen from a monumental inscription in the sixteenth century may be offered from the Church of Stanford in the county of Northampton, thus given by Bridges (vol. I.

* " Fifteenth century, p. cclxii. parag. ult. you have, I observe, noticed on a brass-plate in North Leach Church, a date half in capital letters and half small numerals, 1484."

p. 582): 'Anno D'ni M^o D^o 58; in memory of Sir Thomas Cave.' Folkes, at p. 28, had noticed in the preceding paragraph a groat of the same King, with his style Edward 6, &c. Query is not this the earliest coin on which the number after the name is noted with the vulgar figure 6º. According to Snelling (View of Silver Coins, p. 21,) those of Henry VII. are the first that have the number after the name.

"P. cclx. parag. 4. ' Several dates are read, as if in such numerals, as in Lewis s Faversham, p. 48.'

"P. cclxiv. ' Mr. Lewis speaks of 1115 on the wainscot of a house then lately re-built near the market-place at Faversham.'

"Jacob, in the preface to the History of Faversham, p. vii. supposes Lewis to have been mistaken, the letters being, as he conceives, no other than I. H. S. the common abbreviation of our Saviour's name and title. He further observes, that the adjoining carvings prove it to be done about the reign of Henry VII.

"Dr. Wallis, in Additions and Emendations to his Treatise on Algebra, has produced one more of his specimens and proofs of the use of Arabic numerals in the twelfth century, of which you may not be aware; and as I think it highly probable that you may not have this tome in your library, I will transcribe the whole passage. It is from page 153.

"After citing Censorinus, de die Natali, printed at Hamburgh, 1614, he says, it need not seem strange that in this antient Mantle-tree (at Helmdon) *millesimo* should be expressed in letters, while the latter part of the number, 133, is written in figures.

"A further account of this Mantle-tree may be seen in the Philosophical Transactions, number 154, for the month of December, 1683.

"And Dr. Thomas Smith, now Fellow of Magdalen-college in Oxford, (a reverend and learned person, and a curious observer of antiquities both at home and in foreign countries, as far as Greece and Turkey) hath showed me the copy of an inscription (not much later than that of this Mantle-tree,) which he saw at Bristol, over the great gate of the College there, commonly known by the name of St. Augustine's, ' Rex Henricus Secundus et Dominus Robertus filius Herdini filii Regis Daciæ hujus Monasterii Primi Fundatores extiterunt, 1140.' This date, like that on the Preston-hall buildings, is probably of the retrospective sort. According to Tanner (Notitia Monastica) Robert Fitz-Harding founded this Priory in 1148; and perhaps if the inscription be remaining, it may be discovered that 8, and not a cypher, is the true reading.

"P. cclxvi. Your remark on Rhyming Epitaphs reminded me of what I judged to be a doubtful suggestion of the late Mr. T. Warton, in his inquiry into the authenticity of Rowley's Poems. It is in the section ii. metre, and at p. 38, where he asserts, that the quatrain stanza, with alternate rhyme, was scarcely ever used under any circumstances by the elder Poets except in translation; but I am rather inclined to think, that very many pieces of this kind of metre, for instance ballads, have perished because committed to memory and tradition only; and I am clear it is to be met with in a species of versifying which the Historian of English Poetry has not noticed, and that is the sepulchral. Whilst pursuing the inquiry, I discovered more antient epitaphs in the vulgar tongue than I had expected to have seen; and it added to my surprise that so many of them were in rhyme. I will refer to three in Weever that have the double rhyme, and two of them solely in two quatrain stanzas; and all the three are in the fifteenth century.

"At p. 399, in St. Lawrence Jewrie, for John Pickering and Elizabeth his wife, A. D. 1448; p. 580, in St. Alban's, —— Wyttor and his wyff Grase, A. D. 1406; p. 333, stone near Dartford, Richard Bontfant, A. D. 1459; but in this there are two stanzas and three other lines.

"It is an obvious remark, that these epitaphs were preserved in consequence of their being carved in stone, stone being *ære perennius*, because not fusible, and not so easily transmutable into silver.

"In the Art of English Poesie, (by Puttenham, though anonymously published by Richard Field, A. 1589,) cap. xxviii. is entitled, 'Of the Poem called Epitaph, used for the memorial of the dead;' and lest you should not have met with it, I will send you the following extract, page 45:

"'An Epitaph is but a kind of Epigram, only applied to the report of the dead person's estate and degree, or of his other good or bad partes, to his commendation or reproach; and is an inscription such as a man may commodiously write or engrave upon a tombe in a few verses, pithie, quicke, and sententious, for the passer-by to peruse, and judge upon without any long tariaunce. So if it exceede the measure of an Epigram, it is then (if the verse be correspondent) rather an Elegiac than an Epitaph, which errour many of these bastard rimers commit, because they be not learned, nor (as we are wont to say) their catftes [cr. for *crafts*] masters; for they make long and tedious discourses, and write them in larger tables to be hanged up in churches and chauncells, over the tombes of great men and others, which be so exceeding long as one must have halfe a daye's leasure to read one of them; and must be called away before he come halfe to the end, or else be locked in the Church by the Sexton, as I myself was once served reading an epitaph in a certain Cathedral Church of England. They be ignorant of Poesie that call such long tales by the name of Epitaphes, they might better call them Elegies, as I said before; and then ought neither to be engraven nor hanged up in tables. I have seen them, nevertheless, upon many honorable tombes of these late times erected, which doe rather disgrace than honour either the matter or maker.'

" Wishes of a happy new year await Mrs. Gough and yourself. As to the year so lately departed, it was considered, in a public view, the most sinister I ever knew; and I am now all but sixty-five. When the year 1895 shall terminate, the antiquaries of that period must contemplate with astonishment the occurrences of 1795, with the growing charges on all the necessaries and comforts of life, and at the same time a ready acquiescence in a large decisive majority of both Houses of Parliament to accumulate taxes to the amount of very near three millions a year; the minister at the same time expressing his satisfaction of the state of affairs, and boasting of the flourishing condition of poor old England!

" The public papers announced the arrival of the Prelate of Winton * from his travels, after an absence from his Diocese for I do not recollect how many years. In a letter I received from Maidstone was this article relative to his spouse, ' Mrs. North has brought home an immense quantity of fossils, and three dogs from Vienna, which cost twenty-five guineas each.'

" I remain, dear Sir, truly yours,   S. Denne."

40. " Dear Sir,   Wilmington, Jan. 26, 1796.
" The proofs of the two prefatory sheets †, with the review of which you favoured me, I have returned; and have added only a few words explanatory of the branch of the family of Cole-peper, settled at Preston-hall.

" Of the Preston-hall inscriptions, I have not a doubt that 1102 are the figures carved, and were the figures intended, though proof positive will certainly be wanted, to the application of them to any remarkable æra in the Colepeper family.

" You have my repeated wishes that you may procure a fac-simile of the Helmdon inscription, from a firm persuasion that it will confirm the notion I have formed of the date; and after coolly weighing all that I have read on the subject of antient dates in Arabic numerals in England, I am clearly of opinion, that every such date, prior to the fifteenth century, is spurious, and the reverie of our antique corps, though I may not choose to express myself thus positively in a letter designed to be read to the Society.

" Since I wrote last, I have procured Dr. Record's Arithmetic, which he dedicated to King Edward VI. Unluckily the edition I bought was published in 1658, and cannot, therefore, be quite so satisfactory as the first impression. To my great surprise, he takes not the least notice of the time of the substitution of the vulgar figures for the Latin numerals; but in his

* The Hon. Brownlow North.   † Of the Sepulchral Monuments.

preface he refers to other books written of arithmetic, concerning which I propose to solicit some intelligence from Mr. Urban's correspondents.

" Neighbour Latham, on Thursday evening last, appeared at Somerset-place, in the double character of F. A. S. and F. R. S. In the apartment of the antiquaries he tells me was exhibited a bill, knife, or I know not what to style it, of gold tipped with amber, that was said to have been an instrument used by the Druids in severing the misletoe sprig. How unluckily was it that the Arch-Druid* of the Old House never met with this choice relic! Mr. Latham likewise informed me, that I was a contributor to the amusement of the evening, as Secretary Brand produced the abstract of the Memoirs of Phineas Pett, which I formerly apprised you I had engaged to communicate to Mr. Wrighte, that it might be read when there was a want of papers of more consequence. The curious part of it is that which recites King James's presiding in a Court of Inquiry held at Woolwich, on a charge against Pett of ignorance and neglect whilst building the famous ship the Prince Royal †.

" To the query inserted in the Gentleman's Magazine, touching the original picture of the reputed Great Harry ship of war, no answer has been given by any one of Master Urban's readers ‡; and I much fear not any will ever be given. I must own that I concur in opinion with Mr. Topham, that the picture represents the Prince Royal, though I a little suspect the print of it may not be a fac-simile, and that this circumstance may have occasioned the difficulty in appropriating it.

" The paragraph in the newspapers that mentioned the fire at the cotton manufactory at Dartford, was, I understand, correct. The cause of it is not certainly known; but it is believed it began in a flue of the chimney in the room that was over the apartment in which one of the proprietors slept.

" I remain, dear Sir, yours very truly,　　S. DENNE."

———————

41. " DEAR SIR,　　　　　Wilmington, Feb. 4, 1796.
" For the two letters of Ducarel and Allen, relative to the supposed Great Harry ship of war, I am much obliged to you, as they may serve as a clue to a discovery of the original picture from which the print published by Allen was drawn; but, with submission, may it not be advisable to defer the communicating of them to Master Urban till the Council of the Society of Antiquaries shall have determined whether they shall or shall not insert in the Archæologia the paper I mentioned in my last? It was delivered to Secretary Wright as a readable paper only in a time of dearth. It was compiled from copious extracts I made from a self-writ-

* Dr. Stukeley.
† See the Archæologia, vol. XIV. pp. 217—296.
‡ See, however, Gent. Mag. Supplement, vol. LXV. p. 1072.

ten Memoir of the Life of Phineas Pett, which is in the British
Museum, or rather from a copy of that MS. lent me several
years ago by the late Mr. Fisher, of Rochester; and he, I think,
borrowed it of a Mr. Gray, who was the master builder in
Chatham Dock-yard. This book of extracts is at present in the
hands of a kinsman and friend, who lives in New Palace-yard;
and you are welcome to the perusal of it. To the paper delivered to Mr. Wrighte, I have had it in my thoughts to add a
page or two touching the Great Harry, as it is called, improperly;
for, as Mr. Topham has well observed, it bears no sort of resemblance to the ship so denominated that is in the Pepysian Library, and I concur in opinion with him, that it is more likely
to be an engraving of the Prince Royal built by Pett. My discussion on Arabic numerals is in such a state of forwardness
that I think I can put the finishing stroke to it in a trice, after I
shall be favoured by Mr. P. Rashleigh with the drawings of the
inscriptions on the Preston-hall barn and oast-house; and I am
willing to believe that between us we shall elucidate a question
in which some of our corps have bewildered themselves.

" In your letter of January 7, you observe, that William de
Soana de Rhetorica was one of the first books printed at St.
Alban's, and that in the title-page 1418 is engraved in fac-simile
in Ames and Herbert; but if in that title-page the modern 4
appears, the type is of a different form from that of the figure
which is a part of Caxtons cypher, and in Mr. Boys's seal,
and in MSS.; and in another of your letters you have intimated
that the modern 4 was not adopted before the sixteenth century.
Query, therefore, were not Ames and Herbert mistaken in the
specimen they have given of this figure?

" A chatty epistle from Archdeacon Law contains this query
and subsequent remark, ' Did you ever hear that Mr. Coxe the
traveller, is deputed by Lord Orford to write the History of Sir
Robert Walpole's administration? The work is in forwardness,
and its publication was expected in the course of this winter,
but further delay is required. The character of Sir Robert is
now less the object of admiration and censure than heretofore;
the two noted parties of Whig and Tory are so divided and sub-
divided that the champions of either of them will be received
with indifference. One ill effect may arise from such a publication as tending to infix a bad opinion of the pretensions to
patriotism.' Novel was this intelligence to me; and on reading
it, I was inclined to think that the noble Earl had not selected
the most proper person for this employment, Mr. Coxe being
Chaplain to the Bishop of Salisbury, and having been preferred
by him; and Bishop Douglas was the Cleve of Pulteney, the
grand opponent of Walpole. As to Sir Robert, I was trained
to have a favourable opinion of him; and it was with satisfaction I read that even the Tory, or rather Jacobite Samuel Johnson bore testimony to his merit, and thus characterised him in

his energetic style, 'Walpole was a fixed star, Pitt a meteor.'
This anecdote is related by Boswell, whose opinion of Sir Robert
was, ' that he was a wise and benevolent minister, who thought
that the happiness and prosperity of a commercial country like
ours would be best promoted by peace, which he accordingly
maintained with credit during a very long period.' Happy
would it have been for old England had his successors trod in
his steps !

" Had the biographer of Johnson lived to read the epitaph of
Anna Seward on the philosopher he idolized, he must have been
sorely mortified ; and yet both Johnson and Boswell were much
to blame in perpetuating the weaknesses of the father of this
celebrated Poetess. By-the-bye, however, if the epitaph I read
in the General Evening Post was correctly printed, there is, I
think, a word in the second line that was not well chosen, 'great'
and 'colossal' being a tautology which might have been avoided
by substituting ' thou ' or ' sage ' for ' great critic.'

" On a revisal of the letters of Dr. Ducarel and T. Allen, I
have altered my mind, and am now inclined to send another billet of inquiry to Master Urban after the good ship Harry, (I
would it were advertised for sale by the candle !) and shall submit it to your inspection. There is, as appears to me, evidence
satisfactory from two persons, Allen and Crespigny, that there
was a picture existing from which Canot's print was engraved ;
though I am convinced that it was not a painting of the Great
Harry, and I have my strong doubts whether the picture had
ever belonged to the Monks of Christ Church Priory. Has Mr.
Deputy of the Ward of Farringdon Extra, any acquaintance
with Dr. Crespigny, the Member for Sudbury, or with his kins-
folk ? if he has, I wish him to ask for anecdotes touching this
picture, as Philip Crespigny mentioned by Dr. Ducarel might
often talk of it in his family, after having given himself the
trouble to search the Pepysian library.

" Mr. Deputy N. as well as his brother Birch, was, I doubt
not, mortified at not being permitted to enter Carlton House ;
and to partake of a slice of cake and a cup of caudle. Alas,
poor Prince ! and alas, poor Deputies ! in this time of dearth !
I trust, however, that at the Mansion House gala, all the pastry
served up had *quantum sufficit* of the flour of barley, the right
worshipful the Lord Mayor having subscribed the self-denying
ordinance of Parliament *. Yours truly, S. DENNE."

42. " DEAR SIR, *Wilmington, Feb.* 13, 1796.
" The testimonial of candidate Clarke † is drawn up verbatim
according to the form you favoured me with ; but, with submission to Mr. Director, the words, ' our personal knowledge,' were

* An Act restricting the use of Flour.
† For the Society of Antiquaries ; see p. 613.

not absolutely requisite, there being a qualifying 'or' in the statute (chap. vi.) ' of the election and admission of Fellows into the Society of Antiquaries,' the words running either upon the personal knowledge of the three propounders, or on his being known to the Society by his works;' and Mr. Clarke has certainly appeared to advantage in Archæologia, vol. XI. But the testimonial must be signed by three Fellows; and it was my intention to have procured the signature of brother Latham, but I find he has taken a trip to Romsey, and that he is not likely to be back again for more than a week. You will be pleased, therefore, in my name to apply to our friend Mr. Craven Ord; and I shall give him a preference, because he and the candidate are investigating the same subjects of antiquity, viz. the remains of those in Churches; and should they have an intercourse with each other, which it is likely they will after Mr. Clarke become F. A. S. they may aid each other in the favourite pursuit. The more readily do I recommend ' Investigator Roffensis,' from a persuasion that he will not be a sleeping partner, though at times I have discovered a degree of backwardness in him that may be, however, partly owing to occasional bodily infirmities, he being, as I suspect, of what is termed the nervous class. Of his inclination to the study of antiquities, an extract of his letter in which he consulted me about his purpose to belong to our corps, is an additional specimen :

" ' On Gothic Architecture little can be said after Barry, Ledwich, and Dr. Young, who has given an excellent paper on this subject in the Irish Transactions of 1789, which I purchased on that account; and if you have not seen them, I beg I may be permitted to send them. Mr. Pownall has also said much, but his principles to me are not well founded, for as it is easy to trace every specific difference between the Gothic and Grecian styles to the corruption of the classic model which took place in the Lower Empire, and yet appears in many Churches in Rome, &c. so it is evident the carpenter followed the mason instead of the contrary. Yet the Governor has given many curious articles of information, and I thank him for many hints on the affair. Yet I am fearful of venturing them more than for my own amusement, ' Nam de Carthagine silere melius puto quam parum dicere,' as says an old Roman. In a work aimed at as complete, no system ought to go unexamined; and much more should be seen than it is possible for me at Gravesend to get at. Nor does even the Museum Library afford such books as I want; the Ely and Worcester are not there to be found; and I have had for the sake of a more extensive opportunity some inclination to attempt becoming a member of the Antiquarian Society, but as I am not an Alumnus in any University, and possess no decent paternal estate, I have given it up hitherto; and as vanity makes up no part of the reason for such a wish, if you will unreservedly give me your opinion on this head, I shall thank you; and believe me my object is confined to consulting their library, being possessed of their valuable productions, and sometimes attending their public meetings; the rest with me, I mean the honour of the F. S. A. would from proper motives be passed over.' When F. S. A. shall be annexed to the name of my correspondent, I have it in my thoughts to set him a task by way of an initiatory lecture; and I shall give him for a thesis a point to be discussed, in which, if I am not mistaken, he will find himself at home, as the phrase is.

" The advice, *per* Master Urban, that the supposed Great Harry ship of war was moored in the Isle of Wight, did not escape my notice; nor do I think it at all improbable that Hans Stanley might have the picture from T. Allen's worthy friend in Westminster for a valuable consideration, by whatever means it might have been conveyed from Canterbury to Westminster. Not but that there is a traditional tale at Greenwich Hospital, that Henry VIII. was so partial to this warlike vessel that was called by his name, that Hans Holbein was ordered to paint four representations of it, and that one of the fac-similes was for some years at Hempsted-house, in the Weald of Kent, in the possession of Sir John Norris. What became of it when the goods and chattels of his worthless thoughtless grandson passed under the hammer, I have not been able to trace.

" Considerate and kind was it in you to favour me with the reading of the three tracts touching the modern antique Shakspearian MSS. so fortunately brought to light, after an interval of almost two centuries; though I had before made up my mind upon the question on perusing the extracts published in the newspapers, which so evidently betrayed anachronisms.

" This find brings to my recollection a loss of precious MSS. sustained by the Dean of Rochester, related as follows by Mr. Archdeacon, though one may easily believe that the loser is better pleased that the to him no laughable tale has not found its way into a newspaper or magazine. 'Our Dean (quoth my correspondent) has been singularly unfortunate in the commencement of his London residence. During his temporary abode at Ibbotson's hotel in Vere-street, a writing-desk belonging to Mrs. Dampier was stolen from the room, containing nearly eighty guineas and seven choice Sermons. A muff and tippet were likewise taken away, so that the undetected thief made an entire clearance. The Dean finds that his story, when recited by him, excites little pity, and the loss of the money is forgotten on the mention of the robbery of Sermons; but I cordially sympathise with him, knowing that I should sensibly feel the privation of any of the feeble labours of my brain.' The remark of the Vicar of W. and D. on this serio-comic narration is, that it does not surprise him that a funny Etonian, if a layman, should smile at the pillage of what he may deem waste paper, and that such a diminution of stock in the tin-box would, for a special reason, have been more felt by Mr. Archdeacon than Mr. Dean, because the Rector of Westmill and Minister of Chatham, be he resident at Westmill or his Prebendal-house, has a pulpit to supply, independently of his turns of preaching in Rochester Cathedral; whereas the Master of Sherburn Hospital, *juxta* Durham, is, by the statute of the founder, precluded from being the proprietor of a parochial tribune.

" When the plates of Paper Marks shall arrive (and Mr. Deputy promises they will be inclosed in the next packet) S. D. will forthwith compare them with the specimens taken from what Mr. G. properly terms Dr. Lort's farrago. Mr. Vice-President was an assiduous collector; but came under the description of those procrastinating Antiquaries who never finish any work out of the materials they amass, as was well noticed by the editor of the Paston Letters.

" I remain, dear Sir, yours truly,   S. DENNE."

---

43. Mr. DENNE to Mr. NICHOLS.

" DEAR SIR,   *Wilmington, Feb. 24, 1796.*

" Since I revised the proof sheet, in which were Staveley's Memorials of the Monks and their Monasteries, it occurred to me that I scribbled some memoranda relative to the medical skill and practice of that class of Ecclesiastics, whilst I was arranging the notes I transmitted it to Mr. Nasmith for his edition of Notitia Monastica. As, however, it was not his design to make any addition to Tanner's original preface, the physical inuendos were not of any use to him; and whether they may be worthy the regard of the Historian of Leicestershire Mr. Deputy is the most proper judge. However, if they do not coincide with his plan, the copying of them has not given me much trouble, and the perusal will be still more easy to you; and I shall, therefore, inclose them in a parcel, intended to be sent to-morrow to a friend in New Palace-yard, Westminster, who will, I doubt not, readily convey it to you, together with some extracts from the MS. Memoirs of Phineas Pett, that I left with my friend Mr. Grant when I was last in town, *viz.* Aug. 25, 1795. Probably it is not new to you, that extracts of these extracts have been lately read at Somerset-place; and I have reason to infer they were thought to be amusing by my brethren, as Secretary Brand, in his letter of acknowledgment and thanks, termed them very curious. It is, however, high time to have done with my *omnium.* That, in the Stock-exchange at Cicero's Head, the whole stock may not be deemed under par, is the wish of a mere literary broker, who, not being a bull or bear, is, dear Sir,

" Truly yours,   S. DENNE."

44. Dear Sir, *Wilmington, Feb. 25, 1796.*

" The return of the proof sheets of the History of Shoreditch might suffice to show the safe arrival at Wilmington Vicarage of the Paper Mark engravings; but I take up my pen to assure you that when the time of my rustication shall be expired, and I be an ocular witness whether London be *in statu quo*, I shall certainly not fail to inquire, *in propria persona*, after the welfare of Mr. Deputy of Farringdon Extra, and to discharge my bill to Messrs. Fox, together with some addition to it. My meaning is, that I wish to have some plates of the jolly Scaramouch toper exhibited on the porch of Chalk Church, because without a facsimile of it the letter-press on Giveales, &c. will not be quite intelligible to some of my friends.

" A Register of Benefactions to the Parish of Lambeth, compiled like that of Donations to St. Leonard, Shoreditch, was delivered to Rector Porteus, and is now in the close custody of Rector Vyse; but unfortunately I neglected to keep the loose sheets from which I copied the contents fair into the book before the surrendry of it to the successor of Rector Denne; the consequence of this omission was, that it was not in my power to make some curious additions to ' Addenda ' which some of the early gifts would have supplied; but in 1769 I was not even an Antiquariolus. Oh that the mantle of the lately departed Patriarch of Whittington was now my portion! This melancholy incident must fill a page or two in the Miscellany to which he was so bounteous and so entertaining a contributor; but I trust that a memoir of him of far greater consequence will pass from Enfield to the Cicero's Head. One evening at least ought at Somerset-place to be devoted to an Eulogy of F. A. S. there being in Archæologia fifty articles, save one, under the signature of Sam. Pegge. Yours truly, S. Denne."

---

45. Mr. Denne to Mr. Gough.

" Dear Sir, *Wilmington, March 14, 1796.*

" By the civility of a gentleman who is my next neighbour, I hope in a day or two to have an opportunity of dispatching to Red Lion-passage the folio of Paper Marks and patterns of antique paper. The former have been compared with the engravings from Fisher's drawings; and had I seen them whilst my explanatory letter was in the press, it does not appear to me that they would have furnished any innuendoes of much importance, copious as are the collections of Mr. Ames and Dr. Lort. Ames, in the plate annexed to Lewis's Life of Caxton, has omitted only two specimens exhibited in his folio; but I am inclined to infer from his dates of illustration that the veteran printer found some difficulty in procuring paper, there being in the same impression of the same book, and that a small volume, sheets of paper with the water-marks widely different. There are three marks to the paper used by Peter Schoiffer for Justi-

nian's Institutes, Mentz, 1476. To the number I have added
one only on blue paper. The emblem is a lion rampant, crowned,
with a bundle of arrows in the dexter paw, and a staff with the
cap of liberty in the sinister. Mr. Fisher supposes this device
originated in Holland, although the crown does not coincide
with that idea.

" Ere this my kinsman and friend, Mr.'Grant, of New Palace-
yard, has probably committed to the care of Mr. Deputy Nichols
for Richard Gough, Esq. the extracts taken from the Memoirs of
the Life of Phineas Pett. Mr. Director is doubtless apprised
that Messrs. Ord and Douce have collated my extracts from the
extracts with the MSS. in the British Museum, and found differences between them. To the application from Mr. Secretary
Brand whether I would consent to the corrections, my answer
was in the affirmative; that as in the paper ordered by the Council to be inserted in Archæologia, there was a reference to the
MS. in the British Museum, it ought to be printed conformably
to it; not but that I have my doubts whether the MS. in the
Museum be not a copy, and if so, whether the copy from which
I made my extracts, and which at that time belonged to the
builder at the Chatham Dock-yard, might not be a transcript
from the original preserved in the family. If the proof sheets
are sent to me for revisal, I shall wish to have at hand my book
of extracts, there being in it some notes concerning the Pette
family. Unless my memory deceives me, I have hinted that
there is a Student of Christ Church, and a Chaplain to the
Bishop of Oxford, a descendant of this famous builder, and
called after his names, Phineas Pett*. King James's presiding
at the trial of this persecuted shipwright, is a curious part of the
Memoir that ought to have before made its appearance.

" Though neither of us met with the Address from the University of Cambridge on the King's happy escape on the day he
opened the present Session of Parliament, I have, by favour of
Messrs. Currey, been so fortunate as to peruse the congratulatory
compliments tendered by our Alma Mater on the safe delivery
of the Princess of Wales, and the birth of a Princess. It was
published in the Cambridge Journal; and Mr. Jas. Currey, imagining that both his father and myself might wish to read it,
was so obliging as to dispatch it to Dartford per post. The
Address had the repute of being drawn up by the Master of
Corpus Christi as Vice-chancellor†.

" In another column of the same Journal, honourable mention is made of another Bene't-college disciple. It is a long
extract from a charge delivered to the Grand Jury at the last
Quarter Sessions held for the county of Cambridge, by the
chairman, the Worshipful and Reverend James Nasmith. The
subject of it is the newly passed Act of Parliament to prevent

* Now (1830) Canon of Christ Church, and Archdeacon of Oxford.
Having been tutor to Mr. Canning, he was offered in 1827 the Bishopric
of Carlisle, but declined it. † Philip Douglas, D. D.

seditious meetings, which the chairman clearly and elegantly
expounds and extols, after previously averring that 'the inquest
would hear from him the sentiments of one unbiassed by party,
uninfluenced by prejudice, and who professes to acknowledge
no political attachment but to his Sovereign and the constitution of his country.'

" A few lines more shall be added on another Benedictine
Orator, who is, I conclude, the father of the existing members
of the old House ; I mean the Right Reverend Sir William Ashburnham. When I read in the newspaper that the Bishop of
Chichester had preached a Lenten Sermon before the King, I
was inclined to believe the duty might have been discharged by
proxy ; but it was, I am assured, really so. His Lordship, as I
understand, came to town on Saturday, made his appearance the
day following in the pulpit of the Chapel Royal, and returned on
Monday to his Palace in Sussex ; and, as this was performed with
ease by his Lordship, and to the satisfaction of his hearers, the
inference is that, though the Prelate must be almost, if not
quite, half-way between four score and ninety, there must be
mens sana in corpore sano *.

" In the aforesaid Journal was a list of Doctors who this year
preserved *senioritatem in prioribus comitiis*, and it exhibited a
difference between the former and the present times. Whilst I
was a Scholar and B. A. the number of Wranglers never exceeded
a dozen, and rarely were there as many more inferior Senior
Optimes ; whereas there were, at the late Bachelor's commencement, sixteen of the upper class, and eighteen of the lower, and
Ds. D'Oyly, of Corpus Christi-college, was the thirty-fourth. His
Christian name is John, the son of Matthias, eldest son of Archdeacon D Oyly, and consequently great-great-nephew of Matthias Ely. He was the Captain of the Scholars in St. Peter's-
college, Westminster ; but not accepted at the election by either
the Master of Trinity-college, Cambridge, or the Dean of Christ
Church, Oxford, being under a suspicion of a democratic taint.
Mr. James Currey has always made a favourable report of his
classical acquirements ; and I think he has obtained a prize for
a Greek or Latin copy of verses. Whether he be a candidate for
the Chancellor's Medal I have not heard. As his name is endorsed upon the first tripos, he is not disqualified from being a
Fellow of Bene't, supposing that preferment worthy his notice †.

* Bishop Ashburnham died in 1797, aged 87.

† Mr. John D'Oyly obtained Sir William Browne's medal for the
Latin Ode, 1795 ; the second Chancellor's medal, 1796 ; proceeded M.A.
1796 ; and was a Fellow of Bene't. He afterwards became Resident at
Candy, and held other appointments in the Island of Ceylon. His
younger brother, George, also Fellow of Bene't, and Christian Advocate,
is the present learned and much esteemed Rector of Lambeth. Of their
father, who, like his father, was for some years before his death Archdeacon of Lewes, a memoir will be found in the Gentleman's Magazine,
vol. LXXXV. pt. ii. p. 478.

" As he was the junior of the Senior Optimes, I a little suspect he may have been the person so named by the Vice-chancellor, according to antient usage, Mr. James Currey having
informed me that the bent of this young man was not to Mathematics and Natural Philosophy. From the want of a Senior
Optime, the now Professor of Modern History undoubtedly
missed a medal, and it was a mortification he partly deserved,
because from vanity and conceit he was in the habit of decrying
Geometry and Algebra, Euclid and Saunderson, and even Newton ; and I well remember that in the theatre, when whiffled by
Brocket of Trinity, who was no less proud and supercilious, the
whiffler completely posed the examinant by suggesting out of
the way questions in chronology from Greek writers.

" Not to offer a reflection of condolence on the recent decease
of the Patriarch of Whittington, who was all but the father of
our corps, would be inexcusable in a letter from a F. S. A. to Mr.
Director. That a man who had for twenty-two years been
walking upon the broken arches at the further end of Mirzah's
bridge, should, with very little previous warning, drop into the
tide of eternity, could not be a matter of surprise ; but as you
made a very favourable report of the health and strength of
your friend after the return of yourself and Mr. Deputy from
your visit to him in the summer, and had not since given a hint
of an approaching change, his departure was not expected.

" Thank you for the perusal of the Catalogue of Herbert's
Library, &c. Had I been in town during the view, I should certainly have looked at those MSS. that particularly relate to
Kent ; though from what I recollect of the authorities cited by
Harris and Hasted, most of them, or at least extracts from them,
had passed under their inspection. It is not unlikely that many,
perhaps most of them, had belonged to Dr. Plot.

" Between this and August, I shall hardly fail of seeing Mr.
James Currey*, because I conclude he will be at Dartford when
his turn comes to predicate at Whitehall, and that is, I think,
in June or July. I will apprise him of its being your wish
to be present at the anniversary gala at the old House ; and most
willingly certify to him, that you are the identical Mr. Gough,
who was a member thereof, and have a high veneration for those
antique walls.   Yours truly,   S. DENNE."

* The Rev. James Currey, the Fellow of Bene't so often mentioned by
Mr. Denne, proceeded B. A. 1791, being the 10th Senior Optime of that
year, M. A. 1794, B. D. 1802. He was appointed a Preacher at Whitehall in 1796 ; was presented by his college in 1811 to the Rectory of
Thurning, Norfolk; and in the following year elected Preacher at the
Charter-house. He died, after a lingering illness, at Epping, August 8,
1823. His father, the Rev. John Currey, who survived him, was of St.
John's-college, Cambridge, B. A. 1758, being the 4th Senior Optime of
that year; M. A. 1761; and for some time Fellow of that Society. He
was presented to the Vicarages of Dartford and Longfield in 1779, by
Dr. Thomas, then Bishop of Rochester, and died Oct. 18, 1825, aged 89.

46. "Dear Sir,   *Wilmington, March 26, 1796.*

"On a cursory perusal of the MS. articles at the end of the Catalogue, which by your direction Mr. Deputy dispatched to me with haste, post haste, I was convinced that the substance of them had been incorporated into a History of Kent; though I frankly own it did not occur to me that they were conveyed from Mr. Hasted to the hammer of Leigh and Sotheby, not having a suspicion that he would dispose of his materials before his work was completed. The prices which some of the lots produced is astonishing, for I should not have been willing to have given half the money asked for the whole previous to the sale, even in better days; I mean when a wheaten loaf was not at a price that the Vicars of the Diocese of Rochester are charged by its Bishop to be sparing in the use of such a luxury. Not but there are some of the MSS. I should have wished to have picked up some gleanings from, had a sufficient time been allowed for so doing. The extracts from the Register of the Priory of Leeds is of the number; and the Register alluded to I take to be that which, according to Notitia Monastica, is in the possession of the Filmer family.

"From your report of the widow of the late highly respectable Dr. Owen, I am not clear whether she be appointed to one of the new apartments, annexed to Bromley-college, or be only a candidate for it. The very heavy charges incurred in building, retarded for a time the appointment; and I was told by Mr. Archdeacon, that there was a longer delay than was needful, because the late Bishop of Rochester was a very intractable person in business. However, near three quarters of a year have passed since I had any conversation with Dr. Law upon the subject, and I have not been at Bromley since Midsummer 1794. You are rightly informed that the allowance to the widows on the new establishment is a third less than to those of the original foundation, which makes a very material difference, considering the advanced charges of several of the necessaries, and of many of the comforts of life, and the prospect there is of their increasing whilst our wise statesmen are regardless of the old adage, that war begets poverty; but I am not aware that a widow of the Betensonian class is precluded from being translated into the Warnerian division in case of a vacancy, provided there be no candidate to whom, by the rules of the College, a preference must be given. This strict propriety does not, as you suppose, extend to three Dioceses, it being confined to the widows of beneficed clerks of the Diocese of Rochester, comprehending the peculiar Deanery of Shoreham. (See Addenda to the History of Lambeth, p. 170.)

"In your letter you term the MS. Memoirs of Phineas Pett, that are deposited in the British Museum, 'original;' are the gentlemen who have given themselves the trouble of being collators quite satisfied that he was the writer of the said MS.? It was my intention to search for the will of this eminent naval architect, as well with the view of learning whether the will itself was an autograph as for the purpose of noticing any biographical anecdotes that might be worthy of attention. The probability is, that the testator might have *bona notabilia* in two Dioceses; and that in course the probate was issued from the Prerogative-office. Secretary Brand was apprised by me, that my friend Mr. Bryant was possessed of an original picture of Captain Phineas Pett; and I think I added, that I believed it was at Cypenham. I also am inclined to believe that the said picture* is what is mentioned in the extracts of the Memoirs that I delivered to Mr. Wrighte. When I was last at Maidstone, Mr. Pett, of that town, regretted that his son Phineas, Chaplain to the Bishop of Oxford, late a Student and Tutor of Christ Church, and now of Chilbolton in Hants †, had not accepted the invitation of Mr. Bryant to take a view of his namesake and progenitor. That Dr. Birch should have so slightly mentioned this famous ship-builder, I agree with you, is a matter of surprise; and I am pleased that I have been the instrument of recalling him from the state of oblivion into which he was in danger of passing before his merit had been fully considered; and it will be an additional pleasure to me, should it be in my power to ascertain that the supposed Great Harry, engraved for Allen, was really the Prince Royal that occasioned its builder so much vexation as well as honour. Archdeacon Law is desired by me to make an inquiry of his friend, and, as I believe, *quondam* ward, Mrs. Hodges, whether any information can be acquired touching the Great Harry that once decorated a room at Hemsted-place. I much fear, however, that it might, as a piece of lumber, have passed under the hammer, and have since perished.

" A letter, dated March 17, brought me this article of news from Chatham : 'On my return from the Dock-yard, I have to impart the unpleasing information of the secession this day of the rope-makers, in consequence of an order from the Navy Board to work up the old hemp (query, old ropes?) This was deemed a grievance; and when the Commissioners referred to former usage, the reply was, that they were more enlightened now than heretofore. Modern illumination promotes neither the peace of society nor the comforts of individuals. The methodists are the most enlightened, and, I believe, the most restless in the three towns.' 'And,' quoth somebody else, 'it is to be feared that the said methodists from their numbers may be the cause of some public turmoil; having lived long enough to be assured, upon observation and experience, that they are not the best men who conceive themselves to be more righteous than other people. It has, indeed, been started as a moot point, whether more evil has not accrued from too much than too

* " In the year 1611, September. About this time my picture was begun to be drawn by a Dutchman, working then at Mr. Prock's at Rochester."   † See Gent. Mag. vol. LXV. p. 798.

little religion; some kinds of superstition are worse than Atheism was once the subject of a discourse delivered in St. Mary's pulpit, Cambridge, by the ingenious and energetic Weston, of St. John's, and which he treated in so free and unguarded a manner, that Dr. Richardson, of Emanuel, the *pro-vice-can.* demanded his notes; and the preacher, therefore, printed them in his own vindication.

" 'Till I received your last favour, I was not aware that no tribute of applause was likely to be paid to the memory of the Patriarch of Whittington, before an assembly whose meetings he had often honoured with his presence and conversation, and who, in absence, had so frequently instructed and entertained them; for, if I have not miscounted, there are fifty papers, save one, adjudged by the Council proper for insertion in Archæologia. The name of Pegge not appearing in the eleventh volume was ominous; and portended that his days were almost numbered. We concur in our opinions, that the reason is not satisfactory which is assigned for not eulogising deceased members of the highest class in the line of antiquarian pursuits; and I really thought that the precedents of such a practice might have been cited from the minutes of our Society.

" I remain, dear Sir, yours truly,　　S. Denne."

---

47. Mr. Denne to Mr. Nichols.

" Sir,　　　　　　　　　　*Wilmington, Feb.* 13, 1796.

" If you are disposed to give yourself the trouble of sending the proof sheets concerning the Abbey de la Pre, I certainly shall not object to the reading of them, being fully satisfied that information and amusement will result from the perusal of whatever passes from the pen of the Historian of Leicester under his types. At the same time it is proper to acquaint you how little matter relative thereto you are likely to have from one who is not of the kingdom of Mercia; and whose ancestors, as far as he can trace, never had the least connection with the town (I beg pardon, the City) of King Leir. The little that has occurred to me since I received the proofs is subjoined; and perhaps that little may not be novel.

" The inclosed billets to Master Urban, and the squib at a Deputy, were scribbled before your packet arrived. I have only to add, that I shall be obliged to you to transmit my answers to part of its contents to Enfield and to Primrose-street.

" It is a mortification to the Vicar of Wilmington when he finds himself under the necessity of keeping a proof sheet to a second and a third day; but the last packet from the Cicero's Head placed upon his table such a profusion of literary viands as could not be speedily digested in the noddle of a person who is more than half way between three-score and three-score and ten, *viz.* Staveley on Monkery, the Abbey de la Pre, the Great

Harry Ship of War, Arabic Numerals, Paper Marks, History
and Antiquities of Shoreditch, the Modern Antique Shakspeare,
more Chattertoniano, &c. &c. a choice *olio et omnium.*   S. D.
flatters himself that, in a cellar of the Abbey de la Pre, the Historian of Leicester may be so lucky as to find a chest containing
the original tragedy of King Leir and his Daughters, by a
British bard.   Yours truly,   S. Denne."

48. Mr. Denne to Mr. Gough.

"Dear Sir,   *Wilmington, April 8,* 1796.
"In my last I apprised you that I might probably have an
interview with Mr. P. Rashleigh in Easter week; and from my
innuendo you might flatter yourself that the long promised
drawings of inscriptions on the out-buildings at Preston-hall
might then be delivered to me.   I had the pleasure of meeting
the Rector of Southfleet at Dartford yesterday, but, alas! you
must wait a few weeks more ere your wishes can be fully gratified; however, the mortification is abated, because I can report
a progress made, as you will see by the inclosed rough sketch of
one of the inscriptions.   The case is, he lately dined at Preston-
hall, but was there so short a time that he could not examine
them with due attention, and his desire is to give you complete
drawings; and I can assure you he has the credit of being expert with his pencil.   He proposes soon to pass a few days at
Preston-hall; and he says, I may depend upon my hearing from
him soon after his return home.
"The inclosed sketch is on the door-case of what is now an
oast-house; and the figures are unquestionably 1102.
                      "Yours truly,   S. Denne."

49. "Dear Sir,   *Wilmington, May 3,* 1796.
"By the removal of Mr. Latham from Dartford to Romsey,
this vicinity has lost an experienced practitioner in the medical,
chirurgical, and clinical line; and I am deprived of the conversation and assistance of a brother F. S. A.   His departure is
the more to be regretted because he had upon his shelves many
books of the antiquarian class to which I had free access; and he
could likewise make good use of his pencil, and was always
ready to employ it.   The settling of his son in Romsey, and the
marrying of his daughter to a surgeon and apothecary in Winchester, was what determined him to transmigrate into the
county of Hants; and as he has taken so long a flight, and is
passed the age of youth and activity, it is not probable that his
visits into Kent will be frequent.   An apology is requisite for
styling him only Mr. he being a Dr. by diploma from Acad.
Cæs. and enrolled M. D. in the lists of the Royal and Antiquarian
Societies of London.

" We clerks of the Diocese of Rochester are to be reviewed by our Prelate* next month ; and this being his Lordship's primary visitation, he has, after the example of his predecessors, issued a paper of articles interrogatory, desiring us to write under each question a distinct and full answer, and to send it to his house in London, before the visitation, or to deliver it to him at his visitation, signed with our respective names. There are twelve queries, but it is the last of them only that has any thing different from what I have seen on former occasions. It is as follows: 'Have you any families or persons in your parish professing themselves Roman Catholics ? In particular, are there any emigrants residing in your parish, and how many of that description ? Among them are there any ecclesiastics; and by what means do they obtain a livelihood ? Do any of them speak the English language readily ? Have you observed that they hold much conversation with the common people?' No concern has the Vicar of Wilmington with this article, there not being in the said parochial district any Papist professed or reputed ; nor to the best of his knowledge and belief did a French emigrant ever find his way into the parish, though situated within a mile of the great road from Dovor to the metropolis.

" The provincial papers of Kent have apprised the public that on Whit-monday the Free and Accepted Masons held their grand anniversary gala at Dartford ; and that an excellent discourse, adequate to the occasion, was preached by the Rev. J. Inwood, Provincial Grand Chaplain. ' Let not your good be evil spoken of,' was certainly an *apropos* text ; and he treated his subject with ingenuity, and with fewer masonic terms than is customary. He is the master of an academy at Greenwich ; and, if credit is to be given to the Kentish Gazette, the Sermon is to be printed at the request of the Society. Some of the congregation objected to the length of the discourse; and I suppose that prayer and sermon took up three quarters of an hour in the delivery. But what would these murmurers have said had they been at St. Paul's Cathedral on the last Anniversary Meeting of the Sons of the Clergy, when the famous preacher, Dr. Rennell, kept me standing for sixty-seven minutes, a minute more or less, and in consequence over-roasted all the beef and lamb that was preparing for the feast in the kitchen of the Merchant-taylors ?

" On Whit-tuesday a new tabernacle was opened at Dartford, under the auspices of Lady Erskine, and another lady called Lady Hill, but who probably is not dignified by any title. They brought with them one of their chosen Pastors, whose name I have not learnt. Whilst standing at some distance from the door, I, though not quick of hearing, could find that as to voice and lungs he was a powerful man in the pulpit ; but I was fully satisfied with the two or three sentences he uttered whilst I stood upon the threshold. He was, I understood, more than an hour

* Dr. Horsley.

haranguing his flock, notwithstanding he had for his text a single word, Bethesda.   Over the door I observed this inscription, 'Zion Chapel;' but report says, that Bethesda will now be added to it.

"We had yesterday a blow at the powder-mills, in this neighbourhood; but happily not a life was sacrificed, nor, I believe, any damage except to the mill itself where the explosion was.   I understand that Mr. Andrews, one of the proprietors of this black work, is a candidate for Bewdley; and it may be presumed that, should he get admission into St. Stephen's Chapel, he will not be clamorous for a speedy peace.   Yours truly, S. Denne."

———

50. "Dear Sir,   Wilmington, June 9, 1796.

"I have it in my thoughts to pass a part of the next week with my friends at Maidstone; and, as I shall in my way thither dine at Preston-hall, I shall have an opportunity of learning from Mrs. Milner, whether Mr. P. Rashleigh has been long enough her visitor to allow him time to draw the inscriptions and coats of arms on the barn and oast-house.   I rather suspect he may not, having been told that he was an active canvasser for the two Baronets who were candidates for Knights of our Shire, with which contest I did not interfere.   You may, or may not, be apprised, that in Kent it was till 1790 a laudable and convenient usage to elect a member from each grand division of our county.   At the last election I was zealous for Mr. Marsham, who had been the western Representative for three Parliaments; but to the disgrace of the freeholders he was dispatched to Coventry.   It was my wish this time to have looked to the west, and to have left the two eastern candidates to themselves and their partisans; but there was in my opinion an insuperable objection to the candidate of the west, and I therefore resolved not to stir from home.   It was a capital objection; and greatly astonished am I that, after the dreadful catastrophe at Yarmouth, there should be any thoughtful freeholder who should not see it in the same point of view.   Mr. Waddington's dissipation of 10 or £.12,000, rapidly acquired by a lucky commercial hit, is not quite an unique; but what shall we say of a gentleman turned of thirty, who shall sell his paternal estate, some say for £.18,000, avowedly for the purpose of squandering the greater part of the purchase-money in a county contest, though not six years before the two winning candidates had paid above £ 30,000 for the honour of being humble servants to the Men of Kent.   Mr. Honywood acknowledges that the last struggle cost him £.18,000.   The amount of Sir Edward Knatchbull's expenses cannot be ascertained, because it now appears that there are long bills in arrear in divers parts of the county.   Had the late Sir Francis Geary left his estate at Polesden in Surrey in the hands of trustees, it would have been a fortunate circum-

stance for his son *. As I am told, the three candidates have
appeared in caricature at the west end of the town; one of the
Baronets being exhibited in a poor-house, the other in a mad-
house, and the Squire in his coffin; but whether the portraits
bear any resemblance to the originals my information was not
apprised. This being the case, it is thought somewhat hard
that the congé d'elire should be thus misapplied; for to be
sure so prevailing is ministerial influence in Kent, that if the
two candidates named in it really join, votes are thrown away
upon a third man; and therefore, as before hinted, one's arm
chair is the seat of credit as well as of ease to a freeholder who
does not love to be in a bustle. During the election it has been
a part of my amusement to inspect former polls, in order to
form a judgment of the number of freeholders, and what proportion there may be of them in the two divisions of our county.
The result of my search is, that at the election in 1734, the
voters amounted to 7,852; in that of 1754 to 7,940; and in
that of 1790 to no more than 6,979. I had imagined that in
West Kent we might have several hundred more freeholders,
perhaps 1000, than there are in East Kent; but am now inclined
to believe there is not so material a difference between the two
districts, all the parishes by the sea, those in the Isle of Thanet
included, having a very large number of houses that are freehold.
                    " Yours truly,   S. Denne."

────────

    51. " Dear Sir,   Wilmington, July 25, 1796.
    " Mr. Currey's preaching commenced at Whitehall Chapel in
the afternoon of the 17th current, there being five Sundays in
the month. But after he shall have delivered his five Sermons
he has the mortification of being repeatedly told that he must
not expect a recompense for his labours for many months to
come, there being an arrear of six quarters in all emoluments
payable out of the Civil List. Dr. Pearce, the Subdean of the
the Chapel Royal, through whose interest with the Bishop of
London Mr. J. Currey obtained the appointment, hinted to the
Vicar of Dartford not long since, that three hundred pounds
were owing to him for his services. This default in the Civil
List Treasury somewhat astonishes me, because economy has
been the boasted word ever since the accession of our gracious
Sovereign to the throne of these realms. The appointment of
a Whitehall Preacher is, it seems, less beneficial than I had imagined it to be. The only emolument is the stipend of £.30,
from which have to be deducted the land tax at 4s. and the place

────────

    * Who sold it to the celebrated R. B. Sheridan ; of whose family it was
purchased by Joseph Bonsor, Esq of London, stationer, who has re-built
the mansion. See Neale's Seats, and Prosser's Views in Surrey.

tax at 1s. in the pound, and this, as already observed, is not a prompt payment.

" The account given in the public prints that the addresses to the King from Alma Mater were read by Mr. Pitt, the High Steward, was inaccurate, for they were as heretofore recited by the Vice-chancellor, in the absence of the Chancellor. You are probably aware that there was a small show at the commencement, partly in consequence of the war, and partly from the election bustle. On my observing it to be unprecedented that the Divinity Professor should not have one son, I was told there was a similar instance about thirty years ago. From a want of a D. D. incept. the Sermon on the Sunday morning at St. Mary's was preached by Mr. Mansel, the Public Orator.

" After an interval of sixteen years, there was at the end of June an episcopal review of the clergy of the Diocese of Rochester by Bishop Horsley. We had concluded we should have been cited a twelvemonth sooner, but for reasons known only to the Prelate, he then made no other than a circuit of confirmation. The Charge delivered was ingenious, learned, and, as was to be expected from a Horsley, energetic. The continuance of it was not, as I believe, precisely marked by any auditor, but it much exceeded an hour; and this was owing to the Bishop's judging it needful to add to the charge originally framed a comment on the statute for the better maintenance of Curates. The principal topic or argument of the original Charge was a comparative statement of the advantages and inconveniences incident to the early preachers of Christianity, and to their successors, in the different periods of its propagation. On the present perilous age you will readily infer there were some sharp pointed strictures. At Dartford, after dinner, the Bishop was entreated, *nem. con.* to transmit to press his wise and spirited instructions and admonition; and a solemn bow was the only token of compliance or refusal. At the Rochester meeting, Archdeacon Law, for self and his brethren there assembled, solicited the same favour; and receiving only the like equivocal token, he signified a hope that silence implied consent. To me it appears probable, that the Charge will be published; and should that be the case, in my humble opinion, the remarks on the above-mentioned Act of Parliament, though most of them may be judicious and stand the test, ought to be added by way of Supplement, there not being, to the best of my remembrance, any affinity between them and the preceding pages.

"On a primary visitation the Bishop always extends his review to the Dean and Chapter of his Cathedral; and at this board of inquest there appeared the very reverend the Dean and four reverend Prebendaries.

" Mr. Rashleigh is obliged to again postpone his visit to Mrs. Milner in consequence of advice received of the death of Major Burville, the brother of Mrs. Rashleigh, on the Island of St.

Domingo. The yellow fever proved fatal to him; though he had before a seasoning in that disastrous part of the world, and was a cautious person in his mode of living.

" I remain, truly yours,   S. DENNE."

52. " DEAR SIR,   *Wilmington, Aug.* 22, 1796.

" Messrs. Ord, Ellis, and yourself have a claim to my thanks for the notes concerning Arabic numerals, communicated in your letter of the 17th current. The memoranda supply me with the additional evidence that Arabic numerals were not in general use for centuries after Professors Wallis and Ward averred their being in common use; and for the no general use of such convenient signs for above a century after they were certainly known in England, I have, in the first part of my inquiry, ventured to hazard a reason, or at least a surmise.

" In compliance with your request, I make the underwritten report of Dr. Philip Twysden, who died Bishop of Raphoe in Ireland, Nov. 2, 1752. He was the younger son of Sir William Twysden, of Royden-hall in Kent, Bart. He was presented to the Rectory of Crayford, in Kent, in December 1737; and resigned it in 1747, on his promotion to the above-mentioned See; and this seat upon the Irish Episcopal Bench was acquired by his being Chaplain to the Duke of Dorset when Viceroy. The first wife of Dr. Twysden, Mary Purcell, died in or about February 1743. I have the same voucher for mentioning that the Prelate of Raphoe was married to Miss Carter March 7, 1750, that he deceased Nov. 2, 1752, and that the lady of the late Bishop of Raphoe was delivered of a daughter Feb. 25, 1753, who was christened Frances, and was married to George fourth Earl of Jersey. The name of the Bishop does not occur among the Predicators in Letsome's Preacher's Assistant, edited by Cooke; nor is it likely that he ever committed to the press any Sermon, though from his high station in the Church he could hardly have avoided delivering a discourse upon some public occasion. On reference to Hasted's History, I find that in May 1745, he was instituted to the Rectory of Easling in Kent, of which the Earl of Winchelsea was then Patron, but he resigned the same year. Mr. Hatton, the now proprietor of Eastwell, presented to it the late Plumian Professor, Dr. Shepherd, who must have had a taste for wine and music, as he had in his cellar, as stated by the gentlemen of the hammer, Skinner, Dyke, and Skinner, ' rich and choice, both of the first growth and flavour, consisting of a pipe of excellent port in the wood, upwards of hundred dozen in bottles of old port of a superior quality, high flavoured claret, excellent Madeira and Sherry, Burgundy, vin de Grave, Tokay, and St. George; also a fine toned double keyed harpsichord, by Kirkman, fine violins and violoncellos, by Cremonensis, Winceslaus, Tieronymus, Amati, Jacobus, Stanier, &c.'; but a *quondam* scholar of Christ's-college, who has calculated many a logarithm by warrant from the Professor for the tables of longitude, has whispered me, that in his opinion the Doctor did not shine more in music than he did in astronomy; and that he was not qualified to play the second Cremona in a concert.

" Alb. Morton is one of the autographs communicated by T. Fisher, and engraved in Archæologia, vol. XII. pl. xx. He was Knight of the Shire for Kent, and is noticed as such by Hasted; but the Historian was not aware that he was Secretary of State to the King, and nephew of the famous Sir Henry Wotton.

" As the Charge delivered at the Primary Visitation of the Bishop of Rochester issued from the Cicero s Head in Red Lion-passage, you had, I doubt not, the earliest notice of its being in print. My Diocesan has sent a copy of it to the Vicar of Dartford, which I have seen; and I trust he will not forget that the Vicar of Wilmington has not a benefice so profitable as that held by his neighbour Mr. Currey. It is, as you may have observed, printed for Robson, whose son * was one of the Chaplains that attended the Prelate in his circuit. He was, I believe, his Lordship's Curate at South Weald.

" In the Kentish Gazette of the past week was inserted an advertisement from the Historian of Kent, concerning the two editions of his labours in that walk; and as the encouragers of the novel edition are desired to send their names to Mr. White in Fleet-street, or to B. Law, Stationers'-court, we are apprised in it that the fourth volume of the folio History is in such forwardness that it is intended to be published a considerable time prior to the two last volumes of the octavo edition. The Maps of Hundreds that are to be given with each volume may contribute to the sale of it both in and out of the county.

" I am, dear Sir, yours truly,   S. Denne."

---

53. " Dear Sir,   *Wilmington, Sept. 6, 1796.*
" Since I wrote last, the perusal of Archæologia, vol. XII. has afforded me much amusement, and some additional knowledge. Mr. Wilkins's paper on Norwich Castle particularly drew my attention; and much is he to be commended for exhibiting so many elegant as well as accurate specimens of the style of Saxon and Norman architecture. Not, however, that I can subscribe to his opinion, that the Keep of that Castle was either of Saxon or Danish construction; and rather suspect that he has here paid too great a deference to what has been advanced by Mr. King upon this subject. Evidence external is unquestionably wanting to prove that it was built by Canute, or any of his countrymen who preceded him; and it is suggested by him that

---

* The Rev. George Robson, of Queen's-college, Oxford, M. A. 1798; he was preferred by Dr. Horsley, when Bishop of St. Asaph, to a Prebend of that Church in 1803; the Vicarage of Chirk in 1804; and the Rectory of Erbistock in 1805.

King Swane in 1004 utterly destroyed both castle and town. As to the internal marks, they bear so close an affinity to the style of Gundulph in his castles, that I think it not unlikely that Roger Bigod might employ an architect trained in the Norman school.

"Full credit am I disposed to give Mr. Wilkins for his position, that neither in the Saxon or the Norman architecture an instance occurs of the three specimens of mouldings noticed at p. 174; and, if he be not mistaken, it is a good criterion by which we may form a decisive judgment on buildings of an earlier or later period in which these marks were discernible. The principles, mathematical or geometrical, of the Gothic style, it was not a part of his plan to discuss; but in the Transactions of the Royal Irish Academy, 1789, is a paper on the Origin and Theory of the Gothic Arch, which Mr. Clarke desired me to read, and so I did with attention and with approbation, as far as my limited knowledge of the mathematics would allow. 'His paper, writes Mr. Clarke, 'I will say, is the best thing on the subject I have ever yet seen; he there more than hints the derivation of the Gothic from the Norman. This you may recollect me to have mentioned more than two years before I met with the Doctor's work, which was not till June 1794; and, though the originality of my idea is done away, yet, as it receives a strong support in this excellent writer, I am not at all sorry. Had he compared the piers of circular and pointed arches, he had done every thing for showing why they were preferred so generally; and had opened the door to a general explication between the Norman and the later Gothic.' You will readily conclude that my advice will not be wanting to induce my correspondent to complete Dr. Young's plan, and to lose no time in digesting the fruits of his researches. He promises fair; but I am apprehensive he may have taken too wide a scope, and that he will find more trouble and less satisfaction in methodising than he had in pursuing his inquiries.

"Were I sitting near Mr. Wilkins, I might be tempted to put a few questions to him concerning the remains of a Saxon Church at Dunwich, which he says consists of three divisions, like that of Ely; 'not much unlike the primitive Eastern Churches, consisting of the sanctuary, the temple, and the anti-temple.' Now, as it appears to me, Dunwich Church, as well as in the Churches of Kiddington and Darent, what is now the lower chancel (by which I mean to draw a distinction between what he terms the altar and the chancel) was the nave of the original church, but added to the chancel when it was found expedient to enlarge the church. The marks of Saxon architecture, which he specifies, are from the altar and the chancel, but he notices not any in the nave. Query then what is the style of the architecture of the nave? does it not show traits of a later period? Did Mr. Ord ever inspect these ruins?

" Unless I misheard Mr. Ellis, he had not seen ' The City Gardener' the last time we conversed upon the Shoreditch History.
Pleased am I that he has been so lucky as to borrow the book,
as I trust he has not omitted noticing any improvements that
were made by Fairchild in that branch of horticulture.   An
account of the lecture he instituted in the Church of St. Leonard, may, from the hints already suggested to the young antiquary, form a chapter in his volume somewhat curious, and impart a few things not generally known that reflect credit on the
founder and promoters of the plan.   Three pounds were thrice
paid by me to the venerable Druid of Kentish-town * for the discourse he preached at my solicitation.   He published all the Sermons ; and they are the three first articles in what was termed
by him Palæographia Sacra, and which he dedicated to her
Royal Highness Augusta Velleda Archdruidess of Kew.   He
presented a copy to my father, of which I am possessed ; and
I think I have seen the book in the library of the Society of
Antiquaries.

    " Thankfully do I accept your kind offer of the loan of the
Description of Oxford Castle, and of the stones supposed in all
ages to be falling from the clouds.   Of edifices in nubibus a
certain *ci-divant* President† of our corps seems at different times
to have read much and imagined more ; however, as an useful
and ingenious labourer in the antique vineyard, he certainly has
more merit than some other Presidents and Vice-presidents,
whom it might be invidious to particularise.

    " In the Kentish Gazette are announced to be sold to the
highest bidder, on Sept. 15, all the Old Castle of Canterbury,
with the stowages, rooms, and appurtenances, together with a
messuage, and garden, and appurtenances ; and also two pieces
of garden ground, containing two acres, situate within the precincts of the said Old Castle, all which premises are freehold.
In the Canterbury ' Walk,' Mr. Gostling mentions, on the authority of Mr. Batteley, that the yards and dykes about the Castle
contain four acres and one rood of land.

    " Has not Mr. Majendie, towards the conclusion of his well-
penned description of Hedingham Castle (Vetusta Monumenta,
vol. III. pl. xliii. p. 12,) from inadvertency considered *Dungeon*,
a *Donjon* Tower, as terms synonymous ; whereas the keep, or
fortress itself, was for a long time called the *Donjon*, and, if not
constructed on a natural eminence, generally erected on a mount
artificially raised.

            " I remain, dear Sir, yours truly,   S. Denne."

    * The Rev. William Stukeley, M. D.   † Edward King, Esq.

54. " DEAR SIR, *Wilmington, Oct. 28, 1796.*

" Mr. Todd has favoured me with an answer to the query communicated to him ; and the under-written is a copy:

" ' Mr. Todd presents his respects to Mr. Denne, and acquaints him that he can hear of no evidence, written or oral, that the Church of Canterbury possessed the picture mentioned by Mr. Denne. Mr. Todd inquired also of old Mr. Flackton, bookseller of this place, a very curious and intelligent gentleman, who never remembers to have heard any thing of such a picture here; and the persons who show the Cathedral know nothing of it. Mr. Todd, however, has heard, that at Deal a painting of the Great Harry is said to be in some gentleman's family. Mr. Todd wishes he could have sent Mr. Denne a more satisfactory answer. In Somner's MSS. Mr. Todd is almost confident that no allusion exists respecting it. If Mr. Todd was not closely engaged in a literary undertaking, he would go through those MSS. ; and will yet, if Mr. Denne thinks it absolutely necessary to his purpose, the earliest opportunity.

" ' Over Sir James Hales's monument in St. Michael's Chapel (see the plate preceding p. 79, in Dart's History of the Cathedral) is a ship of war in relievo, with four masts, and is therefore said to have a resemblance to the Great Harry. Mr. Denne having done Mr. Todd the honour to quote his little book in his ' Addenda to the History of Lambeth, p. 344,' Mr. Todd supposes Mr. Denne to have the ' Deans,' and therefore respectfully sends him a page of ' corrections,' printed long since, and which he is very desirous to present to every possessor of the book. Mr. D. will also have the goodness to allow Mr. T. to state, that Turner (see ' Addenda,' p. 219) could not be the person who had the Prebend of Lincoln, as stated by Browne Willis, for the reasons given by Mr. Todd. See Deans of Canterbury, pp. 117, 118.'

" Supposing the plate in Dart's History to be a fac-simile of this ship of war, it ought to be examined how far it corresponds with Allen's print of the supposed Great Harry. The ship in St. Michael's, alias the Warrior's Chapel, being denominated the Great Harry because it has four masts, cannot be deemed a satisfactory inference ; because in the picture at Windsor Castle, representing the embarkation of King Henry on board his darling, there is another ship that has four masts ; and I am much mistaken if I have not observed delineations of ships of a later date that have had the same number of masts. Amazing is it that such a curious piece of old sculpture, especially if called in former days the Great Harry, should be unnoticed by such a trio of antiquaries as a Somner, a Batteley, and a Gostling ; and much is it be regretted that there should be a want of evidence, both written and oral, to show who was the artist, or what he designed to memorialise.

" My kinsman, Mr. Harvey, of Ramsgate *, has presented me

* See before, p. 627.

with the second print of the Brunswick's valiant engagement on
the illustrious 1st of June; it is in my judgment an excellent
print, and not to be viewed without regretting the departure of
the brave Captain, who was an honour to himself, his family,
friends, and country.   In the postscript of the letter of thanks
to Mr. Harvey, who is one of the six Preachers of the Cathedral,
I signified a wish to be informed in what literary work the biographer of ' The Deans' was so closely engaged; and perhaps
Mr. Director or Mr. Deputy may be able to gratify my curiosity.
        " I remain, dear Sir, truly yours,   S. Denne."

55. " Dear Sir,   *Wilmington, Nov.* 4, 1796.
    " A resumption of the subject of Paper Marks has not, as yet,
been judged expedient by me through a want of new light.   I
will, however, trouble you to apprise Mr. Ord, that Mr. Tracy,
since I communicated to him the paper in Archæologia, has
turned over some old MSS. wherein he has found water marks
of a like kind; and some different, though bearing an affinity.
You may likewise acquaint our friend that Mr. Boys has informed
Dr. Latham, that he met with dissimilar marks.   How far it
may be requisite to exhibit specimens of those that are totally
different, merely because they are so, I do not presume to determine; but I think they will appear to more advantage if the
age of the paper can be clearly ascertained, and the place where
it was manufactured.

    " On the subject of Stone Seats I have written a great deal; and
unluckily have not yet been able to discover a single passage in
an antient MS. in which they are explicitly mentioned; and, as
Mr. Clarke has not been more successful, I begin to apprehend
that our researches will be fruitless, strange as this absolute
silence must appear, considering the great number of these
sediles that have been discovered.   But we retain each of us his
own sentiment respecting the pristine use of them; and in the
last proof sheet of the History of Leicestershire which I revised,
I hinted to Mr. Deputy that there were in a side isle in one of
the Churches in Leicester, three seats that rather corroborated
my surmise than that of my ingenious correspondent at Gravesend, because they were placed near an altar that had unquestionably only one officiating priest, to whom a certain gild or fraternity paid a yearly stipend; and it was likewise in evidence
that three persons, I think styled a Steward or President, and
two Wardens, were the leading members of the said gild.

    " Not in the least apprehensive am I of a want of employ-
ment in the antique line, for after, with the leave and concurrence of the Rector of Southfleet, I shall have transmitted part
the first of my Observations, Queries, and Surmises, touching
the no early general use of Arabic numerals in England, I have
in petto addenda to the same, to be furnished out of your survey

of the Helmdon mantel-piece, and a revisal of the figures in
Textus Roffensis, obligingly undertaken by the Archdeacon of
Rochester and Mr. Secretary Wrighte, Vicar of St. Nicholas.

" Besides, you will be pleased to recollect that the Journals of
our cruises after the Great Harry ship of war, or of a man of
war erroneously so styled, must be extracted from each of our
log-books; and since you had any advice from other persons of
the said ship, you have had intelligence from me of a picture
said to be at Deal, and of a four-mast ship in relievo in Canterbury Cathedral, and engraved in a plate exhibited by Dart.

" As to your inquiries ' after the Roman, or any other gate, at
Canterbury, and the leaning and standing tower of St. Ethelbert, within the precincts of the Abbey of St. Augustin,' why
not submit them to the consideration of some antiquary on the
premises, if any such can be found? Mr. G. Wall has not, I
am persuaded, a bias to that kind of lore; and I am apt to suspect that the reverend Biographer of the ' Deans' may be much
more versed in the works of the pen than of the chisel, judging
from his favouring me with his ocular report of the Great Harry.
Are Mr. Deputy of Farringdon Extra, and Mr. Alderman (I
beg pardon, Captain) Simmons, of the volunteers, Canterbury,
quite strangers to each other? As they are brethren of the type,
I imagine they may have had a correspondence. I am not long
since informed, though I cannot just now remember through
what channel, that a material alteration was soon to be made, if
it were not made, in the old arch of Worthing-gate, alias Win-
cheap-gate, near the Old Castle, noticed in Gostling's Walk,
pp. 7, 13, 59, 365; and I have been told that Mr. Simmons has
converted the Dungel-hill, and the adjoining grounds, into an
elegant promenade * Yours truly, S. DENNE."

---

56. " DEAR SIR, *Wilmington, Nov. 14, 1796.*
" For your notes from Dart and Lediard, and for your sketch
of the four-mast ship exhibited in the Warriors' Chapel in Canterbury Cathedral, above the ship from which Sir James Hales,
in a coat of mail, is displayed as dropping into the sea, I am
obliged to you ; and it is likely that I may avail myself of your
remarks, should the time come for my bringing the Great Harry
into port. Touching this famous ship, I have now reason to
believe that it was in the reign of Edward VI. described by a
juvenile bard, *viz.* by Puttenham, the author of the English
Art of Poesie, from which treatise an extract has been transmitted for insertion in the Gentleman's Magazine; and, if it

---

* Of James Simmons, Esq. of Canterbury, memoirs and a character are
given in " Literary Anecdotes," vol. III. pp. 443—445 ; and prints of these
walks may be seen in Hasted's Kent, vol. IV.; and the Gentleman's Magazine, vol. LXXVIII. p. 481.

shall so please Master Urban, I have it in contemplation to supply
him with more extracts and a commentary upon them. But,
alas! of the poem alluded to there are not half a dozen lines,
I fear, remaining; and of these one only that in my opinion
refers to the Great Harry. The writer of them, by his own
account, was but eighteen years old when he undertook to specify to his Sovereign, King Edward VI. all the parts and tackle
of a ship.

" Upon the authority of the same writer, I shall be able to
offer, as I apprehend, decisive evidence that the roundels of beech
wood, ornamented and posied, about which much was advanced
in the Gentleman's Magazine, vols. LXIII. and LXIV.* were no
other than Desert Trenchers, notwithstanding one of Mr. Urban's correspondents treated it as a ridiculous idea. Puttenham will likewise warrant a suggestion, that in his days the ladies,
who painted were, laid only a crimson tainte upon the lips, or
right in the centre of the cheek ; and that Queen Bess had,

> ' Two lips wrought out of rubie rocke,
> Like leaves to shut and to unlock.'—And that,

> ' Her bosom sleak as Paris plaster,
> Held up two balls of alabaster;
> Each byas was a little cherrie,
> Or els I think a strawberie.'

" The following anecdote of the late respectable T. Row, is
communicated for the amusement of two of the surviving recent
friends of the deceased : Whilst Mr. Pegge was Vicar of Godmersham, he was occasionally a preacher in Canterbury Cathedral on Saints' days for one of the six Preachers ; and on these
holidays, the appearance of the scholars of the King's school
being required, S. Denne might be again and again one of the
congregation who ought to have been edified; but it must be
acknowledged to his discredit, that he was less attentive to matter than to manner, and more observant of the voice and action
of the preacher than of the good sense and reasoning of what
he spoke. The plea he has to offer by way of extenuation is,
that he was a school-boy; and that the tone and toss up and
down of the reverend orator were peculiar in the extreme, and
so striking, that young Sam. Pegge, who was a King's Scholar,
and had a turn for Footism, could not forbear, for the diversion
of his Fellows, to take off Papa. Not long since, on mentioning this occurrence in Scotland-yard, S. D. could perceive that
his namesake seemed to be unwilling to be reminded of his
having been such a naughty boy; however, after a little pause,
he recollected that the innuendo was not groundless, and added,
that the old gentleman had considerably rectified this awkward

* See also Gent. Mag. vol. XCVII. ii. pp. 501, 592; XCVIII. i. pp.
133—137.

habit; and in the memoir of his life it is only observed, that
' from the weakness of his voice he was heard to a disadvantage
in a large church.'

" That what is above related is not a Canterbury tale,
might have been proved by the testimony of the facetious and
sarcastic *Walker* * in and about that city; and may be authenticated by the evidence of two females, daughters of George
Lynch, M. D. and brother to Dean Lynch, by whose interest Mr.
Pegge became a Kentish Vicar.

" On one of the preaching days alluded to, when the auditors
were passing from the choir, quoth Master Gostling (with a significant shake of his poll, and twirling a key between his thumb
and finger, which were his habits), ' in troth, our friend Pegge
has studied a bad delivery till he is completely master of it.'
And when Mr. Pegge was on a visit for some days to Dr. Lynch,
being in a parlour with Mrs. Lynch and her daughters, who were
employed with their needles, and a new dramatic piece lying
near the work-baskets, the guest complaisantly offered to read
to them the farce, which S. Denne thinks was Garrick's Lethe,
a civility the company rather wished to decline, because apprehensive of the risible consequences that might and did follow.
It was, however, accepted; and the play being as it were enacted
with the very same tone and air that the young ladies had
noticed and admired in the performer when he was in the pulpit,
an immoderate and unseasonable fit of laughter ensued, either at
Lord Chalkstone or his representative.

" I remain, dear Sir, yours truly,   S. DENNE."

---

57. " DEAR SIR,   *Wilmington, Dec. 29, 1796.*
" Having had repeated intelligence that the Great Harry was
moored at Deal, it occurred to me that it must be known in
what part of the harbour by the Historian of Sandwich, whose
knowledge of things curious in every limb of the Cinque Ports
was so extensive. An epistolary corvette was therefore dispatched
to him; but, alas! the result is, that Mr. Todd had been amused
with a Canterbury tale. Mr. Boys's answer to my inquiry is
dated from Walmer near Deal, and is as follows: ' Dear Sir, I
left Sandwich about four months ago, and reside at this place,
within a short distance of the hospital, of which I have the
medical care, and which is situated at the northern extremity of
this parish, close to Deal Castle. I have been traversing the
whole district of Deal in different parallels of latitude and longitude, in chace of the painted Great Harry; twice I have thought
myself sure of success, but both times was led astray by fog
banks, as the great Cook, and other *investigatores acerrimi*, have
been before. In short, I find many people who ought to know
better, scarcely acquainted with the distinction between a paint-

* Mr. Gostling.

ing and a print; and I suspect that Mr. Todd has met with some of these ignoramus's, and has innocently misled us.

" 'I wish I had known of your intention to write on Paper-marks, as I think I could have furnished you with some older ones than you have been able to procure.   The records of Sand-wich begin in 1431, and are in fine preservation.   If you should resume the subject, command my services.   Hasted's fourth volume goes on briskly; and his octavo edition of the History of Kent, ridiculous as the plan appeared to me, I find is likely to succeed much better than could in reason have been expected.'

" To the account above given of the reduced History of our great County, I have to add, that a son of Mr. Hasted, who is clerk to a brewer of Dartford, has lately circulated his father's proposals, and solicited subscriptions, not without success, as I am told; and as the first volume is to extend to Dartford, this is an encouragement to those among us who take any delight in a work of that kind to advance their shillings.   There are likewise, it is probable, some who will be contributors from a motive of kindness towards one who resided several years in the neigh-bourhood, and was an acting Magistrate and eke Commissioner of Sewers and Taxes.

" With respect to the erroneous advice touching the Great Harry, a disappointment is not novel to either of us; and it is most likely that we shall again, again, and again steer a wrong course ere we fall in with that famous ship.   Luckily the very first signal thrown out to speak with the Prince Royal was an-swered soon and well.   From the report J. J. has made *, there seems to be so little resemblance between his picture and Allen's print of what, without authentication, he termed the Great Harry, that Allen's ship can hardly have been designed to exhibit the Prince Royal, which I must own I thought was a probable conjecture.   It is, however, a point gained, to be assured that there is extant a representation of the man of war built by Phi-neas Pett.   If J. J. still continues to be a picture connoisseur, as it may be presumed he does, I think he will give himself the trouble of inquiring after the portrait of the master shipwright who constructed it.

" I remain, dear Sir, truly yours,   S. DENNE."

58. " DEAR SIR,   *Wilmington, Jan.* 12, 1797.
" Hever being in the Deanry of Shoreham, its Rector is of course a peculiar clerk, or, as heretofore hinted to you, one of those whom Master Duncombe was wont to style his Grace's Odd Fellows; and as I, as Vicar of Darenth, am of the same corps, I have now and then seen the late Rev. Stafford Newe†, at a visita-tion in Sevenoaks Church, and heard him answer to the call when

* See Gent. Mag. vol. LXVI. p. 900.
† The Rev. Stafford Newe died at Hever, Nov. 30, 1796, aged 70.

summoned to testify his subjection to the Dean of the Arches; but he never once, when I was of the party, dined with his brethren, and his absence was imputed to his being in the extreme a shy man. In the year 1769, which was the first visitation I attended, he had a notice in turn to be the preacher, but solicited Sir George Hay that he might be allowed to officiate *per alium*, and the Curate of Sandwich was his proxy. Of his birth, parentage, and education, I have not at present any knowledge, but will, when an opportunity shall offer, consult some of my brethren of the Peculiars; and for a reason which I need not suggest, I own I am not so well acquainted with my Peculiar brethren as I am with those who are more strictly speaking of the Diocese of Rochester. According to the list of incumbents in the Kentish Companion (an annual publication), the late Mr. Newe was presented to Hever by the Rev. Mr. Hamlyn.

" Mr. Boys is the son of Commodore Boys, who experienced such great perils by sea. He died Lieutenant-Governor of Greenwich Hospital; and my kinsman, Rear-Admiral Harvey, who has the command of the Fleet at the Leeward Islands, married his daughter. Mr. Peete tells me, that Mr. Boys has two sons likely to do credit to themselves and their father; one of them is of the medical profession, and, as I believe, the other in the agricultural line.

" Dean Cornewall is certainly to be the new Bishop *vice* Courtenay; though, as it is agreed, his income will be diminished by quitting his Decanal Stall at Canterbury for the Episcopal Throne. It is, however, suggested, that he has his eye to a translation to Hereford, the Prelate of which is very far advanced in years, and has infirmities that may shorten his days; and it seems, if Dr. Cornewall is not a native of Hereford, he has connections with that part of the kingdom that incline him to wish to obtain a post of pre-eminence among them *. Are we to infer that the interest of the Earl of Liverpool with the Minister prevailed over that of Lord Harrowby, or that the successful candidate was willing to cast better preferment into the Premier's promotion scale than might be convenient to Archdeacon Hamilton to part with, who is doubtless the greater pluralist of the two competitors? The Deanry of Canterbury has of late been a principal step to a Bishopric; and I question whether the ecclesiastical annals of this country will furnish, in any other Cathedral, instances of six Deans in succession † being elevated from it, and that within a quarter of a century. At Canterbury the rumour is, that the Master of the Temple, or Dr. Paley, will succeed the now Dean ‡.

" I remain, dear Sir, yours truly,   S. DENNE."

* Dr. Cornewall attained the mitre of Hereford in 1804, but was tempted to re ign it for Worcester in 1808. With the exception of the Archbishop of York, he is now (1830) the senior of the Bench.

† North, Moore, Cornwallis, Horne, Butler, and Cornewall.

‡ The Rev. Thomas Powys, of St. John's-college, Oxford, M.A. 1760,

59. "DEAR SIR,   *Wilmington, Jan.* 18, 1797.

" Mr. Boys says in his last letter: 'From the moulds of seals given me by Mr. Hasted, I took impressions, some in plaster of Paris, some in wax. The collection comprehends a very great number of royal, archiepiscopal, episcopal, conventual, municipal, public and private, British and foreign Seals, many of which are very antient, and in fine preservation.'

"Supposing Mr. Boys's packet to you to have been sealed with his coat of arms, had you attended to the inscription you would have concluded that he was the son of the Captain who had so narrow an escape; for thus it runs: 'Preserved by Providence from fire, water, and famine;' and I have understood that the Governor kept one day in the year with the strictest abstinence in commemoration of his deliverance; and Scrimsour the surgeon, who was of the party, was for some years one of my parishioners in Darenth. He afterwards removed to North Cray, and is interred in that church-yard, together with his wife, who was of Lethieullier family.

"Till I read in the Gentleman's Magazine for December the list of the late Dr. Pegge's communications to that Miscellany, I was not aware that the letter in vol. XXXIII. p. 441, against Dr. Ducarel's Repertory of the Endowments of Vicarages, under the signature of Vicarius Cantianus, was written by a *quondam* Vicar of Godmersham. At the time of its appearing, I well remember I thought that the strictures were not well founded; and observation and experience have satisfied me that I was not mistaken in my opinion. Between Impropriators and Vicars, the words of the ordination are conclusive as to their respective claims; and it is from a want of knowing whether *omnimodæ minutæ decimæ* were allotted to a vicarage that so many little Vicars are deprived of sundry articles of tithes. This, indeed, is not a difficulty that the Vicar of Wilmington and Darenth has to encounter; but he is strongly prepossessed, that in another instance he is a sufferer from not being able to ascertain all that Bishop Gilbert de Glanville assigned to the Vicar of Wilmington. Could the original deed be discovered, he has hardly a doubt but that without a demur he should legally support his pretensions to a stipulated boon of corn from the Parsonage-barn of Sutton *cum* Wilmington, for which, by the supineness of those who have gone before, he receives only 16s. a year. With the evidence obtained, he made out so strong a case that the late Mr. Dunning apprehended his pretensions in Westminster-

B. and D. D. 1795, a Canon of Windsor 1796, resigned for Canterbury Deanery 1797. He also was Rector of Fawley in Buckinghamshire and Silchester in Hampshire; and died at the Deanery-house, Canterbury, Oct. 7, 1809, aged 73. His elder brother, Philip-Lybbe Powys, Esq. of Hardwick-house in Berkshire, a Magistrate and Deputy-lieutenant for that county, had been drowned by falling into a pond through missing his way in the dark, on the 12th of April preceding, in the 75th year of his age.

hall, would the difference in value compensate the charge of a litigation, which it certainly would not; and, therefore, till the ordination shall be found, it is impolitic in the Vicar to acquiesce. Yours truly, S DENNE."

<hr />

60. " DEAR SIR,   *Wilmington, Feb.* 10, 1797.

" Did I not intimate in my last letter, that I should request the juvenile antiquary * of St. John's-college, Oxon, to search for Arabic numerals upon the shelves and in the boxes of the Bursar's rooms in some of the principal colleges? He has already reported the progress he has made under this commission, and in a clear and satisfactory manner, with a promise that he will, in eight or ten days, transmit to me a faithful detail of whatever may occur relative to this subject in the bursary and other accounts of the remaining colleges. Judging from the specimens he has sent me, I think I shall, with the evidence to be produced, wind up my additional remarks on the knowledge and use of the vulgar figures of arithmetic in former days. Wishing, however, that some person or persons who may have it in their power, will be so obliging as to examine the books of the mercantile fraternities in London; and particularly of those companies who were engaged in the Levant trade.

" By favour of my correspondent at Rochester, I have this account of what may, or what may not be, the Minister's mode of gratifying the wishes of some of the candidates for ecclesiastical dignities: Our Dean,' writes Mr. Archdeacon, ' on his late visit to Canterbury, saw or heard the contents of Bishop Pretyman's letter to Dr. Cornewall, tendering the See of Bristol on the resignation of the Deanry of Canterbury, and intimating the probability of a speedy vacancy in the See of Hereford. If honour were not more the object of desire than profit, Dr. Cornewall's exchange would reasonably be censured. Our Dean conjectures, that the Deanry of Canterbury may be offered to the Bishop of Chester, whose translation to a more eligible See is obstructed by the supposed pretensions of Bishops Beadon, Stewart, &c. I do not allot this preferment to Dr. Pearce; the Deanry of Ely has been long assigned to him. Who will be the successor I little care, as the boon is not likely to be conferred on any friend of mine. Dr. Hamilton has never, I well know, made the least exertion to obtain the honours of episcopacy. He has an ample private fortune and productive preferment; and, though he would not decline the offer of a seat in the House of Lords, he never, I am confident, will solicit it. Bishop Courtenay is satisfied that his removal to Exeter is fixed upon; though the Minister has never given any information to him on the subject. The value of the See of Exeter is under-rated by Mrs. Templer; Bishop Ross admitted to our Dean, in conversa-

* Henry Ellis, Esq. F. R. S. Sec. S. A.

tion, the produce to be £.1,400 *per annum;* and other well-founded reports, formed from a calculation of thirty years, enhances the value. Much of the preferment, in the patronage of the Bishop, has recently been given to young men, or, at least, to those of a middle age; but calculations on lives are, as you justly observe, uncertain; and the vacancy at Exeter is an additional proof of your remark.'

" More information has been obtained concerning the late Stafford Newe, Rector of Hever, than could have been expected from the recluse life which he always led; it was communicated to Mr. Richard Williams, Vicar of Horton Kirby, by Mr. Saunders, Vicar of Farningham, who has been my fellow traveller to Sevenoaks for the two last years; when, as Vicar of Darenth, I have been cited to make my obeisance to Sir William, Dean of the Arches, whose province it is to visit the Archbishop's Odd Fellows. ' You wish,' quoth Mr. Williams's correspondent, ' to have some account of the late Stafford Newe from me. I knew him when a little boy; we were play-fellows. He was born at Oxford; and, as I believe, in the parish of St. Giles's. His father was a gentleman; Mr. Newe was a Commoner of Baliol-college. He stood for a Fellowship of Oriel in the year 1746, but did not succeed. He took his degrees, and came to the Curacy of Hever many years ago; after which time I never saw him till I met him at our visitation. He was a close man, had a good income; and, as I hear, died rich. His fortune, I am told, is left to a person at Oxford. Further this deponent saith not.'

" As to Hever Rectory, if you turn to Hasted's Kent, vol. I. you will find that the advowson was in 1721 in George Lewis, who was also Incumbent of the same, and eke Vicar of Westerham. On his death, the Lewis family disposed of the advowson to Mr. Hamlyn, who bought it with the intention of placing a son in the Rectory. Mr. Newe was presented to hold it during the minority of young Hamlyn; but, as he died before he was of age to be ordained priest, Mr. Newe kept possession, though it has been surmised that he ceded some part of the profits of the living to the widow of the patron. Mr. Marmaduke Lewis, Rector of Lullingstone, and son of the aforenamed George Lewis, is my voucher for this report.

" George Currey, of Trinity-college, Cambridge, noticed in the public prints as one of the A. B.'s lately capped, is the fourth son of the Vicar of Dartford*. He acquired his degree with

* George Gilbert Currey, 15th Wrangler 1797; M. A. 1800; F. R. S. 18... He was for many years an eminent physician in Half-moon-street, a Fellow of the College of Physicians, and a Commissioner for licensing Madhouses. He contributed to the Medical Transactions, "A Case of Tetanus arising from a wound, in which the affusion of cold water was successfully employed." Vol. IV. p. 166. 1813. In 1822 he went down to Cornwall, to marry Mary, only child of the late John Dennis, Esq. of Alverton, Penzance; the marriage took place at Madron Church, Nov. 18, and the bridegroom died on the 11th of the following

credit to himself and his tutor, for you know in our Alma Mater a Wrangler is an honourable appellation. There were, I observe, eight new Bachelors of the old House, which is a large number. Yours truly, S. DENNE."

61. "DEAR SIR, *Wilmington, Feb. 23, 1797.*

"Obliged am I to you for your intelligence that some of the Ducarelian vicarial notes are deposited in the library at Somerset-place, though I have not the shadow of a hope that the ordination of the Vicarage of Sutton, *cum capellâ de Wilmington*, is among these MSS. The fact is that, whilst I was in pursuit of this choice relic of antiquity, I paid a visit to the collector at his chambers in the Commons, with the view of discovering whether he might have any other knowledge of the rights and profits of my little benefice than what I had communicated to him from my father's papers; and, being aware of the mercenary motives which too often influenced him, I tendered him a fee of one pound and one shilling, which he pocketed. I ought to add, however, that it was offered as for his legal opinion and advice upon the state of my claim. The case was resumed in a few days with an opinion subscribed by him, though, as I strongly suspect, composed by some other Doctor or a Proctor; but it was not to me worth a shilling, as I had previously consulted Doctor, now Sir William Wynne, and as I could not pick up any tidings of an original endowment, which will, I fear, be ever a desideratum.

"I have received a very civil letter from J. J. *i. e.* from Capt. J. Jackson, of Godmanchester, touching the picture of the ship of war inquired after in the Gentleman's Magazine. It is called 'The Prince,' and not 'The Prince Royal.' The two sternmost of the four masts are lower masts only, having no top-mast to them. The shield (heart-shaped) is so far shown on the stern as to give St. George, the horse, and dragon perfectly; the dragon has green scales, the horse is white, with netted armour over him. And most certainly I shall take the liberty of soliciting the Captain to inform me, in what points there may be a resemblance, and in what a dissimilitude between 'The Prince' in his sea-piece, and Allen's print of the supposed Great Harry; being still of opinion that the print must represent a ship of war built in the reign of James the First, or in that of his son Charles.

"The perils by fire, water, and famine, which the late Governor Boys escaped, were when he was first mate of a merchant ship. In the Obituary of the Gentleman's Magazine, vol XLIV. p. 142, where his death is mentioned, there is a very concise account of them. I once read the detail of them compiled by

month at Ivy Church in the same county. — Mrs. Currey, his mother, wife of the Rev. John Currey noticed in p. 668, was the author of some small tracts for the use of young persons. She died Oct. 1, 1788, aged 42. Her maiden name was Elliot.

the surgeon, whose name was Scrimsour, who for several years was a practitioner at Dartford; but on marrying a Lethieullier, who was an old maid, with a competent fortune, he retired from business; and resided first at Darenth, and afterwards at North Cray, in the church-yard of which parish they now sleep.

"Mr. Hasted's dedication of the first volume of his octavo History is to Lord Romney, ' in whose generous protection the distressed and the unfortunate are sure to find both succour and relief;' and the author intreats his Lordship to pardon this effusion of gratitude, and to condescend to accept it as the only acknowledgment in his power. If you turn to the folio title-page, you will find that the motto there is *Servabo Fidem*, or *Fidem Servabo*; but, in lieu thereof, in the octavo edition the motto is, *Le bon temps viendra*. Most cordially do I wish that these better times may come to Mr. Hasted; though the prevailing opinion is, that with respect to his affairs *nil desperandum* would not be an apt motto. Query, is it the practice to change a motto? My opinion has long been that, upon the whole, it is as well not to affix a motto, considering the chances and the changes in things and persons. His letter to me of the 7th current, contained sundry queries about Wilmington, to almost all of which I was able to return answers explicit; and with them I transmitted a medley of extracts and hints. To his discretion it was left to select such as might coincide with his plan; and I let him know that I was well aware that many articles which were interesting to persons resident in a parish, might be deemed otherwise by those who were not connected with the district.

"On talking a few days since with Mr. Marmaduke Lewis, who joined in the sale of the advowson of Hever to Mr. Hamlyn, I do not understand that any clerk has been instituted Rector since the demise of Stafford Newe; but it is thought that Mr. Nott will be presented, as he married a daughter of Mr. Hamlyn.

"In the Rectory of Ditton, John Roberts was the successor to my friend Mr. Milner, who died July 26, 1784; but Mr. Roberts vacated that living for a benefice in Wales, with which the Bishop of Bangor was glad to accommodate him, that Dr. Bishop might have Ditton, which was within distance of St. Martin Outwich. This *quasi* change took place in 1786. Mr. Roberts is also Archdeacon of Merioneth *; and to the best of my recollection he was in the suite of his diocesan, when an entry was made into the Register-office, *cum fustibus*, and possession maintained *cum fistibus*. I do not find that I have entered the name of Mr. Ward, Dr. Bishop's successor, in my repertory of the Diocese of Rochester; and I conclude I waited till I had learnt his Christian name, which is yet unknown to me. He was a Fellow of King's College, Cambridge, till he became Benedict the married man.

"Yours truly,   S. DENNE."

* He died possessed of that dignity, and of the Rectory of Llanbedrog in Lyne, Carnarvonshire, in 1802. He was of Brazenose-college, Oxford, M.A. 1753.

62. " DEAR SIR, *Wilmington, March* 25, 1797.

" By Dr. Latham, F. R. S. and F. A. S. who on Thursday the 23d of February attended the meeting of both those fraternities, I had advice, that on that evening was read to the Antiquaries a discussion on the date of the Preston-hall barn window-frame, &c. in a letter from Samuel Denne to Mr. Director; and to the best of my remembrance, I promised that within a month after such a paper, &c. should have been introduced, it should be followed with additional remarks on the Helmdon mantle-tree and Arabic numerals. For the delay of a few days I beg leave to assign as a sufficient reason, that when I engaged for a month I had not a thought of scrutinising the voluminous but useful collection of Ames and Herbert; and that some days were requisite for a due arrangement of the evidence resulting from them must be allowed. The task is, however, finished.

" It was not possible to survey the laborious researches of the deceased Mr. Herbert without regretting that we had not him for a living coadjutor in our inquiries after the progress of Arabic numerals, for I am fully persuaded he would have illustrated the subject. The title-pages of some of the books he had traced were, you will find, of use to me; and I trust that I have availed myself of the chief articles of information that Record affords in his ' Ground of the Arts.' Perhaps it may be new to you, that this learned M. D. and mathematical author had it in contemplation to be a precursor of the immortal Camden and of Speed in the Britannia line. Towards the conclusion of his preface to the reader, he thus expresses himself: ' If I shall perceive that all his Majesty's loving subjects shall receive my book (on Arithmetic) with as good will as it was written, then will I shortly, with no less kindness, set forth such introductions into geometry and cosmography, as I have at times promised, and as hitherto in English hath not been enterprised, wherewith I dare say all honest hearts will be pleased and all studious wits greatly delighted.' The Doctor was, I apprehend, a free and accepted mason; the last sentence of his preface being in the style commonly used by that fraternity. ' And (writes he) thus for this time I will stay my pen, committing you all to that true Fountain of perfect number which wrought the whole world by number and measure; he is Trinity in unity and glory. Amen.'

" Obliged am I to Mr. Ayscough, or to Mr. Deputy, perhaps to both, for a note or two respecting the Colepeper family from MSS. in the British Museum; though I was mortified to find the name not mentioned in any *carta* previous to the reign of Edward the Second. There was, it seems, a petition to Charles the Second from Col. Colepeper *, the representative of a family which had held forty manors in Wiltshire, Northamptonshire,

---

* See a letter on that very singular document in the Gentleman's Magazine, vol. XCVII. pt. ii. p. 296.

&c. for a pension for support. I have not looked over Hasted's genealogical minutes of this family, to see whether the said Col. C. might be the Colepeper recorded by Pope;

> ' Who, had his wealth been hops and hogs,
> Could he himself have sent it to the dogs.'

" During the course of next summer I think I shall be along-side the Great Harry, said to be in port at East Malling, and under the charge of a kinsman of Admiral Norris, who took it from a Spaniard.

"I am, dear Sir, yours truly, S. Denne."

63. " Dear Sir, *Wilmington, April* 5, 1797.

" On perusing, in the Gentleman's Magazine, Feb. 1797, p. 139, the review of Dr. Whitaker's Sermon for the General Infirmary at Leeds, it occurred to me that, when the late Master of Bene t* preached a Sermon in support of Addenbroke Hospital, the History of the Charitable Institutions was the subject of his discourse, and that his friends regretted he could not be prevailed upon to send it to the press. The report I had of it was from my friend Dr. Milner; and I believe that Dr. Colman permitted him to read it. Milner was at that time an inmate at the lodge previously to his taking his degree of D. D.

" Dr. Radcliffe has published his *Concio ad Synodum* †, but the subject thereof is not mentioned in the advertisement. By the promotion of Dean Cornewall to the See of Bristol, the Lower House of Convocation will be *sans* Prolocutor, it not being now the practice to supply the vacancy; and to be sure a Prolocutor is an useless office in a silent meeting.

" I have in petto two or three billets for the Miscellany of Sylvanus Urban. One is the copy of an excellent form of prayer directed to be used repeatedly in 1692, when there was an alarm of an invasion, though I think from Bishop Burnet's account of the events of that year in the History of his Own Times, the French had not then any real design to transport an army to Great Britain; we may, however, infer, from an expression in this prayer, that the French nation are to be deemed a common enemy and oppressor, whether the executive power be vested in one despot, or in five despots, under the appellation of a Direc-tory. The presumption is that the prayer was composed by Archbishop Tillotson, and was wisely calculated to show that an invasion of our island is not so easily to be effected as ministers at sundry times have endeavoured to have it thought it is, and

---

* Dr. Colman.

† Archdeacon Radcliffe, of whom before, p. 650. " Concio ad Clerum Provinciæ Cantuariensis in Synodo Provinciali ad Divi Pauli, iv kal. Oct. A. D. 1796." 4to, 1797.

have from that circumstance created alarms that had better have been avoided.

" Just as I was preparing a wafer for my scroll, I was favoured with a letter from my friend the Archdeacon of Rochester, in which are the following articles of intelligence: 'Mr. Jacob Marsham (Lord Romney's brother) was yesterday installed into the Prebend vacated by the promotion of the Bishop of Exeter. He seems much pleased with the preferment. You will deem me a bold man when I acquaint you that I have undertaken to preach the Anniversary Sermon this year at the Asylum. I had promised my aid to Dr. Vyse some time since; and when I received the last application I requested procrastination. My request was not, indeed, refused; but an intimation was given by the Chaplain of extreme difficulty in procuring a Preacher, and Dr. Vyse reported that my attendance would be doubly agreeable in this year.' The Archdeacon is also engaged to preach the Sermon at St. Paul's on the Anniversary Meeting of the Trustees of the Charity Schools *. I remain, dear Sir, truly yours, S. DENNE."

* The Rev. John Law, D.D. (the communicative correspondent from whose letters Mr. Denne makes such frequent extracts, and who was) Archdeacon of Rochester for the almost unprecedented period of sixty years, was son of Stephen Law, Esq. of Broxbourn in Hertfordshire, at one time Governor of Bombay. He was of Emanuel-college, Cambridge, B.A. 1760, being the fourth Senior Optime of that year; M.A. 1763; D.D. 1778; and was for some time a Fellow of that Society. He was appointed Archdeacon of Rochester by Bishop Pearce in 1767; presented to the Vicarage of Shorne by the Dean and Chapter of that Church in 1770; to that of Westmill in Hertfordshire in 1771 by Ralph Freman, D.D.; to that of Great Easton in Essex in 1776 by Viscount Maynard, upon which he resigned Shorne; and to the Perpetual Curacy of Chatham in 1784 by the Dean and Chapter of Rochester. He published Charges delivered to the Clergy of his Archdeaconry in the years 1779, 1782, 1798, 1802, 1806, 1811, 1817, 1820, and perhaps others; and also the Sermon (above announced by Mr. Denne) delivered at the Anniversary Meeting of the Charity Children in St. Paul's in 1797. He died at Rochester, Feb. 5, 1827, in his 88th year; being the oldest dignitary of the Church of England. At a Chapter holden on the 17th of the same month, it was unanimously resolved that "the Dean and Chapter, sensibly affected by the loss which they have sustained in the death of Dr. John Law, Prebendary of this Cathedral Church, and Archdeacon of the Diocese of Rochester, they deem it a duty which they owe to his memory, to themselves, and to the Church, to record their sentiments and feelings towards him. The dignity and affability with which, during a period of nearly sixty years, he supported and graced the station which he held in this Cathedral Church; the unremitting diligence and fidelity, the wisdom and firmness, the urbanity and moderation, with which he watched over its interests and sustained its credit; together with the zeal and vigilance with which he engaged in the administration of its spiritual concerns, were such as at once to excite admiration, respect, and love, and to throw a brilliant lustre over his name and character. The present Dean and Chapter can never lose the recollection of his long and faithful services, nor of his numerous and estimable Christian virtues; and they have the highest gratification, in the midst of their regret, in placing upon record this memorial of his excellence, and this tribute of their esteem and affection." The clergy of the Archdeaconry had, some years before, presented a vase thus inscribed:

64. " Dear Sir, *Wilmington, April* 11, 1797.

" Who transmitted to the Obituary, p. 261, the account of the late Commissioner Hey? I think not R. G. because I have a notion he would have mentioned that the deceased, though not a graduate of Alma Mater, was a member of the old House*. That you and he were contemporaries I am clear, though you could not have been together in the lecture-room of Tutor Masters when the under-written occurrence happened, which may in the reading amuse a Benedictine, and yet not be unquestionably of sufficient importance to fill half a column in the Gentleman's Magazine. At an algebraic lecture, present Aynsworth, Hey, and others, a problem was delivered from the chair, that the lads were to solve if they could. Will. seemed to be as busy with his slate and his pencil as either one of the party; but, alas! upon the tutor's asking for the slate, to see in what manner the proof was worked, he was struck with astonishment; and after uttering some of his shrill hems, quoth he, ' I perceive, Hey, that with you x is equal to a flight of birds!' The case was, that Will. who was an excellent shot, had been sketching not $a+b$ and $c-d$, but himself with a gun levelled, a pointer in an attitude proper, and a covey of partridges on the wing. Such an abuse, such a profanation of a lecture-room, merited a severe imposition ; and the task enjoined was, that Hey should the next morning repeat a hundred lines in Homer to the indignant tutor. The culprit, in a tone of humiliation, asked where he was to begin. Homer was brought from the shelf in the adjoining gallery, and after some demur the verse was marked at which the punishment was to commence; but no sooner was the catch-word sounded, than Will. who had a retentive memory, improved by practice at Eton, repeated the verses more expeditiously than Masters could read them, for I need not remind you that Bobby had not the credit of being an expert Greek scholar. The

---

" Joanni Law, S. T. P. Archidiacono Roffensi, Ecclesiæ Anglicanæ, cujus purioris disciplinæ rationem, cujus officia et fidem, tum conciunandi gravitate et copia, tum vita et moribus illustravit, Defensori spectatissimo ; venerando huic eidem suo plus quadraginta octo annos Fantori, Monitori, Duci, unde nec viduis, quod solitudini opem ferat, nec liberorum orbitati ad quod confugiat, deest, Archdiaconatus Roffensis Clerus hoc pii et grati animi munus, observantiæ ergo, D. D. D. A. D. MDCCCXV."—Of Dr. Law's family further notices will be found in some subsequent letters.

* William Hey, Esq. (younger brother to the Rev. Thomas Hey, noticed in p. 700) was admitted of Bene't-college in 1751. He was at one period Chief Justice of Quebec. In 1763 he was elected Recorder of Sandwich, and in 1774 returned to Parliament for that borough, but vacated his seat in 1776, on being appointed a Commissioner of the Customs, which office he held to his death. He was a great favourite with Lord Chancellor Thurlow, and, it is said, was dining with him when the great seal was stolen in 1785. He had a country house at Coxheath in Kent; but died at his town-residence in Park-place, St. James's, March 3, 1797, in his 64th year. He married April 5, 1783, Miss Paplay, of Jamaica, whom he left his widow, without children.

penalty, however, being paid, the offender had a right to a dismissal; and thus ended a scene that was somewhat farcical.

"Master Urban, or his correspondent, may have a voucher for the intelligence, that the Commissioner was dining with the late Lord Chancellor when the Great Seal was stolen, though I do not remember to have heard that circumstance; but of this I am satisfied, that he is mistaken in his suggestion that the deceased had ' a fine seat on Coxheath ;' for it is a very ordinary mansion, and is placed below the heath. Boughton Mount, is, I observe, the appellation given it by Mr. Hasted; when that gentleman made his collections, it must have been inhabited by a gentleman of the name of Savage, who was the proprietor of it; and to one of his relatives, I suppose, it still belongs, for Mr. Hey was only a tenant, as was Mr. Rashleigh before him.

"Who could have supposed that the pen of my second tutor at Bene't-college should have had so powerful an effect * as it is averred to have had in the Gentleman's Magazine for March, p. 258, col. 1. par. 1. The ' Historic Doubts,' though they issued from Strawberry-hill, did not, in my opinion, obviate the doubts that many had entertained upon the part of English History which Mr. Walpole with much ingenuity laboured to illustrate. Were there any of the Paston letters published in the last volumes that afforded a gleam of light? Among the posthumous works alluded to by Urban's obituarist, p. 259, there is an innuendo of the expected publication of the letters from Horace Walpole to Sir Horace Mann must; which I should suppose, be interesting as well as amusing. He has, I observe, bequeathed a legacy of £.5,000 to the present Sir Horace Mann ; and I understand that the Baronet had his *prænomen* from the testator, who was his sponsor. Yours truly, S. DENNE."

---

65. " DEAR SIR,   *Wilmington, Easter Eve,* 1797.

" Mr. Archdeacon Law is the person who has boldly engaged to mount the rostrum in the same year, at the request of the Trustees of the Charity Schools and of the Committee of the Asylum Institution ; and you will see by the inclosed, that the Secretary of the Asylum has clenched the business. An application to myself would have surprised me; and it is one of the advantages that we rusticated clerks enjoy, that a country vicar is not thought to be an orator of sufficient dignity and importance to be announced in an advertisement for any public sermon. As the son of a late Rector of Lambeth, it is true that Dr. Vyse hinted, I ought to preach a Charity Sermon for the Boys'-school of that parish; but I parried the solicitation by

---

* " Some Remarks," by the Rev. Robert Masters, on the Historic Doubts, printed in Archæologia, vol. II. " provoked Mr. Walpole to withdraw himself from the Society of Antiquaries."

observing what was literally true, that I had not passed a Sunday in town since Midsummer 1781.

" Mr. Douce, by his answer to you, does not seem to be thoroughly apprised of the main drift of my pursuit. The time of the introduction of Arabic numerals into Europe, will ever be, as I suspect, a desideratum; the progress of them may, however, be traced; and I am inclined to believe that a little light may be cast upon it by every book on the subject that was printed before the middle of the sixteenth century.

" Mrs. Berkeley, in her memoir of the son, George-Monck Berkeley, is not very accurate in her report of the promotion by Lord Thurlow of the present Rector of Gravesend.   Mr. Tucker was the son of Mr. Tucker, who was Usher of the King's School at Canterbury when his Lordship and self sat in the same form * ; and after our removal to Cambridge, the said Usher became Under-master by the death of Mr. Gurney, whose eldest daughter he married. Thurlow was intimate with the Gurneys † ; and kind

* The Rev. John Tucker, of Trinity-college, Cambridge, B A. 1743; M.A. 1751; was appointed Second Master of Canterbury school in 1755; and in the same year presented, by the Rev. Richard Monins Eaton (son of the Rev. Richard Monins, who had been Head Master of the same school) to the Rectories of Charlton by Dovor, and Ringwold also in Kent, both of which he resigned in 1758 in favour of the patron. In 1757 he was presented, by the Dean and Chapter of Rochester, to the Vicarage of Sheldwich; in 1764 collated by Archbishop Secker to the Perpetual Curacy of Thanington; and in the same year presented by Philip Honywood, Esq. to the Rectory of Milton near Canterbury, which he resigned in 1770, on being again presented by John Monins, Esq. to the Rectory of Ringwold. He died Dec. 12, 1776, and was buried in the vault of his wife's family in the chancel of Westwell Church, where a flat-stone is thus inscribed: " M S. Johannis Tucker, M.A. Regiæ Scholæ Cantuariensis Hypodidasculi, Rectoris de Ringwold; qui obiit 12 die Decembris 1776, ætatis 53." Mr. Tucker was a most worthy cha- racter; his benevolent disposition and goodness of heart, the honesty of which was open and undisguised throughout life, gained him universal love and esteem.—His son, the Rev. John Tucker, was also of Trinity- college, Cambridge, B. A. 1779, being the eighth Senior Optime of that year; M. A. 1782. His preferments are noticed by Mr. Denne above; he died at Wingham, Kent, Feb. 26, 1811, aged 53, having retained to his death the Rectories of Gravesend and Luddenham.

† The Rev. William Gurney, " of Kent," was admitted of Bene't- college, Cambridge, in 1716; proceeded B. A. 1719; M. A. 1723; he was presented in 1726 by Sir John Shelley, Bart. to the Rectory of Hurst, and in 1730 collated by Archbishop Wake to the Rectory of Westwell, both in Kent. He died in 1755, and was buried at Westwell, where there is, in the chancel, a marble tablet to his wife Jane, who died April 26, 1731, aged 24.—In January 1755 we find the Rev. John Sharp (after- wards D. D.) writing to Mr. Denne: " I shall probably be at Cambridge time enough to pay my respects in the theatre to our Canterbury school friends that take their B. A. degrees this year. I think there are five of them, which is more than I ever remember from our school on this occasion. They are Monins [10th Wrangler, and afterwards Fellow], Taylor, and Leightenhouse of John's, with Bedford of Clare-hall, and Gurney of Bene't. I believe Monins is the first man; but I can assure

to the family after his elevation. The eldest son (who was of Bene't, and kept there a noted dog called Boguy) he presented to the Rectory of Luddenham, not far from Feversham; and Gravesend was kept vacant for young Tucker during his minority, though not for much more than half the time averred by the memorialist, as Mr. Crawley, the predecessor, died in December 1780, and Mr. Tucker was instituted April 5, 1782, being at that time the Head-master of Canterbury-school. The Chancellor also presented him to the Rectory of Luddenham on the death of his uncle Gurney in 1784; and this, perhaps, might occasion Mrs. Berkeley's surmise that four years' vacancy had preceded the promotion. Her anecdotes about the great uncle of the Earl of Aylesford shall be inquired into when I see my friend at Preston-hall, which is not half a mile from the Friary, now inhabited by the Countess dowager; and her Ladyship and Mrs. Milner often exchange visits, and I have a notion dine at each others' houses.

" It is not in my power to accommodate you with the loan of the tracts written by Mayhew and Apthorpe against and for Episcopacy in America. Particular notice is taken of this controversy by Drs. Porteus and Stinton, in the Life of Archbishop Secker, prefixed to the first volume of his Sermons.

" I remain, dear Sir, yours truly,   S. DENNE."

66. " DEAR SIR,   *Wilmington, May 12, 1797.*
" When we talked at Mr. Ord's about the Benedictine Heys, I believe I forgot to mention that Thomas, the elder and the surviving brother, had lately had a considerable windfall, as the phrase is, on the decease of Mrs. Cosnan, of Wingham-house, situated not far from Canterbury, on the road to Deal. This house, with an estate, as I understand, of hundreds a year, formerly belonging to Sir Thomas Palmer, was bequeathed to Dr. Hey by Sir Thomas's daughter; and her motive for giving the same to him was, that he was the son of Lady Palmer, her

you with pleasure, that our worthy Master Gurney's son will not be the last." This was the elder son, the Rev. William Gurney, B.A. 1755, M.A. 1761. He was presented in 1763 by Lewis Lord Sondes to the Vicarage of Sellinge, but resigned it in the same year for the Rectories of Badlesmere and Leveland in the same patronage, and which were united during his incumbency in 1780; in 1772 by Sir Edward Dering to the Vicarage of Bredgar, which he resigned in 1780 for the Rectory of Luddenham, to which Lord Chancellor Thurlow preferred him. He died at Badlesmere, April 8, 1784.—The Rev. Thomas Gurney, the younger brother, was also of Bene't-college, B.A. 1760, M.A. 1765; was presented to the Vicarage of Seasalter by the Dean and Chapter of Canterbury in 1764; in the same year by the Dean and Chapter of Chichester to the Vicarage of Bapchild, which he resigned in the following for the Rectory of Whitstaple, to which he was collated by Archbishop Secker. In 1770 he was presented by John Monins, Esq. to the Rectory of Charlton by Dovor, and he died June 12, 1774.

step-mother, who, after the death of Sir Thomas, wedded Mr. Hey's father *. This and more will probably be related concerning the family in the concluding volume of Hasted's History of our County; and possibly before that shall be finished the estate may pass into other hands, for my school-fellow and fellow-collegian has a consumptive habit of body, and finds it necessary to make frequent journeys to Bristol. He is now there for the benefit of the waters; and he means to prolong his residence there till the end of the month. It was surmised that Mr. Hatton, of Eastwell, would, as heir-at-law to Sir Thomas Palmer, contest the will of Miss Palmer as to a part at least of the estate; but, if he ever intended a litigation, he now acquiesces, and Dr. Hey will probably, during the course of the summer, remove from the Parsonage-house of Wickham Breaux to Wingham-house. The household effects of the late widow Cosnan are, I see, to pass under the hammer this week. She was a daughter of Sir Thomas d'Aeth, of Knowlton; and her first husband was Herbert Palmer, once a Captain of Marines. Unluckily for him, he made his appearance in the world before his father could be prevailed on to make an honest woman of her who afterwards became Lady Palmer †.

" On looking into the list of Members of Corpus Christi-college, Cambridge, I perceive that the Historian has mis-spelt the name of Hey, styling him H*ay*. I observe, that he was born in London, whereas I supposed him to have been a man of Kent, and had imagined that he was born in Wingham-house, where the presumption is, that he will now terminate his days, unless he should be carried off the stage at Bristol, whilst in pursuit of health. My *quondam* tutor notices his being A. B. 1749. Were the list to be reprinted, if D. D. were subjoined in a note, it would be with a mark of contempt that he was only a Lambeth Doctor.

" Perhaps it may be new to you, that Mr. Cooper has, *quasi voluntarie*, resigned his Prebendal Stall in Rochester Cathedral;

---

* Sir Thomas's second wife, " Mrs. Cox."

† This lady, who was third wife of Sir Thomas Palmer, the fourth Baronet of Wingham, is called in the Palmer pedigree " Mrs. Markham." The Rev. Thomas Hey, D. D. was the eldest son of her subsequent marriage; he was of Bene't-college, Cambridge, B. A. 1749, M. A. 1753. He was presented in 1755 to the Rectory of Wickham Braose and the Vicarage of Eastchurch in Kent, the advowsons of both which livings had belonged to the Palmers; and in 17.. was collated to a Prebend of Rochester. In 1770 Mrs. Frances Palmer (daughter of Sir Thomas by his second wife) devised to him the college estate at Wingham; and also the fee of the manor of St. John's in Irvingfield, where he afterwards in 1777 purchased the estate, then in Chancery, and in 1787 the fee-farm rent from the Crown. He died at Wingham, in Nov. 1807, aged 80; and his widow, at the same place, Oct. 18, 1814. His only son, John, died a student at Christ Church, Oxford, April 28, 1778. His daughter, Clementina-Paget, was married Nov. 28, 1815, to the Rev. Henry Plumptre, Rector of Clayton near Newark.

but who was likely to be the successor was doubtful when I had my last interview with Archdeacon Law. Many persons in the vicinity of Rochester and of Maidstone have suggested that Lord George Murray will be the fortunate clerk; but I understand that he has weakened his interest by refusing the boon of £.1000 for his telegraph services, and claiming, as well as receiving £.2000. His Lordship, however, in a recent letter to Dr. Law, relies on the accumulated promises of the Minister for ecclesiastical promotion; and by an agreement between the Chancellor and the Premier, Mr. Pitt is, it seems, to nominate the person for the vacant Prebend. Mr. Cooper will, I should suppose, in future resume the lay habit; and he can the better afford to part with his clerical income, as by the death of James West, Esq. Auditor of the Land Revenue of almost all the counties of England, the reversionary grant by patent to Cooper takes place. It is the opinion of my informant, that the net profits of this sinecure place amount to upwards of £.2000 a year; but it is supposed that Sir Grey Cooper is a sharer with his son in the emoluments thereof. Lord Cadogan was lately in such a dangerous state, that extraordinary exertions were made to procure the completion of the Divorce Bill; and as it might certainly have been retarded by her Ladyship, she was induced to decline all opposition by a stipulation that she should have an annual allowance of £.600. She cannot, however, marry her gallant, he being still *sub vinculo matrimonii*.

"The correspondent in the Gentleman's Magazine (signature B.) who communicated the facetious nomenclature of the Navy Royal *, I had imagined to be R. B. (Richard Bathurst) one of the Minor Canons of Rochester, there being in the epistle referred to some traits of his style of writing; but as B. in his elucidation of Naval Medals perseveres in his dating letter from Chatham, I am now apt to suspect they both are from the pen of a Mr. Burton, Store-keeper of the Victualling Office, who not long since published some Lectures on Female Education. Whoever may be the author of what has afforded instruction and entertainment to the readers of Urban's Miscellany, he is certainly a man of sense, with a large portion of acquired knowledge. His remarks on the Medals are pertinent; and well-founded are his censures on the folly of the insulting kind, as many direful evils have unquestionably resulted from them. And with becoming deference to superiors, are not the current Spanish dollars, which display the effigies of the King of Great Britain impressed on the neck of the King of Spain, open to this stricture? As this may be not improperly termed the Coronade war, in which this country has taken a principal part, ought there to have been any mark of contempt pointed at royalty?

* Vol. LXVII. p. 26; Mr. Denne appended some antiquarian remarks on the same subject in the next number, p. 116.

" If the late Rector of Welwyn lived to be 82, as you hinted, he must have been many years older than his brother Richard Bathurst, Master Urban's correspondent under the signature R. B. for I rather question whether he may have attained to threescore years and ten. R. B. was of Tunbridge School; I think he was of Oxford, but of what college I do not recollect *.

" Mr. Ord may possibly have apprised you, that on the morning before I left town, I stepped into the reading-room of the British Museum, and discovered in the Catalogues some of the treatises on Arithmetic mentioned in a former letter. I had not time to ask for a single book; but I have it in my thoughts to take my second spring trip to the metropolis on Monday the 15th current, and shall be disappointed should I not be able to repeat my visit to Mr. Ayscough, or his associate. Bradwardin's Arithmetica Speculativa is in the collection, not so Arithmetica Practica, which is also wanting in the Bodleian Library; and if it be not in Lambeth-house, probably it is not to be found in England. From the Museum I proceeded to Sion-college Library, and passed there half an hour in cursory perusal of Buckley's Arithmetica Memorativa, *versu*, and of Mulcaster's Positions. I wished to have conveyed both books to Wilmington Vicarage for a fortnight; but, not being one of the London clergy, it was a liberty I did not think myself warranted to assume. There is one incident in Mulcaster's Positions concerning Sir John Cheke, that is not, as I believe, particularly noticed by Strype. ' He sent down to King's-college (writes Mulcaster) from the Court, Maister Bukley, some time Fellow, and very well studied in the mathematics, to read arithmeticke and geometry to the youth of the college; and, for the better encouraging of them to that studie, gave them a number of Euclides at his own coast. Maister Bukley had drawn the rules of arithmetike into verses, and gave the copies abroad to his hearers. Myself am to honour the memorie of the learned Knight, being partaker of

* The Rev. Richard Bathurst was the youngest son of Edward Bathurst, Esq. of Finchcocks in the parish of Goudhurst, Kent, who died in 1772, at the advanced age of 92. In 1767, on the death of Mr. Charles Bathurst, to whom Finchcocks had been conveyed by his father, his brother, the Rev. Richard Bathurst, succeeded to that estate, which was for some time his residence, but he sold it before 1797. He died at Rochester in February 1803, then holding his Minor Canonry and the Vicarage of St. Margaret's in that city.—His half-brother, the Rev. Thomas Bathurst, the Rector of Welwyn above-mentioned, was of All Souls' college, Oxford, where he took the degree of M. A. in 1740, and by which Society he was presented to Welwyn, on the death of Dr. Young, the author of Night Thoughts, in 1765. In the chancel of that Church is the following epitaph: " Under this monument rests interred the body of the Rev. Thomas Bathurst, Rector of this parish, and Fellow of All Souls'-college, Oxford. He was the youngest son of Edward Bathurst, Esq. late of Finchcocks, in the county of Kent, and Elizabeth his wife, daughter of Stephen Stringer, Esq. of Triggs, in the same county, and departed this life April the 17th, 1797, aged 82."

his liberal distribution of those Euclides, with whom he joyned Xenophon.'

" In the postscript of a paper addressed to Sylvanus Urban, within which this letter will be inclosed, a doubt is started by W. and D. whether there may not be an anachronism in the surmise that the present worthy Bishop of Waterford be the Prelate noticed by Boswell in his Life of Johnson, pref. p. *viii. ; and an innuendo is offered that Drs. Maxwell and Johnson might allude in their conversation to Primate Stone. The sceptic has not any biographical notes to support his conjecture; and trusts only to memory for his having understood that the said Primate encouraged the building of parsonage-houses in his Diocese. When did his brother, Andrew Stone, depart ? and were not the Primate's good deeds mentioned in the account then given of the Stone family ?

" I am, yours truly,   S. DENNE."

---

67. " DEAR SIR,   *Wilmington, June 5, 1797.*

" By the civility of Mr. Peete, I had the first cut of the little dish of Mr. Hasted's History of Kent, and the morsels of new matter were so few, that it was easy to digest them all without loss of time; nor I must own had I room to expect a more plentiful repast after the perusal of the last epistle he wrote me, and which was submitted to your perusal. In page 342, note ʳ, this fulsome compliment is paid to the Vicar of Wilmington: ' A gentleman to whom literature in general, and the editor of these volumes in particular, is highly indebted for his liberal communications ; and yet I will venture to say, that in the two volumes octavo he has not inserted communications that would cover half a sheet ; and under Darenth in particular there are errors that I am confident were not communicated by me. It was hinted to him in my letters, to have an eye towards Custumale Roffense and the Kentish Traveller's Companion, with the hope that he would discover, in both these publications, there were some mistakes in the folio edition of his History that ought to be corrected. They are, however, repeated in octavo. I will instance one, *viz.* that the great window of the chancel of Dartford Church was constructed by Bishop Thomas de Woldham, whereas there is proof direct it was put up at the expense of Bishop Haymo de Hethe, and a bust, commemorative of him, is extant in good preservation. Mr. Hasted had also an innuendo from me, that the lodge of the Royal Kentish Bowmen upon Dartford Heath was worthy of particular notice; and I am still of opinion the description of it in full would have amused many of his readers ; he has, however, compressed his account into about ten lines, and of the encored direful catastrophes at the powder-mills in this vicinity not a word is written. The first volume was dedicated to Lord Romney; the patronage of

Viscount Sydney is solicited to this second tome. And he observes, that 'to enumerate his Lordship's public as well as private virtues would not only give offence, but would exceed the limits of this volume;' though it consists of 578 pages. Fuller, you may recollect, found out a patron for every century of his Church History. I think the Historian of Kent would not have judged amiss had he contrived to address every hundred to some person of consequence resident within the district. Mr. Hasted promises a third volume in September; and before I pass to another subject I ought in justice to observe that he is to be commended for attempting, in this diminutive work, to ascertain the number of acres of land there are in many of the parishes.

"I wish to acquire some intelligence, besides what I have procured in Wottonianæ Reliquiæ and Rymer's Fœdera, concerning Sir Albertus Morton, nephew of the famous Sir Henry Wotton, and Secretary of State to King Charles the First. That he was Knight of the Shire for Kent in the first Parliament of that King is the whole of what is said of him by either Harris or Hasted; but I have the copy of a curious letter concerning his being elected, which I design to transmit to Master Urban's Miscellany as soon as I shall have collected other information of him. How he became the nephew of Sir Henry Wotton I am as yet somewhat puzzled to explain; and you may perhaps have it in your power to dispel the mist. I have reason to believe there was in Dorsetshire a family of the Mortons of some note; and if there were, you from the History of that County can easily trace whether the said Sir Albertus Morton might be of that branch. He died at Southampton in 1625, and was there buried; and the elegiac tears which Sir Henry Wotton shed over the grave of his beloved nephew are printed in the Reliquiæ Wottonianæ.

"He is mentioned at pp. 108, 131, of the Life of Wotton by Walton, edit. 1675; and something more may be said of him in the new edition of Walton's Lives of Donne and others, by Zouch. I remain, dear Sir, yours truly,   S. DENNE."

---

68. "DEAR SIR,   *Wilmington, June* 17, 1797.
"Of Sir Albertus Morton Dean Dampier has communicated sundry items, of which some, however, do not appear to be quite accurate. He had them from the memoranda of one Anthony Allen, formerly Fellow of King's-college, and afterwards a Master in Chancery, who 'compiled in five large folio volumes every thing that could be collected concerning the Members of both Colleges, as well from historical books as from the private ledgers of the Societies;' but the Dean hints that he was sorry to find that he gave but few additional notices, except of men whose names are not likely to find their way into our Histories.

" Rushworth, and on his authority Rapin and Mrs. Macauley, with probably other historians, have, as appears to me, assigned a speech in the first parliament of Charles the First, after its removal to Oxford, to Secretary Cooke instead of to Secretary Morton, if any Secretary of State, who was a Commoner, ever delivered the speech alluded to, which I rather doubt. Anthony Allen's notes mention Albertus Morton as having been returned to that parliament by the University of Cambridge; but Carter (History, p. 464) must be an error in his suggestion, that Albert Morton was likewise a representative for the University in the third year of that reign, as he deceased in 1625. Allen says, that he died in St. Margaret's, Westminster; but he was certainly buried at Southampton. On a revisal of a no short note in Hasted's account of Chilham (Kent, vol. III.) I have discovered that Sir Albertus was a demi-nephew, by the mother's side, to Sir Henry Wotton; and I have it in my thoughts to write to Mr. Jarvis Kenrick, Vicar of that parish, for information, whether his baptism be there registered. Mr. Kenrick was, you know, of the old House; and, should I transmit an epistle to him, I shall not fail to hint that Benedictines are presumed to be of the antiquarian cast.

" The commission of public censor of the diminutive edition of the History of our great County, I must be so free as to decline, for these among other reasons : first, that, though I address my letters to the author at a coffee-house in the Strand, I do not forget that he is an inmate in a large house *trans Thamesin;* second, that I cannot well become a criticiser without laying myself open to an imputation of betraying the secrets of a confidential correspondence; third, that the said octavo historian is incorrigible.

" Poor Mr. Clarke, of Gravesend, has been in a pitiable state in consequence of the mutiny at the Nore. He thus feelingly expresses himself, ' From a man in the heart of a besieged city, as it were, little is to be expected. We are here in high military array, and our peaceable green is converted into a camp, and disturbed with perpetual noise, and for many days with continual alarms. The town is full of troops of all regiments and sizes ; and exhibits a scene so new in every thing to such a hermit as myself, that I seem as if affected with a kind of vertigo; and desire most heartily a return of the comforts of repose, and of the business in its ordinary course. Whilst I breathe, may it never again be my fate to see any thing like the inside of a place prepared to stand a siege ; or to feel the anxiety of sending off my infant and his mother at an instant; and the fear of our property being ruined by the shot from the shipping which threatened to pass this place, and which was to have been attacked with all our might!' As Mr. Clarke is a person who prefers the pen to the sword, and is apt to be nervous, I do not wonder at his being so much distressed. He thus concludes his letter, ' I will just acquaint you, that Mr. Pocock has got his History in great forwardness in the press ; of its quality or quan- tity I can say nothing, as we are not acquainted.' Mr. Pocock is a printer ; and the work in which he employs his pen and his types is the History of Gravesend and its environs. So many years have passed since I became a subscriber to it, that I do not recollect what is to be the money paid on delivery ; for if I made a deposit, I have unluckily lost both receipt and proposals. This I remember, that I communicated to him a long list of the Rec- tors of Gravesend, and perhaps of Milton, the contiguous parish ; and that in his letter of acknowledgment he noticed the names of a few incumbents that had escaped the researches of Dr. Thorpe and my father.

" The bequest from Joseph Wilcocks, Esq. (son of Bishop Wilcocks) of £.2,700 towards an hospital, has been frequently encored in an advertisement in pursuance of the testator's will. If not claimed within a certain number of years, it becomes a lapse legacy, as I think, towards some other charitable institu- tion ; and there is little doubt of its devolving, as there is not a probability of an hospital being established within three miles of Rochester. The trustees of the Kent and Canterbury hos- pital, by erecting their building near the dilapidated Abbey of St. Austin, placed it out of distance. As this hospital is not in a flourishing way, they wished, but in vain, to have found a clause in the will that would have allowed of the executors transferring the stock to their use ; it is in the 3 *per cent.* Consolidated Bank Annuities.

" I remain, dear Sir, yours truly, S. Denne."

69. " Dear Sir, *Wilmington, July* 21, 1797.
" In my late passage to Maidstone, I was within half a mile of the Great Harry, safely moored at East Malling ; but being in a vehicle that might take for its motto *labere pennis*, it was not in my power to bring the ship within view. I trust, how- ever, that in my week's tarrying at Preston-hall on this side Michaelmas, I shall be along side this famous vessel ; and I am the more sanguine, because I understand that Mrs. Milner occa- sionally visits Mrs. Norris, who is the owner of this picture, copied from the picture Sir John Norris met with in a Spanish prize. A lady who has seen it told Mr. Pett, the father of Chan- cellor Phineas Pett, and a descendant of builder Phineas Pett, that it was a most awkward vessel ; and in what points it may differ from Allen's print of the supposed Great Harry, an exa- mination will, I trust, be made by a person better skilled than myself in naval architecture.

" To my letter of inquiry after Sir Albertus Morton, I had a speedy and a polite answer from Mr. Jarvis Kenrick, Vicar of Chilham ; and I transmit these extracts from it : ' I have carefully looked over my Register-book from 1558 to 1676, and do not find any one of the family of Moreton baptised in all that time. I then looked over the marriages and burials for the same time, to see if I could find any mention made of any person of that name; and the only persons of that name taken notice of are amongst the burials, and them only two, *viz.* Sir Robert Moreton, Knt. buried 10th April 1637; and Ann, the lady of Sir Robert Moreton, Knt. buried 22d Feb. 1637-8. There is no monument, or other memorial, to the above persons; nor can I trace any account of the family, but what is mentioned in note m, p. 136, of Hasted's vol. III. folio, under the article of Esture, which you of course have seen, as you mention his omission of Sir Albertus in his list of Knights of the Shire. As Sir Robert Moreton is mentioned by Hasted (as also in The Topographer, No. XXIII. for Feb. 1791, printed for Robson,) as being buried in the church of Chilham, I should suppose there must have been formerly some monument, or other memorial of him, in the church, as in the register there is nothing more recorded than what I have mentioned.'

"The Master and Fellows of Bene't have agreed to my tutor Masters's resignation of the rectory of Landbeach in favour of a son-in-law elect, who is a senior Fellow of Caius, on condition that the humble servant of the young lady shall cede to Mr. Dickson the presentation to Broadway, co. Dorset. Burroughs is the name of the lover. Miss Masters is mentioned by Mr. James Currey as being a woman of good sense, and of merit in other respects. I had imagined that the Master himself might have an eye to this Rectory, as being within the legal distance of the vicarage of Gedney; but Mr. James Currey says, that the Master is precluded from taking any living in the patronage of the College, St. Mary Abchurch excepted; but whether this preclusion be by the statutes, or by any special deeds, I am not apprised.

"Knowing that the Hon. and Rev. Jacob Marsham was a graduated nobleman of Christ Church, Oxford, it was with some surprise I learnt that he had emigrated to King's-college, and commenced D D. at our Alma Mater; nor have I yet heard a reason assigned why he did not adhere to his old corps. He was presented by the Public Orator.

"There is not as yet any successor appointed to the stall in Rochester Cathedral, vacant by the *quasi* voluntary dereliction of Mr. Cooper. One of the Papillons has, it seems, been named for it in public; but Mr. Papillon, Vicar of Tunbridge, expressed his surprise to Archdeacon Law, at the information of the supposed allotment of this prebend to one of his family, as he had not received the least innuendo of the circumstance. Some have imagined that the other members of the Church had not any cause personally to regret the want of a sixth brother at the time of their Midsummer chapter harvest; but that is a mistake, for the Dean and the five Prebendaries do not appropriate to their private benefit the dividend of the open stall,—it is expended upon the fabric.

" The Bishop of Bangor * has, it may be presumed, disappointed a successor expectant, as for some days a report prevailed that the Prelate was likely soon to follow his brother. A sharp humour on the right side of the face created the alarm; and supposing it had been cancerous, as it was suspected, it might be death would have speedily ensued. He is, however, so far recovered as to be able to move to a villa which he has near town.

" Have you read the last anniversary Propagation Sermon, by Bishop Sutton? Well drawn is the character of the illustrious Washington; but I understand it was with a degree of admiration that it was heard from the pulpit of St. Mary-le-Bow, and from the tongue of a Prelate, it being within memory when there were not more than two or three of the Episcopal Bench who did not regard Washington as a rebel destined to the cord. The well-regulated ambition of this country Esquire, the first of his class on either side of the Atlantic, is a pertinent epitaph; and happy would it be for the world were it applicable to more of the Rulers of the world, by whatever style or title they and their agents may be distinguished and dignified.

" Is it new to you, that the Sermon at St. Mary's, on the commencement Sunday, was by Dr. Nasmith, of Corpus Christi? I do not understand that it is to be published; and I regret its being kept in the tin-box, as I am fully persuaded that it might be perused to the edification of the reader, and to the credit of the writer, and to that of the old House, of which he was, and may still be, a member.

" I am, dear Sir, yours truly,   S. DENNE."

---

70. "DEAR SIR,   *Wilmington, Aug.* 7, 1797.
" Should it be in Dr. Latham's power to procure any satisfactory answers to the proposed queries about Somerley, Pile, and Willis, from his Hampshire acquaintance, I doubt not of his readiness to oblige Mr. Urban's correspondent; though ornithology is a more favoured hobby than antiquities. In a letter I had from him in May, he thus expresses himself, ' In respect to natural history and antiquities, I compare myself to Garrick between tragedy and comedy; and, though not so great a man, I cannot help, like him, squinting towards that which pleases me best.' He not long since communicated to his Linnean brethren an essay of forty or fifty pages of letter-press, and drawings for seven quarto plates, concerning the Trachea Avium, or what is vulgarly called the wind-pipe, which in certain species exhibits

---

* The Right Rev. John Warren ; he survived to 1800.

unlooked for circumstances. He thinks the Linnean Society will deem it of sufficient consequence to print it. Not having heard from him for several weeks, I apprehend he has taken a flight from Romsey into Wales, on a visit to Mr. Pennant, his friend and fellow-labourer in the bird line.

" Mr. Ellis's letters brought me the following advice concerning a MS. of Ingulphus. In his first letter he mentions there being an index to forty-four quarto volumes of original letters in the Bodleian Library, and that he found a reference to one, wherein Mr. Obadiah Walker is reproached with stealing a MS. of Ingulphus; and in a letter of the next day's date, Mr. Ellis apprises me of his having found the letter wherein Obadiah Walker is accused, and that it is in the fifth volume of Ballard's Collection of Letters, No. XXIX. and in the hand-writing of Bishop Gibson. He adds, that it is also therein asserted, that Mr. Walker frequently declared Sir John Marsham had given it to him; and that Sir John as frequently complained of Mr. Walker's unkindness in purloining it. In his opinion, however, Mr. Walker was conscious of the theft, as he afterwards presented the MS. to Dr. Arthur Charlett, to be lodged in the library of University-college; but requested that Sir John might not be acquainted with it. When Mr. Ellis wrote, he had not had an opportunity of examining whether it be still extant.

" Lord Romney, with much politeness, presented my poor brother with a copy of the new Musæ Etonenses; and from that circumstance I had an opportunity of perusing them. I cannot say that they afforded equal pleasure with the Musæ Etonenses that were published not long before I was admitted a scholar of the old House; but the case is certainly altered, between a lad not out of his teens, and in the habit of reading Latin verses, and a man drawing towards threescore and ten, and who has the honour of being F. A. S. And even of the classical Atterbury, it was declared by Addison, in Spectator, No. 447, ' I have heard one of the greatest geniuses this age has produced, who had been trained up in all the polite studies of antiquity, assure me, upon his being obliged to search into several rolls and records, that, notwithstanding such an employment was at first very dry and irksome to him, he at last took an incredible pleasure in it, and preferred it even to the reading of Virgil or Cicero.' With several of the pieces in Nov. Musæ Etonenses I was, however, not a little diverted; and particularly with three improperly said to be written by Lord North, because, when he was under the tuition of Master Sumner, he was not by courtesy entitled to the appellation of Lord. The three copies of verses alluded to show, that he had at school that turn for humour which enabled him, when Premier, to set the House of Commons in a roar; and to retort with admirable success the facetious strictures of his political opponents. There are ten copies by the present Earl of Mornington, then Wellesley, which reflect credit on his Lordship's versifying talents. I remain, dear Sir, yours truly,   S. Denne."

---

71. " Dear Sir,   *Wilmington, Aug.* 21, 1797.
" Mr. H. Ellis, in a letter conveyed in Mr. Nichols's parcel, writes, that he cannot immediately lay his hands upon his extract from Dr. Gibson's letter, touching the charge brought against a quondam non-juror, who was Master of University-college; but he observes that, should a jury be summoned to hear and determine the merits of the cause of Marsham *versus* Walker, he is confident they would decide in favour of Sir John against Obadiah, who appears to have been notorious as an antiquarian purloiner; and he cites in evidence a note from the fifth volume of the Biographia Britannica (article Elstob), Walker's being accused of cutting out several leaves from a MS. that contained Sir John Cheke's remarks against Popery. The letter of Elstob to Strype, printed in the Life of Cheke, has in it this sentence, ' And it is no wonder, if he who had so good a knack at concealing as to hide his religion for so many years, should afterwards manifest an equal dexterity in suppressing arguments against it.' To have applied the scissors with the same view to the Ingulphus MS. would have been an endless task.

" You notice your having long wished to investigate the forty-four volumes of letters in the Bodleian Library. If I am not mistaken, a correspondent in the European Magazine for May last has revised some of them. I allude to those in the section, under the quaint appellation of Drossiana, that were addressed to Dr. Charlett, Master of University-college.

" The County Chronicle, which announced the proceedings against the mutineers belonging to the St. George, states, that they were condemned on Saturday the 8th of July, and executed on Sunday the 9th; surely this must be an error of the press. Sunday does not shine a Sabbath day to the *sans culottes* of France, and therefore it is not unlikely that the guillotine might often be worked on that day at Paris; but much mortified shall I be, if it can be averred with truth, that Sunday, or the Lord's-day, is become a hanging day among Englishmen. By the Act of Parliament which enjoins the speedy execution of persons convicted of murder, if sentence is passed on Friday, there is a respite of it till Monday. Willing, therefore, am I to believe, that there must be a mistake in this paragraph.

" A son of my parishioner Mr. Campbell having been a subscriber to Staunton's Embassy to China, the two volumes, but not as yet the prints, have found their way to Wilmington; and I am not without some hopes that, before he carries them back to town, I may have an opportunity of skimming their contents. From Mr. Dugald Campbell the elder son's report of

them, there are grounds for inferring they exhibit, notwithstanding they cost six guineas, too many traits of author-craft and
book-craft. He in particular suggests, that two thirds of the
first volume are taken up with an uninteresting detail of the
voyage; and with descriptions of places well known to every
reader of voyages. Two thousand are said to be the number of
copies printed; and I understand that there are booksellers who
subscribed for several copies, and flatter themselves that they
shall make an advance of four guineas on the subscription price,
but I think they must wait till better times shall come.

" Mr. Ord's having his country villa at Epsom, instead of
Enfield vicinage, is a disappointment, as it is likely you have not
in your neighbourhood another antiquarian acquaintance with
whom, after a morning ride, you can interchange discoveries and observations. You mention our worthy friend's having found in Epsom vicarage Mrs. Thomas, the daughter of
Mr. Parkhurst, revising a new edition of her father's Lectures
through the press. I had heard of one daughter, and of one
only, as I understood, who married the late Mr. Altham, Rector
of St. Olave, Jewry, with whom I had a slight acquaintance; and
who was not, to the best of my recollection, in the upper class
of learned divines, as his father-in-law undoubtedly was *.

" Yours truly,   S. DENNE."

72. " DEAR SIR,   *Wilmington, Sept. 7*, 1797.
" Dr. Latham is returned from his tour into Wales, where he
passed a fortnight with his ornithological fellow-labourer Mr.
Pennant; and in his trip he says he saw most of the lions in
Oxford, Birmingham, &c. &c. On mentioning the new window of
the anti-chapel in New-college, designed by Sir Joshua Reynolds
and painted by Jervis, he observes, that the portraits of these
two eminent artists are well represented in the persons of two
shepherds, a circumstance that may not be novel to you;
though, if I had before heard it, it had slipt my recollection.
He says, that in his way to the Hall of Lleweny, he and his
friend made a stop at a seat of Mrs. Piozzi, a pretty little box,
said to have cost £.10,000.

" Art. XI. of the Monthly Review of July last notices the
History of the Principal Rivers, vol. II. in which there is, it is
said, an excursion to Maidstone, Penshurst, and even to Tunbridge; and it is observed by the Reviewers, on taking leave of
the production, that the plates greatly contribute to its magnificence, its entertainment, and its utility. But according to
the report of Mr. Jefferys, Mayor of Maidstone, who has, with
his pencil in his hand, surveyed the banks of the Medway from
Tunbridge to Upnor, there are in these plates many capital mis-

---

* Milicent, wife of the Rev. Joseph Thomas, was Mr. Parkhurst's
daughter by his second wife; see the pedigree of Parkhurst in Baker's
Northamptonshire, vol. I. p. 289.

takes. When I was last at Maidstone, Mr. Jefferys showed me several of his drawings; and he said, if time allowed, he had it in contemplation to extend his views to Sheerness; though he had his doubts, and so have I mine, whether it would be prudent to risk the expense of their passing under the burin.

" The town being thinned by the elopement of the great, and would be thought great folk, Dr. Pitcairn has arrived at a small ellinge cottage he has hired just without the bounds of Wilmington parish; and I was lately told an anecdote not unamusing, concerning my new neighbour. Very soon after Abraham Newland had issued one of his new one pound notes, it was announced in the public prints, that the late Dr. Warren, having received from a veteran female patient of quality one of these notes, together with a shilling as a make weight, hastily cast the note into the fire as waste paper, and put the silver among the golden fees. Far more fortunate was his friend Dr. Pitcairn, for on emptying his pockets, after making his forenoon rounds, he found a ten pound note; but recollecting that the only note he had received was from Lord Beaulieu, and conceiving that it must have been put into his hand for a one pound, he thought himself bound in honour to apprise his Lordship of what had happened. My Lord smiled, when the tale was told, but declined acceptance of the note, as it was not customary for physicians to return fees to those who could afford to give them; and that his Lordship was in this predicament must be concluded, for not long before the Doctor drew this ten pound prize, Lord Beaulieu, in reciting his ailments, mentioned as one, a want of rest in consequence of his having in his escretoire, &c. a superfluity of pelf; and on the Doctor's being employed to examine it, he made the sum total, in notes and cash, to amount to upwards of eleven thousand pounds. The Doctor immediately advised the sending for a banker to take the charge of it; and by this prescription being followed, a nap was procured to the noble patient!

" The panegyrist of the Secretary of the Society for Promoting Christian Knowledge, is, I doubt not, the Rev. George-Henry Glasse, under the signature of initials (Gent. Mag. Aug. p. 660); but I must confess, notwithstanding all that Mr. Glasse has written, that he has not convinced me that Mr. Jones, in his elegant dedication of his Sermon to Dr. Gaskin, in the phrase the ' business of Christianity,' did make the most happy choice of a word, according to the common acceptation of the term business.

" The True Briton announced the publication, price 3s. ' On the Means of Saving our Country,' by Henry Redhead York, Esq. What may be the scheme that is to effect this patriotic purpose? Since the writer, by a prescription from Dr. Kenyon and Co. became a patient in the penitentiary limbo at Dorchester, I do not recollect that his name has been inserted in the public prints. In his solitary cell he has certainly time to make use of pen and ink. Mr. James Currey, a contemporary at Bene't-college, makes an unfavourable report of his literary acquirements. I remain, dear Sir, yours truly, S. DENNE."

73. " DEAR SIR, *Wilmington, Sept. 25, 1797.*
" Hardly can it be new to you, that the third volume of the diminutive History of a great County is published; and that printer Bristow has assigned his reasons for the unpleasant task he is under, of representing to the numerous subscribers the necessity of adding a shilling *per* volume to the first stipulated price. He, however, contends, that the book at 8s. 6d. in boards will be the cheapest of its kind, considering the size and engravings contained in it, of any at this time published; and hoping that the trifling advance will not be thought exorbitant, he promises that no further alteration shall be made in the terms.

" Not long since, I believe, I apprised you that the Bishop of Rochester * was said to have preached a fervent political Sermon in Bromley Church pulpit. On further inquiry I learn, that there was a little, and very little, of politics in the discourse, but it was distinguished for the length of it, which was extended to one hour and a quarter. ' The people wondered,' was the text; and prophecy the subject treated on, particularly those predictions which are likely to receive their completion in this age of wonders, with some strictures on the false prophets that have arisen. I had my information from Mr. Currey, and he from a niece of the late Mr. Hawksworth, one of the hearers; and she observed that, though it was not without some surprise, the clock was heard to strike the hour of one, whilst the right reverend preacher was in the pulpit, she does not think there was one of the congregation dissatisfied with the uncommon length of the Sermon energetically delivered. The Bishop, it seems, is at one of the watering-places in Sussex, I believe Worthing; having left Bromley-house and a single cow under the care of one female domestic.

" On the 3d of September I repeated ' dust to dust ' over the remains of Bob. Shenstone, who deceased at half past seven. He was in youth, and in his prime, a poacher and game-keeper *(aliudque et idem)*; but failing when an *emeritus miles* in the service of Sir Nicholas Carew, he was, by an order of two Surrey Justices, removed as a pauper to Wilmington. Being told that he had a twin-brother, now game-keeper to the 'Squire of Sutton-place, and thinking it very extraordinary that there should be two twins (as speak the vulgar), who had attained to such an age, I applied to the Vicar of Horton for evidence, as they were natives of that parish; and the transcript he sent me is decisive. ' Robert and Richard, sons of Robert Shenstone,

* Dr. Warren.

husbandman, were baptised March 3, 1722-23.' This instance
of a protracted coevalty in the brothers is the more striking,
perhaps an unique *, as they must often have laboured by night
and by day in their vocation, and consequently have lived more
than all the days of their lives. 'Two twins' I have marked for
a vulgar phrase, though it must be admitted that is a vulgarism
used by authors who ought not to have given a sanction to a
term so incorrect. 'Two twins' occur again and again in Chambers's Dictionary, under the article Twins; nay, he adds still
more preposterously, 'Sometimes there are born *three* twins, as
in the instances of the *Horatii et Curiatii*; and sometimes there
have been *four*, or even *five*†.' And Dr. Johnson, in his Dictionary, has cited, without any disapproving comment, these
lines from Cowley,

> ' No weight of birth did on one side prevail,
> Two twins less even lie in Nature's scale.'

" It ought, however, to be observed, to the credit of Shakspeare, that in his Comedy of Errors, though the Gemini, Gemini, are the principal dramatis personæ, he has avoided this
error in language.

" I remain, dear Sir, yours truly,   S. DENNE."

74. " DEAR SIR,   *Wilmington, Oct. 4, 1797.*
" By the civility of Mr. Peete, I have had the perusal of the
third volume of the History of Kent in octavo; and sorry,
though not surprised, was I to find that, notwithstanding there
is an advance in price, the value of the performance is not increased. To me it seems probable, that there is not a sheet, a
half sheet, possibly I shall not deviate from the truth, if I should
say, not a quarter of a sheet, of additions and corrections, when
he certainly might have been indebted, under these two articles,
to Thorpe's Antiquities in folio, and to that more diminutive
tome, the Kentish Traveller's Companion. When at the Spring-
head in Southfleet, he again mentions the long-contested antiquarian question, the site of the Vagniacæ Station. He takes
not the least notice of the learned, ingenious, and pertinent letter upon the subject from Mr. Landon to Mr. Thorpe; and for
the grotesque figures upon the porch of Chalk Church, he refers
to the plate in the Bibliotheca Topographica Britannica, No. VI.;
when being an F.S.A. he must be aware, that there is in Archæologia, vol. XII. a more correct engraving of the jolly toper and
his laughing companions, with an attempt to illustrate the design of this preposterous decoration of a sacred edifice. Sir

* While this sheet is printing, a similar case occurs: " 1830. Jan. 3.
At Maulden Mill, Beds, died Mr. Edward Pennyfather; and Jan. 11,
at the same place, Mr. Isaac Pennyfather. They were twins, and lived
to be nearly 77 years of age."
† " Mem. These paragraphs are judiciously omitted in the new edition
of Chambers's Dictionary. S. D."

John Henniker, Bart. of Newton-hall and Stratford-house, in
the county of Essex, is the Mecænas to whom this volume is
addressed; and, in justice to the author, the dedication is not
penned in that extravagant style which distinguished that prefixed to the second volume.

" You could not avoid noticing in the public prints, that the
Master of Bene't * was, by a decisive majority of thirty-one,
foiled in his attempt to be the Principal Librarian of Alma
Mater, vice the late Dr. Farmer; but perhaps you may not be
fully apprised of the manœuvres that left him in such an unexpected minority, for, before the poll or ballot commenced, an
opinion prevailed that it would be a close contest. The account
I had from Fellow Currey was to this purport: It seems that
the practice is for the Heads of Houses to put two persons in
nomination; and, as they are generally partial to one of their
own corps, the scheme is to start against him one who is not
likely to be a formidable competitor. Mr. Davies, of Trinity,
not coming under this predicament, his name was not returned
to the Senate; but not being aware that he should be thus excluded the chance of a poll, he had applied to his distant friends
to come in and support him, nor was there time allowed to stop
their progress. The consequence was, that they resented the
trick that had been played off to the prejudice of their friend,
and espoused Mr. Kerrich. Mr. Currey says, that our Master,
from an indolence that is habitual to him, was too remiss at the
beginning of the canvass; and he adds, that he is very much
disappointed with his ill success, for, not aware how many there
were upon the road on the solicitation of Mr. Davies, he and
his managers had flattered themselves, that among the resiants
he should secure so many votes, that a few outlyers would be
sufficient; and, I understood, he had every vote in St. John's-
college except one. His nuptial union with a niece of Mr.
Mainwaring certainly gave him a great advantage in that Society.

" When I returned Ascham's School-master, I believe I forgot to mention that, though Camden has noticed him as an
amateur of cock-fighting, and, though he himself refers to a
treatise written by him on that barbarous sport, these are circumstances omitted by the late Dr. Pegge in his Memoir on
Cock-fighting, printed in Archæologia. I think it does not
appear, that the treatise was ever published; nor do I find, from
Tanner's Bibliotheca Britannica, that the MS. copy is extant.

" At p. 76 of the School-master, Ascham has sketched the
character of Watson, Bishop of Lincoln; and the editor has
subjoined this note, ' This learned Prelate has left nothing behind him, that I know of, but a copy of Latin verses, to recommend Mr. Seton s Logic to the world.' But Upton was mistaken, as you may be satisfied, by turning to Tanner's Bibliotheca Britannica, p. 754.

* The Rev. Philip Douglas, D. D.

" Mr. Woodhouse, whom the Chancellor has, as keeper of the King's conscience, presented to the Stall in Rochester Cathedral, vacant by the resignation of Mr. Cooper, was tutor to Earl Gower at Christ Church, if not when he was at school. As Mr. Woodhouse has two parochial benefices in Shropshire, a Stall at Gloucester, or at Bristol, would be more convenient; and perhaps, through the interest of his pupil, or his pupil's sire, the Marquis of Stafford, an exchange may be obtained.

" In the Maidstone Journal of this week it is announced, that the Histories of Gravesend and Milton, by Pocock, will be published in the current month. With the literary talents of the author, I have so small an acquaintance, that I am not competent to form a judgment how much or how little information is likely to obtained from his work.

" I am, dear Sir, yours truly, S. DENNE."

---

75. " DEAR SIR, *Wilmington, Oct. 26,* 1797.

" The pen is resumed to thank you for your communications in two well filled sheets of letter-post; and to make for them the best return in the power of a recluse rustic, who can know but little of what is passing in the learned, the busy, and the gay world.

" As a quondam Benedictine, I heartily congratulate you that there is now one Fellow of the old House of the antiquarian cast. With such a treasure as the Society are possessed of, by the munificence of the illustrious Parker, there ought ever to be of that school one disciple at least as conversant in the MSS. as in a, b, c. To your *entre nous* innuendo, concerning another Fellow, I pen in a whisper my assent, being satisfied that neither *Nulla dies sine linea*, nor *Sic curre ut capias*, could be a suitable motto to his armorial shield; and I regret the unaptness, because it cannot be denied that there is much capability in the person alluded to; but we must both of us have observed, that pupil-mongers are not always the most studious men, or patterns of industry to the lads. Who could have a stronger propensity to a lounge than tutor Barnardiston? nor was there, as I have understood, an alteration for the better, after he became Master of Bene't and Librarian Principal of the University: however, as in duty bound, I ought to allow, that my last tutor was ever busy, though to be sure he was very often about it and about it.

" Very different is the account I have had of the predicating talents of the titular Bishop of Waterford; but it is to be considered, that it was indirectly from those who could believe *quia impossibile est,* who saw no objections to tenets preposterous, which the preacher attempted to illustrate. As to your question about the antiquity of Sermons in the vulgar tongue, are there not some Saxon homilies in print, and a great many in MS.? As Prelate Gundulph occasionally preached *ad populum*, it must be presumed that he addressed them in the language of the country in which they were born, and not in Latin or French. It appears, however, that the congregation were more affected by the action of the Bishop than by his expressions; and that on his display of the character of Mary Magdalen, they wept because he shed tears. ' Cessabant verba, lacrimæ Sermonem explebant. Hoc autem maxime fiebat, cum in festivitate Mariæ Magdalenæ de ejus pœnitentiâ vel lacrimis Sermonem ad populum faciebat. Recitans illius lacrimas, lacrimans et ipse cæteros ad lacrimas succendebat.' A. S. vol. II. p. 286, ' Si vis me flere, dolendum est primum ipse tibi,' was the rule given by Horace; but perhaps the right reverend builder of churches and of castles, (of temples dedicated to the Saviour and Prince of Peace, and of fortresses for the abode of the agents of war and the destroyers of mankind,) might be better read in the De Architectura of Vitruvius than in De Arte Poetica. Thus much about a preacher of the higher class, and in a cathedral; as to pulpits in country churches, rarely was the word of God delivered from them in consequence of the ignorance of Rectors, Vicars, and Curates; and, in order to obviate this difficulty at the time of the Reformation, Itinerant Clerks from the two Universities had a special warrant to preach to the people; but within a century what an alteration ensued, as the hypochondriac author of the Anatomy on Melancholy forebore printing the many Sermons he had in his tin-box because there was then such a number printed that whole teams of oxen could not draw them!

" Since I wrote last, I have had, after a suspension for almost twelve months, a long letter from my ingenious and learned correspondent at Gravesend *, upon the subject which has for a much longer period engaged his thoughts, viz. an inquiry into the origin and progress of what is called, for a reason not clearly known, the Gothic Style of Architecture, and the principles on which it was founded. I would I could add, that he was near bringing his proposed treatise to perfection; but he has formed a plan upon so extensive a scale, that it does not seem likely he should complete it, whilst, in the Ordnance department its officers have such a multiplicity of business; and till the war shall be at an end (of which who can prognosticate the termination?) there must be much to do, and a close confinement.

" Having been a kind of sponsor that Mr. Clarke, after he became F.A.S. would become an acting, instead of a sleeping, partner, I was pleased to see that he had not forgot what I had promised for him to yourself and Mr. Ord. And thus he writes, ' Let me now make known to you, that I have not, by any means, given up the subject recommended by a gentleman at Wilmington, viz. an explanation of the title of a chapel at the Old Palace at Westminster, denominated the Chapel of St. Mary

* Mr. Clarke.

of Pity of the Piew;' and in another page of his letter he
acquaints me, that he has two drawings which he proposes to
exhibit at Somerset-place. One of them is of a four sided
mitre, from the Church of Bobbing near Sittingbourne; the
other, of a not inelegant female bust, surmounted with a crescent lunette, on the capital of a pillar in the Church of Muck-
inge in Essex. This appears to us to be an unique ornament;
and if it be so, it will not be easy to determine what the artist
might mean by it. Query then, did the like ever occur to you in
stone, or in any illuminated figure in a missal, or other devotional MS.? Should Mr. Clarke submit the latter drawing to the
inspection of the Society, I rather suspect he will take the
opportunity of controverting Mr. Ledwich's explanation of the
hieroglyphical devices on the capitals of the pillars in the crypt
of Canterbury Cathedral, as published in Archæologia, vol. VIII.;
for though he professes to entertain a just regard for the writer
of that paper, and obligations for knowledge acquired from it,
I perceive he differs in opinion from him, that many of the
symbols, or emblems, are of a Paganish cast, and borrowed from
Egyptian temples.

"His Grace of Richmond has, I observe, been complimented
by the Premier with the nomination of his eleve Clerk * to the
See of Chichester. The promotion certainly throws some
weight into the Duke's scale of interest in the county of Sussex,
though not so much in the present days as heretofore.

"Yours truly,   S. Denne."

76. "Dear Sir,   Wilmington, Nov. 4, 1797.
"Dr. Latham has not been returned many days from a tour
into Wiltshire, where he passed more than a fortnight near Chip-
penham, with Colonel Montagu †, of the Linnée cast. This

---

* Dr. Buckner.

† The Montagus of Lackham are descended from James, the third son
of Henry first Earl of Manchester, who acquired the estate by marriage
with the heiress of Baynard, which family enjoyed it for two centuries.
George Montagu, Esq. for many years a Lieut.-Colonel in the Wiltshire
Militia, was fifth in descent from James. His mother was Eleanor, daughter and co-heiress of Thomas Hedges, Esq. of Alderton in Gloucestershire, and grand-daughter of Sir Charles Hedges, Secretary of State to
Queen Anne, many of whose papers descended to Col. Montagu; and
after his death, on the 6th of August 1816, upwards of three hundred
letters of John Duke of Marlborough, and including three notes of the
Queen, were sold by public auction, and produced 570 guineas (see an
account of these MSS. in the Gentleman's Magazine, LXXXVI. ii. p. 135.)
The Colonel was author of an "Ornithological Dictionary; or, Alphabetical Synopsis of British Birds," 2 vols. 8vo. 1802, Supplement 1813
(reviewed in the Gentleman's Magazine, vol. LXXXIII. pt. ii. p. 255);
"Testacea Britannica; or, Natural History of British Shells, marine,
land, and fresh-water, including the most minute, systematically arranged,
and embellished with figures," 4to, 1803, Supplement, 1809, (reviewed
ibid. vol. LXXIX. p. 51); and also contributed to the Transactions of the

gentleman has been left by his brother a noble house built within five years; situated in the midst of a good estate, and the manor extensive to the river Avon, meandring by a considerable part of it; and which, with a very few modern improvements, might be made a charming place. ' I found,' continues the Doctor, ' at Lackham, a library of between four and five thousand books; but scarcely any in the line of my friend's pursuit, which is that of Natural History, chiefly old law and divinity, with some respectable books of antiquities, likewise very many on Heraldry, collected by one of the family, a Mr. Gore. These the Colonel means to keep; most of the others will come under the hammer, and the produce to purchase Natural History, Travels, &c. I forgot to say, that there is also a very good and large collection of Roman and Greek Coins, which the Colonel would dispose of if he knew how to set about it; but I could not advise him in this particular, and it must be left for future consideration.' I have copied this confession of incapability in the Doctor, with the view of affording a knowing gentleman an opportunity of setting the Colonel about the right way of disposing of his antique pieces of money, supposing, in the present scarcity of a circulating medium, this should be deemed an advisable season for offering them to sale.

" Whilst the Doctor, on his return home, was meditating in the Abbey Church at Bath, his eye caught another brother Linnean; and he adds, that he saw with concern, that his friend looked very poorly, and that he understood that he was at Bath for the benefit of his health, having much declined since July, when the Doctor paid him a visit at Downing. May there not then be some reason to apprehend, that poor Pennant will not utter many more ' Last Words?' He must be now in the 72d year of his age, for he was half past 67 in 1792, when he an-

Linnæan Society, of which he was a Fellow, in 1796 "Descriptions of three rare species of British Birds;" in 1802 "Description of several marine animals, found on the south coast of Devonshire;" in 1803 "On some species of British quadrupeds, birds, and fishes;" in 1805 "Of the larger and lesser species of Horseshoe Bats, proving them to be distinct; with a description of Vespertilio Barbastellies, taken in the South of Devonshire;" in 1807 "On the natural history of the Falco Cyaneus and Pygargus;" in 1811 "Of several new or rare animals, principally marine, discovered on the south coast of Devonshire;" and "Of some new rare marine British shells and animals;" in 1815 "Some Remarks on the Natural History of the Black Stork, for the first time captured in Great Britain;" and (after his death, communicated by Dr. Leach) in 1817 "Descriptions of five British species of the Genus Terebella of Linnée." Col. Montagu chose a beautiful retirement in Devonshire for the promotion of his studies in the works of nature. He died at his seat there, called Knowle House, Aug. 28, 1815, in his 64th year. Colonel Montagu married Anne, daughter of William Courtenay, Esq. by Lady Jane Stuart, sister to John Earl of Bute, the celebrated Prime Minister. She died at Bristol Hotwells, Feb. 10, 1816, and was survived little more than a month by her brother John Courtenay, Esq. a distinguished Member of the House of Commons, where he sat for upwards

nounced the period of his literary life, well termed by the
Monthly Reviewers 'only a fit of suspended animation.'

" Since Michaelmas my pen has been occasionally employed
in endeavouring to elucidate a miraculous incident recorded in
the Gospel, which has, as appears to me, been misconceived from
a want of close attention to the context; and among the erroneous expositors alluded to, is a clerk now living, high in rank
and in repute. I have made up my mind upon the subject; but
am sensible that I ought not to obtrude my thoughts upon the
public, unless convinced, after mature deliberation, that I may
not do more harm than good by letting them transpire.

" In a letter from Mr. Archdeacon Law, dated Oct. 24, was
this paragraph, ' The Dean announces the death of the Provost
of King's *. He died at Bath in the preceding week. A too long
continuance in the damp situation of Denham (the Provost's
living) is assigned as the primary cause of his indisposition; but
I admit not the cause, as a mortification was, on examination,
found on his back three days before his death. Drs. Sumner,
George Heath, Foster, and Mr. Goodall, are the candidates for
the Provostship. The contest is expected to be between the two
former; and it is suggested by the Dean, that the third is only
started with the view of serving Heath; but according to the
London Herald of Nov. 5, the Master fled the pit, and left it to
the other two to fight the battle. Who may be the victorious
wight you may know, though I am ignorant.' My correspondent
adds these particulars concerning vacant stalls : ' The Master of
Jesus-college, Dr. Pearce, has long been named for the Deanery
of Ely. The Dean asserts, that the prehend of Westminster,
vacated in the preceding year by the demise of Dr. Wake, is not
yet filled up; though Mr. Lukin, a near relation of Mr. Windham †, has been invariably named for the successor.' The Arch-

of thirty years, and author of an Essay on the character of Dr. Johnson,
and several other literary productions (see Gent. Mag. vol. LXXXVI.
pp. 375, 467). Colonel Montagu was succeeded in his estates at Lackham and Alderton by his son, the present George Conway Courtenay
Montagu, Esq. and left also two daughters, Louisa-Matilda, married to
Matthew Crawford, Esq. and Eleonora.

* William Cooke, D. D. Dean of Ely, of whom a memoir is printed in
the " Literary Anecdotes," vol. IX. p. 629; and see also vol. VII.
pp. 94, 541.

† The Very Rev. George William Lukin, Dean of Wells, was half-brother to the Rt. Hon. William Windham. He was of Christ's-college,
Cambridge, LL. B. 1797, incorporated of St. Alban-hall, Oxford, June 21,
1798, and proceeded D. C. L. two days after; was preferred to a prebendal
stall at Westminster in 1797, and to the Deanery of Wells in 1799. He
died at Wells, Nov. 27, 1812, possessed of that dignity and the Rectories
of Felbrigge and Aylmerton, Norfolk, which were in Mr. Windham's
patronage. He left a widow, who died at Brighton, April 15, 1814; and
three sons, 1. William Lukin, R. N. to whom, after the death of his
widow, Mr. Windham left his estate, amounting to £.6000 a year; he
married in 1801, Anne, daughter of Peter Thellusson, and aunt to the present Lord Rendlesham, and has a numerous family; he has taken the

deacon then notices its being said, that the King is very urgent to have a day of thanksgiving on account of our late victory, and to go to St. Paul's on the occasion; but that the latter being objected to by some, the adoption of it is doubtful.

" Yours truly,   S. DENNE."

---

77. " DEAR SIR,   *Wilmington, Nov.* 28, 1797.

" The sentence against poor Bridgen, the Curate of Shoreditch, was very severe, as he was not chargeable with any immoral offence; the utmost that could be imputed to him was a want of consideration in neglecting to inquire of the parties whether they were of age; for if this question had been put, and a true answer not returned to it, the Judge who presided in the Court of the Bishop of London, whether he were the Chancellor himself I do not recollect, declared he should have dismissed the libel; and it was in consequence of this suggestion, that some waggish friends of Mr. Bridgen were wont, when required to perform the ceremony, to ask the bride whether she was of age, though all her teeth marks were out of her mouth. From my father's silence as to Mr. Bridgen's not preaching again after the three years' suspension was expired, I must own I somewhat doubt your having been truly informed in this particular; but of one thing I am confident, that my father and his other friends gratuitously supplied for him the pulpits into which he was prohibited entering whilst under sentence.

" Much obliged shall I be to you for the loan of the Lusiad of Camoens, by Mickle, because I am assured there is in the preface and notes not a little historial intelligence; and I may elicit a spark on the emblem and motto so frequently displayed in the proposed mausoleum of Emanuel at Batalha. Since, in Fanshaw's translation, of which I had a transient glimpse in the library of Sion-college, I thought I discovered a few words to the purport I have in contemplation. Entirely do I agree with you, that there are not any such letters as *C* or *Y*, and that *E* is the only letter discernible; but, with submission, though you burn a little, as the phrase is, there is a device that has not

name of Windham, and is now a Rear-Admiral : 2. Robert Lukin, Esq. now First Clerk of the War Office; he married in 1808 Catherine, daughter of Bishop Hallifax ; 3. the Rev. John Lukin, of Oriel-college, Oxford, M. A. 1807 ; he was collated to the prebend of Combe in the Church of Wells in 1807 by Bishop Beadon ; presented to the Vicarage of Combe St. Nicholas, co. Somerset, by his father as Dean of Wells in 1809, and collated to the rectory of Nursling, Hants, by Dr. North, Bishop of Winchester, in the same year. He married in 1810 Miss Emma Jenner, of Etchingham, Sussex, who died April 30, 1813. Mr. Lukin is now Prebendary of Wells, and Rector of Nursling.—Robert Lukin, Esq. brother to the Dean, died in Dorset-street, Portman-square, Oct. 19, 1816, aged 82. His only daughter was married in 1794 to George Whalley Risdale, Esq. of the Inniskilling dragoons.

made the same impression upon your eye it has done upon mine. Indeed, of the device here alluded to, I do not despair of giving a satisfactory solution; and I trust I shall be more lucky in my surmise, touching the words within the rings, than was Father de Sousa, who hardly merits the title of Antiquariolus.

" In a letter last week from my correspondent at Gravesend was the following: ' The Mucking Head I fancy myself convinced to be a portrait of Mary Abbess of Barking, 1173, figured under the representation of the Patroness of herself and of her house, the Virgin Mary. This notion, supported as well as I am able, is designed as a scrap for Somerset-place, as my essay on our Lady of Pity is shortly to be consigned to your pleasure.' In another page of his letter, Mr. Clarke wishes for some information concerning an altar to our Lady of Pity in the Galilee of Durham Cathedral, as noticed by Hutchinson; and to the extracts desired, I have subjoined five pages of notes collected of altars of Pity, and of images and pictures appertaining to the same. It were to be wished that the Chapel of La Pieu, by St. Stephen's Chapel, were re-surveyed by a person of judgment; and, in my opinion, the site of it ought to be fixed with precision, and an attempt made to determine when this beautiful chapel was first converted into a kitchen, and annexed to the mansion of the Auditor of the Exchequer.

" Considering the season of the year, the designed voyage of the Sovereign to the Nore and Blackstakes had not my concurrence; and happy was I to find, that the new Knight Banneret had safely re-landed at Greenwich his inestimable passenger. Winds and waves are of a democratic cast; or, to borrow a line from the Tempest of Shakspeare,

' What care these *roarers* for the name of King ?' "

---

78. Mr. Gough to Mr. Denne.

" Dear Sir,   Dec. 12, 1797.

" What a foolish question must I appear to have asked you about suspension and the case of Bridgen, when I might have answered myself respecting both from Burn's Ecclesiastical Law and Ellis's History of Shoreditch.

" I shall wait with as much patience as I can for your and Mr. Clarke's respective papers. The application of the Virgin Mary's portrait to any of her namesakes is not novel. Hearne conceived she furnished a model for the Queen on the Eleanor crosses; and some such crosses, between Paris and St. Denis, where the body of St. Louis rested, were called Maries. In some late review, a French writer is quoted for saying, that several antique images of Iris in basalt, in some monastic museum, were destroyed as black Maries.

" Hutchinson's account of the Lady of Pity's altar in the

Gallilee at Durham, is taken *verbatim* from Davies's Rites of Durham. It seems thereby, that this was the style of the Virgin Mother holding her dead son on her knee, in contradistinction to her holding him living in her arms. *Pieu* is old and modern French for *palus*, a stake. If you have authority for giving this term to the Cross, which in the New Testament is called a tree, q. d. *stipes;* Greek Ξυλον, our Lady of the *Pieu* will be equivalent to our Lady of the Crucifix. Du Cange, in *furca,* joins *palus* with *furca;* but there *palus* is the post wherein the quarters were fixed after the body was taken down from the *furca.* I cannot, at present, pursue the inquiry further; but what light can be derived from the Chapel of that name at Westminster, I do not immediately see.

"Since the Sovereign will neither hear us nor the Church against his going publicly to Church in the depth of winter, and I have heard the thanksgiving prayer read its full number of times, I shall be boy enough to make an effort to see the procession, having always been fond of such pageants.

"Whether Mr. Pinkerton's plan in the last Gentleman's Magazine supersedes mine, or whether either of us will have the honour of introducing Matthew Paris into the world under a a new form, is uncertain.

"Much as I may wish to read your and Mr. C.'s papers, they must not be addressed to me either as Director or F. A. S. for I have resigned both titles at the Council this day*. The act of this day is the result of premeditation, I having served the Society of Antiquaries long enough.

"A thirteenth volume of Archæologia was ordered to be put on the stocks; now you have some prospect of figuring in it.
                    "Yours truly,   R. Gough."

_____

79. Mr. Denne to Mr. Gough.

"Dear Sir,   *Wilmington, Dec.* 19, 1797.
"Of the death of my sister Denne you will possibly be apprised before this letter reaches Enfield; and, in consequence of this melancholy event, on me has devolved the sole care of my grievously afflicted brother, and the management of his affairs. He is in the same state in which he has been upwards of twenty years; one day quite composed and perfectly sensible, and the next day much agitated and deranged. Perhaps hereafter I may state to you more circumstantially this singular case; at present I had rather decline dwelling upon a subject that is very painful to me.

_____

* "Not in person, as Mr. Craven Ord seems to think you encouraged him to believe; for I must have expressed myself very ambiguously indeed in a former letter to you respecting your Arabic numerals, which I never intended to re-demand in person."

" Since this change in our family, there has of course been
an entire suspension of my literary and antiquarian pursuits;
and I must frequently be moving to Maidstone, and have there,
whilst not conversing with my brother in his tranquil hours, a
variety of business to engross my attention.

" Your resignation of the office of Director S. A. did not surprise me, considering what is said to have passed between yourself and the Council, or, rather, a junto thereof, some years
since; but, with submission, as the offence was not imputable
to the corps in general, in my opinion you was not warranted in
withdrawing yourself from the Society. Had I been aware of
your having such a design in contemplation, I should have been
tempted to have hinted to you that your friend Mr. King was
still F. S. A.

" Mr. Clarke, ten days ago, left for me at Dartford his Dissertation on the Chapel of our Lady la Pieu; but I have not been
able to pay it a due attention, and fear I shall not for a week or
ten days to come. As you joined with Mr. Craven Ord in starting the subject, you shall have the perusal of it before our
friend conveys it to Secretary Brand.

" By the post this morning, I was favoured with a long letter
from my correspondent at Rumsey, in which are the under-
written articles that may afford you some intelligence and
amusement:

" ' Col. Montagu's books and coins will come under the hammer about February next *. Of the former there are some good
things, and much trash; and the same of the latter. Mr. Miles
looked over the coins in my presence; and he thinks that many
of them will go at a pretty high rate, and would have risen
higher were it not for the deluge sent to London from France
for disposal within a year or two past.

" ' I had the honour of calling on the author of the China
Embassy†, and thanking him for my copy of the same. I learn
that it sells for a greatly increased price; so far I am safe.

" ' A copy of Pocock's Gravesend overtook me in York-street.
All I can say is, that I find it much better than I expected.

" ' At my return from town, I found a letter from the editor
of the Cyclopedia Britannica, wishing my opinion whether a
supplement to that work will be well received. I have before
given my affirmative, and as they wished, shall certainly say so
a second time; for there are many articles which they mean to
mend, and I am sure stand much in need of correction.

" ' The Linnean Society increases rapidly; more than 250
members; and we mean to publish a volume annually. The
fourth is in great forwardness.'

" I remain, dear Sir, yours sincerely,   S. DENNE."

* Two sales, one of Col. Montagu's library and the other of his coins,
took place at Leigh and Sotheby's in 1798; a third, of " Greek coins
and English medals," after his death in 1815.
† Sir George Staunton.

80. " Dear Sir, *Wilmington, Dec.* 31, 1797.
" Be pleased to accept my thanks for the loan of the two
works, great and little. I have not a doubt I shall acquire much
knowledge and amusement from Mr. Mickle's labours; though I
may miss obtaining that particular article of information that
occasioned my inquiry after the Lusiad. But my progress in so
thick a quarto must now be very slow; for you are little aware
in what a series of perplexing business I must be unavoidably
involved by the late change at Maidstone. Since the melancholy
event, I have been already three times to visit my afflicted brother, and to superintend the management of his affairs; and to-
morrow, after making an early breakfast, I shall be travelling
the same road; nor shall I return till Friday, being willing to
converse with my brother on two of his tranquil days; and on
those I sit with him from between two and three o'clock to
eleven, with an exception to about an hour after dinner, when
he is in the habit of taking a nap of refreshment and forgetfulness. To debar him of the comfort of these hours would be
most unkind, as he is always perfectly sensible and communicative, though at the same time it prevents my attention to his
business.
" In June last the implements of archery were cast aside by
the Royal Kentish Bowmen, and the sock and buskin assumed
instead thereof; since then their theatre has been considerably
enlarged and embellished. Twice in the last week they enacted
the Merry Wives of Windsor, with the Children in the Wood;
Master Ford by my 'Squire of Wilmington-common; Falstaff by
the second son of the late Counsellor Maddox; and Parson Sir
Hugh Evans by Parson Dodd. To the discredit, or the credit
of the females in the purlieus of Dartford Heath, there not
being two merry wives to be found who chose to appear upon
stage boards, Dames Ford and Page, and eke Anne Page, were
brought from the vicinity of Drury-lane and Covent-garden.
" The date of the letter I am finishing being the last I shall
write to you in the year that is so near expiring, I shall conclude with a tender of my fervent wishes, that the approaching
year may be prosperous to Mrs. Gough and yourself. For the
reasons again and again assigned, it must be a year of perplexity
to, dear Sir, yours truly, S. Denne."

---

81. " Dear Sir, *Wilmington, Feb.* 6, 1798.
" Biddenden, not Boddington, is the name of the parish to
which his Grace of Canterbury has collated Mr. Nares, son-in-
law of the Duke of Marlborough. It will be lucky for him,
and unexpectedly so, should he find his benefice worth £.400
a year; but half what is commonly said, may in this instance,
as in most cases, be nearer the truth. The Rectory of Bidden-

den is in Liber Val. rated high, very high, *viz.* at £.35 *per* year;
but in this parish, as in many parishes in Romney Marsh, there
is a *modus* established upon the marsh land.

"Yours truly,   S. DENNE."

82. " DEAR SIR,   *Wilmington, March* 8, 1798.
" On Friday last I was favoured with Mr. Ord's report of his
inquiries after the authorities cited by Newcourt, &c. touching
the appointment of Priests to officiate in the Chapel of la Pieu,
and unluckily *non invent.* was the return ; and a week before,
my correspondent of the Ordnance Office, Gravesend, apprised
me, that he had not succeeded in his Bullarium pursuit.   From
his letter I will transmit the following paragraph : ' You are
now also to be acquainted a Bullarium has been searched.   Not
a mention occurs of Earl Rivers, or his Chapel, among the entries
under Sextus IV. ; and I am disposed to think, that grants of
indulgences were not always thought of sufficient consequence
for forming a part of this *opus absolutissimum.*   The bookseller
went after me with better success.   He had been Librarian to
the University of Caen ; a priest, a friendly man, and has a
good assortment of books in a line I am pleased with, huddled
together at the sign of the Green Dragon, King-street, Golden-
square, where the curious are made to pay not immoderately
for being gratified. Here I met with a Ceremoniale Episcoporum,
with wood-cuts (Romæ, 1600), a work which completes my
collection on that head.`
" It is the opinion of Mr. Wrighte, to which S. Denne accedes,
that the Chapel in question was not dedicated to the Blessed
Virgin, but to St. Mary, the sister of Lazarus and Martha ; and
therefore I wish to peruse the memoirs, authentic, or legendary,
of the said Saints.
" Part of my employment, during my stays at Maidstone, has
been to read and to destroy family epistles.   Not fewer than a
1000 scribbled by me, for the amusement of my poor brother
since his calamity befel him, have been committed to the flames.
In my last visit I met with a parcel from my father to my mother,
which, also, are now out of sight ; but from two or three I
could not forbear making short extracts.   A copy of one I now
transmit, because I know you will be amused with an anecdote
of a *quondam* Head of a House of our Alma Mater.   The letter
bears date Sept. 10, 1750, and was written by my father when
he and my brother were Bishop Mawson's guests in the Episcopal Palace at Chichester. ' We have,' he observes, ' dined at
Mr. Hamilton's, who is one of the principal among the Counsel
in Chancery, and Recorder of this City *.   He has an exceed-

* William Hamilton, Esq. father to the Right Hon. William Gerard
Hamilton, of "single-speech" memory. (See the Gentleman's Maga-

ingly pleasant seat about four miles off, which, with a very good
estate around it, came to him by his lady, who is a most agreeable woman. The Bishop of Ely, it is said, made his addresses
to her whilst Dr. Gooch and Residentiary of this Church, before
he married Cæsar's wife. The courtship came (says report) to
this short poetical issue,

'Madam, will you please,
To have and to hold the Master of Keys?'

This was cut with a diamond upon a glass; for which another was returned, thus inscribed:

' Dr. Gooch, I should please,
(Was you not so old)
To have and to hold
With the Master of Keys.'

"My communicative correspondent, Mr. Archdeacon Law,
tells me, 'The contest about the See of Chichester is terminated;
and St. Giles's is to be holden *in commendam.* The Bishop*
was consecrated last Sunday; Dr. Napleton, a man of literary
character, was the Preacher on the occasion †. You have doubt-

zine, vol. LXXIX. p. 529.) The lady was Miss Mary Smyth, his second
wife, who was the heiress of Apuldram near Chichester, and died s. p. in
1755: but bequeathed the estate to her celebrated stepson. See Dallaway's History of Sussex, vol. I. p. 97.

* Dr. Buckner.

† The family of Napleton probably derived its name from a hamlet in
the parish of Kemsey, Worcestershire. Marsh Napleton, Esq. of Ten-
bury, in that county, died in 1768; as about the same time did Neal
Napleton, Esq. merchant in London. There was a Stephen Napleton, a
physician, of All Souls'-college, Oxford, M. A. 1688; M.B. 1697; M. D.
1700; and a Thomas Napleton, of Oriel-college, M.A. 1712. There have
been also of the same University three bearing the name of John; the
first of Magdalen-college, M. A. 1676; the second of Corpus Christi,
M.A. 1712; B.D. 1721; the third of Brazenose, M.A. 1761; B. and
D. D. 1789. The last is the literary man mentioned in the text. He
was for some time a Fellow of Brazenose; and was presented to the Rectory of Wold in Northamptonshire by that Society in 1777. He became
Chaplain to Dr. Butler, Bishop of Hereford, who preferred him to a
Canonry of Hereford, and he was possessed of that dignity when called
upon to deliver "A Sermon, preached in the Cathedral Church of Here-
ford, at the Meeting of the three Choirs of Worcester, Hereford, and
Gloucester, September 9, 1789," afterwards printed; as was "A Sermon, preached in St. Mary's Church in the University of Oxford, at
the anniversary meeting of the Governors of the Radcliffe Infirmary,
June 19, 1792." Dr. Napleton married Dec. 4, 1793, Miss Daniell, of
Truro. In 1795 he published, in an octavo volume, "Advice to a Student in the University, containing the qualifications and duties of a
Minister of the Gospel in the Church of England;" a work excellently
adapted to its object, and which is noticed in the review of the Gentleman's Magazine, vol. LXVI. p. 136. In 1796 he was collated by his
friend Bishop Butler to the Chancellorship of the Diocese of Hereford.
In 1798 he published, by command of the Archbishop, the Sermon he
preached at Lambeth on the Consecration of Dr. Buckner to the See of

less heard, that the Bishop of London* gives Lectures at St. James's Church on each succeeding Friday in Lent, Good Friday excepted. Our Dean means to be a regular attendant. With the introductory Lecture he was highly pleased; it contained a summary of the contents of the Bible from Genesis to the Revelations, and he describes it as being peculiarly neat and clear, and as far exceeding his expectations. I have had no other account of the second Lecture than that it was numerously attended, not only by the Clergy, but by many of the high orders of laity. I remain, dear Sir, yours truly, S. DENNE."

---

83. "DEAR SIR, *Wilmington, March 20, 1798.*
"To Mr. Ord's doubt whether the Speaker's kitchen was ever the Chapel of our Lady la Pieu, I cannot readily subscribe, because, if Froissart's evidence is to be relied on, there was a little detached Chapel in which Richard the Second was present at Mass, and made his offerings to the image of our Lady that worked miracles; and because, if Weever was not misinformed, this Chapel was re-built by Antony Earl Rivers. Obliged am I to you for your citation from Tanner's Monasticon, p. 320; and I shall be obliged to Mr. Ord to examine whether Pat. 16 Rich. II. be correctly cited.

"Your not finding in Butler or Villegas the devout Mary, as well as the much cumbered Martha, enrolled among the Popish Saints, has again, as you express it, put us out to sea; I therefore propose a question to be answered by you or Mr. Ord, either from printed evidence, or from the *viva voce* evidence of some emigrant Priests,—whether there are, or rather whether there were not lately, in France and in Flanders Churches and Chapels,

Chichester (see Gent. Mag. vol. LXIX. p. 967); in 1800 "The Duty of Churchwardens respecting the Church," 12mo. (ibid. LXX. p. 645); in 1804 "Advice to a Minister of the Gospel in the United Church of England and Ireland; being a continuation of 'Advice to a Student in the University.' To which is added, A Sermon on the Pastoral Care," (ibid. LXXIV. p. 1039); and in 1806 "Sermons for the use of Colleges, Schools, and Families," two vols. 8vo. In 1810 Dr. Napleton was presented by the Dean and Chapter of Hereford to the Vicarage of Lugwardine; and in the same year he was collated by Bishop Luxmoore to the office of Prelector in the Cathedral of Hereford. He died holding those preferments, together with the Rectory of Stoke Edith, and the Mastership of Ledbury Hospital, Dec. 9, 1817, in his 80th year. His sister, Miss Napleton, of Hammersmith, died at Newbury, July 13, 1807, aged 60; another died unmarried at Tockington, Gloucestershire, in 1822, aged 80; (a third, it is presumed) Elizabeth, wife of William Mullen, Esq. of the Bank of England, and third daughter of the late Rev. John Napleton, Rector of Pembridge, Herefordshire (the member of Corpus Christi-college named at the commencement of this note), died March 20, 1805.—There was another clergyman of this uncommon name, Timothy Napleton, of Trinity-college, Cambridge, M. A. *per saltum* 1785, Rector of North Bovey, co. Devon, 1802, and also Rector of Powderham, where he died Jan 16, 1816, aged 59. * Dr. Porteus.

or Monasteries for Monks or Nuns, or Hospitals, dedicated to
St. Mary the Pious. When Mr. Wrighte was abroad, he understood that the said St. Mary was revered as the Patroness of some
religious edifices, or of some charitable institutions; and he
imagines, that the Mary here meant might be the sister of
Martha and Lazarus.

" Before I had your letter, Mr. Clarke had apprised me of the
order of the Council for a less liberal use of the books in the
library, or rather out of the library of the Society of Antiquaries, than the members of the Society had been accustomed
to for some years; and the revival of such an order, I must
own, has not my approbation, as it must prevent my taking any
book to my lodgings, if in town, from a Monday to a Thursday
evening, and that was often my practice.

" Till you reminded me, it had slipt my memory that Bishop
Gooch's first wife was of the house of Sherlock; and I have
no doubt that she was the wife of Cæsar alluded to in my
father's letter. From what circumstance she acquired the appellation, I may have heard, and probably often did hear my father
and mother relate; but here is another lapse of memory, nor
does my brother recollect, though very frequently he is an
assistant to me when chatting on the days that are past.

" I remain, dear Sir, yours truly,   S. DENNE."

84. " DEAR SIR,   Wilmington, March 31, 1798.
" Mortifying is it, that four investigators antique should be
foiled by a monosyllable; and yet it should seem that you begin
to despair lest la Pieu should not be traced to its origin. Secretary Wrighte spoke confidently of his having, while in France,
heard of Religious Houses and Hospitals, which had for their
Patroness St. Mary the Pious. In my proposed return through
Rochester on Thursday, it is probable I may not have it in my
power to wait upon him.

" From Mr. Archdeacon Law I have had this piece of Cambridge intelligence, that the late Dr. Peckard * bequeathed to

* The Rev. Peter Peckard, D. D. was educated at Oxford, as a scholar
of Corpus Christi college, where he attained the degree of M.A. in 1741,
and was elected Fellow. In 1766 he was appointed Chaplain to the first
troop of Grenadier Guards; he served with the army in Germany, and
was then a convivial man; but when, through the patronage of Lord
Carysfort, he had become Rector of Fletton in Huntingdonshire, he
resided there with the strictest economy, and, after his elevation to the
Deanry of Peterborough, only gave one annual dinner to his Chapter. The
Deanry was then valeud at £400, the Rectory at £100. In 1777 he
had a dispensation to hold the Rectory of Fletton with that of Tansor
in Northamptonshire, to which he was presented by the Dean and Chapter of Lincoln; and he appears as a Prebendary of that Cathedral, when
admitted in 1781 to the Mastership of Magdalen college, Cambridge, on
the nomination of Sir John Griffin Griffin, K. B. He served the office of
Vice-Chancellor at Cambridge in 1784, and was admitted D. D. *per lit.*

Magdalen-college, the chief, if not the whole, of his fortune, after the death of his wife, who is aged; and that there is to be a

Reg. in 1785; and was appointed Dean of Peterborough in 1792. Dr. Peckard was author of the following works : The popular Clamours against the Jews indefensible ; a Sermon, preached at Honiton (1 Cor. ix. 20), Oct. 28, 1753, 8vo.; A Sermon on the Nature and Extent of Civil and Religious Liberty (1 Pet. ii. 16), 1754; A Dissertation on Rev. xi. 13, in which there is attempted to be shown that there is some reason to believe this Prophecy completed by the late Earthquake at Lisbon, 1755, 8vo (a review of which in the Gent. Mag. vol. XXVI. p. 138, was answered by Dr. Peckard in a subsequent number, p. 213) ; Observations on the Doctrine of an Intermediate State between Death and the Resurrection, with some remarks on Mr. Goddard's Sermon on the Subject, 1756; Further Observations on the doctrine of an Intermediate State, in answer to the Rev. Dr. Morton's Queries, 1757; Observations on Mr. Fleming's Survey, &c. 1759; The proper style of Christian Orations, a Sermon at Huntingdon (1 Cor. i. 21), Jan. 7, 1770; A Sermon at the Visitation of Archdeacon Cholwell, at Huntingdon (Rom. ix. 28), May 19, 1772; A Sermon on the unalterable nature of Vice and Virtue, against Lord Chesterfield's Doctrines (Isaiah, v. 20), preached at St. James's, Westminster, April 4, 1775, (see Gent. Mag. vol. XLVI. p. 132); The nature and extent of Civil and Religious Liberty, a Sermon, preached before the University of Cambridge, Nov. 5, 1781; Piety, Benevolence, and Loyalty recommended, another Sermon before the same University, Jan. 30, 1784 (Gent. Mag. vol. LIV. p. 611) ; A third Sermon before the same, intituled, Justice and Mercy recommended; and a fourth, The neglect of known Duty is Sin (on James, iv. 17); these were directed against the slave trade; and, on Dr. Peckard's becoming Vice-Chancellor in 1785, he proposed the ensuing question : " Anne liceat invitos in servitutem dare?" Memoirs of the Life of Mr. Nicholas Ferrar, 1791 (see a long review in Gent. Mag. vol. LXI. pp. 456—460) In the fifth volume of Wordsworth's Ecclesiastical Biography is a life of the same personage published, but not without some omissions, from Memoirs of the Life by Peckard. " The present edition," however, " it is presumed, is greatly increased in value by a large accession of very interesting papers, transcribed from the Lambeth library, which appear to have been written by Mr. John Ferrar, eldest brother of Nicholas, and the compiler of the original MS. from which Dr. Peckard's Memoirs are taken. They were written probably in the year 1653, but to whom they are addressed it does not appear." National Crimes the cause of National Punishment ; a discourse delivered in the Cathedral Church of Peterborough, on the Fast-day, Feb. 25, 1795 (reviewed in Gent. Mag. vol. LXV. p. 496). Dean Peckard lost his life by imprudently, three years before his death, cutting off a small wen on his cheek when shaving himself, after having for many years endured the trouble of avoiding it with his razor. It turned to a cancerous complaint, which the advice of London surgeons, and Dr. Kerr, of Northampton, could not relieve. He died Dec. 8, 1797, in his 83d year, being then Master of Magdalen college, Dean of Peterborough, Prebendary of Southwell (and Lincoln ?) and Rector of Fletton and Abbot's Ripton, Hunts. Lord Carysfort, the patron of Fletton, permitted him to name for his successor there the Rev. Richard Buck, Fellow of Magdalen college ; who allowed Dr. Peckard's widow to reside in the house, and enjoy the gardens, which she had much improved. She died at Fletton, Jan. 14, 1805, having in perfect health entertained a large party of friends on the preceding day.—After the death of Mrs. Peckard, the Dean left his fortune to augment the incomes of the Master and Fellows of Magdalen college. The two Scholarships he founded are called the

considerable accession to the revenue of the Master, and two Scholarships instituted of fifty pounds a year each. I had not imagined that it was in the power of the Doctor to amass so much wealth as is here suggested; and I imagined that he was a widower. The widow certainly cannot be on the bright side of threescore and ten, as pretty Miss Farren was a fashionable toast among the Cantabs above half a century ago.

"I am, dear Sir, yours truly,   S. Denne."

---

85. "Dear Sir,   *Wilmington, May* 10, 1798.
"Further inquiry after Mary the Pious, sister of Lazarus, and averred by Baronius of the Church of Rome, and Lightfoot of the Church of England, to be the same with Mary Magdalen, and of the number of religious and eleemosynary buildings dedicated to her honour, is, for the present, needless; but I am much inclined to believe, that my correspondent at Gravesend will not relinquish *la Pieu* for *de la Peur*, the holy well near the scullery, for what is styled by Dr. Wells, in our Saviour's journeyings, the Mountain of Precipitation; upon which, writes Maundrell, the Empress Helen, mother of Constantine, built a church.

Ferrar's Scholarships; they are worth *£.*65 *per annum*, and are perfectly open. In the Gentleman's Magazine for April 1799, appeared the following poetical "Essay towards a characteristic Epitaph on the late Dean of Peterborough:

> "If ' peace on earth, good-will tow'rds men,' may claim
> The blest distinction of the Christian name,
> Behold a Christian here; whose hallow'd dust
> Shall rise to glory with the good and just;
> Whose living energies were all supplied
> From the pure stream of Mercy's healing tide;
> Whose ardent pen, and latest breath, display
> Thy blessings, Peace! and War's destructive sway,
> While bright conviction proves thro' every line,
> The hands, tho' human, had a guide divine;
> Witness his zeal to stay the mad career
> Of hard Oppression, and to dry the tear
> Of weeping Slavery, and from Rapine's hand,
> Devoted Afric! free thy groaning land.
> Should Chance, in the eventful round of Time,
> Bring some poor wanderer from thy sultry clime,
> (To whose fond ear his grandsire had reveal'd
> The tale of Freedom, nor his name conceal'd
> Who plann'd the glorious scheme,) and tow'rds this tomb
> Direct his steps along the cloister'd gloom;
> Here shall he stop—while grateful sorrows break
> From his full heart, and wet his sable cheek;
> The silent drops, unconscious as they flow,
> Embalm the sacred dust that sleeps below,
> While with clasp'd hands, and deep regretful sighs,
> His quiv'ring lips pronounce—here Peckard lies."

" It can hardly be new to you, that the Primates and Prelates had a few days since a meeting at Lambeth-house, in order to take into consideration what ought to be the conduct of the Clergy in this arming period ; but you may not have heard, that my Diocesan * was singular in his opinion at first, and zealous in maintaining it, that his Brethren ought forthwith to be trained to the use of arms, and that he was with dignity answered by the Archbishop of York, and a resolution in course adopted unanimously, 'That it would not conduce, in any considerable degree, to the defence and safety of the kingdom, and would interfere with the proper duties of the profession, if the Clergy were to accept commissions in the army, be enrolled in any military corps, or be trained to the use of arms.' Certainly it was high time for our ecclesiastical rulers to check the arming influenza of their inferior brethren ; for, in the vicinity of Maidstone, there were four who were to be recruiting Captains, with cockades instead of roses in their beavers, viz. the Right Hon. Lord George Murray, Rector of Hutton† ; the Hon. Charles Marsham, Prebendary of Rochester ; Robert Foote, another Prebendary of the same Cathedral ; the Rev. William Horne (brother of the late Prelate of Norwich), Rector of Otham ; and to these four may be added one Clerk from East Kent, viz. Edward Tymewell Brydges, Master Urban's correspondent. Circular letters are issued from the several Bishops to the Clergy of their respective Dioceses ; and upon this point the Bishop of Rochester declares he means ' to speak out his own mind very plainly, and that he desires to be fully and clearly understood.' It is, that in a dangerous crisis ' his country will have a right to his best services, in any and in every way, even if the best service to be performed by him should be to level the musket or trail the pike.' Happy, however, is the Vicar of Wilmington to find, that it is not now expected of him to accept a military commission, or to submit to be drilled in the ranks !

" Robert Foote, clerk ‡, above mentioned, was a few months

* Dr. Horsley.

† Afterwards Bishop of St. David's, and father of the present Bishop of Rochester.

‡ The Rev. Robert Foote was the second son of the Rev. Francis Hender Foote, Rector of Boughton-Malherb in Kent, who died Jan. 27, 1773, by Catharine, daughter of Robert Mann, of Linton, Esq. and sister to the celebrated Sir Horace Mann, K.B. and first Baronet of that name ; and was consequently uncle to the present Robert Foote, of Charlton-place, near Canterbury, Esq. (who married Charlotte-Augusta, daughter of the Hon. and Right Rev. Frederick Keppel, Bishop of Exeter, and was Sheriff of Kent in 1816) ; and elder brother to the present Vice-Admiral Edward James Foote. He was of University-college, Oxford, M. A. 1782 ; his preferments are mostly mentioned by Mr. Denne above ; and the living to which he afterwards succeeded (as Mr. Denne anticipated) through the patronage of the Dean and Chapter of Rochester, was the Vicarage of Shorne. He married Anne, daughter of Robert Dobbin Yates, Esq. ; but died without issue at Boughton-Malherb, Oct. 21, 1804, greatly lamented by all his acquaintance.

since a Canon Residentiary of Lichfield Cathedral, but translated to Rochester by exchange with Mr. Woodhouse, for their
mutual benefit in point of situation, Mr. Woodhouse having two
parochial benefices on the confines of Staffordshire, and Mr.
Foote the Rectory of Boughton-Malherb, and the Vicarage of
Linton in Kent, and not many miles from Maidstone. Concerning this change, Archdeacon Law thus expresses himself: ' Your
ideas of the relative value of the Prebends of Lichfield and Rochester were entirely consistent with mine. An Act of Parliament, obtained within these three or four years, has much augmented the former, by annihilating some of the Prebends, and
adding their produce to the income of the Residentiaries. If I
recollect rightly, the number of the Residentiaries is increased
to six. From Mr. Foote's report, the difference in the produce
of the Prebends is very inconsiderable. He has left behind him,
indeed, a very good house, and succeeds to a wretched one here,
as you well know.' And well also is it known to S. Denne, that
almost all the livings in the patronage of the Dean and Chapter
of Rochester, are within the statutable distance of the Rectory
of Boughton; and that of course in due time Mr. Foote will
have the option of a living more advantageous than the Vicarage of Linton, which does not produce more than £.100
per year. I remain, dear Sir, yours truly,   S. DENNE."

" *Extracts of a Letter from Mr. Charles Clarke to Rev. Samuel
Denne, March 27, 1798.*

" DEAR SIR,

" I am now convinced Earl Rivers never brought Le Puy
across the channel with him from his pilgrimage, although centuries before his time it came that way ; that it is not derived
from Preuse, nor has any relation in sense to *Piete della Picta,*
&c. either in shape of substantive or adjective. In consequence
I wish my strictures on its name and thing withdrawn, and trust
so much indulgence may be obtained, for it appears very far
from evident that it was ever dedicated to the Virgin of Pity.
Strype is the only authority who calls it Pity of the Pieu ; and
Mr. Gough's citation from Froissart is of too much consequence
not to have a place and consideration in the body of its history.

" If we were in Westminster hall, I could take you through
an alley of Chambre's beautiful cloister, under and over Pontem
Reginæ; its screen or front is delineated slightly in Carter's
St. Stephen's; and at the entrance of the passage leading to
(I think) the Cotton-garden, where stands a venerable scrap of
the twelfth century by Becket when Chancellor, the Queen's
painted chambers, and facing the arches of this bridge is a stair
up to the Court of Requests, &c. It was long before I could
comprehend a bridge not over a water, so closely has habit
enlinked certain ideas; yet I fancy such a passage was usually

so named. I find about the same time an Abbess of Soisson
making a bridge across the street from her Monastery to the
hospital.

"But what is there in the notion of a closet which should
occasion a suspicion the present elegant kitchen appendage was
not the Chapel in question of le Pieu. Might it not be so
named from its small size? Might there not have been an
adjoining tribune for the royal family so named; and the jewels,
&c. have been stolen from the famous image of the Virgin.
Such were annexed to Churches, and those adjoining the Chapel
of the temporary Palace for the interview of Henry VIII. and
Francis I. described by Holinshed, are curious instances, and
may be deemed in point; but whatever remained of that edifice
is gone. The present is placed within the secular part of the
Palace, as I judge. Its vaulted roof with me renders it highly
probable that it may be the successor of one destroyed by the
flames."

86. " DEAR SIR,   *Wilmington, June .., 1798.*
" On the 12th I had a sheet from Mr. Clarke, from which I
make these extracts, 'As I find there will be no Archæologia
this year, there will be ample time for doing my best, such as
it is, since my vanity induces a supposition, that Messrs. the
Council will think it worthy a place in their thirteenth volume*.
Such was the effect of Mr. Wrighte's second notion, that,
had not a well made itself manifest, I should with pleasure have
subscribed to it; and that as much from a desire to rest conjecture somewhere, as owing to the merit of the supposition.'
" Notwithstanding a sturdy veteran Peer (my old school-fellow
Thurlow) averred in the House of Lords, that the Memoirs
of Sir Robert Walpole is a miserable stupid book, I rather wish
to have the perusal of it, as well because I am told the volumes
contain much original matter, as that it will bring to my remembrance the sentiments of persons, whose memory I revere, on
the merits of that truly great Minister, who kept his country at
peace for a number of years; for Archbishop Herring and my
father were staunch Walpolians, and of course not well affected
to Pulteney and the Tory party, who drove the Minister into a
war. I remain, dear Sir, truly yours,   S. DENNE."

87. " DEAR SIR,   *Wilmington, June 12, 1798.*
" Highly pleased was I with the perusal of your late tour,
which, as you say, was fraught with pleasures unalloyed; and
much obliged am I to you for your circumstantial detail of what
you saw and heard at Cambridge, Chesterton, Peterborough,

* No article on the subject ever appeared in the Archæologia.

Barkway, &c. &c. These particulars were the more grateful to me at present, because, in the too many elopements I am under a necessity of making from home, there is, unhappily, a very large portion of solicitude, perplexity, and distress of mind, on account of the state of the dear and near relation whom I am so frequently called to visit in his affliction.

" It was a satisfaction to me to be assured, that our old Fellow-collegian Fisher, of Barkway, enjoys so many domestic comforts. Very near forty years have passed since we saw each other, for, to the best of my recollection, the last interview we had was on the day after the King's Coronation, in September 1761.

" Your copious extracts, relative to Arabic numerals, shall be duly attended to, and deposited with your other notes upon the same subject; and perhaps the time may yet come, when I shall be more at liberty than I now am, to digest and apply them; but I must beg leave to remind you, that the slow progress in England, in the use of these vulgar figures, was my principal pursuit; and that I never presumed to flatter myself that I should be able to ascertain the origin of these inestimable characters. In the cursory chat we had lately at Cicero's Head, I hinted to you, that Dr. Robertson, in his Disquisition concerning India, had a pertinent remark upon this long agitated question; and, to save you the trouble of turning to the book, I inclose a copy of the paragraph alluded to :

" ' In all the sciences which contribute towards extending our knowledge of nature in mathematics, mechanics, and astronomy, arithmetic is of elementary use. In whatever country then we find that such attention has been paid to the improvement of arithmetic, as to render its operation most easy and correct, we may presume that the sciences depending upon it have attained a superior degree of perfection. Such improvement of this science we find in India; while among the Greeks and Romans the only method used for the notation of numbers was by the letters of the alphabet, which necessarily rendered arithmetical calculation extremely tedious and operose. The Indians had, for time immemorial, employed for the same purpose the ten cyphers, or figures, now universally known; and by means of them performed every operation in arithmetic with the greatest facility and expedition. By the happy invention of giving a different value to each figure, according to its change of place, no more than ten figures are needed in calculations the most complex, and of any given extent; and arithmetic is the most perfect of all the sciences. The Arabians, not long after their settlement in Spain, introduced this mode of notation into Europe; and were candid enough to acknowledge that they had derived the knowledge of it from the Indians. Though the advantages of this mode of notation are obvious and great, yet so slowly do mankind adopt new inventions, that the use of it was for some time confined to science; by degrees, however, men of

business relinquished the former cumbersome method of computation by letters, and the Indian arithmetic came into general
use throughout Europe *. It is now so familiar and simple, that
the ingenuity of the people, to whom we are indebted for this
invention, is less observed, and less celebrated than it merits †.'

" It is here explicitly averred, that the Arabians, who introduced this mode of notation into Spain, were so candid as to
acknowledge that their countrymen borrowed it from the Indians; and the main point to be considered is, whether Montucla had competent authority for this fact. Of the early use of
these characters by the Arabians themselves, we cannot have
better evidence than what is to be procured from MSS in that
language; and therefore it were to be wished, that the very few
who are conversant in it would give themselves the trouble of
examining these MSS. of which there must be in the libraries at
Oxford and Cambridge, particularly in the former, several that
are unquestionably very antient. In the London Chronicle of
Oct. 27—30, 1764, which I accidentally met with in one of my
brother's drawers, was this article of literary intelligence. ' The
King of Denmark has received a mail from the Society of
learned men, whom he sent into Arabia. This mail contains
five hundred volumes, extremely antient, all wrote in Arabic;
and amongst them are several Bibles, one of which was written
above 1000 years ago.' Supposing this to be true, and supposing the Arabians, above a thousand years ago, to have had
the use of these cyphers, it will be strange indeed, should they
not occur in divers verses of the Bible; but to whom can one
apply with the hope of a satisfactory answer to the question,
whether these suppositions be well founded?

" Architect Alexander, agreeably to his plan and his engagement, has already made the passage over Rochester-bridge much
more commodious; and a resolution is lately taken by the
Warden and Assistants, to make only one arch of the fifth and
sixth arches, one of which had within it the old draw-bridge.
The following advertisements, relative to this improvement, are
from the Maidstone Journal, May 15, 1798:

" ' Notice. A Meeting of the persons interested in the Navigation of the River Medway, is appointed for Saturday next, the
19th instant, at the Town-hall in Maidstone, at eleven o'clock
in the forenoon, to take into consideration the proposals of the
Noblemen, Gentlemen, and Bridgewardens of Rochester-bridge,
for taking down the fifth and sixth arches of the said bridge,
and converting the same into one; and for returning an answer
to the said proposals on or before the 31st instant.

" ' May 14, 1798.   J. Roffe.'

" The second advertisement from the same Journal:

" ' Maidstone, May 19.—At a Meeting this day, holden by

* ' Montucla's Hist. des Mathemat. tom. I. p. 360.'
† Robertson's Disquisition concerning Antient India, Appendix, p. 301.

appointment, in the Court-hall in this town, to take into consideration the proposals made to them by the Noblemen and Gentlemen, Bridgewardens of Rochester-bridge, for the loan of
£.5000 towards the charge of taking down the fifth and sixth
arches of the said bridge, and laying the same into one, for the
better improvement of the navigation of the river Medway
above the said bridge, the sum of £.3500 was immediately
subscribed; and a Committee appointed to attend to a further
subscription for completing the same.

"' Sir William Bishop, Chairman.

"'' Resolved unanimously, that the thanks of this Meeting be
presented to the said Noblemen and Gentlemen at their next
Meeting, for their honourable and candid proposals transmitted
to us for the above purpose.

"'' Resolved, that the thanks of this Meeting be given to
Daniel Alexander, Esq. surveyor and architect, and Sir William
Bishop, the chairman, for their attendance and assistance at this
Meeting.'

"The loan is for ten years, at 5 *per cent.* interest.

"Master Urban, in the Obituary for May, has truly suggested,
that the late Master of Trinity-college * was accounted one of
the best mathematicians in the University. There was an hour,
in the days of my ladship, when I experienced his superiority
in that science, for in the first act I kept in the Sophs' schools,
under Moderator Barford, Postlethwaite of Trinity was first
opponent to Denne, of Corpus Christi-college, respondent, who
soon perceived that he had not been well advised by his friend
Byrch, to take the movements of the Lunar Apsis for one of his
questions; however, I scrambled through it as well as I could,
and was, at the end of the year, not a little pleased to have my
name inserted with that of my more able opponent at the back
of the tripos among those ' quibus senioritas reservatur in prioribus comitiis.' Disney, of Trinity †, was our Senior Wrangler;

---

* The Rev. Thomas Postlethwaite, D.D. a native of Lancashire, of
Trinity-college, Cambridge, B.A. 1753, (third Wrangler or Senior Optime,—in that year, for the last time, one class,) M.A. 1756, B.D. 1768,
D.D. *per lit Reg.* 1789, Fellow 17.., Master 1789, on the resignation of
Bp. Hinchliffe. He was presented to a living in his native county by the
Earl of Derby, who had been his pupil in the University. He published
only a single " Discourse, in two parts, on Isaiah, vii. 14—16, preached
before the University, on Sunday, Dec. 24, 1780." (See Gent. Mag.
vol. LI. p. 179.) He died at Bath, May 4, 1798, where a tablet in the
north aisle of the Abbey Church merely records his name and date of
his death. He left £.2000 and some books to his college; his landed
property to his brother, with reversion to his son; and his funded property to his two nieces, one of whom kept his house, and attended
him to Bath; and £.100 and some books to his executor, the Rev. Mr.
Davies, Fellow of Trinity, and Public Librarian.

† William Disney, D.D. was fourth cousin to the Rev. John Disney,
D.D. the subject of the article in the present volume, pp. 478—489;
being (as appears by the pedigree there mentioned) descended through

and friend Fisher * distinguished by a Senior Optime. It so hap‑
pened, that I had not an interview with Postlethwaite from the
time of my drinking tea with him at his rooms, when I commenced
M. A. Three or four years ago, he was a steward at the Anni‑
versary Meeting of the Sons of the Clergy; and I had flattered
myself, that we should have renewed our acquaintance in Mer‑
chant‑taylors'‑hall, but I had the mortification of hearing, that
he was prevented appearing with his white wand by a sprain,
in consequence of a slip of his foot when getting in or out of
a carriage. By the Dean of the Arches, at the Visitation of the
Peculiars at Sevenoaks, I was told, that the Doctor was not
very active after he became Master of the College, i. e. as
we agreed, he soon discovered that, if he was alert, he and the
Seniors should be at variance, according to antient usage; and
as he was advancing in age, he therefore thought it would be
more for his ease to keep within his lodge, and to enjoy the
company of his brother Head of St. John's; for Masters Pos‑
tlethwaite and Craven (who were of the same year) it seems
chose to dine at each other's lodges one day in a week at least.

three generations of divines from a common ancestor, Sir Henry Disney,
of Norton Disney, Knt. who died in 1641. The Rev. John Disney, son
of Sir Henry, was Rector of Stoke Hammond, Bucks, and father of the
Rev. Matthew Disney, Rector of Blechley in the same county; whose
son, the Rev. Joseph Disney, Vicar of Cranbrook and Appledore in Kent,
was father of the Rev. Matthew Disney, B. D. Fellow of St. John's‑col‑
lege, Oxford, who died unmarried March 9, 1768, and of the Rev. Wil‑
liam Disney, D. D. William Disney was a Fellow of Trinity‑college,
Cambridge, B. A. 1753, M. A. 1756, B. D. 1768, D. D. 1789. He was
chosen Regius Professor of Hebrew in 1757, and held that chair till 1771.
In 17.. he was collated by his collegian and friend Bishop
Hinchliffe to the rectory of Paston in Northamptonshire; which in 1777
he exchanged with Mr. Jones, afterwards of Nayland, for the rectory of
Pluckley in Kent. He published "A Sermon preached before the Uni‑
versity of Cambridge, June 28, 1789, with some strictures on the licen‑
tious notions avowed or insinuated in the three last volumes of Mr. Gib‑
bon's Roman History" (noticed in Gent. Mag. vol. LX. p. 58); and "The
Superiority of Religious Duties to Worldly Considerations, 1800," 8vo.
Dr. Disney married Jan. 9, 1782, Anna‑Maria, daughter and co‑heiress
of John Smyth, of Chart Sutton in Kent, Esq.; but had no family, and
on his death, which it is believed occurred about 1816 (when an incum‑
bent was collated to Pluckley), his branch of the family became extinct.
    * Edmund Fisher, "of Norfolk," admitted of Bene't‑college, 1749,
B. A. 1753, M.A. 1756, and Fellow of Bene't. Mr. Denne (in p. 755) has
called him of Barkway, why it is not known, unless he was Curate there
before he obtained the rectory of Dunford St. Peter's, Cambridgeshire, to
which he was presented by his college. He died in 1819, in his 90th
year. Mr. Fisher is mentioned by Mr. Gough among his college friends
(see the "Literary Anecdotes," vol. VI. p. 617; where, however, his
Christian name is misprinted;) and the person remembered in Mr.
Gough's will was his son (also not Edward, but) Edmund. He, as his
father, was of Bene't‑college, B. A. 1797, M.A. 1800, and collated to
the vicarage of Linton, Cambridgeshire, in the latter year by Dr. Yorke,
Bishop of Ely. He is still resident on that living.

" The next time I write to my correspondent of the Ordnance-office, Gravesend, I shall apprise him of your remark, that
you have discovered, in your late visit to Churches in the county
of Huntingdon, many stone stalls in the south ailes, but do not
remember seeing any in the north ailes. Query, may not this
difference have proceeded from the convenience afforded by the
south walls admitting easily such recesses; and the south sides
of the north ailes generally communicating with the nave by
open arches? That there were chantries, or private altars, in
both ailes, may be easily proved in many churches.

" Yours truly,   S. DENNE."

---

88. " DEAR SIR,   *Maidstone, July* 17, 1798.

" From your letter I had the first advice of the departure of
my *quondam* tutor Masters. The office of biographer, which
you are pleased to assign to me, I shall beg leave to decline, for
a reason already suggested; and because I really have not so
many circumstances relating to his life and conversation, and
literary abilities, as a certain collector of Benedictine notes may
be possessed of; not but that I may be tempted to scribble an
addendum to the Obituary of Sylvanus Urban, where the merits
and demerits of the deceased will doubtless be recorded, though
I may not choose to communicate for insertion, the under-written
anecdote, which I have heard my brother frequently repeat. The
libel to be communicated had for its framers Denne, Green,
Clagett, and perhaps there might be others of the junto; and
it had its rise in Toby Masters's worrying the lads of the old
House, by obliging them to attend an afternoon Lecture when
they wished to be gossiping over their tea, and by constraining
them to come to Chapel at half past six in the morning, when
they wanted to lengthen their nap. In order to mark a Fellow
who was thus troublesome, the junto chose to pen the following
paraphrase on a passage in the Psalms, and to place it in the
prayer-book of Mr. Dean, ' Quoth David of his enemy, He
worketh mischief, he has conceived sorrow, and brought forth
ungodliness,' or words to that purport; but, quoth the commentators, 'Toby worketh mischief, he hath conceived dullness,
and brought forth stupidity.'

" Sir Henry Wotton's sentiments must correspond with the
feelings of every thoughtful person who has a satisfaction in
reflecting on the days of his youth. Would it suit my convenience, I should choose to pay a yearly visit to a room on the
south side of the Mint-yard at Canterbury; and to traverse my
removes, from form to form, till seated in the highest class with
a *ci-devant* Lord Chancellor, and with divers whose places are
not any where to be found. Gray, having in his view of Eton-
college cited the text, ' Sufficient to the day is the evil thereof,'

3 B 2

was one of the several lines which struck me with the notion,
that the Poem originated from the epistle of a Provost of that
College. You refer to the saying of a Primate, who had his last
translation about thirty years ago; and I therefore conclude
Archbishop Secker to be the person meant. His having made
the remark you attribute to him was new to me; and I wish
to know, for a special reason, whether it can be authenticated.

" To your question, whether the *holy brede* is not an unusual
term for the *Host?* I will refer you for a solution to a clause in
a statute of Edward VI. where it is enjoined, ' that in such
Chappeles annexed, where the people hath not been accustomed
to pay any *holy bread,* there they must either make some charitable provisions for the beryng of the communion, or els (for
receyving of the same) resort to their parish Churches.' It was,
perhaps, more frequently called, the Paschal Pence; and after
the Reformation acquired the new term of Communion Pence.
See Addenda to the History of Lambeth Parish, p. 374, note a.
" 1558. At Ester for the holye loff, 34s." Archæologia, I. 13.

" A trait of the peculiarity of a *quondam* Master of the old
House shall be added to this scroll; and the Master meant is the
person, who, according to tradition, was conveyed by his coach-
man to Drury-lane Theatre, in consequence of the order received
from his master to drive to 'the old House.' For the authenticity
of the tale I have to relate I can vouch, as I have found it
recorded in a letter I wrote to my brother from Vauxhall, on
Feb. 25, 1759, in which was this passage:

" ' After I had finished my letter last night, we were favoured
with a visit from my good Lord of Ely *. We thought his Lordship paid my father a rather late visit; and we found he designed
to have travelled back to Kensington, and by the pale light of
the moon. The Bishop had, however, forgot that the moon was
past the full, and would not rise till nine o'clock; he was therefore obliged to put himself to the expense of a flambeau; and
what was still more unlucky, he had not a single farthing in
his pocket to satisfy the demand of any gentleman of the road.'
This John gathered from the conversation which passed between
the Bishop and his foot-boy, whilst the Prelate was stepping into
his chariot. ' Boy,' quoth he, ' Have you got any money in
your pocket?' ' Yes, my Lord.' ' Give me all you have. What
have you given me?' ' Four and sixpence, my Lord.' A very
small sum, brother, for a Bishop of Ely to tender to a highway-
man; and I am apt to suspect that, should a Macheath, or a
Jemmy Twitcher, have paid his respects to his Lordship, he
would, by way of frolic, purloin the feather-top wig, not unfrequently denominated by the lads of Bene't, Madingley Gap.'

" When Master Urban's Obituarist shall characterise Tutor
Masters, he doubtless will not forget to inform the public, that
in October 1745, in the perilous days of jacobitism, when the

aid was required of 'all heads, hands, and hearts, for the support and preservation of our present happy constitution, the zeal of the deceased prompted him to excite the Wilbrahamites, great and little, towards so good a work; and that the Preacher 'flatters himself that, by publishing his discourse, it would become more effectual and extensively useful.' In the concluding paragraph he alludes to the valour and bravery of the ancestors of his flock, but without specifying any instance. Can any be produced by the Editor of Camden's Britannia?

" Yours truly,   S. Denne."

---

89. " Dear Sir,   *Wilmington, Aug.* 18, 1798.

" The following are extracts from a letter of Mr. Clarke:

" ' For notices from Mr. Gough's Cambridge excursion you receive my acknowledgments, as well as for the contents of a certain detached piece inclosed. True enough I have driven conjecture every where within my reach, on the subject of the delightful, yet abused, little oratory of our Lady; and I hope perseverance will elicit truth by presenting such existing circumstances as may go towards giving preponderance to one of my conjectural experiments.

" ' I am not certain as to the antiquity of the well. One about thirty years ago was sunk, the man yet living who did the work; a body was removed. It is opposite what I believe Pennant supposes a representation of the west front of the great Chapel, of the same kind as that on the roof of the cloister, and Mr. Capon supposed a holy water niche; but, in reality, a little monument, robbed of its brass plates*, likely that of Dr. Chambre, Dean of the Chapel, the builder of the cloister itself, at 11,000 marks, who was interred beneath. But with regard to the object of pursuit, the well under the servants'-hall, for no stone with a ring appeared, I am led to suppose it a refitting and enlargement of one of an antient date. The room over the Chapel has had a beautiful finished tracery about its walls; it is named the King's Confessionary, and served probably enough that purpose; but I did not find the Chapel below called the Monks'. The King's Confessionary is a repository for a press-bedstead, is kept clean, and has had a chimney formerly; and the Speaker here puts on his robes. The ceiling is flat and plastered; once probably wainscoted and panelled. The galleries over the cloister have beautiful windows enough, the opposite side and ceiling plain and plastered. Were these not once painted for the recreation of Mr. Dean and his brethren, the Canons of St. Stephen's, to walk and study in?

" ' Mr. Gough does not, you tell me, recollect finding any stalls repeated in the north ailes of the Churches he visited, but

---

* See it engraved in Smith's Antiquities of Westminster.

only in the south, such as we find is at Northfleet, in St. Paul's
at Bedford, &c.   You have noticed the south, or right hand side,
as the most honourable ; is it not likely the Chapels of the Virgin were there placed ?   They were annexed to parish Churches,
and had the regular offices of matins, vespers, &c.   See a will of
William Bruce, Garter King at Arms, dated 1449, in Nichols's
" Illustrations of the Manners and Expenses of Antient Times,"
4to, p. 134.   In the same will you will find a legacy for
puyng the said Church (of Stamford), and paving it with
Holland tile.   Pew thus appears a term more than a century older than 1561, when Lord Bacon was born.   See on the
word Podium, Junius in his Etymologicon, and it will be evident
it is not of Dutch extraction, but the *pui*, or the letter of the
French.   By Matthew Paris a choir stall is named Podium ;
but this has nothing to do with our affair at Westminster.'

" In a day or two the receipt of Mr. Clarke's letter shall be
acknowledged, and he informed that an extract has been forwarded to Enfield, and a wish expressed, that both Mr. Gough
and Mr. Ord may be at liberty to meet him in the *quondam*
Chapel; and the more I consider the apartments to be examined,
the more satisfied I am that six eyes will be preferable to two,
and that all preconceived ideas should be dropt at the door.
Supposing Mr. Clarke to have discovered the place where Dean
Chambre was interred, and the brassless memorial of him, that
will doubtless be minuted by the author of Sepulchral Monuments.

" A collection of C. C. C. Ana, local as well as personal,
is upon the tapis; and will, within a few weeks, be on its way
to Enfield.   They are nearly fifty years old ; and the find of
them was lucky and unexpected.   Yours truly,   S. DENNE."

———

90. " DEAR SIR,   *Wilmington, Aug.* 25, 1798.
" No sooner had I cut open the leaves of the Magazine for
July, than I turned to the Obituary for article Masters, not
having a doubt but that I should find a copious detail of the
parentage, birth, education, life, and learned works, of my *quasi
quondam* tutor, from the pen of a Benedictine ; nor was I disappointed.   One circumstance was, however, new to me, and so
it is, I believe, to my brother, that the deceased was the great
grandson to a Baronet ; not so to either of us, nor yet to yourself, is it, that his father was a vender of ale in a small village
juxta Norwich.   Perhaps it may be novel that there was in this
respect a rather strange coincidence between the genealogies
of the two co-tutors, tutor Heaton's sire being of the same
occupation, but in a higher style ; for, if I did not mishear my
brother, his old friend was the son of an eminent inn-keeper in
Doncaster.

" Some more Bene't Ana I have lately picked up quite unex-

pectedly at Maidstone, my brother having omitted to commit
to the flames sundry gossiping epistles he received from Sharpe
in the years 1747—1755. To a Member of the old House, some
of these tales told may not only be amusing, but a little interesting *.

"In addition to your anecdote of the deceased Primate, founded
upon the authority of Lord Chancellor Bowes, my brother observed, that when Dr. Robert Lynch, his brother-in-law, was at
Leyden, he read the thesis or exercise penned by Secker, whilst
he was a student or pupil in the clinical line, and that it principally treated of the puerperal fever †. His Grace's biographer
has not noticed what was probably the publication of his most
reverend patron.

"I remain, dear Sir, yours duly and truly,   S. DENNE."

---

91. Mr. CLARKE to Mr. DENNE.

"DEAR SIR,   *Sept.* 10, 1798.

"Gratified as I must have been on a survey, in company with
Mr. Gough and learned friends, of the beautiful things preserved
about the Speaker's mansion, I was under the necessity of availing myself of the opportunity I had some time been forming, as
I foresaw that, if I did not, it might be long before I should be
free to employ the leisure requisite for obtaining the plan and
sketches I proposed. At the same time, I trust I have in reserve
the satisfaction of attending those gentlemen; and my long
visit to the cloister has enabled me to offer to their notice several
things which might escape a cursory view; and I hope also to be
favoured with their sentiments on one or two particulars about
that secluded spot. I can assure them, if they are strangers,
there are few remains in our nation, the genuine seat of Gothic
Architecture, which will afford more pleasure; although I cannot say with Mr. Pennant, they bear away the palm from that
superbly finished edifice, the Chapel of Henry VII. What my
adventures were the annexed scraps will unfold. Two days were
spent in measuring and drawing. The whole is laid before you
as soon as I could put my papers into an intelligible form; a
long description was intended, but my pencil remarks, copied on
the plan, &c. drawn at large for the sake of elucidating every
particular, are more capable of leading to the comprehension of
the place, rendered intricate by the modern addition of dirty
offices, the work of Kent, under the Duke of Newcastle. In
the plan of the western alley it will be found, that La Piew is
seated between the massives of two of the vast buttresses of
Westminster-hall; the breadth of the cloister is exactly the
length of the butting arches, which cross the corridor above;
from each it is four feet distance. In the space between the
chapel and the northern buttress is a small room, six feet by

---

* Some of these will be inserted hereafter.

† There was some dispute on this point in the Gentleman's Magazine
for 1798; see that Miscellany, vol. LXVIII. pp. 559, 931, 1106.

four ; a door has been unmercifully (the whole treatment here
has been with a barbarian hand) cut through the wall of the
Chapel into this place; it is through the first arch on the left
hand in Carter's Views, who has re-placed it, and thus it should
seem he deems it not original. At first, from the strength of
the appearance, I imagined it a sacristy: but in that case it
would, as no inconvenience attended the choice, have been
placed on the opposite side, and have had an entrance from the
Chapel. Its eastern boundary is a wall two feet thick, a continuance of a buttress. On the west an elegant door opened into
it from the cloister, the only one it had ; and for the sake of
uniformity, equal to the one through the screen of the Chapel
adjoining. The further state of this apartment may be seen
from the plan and remarks ; its use is also there hinted at, and a
like was seen at Walsingham by Erasmus ; and so common were
wells, cisterns, &c. in the cloisters, there can be very little doubt
that what it contained is explicated by the old French word.

"There are one or two other particulars worthy regard.
Upon the first glance I had of La Piew, it appeared by far too
small for the devotion of the faithful; I expected it might be
latticed off from the cloister, as a chancel from the body of the
Church. On a visit to the Speaker's coal-cellar, I was struck
with the appearance I expected ; a screen was found which yet
seemed closed. After prying in the dark, (the light which enters
this once remarkable spot is through a break over it,) I discovered a slit in the lathing and plastering, an iron bar became
also manifest with the upper part of the architrave, or rather
cima, of a low door, for the coals were fortunately reduced. The
wooden door was yet in its place, a neat and delicate piece of
framing ; a drawing is given of what was thus found. With
the screen, fine vaulting, painted windows, lights, jewels, and
habits, you may figure to yourself such another habitation of
the Virgin as described at Walsingham and Canterbury. The
step without was pressed by the knees of the devout of low degree, while the cells of the screen supported their clasped hands;
within, the great saluted our Lady with a *Salve, Regina*, and *Tota
pulchra es, Maria*, amidst the blaze of whatever the arts and piety
of the day could bestow on the universal Patroness. After the
general beauty of the cloister and chapel, the sculptures on the
key-stones present the greatest pleasure and instruction. Those
above the spot demand a few moments for explaining a certain
sense they seem to contain ; and if I am happy enough to penetrate sufficiently into the sentiments of those times, it was as
follows: In 1353, Edward III. bestowed the ground, on which
the Canons erected a cloister and houses, with the grant of an
entrance through the Hall ; this had been unnecessary, had there
been access, as at present, on the Exchequer side. The key-
stone, or knob of the bust (query?), into which this passage opens,
contains a large C on an entwinement of rose and pomegranate.
Next we see our Lady with her infant as pointing out the limits

of her domain. From the infant state of our Lord, he next appears in majesty in the clouds, surrounded with rays of light; this is over the Chapel door; and, lastly, as an object worthy the regard of the antiquary, Dr. Chambre himself is seen, supported by two pages, or possibly keepers, of the treasures here deposited. He is in his Dean's *super-humerale*, an old man of a mild countenance, with uplifted hands, praying to our Lady. Probably he was interred beneath. These forms seem to comport so ill with the dolorous appearance of the image of Pity, that I conceive them, particularly the second, as a kind of internal evidence of that composition having had no place here. Of what I deem the founder I have sent a sketch. It will afford me much pleasure if it should turn out that I have discovered the portraiture of a man who has amassed such a profusion of elegance to the honour of his Deanery; and much obliged shall I be to you if you will hint where I may learn his history, and for appropriating any of the coats of arms noticed on the plan. In my development of principal lines in the plan and elevation of La Piew, as distributed on an opening of a bay of the cloister, I am so unfortunate as to lessen the value of the Chapel by destroying the relation which subsisted between it and the Earl of Rivers; but such is the evidence, on a comparison of the cloister and the oratory of our Lady, that it must appear the same design and execution was common to them both."

---

92. Rev. Samuel Denne to Mr. Clarke.

"Dear Sir,   *Wilmington, Sept.* 21, 1798.

"On my return from Maidstone on Friday the 14th current, I found upon my table your long parcel filled with excellent matter. The drawings, with the descriptions, cannot but be acceptable and pleasing to all our antique corps, though possibly some of the conjectures may not be quite satisfactory; nor is it in reason to be expected that they should, considering the amazing changes in the spot surveyed, and that what was centuries ago resorted to by persons opulent, noble, and royal, is now a scullery and a receptacle for coals.

"It is at your request that I with freedom communicate my sentiments, and to your candour I submit these circumstances, in which I may express a difference in opinion from you. Fortunate are you in having discovered, as I firmly believe, the portrait of Dean Chambre, the constructor of the western cloister; but to your suggestion, hinted with regret, that this eminent ecclesiastic and physician was, and that the ill-fated Earl Rivers was not, the builder of the Chapel of our Lady la Piew, I must beg leave to demur. It is unquestionable that the west cloister of St. Stephen's College was built by Dean Chambre; the marks expended are also specified; and I have a notion I have heard Mr. Ord mention his having perused, among the accounts remain-

ing in the Exchequer, several items of the charges *. The cloister alone is, however, named as the work of Chambre; and is it
likely that a Chapel so elegant and beautiful should have been
omitted, had it been constructed under the Dean's direction?
But this being evidence rather of a negative kind, it is next to
be observed that there is proof strongly implied, if not expressed, that the Chapel was built by the Earl of Rivers, who
was beheaded in 1483. This does not rest merely upon the *ipse
dixit* of Stow, but may be collected from the Earl's will. The
will at least shows, that there was then subsisting a Chapel,
called La Piew, unless my memory deceives me; and it is not by
any means probable that that Chapel should have been taken
down and re-edified by Chambre.

"Let us next turn to what may be deemed the internal
proofs, the supposed similarity in the style of architecture. The
form of what you term the Tudor arch has weight with you;
and certainly the screen and the door, so accurately drawn by
your pencil, exhibit that flat kind of arch; but, judging from
Carter's view of the Chapel, every arch within the Chapel is
much more pointed; and I am rather inclined to believe on this
score, that the screen might be raised under the direction of
Chambre, and not any other part of the Chapel.

" But the difference in the decorations of Chambre's cloister
and of the contiguous Chapel, ought to be particularly noticed.
On the key stones of the former there are pomegranates and
roses slipt, wreaths of pomegranates, roses, and thistles, a shield
with royal arms, capital letters, and portraits. Whereas, as you
observe, all the shields of the principal key-stones of the Chapel
are like the one at Windsor (Archæologia, vol. XII. p. 415).

" Concerning the title La Piew, which has been so long our
crux, I have now a few more words to offer. To my information of the conjecture of Secretary Wrighte, that it meant our
Lady of Fear, your reply, if I mistake not, was, that you should
have acceded to it, had you not previously adopted that of *Puis*,
a well. I perceived he was sanguine, very sanguine, and as I
really think, on competent grounds, that he had brought forward
a successful etymology. He, it is true, had relied only on the
English edition of Le Bruyn's Voyage to the Levant; but if La
Peur be the word in the original, as it probably is, that indisputably signifies *fear*; and as in French the final *r* is seldom pronounced, it is easy to account for the omission of it in a MS.
where the Chapel of La Pieu is mentioned. He recommends it
to you to consult the travels of Le Bruyn and Thevenot; and
indeed all books of travels through the Holy Land in which

* At the second sale of Mr. Ord's MSS. Jan. 29, 1830, appeared the
Compotus Nicholai de Tickhull, containing minute accounts of the
works and repairs at the Palace of Westminster and the Tower of London, in the 5th Edward II. It was sold for £.73 10s.; and is now in the
large collection of Sir Thomas Phillipps, Bart. F. S. A.

notice is taken of the various sacred edifices that have an allusion to the acts, sufferings, and deliverances of our Blessed Lord
and the Virgin Mary.' That the Chapel of our Lady la Peur, or
of Fear, near the Mountain of Precipitation, in the way from
Nazareth to Akari, was probably the origin of *all* the chapels
dedicated to Mary under that appellation. It was the word *all*
that struck me, as only one Chapel so denominated has been
hitherto noticed in England, nor could Mr. Wrighte refer me to
any Chapel so called in Italy or in France. Should you in your
reading meet with any edifice so called, I am persuaded you will
not fail to notice and to note it.

"With respect to your innuendo, that La Pieu might mean
La Puis, a well, I suspended my opinion till you had surveyed
the Chapel and its appendages; but since you have not discovered any well within the Chapel, and are fully satisfied that the
supposed lavatory apartment could not originally have had a
direct communication with the Chapel; and as there is not any
legendary vestige of a Holy-well within the precincts of St. Stephen's College, like the Holy-well in Shoreditch, or the Holy-
well of Clerkenwell, or the still more wonder-working well that
had the imaginary St. Winifred for its Patroness, I am rather
apt to suspect that your surmise, however ingenious and plausible, may, if weighed in the true matter-of-fact antiquarian
balance, be found wanting.

"There is in Wood's Athen. Oxon. vol. I. p. 682, a memoir of
Dean Chambers, and in Newcourt's Repert. vol. I. p. 747, it is,
in part at least, re-printed with a correction.

"I am, yours truly,   S. DENNE."

---

93. Mr. CLARKE to Mr. DENNE.

"DEAR SIR,   *Oct.* 2, 1798.

"The objection I offered to Mr. Wrighte's etymological idea
was, that the word *Peur*, so written, was not in the French contemporary with the appellation of our Chapel, it being derived
from the Latin *Pavor*. By Ivenville it is written *Poour;* La-
combe, from two authors, *Paour;* Kelham, *Poeur, Poieu,* and
Pavur, and *Paiou.* I will add, that I suspect when the French
Le Bruyer is consulted, it will be found, should Crainte not be
preferred, not *N. Dame de la Peur,* but *N. D. de Peur,* as *N. D.
de Pitie de recouverance, de consolation, de grace,* &c. for the reason I will refer to the better writers on the French language.
For the final *r*, in this particular word, I am led to suppose it
pronounced. Were a French gentleman long since applied to
for the sound he gave it, I might expect his Peor or Peaor, in
our own letters. Of seventy-one Churches of our Lady in
Rome, in which there is a *S'ta Maria del Pozzo,* not one is dedicated to her as under the impression of fear; nor in all the
variety of patterns seen during about two years past has such a

title occurred to me any more than to yourself or the Vicar
of St. Nicholas. In Moreri, article Nazareth, the Church of
the Precipitation is passed by, as it is in Sandys's Travels; nor did
St. Lewis visit it, although he did those of the Virgin, with
great solemnity and devotion. I am, therefore, disposed to
entertain some doubt on the repute of the thing at home; and
whether it was ever repeated in Westminster, or at all in
Europe.

" To my own notion of a well in old French, so like our
Westminster term, notwithstanding its probability, from their
being as common nearly in the cloister as in the court of a private dwelling, I am willing enough to part with it, and assign
my lavatory to some other purpose ; and seek again, within the
limits of the probability marked out by the terms, *Notre Dame
de le Pew*, our Lady in the *Piew, Pue*, &c."

<hr>

94. Mr. DENNE to Mr. GOUGH.

" DEAR SIR,   *Wilmington, Sept. 24, 1798.*
" Mr. Nichols has doubtless apprised you of his having delivered into my hands your three well filled sheets, for which be
pleased to accept my hearty thanks and a brief reply. By Mr.
Nichols it may be presumed, that you are likewise informed of
my having received a large packet from my indefatigable correspondent at Gravesend, and that I promised I would give you
some account of its contents, if possible, before my next excursion to Maidstone. The inclosed two sheets will show you what
has been drawn and written by Mr. Clarke concerning the
Chapel of La Pieu or Pieur, and my comments upon the same;
but when the drawings and explanations will reach Enfield I
am not warranted to make report.
" I remain, dear Sir, yours truly,   S. DENNE."

<hr>

95. " DEAR SIR,   *Wilmington, Nov. 2, 1798.*
" In pursuance of my promise, you now receive more Bene't
Anas, some from a letter written by Sharpe *, and some from a
very long epistle from Denne to Crayford. Their friendship
began at Canterbury-school; and their correspondence, whilst
the former was an academic, and the latter still a disciple of Master Monins, for though they were of the same year at Bene't,
my brother, by residing as a *Non Ens*, passed one year more in
College as Under-graduate. Crayford was a young man of
exemplary morals, and a hard Student ; of sound judgment, but
had not brilliant parts. He died of the small-pox, Dec. 20,
1748, in my nonentity term; and I was by that means deprived
of his advice at a very critical period. The poor man who dated

* See some of these hereafter.

his epistle from Chichester * had the pen of a ready writer,
and was a lively correspondent; but to repeat a few Latin words
quoted by himself, ' Quantum mutatus ab illo,' for since he was
seized with the ague of the mind, it is with reluctance that he
takes a pen in hand even to subscribe his name, and rarely will
he cast his eye over a page in a book.   On his tranquil days he
is, however, very conversible, intelligent, cheerful, and fortunately his memory is not much impaired.   To be sure, like most
people who are not on the bright side of seventy, old tales please
him most ; and this is the more to be expected in him as he has
been for twenty-one years sequestered from the world.   From
his report of the initiatory Sermon delivered by the Bursar at
Whitehall Chapel, you will perceive that he had a knack for that
kind of exercise, which was more commonly practised in days
of yore than in modern times ; and I have not a doubt but that
I should discover, were I to pump him, which I probably may in
some future interview, that he has a perfect recollection of the
substance of the Sermon alluded to; for not long since, having
met with the syllabus of an excellent discourse delivered by
Dean Lynch at Rochester Cathedral in 1744, when he was visiting my father, I found. upon striking the key, that my brother
could repeat what he had communicated to his friend above half
a century ago.   The purchase of two lottery tickets towards de-
fraying the charge of erecting a new college in the air was a
quaint conceit in the *quasi* delineator of the plan : and was,
strictly speaking, a new anecdote to me, though you who are a
closer investigator may have picked it up.   Hereafter I may take
an opportunity of inquiring of my brother what was the event;
though, from nothing having generally transpired, I see no reason that blank, blank,' were not the words sounded in Guildhall.
Had they been 'ten thousand pounds principal money,' there certainly would not have been occasion to suspend the work, because a succession of wars had lowered the stock appropriated for
this purpose ; and such was the reason Master Colman gave me
for his being the Head of nothing but the *old* House.   Crayford,
of this old House, being mentioned in the first page of this sheet
and purporting to put into the packet an excellent letter, as well
in composition as in penmanship, from the disconsolate parent
on the irreparable loss she sustained by his premature decease,
you may possibly have a wish to know something more of the
family.   The father was Recorder of Canterbury and Faversham,
a lawyer deservedly eminent for his talents, natural and acquired,
but carried off in the prime of life by a violent fever.   He left
a widow and three sons, with rather a scanty provision.   Robert,
above-mentioned ; William, who became a seaman in the royal
navy, and died of the small-pox a midshipman on board the Bur-
ford Man, very much esteemed by the Captain and the other
officers ; and Edward, still living at Canterbury, of which city

* Mr. Denne's brother; see the " Literary Anecdotes," vol. III. p. 527.

he was for a few years an Alderman, but in a pet threw aside his
scarlet gown. He was a practitioner at Sittingbourne in medicine, chirurgery, and midwifery, but having acquired a com-
petency declined business. The Crayfords were long a family of
repute in East Kent, and had once more landed property than
appertained to their descendants. Mrs. Crayford's maiden name
was Cumberland; her father was a most respectable divine, and
Rector of St. Andrew's in Canterbury, of which you know our
friend Duncombe was incumbent by favour of Archbishop Herring. The Rev. Robert Cumberland was a Minor Canon of Canterbury, and Rector of Hastingleigh.

" Thanks to you for your list of the Treasurers of the Exchequer, of which, perhaps, some use may be made in the purposed
Memoir of the Chapel of La Piew. Since I wrote last, I have
not had any letter from Mr. Clarke, and am therefore not
apprised whether he has by himself repeated his visit to the
the cloister constructed by Chambre, or rather Chambers, for
so he wrote his name (vide Fuller's Church History, cent. xvi.
book VII. p. 422.) Browne Willis has not cited his voucher for
his assertion that this Dean of St. Stephen's was buried in
that chapel.

" At my request Mr. Ellis has transmitted to me from Mr.
Cherry, Henshall's two publications *, and I thought myself warranted in applying for the loan of them, as on a short interview
I had with Mr. Cherry in one of his trips through Rochester, he
mentioned these tracts, and with expressions of applause. When
in town in May, I saw the ' Specimens and Parts ' in Rivington's
shop; and as the title-page held forth that it contained a History of the County of Kent, I was nearly tempted to become a
purchaser without examination. I do not, however, regret my
having prudently determined to wait till I had some advice
whether the book were worth ten shillings; and I must own,
from your silence concerning it, I began to have my doubts increased. The only notes I have taken from the book have a
reference to the number of churches recorded in Domesday, in
which I presume he may be correct; but I cannot accede to the
opinion of the fanciful compiler, that ecclesiastics were meant
by *Pervi*, a word that so frequently follows *Ecclesia*. As to the
author's reciprocal illustration of the Saxon and English languages, I am much mistaken if he has not a host of critics to
contend with; and I utterly disapprove of blending political
subjects of the present day and personal remarks with antiquarian and literary topics. The Diversions of Purley, and the
merits or demerits of Επεα πτεροεντα, are surely quite foreign
to the trial of Horne Tooke at the Old Bailey; and why need

---

* " Specimens and Parts of the History of South Britain ; " and "The
Saxon and English Languages reciprocally illustrative of each other."
The latter is ably and severely criticised by Mr. Gough in the Gentle-
man's Magazine, vol. LXVIII. p. 861.

the author have inserted another long note censuring the President of the Antiquarian Society for not choosing to be a subscriber to a continuation of Specimens and Parts of Domesday. The note a at p. 40, with the note explanatory subjoined, in which reference is doubtless made to the living successor of Bishop Gibson in the See of London, cannot have escaped your notice; and I am convinced I am not the only reader of the contrast between the two Prelates, who must attribute the compliment paid to the memory of one at the expense of the other, to Bishop Portéus's having dismissed a certain person from the Curacy of Spitalfields from a justifiable motive.

"You might have in your newspaper the article which mentions the Prince of Wales being at the gala assembly at Canterbury after the account arrived of Lord Nelson's victory. The private account I have of the same shall be communicated to you: 'Oaks, Oct. 15, 1798. Every body this day is making preparations for the ball this evening, in honour of the brave Admiral of the Nile. The milliners are provided with bandeaus, ribbons, fans, &c. on which are painted, Nelson and Victory; and the mantua makers, it is to be hoped, are equally provided with laurels, as the ladies' garments are to be festooned with that and myrtle. The Prince of Wales has notified his intention of honouring the company with his presence in the ball room at nine; at twelve o'clock his Royal Highness, and Prince William of Gloucester also, whom I ought to have mentioned before, repair to the Fountain, where a supper is ordered for them, and any company at the ball that chooses it, at the expense of another half guinea, which I dare say most of the company will not object to pay.'—P. S. To a letter from the same correspondent, Oct. 22. 'The two Miss Thurlows dined at Charlton-place the day of the ball; and came with his Royal Highness in the evening to Delmar's rooms, with the rest of the company who had been his guests.' His Royal Highness, I understand, viewed some of the monuments in Canterbury, and blamed the want of attention shown to Archbishop Warham; but I was somewhat surprised that the Blue Prince, though a military Knight, girded with a scymitar, should not have desired to see the portrait of the Black Prince, and the armour he wore, as it is said, when he conquered the French. Yours truly, S. DENNE."

---

96. Mr. GOUGH to Mr. DENNE.

"DEAR SIR, *Enfield, Nov. 12, 1798.*

"Much was I entertained and informed by the various Ana of your last, which came to my hands *via* Nichols yesterday, on my return from Wormley, (to which Rectory, five miles distant, I had lately the great satisfaction of inducting my friend M'Culloch, and whither and to his Curacy of Cheshunt, two miles nearly, I follow him *alternis vicibus;*) and finding some

friends ready to take their places at my table, and some press-
work to correct when they were departed, I could not attend too
so soon as I eagerly wished.   How much do I regret that distance prevents my having the opportunity of seeing and hearing the originals of many more Ana C. C. C. C. before you
' commit them to the custody of Mister Vulcan.'   They set
all my early academic days before my eyes, and carry me back
to scenes I only knew by hearsay.   Yours, &c.   R. GOUGH."

***

97. Mr. DENNE to Mr. GOUGH.

" DEAR SIR,   *Wilmington, Nov. 26, 1798.*
  " When I conveyed to you the drawings by Mr. Clarke of the
ground plot of the Chapel of our Lady la Piew, and his remarks
upon the cloister contiguous to it, that was built by Dean Chambers, alias Chambre, I hinted that I was in hopes I might have it
in my power to give the delineator a chance of discovering the
portrait of the Dean among a group of figures painted by a
contemporary artist.   Hans Holbein's picture of the delivery of
the charter to the Company of Barber-surgeons was the picture
I had in my thoughts; and Mr. Walpole, in his Anecdotes of
Painting, having mentioned that Dr. Butts was there exhibited,
I had hardly a doubt but that Chambers, who was likewise a
physician to King Henry VIII. was there also represented; and
if you look into the well-known print of this picture, you will
perceive that he is kneeling near the Sovereign's footstool, and
marked No. 3.   Whether this picture bears a resemblance to the
portrait of the key-stone in the cloister of St. Stephen's Chapel,
it will be Mr. Clarke's business to examine.   Though your search
in the Prerogative-office after the Dean's will has been fruitless,
some tidings concerning it may be had from Merton-college;
supposing him to have been, which is not unlikely, a benefactor
to the Society of which he was several years Warden.
  " For several years I was well acquainted with Mr. Harwood,
the late Vicar of Dartford.   I am inclined to believe he might
be of a family co. Chester, though I rather suspect him to have
been a native of the Metropolis *.   He certainly was a Fellow
of Merton-college; but in an early part of life became domestic
Chaplain to Dr. Wilcocks, Bishop of Rochester, who presented
him in October 1743 to the Rectory of Ibstock, in the county of
Leicester; and for some other living he got the Rectory of
Uppingham, co. Rutland, which he held with Ibstock.   Being

---

* The Rev. James Harwood was younger brother to ——— Harwood,
Esq. of Crickheath in Shropshire.   He married a daughter of Thomas
Chase, Esq. of Bromley in Kent, sister to Sarah, wife of the Hon. and
Rev. St. Andrew St. John, D.D. Dean of Worcester.   Mrs. Harwood, after
her husband's death, was, with her seven children, resident at Rochester.

desirous, however, of settling in Kent, and the Vicarage of
Dartford becoming vacant, he at length effected a change for
Ibstock and Uppingham; and, if you turn to Hasted's Kent, you
may see when he was collated to Cliffe in the Hundred of Hoo.
I well recollect that I inducted him into this Rectory; and that,
from being wet through, I caught a cold which rendered me deaf.
He died Feb. 15, 1778, aged 64. I saw his remains deposited
in a vault in the burial ground on the top of Dartford-hill, heretofore called the Cemetery of St. Edmund; but there is on the
east wall of the south chancel of Dartford Church, an elegant
marble tablet, with a very short inscription in memory of him;
and, if you turn to the engraving of Bromley-house, published
in Hasted's Kent, you will see Bishop Wilcocks and his Chaplain. The size and air plainly show, to those who knew Mr.
Harwood, that he was the clerk exhibited in his gown, *sans
chapeau*, though the back is to the spectator.

"Not being expert in the science of Heraldry, I shall not
presume to comment upon the sundry devices granted as an
augmentation to the armorial coat of the Hero of the Nile; but
on the change of motto on the shield, or, to write more correctly,
on the motto of the shield he bore as Knight of the Bath, I cannot forbear suggesting a remark *. The words were *Faith and
Works*, a motto in my opinion better adapted to a clergyman,
and to the son of a clergyman who is of his father's profession,
than to a son who wears a sword; as it is hard of belief that,
when St. James argued upon faith shown by works, he could
ever mean martial deeds from a carnal weapon. The paternal
coat of Sir Horatio Nelson, with this motto, is at the bottom of the print of this illustrious naval officer by Barnard;
and I was led to pay the more attention to it because this young
artist is the only son of the eldest daughter of my predecessor
in the Vicarage of Wilmington †. As far as my little judgment
is competent to determine, it is a neat well-executed engraving;
and I trust it will be ultimately to the material advantage as well
as to the credit of Barnard. Yours truly,   S. DENNE."

---

98. " DEAR SIR,   *Wilmington, Dec. 17, 1798.*
" Not long after I had noticed your application for intelligence
concerning the late Vicar of Dartford, it occurred to me that
above two years since I had received a letter of inquiry from
Mrs. Harwood about the family name of her deceased husband.
This letter I have transmitted to you, as it is in your line of pur-

---

* See a letter by Mr. Denne in Gent. Mag. vol. LXIX. p. 197. The
motto given by royal authority, was " Palmam qui meruit ferat," from
a Latin ode by Dr. Jortin.—It has been remarked that no more appropriate motto could now be placed under the Nelson shield, than the
uncommonly apt anagram of " Horatio Nelson,"—*Honor est a Nilo.*

† The Rev. John White was for forty years incumbent of Wilmington,
from 1726 until his death in 1767.

suit, though possibly, in consequence of the Harwoods being not only your cater cousins, but of your acquaintance, the same etymological and genealogical queries may have been submitted to your consideration. The answer I returned I do not well recollect; but I think I gave no countenance to the notion, that my friend could trace his descent from Hereward, the Saxon chief, who showed a spirit similar to what prompted the men of Kent to resist the attempt of the Norman invader.

"Dr. Latham's new *cara spousa*, it appears, is a helpmate literally in his epistolary correspondence; and I have a notion I might hint to you before, that Mrs. Latham, whilst Miss Delamotte, was for a few years one of my flock as Vicar of Darenth.

"Mr. Weston * has at last acquired the object of his wishes. On the demise of Dr. Farmer, he was sanguine that he should then be removed from Canterbury to St. Paul's; and not a little mortified when he found, that the united interest of the Premier and the Earl of Hardwicke could not prevail over the royal interference in favour of Dr. Majendie. He was obliged to take two journeys to town before he was admitted to kiss the King's hand on his promotion, the Minister having failed in the levee etiquette to apprise the Lord in waiting of his having nominated Mr. Weston to the vacant Stall. He was disappointed also on a view of the house appropriated to it, having been told it was a very good one, and finding it the reverse. Concerning these three mansions, I am not competent to form an opinion, not having entered the door of either one; but I had imagined that within they were suitable and comfortable abodes, and that the grand objection was to the site of Amen-corner. It was generally supposed that the Speaker's Chaplain would have been Mr. Weston's successor; but the papers must have informed you that Mr. Norris, tutor to Earl Spencer at Trinity-college, Cambridge, is the fortunate clerk †. He is the son of Mr. Norris, who was formerly Vicar of Brabourn, near Ashford, and the grandson of Mr. Norris, for so many years Chapter-clerk and Auditor to the Dean and Prebendary of Canterbury, one who both in and out of office was intelligent and respectable, and not unworthy to be a successor of antiquary Somner.

"On Saturday the 15th current, died two of the quondam boys of the King's School, Canterbury, and I have a notion they might be in the same form, *viz.* Ned Taylor, of Bifrons-house, and Rector of Patricksbourne, and Sir Edward Dering, of Surrenden Dering, Baronet. Mr. Taylor was seized with a paralytic stroke about two months ago, and Bath water was prescribed, under a notion that because it was hot it would brace up the relaxed nerves. He was said to be better from the use of it,

* The Rev. Samuel Ryder Weston, B.D. was in 1798 appointed Canon Residentiary of St. Paul's.

† The Rev. Charles Norris, M.A. is living, a Prebendary of Canterbury, and Rector of Aylsham and Fakenham, Norfolk.

but relapsed upon the road on his return home. From the accounts of his sufferings it may be allowed to be a happy release *. The Baronet has long had a battered constitution, but his departure was rather sudden and unforeseen; for, purposing to take a walk, his servant was assisting to put on his great coat, when he dropped down and soon expired. It is observable that Edward, Mr. Taylor's son and heir, and Cholmeley, the eldest son of Sir Edward Dering, by the present lady, are both in Ireland on military service. The former is Aid-de-camp to Marquis Cornwallis, the latter Captain of the Romney Fencibles. Mr. Taylor was of St. John's-college, Cambridge, as were his father and his brother Herbert; and the father was, by Archbishop Wake, collated to the Rectory of Hunton, near Maidstone, and appointed one of the Six Preachers of Canterbury Cathedral. Mr. Edward Taylor unhappily lost a son about a year ago, being drowned when up the Thames near Richmond, on a party of pleasure; but he has fortunately well married two of his daughters, one of them to the opulent Wilbraham Bootle.

"This being the last time of writing on this side of a new year, I will transmit to Mrs. Gough and yourself my congratulations and wishes of *multos et felices.* To myself, the year *penult.* of the eighteenth century has been, in divers instances, very trying and vexatious, may the year *ult.* be more propitious; but I own I find it difficult to discern a glimpse through the gloom, public or private. Yours truly,   S. DENNE."

* The Rev. Edward Taylor was the younger son of Herbert Taylor, of Bifrons-house, Kent, Rector of Hunton and Vicar of Patricksbourne, by Mary, daughter of the Rev. Edward Wake, Prebendary of Canterbury, and first cousin to Archbishop Wake. The Rev. Brook Taylor, D.D. Sec. R.S. author of an essay on linear perspective, and other scientific treatises (of whom, and his writings, a memoir is given in the "Literary Anecdotes," vol. I. p. 171), was his uncle. Edward was educated (as Mr. Denne informs us) at Canterbury school and St. John's college, Cambridge, where he proceeded B.A. 1755, M.A. 1758. On his father's death in 1763 he was presented by his brother, Herbert Taylor, Esq. to the vicarage of Patricksbourne; and on that gentleman's death in 1767 he succeeded to Bifrons, and his father's other lay property in that parish. He re-built the mansion, and died there, Dec. 8, 1798; when he was characterized as "a man of an enlarged intercourse with society, who had lived some years in Germany and Italy, and whose name may be found both in the domestic tours and foreign travels of Mr. Arthur Young." Mr. Taylor married in 1769, Margaret, daughter of Thomas Turner, afterwards Payler, of Ileden in Kent, Esq.; and by that lady, who died at Brussels in 1780, left four sons: 1. Edward Taylor, Esq. 2. Lieut.-Gen. Sir Herbert Taylor, K.C.B. and K.G.H. well known as the much attached Secretary of the late Duke of York, and now Adjutant-general; 3. Brook (whose twin brother, William, was the son drowned as mentioned by Mr. Denne); 4. Bridges, R.N.; also three daughters, 5. Mary-Elizabeth, married April 19, 1796, to Edward Wilbraham Bootle, Esq. M.P. who was created Lord Skelmersdale in 1828; 6. Charlotte, married to the Rev. Mr. Northey, Rector of Kinlet, Salop; and 7. Margaret.—Bifrons was sold by the Taylor family in 1830 to the Marquis of Conyngham; the price is stated to have been £.100,000.

99. " Dear Sir,   *Wilmington, Jan.* 8, 1799.

" Among some academical news sent me by Mr. Archdeacon Law, are the following items : ' The present Master of Trinity has formed the resolution of not admitting any more members than could be contained within the college walls. Such a determination meets with my cordial approbation. When young men are resident in private lodgings, there cannot be any superintendance of conduct. It is reported, that the example will be followed by St. John's. In this latter college, however, there was more propriety than in Trinity; for at St. John's none were allowed to live in lodgings before the Soph's year; at Trinity the young men were left to themselves immediately on admission. I expected to have heard, before this time, of some motion in the Court of Chancery relative to the election of a Master of Catharine-hall. The Lord Chancellor is the Visitor. There are only five electors, the Fellows on the new foundation having no right to vote. Mr. Waterhouse had his own vote, and that of another Fellow ; Dr. Gardiner had a vote, as had Dr. Hey, who was originally a Member of the Society. A fourth person was, I believe, named. Waterhouse is not defective in point of abilities; but is represented as coarser in his manners and in his habits of life than Parson Trulliber *. The question,

---

* The eccentricities of this unfortunate gentleman, and his tragical murder in 1827, are fresh in recollection. He discharged the University office of Proctor in 1783 ; and when candidate for the Mastership of Catherine-hall, had for some years been a Fellow. Anecdotes of his eccentricities, and the circumstances of his unfortunate death, will be found in the Gentleman's Magazine, vol. XCVII. pt. ii. p. 279 ; the following extract from a private letter, soon after written, gives a copy of the epitaph which was erected by some illiterate relatives of the deceased :

"A tomb is about to be erected over the remains of the late singular and unfortunate Rector of Little Stukeley, and is now exhibited on the premises of the lapidary artist at Huntingdon. According to immemorial wont and usage, a copy of verses is appended to the inscription, which, in point of style, taste, and orthography, are on a par with the ' uncouth rhymes' alluded to by Gray.— This branch of English literature has certainly remained stationary during the last century. I transcribe the whole of the inscription :

' Sacred to the Memory of the Rev. Joshua Waterhouse, B. D. nearly 40 years Fellow of Catherine-hall, Cambridge, Chaplain to his Majesty, Rector of this parish, and of Coton, near Cambridge, who was inhumanly murdered *in this parsonage-house*, about ten o'clock on the morning of July 3rd, 1827, aged 81.

' Beneath this Tomb his Mangled body's laid,
Cut, Stabb'd, and Murdered by Joshua Slade ;
His ghastly Wounds a horrid sight to see,
And hurl'd at once into Eternity.
What faults you 've seen in him take care to shun,
And look at home, enough there 's to be done ;
Death does not allways warning give,
Therefore be carefull how you live.'

" (I have adhered to the capitals and spelling of the original) "

LETTERS OF REV. SAMUEL DENNE, F.S.A. 757

I believe, is, whether a majority of the electors who were present is not necessary ; if it be not, Waterhouse must succeed, however unworthy of the situation.' Since the receipt of this article of information, I noticed in the public prints that the Lord Chancellor had declared the election void; though I must own I had my doubts whether such might be the power given to the Visitor, having known so many instances in which the founders of colleges and the framers of statutes had shown more zeal than knowledge. The adjudication of the Chancellor was differently stated in different papers; but, supposing him to have ordered a new election, it may be presumed that he has issued a peremptory injunction for all the electors to attend; there being no more than five, surely it was expedient that the privilege should have been allowed to all the Fellows of the new foundation.

"In a parcel I received on Monday from the Ordnance-office in Greenwich, was a pamphlet of twenty-five pages in quarto, intituled, 'Observations on the Intended Tunnel beneath the River Thames, shewing the many defects in the present State of that Projection ; by Charles Clarke, F. S. A.; ' with the motto, ' Haud Inscia, ac non Incauta Futuri.' Hor.—The body of the essay contains further remarks, in addition to those inserted in the Gentleman's Magazine *, on the form of the arch that will be necessary to guard against the influx of the river, beneath which the tunnel is to be constructed; but there is a postscript by a gentleman of Rochester, in which the futility of the whole scheme is clearly shown ; and I must own that, from the first suggestion of it, I have always conceived it to be of the *Dodd* Quixote cast. It has often struck me, that there is not, either in an agricultural or in a commercial view, such an intercourse between the two counties as to warrant the risk of so large a sum of money as will be wanted to carry the plan into execution. It is also certain, that the market of the two counties is the metropolis; and justly it is observed by the Rochester gentlemen, that the surface of the river is the cheapest road to London. He also avers, and I think truly, that Essex possesses no one commodity which Kent wants ; and that, the only trade now subsisting between the two counties is for the chalk which Kent sends to Essex ; and that, as long as a barge can swim, it will always be cheaper to convey bulky commodities from shore to shore, on the surface of the water, than by land under it. Mr. Clarke, in his letter hints, that he did not choose to run the risk of the expense of publishing the pamphlet, but that this was undertaken by a Gravesend acquaintance ; and, as I suspect,

* Vol. LXVIII. p. 565 ; Mr. Clarke's pamphlet is reviewed, vol. LXIX. p. 1056.—In 1812 Mr. Clarke (who is living 1830) communicated to Mr. Britton, " An Attempt to ascertain the age of the Church of Barfreston in Kent, with remarks on the architecture of that building," printed in the " Architectural Antiquities," vol. IV. pp. 19—51.

by Pocock, the historian and printer of that town. He mentions his having heard, that Dodd is to be put out of the business, and the work to be conducted under Col. Twiss ; and that this intelligence came some days since from Lord Darnley. It is mentioned by Mr. Clarke, as one motive for his engaging again in controversy *versus* the tunnelist, that he wished to divert his thoughts, and to abate the chagrin he had suffered from the unsuccessfulness of another attempt to amend his situation and circumstances ; and he explains himself by alluding to a refusal of his services to accompany Major Holloway to Constantinople, and indeed through the Turkish empire. He thinks himself not to have been fairly treated in the negociation, but he casts not the least imputation on the Major, who honoured him with his friendship and influence, and who he represents to be the only friend he had ever formed from his Ordnance connections.

"To La Piew and Dean Chambers my correspondent passes from the tunnel subfluvial ; and he labours to justify the change of profession in a man, who is with him a very favourite character. 'I am certain, he says, ' no sense of duty, or even common propriety, was violated by that good man, whose sanctity did not consist only in externals.' But my opinion is, that in this instance, as in that of Linacre, whose becoming an ecclesiastic was much censured by his contemporaries, a regard to interest was the *primum mobile ;* and well was he paid for the transmutation, by being appointed Dean of St. Stephen's Chapel. The quotation from Mr. Clarke's letter is followed by this article of information, which, I have a notion, will be as pleasing to you as to myself. ' Dr. Chambre's portrait, cast in plaister, has long been promised me by a person employed by the engineers at Gravesend, who has been known and worked at the Speaker's. He was induced to undertake it on the sight of my rough plan ; and, whether the notion of a well has been communicated to the superior or not, I find it is intended to make a strict search after one about La Piew, which I have since visited, and drawn the habit of the Doctor, but whether it be of Priest or Deacon I can scarcely decide.'

"I remain, dear Sir, yours sincerely,   S. DENNE."

---

100. "DEAR SIR,   *Wilmington, Feb.* 10, 1799.
"Not any regular series of Lambeth Doctors has ever been published, as I believe ; it would be very voluminous for a course of 267 years, for it was by the statute of the 25th Henry VIII. cap. 21, A. D. 1533, that the power of dispensations was taken from the Pope and vested in the Archbishop of Canterbury ; and, as Bishop Gibson has observed in a note, the right of conferring degrees of all kinds is given to the Archbishop by this statute, and that this power hath not been abro-

LETTERS OF REV. SAMUEL DENNE, F.S.A. 759

gated or touched by any succeeding law. The edition of the
Codex which I cite is that published in 1713; and the part of
the note alluded to is in vol. I. p. 106.

 "Schoolmaster Carter's History of Cambridge University, in
which he has given the list of Proctors from 1600 to 1752, with
a circle of the Proctors for fifty years, commencing 1751, was
consulted by me before I proposed the query to you, when the
cycle might have been originally settled, and on what mode of
computation the arrangement was made, as nothing can be collected from Carter, nor unfortunately either from Fuller in his
History of Cambridge, or from Le Neve's Fasti. Carter's Circle
is, I have a notion, a copy from that printed with an Abridgement
of the Statutes; subjoined to it is this note concerning Trinity-
hall: 'This house having but few divines, it affords a Proctor
but once in fifty years, unless one dies in that office, when the
remaining part of the year is supplied from thence.' But the
list given does not correspond with the period of fifty years, as
is plain from the following items: 'A. 1601. Robert Naunton;
A. 1645. Charles Eden; A. 1696. William Tindall; A. 1747. William Ridlington; A. 1798 John Vickers. Between Naunton
ton and Eden there was an interval of no more than forty-four
years; and since 1747 there has been an interval of fifty-one
years. My brother having become B.A. when the Proctor was
last of Trinity-hall, occasioned his starting the subject; and it
is the less to be wondered at that it should have made a lasting
impression upon his mind, as Proctor Ridlington was as rigid
and perverse in his office as any man who ever traversed the
theatre with his book and gold chain, and as he had for his Deputy or Moderator the martinet Ross *. What a contest did these
reformers stir up by a vain attempt to make the disputations
and the declamations of the Bachelors what they termed a
serious exercise! an opposition to which subjected the author of
the Bath Guide to a suspension, 'ab omni gradu suscepto et
suspiciendo,' a sentence that has been in force for more than
half a century, for it was passed a few days before the commencement in 1748; and, if I did not hear it announced, I was
certainly in the Law-schools pending the trial before the Delegates, on an appeal against the jurisdiction of the Vice-Chancellor.

 "'Have you seen (asks Dr. Latham) the pamphlet about the
antient Clausentum at Southampton †? I have not been there,
but Lord Palmerston and Sir Charles Blagdon have; and tell
me that they can make it all out (vide Gough's Camden's Britannia, which gives a very good account.) Many coins are continually turned up by the plough as low as the Emperor Gor-
dianus. I know no more about it myself than what I have said
above.'

* John Ross, afterwards Bishop of Exeter; see "Literary Anecdotes,"
vol. II. p. 184.   † By Sir Henry Charles Englefield, Bart. F.S.A.

" To the inquiry I made whether there was likely to be any posthumous publication from the escrutoire of the voluminous writer Pennant, the answer was, ' By what I saw at my late friend Pennant's when at Downing, there is at least as much yet unpublished in manuscript as has yet come from his pen; no less than twenty-two volumes in folio, *viz.* Outlines of the Globe, of which only the View of Hindostan has yet made its appearance; and these seem to be fit for publication, being written out in a very fair hand, and, except in selection of necessary plates and other decorations, seem to be fit for the undertaking of any bookseller who may dare to attempt it. As to his son, I never heard a hint of his having written any thing with an intent of publishing; but I believe he furnished his father with much matter during his travels in Switzerland, and other parts, where he was for some time.'

" In what year was it that Mr. Wedderburne moved in the House of Commons for leave to bring in a Bill to empower Companies, Hospitals, and other Corporate Bodies, to alienate their estates, and to vest the purchase money in the public funds? If I am not mistaken, the scheme was opposed with spirit, and rejected by a considerable majority; though now, under the new act for the redemption of the land tax, all persons whatever possessed of lands in mortmain may dispose of a part thereof for this purpose. Mr. Wedderburne was at the time Solicitor, if not Attorney-general; but supposing my school-fellow, Mr. Thurlow, to have been then the Attorney-general, I imagine that he was a sturdy objector to this innovating project. To me it seems far from being very improbable that the year will soon come, when the parochial clergy will be encouraged, and many of them induced to accept, as a commutation for their tithes, stipends arising from the public funds, because the stock, when thus appropriated, will not be vendible, nor of course have any effect upon the market.

" Being second cousin to Mrs. Harvey, mother of Mr. Harvey (Vicar of Eastry, and late Vicar of St. Laurence, which, by permission, he resigned in favour of his son, though he continues to officiate in the new chapel at Ramsgate,) he apprised me of her death on Monday, 14th of January, in the eighty-third year of her age; and he also adverted to the death of his father on the 20th of February last, in his 84th year (see Obituary of the Gentleman's Magazine for March, p. 260), with this somewhat remarkable circumstance, that he deceased on the anniversary of his wedding-day, having lived with his wife in the utmost harmony and affection sixty-four years complete. My friend Harvey, who was, you will recollect, a Benedictine, is the only clergyman named as a Commissioner for the redemption of the land tax in the county of Kent; and, as it may be inferred that the appointment had the concurrence of the Lord Warden of the Cinque Ports, to whom Mr. Harvey must have been introduced as an acting magistrate in the Isle of Thanet, and as the elder brother of Admiral Henry Harvey, Commander-in-chief at the Leeward Islands, and to the gallant Captain John Harvey, of the Brunswick, there is room to hope that he may in due time receive some more lucrative post in the line of his profession; perhaps a Stall at Rochester, if not in Canterbury Cathedral, of which Church he is one of the Six Preachers, an office he always performs to the satisfaction of his hearers; and, according to the opinion I have been able to form of his brother Commissioners, he is as well qualified as either one of them to carry the Redemption Act into execution, should the scheme under the new Bill be rendered practicable.

"I remain, dear Sir, yours truly,   S. DENNE."

---

101. Mr. DENNE to Mr. NICHOLS.

"DEAR SIR,   *Wilmington, Feb.* 14, 1799.

"To your inquiry concerning the time when the Prelates of London discontinued their residence in their Episcopal Palace *juxta* their Cathedral, I can at present only refer you for information to Wharton de Episc. Londinen. and to Sir Henry Spelman's English Works, part II. p. 213. From the latter volume I have occasionally met with intelligence material concerning the houses or places of abode belonging to the Bishops of other Dioceses, but I cannot from memory make any report of the houses of the Bishop of London: and the book of which my father was possessed, and which he has frequently cited in his interleaved Le Neve's Fasti, is among my brother's collection.

"Obliged am I to you for the proof sheets of Appendix to Atterbury's Epistolary Correspondence, which shall be properly revised; and for your giving me such a gentle tap touching the long promised miscellaneous remarks on the Arrii and Sebosi you are entitled to my thanks. My notion concerning the cause of Atterbury's allusion to Arrius and Sebosus is, that there was between him and Cicero such a resemblance as to talents, views, and conduct political, that he found himself to be, when retired to Bromley-house, in a similar situation with Tully, while at his villa, after the downfall of the party to which he was so strongly attached; and both these able men had reason to regret that they chose to be ruling statesmen instead of taking the lead as philosophers and literary characters. The choice was the more inexcusable in the Prelate, because he was a Christian divine.

"The Vicar of Wilmington and Darenth envies not the self-denying Common Councilman * of the Ward of Farringdon Without in his appointment to be elected a Commissioner of Taxes, for he is persuaded that he shall be obliged to employ enough of his time in ascertaining how deep the new financial gauge will dip

* Mr. Nichols, who had accepted the office of Commissioner of the Income Tax.

into the purses and note books of the trio, his brother, his sister, and self; and the more irksome will be the task, as he continues to be a polemophobist, and an advocate of course for a speedy peace; but, alas! that is not the ruling passion of the people of either France or of old England, though it may be easily proved that both countries suffer extremely by war.

"Yours truly,   S. Denne."

---

102. Mr. Denne to Mr. Gough.

" Dear Sir,   *Wilmington, Feb. 28, 1799.*

" Seldom hath a budget been dispatched from Wilmington to Cicero's Head without some scroll addressed to Enfield; but in the packet sent a few days ago to Mr. Nichols, there certainly was not for you a scrap of antiquarian or other intelligence, because I was unwilling longer to delay transmitting the promised reveries touching *Arrii et Sebosi* that are to be attached to the Memoirs of Bishop Atterbury, who was so unpolite as to apply, in a letter to Pope, these names rather contemptuously to the gentlemen in his time resident in the vicinage of Bromley-house.

" Having in a letter to Archdeacon Law expressed a wish that some member of every college would so far follow the example of Mr. Masters as to compile at least a catalogue of members for the use of any person who might be disposed to form *Fasti Cantabrigienses*; this was the answer I received: ' On your mention of Mr. Masters's list of the Members of his College, I recollected that my late valued friend Dr. Farmer talked to me of an account that he had kept of his contemporaries at Emanuel. I shall, when I have an opportunity, inquire whether this manuscript be existent, and into the accuracy of its information. He professed to me, that he had noticed the situation of the members of our college, pointing out any changes in it, and an account of their literary productions. I shall be deemed, I fear, an apostate, having just entered my son at St. John's*. I now

---

* Henry Law, of St. John's-college, Cambridge, took the degree of LL. B. in 1806; he is now Vicar of Standon in Hertfordshire, to which he was presented in 1811 by William Plumer, Esq. formerly M.P. for that county, who married in 1760 the Hon. Frances-Dorothea Carey, aunt to Mr. Law; but lost her after a union of only sixteen months. Archdeacon Law's wife was her next sister the Hon. Mary-Elizabeth Carey, third daughter of Lucius-Charles sixth Viscount of Falkland, by the Right Hon. Jane dowager Viscountess Villiers (widow of James-Fitzgerald Viscount Villiers, who died in the life time of his father John Earl of Grandison,) and daughter and heiress of Richard Butler, of London, Esq. The following epitaph by the Archdeacon to the memory of his brother, wife, and father, appears on an altar tomb in Broxbourn church-yard, at the east end of the church: " Under this stone are interr'd the remains of Henry Hoadly Law, son of Stephen and Martha Law, who died Septem-

know nothing of the Society at Emanuel; and, attached as I still feel myself to it, yet such partiality is not to operate in the momentous concern of a son's education. Mr. Smith, one of the Tutors of St. John's, is the very particular friend of Mr. Dampier; is thence well known to me, and his merits are universally allowed.'

" Other articles of family and public intelligence, shall, for your amusement, be extracted from two letters of my chit-chat correspondent :—

" Mr. Archdeacon thus begins his letter of Feb. 14: ' You will not wonder that my attention is primarily directed to the marriage of my daughter. The union, that was completed on Tuesday last, met with my entire approbation. My acquaintance with Mr. Biscoe * has been short; but every thing that I have seen has been satisfactory, and more ample testimonies of character I could not have wished for. I trust that he will be happier in this connexion than in a former one; if I may be allowed to commend my daughter, I would assert, that a milder and a more accommodating disposition is not to be met with. I must regret the separation from her; and if her two maiden sisters should follow her example, I shall feel myself in a very forlorn state, however anxiously I ought to wish for their advantageous settlement in life. Our Dean has now left Rochester; he was so good as to prolong somewhat his stay here, in order to perform the marriage ceremony at St. Margaret's Church.'

" Stephana being the Christian name of the bride, I have no doubt that she received it at the font in compliment to her grandsire; and from the report made of her by her father, she appears to be, happily for herself and the bridegroom, endowed with a large portion of those amiable qualities for which Governor Law was distinguished and honoured. The maiden name of the wife, to whom Mr. Biscoe was before unfortunately wedded, I have not been able to discover. G——, who acquired opulence in the East Indies, is that of her gallant. They still cohabit, but where I know not. An intimacy between Miss S. Law, and a sister of Mr. Biscoe, who is a married lady advantageously settled †, brought on the acquaintance of the nuptial pair.

ber the 7th, 1768, aged 19 years. Of the Hon'ble Mary-Elizabeth Law, daughter of Lucius Viscount Falkland, and wife of the Rev. John Law, D. D. who died October 1, 1783, aged 44 years. And of Martha Law, wife of Stephen Law, Esq. who died February 9, 1785, aged 77. As a testimony of fraternal, conjugal, and filial affection, this stone is inscribed by the relation who was united by these several ties to the above justly valued and beloved, and who feelingly deplores their loss."

* Joseph Seymour Biscoe, Esq. of Pendhill, Surrey, only son of Vincent Biscoe, of Austin Friars, Esq. by Lady Mary Seymour, only daughter of Edward eighth Duke of Somerset; he was elected F. S. A. about 1797. His daughter Mary was married in 1820 to Sir Robert-Harry Inglis, Bart. F. R. S. and S. A. now M. P. for the University of Oxford; and Frances in 1830 to George Basevi, Esq. F. S. A.

† Mary (only daughter), married in 1798 to William Bensley, Esq. a

" Hasted, as an advertisement may have apprised you, has let off another squib from his compressed History of our County, and a copy of the dedication thereof: ' To Joseph Musgrave, Esq. of Kypier, in the Bishopric of Durham,' is, as usual, sent for your perusal, being aware that otherwise you may not have the reading of it. ' Sir, Be pleased to accept this tribute of grateful respect for the friendship you have honoured me with, a friendship begun in our early days, when we first imbibed the rudiments of our education at the same seminary of learning in the county of Kent, whilst we were under our respective paternal roofs in the same neighbourhood. Your property in the county, your encouragement of learning, and of this History in particular in the earliest publication of it, joined to your well known liberality of sentiment, will, I am certain, induce you to continue your patronage to this edition, and to the author of it, which will add to those favours you have already conferred on him, who is, with much respect, your most faithful, &c.

 ' *London, Dec.* 10, 1798.   Edward Hasted.'

" The King's-school, attached to the Dean and Chapter of Rochester, must be the seminary alluded to, Mr. Hasted's father having at the time a house in Chatham, and the father of Mr. Musgrave being Store-keeper to the Office of Ordnance in that place. Mr. Musgrave has property in Borden, not far from Sittingbourne; and under that parish, as he has the advowson of the Vicarage, there is probably an account of him and his connexions. He is a man of very different character from his school-fellow, being discreet, and possessed of many engaging qualities; and I doubt not of the Historian's having often experienced the liberality of his disposition.

  " I remain, dear Sir, yours truly, S. Denne."

---

 103. " Dear Sir,   *Wilmington, March* 18, 1799.

" Acceptable was the intelligence that the now Director S. A. had communicated a billet to his indefatigable predecessor; and pleased was I to learn that the memoir on Arabic Numerals was not to be consigned to Coventry, because the compiling of it really cost us both much time and research; and, though it does not aim to fix the time when these symbols of arithmetic were first used in England, and much less to ascertain the original inventors of them, it will clearly show how astonishingly slow was the progress of them in common use after their excellency must have been understood.

" Obliged am I to you for a copy of the sepulchral inscription over the remains of a quondam Vicar of Town Malling; and the remark I have to offer on one of the lines, which is

Director of the East India Company, who was created a Baronet in 1801, and died in 1809, s. p. Lady Bensley died Feb. 28, 1830; see Gent. Mag. vol. C. i. 281.

somewhat quaint, is, that it implies there was a vulgar garrulity afloat that was not to the credit of the deceased Vicar of
Cheshunt. By way of return you shall have a copy from my
father's Repertory of Incumbents of the Diocese of Rochester
of what he has perpetuated concerning Mr. Browne.
  "'Carolus Browne, A. M. instit. ad Vic. Malling Occident.
March 13, 1730, per mortem Sim. Babbe, Patron. Tho. Twisden,
Baroneto (E Reg^ro Sam. Bradford, Ep^i.) ; admiss. in Diac.
Ord. Sept. 25, 1715, et in Presbyt. Sept. 22, 1717. (E Reg^ro
superscript.) E Coll. Trin. Cantab. Vicar. etiam de Cheshunt,
Hertf. comitat. obiit Maii 27, 1748, et sepult. est apud Cheshunt.'
From some other notes in English, minuted by my father in a
different book, it is plain that Mr. Browne was for several years
Curate of Town Malling, from which circumstance he became
acquainted with the Patron. Nov. 23, 1716, he was licensed to
the Curacy, with a stipend of £.40 and surplice fees, provided
they did not exceed £.10 *per annum ;* and he was to read morning prayers all Litany and Saints' days, and to catechise three
times a week during Lent. At the primary visitation of Bishop
Bradford, Mr. Browne returned an answer to the Prelate's injunctions concerning the benefactions to that parish, dated
Sept. 28, 1724; and from the term 'injunctions' being used, it
must be concluded that he had not taken proper notice of the
previous article of inquiry. On looking into the Preacher's
Assistant, I observe that he published two Sermons preached at
the Assizes at Hertford in the year 1740. Simon Babb, Mr.
Browne's predecessor at West Malling, had a dispensation of
absence granted to him Oct. 11, 1717, upon his going to the
Isle of Providence in North America, but he returned to England, and became Curate of St. Giles's-in-the-Fields.
  " Somewhat mortified, but not in the least surprised, was I,
when I read the complaint of your sensible clerical correspondent in Dorsetshire, that he could obtain no satisfactory
account concerning the organs used in so many churches before
the reformation, as I have hitherto in vain pursued the like
inquiry. The estimated weight of the iron, mentioned in the
return of the church utensils at Buckland Newton, was, I suppose, noticed in order to its being sold ; as to the 'pair' of organs,
that was the customary mode of expression, meaning a set ; and
the same phrase was used for a pair, or pack, of cards. In
country parish churches, even where the district was small, there
was often a choir of singers, for whom forms, desks, and books
were provided ; and they probably most of them had benefactors
who supplied them with a pair of organs, that might more pro-

---

* "M. S. Caroli Browne, A. M. hujus ecclesiæ, necnon ecclesiæ de
Malling Occiden. in agro Cant. nuper Vicarii. De cujus vita moribusque
sileat hoc marmor, garrulus loquatur populus, pronunciabit vero Christus.
Obiit annum agens quinquagesimum quintum 17 kalendas Jun. 1748." —
Mr. Browne was presented to Cheshunt by James Earl of Salisbury in 1734.

perly have been termed a box of whistles; and to the best of
my recollection, there were in some of the Chapels of the Colleges in Cambridge, very, very indifferent instruments. The
organ of the Chapel belonging to our old House was removed
before I was admitted. If you cast your eye on " Addenda to the
Histories of Lambeth Palace and Lambeth Parish," p. 272, you
will see that in 1565, ' an olde paire of organs in that Church
was sold for £.1. 10s.' It is also mentioned in the Churchwardens' accounts, that in 1517 there was a payment of 10s. to
Sir William Argall for the organs; and that in the year 1568 a
fee of 8s. was paid for keeping the organs one yere, and new
organs must be meant.

" From the small Rectory of Keston to the Parsonage of
Berewick in Elmet *, is a very advantageous translation. The
Rector of Keston being one of us peculiar Clerks of Shoreham
Deanery, it was Mr. Hodgson's duty to have made his appearance
at the visitation of Sevenoaks, but, as he lived at Croydon, he
was, I believe, in the habit of making his bow there to the
Dean of the Arches; at least I do not recollect the seeing him
among us but when he was in course the Preacher and he then
appeared to me to be a brother who had not been an assiduous
labourer in his pædadogish occupation. Keston must be a convenient *commendam* to the Vicar of Croydon. Of Mr. Ireland's †
Sermons I know nothing more than I learnt from the Monthly
Review, vol. XXII. p. 350.

" I remain, dear Sir, yours truly,   S. DENNE."

----

104. " DEAR SIR,   *Wilmington, April* 1, 1799.
" From my correspondent at Rochester I have had, since I
wrote last, a very communicative epistle; but, alas! Mr. Archdeacon Law was obliged to begin it with a plea for his delay in
not writing to me, owing to his having been detained eleven
days on a visit to his brother-in-law, Mr. Cartier, of Bedgbury,
' who on the 22d of February was suddenly seized, while sitting
with two friends after dinner, with a paralytic stroke. The use
of the left side is nearly taken away.' Truly do I sympathise
with Mr. Archdeacon on this severe attack, which must inevitably render life a burden to a friend and relation so deservedly
dear to him. Mr. Cartier was a nonpareil East India Governor;
and his conduct since his retirement into the country so excellent that his continuance in life is the anxious wish of his neighbourhood ‡.

* Rev. James Hodgson, collated to Keston by Archbishop Cornwallis
in 1774.
† Rev. John Ireland, D. D. Vicar of Croydon, and now Dean of Westminster.
‡ John Cartier, Esq. was Governor of Bengal for two years previously
to the appointment of the celebrated Mr. Hastings. In 1774 he married his second wife, Stephana, daughter of Stephen Law, Esq. of Broxbourn, formerly Governor of Bombay, and sister to the Archdeacon of

"My Rochester correspondent mentions the underwritten relative to an inferior member of that Cathedral. ' Did you ever hear of the appointment of a Minor Canon to a King's Chaplainship? Mr. Menzies is, I believe, the only instance. He avers that he did not now wish for this distinction; that the honour had been solicited about eight years since by the Marchioness de Grey, at which period he had entertained hopes of accessional preferment.' The answer I returned was, that I knew not of a single precedent; and I have further to observe, that Mr. Menzies has, in my opinion, cause to regret the appointment, for that to a royal scarf there is a constant and unavoidable charge attached that will draw deep upon the slender revenue of a Minor Canonry.

"Not without some exertion, under a pressure of business in some points perplexing, after a much longer interval than usual, ' W. and D. ' has revived his correspondence with Sylvanus Urban; and he is inclined to believe that the curious comment in an original letter written by Garter Anstis on King Jemmy s motto on the medal of the Order of the Bath, published in the March miscellany *, will afford entertainment to ' D. H.' Two papers are likewise forwarded for insertion in a subsequent Magazine. In one of them is ascertained, on evidence hardly controvertible, who was the unprecedented grand bankrupt in 1718, stigmatised by Bishop Fleetwood in his short address to the Citizens of London, prefixed to the Sermon he published that year, ' On the Justice of Paying Debts †.' Crito, in the Supplement to the last volume, by questing on the scent of the clerical second editor of that Sermon, was quite at fault, as the sportsmen style it; and it is left to the guess of a quondam member of the old House to name the Benedictine who furnished to W. and D. this authentic information. In the other paper reasons highly probable are assigned for supposing that Margaret Vernon, whose imploring and interesting epistle filled half a page in the January Magazine, was, on ceasing to be the Prioress of a little Convent co. Bucks, raised to the presidency of the Nuns of her order in the Great Abbey of West Malling ‡. The year of her death cannot be precisely fixed, but, as she was not in the list of pensioners in 1553, noticed by Willis as being then existing, it may be fairly concluded that the term of her natural life was ended. W. and D. has it also in contemplation to *hitch* in a few lines concerning a word much more commonly used than Lexicographer Johnson seemed to imagine §. Did D. H. ever meet with it in Hudibras? for

Rochester. He resided at Bedgbury, in the parish of Goudhurst, near Tunbridge Wells, from that time till his death, which took place Jan. 23, 1802, in his 69th year (when a memoir of his life was published in the Gentleman's Magazine, vol. LXXIII. p. 183.)
* See the Gentleman's Magazine, vol. LXIX. p. 194.
† Sir Joshua Hodges; vide ibid. p. 288.
‡ Ibid. p. 292; and corrections, p. 392.   § Ibid. p. 451.

it is rather strange that Butler should not frequently have *hitched* in a term so quaint, and yet so apt in his doggrel rhymes and in his display of ludicrous characters.

"On talking with Mr. Peete, F. L. S. on the subject of Mr. Ord's letter, and on the address circulated by Leicester, P., I understand that Lord Lewisham, to whose name these three initials are subjoined, is a meritorious disciple of Linnée, being a naturalist and particularly fond of botany, in the specimens of which he has made collections. This pursuit, however, is not likely to forward his researches in the antiquarian line *; and I am yet to learn whether he has ever laboured in the hive surmounted by a lamp that has for its motto *Non extinguetur*.

"Dufresne I take it for granted was examined by your learned clerical correspondent co. Dorset, touching *v. Organum*, and if so, that he must be apprised of a passage cited from William of Malmesbury, noticing that warm water was used in order to excite a violent wind that filled ' concavitatem barbiti et per multiforatiles transitus æneæ fistulæ modulatos clamores emittunt.'

"Ere this, most probably, the pipes of the organ in the chapel of King's college have sounded a dirge in compliment to the veteran who was the mover of the keys †. On the Commencement Sunday, when I took the degree of M. A. Dr. Randall kept his music act; and on Tuesday, as Professor, he in a motley coloured gown presented a Bachelor of Music to that first degree in the science, the Doctor having in his hand the form written in English, for he certainly was not a Latin scholar. I also remember that, though he was a Doctor, and eke a Professor, he was not admitted to a place among the literati of that denomination, but took his seat among the A. M.'s. He was, however, stared at and admired while walking upon the Clare-hall piece, because he had on a robe that was novel to the academics in general. To the best of my recollection, he was trained in the King's Chapel; and he attained to a far greater age than there was reason to believe he would, as he was in his juvenile days a very free liver. I have understood that, what rarely happens, he was a rake reformed by marrying a discreet woman, for whom he had deservedly a high regard.

"I think I heard Catharine Boys speak of his having children, and that they were daughters. Did Mr. Professor acquire much credit by the music he composed for Gray's Ode on the installation of the Duke of Grafton as Chancellor; and in particular were there affecting sounds in the notes applied to the still small voice of Gratitude?

"I am, dear Sir, yours truly,   S. DENNE."

* Some persons at this period wished to place Lord Lewisham in the chair of the Society of Antiquaries, in the room of the Earl of Leicester.

† John Randall, Mus. B. 1744, Professor of Music 1755, Mus. D. 1756; died at Cambridge, March 18, 1797, in his 84th year.

105. " Dear Sir, *Wilmington, April* 10, 1799.

" Adam Wall's note concerning the mode of appointing Proctors at Cambridge has obviated the principal difficulty that puzzled my brother and self. To the cycle printed with the excerpta from the statutes, published for the information of the young academics, the term fifty years was subjoined, and therefore Historian Carter is not to be blamed for circulating it. What is still wanting is the date of the decree referred to by Wall ; and I shall add only one remark more, *viz.* that it seems rather unfair that, when one of the Proctors is of a large college, he should be always the senior Proctor, supposing there may be an additional pecuniary emolument to the senior above the junior Proctor. I may, however, in this point have been misinformed.

" To the notice taken in the Pursuits of Architectural Innovation, No. VIII. (Gentleman's Magazine, March, p. 189) of the regalls, or small organs, and the large organs, I am persuaded that neither yourself nor your sensible clerical correspondent of co. Dorset, has been inattentive. That the writer and able delineator * has not met with a fac-simile of one or the other, on stone, wood, or paper, may be reasonably presumed ; because, if he had, he would have exercised his pencil, as he reports he has done upon the seventeen specimens of the instruments in the hands of figures over the columns in Beverley Minster. But has not ' An Architect*' been rather precipitate in the opinion he has formed, that all these musical instruments must have been in common use in England, because they are here represented ? Might not the sculptors be foreigners ; or, if natives, might they not carve from copies of ornaments prepared for the instruction and assistance of artists ? He mentions, that on the thirteenth figure there was a small harp of an uncommon form ; and that in the sixteenth compartment an angel held a small harp of a still more uncommon form ; statue ninth exhibits a man with a bass, or double bagpipe ; but, notwithstanding this may have always been a favourite instrument with the Scots, is there any collateral evidence that in England it was employed to accompany the voices of any choir, cathedral, collegiate, or parochial ?

" Eton-college have come to a resolution to part with the Manor of Baldwins, situated upon Dartford Heath ; and Mr. Fraser, the lessee, is in treaty for the purchase of it. Mr. Hulse was for several years after I came to Wilmington the lessee ; and he has told me that, on his hinting to Dr. Barnard that he conceived the College were too sharp in their demands of fines of renewal, the Provost was wont to reply with some humour that Mr. Hulse did not know the real value of the estate, for that by the generosity of Henry VIII. the College had it in lieu of a tract of ground in and near Pall Mall. It is, however, upon the

* Mr. John Carter, F.S.A.

whole a vile farm; nor do I think that the most skilful and industrious man could acquire a comfortable livelihood by cultivating it.

" Little did I think that my name, and my desultory lucubrations in one branch of science, would ever be deemed of such importance as to be hitched into metre; however, I really think that the satirical author of the Pursuits of Literature has paid me a high complment by placing me in the same verse with an antiquary of the uppermost class *. To this Dunciader's (whoever he may be) eulogy on the rising planet I in part agree; as allowing Mr. Lysons to be an expert antiquary in Roman matters, and to have a sufficient knowledge of the classics for illustrating the remains he has so elegantly delineated. But English antiquities do not appear to me to be his forte, from a want of knowledge in books, printed or manuscript, relative to them, as eke from a want of capability in starting a happy surmise. In his description of the south door of Quenington in Gloucestershire, published in Archæologia, there is, as I imagine, a material mistake. Some remarks upon it were at the time scribbled by me; and if I can find the small piece of paper which contains them, you shall have a copy. From the distich sent, I am convinced that the writer is a Cantab., and I think it likely he has his prejudices against the old House, though we, who were there trained, glory in its having been a seed-plot of antiquaries. Of what college is Mr. Mathias, and what may be his general character?

" Having communicated to my correspondent at Rochester † Mr. Wilberforce's excuse for not continuing to the veteran Curate and Lecturer at Betchworth the allowance that had been paid to him yearly by Mrs. Bouverie for his extra duty on a Saturday, he adds this article of intelligence concerning the property of that opulent lady: ' It comes (he writes) from Mr. Hallett, who is a great collector of news, and who reports, that Lord Radnor, as heir-at-law, disputes that part of the will which concerns Sir Charles Middleton, on the ground of its having been obtained by misrepresentation. The ground must surely be a very feeble one to stand upon, especially as the will was made in 1784 (query 9 ?). Mr. Hallett, however, avers that a Bill is already filed in Chancery. I may probably have before conveyed to you my disapprobation of the allotment of the Teston estate. Where property comes by succession, it seems not right to me to convey it from the heirs-at-law. Sir Charles might have been accommodated with the property for his life; but I object to his right of bequeathing it.'—To the pertinency and strength of Mr. Archdeacon's reflections on the impropriety of alienating to a no-relation an estate to the prejudice of an heir-at-law, I readily subscribe; and I likewise coincide in opi-

* " For now the Dennes and Stukeleys of the day
Must yield to Lysons' more enlightened ray." † Archdeacon Law.

nion with him that, if there has been a misrepresentation, it will be but a weak plea to urge against a devise made with deliberation and so long adhered to. As the Baronet is a shrewd North Briton, there having been a misrepresentation is a probable surmise, particularly as Mrs. Middleton, afterwards my Lady, who, it is notorious had acquired a paramount influence over her friend the testatrix, was own sister to Admiral Gambier; but I rather demur, and so perhaps may my informant, on Lord Radnor's having really commenced a suit in equity with such a little prospect of success, if the fee of the estate was in Mrs. Bouverie; and it has been generally understood that there was a compromise settled between her and the heir-at-law.

"Many weeks have passed since I heard from my correspondent at the Ordnance Office, Gravesend; in consequence I am not apprised whether he has employed his pen and his pencil on subjects of antiquities, or in controverting the novel attempt of a subaqueous communication between the counties of Kent and Essex. The Monthly Reviewers observe, that Mr. Dodd has met with a severe opponent in Mr. Clarke, who attacks him in all points; and in the Gentleman's Magazine for March * this preposterous scheme was humourously and well exposed, though no trait given from what quarter.

"Of the late Mr. Justice Boys, of Hawkhurst, I can advance nothing with certainty, but that he was not a son of Commodore Boys; and I have understood that the eminent practical agriculturalist of that name at Betshanger, does not bear any relation to the Historian of Sandwich, who was unquestionably the eldest son of the Lieutenant Governor of Greenwich Hospital. I remain, dear Sir, yours truly,   S. DENNE."

106. "DEAR SIR,   *Wilmington, April 19*, 1799.
"Since I transmitted to you my last, I have been favoured with a sheet replete with miscellaneous matter, chiefly of the antique cast, from my correspondent at the Ordnance Office in Gravesend. He was at a meeting of the Antiquaries when President Leicester announced from the chair, that, in consequence of his appointment to the Stewardship of his Majesty's Household, he had altered his mind about declining the seat of preeminence in which he was then placed. 'In a speech from the chair of some length, his Lordship assured the numerous Fellows then present, he was willing, if offered, to accept, for the ensuing year, the office he has hitherto held. This condescension gave occasion to a general approbation; it was communicated to his Lordship by the Heads and Canes of the Society, who replied with the usual numbers of low bows.' Mr. Clarke next mentions, that on the same evening a Mr. Meredith, of Islington, was put to the ballot, and that his recommendation was, *inter alios*, signed J. Wyatt; and that at the conclusion a mino-

* See Gent. Mag. vol. LXX. p. 200.

rity of forty-five was discovered, while the author of the History of Evesham * had admittance without a dissentient ball. Then follows this remark, ' I notice these trifling circumstances because they appear connected with a certain iterated ballot, and a secession. I do not say in consequence, but yet much to be lamented ; although the eminent author of the Pursuits of Literature, in some of his valuable notes, declares Mr. Lysons (whose Directorship I have heard was a job of Sir J. Banks) to be the best of antiquaries, and J. Wyatt the finest of architects ; and throws his gauntlet against gothicisms, and those who support and love them.' Mr. C. afterwards notices Mr. Secretary reading an explanation of the drawing of a figure on a monument in Staindrop Collegiate, now dispersed with others about the Church, and that it raised the smile of many. Mr. Carter, he says, considers it equal in beauty to any thing of any country and age; and recommended it as a model. But, though my correspondent does not fully subscribe to this notion for some reasons he has offered, he seems much pleased with the declaration of ' An Architect ' in the Gentleman's Magazine, that ere long will be fully considered the transition from the Saxon to the Norman style of architecture ; and I did not wonder at the satisfaction expressed by Mr. Clarke, because aware of there being a similarity in their notions upon the subject, though in one point, if I am not mistaken, he goes further than Mr. Carter seems to have done, as he supposes that the architects of that period were theoretical as well as practical mathematicians, and that it was from their skill in that science they adopted the angular arch, as being most suitable to the plan of the edifices they were constructing. Before Mr. Carter delivers his sentiments, I wish that his friend at Enfield, or some other person more conversant with books than himself, may be able to ascertain who were the earliest writers, both foreigners and natives, who made use of the phrase *Gothic* architecture. As the buildings erected were certainly formed on a scientific plan, and as the ornaments of some of them are unquestionably beautiful, and *prima facie* very striking to the eye of an unprejudiced spectator, I hold the term to be highly improper; and I attribute the origin of so degrading an epithet to some fastidious traveller, who imagined he could not better show his taste and his admiration of the Grecian structures he had lately viewed.

" Mr. Clarke is apprehensive that the Chapel of La Piew is gone to rest, from my long silence upon that subject; a fear which I have discouraged, in consequence of my having hinted to Mr. Ord, that in my opinion there ought to be an engraving of the ground plot from Mr. Carter's delineation, as also of some parts of the contiguous cloister. Mr. Carter has got a cast, though a rough one, of the whole key stone, containing the figure of Dr. Chambre, and of his two supporters ; but he adds, unfortunately, the nose of the Doctor, that is a little

* The Rev. William Tindal.

damaged in the original, has been further hurt in the carriage down to Gravesend. He, however, observes, that he can yet perceive the same face, at about the age of forty, that the head of Holbein represents in his picture, where the King is exhibited as delivering the charter to the College of Physicians. From Mr. Tracy Mr. Clarke has procured some illustrations of the armorial shields upon the key-stones of the St. Stephen's cloister, &c. that may be of use.

"By favour of the officers of Meopham parish, Mr. Clarke has so long had the perusal of the old Churchwarden's book as to allow him time for nearly copying the articles in which he takes much delight, as he says particulars of old church furniture are with him always acceptable; and he particularly notices that, our Lady's vestment of a Priest, Deacon, and Subdeacon, and appurtenances ('kept a sounder') with a vestment of crimson satin of Bruges, were cut into carpets, and made into 'a pyllowe for the chyldwyfe's seat.' According to him, the Historian of Gravesend has likewise got the old Book of Shorne; and from it had learnt that the oratory mentioned by Thorpe in Antiquities, p. 247, and of which there is an engraving, pl. xx. fig. 3, was a Gild Chapel of Corpus Christi. As Mr. Thorpe was well acquainted with Mr. Perfect, the veteran Vicar of Shorne, and with the ruling persons in that district, he could have found no difficulty in procuring a sight of that book; but, if I am not mistaken, whilst resident at Bexley, he confined his researches to the Register, though it is obvious that more parochial anecdotes in general he acquired from the Churchwardens book of accounts. One more extract from Mr. Clarke's letter shall be given, 'On the tunnel (he writes) you might expect some information, and should have it on a subject so curious; but the colonels and engineers, civil and military, keep all under a snug and close management. It was their opinion, and also that of the committee, that Mr. Dodd had not sounded the bed, and this was hinted in a certain pamphlet that issued from the wretched press of this town.'—Surely no colonel, no engineer, civil or military, will ultimately give a sanction to a scheme so preposterous and so extensive as a subaqueous communication between two counties that cannot be of the least use to the inhabitants of either; but motives are too obvious for their not too hastily bringing the question to a conclusion.

"I am led to notice, from a long paragraph in the Times, in the demise of the Rev. Clayton Mordaunt Cracherode, the setting of a much admired literary sun in Queen's-square, Westminster. The paragraph alluded to is doubtless written *con amore*; and it is a very laboured panegyric. From it, however, it appears, that his literary supellex was large, curious, and valuable, whether we consider the books, the collection of medals, the specimens of minerals, or the assemblage of prints and drawings; but as to the use he himself made of all or any of these articles *non constat*. Whilst I resided at Vauxhall above forty years ago, I had often seen him at Tom Payne's literary gallery, or literary coffee-house, and since I became F. A. S. have frequently met him at Somerset-place; but, notwithstanding my various attempts to discover what there might be in him more than in his contemporaries to give him the *eclat* he had acquired, I was not ever so fortunate as to trace a vestige. When in his small circle of friends, who were remarkable for their taste, abilities, and learning, he might be communicative and shine; but, from his reserve in public, I rather suspect that he did not duly consider that a man who is really possessed of knowledge ought to show to others that he has this gift. His encomiast has cited this line,

"Nil actum reputans, si quid superesset agendum,
and I will add another quotation,

"Scire tuum nihil est, nisi te scire hoc sciat alter.

"In consequence of his enjoying an affluent fortune, he sought no preferment in his professional department, not even a parochial benefice in the country to which he might have retired for change in the summer months: and an option of divers vicarages he must have had that are in the presentation of his college. It is admitted that he kept his Studentship of Christchurch; and, as it may presumed, from the inclination he had to preserve his connection with the men of learning in Oxford. From the high esteem the Presidents of the Royals and of the Antiques had of him, he was again and again upon the House List of Council of the two Societies, of which he was a Fellow; but was he not always a sleeping partner? at least I do not recollect any paper in Archæologia, or in Vetusta Monumenta, subscribed C. M. Cracherode. His being appointed a trustee of the British Museum shows he had a strength of interest among persons in the great world; and it will reflect a lasting honour upon his name; for, as it is related by the editor of the Anecdotes of Bowyer, 'Demosthenes Taylor counted the office of the Curator of the British Museum, the blue ribbon of a scholar; though he died without it. Diis aliter visum est.'

"Another illustrious character in the literary world, who was also a Fellow of the two Societies, is, I observe, recently departed; but Mr. Strange* was, in one respect, a different man from Mr. Cracherode, as he did not keep his talent wrapt up in a napkin. His Museum will yield benefit tickets to not fewer than four of the Peter Puffs with their hammers, *viz.* to Leigh with Sotheby, to Christie, and to King.

"On being favoured with the perusal of the entertaining Pursuits of Literature, I perceive that in the first part Mr. Cracherode is recorded as one of the frequenters of the Literary Coffee-

---

* See the "Literary Anecdotes," vol. VII. pp. 400, 683.

house, near the Mews-gate; and that there is a brief trait of
his character.

" Or must 1 as a wit with learned air,
Like Dr. Dewlap, to Tom Payne's repair,'
Meet Cyril Jackson, and mild Cracherode.

' Hold ! cries Tom Payne, that margin let me measuie,
And rate the separate value of the treasure ;
Eager they gaze—well, Sir, the feat is done,
Cracherode's Poetæ Principes have won.

" ' Note.—The Reverend Clayton Cracherode, M. A. Student
of Christ Church, Oxford, and one of the Trustees of the
British Museum. A rich, learned, and most amiable man, (to
use the words of the son of Sirach,) furnished with ability,
living peaceably in his habitation. His library is allowed to be
the choicest in old Greek and Latin authors of any private collection in this country.'

" Grateful is the return of the deceased for the honour conferred on him by electing him a Curator of the British Museum,
in bequeathing to it all his books, prints, drawings, coins, and
medals *; and it would have been a subject of regret had so
chosen a collection been dispersed. He has, however, it seems,
excepted a Polyglott Bible given to the Bishop of Durham; and
the first edition of Homer to his friend the Dean of Christ
Church, who is placed in the same verse with him as a resorter
to Tom Payne's Conversation-gallery.   Yours,   S. DENNE."

* "One of the most conspicuous and valuable accessions by gift to the
British Museum is the fine collection of books and prints bequeathed by
Mr. Cracherode. The library occupies a distinct room, under the title of
BIBLIOTHECA CRACHERODIANA, and contains the most choice copies in
classical and biblical literature; many of which are printed on vellum.
The editions of the fifteenth century Mr. Cracherode used modestly to
call a *specimen* collection; they form, perhaps, the most perfect *collana*,
or necklace, ever strung by one man; several of these volumes were formerly in the possession of the celebrated Grolier—a French *savan*, who
died in 1565, but his library was not sold till 1675. Mr. Cracherode's copy
of Walton's Polyglott Bible was left to the Bishop of Durham (Dr. Barrington), and the first edition of Homer to Dr. Cyril Jackson, late Dean of
Christchurch; the book, by the Dean's express order, has been restored
to the collection [as since has been Bishop Barrington's; see his will in
vol. V. of this Work, p. 625.] The printed books were valued at £.10,000,
and the prints at £.5,000. A catalogue drawn up by Mr. Cracherode, and
in his handwriting, is attached to the collection; from this catalogue our
selections have been made.—Mr. Cracherode was an elegant scholar and
an amiable man; his passion for collecting was strong even in death,
and whilst he was at his last extremity, Thane was buying prints for him
at Richardson's. In his final visit at Payne's shop, he put an Edinburgh
Terence into one pocket, and a large paper Cebes into the other; and
expressed an earnest desire to carry away Triveti Annales, and Henry
Stephens's Pindar, in old binding,—both beautiful copies." Clarke's
Repertorium Bibliographicum; where there is an engraving from the
portrait of Mr. Cracherode drawn by Edridge. See the "Literary Anecdotes," vol. IX. p. 666.

107. " DEAR SIR,   *Wilmington, April* 23, 1799.

" On St. George's-day this is scribbled, when all F. S. A.'s, who have the credit of their Society at heart, ought to have been, if practicable, at Somerset-place ; but it was really not in my power to give my attendance ; and all I have to hope is, that the job work (as Mr. Clarke terms it) of the Præses of the Royals may have been scouted effectually. However, let the contest have ended as it may, one thing is certain, that there is a spirit of disunion raised among the members that will not soon subside ; and that in consequence the pursuits of antiquities will meet with an interruption. Not that for some time past they have been encouraged as they ought to have been, and, though the plates of St. Stephen's Chapel and of Exeter Cathedral reflect an honour upon the corps, I must beg leave to repeat that to such fine engravings there ought to have been added some more account than passed the letter-press ; nor, as I ima- gine, would it have been an arduous task to have collected and digested sufficient materials.

" Dean Dampier was a zealous espouser of the Viscount *, and applied to Dr. Law to request he would solicit the ballot of Mr. Biscoe ; but, as the Archdeacon had before been rather pressed by Archdeacon Hamilton, to influence the same vote in favour of the Earl, he felt himself, under these circumstances, con- strained to maintain an entire neutrality ; so that whether his son-in-law was for or against the House List, I know not.

" In the Obituary of the Gentleman's Magazine for the cur- rent month, there will, it may be presumed, be a copious detail of the late great collector, whose Museum was in Queen-square, Westminster. That he was in very good circumstances it was reasonable to infer ; but that he was so affluent as some of the papers have represented him to be, I had not a suspicion. Pro- bably Master Urban will be able to apprise his readers, what might have been the original basis of such a column of wealth. The account you give me of him corroborates the surmise I had formed, that Mr. T. C. Cracherode was a very, very reserved man as to his diffusion of the knowledge he had acquired from the various curious articles he possessed of the book and coin cast, and of the natural specimens, and artificial drawings and prints, he is said to have selected with judgment and taste. Your report that there was a superfluity of bile, increased by the fear of an invasion, that proved fatal to him, was quite new to me.

" I am, dear Sir, yours truly,   S. DENNE."

108. " DEAR SIR,   *Wilmington, May* 13, 1799.

" Mr. Ord not having been at leisure to communicate to me his detail of the proceedings at Somerset-place on St. George's- day, I was much obliged to you for your favour received by the

* Lewisham.

post on Sunday; and join heartily with you in the congratulation on the victory obtained over Magog Banks. Not that I think, any more than yourself, that the re-elected Præses of our corps will be that active and useful person he ought to be, whilst seated in the chair of a literary corps; and at the same time I think that no true antiquary could consistently espouse his competitor, when even his advocate admitted, as was announced in the Morning Herald, that Lord Lewisham had not yet recommended himself by any very considerable attention to antiquarian pursuits. The science of heraldry, in which it is agreed the Earl of Leicester has acquired some knowledge, is doubtless a branch of antiquities; it will, however, require some pains to show, that there is likely to be a sprig of them, from the closest attention to Botany, and to other articles of Natural History; but I must own I have long wished, and I am persuaded so have you, that rank and title should not be made the primary motive in the choice of a Præs. S. A. It was a drawback to the pleasure I had in being assured of the victory obtained by the Earl, to learn that Mr. Craven Ord had not retained his seat in the Council, as the President must expect to be perpetually thwarted and opposed by the officers who have hitherto been so inimical to him; and besides we shall, in consequence of Mr. Ord's not being one of the conclave, find a difficulty in learning what is going, or rather perhaps what is not going forward in the pursuit to which we are both of us so strongly inclined. Concerning the late contest I shall at present make only more remark, *viz.* that, as the Earl was the favourite candidate with his Majesty, it is not a little strange that the Knight encircled with a red ribbon, and of the King's most honourable Privy Council, should choose to adopt so decisive a part in favour of the Viscount. One would rather have thought that a preference would have been given to the Steward of his Majesty's Household, before one of the principal officers upon the establishment of the Heir Apparent.

"The question started by Mr. Ruggles concerning the misletoe, merits a closer investigation; and I shall certainly make it my business to inquire of those who know more of woods than I profess to do, whether there are not proofs to be brought of the growth of that Druidical plant upon the oak. In the Weald of Kent there are so many trees, and those of all ages, that surely the fact may be ascertained; and, should the result be in the negative, it must, as you express yourself, be a deadly wound to a leading trait in the History of Druidism. From what I recollect, Arch-druid Stukeley never hinted a doubt upon this point; and I am apt to suspect Mr. Ruggles may be mistaken.

"During the last watering season upon Thanet Isle, Lord Thurlow had a house at St. Laurence, to which Ramsgate was heretofore a small appertaining fishing hamlet, though now increased to the size of a townlet. An intercouse ensued between his Lordship and the Chaplain of Ramsgate, my intelligent and worthy friend Mr. Harvey. The sternness of countenance and of behaviour by which his Lordship has been often characterised, was entirely removed; many agreeable hours did they pass together, and what attached the Peer and the Chaplain to each other was, their having been of Canterbury school, and consequently well acquainted with the striplings trained in that seminary. On application for topographical books relative to that quarter, Mr. Harvey supplied Lord Thurlow with Lewis's Thanet and with Boys's Collections for Sandwich, and with other smaller tracts; and upon them were made some pertinent remarks that I should not have expected, as I have understood the noble Lord has rather held in contempt antiquarian lore. But what struck Mr. Harvey as more extraordinary was, that he noticed his Lordship to be strictly re-teaching himself Greek; for that he had before him Aristophanes, and on one hand a Greek grammar and on the other a Lexicon. Lord Thurlow's two unmarried daughters were with their father, but unaccompanied by their mother. To his lasses my Lord seemed to show a proper regard, though Mr. Harvey thought he could perceive that there was somewhat of partiality towards the younger; they are sensible and well-behaved young women, and with a competent share of personal charms.

" By Dr. Law I was informed, that the new Prebendary of Westminster had been Chaplain to the House of Commons, and for some time in expectation of a reward for his services in that department. Mr. Archdeacon added, that Mr. Causton * had lately officiated for a friend in the Weald of Kent, where his praises had been generally celebrated. It was no small disappointment to him that he did not succeed Mr. Weston at Canterbury, on the promotion of that gentleman to the Residentiaryship of St. Paul's; but the mortification of so short a delay before he had a recompense for his labours must be now matter of joy, for, considering all the circumstances of the two Stalls, I am fully persuaded that that in the Abbey of St. Peter's is the most profitable and the most convenient.

" Noticing in the Obituary of the Gentleman's Magazine that the father of the late Mr. Cracherode was a circumnavigator with Anson, I examined the History of the Voyage erroneously attributed to Chaplain Walter, to see what was said upon the subject; and on inquiry I found that the Lieutenant-Colonel had the command of the invalids and marines, so thoughtlessly sent upon the expedition, under the denomination of land forces; but in another column of the Obituary there seems to

* The Rev. Thomas Causton, of St. John's college, Cambridge, B. A. 1791; M. A. 1794; D. D. 1820. He is now the senior Prebendary of Westminster; and holds the Rectory of Turveston in Buckinghamshire, to which he was presented by the Dean and Chapter of Westminster in 1804.

be an implication that will hardly stand the test, as it rather presumes that the Colonel laid the basis of his very large fortune from his acquisition in that voyage, for it appears from p. 483, he was not on board the Centurion at the time of the capture of the great prize, having returned to England in one of the Company's ships. The case I am satisfied was, as I purposed hinting to you in a former letter on the credit of a Westminster whom I have generally found correct in his report, that General Cracherode became possessed of a very large fortune by the death of an intestate relation at Clapham; and, I observe that Clapham was one of the few places occasionally visited by his son, though he did not choose ever to cross the back of a horse.

"With the ingenious, very ingenious Essay of Sir James Hall *, with his perspicuous mode of delivering his sentiments, and often with elegance, and with the correct and beautiful engravings that are subjoined to the volume, he must be a most fastidious reader who does not find a pleasure in the perusal; but it must likewise be confessed, that his notion of the origin and principles of Gothic architecture are too fanciful to be entitled to the approbation of any person of a moderate judgment in the science.

"Obliged am I to you for the loan of ' The Shade of Pope,' which I really think is inferior to the other works of the celecrated author of the Pursuits of Literature; and as the Bard was raised from the tomb chiefly to bewail the residence of Seceder Grattan at Twickenham, and to give the new Dunciader an opportunity of criticising the jacobinical publications of Godwin and other writers of that stamp, I must own I cannot discover either rhyme or reason in hitching in the distich against the antiquaries of the old House, unless it was done with the view of giving Director Lysons a little hoist in the expected contest on last St. George's-day.

"Bath †, of which you make repeatedly such a favourable report, is not yet arrived; but I have had from Mr. Lysons two proof sheets of my first paper on arabic numerals. But query when the second paper, with the additional remarks, shall be printed? will it not be advisable that you should examine the proof sheets, as you took the trouble of a journey to Helmdon, in order to survey the famous mantle-piece ‡.

"Mr. Clarke's pamphlet in quarto upon the Tunnel, and which was a kind present from the author, I shall wish to keep, as I may have occassion to consult the latter pages of it; the mathematics in the former being, I freely own, now above my compass, though possibly heretofore, when I occupied a chair in Tutor Masters' apartment, I might have understood the jet of

* On Gothic Architecture, published in 1796 in the Transactions of the Royal Society of Edinburgh, of which Sir James was President, and afterwards in a quarto volume, 1813.
† Carter's Views, &c. of Bath Abbey, published by the Society of Antiquaries. ‡ See it in the Gentleman's Magazine, vol. LXX. p. 1232.

the demonstration. Pertinent as is your remark about John
Bull's running mad about something or other, whether it be a
canal above or under ground, it seems that *Dodd* Quixote's
scheme of a tunnel between the two counties of Kent and Essex
is not a spick and span notion, there being in my last letter from
my correspondent at Rumsey the underwritten paragraph.

" ' Apropos, in respect to Mr. Pocock, I see the History of
Gravesend reviewed in a late Monthly, in which it was not
highly extolled. (Mem. It struck S. D. that the critical corps
had been as favourable in their report as could in reason have
been expected, considering that it was avowedly a mere compilation from books chiefly in print.) As to the subaqueous
excavation there to be carried on, whether it will succeed or not,
the thought is not new, for I remember Mr. Calcraft's father,
twenty-five or thirty years ago, was reported to have said, that such
an undertaking would be a good thing; and at Greenhithe the
lower people verily believed he was going to build a bridge
under the Thames, for so they expressed themselves, but the
moderately thinking people scouted the idea. I never thought
to hear more of it.'

" I remain, dear Sir, yours truly,   S. DENNE."

109. "DEAR SIR,   *Wilmington, May* 29, 1799.
" For your two communicative and entertaining epistles, one
dated the 15th and the other the 20th current, my gratetul
acknowledgments are due: and the favour conferred ought to
be deemed the more acceptable and meritorious, because, at present, I do not find myself capable of making any thing like an
adequate compensation. The case unhappily is, that the bilious
complaint with which I have been so long visited has left such a
weakness and such a listlessness that I cannot scribble to my
absent friends with my accustomed satisfaction; however, after
the pains you have taken to amuse me, I ought not to decline
doing what is in my power, and I will therefore duly notice
divers of the particulars in your letters.

" The majority in favour of the re-election of the Earl of
Leicester to be Pr. A. S. exceeds by twenty more than had been
represented to me, or rather the majority in support of his
Council list. In the list of Councillors from the old Council,
I missed the name of a person who had, I have a notion, kept
his chair there ever since 1 was F.A.S. Mr. Astle is the person
alluded to; and I wish to know whether, like Mr. Ord, he was
out-manœuvred by being in two lists, or whether his name was
not inserted in the Earl's list from his being suspected to have
a predilection for the Bankites, the Tophamites, and the Ly-
sonsites. Mr. Aubert is a very proper person for the office of
Vice-president; and I think it not unlikely he may be a contributor to Archæologia, unless the multiplicity of business in

which he is engaged should prevent his employing his pen on antiquarian lore. But are you not mistaken in your computation, that another Vice-president will soon vacate his seat upon the same bench, from his being upwards of seventy? a number that rather implies that his Lordship is only a little turned three score and ten, whereas I should suppose he must be at least half way towards fourscore. For let us only recollect how many years have passed since the commencement of the controversy between Douglas and the infamous Lauder.

" Since Director Lysons dispatched to me the proof sheets of my first paper on Arabic numerals, I have found time to revise some of my miscellaneous notes that were scattered here and there; so that I trust I shall, in the further correction of these proofs, find less difficulty than I had in the review of what he sent me. As to referring to the different black-letter books of arithmetic, I have not quite made up my mind, whether they be of sufficient importance to be noticed. From what I at present recollect,'Record's Treatise will afford sufficient information.

" Your report of the excellent Visitation Sermon, preached by Mr. Nicholson, on Acts, xxvii. v. 22, brought to my remembrance my having heard from the Master of Bene't, Professor Green, in the Chapel of the old House, the first part of a discourse upon the same text, and many judicious remarks there were in it; a second part was promised, but whether ever delivered I know not, perhaps not, as the Doctor was of a very indolent turn of mind. His attack upon Berridge he left unfinished; it was whispered that his plea was, that Archbishop Secker did not approve of the Methodists being so closely pressed.

" To your sheets of the Household-book of Sir William Fitz-William *, I have attended; but, as you will perceive, Kersey's Dictionary has added very, very little to your citations from Bailey. The articles relating to Garden-seeds and Plants appear to me to be as curious as any; though I am rather at a loss to account for the high price many of them fetched, as in the beginning of the seventeenth century there were such men employed in horticulture as the Tradescants.

" Having such an imperfect knowledge of a late Curator of the British Museum †, it was hardly fair to throw out the innuendoes I suggested in former letters; but prejudices will sometimes spring up, and I must own I had formed a notion that he might have obtained more than the full degree of applause to which he was entitled on the score of his literary abilities, natural and acquired. His verses in *carmina quadrigesimalia* I have not yet had an opportunity of reading, but am promised the loan of the book from one of his contemporaries.

" Yours truly,   S. Denne."

* Printed in Mr. Gough's History of Castor, Northamptonshire, 4to.
† Mr. Cracherode.

110. " Dear Sir,   *Wilmington, July* 10, 1799.

" In the lamentably weak condition, which I look upon as desperate, to which I am reduced by a tedious indisposition, the use of a pen is not merely irksome, but a fatigue to me. I adhere to my former opinion, that Milton has accurately defined my complaint, by his significant expression in his Lazar House, ' a pyning atrophy; ' particularly as I yet take, during the twenty-four hours, a competent portion of the supposed neces-saries of life without the least nutrition, and there are days in which I have not lost my relish for what I eat and drink. When nature shall be exhausted, and a powerless body have a tempo-rary release from its old companion and better part, it is not for me to prognosticate ; but in case of a fatal separation, my exe-cutrix will have instructions to forward to Enfield all bundles of letters endorsed Richard Gough, Esq. ; and in so copious a col-lection, should there be found any differently marked, I am well satisfied that you will attend to the proper rule of *suum cuique*. With my wonted busy mind, and in the way of amusement, my bent towards a certain science that has occasioned a frequent correspondence between us, it may be presumed that I have sundry ideas floating in my mind; but such is my debilitated state that I really want power to fill up all traits in a subject that is not as clear as a b c. For a day or two I have been rumi-nating on the preservation of a book and a picture ; and to your consideration it shall be submitted, because you was a Bene-dictine. According to my notion, my father's collated copy of the Textus Roffensis cannot be more properly deposited than in the MS. Library of Bene't-college; but, supposing I present this valuable book to the Society, as one good turn merits an-other, shall I not be fully warranted in desiring that they will likewise give admission to my father's picture. It is the only portrait there is of him ; and no print has been taken of it, nor is it likely it should be now engraved. That Dr. Denne through life had the interest of the College at heart is unques-tionable ; and it certainly merits due notice that he was joint tutor with Mr. Herring, afterwards Archbishop of Canterbury. Not that I am solicitous that the picture in question should have a place within the Lodge among Archbishops, Bishops, Judges, and the Masters of the College ; Dr. Denne having been only a Fellow and Tutor, it will be deemed sufficient if it be suspended on a wall in the MS. Library; or why not fixed to one of the doors of the presses, should there be any danger likely to accrue from the dampness of the wall ?

" Before my strength departed from me, which it literally is, I had not the least conception of the burden of extreme weak-ness; but a sufferer as I have been, and still am from it, what a want of feeling should I betray did I not tender my fervent wishes, that health and strength may be for years the portion of Mrs. Gough and yourself; and having mentioned these ines-

timable blessings of life, with a desire that you may enjoy as
many other comforts as can reasonably be expected in this fluc-
tuating scene, I will subscribe myself,
"Your true friend,   S. DENNE."

---

111. The Rev. JOHN CURREY to Mr. GOUGH.

"SIR,   *Dartford, July* 11, 1799.
"It is only with concern I can speak of our worthy friend's
health. About four months ago he had a violent bilious attack,
his legs swelled much, and soon after began to discharge; the
discharge, however, ceased, and some favourable symptoms appeared, but the constitution was too feeble to rally. Ever
since he has grown weaker and weaker; and is now in so totally
debilitated a state as not to be able to change his room without
assistance. His legs are again much swolen; and he told me a
few days since that he thought he began to fill higher. His
mind is still vigorous, and his spirits easy, though perfectly sensible of his situation. I shall mention to him that his silence,
and having spoken to you of his want of health, had led you to
favour with your friendly inquiries after him,
"Sir, your most obedient servant,   JOHN CURREY."

---

112. Mr. GOUGH to Mr. DENNE.

"*July* 15, 1799.
"Believe me, my dear Sir, it was a pleasure to me to see your
letter of a date prior to that which I addressed to Mr. Currey to
inquire into the cause of your silence. Not to importunate you
with inquiries, I will still cherish a hope that you may be restored
to your former energy of mind and body; but, should it be otherwise ordered by the Supreme Disposer of all events, I will assure
you of my hearty concurrence in the execution of any wish of
yours at Cambridge or London. I am sure the Benedictines will
be very ungrateful if they do not place the portrait you mention
in their Lodge instead of burying it in a cellar not opened four
times in the year, and then perhaps to strangers.
"The very happy revolution in public events will certainly be
welcome to you in common with us all.
"Adieu, my dear Sir, and assure yourself of a place under
all circumstances in the truest regards and best wishes of your
sincere friend,   RICHARD GOUGH."

---

113. Mr. DENNE to Mr. GOUGH.

"DEAR SIR,   *Wilmington, July* 30, 1799.
"One more scrap of antiquary fare, which shall be appellated
cheese, is purposed to be sent from Wilmington Vicarage to

Cicero's Head, though it is much to be feared that, from the minutes relative to them being in confusion, and from his not being able to move up and down stairs, the purveyor will not have it in his power to serve up his little plate in the manner he wishes. Batalha, or, rather, the intended sepulchral tomb erecting by King Emanuel, but left in a dilapidated state, will be the leading subject, and especially those pages on which a learned Spanish Dr. —————— figured as an illustrator of the sphere, which was Emanuel's chosen device, and his translation of the mottoes. Now on both these points I differ from the Doctor as far as I can comprehend his meaning; and I am sure that he might, with a small degree of consideration, have rectified the error into which he has slipt, concerning some of the ornaments of the sphere. Unless my memory deceives me, I suggested the fundamental mistake a few months ago; but I will be now more explicit. The three complete horns affixed to the lower end of the sphere, are the embellishments alluded to; and that horns are generally to be deemed tokens of power and authority we have the sanction of writers, both holy and profane, as you may easily satisfy yourself by even a cursory perusal of Newton's Dissertation on the Prophecies; and in Bruce's Voyage for the Discovery of the Sources of the Nile are sundry proofs of the notion formed by different nations of the reputed power of horns, with divers apt illustrations from Holy Writ. Concerning the three horns under review, it ought to be further noticed that the caps of them all exhibit crowns upon them, and that of course they are to be looked upon as emblems of monarchical power; and can there then be a doubt but that the framer of this device, which was upon a sphere that he was partial to, meant by the device to announce to all people that he had royal dominions in three quarters of the then known parts of the world; and his Majesty of Portugal possessed such dominions in Europe, *jure paterno,* and in Africa and in the East Indies by the right of the gun and the sword; nay, a few years afterwards, when the Brazils were annexed to the throne of Portugal, the newly discovered continent of America acknowledged Portugal to be one among its sovereigns, and perhaps there may be spheres upon which four coronetted horns are displayed.

" Admitting, therefore, the opinion I have adopted concerning these horns to be well founded, and I profess I am not aware of there being any reasonable objection to it, not any difficulty do I see in correcting the mistake of the Spanish Doctor; but as to his comment upon the mottoes, I am not apprised how he is to be extricated from the error that bewilders him, because, as far as appears, he had not the mottoes before him, and of an uncertain motto the reading or explanation must be vague. The want of an accurate copy of the motto might have its origin in the expertness of the carver to insculp it on different parts of the mausoleum, or the Doctor himself might mistake from having placed himself at too great a distance when he attempted to read it, or the persons employed to take a fac-simile might be inattentive. It appears, however, from the Doctor's own report, and from his mode of construing the mottoes, that the mottoes themselves were not to be depended upon, and therefore it would be presumption to think of offering any explanation that shall be clear and convincing; but to antiquaries is generally allowed an opening for surmise, and therefore into this wide and not unpleasant field I shall take a short trip. Almost all that I could collect from the Doctor was, that the characters of the mottoes were Grecian, a circumstance that might of itself rather embarrass the commentator; but it is on this surmise, and one other, that I shall suggest what I have to offer, that the word or words forming the mottoes had a reference to *the East*, because at that period there were many nations, and of these the Portuguese principally, who were intoxicated and infatuated with eastern notions and views. Read but the Annals of the Portuguese, and not a book, hardly a page in a book, which will not prove to a demonstration how predominant were eastern words, and how impatient they were to be incorporated with the country that was to the east of them. What fatigue and immense anxiety did they not encounter in their voyage round the Cape of Good Hope to this eastern land, in which their hearts were placed; and with what a high tone of exultation did they triumph on finding they had acquired eastern territories, though afterwards they turned out to be a bane and a curse to the conquerors, as the same country had previously been to other nations; and as it may ultimately be a source of ruin to other countries, who, though they stand upon a perilous fabric, think they have established a system that must reflect honour on the devisers of it, a system that must directly or indirectly bring in an augmenting flux of wealth to the public and to individuals, whilst a good government can be supported in any part of the world.

" Had not almost all my antiquarian researches been impeded by an indisposition, severe and tedious in the extreme, I think it not unlikely I might have carried into execution the plan I had formed of revising, with the closest attention, the extracts I had made from the Luciad of Camoens by Milton, and divers other notes, with the view of preparing a readable paper for the Society on the Sepulchral Chapel constructed at Batalha by the illustrious Emanuel of Portugal; and it was my design to have addressed it to Craven Ord, and to have left it to his discretion whether it should be put into the hands of Secretary Brand. But circumstances are so altered that, if the scheme shall be pursued, it must be by Mr. Ord himself during his recess in the country, provided he can fill up the sketch I have delineated. And query ought he not maturely to weigh, that a paper of the cast given, would not be out of season in November, in

order to parry the sarcastic cantos then announced for publication, that will be entitled Ajax and Ulysses. With such a paper
upon his cushion, Ajax may feel his spirits return, and Ulysses be
again defeated by his competitor. For what reason the Bard
styled the Earl Ajax and the Viscount Ulysses, I have not yet discovered; but of this I am certain, that he must be a minor Poet,
who is not well versed in twisting and metamorphising, who
cannot display with the same pen a great man and a little man,
a man passionate and outrageous and one who has a tranquil
temper and can dissemble his thoughts. Is it not thought by
many, that the sly Peter Pindar is the person who has it in contemplation to hold out F. S. A.'s as the proper subjects of satire
and ridicule? If he be the man *in petto*, who has taken so
many weeks to ruminate on the questions, and on the persons
who are to be exposed by the cutting cantos of a waggish Poet,
who is said to have acquired a competent sum of money by
creating a laugh at the expense of his neighbours of all distances and degrees.

" Aware I am, in the proposition submitted to the deliberation
of Mr. Ord, there is still wanting a grand desideratum, as that
without obtaining the mottoes no satisfactory solution can possibly be obtained; but is there a perpetual bar against every
method of tracing what might have been the designed mottoes?
By historians and memorialists it is averred, that different Kings
of Portugal established many religious houses and constructed
many sacred edifices; and, if my recollection does not deceive me,
there are some of the Historians who have suggested they were enabled to effect these pious and eleemosynary acts by means of the
wealth acquired in the east; though how acquired it has not in
general been deemed proper to record. Of these buildings
several must have been destroyed by the earthquakes, and others
have become ruinous in the ordinary way; but still vestiges of
these mottoes may still be traceable, and the dilapidations themselves even afford an opportunity not before to be had of procuring something that may resemble a fac-simile. The point is,
whether Mr. Ord may have in Portugal any antiquarian correspondent inclined to execute such a commission. A sphere, as
before-mentioned, was a favourite, and, as it is believed, an emblem never forgotten by the great Emanuel, after his success in
so many places. Should it have been continued in the edifices
constructed by subsequent Kings of Portugal, and should there
be found attached to them horns coronetted, I am confident that
the explanation offered of the device will stand the test.

" Thus, after a delay not formerly gratified, have I stated the
tenor and the purport of two antique topics, which it is my
real wish Mr. Ord would fully weigh, being convinced that from
one of them at least, even *in statu quo*, he might set Ajax en-
compassed with horns at defiance, and compel the mild and the
crafty Ulysses to be perfectly quiet at the opening of the next

campaign. Not a doubt have I of his being soon able to exhibit, not only a readable, but a plausible, sheet for the amusement of his brethren; and I trust that he will avail himself of my innuendo. Far was it from me to cast the task upon him; and to satisfy him that it was not, be it known unto him that, I had provided not only a drawing of the sphere of the great Emanuel of Portugal, from Murphy's Batalha, but also delineations of the best copies I could acquire of the mottoes. A piteous atrophy impeded my progress; and I begin to be not a little apprehensive that asthma will soon be an additional malady, having experienced for more than a fortnight a shortness of breath, to which, in the days that are past, I was a total stranger. It becomes me, however, to be grateful that I can still, under my own sign manual, subscribe myself, dear Sir,

"Yours truly,   S. Denne."

---

114. Samuel Hawkins, Esq. to Mr. Gough.

"Sir,   *Wilmington, Aug. 7, 1799.*

"It is with the truest concern I acquaint you with the great loss we have sustained by the death of our excellent and ever-to-be-regretted friend! which happened about four o clock on Saturday morning last. We have long had too much reason to expect it, though it may appear more sudden than from the last accounts, perhaps, we might have been given to hope, a circumstance not unusual in such cases. I have the satisfaction, however, of assuring you, a melancholy one indeed it must be confessed, that he departed with a calmness which truly indicated that all within was peace!

"Poor Mrs. Denne *, than whom none will have a greater loss, nor feel it more, seems to bear it upon the whole as well as may be; and I sincerely wish it may not afterwards be felt more by her. She desires me to express her wish that I should say every thing that is proper for her. I have the honour to be, Sir,

"Your most obedient humble servant, Samuel Hawkins."

---

115. "Sir,   *Pall Mall, Aug. 22, 1799.*

"I have had the pleasure of both your favours, and cannot see that there can be any objection to your having the refusal of your late friend's library; but, on the contrary, it is what I had intended considering as a compliment to be paid you if I had been able to find the will, but after most tedious searches at different times, no where is it forthcoming; and the only chance there is of discovering one is among the leaves of the different books which he may lately have had in use, and wherein he may inadvertently have left it. I am, Sir,

"Your most obedient servant, Samuel Hawkins."

* Mr. Denne's sister; see the "Literary Anecdotes," vol. III. p. 527.

*The following letters and extracts were communicated to Mr.
Gough by Mr. Denne from the papers of his father and bro-
ther; chiefly as containing anecdotes of members of Corpus
Christi or Bene't college, Cambridge:*

Extracts of letters from the Rev. THOMAS GREENE, D. D.
Archdeacon of Canterbury, and afterwards successively Bishop
of Norwich and Ely, and who had been Master of Corpus Christi
college, Cambridge, to JOHN DENNE, a Fellow of that college.

" 1716, June 23.   I have recommended you as tutor to young
Mr. Barrett, your quondam school-fellow, whom his uncle Dr.
Boyce will very shortly send to your college to be a Fellow Commoner there.   The Doctor and Mrs. Barrett will stick at nothing
to reward your care, provided you will take a more than ordinary care of him.   The young man is no great scholar, nor do
they expect very much in that way.   He is now innocent, a
thorough Whig, and that they desire he should continue, for
which reason they would not have him much acquainted with
his school-fellows either of St. John's or Pembroke.   They could
wish that either he might keep in the chamber with you, if that
might be, or as near you as possible, and that he might have
your company as much as may be with your convenience; and,
as I said before, whatever you shall ask for your trouble and care
shall be granted.   They desire he may be acquainted with Castle,
who, also, if he will take some pains, and assist him in his studies,
shall have a reward for it.

" And now, dear Sir, give me leave as a friend to add a word
or two more.   You are now setting out in the world, and cannot
but be sensible of what great consequence it will be to your
future advancement in it to begin well and prudently; and
therefore let me advise you to be very cautious of your conduct,
and set Mr. Laughton, of Clare hall, as a pattern before you for
the management of your pupils.   You see what an universal
credit he has gained thereby.   By all means avoid that tippling
way of drinking wine every night at a townsman's house, which
is both scandalous and chargeable, and draws into many other
inconveniences.   Give good example to your pupils, by keeping
constantly to Chapel in the morning as well as the evening; and
be as seldom out of the gates at night as possibly you can.   I
am sure you will thereby recommend yourself to your most
excellent Master *, who is a pious good man, and will nev erlike
such practices as I just now mentioned; and what is most of all
to be desired, will have the blessing of God upon all your undertakings, who will never fail to prosper your piety and diligence.

* John Bradford, D. D. afterwards Bishop of Carlisle and of Rochester,
and whose daughter Mr. Denne married in 1724, and thus became an
Archdeacon,—had at the date of this letter recently succeeded its writer
in the Headship.

I have a mighty desire to see you prosper in the world, to which you may assure yourself of my assistance to the utmost of my power. I have conceived great hopes of you and Mr. Herring*, and should be sadly baulked if I should be disappointed. Pray remember me to him in a particular manner, to whose acquaintance also I will recommend Mr. Barrett when he comes."

"1716, Oct. 17. I have been in a good deal of hurry for some time, or you had sooner received my thanks for your very kind letter, as had also Mr. Barrett, to whom pray give my service; and tell him as soon as I am a little more at leisure, I will thank him myself. I am mighty glad to hear he goes on so well with you. The Master, in his letter to me, spake very kindly of him for his regularity and sobriety. His friends here are all wonderfully pleased to hear so good an account of him; and I hope it will be to your advantage as well as satisfaction, if he should come very well out of your hands, as I see not the least reason yet to doubt but he will; it may be of very good service to you by bringing more to you. By all means take care of the morals of those which shall be committed to you. Set Mr. Laughton as a pattern to you, and you cannot do amiss."

"1716-17, March 14. Your Master gives me a very good account of your charge Mr. Barrett, which I am extremely glad of. Pray give my service to him. Be so kind as to tell me sincerely how my nephew Vertue behaves himself in the college. I wish him well, and will make the Master his friend if he deserves it. I am afraid he is a little Toryish; I should be glad if you could bring him off from it."

"1717, April 19. I am sorry my nephew Vertue is not more sensible of his interest. I always thought him such as you represent him. Assure yourself, by what I hear from several, he is not to be depended upon for any zeal to that interest which I wish may always flourish in the college, and therefore I desire no favour for him from you against your inclination. If I were there again, I should have no regard to him whilst Mr. Genning and the rest of that interest were his advisers and confidents.

"It is a great pleasure to hear that the college flourishes so much. There is a young man coming from this school (Canterbury), one David Comarque, whom I have recommended to your care. It seems he has a brother too, who would come to study physic. They will be pensioners.

"I hear much of Castle to his reputation †. I am glad to hear Mr. Barrett goes on to yours and his friends' satisfaction. Pray give him my service."

* Thomas Herring, afterwards Archbishop of Canterbury, was a fellow-tutor of Bene't college with Archdeacon Denne.

† Edmund Castle, B.D. afterwards Dean of Hereford, succeeded Bishop Mawson as Master of Bene't in 1744-5, and was succeeded by Dr. John Green (afterwards Bishop of Lincoln) in 1750; for his biography see the "Literary Anecdotes," vol. VII. pp. 65, 530.

On these extracts Mr. DENNE offered Mr. GOUGH the following
observations :

"Fellow-commoner Barrett was, you know, a collector of
antiques*, but not supposed to be so well instructed in that kind
of lore ; nor probably did he much improve the little scholarship
Archdeacon Greene intimates he possessed, when he left the seminary in the Mint-yard, Canterbury ; as his intellectual talents
were not naturally above par.   There is also reason to suspect
that, maugre the wishes of his uncle and aunt, and of Dr.
Greene, and the instructions impressed by his tutors, he afterwards
became rather Toryish, for at the great election of Knights of
the Shire for Kent, when Watson and Fairfax, as Whigs, obtained a decisive victory over the Tories, Thomas Barrett, Esq.
gave a plumper for Sir Edward Dering ; though, from an indolence of disposition, he had not the repute of being a zealous
partizan, and he certainly had the merit of being in other points
a respectable country gentleman.   He presented to my father
a picture of himself, which hangs over the chimney-piece in my
chamber.   I offered it to my late sister Denne, who was his God-
daughter, but she declined accepting it, because it did not in
her opinion bear any resemblance to her sponsor at the font.

"James Vertue, though a Tory, was presented by his uncle,
Bishop Greene, to the Rectory of Glemsford in Suffolk (Masters's List, p. 49), who, while Bishop of Norwich, seems to have
given him the Rectory of West Halton, co. Lincoln ; and, on
the removal of Vertue to the Rectory of Feltwell in 1732, may
not David Comarque, who succeeded to Halton, have obtained
that living through the interest of Bishop Greene, who had
recommended him to Bene't † ?

"But of the extracts from a quondam Head of the old House,
(who, by-the-bye, was not an epistolary correspondent of elegance) apart not the least curious is, that which alludes to the then
habit of some of the tutors at Cambridge in tippling wine every
night at the houses of townsmen ; and, unless the town had a
more respectable set of inhabitants in 1716 than it had between
forty and fifty years afterwards, it was not to the credit of the
tutors that these were places of call.   But who would have surmised that, not far from the commencement of the present century, a late Head of a College should deem it expedient to caution tutors Denne and Herring not to be absent from Chapel in
the morning, and to avoid having their names entered in the
gate-bill ?

* A juvenile portrait of Thomas Barrett, Esq. from a miniature executed by Zinke in 1725, is beautifully engraved in Dibdin's Decameron,
vol. III. p. 456, accompanied by notices of his collections, and of his son,
the inheritor of his name, his fortune, and his taste.

† The Rev. David Comarque proceeded B. A. 1720; M.A. 1726 ; and
married Jan. 23, 1732, "a daughter of the late Peter Raneu, Esq."—
His brother Reynald Comarque, the student in physic, took the degrees
of M. B. 1728, and M. D. comitiis regiis the same year.

" From these extracts we see that Laughton, of Clare *, was the pattern tutor; nor was his name forgot when I was an academic, though Courtail† might be willing to throw his predecessor into the back-ground. In the Political Register of 1723, which notices Laughton's death on Sunday July 28, he is styled a tutor celebrated for the great number of the nobility and gentry educated under his care, and a person eminent for his learning; but no other specimen in print did he exhibit of his literary acquirements than a Sermon delivered before the King in King's-college Chapel, anno 1717, and when I read that discourse some years ago, I do not remember that preaching was the forte of this illustrious tutor; and I think it is an observation not unfrequently made, that schoolmasters and tutors, who are accustomed to write in Latin, but seldom appear to advantage in English exercises. The Consecration Sermon preached by Dr. Markham, when his friend Bishop Johnson was raised to the See of Gloucester, has been by some critics termed pedagoguish, because it reads like a translation from the Latin into the vulgar tongue."

Extracts from a letter of J. Denne to T. Stephens.

" Bene't college, Jan. 28, 1747-8.   Mr. Hervey is with us; and from the little acquaintance I have the pleasure to have with him, is become a great favourite of mine. There seems as much good nature in him as politeness ; and the manner in which he spends his time seems to show that he is inclined to improve those good qualities he has brought from Westminster; a disposition the more commendable as it is the more unusual among the politer part of the University."—As Frederick Lord Bishop of Derry and Earl of Bristol is the Mr. Hervey here described, S. Denne has more than once commended the superior sagacity of J. Denne in making choice of so favourite a character to be a subject of praise. — J. Denne thus proceeds : " Green has got £.500 in the lottery, which makes me inclined to think that Fortune is not so blind as she is represented, since she can bestow her favours upon a deserving man. I am myself equally happy with an university degree, which has put a very agreeable period to all my philosophical labours. I have been, I must own, a little impatient under the discipline that is necessary to attain it ; and could almost compare the last year to a state of subjection and confinement in which the mind is embarrassed with rules, subdued by authority, and habituated only, as it were, to one track of thinking; but I can now, without any restraint, pursue those studies which are most suitable to my mind."

* Richard Laughton, D. D. of whom see the " Literary Anecdotes," vol. V. p. 420; and also the references in vol. VII. p. 222.
† John Courtail, a Fellow of Clare, B. A. 1735, M. A. 1739.

From T. Stephens to J. Denne.

" Bene't-college, Feb. 16, 1748-9.   I am now trembling with
the thoughts of the Second Tripos, which falls to my share.
My subject is, ' Inclinatio Axis Telluris ad Eclipticam in melius mutari nequit.'   I should be extremely obliged to you if you
would send me what poetical thoughts occur to you on that
subject."

From T. Stephens to J. Denne, after the publication of the Second Tripos.

" I am much obliged to you for the good opinion with which
you was prepossessed in regard to my poetry; but although it
gives me pleasure in one sense, viz. as I perceive it arises entirely
from your friendly prejudices in my favour, yet in another
respect it gives me concern, as I have great reason to fear that
upon the perusal your opinion is much altered, for I own to you
they savour greatly of the school-boy.   I did intend to have
addressed them to Lord Anson; and had accordingly made an
introduction, in which I endeavoured to pay him a compliment
upon the success of his voyage; but on reading it over carefully,
I found the verses by no means equal to the subject, and therefore
thought it more advisable upon the whole to say nothing of his
Lordship than,

" Laudes egregias—
Culpa deterre ingenî.

" I have scarce read any thing since I came down but what
has related to poetry, so that mathematics and philosophy have
been in a manner quite laid aside; and, indeed, were I not convinced of the necessity of gaining some sort of knowledge of
those sciences, I should not be persuaded to leave the more
agreeable studies of the classics."

Remarks by the Rev. Samuel Denne addressed to Mr. Gough.

" The names of Ds. Crayford and Ds. Denne, among two of
the B. A.'s ' quibus reservatur senioritas in Prioribus Comitiis,'
Feb. 25, 1747, would perhaps have been deemed a sufficient reason of itself for sending the Tripos to Enfield, even though it
will be accompanied with an extract of a letter from S. Denne,
in which he complains of his being obliged to work against the
grain in order to obtain this academical honour; but there is one
of the two Poems that seem to me to be entitled to notice for
a special reason.   Graham, of King's, the ingenious and elegant
Bard, who chose to expatiate on ' Mundus non fuit ab æterno,'
was, I imagine, the Graham of Lincoln's-inn, who was rising in
practice at the Bar, and who, had he not been removed by a premature death, was expected to be one of the first men of his
days in the law line.   Robinson, of Trinity-hall, is a brother of

the ingenious and learned, but very eccentric, veteran, Lord Rokeby *.

"Is 'Insula Tiniana' new to you? Tom Stephens, the writer, is mentioned in the Gentleman's Magazine for 1781, p. 366, note, and I think it not unlikely that the account might be communicated to Master Urban by Duncombe †. Till I met with letters from Stephens to my brother, from which extracts are inclosed, I was not aware that the island of Tinian was not designed primarily to be the Thesis. Not having duplicates of either of these Tripos's, you will be pleased to return them at your leisure. Stephens, the *in statu pupillari* Usher of Westminster-school, was one of the best, if not the best young man I was ever acquainted with; and this notwithstanding his being trained in that perilous seminary, and his being intimately acquainted with and esteemed by some of the bucks his contemporaries. Gilpin, I have a notion, has published in his Poems a humourous copy of verses upon the Powder Plot; and at Bene't, in 1748 or 1749, when it was the practice to have verses by the lads hanging in the Hall near the Fellows' table on that gala, Stephens tendered a copy of a humourous cast that was much admired. It was a translation into Latin, rather paraphrastically, of the vulgar begging lines of ' Pray remember the fifth of November;' but, unfortunately, a copy of the same was not preserved. He also sported a copy in which he drew the characters jocosely of four of his fellow-collegians, *viz.* Lynch, Denne, Knowles, and Herring, of which the two first lines were,

" Stat, quâ Camus agros torpenti flumine lambit,
     Antiqua antiquo nomine nota Domus;

and the old House is still its proper name, maugre the wishes and the attempts of the lately departed Historian to have a *new* building upon any plan that shall be thought advisable by the best architects.

"Most probably there are among Mr. Masters's collection, sundry letters, and other papers, written by my father, and I am possessed of several he wrote to his coadjutor in this work; and I find in some of them that the Historian complains, and I think not without cause, that he was not encouraged so much as he

* Of the Rev. William Robinson see a memoir in the Gentleman's Magazine, vol. LXXIII. p. 1192.

† The following particulars are derived from that source. Thomas Stephens was the only son of the Rev. Thomas Stephens, Fellow of Bene't-college, Rector of Sherfield in Hampshire, and Lecturer of the New Church in the Strand, by Winifred, niece and heiress of the Rev. James Johnson, D.D. Chancellor of Ely (of whom there is a long memoir in Gent. Mag. at the place referred to in the text). Thomas was " a very deserving youth, educated at Westminster school, and made one of the Ushers there before the time of taking a B. A. degree. But he was almost immediately cut off, by consumption, at the age of 20, Dec. 25, 1750." His mother was re-married (after the death of her husband in 1747) to the Rev. Joseph Sims, Prebendary of St. Paul's and Lincoln, Rector of St. John's, Westminster, and Vicar of Eastham; of whom see the " Literary Anecdotes," vol. III. p. 631; vol. V. p. 515.

ought to have been, not only by the Benedictines, but also by
members of other colleges, and by persons of the antiquarian
cast; and I think it is to be regretted that collections at least
for the Histories of other Colleges, are not made by some judicious and assiduous member of each Society. A list of the
members of each, from the earliest time, would be a considerable acquisition; and is the more wanted at Cambridge, because
the oldest Register of Graduates in the University is modern in
comparison, and consequently there is no scope for an A. Wood
to publish Athenæ et Fasti Cantabrigienses.   S. DENNE."

ARCHBISHOP HERRING to the Rev. Mr. HEATON, &c.

"GENTLEMEN,   *Lambeth, June 16, 1750.*
" As you have been pleased to apply to me for my advice on
a very important occasion, I will give it you as becomes a friend.
In this view, and in this view only, agreeably to your 3d, 5th,
8th, and 14th statutes, I would recommend to your choice,—as
the fittest person to succeed your late excellent Master,—the Rev.
Dr. Green, of St. John's college, Regius Professor of Divinity.

" Dr. Green knows nothing of my design; and no consideration whatever but that of his character has induced me to name
him to you on this occasion. The goodness and integrity of
that, his distinguished learning, the dignity of his situation in
the University, his faithful attachment to the King and his Royal
Family, and the great excellency of his temper, joined with prudence, are the qualities which concur to recommend him to me;
and I have the best hopes that, under the conduct of such a
Head, if you think fit to choose him, the interest of the old
House, and the credit which I observe with singular pleasure it
maintains at present, will be supported and augmented, and the
affairs of it conducted with unanimity in the best and most prudent order.

" May it please God to bless and direct you. You may be
assured that, on all occasions which should call for any help
from me, I shall be ready to afford it to the college with the zeal
and fidelity of a true friend,   THO. CANTUAR."

" The 'Cappadocian' members of the old House (remarks Mr.
Denne) resigned their freedom of election to the Pope of Lambeth-
house, and were so mean as to consent to be governed by a
foreigner, who had as many Yorkshire tricks as most of his
countrymen. Had it not been for my brother, I am confident
he would never have been chosen Master of Bene't; but after
he was seated in a lodge that probably prepared the way for his
elevation to the Episcopal Bench *, he did not remember Joseph,
alias John, but forgot him, and never conferred upon him the
smallest favour. Often do I hint to my poor brother, that he
merited such treatment because he was a Cappadocian!"

* Dr. Green became Bishop of Lincoln in 1761; he has very frequently occurred in the " Literary Anecdotes;" see the Index, vol. VII.
pp. 161, 581.

1. The Rev. JOHN GREEN, D. D. to the Rev. J. DENNE.

"DEAR SIR,   *Cambridge, March* 29, 1753.

" I take this opportunity of sending you, which indeed I
should have been earlier in making, my sincere congratulations
on two late happy events, your recovery from the small-pox and
your preferment. I hope the latter is likely to place you in a
situation that is agreeable to you ; and which I find you are very
soon to enter upon. This I shall be much rejoiced to hear, as I
shall always find a great and sensible pleasure from any instance
of good succees that befalls you. I think of seeing London
soon ; and shall be glad of waiting upon you, if the duties of
your parish do not call you away before that time. It is, I dare
say, a great satisfaction to you, and does much credit to the old
House, that your brother* has acquitted himself so much to his
honour in taking his degree. Two or three of our number are
shortly leaving us, so that we are likely to be the next year a
thin Society. You will be pleased to pay my respects to Mr.
Archdeacon. I am, dear Sir,
          " Your very faithful humble servant,   J. GREEN."

2. " DEAR SIR,   *Barrow, Oct.* 20, 1754.

" I was favoured lately with a letter from your father, which
contained a very obliging message from you ; and for which I
send you, as I ought, my most thankful acknowledgments. It
was that you were ready ' to put the resignation of your fellowship into my hands when I should think it convenient.' This
mark of your regard and friendship obliges me to give you my
sentiments freely on this subject. D^s. Herring† is, I have reason
to suppose, disposed to return to College soon, and to make
some stay with us ; this I apprehend he would do with more
pleasure if he had a settlement with us, and a nearer relation to
the Society. This he cannot have before the vacancy of your
fellowship without slurring, and finally rejecting one three years
his senior ; and, as far as I know, of an unexceptionable character, which I should look upon as a hard thing. As the year
is now concluded, the income of your fellowship, while you have
a right to keep it, will be inconsiderable ; no fines are set yet,
nor do I hear of any who talk of renewing but one, and I much
question whether that will soon take place. But you would be
offended with me for dwelling longer on this topic, when I further tell you, that the giving up this small portion of your right
to facilitate and quicken the election of Herring, would, I have
reason to suppose, be doing an acceptable thing to his Grace of
Canterbury. I dare say I need not suggest anything more, either
to dispose you to, or satisfy you about, the propriety of this measure. If, therefore, you are pleased to send me your authority

* The Rev. Samuel Denne.
† One of the Archbishop's nephews, either Henry or Thomas, who were
both Fellows of Bene't.

to vacate your fellowship, it is probable that I may make use of it in ten days' time, for within that time I expect a sufficient number in college to make an election; but then I will not make use of it, unless there be such a number, nor till the time that number can be got together, which, in our present straggled state, is not always to be done. I am under no apprehensions of being thought hasty in this affair, or wanting in a proper regard to you and your interest, as it is what I should advise my own brother to under the same circumstances. It is doing a right thing, and paying a proper piece of respect, where I am sure you would choose to pay it. I am, dear Sir, with very true respect, your faithful humble servant,   J. GREEN."

——

Mr. DENNE's remarks on this letter to Mr. GOUGH :

" Dr. Green's contrivance in electing Herring into the Fellowship that became vacant by the resignation of Denne, was properly termed by Dr. Denne, one of Dr. Green's 'Yorkshire tricks.' The case was, immediately after he was chosen Master, he declared that no scholar should be elected who did not reside in the winter terms, in consequence of which Herring and Samuel Denne did reside, as if they had been Under-graduates; and large must have been the expenses incurred by their fathers to defray this useless plan of regulation as it turned out to be. For Ingram did not reside a day; and Herring, the senior, ought to have been elected into the Fellowship filled up by Ingram, had the Master been really in earnest about paying a proper compliment to Herring and to the great man at Lambeth. When my father perceived how shuffling Master Green was, he prudently determined that his son Samuel should not run any risk of losing a Fellowship hereafter by Fellow John's hastily resigning his Fellowship, and therefore kept possession for months, notwithstanding clergymen of rank (S. Denne has a notion an English and an Irish Bishop) might be employed to procure his resignation; and the plea urged by them was that the Archbishop had a right to expect that a becoming mark of respect to him and his family should not be withheld. The drift of the Master was, however, clearly understood by the Archbishop, and he did not interfere. The manner in which he endeavoured to prove that J. Denne, by ceasing to be a Fellow, and becoming a Scholar, would sustain a loss so trivial, that it ought not to have any weight in the scale, considering the especial purpose for which he was solicited to accommodate Herring, will not stand the test of an inquiry. For, had he kept his Fellowship to the day of his marriage, as by the statute of the college he might have done, it is clear there would have been in his favour a considerable difference. With the clue here offered, Mr. Gough may read and understand the Jesuitism of a Master of Bene't; and it is the opinion of S. Denne that he would have made a distinguished figure among the disciples of Loyola."

3. " Dear Sir,   *Cambridge, Nov.* 26, 1754.

" I ought sooner to have made my very thankful acknowledgments to you, for the authority you were so kind to give me by your last, and to have acquainted you, what use I had made of that authority. I should certainly not have suggested it to you, had I not myself been clearly satisfied as to the propriety of such a step, and thought it was doing a respectful thing to that family (as Sr Herring's election was by that means quickened) at an easy expense. As your fellowship would have been vacant of course in a little time, and but little emoluments would have come to you by continuing it for the whole time, I think you acted perfectly right in making this compliment. It is what I would have done myself, or what I would have advised my brother to do. Under any other circumstances you may be assured, I should neither have had, nor shown the least inclination for your quitting our Society a moment sooner than you must have done, as I shall always preserve the truest regard for you, and set the greatest value on your friendship.

" Your Fellowship was declared vacant the 9th, and filled up by Sr Herring the 11th instant; in which choice the Society unanimously concurred. He came to be admitted last week; and proposes to spend (as I knew he designed to do if this event took place) the whole winter with us. I read your affectionate letter to the Society; and all of them, I believe, are persuaded of your kind inclinations towards us, and all, I hope, will be ready to show a return of the same good-will and regard towards you. I am, dear Sir,

     " Your affectionate humble servant,   J. Green."

Rev. John Duncombe * to the Rev. John Denne.

" Dear Sir,   *Sundrich, March* 30, 1754.

" Your very friendly letter found me here; and was the more agreeable as it was unexpected. It was a testimony of your regard, and on that account more valuable than if it had been a regular critical panegyric on my Poem. Your commendation of the Feminead † is much more than nought. Praise from such as you is all that I desire; for believe me I write not for the critics, but for my friends.

" And now to answer your inquiries. In the lines you mention, I certainly drew the mistress of my fancy, the Sacharissa I should choose, but no real person; though the picture has more likenesses than one in the Poem. You are right in your conjectures about Flavia, Florimel, and Delia. Cornelia is intended for Mrs. Madan, Col. Madan's wife, and Spencer Cowper's daughter, and Eugenia is Miss Highmore.

* One of the translators of Horace; of whom see the " Literary Anecdotes," vol. VIII. pp. 271—278; also vol. VII. pp. 118, 556. He was at the date of this letter Curate of Sundrich in Kent.

† Vide ibid. vol. VIII. p. 276.

" I was in London some time ago to meet Green and Barnardiston, ambassadors from the college to the two new Bishops. We dined with them both; and at Kensington met (among other company) your father and our Historian. He begun to say something to me about publication, but I soon stopt him short by wishing him joy of his degree at Oxford. Charles Thomas too was present, for whom I have lately hoisted up in Drury-lane.

" Your ministerial office, indeed, is truly melancholy; and surely this is one of the worst circumstances that attends your cure. Such prison scenes as these must shock humanity.

" Soame Jenyns has published an excellent Ode on Mr. Pelham's Death, and I think it may be fairly said to speak the language of the heart; nothing but what every lover of his country will concur in. This is a loss which I fear we shall be more and more sensible of every day; and it is a melancholy circumstance to reflect that our good King should be obliged to enter into new measures with a new set of people at a time of life when, even in a private station, repose and quiet are the most that can be expected. When the Chancellor was lately indisposed, the King insisted on his keeping within, and appointing Lord Delawarr Speaker; for, says he, I have lost too many of my old servants not to take care of the rest. Lord Bolingbroke's works will surprise you. What he there advances, unsupported by argument, and attended with the grossest scurrility and abuse, is amasing. Pity that a man, endued with such talents, should so pervert them; and, like the giants of old, attack that Heaven which furnished him with arms. Another noble author will soon entertain us in quite another way. I mean a MS. History of Lord Clarendon's, left by Lord Hyde, one part containing the private history of his own life, and the other that of King Charles the Second's Court and Ministers, whom he has drawn even in blacker colours than Bishop Burnet has, yet not blacker, I believe, than they deserve. Lord Hyde had left it to found a riding-school at Oxford; but he dying before his father, it goes to Lord Clarendon's heirs-at-law.

" What you say of ' Sir Charles Grandison ' gives me a meaner opinion than I would wish to have of the good parish of Maidstone. Indeed the ladies in general are dissatisfied with the conclusion ; but the author has drawn up a letter in defence of it, which I believe he will print, and which I think will effectually silence all scruples.

" The day of battle is now approaching when the candidates take the field; a time that I heartily wish was well over.

" Our Master * is in town, and preaches at Court next Wednesday. No longer to detain you from parochial duty, I will subscribe myself, dear Sir, yours very sincerely, J. DUNCOMBE."

* Dr. John Green.

Rev. JOHN SHARP to Mr. DENNE.

1.   "*Aug.* 29, 1751.

" Jortin was here yesterday ; and I had the pleasure of attending him to our MS. library. Masters, I believe, took him
for some country parson, and prosed accordingly ; and seemed
much surprised when I told him afterwards with whom he had
been conversing. He came to the Master, but he being out of
the way, the greatest man in the College was next applied to."
— " Sharp has not suggested," remarks Mr. Denne, " what
might be the particular object of Jortin's search, but I think
it likely that he was in pursuit of materials for the Life of
Erasmus."

———

2.   " *Dec.* 3, 1751.

" The monastic life of an academic is not without the most
exquisite enjoyments. Here certainly we may learn to think
most justly, and to write most exactly, by studying the best patterns of imitation ; here, too, we might learn to converse,
though not by studying the models that are before us, and to
read, though not following the dull systems that are encouraged
amongst us. You, my friend, have all the advantages of an
academic life, in your present retirement, without its inconveniences ; you have the same opportunity and authors that teach
to think and to write ; and the necessary engagements in a
domestic life, and being in the world, afford you the best opportunities for reading and conversing in the most useful and improving manner.

" I am much pleased with your sentiments on conversation ;
and, had I time, I would in return give you some of my thoughts
on the same subject, not extemporaneous ones, but such as I
have already collected, and which are drawn from nature and
observation, from close reflection, particular reading, and general experience.

" Conversation is much degenerated ; sportsmen, games, and
the itch of trifling novelty have given it a fatal blow ! but you
shall have my MSS. on these and other subjects in a course of
letters, which I hope your friendly returns will encourage me to
send you this winter. In the mean time, if you are desirous of
seeing any of my printed performances, trifling indeed as they
are, I must refer you to a paper intituled, the Inspector, printed
in a newspaper called the London Daily Advertiser. In the
paper for July 17, is a letter on a Plan of Life for a family in
the Country during the Summer Months, signed Pharesio ; in
that for August 27, an Essay on Pedantry, signed Phares ; in
the paper for September 13, an Essay on the Moral Use of Newspapers ; and last of all, in the paper for last Wednesday,
Nov. 27, is a letter containing Observations on Lord Orrery's
Remarks on the Life of Dr. Swift. All are of my minting ; and
on which I should be glad of your animadversions. The three

last are signed Phares, which is the stamp I give all my compositions of this sort; and it is no more than a mixed transposition of the letters of my name, { SHARPE. PHARES."

---

3. "DEAR SIR,   *Cambridge, April* 1, 1752.
" I am resolved to begin this month well; and I cannot begin it better than by discharging the duties of friendship and gratitude in acknowledging the great pleasure I received the last month from you, though I hope you received two packets of printed papers, which I dispatched soon after the arrival of your last letter, which I am now to answer. I have read your letter over and over again with pleasure, with improvement, with sympathy. Our sentiments of men and manners accord very friendly; and the exchange of them will, I hope, ever continue to be the arguments of our correspondence and conversation till death.
" I am glad to find Mallet is a favourite author with you. You know my sentiments of him by what I wrote of his Life of Lord Bacon (by-the-bye Birch was never my favourite, and his name was foisted into my paper by his friend Hill). But what say you now to the posthumous works of Mallet's patron ? I have read over his Reflections on the Use of Retirement and Study, and those on Exile; I was charmed with both, and felt them, I believe, as much as the writer, for I believe he never felt them but in theory ; in short, I look upon Lord Bolingbroke to have been more of a philosopher in speculation than in practice, to have had in his disposition more of the Heathen than the Christian, more of the enthusiast than the wise man. His remarks on History are in my humble opinion ingenious, but subtle and delusive ; and what he says of the Scriptures, though a man who is not a Christian might think as much, yet as a Briton, he is not I think to be forgiven for this any more than he is for his apostacy in political principles. Such is my real opinion of this vain man ; and I would sooner be the despicable book-worm he describes all my life-time, than to be all my life-time, at my death, and, oh ! what is beyond, to find myself at my resurrection a Bolingbroke !"

---

4. "Oct. 17, 1752. I believe all competitions between the two tutors of the old House are near at an end, and Mr. Masters has declared that he shall take no more after Michaelmas, and that he shall shortly go to Paris to reside there for three years. As Mr. B. (Barnadiston) and I are not on the best terms, I cannot tell you more of these affairs at present.' "
On the above Mr. Denne remarks to Mr. Gough :
" The cause of the misunderstanding between Barnadiston and Sharp was not what you have suggested it to have been ; for it appeared from one of the letters which I have destroyed,

that the former was offended on his being told that the latter
had been the instrument of introducing a suitor to Miss Powel
(the sister of her who was afterwards the Mistress of Bene't-
lodge), with whom an alliance was not desirable. The name
and connexions, and something of the character, of the lover
were specified, but they not being matters in which I felt myself
at all interested, I took no notes of them ; but this I well
remember, that Sharp positively denied the charge, and that
Barnadiston was afterwards convinced it was without foundation."

5. " DEAR SIR,   *Cambridge, March* 14, 1755.
 " I intend to set out from this place on the 14th of April,
and to go immediately into Kent, where, in the three weeks
that I intend to pass there, I shall hope to see you often, and
certainly to visit Maidstone. Our friend at Sundrich *, too, expects me there; and our other reverend acquaintance, the Curate of Downe and Cudham,—the little Colman †, with whom I
breakfasted when in town at the Chaplain's apartment in Ely-
house with Sir Gilbert Knowler and one Parson Jefferis, a Norfolk divine, a quondam Member of ours ‡, but now married to a
daughter of the unfortunate Mr. Kirby, of Norwich, and in
possession of a Vicarage something under fifty pounds a year,
for the support of his family.
 " I know you will ever retain a love to the old House, and
your particular friends in it. We are at present six in number
here, but, as usual, divided. Our new Fellows are the worthiest
of men ; Fisher § is an amiable and ingenious young man, and
Herring one of the best sort of men to live with that ever I
came near ; I am sorry we shall lose him so soon. Mr. Masters
and I are on very good terms, visit and ride out together frequently. I believe he acts upon the principles of integrity,
though he is so unhappy as frequently to have a very wrong way
of being in the right. What think you of our intention to
spend the first vacant month in the MS. library ; and of seeing
an advertisement somewhat like the following, some years hence?
 " ' This day is published, proposals for printing a work, entitled,   ' Antiquitates
                  Desideratæ et Curiosæ
                       ex &c.
        Celeberrimâ MSS. C. C. C. Bibliothecâ.
                     Editoribus
        R. Masters, S. T. B.   J. Sharp, A. M. Collegii Sociis.
                    Cantabrigiæ,
 a R. M. invenit et legit.)   &c.   (J. S. delineavit et pinxit.'
 a You 'll observe this is to guard against an *Essex* controversy.

 * The Rev. John Duncombe.
 † Of William Colman, D.D. see the " Literary Anecdotes," vol. VII.
pp. 91, 540.   ‡ John Jefferis, entered at Bene't 1747, but took no degree.
 § Edmund Fisher, of whom before, p. 738.

" The papers tell you of all the University news, which has of late been a great article there ; what with the King of Naples, the Duke of Newcastle, Lord Townshend, &c. The other day the Chancellor's medals were adjudged to the new Bachelors, who were Apthorp* and Castley†, both of Jesus-college; Castley Senior Wrangler. There were six other candidates, all of great merit. Dr. George‡, after examining one of them in Demosthenes, harangued some time on that orator ; on which Meredith, of Trinity, the Senior Westminster, went up and told the Provost, they were not to examine him but the lad, and he desired to take him now himself !

" The Earl of Strathmore§, a Scotch Peer, is admitted at Pembroke, and is a pretty young fellow. I have a private pupil, an American ; and Jamaica is like to do me more credit than Barbadoes did. They are sitting at St. John's for Fellowships ; I fear Monins will yield to Abbot ||.

" The Master goes to London in a few days ; and enters on waiting at Court the beginning of April, as my brother does at Whitehall at the same time ; and we propose to dine one day with the Master at the Chaplains' table. Your friend George Lynch¶ is well and behaves well ; is so good a kind of man, and so much esteemed among us, that we are very sociable with him, and hope to have him one of us in very good time. Harvey** is a very regular, industrious, and good lad, deserves our notice and favour as often as we can show it. One Lorton, a friend of Herring, was admitted a few days ago, and my pupil a little before. We have three Kenricks††; and expect the two Stanleys very soon.

* East Apthorp, D.D. memoirs of whom will be found in the "Literary Anecdotes," vol. III. p. 94 ; vol. VII. pp. 11, 503.
† Thomas Castley, Fellow of Jesus, B.A. 1755, M.A. 1758. He was for many years Chaplain at Castletown in the Isle of Man, and Master of the Grammar-school there, at which nearly all the next generation of Manks clergy were his pupils. His wife died at Castletown, May 18, 1804 ; and he at Islington, near Liverpool, in 1808, aged 78.—His son, of the same names, and also a Fellow of Jesus-college, proceeded B.A. in 1787, as eighth Wrangler, and M.A. 1790. He was presented by that Society in 1808, to the Rectory of Cavendish in Suffolk, where he still resides ; and announced for publication in 1810, " Essays and Dissertations in Philology, History, Politics, and Common Life."
‡ William George, D.D. Provost of King's.
§ John the ninth Earl, who married the great heiress Miss Bowes, and died in 1776, aged 38.
|| Richard Monins (of whom before in p. 698) and William Abbot both became Fellows of St. John's. The latter was Senior Wrangler in 1754, and proceeded M.A. 1757, B.D. 1764. He was collated by Archbishop Drummond in 1767 to the Prebend of Fridaythorpe in the Cathedral of York, and was the oldest member of that church at his death, which took place at Ramsgate, Jan. 15, 1826, at the age of 93.
¶ See before, p. 612.
** Richard Harvey, B.A. 1758, M.A. 1761.
†† John, Matthew, and Jarvis, sons of Matthew Kenrick, Esq. Commissioner of Stamps and of Bankrupts, and nephews to Scawen Kenrick, D.D. of whom in Masters's History of Bene't-college, p. 326. Jarvis Kenrick, B.A. 1759, M.A. 1763. Matthew Kenrick, LL.B. 1762, LL.D.

" Clagett * writes seldom; I have heard nothing of him since
he left us after our audit. He is the same worthy, friendly, pleasant sort of man he ever was. Duncombe is an excellent correspondent and a most valuable friend; I hear from him every
week, and enjoy a very improving and entertaining correspondence with him. For society and conversation I am often
obliged to look abroad, as it is not always confined to the walls
of Corpus Christi college. We have one or two very agreeable
clubs, consisting of some of the cleverest M. A. in the University,
of which I will tell you when we meet. Being ever, dear Sir,
                    " Your sincere friend,   J. Sharp."

6. " Aug. 29, 1755. The old House will ere long be very populous, for we can scarce provide apartments for our Members.
Since the commencement, we have admitted the Hon. Mr. Scott,
brother to the Earl of Deloraine, now resident with us as a Fellow Commoner†. He was sent here by Lord Anson, his guardian,
and recommended by Mr. Charles Yorke. Since this we have
had the son of the late Mr. Brock Rand admitted ‡; and yesterday
came the worthy Mr. Stanley, and entered both his sons in the
good old House, to which they bid fair of being as great a credit as
their father and grandfather before them §. The Master informs
me, that Mr. Webb, Member for Haslemere ||, proposes to send
his son quickly to Bene't; and he has offered to recommend me
as his private tutor. Thus flourishes the ancient House. We
have this vacation repaired the library, had the books put into
better condition by a binder in the College; and when the

1776. He died Rector of Blechingley in Surrey in 1803, and was father
of William Kenrick, Esq. the Welch Judge, who died in 1829, and of
whom in Gent. Mag. vol. XCIX. ii. p. 565.
    * William Clagett, Fellow of Bene't, B. A. 1749, M. A. 1753.
    † The Hon. John Scott was a Commissioner of Bankrupts and died in
1788, aged 50; see Douglas's Peerage of Scotland, by Wood, vol. I. p. 410.
    ‡ Also named Brock, and proceeded B. A. 1760, being sixth Wrangler,
M. A. 1763. See the " Literary Anecdotes," vol. VI. p. 106.
    § The grandfather was William Stanley, D. D. Dean of St. Asaph,
Archdeacon of London, and Master of Bene't from 1693 to 1698. He
was a nephew of Bishop Beveridge, and, having been a native of
Hinckley, has a long memoir in the History of Leicestershire, vol. IV.
pp. 742—744. His son, the Rev. Francis Stanley, was for a few years
Vicar of Shoreditch (where he preceded Archdeacon Denne), and afterward Rector of Hadham in Hertfordshire. The grandsons Richard and
Francis entered at Bene't in 1755; they both took their B.A. degree
in 1760, when they ranked together as second and first Senior Optime;
Richard M. A. 1763, was a barrister; elected Recorder of Hertford 1780,
and died holding that office, and being a Senior Bencher of the Inner
Temple, at Much Hadham, Aug. 5, 1810. Francis, M. A. 1763, was presented to the vicarage of North Weald in Essex, in 1764, by Dr. Plumer,
and to the rectory of Eastwick in Hertfordshire by the son of the same
patron, in 1781. The latter he resigned about three years before before
his death. Having succeeded to the family estate at Much Hadham on
his brother's death, he died there, April 18, 1827, aged 90.
    || Philip Carteret Webb, Esq.
                    3 F 2

whole is finished they are to be new classed, &c. The library
and chapel look very smart to the garden; the former new
slated, and with new windows. These particulars relating to
the whole House, will, I dare say, be not unacceptable to you,
who will not forget your former relation thereto; but be as
zealous as the worthy Archdeacon in its service. Have you found
time to read through the second part of our History? The
account of Dr. Scawen Kenrick I find has given offence; and,
as we suppose, the cause of it may easily be accounted for, as
well as the first author. At my leisure I have made some MS.
observations on the book, have continued the Catalogue of
Names, am writing a copy of the College Statutes, with a list of
the Fellows in their successions in each Fellowship, with other
things towards another MS. volume.

" When I have the pleasure of seeing you, I shall tell you a
great deal about Norwich. I was at their new assembly twice.
The apartments were designed by the Master of Caius * ; but
there is a room in them sacred to the Corporation, and other
jolly fellows, no other than a combination-room, well stored
with pipes, port, and tobacco, for which you pay one shilling at
your admittance. The ladies were very brilliant ; but disgusted
me a good deal with their Norfolk dialect, the very reverse of what
is elegant and harmonious. We were last week at Ely on a visit
to the good old Prelate † there, who looks very well, and received
us very graciously. We met Soame Jenyns there, and were invited to supper, though we were in the first part of the evening
at the Ely Assembly in our canonicals ; but to describe this truly
bread and cheese club would require Hogarth's pencil. We met
there Mr. Gooch and his lady, and others of the Ely Clergy.
The tickets are one shilling ; for which you are entitled to as
much tea and coffee, or ham and chicken, as you please. They
play very low. The Rev. Mr. Watkins, a large Minor Canon,
was there in his night-gown. He never plays beyond three-
pences ; and keeps store of the small silver coin for prompt
payment."

7. From a letter dated Nov. 29, 1755. " How Barnadiston's
interest stands at Lambeth I cannot tell. People here seem to
wonder at his staying so long at College in such circumstances,
and begin to set him down for a College living. His income is
very considerable from the pupils, the College being very full,
within one or two of threescore. Mr. Burnaby, one of the
Clerks of the Treasury, admitted his son Fellow Commoner with
us a few weeks ago, when the Master was so kind as to recommend me for his private tutor."

8. " Corpus Christi college, Camb. Feb. 13, 1756. At our audit it was unanimously agreed to face the Hall of the College with

* Sir James Burrough, Knt.   † Dr. Green.

·stone, after the manner of some other Colleges. The historian presented a plan for that purpose; but within these few days his working brain has projected another, which is no other than making a new court of the Pensionary one; that building to be removed to the west end of the Chapel, and a new building to run across from the kitchen side, which is to be lengthened. By this means, he says, we shall have more apartments for our increase of members; and the scheme will not cost more than a quarter of what the plan before his History would have amounted to. In this case, the Master's Lodge, as on one side of the Court, is to be new fronted. We talk of beginning to case the kitchen side by Lady Day. I was surprised the other morning at going to the garden to find the great man in a night cap and a great coat, measuring with poles set up round the Pensionary. You are to know, perhaps, that our Historian indisputably pays his addresses to Miss Conny Cory, of Free-school-lane, granddaughter of the celebrated antiquarian Master Cory, the quondam Rector of Landbeach."

—

9.   " *March* 12, 1756.
" Our new Bachelors are now contending for the Chancellor's medals. Webster * is a candidate, and superior to any of them in academical learning; but, as this matter is to depend on the knowledge of languages and composition, the Etonians and Westminsters will be formidable competitors.

" Mr. Gray, our elegant Poet, and delicate Fellow Commoner of Peter-house, has just removed to Pembroke-hall, in resentment of some usage he met with at the former place. The case is much talked of, and is this. He is much afraid of fire, and was a great sufferer in Cornhill; he has ever since kept a ladder of ropes by him, soft as the silky cords by which Romeo ascended to his Juliet, and has had an iron machine fixed to his bed-room window. The other morning, Lord Percival and some Petrenchians, going a hunting, were determined to have a little sport before they set out, and thought it would be no bad diversion to make Gray bolt, as they called it, so ordered their man Joe Draper to roar out fire. A delicate white night-cap is said to have appeared at the window; but finding the mistake, retired again to the couch. The young fellows, had he descended, were determined, they said, to have whipped the butterfly up again.

"At Bene't, Mr. Masters, in the midst of as much mortification, opposition, and disappointment as ever, has sat for his picture †. Numbers resort to it; and he is allowed to be neighing on the very canvas. Many people inquired if there is not a miniature piece for a lady's watch, others of a copper-plate

—

* John Webster, of Bene't; see " Literary Anecdotes," vol. VI. 615.
† This extract (observes Mr. Denne) ascertains the date of the portrait by Kerrich, supposing it to be what is mentioned in Urban's Obituary.

for the History; and others why an old abbey, or a distant
prospect of Free-school-lane, is not drawn near him."
[There is a letter of the Rev. John Sharp in 1765, relating
some particulars of Dr. Johnson's visit to Cambridge in that
year, printed in Gentleman's Magazine, vol. LV. p. 178; see
also vol. C. i. 295.]

Rev. SAMUEL DENNE to Rev. JOHN DENNE.

"DEAR BROTHER,   *Vauxhall, Feb. 17, 1757.*

" I was not at home on Tuesday, or I would have returned an
immediate answer to that part of your letter which relates to
the man who was formerly an Anabaptist. I have communicated it to my father, who is of opinion that, unless the young
fellow's scruples can be removed, and he convinced in his conscience that immersion is not absolutely necessary, the Archbishop cannot dispense with the form. You must, however,
consult his Grace on the affair. My father does not apprehend
how the ceremony can be decently performed at Maidstone, as
you have no proper place for dipping in the Church, and your
river is so much exposed, and therefore thinks you ought to
look out for some small church contiguous to the river; but, for
my own part, I am of opinion it will be most advisable to let
his Grace determine the place and manner.

" My mother told you, that I had officiated as Chaplain to
Mr. High Sheriff*. We had a city dinner. Our company consisted chiefly of persons who had done honour to their country
in that office, inhabitants of Southwark and Bermondsey; and,
as far as I can find, I shall meet but few gentlemen at the
Assizes who do not live in the neighbourhood of London.
There are so many merchants, &c. who are proud of appearing
before my Lords the Judges, that the country gentlemen are not
afraid of being fined for non-attendance.

" The evening papers will probably tell you the unanimous
opinion of the Judges concerning Mr. Byng's sentence, that it
is a legal one. If this be true, he seems to be in imminent
danger. Lord M———d's character as a lawyer is not a little
sullied by an affair which happened last week. Lady Ferrers
appeared in the Court of King's Bench to swear the peace
against her Lord; upon which a motion was made by her
Counsel, for an attachment to bring his Lordship into Court.
Upon this the chief demurred, as thinking he had no power over
a Peer of Parliament till the opinion of the House of Lords
should be known. It was by them adjudged that, in all cases
where the peace is violated, not only the King's Courts, but
every Justice, has a power of securing the persons of Peers.
The other Judges, especially Foster, were much chagrined at
seeing the dignity of their Court questioned by one who ought
to have supported it. I am, most sincerely yours, S. DENNE."

* Sir Joseph Mawbey, of Kennington, Bart. Sheriff of Surrey.

Rev. THOMAS KERRICH, F. S. A.

The Rev. Thomas Kerrich, M.A. F.S.A. Principal Librarian of the University of Cambridge, Prebendary of the Cathedrals of Wells and Lincoln, and Vicar of Dersingham, Norfolk, was descended from a Norfolk family of great respectability, and which has been particularly productive of ministers of religion *.

* Of these the following notices have been collected:
The Rev. John Kerrich, son of John, of Mendham in Norfolk, was admitted a Scholar of Corpus Christi college, Cambridge, in 1681. He took the degree of B. A. in 1684, and died Rector of Sternfield in Suffolk May 14, 1691, aged 28.
John Kerrich, M. D. was a Fellow of Caius college, Cambridge, (M. B. 1717, M. D. 1722) ; and he had a son John, also of Caius college, B. A. 1728, M. A. 1732, and who was instituted Rector of Banham in Norfolk in 1735. His son, the Rev. Thomas Kerrich, also of Caius college, B. A. 1758, was presented to the Vicarage of Tibenham in 1759, and to Banham in 1772, and retained both those livings until his death in 1812.
The Rev. Charles Kerrich, Curate of Redenhall, became in 1749 Vicar of Kenninghall and Vicar of Wicklewood in 1750. He published in 1746 a Fast Sermon on 1 Kings, xii. 10, 11. 8vo.
One of the name became Rector of Winfarthing in 1749, and died in 1774.
The Rev. Thomas Kerrich, of Trinity hall, Cambridge, LL. B. 1780, died Rector of Great and Little Horningsheath, Jan. 10, 1814, aged 71.
More eminent than any of the above was the Rev. Walter Kerrich, who was Fellow of Catherine hall, Cambridge, B. A. 1758, being the fifth Senior Optime of that year, and obtaining the second Chancellor's and second Browne's medals, M. A. 1761. He was presented to the Rectory of St. Clement's, Eastcheap, London, in 1760; to the Vicarage of Chigwell, Essex, in 1765; to the Curacy of Stratford-sub-Castro by the Dean and Chapter of Sarum in 1789; and died in possession of those preferments, and of a Residentiary Canonry of Salisbury, in 1803. He published "A Sermon preached at the Cathedral Church at Sarum. London, 1780," 4to; and a "Fast Sermon, on Joel, ii. 12, 13. 1781," 4to.
His son, the Rev. Walter John Kerrich, was formerly Fellow of New college, Oxford, M. A. 1795. He was presented by Bishop Douglas. in 1792, to the Prebend of Alton Australis in

His father, the Rev. Samuel Kerrich, was educated at St. Paul's School, London; admitted Scholar of Corpus Christi college, Cambridge, in 1714,
and elected a Fellow in 1719. He proceeded B.A.
1717, M. A. 1721; was presented by the College to
the Vicarage of St. Bene't, Cambridge, in 1726, which
he resigned in 1729 for that of Dersingham in Norfolk; and was presented to the Rectory of Woolferton in 1731. In 1735, on proceeding to his Doctor's degree, he published a Sermon preached before the University on 1 Pet. iv. 10, 8vo, and in
1746, " A Sermon preached in the Parish Churches
of Dersingham and Woolferton, in the County of
Norfolk, on Thursday, Oct. 9, 1746, being the day
appointed for a General Thanksgiving to Almighty
God for the suppression of the late unnatural Rebellion, &c. Ps. cxxiv. 7. Cambridge, 1746," 8vo.

Dr. Kerrich " had been engaged," says Cole, " in
the former part of his life, to a young person at
Cambridge of the name of Newton, who left him
her fortune and estate, and for whom he composed
an epitaph in Bene't churchyard, Cambridge*." He

the Cathedral Church of Salisbury; and by his College, in 1818,
to the Rectory of Paulerspury, Northamptonshire. He married,
at East Hendred, Berkshire, May 23, 1823, Emma-Elizabeth,
daughter of C. W. Wapshare, of Salisbury, Esq.; and is living
1830.

* " On an altar-tomb of white marble," says Blomefield, in his
Collectanea Cantabrigiensia, " neatly adorned with a marble urn
at top, and railed in with iron palisadoes:

M. S.
Saræ filiæ Samuelis Newton,
nuper de hac parochia Generosi,
Quæ eximiâ vultûs morumque suavitate,
Patre, matre,
Sorore, Sororisque Filio,
uno fere quinquennio abreptis,
ita ut doloris nulla dareter intermissio,
sola tandem relicta,
luctibusque heu nimium indulgens,
ex vitâ,
quam per xxx annos castè ac pudicè egerat,

was afterwards twice married, first to Jane, daughter
of the Rev. John Kitchingman, Master of the Free
School at Cambridge, who with her first infant died
soon after its birth; and secondly, to a daughter of
the Rev. Matthew Postlethwayte, Archdeacon of
Norwich *.

ix Febⁱⁱ A^o D'ni. MDCCXXIV.
placidè discessit,
feliciore,
nisi fallit animus,
potitura.
Charissimæ Virginis reliquias
subter hoc tumulo depositas voluit,
qui ardebat vivam,
mortuam deflet."

The singular case of mortality to which this inscription alludes, is thus particularized on an adjoining altar-tomb:

"Samuel Newton died Sept. 27, æt. 64, a^o 1718. Here also
lie 9 of his children, 6 sons and 3 daughters; and also Eliz. his
daughter, wife to Benj. Watson, ob. Febr. 2, 1721, æt. 36.
Here also lyes Eliz. wife of Mr. Sam. Newton, ob. 21 Aug. 1723,
æt. 56. Benj Watson died March 6, 1717, æt. 47; his daughter Sarah, and Samuel their son, ob. Feb. 12, 1723, æt. 22."

* The Rev. Matthew Postlethwayte, born at Millom in the
County of Cumberland, was educated at St. Paul's school, London, by his worthy uncle the Rev. John Postlethwayte, of whom
there is a full memoir in Knight's Life of Dean Colet, pp. 384
—387. He was admitted at Corpus Christi college, Cambridge,
under Mr. Kidman, April 3, 1699; and on the 23d of June
following he was appointed by the Master to Dr. Spencer's
Scholarship, which he resigned upon his removal to St. John's
college, Dec. 28, 1702. He there proceeded B. A. 1702, M. A.
1706, went into Holy Orders, and became Vicar of the Shot-
teshams in Norfolk in 1708. He was likewise instituted in
1714 to the Rectory of Denton in that county, the patronage of which his uncle (who died Sept. 26, 1713) had purchased of the Duke of Norfolk, and bequeathed to the use
of Merton college, the place of his education, with £.200
for repairing and adorning the chancel. This was expended
by his nephew and executor with a considerable addition of
his own (see Knight's Life of Colet, *ubi supra*); and who
also built an elegant and spacious parsonage-house upon the
glebe, notwithstanding his own estate abutted upon it, and the
advowson was given away from the family,—a benefaction which
was supposed to have cost him at the least £.2000. He also
gave in 1714 £.200 to augment the Vicarage of Millom, the

Their son, the Rev. Thomas Kerrich, was of
Magdalen college, Cambridge; and in 1771, having

place of his nativity. He published in 1715, a Sermon on
Heb. v. 12, preached at the School feast; and in 1718, another
on Acts, xxvi. 9, intituled, " The Moral Impossibility of Protestant Subjects preserving their Religious or Civil Liberties
under Popish Princes, who act according to the Laws, Ecclesiastical or Civil, made against Protestants by the Church of
Rome. Preached at Norwich Cathedral, Nov. 5, 1710." His
first wife was Elizabeth, daughter of the Rev. Robert Rogerson,
M. A. his predecessor in the Rectory of Denton, by Barbara,
daughter of William Gooch, of Mettingham, Esq. and his second,
Matilda, her cousin-german by the mother, and a sister to Thomas
Gooch, D. D. who, when Bishop of Norwich, collated Mr. Postlethwayte to that Archdeaconry, July 13, 1742, and a few months
after to the Rectory of Redenhall cum Harlston. He enjoyed
these additional preferments, however, but for a short time,
dying in 1745; when he was buried in the church of Denton,
and the following epitaph was written for him by his son-
in-law Dr. Kerrich:

H. S. E.
Matthæus Postlethwayte, A. M.
Hujus Ecclesiæ multos per annos vigilans Rector,
deinde etiam de Redenhall cum Harlston,
Archdiaconus haud ita pridem Norwicensis,
Dignius cui hi parietes sustineant monumentum,
per quem ipsi sustentabantur, ornabantur.
Pietatem in Deum et Ecclesiam testantur hi cancelli,
testantur et testabuntur olim
ædes in proximo firmæ pariter et elegantes,
quas successoribus quàm hæredibus extrui maluit,
rebus Æcclesiæ postabens suas.
[Qualis fuerit moribus et charitate evangelicâ,
ab ipsis qui hâc in viciniâ degunt
ab Ecclesiâ Anglicanâ dissentientibus,
quibus charus vixit, obiit desideratus, discas.]
Eruditione haud vulgari
Latinis Græcisque literis penitùs imbutus,
Orientalibus, Occidentalibus minime hospes,
magnum illum Postlethuatium patruum suum,
Scholæ Paulinæ apud Londinenses Archididascalum,
passibus non iniquis secutus.
[Primis nuptiis uxorem duxit Elizabetham
Roberti Rogerson, A. M. hujus Æcclesiæ quondam Rectoris filiam,
quâ matre marmor ex adverso docet;
Secundis priori consobrinam Matildam,
D. D. Thomæ Episcopi Norwicensis sororem,
Goocheorum de Mettingham in agro Suffolciensi

in that year taken the degree of B.A. with the rank
of second Senior Optime, was elected one of Worts's
Travelling Bachelors *. He was at the same time
tutor to Mr. John Pettiward, Fellow Commoner of
Trinity college, the eldest son of Dr. Roger Mortlock, afterwards Pettiward, a Fellow of that College, and Chancellor of Chichester, who changed
his name from Mortlock to Pettiward on a very
large fortune being left him by an uncle †. Mr.
Kerrich travelled with his pupil through France
and the Low Countries, settled at Paris for six
months, and at Rome for two years ‡. The extent

perantiquâ familiâ oriundam.
Elizabetha reliquit Joannem filium,
Barbaram et Elizabetham filias, superstites.]
Adjacent exuviæ uxoris Elizabethæ,
omnibus, quæ secundùm Divum Paulum
Presbyteri conjugem decent, virtutibus ornatæ.
[The parts within crotchets are omitted on the monument.]

His son John Postlethwayte, was of Merton college, and
from gratitude to their benefactor his great-uncle, and respect
to his father, that Society, immediately on his father s death,
recommended him to the Archbishop of Canterbury as a successor to Denton, which living he held united with that of Thel-
ton in the same county.

* At this period the Rev. William Cole thus addressed " Mr.
Alban Butler at the English-college in St. Omer's, Artois:

" DEAR SIR, *Milton near Cambridge, Nov.* 17, 1771.

"The bearer, a friend of mine, Mr. Kerrich, one of the Fellows of Magdalen college in this University, setting off on his
travels on Tuesday, with a design to pass this winter at Brussels,
I thought that I could not show him a greater mark of my
friendship than by introducing him to the knowledge of a person who does so much credit to the English name abroad, at the
same time that I was desirous to testify to you my unalterable
esteem, with my gratitude for the very kind and hospitable
reception that I met with in your College. Mr. Kerrich is lately
chosen Fellow of his House, and since that elected by the University into one of the Travelling Fellowships, founded among
them, for a certain term of years. He is an ingenious young
man, a brother antiquary, and a most excellent draftsman. If,"
&c.—To Mr. Cole's copy of this letter is appended this note :
" This is the last letter I wrote to this honest, worthy, and learned
man, who died about May, 1773. Mr. Kerrich made no use of
it, not going through St. Omer's, or not calling on Mr. Butler."

† Restituta, vol. IV. p. 407.   ‡ Ibid. vol. III. p. 79.

of his scientific research, as well as his travels, will
appear by what is hereafter mentioned. In 1776 we
find the Rev. Michael Tyson thus writing from
Cambridge to Mr. Gough : " Mr. Kerrich and myself are busy every morning making a catalogue of
the prints in the Public Library. Mr. Kerrich has
the Travelling Fellowship, has been some years in
Italy, and was rewarded at Antwerp, at the Academy
of Painting, with a [silver*] medal for making the best
drawing. He has a fine collection of drawings from
old monuments in England, France, and Flanders
—so good that I shall be ashamed ever to draw
another †." There are allusions to Mr. Kerrich in
others of Mr. Tyson's letters; and in 1782 Mr.
Gough was thus addressed by Mr. Cole : " Besides
these four full sheets of paper, I send you Mr. Kerrich's draft of Sir —— de Trumpington, his drawing of Thomas Peyton, of Iselham, Esq. temp.
Edw. IV. with two others of his two wives, most
admirably done, and showing the dress of the times;
and a fifth of the tomb, or figure rather, of Sir
Thomas de Sharnborne, of Sharnborne in Norfolk,
by the same excellent hand; all which I trust to
your care, and shall be glad to have returned when
done with. I could have wished he had been more
exact in giving draughts of the monuments, arms,
inscriptions, &c. I am afraid he will disappoint
your expectations of any account of foreign monuments and habits; he seemed to me to have only
one object, that of cross-legged knights, and perhaps a few pillars in Churches ‡." From this it
appears that Mr. Kerrich's attention was especially
directed to the effigies. Mr. Gough, in his preface
to the first volume of his " Sepulchral Monuments,"
in 1786, expressed himself " happy in testifying

---

* Not "gold," as Mr. Tyson writes.
† See the "Literary Anecdotes," vol. VIII. p. 621. That
Mr. Tyson was himself eminently skilful in drawing, painting,
and etching need scarcely be here repeated.
‡ See "Literary Anecdotes," vol. I. p. 695.

his acknowledgments to Mr. Kerrich for several
highly finished drawings *."

Mr. Kerrich proceeded M.A. in 1775, and about
the same time was elected Fellow of his College.
In 1784 he was presented to the Vicarage of Dersingham (late his father's living) by D. Hoste, Esq. In
1793 he served the University office of Taxor, and
in 1797 he was elected Principal Librarian on the
death of the celebrated Dr. Farmer†. In 1798 he
was presented by Bishop Pretyman to the Prebend
of Stow Longa in the Cathedral of Lincoln, and in
1812, by Bishop Beadon, to that of Shalford, in
the Cathedral of Wells.

In 1797 Mr. Kerrich became a Fellow of the
Society of Antiquaries; and during the remainder
of his life he furnished some important articles to
its Archæologia. The first of these was in 1809,
" Some Observations on the Gothic Buildings abroad,
particularly those in Italy; and on Gothic Architecture in general," illustrated by eighteen plates of
sketches and sections of the Cathedrals of Placentia,
Modena, Parma, Milan, &c.‡ In 1813 he communicated to the Society an " Account of some lids
of Stone Coffins discovered in Cambridge Castle in
1810," with two plates §; and in 1824, " Observations upon some Sepulchral Monuments in Italy
and France ||," accompanied by eight plates, either
etched by Mr. Kerrich himself, or copied from his

---

* As engraved in the work may be specified: two views of the effigies of Sir Hugh Bardolph, at Banham in Norfolk, accompanied
by a description in Mr. Kerrich's own words, at vol. I. p. 36;
one of that of Sir Robert du Bois, ibid. p. 79; brasses of Sir
John Creke and Lady, ibid. 142; Sir John de Freville, ibid. 170;
Sir Thomas Shernborne and lady, vol. II. p. 185; and Thomas
Peyton, Esq. [not a Knight] and his two wives ibid. p. 286 (it
has incorrectly the name of M. Tyson.)

† See the circumstances of Mr. Kerrich s election related by
Mr. Denne, p. 715 antea.

‡ Printed in vol. XVI. of that work, pp. 292—325. — Many
years before, Mr. Kerrich drew, from the Pepysian library, the
great ship Harry Grace à Dieu, engraved in Archæologia,
vol. VI. plate xxii. § Vol. XVII. 228. || Vol. XVIII. 186—196.

etchings. It was the sight of these and other specimens of Mr. Kerrich's skill in delineating monumental effigies, that induced that excellent artist,
Mr. C. A. Stothard, F. S. A. to undertake his beautiful work on those very interesting remains of antient art, and undoubted authorities for the features
and costumes of the mighty in former ages. "There
are," says Mr. Stothard, in his prospectus, " though
not generally known, as they have never been published, a few etchings by the Rev. T. Kerrich, of
Cambridge, from Monuments in the Dominicans'
and other Churches in Paris *, which claim the
highest praise that can be bestowed, as well for
their accuracy as for the style in which they are
executed ; these are mentioned as a tribute which
they deserve, and as a sight of them induced the
proprietor of this work to execute the etchings for
it himself."

Desirous of obtaining the critical remarks of Mr.
Kerrich, Mr. Stothard anxiously conveyed to him
the first number of his work. "Of this gentleman,
who is still living, delicacy," says Mrs. Stothard, in
her admirable sketch of the Life of her husband, "forbids me speaking all I feel ; but gratitude for the
friendship and kindness he evinced towards my hus-

* Perhaps a list of those subjects etched by Mr. Kerrich, as
far as they have been ascertained, will be interesting and useful :
1. Effigy of Peter Earl of Richmond, in the Church of Aquabella in Savoy (two plates) ; 2. Peter de Aquabella, Bishop of
Hereford, in the same Church : 3. Equestrian Statue of Ber-
nabo Visconti, at Milan (several plates) ; 4. Monument of Matteo
Visconti, at the same city ; 5. Louis Earl of Evreux 1319, in the
Church of the Dominicans at Paris ; (all the preceding are in
the Archæologia ;) 6. Charles Earl of Anjou and King of Naples,
1285 ; 7. Philip d'Artois, 1298 ; 8. Robert Earl of Clermont
1317 ; 9. Louis Earl of Clermont and Duke of Bourbon, 1341 ;
10. Peter Duke of Bourbon, slain at Poictiers, 1356 ; and 11.
Charles Earl of Valois, all from the Church of the Dominicans
at Paris ; 12. a Bishop at Pavia ; 13. a Harsyck, from South-
acre Church, Norfolk ; 14. a broken effigy at Stamford ; 15,
16, two portraits from paintings by B. Gozzoli. These were
mostly etched about the years from 1782 to 1785.

band during his life, and towards myself since his decease, forbids my being silent. Mr. Kerrich was one of the earliest and most zealous friends Charles ever found. To great antiquarian knowledge he united the most accurate skill as a draughtsman. Of his judgment my husband entertained the highest opinion, and always declared that to his just and candid criticism, during the progress of the work, he felt greatly indebted for much of its improvement. Mr. Kerrich, he would say, was a severe judge, but one who never bartered his sincerity for compliment, and whose praise was worth receiving, as it was the commendation of judgment without flattery *."

And again, speaking of his work, Mr. Stothard himself says, " You, amongst other things, say that you think my etchings superior to those of Mr. Kerrich, but you are not perhaps aware that, if they really are so, it is in consequence of the judicious remarks and criticism I have received from that gentleman from time to time; and it was the very severe opinion that he gave me on my first number, which induced me to endeavour at acquiring that sort of excellence he then pointed out, and to which I look forward still with anxious hope †."

In 1815 Mr. Kerrich exhibited to the Society of Antiquaries, an urn discovered by some workmen employed to remove one of the barrows on Newmarket Heath ‡.

In 1820 he communicated some " Observations on the Use of the mysterious figure called Vesica Piscis, in the Architecture of the Middle Ages, and in Gothic Architecture §." This is accompanied by fifteen plates, containing no less than 65 draughts of the ground-plans and arches of antient ecclesiastical edifices, both abroad and at home.

* Memoirs of Stothard, p. 37. † Ibid. p. 129.
‡ See it engraved in Archæologia, vol. XVIII. p. 436.
§ Vol. XIX pp. 353—368.

To Mr. Kerrich's other attainments in the arts, was added that of taking portraits. The heads of Robert Glynne, M. D. 1783; Rev. James Bentham, F. S. A. the Historian of Ely, 1792; the Rev. Robert Masters, F. S. A. the Historian of Bene't-college, 1796; the indefatigable Rev. William Cole, F. S. A.; were all engraved by Facius, from drawings by Mr. Kerrich. Dr. Glynne Cloberry (such was latterly his name), on his death in 1800, left Mr. Kerrich his executor and residuary legatee, with a legacy of £.2,000 *.

In 1823 a considerable bequest devolved on Mr. Kerrich, on the death of Mr. Nollekens the sculptor, who appointed him one of his residuary legatees. Mr. Nollekens in his will, dated March 21, 1818, mentioned Mr. Kerrich thus: " I give to my worthy friend the Reverend Mr. Kerrich, one hundred pounds; and I desire that he the said Mr. Kerrich do select from my prints of Rubens, twelve of them for his collection, and which twelve prints I hereby bequeath to him." It was in a codicil dated Jan. 29, 1819, that Mr. Kerrich was appointed a residuary legatee with Francis Russell Palmer, Esq. Francis Douce, Esq. and the Rev. Edward Balme.

Mr. Kerrich married Sophia, fourth daughter of Richard Hayles, Esq. surgeon at Cambridge. He died in the University, May 10, 1828, aged 80, leaving that lady his widow, one son, Richard Edward Kerrich, Esq. M. A. of Christ's college, Cambridge, elected F. S. A. in 1830; and two daughters. One of the latter is the wife of the Rev. Charles-Henry Hartshorne, M. A. author of " Book Rarities of the University of Cambridge, 1829," 8vo.

A posthumous publication by Mr. Kerrich is intituled, " A Catalogue of the Prints which have

* See the Memoir of Dr. Glynne Cloberry in the " Literary Anecdotes," vol. VIII. p. 211; and letters in the present Work, vol. III. p. 221.

been engraved after Martin Heemskerck; or rather,
an Essay towards such Catalogue," 8vo, pp. 126.
Of the works of Heemskerck, who has been termed
the Raphael of Holland, Mr. Kerrich was an ardent
admirer, almost from his childhood; having become
possessed of some of the prints after that master at
a very early age.

Mr. Kerrich possessed a somewhat extensive
library, particularly rich in old wood-cut books.
His very curious collection of antient paintings in
panel he bequeathed to the Society of Antiquaries;
and his extensive manuscript collections and sketches,
for a History of Gothic Architecture, and on Ancient
Costume, to the British Museum *.

A very good portrait of Mr. Kerrich, taken by
H. P. Briggs, was engraved by G. S. Facius, in
folio, and is copied in the present Volume (p. 552).
There is an etching by Mrs. Dawson Turner, representing him at a more advanced age.

---

*List of the Pictures bequeathed to the Society of Antiquaries
by Mr. Kerrich.*

1. An antient Portrait on board, representing a person of
colour in a scarlet cap furred, dressed in a robe of cloth of
gold, with an ermined collar. It is probably an imaginary portrait of the fifteenth century, as upon the frame is written
the name CHARLE MAINGNE. This, with the eight pictures
which immediately follow, all upon board, are arched at the top.

2. A Portrait of Ferdinand King of Arragon, in a dress of
cloth of gold, the under-dress black, with a cross of gold and
pearls, pendant by a red string from his neck. On the frame
are the words *Fernandus Hispaniæ Rex.*

3. A Portrait of Louis the XIIth of France, in a cap or
head-dress fitted close. His dress consisting of a scarlet robe
furred, with an under-dress of cloth of gold. Louis the XIIth
of France was husband of Mary, sister to King Henry the VIIIth,
and afterwards Duchess of Suffolk. She became the bride of
Louis the XIIth on the 10th of October 1513, and in eighty-two
days became his widow. The frame is inscribed *Le Roy Loys.*

4. A Portrait of Francis the Ist, the successor of Louis the
XIIth, young and without a beard. He is dressed in a robe of
scarlet, with a black square cap upon his head, richly ornamented, and a fleur-de-lis of gold pendant by a black string

* They are contained in forty-eight volumes of various sizes,—Additional MSS. 6728 to 6773 inclusive. The volumes 6760 to 6773 are
architectural MSS. of Mr. Essex.

from his neck. His shirt is edged with a border of gold, and his under-dress is of cloth of gold. The face looking to the left.

5. Edward the IVth of England *, in a black cap, with a rich ornament and pearl above the forehead. His outer dress cloth of gold, with an under-dress of black, ornamented with rows of pearls and pendants. In his right hand the rose of York. On the frame is inscribed in antient characters, *Edward' Rex quart'*.

6. Richard the III^d of England †. This Portrait is a companion to the former. He wears a black cap with a pearled ornament; his hair brown and long. His robe cloth of gold, with an under-dress of scarlet; the right hand engaged in placing a ring upon the third finger of the left hand. The inscription, in part obliterated, *Ricard' Rex terci'*. Mr. Kerrich became possessed of this and the preceding Portrait, with the Numbers 2 and 3, in 1787.

7. Is an antient Portrait, well painted, and probably executed in the early part of the 16th century, inscribed in a very old character, LE ROY DE DENEMARQVE. It is possibly a portrait of Christian the Third. The king, whoever he was, is represented in an ornamented robe of cloth of gold furred. His beard large and red. A collar, probably of some Order, round his shoulders; a pink in his right hand. .

8. Is the Portrait of a person of middle age, in a square black cap with an ornament and pearls pendant in front. His robe dark; the collar of the Golden Fleece suspended from his shoulders; a cross and pearls below. A book in the left hand. An old inscription on the frame assigns this portrait to MONSOVR DE NASSOV.

9. Represents a Figure in a black dress and cap, the gown furred; a chain of gold with a pendant round the neck; a roll of paper in the left hand. On the lower part of the frame, the name MONSOVR DE RAVESTEIN.

Freher, in his Theatrum Virorum Eruditione Clarorum, mentions one Jodocus Ravesteyn, a Fleming, an eminent scholar and theologian; he was a Canon of the Collegiate Church of Louvain, Provost of Walcheren in the diocese of Namur, and one of the defenders of the Council of Trent, who died in 1570. Possibly the same. The picture might have been painted much earlier.

---

* An engraving of this picture, from a drawing by Mr. Kerrich, forms, the frontispiece to the fourth volume of the Paston Letters.

† Printed in lithography in the fifth volume of the Paston Letters, where it is remarked in the preface, "The head of Richard is a very antient picture; and in addition to its own intrinsic merit and strength of expression and character, it possesses this circumstance which renders it particularly interesting in the present work. It was formerly the property of the Paston family; and was sold, with many others, at Oxnead in Norfolk, once the magnificent seat of that family, after its property had been dissipated by the extravagance of the last Earl of Yarmouth of that name. Many valuable pictures of more modern date were sold at the same time, some of the principal of which are now in the possession of Sir Robert Buxton. The portrait in question was probably an original, — or at least a contemporary picture, and had been in the possession of the Pastons from the time of its being painted."

10. Is another Portrait of King Richard the III^d, with a dagger or short sword in his right hand. A very antient picture, half-length. He is dressed in a black robe with sleeves of black and crimson, apparently wearing an under-dress of cloth of gold; a small black cap upon his head. The dimensions of this picture, one foot seven inches by fourteen inches. Mr. Kerrich became possessed of this picture in 1783.

11. Henry the VIIth, in a cap with a pearled ornament in front, a robe of scarlet, with a collar of roses. Half-length; on board. The rose of Lancaster in his right hand.

12. Another Portrait of Henry the VIIth, similar to the former, but apparently of more advanced age. The right hand also holding the red rose.

13. Henry the VIIIth, in advanced life, with hat and feather, in a black robe furred, the sleeves having slash openings; under-dress of scarlet. A half-length, on board.

14. A smaller Portrait of Henry the VIIIth, similar in dress except that the under-robe appears of cloth of gold.

15. A half-length Portrait on board, companion to the preceding, supposed of Queen Anna of Cleve *. The head-dress and gown of cloth of gold. This and the last-mentioned portrait of Henry the VIIIth were purchased by Mr. Kerrich in 1781.

16. A very fine Portrait, three-quarter-length, of Queen Mary the First, richly dressed; a hood upon her head; at the lower corner on the right of the figure is the monogram of Lucas de Heere, HE, with the date 1554. This portrait Mr. Kerrich bought in February 1800 from the collection of Mr. Smith, of Boston in Lincolnshire, which was then sold in London. It is said formerly to have come from Kensington Palace.

17. A small half-length, on board, of Philip the Good, Duke of Burgundy. He is dressed in a black robe and cap, and wears the collar of the Order of the Golden Fleece.

18. Mary Queen of Hungary, in a rich dress of cloth of gold, with a large head-dress profusely ornamented. Inscribed, *Maria Regina*, 1520, on one side of the head; and the words, *Anno Etatis* 14, on the other.

19. Is a small round Portrait of a Man with a red beard, dress of black, and sword. At the sides of the head, ANNO D'NI 1558, and ÆTA. SUE 45. Round the edge of the frame,

MATER QVÆ QVONDAM NVNC EST FORTVNA NOVERCA,
SED DEVS EST IDEM QVI FVIT ANTE MEVS.

20. A round Picture in a square frame, the size of life, on board; inscribed in a character of the time, " ANT. MORVS, PHI. HISP. REGIS PICTOR, IO. SCORELIO PICTORI. A^o. MDLX." John Schorel or Schoreel, so called from the village of that name in Holland, was born in 1495. He studied for a time as a

* Misnamed Jane Seymour in the Archæologia, vol. XXII. p. 450.

painter under Mabuse and Albert Durer, and afterwards pursued his art during a pilgrimage to Palestine. He is said to have been the first of the Flemish painters who introduced the Italian taste into Holland. He died in 1562. Sir Antonio More, who painted this picture, was a pupil of Schorel.

21. From a half obliterated inscription at the back, is appropriated by Mr. Kerrich, as the Portrait of Bartolomeo Liviano de Alviano. It is large, and on board, and similar in dress and appearance to some of the figures in the pictures of Raphael.

22 and 23. Two Pictures, each in two compartments, formerly belonging to the old conventual Church of Ely, and representing a portion of the legend of St. Etheldreda, the Foundress of that Monastery. The first or upper compartment of the first picture, represents the marriage of Etheldreda with her second husband Egfrid King of Northumberland. The second represents her as overlooking the workmen who are carrying on the buildings of the Church of Ely. In the upper compartment of the second picture, Etheldreda is seen obtaining Egfrid's consent to depart the court, whence she is said to have retired to the Abbey of Coldingham. Beneath are the words,

Hic Rex dat votum, quod Sancta petit fore totum,
Extans corde rata, permansit Virgo beata.

Etheldreda is stated to have persevered with both her husbands to live in a state of virginity.

In the last, or lower compartment of the second picture, her interment is represented. Not the first interment in a wooden coffin in the common cemetery of the Nuns of Ely in 679; but that which is so minutely described by Bede in his Ecclesiastical History, consequent upon the translation of her body by the Abbess Sexburga into the Church of Ely in 695, when it was deposited in a marble coffin.

From the general appearance of these pictures they may be ascribed to a date at least as early as the reign of Henry the Sixth.

24. Is a Picture upon board of the Martyrdom of St. Erasmus.   At bottom, in the old English letter, *Per fr'em Jo'm Holynburne Aº D'ni* 1474.

25. Is an antient Picture painted upon canvass laid upon board ; and was brought from Palestine by the late Dr. Edward Daniel Clarke of Cambridge, by whom it was presented to Mr. Kerrich. At the back of this picture is the following account of it in Dr. Clarke's hand-writing:

" This Picture was found by Dr. Edward Daniel Clarke on the 3d day of July 1801, at the Church of Safouri or Sephori in the Holy Land, about five miles from Nazareth, and between that place and St. John d'Acre. The Church, once a magnificent building in the form of a Greek cross, is now in ruins. It was in a vaulted stone chamber, where the natives now keep their empty bee-hives, that this picture, with others, formerly a part

of the sacred ornaments of the church, were discovered under
a heap of rubbish. One of them had been taken out, and
placed on a rude temporary altar among the ruins formed of
loose stones. It is not certain when the Church of Safouri
was destroyed. It was dedicated by the primitive Christians to
St. Joachim and St. Anne, the parents of the Virgin ; who were
said to have resided there. E. D. C."

26. The last Picture is a Portrait of Henry the Sixth, marked
Henricus Sextus, but certainly not so old as his time *.

------

1. Mr. KERRICH to the Rev. WM. COLE †.

" DEAR SIR, *Magdalen college, Cambridge, Dec.* 27, 1780.

" The view of the Play-house in Dorset-gardens that is in our
Library is not a drawing but a print ; and the letters are cut off,
so that there may be some reason to doubt whether or not it be
really that theatre.

" The other views Mr. Walpole speaks of, are, I apprehend,
six small drawings with a pen by Hollar. They are rather slight,
little more than outlines; but may probably enough be really by
Hollar, and, if they have not been engraved, I should guess are
curious.

" 'Suffolk House ; York House ; Durham, Salisbury, and Worcester Houses ; Savoy; Somerset House ; ' are written on them;
but in a hand more modern than the drawings themselves. I make

* Of this also a lithographic plate is published in the fifth volume of
the Paston Letters. " It is certainly a very early portrait, if not an
original ; and it possesses this peculiarity which renders it valuable, that,
while the expression of the countenance indicates the vacancy of mind
and weakness of character which belonged to the amiable but unfortunate original, it contains more of marked individuality of character than
the other representations of his countenance which have been transmitted to posterity."—" These two engravings have been recently executed in lithography from drawings made [in Nov. 1821 and Jan. 1822]
by the very spirited and correct pencil of Mr. Kerrich." The editor,
Mr. Frere, previously remarks that " This gentleman's taste and judgment in the arts of Engraving, and knowledge of Antiquities, particularly those connected with Architecture, have long been well known to
the world. He is to be enumerated among the distinguished characters
whose friendship Sir John Fenn possessed. This circumstance led him
to contribute a portrait of Edward the Fourth to the former part of this
work ; and I have to express to him my best thanks for the great kindness and liberality with which he has supplied the three portraits to the
present volume."—The third is a head of Margaret of York, Duchess of
Burgundy, the " Dido" of the history of King Henry the Seventh.
This painting is inscribed, MARGAR' DE ORC. 3 UXOR CAROLI DUCIS
BOURGON'. It was engraved by Facius (from a drawing by Mr. Kerrich) and published by Richardson in 1804; and the same plate was purchased for the " Paston Letters" at Mr. Kerrich's suggestion. This
painting was not included with those sent to the Society of Antiquaries
the wood being so completely decayed as scarcely to bear a touch

† From the British Museum, Additional MSS. 6401.

no doubt but our Society would be very happy to oblige Mr. Walpole with copies of them, if from this account he should think them worth his notice *. As to the making the copies my pencil shall be at Mr. Walpole's and your service. But, as it is not customary, on any account, to take the books in which the drawings are, out of the library, one can hardly set about this matter till the weather is warmer.

" The picture given by Lord Carlisle to King's college is a very capital one of the Florentine school, they say by Daniel de Volterra. The subject is a dead Christ in the arms of Joseph of Arimathea, &c.—ten figures as large as life, two of them apparently portraits †. It seems scarcely credible that so considerable a picture as this, if really by Daniel de Volterra, should not have been mentioned by Vasari in his Life of that painter.

" Your obedient servant,   T. KERRICH."

---

2. Mr. KERRICH to RICHARD GOUGH, Esq.

" SIR,   *Magdalen college, Cambridge, July 29, 1782.*
" I have just received your roll of prints, on my return to College, for which accept my best thanks.

" It seems to me, that the only merit such prints as these ought to aspire to, is a mere servile imitation of the objects they pretend to represent ; and all attempts of the artist, either the designer or engraver, to show his own abilities, are impertinent ; and, indeed, in this case insufferable. I own your prints do not appear to me entirely free from faults of this kind ; the two from brasses particularly have too much of touch and slight *maestria* in them, the very reverse of the firm dry manner in which those figures are always executed. I would not be understood here to blame your engraver ; I know my poor friend Tyson's haste and want of patience to imitate the manner of his originals with the painful exactness I require ; and it is probable all the faults I complain of were in the drawings.

" In the figure of the gentleman in St. Mary Overy's Church, I should apprehend the stern bluff character of the countenance to be a mere interpolation of the artist who copied it ; indeed the whole head, and the whiskers especially, have more the appearance of a portrait from the life than a drawing of a statue. The drapery, too, as the painters say, is not understood, and the habit is that of no time ; that part of it about the knees, I will venture to assert, (though I never saw the figure,) is false.

" I made, several years ago, slight drawings of all the Knights in the Temple-church, merely with a view to their habits ; and I

---

* The three first subjects are engraved in Wilkinson's Londina Illustrata ; of the two latter several views have been preserved.

† " It has nothing to do with his famous picture of the Descent from the Cross, which is at Rome."

think I can, when I have the pleasure of seeing you, point out several mistakes in your prints of them, which it would be worth while to have corrected before they are published.

" I ought now to apologise for the freedom of my criticisms; perhaps it may be sufficient to refer to your letter, which gives me leave to speak my sentiments without reserve. I am, Sir, your obedient and very humble servant,   T. KERRICH.

" I believe Mr. Cole knows nothing of De Arche more than the name which he gathers from the arms on his shield. As I see in your plates you give the whole stone with all its ornaments, it is but right to inform you that this, Sir —— De Arche has his lady by him, and several Gothic ornaments, in very good taste about him * ; and I fear my drawing may not answer your purpose. It is not at Weston Colville, but Weston Waterless, a village not far from Newmarket. I think we may ascertain its date pretty nearly,—the early part of Edward the Third's reign, before the introduction of the cuirasse."

3. "DEAR SIR,   Burnham, Norfolk, Feb. 17, 1783.
" I received your kind present of Mr. King's long-expected Castles here at the most northern point of Norfolk, where I have been some weeks ; and beg you will be so good as to thank him in my name for them. By-the-bye I must take the liberty to remind you of some twelve shilling antiquities you were to procure for me, and a seal of an Earl of Chester, and some other works of Mr. King's, the Great Harry ship business, with the print from the drawing in our library †, &c.

" What shall I do with Mr. Basire ? If he can neither copy correctly, nor correct his blunders, what hopes are there of his producing any prints that can be at all to the purpose ? As I have not my drawing with me here, I must postpone my new corrections to my next letter ; and shall only observe in this, that his alterations are so very clumsy, that both the new and old lines appear in the print, and do confuse the figure most gloriously.

" I really thought I had long ago thanked you for Croyland Abbey. It is certainly an elegant print, and I am much obliged to you for it ; you are to answer for its correctness.

" I just looked over your Camden, but not so carefully as I mean to do on my return to College. The only observation I recollect to have made was, that you seem to have given nearly the same account of Castle Acre, twice over, in different words. You may, if you please, look at it, and see whether it be so.

" Dear Sir, your most obedient servant,   T. KERRICH."

* This monument Mr. Kerrich afterwards appropriated to Sir John Creke and his lady ; see p. 813.
† See the note in p. 813.

Magdalen college,
4. "DEAR SIR,   *Cambridge, April 23,* 1783.

" I beg your pardon for not returning the proof of your new edition of Camden sooner; but I was so long confined in Norfolk, and have been so much engaged since my return to College, I had not time to read it over with the attention that I ought. I have taken the liberty to offer some slight alterations in the margin, which I submit to your consideration; you receive with it the two prints of Bardolph. Basire certainly has employed his boys about them; however, I have endeavoured to correct them, as far as they seem to me capable of correction. I shall be obliged to you for them again as soon as he has altered the plates.

" I send you too the best plan I could make up of Castle-Acre Castle, because I promised it; but can by no means advise you to have it engraved. All the parts west of the Castle itself (which Parkin calls the Barbican), I know are not correct; particularly, I am not sure how far towards the north the north-gate should be placed.

" I received, some weeks ago, Mr. Carter's Antiquities, and am much obliged to you for directing him to send them. I will not trouble you to pay him for them, as it is probable I shall be in London myself in the course of the summer.

" Dear Sir, your obedient servant,   T. KERRICH.

" P. S. If I should go into Norfolk again this summer, I will endeavour to get a more accurate plan of Castle-Acre Castle, if you wish to have one to engrave, and can stay for it. I forgot to say, that I cannot help thinking there was an outwork on the west of the Castle similar to that on the east, but larger; and that the street of the present town is almost all, if not all of it, in the ditch."

---

5. "DEAR SIR,   *Magdalen college, March* 28, 1786.

" The parson of Banham *, I hear, has it in contemplation to paint Sir Hugh Bardolph's effigy all over of a stone colour. I wish much to prevent him, if possible, because it will destroy the little that remains of the antient paint, which constitutes one great part of its value. Perhaps if he were to see your prints of it, and know the pains that have been taken to copy this very paint accurately†, it might be a means of stopping his hand. I should, therefore, be much obliged to you for a few of the impressions, that I might send him one of each.

" How our correspondence has been interrupted I do not very well know; but I fear it has been my fault. I was so ill when

---

* Mr. Kerrich's namesake; see p. 807.

† Mr. Kerrich's coloured drawing of this effigy is among his MSS. at the British Museum (6728, p. 25). The engraving is in the Sepulchral Monuments has been mentioned in p. 813.

I received your last letter, that I am totally ignorant what became of it, but I think poor Mr. Essex answered it for me*. I should be glad to hear how your " Monuments " go on ; and whether your engraver is ready for any more of my drawings. I do not wish them to be better executed than that of Du Bois is ; and am at leisure at present to prepare them for him.

" I scarce need add, that I should take it as a particular favour that you would send me the prints immediately, else they may be too late to do any service. Dear Sir,
        " Your most obedient servant,   T. KERRICH."

6. Mr. GOUGH to Mr. KERRICH.

" DEAR SIR,   *Enfield, April 7, 1786.*
" The parson of Banham (be he Bishop, Priest, or Deacon) deserves to be made a whited wall for his irreverent intentions towards a monument on which you have bestowed so much attention. If the prints of it herewith sent aver this barbarous purpose, I shall be happy.

" Our correspondence ended, as you truly say, with yourself ; and so long ago that I have entirely forgotten with what parts of your collections you intended to favour me. Though I am drawing to a conclusion as fast as the nature of the work admits, I shall always be ready to receive the communications of my friends, and none will be so acceptable as those from your pencil. I am, dear Sir, yours sincerely,   R. GOUGH."

7. Mr. KERRICH to Mr. GOUGH.

                                    Magdalen college,
" DEAR SIR,   *Cambridge, April 22, 1786.*
" Mrs. Essex has been so obliging as to search for the plan of Sturbridge Fair in question †, and has found two impressions of it ; the one corrected, the other not. I here send you the corrected one for Mr. Nichols by her leave.
     " Dear Sir, your obedient servant,   T. KERRICH."

8. " DEAR SIR,   *Market Weston, July 29, 1788.*
" I left, I think, twelve drawings packed up to be sent to you the other day, on my leaving College, which I hope you have received safe, and of which I beg your acceptance.

* On the 29th of February 1784, Mr. Essex wrote to Mr. Gough : " Mr. Kerrich has had a bad fall upon a stone pavement, which has much hurt his head ; but, as there is no fracture, we hope is now out of danger. I saw him this morning before I received your letter ; but, as he is forbid reading, writing, and drawing, I thought it would not be proper to trouble him again this day." On the 14th of March the same correspondent says : " Mr. Kerrich is better, and abroad again."
† See Bibl. Top. Brit. No. XXXVIII. p. 73.

" Bad health, some misfortunes, and, above all, weakness in my eyes, must excuse me for not having made these drawings long ago ; indeed I was afraid they would have come too late for your purpose ; but at length I have got a sight of your book, and find that all of them but one will be in time for the second volume.

" You have now all the drawings which you marked in my collection, except one, which is part of De Freville's monument, and which you shall have, if it will be of any use to you. You may recollect it is of the time of Edward the Second. You should have had it with the rest, but I was sent for into Norfolk in haste to a friend who was very ill, just as I was going to begin it.

" I shall be in College again in about ten days, and shall be obliged to you to favour me with a letter, to let me know that you have received the parcel; and when the drawings are engraved, I must request that I may have an opportunity of correcting the proofs before they are published. I am, Sir,

" Your obedient servant,   T. KERRICH."

---

9. Mr. KERRICH to the Rev. EDWARD BALME *.

" DEAR BALME,   Cambridge, Nov. 27, 1804.

" Can your friend —— give a plausible account of the object of his pursuit ? Is he sure that he is not hunting a shadow or an *Ignis fatuus ?* If he is only going to prove that Gothic architecture was not invented here in England, surely he might as well spare his time and labour; let —— or any body prove that it was. The attempt will be quite harmless, so he do not perplex us with new names for things that have names already well established and generally received; but if he is going to search, and endeavour to find out and demonstrate to us where and when Gothic Architecture was invented, he will, I think, if possible, be still more hopelessly employed. Gothic Architecture was not invented or discovered in any one place, nor did it come ready made into the world at any one certain period of time. It began almost imperceptibly from the old, heavy, clumsy architecture of the middle ages, and grew up by slow degrees to the exquisite beauty and elegance which we now be-

* The Rev. Edward Balme was a Fellow of Magdalen college, Cambridge, where he proceeded B. A. 1775, and M. A. 1778. He was elected a Fellow of the Society of Antiquaries in 1794, being then resident at Finchingfield in Essex ; and of the Royal Society in 1801. He was chosen of the Council of the former in 1820. He died in Russell-place, December .., 1822 ; and was buried at St. Pancras new Church. His valuable and extensive library was dispersed by auction by Mr. Evans. Mr. Balme, like his friend Mr. Kerrich, was one of those selected by Mr. Nollekins to benefit by his large property. He was appointed an executor with a legacy of £.500, and one of the three original residuary legatees; but dying before the testator, his family were not benefitted by the bequest.

hold with delight and astonishment in the best productions of it. It never was at one stay; it was continually increasing, improving, refining, and altering, by the constant addition of new beauties, new forms of elegance and delicacy, and sometimes new absurdities, invented at distant times and in different countries of the world; and it would require more than the life and industry of one man to discover and ascertain the birth-place of each; and every one of them, wherever it was produced, seems to have been carried with most wonderful celerity into all the other countries of Europe. It is much to be wished that somebody could solve that strange phenomenon of Gothic Architecture being so generally and widely spread over the world, and that there should be such an almost perfect uniformity of style at the same time in all the several countries, however distant, where it was known. And here I feel much inclined to venture upon an observation, if I did not suspect it to be nonsense; but no matter if it is, that the disagreeable, inelegant, ugly forms (wherever produced) did not meet with a general reception in the different countries, but the elegant and graceful did. I cannot help thinking that I have seen in the Great Church at Milan, at Ely, and in other places, particular forms of deformity, which, if not peculiar to those places, are at least such as we do not commonly meet with elsewhere, a sort of provincial style of absurdity or ugliness. I have observed none such of beauty.

" I hope your friend means to have the drawings you speak of engraved and published; that must always be to the purpose, provided it be done fairly, and that they are not warped or altered to make them favour some particular theory. Persuade him, if you can, to let them be had separate from his book, after it has had its sale; that will make them doubly and trebly useful.

" If he be going to look after the origin of the Gothic (impointed) arch, I heartily wish him good luck. There are evidently two questions, how it was invented, and when and where it was invented ?

" About the first old Bentham and Mr. Essex always were at daggers drawing ; neither of them made much of the matter, and two or three other theories, how it might have been hit on on or invented, may easily be produced, just as plausible as either of theirs ; but how a thing might possibly have been done, and how it actually was done, are two very different inquiries; and here it was that Sir James Hall split. As to the other question, when and where it was discovered, there seems to be no hope of our getting a satisfactory answer. Euclid taught us how to make the figure, it is the first proposition in his book; but where and when an arch of that figure was actually built of real stone and mortar is a different matter; as it also is, who they were that first of all men put an arch of that figure into a design for building. If I were obliged to guess at this matter,

I should say these things were probably first done somewhere in Germany. The Italians have always called architecture of this sort, which we call Gothic, German Architecture, to distinguish it from the old heavy kind, which they call Lombard; they have not a great deal of it south of Lombardy. They retained the round arch much longer, I think, in Italy, than in Germany, France, or England, but they applied the delicacies of the Gothic style to those arches; see the Cathedrals of Venice, Florence, Orvieto, and Siena. Perhaps if we had a mind to indulge conjectures, and yet wish to avoid talking sillily, we might venture to suppose, by way of a general notion, that the Pointed Arch, that great foundation and criterion of Gothic Architecture, was of Northern original; and that most or many of the delicate, tender, elegant members of it, or at least the taste for lightness, slenderness, and subtilising, came to us from the East. So if any part of this appears to be sense, you are at full liberty to communicate it to your friend, or whom you will.

" Pray who managed the book about St. Stephen's Chapel ? I like that best of all that the Antiquaries have published; there is more detail of the parts, which are the life and soul of the things *.   Yours sincerely,   T. KERRICH."

10. " DEAR BALME,   *Burnham, May* 6, 1820.
" You have pleasure in reading letters, so here is another; and I will try to make it such a one as you wish to have from me.

" My great object in all that I have ever done, or thought, or written about Norman and Gothic Architecture, was to recover, if possible, the rules and principles of the science or art (whichever you may choose to call it), which are lost; and this I should not despair of seeing effected if men would seriously examine and study the buildings in those styles that are left, so as to understand them, and not waste their time in frivolous disputes as to what they should be called, or fruitless inquiries from whence Gothic Architecture was brought, and hopeless guesses concerning the origin of the Pointed Arch. All these I have endeavoured to discourage as much as I could in the former dissertation I sent to the Society, which was meant as a mere introduction to that now before them, which is the result of many years' study, and a patient examination of a great number of buildings. I in that made some remarks upon the particular nature of Gothic Architecture, the simplicity of its leading forms, the astonishing variety of which it is capable, which exceeds infinitely every thing that could possibly be done in the Antique, or, as it is called, regular Architecture. I hinted the use which had been made of a mysterious figure (for which we had no name) by the old architects in making their designs, long

* The account of St. Stephen's Chapel, which accompanies Mr. Carter's drawings, was written by John Topham, Esq. Treas. S.A. A Supplement to it was afterwards published, with Mr. Smirke's drawings.

before the Pointed Arch was in vogue. I observed its having been used for the form of ecclesiastical seals, and other things designed for sacred purposes; and said, that on accidentally looking into Albert Durer's book of Geometry, I had found that he named it Vesica Piscis. He must therefore answer for that name; I only adopted it as better than Gothic Oval or Gothic Ellipsis, which is absolutely intolerable, but I have heard it called by both these names; and I believe I went so far as to assert, that the influence of this figure was very extensive. This I meant to show, so far as architecture is concerned, in the present paper, which I then meditated, and have now sent.

"There was some other loose matter in the former dissertation, I fancy of no great consequence, which I do not recollect, and I have it not here with me; but I remember full well I ended it with some foolish popular stuff about the Great Church at Milan, which I heartily repent having ever written; there is nothing in it but what the silliest man upon earth who had been at Milan might have told us; and I have had the mortification to find it was so well relished by some of my readers that they attended to nothing else, and seem to have overlooked, or rather skipped every thing in the Dissertation that had any sense in it.

"I was determined not to fall again into the same error; and in the present paper have adhered strictly to my purpose, which was to show the truth of what I had before asserted concerning the use of this mysterious figure, which A. Durer calls *Vesica Piscis*; so far as relates to Gothic Architecture and the Architecture of the Middle Ages. Perhaps one might say the Architecture of Christian nations; but I believe it had better be omitted, so we will let the matter stand as it is. If the notions produced in this paper have any foundation; if they are right, or nearly right, which there is surely good reason to believe they are, one very considerable step is gained, for we have discovered the rule by which the old architects formed many of their designs of plans, doors, windows, &c. &c. and the mode in which they proceeded to adjust their proportions. I do not pretend that I have found out all their rules, much less that I have arrived at the principles of their architecture; that is the very pinnacle we are striving to attain; but I do think I have here pointed out a track, which, if pursued, may lead men so nearly right that there is no reason to despair of their attaining the high point we have or ought to have in view. Rules are for workmen, principles are the object to men of sense and philosophers.

"Now you may do exactly as you please with all this; you may communicate the whole, or as much of it as you think proper, to our brother Antiquaries.

"Yours sincerely, T. KERRICH."

SIR JAMES EDWARD SMITH, M. D. F.R.S.

was President (from its establishment) of the Linnæan Society; Honorary Member of the Horti-
cultural Society; Member of the Academies of
Stockholm, Upsal, Turin, Lisbon, Philadelphia,
New York, &c. the Imperial Academy Naturæ
Curiosorum; and the Royal Academy of Sciences
at Paris.

He was born in the City of Norwich, Dec. 2,
1759, the eldest of seven children, whose father, a
Protestant Dissenter, and a respectable dealer in the
woollen trade, was a man of much intelligence and
vigour of mind. His mother, who was the daughter of a clergyman, lived in Norwich to the advanced age of eighty-eight, revered for the benevolence, cheerfulness, and activity of her character.
It is probably to the locality of his birth that we
are to attribute his early predilection for natural
history; for at Norwich he associated with some of
the earliest and most devoted disciples of the great
Linnæus. That city has, for more than two hundred years, been famous for its florists and botanists.
There lived and flourished Sir Thomas Browne, the
author of "Vulgar Errors," and "The Garden of
Cyrus; or the quincuncial, lozenge, or network Plantations of the Ancients, artificially, naturally, and
mystically considered." A weaver of that commercial place claims the honour of having been the first
person who raised, from seed, a lycopodium; as a
Manchester weaver was the first to flower one of our
rarest jungermanniæ. During the middle of the
last century, Mr. Rose, the author of the "Elements of Botany," Mr. Pitchford, and Mr. Crowe,
names familiar to every botanist, took the lead in
botanical science in their native city; and instilled
into the youthful mind of the future President an
ardent attachment to their favourite pursuit, and the

Sir *J.E.Smith*, Knt

M.D. F.R.S. Pres. L.S. &c. &c.

Born 1759 — Died 1828.

Published by J.B. Nichols & Son, Jan.1.1831.

skill in discriminating species for which these gentlemen were so eminent.

Having remained the usual time at a school in
Norwich, he went in the year 1780 to the University
of Edinburgh, where he distinguished himself by
obtaining the gold medal given to the best proficient in Botany.

Upon leaving Edinburgh, he came up to London
to finish his studies, and soon became acquainted
with the late Sir Joseph Banks. This acquaintance,
and the access it obtained for him to men of science,
only riveted more firmly his ardent attachment to
natural history; and, accordingly, we find Sir Joseph
recommending him, as early as 1783, to become the
purchaser of the Linnæan collection. As this circumstance laid the foundation of the President's
future fame, the history of the transaction shall be
detailed.

The younger Linnæus had died suddenly, Nov. 1,
1783; and his mother and sisters, desirous of making as large a profit as they could by his museum,
within a few weeks after his death, offered, through
a mutual friend, the whole collection of books, manuscripts, and natural history, including what belonged to the father as well as the son, to Sir Joseph
Banks, for the sum of one thousand guineas. Sir
Joseph declined the purchase, but strongly advised
Sir James Smith to make it, as a thing suitable to
his taste, and which would do him honour.

Sir James, in consequence, communicated his desire to become the purchaser, to Professor Acrel, the
friend of the family of Linnæus, and who seems to
have conducted the negotiation with scrupulous
honour. The owners now began to suspect they
had been too precipitate; having received an unlimited offer from Russia, while also Dr. Sibthorpe
was prepared to purchase it, to add to the treasures,
already famous, of Oxford. They wished to break
off their treaty with Sir James Smith; but the

worthy Swedish Professor would not consent to it, and insisted on their waiting for his refusal.

In consequence of the subtraction of a small herbarium made by the younger Linnæus, and given to a Swedish Baron to satisfy a debt he claimed, a deduction of one hundred guineas was made in the purchase-money; and in October 1784 the collection was received in twenty-six great boxes, perfectly safe. The whole cost, including the freight, was £.1,029. The duty was remitted on application to the Treasury. The ship which was conveying this precious treasure had just sailed, when the King of Sweden (Gustavus III.), who had been absent in France, returned, and hearing the story, sent a vessel in pursuit, but happily it was too late *.

* The collection consists of every thing possessed by the great Linnæus and his son, relating to natural history and medicine. The library contains about 2500 volumes. The old herbarium of the father comprehends all the plants described in the " Species Plantarum," except, perhaps, about 500 species (fungi and palmæ excepted), and it had then, perhaps, more than 500 undescribed.

The herbarium of young Linnæus appears to have had more attention bestowed upon it, and is on better paper. It consists of most of the plants of his " Supplementum," except what are in his father's herbarium, and has, besides, about 1500 very fine specimens from Commerson's collection, from Dombey, La Marck, Pourrett, Gouan, Smeathman, Masson, &c. and a prodigious quantity from Sir Joseph Banks, who gave him duplicates of almost every one of Aublett's specimens, as well as of his own West India plants, with a few of those collected in his own voyages round the world.

The insects are not so numerous; but they consist of most of those that are described by Linnæus, and many new ones. The shells are about thrice as many as are mentioned in the " Systema Naturæ," and many of them very valuable. The fossils are also numerous, but mostly bad specimens, and in bad condition.

The number of MSS. is very great. All his own works are interleaved with abundance of notes, especially the " Systema Naturæ," " Species Plantarum," " Materia Medica," " Philosophia Botanica," " Clavis Medicinæ," &c. There are also the " Iter Lapponicum" (which was afterwards published), " Iter Dalecarlicum," and a Diary of the Life of Linnæus, for about thirty years of his life. The letters to Linnæus (from which a

This splendid acquisition at once determined the bent of the proprietor's studies. He considered himself, as he has declared, a trustee only for the public, and for the purpose of making the collection useful to the world and to natural history in general. He had no sooner obtained quiet possession, than he began to fulfil his engagement; for we find him, in the year 1785, making his first appearance as an author, by translating the Preface to the " Museum Regis Adolphi Friderici" of Linnæus, being succinct and admirable reflections on the study of nature.

In the year 1786 he prepared himself for an extensive tour on the continent, in which his chief object was to examine into the state of natural history in the different cities and towns he might pass through, not neglecting the incidents, especially the fine arts, which usually engage the attention of travellers. At Leyden he graduated in medicine; but it does not appear that he tarried there a longer time than was necessary for this purpose. On this occasion he published his thesis " De Generatione." His " Sketch of a Tour on the Continent," in three vols. 8vo. 1793, though long superseded as a companion to the tourist, is still curious to the naturalist, as showing the state of science at that time. It contains, too, a fund of good sense expressed with facility; and, to those who enjoyed the acquaintance and friendship of the author, will always remain valuable, as furnishing the truest image of his mind,

selection was also published by the President; see pp. 839, 850) are about three thousand.

On the Anniversary of the Linnæan Society following Sir J. E. Smith's decease, the Secretary stated to the members, that the executors of Sir J. E. Smith had offered his valuable library botanical and other collections, to the Society, for the sum of £.4,000. The library embraced the original collection of Linnæus, containing 2.500 volumes. The sum of 3000 guineas was ultimately agreed to be paid for the entire Collection and Library; and a subscription was made, as the best and speediest plan for realizing the purchase-money.

reviving his liberal opinions in their recollection, and his easy and elegant manner of communicating them.

In the year 1788, when he had returned and was settled in London, he, with some other naturalists, projected the establishment of the Linnæan Society, which had for its object the cultivation of natural history in all its branches, and especially that of Great Britain. This Society, which has grown now into considerable importance, was a scion of the Royal Society, and had its origin in the jealousy which some of the members of the parent Society entertained of the preference which, they alleged, was given to natural history in their "Transactions;" while its then President was thought to favour the subject, to the exclusion of others of equal, if not of greater, importance. There are still some who recollect the argumentative and vehement eloquence by which this side of the question was supported by Bishop Horsley.

It was during this stormy period that Sir James Smith, in conjunction with Dr. Goodenough (the late Bishop of Carlisle), Sir Joseph Banks, and others, laid the foundation-stone of the Linnæan Society *. Its first meeting was held, April 8, 1788.

* There had, however, previously existed a " Natural History Society." This was established in London 13th October 1782. The original members were, Mr. Isaac Dalby, Mr. William Forsyth, Mr. Charles Harris, Mr. George Prince, Mr. John Prince.

"The officers of the Society in 1791 were, Viscount Lewisham, President; Dr. Ash, Rev. Edmund Poulter, Vice-Presidents; Mr. Francillon, Treasurer; Rev. John Hadley Swain, Secretary; Dr. George Fordyce, William Forsyth, Esq. Everard Home, Esq. John Woodd, Esq. James Agar, Esq. Mr. George Prince, and Mr. Day, Committee. The number of members in 1791 was 110, and honorary members 50. The members met originally at a house in Golden-square, on the second and fourth Monday in every month, except August and September, at seven o'clock in the evening, and when five members (the original number) were present, they proceeded to business. The subscription was one guinea a year, and one guinea admission; and nine guineas, besides the admission fee, exempted members from all future

The Society then consisted of fifty Fellows, and as many more foreign members, Dr. Smith being the first President, Dr. Goodenough the first Treasurer, and Mr. Marsham the first Secretary.

At the first meeting the President delivered a Discourse, judicious and appropriate, " On the Rise and Progress of Natural History." We find him also, about this time, producing a paper which was read before the Royal Society, intituled, " Observations on the Irritability of Vegetables." It chiefly regards the mode of impregnation in the barberry ; and attracted considerable attention at the time, being translated into other languages, and appearing in different publications.

The next considerable work which we find him undertaking is, the re-publication of the wooden blocks of Rudbeck, which had fallen into his hands with the Linnæan collections. Linnæus was pos-

payments. The anniversary was kept on the second Monday in March. None of their communications were ever published. When the Linnæan Society was established in 1788, many of its members quitted, and joined that Society. From that time it dwindled away. The members gave up their house in Golden-square, took apartments in Warwick-street, and afterwards held their meetings at the York Coffee-house in St. James's-street. Their meetings finally ceased in 1794 or 1795. The following are all that are now [1828] living who were members in 1791 : James Agar, Esq. Hare-court, Temple, 1787 ; Joshua Brooks, Esq. Blenheim-street, 1786 ; Montagu Burgoyne, Esq. Upper Brook-street, 1791 ; Everard Home, Esq Leicester-square, 1785 ; Rev. Rob. Nares, James-street, Westminster, 1789 [died 1829] ; William Smith, Esq. Aldermanbury, 1789 ; Rev. Dr. Robert Thompson, Kensington, 1786. These were their residences, &c. at that time. Dr. J. E. Smith had only lodgings at Chelsea ; about 1790 he had a house in Great Marlborough-street, where he remained till the year after his marriage, 1797, when he retired from London to reside at Norwich. Of the original members of the Linnæan Society, now living, are, Robert Barclay, Esq. Clapham ; Sir T. Gery Cullum, Bart. Bury ; Sam. Galton, Esq. Birmingham ; Aylmer B. Lambert, Esq. ; Dr. John Latham ; Mr. Arch. Menzies ; R. A. Salisbury, Esq. [died 1828]."
—A letter signed " M. H." in the Gent. Mag. XCVIII. i. 582

sessed of about 120 of these blocks, which had
escaped the fire at Upsal, where almost the whole
impression of the second volume, and all but three
copies of the first, were burnt. As Rudbeck was
the founder of a school at Upsal, destined afterwards
to give laws to the rest of the world, the re-publication of this fragment of his great work was a tribute of gratitude to his profound and varied learning.

From 1789 to 1793, our author was engaged in
various publications relating to his favourite science.
Most of them terminated in being only fragments,
for want of patronage by the public. Such were his
" Plantarum Icones hactenus ineditæ ; " "Icones pic-
tæ Plantarum rariorum;" "Spicilegium Botanicum ; "
and " Specimens of the Botany of New Holland."
One of these literary projects, " English Botany,"
however did not suffer the shipwreck experienced by
the others, but has received the encouragement it
deserved. This is not attributable to its execution
being superior to the other works which have failed,
but because it treats of the plants of our own country, in which all are interested. It had the singular merit of being the only national Flora which had
given a figure and description of every species native
to the country whose productions it professes to
investigate; and while other works of a similar
kind enjoyed the patronage of foreign Crowns, and
were even supplied with funds to carry them forward in their tardy progress, this work was rendered complete by the patronage of the public
alone; and, having been commenced in 1790, was
brought to a successful termination in 1814, by the
united efforts of the President of the Society, and of
Mr. Sowerby, the draughtsman and engraver. This
work extends to thirty-six volumes, and contains
2592 figures of British plants.

In 1792, Dr. Smith had the honour of giving
some instruction in botany to the Queen and Prin-
cesses at Frogmore. As a lecturer, he was particu-

larly admired for his ease and fluency, and for the
happiness of his illustrations, as well as for the
extent and variety of his knowledge. This will be
testified by all who heard him at the Royal Institution in London, at Norwich, Liverpool, Bristol, &c.

In the year 1793 appeared in the Memoirs of the
Academy of Turin, of which he was a member, his
essay, " De Filicum Generibus dorsiferarum," and
which was re-published in English in his " Tracts
on Natural History."

In the year 1796 Dr. Smith married the only
daughter of Robert Reeve, Esq. of Lowestoft, in
Suffolk; and in the following year he removed to
Norwich, his native place, where he continued to
reside, paying occasional visits to London, for the
remainder of his life.

The next considerable work upon which the reputation of our author is built is the " Flora Britannica," which appeared in the years 1800—1804.
It is remarkable, like all his other labours, for accuracy in observing, accuracy in recording, and unusual accuracy in printing. It comprises descriptions of all the phænogamous plants, of the filices
and the musci; and every species has been carefully
collated with those which Linnæus described.
Being written in the Latin language, the information is condensed into a small compass; while it has
the rare advantage of having had every synonym
compared with the original author.

The "Compendium Floræ Britannicæ" has gone
through four editions, and is become the general
text-book of English botanists. It is perhaps the
most complete example of a manual furnished on
any subject.

While he was engaged in the " Flora Britannica," the executors of Professor Sibthorpe selected
him as the fittest person to engage in editing the
splendid posthumous work of that liberal patron of
science; a task for which the unrivalled attainments

of the President, and his personal friendship with
the Professor, peculiarly qualified him. The drawings, which were made by Ferdinand Bauer, and
the letter-press, which was written by Sir James
Smith from scanty materials furnished by Dr. Sibthorpe, are both worthy of so munificent an undertaking.

In 1806 the first part of the " Flora Græca" appeared. Its publication was continued in parts
until it reached six folio volumes, with one hundred
coloured plates in each. To complete the work,
which is to consist of ten folio volumes, Dr. Sibthorpe bequeathed a freehold estate at South Leigh,
in Oxfordshire; which, after the completion, is to
be charged with the support of a Professor of Rural
Economy in the University of Oxford.

There was also a " Prodromus" of the same work,
in two volumes 8vo. without plates.

The " Introduction to Physiological and Syste-
matic Botany," which appeared in 1807, was a most
successful publication, having passed through five
editions. It is indebted for its popularity to a
happy method which the author had of communicating knowledge, to the good taste he every where
displayed, and to that just mixture of the *utile* with
the *dulce,* which he knew so well how to apportion.

In 1810 appeared, in a magnificent folio volume,
his "Tour to Hafod," the seat of his old and accomplished friend, Thomas Johnes, Esq. the translator
of Froissart; and, in 1811, his " Translation of
Linnæus's Tour in Lapland."

In 1814 he received the honour of knighthood
from the hands of his present Majesty, on the occasion of his present Majesty consenting to become
the patron of the Linnæan Society, and granting
them a charter.

About 1818 Sir James was deputed by Professor
Martyn to deliver lectures from the Botanical chair
in the University of Cambridge,—an arrangement

which might naturally have led to his being elected
Mr. Martyn's successor. He obtained the countenance of many of the Heads of Houses, and of
several of the first Dignitaries of the Church; but,
unfortunately, a controversy was raised by interested
persons respecting his religious opinions, (those of
the Unitarian Dissenters,) of which congregation at
the time of his death he was one of the Deacons;
which opinions (like his illustrious predecessor, Ray,
who was deprived of his fellowship for a similar
cause,) he could not compromise. It produced two
small tracts from his pen, intituled, "Considerations respecting Cambridge, more especially relating
to the Botanical Professorship," &c. 1818; and,
" A Defence of the Church and Universities of England against such injudicious advocates as Professor
Monk and the Quarterly Review," 1819.

In 1821 his " Grammar of Botany" appeared;
and in the same year, selected from his copious
stores of original MSS. two volumes of the " Correspondence of Linnæus, and other Naturalists *."
These volumes abound with particulars interesting
to all literary men, but especially so to Naturalists;
and we know it was the intention of Sir James
Smith to have favoured the public with a continuation, had the success of the first two volumes answered his just expectations. But naturalists are by
no means all readers; their studies are rather in the
book of nature than in the book of the author. They
would not, however, be less fitted for their pursuits,
if they were more accustomed to add past experience to modern practice, by the perusal of works
similar to that now noticed.

During a large portion of his literary life, Sir J.
E. Smith was in the habit of writing articles for Dr.
Rees's " Cyclopædia" on different subjects in botany and biography connected with it. Many of
these biographical memoirs are choice morsels of
original information; and we need only refer to the

* See the letters relative to this Work, hereafter, p. 849.

words Collinson, Curtis, Dombey, Hudson, Linnæus, Ray, Sibthorpe, Tournefort, &c. in justification of our assertion. Most of his articles will be
found marked with the letter S, it being his undeviating rule never to publish any thing on anonymous authority in science. Even some reviews
which he had written early in life, he afterwards
avowed, by re-publishing them in his " Tracts."

The second volume of the Supplement to the
Encyclopædia Britannica is indebted to our author's
pen for a Review of the Modern State of Botany,
an article which supplies some deficiencies in his
Introduction, though chiefly an abridgement of the
Prælectiones of Linnæus, as published by Giseke.

During the whole of his literary career, he occasionally contributed papers to the Linnæan Transactions. But the last and best work of the distinguished President is the " English Flora," consisting of four volumes octavo, and describing the phænogamous plants and ferns of Great Britain, though
its title may imply a more limited range. *Finis
coronat opus.* There is no Flora of any nation so
complete in flowering species, and none of any
country in which more accuracy and judgment are
displayed. If any person should in future contemplate a work of this kind, whatever the originality
of his information, whatever the novelty of his subject, let him imitate this illustrious author in careful
remark, in taking nothing upon trust, in tracing
every synonym to its source ; and, lastly, in arranging his matter in such a manner, by the aid of different types, at shall render it easy of reference, and
point out at a glance the nature of it. However
mechanical some of this may appear, it is absolutely
essential to be attended to in natural history, where
the subjects are infinite in number, and where aid
must be derived from every mode of generalizing
particulars.

To this work Sir James Smith had devoted much
of his time during many years. It was pursued

with ardour, in spite of the interruptions of declining health, with the anxious desire, often expressed, that he " might live to finish it." On the very day when he entered his library for the last time, the packet containing the fourth volume of the " English Flora," reached him. The following remarks, at the close of that volume, will be read with melancholy interest :—

" Several circumstances have caused a long delay in the publication of the present volume, which, if their recurrence should not be prevented, may render the completion of the work, according to its original plan, very precarious. In the meanwhile, the number of volumes originally proposed is now finished, and the first twenty-three Classes are completed, as well as the first Order of the twenty-fourth, Cryptogamia Filices, the only one that required more study and emendation than it has hitherto received.

" If our bodily powers could keep pace with our mental acquirements, the student of half a century would not shrink from the delightful task of being still a teacher; nor does he resign the hope of affording some future assistance to his fellow-labourers; though, for the present, 'a change of study,' to use the expression of a great French writer, may be requisite, ' by way of relaxation and repose.'"

Sir James Smith had, by nature, a delicate constitution, and struggled, in the course of his life, with many attacks of an inflammatory kind. To her whose tender affection, aided by her vigilance, good sense, and gentleness of manner, had so large a share in the preservation of this valuable man through many years of feeble health, no consolation is wanting which memory can bestow *. For some years past he had been losing strength, and suffering from the increase of painful and distressing symp-

* A biographical memoir of her husband, with a selection from his extensive correspondence, has, we learn, for some time occupied her, and is now in the press.

toms. He had generally, however, kept his annual engagement with the Society, at the anniversary and other meetings, at which he felt proud and happy to preside. But in the year 1827, his hopes of reaching London were frustrated by the state of his health. Some amendment afterwards took place; the return of spring renewed his earnest wishes to meet his old friends again, and he had actually laid his plans for once more visiting the metropolis.

On Saturday, March 15th, 1828, he walked out as usual, and apparently without much fatigue; but in the evening he was attacked by such an alarming fit of illness, as almost immediately forbade the hope of his recovery. He continued sinking until six o'clock on the Monday morning following, when he quietly resigned his breath, and his spirit returned to Him who gave it.

His remains were deposited in the vault belonging to Lady Smith's family, at Lowestoft, in Suffolk.

The scientific character of Sir James Smith may be comprised in a few words. As a naturalist, he contributed greatly to the advancement of science; and stood pre-eminent for judgment, accuracy, candour, and industry. He was disposed to pay due respect to the great authorities that had preceded him, but without suffering his deference for them to impede the exercise of his own judgment. He was equally open to real improvement, and opposed to the affectation of needless innovation. He found the science of botany, when he approached it, locked up in a dead language; he set it free, by transfusing into it his own. He found it a severe study, fitted only for the recluse; he left it of easy acquisition to all. In the hands of his predecessors, with the exception of his immortal master, it was dry, technical, and scholastic; in his, it was adorned with grace and elegance, and might attract the poet as well as the philosopher.

His moral and religious qualities are likewise deserving of the highest praise. The uprightness and liberality of his mind appeared in the uniformly candid expression of his sentiments. It was his constant, earnest desire, to banish jealousy and rivalship from the pursuits of science, and to cultivate a union and good understanding between the botanists of all nations; exhorting them to adopt, with a readiness and ungrudging alacrity, of which he set the example, the suggestions of foreigners, whenever the interests of science were concerned.

The same steadiness and constancy with which, from a conviction of its excellence, Dr. Smith devoted his life to the illustration of the scientific system of Linnæus, he equally evinced in the support of those principles, both religious and political, in which he had been brought up. His liberal education, and his intercourse with men of all countries, holding various opinions, served but to settle his own; and they were established on the only firm basis, that of investigation and reflection.

When he took up his final abode in his native city, in 1797, it was after an absence of seventeen years. In the course of those years he had formed many friendships; he was known, honoured, and courted by celebrated men of all countries, and of all parties in his own; and he returned to Norwich full of information, rich in fame, and loaded with honorary titles; besides the substantial possession of his great prize, the Linnæan collection. Yet he came, unspoiled by honours, and uncorrupted by travel, to sit down among the friends of his youth; willing to give and to receive pleasure from the most attainable and simple objects. It is obvious to remark, that, if a residence in London presents more attractions to a man of science than a residence in a provincial metropolis, he is often abundantly rewarded, for resisting them, by the closer friendships which local circumstances permit him to form, and by the delightful consciousness of being the means of improving the tone of society around him.

An individual, eminent for knowledge, and conciliating in manners, is, in such a situation, a treasure of inestimable value; he is the stay and support of his contemporaries; and, to the young, his industry and attainments, his elegant tastes and pure morals, are held up as examples of the manner in which nature rewards those who have not wasted their hours in sloth, nor frittered away their best powers in dissipation. Such a support and such an impulse the late President of the Linnæan Society assuredly gave by his connection with Norwich; and, had his health permitted, they would have been given in a yet greater degree. He never appeared to be happier than when surrounded by young people, for whom he readily unlocked his cabinet and displayed his mental stores, imparting knowledge in the most familiar and captivating manner.

With regard to politics, he was to the last an ardent lover of liberty; and, though of the gentlest and most retiring disposition, he always gave his public countenance and support to Whig principles in his native city and county. Placed in a scientific station of eminence, he did not obtrude his own religious and political sentiments where they would have been out of place; but through life, no honours or distinctions, or fear of unpopularity, or devotion to scientific pursuits, could deter him from the most unreserved and steady avowal and support of his principles, both religious and political.

His poetical compositions are distinguished by elegance, and by frequent allusions to that world of nature towards which his thoughts perpetually turned, when in search of objects for love and grateful praise. At the same time, let it not be thought that Christian topics were forgotten. Upon these his compositions were less numerous, but upon none, perhaps, were they so beautiful. Many elegant specimens of his poetical powers are in the hands of his surviving friends. Several of these are to be found in a volume of " Hymns for Public Worship, selected for the Use of the Congregation assembling at the Octagon Chapel, Norwich " (1826).

On Wednesday, the 19th March 1828, at the meeting of the Linnæan Society, the intelligence of Sir James Smith's decease was communicated; when the members, as a tribute of respect to their friend and President, immediately retired. At the next meeting of the Society, which took place on the 1st of April 1828, Lord Stanley in the chair, his Lordship opened the proceedings by adverting, with much feeling, to the great loss which had been sustained by the country and the world, and more especially by the Society, in the death of its illustrious and beloved President, Sir James Edward Smith, who from its first establishment, in which he had taken an active part, had been called upon to preside over it by the annual and unanimous votes of its members, and had greatly contributed to place the Society in the distinguished rank which it had attained, by his great talents, indefatigable industry, sound judgment, and enlarged views as a naturalist; by the high estimation in which he had long been held by men of science all over the world; by the excellence of those valuable and accurate works in which he had done so much to promote and improve the study of natural history; and especially by the qualities of his heart, mind, and temper, for which his memory would long be revered by those who had enjoyed the happiness of his friendship. His Lordship could not forbear expressing what he felt on the occasion, especially with reference to the particular moment of his loss, at a time when those considerations of religious distinction were about to be removed, which had seemed to have a tendency to deprive those who, like this excellent and distinguished man, differed from the established religion, of the rank in society due to their talents or their worth *.

His Lordship expressed his anxiety that whatever choice might be made by the Society to fill the vacancy in its Chair, should be such as would contribute to its prosperity, however impossible it might be adequately to supply the loss which it had now so much to regret †.

Lord Stanley, then adverting to the last volume of the English Flora, which had been received from Sir James Smith but a few days before his death, and was among the presents on the table, related that, showing it to a friend, Sir James had exclaimed, " This is the close of my labours."—As its distinguished author was now removed from the possibility of receiving the customary vote of thanks, his Lordship concluded by proposing that the grateful feelings of the Society might be expressed to Lady Smith for this last gift of their revered President. A marble bust ‡ of Sir James, executed by Mr. Chantrey, was placed in the meeting-room of the Society previously to the next meeting.

The following is a list of Sir J. E. Smith's papers in the Transactions of the Linnæan Society:

On the Rise and Progress of Natural History, vol. I. p. 1. —Descriptions of two kinds of Lichen, collected in the South of Europe, p. 81.—On the Festuca spadicea and Anthoxanthum paniculatum of Linnæus, p. 111. — Remarks on the Genus Veronica, p. 189. — Remarks on the Abbé Wulfen's Descriptions of Lichens, (1789,) vol. II. p. 10. — Additional observations on the Festuca spadicea and Anthoxanthum Paniculatum, (1792,) p. 101. — Remarks on the Centaurea solstitialis and Centaurea Melitensis, p. 236. — Remarks on the Genus Dianthus, (1793,) p. 292. — The Botanical History of Mentha exigua, (1794,) vol. III. p. 18.—Botanical Characters of some Plants of the Natural Order of Myrti, (1796,) p. 255. —Characters of a New Genus of Plants named Salisburia, p. 330.

* Alluding to the proceedings in Parliament for the abolition of the sacramental test.
† At the next Anniversary meeting of the Society the choice of the Society for the Presidency fell on his Lordship.
‡ There is a beautiful etching by Mr. Dawson Turner, from a bust by Bullock, 1810.

— Remarks on some Foreign Species of Orobanche, (1797,) vol. IV. p. 164.—The Characters of Twenty New Genera of Plants, (1798,) p. 213.—Observation son the British Species of Bromus; with Introductory Remarks on the Composition of a Flora Britannica, p. 276.—Description of Sowerbæa Juncea, a Plant of New South Wales, (1799,) vol. V. p. 159.—On the British Species of Mentha, p. 171.—Of five New British Species of Carex, p. 264. — On the Genera of Pæderota, Wulfenia, and Hemmeris, (1800,) vol. VI. p. 95.—On some British Species of Salix, (1801,) p. 100. — Botanical Characters of four New Holland Plants of the Natural Order of Myrti, p. 279.—Of the Fruit of Cycas revoluta, p. 312.—Of the Grass called by Linnæus Cornucopia Alopecuroides, (1803,) vol. VII. p. 245. — On the Generic Characters of Mosses, and particularly of the Genus Maimm, p. 254.—Biographical Memoirs of several Norwich Botanists, (1804,) p. 295.—Account of the Bromus Triflorus of Linnæus, p. 276.—Three New Species of Boxonia, p. 282.—A Botanical Sketch of the Genus Conclium, (1806,) vol. IX. p. 117. —Inquiry into the Genus of the Tree called by Pona, Abelicæa Cretica, p. 126.—An Inquiry into the real Daucus Gingidium of Linnæus, p. 131. — Inquiry into the Structure of Seeds, (1807, p. 204.—Respecting several British Species of Hieracium, (1808,) p. 225.—Specific Characters of the Decandrous Papilionaceous Plants of New Holland, p. 244.—Of the Hookeria, a New Genus of Mosses, with Descriptions of ten Species, p. 272.—Characters of Platylobium, Bossiæa, and of a new Genus named Pirretia, p. 301.—Of a new Liliaceous Genus called Brodiæa, vol. X. p. 1.—Remarks on the Sedium Ochroleucum, p. 6.—On the Synonyms and Natural Country of Hypericum calycinum, (1809,) p. 266.—Of a new Genus of New Holland Plants named Brunonia, (1810,) p. 365.—Description of Duchesnea fragiformis, p. 371.—On the Iris Susiana of Linnæus: and on the Natural Order of Aquilaria, (1812,) vol. IX. p. 227. — On the Genus Teesdalia, (1814,) p. 283.—Remarks on the Bryum Marginatum and Bryum lineare of Dickson, p. 290. — Some information respecting the Lignum Rhodium of Pococke's Travels, (1815,) vol. XII. p. 1.—A Botanical History of the Genus Tofieldia, (1817) p. 255.—Characters of two Species of Tordycinum, p. 345.—An Account of Rhizomorpha Medullaris, a New British Fungus, p. 372.—Remarks on the Hypnum recognitum, and on several new species of Roscoea, (1820,) vol. XIII. p. 459.

Extracts from a letter of Professor Schultes, of Landshut in-Bohemia, to the celebrated Naturalist Count Sternberg; de scribing a visit to Sir J. E. Smith in 1824 *.

" On the 27th of August, about noon, we proceeded in the mail coach from Ipswich to Norwich, where, by a fortunate cir-

---

* First published in the Botanische Zeitung for 1825.

cumstance, we accomplished the object of our journey thither.
Sir James E. Smith, to whom we made this pilgrimage, had just
returned home from the country, and was on the point of again
visiting his friends when we called on him at his beautiful house.
Our joy was great at finding this most respectable man so far
recovered from the severe illness which had threatened his life,
as to be again enabled to devote his leisure hours to the *amabilis
scientia.* He was then employed in revising some printed sheets
of the third edition of his Introduction to the Study of Botany.
Sir J. E. Smith displayed to us the treasures of his collection,
(in reality the only one of its kind,) with a courtesy and kindness which are peculiar to great and well-educated men ; and
which in this truly noble person are heightened by such charms
of gentleness and affability, as cannot fail to attract to him most
forcibly even such individuals as have but once enjoyed the privilege of his society. The books of Linnæus, with their margins full of notes in the handwriting of the immortal Swede ;
many valuable MSS. of his, not yet published ; the Linnæan
Herbarium, in the same order and even occupying the very cases
which had contained it at Upsal, (little as the old-fashioned form
of these cabinets corresponds with the elegant arrangement of
Smith's museum) ; the collection of insects, shells, and minerals,
which had belonged to this second creator of Nature ;—all these
are arranged and preserved by Sir James with a scrupulous care
which almost borders on a kind of religious veneration. The
relics of Mohammed are not enshrined with more devotion in
the Kaaba at Mecca, than are the collections of Linnæus in the
house of Sir J. E. Smith at Norwich.

" Besides the Linnæan herbarium, Sir J. E. Smith has a large
collection of plants of his own formation, which is especially
rich in the productions of New Holland and Nepaul. The
worthy Professor Wallich at Calcutta, whose health has lately
suffered from an Indian climate, has greatly contributed towards
the latter. The Linnæan specimens, as well as Sir James's private herbarium, are very well preserved ; and after the old plan,
which is now seldom followed on the continent, they are fastened
down on a folio sheet of paper, and washed over with a solution
of corrosive sublimate. Sir James has also under his care the
plants of Sibthorpe, to aid him in the publication of his *Flora
Græca,* which is now nearly completed.

" Among the papers of Linnæus, their present possessor
found a number of copies of two pamphlets by this illustrious
man, which do not appear to have been ever published. One of
them bears the title of ' C. Linnæi Observationes in Regnum
Lapidum,' and contains a view of the mineral kingdom, so far
as it was known at the time of its being printed ; the other is
intituled, ' Orbis eruditi Judicium de Caroli Linnæi, M. D.
Scriptis.' Both fill a complete sheet of letter-press. Sir James
was so kind as to give a copy of each to my son and myself,

with his own signature affixed. The latter of these pamphlets, *sine loco et anno*, like the first, appears to be a defence of this illustrious man extorted from him by some of his envious and prejudiced contemporaries. But what redounds as much to the honour as it must have done to the peace of the cautious and amiable Linnæus, is, that after having composed this paper, which consists entirely of the testimony which was borne to his character by the principal naturalists of his time,—such as Boerhaave, Burmann, Sloane, Dillenius, Jussieu, Haller, Gesner, Gleditsch, Breynius, &c. &c. — he afterwards entirely suppressed it ; and thereby deprived his opponents of those fresh subjects of disputation, which are sure to arise on such occasions, and which only furnish ground for sincere pity for the contending parties. It would appear as if the motto which Linnæus had chosen for this paper,

' Famam extollere factis
Hoc virtutis opus,'

had animated him with this feeling even while composing it.

" The few hours which Sir James Smith's kindness induced him to devote to me, though he was ready prepared to set off on a journey to join his Smithia, (a lady of rare talents,) passed away like a moment of time; just as the sweetest periods of life seem to fleet upon the swiftest wings. I have rarely beheld a more noble countenance ; one indicative of such candour, simplicity, and kindness, united with so much clearness of intellect, as that of Sir J. E. Smith ; and the expression of his features will never be obliterated from my memory."

---

1. Sir J. E. Smith to Mr. Nichols.

" Sir, *Norwich, Jan. 22, 1819.*

" Having been reading, with infinite pleasure and information, your first volume of " Illustrations of the Literary History of the Eighteenth Century," as well as the various publications of your venerable friend Mr. Hutton, I feel so little a stranger to your character, though entirely so to your person, that I am encouraged to take the liberty of addressing you upon a subject I have long had in my mind.

" When I became the proprietor, by a fortunate purchase, of the Library and Museum of the great Linnæus in 1784, I acquired also his original correspondence — amounting perhaps to 500 letters. I have often wished to communicate what was proper of this store of information and amusement to the public, but could never hit on an eligible way of doing this. I therefore frankly confess that my motive for troubling you with this letter is to ask your advice and assistance in a matter which I trust you cannot but approve.

" The letters of his English correspondents (mostly in English) would at least come under the plan of your work. Those of the celebrated Ellis, whose life I have written in Dr. Rees's Cyclopædia, and those of Peter Collinson, whose life in that work is also of my writing, are peculiarly interesting. I have also Ellis's own correspondence entire, and copies of the letters he wrote, all given me by his daughter — the late Mrs. Watt, highly curious.

"Can you suggest any means of publishing a selection of these? I would supply needful explanations and notes.

"What could be done with Latin letters? I would translate them if you thought it best. Was Gronovius's letter, in your vol. I. p. 815, written in Latin or English? It is from 'the great author' himself, the friend of Linnæus, not from 'a descendant.' I have numerous Latin letters of his, as well as many from Boerhaave, Hallen, Dillenius, Garden (see Rees's Cyclopædia, G.).

" My name probably is not unknown to you. I visit London for a few weeks every spring; and shall be happy to confer personally with you some time in April or May next. Meanwhile allow me to subscribe myself, Sir,

" Your very faithful servant,   J. E. SMITH."

---

2. To Mr. J. B. NICHOLS.

" DEAR SIR,   *Norwich, Jan.* 22, 1828.

" Your accompt of the ' Linnæan Correspondence' is deplorable*. I relied originally on your promoting the sale of this work as a sequel to what you had previously published, especially to the letters of Sherard. I know the work is much esteemed by scientific people. The very good review of it in the Gentleman s Magazine I should have thought must have insured the sale of any book. There is much besides Natural History that is curious, especially about the beginning of discontents in America; and I hear from that country that the families of Colden, Garden, and others are much interested in reading some of these letters. I believe I could get from thence some corresponding letters, if our undertaking had prospered.

" I could do nothing with the work myself, being no bookseller, nor in mercantile connexion with any. It were absurd for me to dictate to you in a matter of which you know so much more than I can. I have deeply lamented your worthy father. His name will live! Believe me, dear Sir,

" Your faithful and obedient servant,   J. E. SMITH."

* See p. 839.

BIOGRAPHICAL NOTICES

DAWSON FAMILY.

If, according to a remark of an eminent moralist, "a life has rarely passed, of which a judicious and faithful narrative would not be useful," the following Notices respecting the Family of Dawson, which will serve to concentrate, extend, and corroborate the accounts that have already appeared in the " Literary Anecdotes of the Eighteenth Century *," the " Monthly Repository of Theology and General Literature †," and Wilson's History and Antiquities of Dissenting Churches ‡," may, with confidence, be presented to the public, as neither useless nor uninteresting.

The first of this family, of whom there is any notice on record, is the Rev. JOSEPH DAWSON, who was ejected in 1662 from Thornton Chapel in Yorkshire. After his ejectment he resided in the vicinity of Halifax, and preached near Burstall. In the year 1688 he was chosen Minister of the Chapel at Morley, about four miles distant from Leeds; a chapel which has this peculiarity belonging to it, viz. that it was for many years the parochial church; but in the year 1650 the Earl of Sussex, then Lord of the Manor and Impropriator, granted a lease for five hundred years to a number of feoffees of the chapel, chapel-yard, parsonage-house, and two small closes, for the use of a preaching minister, on payment for the same of twenty shillings *per annum*.

---

* Vol. VIII. pp. 380, 381 ; vol. IX. p. 694.

† Vol. V. pp. 324, 474. This account of the Dawsons was communicated by an accurate and laborious writer, the Rev. William Turner, of Newcastle-upon-Tyne, with memoirs of other gentlemen who had been pupils of Dr. Rotheram, of Kendall.   ‡ Vol. IV. p. 315—317.

Mr. Dawson died in June 1709, and in the 73d
year of his age.   He was a very pious and learned
man ; of a venerable aspect and a good report, being
greatly esteemed for his prudence and integrity, his
humility and meekness.   He was a severe student
and an affectionate preacher ; unwearied and successful in his ministerial labours, and naturally solicitous for the welfare of the souls entrusted to his
care.   Even in his advanced age he travelled to a
considerable distance at all seasons of the year to
preach to a poor people, whom he took as much
care to serve as if they had paid him the largest
salary.   He suffered considerably from the narrow-
ness of his circumstances, having a numerous family;
yet he never repented of his non-conformity, but
was ever distinguished for his patience and submission, his faith and self-denial.

Mr. Dawson brought up four sons to the ministry, viz. Abraham, Joseph, Samuel, and Eli ; and
three of them survived him*.   The youngest of
these,

The Rev. ELI DAWSON, was minister at Halifax,
or at Little Horton near Bradford ; but I suspect
that he had the charge, in whole or in part, of both
these Societies of Dissenters.   He had seven sons ;
and the order of their births stands thus, according
to the Baptismal Register of their uncle, Joseph
Dawson, who was the Minister of Rochdale, viz.
Samuel, born in 1713 ; Abraham in 1714; Joseph
in 1719 ; Eli in 1723 ; Thomas in 1727 ; Benjamin in 1729 ; and Obadiah in 1731.

The six eldest of these sons were educated for the
ministry, at a very great expense to the funds possessed for that purpose by the Dissenters ; and all
of them deserted the profession: and what is more
remarkable, four of them conformed.   I have heard,
says Mr. J. Hunter, that Dr. Leigh, the Vicar of Ha-

* Palmer's Non-Conformists' Memorial, vol. III. p. 452.

lifax, was the principal instrument in reclaiming the conformists of this family to the Established Church. He was once asked by a Dissenter, "Why he did it; and if it was to make them better men?" To which he immediately and handsomely replied, "No, Sir, it was to make us better."

I shall now notice each of these sons according to their respective priority.

I. SAMUEL was born in 1713; and, after his conformity to the Established Church, kept a school, and is complimented by one of his pupils, the late Mr. Scholefield, of Birmingham, in the dedication of a Sermon preached at Cockermouth in 1769, as "one of the Clergy of the Establishment, from whose exertions a reformation in the Church might be expected." He expired in an apoplectic fit, whilst sitting at the table of his brother Thomas, during a visit to him at Hackney. Whether he had any preferment I know not; but he seems to be the person mentioned in the Obituary of the Gentleman's Magazine, vol. LI. p. 444, as follows: "Sept. 26, 1781. Rev. Mr. Dawson, late Rector of Ightham in Kent," to which, according to the Historian Hasted, he was presented by William James, Esq. in 1763.

II. ABRAHAM was born in 1714; and, after his conformity to the Established Church, was presented in 1755, by Miles Barne, Esq. to the Rectory of Ringsfield, with Redisham annexed; in 1786, by the same patron, to that of Satterley, both in the County of Suffolk; and in 17... was licensed, on the nomination of the Dean and Chapter of Norwich, to the Perpetual Curacy of Aldeby in Norfolk. He deceased on the 3d of October 1789, and was interred in the Church-yard of Ringsfield, but without any memorial, as he had expressly ordered, to designate the place of his interment.

Mr. Dawson was one of the Secretaries to the

Meetings of the Petitioning Clergy at the Feathers
Tavern in London *.

He published, at three different periods, a new
and valuable translation from the original Hebrew,
by way of specimen, of the first eleven chapters of
the Book of Genesis, with notes critical and explanatory, in which he ably attacks the doctrines of
the Trinity and of original sin. The first part was
intituled, " A New English Translation from the
Original Hebrew of the three first Chapters of Genesis ; with Marginal Illustrations, and Notes Critical and Explanatory. London, 1763." 4to.

" I have endeavoured," says Mr. Dawson, in his Preface, " to
translate faithfully and exactly my author, whoever he was; and
whether you suppose him to have written the following account
of the formation of things, and of the state of our first parents,
under the immediate direction and inspiration of God, or not.
The discussing these, and the like theological questions, was no
part of my design, much less was the presuming to decide them.
What I have attempted is merely to give a new English version,
as accurate a one as I could, of the three first Chapters of Genesis; and in the notes to account for, and justify, that version."

A view of the work itself can alone afford a just
and complete idea of the manner in which this de-

* In 1772 a Society was formed at the Feathers' Tavern in
London by numbers of the Clergy of the Established Church, to
frame a Petition to Parliament for the removal of all subscrip-
tions to Human Formularies of Religious Faith. The Petition
was agreed on, and signed by the following Clergy of the County
of Suffolk, viz. John Boldero, A. B. Rector of Ampton; John
Carter, A. M. Rector of Hengrave; Abraham Dawson, A. M.
Rector of Ringsfield ; Benjamin Dawson, LL.D. Rector of
Burgh; William Fonnereau, LL. B. of Christ Church, Ipswich ;
John Gent, A. B. Vicar of Stoke juxta Neyland; Christopher
Holland, LL. B. Rector of Cavenham; William Holmes, A. B.
Curate of Holton; John Jebb, A. M. Rector of Homersfield ; Jo-
seph Lathbury, jun. A. M. Rector of Livermere; James Lam-
bert, A. M. Fellow of Trinity-college, Cambridge; Michael Mar-
low, A. M. Rector of Lackford; Thomas Pudden, M. A. Bungay;
Humphrey Primatt, A. M. Minister of Higham St. Peter; A.
Luther Richardson, LL. B. Rector of Felsham; George Rogers,
A. M. Rector of Horningsheath, who, in a green old age, and
in the full enjoyment of his intellectual faculties, is now (1830)
the only one surviving.

sign is executed. The author shows himself to be
a masterly interpreter of the Hebrew tongue, and a
very just critic; nor will his fidelity, with respect
to altering the text, his care in comparing it with
the ancient versions, and his ingenious caution not
to mislead his readers, be found at all inferior to the
following representation, given in his own words:

"I have carefully," says he, "compared the present Hebrew
with the Samaritan text, and with the ancient versions, and I
have noted the variations; not indeed all, but such as I judged
to be the most material, and to afford a better reading than, or
at least equally good with the present Hebrew; nor have I once
ventured to suggest, much less have I made, any alteration in the
text, without giving fair notice of it, and accounting for it; nay,
so scrupulous have I been in this respect, that I have not, to the
best of my knowledge, inserted in the translation a single word,
how necessary however, to complete the sense, to which there is
not a corresponding word in the original, without remarking it
in the notes; and wherever any words are inserted from the
Samaritan, Septuagint, &c. as containing a reading different
from, and, in my judgment, preferable to, the present one, such
words are distinguished by being put in small capitals. I have
also generally translated the same Hebrew by the same English
word; but as this is impossible always to be done, when I have
found myself obliged to depart from what is said to be the usual
and primary signification of the Hebrew word, I have almost
every where observed it in the notes.—Some, perhaps, may object that I have been too minute and particular in these instances.
It may be so; but I had much rather be blamed on this head
than for rashness, and taking too great liberties with ancient
and venerable writings, with sacred and inspired ones, or at least
deemed to be so."

In 1772 he published the second part, under the
following title, viz. "A Fourth and Fifth Chapter
of Genesis, translated from the Original Hebrew;
with Marginal Illustrations and Notes, Critical and
Explanatory. Lond." 4to. The strict attention and
care which had been bestowed upon the former publication, appear likewise to have been observed in
regard to this performance; and the writer still finds,
as he had done before, several occasions to differ
from our common English version. It should be
observed that, though the title of this pamphlet
mentions only a fourth and fifth chapter of Genesis,

the translation extends to what, in the common
English Bible, is the eighth verse of the sixth
chapter. It contains several interesting observations
on the longevity of the antediluvians, with the size
and strength of their bodies, on chronology, the
state of the earth, and various other subjects, which
cannot fail of affording entertainment and satisfaction to those who love to inquire critically into
these parts of Scripture. Mr. Dawson uses no
ceremony with those commentators whom he has
occasion to mention; he pays them no compliments,
and sometimes, perhaps, is rather cavalier. Le
Clerc, Patrick, Kidder, Shuckford, Sherlock, Robertson, &c. are in some instances pretty freely censured; but he persuades himself, that he shall only
be found to have used an honest freedom in examining the criticisms and arguments offered on particular subjects.

The third part was published in 1786, under the
following title, viz. " The Sixth and Eleven following Chapters of Genesis, translated from the Original Hebrew; with Marginal Illustrations and
Notes." 4to.

The author proceeds on the plan which he had
before laid down; and the reader must be inclined to
credit him when he tells him that, " He can truly
say, that he has given all the attention to his subject,
and taken all the pains in his power."

Several of the notes in this work are merely hints,
such as a student might be supposed to enter into
his memorandum-book; they answer the end in the
present form, but a little enlargement might have
rendered them, to the generality of readers, more
easy and acceptable. Others are long, and some
very considerably so, particularly those concerning Noah and his sons.

Mr. Dawson is inclined to discard, in some instances, explications that have been long established;
and dismisses the many typical significations and

mysteries to be met with in Augustine, Ambrose, and other writers, ancient and modern, which are, he says, to be regarded merely as the issue of a wild and luxuriant imagination, too whimsical and extravagant to stand in need of confutation, or to merit the slightest attention. He enters into no geographical disquisitions, or attempts to assign habitations and settlements to the first inhabitants and prophets of the earth after the flood. In the Preface he does not appear to be any great advocate for a new English version of the Scriptures; but adds, " There is another work, which would be a much less arduous one, and in which there would be much less danger of committing any material faults, and which would be, in my opinion, of much greater, because of more general utility; and that is, a revisal of our Book of Articles and Liturgy." This he strenuously recommends in the words of Dr. Durell and his own.

Mr. Orme, in his " Bibliotheca Biblica," thus notices these translations:

" Dr. Geddes compliments the author of the above works with the quaint title of ' honest Abraham Dawson.' He was certainly tinctured a little with the Doctor's liberality, or rather scepticism, on some points. He denies the prophetical nature of Noah's prophecy, and the reference to the Messiah in the blessing of Abraham ; and seems to think, that the Mosaic account of various early occurrences is little better than a piece of ancient mythology. In some passages he improves upon the common translation ; but, on the whole, his works add nothing of great importance to our biblical apparatus."

III. Joseph was born in 1719, and was one of the Divinity Students in Dr. Rotheram's academy at Kendal; and, on quitting it, settled at Hull. He conformed to the Established Church ; and soon after was presented to the Vicarage of   near that town.

IV. Eli was born in 1723. He likewise conformed to the Established Church, and was for some time Chaplain to his Majesty's ship the Stirling

Castle. He preached the first Protestant Sermon
in Quebec; and afterwards obtained a living in the
West Indies, where he died. He was the author of
the following Discourse, *viz.* " Sermon at Quebec,
in the Chapel belonging to the Convent of the Ur-
sulines, Sept. 27, 1759; occasioned by the success
of our arms in the reduction of that capital. Preached
at the request of Brigadier-General Monckton, and
by order of Vice-Admiral Saunders, Commander-
in-Chief. By the Rev. Eli Dawson, Chaplain of
his Mjesty's Ship Stirling Castle; on board of
which the Vice-Admiral hoisted his Flag during the
Siege. 1760." 4to. A Sermon preached by an
English Protestant in a Popish pulpit, by British
authority and in the capital of the noblest province
of France, was a circumstance that, at the time,
attracted considerable notice.

V. THOMAS was born in 1727. He was a Student at Dr. Rotheram's academy at Kendal; and
was either a fixed or an occasional Minister of the
Gravel-pit Meeting in Hackney, some time between
the years 1750 and 1757. Afterwards he retired
from the ministry, and became M.D.; and practised with success for many years at Hackney. He
was one of the Physicians to the London Hospital
before, in, and after the year 1768. He continued
among the Dissenters till his death; and very
honourably repaid to the funds the money which
had been expended on his education. After he
became M.D. he attended his neighbour, Miss Cor-
bett, of Hackney, who was indisposed, and found her
one day sitting solitary, piously and pensively
musing upon the Bible, when, by some strange
accident, his eyes were directed to the passage where
Nathan says to David, "Thou art the man." The
Doctor profited by the kind hint; and after a proper time allowed for drawing up articles of capitula-
tion, the lady, on the 29th of May 1758, surrendered herself up to all his prescriptions, and the

Doctor very speedily performed a perfect cure. He
died April the 29th, 1782, having never recovered
the shock which he received by his brother Samuel's
sudden death *. The Doctor was the author of
the following professional publications, *viz.* " Cases
in the Acute Rheumatism and the Gout; with Cursory Remarks and the Method of Treatment, 1774,"
8vo; second edition 1776. This pamphlet contains
an account of the effectual and speedy relief which
has been given in several cases of the acute rheumatism and gout by the exhibition of large doses,
to the amount of half an ounce each, of the vola-
tile tincture of guaiacum.

Several of these cases are minutely related, each
accompanied with a particular commentary, and
with judicious remarks relating both to the general
treatment of these disorders, and the proper seasons
of exhibiting the medicine here recommended.

" An Account of a Safe and an Efficacious Medicine in Sore Eyes and Eye-lids. Lond. 1782." 8vo.
The purpose of this pamphlet is to recommend an
external application in sore and inflamed eyes,
which is an ointment composed of a solution of
mercury in aqua fortis, and a due proportion of
fresh butter, with some oil and camphor. In the
use of it we are directed, firstly, to abate the inflam-
ation by bleeding, &c. and then to apply a little of
the ointment warmed, with a camel's hair pencil, or
the tip of the finger, on the edges of the eye-lids
every night.

In the "Literary Anecdotes," vol. III. p. 750—1,
are inserted some additions to Jones's Account of
Archbishop Secker by the Doctor.

* Dr. Dawson was on terms of the strictest friendship with
the Rev. John Jones, the learned author of " Free and Candid
Disquisitions ;" many, if not all of whose MSS. passed into his
hands after Mr. Jones's death, and were by him ultimately deposited in the Dissenters' Library in Redcross-street.

He left a son, Mr. S. T. Dawson, who is now
resident at Botesdale in Suffolk.

VI. BENJAMIN was born in 1729, and pursued
his studies for the ministry under Dr. Rotheram at
Kendal. From thence he removed to Glasgow,
where in 1750 he proceeded to the degree of M. A.
on which occasion he defended a Thesis "de Summo
Bono." His first settlement was at Congleton in
Cheshire, where, however, he continued only a short
time. About the year 1754 he removed from
thence to St. Thomas's in Southwark. In 1758 he
proceeded to the degree of LL. D. In 1759 he
quitted the Dissenters and conformed to the Established Church; and, in the following year, was
presented by Miles Barne, Esq. in whose family he
was engaged as tutor, to the Rectory of Burgh in
Suffolk. In 1759 he published an excellent Sermon
under the following title: "Some Assistance offered
to Parents with regard to the Religious Education
of their Children, in a Discourse from Proverbs,
xxii. 6. London," 4to, to which is prefixed the following affectionate and appropriate dedication to
his mother:

" HONOURED MADAM,
" In dedicating this small performance to you, I break through
the general custom of authors, who seem to think none worthy
to patronize their works, but those that are distinguished by
birth, title, or fortune. Their reason for this they generally
acknowledge to be some particular favours received, for which
they consider a dedication as a kind of genteel receipt. Allow
me, Madam, the same privilege; and to present you with this,
as a testimony of filial gratitude for a liberal and pious education : a favour, for which as I shall ever be thankful, so I esteem
it greater than any which the most conspicuous for birth, title,
or fortune are able to bestow upon me.
" Permit me also, Madam, to beg your patronage of these few
pages; since, as narrow as your sphere may seem, if a work of
this nature gain your approbation, I am certain it will, on that
account, find an easy access into many worthy families. For they
are not a few to whom your affectionate and judicious endeavours
in training up a numerous family in the principles of religion

are well known, and to whom your exemplary piety, prudence, and virtue have rendered you long respectable. That a life so valuable may be continued for many years, that the wisdom and virtue of your children may do honour to your instructions, and that your grey hairs may at last descend with peace and comfort into the grave, is the most ardent prayer, and shall be the constant endeavour of, Madam,

" Your ever dutiful and affectionate son,   B. Dawson."

This discourse well merits the attentive perusal of every Christian parent. It is drawn up in a very judicious manner, and the language possesses a plainness and simplicity well suited to a subject so universally useful. A second edition of it was published in the following year.

Soon after this he published, " A Family Prayer," in the preface to which he offers a very free explanation of the phrase, "through Jesus Christ." In 1761 appeared his " Reformation of Manners shown to be the only ground of Confidence towards God ; a Sermon preached on occasion of the General Fast, February 13, 1761," 4to, a plain and sensible discourse ; and, "The Duty of Charity to the Poor, a Sermon preached at St. Paul's, Shadwell, July 26, 1761," 4to. In 1762 he published, "The Efficacy of Divine Aid, and the Vanity of confiding in Man; a Sermon from Psalm cviii. preached on Occasion of the late General Fast, March 12," 4to. In 1764 he preached the Lectures founded by Lady Moyer in defence of the Trinity, and afterwards published them under the title of " An Illustration of Several Texts of Scripture, particularly those in which the Logos occurs. The Substance of Eight Sermons preached in the Cathedral Church of St. Paul in the years 1764 and 1765. At the appointment of Mrs. Heathcote, and by permission of the Lord Bishop of London, for the Lecture founded by Lady Moyer. To which are added, Two Tracts relative to an Intermediate State. Lond. 1765," 8vo, in the preface to which he says, the Trinity is indeed defended " in a manner perfectly new." The book

862   ILLUSTRATIONS OF LITERATURE.

is, in truth, completely Unitarian; and is rather an
attack on the Arian hypothesis than a defence of
any scheme of the Trinity, upon which point the
author's views inclined him to Sabellianism.   In this
work, the texts usually alleged in favour of our
Lord's pre-existence are, perhaps, more satisfactorily
explained than in any other places.   In the appendix the Doctor ably defends Bishop Law on the
question of an Intermediate State.   In 1766, on
the publication of " The Confessional," he took an
active part in that highly-interesting controversy
with Rotheram, Rutherforth, and others, and by his
publications on this occasion obtained from Archdeacon Blackburne the character of " an incomparable writer."   During this controversy, between
seventy and eighty pamphlets were published by
the contending parties, eight of which were the
production of the Doctor's pen, *viz.* " Examination
of Dr. Rutherforth's Argument respecting the Right
of Protestant Churches to require the Clergy to subscribe to an Established Confession of Faith and
Doctrine, Lond. 1766," 8vo.   "An Examination
of Rotheram's Essay on Establishments in Religion;
with Remarks upon it, considered as a Defence of
the Church of England, and as an Answer to the
Confessional; Lond. 1767," 8vo.   " An Address
to the Writer of a Second Letter to the Author of
the Confessional; containing a Vindication of the
original Principles of the Reformers, as laid down in
the Confessional; and a Confutation of the Principles on which the Letter Writer has founded his
Argument for Subscription to Established Articles
of Religion, 1767," 8vo, an address containing some
very sensible observations on the principles of the
reformers.   " A Short and Safe Expedient for ter-
minating the present Debates about Subscription,
occasioned by a celebrated performance entitled the
Confessional. Lond. 1769," 8vo.   " An Answer to
Letters concerning Established Confessions of Faith;

in Vindication of the Confessional. Lond. 1769,"
8vo. "Free Thoughts on the subject of a further
Reformation of the Church of England, in Six
Numbers; to which are added the Remarks of the
Editor, 1771," 8vo. "Free and Candid Disquisitions on Religious Establishments, occasioned by
a Visitation Sermon. Lond. 1772," 8vo. "A Letter to the Clergy of the Archdeaconry of Winchester, being a Vindication of the Petition presented the
last Session of Parliament to the Legislature for the
removal of Subscription to human formularies of religious faith and doctrine, from the misrepresentations of Dr. Balguy, in a late Charge to the Clergy
of the Archdeaconry. In which also the Question,
Whether Subscription to the Thirty-nine Articles
of the Church of England be constitutionally required of the Clergy, is occasionally discussed. Lond.
1773," 8vo. This is a very sensible, spirited, and
manly answer to Dr. Balguy's celebrated Charge.
After a short and pertinent address to the Clergy of
the Archdeaconry of Winchester, Dr. Dawson proceeds to show, in a very satisfactory manner, that
every thing which Dr. Balguy has said in dispa-
ragement of the petition is either mere aspersion,
or proceeds from the grossest misconstruction of its
nature, or rests on such reasonings as must discredit
the understandings of those who can be imposed
upon by it. He confines his remarks to the first
fifteen pages of the Charge, the remainder of it
referring for the sentiments of what Dr. Balguy terms the Party, to a printed paper unautho-
rised by the Petitioners. In 1780 he published
"National Depravity the Cause and Mark of Divine Judgment upon a Land, from Luke, xiii. 3,
preached on occasion of the late General Fast, February 4, 1780. Lond." 4to. This discourse contains some good observations on the propensity, too
common with mankind, to conclude from particular
events that great sufferings are the immediate con-

sequences of divine judgments. The conclusion, when it relates to individuals, is generally the effect of ignorance, bigotry, and personal hatred. After guarding his hearers, according to the example of our Saviour, in the verses which precede the text, against rash and uncharitable judgment, the Doctor observes that, " though we have no right to pronounce when and on whom the judgments of God are brought from any calamities that befal others, yet that sin and wickedness tend to bring them upon a land and nation, and that the text shows us, in a very awful declaration, how afflictive visitations of Heaven should assist us and be improved by us." The concluding part of this discourse is more of a political than of a practical nature *. In 1781 he published "A Sermon from Psalm xxvii. 8, preached on occasion of the late General Fast, February 28, 1781. Ipswich," 4to, a plain and well-written discourse. In 1783 he published a Dialogue on the question of Liberty and Necessity, under the title of "The Necessitarian ; or the Question concerning Liberty and Necessity stated, in Nineteen Letters. Lond." 8vo. In these letters the Doctor has brought forward the leading and essential objects of this curious controversy with equal judgment and perspicuity, and arranged them with such accuracy and precision as to give the reader a very clear view of the several arguments by which the doctrines of liberty and necessity have been supported by their respective advocates. He has particularly exposed the fallacy of the common objections to necessity, drawn from a supposition of its being inconsistent with merit; and has fully established his proposition, that the will is always impelled by motives, and that it is the quality of an

* This Sermon was dedicated " To the Rev. Mr. Blackburne, Archdeacon of Cleveland, Yorkshire, the firm, strenuous, and consistent Assertor of Religious Freedom," and went into a second edition.

act that constitutes the ground of merit or demerit. The ingenious author has only discussed the subject on moral and metaphysical principles.

In 1789 he published "The Benefits of Civil Government, a Ground of Praise to God. A Sermon preached on occasion of the late General Thanksgiving, for the Restoration of His Majesty's Health, April 23, 1789. Ipswich," 4to.

In 1795 he published "The Efficacy of Divine Aid, and the Vanity of Confiding in Man, a Sermon preached on occasion of the late General Fast, March 25, 1795. Cambridge," an excellent and pious commentary on the text, Psalm cviii. v. 12, with very judicious applications to the appointment of the day and the emergency of the times. The topic is well illustrated ; and if the Doctor has deviated a little into party politics, the good sense and real piety, which pervades the whole of the discourse, may plead in his excuse. He paints, in a strong light, the evils attendant on that spirit, which delights to rest on the wickedness and impiety of a foreign enemy ; and thinks that mankind may be better employed in the examination of things at home.

In 1806 he published a specimen of an English Dictionary upon a new plan, under the title of " Prolepsis Philologiæ Anglicanæ; or Plan of a Philological and Synonymical Dictionary of the English Language. Ipswich," 4to. This was dedicated by permission to the Right Hon. Alexander Lord Loughborough, Lord High Chancellor of Great Britain, and one of his Majesty's most Honourable Privy Council. In the same year he commenced the publication of it in parts, under the following title, " Philologia Anglicana ; or a Philological and Synonymical Dictionary of the English Language, in which the Words are deduced from their Originals, their sense defined, and the same illustrated and supported by proper Examples and Notes, Critical and Explanatory. Ipswich," 4to, a work of considerable promise, and which it is greatly to be lamented that the author did not live to complete. This publication was the amusement of the latter years of his life, and extends only to a part of the letter A. *viz.* Adornment. It contains, however, five hundred pages ; and would, if it ever had been completed, have extended to an immeasurable length. Whether the Doctor left at his decease any materials for the further progress of this work, the writer of these " Notices" is not informed. In chapter eight of the " Prolepsis" is given the following " Summary View of the Object of the Work and Manner of its Execution: "

" The statement made in Chapter VI. of what is requisite to constitute a full and accurate explanation of a word is to be understood of its literal sense. For that only we purpose to investigate and set forth in the explication. The Philologist is not concerned with the figurative senses in which a word may be used, any further than as attention to, and examination of the propriety or impropriety in the use of it may serve to elucidate its literal or proper signification. The technical use of a word is also no further than this, in the plan of our undertaking ; and we scarce need to advertise the reader, that he is not to ex-pect from us an account of all the words in our language. Pro-per names of persons, places, officers, terms appropriated to par-ticular arts, sciences, professions, orders, ranks in society; in short, whatever words regard not human intercourse at large, or serve not the purpose of general communication, will be either wholly omitted, or so far only considered as they are con-nected with the general principles on which we purpose to pro-ceed; and many of those words, which might fall properly within our plan, we shall find ourselves under the necessity of omitting, not less for want of time and leisure from occupa-tions more immediately incumbent upon us thoroughly to inves-tigate, than, alas! for want of ability to explain with that pre-cision and certainty which we could wish, and have attempted in what has been done.

" To our account of a word, and the authorities adduced in support of it, we have not unfrequently (indeed we have almost constantly) subjoined notes and remarks upon both. This seemed necessary, as well more fully to convey our meaning (for which the conciseness used in a formal definition, though aided by proper examples, is not always sufficient) as in justification of the sense given, and to contrast it with what we apprehend to be an erroneous or less accurate account.

" In this part of our work we have gone into a minuteness and prolixity which may appear unnecessary, and to readers of a certain complexion we fear will be disgusting. For this we shall not stay to apologise further than to say that, on a subject of this nature we know not how to dispense with it without erring on the other hand, and incurring danger of censure for deficiency of discussion, and not doing our utmost to satisfy the more critical inquirer, whose approbation we chiefly covet, and cannot hope to merit but by industry of research and elaborate investigation."

With this publication the Doctor closed his literary labours; when, after a long life spent in a faithful discharge of his ministerial duties, he finished his earthly career in the Glebe-house at Burgh near Ipswich, on the 15th of June 1814, in the 85th year of his age. His remains were interred in the chancel of that church ; and on a flat-stone is the following inscription to his memory :

In memory of
MARY DAWSON,
wife of the Revᵈ Benjamin Dawson, LL.D.
She died the 22d of June
1805, aged 80.
Also of the
Revᵈ BENJAMIN DAWSON, LL. D.
54 years Rector of this Parish,
who died the 15th of June
1814, aged 85.

Dr. Dawson's manners were peculiarly mild and unassuming; and he possessed, in an eminent degree, those virtues which form the chiefest ornaments of private life. His benevolence was of the largest and most liberal cast ; and though so deeply engaged in the various controversies, which at different periods of his life strongly agitated the public mind, his writings never breathe the spirit of acrimony, or are disgraced by unjust censure and personal remark. No one was more industrious and indefatigable in the investigation of scriptural truths; more zealous in exposing error and superstition ; or

more earnest in enforcing the spirit and simplicity
of the Gospel. As a divine, he was eminent for an
extensive acquaintance with every branch of theology; as a critic, for the correctness of his strictures
and the perspicuity of his remarks; and as a philologist, not less distinguished for the accuracy of his
judgment and the depth of his research. A zealous
advocate for religious and civil liberty, as well as a
decided enemy to every encroachment of human
authority in matters of belief, his sentiments were
liberal, candid, and enlarged; and although such
sentiments in the present day too frequently expose
those who entertain them to obloquy and censure,
yet, on every occasion, he fearlessly espoused the
cause of free and genuine toleration, and boldly
acted up to its principle with firmness and consistency. In 1772, when the petition for affording
relief from Subscriptions to Articles of Faith was
presented to Parliament, it received his steady and
decided support. Throughout life he was ever employed on some subject of theology or criticism,
which is fully evinced by the many interesting treatises which he published on these subjects, the style
of which is plain and perspicuous, and the reasoning
close and conclusive. But the chief work on which
he had been long engaged, and of which a very
small part only was published, was his " Philologia
Anglicana;" a work, which evinces a profound knowledge of the theory of language, and which, as far
as it extends, has advanced the bounds of philological science, and enriched, in no inconsiderable
degree, the stores of etymology.

The Doctor was highly respected and esteemed
by a select circle of friends in his immediate neighbourhood, among whom I may be allowed to parti-
cularize, the Rev. William Layton, Rector of St.
Matthew in Ipswich; Rev. George Rogers, Rector
of Sproughton; Rev. John Higgs, Rector of Grun-
disburgh; Rev. William Talbot, Rector of Elm-

sett; Rev. William Fonnereau, of Christ Church,
Ipswich ; Rev. Charles Haynes ; and the Rev. James
Coyte, Minister of St. Nicholas in Ipswich. Of
each of these individuals a brief notice is appended
in the concluding note *.

VII. OBADIAH, the youngest son, was born in
1731, and was for many years an eminent merchant
at Leeds, in which town he died about the year 1790.
He left two daughters, who resided with their uncle,
Dr. Benjamin Dawson, for some years previous to
his decease.

* The Rev. WILLIAM LAYTON is a native of Sproughton in Suffolk, and received the rudiments of his education, first, at Richmond in Yorkshire, and afterwards at St. Paul's-school, London,
then under the judicious superintendence of that very able and
accomplished scholar, George Thicknesse, Esq. From thence
he was removed to Trinity-college, Cambridge, where he proceeded to the degree of A. B. in 1773, and to that of A. M. in
1776. In 1774 he was licensed, on the nomination of George
William the second Earl of Bristol, to the Perpetual Curacy of
Playford in Suffolk ; and in the following year was presented by
the Crown to the Rectory of Helmley in the same county, and
to that of St. Matthew in Ipswich.

The pages of these " Illustrations," as well as those of the
" Literary Anecdotes," are enriched with many of this gentleman's valuable and judicious remarks; and his name is honourably recorded by the late Mr. Nichols in his advertisement to the
Eighth Volume of the " Anecdotes;" and in his preface to the
Fourth of this Work, as " one of those friends and excellent
correspondents to whom he returns his sincere acknowledgments
for continued assistance, and to whom his warmest thanks are
particularly offered."

In the advertisement to the First Volume of this Work, the
Editor acknowledges his " having been favoured by his worthy
and intelligent friend, the Rev. William Layton, with the Memoirs of Mr. Midgley and Mr. Archdeacon Pearson, and the
portrait of Mr. Midgley," which appeared in that volume.

> " Fortunate Senex ! ergo tua vita recedit,
> Et tibi longa satis, quia non sine laude peracta.
> Ergo nec lethi, qui cætera territat, horror
> Mente quatit solidâ. Pauli jam cerno triumphum
> Morte superdomitâ et vacuum terroribus orcum."

The REV. GEORGE ROGERS, a venerable and liberal-minded divine, was a native of St. Edmund's Bury in Suffolk, and received the rudiments of his education at the Free Grammar School in that town, then under the superintendence of that accomplished scholar the Rev. Robert Garnham, A. M. From thence he was removed to Trinity-college, Cambridge, of which Society, on proceeding to the degree of A. B. in 1764, he was elected a Fellow. In 1767 he proceeded to that of A. M. In 1766 he was presented by Sir Charles Davers, Bart. to the Rectory of Welnetham Parva, which he resigned, on the presentation by the same patron, to that of Horningsheath in 1767. In 1784 he was presented by Frederick the fourth Earl of Bristol and Bishop of Derry, to the Rectory of Sproughton, when he relinquished that of Horningsheath.

Mr. Rogers is known to the literary world by the following publications, *viz.* "The Place, Object, and Nature of Christian Worship considered, in a Sermon, preached at the Archdeacon's Visitation, April 23, 1790, in the Parish Church of St. Mary at Tower, Ipswich." 8vo.; and "Five Sermons on the following subjects, *viz.* The true Nature of the Christian Church, and the Impossibility of its being in danger. The Scripture idea of Heresy. Mysteries made plain. The Scriptural Doctrine of Atonement. The Place, Object, and Manner of Christian Worship. Lond. 1813." 12mo. In 180.. he edited the Sermons of his intimate friend the Rev. Edward Evanson, in two volumes octavo, to which he prefixed a short but well-written memoir of the author.

The Rev. JOHN HIGGS was a native of London, and received the early part of his education at the College School of St. Peter's, Westminster. From thence he was elected to Trinity-college, Cambridge, where he proceeded to the degree of A. B. in 1750; to that of A. M. in 1754; and to that of S. T. B. in 1768. In 1752 he was elected a Fellow of his Society, as the Senior Westminster of his year, together with Dr. Spencer Madan, successively Bishop of Bristol and Peterborough, the celebrated Mr. Richard Cumberland, and Mr. John Ord, afterwards one of the Masters in Chancery. In 1780 he was presented by the College to the Rectory of Grundesburgh in Suffolk; a preferment at that period tenable with his Fellowship, and on which he constantly resided till his decease, which took place on the 6th of October 1816, in the 89th year of his age.

Mr. Higgs was for many years a Senior, and most probably for some time previous to his death the oldest Member, of the College. Throughout life he was on terms of the strictest intimacy with many of his celebrated contemporaries at Trinity, *viz.* Dr. John Hinchliffe and Dr. Spencer Madan, successively Bishops of Peterborough; and Dr. Richard Watson, Bishop of Landaff. He possessed an extensive and valuable collection of engravings by the old masters, principally proofs, which he had selected with much taste and judgment; these were dispersed by public auction on the 24th of March 1817, and produced very large prices.

His remains were interred in the chancel of the Church of Grundesburgh, where, on a mural tablet against the south wall, is the following inscription to his memory:

M. S.
JOHANNIS HIGGS, S. T. B.
hujusce ecclesiæ per Annos xxxvi Rectoris,
qui
propter morum facilitatem
et animi candorem omnibus acceptissimus
legum Angliæ municipalium interpres et assertor
fidelis, incorruptus, strenuus,
et publicas et privatas vitæ partes egregiè sustinuit.
Natus in civitate Londinensi, in scholâ regiâ
Westmonasteriensi bonis literis haud mediocriter
imbutus, et inde Collegium S. S. Trinitatis
apud Cantabrigienses electus;
mox in ordinem Sociorum ejusdem cooptatus,
inter quos denique primum gradum
tenens, et annum agens LXXXIXm.
Animam Deo reddidit pridie non: Octobris,
Salutis Anno
MDCCCXVI.

The late Mr. Cumberland, who was contemporary with Mr. Higgs both at school and at college, and with whom he ever continued through life on terms of the strictest friendship, thus feelingly delineates the virtues and character of his friend, in his own "Memoirs written by himself:—"

"The Senior Westminster of my year, and joint candidate with me for a Fellowship at this time, was John Higgs, now Rector of Grundesburgh in Suffolk, and a Senior Fellow of Trinity-college; a man, who, when I last visited him, enjoyed all the vigour of mind and body in a green old age, the result of good humour and the reward of temperance. We have spun out mutually a long measure of uninterrupted friendship, he in peace throughout, and I at times in perplexity; and if I survive to complete these Memoirs, and he to read this page, I desire he will receive it as a testimony of my unaltered regard for him through life, and the bequest of my last good wishes at the close of it."

Whilst resident in town, as Private Secretary to the Earl Halifax, then first Lord of Trade and Plantations, Mr. Cumberland details the kind attentions of his friend in the following affectionate terms: "I read and work incessantly, and should have been in absolute solitude but for the kind visits of my friend Higgs, who, not forgetting our late intimacy at college and at school, nor disdaining my poor fare and dull society,

cheered and relieved my spirits with the liveliness and hilarity
natural to him ; these are favours I can never forget, for they
supported met at times when I felt all the gloominess of my situation, and yet wanted energy to extricate myself from it, and
renounce those expectations to which I had devoted so much
time in profitless dependence."

In the " Supplement" to his " Memoirs," Mr. Cumberland
again reverts to his old and intimate friend, " As I now (1807)
find myself once more under the hospitable roof of my old
friend Mr. Higgs, I am likely to wind up this Supplement of my
Memoirs in the very spot, where, fifteen years ago, I concluded
my Poem of Calvary. This companion of my youth, though
far advanced into the vale of years, is still enjoying the reward
of temperance, a sound mind in a healthful body. He performs
all the duties of a parish priest in an exemplary manner, executes
the laborious office of an acting Justice of the Peace with that of
a director of the poor-house, established at Nacton in this county
of Suffolk. When I fell ill at Ramsgate, and he was made
acquainted with my situation, he wrote a letter, that convinced
me his affection had suffered no abatement by the lapse of years
since I had seen him, and he took a journey of a hundred and
forty miles to visit me in my convalescence. He was of the
same year with me at Trinity, and we have not a Senior to us in
the College now living."

The Rev. WILLIAM TALBOT was a native of Bedfordshire, and
was born on the 15th of Jan. 1720. In 1738 he was entered a
Pensioner of Clare-hall, Cambridge, where he proceeded to the
degree of A. B. in 1742, and to that of A. M. in 1746. In 1744
he was elected a Fellow of his Society. In 1766 he was presented by the College to the Rectory of Elmset in Suffolk ; in
1768 to that of Teversham near Cambridge, by the Bishop of
Ely; and in 17.. was installed Chancellor of the Church of
Salisbury. He married Miss Mary Kirke, one of the executors
to Dr. John Newcome, Master of St. John's college, Cambridge,
Lady Margaret's Professor of Divinity, and Dean of Rochester,
with whom, after the decease of his wife, she resided, and to
whom he bequeathed a large portion of his fortune *.

Mr. Talbot deceased on the 25th of November 1811, having
survived his wife six years, and was interred in the Chancel of
the Church of Elmsett, where, on a flat-stone, is this inscription
to their memories:

In Memory of
Mary Talbot,
wife of the Rev. WILLIAM TALBOT,
Rector of Elmset,
she died 8th November 1805,
aged 78 years.

* See " Literary Anecdotes," vol. I. p. 564.

Also Sacred to the Memory of
the above Rev. WILLIAM TALBOT, M. A.
Chancellor of the Church of Salisbury,
and upwards of 45 years Rector of this parish.
He was born January 15, 1720,
and died November the 25th 1811,
aged 91 years.

Cole, in his MS. Collections, describes Mr. Talbot " as a very
little thin man ; " and says that he " was a candidate for the
Mastership of Clare-hall against Dr. Goddard ; was born in Bedfordshire, and bred among the Dissenters."

At the time of his death, Mr. Talbot was the oldest incumbent in the Dioceses of Norfolk and Ely ; and the oldest member
of the Society for Promoting Christian Knowledge.

A mural tablet has been since erected to his memory, with the
following curious inscription :

" Sacred to the Memory of
the Rev. WILLIAM TALBOT, M. A.
Chancellor of the Church of Salisbury,
and upwards of 45 years Rector of this Parish.
He was born January 15th, 1720,
and died November the 25th, 1811,
aged 91 years.

" *Extract from his last Will and Testament.*

" I desire that my executors will place a mural tablet against
the wall within the Church of Elmsett, where it may be most
easily seen, and the inscription upon it best read ; and that there
be inscribed thereon my name and age, and the day of my death ;
and my earnest and most affectionate exhortation to my beloved
parishioners to be unceasing in their prayers for the grace of
God, to enable them to prepare themselves, through the merits
of our blessed Redeemer, for a happy immortality, and particularly recommending to the young people to remember their
Creator in the days of their youth, a practice that will secure
their comfort here and their happiness hereafter ; and that it be
expressed upon the tablet, that I earnestly beg the parishioners
of Elmsett will read the inscription every time they go into the
Church, that so I may hope to be as useful to them when I am
dead as I have endeavoured to be in my life-time ; and that one
speaking to them as it were from the dead, they may repent."

" In pursuance of the above direction this tablet was erected by
Richard Lord Bishop of Bath and Wells, and George Brooks, Esq.
the executors ; by whom it is earnestly requested and confidently
hoped, that the future Rectors and Churchwardens of the parish
of Elmsett for the time being will endeavour to promote and
perpetuate the excellent design of this pious and exemplary pas-

874 ILLUSTRATIONS OF LITERATURE.

tor of his flock, by preserving the tablet free from injury, and
keeping the inscription thereon in a perfectly legible state.
1812."

The Rev. WILLIAM FONNEREAU was the son of the Rev. Claudius Fonnereau, LL. D. of Christ Church in Ipswich; and received his academical education at Trinity-hall, Cambridge,
where he proceeded to the degree of LL. B. in 1755. In 1773
he was presented by the Lord Chancellor Apsley to the Rectory
of Great Munden, Herts.

As a companion, Mr. Fonnereau's manners were peculiarly
mild and easy, bland and unaffected; and his was that infantine
gaiety of heart which the Poet happily styles " the sunshine of
the breast," and which long endeared his memory to the circle
of his intimate acquaintance. In his general intercourse with
others his address was free and open, affable and facetious; and
of so attractive a nature were his colloquial powers, that to the
gay and the grave, the young and the old, he was a most delightful and engaging companion. Throughout a long life his
conduct was manly and simple, and his sentiments liberal and
enlarged; and it may be truly said, that he presented a genuine
picture of the gentleman of the old English school. An innate
love of freedom and independence, and a thorough indignation
of corruption and venality, whether in rank or in power, were
his peculiar characteristics; and from the open avowal of these,
even in the worst and most dangerous times, he never shrunk,
but on all occasions dared to think and to act for himself, as became a free and independent man. From mean and narrow
bigotry he was utterly exempt; and for the exercise of private
judgment in matters of religion, and in the investigation of
truths that point to eternity, he was a most firm and decided
advocate. After a long life, which he enjoyed to the last, spent
in the service of God and of man, he resigned his soul into the
hands of its Creator with a hope full of immortality, and with
the bright prospect of being united to him in the glories of another and a better world, on the 28th of February 1817.

His remains were interred in the family vault, in the Church
of St. Margaret, Ipswich; and, on the north side of the chancel, a mural tablet, commemorative of his virtues, is erected to
his memory:

In his family vault
east of this monument, is deposited
the remains of
the Rev. WILLIAM FONNEREAU, of
Christ Church in this parish.
Enjoying a constant flow of cheerfulness
and good humour, with a body and mind
actively engaged in manly and
rational pursuits, and never allowing himself

to view the crosses and disappointments
of life through a discouraging medium,
he calmly passed through the last
awful and trying scene February 28th 1817,
in the 85th year of his age,
in a full confidence of the mercies
of God towards his frail and
degenerate creatures.

Psalm xxxvii. v. 38, " Keep innocency and take heed unto the thing that is right, for that shall bring a man peace at the last."

The Rev. CHARLES HAYNES was born at Elmsett in Suffolk, in 1739, and was the fourth son of the Rev. Hopton Haynes, A. M. the Rector of that parish, who was a son of Hopton Haynes, Esq.* Assay Master of the Mint, and principal Tally-writer of the Exchequer, a strenuous advocate for Socinianism, and the author of a tract relating to the prerogatives of his office, and of several publications on religious subjects ; and an elder brother of Dr. Samuel Haynes *, Canon of Windsor, the learned editor of " A Collection of State Papers," transcribed from the Cecil MSS. at Hatfield-house, 1740, folio.

Mr. Haynes received the rudiments of his education at the Grammar-school of Dedham in Essex, and from thence removed to Clare-hall, Cambridge, where he proceeded to the degree of LL. B. in 1765. In the year following he was presented by Thomas Pelham Holles, Duke of Newcastle, to the Vicarage of Damerham in Wilts, as an accommodation to the celebrated preacher, Dr. Ogden, and in exchange for the Rectory of Stansfield in Suffolk, which had been promised Mr. Haynes by the Lord' Chancellor, and which was then vacant by the decease of his father. This living he held at his death ; and it is a circumstance worthy of remark, that during the fifty-six years of his incumbency, the Crown presented four several times to the Rectory of Stansfield, while two Dukes of Newcastle passed away without presenting to Damerham.

As a member of the Established Church, Mr. Haynes was firmly attached to her doctrine and discipline; and for many years officiated as a Curate in his native county. A scrupulous obedience to the divine commands, and the keeping a conscience void of offence towards God and man, were the rules that regulated his life. His religion was without bigotry, and his piety without enthusiasm. As his sentiments were distinguished by candour, freedom, and liberality, he was a firm and decided advocate for the exercise of private judgment in matters of religion and on points of doubtful disputation †. Of a humane

* For brief memoirs of both these persons, see " Literary Anecdotes," vol. II. pp. 140, 141.
† In corroboration of these remarks on his character, I have extracted

and benevolent disposition, he performed without ostentation many generous and charitable actions (more particularly to the family in which he resided) that would have dignified a more ample fortune.

In his intercourse with others, his manners were mild and humble, friendly and unassuming ; yet his humility was without meanness and his friendship without dissimulation; these qualities, therefore, ensured him the respect and esteem of his acquaintance. Naturally of a shy and timid disposition, the tenor of his life was retired: he mingled but little in promiscuous company, excepting at particular periods, when he was the life and soul of the party in which he joined.

The powers of his memory were great indeed ; and whatever had pleased or interested him, either in the perusal of books or the remarks and observations of others, he made his own entirely, and could bring forth his stores, as occasion offered, with the greatest facility and effect. In history and geography, his favourite pursuits, his knowledge was extensive ; and his recollection of names, dates, and places, truly surprising. The writer of this brief memoir, who revered his character, and who has been often gratified in his society, heard him, when at the advanced age of seventy-six, repeat, without hesitation, the regular accession of our English Monarchs, with the precise year and month of their accession to the throne, as well as of the day and year of their decease; and what is still more surprising, this stretch of memory was followed by a similar recital of the Roman Emperors.

He possessed a strong vein of pleasantry, and a considerable share of humour ; and to a pun was by no means an enemy. In all parties, where the company accorded with his taste and incli-

from "The Monthly Repository of Theology," vol. II. p. 336, the following conversation, which passed between Mr. Haynes and the Rev. Samuel Say Toms, of Framlingham, as detailed by the latter gentleman : "Some years since," says Mr. Toms, "visiting at a friend's house near to Witnersham, Mr. Haynes's present residence, I met the old gentleman, and, entering into conversation, I mentioned that I had often heard my mother speak of a clergyman of his name at Elmsett, he replied, 'He was my father ;' and of Mr. Hopton Haynes, 'Yes, he was my grandfather ;' and said, his writings were very differently thought of now from what they were at their first publication, and some years after. They are now in high repute with many, as giving a just and rational interpretation of the Scripture doctrine concerning Jesus Christ. There were warm contenders on both sides of the question. It became every one to examine and think for himself, and speak and act from conviction; but some were of opinion, that religion was a plain simple thing, and that it was of more importance to insist on it practically than to enter upon the minutiæ of controversy. 'He hath shown thee, O man, what is good, and what,' &c. 'Thou shalt love the Lord thy God,' &c. 'The grace of God, which bringeth salvation, hath appeared unto all men, teaching,' &c. On these things hang all the law and the prophets; and those persons think they best preach Christ, who lay the main stress on them."

nation his conversation was animated and amusing, teeming with repartee and pointed with wit ; enriched by anecdote and enlivened by story. His recitations of passages from various authors, whether serious or humourous, were given, on such occasions, with great tact and spirit, and will be long remembered by those who have ever had the pleasure of hearing him. Many pleasing anecdotes respecting him are in the recollection of his friends, to whom his attractive and engaging qualities had long endeared him, and whom he had entertained with as many good puns as had ever emanated from the most celebrated wits of the day.

Mr. Haynes departed this life at Claydon, on the 17th of April 1822, in the 83d year of his age, and in the full enjoyment of his faculties even to the last.

At his particular request his remains were interred in the Church-yard of his native village, Elmsett, under a tree, which he had specified, and which he had often visited ; having always strongly decried the indecency of interment in Churches, wisely observing that " the Church was intended for the living and its yard for the dead."

Mr. Haynes was never married ; and his niece, Charlotte-Catherine-Anne, the sole daughter and heiress of his elder brother, Colonel Samuel Haynes, was married on the 14th of Jan. 1783, to John-William Egerton, the seventh Earl of Bridgewater *. Her Ladyship was left a widow, Oct. 21, 1823, and is living 1830.

The following simple inscription, suggested by Mr. Haynes himself, marks the place where his remains are deposited :

Hic jacet CAROLUS MEIN HAYNES, Clericus,
in expectatione diei supremi.
Qualis erat, dies iste indicabit.
Ob. Apr. 17, 1822, æt. 83.

JAMES COYTE received his academical education at Caius-college, Cambridge, and proceeded to the degree of A. B. in 1771. In 1779 he was presented to the Rectory of Cantley in Norfolk ; and in 1785 was licensed, on the nomination of the parishioners, to the Perpetual Curacy of St. Nicholas in Ipswich. He deceased on the 13th of June 1812 ; and was buried in the Chancel of the Church of St. Nicholas, where, on a mural-tablet, is this inscription :

In memory of the Rev. JAMES COYTE, twenty-seven years minister of this parish, and Rector of Cantley in Norfolk. He died June 13, 1812, aged 63. Also of ANN, his wife, who died February 18th, 1820, aged 60.

His elder brother, William-Beeston Coyte, was educated at Queen's-college, Cambridge, where he proceeded to the degree of M. B. in 1763. Being originally designed for the Church, he was ordained a Deacon ; but, afterwards embracing the medical profession, he practised for some years in the town of Ipswich.

* Gentleman's Magazine, vol. XCII. pt. i. p. 373.

He was much attached to the study of botany; and in illustration of his favourite pursuit, published the following works:

"Hortus Botanicus Gippovicensis; or a Systematical Enumeration of the Plants cultivated in Dr. Coyte's Botanical Garden at Ipswich in the County of Suffolk; with occasional Botanical observations. Also their Essential Generic Characters, English Names, the Natives of Britain particularised, the Exotics where best preserved, and their duration. To which is added an Investigation of the natural produce of some Grass Lands in High Suffolk. Ipswich, 1795," 4to; and, "Index Plantarum, or an Alphabetical Arrangement of all the Genera and Species of Plants hitherto described, with references to original authorities for each Genus and Species, and to Plates of such Plants as have been figured. To which is added an Index of the Natural Order, and an Appendix containing Observations upon the Medicinal Virtues of the British Plants, London, 1807," 8vo.

The first volume only of this work was published, containing Class 1.—XVI.

He was also the writer of "The Consequence of a Crown Piece swallowed by an Epileptic man, and vomited after many months," inserted in the Medical Transactions, vol. III. p. 30, 1785.

In 17.. he was elected a Fellow of the Linnæan Society.

He deceased on the 3d of March 1810, and was interred in the chancel of the Church of St. Nicholas in Ipswich, where, on a mural-tablet, is the following inscription:

"In memory of William Beeston Coyte, M. D. and Sarah his wife; he departed this life March 3, 1810, in the 69th year of his age; she died Sept. 21, 1776, aged 36. In the same vault are deposited the remains of Hesther, his second wife, who died July 21, 1820, in the 81st year of her age; also three children, who died in their infancy. This tablet is erected as a tribute of respect to his departed ancestors, by William Coyte Freeland and their grandson.

Their father, William Coyte, was the son of the Rev. William Coyte, Rector of Brantham, with East Bergholt annexed, in Suffolk, and —— his wife, the daughter of the Rev. Edmund Beeston, Rector of Sproughton, in the same county. He received his academical education at St. Peter's college, Cambridge, where he proceeded to the degree of M. B. in 1732. He practised at Ipswich for many years, and dying there on the 4th of August 1775, was buried in the nave of the Church of Bentley in Suffolk.

Edmund Beeston, the father of Mrs. Coyte, was educated at Trinity-college, Cambridge, where he proceeded to the degree of A. B. in 1688; and to that of A. M. in 1699. In 1690 he was presented by Adam Felton, Esq. to the Rectory of Sproughton, which he resigned in 1732; in 1704 he was appointed Town

Preacher by the Free Burgesses of Ipswich; and in 1711 instituted to the Rectory of Whatfield.   He deceased in 1735, and
was interred in the chancel of the church of Sproughton, where,
on a mural-tablet, is the following family inscription to his
memory :

"Arms : arg. a bend sab. between six bees volant of the
second.

"Here lies Edmund Beeston, M. A. Rector of this Church, a
man of primitive integrity (ob. 1713) ; and Mary, his good and
virtuous wife, ob. 1724 ; also Edmund, their eldest son, M. A.
Rector of this Church; a man of universal esteem for his humanity and charity, and all the virtues of a steady friend, sound
divine, and good Christian, ob. 1735; also Shelton, their third
son, Batchelor of Music, who died 1713; and George and Mary,
who died infants."

After his decease were published his " Practical Sermons and
Discourses upon several Subjects.   London, 1739," 8vo.

His younger brother, William Beeston, received his academical education at Trinity-college, Cambridge, where he proceeded to the degree of M. B. in 1692; and to that of
M. D. in 1702.   He was an able physician and an eminent
botanist; and, having practised in Ipswich for many years
with considerable success, acquired a handsome fortune, which,
upon his decease without issue, he bequeathed to his relations.   He died at Bentley in Suffolk, on the 4th of December
1732, and was interred in the nave of that church, where, on a
flat-stone, is the following inscription to his memory, as well as
to that of his nephew Mr. Coyte :

In Memoriam
GULmi BEESTON, M. D.
ob. 4o die Dec. 1732,
æt. 60,
etiamq. in memoriam
GULmi COYTE, M. B.
qui artem medicam
per multos annos feliciter exercuit
Gippovici.
Ob. 4o die Augti 1775,
æt. 67.

In a letter from Dr. William Sherard to Dr. Richardson,
dated July 24, 1722, and inserted in the First Volume of this
Work, p. 381, is a notice of Dr. Beeston.

The Rev. GEORGE BURTON, A. M.

George Burton *, the subject of this notice, was the second son of George Burton, of Burton Lazars in Leicestershire, Esq. and the younger brother of Philip Burton, Esq. the father of Mrs. Horne, the wife of that amiable, accomplished, and learned Prelate, Dr. George Horne, Bishop of Norwich.

He was born in 1717, and received his academical education at Catherine-hall, Cambridge, where he proceeded to the degree of A. B. in 1736, and to that of A. M. in 1740, being then a Member of King's college in that University. In 1740 he was presented to the Rectory of Elvedon, and in 1751 to that of Herringswell, both in the county of Suffolk. He married a sister of William Reeve, of Melton-Mowbray, Esq.; and, dying at Bath on the 3d of November 1791, was interred in the Church of Walcot.

Mr. Burton was a person of great industry in his favourite study of Chronology; and had generally three or four boys boarding in his house for instruction. He built, and again entirely re-built, the Glebe-house at Elvedon, which, unfortunately, had been burnt down by some fire, brought from a farm-house then in flames a mile distant, and which lighted on the thatched roof of a well that joined the dwelling, and which was the only thatch about the premises.

Mr. Burton was the author of the following works *viz.*: "An Essay towards reconciling the Numbers of Daniel and St. John, determining the Birth of our Saviour, and fixing a precise time for the continuance of the present Desolation of the Jews;

* In vol. III. pp. 394—399, of this Work, are inserted three letters from Mr. Burton to the learned antiquary Dr. Ducarel. For an account of the Burton family the reader is referred to Nichols's " History of Leicestershire,' vol. II. p. 268.

REV. GEORGE BURTON, A. M.   881

with some Conjectures, pointing out the year 1764
to have been one of the most remarkable Epochas
in History. Norwich, 1767." 8vo.*

" A Supplement to the Essay upon the Numbers
of Daniel and St. John, confirming those of 2436
and 3430, mentioned in the Essay, from two Numerical Prophecies of Moses and our Saviour. 1768."
8vo.; in which the author says that, " when he
published his Essay, his utmost hopes were to offer
a few hints that might be rendered serviceable to
religion, when improved by some able writer, but
had since happily succeeded in discovering what
seemed to carry conviction along with them †."

" The Analysis of Two Chronological Tables,

---

* In the preface Mr. Burton thus expresses himself: " If in
the course of this Essay towards fixing the æra of events, which
have hitherto been looked upon as in a great measure inexplicable, I have erred, the public, I hope, will kindly throw a veil
over the mistakes, as arising from an earnest zeal for advancing
the honour of God, and a hearty endeavour to render even the
difficult parts of the Holy Scriptures more universally intelligible; and the severest critic will indulge me with that favourable sentence pronounced by the Heathen moralist, *humanum
est errare*. Whilst I conduct myself with that decorum in the
course of these inquiries, which should ever be strictly observed
by those who write in defence of the best of religions, in favour
of a gospel of peace, I promise myself the candour of the
public voice, a well known voice for distinguishing justly between the pedantry of the mere scholar and the sober inquiries
of a real searcher after truth; especially as I profess not to interfere with the opinions of any man, and only mean to express
my own private sentiments, which, I hope, may be rendered useful to the interests of religion, when impressed upon, and regulated by an abler pen."

† According to Mr. Burton's calculations, the conversion of
the Gentiles and the Millenium will commence in the year 2436;
the battle of Gog and Magog will begin in 3430; and the Millenium terminate in 3436. It will shake the confidence of the
reader in our author's wisdom and calculations, when he is informed that the numerical prophecy of Moses referred to is
Lev. ch. xxvi. v. 18—28, " I will punish you seven times more for
your sins," &c.; and that of our Saviour, Luke, ch. xvii. v. 4,
" If thy brother trespass against thee seven times in a day," &c.
Orme's Bibliotheca Biblica, p. 69.

VOL. VI.   3 L

submitted to the consideration of the Public. The
one being a Table to associate Scripturally the different Chronologies of all Ages and Nations; the
other to settle the Paschal Feast from the Beginning to the End of Time. 1787." 4to.*

The following character of this eccentric divine
is from the pen of that ingenious antiquary, the
late Rev. George Ashby, B. D. F. S. A. Rector of
Barrow and of Stansfield, in the county of Suffolk,
who appears to have been well acquainted with Mr.
Burton, and to have pourtrayed his talents and foi-
bles with accuracy and discrimination. It is transcribed from the blank leaves of a MS. to which is
prefixed the following title, viz. "A Table of Julian, Lunar, and Solar Years, for the Term of the
Julian Period. To the Rev. Mr. Ashby. The
gift of the author, George Burton."

"Mr. Burton was a person of great industry in

* In the dedication to the Bishop of Norwich, we are informed
that Mr. Burton had arrived at the "age of well nigh three
score and ten, with a constitution enfeebled with many infirmi-
sies;" and in the preface we are further informed that the author
had struggled under many adversities; among others, that he
was obliged to "re-build his Parsonage-house, which was burnt
to the ground soon after he had in a manner re-built it." He
adds, "a natural concern for an increasing family of ten grandchildren, together with the infirmities incident to his years, and
too sedentary a life, had further discouraged him;" having,
however, completed his work, and by the assistance of his friends
brought forward this Analysis, he hopes "it will meet with such
an indulgent reception as may countenance and encourage the
end of all his wishes, namely, the publication and happy success
of his Tables."

He says that, "very few leading principles are wanting to
govern the Chronological Tables. — We are instructed in many
parts of Scripture, that there is a fixed period when time shall
be no more; and such a period is the first principle to be established. The second principle is the lunar year; to explain the
extent of that period, which is of so much consequence to us all,
namely, 7980 years. The third principle is the solar year; by
which may be presumed, a shortening of that period for the
elect's sake. The fourth principle is an acquired period; by
which the Easter limit is to be ascertained for ever; and the
second ascension, towards a final judgment, is pointed out."

his favourite study of Chronology, as appears by the many copies of the following pages, which he took the pains to transcribe over and over again ; but I could never perceive what the principles or foundations were, although I have attended in hopes of learning them. Mr. Burton would often repeat, turning over the following leaves, ' All this is quite certain and indisputable, figures cannot deceive; you know fifty and fifty make an hundred, and an hundred and hundred make two hundred.' To this I was necessarily obliged to assent ; but when I asked him, 'Why do you assume fifty and fifty, and an hundred and hundred?' I never could get an answer from him; nor does he seem to have settled a single æra, or cleared up one point of the many doubtful ones in this branch of science. He ever seemed greatly deficient in the books on the subject, as I do not remember to have seen more than an English Helvicus, which does not give a regular series of years, as Isaacson, Tallent, Marshall, and Blair do, and Playfair has since. Either of these books would have saved him a vast deal of trouble in writing; indeed, he seems to have been misled from the first by two expressions of Bishop Beveridge, who, when thirty-three years old, published in quarto, 'Ars Chronologica,' in which the learned writer, speaking of the Julian period, says, ' Egregia hæc Periodus (cujus utilitates in temporibus distinguendis opinionem superant) Juliana dicitur ; ' and again, ' Hic enim, cùm probè noverit quantum conducunt Cyclus solis et lunæ et indictionis *ad annum unum ab aliis secernendum*, istos tres cyclos in se invicem multiplicavit, cujus productum 7980 periodum Julianum nominavit.'

"These two sentences seem quite to have disconcerted my friend, who, not content with the general opinion that prevailed in the Bishop's time of the vast utility of this period in Chronology, firmly believed that it pointed out the exact beginning and end of the world; whereas Scaliger, the inventor, meant no more than to form a cycle or number of years, that should comprehend the year of the creation of the world, according to the various opinions of learned writers on this subject; and extend far enough for any use that the men of this generation could have for such a scale. He thought he had taken room enough, but even in the first particular he was sadly disappointed, as he was immediately told that the three Christian Churches of Constantinople, Alexandria, and Antioch, ascribed a still higher origin to this grand event; placing it 796, 799, and 780 earlier than the commencement even of his period, in the 765th year of which he had placed it. As to the latter particular, or end of the world, as it never entered Scaliger's head to fix that, the less that is said about it the better.

"Mr. Burton's researches seemed to have been confined to prophetic and visionary chronology in a degree hardly credible. Once, when he had talked a great deal, I thought it was proper to say something. 'You seem, Sir, to be very fond of these studies; have you ever paid any attention towards endeavouring to reconcile the discordant accounts of the Samaritan, Hebrew, and Septuagint Chronology?' He affirmed over and over again that he had never heard of any such difference; but added, that he would consider it, and did not doubt but that he should succeed. Some time after, on my meeting him at the Generals *, or Archdeacon's Visitation, at Mildenhall, he came and stood behind my chair, and said, that he had reconciled the differences completely. I only remarked, that he was doing great service to the Scripture Chronology. Soon after this, a paragraph appeared in the Bury Post, that a learned clergyman in that neighbourhood had reconciled the above differences; but

* The term used for the Archidiaconal Visitations in the Diocese of Norwich. See Forby's Vocabulary, p. 130.

I never heard any more of it, and cannot persuade
myself that he had had better success than the
whole body of Chronologers. There could be little
doubt of this paragraph having come immediately
from my friend, as the time agreed exactly ; and as
about the same time another appeared of a *flint* in
his (but nameless) possession, which exhibited a
wonderful representation of a volcano, &c. upon it.
This was no more than a beautiful flint stained with
a deeper red than common; but which had no more
reference to a volcano than to the man in the moon.
I have one or two somewhat like this, but not so
strongly coloured. He had besides a beautiful *echi-
nite* adhering to a flint, with one spine fallen off and
fastened to the flint; also one of the short antique
swords, broken in two, and an intermediate part
wanting.

"At another time I mentioned to him that there
were ten or eleven years difference not accounted for
between the reigns of the Kings of Judah and Israel.
He instantly replied, 'Oh! those are the years, to be
sure, that I want to make my system complete!'
How he could be perfectly ignorant of two such
well-known facts in chronology, is utterly inconceivable, at least unaccountable by me.

"He possessed also a curious book on Chinese Gardening, which, being vastly romantic, and quite different in the engraving from any thing done in
Europe, he concluded must be a Chinese production.

"He was a friend of Dr. Stukeley, from whom he
received as a present Bertram's 'Richard of Cirencester,' with the map, as he had noted in the blank
page. This copy I bought, after his death, at
Deck's, the bookseller of Bury.

"He had also several medals, which had been
found at different times at Icklingham; these were
consumed when his house was burnt which he had
built, and had to re-build again.

"In the latter part of his life, he had a cabinet of

medals by the decease of a brother, or some near
relation. When he showed me these, he kept lift-
ing up his hands, and crying out that, as he had no
reason to believe that his brother knew any thing of
these matters, he was astonished to think how he could
have collected so many fine things; that they must
be of great rarity, for that he could find few or none
of them in books; and truly no wonder, for they
were the most grossly false and spurious that could
possibly be. Of medals he knew little, as may be
inferred from this specimen of his abilities; and in
his favourite study of Chronology, he could never
make himself intelligible to, or convince a single
person. What Mr. Burton meant by the Julian
period being that alone which equates time, is not
easily understood; for, if the years of the vulgar
æra run parallel with it, must they not be both of
the same length; and, if so, does not one equate
time the same as the other? This is certainly not
the case with the vulgar æra and the Mohammedan
Hegyra; the difference between which is continually increasing."

The Editor of these volumes is in possession of a
MS. " Common-place Book, collected by George
Burton, of Elden, in 1744-5; consisting of Extracts
from various Authors." It contains nothing inte-
resting in it, but the particulars of a tithe cause at
Lakenheath.

In the first sale of "the Curious and Valuable
Library of Craven Ord, Esq." dispersed by public
auction in 1829, were the following MSS. in the
handwriting of Mr. Burton, viz.:

" Registrum Monasterii St. Edmundi, anno 1280; a tran-
script from the Album Registrum, folio." Sold for £.3. 6s. to
Thorpe the bookseller, and now in the extensive collection of
MSS. belonging to Sir Thomas Phillipps, Bart. F.S.A.

" Album Registrum, sive Chartularium Sancti Salvatoris in
Buria, transcribed by G. Burton," 4to. Sold for £.11 to Thorpe,
the bookseller; now *penes* Sir Thomas Phillipps.

" Consuetudinarium Sancti Ædmundi, ex codice pergamensi

penes Comitem de Cornwallis; compilatum a monacho Buriensi circiter A. D. 1234, transcriptum et collatum per me Georgium Burton, A.D. 1762," folio. Sold for £.12 to John Gage, Esq. Director S. A.

"Registrum Curteys, olim pertinens Abbatiæ S^{ci} Edmundi, by G. Burton, Rector of Elvedon, folio." Sold for £.7 to Cochran the bookseller; now *penes* Sir T. Phillipps.

"History of the Hundred of Elvedon*, Suffolk, by G. Burton, Rector of Elvedon. The original MS. with numerous papers and letters inserted, folio." Sold for £.21. 10s. to Cochran; now *penes* Sir Thomas Phillipps.

MR. JOHN MOLE.

" A Shepheard's boy, no better doe him call." SPENSER.

Mr. John Mole, deservedly eminent for his skill and knowledge in the science of Algebra, was descended from poor yet respectable parents, and was born at Old Newton, near Stowmarket, in the county of Suffolk, on the 10th of March 1743, O. S. His father was bailiff to John Meadows, Gent. of that parish; and, having a numerous family of children, was unable to give them the benefit of a school education. Fortunately, however, the mother, whose maiden name was Sarah Martin, had it in her power to remedy, in some measure, this disadvantage. During her intervals of leisure, she taught them their letters, as well as to read a few easy lessons; and thus unconsciously laid the foundation of her son's future celebrity. At thirteen years of age, young Mole was placed with Mr. John Cooper, a farmer in his native village, where he remained two years. He then resided with Mr. Thomas Riches of the same place; and from thence removed to Mr. William Harpur's, of Donham-bridge farm, in the vicinity of Ipswich. Here it was that Mole,

* There is no such hundred in the county. The parish of Elvedon is in the Hundred of Lackford.

who had now attained his twenty-seventh year, first
evinced a predilection for his favourite pursuit. One
of those accidents occurred, which, as Dr. Johnson
observes in his Life of Cowley, produce that particular designation of mind and propensity for some
certain science, commonly called genius, and which
Mole, in after life, was very fond of relating. Having
been sent with a waggon to the shop of a neighbouring carpenter for a load of timber to repair his
master's premises, one of the workmen asked him, if
he could tell him how many cubical quarters of inches
could be cut out of a solid foot of timber; when
Mole replied, that he could inform him how many
cubical quarters of inches could be cut out of ten
thousand solid feet. The carpenter betted him a
trifling wager that he could not; but Mole soon
satisfied him of his mistake, and won the wager.
Some other questions were then started; one of
which was, how many farthings there were in a
million of moidores of the value of twenty-seven
shillings each. These Mole as readily answered;
and, in lieu of the wager he had won, asked the
carpenter to teach him the method of multiplication. The carpenter asked him, if he was acquainted
with that of addition, which Mole told him he was
not; he then showed him how to multiply a small
number by twelve, making two lines of the pro-
duct, and the manner of adding them up. Our
young arithmetician had previously made himself
acquainted with numeration by setting down figures
with chalk, and then asking some one of his fellow-
servants to read and decypher them to him. Having
quickly mastered the rules of multiplication, and
made a rapid progress in solving such questions as
it would reach, he resolved to follow the bent of his
inclination, and accordingly applied himself with
diligence to figures. He soon acquired, by his own
exertions, a thorough knowledge of the rule of three;
and his residence being situated within a short dis-

tance from Ipswich, he applied to Mr. Carter*, who
at that time kept a school there, to teach him,
during the summer evenings, vulgar and decimal
fractions as well as the extraction of the square and
cube roots. In the science of Algebra, however,
he was not indebted to the instruction of others;
but acquired his intimate knowledge of that difficult branch of arithmetic solely from himself.

He now relinquished his occupation as a farmer's
servant, and applied himself most diligently to his
studies; and, in 1773, at the suggestion of some
friends who had kindly interested themselves in his
behalf, commenced the superintendence of a school
at Nacton. In 1788 he published in octavo his
" Elements of Algebra; to which is prefixed a
choice Collection of Arithmetical Questions, with
their Solutions; including some new improvements
worthy the attention of Mathematicians. London;"
a work, which, as an introduction to that science,
possesses considerable merit. It gives the notation
and common rules with great ease and perspicuity,
diffusely explains the several methods of solving
affected equations; and comprises, in one view, all
that is necessary to be known for solving infinite
terms for quadratic, cubic, and biquadratic equations,
where such solution is possible. The common rules,
likewise, are given with the utmost perspicuity; and
the principles on which they are founded clearly
demonstrated. Both the Monthly and Critical Reviews of that period expatiate largely on the merits
of this treatise; and speak of it in terms of the
highest commendation. After the publication of
this work, Mr. Mole was sent for by several schools
in Ipswich to teach them Algebra; and, what is
somewhat remarkable, he instructed in that branch
of science, as well as in the solution of astronomical
problems, the then master and ushers of the very

* The author of an excellent English Grammar for the use of
schools.

school in which he himself had first been taught the use of vulgar and decimal fractions. In 1793 he relinquished his school at Nacton, and removed to Witnesham, a village situate a few miles on the other side of Ipswich, where he again commenced the drudgery of tuition. In 1809 he published in octavo, " A Treatise on Algebra for Schools." In 1811 he quitted Witnesham, and returned to his former residence, where he remained in the exercise of his profession until his decease, which occurred on the 20th of September 1827, in the 85th year of his age.

Mr. Mole was a contributor to the pages of the " Ipswich Magazine," the first number of which appeared in February 1799, and which was continued until that month in the following year. The following is a list of these contributions: " An Elegy on the death of Charity Kent, who died of the Small Pox at Nacton, in the 17th year of her age." " Thoughts on whether the Discovery of America has added to the sum of happiness or not." Four Essays "On the Vanity of Human Wishes;" "On Emulation;" " On Justice;" and "On Dissimulation;" and " A Description of the Consternation of a simple and inoffensive people, on descrying a formidable Fleet approaching their Coast with hostile intention, their imprecations for the confusion of the insulting Foe, &c." in verse; all of which have considerable merit.

Mr. Mole, like every other man, had his virtues, his failings, and his defects. He was, in the strictest sense of the term, a self-taught genius; and, in the study and pursuit of his favourite science, had deservedly attained considerable celebrity. At the commencement of the French Revolution he became an ardent admirer of its principles, and was by no means over-sedulous in concealing his opinions. To the exercise of free inquiry he was strongly addicted ; and, as it has been well observed and

lamented that minds merely mathematical are apt to
tend to scepticism and infidelity, because, always
accustomed to demonstrate proofs, and wholly engaged in a science which admits of them at every
step, they will not readily acquiesce in a series of
probabilities where investigations of another kind
are presented, and perhaps will not have patience to
examine circumstances deeply enough to ascertain
on which side there is a preponderancy of evidence
amounting to demonstration,—in religious belief
Mr. Mole was far from orthodox. The writings of
Woolston, Hobbes, and others of that school, he
had perused with deep attention; and, while nar-
rating their heterodox opinions, would chuckle over
them with much seeming delight; but at the same
time he frankly admitted that Pope, Johnson, and
more especially Montaigne, whose writings he delighted in, were his favourite authors; and these
he would occasionally quote with much effect.
Throughout a long life his conduct was strictly
moral, virtuous, and correct; his manners mild and
unassuming, and his habits frugal, temperate, and
plain; like Emerson, indeed, for whose memory he
entertained the highest veneration, he was fond of a
jug of ale, but in the occasional indulgence of this,
their favourite beverage, he seldom exceeded the
bounds of sobriety. He possessed a firm independence of mind, and a genuine, nay, an ardent love of
truth. His honesty and integrity were unimpeached;
and it afforded him the greatest pleasure to promote, as far as his slender means would allow, the
welfare and happiness of those around him.

Mr. Mole was twice married, but left no issue.
His second wife, who survived him, was a person
whom he, from motives of charity, had brought up
and educated.

892

ADDITIONS AND CORRECTIONS.

P. 116, line 11, the punctuation should be, "My *sarvis* to your cousin of Londonderry; as he was so civil to request it [that is, Lord Camelford's acquiescence in Mr. Stewart taking his title from Londonderry], I could not," &c.

P. 137, line 3 from bottom, read, "It is not a *lion* in the toils; but," &c.

P. 146. In the Gentleman's Magazine, vol. LXX. p. 436, are anecdotes of Robert Forster, the Flying Barber of Cambridge, by the Rev. B. N. Turner.

P. 154, line 5. The reference in the 2d volume of the New Monthly Magazine, p. 525, is to the Gentleman's Magazine for March 1785, vol. LV. p. 178—the same letter of Dr. Sharp as is referred to in the present Volume, p. 147 and p. 806.

P. 191, line 22, read viduata est.

P. 248, line 18, for Antiquarian read Linnæan.

P. 249, note, 8 from bottom, for 17.. read 1790.

P. 253. Ewan Law, Esq. died at Horsted Place, Sussex, April 24, 1829, aged 82. He was M.P. for Westbury from 1790 until Jan. 1795; and one of the Commissioners of Naval Inquiry appointed in 1802.

The following epitaph to the Rev. Henry Forster Mills is placed on a tablet on the south wall of Brancepeth church, Durham: "To the memory of the Rev. Henry Forster Mills, A. M. Chancellor of the Cathedral of York and Rector of Elmley in that diocese. He was the eldest son of Henry Mills, Esq. of Willington in this parish, and after an illness of above twenty years, which he bore with exemplary patience and pious resignation, died at Bath April 27, 1827, in the 58th year of his age. In te, Domine, speravit."—Lieut.-Colonel Robert William Mills, brother to the Chancellor of York, was returned M. P. for Bletchingly at the general election in 1830.—In Brancepeth church is also another tablet: "To the memory of William Forster, Esq. of the City of Durham, who died January 6, 1766, aged 50, and lies interred in the yard near the south wall of the church, Henry Mills, Esq. his affectionate nephew, erected this monument."

P. 267. A monument to the memory of Mr. Wilmot, by Richard Westmacott, is erected in Berkswell church, Warwickshire. It bears the following inscription: "Sacred to the memory of John Eardley Wilmot, Esq. (second son of the Right Hon. Sir John Eardley Wilmot, Knt.) Master in Chancery, Member of Parliament, Commissioner for granting relief to the American Loyalists and to the French Refugees. He died June 23, 1815, aged 66 years. 'He was a father to the poor; and the cause which he knew not he searched out. The blessing of him that was ready to perish came upon him, and he caused the widow's heart to sing with joy.' Job, c. xxix."

Other epitaphs to the Wilmot family in the same church will be found in the Gentleman's Magazine, vol. XCVII. i. 577.

P. 309. Miss Essex was the first wife of John Hammond, Esq. M. A. who resigned a Fellowship of Queen's for her hand; but she did not live long after marriage. Mr. Hammond survived till June 7, 1830; and has a memoir in the Gentleman's Magazine, vol. C. pt. ii. p. 88.

P. 373, first line of note, read, " met his."

P. 455. The Rev. James Douglas, F. S. A. succeeded the celebrated clerical artist the Rev. William Peters, R. A., in the rectory of Litchborough, Northamptonshire ; to which he was instituted Nov. 17, 1787, on the presentation of Sir William Addington, Knt. He was appointed one of the Prince of Wales's Chaplains towards the end of 1787 (together with the Rev. Robert Lewis, who is noticed in vol. V. of this Work, p. 848.) Mr. Douglas resigned Litchborough in 1799, when presented by the Lord Chancellor, through the recommendation of the Earl of Egremont, to the Rectory of Middleton in Sussex. Mrs. Douglas was sister to James Oldershaw, M.D. of Stamford, and to the Rev. John Oldershaw, B. D. Archdeacon of Norfolk, and F.R.S.; and twin sister of Martha, wife of Sir Richard Glode, of Mayfield-place, Kent, who was knighted when Sheriff of London and Middlesex in 1793. Their daughter Margaret was married in 1811 to M. Tucker, Esq. The relics found by Mr. Douglas in his excavations, and engraved in the Nænia Britannica, were sold by his widow to Sir Richard Colt Hoare, Bart. F. R. S. and S. A. who in 1829, with his wonted munificence, presented them to the Ashmolean Museum at Oxford, where they are now arranged for public inspection.

P. 492. " In the Museum of Marischal college, Aberdeen, is preserved the elegant gold box presented by the Earl of Buchan to the college, in the year 1769, inclosing a silver pen, for which an annual competition takes place among the students of the Greek class. The successful candidate is rewarded by a donation of a book; and a small silver medal, with his name inscribed upon it, is appended to the pen." Kennedy's Annals of Aberdeen, vol. II. p. 110.

P. 494. The Earl of Buchan, among his other tributes to the memory of Thomson, placed the brass tablet in Richmond Church, Surrey, which bears the following inscription :

" In the earth below this tablet are the remains of James Thomson, author of the beautiful poems, intituled, The Seasons, The Castle of Indolence, &c. who died at Richmond, Aug. 22, 1748, and was buried here the 29th, 1748, O. S. The Earl of Buchan, unwilling that so good a man and sweet a poet should be without a memorial, has denoted the place of his interment for the satisfaction of his admirers, in the year of our Lord 1792

> Father of light and life, thou Good Supreme !
> O teach me what is good, teach me thyself ;
> Save me from folly, vanity, and woe,
> From every low pursuit, and feed my soul

With knowledge, conscious peace, and virtue pure,
Sacred, substantial, never-fading bliss! "

P. 597.   Mr. Turnor's pamphlet on Wool was first printed in
1782, and was extracted from the Pamphleteer, no. XLVI.—
Mr. Turnor is thanked in the preface to Bromley's Catalogue of
Portraits.

P. 605, penultimate line of text, for "Sir Frederick," &c.
read " Sir Ludovick Grant, of Grant, Bart. by Lady Margaret
Ogilvy, daughter of James Earl of Findlater and Seafield; and
aunt to Sir Lewis-Alexander Grant, who succeeded his maternal
uncle in the latter Earldom in 1811, and is the present Peer."—
There is a large 4to portrait of Dean Waddilove, engraved in
mezzotinto by W. Ward, from a painting by George Marshall,
of York.

P. 666.   Archdeacon Pett died at Oxford, Feb. 4, 1830.   The
family of Pett was, for several generations, engaged in the
superintendance of the royal dock-yards, having been raised to
eminence in that employment by Phineas Pett, who was shipwright to King James the First, and from whose diary some interesting extracts were communicated by Mr. Denne to the
Archæologia, vol. XII. and several others are interspersed
in Nichols's " Progresses of King James I."   Dr. Pett's father
resided at Maidstone.   He was educated at Westminster, where
he was admitted King's scholar in 1770, and elected to Christ
Church, Oxford, in 1774*.   He proceeded M.A. 1781, B.D.
1791, D.D. 1797; and served the University office of Proctor,
together with Dr. Routh, now President of Magdalen college, in
1785.   At the close of 1788 he was appointed one of the Whitehall preachers.   In 1789, being then Chaplain to Dr. Smallwell,
Bishop of Oxford, he was collated by that prelate to the vicarage
of Orton on the Hill, in Leicestershire; but exchanged in the
same year for that of Cropredy in Oxfordshire, which is in the
same patronage.   In 1795 he was presented by his college to the
rectory of Wentnor in Shropshire; and in the same year was
collated by the Hon. Dr. North, Bishop of Winchester, to the
rectory of Chilbolton in Hampshire, which he retained until his
death.   In 1796 Bishop Smallwell appointed him Chancellor of
the diocese of Oxford, and in the following year Archdeacon.
In 1801 he was collated by Bishop Fisher to the prebend of
Grimston and Yetminster in the church of Salisbury; and in
1802, by Archbishop Moore, to the rectory of Newington in
Oxfordshire.   In 1801 Dr. Pett was elected Master of St. Mary
hall, which office he resigned in 1815, when he was appointed a

* The scholars elected to Christ Church in 1774 were five: the Hon.
Percy Charles Wyndham; Multon Lumbarde (of Sevenoaks, Esq.);
Thomas Andrew Strange (sometime Chief Justice of Madras, and
knighted); Phineas Pett; and William Frederick Browne (now D.D.
and Prebendary of Wells).   All these, after the lapse of fifty-five years,
were living until the death of Archdeacon Pett.

Canon of Christ Church. Dr. Pett was tutor to the late statesman, Mr. Canning. On the death of Bishop Goodenough in 1827, King George IV. wrote an autograph letter to Lord Goderich, in which he stated that, as he knew it was the intention of the late Premier to appoint his tutor Dr. Pett to the first vacant Bishoprick, the death of the Bishop of Carlisle would, if Lord Goderich saw no objection to it, supply the opportunity. The offer was in consequence made; but Dr. Pett without hesitation declined it, being perfectly content with that station in the church he already so honourably filled. From the decided manner in which he had expressed himself, the Doctor expected the affair would have at once been set to rest; three weeks afterwards, however, his Majesty ordered the offer to be repeated, observing, "That no steps had been taken till the Doctor had had time to reconsider his refusal, and that the Bishoprick was still at his service." Dr. Pett, however, although entertaining the most grateful sense of His Majesty's liberality and condescension, persisted in his first resolve, and the See passed into the possession of the Hon. Dr. Percy, Bishop of Rochester. It is difficult to say which part of this transaction is the most rare —the second offer or the second refusal. Dr. Pett passed a long and useful life, excepting one short interval, within the precincts of the University of Oxford, beloved for the benevolence of his disposition, admired for his taste, wit, and scholarship, and respected for his integrity. There is a portrait of Dr. Pett, by Owen, at St. Mary's hall, Oxford, taken at the expense of the members of that Society; as was a fine engraving which has been published from it.

P. 667, line 21, for Doctors read Domini.

P. 668. In Dartford church, on the north wall of the chancel, is a very handsome mural monument by Milligan, erected by subscription to the memory of the late Vicar. It consists of a large square tablet, on which is the inscription, surmounted by a pyramid of black marble, bearing a medallion profile the size of life, below which appear several books. The inscription:

"Sacred to the memory of the Rev. John Currey, M.A. forty-seven years Vicar of this parish, Rector of Longfield, and formerly Fellow of St. John's college, Cambridge; who departed this life on the 18th day of October 1824, aged 89 years, and lies buried in Northfleet church.

"For a perpetual remembrance of his virtues, to record their deep sense of his worth, and their heartfelt sorrow for their loss, his parishioners have caused this monumental tablet to be erected.

"We saw in him benevolence tempered with discretion, zeal controlled by sober judgment, piety adorned with simplicity approaching to almost that of the apostolic age."

Below is sculptured a shield of arms: Gules, a saltire Argent, in chief a Rose. Crest, on a wreath, a Rose.

P. 695. Stephen Law, Esq. formerly Governor of Bombay,

and one of the Directors of the East India Company, died at
Bedgebury, the seat of his son-in-law Governor John Cartier
(of whom in p. 766), Dec. 25, 1787, aged nearly 90; his lady
died at Broxbourn, Feb. 2, 1785, aged 77. Soon after his death
the following warm eulogy appeared in the Gentleman's Magazine, in the words of an old correspondent : " If complacency
in manners, extensive benevolence, inflexible integrity, and submissive piety are virtues beneficial to mankind, and acceptable
to God, no one could more justly command the esteem of
his fellow-creatures, nor more assuredly hope for an eternal
recompence of reward, than this most excellent man.—It ought
to be recorded, to the lasting honour of the deceased, that,
though a Governor of an East India settlement, he returned to
England with clean hands,

> —————— "Faithful found
> Among the faithless ————
> Among innumerable false, unmov'd,
> Unshaken, unseduced ————."

P. 700, last line, for Clayton read South Claypole.

P. 713, note, in most copies, for Warren read Horsley.

P. 718. Mr. Montagu was born at Lackham; and, being a
younger son, entered the army, and served as a Captain in the
fifteenth regiment of foot during the war with the American
colonies. His father died in 1790; his brother James was appointed High Sheriff of Wiltshire in 1795, but died soon after;
upon which he inherited the property. His death (which took
place June 19, not Aug. 28, 1815) was from a locked-jaw,
caused by a rusty nail wounding his foot. A very extensive and
finely preserved collection of birds and other animals, which he
had made, was purchased by the British Museum. His first
publication was, " The Sportsman's Dictionary; or, a Treatise
on Gunpowder and Fire-arms, &c. London 1792;" re-printed
1803.—He lost a son, Frederick, at the battle of Albuera.

P. 720. The Rt. Hon. William Windham was born in 1750,
the only son of William Windham, Esq. by Sarah, *widow* of Robert
Lukin, Esq. See epitaphs of the Rt. Hon. W. Windham and
his lady, at Felbrigg, in the Gent. Mag. vol. XCIX. pt. i. p. 230.

P. 738. Dr. Disney died at Pluckley, March 28, 1807, aged
75; and his remains were interred in the family vault at Cranbrook. His widow survived until the 18th of May 1820, when
she died at Ashford, aged 84; and was buried at Cranbrook.
" A portion " of Dr. Disney's library was sold, together with a
gentleman's library from Canterbury, by Messrs. Wheatley and
Adlard, in Piccadilly, Nov. 16, 1829, and five following days.

In note on Mr. Fisher, for 755 read 735; and for Dunford
read Duxford.

J. B. NICHOLS AND SON, 25, PARLIAMENT STREET.

CPSIA information can be obtained at www.ICGtesting.com
Printed in the USA
LVOW11s1129301214

420816LV00002B/210/P